Using **Simply Accounting**® M. PURBHOO

by Sage Premium 2010

Covers both Simply Accounting® Premium 2010 and Simply Accounting® Pro 2010

D0619217

Pearson Canada
Toronto

LIBRARY AND ARCHIVES CANADA CATALOGUING IN PUBLICATION

Purbhoo, Mary, 1949–
   Using Simply Accounting by Sage Premium 2010 / M. Purbhoo.

Includes index.

ISBN 978-0-321-70165-7 (college ed.)
ISBN 978-0-321-70166-4 (trade ed.)

1. Simply Accounting for Windows (Computer file). 2. Accounting–Computer programs. I. Title.

HF5679.P8994 2011   657'.0285536   C2010-902856-2

This edition is also published as Teach Yourself Simply Accounting® by Sage Premium 2010.

ISBN: 978-0-321-70165-7 (college ed.)
ISBN: 978-0-321-70166-4 (trade ed.)

Vice-President, Editorial Director: Gary Bennett
Editor-in-Chief: Nicole Lukach
Sponsoring Editor: Don Thompson
Executive Marketing Manager: Cas Shields
Developmental Editor: Madhu Ranadive
Production Editor: Heather Sangster, Strong Finish
Copy Editor: Heather Sangster, Strong Finish
Proofreader: Suzanne Needs, Strong Finish
Project Manager: Sarah Lukaweski
Page Layout: Mary Purbhoo
Art Director: Julia Hall
Interior and Cover Design: Anthony Leung
Cover Image: ShutterStock Images

Credits
Photo of the body fat scale used in the data files on the Student DVD: Courtesy Tanita.
Page 474, screen shot from Canada Revenue Agency Web site: Canada Revenue Agency and the Minister of Public Works and Government Services Canada, 2010.

2 3 4 5   14 13 12 11 10

Printed and bound in the United States of America.

CONTENTS

Part 3: Advanced Premium Features

PREFACE

Using Simply Accounting® by Sage Premium 2010 provides full coverage of the Simply Accounting program for the Premium and Pro version features. The 2010 Student version (Release A) is also a Premium version program, so all users can learn the program using the same release the author used to create the data files, screens and keystrokes. Although we do not address the Enterprise version of Simply Accounting, the book is also compatible with this version. Because Sage now offers the Simply Accounting 2010 Student version program only as a download from its Web site, we do not provide a CD with the Student version program. Instead, we include simple download instructions in an access card packaged with this book and detailed instructions for downloading, installing and activating the Student version in Appendix A.

In this edition, we continue to work with module windows in the Enhanced view throughout the text, create user-specific customized shortcuts to access journals in other modules and use the industry-specific terms for the different applications. As in the past, we provide margin notes for the traditional Classic view.

We maintained the aspects of the book that have been well-received in previous editions:
- the diversity of companies and business situations, including non-profit, service and inventory businesses
- comprehensive and current tax coverage for different provinces, including remittances and the recent implementation of the Harmonized Sales Tax (HST) in Ontario and British Columbia
- the realistic approach
- easy-to-follow, step-by-step keystroke instructions and screen illustrations, updated for Version 2010
- the currency of our information (although keeping up with fluctuating currency rates and sales tax changes provides ongoing challenges)
- several company setup chapters increasing in complexity and a separate setup for payroll, all with keystroke instructions
- delayed introduction of advanced Accounts Receivable and Payable topics
- realistic source documents that give you the "feel" of actual company transactions throughout the text

We have also introduced some changes.

Although we used the same companies as in the previous edition, we made a few changes to update the sales taxes. Five provinces have now adopted the single HST to replace the separate federal and provincial sales taxes. For companies in Ontario and British Columbia, we changed all tax codes and recalculated all amounts. Alberta and the three territories have only the single GST. This leaves only five provinces with separate provincial taxes. Therefore, to maintain a broad coverage of provincial tax differences, we "relocated" some HST province companies to provinces that still have separate provincial sales taxes.

Two new supplementary appendices have been added to the Student DVD: one covers Sage's Simply Accounting HR Manager, a program that links with Simply Accounting data and manages the non-payroll aspects of human resources, and the other outlines a complete accounting application for cash-basis accounting, including source documents. Both include detailed keystroke instructions.

The Student DVD with Data Files has the following additional resources:
- review questions and cases for each chapter (Appendix E)
- additional appendices with supplementary materials
- the interactive Accounting Cycle Tutorial, which introduces basic accounting terms and concepts

The data and supplementary files are now on a single DVD instead of a CD. This move was necessitated by the data and appendix files we added for this edition and the desire to maintain flexible data instalment options. We believe that because CD/DVD drives are common enough, this format should present no new issues. However, if any user does not have access to a PC with a CD/DVD drive, we can make the data and supplementary files available for downloading.

Because of previous concerns about the difficulty of using backup data files we continue the three options for installing data. We offer backup data files for both Premium and Pro versions, and we include full Premium version data files for all source document applications in the text. Pro version and supplementary Premium version data files (optional files for company setups and bank reconciliation) are provided only as backup files. Of course, we still provide detailed instructions on restoring backups. This decision has additional advantages — if computer speed and time permit, users can install the full data files; otherwise, the smaller backup files can be copied quickly or backup files can be restored to your hard disk directly from the DVD one at a time. Premium version users can even install both the full and backup sets of files with the advantage that the same backup files can be installed once and restored as often as needed without reinstalling. As usual, the DVD includes automatic installation for each of these options.

The removable page-length bookmark attached to the back cover has a mini index and a ruler-marked edge to help you refer to specific lines on a page. Combined with the ⟲ symbol, the bookmark should help to manage the page-flipping that is inevitable with a keystroke text.

The basic organization of the text is unchanged. Part One provides an overview and introduction to Simply Accounting and sales taxes. Data applications that can be completed with both Pro and Premium versions are located in Part Two. We introduce the six ledgers of the Simply Accounting program (General, Payables, Receivables, Payroll, Inventory and Division) in separate applications. Budgeting and account reconciliation procedures are covered in two more applications. Advanced Receivables and Payables features (orders and quotes, tax remittances, sales to foreign customers and Internet links) are demonstrated in two other separate chapters. An online banking simulation allows you to download a bank statement that integrates with data from the text. The required data files for all these chapters are set up in advance, and for each new type of transaction we provide detailed keystrokes and matching screens.

Four applications cover setting up a computerized accounting system using Simply Accounting. Again, detailed instructions with screen illustrations are given for each setup as you learn to convert, design and implement a complete accounting system.

- In Chapter 4, you set up a non-profit organization that uses only the General Ledger.
- In Chapter 7, you set up a service organization using the General, Payables and Receivables Ledgers.
- In Chapter 9, you add payroll to a data file that already has the General, Payables and Receivables Ledgers.
- In Chapter 16, you set up a comprehensive retail organization that uses the General, Payables, Receivables, Payroll and Inventory Ledgers.

In the final application in Part Two (Stratford Country Inn, Chapter 17), you set up a computerized accounting system on your own. All source documents in this chapter are realistic and descriptive.

Time & Billing and Departmental Accounting, advanced features available only in the Premium version, are covered in Part Three. Separate chapters and data files are prepared for these. All Part Three pages are edged with a blue stripe so that you can find them quickly.

Fourteen appendices are provided for reference or further study — four in Part Four of the text and ten on the Student DVD. By placing some material on the Student DVD, we were able to keep the length of the printed book unchanged while still covering extra features. The text includes the following appendices:

- A: Installing Simply Accounting (includes downloading, installing and activating the Student version)
- B: Windows Basics, Shortcuts & Terms (includes chart of Simply Accounting keyboard shortcuts; accounting vs. non-accounting terms; terms used for different types of industries)
- C: Correcting Errors after Posting (descriptions and screen displays for reversing entries)
- D: Working in Multi-User Mode

The remaining ten appendices in PDF format on the Student DVD are available for you to read or print:

- E: Review Questions and Cases for all keystroke chapters
- F: Customizing Reports
- G: Customizing Sales Invoices
- H: Setting Security and Passwords (entering and removing users, access rights and passwords)
- I: Air Care Services – Cash-Basis Accounting (including source documents and keystroke instructions)
- J: Integration with Other Software (linking with Microsoft Office documents, exporting GIFI financial reports and payroll T4s to Canada Revenue Agency, importing customer or vendor data, accounts and transactions)
- K: Online Banking (including a complete simulated online bank account)
- L: Online Billing with Billing Boss (with setup keystrokes and accounting examples)
- M: HR Manager (with setup keystroke and examples)
- N: Review of Basic Accounting

USING THIS BOOK

The accounting applications in this text were prepared using the Premium 2010 and Pro 2010 versions (Release A) of the Simply Accounting software published by The Sage Group PLC. Windows Vista, 7 and XP operating systems were used to create and test the screen images and keystrokes.

You must have a hard disk and CD/DVD drive, or a network system with Windows installed. If you do not have your own copy of the Simply Accounting program, you can download the Student Premium software from the Simply Accounting Web site (refer to Appendix A). Network system users should work with the site administrator to ensure complete data access.

In addition, you should have a standard accounting text for reviewing accounting principles. The text provides some accounting principles and procedures, and the Review of Basic Accounting (Appendix N) and the Accounting Cycle Tutorial on the Student DVD also provide an introduction. However, these are not intended to replace the breadth and depth of most standard accounting texts. You should also consult the built-in Help features and the Simply Accounting manuals on the program CD.

The text is as simple and straightforward as we could make it, but you will still need some familiarity with computers before you work through it. Your life will be easier still if you have acquired some of the fundamentals of troubleshooting.

Instructors can order an Instructor's Resource CD-ROM that includes an Instructor's Resource Manual with answers for all the cases in the text and a Test Item File. In addition, Simply Accounting solutions for each application after all transactions are completed can be downloaded from the Instructors' Resource Web site. The testing resources and Instructor's Resource Manual can also be downloaded from this site. By locating these resources on a Web site, we are able to make them available earlier and post changes or notifications about corrections as soon as they are discovered. Instructor packages to accompany this text or information about access to the Instructor's Resources Web site can be obtained from your Pearson Education Canada sales representative.

The Student DVD with Data Files

Because the text is used with the Pro version as well as Premium, we have tried to make version differences, such as differences in features, terminology and labels, as clear as possible. Margin notes in the text for the Pro version and separate data sets should make it easy for all users to follow the text.

The Student DVD has an autorun feature that should open the Student DVD homepage automatically when you insert the DVD into your CD/DVD drive. From this homepage you can choose to install data files, view the supplementary appendices in PDF format, run the Accounting Cycle Tutorial or browse the DVD. The Student DVD homepage will remain open for you to make another selection until you close it.

If the Student DVD does not start automatically,

Choose the **Start icon** (or menu). **Type** Run and **press** (enter) (or click Run in Windows XP).

In the Run window filename field,

Type d:\start.exe (where d: is the drive letter for your CD/DVD drive). **Click OK**.

Click **Exit** to close the Student DVD after making all the selections you want.

The separate installation programs will help you install the data set you need. To choose the correct data set, you must know what version you are using. You can get this information from the program package, from the program CD or from the Select Company window in the program. SIMPLY ACCOUNTING BY SAGE PRO or SIMPLY ACCOUNTING BY SAGE PREMIUM appears in the Home window title bar for all data files. If you accepted the default installation settings, the program folder name in Program Files also matches the version.

Use the following chart to help you install the data set you need from the Install Data screen.

FOR PROGRAM VERSION	CLICK INSTALL BUTTON	DATA SET (FOLDER ON DVD)
Pro Version 2010	Install Pro Version Backup Files	Pro_Backup_Version

FOR PROGRAM VERSIONS	CLICK INSTALL BUTTON	DATA SET (FOLDER ON DVD)
Student Premium Version 2010	Install Premium Version Full Files	Premium_Full_Version_Data
Premium Version 2010	or	
Enterprise Version 2010	Install Premium Version Backup Files	Premium_Backup_Version

All installation programs create a data folder named SimData10 on drive C (Local Disk C: or [OS] C:). If you need to work with another location for your data files, refer to page 6 in this text. You can install the data as often as you need to. However, the new installation of full data files will overwrite the previous data files unless you first copy them to another folder or location or change the name of the folder containing the older files.

You can restore backup files directly from the Student DVD to your hard disk. However, we recommend installing the backup files to your hard disk and keeping the original DVD safe for later use.

If you are using the Enterprise version, the Simply Accounting data conversion wizard will convert the Premium data files when you open them or restore them. Because the DVD files remain unchanged, you can install the same files later and use the Premium version.

Supplementary Data Files

In addition to the data files needed to work through the keystroke applications in the text, we provide several supplementary files in backup format with all installation options. These backup files will be located in the Setup, Bank and ACCOUNTANT folders in SimData10 when you install the data files. The Setup folder backup files have the setup already completed for chapters 4, 7, 10 and 16, allowing you to enter only the source documents for these chapters. Three backup files are included for Chapter 16, allowing users to begin the source documents at the start of any of the three months. The Setup folder also includes some company and inventory logos for the setup chapters and new inventory items. The Bank folder has three backup data files for reconciling bank accounts: one for Tesses Tresses in Chapter 15 for the month of February, one for online banking in Appendix K on the Student DVD and one for Chapter 16, Case 8 in Appendix E on the Student DVD. The ACCOUNTANT folder has the backup and text files you need to import accounting transactions from an Accountant's Edition (Chapter 12).

Passwords

We have not added passwords to any data files to ensure maximum accessibility. However, if you are using the program in a multi-user or network environment that includes users and passwords, you will need to enter your user name and password before you can open the data files. Ask your instructor or site administrator for the user name and password that you should use. Refer to Chapter 16, page 678, and Appendix H on the Student DVD for instructions on working with passwords.

Windows Version

We used Windows Vista for the primary screens and keystrokes for this text and worked with both Windows XP and Windows 7 while creating and testing the data files. Fortunately, the screens and functionality of Simply Accounting are the same for these three versions of Windows. They differ only at the interface between Windows and Simply Accounting — in the screens for browsing, opening and saving files. For example, My Computer and its File menu in Windows XP are named Computer and Organize menu in Windows Vista and Windows 7. A basic Windows text will include the information you need to successfully complete this text.

Working with Different Versions of Simply Accounting

You can use the Student DVD data files with the 2010 Pro, Premium, Enterprise and Premium Student versions of Simply Accounting, Release A or later.

Student Version

The Student version is a fully functional Premium version that you can use for 14 months after installation, but you cannot restore or open data files from previous versions with it. If you have already installed a Trial version, the date you installed it will count toward this 14-month limit. You can install only one version of Simply Accounting 2010 on your computer. If you are using the Pro version or a Trial version and you want to install the Student Premium version, you must first completely uninstall the Pro or Trial version from the Control Panel in Windows (refer to Appendix A, page A–17). After you use a data set with the Student version, this data set will expire after 14 months as well. You must then use a regular retail licensed version of the program to access that data.

None of the data files were created with a Student or Trial version, so the data itself will not expire until you have used the data with a Student version for 14 months.

If you see a message that the program has expired when you try to install it or to open a data set, and you have not yet used the program for 14 months, you should refer to page A-17 and ask your instructor for assistance.

Please refer to Appendix A in this text for detailed instructions on downloading, installing and activating or registering your Student version of Simply Accounting.

Earlier Versions

If you try to access the data files with earlier versions of Simply Accounting (2009 and earlier), Simply Accounting displays an error message. In this case, you should download and install the Student version. Refer to Appendix A, page A–10, for information on downloading and installing the Student version.

Later Versions

Although the data files can be used with later versions of the software, you may see changes in screens, keystrokes and payroll tax amounts. Before you open a data file with a later version, the Simply Accounting conversion wizard will update the data file to match the program version you are using. Always refer to the manuals and update notices for later versions. Once the file has been updated, you will no longer be able to use it with the earlier version or release, unless you reinstall the data files from the Student DVD.

We recommend that you turn off the Automatic Updates feature so that you do not update your program beyond Release A until you have finished working with the data files in the text. Refer to Appendix A, page A–10, for information on automatic updates. Automatic updates are not available for the Student version.

Enterprise Version

This text can be used with the Enterprise version of Simply Accounting. All the features covered in the text are available in the Enterprise version, though you may see small variations in the screens. The Enterprise version includes features that are not available in the Premium version — these advanced features are not covered in this text. If you are using the Enterprise version, the Simply Accounting data conversion wizard will convert the Premium data files when you open them or restore them. Because the DVD files remain unchanged, you can install and use the same files later using the Premium version.

Working Through the Applications

Keystroke Instruction Style

We have incorporated different paragraph styles for different kinds of statements in the text to help you identify the instructions that you must follow to complete the transactions correctly and see the screens that we present. These different styles are illustrated below:

Press   `enter` or **press** the **Add button** to start the Add Account wizard. (Keystroke command line — command word is in bold and the object of the command, what you press, is in colour. Lines are indented and spaced apart. Additional text or information for the line is shown in plain text.)

Type   West Carbide Tools (net 30)   (Command line with text you type in a special font.)

Or you can click the Comment field to advance the cursor. (Alternative keystroke sequence that you may want to use later. Paragraph is indented in block style and plain text style is used.)

Regular text is presented in normal paragraphs like this one. **Key words** are shown in colour to make it easy to identify the topics covered in the text. Names of icons, fields, text and tool buttons that you will see on-screen in the program have all initial letters capitalized in our text (for example, Adjust A Previously Posted Invoice tool or Display A Reminder If Exchange Rate Is One Day Old). Account names included in regular text paragraphs are italicized (for example, *Revenue from Sales* or *Cost of Goods Sold*).

The symbol we introduced in the previous edition indicates that you must return to the source documents because no keystroke instructions are included for the next transaction or group of transactions. For example,

 Enter   the **next sale transaction**.

☑ **Cheque Copy #171**   **Dated Aug. 2/12**

122   To Fundy Gift House... (Source document that you should enter using Simply Accounting. The ✓ in the check box indicates that keystroke instructions are provided. The number in colour below the check box shows the starting page for these instructions, page 122.)

☐ **Memo #14**   **Dated Aug. 9/12**

From Owner... (Source document that you should enter on your own using Simply Accounting. No keystroke instructions are provided — the check box is empty).

The text also uses Notes and Warnings that contain additional important information and cautions.

Order of Applications

Setup applications are introduced early in the text. Advanced users should have no difficulty working through the applications in the order given and may even choose to skip some applications. However, at a minimum, we recommend working through all keystroke transactions (the ones with a ✓ beside them) so that you become familiar with all the journals before starting the more comprehensive applications.

There are alternatives if the text is used at introductory and advanced levels for different courses. In this case, students can complete the General, basic Payables, basic Receivables, Payroll and Inventory transaction applications (Chapters 3, 5, 6, 8 and 10) in the introductory course and the remaining chapters later. Chapters 11 and 12 may be completed at any time after Chapter 6 because these chapters do not have payroll or inventory transactions. Students can also complete the transactions for the four setup applications separately from setting up these data files because we provide backup data files for these setup chapters as well (except Stratford Country Inn, Chapter 17). Chapters may also be completed in a different sequence, outlined below and on the following page.

1. Read and work through the two Getting Started chapters in Part One.
2A. Complete the ledger applications in order: Missoni Marbleworks (General), Chai Tea Room (basic Payables), Air Care Services (basic Receivables), Helena's Academy (Payroll), Adrienne Aesthetics (Inventory), Andersson Chiropractic Clinic and Maple Leaf Rags (advanced features of the first three ledgers) and Truman Tires* (Division or Project).
2B. (Premium version only) Complete the Part Three applications in any order: Flabuless Fitness — Time & Billing and Able & Associates (Departmental Accounting).
3. Complete the account reconciliation (Tesses Tresses) and budgeting (Village Galleries) applications.
4. Complete the four setup applications in order: Toss for Tots (General), Dorfmann Design (three ledgers), Lime Light Laundry (adding the Payroll ledger) and Flabuless Fitness (six ledgers).
5. Complete the Stratford Country Inn setup application with realistic source documents. Users may want to attempt this setup with the help of the setup wizard from the Setup menu in the Home window.
6. Complete the cash-basis accounting application in Appendix I at any time after Chapter 6.

* Truman Tires (Division Ledger, Chapter 13) may be completed after all other chapters because it does not introduce keystrokes required for any other application.

This order is shown graphically in the chart on the following page:

AN ALTERNATIVE SEQUENCE FOR WORKING THROUGH THE APPLICATIONS

Getting
Started

Ledger
Applications

Advanced Features

Setup
Applications

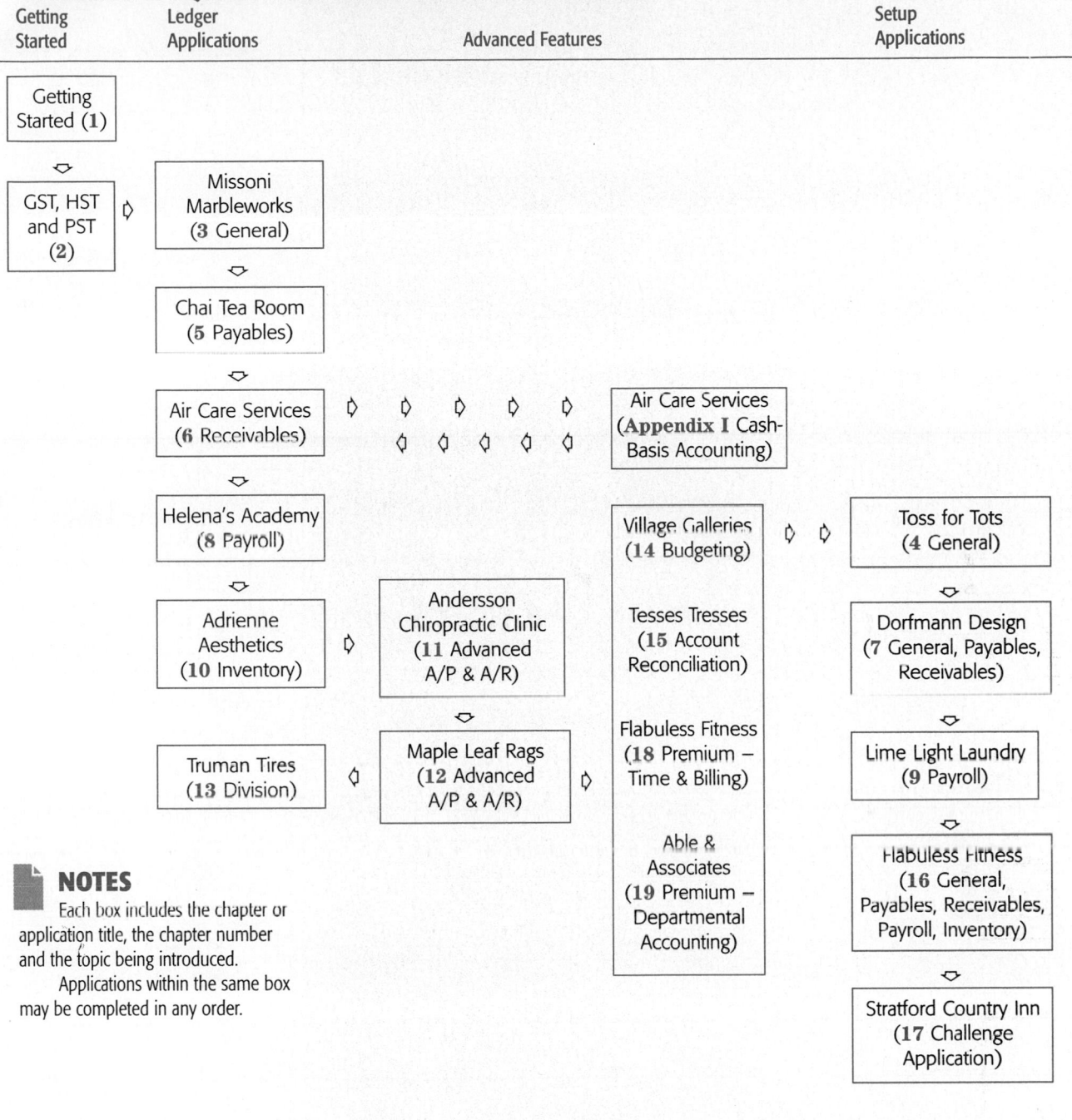

NOTES

Each box includes the chapter or application title, the chapter number and the topic being introduced.

Applications within the same box may be completed in any order.

ACKNOWLEDGMENTS

How can I thank thee? I cannot begin to count the ways I need to thank the many individuals who play such an important and often silent role in bringing this project to completion — on time with high standards of quality. But I must try.

Over the past twenty-three years, I have developed a large network of support at Pearson Education and Sage. Living within an easy drive of the Pearson offices and attending numerous Sage conferences has put faces on this network map of names, so that even though both organizations are in a constant state of flux with people assuming different roles, there are always some familiar friendly faces. If fact, I had worked with two people on this year's team more than a decade ago, in the Addison Wesley era, when their roles were different. It has been a pleasure to renew these relationships with Madhu Ranadive and Don Thompson. Both have offered a large and needed measure of stability and support in an uncertain environment.

It has also been reassuring to know that Nicole Lukach and Gary Bennett are sincere in their generous offers to jump in if bigger issues arise.

Sarah Lukaweski, also in a new role, was again central to the project, efficiently and effectively coordinating the details of the production with internal and freelance team members.

I also appreciate the work completed by Norbert Mantik, who prepared the Student DVD, and his quiet, "no problem" attitude to my needs and requests. Michael Kelley has again spent several hours sorting out the bugs of creating print-ready documents. One day we may get these bugs sorted out, but in the meantime, we seem to have an annual date to keep trying.

I am pleased once again with the cover Anthony Leung designed that creatively links the text to the latest version of the Simply Accounting software.

Jim Collins at Sage continues to be a mainstay. Jim is a very busy person, yet he allows me to rely heavily on his professional and friendly assistance to resolve software problems. Thank you, Jim.

Cas Shields, executive marketing manager, has been involved with this book in some way since the early days. Her customer contacts offer new challenges as we try to meet increasing customer demands and expectations, but they also ensure that meeting these needs will be rewarded.

Although I am quite particular about accuracy of fact and content, I easily overlook other details and create stylistic or formatting inconsistencies. Several people have been integral in locating and correcting these errors, and I rely on them heavily to do so. Efren Barrato again completed the technical check of all the instructions and numbers, and did an excellent job of finding the little, and some not-so-little, things I missed. In addition, Heather Sangster and her team at Strong Finish, who copy edited and proofread the text, further added to the quality and accuracy. These extra sets of eyes check this text in painstaking detail. Of course, any remaining errors are my responsibility, but their effort greatly increases my confidence.

Many others at Pearson Education and Sage Software's customer support have provided essential telephone technical support that helped to keep me working on schedule. Several federal and provincial Ministry of Finance personnel, whose names I do not know, also provided valuable and timely information about proposed tax changes in Ontario and British Columbia long before these taxes were officially enacted and implemented and many were satisfied to answer my questions with a "do not know yet" response. The additional assistance from these sources saved valuable research time and provided a degree of confidence that the information in the text would be accurate.

And, finally, direct feedback from users continues to be important. The errors they report and their questions or problems all spark a problem-solving process that inspires changes to improve the book.

Each year the book gets a little bit bigger — two chapter-sized appendices were added to the Student DVD this year — so there is more for everyone to do, on this and their many other projects. Yet no extra time has been added to the eight months we have to finish it all. So thank you to everyone for helping to meet all the deadlines that seemed so impossible just a short while ago, and making that journey a more pleasant one.

Part 1
Getting Started

CHAPTER ONE

Getting Started

OBJECTIVES

After completing this chapter, you should be able to

- ■ *access* the Simply Accounting program
- ■ *open* a working copy to access the data files for a business
- ■ *restore* backup files to access data files for a business
- ■ *understand* Simply Accounting's help features
- ■ *save* your work
- ■ *back up* your data files
- ■ *finish* your session
- ■ *change* default date format settings

GETTING STARTED

Data Files and Abbreviations

The applications in this workbook were prepared using Windows Vista, XP and 7 versions and the Simply Accounting Premium 2010 and Simply Accounting Pro 2010 (Release A) software packages produced by Sage Software. You will be unable to open the data files with Simply 2009 or earlier versions. Later releases and versions of the software use later income tax tables and may have changes in screens or keystrokes. If you have a version other than 2010 Release A, you can download and install the Simply Accounting by Sage 2010 – Student Version (Release A) program to work through the applications. Refer to Appendix A, page A–10, if you are installing the Student version — also a Premium version.

The instructions in this workbook have been written for a stand-alone PC, with a CD/DVD disk drive and a hard disk drive with Windows correctly installed. Your printer(s) should be installed and accessible through the Windows program. Refer to Windows Help and manuals for assistance with these procedures.

This workbook reflects the author's approach to working with Simply Accounting. There are alternative approaches to setting up company accounts and to working with the software. Refer to Simply Accounting and Windows Help and manuals for further details.

DATA APPLICATION FILE NAMES AND LOCATIONS (All folders and files are located in C:\SimData10\)

Company	Full File Installation	Backup File Installation	Chapter
Getting started	Start\start.SAI	start1.CAB	1
Missoni Marbleworks	Missoni\missoni.SAI	missoni1.CAB	3
Toss for Tots	Template\skeleton.SAI (Setup\toss1.CAB)	skeleton1.CAB (Setup\toss1.CAB)	4
Chai Tea Room	Chai\chai.SAI	chai1.CAB	5
Air Care Services	Aircare\aircare.SAI	aircare1.CAB	6
Dorfmann Design	Setup\dorfman1.CAB	Setup\dorfman1.CAB	7
Helena's Academy	Helena\helena.SAI	helena1.CAB	8
Lime Light Laundry	Limelite\limelite.SAI	limelite1.CAB	9
Adrienne Aesthetics	Adrienne\adrienne.SAI	adrienne1.CAB	10
Andersson Chiropractic Clinic	Anderson\anderson.SAI	anderson1.CAB	11
Maple Leaf Rags	Maple\maple.SAI	maple1.CAB	12
Truman Tires	Truman\truman.SAI	truman1.CAB	13
Village Galleries	Village\village.SAI	village1.CAB	14
Tesses Tresses	Tess\tess.SAI	tess1.CAB	15
Flabuless Fitness	Setup\flab-apr1.CAB	Setup\flab-apr1.CAB	16
	Setup\flab-may1.CAB	Setup\flab-may1.CAB	16
	Setup\flab-jun1.CAB	Setup\flab-jun1.CAB	16
Stratford Country Inn	user setup	user setup	17
Flabuless Fitness (Prem.)	Time\flab-time.SAI	flab-time1.CAB	18
Able & Associates Inc. (Prem.)	Able\able.SAI	able1.CAB	19
Air Care Services (Cash-Basis)	Cash\air-cash.sai	cash1.CAD	Appendix I

The applications increase in complexity. Each one introduces new ledgers, setups or features as shown in the following chart.

DATA APPLICATION	LEDGER USED						OTHER
	GL	AP	AR	PAY	INV	DIV	
Missoni Marbleworks	*						
Toss for Tots	*						2
Chai Tea Room	*	*					
Air Care Services (Chapter 6)	*	*	*				3
Dorfmann Design	*	*	*				2, 3
Helena's Academy	*	*	*	*			
Lime Light Laundry	*	*	*	*			2
Adrienne Aesthetics	*	*	*	*	*		3
Andersson Chiropractic Clinic	*	*	*				
Maple Leaf Rags	*	*	*				3, 4, 7
Truman Tires	*	*	*	*	*	*	3, 7
Village Galleries	*	*	*	*	*		3, 5, 7
Tesses Tresses	*	*	*		*		6
Flabuless Fitness (Chapter 16)	*	*	*	*	*		2, 3, 4, 7
Stratford Country Inn	*	*	*	*			1, 3, 7, 8
Flabuless Fitness (Chapter 18)	*	*	*	*	*		PREMIUM 1
Able & Associates Inc.	*	*	*	*	*		PREMIUM 2
Air Care Services (Appendix I)	*	*	*				9

LEDGERS

GL	= General Ledger	PAY	= Payroll
AP	= Accounts Payable	INV	= Inventory
AR	= Accounts Receivable	DIV	= Division or Project Allocations

Other:

1 All realistic source documents (most chapters have some realistic source documents)

2 Setup application with keystrokes	5 Budgeting	8 Setup application without keystrokes
3 Credit cards	6 Account reconciliation	9 Cash-basis accounting
4 Internet links	7 Foreign currency transactions	

PREMIUM 1 Time & Billing; Build from Bill of Materials; Inventory locations (Premium version only)

PREMIUM 2 Departmental Accounting (Premium version only)

NOTES
For users who do not want to complete their own setups, additional backup files are provided for Toss, Dorfmann, Lime Light Laundry and Flabuless Fitness in the Setup folder.

NOTES
The applications in Chapters 1 through 17 can be completed with both the Pro and the Premium versions. For the applications in Chapters 18 and 19, you must use the Premium version.

The Stratford Country Inn file is not set up in advance for you. You must create that file on your own.

The Student DVD also includes data files for cash-basis accounting in Appendix I (Cash folder or cash1.CAB backup file) and a Bank folder with backup data files for bank reconciliation in Chapter 15 and Review Case 8 for Chapter 16 in Appendix E, and for online banking in Appendix K (Appendices E, I and K are also on the Student DVD as PDF files.)

The Simply Accounting Program

Simply Accounting is an integrated accounting program with many features that are suitable for small- and medium-sized businesses. It includes several ledgers and journals that work together so that data entered in one part of the program will be linked and available in other parts of the program. Thus ledgers are automatically updated from journal entries, and reports always include the most recent transactions and ledger changes. A business can use one or more of the accounting modules: General, Payables, Receivables, Payroll, Inventory, Project and, for the Premium and Enterprise versions, Time & Billing. You need to set up only the features you use. Thus, if payroll is not used, there is no need to set up the Payroll module, and it can be hidden from view. A more complete description of the program and its features is presented in Chapter 16, pages 614–615.

Simply Accounting Program Components

When you select the Typical Installation option, several components will be installed:

- **Simply Accounting Program**: the Simply Accounting software you will need to perform the accounting transactions for your company. It will be placed in the main Simply Accounting Premium 2010 folder in the Program Files folder or the folder location you selected.
- **Samples**: complete company records for a sample company — Universal Construction. They will be placed in a folder called Samdata under Documents and Settings\All Users\Documents\Simply.
- **Templates**: predefined charts of accounts and settings for a large number of business types. These files will be stored in a folder called Template under Simply Accounting Premium 2010. Two starter files with only charts of accounts also appear in this folder.
- **Crystal Reports Print Engine**, **Forms** and **Management Reports**: a variety of commonly used business forms and reports that you can customize to suit your own business needs as well as the program to access and print them. They will be placed in a folder under Simply Accounting Premium 2010 called Forms.
- **Customizable Forms** and **Microsoft Office Documents**: a variety of documents designed for integrated use with Simply Accounting. They will be placed in a Reports folder under Simply Accounting Premium 2010.
- **New Business Guide**: a number of checklists showing the steps for setting up a new business, customized for a variety of business types in different provinces. This guide includes addresses and phone numbers as well as Web addresses that you can access for further information.
- **Manuals** & **Tutorials**: documentation and videos to help you learn how to use Simply Accounting.

The Student Data DVD

Before you begin the applications, you must copy the data to your hard disk drive. The Student DVD has both full data files and Simply Accounting backup files. The full data files are large and may take a long time to install, so we provide backup files for supplementary data files (refer to page xi) and for Pro users. Furthermore, you cannot work from CD or DVD files because they are read-only files. Keep the DVD in a safe place in case you need to start over from the original files. The following instructions will copy all the files to your hard disk drive and create the necessary folders.

Installing Your Data

The Student DVD contains Pro and Premium versions of the data files and several supplementary files for the book. It also has programs that will automatically copy the data to a new SimData10 folder on your hard drive (drive C:). If you want to use a different location for your data files, proceed to page 6.

You must work with the correct version of the data set. If you are working with the Pro version, install the Pro data files — you cannot open Premium version files. If you are working with the Premium (or Student) version, install the Premium data files.

If you are using the **Pro version**, refer to sidebar notes throughout the text for the differences between the Pro 2010 and Premium 2010 versions.

Insert   the **Student DVD** into your CD/DVD drive. The homepage appears:

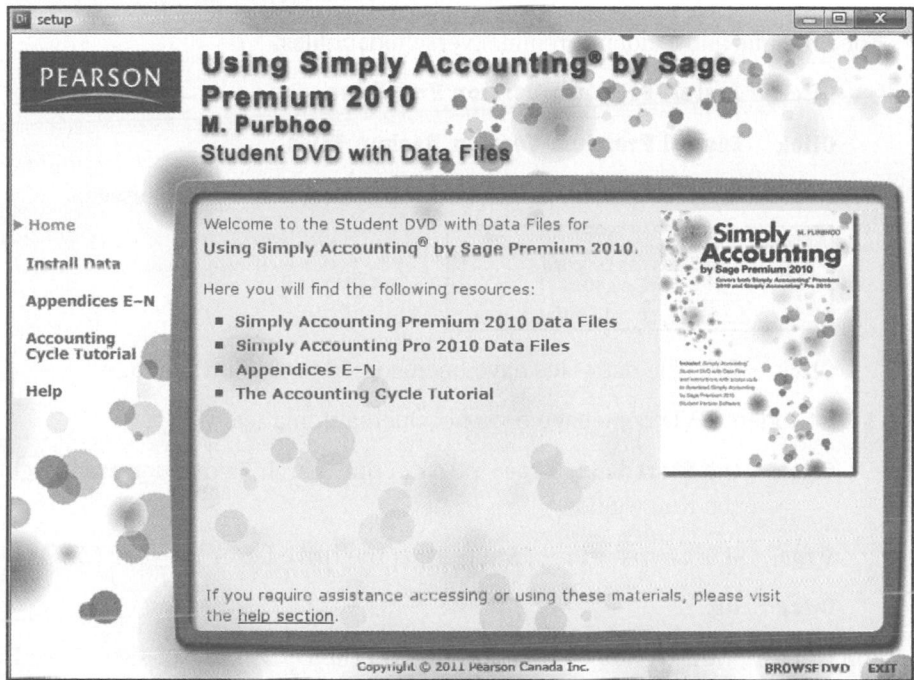

This page shows your options for installing data files and viewing the additional resources and allows you to access these options from the left-hand side pane.

Click   **Install Data** to see your data installation options:

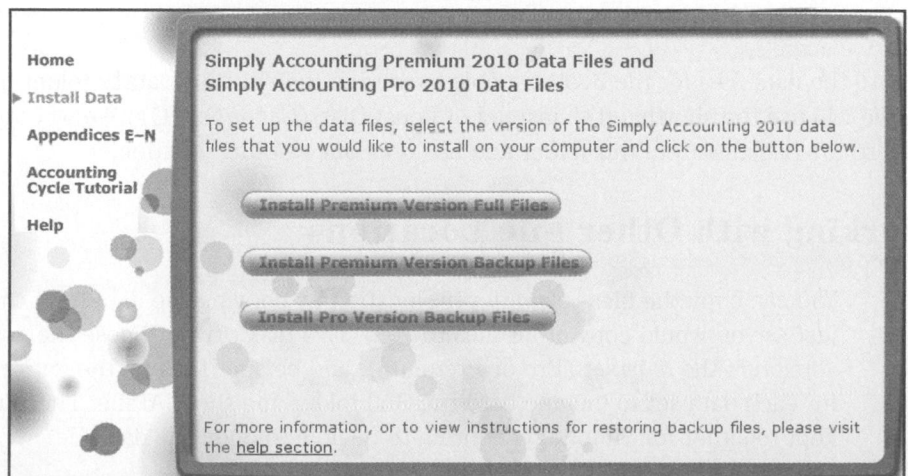

All data installation options will create the SimData10 folder on your hard drive Local Disk C: or (OS) C:, and all files will be placed in this new folder.

⚠ WARNING!
Unless you have experience working with Windows folders, we recommend using the autoinstall option on the Student DVD to install your data set.

📄 NOTES
If you are working with the Enterprise version, you should install the Premium version files. Your program will automatically upgrade the files to the Enterprise version when you open or restore them.

📄 NOTES
If the Student DVD does not start automatically, open your Computer or Windows Explorer window. Right-click the DVD and click Explore. Double click Setup.exe to run the DVD.
  Clicking Browse DVD on the DVD homepage (in the lower right-hand corner before Exit) will open the DVD directory and list all the files on the Student DVD.

📄 NOTES
The Student DVD includes an appendix that reviews accounting principles and an interactive Accounting Tutorial that introduces basic accounting procedures for manual accounting.

📄 NOTES
If you need to reinstall the data files, the new installation will overwrite (replace) the previous files. If you want to keep the first set of data files, you can rename the folder to SimData10-old before you install the data files again.

The **Install Premium Version Full Files** option (~550 MBytes) will copy folders and files for each company data set in the primary keystroke chapters. In addition, you will have backup files for chapters that have options such as completing only the bank reconciliation or only source transactions and omitting the setup for a new company. This installation requires substantially more time for copying the files.

The **Install Premium Version Backup Files** option (~60 Mbytes) will install backup files for all the applications in the text. When you restore these with Simply Accounting, the default location will be the same as that for the Full File Installation option. If you are working on a slower computer, we recommend this option.

The **Install Pro Version Backup Files** option will install backup files for all applications for Pro users. Pro version files are provided only in backup format.

Instructions for restoring backup files are provided on page 20.

Click   **Install Pro Version Backup Files** to copy the data set for Pro 2010.

For Premium and Student Premium version data files,

Click   **Install Premium Version Full Files**, or

Click   **Install Premium Version Backup Files**.

When all the files have been copied, you will see the following message:

Click   **OK**. The data files have been copied to C:\SimData10.

If the Student DVD homepage does not open automatically,

Click   the **Start icon**. **Type**   run   in the Search field and **press** (enter) to open the Run window.

Type   d:\start.exe   (where D: is the drive letter for your CD/DVD drive.)

Click   **OK**.

You can also view the supplementary files on the DVD. You can save these PDF files to your hard drive or print them if you want.

Click   **Appendices E–N** and then **click** the **file** you want.

Close   the **PDF file** when you have finished viewing or printing it.

Click   **Exit** to close the Student DVD window.

All the data files for the book are now located in the new SimData10 folder in drive C:. We will use the shorthand C: instead of Local Disk (C): or OS (C):. We will open and restore the backups from this folder and use it as our working data folder.

Working with Other File Locations

You can copy the files to a different location by copying the data from the DVD just as you would copy other files to your hard disk drive. Choose the correct version of the data set (Pro or Premium), and be sure to copy the entire folder for each data set to include both the SAJ folder and the .SAI file. These must be kept together for Simply Accounting to be able to open the data file.

You cannot open a Simply Accounting data file directly from a CD or DVD, but you can restore a Simply Accounting backup file from a CD or DVD. You must save the file on your hard disk drive before you can work with the data.

You can also work on a removable USB drive in Simply Accounting because this is a rewritable medium.

Starting Simply Accounting

From your Windows desktop, if you are using the Windows Vista view,

Click   **Start** 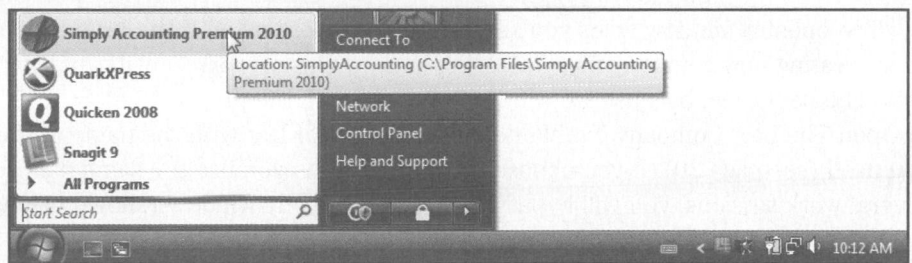 (on the task bar) so the pop-up menu appears.

If you have opened the program recently, its name may be pinned to the shortcuts list above All Programs:

In this case, you can click Simply Accounting Premium 2010. Otherwise,

Point   **to All Programs**.

Point   **to Simply Accounting Premium 2010** and **click Simply Accounting Premium 2010** as shown in the following screen:

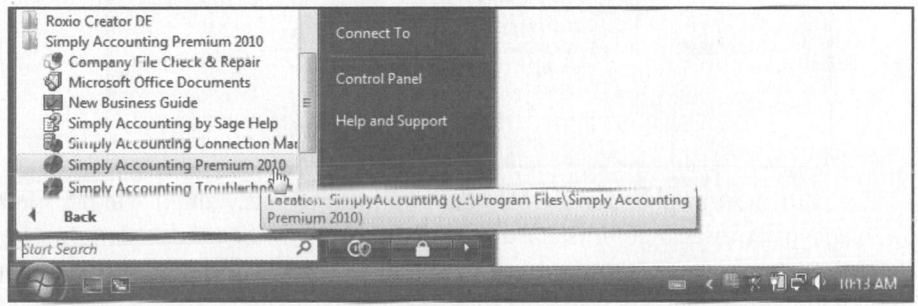

Click   **Simply Accounting Premium 2010** from the submenu.

If you are using the **Classic Windows view**, click Start 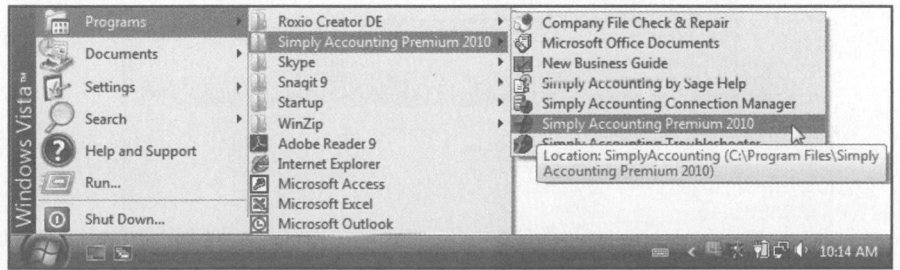 and point to Programs. Then point to Simply Accounting Premium 2010 and click Simply Accounting Premium 2010 as illustrated in the screen that follows:

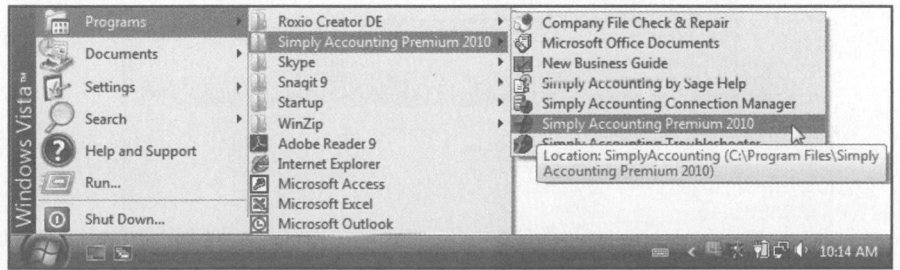

You will open the registration screen the first time you use the program. Otherwise, you will see the Simply Accounting Select Company screen (on the following page).

If you have not yet registered the program, refer to Appendix A, pages A-6–A-9 in the text. Until you register and activate the program, you will be allowed to use the program only for a limited time. The Student version must be activated before you can use it. Refer to Appendix A, pages A-15–A-17.

If you are restoring the backup file, refer to page 20 for instructions.

PRO VERSION

The desktop shortcut is labelled Simply Accounting Pro 2010.

You will point to Simply Accounting Pro 2010 in the Programs list and then choose Simply Accounting Pro 2010 to open the Select Company Welcome screen.

NOTES

If you added a desktop shortcut when you installed the program, you can double click to open the Simply Accounting program.

WARNING!

You will be allowed to use the program only for a limited time before entering the registration validation codes.

Remember to activate Payroll as well. Refer to Appendix A in this text. You must have a payroll ID code in order to use the Payroll features of the program.

You must register the Student version before you can use it, but you will not need to activate payroll.

NOTES

If you are restoring backup files, refer to the instructions on page 20.

Opening a Data File

You will now see the Simply Accounting Select Company Welcome screen:

The opening window gives you several options: working with the sample company files, creating new company files, restoring backup files or working with existing data files. The next time, because we will have worked with the program before, the option to Open The Last Company You Worked On will appear last with the name of the file you used (see page 20). If you choose this option when you use the same data set for several work sessions, you will bypass the Open Company window (shown below).

Click Select An Existing Company. Click OK.

The Simply Accounting – Open Company window appears next:

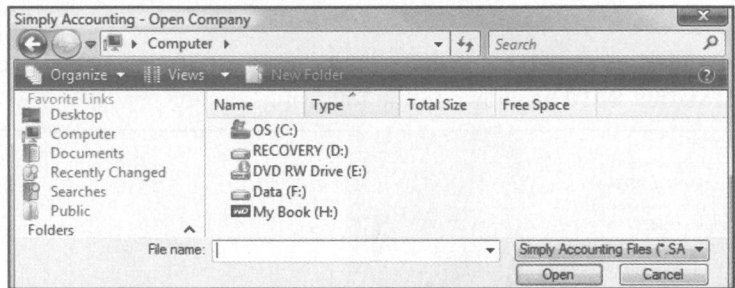

The path shown will be for the file you used most recently and it will be selected for you to accept or to change. If this is the first time you are opening a data file, your path will be determined by your program and system settings. Therefore, the file name you see on your screen may be different from the ones we show.

Click Computer in the list of Favorite Links in the left pane or in the file path field on top to open the screen we show.

Click OS (C:) or the name for the local hard disk drive C: on your computer and **click Open** to list the folders on this drive:

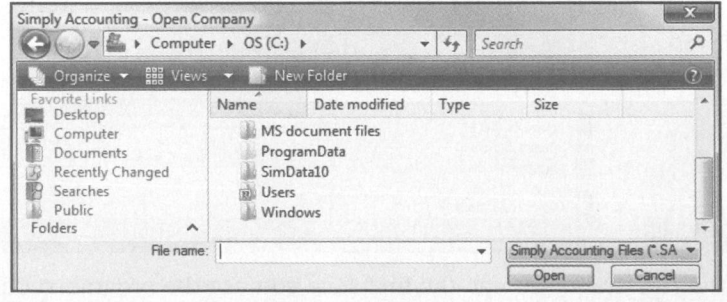

Click SimData10. (Click the SimData10 folder icon if your viewing mode is icons.) Then **click Open** to see the files you installed from the DVD Data Disk:

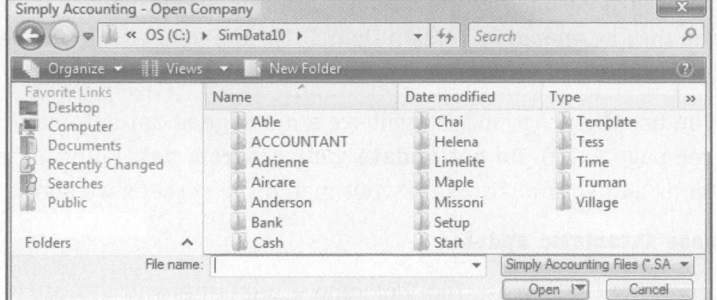

Click **Start** (or its folder icon) and then **click Open** to see the files we need:

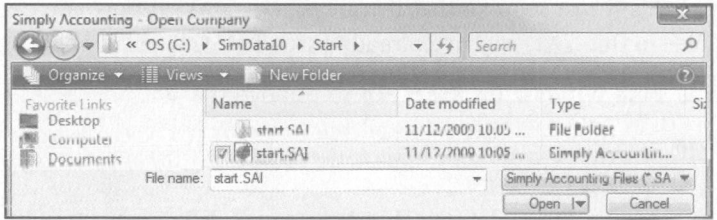

You can gain access to the company records only from the *.**SAI** file. Simply Accounting recognizes this file extension as a Simply Accounting format. The remaining data files for the company are in the SAJ folder. Both the .SAI file and the SAJ folder that are part of the data set must be located in the same folder. The complete data path (OS (C:)>SimData10>Start) is added to the path field near the top of the screen.

Click **start** (or the start icon 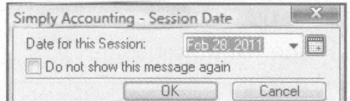), or click **start.SAI** (if you show file extensions) to select it and add it to the File Name field as shown:

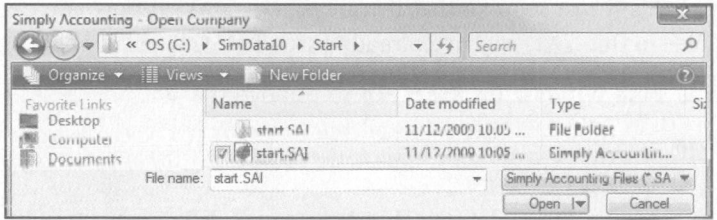

Click **Open** to see the session date screen:

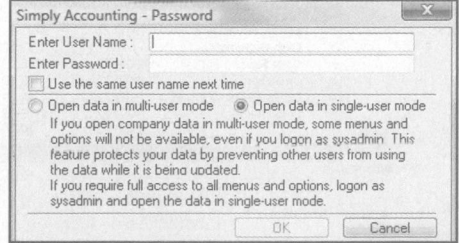

Click **OK** to open the Home window.

If passwords have been set up for the file, you will see this password entry screen before the session date window:

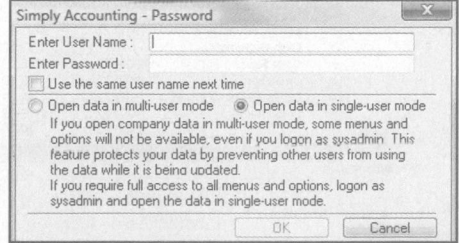

Ask your instructor or site administrator for the name and password to use. Enter your user name and password. Open the file in Single-User Mode. Click OK to open the session date screen. Refer to Chapter 16, page 681, and Appendix H on the Student DVD.

PRO VERSION
pro The first folder on the list is ACCOUNTANT. Refer to page 20 for instructions on restoring backup files.

WARNING!
If you are not showing file extensions, you will click start. Do not click the Start.SAJ folder.

NOTES
We have selected to add check boxes to file and folder names in the Computer windows. You may not see these check boxes.

NOTES
The session date is explained in Chapter 3, where you will also learn how to change the session date.
The session date drop-down list includes the current session date, the end of the fiscal period and the start of the next fiscal period. The list for any date field includes the dates commonly selected.

NOTES
We have not set passwords for any data files in this text, but your site administrator for the network may have done so. Refer to Appendix D for more about passwords.

PRO VERSION
pro You will see an additional message about upgrading to the Premium version of Simply Accounting.

NOTES
If your update is later than Release A, you can use the Student Premium Version Release A program that comes with the text.

NOTES
You can download updates periodically (from the Help menu) when you have finished working through the applications in this text.

NOTES
The contents of the Getting Started screen will change to match the industry or business type of your company data set.

PRO VERSION
The terms Customers and Vendors will replace Clients and Suppliers.

Title bar

Menu bar

Tool/Search bar

Change View command

Open module

Modules pane

Ledger icon

Clients (Customers list)

Tasks panes

Journal activity icons

Reports pane

Shortcuts pane

General Journal shortcut

Related tasks pane

Recent reports list

Status bar

If you see a screen advising that the data has been updated to a new file format, your program may be an earlier version than 2010, and you will be unable to open the data file.

The first time you use the program, you will see a message about automatic program updates (see page A-10). **Do not update your program yet.** Later updates will download later versions and your answers may not match the screens we show.

Do not choose automatic updates.

The Simply Accounting Getting Started Welcome screen opens:

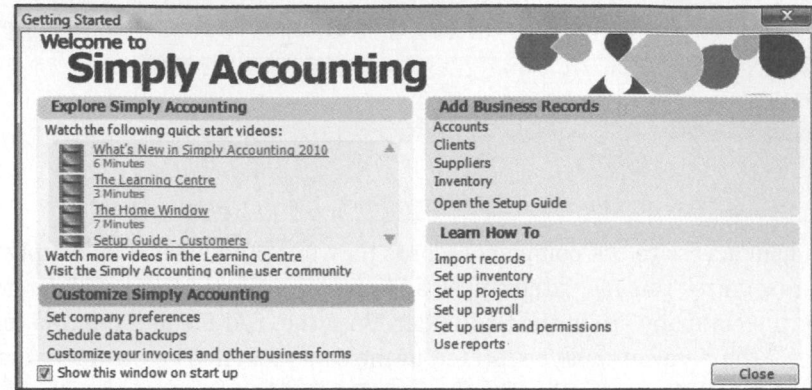

This screen outlines various options for getting assistance with the program. These include brief video tutorials and instructions for some basic steps you might need when setting up data files for a new company. You will see this screen each time you open a data file in Simply Accounting 2010, unless you have turned it off. After reading the options, you can close this screen now so that it will not appear each time you open this file. For other data files in this text, we have already turned off the selection.

Click **Show This Window On Start Up** to remove the ✓.

Click **Close** to continue.

Simply Accounting Window (Enhanced View)

The main Simply Accounting Home window should now be open.
The Receivables module window is the default Home window:

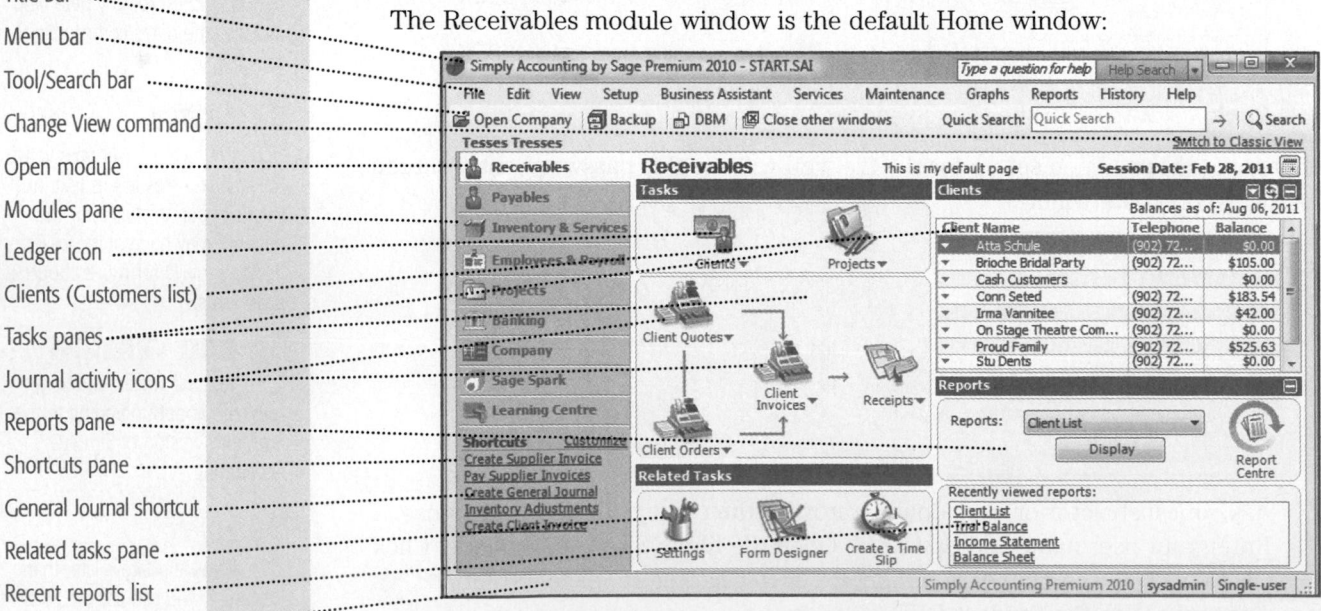

The **title bar** is at the top of the Home window, and it contains the program name, Simply Accounting by Sage Premium 2010, the file name, START.SAI, the Help/Search field, Control Menu icon and the size buttons. The **main menu bar** comes next with the **tool bar** below. Tool buttons provide quick access to commonly used menu items and the **search** function. The Search field enables you to look up information in any journal or ledger. Different Simply Accounting windows have different buttons on the tool bar. Below the tool bar, you will find the command to **Switch To Classic View** (see page 13).

The Home window is divided into several panes. The **Modules pane** lists all the modules available for this company data set. The open module — Receivables in this illustration — has a lighter background. The Receivables module is the default Home window, but you can choose any module as the Home window. Activities for the module are represented by separate icons. The Modules pane also provides access to the **Learning Centre**. To access a function or activity, click the related icon.

Below the list of modules, the **Shortcuts pane** allows one-click access to as many as 10 different tasks and activities that you set up or customize for each user.

The next column has all the icons you need to complete the activities for the module. The **upper Tasks pane** has the **ledger icon** that allows you to create and modify customer records from the Customers (Clients) window and Project records in the Projects window. The **lower Tasks pane** has the icons for **journal activities** or **transactions**. Use these icons to enter the accounting transactions in this text. Clicking the icon opens the journal directly for that type of transaction.

In the Premium version, the icon labels change to suit the type of company. For the service company illustrated here, the ledger icon is labelled Clients.

Many ledger and journal icons have a **shortcuts drop-down list arrow**. Clicking an entry in an icon shortcuts list will access the activity directly and bypass the main task window. For example, you can begin adjusting an invoice to make a correction if an entry was posted in error, bypassing the first step of opening the journal.

> **Click**   the **shortcuts drop-down list arrow for Client Invoices** ⬇ :

> **Click**   some **other shortcuts list arrows** to see the choices.

Below the ledger and journal icons, you will find the **Related Tasks pane**. From the icons in this pane, you can perform other ledger-related activities such as entering settings for the open ledger.

The right-hand column also has three different panes. The first one has a **list of ledger accounts** for the selected module. For the Receivables module, the list shows clients or customers with the phone number and outstanding balance. The Payables ledger will show the list of suppliers or vendors. You can hide the extra details.

Below the list of customers or clients, the **Reports pane** allows quick access to all reports for the ledger from the **Reports drop-down list** and to the **Report Centre**, from which you can access all reports. Reports that you displayed most recently are added to the list in the **Recently Viewed Reports** section. Clicking a report in this list will open the last report you viewed with the report options you selected most recently.

The **status bar** appears last. In the Enhanced View, the status bar shows the program name and version as well as the user's name.

To work with another module, you can click the module you want from the list in the Modules pane.

> **Click**   **Employees & Payroll** in the Modules pane.

This module now becomes the Home window, so its icons for ledger and journal activities are displayed.

PRO VERSION
pro The program name in the title bar is Simply Accounting by Sage Pro 2010. You will not see the Create A Time Slip icon (Related Tasks pane).

NOTES
Appendix B shows a complete chart of alternative terms used in Simply Accounting for different types of industries.

PRO VERSION
pro Icon labels do not change. Customers will replace the Clients label for the ledger icon and list. Sales Invoices replaces Client Invoices.

NOTES
You can hide the telephone number and Balance columns for increased security.

NOTES
In other windows, the status bar describes the purpose of the icon or field that has the pointer.

The ledger icon is now labelled Employees as shown:

In this module, the quill pen symbol 🖋 shows that the Payroll Ledger is not set up — the history is not finished. When ledgers are not finished, you can add and change historical data. When you create new company data files, all ledgers have this symbol.

Your Missoni Home window (in Chapter 3) will show the Company Module with access only to the General Ledger and journals — Chart of Accounts and General Journal. Icons for unused features and ledgers that are not set up will be hidden.

Open and close some of the other module windows to see their activity icons.

Simply Accounting on the Windows Desktop

Click   **Receivables** in the Modules pane list.

Click   **Create General Journal** in the Shortcuts pane list. This will open the General Journal.

Click   the **Edit menu**. Your desktop should now look like the one that follows:

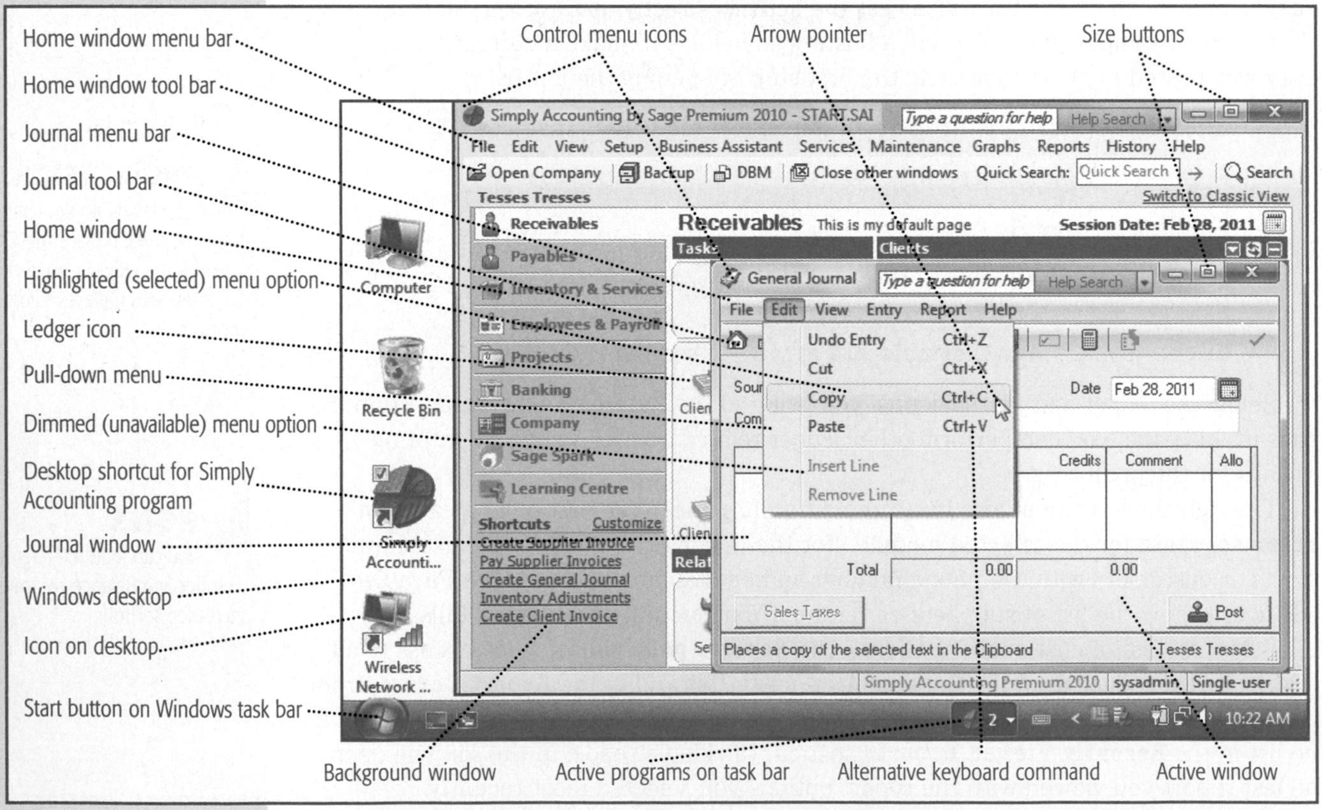

Home window menu bar ·
Home window tool bar ·
Journal menu bar ·
Journal tool bar ·
Home window ·
Highlighted (selected) menu option ·
Ledger icon ·
Pull-down menu ·
Dimmed (unavailable) menu option ·
Desktop shortcut for Simply Accounting program ·
Journal window ·
Windows desktop ·
Icon on desktop ·
Start button on Windows task bar ·

Control menu icons   Arrow pointer   Size buttons

Background window   Active programs on task bar   Alternative keyboard command   Active window

If you need an explanation of terms in this illustration, please refer to Appendix B.

Click   ☒ to close the journal window and return to the Home window.

NOTES

Many Simply Accounting windows include a Home window tool 🏠 that brings the Home window to the front without closing the other windows.

NOTES

We used Windows Vista to illustrate this desktop. If you have a different version of Windows or use different Windows settings, your desktop may look different from the one we show.

Simply Accounting Classic View Home Window

Throughout this text, we will work from the Enhanced view Home window. However, we will provide alternate instructions for using the Classic view in sidebar notes.

Click   **Switch To Classic View** to change the Home window:

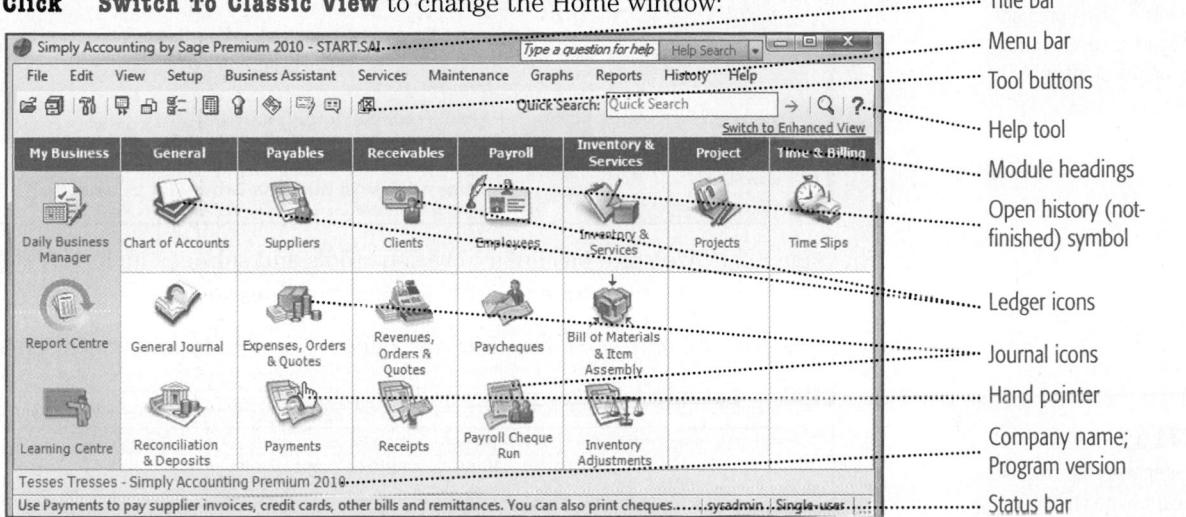

Title bar
Menu bar
Tool buttons
Help tool
Module headings
Open history (not-finished) symbol
Ledger icons
Journal icons
Hand pointer
Company name; Program version
Status bar

The tool bar in the Classic view has more items than in the Enhanced view. The **ledger** or module names come next with their respective icons filling up the major part of the window. The ledgers in the top row are below the ledger or module name, and the **journal icons** are under their respective ledgers in the last two icon rows of the window. All journals and ledgers can be accessed from the icons in this single Classic view Home window. Below the journal icons are two more information lines: the company name and the **status bar**. In this example, the status bar describes the purpose of the Payments Journal because the pointer is on the Payments icon.

The icons in the **My Business tab** allow quick access to the Daily Business Manager, Report Centre and Learning Centre.

Hold the mouse pointer on a tool button for a few seconds to see the name or function of the tool button and the keyboard shortcut if there is one. Hold the mouse over an icon to see its description or function in the status bar at the bottom of the window.

Click   **Switch To Enhanced View** to change Home window views again.

Simply Accounting Help Features

Simply Accounting provides program assistance in several different ways. You can display or print Help information on many topics. General accounting information, advice topics and Simply Accounting software assistance are included. You can access Help from the Home window at any time.

The most immediate form of help comes from the **status bar** at the bottom of many program windows. It offers a one-line description of the icon or field that the mouse is pointing to. As you move the mouse around the screen, the status bar information changes accordingly. The message in the status bar is connected to the mouse position only. This may not be the same as the position of the cursor or insertion point, which is located wherever the mouse was when you last clicked the mouse button.

Many settings or options windows include a **Help button** that offers context-sensitive help for the procedure you are using.

Simply Accounting help can be accessed in several ways.

Click **Sage Spark** in the Home window Modules pane list:

The Sage Spark Web site has links to various tools and services including Billing Boss, a free online billing program suitable for small businesses.

To access the site, start your Internet connection and type www.sagespark.com.

Click **Learning Centre** in the Modules pane:

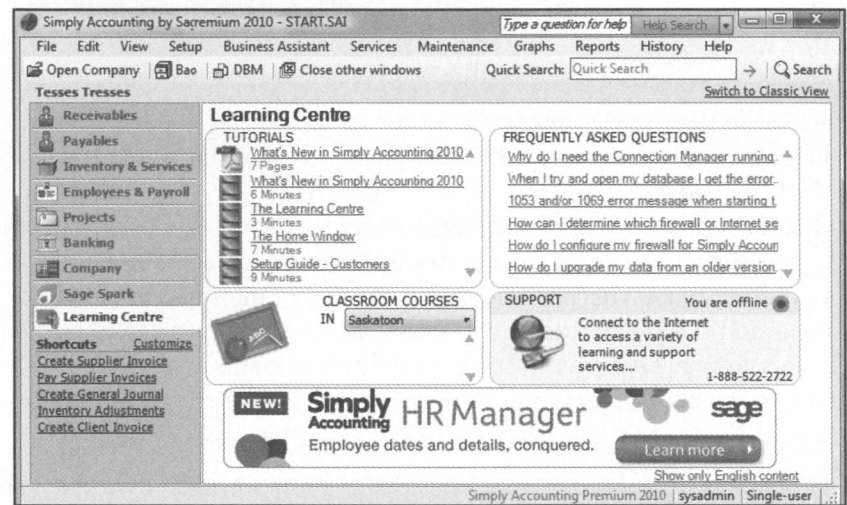

From this centre you can get different types of assistance: online assistance, run a tutorial, learn about courses and training, look for answers to frequently asked questions, contact a Simply Accounting expert or provide feedback to Sage Software.

You can also use the program's built-in Help.

Click the **Help menu** in the Home window as shown:

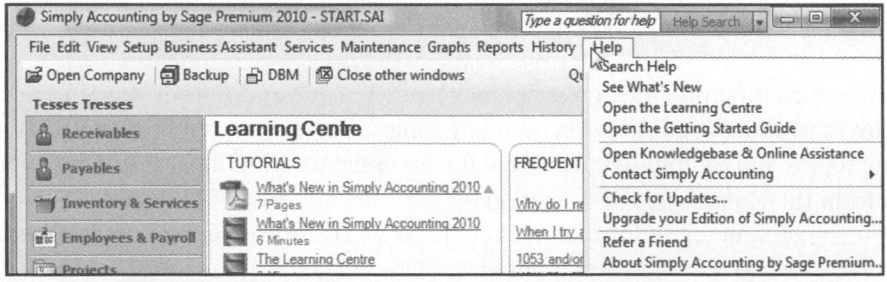

The options on this menu include access to Help, the Learning Centre and its options, a description of new features for version 2010 and the Getting Started Guide manual. In addition you can update the program to a later release, upgrade the program to Premium from Pro (or to Enterprise) and see the version number and serial number for your program (About Simply Accounting by Sage Premium).

Choose the **Help menu** and **click Search Help** as shown above or **press** _f1_ to open the Simply Accounting Help Welcome screen:

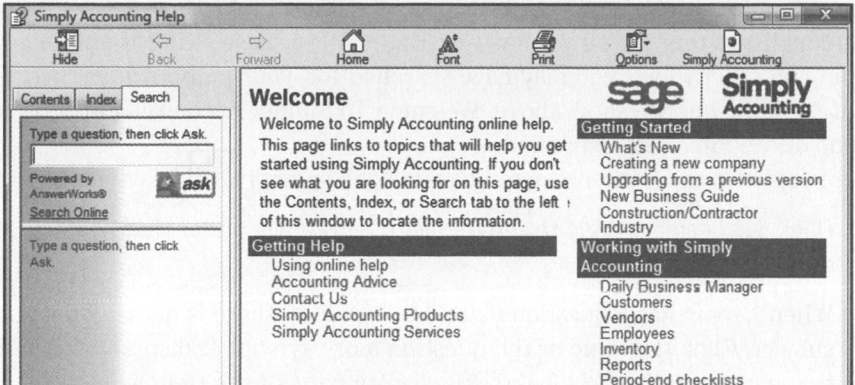

NOTES
You may see a warning about Internet security because many parts of the Learning Centre use Internet access. The Ask portion does not require an Internet connection.

The Help Welcome screen opens with links to several introductory topics and sources of assistance. The Search tab is selected and the Search pane is added on the left.

Click   the **Type A Question field** in the Search pane.

Type   purchase orders **Click** the **Ask button**:

Several topics related to purchase orders are now listed in the Search pane. The topics are shown in order of likely relevance — their **Rank**.

Click   **Enter A Purchase Order** to display information for this topic:

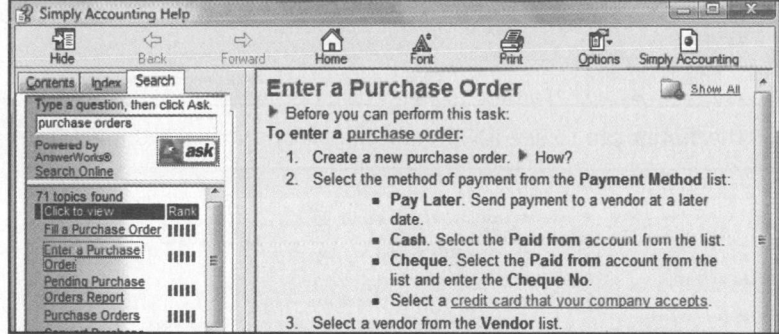

Click any underlined topic in the Search pane or in the information display pane to display the information for that newly selected topic. Clicking an arrow ▶ beside a topic in the right-hand side display pane expands the list of topics.

Click   the **Contents tab** in the Search pane:

NOTES
If a topic has subtopics (an indented list), you must choose a subtopic to display. If there are still multiple entries, you can choose from the list that Simply Accounting offers at this stage.

The help information from your previous search is still displayed. If you scroll down the contents list of topics, you will see that Enter A Purchase Order is still selected. Depending on other topics you may have searched for, your pull-down list may be different from the one we show above. Welcome To Simply Accounting may be selected with none of the topic lists expanded.

Major topics in the Contents menu have a book symbol ![book] beside them.

Click ![plus] beside a topic to see the list of subtopics under that heading (or double click the topic).

When a topic has a question mark ![?] beside it, there is detailed help on that subject. Click the topic or the question mark symbol to display information on that subject in the right-hand side display pane of the Help window.

Click a book title or click ![minus], the boxed minus sign beside it, to close the book and hide the list of subtopics.

Click **Vendors**. The list expands with several subtopics.

Click **Purchases** to view the second list of subtopics.

Click **Paying Vendors (Payments)** to view the next list of subtopics.

Click **Paying A Vendor** (with a question mark ![?] beside it).

You will see the help information on this topic:

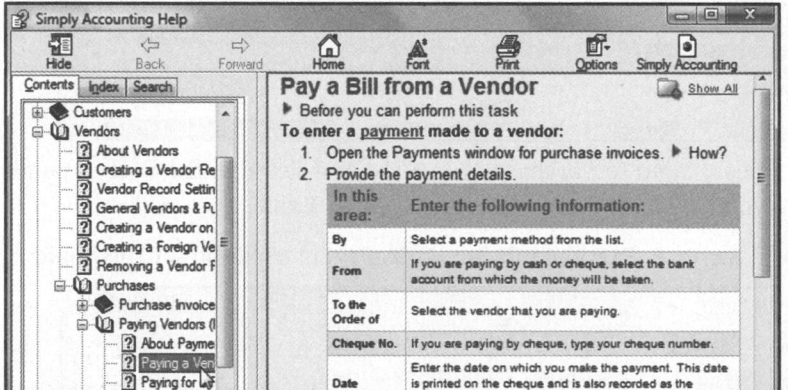

Click the **Index tab** to see an alphabetic list of entries as shown here:

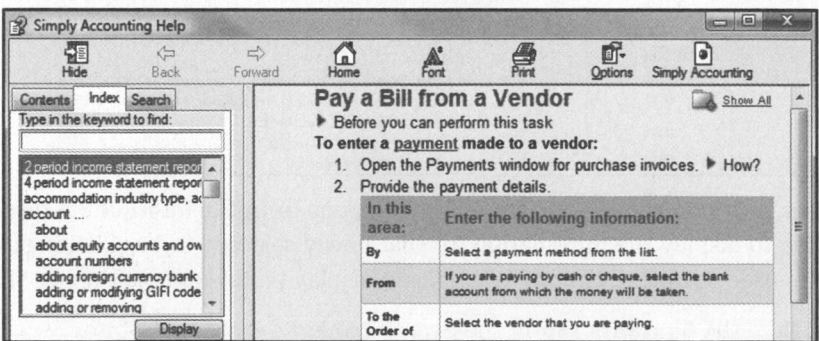

Notice that the previous topic remains on display until you select a new topic.

Click an index topic and then click Display to open the help information. Type a letter in the field above the list to advance the alphabetic list quickly.

Search for information on other topics in the different tab screens.

Close the **Help windows** when finished.

The Simply Accounting program also includes **Advice** on a number of topics.

Choose the **Business Assistant menu**, then **click Business Advice** and **All Modules** as shown:

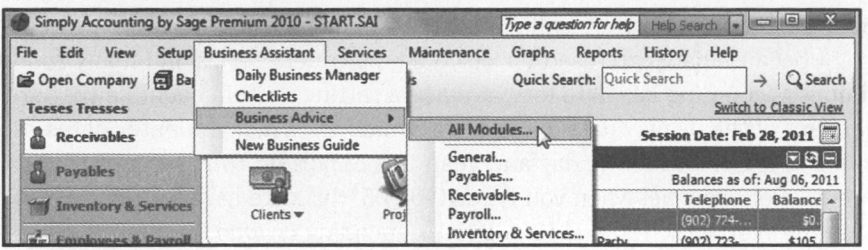

A list of topics opens:

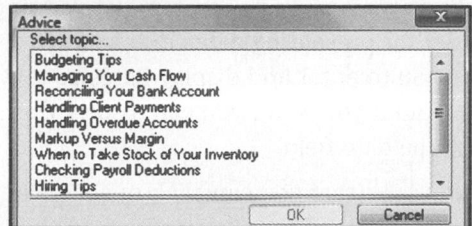

These topics provide general business information or accounting practices.

Management Reports, available from the Reports menu in the Home window, also provide advice, but the information is specific to the company data set that is open.

Management Reports are available only for ledgers that are not hidden, so the list you see is not always complete. These reports combine the company data with forms and reports provided through the Crystal Report Engine. Management Reports are covered with other reports for each module in the following chapters.

Click the **topic** you want and then **click OK**. **Close** the **advice report windows** when finished.

A final source of general assistance is available as **automatic advice**. This feature can be turned off from the Setup menu (User Preferences, View, shown on page 83) in the Home window if it is not needed. We recommend leaving it on. When it is turned on, the Simply Accounting program will provide warning statements.

For example, when you choose a customer who has exceeded the credit limit, you will see this warning:

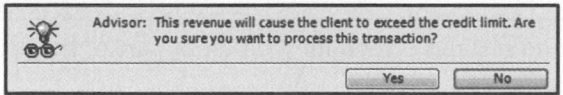

To proceed, you must close the advice screen. In the example shown here, you can click Yes to proceed with the sale, or No to make a change (perhaps by asking for a deposit).

The following warning about a customer appears when you choose a customer with a history of making late payments:

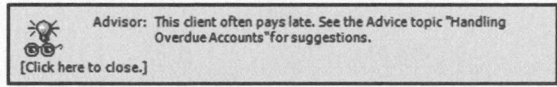

To close this message, click the Advisor icon as indicated [Click Here To Close].

The program also warns when year-end is approaching and it is time to complete year-end adjustments, when your chequing account is overdrawn or when inventory items reach the reorder point.

CLASSIC VIEW

In the Classic View, you can click the Advice tool.

Both General Advice and Management Reports will be available.

If a Home window ledger or journal icon is selected when you click the Advice tool, you will see the list of Management Reports for only that module or ledger.

NOTES

If you have not installed the Crystal Report Engine and the customizable forms, these reports will not be available.

PRO VERSION

Remember that you will see the term Customers instead of Clients.

NOTES

If you try to post a sale (client invoice) for any of the listed customers for $10 000, you will see the message about credit limits.

If you try to enter a sale to Irma Vanitee, you will see the message about the customer who pays late.

Date Formats and Settings

NOTES
Simply Accounting allows you to enter earlier session dates but warns you first. If you have advanced the date incorrectly, you can reverse the decision as long as you have not moved to a new fiscal year. Warnings are also given when you advance the date by more than one week or when you try to move to a new fiscal period. These warnings should serve as signals that you may have made a mistake.

NOTES
Simply Accounting always uses three letters for the month when the Long Dates text option is selected. Therefore June 5, 2010, is displayed as Jun 05, 2010.

CLASSIC VIEW
Right-click the Chart of Accounts icon and then click the Setup tool icon to open the General Settings window. Click Company.

NOTES
When you click the ⊞ beside Company, the list expands beneath the heading. You can click Date Format in either list to open the Date settings window.

NOTES
Simply Accounting displays only the first three letters of a month when you choose the long or text date format (shown as MMM in the selection list). Therefore Jun is displayed for June.

Before closing the program we will review date format settings. Date accuracy is very important because dates are used for discounts, payment terms and many reports.

Simply Accounting has date format control settings within each file that are independent of the display date settings for Windows. When you enter dates using a series of two digits for month, day and year, it is important to know how these will be interpreted. For example, when you type 10-06-05, this date may be June 10, October 6 or June 5 in the year 2005, 1905, 1910 or 2010, depending on whether month, day or year comes first and whether your computer defaults to 1900 dates or is preset for 2000 dates. (Refer to Chapter 3, page 66, for information about computer system date settings.) We always use month, day and year as the order for presenting dates in this text.

Fortunately, Simply Accounting allows you to enter and display dates as text. Thus, you may type June 5, 2010, in a date field. And if you want, you can display this date as Jun 05, 2010, even if you enter numbers in the date field.

All date fields also have a **Calendar icon** 📅 that you can click to access a month-by-month calendar from which you can select a date. These two options will help you avoid making date errors from incorrect orders. To access the date settings,

Click   the **Settings icon** 🔧 in the Related Tasks pane, or **choose** the **Setup menu**, then **click Settings**.

Click   **Company** in the list of modules on the left.

The main Company settings window opens:

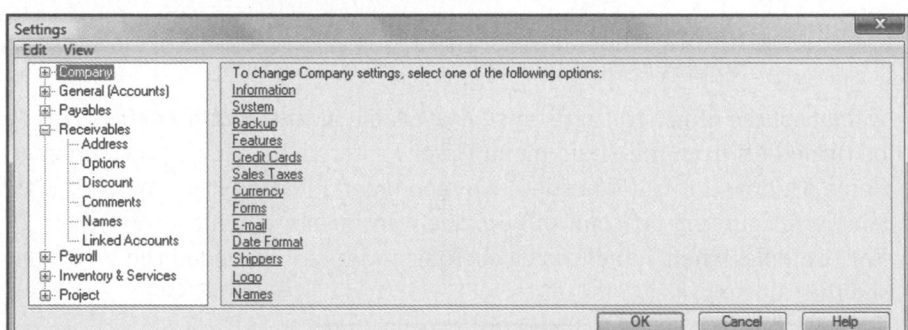

Each entry in the list opens the settings screen for a different part of the program. We want the date format settings.

Click   **Date Format** to open the Settings window for Dates:

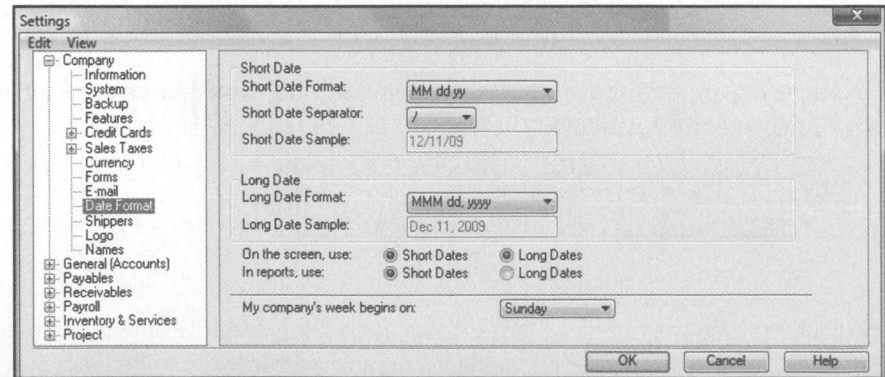

Each field has a drop-down list of format options. The **Short Date Format** uses two digits each for month and day. For the year, you can choose a two-digit or four-digit format. You can choose to begin with month, day or year — the Short Date Format shows which comes first. The **Short Date Separator** character may be a slash, dash or period. This is the character that will appear on the screen regardless of how you entered the date. The sample shows the appearance for the current date from your selections.

The **Long Date Format** shows the month as a three-letter text abbreviation. Either the month or the day can be the first character in the long date style. The sample shows the current date with your selection.

The next section allows you to select the short or long date styles for your screen and reports. You can select different date styles for your reports and screen displays.

We will use the same date format settings for all files to avoid any confusion about dates when the numeric entry might be ambiguous. For reports you can use long or short date formats. For the files we provided in the data set, the month-day-year order is already selected for short and long formats. To change date format settings,

Click   the **Short Date Format field list arrow**.

Click   **MM dd yyyy**. Be sure that Month (MM) is the first part of the entry.

Click   the **Long Date Format field list arrow**.

Click   **MMM dd, yyyy**.

Click   **Long Dates** beside the option On The Screen, Use.

Click   **OK** to save the settings.

Saving and Backing Up Your Work

Simply Accounting saves your work automatically at various stages when you are working with the program. For example, when you display or print reports, Simply Accounting writes all the journal transactions to your file to compile the report you want. When you exit from the program properly, Simply Accounting also saves all your work.

On a regular basis, you should also make a backup copy of your files. The Backup command is described in detail in Chapter 3.

Click   the **Backup tool** or **choose** the **File menu** and **click Backup** to start the Backup wizard.

The wizard will create a separate backup folder inside your current working folder so that the backup will remain separate from your working copy.

While **Backup** creates a compressed copy of the files that must be restored with the Restore command before you can use them, the next two options create new complete working copies of your data files that can be opened directly. Both save the file under a different file name so that you will have two working copies of the files, the original and the copy. You cannot create backups on a CD or DVD with the Backup command.

Save As makes a copy, closes the original file and lets you continue to work with the new copy. Because the new file becomes your working file, you can use Save As to copy to any medium that you can also work from in Simply Accounting — your hard disk drive or a removable memory stick, but not a CD. **Save A Copy** makes a copy of the file and then allows you to continue working with the original file. You can use Save A Copy to save your files to a CD (but not to a DVD). You must copy the CD files back to your hard disk drive and remove the read-only property before working with these files.

Because the data files are very large, we recommend using the Backup procedure described in Chapter 3 rather than Save As or Save A Copy for regular backups.

Choose the **File menu** and **click Save A Copy** to open the file name window.

You can save the copy in the same folder as the original or use a different folder. We recommend using different folders.

NOTES
A final date option allows you to indicate the normal first weekday for the business.

NOTES
Showing a four-digit year will ensure that you see whether you are using 1900 or 2000 year dates. Refer to Chapter 3, page 66, for information about date settings in Windows.

NOTES
You may want to use the Save A Copy or Save As command when you are unsure how a journal entry will be posted and you want to experiment with different methods of entering the same transactions.

NOTES
To remove the read-only property, right-click the file or icon in the Computer window and choose Properties from the pop-up menu. Click Read-only to remove the ✓.

NOTES
You can also create a new folder by choosing the Organize menu and clicking New Folder (in Windows Vista).

NOTES
You can also use the Windows Copy command to make CD copies of your data, but you must close the Simply Accounting data file before you start to copy. Remember to copy the data folders when you copy from Windows to ensure that you keep all necessary files (the .SAI file and the SAJ folder) together.
You must use a DVD writing program to copy your data files to a DVD.
You cannot open the data files from the CD or DVD. You must first copy them back to your hard disk drive and remove the read-only property.

Click   a **different folder in the file path** to change folders.

Double click   a **folder** in the name and folders pane to open it. To create a new folder inside the one that you have open,

Click   **New Folder** (in the tool bar). **Type** a **new name** to replace New Folder, the selected text. **Click Open**.

Double click   the file name **NEW** or **NEW.SAI** if you show file extensions.

Type   the **new file name**. **Click Save**. You will return to your original file and you can continue working.

To save the file under a different name and work with the new file, use **Save As**.

Choose the **File menu** and **click Save As** to open the file name window.

The remaining steps are the same as Save A Copy. Change folders, create a new folder, rename the folder, open the new folder, type a file name for the copy and click Save. Remember to return to your original working copy before entering any transactions if you use the Save As command.

You can also back up all your data files at the same time by using Windows (in the Windows Explorer or Computer windows) Copy and Paste commands. In this way, you can save the files to a different folder on your hard drive or on a CD.

Finishing a Session

Choose the **Control Menu icon** and **click Close** or **click** ⊠ to close the journal input form or display window you are working in.

You will return to the main Home window.

Choose the **Control Menu icon** and **click Close**, or **click** ⊠ or **choose** the **File menu** and **click Exit** to close the Home window. **Click No** to close the backup prompt.

Your work will be saved again automatically when you complete this step. You should now be in the Windows desktop.

Opening a Data File from a Backup

NOTES
The first time you start the program, the option to Open The Last Company You Worked On will not be included. See the Select Company Welcome screen on page 7.

Click   [Simply Accounting Premium 2010], the desktop icon, or **start** the **Simply Accounting program** from the Start icon or menu (see page 7) to open the Select Company Welcome window:

The opening window gives you several options: working with the sample company files, creating new company files, restoring backup files or working with existing data files. If you have worked with the program before, the option to Open The Last

Company You Worked On appears with the name of the file you used most recently (as shown here). We need to restore a backup file.

If your working files are lost or damaged, you will also need to restore backup files. You can also restore files from the File menu in the Home window of any data file, including the Sample Company file.

Click   **Restore From Backup**.

Click   **OK** to start the Simply Accounting Restore From Backup wizard:

Click   **Next** to begin:

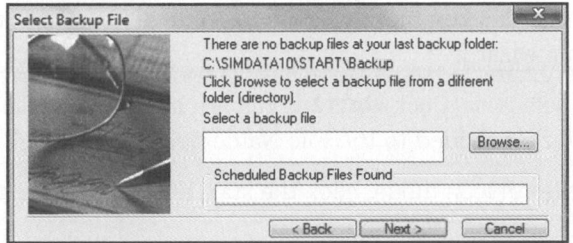

The first time you restore a backup, no default location or backup files are entered.

Click   **Browse** to open the folder you worked in most recently.

The folder names in your Look In field and Browse windows may be different from the ones we show. Simply Accounting 2010 uses a folder under Documents and Settings as the default location for files, so you may see this as the selected folder initially. If you have opened another data file, you may see the folder where that file is stored. To ensure consistency in file names and locations for our instructions, we always work with the folder we created when installing the data files, that is, C:\SimData10.

Click   **Computer** in the path field at the top of the screen or in the left pane list of Favorite Links to see all the drives on your computer:

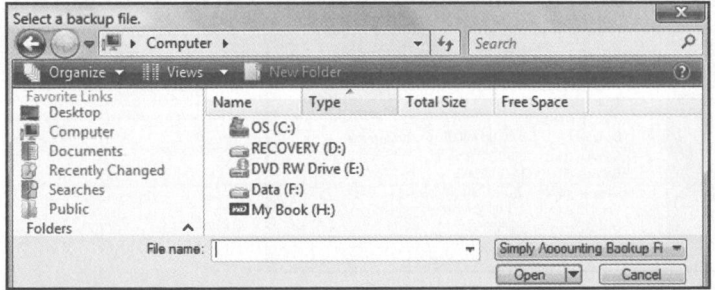

Double click (OS) C: to show the files and folders in this drive:

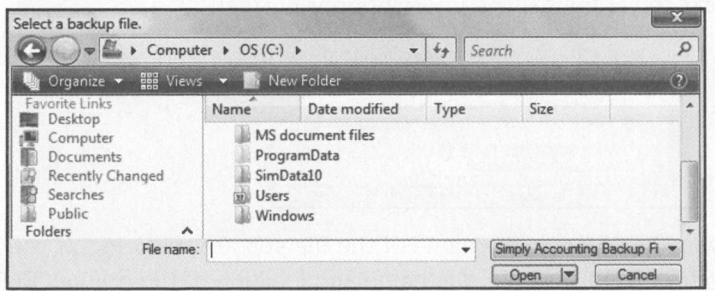

NOTES
We show the default location for the data files from the automatic installation. If you installed the files to a different location, choose the drive and folder for your setup.

NOTES
Your screens may look different if you have selected different viewing options such as displaying the folders as lists or icons. The viewing options can be changed from the Views drop-down menu.

Click **SimData10** to select it. (Click the SimData10 folder icon 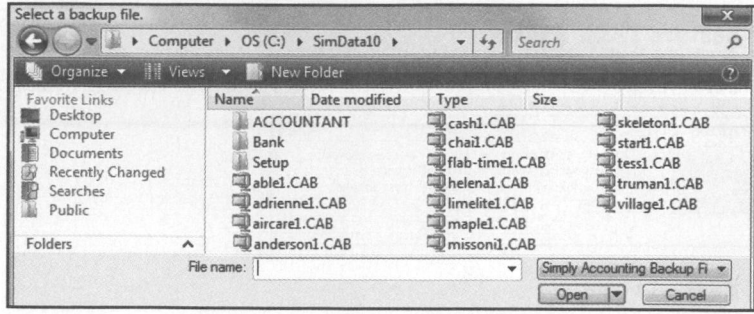 if your viewing mode is icons.) **Click Open** to see the list of files you copied from the Student DVD:

Only Simply Accounting format backup files and folders are listed because we are working with the Restore Backup wizard.

Click **start1.CAB** to select it. (Click **start1** if you are not showing file extensions.) Start1 is added to the File Name field.

If you are viewing the files in icon mode, click the start1.CAB icon.

Click **Open**.

You will return to the wizard. The backup files are now listed in the Select A Backup File text box with start1.CAB selected as shown:

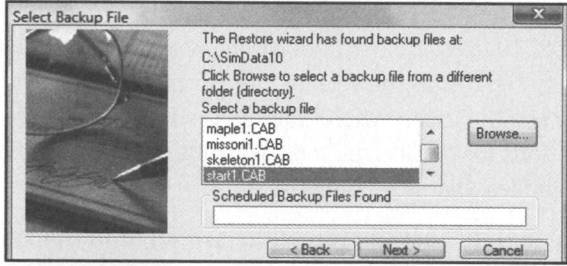

Click **Next** to continue, showing the selections you have made:

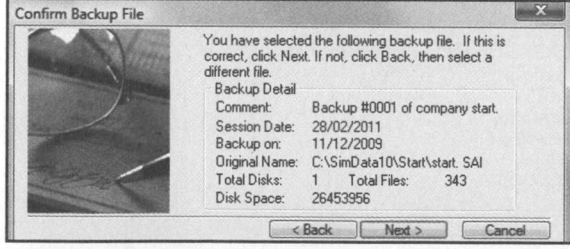

If the information is incorrect, click Back to return to the file selection screen.

Click **Next** to continue if the information is correct:

At this stage, you should enter the name of the file you are restoring. If you have created the backup from your own file, the name and location of the original file from which you created the backup are shown as the default.

We will create a new folder for each data set in this text. We will continue to work in the SimData10 folder. If the name you see is different from the one shown above,

Type   C:\SimData10\Start\start

Click   **Next**.

You can choose a different location and file name by clicking Browse to access your folders. Enter the location and file name you want to use.

You will see a screen advising you that you are using folder and file names that are new. Simply Accounting will create the new folders and files for you:

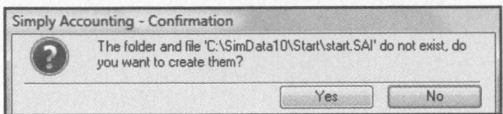

Click   **Yes** to confirm and continue.

If you are replacing a corrupt or unusable file, you will see a warning when you type the file name and location file. Click Yes to accept the replacement.

Simply Accounting now confirms that all the data required have been entered:

This is your last chance to change information by clicking Back.

Click   **Finish** to begin restoring the file. You should see the screen that prompts you to enter the session date:

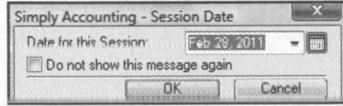

Click   **OK** to open the Getting Started window.

Click   **Show This Window On Start Up** to remove the ✓.

Click   **Close** to continue to the Home window.

Continue with the instructions on page 9.

R E V I E W

The Student DVD with Data Files includes Review Questions for this chapter.

CHAPTER TWO

GST, HST and PST

OBJECTIVES

After completing this chapter, you should be able to

- **understand** the terms relevant to the federal Goods and Services Tax
- **understand** the different methods of calculating the GST
- **understand** Harmonized Sales Tax in relation to GST
- **understand** how to file for GST or HST remittances or refunds
- **understand** other provincial sales taxes in relation to GST

GENERAL TAX INFORMATION

Definition of GST

The Goods and Services Tax (GST) is levied by the federal government at the rate of 5 percent on most goods and services in Canada. Retailers pay the GST to their wholesalers and vendors but are allowed to deduct any GST they pay from the GST they collect from customers. Retailers remit the difference, GST owing, to the Receiver General for Canada or claim a refund with monthly or quarterly returns.

GST Registration   Any business with annual sales exceeding $30 000 per year must register for GST collection and must collect GST on all applicable sales. Registration is optional for most smaller businesses. Businesses that are not registered for GST do not charge GST on sales to their customers, but they also cannot recover the GST they pay on business-related purchases.

Collecting the GST   The business must collect GST for those goods and services sold that are not zero rated or tax exempt. The business must remit GST at regular intervals, filing GST returns monthly, quarterly or annually and paying instalments, depending on annual income and GST owing.

Zero Rated Goods and Services   Zero rated goods and services are those on which the tax rate is zero. These goods include basic groceries, prescribed medical devices, prescribed drugs, exported goods and services, agricultural products and fish products. A business selling only zero rated goods and services does not collect GST on sales, but it can still claim a refund for GST it pays for purchases.

> **NOTES**
> Provinces may or may not include GST in the price on which they calculate Provincial Sales Tax (PST). Provincial tax rates vary from province to province. See page 28.

> **NOTES**
> GST collected on sales is reduced by the GST on sales returns.

Tax Exempt Goods and Services   Tax exempt goods and services are those on which tax is not collected. These goods and services include health care, dental care, daycare services and rents on residences. Most educational and financial services are also included in this group. These businesses are not able to claim refunds for GST paid for business purchases related to selling tax exempt goods and services.

Paying the GST   A business must pay GST for purchases made specifically for business purposes, unless the goods or services purchased are zero rated or tax exempt. The business can use the GST paid as an input tax credit by subtracting the amount of GST paid from the amount of GST collected and remitting GST owing or claiming a refund. GST amounts paid on purchases for personal use do not qualify as input tax credits.

Bank and Financial Institution Services   Most bank products and services are not taxable. Exceptions include safety deposit box rentals, custodial and safekeeping services, personalized cheques, self-administered registered savings plan fees, payroll services, rentals of night depository, rentals of credit card imprinters and reconciliation of cheques. Banks remit the full amount of GST they collect from customers. Because most bank services are not taxable, banks cannot claim input tax credits for GST they pay on business-related purchases.

GST on Imported and Exported Goods   GST is not charged on exported goods. Customers in other countries who import goods from Canada do not pay GST. However, businesses in Canada must pay GST on the items they import or purchase from other countries. The GST is collected by Canada Revenue Agency (CRA) when the goods enter Canada based on the purchase price (plus import duty) and current exchange rates. Businesses must pay this GST and other import duties before the goods are released to them.

Administering the GST

The federal government has approved different methods of administering the GST; the regular method is most commonly used.

The Regular Method

The regular method of administering the GST requires the business to keep track of GST paid for all goods and services purchased from vendors (less returns) and of GST collected for all goods and services sold to customers (less returns). It then deducts the GST paid from the GST collected and files for a refund or remits the balance owing to the Receiver General on a monthly or quarterly basis.

Accounting Examples Using the Regular Method (without PST)

SALES INVOICE Sold goods to customer for $200 plus $10 GST collected (5%). Invoice total, $210.

Date	Particulars	Debit	Credit
02/15	Accounts Receivable	210.00	
	GST Charged on Sales		10.00
	Revenue from Sales		200.00

PURCHASE INVOICE Purchased supplies from vendor for $300 plus $15 GST paid (5%). Invoice total, $315.

Date	Particulars	Debit	Credit
02/15	Supplies	300.00	
	GST Paid on Purchases	15.00	
	Accounts Payable		315.00

NOTES
The input tax credit is reduced by the amount of GST for purchases returned.

NOTES
Visitors to Canada can request a GST refund for GST paid on goods purchased in Canada that they are taking home with them. They cannot claim a refund for goods and services they consumed in Canada, such as entertainment and dining.

NOTES
GST Paid on Purchases is a contra-liability account because it normally has a debit balance while most liability accounts have a credit balance. Therefore, GST Paid on Purchases reduces the total GST liability to the Receiver General.

The GST owing is further reduced by any GST adjustments — for example, GST that applies to bad debts that are written off. If the debt is later recovered, the GST liability is also restored as an input tax credit adjustment.

Other Methods of Calculating GST

Certain small businesses may be eligible to use simpler methods of calculating their GST refunds and remittances that do not require them to keep a separate record for GST on each individual purchase or sale. The simplified accounting method, the streamlined accounting method and the quick method are examples of these alternatives.

Calculating GST Refunds or Remittances

The following example uses the regular method for a retailer who is filing quarterly.

Quarterly Total Sales (excluding GST)	$50 000.00	
Quarterly Total Qualifying Purchases	29 700.00	
5% GST Charged on Sales		$2 500.00
Less: 5% GST Paid on Purchases		
Cash Register (cost $1 000)	50.00	
Inventory (cost $25 000)	1 250.00	
Supplies (cost $500)	25.00	
Payroll Services (cost $200)	10.00	
Store Lease (cost $3 000)	150.00	
Total GST Paid		− 1 485.00
GST Remittance		$1 015.00

GST Remittances and Refunds

The business must file returns that summarize the amount of GST it has collected and the amount of GST it has paid. CRA may require reports monthly, quarterly or yearly, depending on total sales. Yearly reports usually require quarterly instalments.

GST Collected on Sales	>	GST Paid on Purchases	=	GST Owing
GST Collected on Sales	<	GST Paid on Purchases	=	GST Refund

Accounting Examples for Remittances

Usually a business will make GST remittances since sales usually exceed expenses — the business operates at a profit. The following example shows how the GST accounts are cleared and a liability (*Accounts Payable*) is set up to remit GST owing to the Receiver General for Canada. In this case, the usual one, the Receiver General becomes a vendor for the business so that the liability can be entered and the payment made.

Date	Particulars	Debit	Credit
03/31	GST Charged on Sales	2 500.00	
	GST Paid on Purchases		1 485.00
	A/P - Receiver General		1 015.00
03/31	A/P - Receiver General	1 015.00	
	Cash in Bank		1 015.00

Accounting Examples for Refunds

The example below shows how the GST accounts are cleared and a current asset account (*Accounts Receivable*) is set up for a GST refund from the Receiver General for Canada. In this case, the Receiver General owes money to the business; that is, it acts like a customer, so a customer record is set up to record and collect the refund.

Date	Particulars	Debit	Credit
03/31	GST Charged on Sales	1 500.00	
	A/R - Receiver General	500.00	
	GST Paid on Purchases		2 000.00
04/15	Cash in Bank	500.00	
	A/R - Receiver General		500.00

Harmonized Sales Tax: HST

Five provinces have adopted the Harmonized Sales Tax (HST) method of taxing goods and services: British Columbia, Ontario, New Brunswick, Nova Scotia and Newfoundland and Labrador. When HST applies, the GST and provincial taxes are harmonized at a single rate. In all provinces, 5 percent of the HST rate is the federal portion or GST while the remainder is the provincial portion. Provincial retail sales tax rates vary from one province to another, so the HST rates also vary. In British Columbia, the HST rate is 12 percent (7 percent provincial); in Ontario, New Brunswick, and Newfoundland and Labrador, the HST rate in 2010 is 13 percent (8 percent provincial), and in Nova Scotia the rate is 15 percent (10 percent provincial). The HST replaces the former separate GST and PST and unlike those separate taxes, it is administered entirely at the federal level. This removes some administrative work both from the provincial Ministries of Finance and from the businesses that charge taxes to their customers. They have only one tax to calculate and remit.

The full 12, 13 or 15 percent Harmonized Sales Tax (HST) operates much like the basic GST: HST is applied at each level of sale, resale and manufacturing, has the same business registration requirement of annual sales exceeding $30 000, is applied to the same base of goods and services, and is collected the same way. HST returns and remittances are also calculated the same way as GST returns and remittances. The business remits any excess of HST collected over HST paid for its business expenses, or claims a refund when HST paid exceeds the HST collected from customers.

The following example illustrates the application in Ontario (or New Brunswick and Newfoundland and Labrador), where the HST rate is 13 percent.

> **NOTES**
> Prices shown to customers may have the HST included (tax-inclusive pricing), but they must show either the amount of HST included in the price or the HST rate.

Ontario business sold goods on account for $565, including HST at 13% ($500 base price).

HST = (0.13 × 500) = $65
Total amount of invoice = $565

Date	Particulars	Debit	Credit
02/15	Accounts Receivable	565.00	
	HST Charged on Sales		65.00
	Revenue from Sales		500.00

A single remittance for the full 13 percent is made to the Receiver General; the provincial portion of the HST is not tracked or collected separately by the business. The following examples show the journal entries for an HST remittance and an HST refund.

Remittance: A British Columbia business calculates and pays HST Owing			
Date	Particulars	Debit	Credit
03/31	HST Charged on Sales	6 000.00	
	A/P - Receiver General		2 500.00
	HST Paid on Purchases		3 500.00
04/15	A/P - Receiver General	2 500.00	
	Cash in Bank		2 500.00

Refund: A British Columbia business qualifies and applies for an HST Refund			
Date	Particulars	Debit	Credit
03/31	HST Charged on Sales	3 000.00	
	A/R - Receiver General	1 500.00	
	HST Paid on Purchases		4 500.00
04/15	Cash in Bank	1 500.00	
	A/R - Receiver General		1 500.00

Goods and Services Exempt for HST

Under the HST method, all items that are exempt for GST or are zero rated are also exempt for HST or are zero rated for HST. In addition, each province has decided that some items will be exempt for HST and subject only to GST. For example, books and children's clothing are exempt for HST but not for GST. For these goods, the customer pays only the 5 percent GST portion of the tax. At the retail level, for these special items a separate tax code for GST only is applied. When the business files its HST return, it will remit the HST collected plus the GST collected, less the amounts of GST plus HST paid on qualifying business-related purchases on a single return.

The following example shows these calculations for a book seller who also sells music CDs in British Columbia. HST at the rate of 12 percent (including a provincial portion of 7 percent) applies to the sale of CDs while GST at the rate of 5 percent applies to the sale of books.

NOTES

Instead of applying different tax rates, retailers who sell PST exempt goods may also charge the full HST rate, provide an immediate point-of-sale rebate for the customer for the provincial portion. They will then claim an adjustment for the rebate amount on their HST return to reduce the amount remitted.

The net effect of the two methods is the same.

Quarterly Total Sales (excluding taxes)	$92 000	
Quarterly Total Qualifying Purchases (excluding taxes)	$52 000	
HST Charged on Sales (12% × 41 000)	$4 920	
GST Charged on Sales (5% × 51 000)	2 550	
Total GST/HST collected		$7 470
Less: GST Paid on Purchase of books for resale (5% × 21 000)	1 050	
HST Paid on other Purchases (12% × 31 000)	3 720	
Total HST Credits		−4 770
HST Remittance		$2 700

GST and Other Provincial (Retail) Sales Taxes

The rules governing provincial sales taxes vary from province to province in terms of the tax rate, the goods and services that are taxed and whether Provincial Sales Tax (PST) is applied to the GST as well as to the base purchase price (that is, whether GST is taxable). The following examples assume that the item sold has both GST and PST applied.

Although GST is applied at each level of sale, resale and manufacturing, PST is a retail sales tax and, therefore, is paid only by the final consumer of a product or service.

NOTES

If a business purchases inventory for resale but later uses the inventory within the business instead, it must remit PST on this internal transaction. The business has become the final consumer of the products.

Therefore, it is generally referred to as a Retail Sales Tax by the provincial governments and the terms RST and PST are equivalent. Thus, a business purchasing inventory to sell to customers will not pay PST on these purchases. When the same business buys supplies or services for its use in conducting business, it must pay PST because it has become the final consumer of these goods or services.

PST applies only to sales within a province, not to sales to customers in a different province or in a different country. HST and GST do apply to interprovincial sales.

Alberta, the Northwest Territories, Yukon and Nunavut

Alberta, the Northwest Territories, Yukon and Nunavut do not have Provincial Sales Taxes. Customers in these regions pay only the 5 percent GST on their purchases. Thus, the examples provided earlier without PST illustrate the application of GST for these regions.

PST in Manitoba and Saskatchewan

These two prairie provinces apply PST to the base price of the sale, the amount without GST included. In Manitoba, the retail sales tax rate is 7 percent; in Saskatchewan, the rate is 5 percent. The following example illustrates the application in Manitoba.

Manitoba business sold goods on account for $500. GST charged is 5% and PST charged is 7%.

GST = (0.05 × 500) = $25
PST in Manitoba = (0.07 × 500) = $35
Total amount of invoice = $500 + $25 + $35 = $560

Date	Particulars	Debit	Credit
02/15	Accounts Receivable	560.00	
	GST Charged on Sales		25.00
	PST Payable		35.00
	Revenue from Sales		500.00

The full amount of PST collected on sales is remitted to the provincial Minister of Finance (less any applicable sales tax compensation).

Quebec Sales Tax (QST)

Provincial sales tax in Quebec (QST) is also combined with the GST. The provincial tax rate is applied to a broader base of goods and services than PST in other provinces, like the base that has GST applied. The QST is calculated on the base amount of the sale plus the GST. That is, QST is applied to GST — a piggy-backed tax or a tax on a tax.

Quebec business sold goods on account for $500. GST charged is 5% and QST charged is 7.5%.

GST = (0.05 × 500) = $25
QST = (0.075 × 525) = $39.38
Total amount of invoice = $500.00 + $25.00 + $39.38 = $564.38

Date	Particulars	Debit	Credit
02/15	Accounts Receivable	564.38	
	GST Charged on Sales		25.00
	QST Charged on Sales		39.38
	Revenue from Sales		500.00

QST and GST are calculated separately but both are remitted to the ministre du Revenu du Québec. Because the QST is also refundable, businesses can deduct the QST they pay on their purchases from the QST they collect on sales, as they do their GST paid. The QST paid on a few items or services — QST on some telecommunication services and insurance — is not refundable. Therefore, QST paid must be designated as

NOTES
Services may be exempt or taxable for PST. PST is usually charged on services, such as repairs, that are applied to goods that are themselves taxable for PST.

NOTES
Quebec was the first province to introduce a Harmonized Sales Tax. It differs from the model in the Atlantic provinces in that the GST and QST components are both administered by the provincial government. QST is covered in Chapter 14.

refundable or non-refundable at the time of the purchase and when the purchase is recorded.

PST in Prince Edward Island

Provincial sales tax in PEI is applied to the base sale price plus GST. However, unlike Quebec, some items have only GST applied, and some have both GST and PST applied.

PEI business sold goods on account for $500. GST charged is 5% and PST charged is 10%.

GST = (0.05 × 500) = $25
PST = (0.10 × 525) = $52.50
Total amount of invoice = $500.00 + $25.00 + $52.50 = $577.50

Date	Particulars	Debit	Credit
02/15	Accounts Receivable	577.50	
	GST Charged on Sales		25.00
	PST Payable		52.50
	Revenue from Sales		500.00

The full amount of PST collected on sales is remitted to the provincial Minister of Finance (less 3 percent sales tax compensation).

Part 2
Applications

CHAPTER THREE

MissoniMarbleworks

OBJECTIVES

After completing this chapter, you should be able to

- ■ *access* the data files for the business
- ■ *open* the General Journal
- ■ *enter* transactions in the General Journal
- ■ *edit* and *review* General Journal transactions
- ■ *post* transactions
- ■ *create* new General Ledger accounts
- ■ *adjust* journal entries after posting
- ■ *display* and *print* General Ledger and General Journal reports
- ■ *graph* General Ledger reports
- ■ *display* and *print* comparative financial reports
- ■ *customize* reports
- ■ *back up* your data files
- ■ *advance* the session date
- ■ *finish* an accounting session

COMPANY INFORMATION

Company Profile

NOTES
Missoni Marbleworks
66 Allies Avenue
Edmonton, AB T3P 4C2
Tel 1: (780) 763-4127
Tel 2: (800) 455-4127
Fax: (780) 765-4842
Business No.: 743 647 397

Missoni Marbleworks in Edmonton, Alberta, is owned and operated by Maria Missoni, who opened the business after graduating from college and training in Italy with Renaissance Marble Works. She builds stone fireplaces and chimneys, stone porches, patios and stairs and installs ceramic and marble tile floors in homes and fountains in shopping malls. Her love of Italian architecture has led her to repairing old marble in museums, galleries and homes. She hopes to include more art restoration in her work in the future. Missoni also has considerable artistic and creative talents. The marble stands that she carves for statues, masks and vases are sold from her home studio, at local craft shows and to individual customers who commission special pieces.

Some of her customers have set up accounts with Missoni, and she has set up accounts with her regular vendors and suppliers.

To convert her accounting records to Simply Accounting in April, she has used:

- Chart of Accounts
- Trial Balance
- Accounting Procedures

CHART OF POSTABLE ACCOUNTS

MISSONI MARBLEWORKS

ASSETS
1080 Cash in Bank
1200 A/R - St. Albert Museum
1220 A/R - Jasper Gallery
1240 A/R - Stoney Plain Plaza
1320 Prepaid Insurance
1360 Marble Inventory
1540 Computer Equipment
1550 Power Marble Tools
1560 Power Marble Equipment
1570 Van ▶

▶LIABILITIES
2100 A/P - West Carbide Tools
2120 A/P - Marblehead Suppliers
2180 A/P - Chinook Promotions
2650 GST Charged on Sales
2670 GST Paid on Purchases

EQUITY
3100 Missoni, Capital
3150 Missoni, Drawings
3600 Net Income ▶

▶REVENUE
4100 Revenue from Contracts
4150 Revenue from Repairs
4200 Interest Revenue

EXPENSE
5020 Advertising & Promotion
5040 Bank Charges
5060 Hydro Expense
5080 Interest Expense
5100 Maintenance & Repairs ▶

▶5110 Marble Inventory Used
5120 Rental Expenses
5140 Telephone Expenses
5160 Wages Expenses

NOTES: The Chart of Accounts includes only postable accounts and the Net Income or Current Earnings account. Simply Accounting uses the Net Income account for the Income Statement to calculate the difference between revenue and expenses before closing the books.

TRIAL BALANCE

MISSONI MARBLEWORKS

April 1, 2012		Debits	Credits
1080	Cash in Bank	$ 24 000	
1200	A/R - St. Albert Museum	2 400	
1220	A/R - Jasper Gallery	3 600	
1320	Prepaid Insurance	1 000	
1360	Marble Inventory	2 050	
1540	Computer Equipment	2 500	
1550	Power Marble Tools	4 500	
1560	Power Marble Equipment	28 000	
1570	Van	32 000	
2100	A/P - West Carbide Tools		$ 1 200
2650	GST Charged on Sales		1 500
2670	GST Paid on Purchases	940	
3100	Missoni, Capital		85 110
3150	Missoni, Drawings	900	
4100	Revenue from Contracts		21 000
4150	Revenue from Repairs		4 000
5020	Advertising & Promotion	200	
5040	Bank Charges	60	
5060	Hydro Expense	300	
5100	Maintenance & Repairs	400	
5110	Marble Inventory Used	5 400	
5120	Rental Expenses	600	
5140	Telephone Expenses	360	
5160	Wages Expenses	3 600	
		$112 810	$112 810

Accounting Procedures

GST

Missoni has chosen the regular method for remittance of the Goods and Services Tax (GST). She records the GST collected from customers as a liability (credit) in the *GST Charged on Sales* account. She records GST that she pays to vendors in the *GST Paid on Purchases* account as a decrease (debit) to her liability to Canada Revenue Agency. Her GST remittance or refund is calculated automatically in the *GST Owing (Refund)* subtotal. You can see these accounts when you display or print the Balance Sheet. Missoni files her GST remittances or requests for refunds with the Receiver General for Canada on the last day of each fiscal quarter. (For details, please read Chapter 2 on the Goods and Services Tax.)

NOTES
Most bank and financial institution services used in this text are exempt from GST charges.
Alberta does not levy a provincial sales tax.

INSTRUCTIONS

1. **Open** or **restore** the **data for Missoni Marbleworks**. Instructions begin on page 38.

2. **Enter** the **source documents for April** in the General Journal in Simply Accounting using the Chart of Accounts and Trial Balance for Missoni Marbleworks. The procedures for entering each new type of transaction for this application are outlined step by step in the Keystrokes section following the source documents. These transactions have a ✓ in the check box and, immediately below the check box, the page number on which the relevant keystrokes begin. Put your own checkmark in each transaction box after you finish entering the transaction to show that you have completed it.

3. **Print** the **reports and graphs** indicated on the printing form below after you have completed your entries. Keystrokes for reports begin on page 51.

REPORTS	Financials	Management Reports
Accounts	☑ Comparative Balance Sheet dates: Apr 1 and Apr 30 with difference in percentage	☐ General
☐ Chart of Accounts	☑ Income Statement from Jan 1 to Apr 30	**GRAPHS**
☐ Account List	☑ Trial Balance date: Apr 30	☐ Revenues by Account
☑ General Journal Entries: Apr 1 to Apr 30	☑ General Ledger accounts: 1080 2650 3100 4100 from Apr 1 to Apr 30	☐ Expenses by Account
		☑ Expenses and Net Profit as % of Revenue

SOURCE DOCUMENTS

NOTES
Remember that the ✓ in the check box and the number beneath it indicate that keystroke instructions for this entry begin on page 40.

NOTES
☑ Create new Group
45 account 2300 Bank Loan. (See keystrokes on page 45.)

SESSION DATE – APRIL 7, 2012

☑   **Purchase Invoice WCT-161**   **Dated April 2, 2012**

40   From West Carbide Tools, $885 plus $44.25 GST paid for diamond-tip drill and drill bits. Purchase invoice total $929.25. Terms: net 30 days.

☑   **Bank Credit Memo #AT-C3104**   **Dated April 3, 2012**

45   From Alberta Trust Company, $10 000 bank loan secured for purchase of new marble equipment. Loan deposited into bank account. Create new Group account 2300 Bank Loan.

☐ **Sales Invoice #MM-40**   **Dated April 3, 2012**

To St. Albert Museum, $3 800 plus $190 GST charged to build marble display stands for statues as per contract. Sales invoice total $3 990. Terms: net 30 days.

☑ **Memo #1**   **Dated April 4, 2012**

47 From Owner: The invoice from West Carbide Tools was entered incorrectly. The cost of the drill was $900 plus $45 GST paid. The revised purchase invoice total is $945. Adjust the posted invoice to make the correction.

☐ **Cheque Copy #48**   **Dated April 5, 2012**

To West Carbide Tools, $1 200 in payment of invoice #WCT-129.

☐ **Cash Receipt #20**   **Dated April 5, 2012**

From St. Albert Museum, cheque #828 for $2 400 in payment of invoice #MM-37.

☐ **Cash Sales Invoice #MM-41**   **Dated April 6, 2012**

To Rolf Kleinje, $2 100 plus $105 GST charged for replacement of marble kitchen counter and other repair work. Sales invoice total $2 205. Received certified cheque #AT-603 in full payment of account.

☐ **Purchase Invoice #MS-611**   **Dated April 6, 2012**

From Marblehead Suppliers, $6 000 plus $300 GST paid for marble pieces (inventory) of different sizes to complete contracted work. Purchase invoice total $6 300 Terms: net 30 days.

SESSION DATE – APRIL 14, 2012

☐ **Bank Debit Memo #AT-D3691**   **Dated April 8, 2012**

From Alberta Trust Company, $24 for bank service charges.

☐ **Purchase Invoice #WMM-4499**   **Dated April 10, 2012**

From West Mall Mechanical, $300 plus $15 GST paid for repairs and maintenance work on equipment. Purchase invoice total $315. Terms: net 10 days. Create new Group account 2190 A/P - West Mall Mechanical.

☐ **Memo #2**   **Dated April 11, 2012**

Missoni paid her hydro and telephone bills from her personal chequing account. She wrote cheque #49 for $283.50 to reimburse herself for these expenses. The hydro bill was $150 plus $7.50 GST and the telephone bill was $120 plus $6.00 GST.

☐ **Bank Credit Memo #AT-C3421**   **Dated April 11, 2012**

From Alberta Trust Company, $500 semi-annual interest earned on bank account.

☐ **Cash Receipt #21**   **Dated April 12, 2012**

From Jasper Gallery, cheque #58821 for $3 600 in full payment of invoice #MM-38.

☐ **Sales Invoice #MM-42**   **Dated April 14, 2012**

To Jasper Gallery, $2 000 plus $100 GST charged for building of marble pedestals and base units as per contract. Sales invoice total $2 100. Terms: net 30 days.

NOTES
If you use MM-xx as the source for sales, you can apply the report filter we show in Appendix F.

NOTES
If you use Cheque #xx as the source for cheques, you can apply the report filter we show in Appendix F.

NOTES
☑ See keystrokes on
49 Advancing the Session Date, page 49.

SESSION DATE – APRIL 21, 2012

NOTES
Create new Group account:
2210 A/P - Devon Equipment

To: Missoni Marbleworks
66 Allies Avenue
Edmonton, AB
T3P 4C2

DEVON
EQUIPMENT CO.
68 CUTTERS ROAD EDMONTON, AB T4C 3N6
TEL: 780-775-6116

Date: April 15, 2012

No: DE-1141

Description of item	
Marble Cutting Equipment	9,600.00

GST # 651 034 271	**Terms:** net 30 days	**Subtotal**	9,600.00
Signature *M. Missoni*		**GST**	480.00
		Total	$10,080.00

NOTES
Use the General Journal for the payroll transaction in this application.

Missoni Marbleworks
66 Allies Avenue
Edmonton AB T3P 4C2

AT **Alberta Trust**
121 Money Way
Edmonton, AB T3C 4N6

No: 50

Date | 2 | 0 | 1 | 2 | 0 | 4 | 1 | 8 |
Y Y Y Y M M D D

Pay ——— Four Thousand, Two Hundred ——— 00 $ 4,200.00

TO THE ORDER OF
Giovanno Assuri
44 Workman's Way
Edmonton AB   T3T 5T5

PER *M. Missoni*

⑉—⋮—⑉ 40361 ⋅⋅ 050

Re: Wages to assistant for contracted
work to date, $4,200.00

No: 50
April 18, 2012

☐ **Sales Invoice #MM-43**   **Dated April 19, 2012**

To Lindbrook Estates, $1 200 plus $60 GST charged for repairs to fireplace mantel. Sales invoice total $1 260. Terms: net 10 days. Create new Group account 1280 A/R - Lindbrook Estates.

☐ **Cheque Copy #51**   **Dated April 20, 2012**

To West Mall Mechanical, $315 in full payment of account. Reference invoice #WMM-4499.

☐ **Sales Invoice #MM-44** **Dated April 20, 2012**

To Sherwood Park Estates (new customer), $3 000 plus $150 GST charged for contracted new marble tile kitchen floor and walls. Sales invoice total $3 150. Terms: net 10 days. Create new Group account 1260 A/R - Sherwood Park Estates.

☐ **Cash Receipt #22** **Dated April 21, 2012**

From Lindbrook Estates, cheque #189 for $1 260 in payment of invoice #MM-43.

SESSION DATE – APRIL 28, 2012

☐ **Purchase Invoice #BT-2194** **Dated April 23, 2012**

From Beaumont Tekstore, $1 300 plus $65 GST paid for external hard drive for computer. Purchase invoice total $1 365. Terms: net 10 days. Create new Group account 2220 A/P - Beaumont Tekstore.

☐ **Sales Invoice #MM-45** **Dated April 24, 2012**

To Stoney Plain Plaza, $3 600 plus $180 GST charged to install marble floors in public washroom as per contract. Sales invoice total $3 780. Terms: net 30 days.

☐ **Cash Purchase Invoice #BAA-719** **Dated April 24, 2012**

From Bon Accord Advertising, $300 plus $15 GST paid for printing and copying advertising flyers. Purchase invoice total $315. Terms: cash on receipt. Invoice paid in full with cheque #52.

☐ **Cheque Copy #53** **Dated April 28, 2012**

To Fonteyn Dance Studio, $390 for one session of dance lessons for daughter. Use Drawings account.

SESSION DATE – APRIL 30, 2012

☐ **Memo #3** **Dated April 30, 2012**

Missoni used $3 800 of marble inventory to complete projects in April.

☐

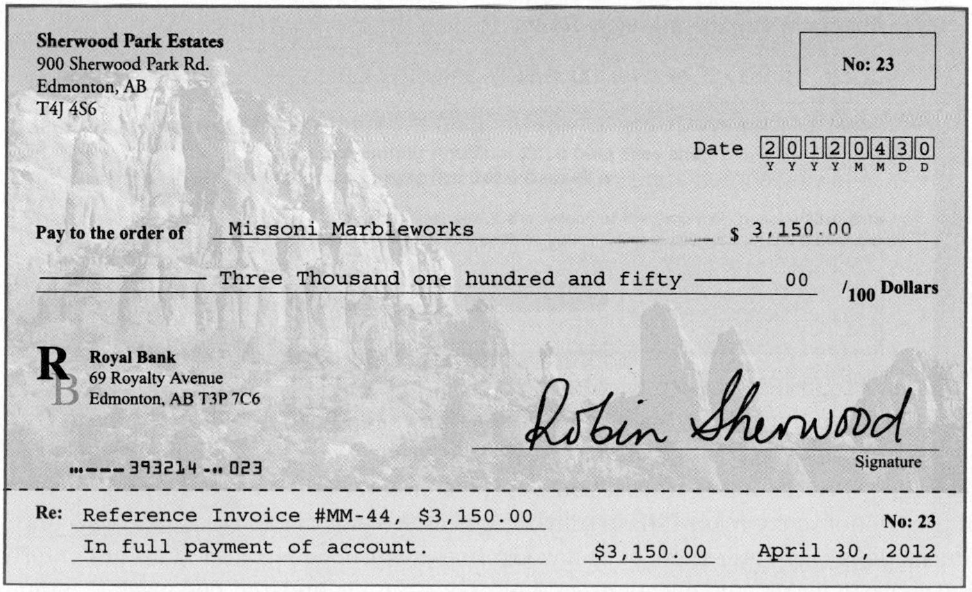

Sherwood Park Estates
900 Sherwood Park Rd.
Edmonton, AB
T4J 4S6

No: 23

Date 2 0 1 2 0 4 3 0
Y Y Y Y M M D D

Pay to the order of   Missoni Marbleworks $ 3,150.00

——————— Three Thousand one hundred and fifty ——— 00 /100 **Dollars**

R **Royal Bank**
B 69 Royalty Avenue
Edmonton, AB T3P 7C6

Robin Sherwood

Signature

⑈⋯─ 393214 ⋅⑈ 023

Re: Reference Invoice #MM-44, $3,150.00   No: 23
    In full payment of account. $3,150.00   April 30, 2012

<table>
<tr><td colspan="3"></td><td>April 30, 2012</td></tr>
<tr><td>Account No.</td><td>40361</td><td rowspan="2">ADVICE TO
ACCOUNT HOLDER</td><td>DEBIT MEMO</td></tr>
<tr><td>Code:</td><td>15</td><td>AT-D4341</td></tr>
</table>

Particulars:

Interest charged on outstanding loan	$70.00

Issued by: *MP*   **Verified by:** *3R*

Missoni Marbleworks
66 Allies Avenue
Edmonton, AB T3P 4C2

A T

Alberta Trust
121 Money Way
Edmonton, AB T3C 4N6

NOTES
In these instructions, our starting point for opening the file is the Start file in Chapter 1 as the last company you worked on.

If you are starting from the missoni1.CAB backup file, click Restore From Backup on the Welcome screen.

Click OK and click Next. Click Browse and locate the folder C:\SimData10 where you installed the data.

Double click the SimData10 folder to open it.

Click missoni1.CAB to select the file you need. Click Open.

Click Next and confirm the details. Click Next and enter the name for your restored file.

Click the Enter The Name field and type C:\SimData10\ Missoni\missoni. (This may already be the default entry.)

Click Next and click Yes to confirm the creation of the new folder and file.

Click Finish. For detailed instructions on restoring data files, refer to Chapter 1, page 20.

NOTES
Many screens include a Cancel button. If you click Cancel, you will return to your previous screen without entering any changes.

NOTES
The Advancing the Session Date section on page 49 will explain how to work with later dates.

Refer to Chapter 1, page 18, and Windows Help for further information on date formats.

Company settings are discussed in Chapter 4.

KEYSTROKES

Opening Data Files

Double click the **Simply Accounting shortcut** on your desktop, or

Choose Start then **choose All Programs** and **Simply Accounting Premium 2010**. **Click Simply Accounting Premium 2010**.

Click   Select An Existing Company and **click OK**.

Locate the folder **C:\SimData10** where you installed the data.

Double click the **SimData10 folder** to open it.

Double click the **Missoni folder** to open it.

Click   missoni or **missoni.SAI** to select the file you need. **Click Open**.

Refer to Chapter 1, page 7, for detailed instructions on opening data files.

The following screen appears, asking (prompting) you to enter the session date for this work session:

The date format on your screen is controlled by the Dates Settings options in Simply Accounting, not by the format you use to enter the date. (Refer to page 18.)

The session date is the date of your work session, the date on which you are recording the accounting transactions on the computer. A business with a large number of transactions may record these transactions at the end of each day. One with fewer transactions may enter them once a week. In this workbook, transactions are entered once a week for most applications so the session date is updated one week at a time. The session date may or may not be the same as the date on which the transaction actually took place.

The session date for your first session is April 7, 2012. Since this is not the default shown on the screen, you must change the date. Every date field has a Calendar icon.

Click   the **Calendar icon** 🗓 to open the calendar:

◀		April, 2012				▶
Sun	Mon	Tue	Wed	Thu	Fri	Sat
1	2	3	4	5	6	7
8	9	10	11	12	13	14
15	16	17	18	19	20	21
22	23	24	25	26	27	28
29	30	1	2	3	4	5

The calendar has the current session date highlighted with a blue background. The calendar for any date field also shows the range of dates that will be accepted based on the settings chosen for the company files. The arrows allow you to move forward to a later month 🕨 or back to a previous month 🕪. The calendar stops at the dates that indicate the range you may use. Click a date on the calendar to enter it or use one of the following alternative formats. For consistency, we use the same order of month, day and year throughout the text. Entering the year is optional in most date fields.

- use different characters to separate numbers: 04-07-12 or 04/07/12
- omit leading zeros: 4/7/12 or 4-7-12
- leave spaces between numbers: 04 07 12 or 4 7 12
- type lower- or upper-case text: April 7, 2012 or APRIL 7, 2012
- use three-letter abbreviations for the month: Apr 7 -12 or apr 7 -12
- use three-letter abbreviations for the month with the day first: 7 apr or 7 Apr
- other non-alpha or non-numeric separating characters may also be used
- in the General Journal and session date window, you can omit the year

We will use a variety of date formats throughout this workbook but we always show the dates on-screen in the text format to minimize entering incorrect dates. Using the calendar to choose a date or using a text version to enter a date will also prevent an incorrect date entry.

Click   **7** on the April date calendar or

Type   april 7, 2012

Click   **OK**.

Your screen shows the following Company module Home window:

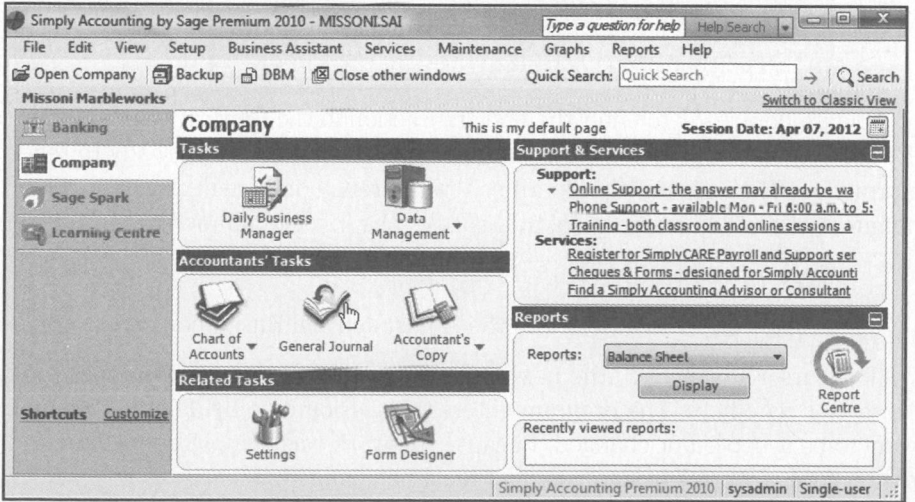

For Missoni Marbleworks, the Company module is the default page. Only the General Ledger and Journal can be accessed for this file. When ledger icons are hidden, all main menu options related to those ledgers are also hidden or unavailable. (Click 🔲 to maximize the window if necessary.) The Home window has the title bar on top with

NOTES

Refer to Chapter 1, page 18, and Chapter 4, page 80, for instructions on changing date format settings.

NOTES

When you click ◀, the dimmed back arrow in the date calendar, nothing happens because the earliest date you can use for Missoni is April 1.

NOTES

When you enter the date using text, the date is not ambiguous, so you can enter the day first. Similarly, you do not need to leave a space between the month and day because there is no ambiguity.

NOTES

Keystrokes that you must use are shown in command statements like these:
   Type   april 7
or
   Click   **OK**
Instruction lines are indented; command words are in boldface; text you type is shown in a special font (Courier); and things that you must click on or select are in colour and bold. This format makes it easy to find the instruction statements in the text.

PRO VERSION

The program name in the title bar will be Simply Accounting by Sage Pro 2010. The status bar will not include the single-user status. The Pro version is a single-user program.

CLASSIC VIEW

The Classic view Home window includes the icon for the Reconciliation and Deposits Journal. In the Enhanced view, Banking is listed as a separate module and the Reconciliation and Deposits Journal is accessed from it.

NOTES

Maximize the Home window if necessary. Refer to Chapter 1 for a more detailed description of the Home window.

NOTES

Although the Banking module is not used, it cannot be hidden if you want to use the General Journal.

NOTES

The Daily Business Manager is used in Chapter 11. The Learning Centre was introduced in Chapter 1.

NOTES

The Refresh tool applies to multi-user use of the program. This feature is not available in Pro version.

NOTES

Source codes can contain up to 20 characters, including spaces.

WARNING!

Unless you change the date, the session date will become the posting date for the entry.
    Remember that you can use any date format listed on page 39 and you may also omit the year in the General Journal Date field.

the program and file names, control menu icon and size buttons; the main menu bar comes next; the tool bar follows. Tool buttons permit quick access to commonly used menu items. The Home window tools (with their alternative pull-down menu locations) include Open Company and Backup (File menu), Daily Business Manager (Business Assistant menu) and Close Other Windows (View menu). The Search function and tool (Edit menu) are located on the far right for easy access.

The major part of the window is divided into three columns of panes or sections — the Modules and Shortcuts panes on the left; the ledger, journal and related Tasks panes in the middle; and the Reports and Support panes on the right. For the Company module, the upper right pane has access to support services for Simply Accounting. For other modules, this pane has the ledger accounts. The session date and the change date calendar icon are located above the Support pane.

Below these panes is the status bar with the program name and version and the user name (sysadmin) and status (Single-user). In most windows, the status bar shows the purpose of the field or icon that has the pointer on it.

Entering General Journal Transactions

All transactions for Missoni Marbleworks are entered in the General Journal in the Accountants' Tasks pane, indicated by the pointer in the following screen:

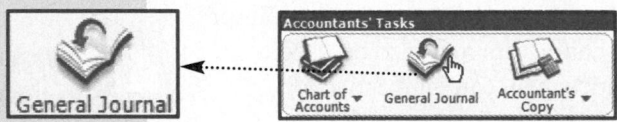

> **Click** the **General Journal icon** in the Accountants' Tasks pane of the Company module Home window to open the General Journal.

The General Journal input form that follows appears on your screen:

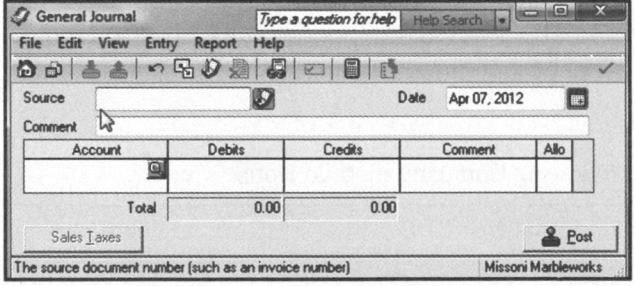

You are now ready to enter the first transaction in the General Journal input screen. The cursor, a flashing vertical line, is blinking in the Source field, ready to receive information. The Source field identifies the reference document from which you obtain the information for a transaction, in this case, the invoice number.

> **Type** WCT-161

> **Press** (tab) to advance to the Adjust Journal Entry icon. **Press** (tab) again.

The cursor advances to the next field, the Date field. You should enter the transaction date here. The program enters the session date by default. It is highlighted, ready to be accepted or changed. Because the work was completed on April 2, 2012, the session date of April 7 is incorrect and must be changed.

> **Type** 04-02

> **Press** (tab) to move to the Calendar icon 🖩.

Notice that the text form of the date is displayed, even though we entered the date as numbers. The year is added to the date.

If you click the Calendar icon in the Date field now, the session date has a frame around it. The current transaction date has a solid blue background.

Press (tab) again to accept the date and advance to the Comment field.

In the Comment field, you should enter a description of the transaction to make the permanent record more meaningful. You may enter up to 75 characters, including spaces.

Type West Carbide Tools

Press (tab).

The cursor moves forward to the first line of the Account field, creating a dotted box for the first account.

Simply Accounting organizes accounts into financial statement sections or categories using the following boundaries for numbering:

- 1000–1999 Assets
- 2000–2999 Liabilities
- 3000–3999 Equity
- 4000–4999 Revenue
- 5000–5999 Expense

This system makes it easy to remember the first digit of an account. Double clicking the Account field will display the list of accounts. If you type the first digit of an account number then double click or press (enter) while the cursor is flashing in any account field, the program will advance the list to accounts beginning with that digit.

Click the **List icon** 🔍, or **double click** the dotted box in the **Account column** to list the accounts.

The following list of accounts appears on your journal screen:

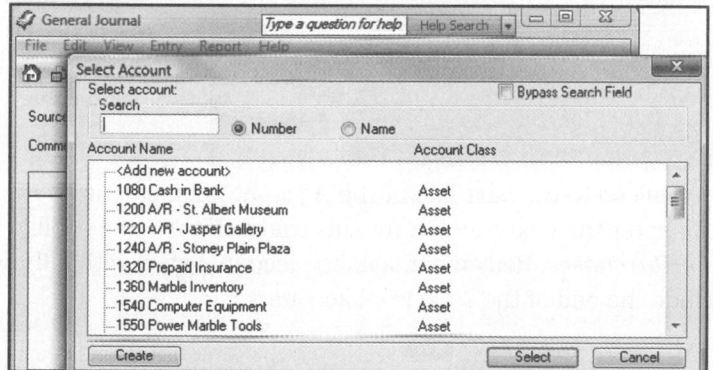

The beginning of the account list is displayed. The list includes only postable accounts, those that can be debited or credited in journal entries. The cursor is in the Search field. If you want to place the cursor in the account list directly from the Account field, you can choose the **Bypass Search Field** option. We will not select this option. Typing a number in the Search field also places the cursor directly in the list. Following usual accounting practice, we enter the account to be debited first.

Click **1550 Power Marble Tools** to select this asset account.

Click the **Select button**. (A darker frame or an inner dotted box shows that a button is selected.)

NOTES
When you press (tab) after typing a date in the Date field, you will advance to the Calendar icon. You must press (tab) again to advance to the next input field. That is, you must press (tab) twice. If you choose a date from the calendar, pressing (tab) once will move the cursor to the next input field.

NOTES
Command statements that are indented but do not have the boldfaced command words show alternative keystrokes or optional instructions.
"If you click the Calendar ..." is an example of an alternative command statement.

NOTES
Although Simply Accounting allows you to use more than four digits for account numbers in the Premium version, we will use only four-digit numbers for the applications in Part Two of the text.

NOTES
Many fields that allow you to select an account or other information from a list have the Select or List icon to provide quick access to the list. Showing the List icon is an option that you select as a user preference setting.
Other fields have list arrows that provide a drop-down or pop-up list.

NOTES
If the cursor is in the Account field, you can also press (enter) to open the Select Account list.

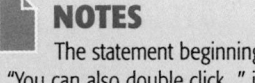

NOTES
The statement beginning "You can also double click..." is another example of an alternative command statement.

You can also double click a selected account or press ⏎ to add it directly to your journal entry form. Instead of using the selection list, you can find the number in the Chart of Accounts, type it in and press ⟨tab⟩.

Notice that the account number and name have been added to your input form, so you can easily see whether you have selected the correct account. If the screen does not display the entire account title, you can see the rest of the account title by clicking anywhere on the part that is showing.

Your cursor is now positioned in the Debits field. The amount 0.00 is selected, ready to be changed. All journals include a **Windows Calculator tool** that opens the calculator directly for easy calculation of amounts if needed.

Click the Display The Windows Calculator tool 🖩 to open the calculator. You can leave it open in the background for easy access.

Type amounts without dollar signs. You do not need to type decimals when you enter whole numbers. The Simply Accounting program ignores any non-numeric characters that you type in an amount field.

Type   885

Press   ⟨tab⟩.

The cursor moves to the Comment field. You can add a comment for each account line in the journal. Account line comments are optional. You can add a comment for each line, for some lines or for none of the lines, but the extra details can be included in the journal report and will give you more information about the transaction.

Type   diamond tip drill and drill bits

Press   ⟨tab⟩. Your input form should now appear as follows:

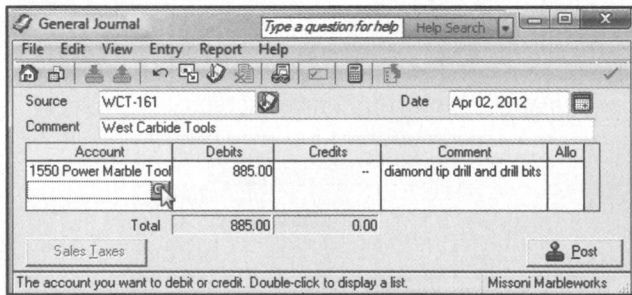

The cursor has advanced to the next line of the Account field, creating a new dotted box so you can enter the next account for this transaction — the liability account *GST Paid on Purchases*. Remember, liability accounts start with 2. However, we will type 3 to include the end of the 2000 level accounts.

Type   3

Click   the **List icon** 🔍 to advance your list to the 3000 accounts as shown:

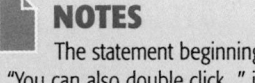

NOTES
If you know that the account you need is closer to the end of its numbered section, typing the next higher number shows you the end of the section you want. For example, typing 3 advances to 3100 and includes 2670 in the display. In this way, your account is more likely to be included in the display. Typing 2 will show the list with 2100 at the end and you will have to scroll down to include 2670.

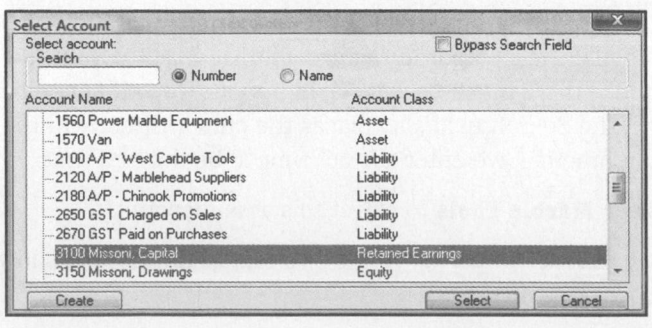

We have bypassed the Search field and selected the first account with the number we typed. This method quickly moves you to a later position in the list.

Click **2670 GST Paid on Purchases** from the displayed list to highlight it. If necessary, click a scroll arrow (▼ or ▲) to move through the account list to include *2670* in the display.

Press (enter).

Again, the account number and name have been added to your transaction form. The cursor has advanced to the Credits field, which shows 885.00 as the default amount because this amount will balance the entry. The amount is highlighted to indicate that you may edit it. This is a compound entry. You must change the amount to separate the GST, and you must delete the credit entry because the GST account is debited.

Press (del) to delete the credit entry.

Click the **Debits field** on the second journal line below 885.00 to move the cursor.

Type 44.25

Press (tab) to advance to the optional Comment field.

Type GST @ 5%

Press (tab). The cursor moves to the next line in the Account field.

Press (enter) to open the Select Account list. The cursor is in the Search field.

Type 2

The list advances to the 2000 accounts. The liability account *2100 A/P - West Carbide Tools* is selected because it is the first 2000-level account. This is the account we need.

Click **Select** to enter it and return to the journal.

The cursor advances to the Credits field again, where 929.25, the amount that will now balance the entry, is shown. The amount is correct, so you can accept it. The total for the Credits column is still displayed as zero.

Press (tab) to update the totals and advance to the Comment field.

Type terms: net 30

Your completed input form should appear as follows:

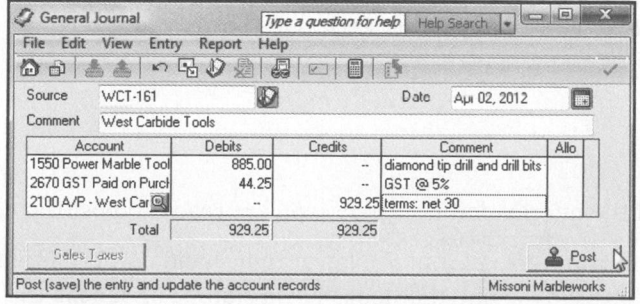

Until the debits and credits of a transaction are equal, you cannot post an entry. Once the entry is complete and balanced, it can be posted. The Store (⬇) button, for recurring entries, is also darkened. Before you proceed either to store or to post an entry, you should review the transaction.

NOTES
Typing a negative number (adding a minus sign) in the Credits field will move the number to the Debits field. Typing a negative number in the Debits field will create a Credit entry.

NOTES
The Sales Taxes button will be covered in Chapter 5. Sales taxes are not set up for Missoni Marbleworks so the button remains dimmed.

NOTES
We will use the Store button in the Chai Tea Room application (Chapter 5).

Reviewing the General Journal Entry

NOTES
Pressing `ctrl` + J will also display the journal entry in any journal. Refer to Appendix B for a complete list of Simply Accounting keyboard shortcuts.

Choose the **Report menu** and then **click Display General Journal Entry** as shown:

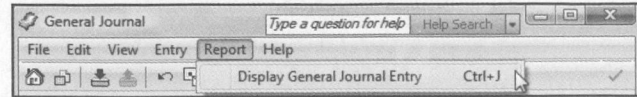

The journal entry for the transaction is displayed as follows:

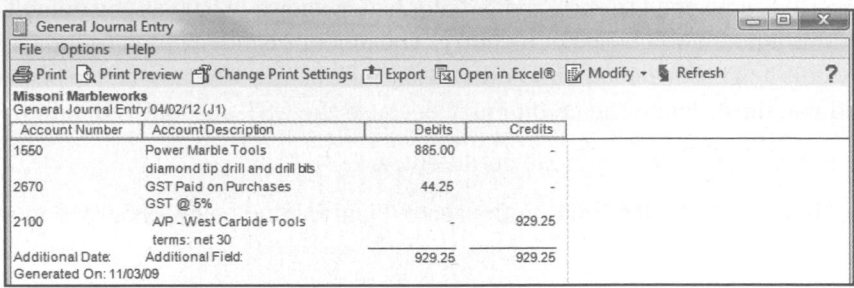

NOTES
If your display includes scroll arrows, you can use them to see more of your transaction.

NOTES
Additional Date and Field can be used to add more information to a journal entry. The Additional Information feature is available in all journals and will be introduced in Chapter 11.

Click the **Maximize button** ⬜ to change your display to full screen size if your transaction does not fit on the screen.

To return to your input form,

Click ⊠ or **choose** the entry's **Control Menu icon** ⬛ and **click Close**.

CORRECTING THE GENERAL JOURNAL ENTRY BEFORE POSTING

Press `tab` to advance to the field that has the error. To move to a previous field, **press** `shift` and `tab` together (that is, while holding down `shift`, **press** `tab`). The field will be highlighted, ready for editing. **Type** the **correct information** and **press** `tab` to enter it.

You can also use the mouse to **point** to a field and **drag** through the **incorrect information** to highlight it. You can highlight a single number or letter, or the entire field. **Type** the **correct information** and **press** `tab` to enter it.

To correct an account number, **click** the **incorrect account number** (or **name**) to select the field. **Press** `enter` to display the list of accounts. **Click** the **correct account. Click Select. Press** `tab` to advance the cursor and enter the correction.

Click an **incorrect amount** to highlight it. **Type** the **correct amount** and **press** `tab`.

You can insert a line or remove a line by clicking the line that will be moved down or removed. Then **choose** the **Edit menu** and **click Insert Line** or **Remove Line**.

To discard the entry and begin again, **click** ⊠ (Close) to close the journal or **click** ↺ (Undo on the tool bar) to open a blank journal window. When Simply Accounting asks whether you want to discard the entry, **click Yes** to confirm your decision.

NOTES
Refer to page 47 for assistance with correcting errors after posting.

⚠ WARNING!
Don't post the transaction until you make sure that it is correct. Always review a transaction before posting it.

Posting

Once you are sure that all the information is correct, you are ready to post the entry.

Click the **Post button** [🔨 Post] in the lower right-hand corner of the General Journal (the one that looks like a stamp) or **choose** the **Entry menu** and then **click Post**.

We have chosen the option to confirm when a transaction is posted successfully, so you will see a confirmation message each time you post or record a transaction:

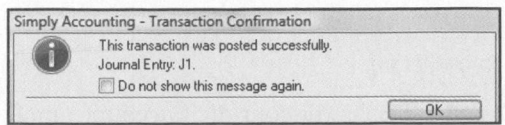

Click   **OK** to open a new blank General Journal input form.

You can now enter the next transaction for this session date.

Adding a New Account

The bank credit memo on April 3 uses an account that is not listed in your Chart of Accounts. Often a company will need to create new accounts as it expands or changes direction. These future needs are not always foreseen when the accounts are first set up. You must add the account *2300 Bank Loan* to enter the bank credit memo transaction. You can add accounts in the Accounts Ledger (Chart of Accounts icon). The Accounts Ledger is explained in Chapter 4. You can also add accounts directly from the Account field in any journal. First, enter the Source.

Type   AT-C3104

Press   `tab` **twice** to advance to the Date field. The date of the previous journal entry becomes the default date until you close the journal.

Click   the **Calendar icon** 📅 and then **click 3**.

Press   `tab` to advance to the Comment field.

Type   Alberta Trust - new loan

Double click the **Account field**.

Double click the **Cash in Bank** account.

Type   10000   (the amount of the loan) as the debit part of the transaction.

Press   `tab` to advance to the Comment field for the account.

Type   loan for marble equipment

Press   `tab` to advance to the Account field on the second journal line.

Click   the **List icon** 🔍 or **press** `enter` to see the Select Account list.

Click   **Add New Account**, the first entry in the list, and **click Select** or **click** the **Create** button.

This will begin the wizard for adding a General Ledger account:

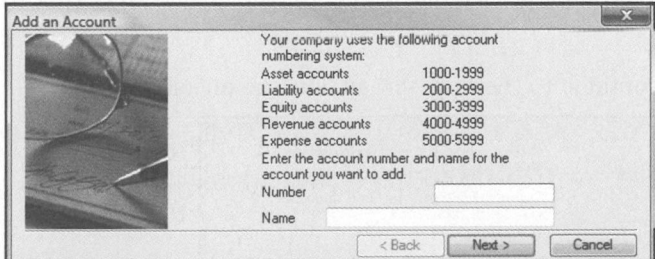

The first screen prompts you for the account number and name. The cursor is in the Number field.

Type   2300

Press   `tab`.

NOTES
When you close the journal and open it later, the session date becomes the default again.

NOTES
Next is selected so you can press ⏎ repeatedly to advance through the wizard screens that you do not need to change.

WARNING!
Account types must be set correctly or you will get the error message that accounts are not in logical order when you display financial reports. If you see one of these messages, you can edit the account type. See Chapter 4, page 91, for help with creating and editing accounts.

Type   Bank Loan

Click   **Next** or **press** ⏎ to continue.

The next screen asks for the **GIFI code**. This is the four-digit account number assigned by Canada Revenue Agency for this category of account for use with electronically filed business returns. GIFI codes are not used in this workbook. They are described in Appendix J.

Click   **Next** to skip this screen and continue.

The next screen asks whether this account is to be used as a **Heading** or **Total** in the financial statements. *Bank Loan* is an ordinary postable account that has a balance so the default selection, No, is correct. A partial balance sheet illustrates account types.

Click   **Next** to accept the default and continue.

The following screen deals with another aspect of the **account type**. Accounts may be **subtotalled** within their group of accounts. For example, if you have several bank accounts, you will want your Balance Sheet report to include the total cash deposited in all of them together. Different account types will be explained fully in the Toss for Tots application (Chapter 4), where you will set up the accounting records for a new company.

Bank Loan is a Group account. It is not subtotalled with any other account so the default selection, No, is correct.

Click   **Next** to continue.

The next wizard screen refers to the **account class**. Account classes are explained in Chapter 7. The default selection is the name of the section. Therefore, for account *2300*, Liability is the section and the default class. Generally, you can accept the default selection.

Click   **Next** to continue.

Now you are being asked whether you want to **allocate** the balance of the account to different projects or divisions. Projects are not set up for Missoni Marbleworks, so the default selection, set at No for Balance Sheet accounts, is correct.

Click   **Next** to continue.

The next setting screen asks whether you want to include or **omit** this account **from financial statements** when it has a zero balance. Choosing Yes means that if the balance in this account is zero, the account will not be included in your financial statements. If you choose No, the account will be printed even if it has a balance of zero. Some accounts, such as *Cash in Bank*, should always be printed in financial statements. In Chapter 4 we explain this setting. The default setting, to include accounts (not to omit), is never wrong.

Click   **Next** to continue to the final screen, like the one shown here:

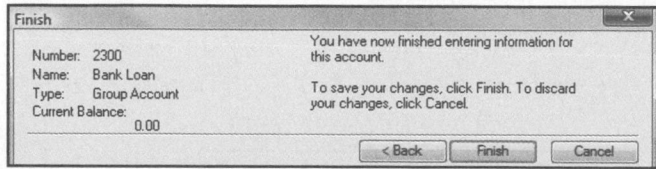

This final screen shows the selections you have made.

Check   your **work. Click Back** until you reach the screen with the error. **Make**
the **correction** and **click Next** until you reach this final screen again.

When all the information is correct, you must save the new account information.

NOTES
You can use the wizard in any account field to create a new account at any time. You do not need to use the account after creating it when you return to the journal.

Click **Finish**.

You will return to the General Journal window with the new account added to the account field. Notice that the cursor has not yet advanced, so you can change your account selection if you need to.

Click the **Credits field**.

Press ⟨tab⟩ to accept the amount and advance to the Comment field.

Type Alberta Trust loan

Display the **journal entry** to see whether it is correct.

Close the **display**. **Make corrections** if you find errors.

Click **Post** ⟨👤 Post⟩ to save the information. **Click OK** to confirm.

↺ **Enter** the **next sale transaction**.

Adjusting a Posted Entry

Sometimes, after posting a journal entry, you discover that it had an error. You can make corrections directly in the General Journal by adjusting the previously posted transaction. Simply Accounting allows you to make the correction by adjusting the entry without completing a reversing entry. The program creates the reversing and correcting journal entries after you post the correction so that the audit trail is complete. The purchase from West Carbide Tools on April 2 was posted with an incorrect amount.

The General Journal should still be open.

Click the **Adjust A Previously Posted Entry tool** ⟨⧉⟩ in the tool bar, or

click ⟨⧉⟩ , the **Adjust An Entry button** beside the Source field, or

choose the **Entry menu** and **click Adjusting Entry**.

The Search screen opens:

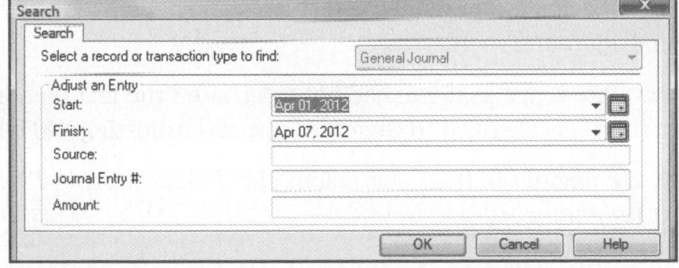

The Adjust Entry and Search functions are combined. Because we selected the Adjust option, the Search section of the screen is dimmed, but General Journal is indicated as the search area. If you begin from the Home window Search option, the cursor will be placed in the Search part of the window. Finding a transaction is the same for both functions. You can select a range of journal entry dates to search. The date we converted the data files to Simply Accounting and the session date are the default start and finish dates for the list. If you know the Source number for the entry, you can enter it in the Source field and access the journal entry directly by clicking OK.

We can accept the default dates because they include the transaction we need.

NOTES
This go-back symbol ↺ directs you back to the source documents for the next transaction because there are no new keystroke instructions for this transaction. Continue in the source documents section until you reach the next page number reference.

NOTES
Pressing ⟨ctrl⟩ + A will also start the adjust entry process in any journal when the option is available.

Click **OK** to list the journal entries:

Select Entry To Adjust				
View entries by: Date ▾		Z...A↓		
Journal Entry #	Date	Source	Comment	Amount
3	Apr 03, 2012	MM-40	St. Albert Museum sale	3,990.00
2	Apr 03, 2012	AT-C3104	Alberta Trust - new loan	10,000.00
1	Apr 02, 2012	WCT-161	West Carbide Tools	929.25

All journal entries are listed with the most recent one at the top of the list (Z...A↓ order). You can choose the way the journal entries are sorted.

Click the **list arrow** beside the Date entry for **View Entries By**:

Select Entry To Adjust				
View entries by: Date ▾		Z...A↓		
	Journal Entry #			
Journal Entry #	Date		Comment	Amount
3	A Source		St. Albert Museum sale	3,990.00
2	A Comment		Alberta Trust - new loan	10,000.00
	Amount			

You can organize the list of entries by journal entry number, date, source number, comment or amount. The Z...A button lets you choose ascending or descending order.

Click **Journal Entry #**.

Click Z...A↓ to reverse the order. The one we want is now first in the list.

Click **Journal Entry #1, WCT-161** to select it.

Click **Select** or **press** (enter) to open the journal entry as it was posted:

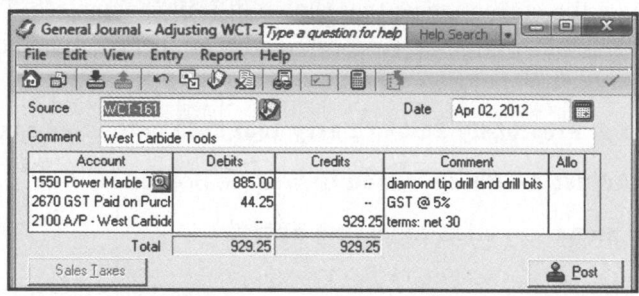

You can also double click anywhere on the line for a journal entry to open the Adjusting General Journal screen.

All fields may now be edited, just as if you had not yet posted the transaction. Notice that the title bar entry has changed to General Journal – Adjusting WCT-161.

Click **885.00**, the amount in the Debit column for *Power Marble Tools*, to select it for editing.

Type 900

Click **44.25** or **press** ⬇ to select the Debit column amount for *GST Paid on Purchases*.

Type 45

Click **929.25**, the Credit column amount for *AP - West Carbide Tools*.

Type 945

Press (tab) to update the totals with the correct amounts.

We will also modify the source to show that this entry is the correction for the memo.

Click the **Source field** before the current entry (**before W**).

Type (COR)

NOTES
You should choose the order that makes it easiest to find your entry. That will depend on what information you entered and what you remember as well as how many entries you have.

NOTES
Although Journal Entry #1 is highlighted, the cursor is still on the A...Z↓ button, so pressing (enter) does not open the journal yet. You must press (tab) or click the entry to advance and select the entry.
You can also double click the entry to open the transaction.

NOTES
Usually clicking a number in a field will select the entire number. Sometimes, however, depending on exactly where you click, only part of the number is selected or an insertion point is added. Double clicking will always select the entire number in the field so that you can edit it.

You can change the date for the correcting entry to April 4 if you want. We have not changed the date for this correction.

Review the **entry** to see the correct transaction and **close** the **display**. **Make corrections** if necessary.

Click   **Post** ![Post] . **Click OK** to confirm the posting. Notice that the entry is J5. (J4 is the reversing entry created by the program.)

When you display the General Journal Report with Corrections selected (refer to page 60), you will see three entries for the purchase invoice — the original incorrect entry, a reversing adjusting entry created by the program (ADJWCT-161) and the correct entry (COR) WCT-161 — providing a complete audit trail for the transaction and correction. See the General Journal Report display on page 60.

REVERSING A GENERAL JOURNAL ENTRY AFTER POSTING

If you need to reverse an entry instead of making changes to it, **click** the **Reverse Entry tool** ![icon] in the tool bar of the General Journal – Adjusting window, or **choose** the **Entry menu** and **click Reverse Entry**. You will see a confirmation message before the action is taken. **Click Yes** to confirm and continue. Simply Accounting does not delete the original entry. Instead it adds the reversing entry to the journal report for a complete audit trail. You can hide reversing entries in journal reports by not showing corrections.

    Continue   with the **journal entries** for the April 7 session date.

Advancing the Session Date

When you have finished all the entries for the April 7 session date, the date for the next transaction is later than April 7. Therefore, you must advance the session date before you can continue. If you do not advance the date before posting the April 8 transaction, you will receive an error message.

Before advancing the date, however, close all open windows and then save and back up your work because you have already completed one week of transactions. Although Simply Accounting saves automatically each time you display a report or exit the program, it is important to know how to save and back up your work directly to a separate file and location or disk because your working files may become damaged and unusable.

Click   ![X] or **choose** the **File menu** for the journal and **click Close** to close the General Journal.

You can save a complete duplicate working copy of the file under a different file name. Choose the File menu and click Save A Copy to continue working with the original files or Save As to open a new working copy of the file. This option requires more disk storage space because the copy is not compressed.

The data files for this workbook have been prepared with the default warning to back up your work weekly. Since we also advance the session date by one week at a time, you will be reminded to back up each time you advance the session date. You are now ready to advance the session date to April 14.

Click   the **Calendar icon** ![icon] beside **Session Date: Apr 07, 2012** on the right-hand side of the Home window:

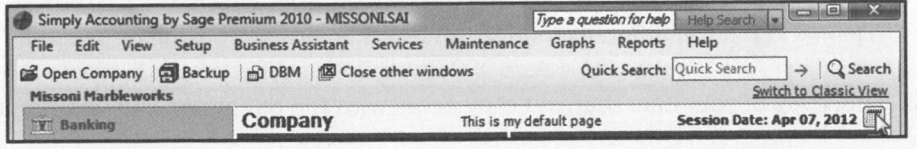

NOTES
The adjusting and correcting entries are posted with the same date – the date you used for the adjusting entry. If you want, you can change the date for the adjusting entry but not for the reversing entry.

NOTES
We have set up the data files for Missoni so that future-dated transactions are not allowed.

NOTES
Refer to page 19 for information on the Save As and Save A Copy commands.
A complete data set is more than 25 Megabytes in size while its backup file is about 2 Megabytes.

WARNING!
You must close all windows before you can advance the session date.
You can click ![icon], the Home window Close Other Windows tool, or close each window separately. You also must be working in single-user mode to change the session date.

Or, **choose** the **Maintenance menu** and **click Change Session Date** as shown:

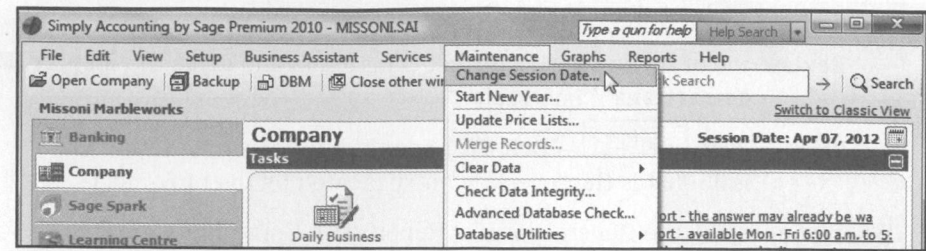

The Change Session Date window opens with the current session date highlighted:

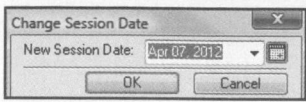

Type   04-14-12 (or click the date calendar and click 14)

Click   **OK** to accept the new date.

The following message advises you that you have not yet backed up your work:

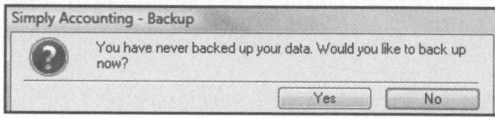

Click   **Yes** to proceed with the backup. The next screen asks for a file name for the backup:

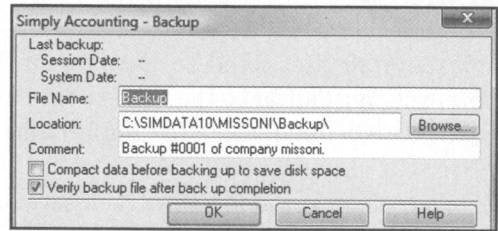

Simply Accounting will create a file named Backup1 inside a new Backup subfolder of the folder that contains your working data files. You can edit the file name and comment. The name Backup is selected so you can change the name.

Type   missoni

If you want to change the location of the backup, click Browse, select a folder and file name and click OK.

Click   **OK** to proceed.

When you name a new folder, you will see the following advisory message:

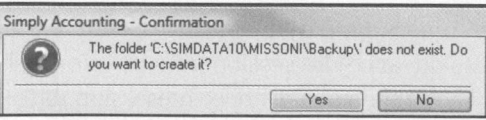

The program recognizes that the name is new and offers to create the folder. If you have typed the correct name and location,

Click   **Yes** to accept the information and continue.

The backup file is different from the one you create by copying or using the Save A Copy or Save As command. The Save A Copy and Save As commands create a complete working copy of your data that you can access with the Simply Accounting program

NOTES
You cannot create backups when working in multi-user mode.

WARNING!
Be sure to back up each time you are prompted to do so or each time you advance the session date. If your files are damaged, your work will be lost unless you have a backup.

NOTES
You may see a backup message that shows the previous backup file name and date. In this case the backup # will also be increased.

WARNING!
You cannot use the same name for the backup and the file if they are in the same folder. If you want to use the same name, you must use a different folder. By using the Backup folder, we can name the backup file missoni.

directly. Backup creates a compressed file that must first be restored before you can use it to enter transactions. This file has a .CAB file extension.

After a brief interval, you will see the message that the backup is complete:

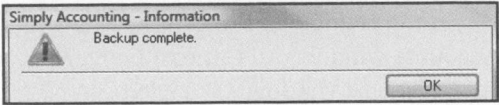

Click   OK to proceed. You may now enter transactions for this session date.

If you have already created a backup for this data file, or when you change the session date again, you will be advised of the most recent backup date when you are prompted to back up again:

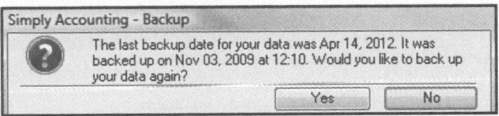

Click   Yes to continue.

NOTES
When you change the session date again, the prompt to back up the file will include the session date and calendar date and time of the previous backup.

Simply Accounting will provide the same file name and location that you used for your most recent backup. The backup number in the Comment field will be updated.

Your backup information screen will look like the one we show, with different dates:

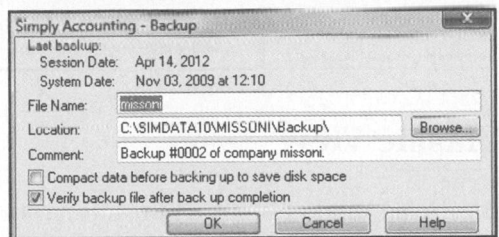

Click   OK, or **make** the **changes** you want. You can change the file name, its location or the comment.

Click   OK.

If you use the same backup file name, you will be asked to replace the previous file:

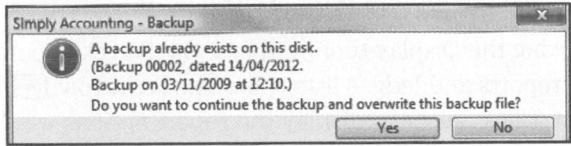

Click Yes to continue with the replacement or click No to enter a different name.

Enter   the **remaining transactions for April**.

NOTES
We recommend updating the backup name by adding a date or number to the name. For example, type missoni2 for the next backup, then missoni3, and so on.

Displaying General Reports

A key advantage to using Simply Accounting rather than a manual system is the ability to produce financial reports quickly for any date or time period. Simply Accounting allows you to enter accounting data accurately so you can prepare the reports you need for reporting to government and investors and for business analysis.

Reports that are provided for a specific date, such as the Balance Sheet, can be produced for any date from the time the accounting records were converted to the computerized system up to the latest journal entry. Reports that summarize a financial period, such as the Income Statement, can be produced for any period between the beginning of the fiscal period and the latest journal entry.

NOTES
Report analysis is beyond the scope of this text.

NOTES
If you have data for more than one fiscal period, you can display and print reports for the previous fiscal periods.

Reports are available from multiple locations: the Accounts window, the Home window Reports menu, the Display tool in the Classic view, and from the Reports list and the Report Centre in the Reports pane of the Home window.

Click the Chart of Accounts icon in the Home window (Classic view or Enhanced view) to open the Accounts window. All General Ledger reports will be available from the Reports menu in this window.

The Reports Menu

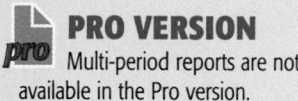
From the Home window Reports menu, most General Ledger Reports are located under the Financials option as shown:

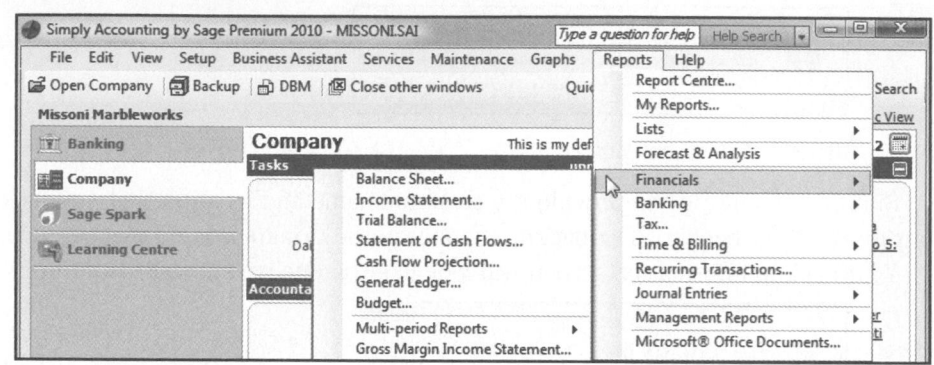

The Display Tool in the Classic View

The Display tool [icon] (on the Classic view Home window tool bar) provides a shortcut to displaying reports related directly to the ledger and journal icons. These include lists related to the ledgers such as the Chart of Accounts, supplier and employee lists, as well as all journal reports. The Display tool works in three different ways.

1. If a ledger or journal icon is selected but not open, the options window for that report is displayed immediately when you click the Display tool. The label for the Display tool changes to name the report for a selected icon.

2. If no icon is highlighted, clicking the Display tool produces the Select Report window that lists all journal reports and ledger lists. Click the list arrow [▼] and choose a report from this list. Click Select to display the report options window.

3. When the Accounts window is open, clicking the Display tool provides a Select A Report window that lists all the reports for the General Ledger. Click the list arrow [▼], choose from this list and click Select to display the report or its options window. In other ledger windows, the reports list will include the reports related to that ledger.

The Reports Pane and Report Centre

The Reports pane allows access to reports in three ways: from the Report Centre, from the list of recently viewed reports or from the drop-down list of reports for the module you have open. The Company module Reports list is shown here:

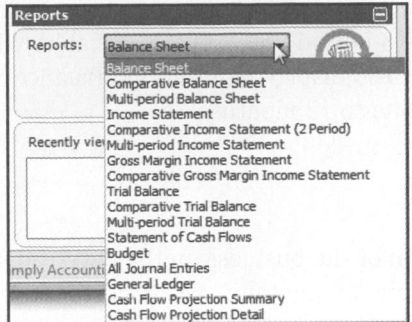

PRO VERSION

pro You will not see Multi-Period reports in the list.

Clicking a report in this list will display it with the default report settings. Once you have displayed a report, it will be added to the Recently Viewed Reports list. Clicking the report in this list will display it with the settings you used most recently. If you have modified a report, using this list provides quick access to your modified report.

We will work from the Report Centre. There are advantages to using the Report Centre: you can either display the report with the default settings immediately or display the Options windows. Furthermore, before opening the report, you will see the purpose and a brief description of the report you want and a display of a sample report.

Click   the **Report Centre Icon** [icon] in the Reports pane.

Click   **Financials** in the Select A Report Type list:

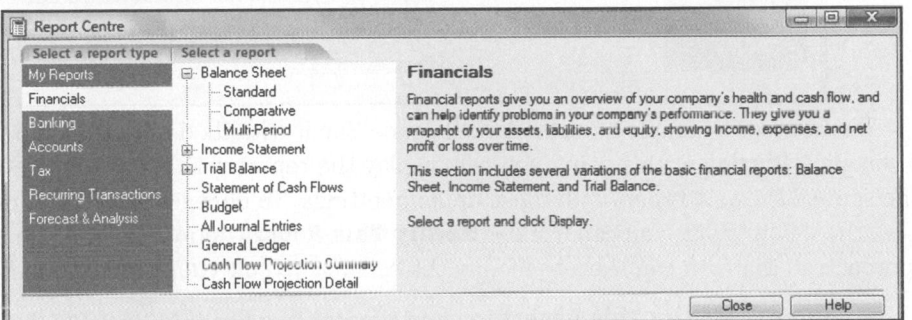

As from the Reports menu, reports for ledgers that are hidden are not available. Financial reports are selected because we started from the Company module Home window, and a list of the different financial reports is added. You can see that several of the reports have a [+] beside them indicating that there are different forms of the report. A brief explanation of Financial Reports appears.

Read   the **description**.

Click   each [+] beside each report type to expand the list.

Click   **Balance Sheet** to see a general description of balance sheets:

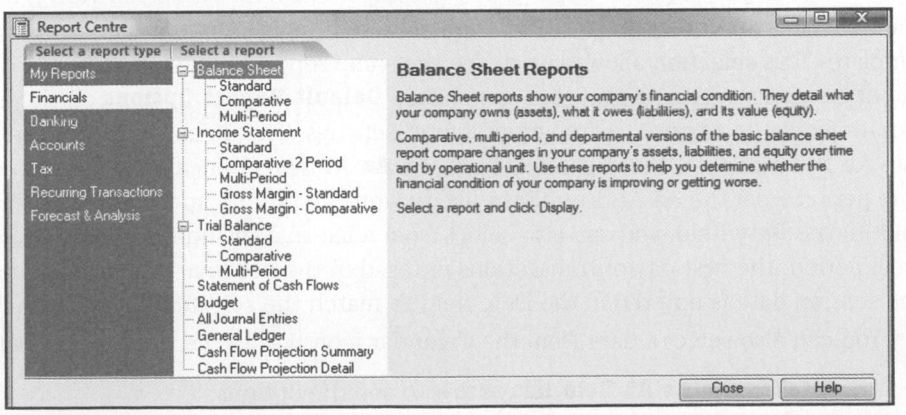

NOTES

When you open the Report Centre from a module window, the first report for that module is selected and you will see the description for it. Balance Sheet – Standard and its description may be displayed initially from the Company module window. Clicking Financials will return you to the general description of Financial Reports and its list.

PRO VERSION

pro The Pro version does not have Forecast & Analysis reports, and you will not see the entry for Multi-Period reports.

PRO VERSION

pro You will not see the entries for Multi-Period reports in the Pro version.

Because Balance Sheet is selected, the description now applies to that report. Standard (single-period) and Comparative (two-period) reports are available. When you have data for more than two months, you can also display Multi-Period Balance Sheets, to compare reports for periods ranging from one to 12 months.

Displaying the Balance Sheet

The Balance Sheet shows the financial position of the business on the date you select for the report. You can display the Balance Sheet at any time.

Click   **Standard** below Balance Sheet:

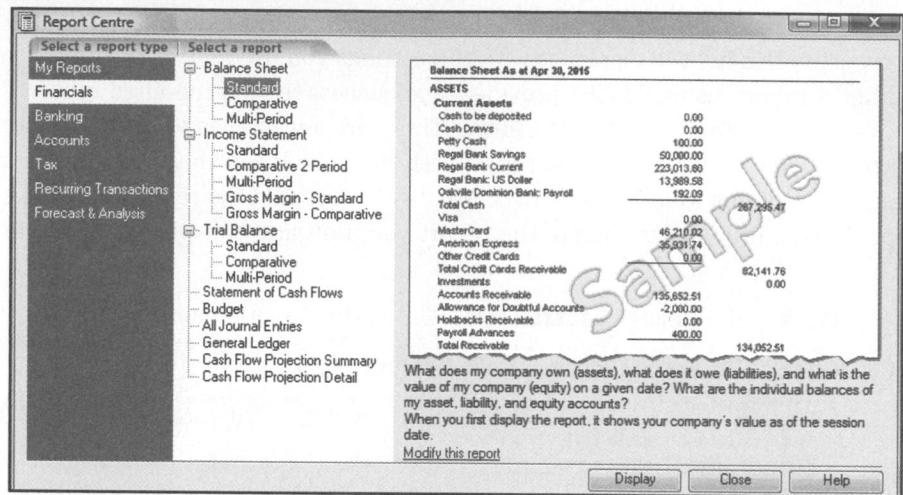

You now see a sample of a standard Balance Sheet with its description and purpose. If you click **Display** at this point, you will display the report with the default settings. The sample shows a report with these default settings. To change the settings or to see what the defaults are, you can use the **Modify This Report** option. We will use this approach so that you can learn to modify the settings to suit your specific needs.

Click   **Modify This Report** to open the Balance Sheet options window:

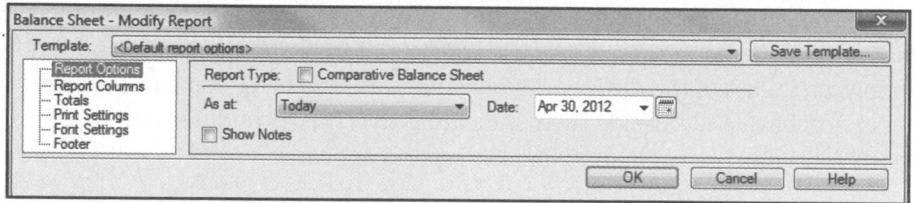

You can also choose the Reports menu, then choose Financials and click Balance Sheet. The report options window will open.

Default Report Options appears as the template the first time you view a report. The next time you open this window, the Last Used Report Options will display as the template. This selection allows you to see the same report without re-entering dates and other options. At any time you can choose **Default Report Options** on the Template drop-down list to restore the program default settings. The default is to use the session date for the report — Today is selected in the **As At** field. You can choose a standard time period from the As At drop-down list, or you can enter a specific date in the Date field. In the **Date** field, you can also select from a list that includes the first day of the fiscal period, the first day of transactions entered in the program or the session date. The session date is entered in the Date field to match the selection in the As At field.

You can also select a date from the Calendar icon  to the right of the Date field.

Click   the **As At field list arrow** to see the options:

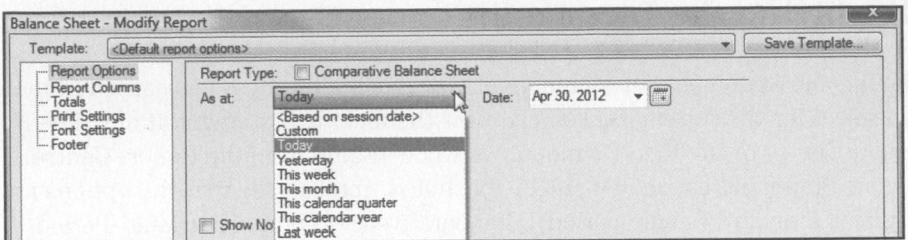

If you want to show the Balance Sheet for two different dates at the same time, you can use the Comparative Balance Sheet. Remember that this was also one of the options in the Report Centre window.

Click   **Comparative Balance Sheet** to select this style of report and open the second date field as follows:

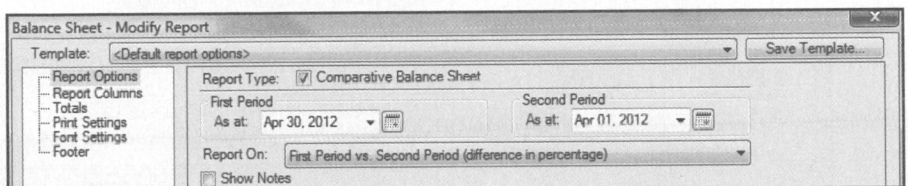

Your most recent session date is displayed in the first date field. The second date is the date on which the files were converted to Simply Accounting, the earliest transaction date.

Press   (tab) to highlight the first date if you want to change it.

Click   the **Calendar icon** [icon] to the right of the date (As At) field.

To enter a date, click [icon] and choose a date, select a date from the list or type the date you want (including the year) using one of the accepted formats.

Press   (tab) or **press** (tab) **twice** if you type the date.

Type   the **second date** (including the year) or choose from the calendar.

Click   the **Report On field** to display the report types in the drop-down list:

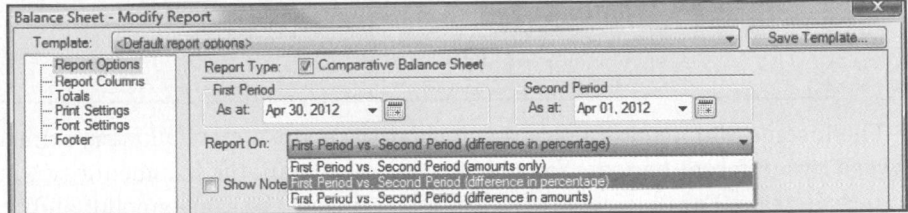

Choose **Amounts Only** if you want only the dollar balances for both dates. Choose **Difference In Percentage** if you want the dollar balances as well as the percentage increase from the second, earlier period amount to the first period amount. Choose **Difference In Amounts** if you want the dollar balances together with the difference between them in dollars. The second, earlier period amount is subtracted from the first to calculate the difference.

Click   the report **contents** you want.

Click   **OK** to display the Balance Sheet.

From any displayed report, you can change report options to create different reports.

Click   the **Modify tool** [icon] or **choose** the **Options menu** and **click Modify Report** to access the report options screen again.

Click   [icon] when you have finished to return to the Report Centre.

Displaying the Income Statement

The Income Statement is a summary of how much a business has earned in the interval you select for the statement. You can view the Income Statement at any time from the Report Centre or the Reports menu. We will continue from the Report Centre. The Income Statement list should still be expanded. You can see that the options are to display a Standard (single-period), Comparative (two-period) or Multi-Period statement. If inventory costs are tracked, Gross Margin Statements that separate the cost of goods sold from other expenses can be displayed.

Click   **Income Statement** and then **Standard** under Income Statement in the Select A Report list to see the report sample.

Click   **Modify This Report** to open the report options window:

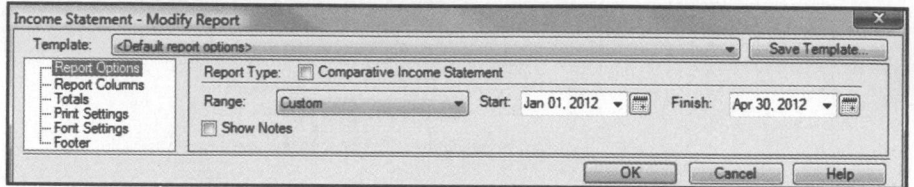

From the Home window, choose the Reports menu, then choose Financials and click Income Statement to open the Modify Report window.

As for the Balance Sheet, you can choose a range of dates from the Range field list or from the Start and Finish field lists. Or you can enter your own choices for the date range (Custom) by typing them in the Start and Finish fields or selecting other dates from the Calendar for those fields. The default range is the fiscal year to date.

Click   the **Range field list arrow**:

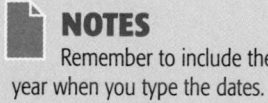
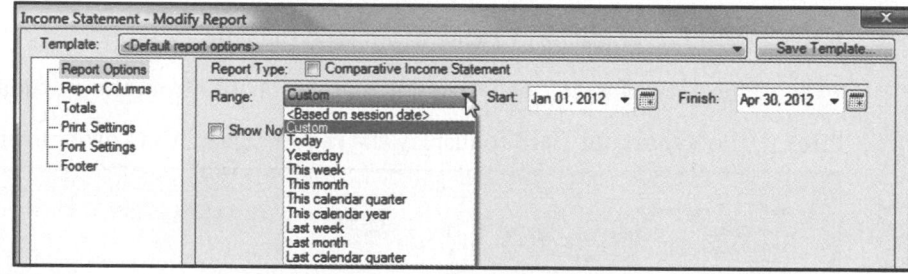

The Income Statement also has a comparative report option, allowing comparisons between two different periods. You might want to compare the income for two months, quarters or years. For the comparative report, you have the same amount and difference options as the Balance Sheet.

Click   **Comparative Income Statement** to select this option:

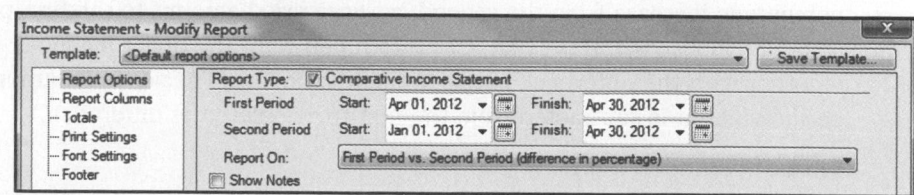

By default, the earliest transaction date is provided as the start date for the first period and the fiscal start is the start date for the second period. The session date is the finish date for both periods when you select the comparative report.

You must enter beginning and ending dates for the period (or periods) you want your Income Statement to cover. You may accept the defaults, choose a date from the calendar, choose from the date field list or type in the dates.

Click	the **Start date field** and **enter** the **date** (including the year) on which your Income Statement period begins.
Press	tab (**twice** if you type the date).
Enter	the **date** (including the year) that your Income Statement period ends.
Enter	the **Start** and **Finish dates** (including the year) for the second period and **choose** the report **content** for comparative reports.
Click	**OK**.
Click	☒ to close the display window when you have finished.

Displaying the Trial Balance

The Trial Balance shows account balances for all postable accounts in debit and credit columns. You can display the Trial Balance at any time while working with the software.

Click	**Trial Balance** and then **Standard** under Trial Balance in the Select A Report list to display the sample Trial Balance.
Click	**Modify This Report** to see the report options window:

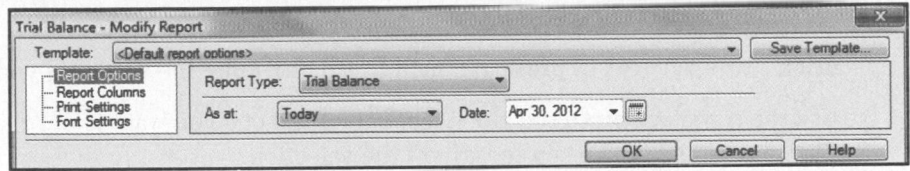

From the Home window choose the Reports menu, then choose Financials and click Trial Balance to open the report options window.

Click	the **default date** and **enter** the **date** (including the year) for which you want the Trial Balance or choose from the calendar.
Click	**OK** to display the Trial Balance.
Click	☒ to leave the display and return to the previous screen or window.

Displaying the General Ledger Report

The General Ledger Report lists all transactions for one or more accounts in the selected interval. You can display the General Ledger at any time.

Click	**General Ledger** in the Select A Report list to display the sample report.
Click	**Modify This Report** to see the report options window:

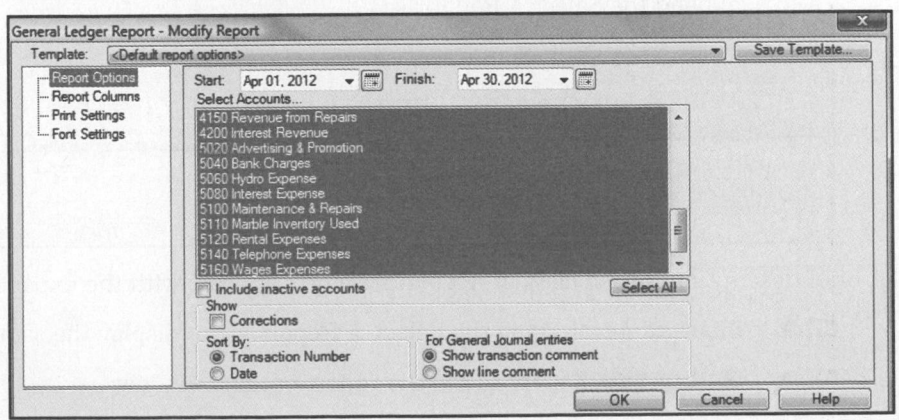

NOTES

The Trial Balance is also available as a comparative report with the same options as the Balance Sheet. Click Comparative Trial Balance, enter the first and second dates, choose the report contents from the Report On list and click OK.

From the Home window choose the Reports menu, then choose Financials and click General Ledger to display the report options.

The General Ledger Report can be sorted in order of the transaction number (journal entry number) or the transaction date. The report includes account balances and transaction or account line comments. The earliest transaction and session dates are the default Start and Finish dates. All accounts are selected for the report initially. You can include the corrections you made to journal entries or omit them with the **Show Corrections** option.

Click   an **option** to select it or to change the default choices.

Enter   the **starting date** for your General Ledger Report (including the year), choose a date from the calendar or choose a date from the Start field drop-down list.

Press   `tab` (**twice** if you type the date).

Enter   the **ending date** for your General Ledger Report (including the year).

The **Select All** option works like a toggle switch. When all accounts are selected, clicking Select All will remove all selections. With one or more accounts selected or with no selections, clicking Select All will include all accounts for the reports.

Click   the **account** or **press** and **hold** `ctrl` and **click** the **accounts** you want.

Use the scroll arrows to see more accounts if the one you want is not visible. Click a selected item again to turn off the selection.

To select several accounts in a row, click the first one and then press and hold `shift` and click the last one you want to include in the list.

You can choose to include the comment for the transaction or for individual account lines in your report. You can also choose to sort the report by date or transaction (journal entry) number.

Click   **OK** to view the report.

Click   ☒ to close the **display window** after viewing it.

Displaying the Chart of Accounts

CLASSIC VIEW
From the Home window, right-click the Chart of Accounts icon to select it. Click ▦, the Display tool on the tool bar to open the report options.

Right-click an icon in the Home window (click the right mouse button) to select it without opening the ledger or journal. Clicking the left mouse button will open the journal or ledger.

The Chart of Accounts is a list of all accounts that shows the account number, name and account type and class.

Click   **Accounts** in the Select A Report Type list (the list on the left) to expand the Select A Report list:

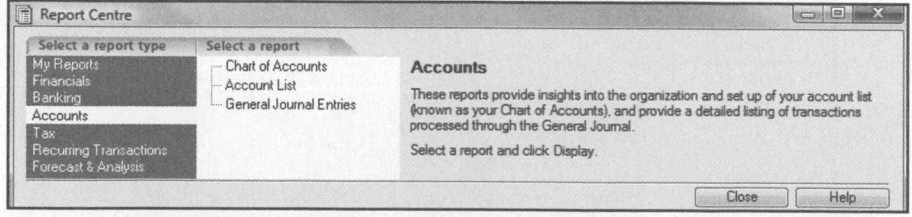

A brief description for the class of Accounts reports appears with the expanded list.

Click   **Chart of Accounts** in the Select A Report list to display the sample.

Click   **Modify This Report** to see the report options window:

Or, choose the Reports menu, then choose Lists and click Chart Of Accounts to display report options.

Choose the **Template** and the **year** (in the Select Fields list).

Click   **OK** to see the chart. **Close** the **display** when you have finished.

Displaying the Account List

If you want to display the Chart of Accounts with account balances or other selected details, you can use the Account List. For example, you could create an account list with only GIFI numbers or account balances as the additional information.

Click   **Account List** in the Select A Report list to display the sample.

Click   **Modify This Report** to see the report options window.

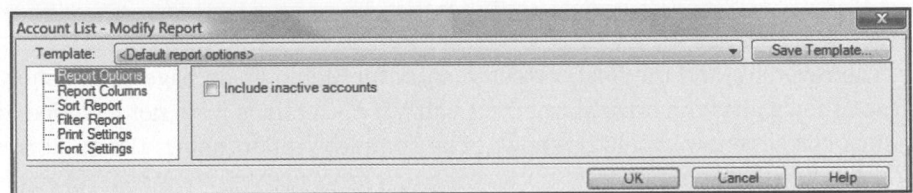

From the Home window, choose the Reports menu, then choose Lists and click Accounts to see the report options.

Click   **OK** to view the report. The default report shows the account number and name, balance, account type and account class.

Click    to close the **display window** after viewing it.

Displaying the General Journal

Click   **General Journal Entries** in the Select A Report list to display the sample.

Click   **Modify This Report** to see the report options window:

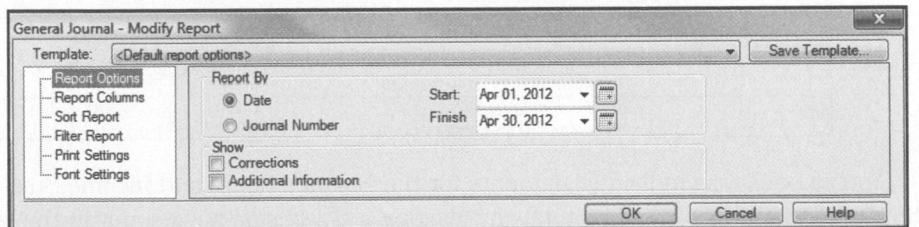

Or, choose the Reports menu. Then choose Journal Entries and click General to display the report options.

Journal reports may include correcting or adjusting entries or may omit them. You may select entries for the report either by the (posting) **Date** of the journal entries or by journal entry number. When you choose **Journal Number**, you must enter the first and last numbers for the entries you want to display. If you do not know the journal numbers, the date method is easier. Furthermore, your journal entry numbers might not

NOTES

Sometimes, depending on who will see the report, you may want to omit the corrections.

match the ones we use if you have made any additional or correcting journal entries. Therefore, all reports in this workbook are requested by date — the default setting.

The earliest transaction and the latest session date are given by default for the period of the report.

Click   Corrections to include the adjusting entries.

You can choose any dates for the Journal Report between the fiscal start and the last journal entry, including postdated entries. Include the year when you type dates.

Accept April 1 and **April 30** as the dates for your journal report.

Click   OK to display the report. A partial report is included here:

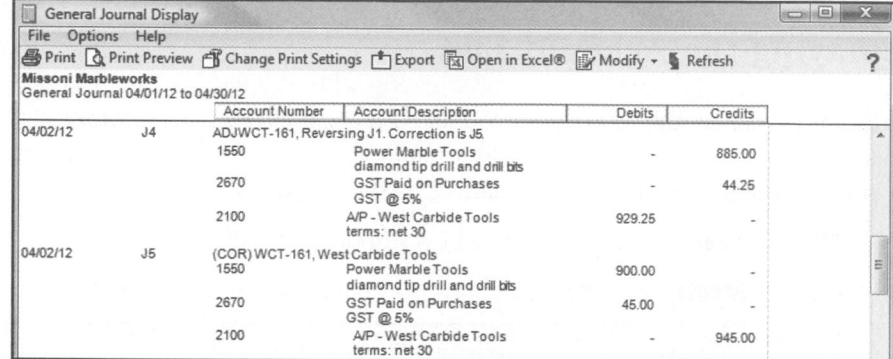

The reversing and the final corrected entry for Memo #1 on page 35 are shown here. J1 (not shown) has the original incorrect entry. If corrections were not included, only J5, the final correct entry, would be shown. The complete report shows the audit trail.

Customizing Reports

NOTES

For example, you could create a journal report that displays only cheques by filtering on the Source field to match the word Cheque (or the entry you used for these transactions).

When we selected dates, comparative options or reversing journal entries, we were customizing reports. Modify Report windows also include customization options in the pane on the left. You can change the columns or fields in the report, sort reports and filter them. Sorting reports changes the order in which data are presented, while filtering reports selects the records to include according to the data fields used as selection criteria. Printing options may also be modified.

Reports already on display may also be modified. You can choose the elements you want to change from the Modify tool drop-down list as shown:

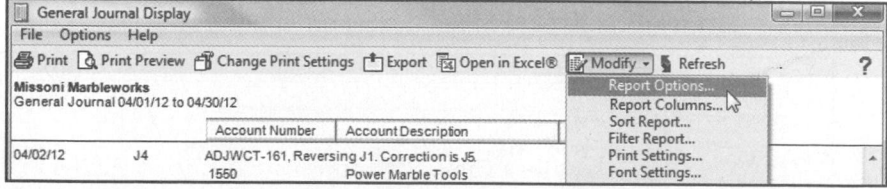

NOTES

Clicking ⊞ beside a collapsed amount will expand the account display again.

You can collapse individual amounts for the Balance Sheet and Income Statement to show only totals, or only some totals by clicking a ⊟ beside an account in the report:

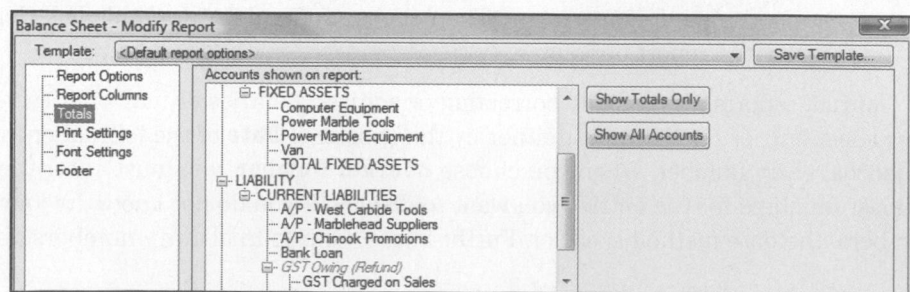

The ⊟ will change to a ⊞ to show the amounts have been collapsed.

You can also modify columns directly in the display. For example, you can widen a column by dragging the header to the right or remove a column by dragging it to the left. Clicking a column head will sort the report by the contents of that column, if the report can be sorted. Report modifications are covered further in Appendix F.

Close the **displayed report** when finished.

Drill-Down Reports

Some reports can be accessed from other reports that you have opened or displayed. These are cross-referenced or drill-down reports.

Whenever the pointer changes to 🔍 (a magnifying glass icon with a plus sign inside it), the additional reports can be displayed. When the other ledgers are used, detailed customer, vendor and employee reports are also available from the General Ledger Report and from the General Journal.

Move the **mouse pointer** over various items in the first report. The type of second report available may change. The name of the second report will appear in the status bar.

Double click while the magnifying glass icon is visible to display the second report immediately. The first report stays open in the background.

The General Ledger Report for a specific account can be accessed from the Balance Sheet, Income Statement, Trial Balance, Chart of Accounts or General Journal when you double click an account number, name or balance amount. The General Ledger record for an account can be accessed from the General Ledger Report.

While you have the additional drill-down report displayed, you may print it or drill down to other reports. (See Printing General Reports on page 62.)

Close the **second report** and then **close** the **first report** when you have finished viewing them. **Close** the **Report Centre**.

Displaying Management Reports

Management reports provide accounting information that is specific to the company data file. When the other ledgers are used, the menu also includes management reports for these ledgers.

Management reports are available from the Reports menu — they are not available from the Report Centre or the Reports drop-down lists in the Reports pane.

Choose the **Reports menu**, then **choose Management Reports** and **click General** to see the display of available reports:

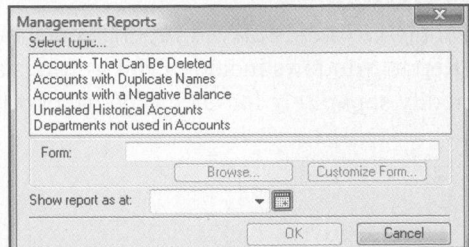

To see a report, click a topic to select it. The date field may de dimmed, depending on the topic selected. If it is not, type the date for the report in the Show Report As At

CLASSIC VIEW
You can also access Management Reports from the Advice tool 💡 in the Classic view Home window tool bar.

PRO VERSION
The Unrelated Historical Accounts and Department reports are not available in the Pro version.

NOTES
Accounts that can be deleted are those that have zero balances and have not been used in journal transactions.

field. The program will select a default report form from the ones you installed with the program. Generally, the default is the best choice. You can click Browse to see other report forms available and select the one you need. If you have the appropriate software program, you may customize the report form. Click OK to display the report.

For example, click the advice topic Accounts With A Negative Balance. Click OK. Your report should include *GST Paid on Purchases* and *Missoni, Drawings* because these contra-accounts normally have negative balances.

Close   the **display** when you have finished.

Printing General Reports

Display the **report** you want to print by following the instructions in the preceding pages on displaying reports.

There are overall print settings for the company file. These are available from the Home window and from any open report. From the displayed report,

Click   the **Change Print Settings tool** or **choose** the **File menu** and **click Reports & Forms** to open the Report & Form Options screen:

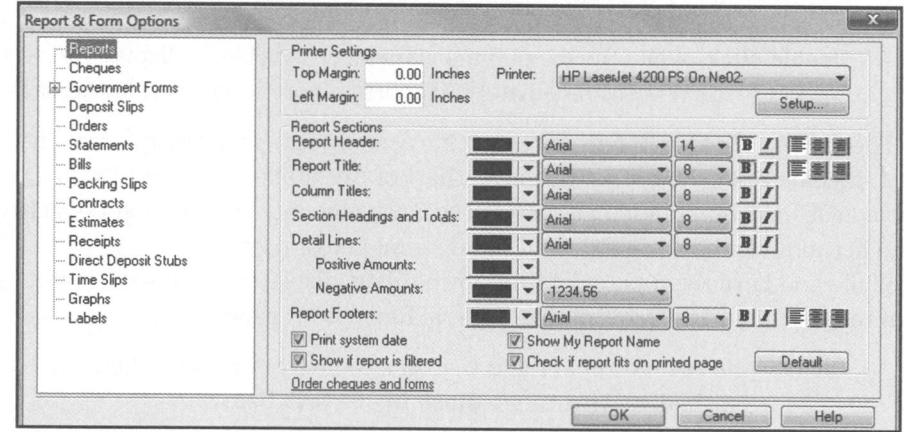

From the Home window, choose the Setup menu and click Reports & Forms.

These company settings become the defaults for all company reports.

From this window, you can select a printer, set the margins and choose the default style for different parts of the report. You can also add the computer system date to the report and indicate whether the report is filtered. The Default button will restore the original program default settings for the report.

Choose   your **printer** from the drop-down list in the Printer field.

Click   **OK** to save your changes and return to the display or **click Cancel** if you do not want to save the changes you made.

If you want to change the appearance only for the displayed report, you should modify the displayed report. The Modify Report windows include Print Settings and Font Settings as elements that you can modify separately for each type of report.

Graphing General Reports

Graphs are available only from the main menu in any Home window.

Expenses and Net Profit as % of Revenue

Choose the **Graphs menu**, then **click Expenses And Net Profit As % Of Revenue** to display the following report options:

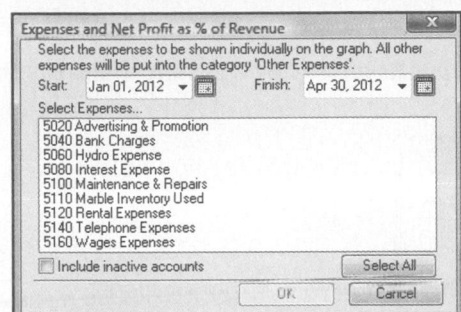

Double click the **default Start date** and **enter** the **beginning date** of the period for your graph, including the year.

Press ⟨tab⟩ (**twice** if you type the date).

Type the **ending date** of the period for your graph, including the year.

Press and **hold** ⟨ctrl⟩ and **click each expense account you want** included in the graph or **click Select All** to include all accounts.

Click **OK** to display the graph:

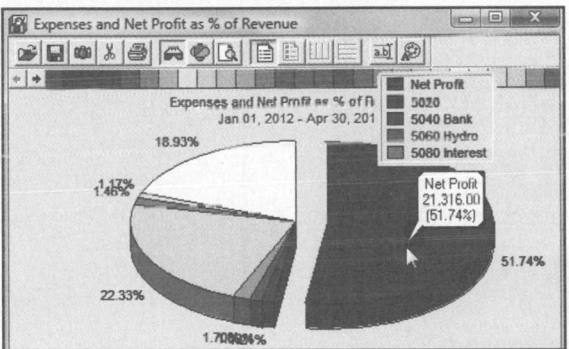

The pie chart shown above includes all expense accounts for the period from January 1 to April 30, and is a form of the Income Statement. You have several options regarding the graph at this stage. The tool bar options are the same for all graphs. By selecting the appropriate button on the tool bar, you can import a graph, export the displayed graph, copy it to the clipboard as a bitmap or a text file, print the graph, change the view from 3-D to 2-D, hide the legend, edit or add titles and so on. Hold the mouse pointer over a tool button for a few seconds to see a brief description of the tool's purpose. Most tool buttons lead to an additional option or control window requiring your input.

In addition, you can change colours by dragging the colour you want to the pie section you want to change; expand or shrink the legend by dragging its bottom border down or up respectively; or pull out a section of the pie chart by dragging it away from the rest of the chart. The graph displayed has the Net Profit portion pulled out for emphasis.

Double click a portion of the graph to see the name of the account, the dollar amount and the percentage of the total.

NOTES
The default start and finish dates for the graph are the fiscal start date and the session date.

NOTES
You can copy the graph as a BMP file to the clipboard and then paste it into the Paint program for full editing capabilities.

Double click the legend to make it larger and to add the account names. Double click the expanded legend to reduce it.

Right-click the legend title to view a set of options for positioning the legend on the graph page. To move the legend to the new position, click the new legend position option. Double click the legend to restore the original size and position.

Close   the **graph** when you have finished.

Revenues by Account

Choose   the **Graphs menu**, then **click Revenues By Account** to display the following report options:

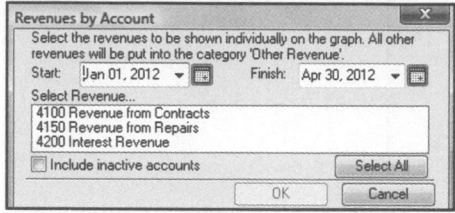

Enter   the **beginning date** of the period for your graph, including the year.

Press   (tab) (**twice** if you typed the date).

Enter   the **ending date** of the period for your graph, including the year.

Press   (ctrl) and **click each revenue account you want** included in the graph or **click Select All** to include all accounts in the graph.

Click   **OK** to display the pie chart as shown:

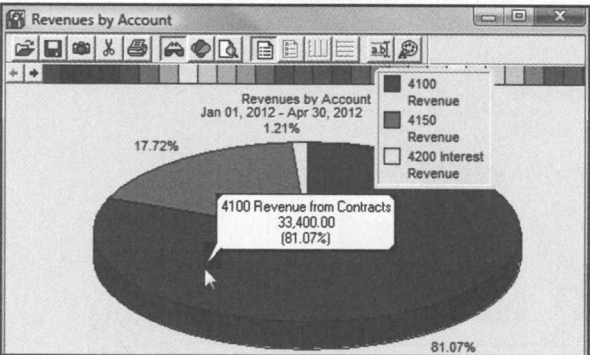

The pie chart has each revenue account represented by a different piece of the pie. You can see that most of the revenue comes from contracts. If you double click a section of the pie, the amount and percentage for that account are shown in a bubble.

You have the same options for this graph as you do for the Expenses and Net Profit as % of Revenue graph.

Double click   a **pie section** to show its amount and percentage.

Close   the **graph** when you have finished.

Expenses by Account

Choose   the **Graphs menu** and **click Expenses By Account** to display the options:

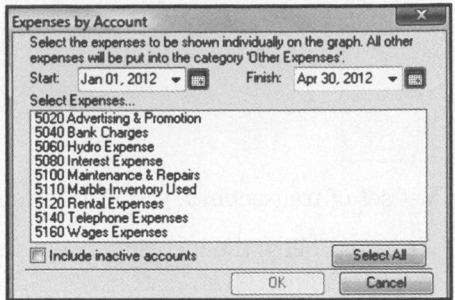

Enter   the **beginning date** of the period for your graph, including the year.

Press   (tab) (**twice** if you typed the date).

Enter   the **ending date** of the period for your graph, including the year.

Press   (ctrl) and **click each expense account you want** included in the graph
or **click Select All** to include all accounts in the graph.

Click   **OK** to see the graph:

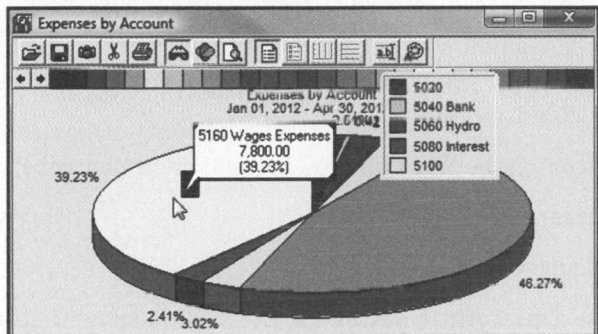

Each expense account that was selected is represented as a separate piece of the
pie. The accounts not selected are grouped together in the **Other** category. The
expenses graph makes it easy to identify at a glance the items that make up the largest
share of expenses — marble inventory and wages in this example.

Close   the **graph** when finished.

Finishing a Session

Finish the last transaction you are working on for this session.

Click   [X] to close the transaction window (such as journal input or display)
to return to the Home window.

You can click the Close Other Windows tool [image] in the Home window if you have
more than one open window. To restore the Home window,

Click   the **Home window tool** [image] in an open journal window. Or,

Click   the **Simply Accounting by Sage button** on the desktop task bar.

Click   the **Close Other Windows tool** [image] in the Home window.

Click   [X] **Exit** to close the program.

You will see the following message about backing up the data file:

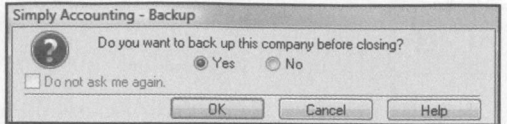

If you did not back up the file after the last set of transactions, you should do so now.

Click   **OK** to start the backup procedure. Follow the instructions on page 50 to complete the backup.

After the backup is complete, the file will close.

The Simply Accounting program will automatically save your work when you finish your session and exit properly. You can now turn off your computer.

Windows Date Format Controls

The default format for some dates in Simply Accounting is taken from your computer's Windows system settings. The default order for dates, whether month, day or year comes first, will be used when you create a new company data set. If you want to see the way your computer system dates are set or you want to change them, you can do this from the Windows Control Panel settings.

Click   the **Start button** on the Windows task bar and **click Control Panel**.

Click   **Clock, Language And Region**.

Click   **Region And Language Options**.

Click   the **Customize This Format button** (or the Additional Settings button).

Click   the **Date tab** to reach the control screen we need:

NOTES
The instructions and screen we show here are for Windows Vista. If you have Windows XP, go to the Control Panel, Regional and Language Options. Then click the Customize button and Date tab to find the date format settings.

NOTES
You can restore the default settings at any time by returning to this screen and clicking the Reset button.

NOTES
Simply Accounting internal database settings also influence whether 1900 or 2000 is selected as the default. These settings may be linked to the version used to create the initial data file and you cannot control them.

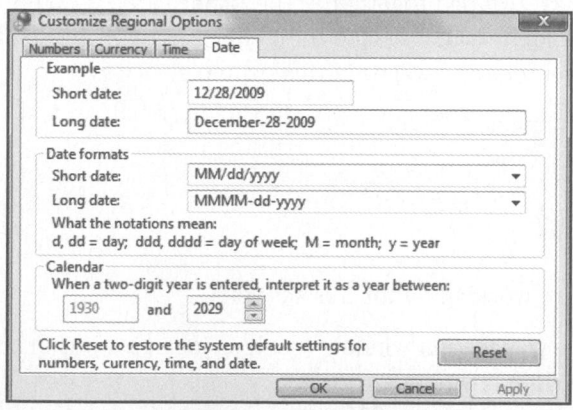

You can choose the format for short and long dates from the two drop-down lists. You can also choose the range of dates that decide the century, either 1900 or 2000, when you enter two digits for the year.

Make your selections and click OK to save them. Click OK again and then close the Control Panel window.

R E V I E W

The Student DVD with Data Files includes Review Questions and Supplementary Cases for this chapter.

Toss for Tots

OBJECTIVES

- ■ *plan* and *design* an accounting system for a non-profit organization
- ■ *prepare* a conversion procedure from manual records
- ■ *understand* the objectives of a computerized accounting system
- ■ *create* company files using the skeleton starter file
- ■ *change* the default home window
- ■ *set up* the organization's accounts
- ■ *enter* historical account information
- ■ *finish* entering accounting history to prepare for transactions
- ■ *enter* fiscal end adjusting transactions
- ■ *close* the books and start a new fiscal period
- ■ *enter* transactions for a previous fiscal period

COMPANY INFORMATION

Company Profile

NOTES
Toss for Tots
North Toronto, PO Box 42665
Toronto, ON M5N 3A8
Tel: (416) 489-2734
Fax: (416) 489-6277
Business No.: 127 362 644

Toss for Tots is a charitable organization created to raise awareness and to support research on cancer in children. One salaried event manager, assisted by a large group of volunteers, organizes a basketball free-throw tournament to raise money for children's cancer research and family support. The tournament uses a ladder-style elimination to determine the championship. During the first two weekends, a first round of 20 free throws determines the basic skill level of each participant for the initial pairing. The subsequent one-on-one free-throw elimination rounds take place over the next two weekends. Two basketball courts are rented, allowing eight participants to play at the same time for the early rounds — two at a time at each end of the two courts. One thousand people are expected to participate in the initial rounds. Professional basketball players are not permitted to compete.

Funds are raised in several ways during the event: each participant pays an entry fee of $50 and receives a $30 tax receipt; each participant is expected to get sponsors who can donate a fixed amount or an amount for each successful

NOTES
Spectators and players can pay $10 for a surprise bag that contains a variety of donated items such as gift certificates, magazines, books and games. The items are hidden from view, and the value of each package is never less than $10.

basketball throw; spectators pay an admission fee to watch the tournament — $10 for one day, $15 for one weekend or $25 for both weekends; snacks and drinks are sold to spectators and participants; surprise bags are sold for $10 each; and photos of participants on the court are sold for $10 each. Prizes, donated by various corporations, are offered to participants who collect large donation amounts, and a cash prize of $1 000 is awarded to the tournament champion.

Volunteers handle all the registrations, monitor the contest and determine placements or pairings for successive rounds on the ladder. Costs are also minimized by the large number of merchandise donations for the surprise packages and prizes. The organization does incur some expenses, including the event manager's salary, rental of the basketball courts, a computer to record all registrations, donations and ladder sequence, office supplies, promotional materials, telephones, drinks, snacks and so on.

At the start of the tournament, many of the participants have already paid their registration fees and most of the merchandise has been purchased or received. The organization has been operating for several months to prepare for the tournament.

The bank account has been set up for the early cash donations and registrations and to write cheques for pre-tournament expenses. Some cash is also kept on hand at the tournament to make change for on-site sales and for immediate purchases. Most of the cash and cheques received from registrations and admissions are deposited immediately for security purposes.

Toss for Tots has decided to use Simply Accounting to keep the accounting records for the tournament in July 2012, partway through its current fiscal year. The charity requires only General Ledger accounts. The following information is available to set up the accounts using the General Ledger:

- Chart of Accounts
- Income Statement
- Balance Sheet
- Trial Balance
- Accounting Procedures

CHART OF ACCOUNTS

TOSS FOR TOTS

ASSETS
1000 CURRENT ASSETS [H]
1020 Bank: Toss for Tots [A]
1100 Cash on Hand [A]
1150 Total Cash [S]
1200 Surprise Bag Supplies
1300 Food Supplies
1320 Office Supplies
1360 T-shirts
1390 TOTAL CURRENT ASSETS [T]

1400 FIXED ASSETS [H]
1420 Fax/Telephone
1450 Computer
1500 Digital Camera
1590 TOTAL FIXED ASSETS [T] ▶

▶LIABILITIES
2000 CURRENT LIABILITIES [H]
2100 Bank Loan
2200 A/P - Designs U Wear
2300 A/P - Quiq Kopy
2350 A/P - Central College
2400 A/P - Snack City
2670 HST Paid on Purchases
2690 TOTAL CURRENT
      LIABILITIES [T]

EQUITY
3000 EQUITY [H]
3560 Accumulated Surplus
3600 Net Income [X]
3690 TOTAL EQUITY [T] ▶

▶REVENUE
4000 REVENUE [H]
4020 Revenue: Registrations
4040 Revenue: Sponsors
4080 Revenue: Surprise Bags
4100 Revenue: Admissions
4120 Revenue: Food Sales
4390 TOTAL REVENUE [T]

EXPENSE
5000 ADMIN EXPENSES [H]
5020 Court Rental Expense
5200 Office Supplies Used
5220 Non-refundable HST
5240 Postage Expense
5280 Printing & Copying ▶

▶5300 Telephone Expense
5320 Publicity & Promotion
5400 Wages - Manager
5420 Miscellaneous Expenses
5440 TOTAL ADMIN
      EXPENSES [T]

5450 MERCHANDISE & FOOD
      EXPENSES [H]
5500 Cost of T-shirts
5520 Cost of Surprise Bags
5550 Cost of Food
5690 TOTAL MERCHANDISE &
      FOOD EXPENSES [T]

NOTES: The Chart of Accounts is based on the current expenses and accounts. Account types are marked in brackets for subgroup Accounts [A], Subgroup totals [S], Headings [H], Totals [T] and Current Earnings [X]. All unmarked accounts are postable Group [G] accounts. The explanation of account types begins on page 86.

INCOME STATEMENT

TOSS FOR TOTS

For the Nine Months Ending June 30, 2012

Revenue
4000 REVENUE

4020 Revenue: Registrations	$20 000.00
4040 Revenue: Sponsors	2 000.00
4390 TOTAL REVENUE	$22 000.00
TOTAL REVENUE	$22 000.00

Expense
5000 ADMIN EXPENSES

5020 Court Rental Expense	$15 000.00
5200 Office Supplies Used	640.00
5240 Postage Expense	450.00
5280 Printing & Copying	2 000.00
5300 Telephone Expense	360.00
5320 Publicity & Promotion	4 000.00
5400 Wages - Manager	6 000.00
5440 TOTAL ADMIN EXPENSES	$28 450.00
TOTAL EXPENSE	$28 450.00
NET INCOME (LOSS)	($6 450.00)

NOTES: Because the event has not yet started, some expenses are still at zero. Because most of the funds have not yet come in, the Income Statement shows a net loss.

BALANCE SHEET

TOSS FOR TOTS

July 1, 2012

Assets
1000 CURRENT ASSETS

1020 Bank: Toss for Tots	$18 550.00	
1100 Cash on Hand	1 000.00	
1150 Total Cash		$19 550.00
1200 Surprise Bag Supplies		500.00
1300 Food Supplies		1 200.00
1320 Office Supplies		750.00
1360 T-shirts		800.00
1390 TOTAL CURRENT ASSETS		$22 800.00

1400 FIXED ASSETS

1420 Fax/Telephone	500.00
1450 Computer	2 400.00
1500 Digital Camera	900.00
1590 TOTAL FIXED ASSETS	$ 3 800.00
TOTAL ASSETS	$26 600.00

▶ Liabilities
2000 CURRENT LIABILITIES

2100 Bank Loan	$ 15 000.00
2200 A/P - Designs U Wear	800.00
2300 A/P - Quiq Kopy	150.00
2350 A/P - Central College	11 300.00
2400 A/P - Snack City	900.00
2670 HST Paid on Purchases	−1 850.00
2690 TOTAL CURRENT LIABILITIES	$26 300.00
TOTAL LIABILITIES	$26 300.00

Equity
3000 EQUITY

3560 Accumulated Surplus	$ 6 750.00
3600 Net Income	−6 450.00
3690 TOTAL EQUITY	$ 300.00
TOTAL EQUITY	$ 300.00
LIABILITIES AND EQUITY	$26 600.00

TRIAL BALANCE

TOSS FOR TOTS

July 1, 2012		Debits	Credits
1020	Bank: Toss for Tots	$18 550.00	
1100	Cash on Hand	1 000.00	
1200	Surprise Bag Supplies	500.00	
1300	Food Supplies	1 200.00	
1320	Office Supplies	750.00	
1360	T-shirts	800.00	
1420	Fax/Telephone	500.00	
1450	Computer	2 400.00	
1500	Digital Camera	900.00	
2100	Bank Loan		$15 000.00
2200	A/P - Designs U Wear		800.00
2300	A/P - Quiq Kopy		150.00
2350	A/P - Central College		11 300.00
2400	A/P - Snack City		900.00
2670	HST Paid on Purchases	1 850.00	
3560	Accumulated Surplus		6 750.00
4020	Revenue: Registrations		20 000.00
4040	Revenue: Sponsors		2 000.00
5020	Court Rental Expense	15 000.00	
5200	Office Supplies Used	640.00	
5240	Postage Expense	450.00	
5280	Printing & Copying	2 000.00	
5300	Telephone Expense	360.00	
5320	Publicity & Promotion	4 000.00	
5400	Wages - Manager	6 000.00	
		$56 900.00	$56 900.00

(handwritten margin note:) ✳ put minus in O/B

Accounting Procedures

HST

Registered charities have two options with respect to the HST. Like regular for-profit businesses, they can register to apply the HST, charge HST on all sales and membership fees and claim all HST paid as input tax credits to reduce the liability to the Receiver General. The second option, used by Toss for Tots, does not require registration or collection of HST but permits a partial rebate of HST paid. Periodically, the charity submits an application for refunds, listing the total of all HST paid toward its operating expenses. Fifty percent of this amount is eligible for the rebate. Therefore, Toss for Tots records all purchases as compound General Journal entries, separating the amount paid for HST from the total and debiting this amount to *HST Paid on Purchases*. This account is cleared with a credit entry as the application for a rebate is submitted. The debit entries to the *HST Refund Receivable* and the *Non-refundable HST* expense accounts (50 percent each) will balance the journal entry.

Bank Accounts

The proceeds from the registrations and from the sale of merchandise are entered into the bank account. This account is used for all cheques to suppliers and to cover operating and administrative expenses and merchandise — drinks, snacks, T-shirts and surprise bag items. During the tournament, a *Cash on Hand* account is set up for day-to-day expenses incurred by the volunteer staff. Transfers are made from the *Bank: Toss for Tots* account to *Cash on Hand* by writing cheques to the Event Manager.

NOTES

On the rebate form, the 5 percent GST paid (federal portion) is separated from the 8 percent PST paid (provincial portion for Ontario) and 50 percent of each is refunded. Thus the total refund is 6.5 percent, half of the 13 percent paid.

INSTRUCTIONS

1. **Set up** the **company accounts for Toss for Tots** in the General Ledger in Simply Accounting using all the information provided in this application. Detailed keystroke instructions follow the instructions.

2. **Back up your work frequently** when working through this application to keep your backups updated.

   You may finish your session at any time while completing the setup. Simply open the Toss for Tots data file again, accept the session date and continue from where you left off.

   If you are using a different location for your data files, substitute the appropriate data path, including the drive and folder for your data setup.

3. **Enter** the **source documents** that begin on page 97 in the General Journal in Simply Accounting using the Chart of Accounts and other information provided.

4. **Print** the **following reports** after you have completed your entries:

   a. General Journal from July 1 to September 30
   b. Comparative Balance Sheet at September 30 and October 1 (amounts)
   c. Income Statement for the period October 1, 2011, to September 30, 2012

KEYSTROKES FOR SETUP

The following are the five key stages in preparing the Simply Accounting program for use by a company:

1. creating company files
2. preparing the system
3. preparing the ledgers
4. printing reports to check your work
5. backing up your files and finishing the company history

The following keystroke instructions are written for a stand-alone PC with a hard disk drive. The keystroke instructions provided in this application demonstrate one approach to setting up company accounts. Always refer to the Simply Accounting and Windows manuals and Help for further details.

Creating Company Files

The following instructions assume that you installed the Simply Accounting data files on your hard disk in drive C: in the SimData10 folder.

Simply Accounting provides both templates and starter files to make it easier to create files for a new company. These files contain different sets of accounts that match the needs of different kinds of businesses. By starting with one of these files, you eliminate the need to create all the accounts for your business from scratch.

There are many templates that work with the setup wizards to define not only accounts, but also a number of settings for the different ledgers. These settings and accounts are suited to the type of business named by the files.

NOTES
If you prefer to enter the source documents before setting up the data files, you can restore the toss1.CAB file in the Setup folder inside your SimData10 folder. In this way, the setup may be easier to complete because you are already familiar with the account structure.

NOTES
Using subsequent versions of the Simply Accounting program may result in different screens and keystrokes from those described in this application.

NOTES
You must work in single-user mode to set up new company files. Access to most settings is restricted in multi-user mode.

NOTES
The non-profit template has many more accounts, modules and features than are needed for Toss for Tots. This file therefore would require substantially more modification to make it match the company profile in this chapter.

NOTES
We want to illustrate different ways of creating company files. Therefore, the method of creating your company files from scratch is described in the Dorfmann Design setup application in Chapter 7.

NOTES
If you use the Skeleton file located in C:\Program Files\ Simply Accounting Premium 2010\ Template\, you will be upgrading from Simply Basic 2005 A to Premium (or Pro) 2010 Release A. Make a backup of this file before changing the settings and accounts. Use the File menu Save As command to create the new file C:\SimData10\Toss\toss.SAI.

NOTES
If you are using backup files, restore SimData10\skeleton1.CAB. to SimData10\Toss\toss. Simply Accounting will create the necessary new folder. Refer to page 20 for assistance with restoring backup files.

If you start from the backup file, you will not need to complete the additional step of saving the file after the Upgrade wizard has completed. You will see the Getting Started window. Click Do Not Show... Close this window and the Daily Business Manager window to see the Home window with Toss in the title bar.

NOTES
In Windows XP, click the list arrow in the Look In field and click SimData10. SimData10 should appear in the Look In field.

PRO VERSION
The file will not be converted. You will see the session date screen immediately.

In addition, Simply Accounting includes two starter files — inteplus.SAI (Integration Plus) and skeleton.SAI. The starter files contain only a set of basic accounts. Starter files are opened like any other company file. You should work with a copy of these files so that you can use the original files for future applications.

The Skeleton starter has only General Ledger accounts, whereas the Integration Plus starter is suitable for a variety of business types because it has the basic linked accounts for all the ledgers.

You will have to customize any of these starter files to your particular company. Rarely are accounts identical for any two businesses. The files that are best suited to the Chart of Accounts for Toss for Tots are the Skeleton starter files (skeleton.SAI). These files contain only a few General Ledger accounts, headings and totals. They contain no linked accounts that link General Ledger accounts to the subsidiary ledgers. This is appropriate for Toss for Tots, which uses only the General Ledger.

The starter files are located in the folder named Template in the Simply Accounting Premium 2010 folder — the folder that contains your Simply Accounting program.

This starter file is a Simply Basic 2005 A version file that must be upgraded before you can use it. The Student Premium version of Simply Accounting cannot open files from previous version years, so we have created a 2010 Pro version of the Skeleton file. We will open this file (skeleton.SAI) from the SimData10\Template folder.

Start   the **Simply Accounting program** to access the Select Company window.

Click   **Select An Existing Company** to access the Open Company window:

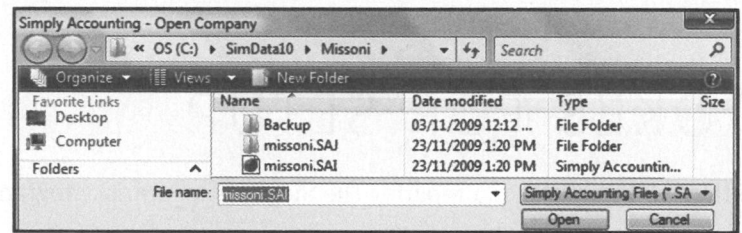

Click   **SimData10** in the file path field to return to this folder and see all the folders you installed from the Data DVD.

Double click Template to open this folder.

Click   **skeleton** (or **skeleton.SAI**) to select this data file. **Click Open** to start the Upgrade Company Wizard:

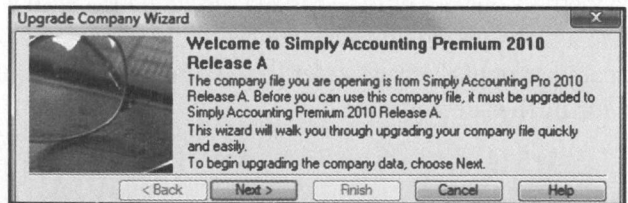

The Pro version Skeleton starter file must be converted to Premium Release A.

Read   the **introduction** to the wizard and **click Next** to continue:

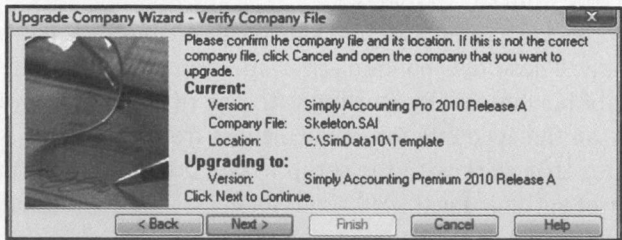

This screen shows the name and location of the working file and the version changes that will be made if you proceed.

> **Click   Next:**

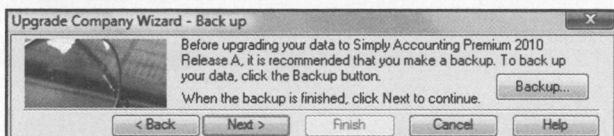

You can now back up the Skeleton file before proceeding. Simply Accounting will check your data file for problems and repair them if you choose this option.

> **Click   Next** to see the final warning about converting files:

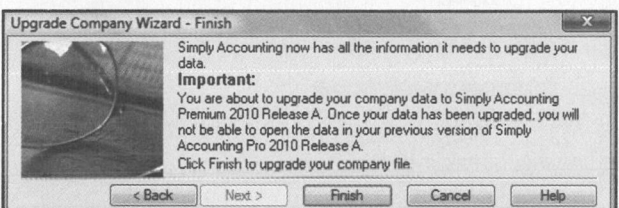

This final screen warns you of the changes you are making. After this step you cannot cancel the conversion. File conversions cannot be reversed — once you convert a file you will be unable to open it in the earlier version.

> **Click   Finish** to begin the conversion.

> **Click   OK** if you see a message about updating your employees' income tax claim amounts. Income tax tables are updated every six months.

You will now be asked to indicate the type of company you are working with. Different company types have different labels in the Premium version.

> **Click   the list arrow beside Other**, the default entry, to see the types:

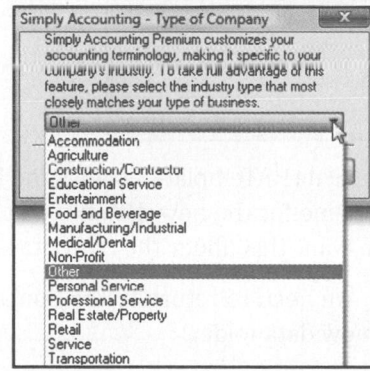

> **Click   Non-Profit** and then **click OK**.

The Session Date window appears with January 1, 2000, as the session date.

> **Click   OK** to accept the date. The Getting Started Welcome screen opens.

> **Click   Show This Window On Startup** to remove the ✓.

> **Click   the Close button** to close the Getting Started window.

> **Click   ☒** to close the Daily Business Manager window.

Click No if you see a message about changing the display settings for the Daily Business Manager. We will change these settings later.

⚠ **WARNING!**
If you make a backup at this stage, it will be a Premium Version 2010 Release A backup.

📄 **NOTES**
When you upgrade to a later release, you will see a reminder about payroll tax changes because new releases of Simply Accounting are tied to tax table changes that usually occur every six months.

PRO VERSION
pro You will not see the Type of Company window. You can select the type on the Company Settings Information screen from the Industry Type field drop-down list (page 76).

📄 **NOTES**
When you upgrade to a later release, you will see a reminder about payroll tax changes because new releases of Simply Accounting are tied to tax table changes that usually occur every six months.

📄 **NOTES**
If you started from the backup file skeleton1.CAB, you will not see the Getting Started and Daily Business Manager windows until the next time you open the data file.

NOTES

If you are using Windows XP, click the list arrow in the Save In field and click SimData10. (Alternatively, click the Up One Level tool.)

Click the New Folder icon when SimData10 appears in the Save In field. (Alternatively, right-click on a blank part of the folders display pane, then choose New and Folder from the pop-up menu.)

The name New Folder is selected. Type Toss to replace the name. Click on a blank part of the display area again to save the new name.

Double click Toss, the new folder, to open it.

Click NEW (or NEW.SAI) in the File Name field .

Type toss to replace the name.

Click Save to return to the Home window.

The Home window opens and all ledgers are available in the list of modules.

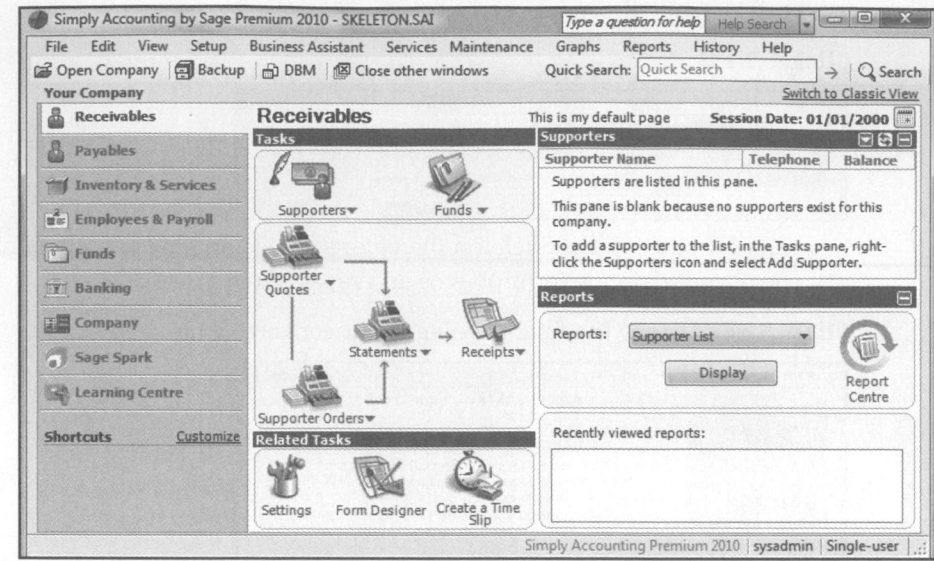

The ledger icon is labelled Supporters because we selected Non-Profit as the company type. For other types of companies, this icon may be labelled Customers or Clients. Projects are labelled Funds for non-profit companies.

The ledgers are not set up. An open history (quill pen) symbol appears beside Supporters, the ledger icon, indicating that you can enter historical data for the ledger. If you open the other modules, you will see the same symbol for each one. Although you can make journal entries at this stage, you should save this file under your company name, enter all the necessary company information and finish entering the history.

First we will copy the template files so we can use this original again if we need to.

Choose the **File menu** and **click Save As** so that we will open the new copy:

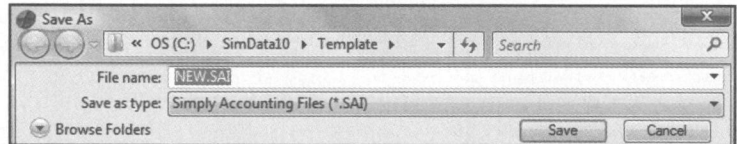

The Save As window opens. The path <C:\SimData10\Template> shows the location of the open skeleton file. NEW.SAI is the default name for the new data file. We need to create a new data folder for Toss for Tots, but we want this under the SimData10 level.

Click   **SimData10** in the file path field. We need to return to the SimData10 folder where we will create the new data folder.

Click   **Browse Folders** to expand the window and include New Folder options:

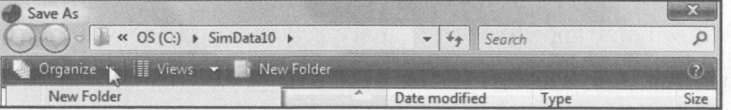

Click   the **New Folder tool**, or **choose** the **Organize menu** and **click New Folder** as shown above. The name New Folder is selected so we can change it.

Type   Toss

Click   the **Toss folder** and then **click Open** or **double click** the **Toss folder**:

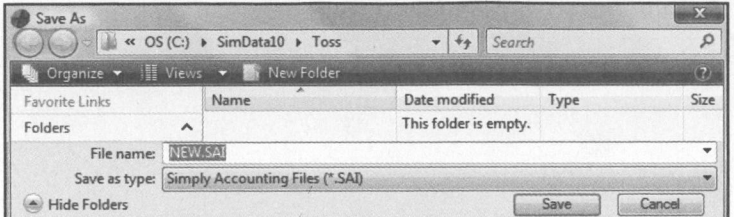

We can now enter the name for the new company file.

> **Click**   **NEW.SAI** to select this text. **Type** `toss` and **click Save**.

You should see the same Home window with the file name TOSS.SAI (or TOSS) in the title bar:

The Receivables module is the default for the Home window. We will change this default because Toss for Tots does not use this module.

Changing the Default Home Window

Toss for Tots uses only the General Ledger (Company module) so we will make this the Home window. The Receivables module has This Is My Default Page below the header.

> **Click**   **Company** in the list of modules on the left to change the Home window.

Now we have the Chart of Accounts and the General Journal available. Notice that the message beside Company has changed to Make This My Default Page. Clicking this option for any module will select the displayed module as the default Home window.

> **Click**   **Make This My Default Page**.

The Company heading now has This Is My Default Page beside it as shown:

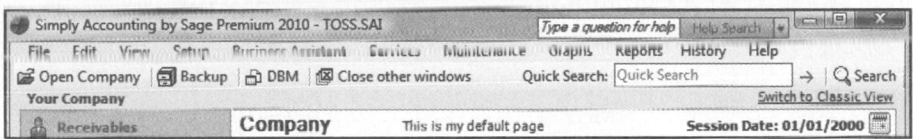

Preparing the System

Before entering financial records for a new company, you must prepare the system for operation. This involves changing the default settings to reflect the Toss for Tots company information such as the company name and address, fiscal dates, screen display preferences and Chart of Accounts. Some initial defaults will not be suitable for Toss for Tots. You must also provide other information, such as the printer(s) that you will be using and the printing formats. This process of adding, deleting and modifying information is called customizing the system.

Changing Default Settings

> **Click**   the **Settings icon** [Settings] in the Related Tasks pane, or **choose** the **Setup menu** and **click Settings**:

NOTES
Simply Accounting includes a Setup wizard that guides you through the company setup with instructions and separate screens for each step. The wizard is not used in this application. To access the Setup wizard, choose the Setup menu, then choose Wizards and click Modify Accounts.

NOTES
You cannot complete the setup in multi-user mode.

The Company Settings main menu window opens:

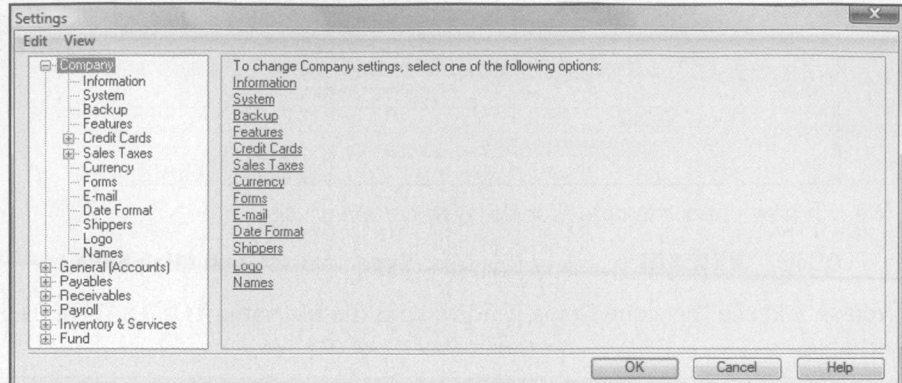

Most settings for a data file are entered from this central Settings screen. Some apply to features and modules not used by Toss for Tots. We will skip the screens that do not apply. They will be introduced in later chapters.

The modules are listed on the left. All have a ⊞ beside them indicating there are multiple settings. The larger right-hand side of the window begins with the same expanded list of entries for the selected module as the expanded list on the left.

Clicking a ⊞ beside an entry will expand the list. Clicking an entry in the list on the left without a ⊞ beside it or in the list on the right-hand side will open the options window for that entry.

Entering Company Information

Company settings apply to all modules of the company for all users of the data file.

Click   **Information** (in either the left-hand side or right-hand side list) to see the following information screen:

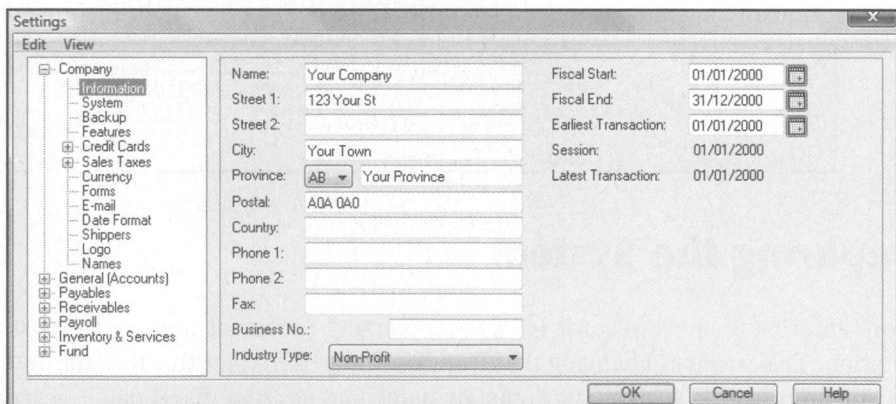

The Name field contains the information "Your Company" to let you know that this is where you should enter the name of your company.

Press   (tab) or **drag through** Your Company to select this text.

Type   Toss for Tots (add your own name)

Press   (tab).

The cursor moves to the Street 1 field, the first address field. You can enter the address immediately because the current contents are already highlighted.

Type   North Toronto

Press   (tab) to advance to the second street address line (Street 2 field).

Type   PO Box 42665

Press   (tab).

The cursor advances to and highlights the contents of the City field.

Type   Toronto **Press** (tab).

The cursor advances to the Province code field. It, too, is ready for editing.

Typing the first letter of the province name will enter the first province beginning with that letter. Typing the same letter again will advance the list to the next province starting with the same letter. You can also select a code from the drop-down list.

Type   O **Press** (tab) to advance to the province name field. ON and Ontario are entered as this is the only province beginning with "O."

Press   (tab) again to accept Ontario as the province.

The cursor is now placed in the highlighted Postal (postal code) field. You do not have to type the capitals or spaces in postal codes. The program automatically corrects the postal code format when you enter a Canadian postal code pattern.

Type   m5n3a8

In this case, all addresses will be in Canada, so we can leave the Country field blank. Now enter the telephone and fax numbers for the business. There is only one phone number so the Phone 2 field will remain blank. You do not need to type brackets or hyphens for phone numbers. Simply Accounting will correct the format when you enter a seven- or ten-digit phone number.

Click   the **Phone 1 field**. The postal code format is corrected.

Type   4164892734

Click   the **Fax field**. The telephone number format is corrected.

Type   4164896277

Press   (tab) to move to the Business No. field.

All companies must use a single Canada Revenue Agency business number that also serves as the HST registration number. All business numbers have an Rx extension that indicates the business area for tax purposes.

Type   127362644 RR0001 **Press** (tab).

There are a number of types of companies to choose from in the program. We selected the type when we upgraded the data file. You can select from the **Industry Type** list to change the type. Changing the company type will also change the icon labels.

Simply Accounting will accept dates after January 1, 1900. You can store 100 years of accounting records.

The **Fiscal Start** field contains the date at which the current fiscal year begins. This date usually defines the beginning of the fiscal year for income tax purposes.

The **Fiscal End** is the date at which the company closes its books, usually one year after the fiscal start, and the end of the fiscal year used for income tax reporting purposes. For Toss for Tots, the fiscal end is two months after the tournament, when all the accounting information for the event has been entered.

The **Earliest Transaction** date is the date on which the company converts its manual accounting records to the computerized system. Entries before this date are historical entries. The earliest transaction date must not be earlier than the fiscal start and not later than the fiscal end. The earliest transaction date will be the first session

NOTES
All provinces and territories in Canada have a two-letter abbreviation code.

NOTES
All postal codes in Canada use the following pattern: Letter, Number, Letter, Number, Letter, Number. Any other sequence, as for other countries, will not be corrected by the program, and you should enter the correct format.

PRO VERSION
pro You should select Non-profit from the Industry Type drop-down list. Icon labels do not change when you select a different company type.
You can store seven years of company data.

NOTES
Companies may use a fiscal period shorter than one year for reporting purposes and close their books more frequently, but the most common period is one year.

NOTES
When we entered various dates, the program accepted dates between 1900 and 3000 without an error message. There appear to be no practical restrictions on the dates you can use.

WARNING!

Type the date as text to avoid number confusion such as entering Jan 10 instead of Oct 1. Type 2012 (use four digits) for the year. If you type 12, Simply Accounting may enter 1912 (refer to page 66).

NOTES
When you view the Company Information again, the session and latest transaction dates will have been updated to match the new fiscal dates.

PRO VERSION
You will not see the warning about changing the industry type because the terminology does not change in the Pro version.

NOTES
Refer to Appendix N on the Student DVD for more information on accrual- and cash-basis accounting. Refer to Appendix I on the Student DVD for an exercise with keystrokes that uses cash-basis accounting in Simply Accounting.

date when you are ready to enter journal transactions. Simply Accounting automatically advances the earliest transaction date when you start a new fiscal year.

Notice that the **default date format** for this file is day-month-year. We will enter these dates in text form and then change the date format for the file. By entering text with four digits for the year initially, we will ensure that we enter the date correctly.

Press (tab) to advance to the Fiscal Start field.

Type oct 1 2011

Press (tab) **twice**. The cursor moves to the Fiscal End field.

Type sep 30 2012

Press (tab) **twice**. The cursor is now in the Earliest Transaction field.

Type jul 1 2012

The session date and the latest transaction date will change as you complete journal entries and advance the session date from the Home window. When the latest transaction date is later than the session date, it indicates there are postdated journal transactions.

You cannot change the earliest transaction date after finishing the history and making journal entries. The company name, address and fiscal end date can be edited at any time. Return to any field with errors to correct mistakes.

You will need to save the fiscal dates before completing the next step.

Click **OK**. If you change the type of company from this Information screen, you will see the following confirmation:

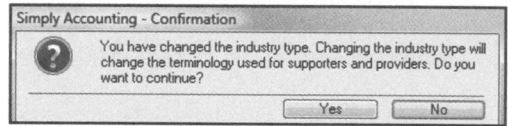

Click **Yes** to accept the changes.

Click the **Settings icon** [Settings] , or **choose** the **Setup menu** and **click Settings** again to resume.

Setting System Defaults

Click **System** in the list under Company to access the options:

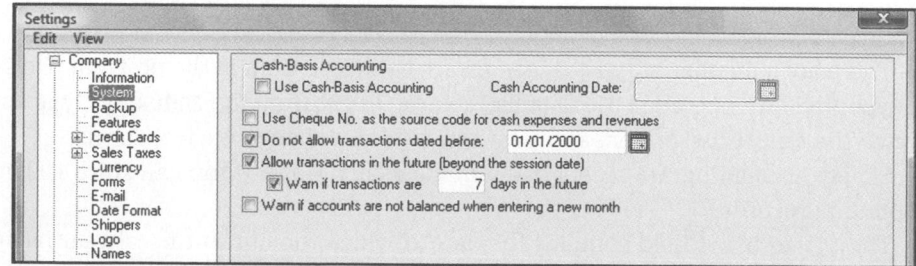

The Company System settings apply to all modules of the program.

This screen has several important settings. The first refers to whether the business is using **cash-basis accounting** instead of the default, **accrual-basis accounting**. The cash basis of accounting records revenues and expenses on the date the money is paid or received. In the accrual method, revenues and expenses are recorded on the transaction date (matching principle). To change to the cash-basis method, click the check box and enter the date on which the change is to take effect. This workbook uses the accrual basis. Do not change this setting.

The next option relates to the use of the **Cheque Number As The Source Code For Cash Expenses And Revenues** in account reconciliation. Since Toss for Tots uses only the General Ledger, this option does not apply. When you are using the Payables and Receivables Ledgers, you should turn on the option.

The next option, **Do Not Allow Transactions Dated Before**, permits you to lock out any transactions for a previous period by entering the date. You can post transactions to earlier dates by removing the checkmark or entering an earlier date in this field. The feature should be turned off only for specific transactions and then turned on again so that you do not post in error with an incorrect date. Similarly, you should not generally allow posting to future periods, beyond the session date, unless you are entering a series of postdated transactions. You can activate the feature for specific transactions when needed so that you do not post with incorrect future dates. You can add a warning for dates beyond a certain period as well. We will restrict transactions before the starting date and not allow postdated transactions.

Remember that the date format is still day-month-year.

Double click the date **01/01/2000**.

Type   Jul 1

Click   **Allow Transactions In The Future** to remove the ✓ and not allow postdating.

Since Simply Accounting allows journal entries before the company setup details are completed, you can add a reminder **warning** as you continue to work with an incomplete and **unbalanced account history**. If you choose to post journal entries before completing the history, you should turn on the warning.

Setting Backup Options

Click   **Backup**:

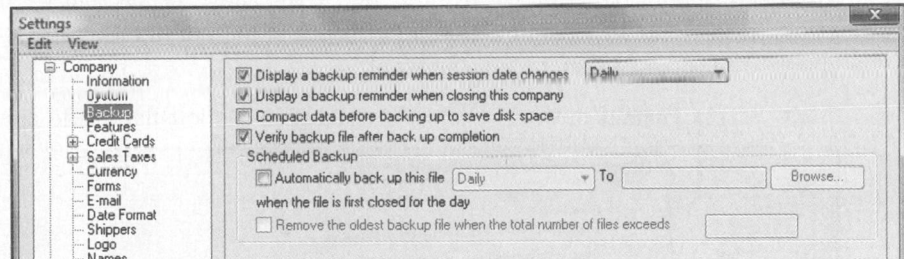

This screen has several options for backing up company files. You can select the **frequency** with which you **back up** your data. Since we usually advance the session date weekly, we will choose Weekly as the backup frequency as well. The program prompts you to back up according to this entry.

Click   the **Display A Backup Reminder field list arrow** and **choose Weekly**.

If you want a specific number of days as the interval between backups, choose Other and type the number in the Number Of Days field that opens.

The next option will show a **reminder** to back up the file each time you close the company file. Leave the option selected because you should back up data files regularly.

You can **compact** the backup files to further reduce the size. You should **verify** the backup files regularly to ensure there are no errors that will prevent you from restoring the data later.

You can also **schedule automatic backups**. You can choose the frequency, the backup file location and the number of old backup files that should be saved.

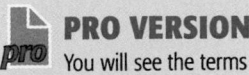

PRO VERSION
You will see the terms Purchases and Sales instead of Expenses and Revenues.

⚠ **WARNING!**
The date you enter for Do Not Allow Transactions Dated Before must not be earlier than the Earliest Transaction Date on the Company Information screen.
If the check box is not checked, you can leave the date field blank. You can also enter the date later.
If you did not save the new fiscal dates, you will see an error message when you enter Jul 1 — the original fiscal dates will restrict the date allowed.

NOTES
Refer to page 105 for details on allowing transactions in a previous year.

NOTES
In general, you do not need to compact the backup files as they are already reduced in size.

Choosing Company Features

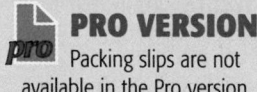

Click   **Features** in the list below Company in the left-hand side panel:

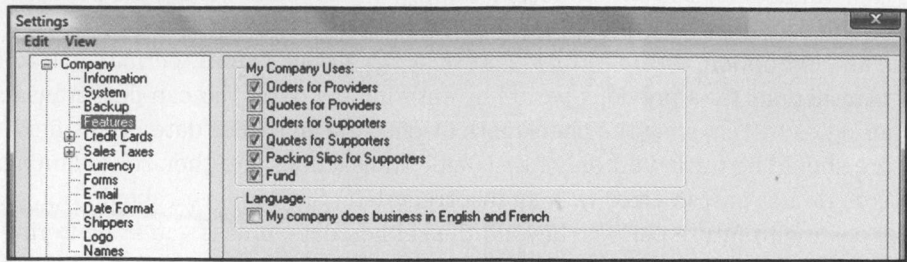

Most of these features (orders, quotes and packing slips) do not apply to General Ledger transactions. The final option refers to languages used. To create forms in both languages, you must choose the option to conduct business in French and English. The Settings option makes the language switch available for many name fields so you can enter names in both languages. The ability to work with the program in both languages is controlled from the View menu (see page 84), not from the Features setting.

Click   **each line** to change all settings. This will remove all checkmarks and
add one to **My Company Does Business In English And French**, the
final option.

Credit cards, sales taxes, currency, e-mail and form numbers, such as for invoices, and quotes, do not apply to the General Journal transactions entered by Toss for Tots. Toss for Tots does not use Shippers or the additional Names fields in the General Ledger, so you can skip these screens as well.

Changing Date Formats

The date formats for the starter file are different from the formats we used for other files. To avoid entering incorrect dates, we will choose the same format that we used for our other data files. We need to change the default setting so that month appears first. You can choose any separator character you want.

Click   **Date Format** in the list below Company in the left-hand side panel:

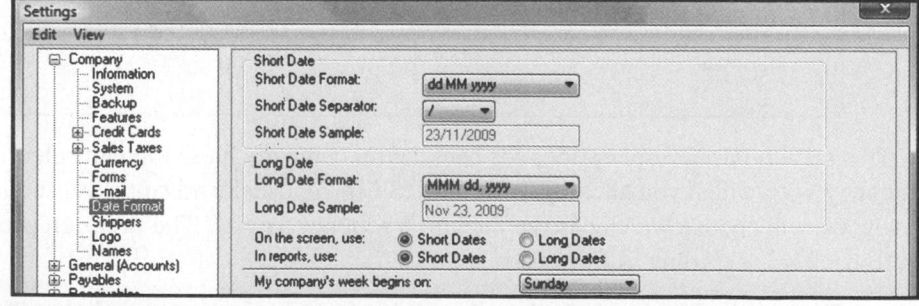

Choose MM dd yyyy from the Short Date Format drop-down list.

Choose another separator symbol from the Short Date Separator list, if you want.

On the screen we will show dates in the long form, text style, to make them as clear as possible. You can choose long or short dates for reports.

Click   **Long Dates** beside the option for On The Screen, Use.

You can also enter the day that is normally the first day of the business week.

Adding a Company Logo

Next we will add the company logo. This logo can be added to invoices or other company documents created in Simply Accounting.

Click   Logo:

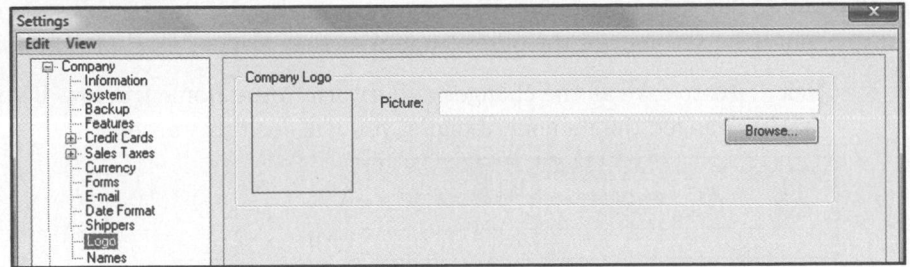

Click   Browse. Click Computer in the left pane. **Double click C:**. Then **double click SimData10**, **Setup** and **Logos** to locate the folder with company logos.

Click   toss.bmp and **click Open** to return to the Logo Settings window with the image and file name added:

Click   the ⊟ **beside Company** to close the expanded Company list.

Setting General Defaults

To change the settings for the General Ledger for Toss for Tots,

Click   General (Accounts) in the list on the left:

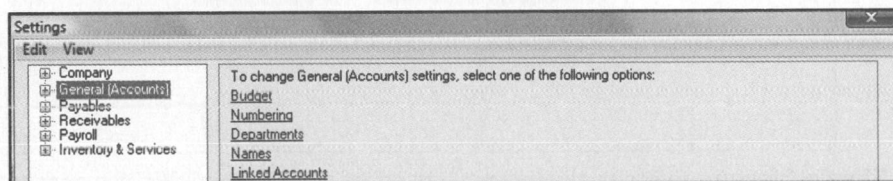

If you want the Simply Accounting program to prepare **budget** reports, click Budget to open the Budget setup options. Then click Budget Revenue And Expense Accounts and choose the budget period from the drop-down list. Each revenue and expense ledger account window will include a Budget tab. Click this tab and then enter budget amounts for the account to include the account automatically in budget reports. You can activate budgeting at any time.

Toss for Tots does not have different **Departments** to track expenses, so we do not need to turn on this option.

Click   Numbering:

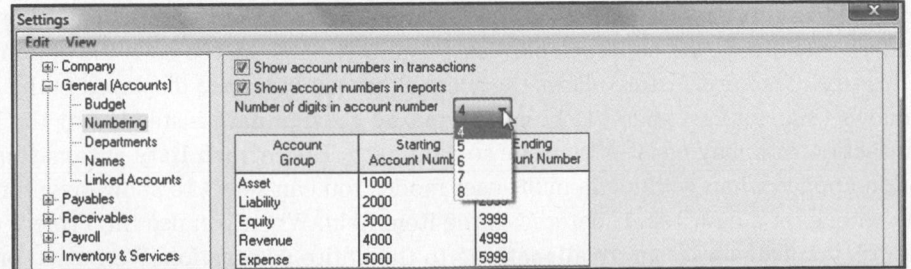

From the **Numbering** option, you can choose not to use account numbers in your reports and journal transactions when the account names are unique; that is, there is no

NOTES
Company logo files are located in the SimData10\Setup\ Logos folder. The default starting point for the Browse is the Forms folder in your Simply Accounting program folder.

NOTES
If you are using WIndows XP, click Browse. Click the Look In field list arrow. Click C:\. Then double click SimData10, Setup and Logos to locate the folder with company logos.

CLASSIC VIEW
From the Home window you can access the General Settings window by clicking the Setup tool bar button and selecting Chart of Accounts. If the Accounts icon in the Home window is already selected, you will access the General Settings directly when you click the Setup tool.

NOTES
The budgeting feature is explained in the Village Galleries application, Chapter 14.
Departments are illustrated in Chapter 19.

PRO VERSION
Departments are not available in the Pro version.
In the Pro version, you cannot change the number of digits for account numbers.

NOTES
In Part Two of this text, we use four-digit account numbers so that the files can be used with the Pro or Premium versions. We introduce five-digit account numbers in Part Three, Chapter 19, for Premium users.

duplication of names. We use account numbers in all the applications in this text.

You can also choose the **number of digits** for your account numbers. Each digit you add to create five- to eight-digit numbers will add an extra zero to the starting and ending number for the account group. When you use six-digit numbers, the Asset accounts will range from 100 000 to 199 900, and the Liabilities accounts will range from 200 000 to 299 900. We use four-digit account numbers in this text. You do not need to change the settings for the other ledgers — they are not used by Toss for Tots.

Click   OK to save all the changes and return to the Home window. If you changed the number of digits, you will see this warning:

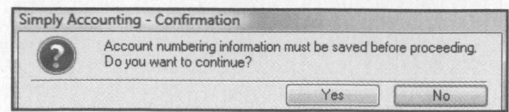

Click OK to save the changes to account numbers.

Changing User Preference Settings

User preferences apply to individual users and indicate the way that person prefers to work with the data files. They do not affect the accounting processes. If you have multiple users who access the files, each user can set his or her own preferences.

Choose the **Setup menu**, then **click User Preferences** to see the options:

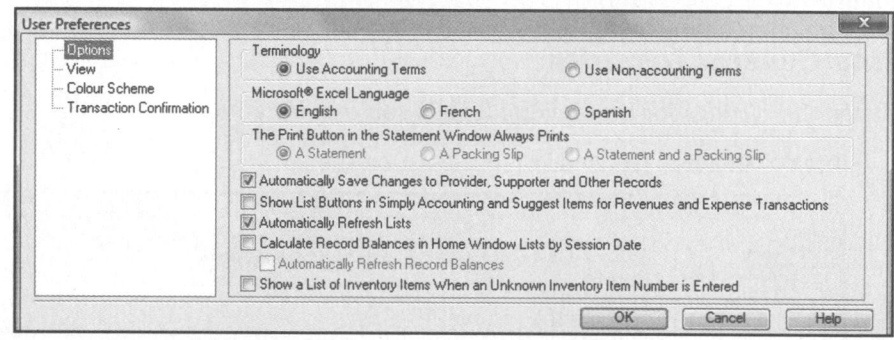

The first feature refers to the language used by the program. We use **accounting terms** throughout this workbook because most people who use accounting programs are familiar with that language. If you choose non-accounting terms, the Payables Ledger will be named Vendors and Purchases in menus and so on. To follow the instructions we provide, you should **Use Accounting Terms**. You can also choose the **language** of your **Excel** program.

Some invoice windows include a **Print button**. If you print these invoices, you can set whether the invoice, packing slip or both will be printed as the default.

If you choose not to **automatically save changes** to ledger records when you close a record window, the program will prompt you to save if you close the ledger record after making changes and give you the option of always saving future changes automatically. **Including the list selection button** in all account fields to select account numbers, vendors, customers, tax codes, employees, inventory items, and so on is the option we use in this text. The next feature allows the account **record balances** displayed in the Home windows (e.g., for customers) to be **calculated by session date** instead of by the latest transaction that may be later than the session date. The **refresh lists automatically** option applies when working in multi-user mode. You can select to show inventory item lists whenever a new item is entered in the item field. When you use the Project (Fund) feature, you can always **apply allocations** to the entire transaction. We turned off Fund in the Features Settings for this company (page 80), so you will not see this option. Inventory and allocations are covered in Chapters 10 and 13, respectively.

PRO VERSION
You will not see the Automatically Refresh Lists option. Packing slips are not available in the Pro version.

NOTES
Appendix B lists all equivalent accounting and non-accounting terms.

NOTES
The Excel language option will apply only if you have installed a non–English-language version of the Excel program.

NOTES
Many account input fields have list buttons or icons like the Account field that you saw in the General Journal in Chapter 3. Other fields have list arrows that provide a drop-down or pop-up list to select from.

NOTES
The Refresh Lists option applies only to the multi-user version of Simply Accounting Premium.

Click   Show List Buttons In Simply Accounting And Suggest Items....

The remaining settings are correct but can be changed at any time by clicking the option.

Changing the View Settings

Several important display or appearance options are controlled from the View option.

Click   View:

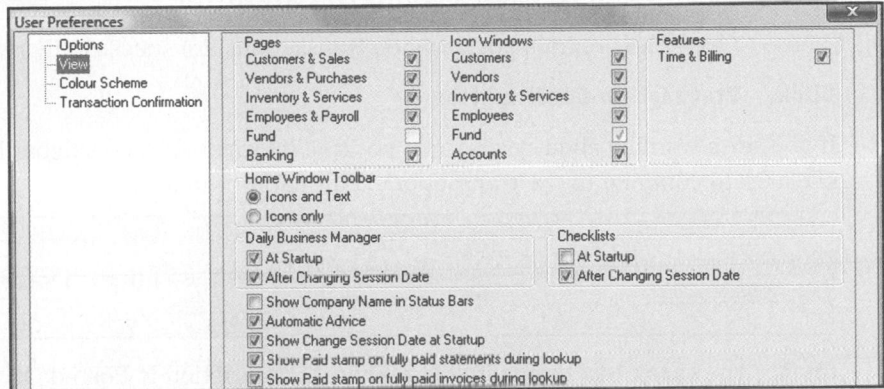

You can **hide**, that is, not display, the icons for **modules** or **pages** that you are not using. We must hide the modules that are not used before finishing the history.

The **Icon Windows** check boxes allow you to hide the accounts icon window for one or more ledgers. If you select the Chart of Accounts icon (or other ledger icon) with this option turned on, account information for the first account will be displayed instead of the list of accounts. Icon windows can be hidden separately only if the module pages are not hidden.

> **Click**   the **Pages check box for Customers & Sales** to remove the ✓. The ✓ for Icon Windows is also removed.
>
> **Repeat**   this step for **Vendors & Purchases, Inventory & Services, Employees & Payroll pages** and the **Time & Billing Feature** so that all these ✓ are removed.
>
> **Do not remove** the ✓ for **Banking**.

The next two options refer to the appearance of the **tool bar** in the Home window. You can display the tools with text or as icons only. The Classic view Home window tool bar never includes text. In our data files, we include the text with the icons.

Simply Accounting has reminders about upcoming activities such as payments that are due, discounts available and recurring entries. The **Checklists** and the **Daily Business Manager** can remind you of these activities each time you start the program, each time you advance the session date or both. Toss for Tots does not use these lists.

> **Click   At Startup** and **click After Changing Session Date** for **Daily Business Manager** to **remove** the ✓s.
>
> **Click   After Changing Session Date** for **Checklists** to **remove** the ✓.

You can **Show the Company Name In the Status Bar** or omit this detail.

Automatic Advice shows advisory messages automatically while you are entering transactions, as, for example, when customers exceed credit limits or the chequing account is overdrawn. Clicking removes the ✓ and the feature. Leave Advice turned on.

We also select to **show the session date** each time we start a work session. If your company has several users who log on frequently during a single day, bypassing this

PRO VERSION
There is no Time & Billing feature in the Pro version, so you will not need to hide it. The term Project replaces Fund.

Classic **CLASSIC VIEW**
You will see two lists: Modules and Icon Windows. Time & Billing is added to the Modules list.

WARNING!
If you do not hide the remaining modules, you will be unable to complete the final setup step of finishing the history because essential information for those modules is missing.

NOTES
The ✓ for Fund is already removed because we turned off the feature.
The ✓ for Time & Billing is automatically removed when you remove Employees & Payroll.

WARNING!
Do not hide the Banking page. If you hide this page, you will be unable to access the General Journal.

NOTES
You can access Checklists and the Daily Business Manager at any time from the Business Assistant menu, even if the automatic display for them is turned off. You can turn on the automatic display again at any time from this User Preferences View settings screen.

step would be efficient. In that case, the system administrator would update the session day for all users at the start of each business day.

Showing the **Paid Stamp** on invoices and payments is another option. If you hide the Vendors & Customers pages, these options will be dimmed because they no longer apply.

You can change the design and colour of Simply Accounting windows from the **Colour Scheme** entry. You can choose backgrounds from a variety of colours and patterns for the different journal windows.

Confirming Posting of Transactions Settings

We will choose to have the program advise when transactions are successfully recorded.

Click   **Transaction Confirmation**.

If you see a warning about losing icon position information (see sidebar Notes), click Yes to continue to the transaction confirmation window:

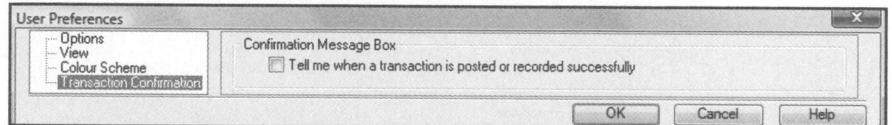

Click   the **check box** beside Tell Me When A Transaction Is Posted Or Recorded Successfully to add a ✓ and turn on the confirmation.

Click   **OK** to save the settings and return to the updated Home window:

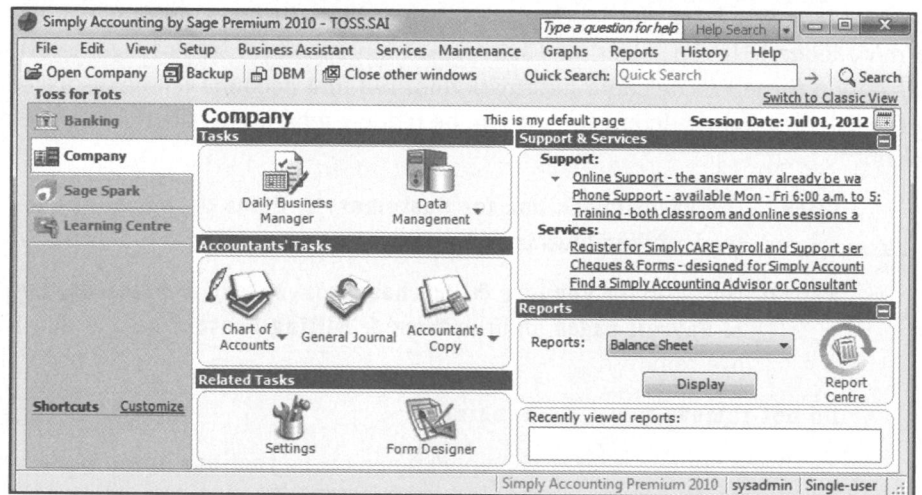

The unused modules (hidden pages) have been removed from the Modules pane list.

Changing View Menu Settings

The View menu controls some of the appearance options for the program:

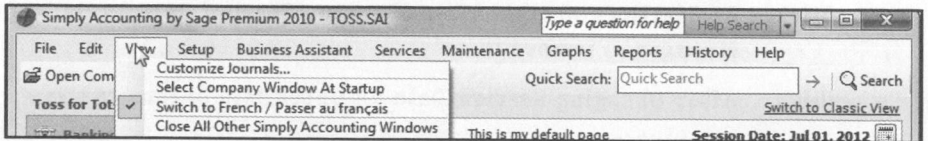

Each journal has optional fields that can be hidden if they are not required by the program and the business. You can also change the order in which journal fields are accessed from the (tab) key, that is, which field is next when you press (tab). You can **customize all journals** from this menu or you can use the customize option within individual journals.

To customize a journal, choose the View menu and click Customize Journals. Click the journal you want. Click Columns or Tabbing Order and click the columns or details you want to change. Hidden fields may be restored at any time by clicking their names again.

Click OK to save the changes and return to the Home window.

The Customize Journal tool in each journal provides the same options as the View menu screen.

You can also customize the order and size of journal columns. To change the order, drag a column heading to the location you want. To change the column size, point to the edge of the column heading; when the pointer changes to a double-headed arrow , drag the column margin to its new size.

The next choice on the main View menu refers to the **Select Company window** that appears when you first start Simply Accounting. There are advantages to showing this window. If you regularly use the same data file, you can bypass the Open Company file window, and open your data file with a single step by selecting Open The Last Company You Worked On. Similarly, you can restore a backup file from this window without first opening another data file. The View menu setting acts as a toggle switch, and you can change it at any time.

Simply Accounting is a fully bilingual program. You can **switch the program language** (choose to work in French or in English) from the View menu. When you are working in French, the View menu (now renamed *Vue*) option changes to *Passer A L'Anglais*/Switch To English.

The final View menu option allows you to **close all other Simply Accounting windows** in a single step, leaving only the Home window open. This menu choice is the same as the one in the tool bar.

You are now ready to make the necessary changes in the General Ledger.

Changing the Printer Defaults

You may select a different printer for customized forms or you may want to change the format of the printed reports. The following instructions should assist you.

Choose the **Setup menu** and **click Reports & Forms** to see the settings screen:

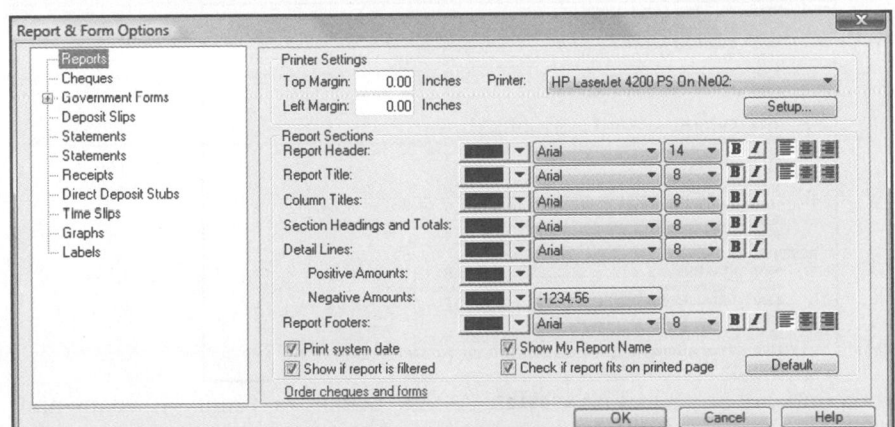

Printer selections are saved with each company file. If you use the file with another computer system or program installation, they may be incorrect. Simply Accounting allows you to set up different printers and settings for reports, graphs, cheques, invoices, labels and so on. Many companies use different printers for their reports and preprinted forms and invoices. Even if you use one printer, you may want to adjust fonts, margins and form selections for each type of printed report or statement.

NOTES
In Chapter 6, we customize journal columns and tabbing order.

NOTES
We have not hidden any fields in any journals used in the applications in this text, except by turning off features, so you can see the full range of input options for each journal.
    We show how to customize journals in Chapter 6 and invoices in Appendix G on the Student DVD.

NOTES
If you have the Select Company window hidden or deselected, you will start from the Open Company window each time you start Simply Accounting. You can turn on the selection again from the Home window View menu in any open data file.

PRO VERSION
You will not see the Time Slips entry.

WARNING!
You need to choose a printer for reports and for each form listed. The default may be incorrect if you have changed your computer setup after installing the program.
    Printer settings may also be incorrect if you use a data file that was created on a different computer.

Choose the printer you will use for reports from the list provided by the arrow beside the field. All printers installed on your computer should be on the list. Change the page margins if necessary. For each part of the report, choose font, type size and how to display positive and negative numbers by clicking the list arrows beside these fields. You can experiment to find the combination that will fit the reports neatly on the page. By default, reports include the computer system date and a message indicating whether filtering is applied.

To modify the printer setup for other outputs, click the relevant form in the list. You can modify printer setup information any time by returning to this screen.

Additional printer settings may be available from the Setup button screen for print quality, paper source, paper size, orientation and so on. The screens and options will vary from printer to printer.

Click   **Cancel** to exit without making changes and return to the Home window. or click OK to leave each dialogue box and save the change.

Preparing the Ledgers

The third stage in setting up an accounting system involves preparing each ledger for operation. For Toss for Tots, this stage involves the following steps:

1. organizing all accounting reports and records (this step has been completed)
2. modifying some existing accounts (you will not need to delete any accounts)
3. creating new accounts
4. entering historical account balance information

Defining the Skeleton Starter Files

When you created the company files for Toss for Tots in stage one, Creating Company Files (page 71), the preset startup accounts were provided.

Print   the **Chart of Accounts** for the current year, as shown here:

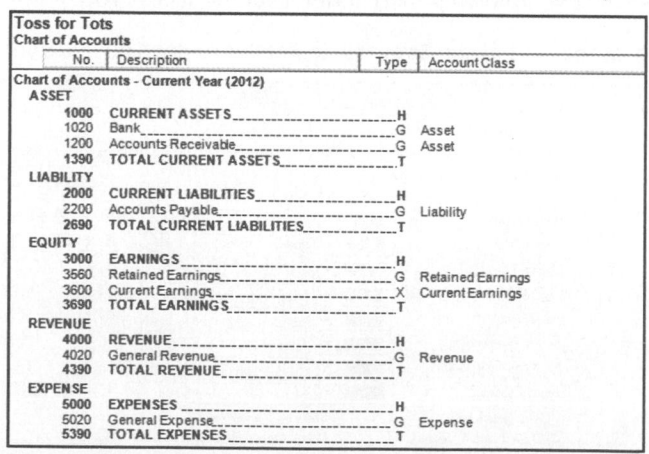

Accounts are organized by **section**: Assets, Liabilities, Equity, Revenue and Expense. The chart also shows the **account type** — such as Heading (H), Subgroup total (S), Total (T), subgroup Account (A), Group account (G) and Current Earnings (X) — and the Account Class. Account type is a method of classifying and organizing accounts within a section or subsection of a report.

Initial account numbers for each account are also shown on the Chart of Accounts.

We are using only four digits for account numbers, so the accounts in this chart follow the sectional boundaries we saw in Chapter 3 as follows:

- 1000–1999 Assets
- 2000–2999 Liabilities
- 3000–3999 Equity
- 4000–4999 Revenue
- 5000–5999 Expense

The Format of Financial Statements

When setting up the complete Chart of Accounts for Toss for Tots, it is important that you understand the composition and format of financial statements in Simply Accounting.

The Balance Sheet is divided into three sections, each with headings: Assets, Liabilities and Equity. The Income Statement is divided into two sections with headings: Revenue and Expense.

Each section of the financial statements can be subdivided into groups. Assets can be divided into groups such as CURRENT ASSETS, INVENTORY ASSETS and PLANT AND EQUIPMENT. Liabilities can be divided into groups titled CURRENT LIABILITIES and LONG TERM DEBT. Equity, Revenue and Expense sections can also be divided. Groups may be further divided by creating subgroups.

Simply Accounting requires that all accounts, including group headings, subgroup totals and group totals, be assigned numbers even if you do not use account numbers in transactions or reports. This is quite different from a manual accounting system, in which numbers are assigned only to postable accounts. Predefined section headings and section totals (e.g., ASSETS, TOTAL ASSETS and LIABILITIES), however, are not assigned numbers by the program.

Financial Statement Sections

The following rules apply to financial statement sections in Simply Accounting:

1. Each of the five financial statement sections has a **section heading** and a **section total**. You cannot change the titles for these headings and totals.

2. A **section total** is the total of the individual group totals within that section. The program will calculate section totals automatically and print them in the financial statement reports. The five section totals are
   - TOTAL ASSETS
   - TOTAL LIABILITIES
   - TOTAL EQUITY
   - TOTAL REVENUE
   - TOTAL EXPENSE

3. The Liabilities and Equity section totals are also automatically added together. **LIABILITIES AND EQUITY** is the sum of TOTAL LIABILITIES and TOTAL EQUITY.

4. In the Income Statement, **NET INCOME**, the difference between TOTAL REVENUE and TOTAL EXPENSE, is automatically calculated and listed under TOTAL EXPENSE.

Financial Statement Account Groups

Financial statement sections are further divided into account groups made up of different types of accounts. The following rules apply to account groups in Simply Accounting:

1. Each group must start with a **group Heading (H)**, which will be printed in boldface type. A heading is not considered a postable account, cannot be debited or credited through transaction entries and cannot have an amount assigned to it.

2. Each group must contain at least one **postable account** and can contain more. Postable accounts are those that can be debited or credited through journal transaction entries. Postable accounts may have an opening balance.

3. Postable accounts may be **subgroup Accounts (A)** or **Group accounts (G)**. Subgroup account balances appear in a separate column to the left of the group account balances, which are in the right column.

4. Postable subgroup accounts must be followed by a **Subgroup total (S)** account. A subgroup total is not a postable account and cannot be given an opening balance. The program automatically calculates a subgroup total by adding all preceding subgroup postable account balances that follow the last group, subgroup total or heading account. Subgroup total balances always appear in the right column. For example, in the previous application, *GST Charged on Sales* and *GST Paid on Purchases* are subgroup accounts followed by the subgroup total *GST Owing (Refund)*. For Toss for Tots, the bank and cash accounts are subtotalled.

5. Each group must end with a **group Total (T)**. All amounts in the right column, for postable and subgroup total accounts, are added together to form the group total. A group total is not a postable account. The program automatically calculates this total and prints it in boldface type.

The following chart summarizes the application of these rules in Simply Accounting:

ORGANIZATION OF ACCOUNTS

BALANCE SHEET

Type	Account Description	Amount	Amount
	ASSETS [section heading]		
H	**CURRENT ASSETS**		
A	Bank: Toss for Tots	xxx	
A	Cash on Hand	xxx	
S	Total Cash		xxx
G	Surprise Bag Supplies		xxx
G	Food Supplies		xxx
	–		
	–		
T	**TOTAL CURRENT ASSETS**		**xxx**
H	**FIXED ASSETS**		
G	Fax/Telephone		xxx
G	Computer		xxx
	–		
T	**TOTAL FIXED ASSETS**		**xxx**
	TOTAL ASSETS [section total]		xxx
	LIABILITIES [section heading]		
H	**CURRENT LIABILITIES**		
G	Bank Loan		xxx
G	A/P – Designs U Wear		xxx
	–		
T	**TOTAL CURRENT LIABILITIES**		**xxx**
	TOTAL LIABILITIES [section total]		xxx
	EQUITY [section heading]		
H	**EQUITY**		
G	Accumulated Surplus		xxx
X	Net Income		xxx
	–		
T	**TOTAL EQUITY**		**xxx**
	TOTAL EQUITY [section total]		xxx
	LIABILITIES & EQUITY		xxx

INCOME STATEMENT

Type	Account Description	Amount	Amount
	REVENUE [section heading]		
H	**REVENUE**		
G	Revenue: Registrations		xxx
G	Revenue: Sponsors		xxx
	–		
	–		
T	**TOTAL REVENUE**		**xxx**
	TOTAL REVENUE [section total]		xxx
	EXPENSE [section heading]		
H	**ADMIN EXPENSES**		
G	Court Rental Expense		xxx
G	Office Supplies Used		xxx
	–		
T	**TOTAL ADMIN EXPENSES**		**xxx**
H	**MERCHANDISE & FOOD EXPENSES**		
G	Cost of T-shirts		xxx
G	Cost of Surprise Bags		xxx
T	**TOTAL MERCHANDISE & FOOD EXPENSES**		**xxx**
	TOTAL EXPENSE [section total]		xxx
	NET INCOME		xxx

H = Group **H**eading
T - Group **T**otal
G = Postable **G**roup Account
A = Postable Subgroup **A**ccount
S = Group **S**ubtotal
X = Current Earnings Account

The Current Earnings (X) Account

There are two linked accounts for the General Ledger — **Retained Earnings** and **Current Earnings**. Both accounts are required and appear under the EQUITY section in the Balance Sheet. You do not need to change the links for these accounts.

The Current Earnings account is the only Type X account in the Chart of Accounts. This account is calculated as follows:

Current Earnings = Total Revenue – Total Expense

Current Earnings is not a postable account, but it appears in the right-hand column with the group accounts. It cannot be removed, but its title and number can be modified (see Editing Accounts in the General Ledger, page 91). *Current Earnings* is updated from any transactions that change revenue and expense account balances. At the end of the fiscal period when closing routines are performed, the balance of this account is added to *Retained Earnings* (or its renamed account) and then reset to zero.

For Toss for Tots, a charitable organization, the *Retained Earnings* account will be renamed *Accumulated Surplus. Current Earnings* will be renamed *Net Income.*

Preparing the General Ledger

Compare the Skeleton Chart of Accounts you printed with the Toss for Tots Chart of Accounts, Balance Sheet and Income Statement provided in this application. You will see that some accounts are the same, and some accounts you need are not yet in the program. You have to customize the accounts for Toss for Tots.

NOTES
You will not need to delete any of the preset accounts for Toss for Tots.

Changing the Skeleton Accounts

The first step, that of identifying the changes needed in the Skeleton preset accounts to match the accounts needed for Toss for Tots, is a very important one. The changes that must be made to these preset accounts are outlined below:

1. Some starter accounts provided by the program require no changes. For the following accounts, the account title, the initial account number and the account type are the same as those in the financial statements:

CURRENT ASSETS	1000	Type H
TOTAL CURRENT ASSETS	1390	Type T
CURRENT LIABILITIES	2000	Type H
TOTAL CURRENT LIABILITIES	2690	Type T
REVENUE	4000	Type H
TOTAL REVENUE	4390	Type T

2. The following accounts have account titles or names that need to be changed. You must also change the account type for *Bank 1020*. (Account numbers are correct.)

FROM (SKELETON ACCOUNTS)			TO (TOSS FOR TOTS ACCOUNTS)
Account Name	Number	Type	Account Name (Type)
Bank	1020	Type G	Bank: Toss for Tots (Type A)
Accounts Receivable	1200	Type G	Surprise Bag Supplies
Accounts Payable	2200	Type G	A/P - Designs U Wear
EARNINGS	3000	Type H	EQUITY
Retained Earnings	3560	Type G	Accumulated Surplus
Current Earnings	3600	Type X	Net Income
TOTAL EARNINGS	3690	Type T	TOTAL EQUITY
General Revenue	4020	Type G	Revenue: Registrations
EXPENSES	5000	Type H	ADMIN EXPENSES
General Expense	5020	Type G	Court Rental Expense

3. The following account requires changes in both the account name and the number:

FROM (SKELETON ACCOUNTS)			TO (TOSS FOR TOTS ACCOUNTS)	
Account Name	Number	Type	Account Name	Number
TOTAL EXPENSES	5390	Type T	TOTAL ADMIN EXPENSES	5440

Creating the Chart of Accounts

NOTES
GIFI numbers and allocations are not used, so they are omitted from this chart.

After identifying the modifications that must be made to the Skeleton accounts, the next step is to identify the accounts that you need to create or add to the preset accounts. Again, you should refer to the company Chart of Accounts on page 68 to complete this step.

The chart that follows shows the accounts that you will need to create. The chart includes account names, account numbers, account types and the option to omit printing zero balances. It lists both postable (group and subgroup) and non-postable accounts (subgroup totals, group headings and group totals).

CHART OF ACCOUNTS TO BE CREATED

Account: *Number	*Name	Type	Omit
1100	Cash on Hand	A	No
1150	Total Cash	S	
1300	Food Supplies	G	Yes
1320	Office Supplies	G	Yes
1360	T-shirts	G	Yes
1400	FIXED ASSETS	H	
1420	Fax/Telephone	G	Yes
1450	Computer	G	No
1500	Digital Camera	G	No
1590	TOTAL FIXED ASSETS	T	
2100	Bank Loan	G	Yes
2300	A/P - Quiq Kopy	G	Yes
2350	A/P - Central College	G	Yes
2400	A/P - Snack City	G	Yes
2670	HST Paid on Purchases	G	Yes
4040	Revenue: Sponsors	G	No
4080	Revenue: Surprise Bags	G	No
4100	Revenue: Admissions	G	No ▶

Account: *Number	*Name	Type	Omit
▶4120	Revenue: Food Sales	G	No
5200	Office Supplies Used	G	Yes
5220	Non-refundable HST	G	Yes
5240	Postage Expense	G	Yes
5280	Printing & Copying	G	Yes
5300	Telephone Expense	G	Yes
5320	Publicity & Promotion	G	Yes
5400	Wages - Manager	G	Yes
5420	Miscellaneous Expenses	G	Yes
5450	MERCHANDISE & FOOD EXPENSES	H	
5500	Cost of T-shirts	G	Yes
5520	Cost of Surprise Bags	G	Yes
5550	Cost of Food	G	Yes
5690	TOTAL MERCHANDISE & FOOD EXPENSES	T	

Account Types: A = Subgroup Account S = Subgroup Total
G = Group Account H = Heading T = Group Total
* Account number and account name are required fields

You are now ready to enter the account information into the Toss for Tots files.

Entering General Ledger Accounts

From the Chart of Accounts icon 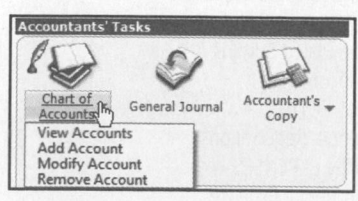 drop-down list, you can make all ledger account record–related changes.

Click the **Chart of Accounts shortcuts list arrow** as shown:

Editing Accounts in the General Ledger

We will change the first account that requires editing, *1020 Bank*. To modify accounts, use the Modify Account option.

Click   **Modify Account** in the Chart of Accounts shortcuts list to open the Search window:

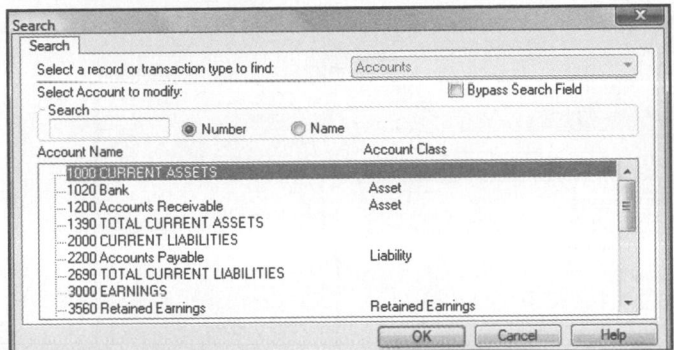

This Search screen is like the one in the General Journal that opens the Adjust Entry feature. Accounts is selected as the search field area.

Click   **1020 Bank** to highlight or select it.

Click   **OK** or double click the account's name to open the account as shown:

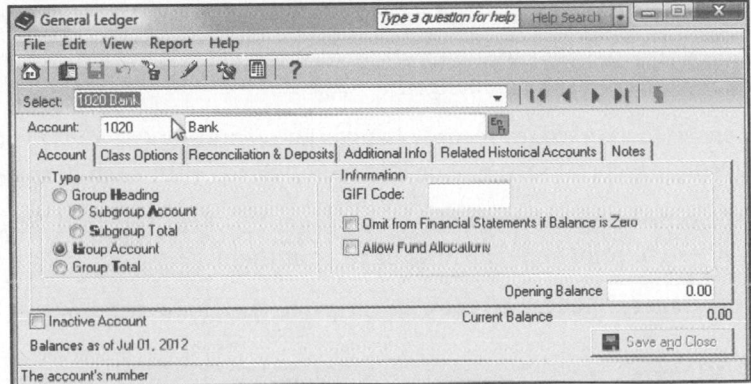

The Account information tab screen is displayed. We use this screen to edit the account name and type. For the bank account, the account number is correct.

Sometimes, it may be appropriate to print an account with a zero balance, although zero balance accounts usually do not need to be printed. In Simply Accounting, you have the option to omit accounts with zero balances from financial statements. You may select this option in the General Ledger.

The balance of bank accounts should always be displayed, so do not select Omit From Financial Statements If Balance Is Zero.

Press   (tab) **twice** to advance to the name of the account and highlight it.

Type   Bank: Toss for Tots

We are not using GIFI codes (Canada Revenue Agency's account numbering system for electronic report filing) or fund or project allocations, so we can leave these options unchecked. The current balance is displayed, but you cannot edit it. It is updated when you enter an opening balance and journal entries. The opening account balance will be added later (see Entering Historical Account Balances on page 95). There is no additional account information. We are not using Account Reconciliation, and we do not need to change the account class, so we can skip these tab screens. On the Related Historical

NOTES
You can advance to a later part of the account list by typing the first number in the Search field. You can also search by account name by choosing this option.

PRO VERSION
The Pro version does not have the Refresh tool or a Notes tab.

NOTES
GIFI codes and exporting GIFI reports are covered in Appendix J.

NOTES
Account class is introduced in Chapter 7.

Accounts tab screen, you can enter the relationship between different account numbers that are used for the same account in multiple fiscal periods. They do not apply here.

Click   **Subgroup Account** to change the account type.

The bank and cash accounts together will be subtotalled. You can now advance to the next account for editing. There are different ways to do this.

Click   the **Select field list arrow** to show the list of all accounts as shown:

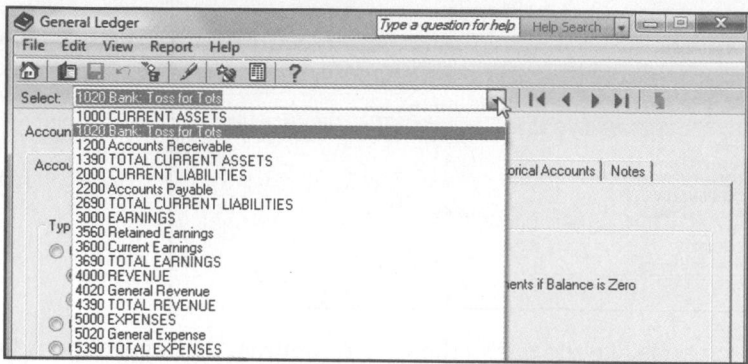

Click   **1200 Accounts Receivable** to display the ledger record.

To open a different ledger record, you can also click the **Next Account tool** to open the ledger record for the next account in numerical sequence.

Or, you can close the bank account window to return to the Home window. Then click Modify Account in the Chart of Accounts shortcuts list again and select the next account to be changed.

Because you chose to save ledger record changes automatically (page 82) you do not need to save an account record (Save tool or File menu, Save) after each change.

Edit   the **remaining accounts** shown on pages 89–90 as required. You may choose to print zero balances or to omit them.

Close   the **General Ledger window** to return to the Home window.

The Accounts Window

Click   the **Chart of Accounts icon** in the Accountant's Task pane to open the Accounts window:

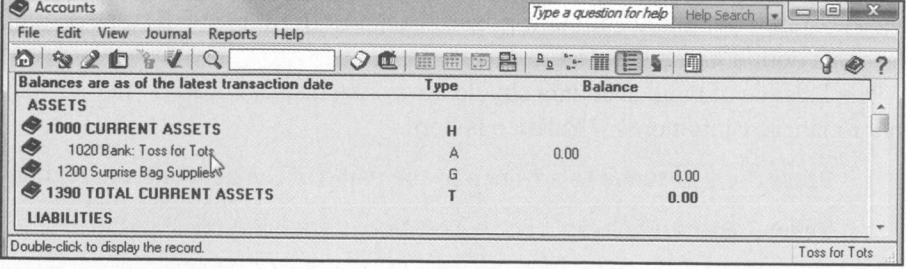

From this window, you can perform all ledger account–related activities as well. The tool buttons and menu options give access to the individual ledger records, and you can modify, delete, add records, display reports, access help and so on.

Click the Maximize button so that the Accounts window fills the screen. This will allow you to display more accounts and keep the Accounts window in view in the background while you are creating or editing accounts. To return the window to normal size, click , the Restore button.

NOTES
To edit an account from the Accounts window, double click the account you want to change, or click the account to select it and then either click the Edit tool or choose the File menu and click Open or press *ctrl* + O.

Several tools control the appearance of the Accounts window. The preset accounts should be displayed in the **Type** format shown above. You can also show the Accounts window in the large or small **Icon** format with icons representing each account. In the Icon view, you can rearrange icons by dragging so that frequently used accounts appear at the top for easier access. New accounts are automatically added at the bottom of the screen, but they can be moved to the desired location. In small icon viewing mode, more accounts can be displayed at the same time.

Another format is available with the **Name** view. Viewing accounts by name shows the account numbers, names and balances in debit and credit columns. Accounts remain in numerical order as new accounts are added.

For entering new accounts and editing a large number of existing accounts, it is easier to work with the accounts listed in numerical order. New accounts are inserted in their correct order, providing a better view of the progress during the setup phase. The addition of account type in the Type view is helpful for checking the logical order of accounts as they are created. You can change the Accounts window view at any time.

If your screen does not show the accounts by Type, you should change the way accounts are displayed.

Click   the **Display By Type tool** or **choose** the **View menu** and **click Type**.

When others are using the same data file, you can click the **Refresh tool** to update your data file with changes that other users have made to accounts. In single-user mode, the tool is dimmed.

We can also check that the accounts are in proper sequence; that is, they follow the rules outlined on pages 87–88.

Click   the **Check Validity Of Accounts tool** or **choose** the **File menu** and **click Check The Validity Of Accounts** to see the message:

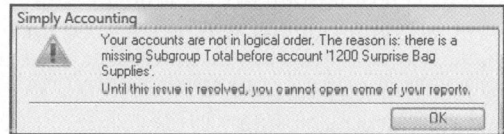

Without the second subgroup account and subgroup total, we have not followed the rules for Groups (page 88, rule 4). The accounts are not in logical order. You can periodically check the validity of accounts while you are adding accounts to see whether you have made errors in your account type sequence that will prevent you from finishing the account history. When we add the remaining accounts, the accounts should be in logical order and the error will be corrected.

Click   **OK** to return to the Accounts window.

Creating New Accounts in the General Ledger

You are now ready to enter the information for the first new account, *Cash on Hand*, using the chart on page 90 as your reference. The following keystrokes will enter the account name, number, type and option to include or omit zero balance accounts.

We are entering new accounts from the Accounts window, and it should still be open.

Click   the **Create tool** on the Accounts window tool bar or **choose** the **File menu** and **click Create**.

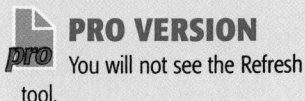

NOTES
You can also press ctrl + N to open a new account ledger form from the Accounts window or from any account's General Ledger window.

NOTES
Depending on your previous step or cursor position, your initial account number and type may be different from the ones we show.

NOTES
When no number is entered, only the Account, Class Options and Additional Information tabs are shown. When you enter a 4000- or 5000-level account number, the Budget tab will be added.

NOTES
Simply Accounting enters an Account Class automatically (Class Options tab screen). For most accounts, the section heading is used (Assets, Liabilities, etc.). For Expense accounts, the default class is Cost of Goods Sold. This selection will not affect the financial statements for Toss for Tots so you can leave it. If you want, you can change the class on the Class Options screen by choosing Expense for these accounts.
Account class is introduced in Chapter 7.

You will display the new account window:

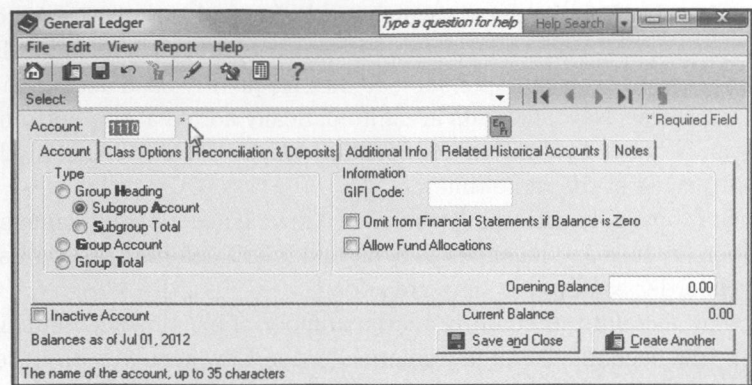

The tabs that appear in the ledger depend on the account section as defined by the account number. If no number is entered initially, only the tabs that apply to all accounts appear. We will create the first account that was not in the Skeleton Chart of Accounts, *Cash on Hand*. The account type is selected as the most likely option for logical account order. The default account type depends on the account record you used most recently. For example, group total accounts are often followed by a group account. The cursor is in the Account number field and the field is selected for editing. The Simply Accounting program will not allow duplicate account numbers.

Two fields are required for accounts: the number and the name. An * appears beside a required field as long as it remains blank. Simply Accounting may enter an account number and type that is the most likely next entry based on the previous selection. If an account number is entered as a default, as in the screen we show, the * will be removed. After the error message, account 1200 is selected in the Accounts window so that you can correct the error. Its preceding account is a Subgroup account, so another Subgroup account most likely follows. The account number will be selected for editing.

Type   1100

Press   tab to advance to the Account name field.

Type   Cash on Hand

Click   **Subgroup Account** to change the account type if necessary.

Leave the option to Omit From Financial Statements turned off. Skip the GIFI field and the Fund (Project) Allocations check box.

Check   your work. **Make** any necessary **corrections** by pressing tab to return to the incorrect field, typing the correct information and pressing tab if necessary.

When the information has been entered correctly, save your work.

Click   **Create Another** [Create Another] to save the new account and to advance to another new account information window.

Both the number and name fields are now marked with an * .

Create   the **remaining accounts** from page 90.

Subgroup totals, group headings and group totals — the non-postable accounts — will have the Balance fields removed when you choose these account types.

Click   **Save And Close** [Save and Close] to save the final account.

Display or **print** the **Chart of Accounts** to check the accuracy of your work.

If you find mistakes, edit the account information as described in the Editing Accounts in the General Ledger section on page 91.

If you want to end your session, close the General Ledger window and close the Accounts window to return to the Home window.

Entering Historical Account Balances

Before completing this step, we will create one more account to use as a test account for our Trial Balance. If you close the General Ledger before entering all the account balances, or if the total debits and credits are not equal, the program forces the Trial Balance to balance by adding the required debit or credit amount to another account.

This automatic adjustment may compensate for other errors that you have made in entering amounts, and you may be able to finish the history with errors in opening balances. You cannot change these balances after finishing the history. To detect this problem, we will create a test account and put all the adjustments into it. If all the balances are entered correctly, the test account will have a zero balance and we can remove the account.

Create the new Group account **1005 Test Account**.

You are now ready to enter the opening historical account balances for all postable (type G or A) accounts. The opening balances for Toss for Tots can be found in the Trial Balance on page 70. Accounts with zero balances are not included in the Trial Balance. You should skip these accounts when entering account balances.

Click the **Select field** list arrow and **choose 1020 Bank: Toss for Tots**. The ledger window opens:

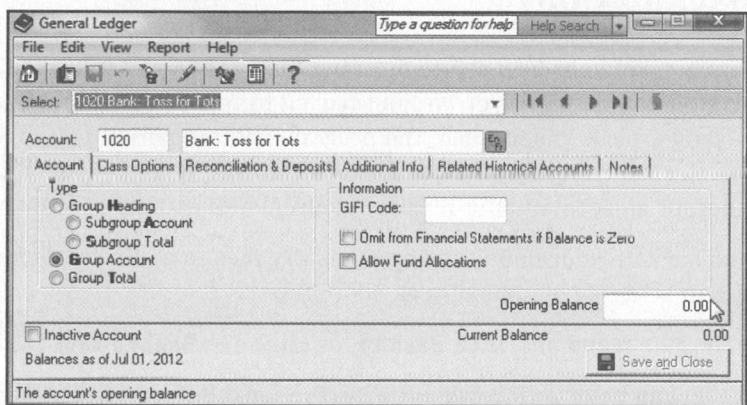

Click the **Opening Balance field** to highlight it.

Type 18550

The Current Balance is updated but you cannot change it directly. Simply Accounting updates this balance automatically from journal entries.

Click the **Next tool** to advance to the next ledger account window.

Enter the **balances** for the remaining accounts.

Remember that *HST Paid on Purchases* has a debit balance (add a minus sign).

If you close the General Ledger window before entering all the account balances, you will see a screen like the following:

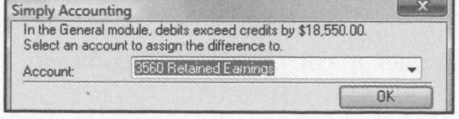

WARNING!
Before you finish the history, the opening balance can be edited. The Current Balance has no data input field because you cannot edit it. Initially, it is the same as the opening balance but it changes when you add journal entries. Because you can enter journal transactions before finishing the history, this distinction is very important. The balance in the Accounts window is the current balance, which may not be the same as the opening balance.

WARNING!
Remember to enter the amount for HST Paid on Purchases with a minus sign to create a debit entry.

The message asks you to choose an account for the difference — an adjusting, balancing entry that will place the Trial Balance in balance. Choose *Test Account* from the drop-down list of accounts. You can choose any account from the drop-down list or accept the default. If you see this warning,

> **Choose account 1005 Test Account** from the drop-down list.
>
> **Click** **OK** to continue.

After entering all the accounts and balances,

> **Close** the **Ledger window** to return to the Accounts window.
>
> **Display** or **print** the **Trial Balance**, **Balance Sheet** and **Income Statement** to check the accuracy of your work.
>
> **Choose** the **Reports menu** in the Accounts window and **click Trial Balance** (or Balance Sheet or Income Statement).
>
> **Check** all your **opening balances** carefully before finishing the history.
>
> **Close** the **Accounts window** to return to the Home window.

Compare your reports with the information on pages 68–70 to be sure that all account numbers, names and balances are correct. The balance for *Test Account* should be zero. Make corrections if necessary.

Finishing the History

Making a Backup Copy

By having a backup copy of your files before finishing the history, you will be able to make changes easily, if you find an error, without having to repeat the entire setup from scratch. After the ledger history is finished, the program will not permit you to make certain changes, such as opening account balances and fiscal dates. You cannot change the account number for an account after making a journal entry to the account.

> You should back up your unfinished open history files to a different folder so that they can be easily identified (e.g., NFTOSS).
>
> **Choose** the **File menu** and **click Backup**, or **click** the **Backup tool** .
>
> **Create** a **backup copy** by following the instructions. Refer to page 49 and page 250 if you need help.

Finishing the General Ledger History

You should be in the Home window.

> **Choose** the **History menu** and **click Finish Entering History**.

The following caution appears:

If you have not made a backup copy yet, click Backup and do so before proceeding. If you have made your backup copy, you should continue.

> **Click** **Proceed**.

⚠ WARNING!
Back up the not-finished Toss for Tots files before proceeding. See Chapter 3 if you need further assistance.

⚠ WARNING!
You can change account numbers only after two fiscal periods have passed if the account was used in journal entries.

⚠ WARNING!
You can finish entering the history when the Trial Balance is in balance. Afterwards, you cannot change opening balances, even if they are incorrect. You will need to make adjusting entries. Simply Accounting always keeps the Trial Balance balanced. Therefore, checking for a zero balance in the Test Account can stop you from proceeding with incorrect account balances.

If you see a different screen at this stage, like the following one, you have errors that must be corrected before you can continue:

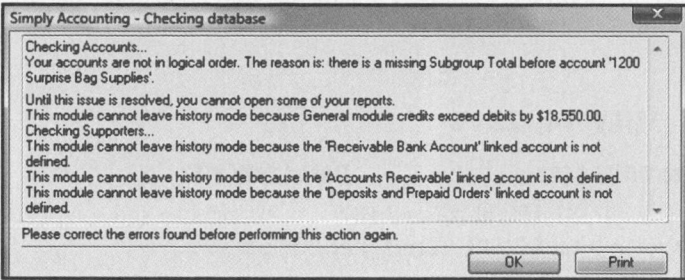

The message describes the mistakes you must correct. If your accounts are out of order, you cannot finish entering the history. If you did not hide the unused modules, you cannot finish entering the history because some essential linked accounts for these modules are not defined.

Read the error description carefully. Print the message for reference when you make corrections. Click OK to return to the Home window.

Make the necessary corrections. Remember to replace your previous unfinished history backup file. Then try again to finish the history.

Notice that the open or not-finished history symbol 🖋, the quill pen, has been removed from the Chart of Accounts icon.

You can now exit the program or continue by entering the source documents. Remember to advance the Session Date. Enter all transactions for Toss for Tots in the General Journal.

SOURCE DOCUMENTS

SESSION DATE — JULY 7, 2012

☐ **Purchase Invoice #QK-2252**   **Dated July 2/12**

From Quiq Kopy, $200 plus $26 HST for photocopying registration and donation forms. Invoice total $226. Terms: net 25 days.

☐ **Purchase Invoice #BC-10116**   **Dated July 2/12**

From Bell Canada, $300 plus $39 HST for rental of cellular telephone equipment. Invoice total $339. Deposit required and balance due at end of month. Create new Group account 2140 A/P - Bell Canada.

☐ **Cheque Copy #167**   **Dated July 2/12**

To Bell Canada, $100 deposit on rental of telephone equipment. Reference invoice #BC-10116.

☐ **Memo #1**   **Dated July 2/12**

From Event Manager: Give T-shirts to volunteers. Cost of T-shirts given out is $120. Reduce T-shirt asset account and increase Cost of T-shirts expense account.

☐ **Memo #2**   **Dated July 4/12**

From Event Manager: Issue cheque #168 for $3 500 to transfer funds to Cash on Hand for snack purchases for the tournament.

NOTES
The first error on this screen states that accounts are not in logical order. The remaining messages refer to missing linked accounts for modules that are not used but are also not hidden.

NOTES
If you want to be sure that the file is correct before making a backup, choose the Finish History option. If the option to proceed is available, click Backup on this screen or click Cancel, make the backup and then finish the history.

NOTES
You can now unhide the unused modules, but you do not need to do so. If you want to set them up later, you must first unhide them, as we show in Chapter 9.

NOTES
In most businesses, the Cash on Hand balance is usually small and is used only for paying small amounts. In this application, we are using the Cash on Hand account to pay for any purchases that normally would require cash or credit card payments. The Event Manager receives cash advances to cover these costs.

☐ **Cash Purchase Invoice #SC-2168**   **Dated July 4/12**

From Snack City, $3 000 plus $390 HST for drinks and snacks for participants and spectators. Invoice total $3 390 paid from Cash on Hand.

SESSION DATE – JULY 14, 2012

☐ **Purchase Invoice #DW-9493**   **Dated July 8/12**

From Designs U Wear, $1 100 plus $143 HST for T-shirts to sell to spectators at tournament. Invoice total $1 243. Terms: net 20 days.

☐ **Cash Purchase Invoice #QAS-4632**   **Dated July 12/12**

From Quarts Arts Supplies, $100 plus $13 HST for bristol board and paint supplies to make signs in gymnasiums. Invoice total $113. Paid from Cash on Hand. (Debit Office Supplies account.)

☐

Toss for Tots   **No: 169**

North Toronto
PO Box 42665
Toronto, ON M5N 3A8

Date 2 0 1 2 0 7 1 3
      Y Y Y Y M M D D

Pay to the order of   Central College $ 11,300.00

———————— Eleven thousand three hundred dollars ————————00 /100 Dollars

TD-CT
2544 Yonge St.
Toronto, ON M4P 1A6

. — — 03544 · 5499 388 169

Marie Gilbert

- -

Re: pay invoice # CC-47221 $11,300.00 **No: 169**
                                               July 13, 2012

☐ **Funds Raised Form #FR-12-7**   **Dated July 13/12**

Cash and cheques received on first two weekends of event. Create new revenue account 4160 Revenue: T-shirt Sales.

Participant registrations	$30 000
Sale of snack foods and drinks	3 500
Sale of T-shirts	1 000
Sale of surprise bags	560

Total $35 060 deposited in Bank: Toss for Tots.

SESSION DATE – JULY 21, 2012

☐ **Purchase Invoice #QK-5306**   **Dated July 18/12**

From Quiq Kopy, $500 plus $65 HST for printing cancer information leaflets for participants and spectators. Invoice total $565. Terms: net 25 days.

☐ **Cheque Copy #170**   **Dated July 18/12**

To Designs U Wear, $800 in payment of account. Reference invoice #DW-6299.

Funds Raised Form #FR-12-8   **Dated July 20/12**

Record $30 200 in pledges to sponsor participants from sponsor forms submitted. Create new asset account 1180 Donations Receivable. (Credit Revenue: Sponsors.)

Cash Purchase Invoice #PH-34982   **Dated July 20/12**

From Pizza House, $250 plus $32.50 HST for pizza and soft drinks for volunteers. Invoice total $282.50. Paid from Cash on Hand.

NOTES
Charge pizza expense to Miscellaneous Expenses.

SESSION DATE — JULY 28, 2012

Toss for Tots

North Toronto
PO Box 42665
Toronto, ON M5N 3A8

FUNDS RAISED FORM:	FR-12-9
Date:	July 27, 2012
Comment:	Cash & cheques received from third & fourth event weekend July 19-27

Description	Amount
T-shirt sales	$ 2 500
Admissions for spectators	11 160
Sale of snack foods and drinks	6 680
Surprise bag sales	1 750
Photo sales	3 900

Deposited to bank account July 27

Signature: *Marcie Gilcrest*

Total	$25 990

NOTES
Create new revenue account 4180 Revenue: Photos.

Funds Raised Form #FR-12-10   **Dated July 27/12**

Record $80 500 in pledges to sponsor participants from sponsor forms submitted by participants. (Debit Donations Receivable.)

Cash Purchase Invoice #PH-39168   **Dated July 27/12**

From Pizza House, $320 plus $41.60 HST for pizza and soft drinks for volunteers to celebrate successful tournament. Invoice total $361.60. Paid from Cash on Hand.

Cheque Copy #171   **Dated July 27/12**

To Sunni Husein, $1 000 for winning tournament. Create new Group account 5430 Tournament Prizes.

Cheque Copy #172   **Dated July 28/12**

To Marcie Gilcrest, manager, $2 000 for wages for one month.

Cheque Copy #173   **Dated July 28/12**

To Designs U Wear, $1 243 in payment of account. Reference invoice #DW-9493.

Tess for Tots

North Toronto
PO Box 42665
Toronto, ON M5N 3A8

M E M O #3

Date: July 28, 2012
From: Marcie Gilcrest
Re: Adjustments required for event sales & supplies used

Cost of t-shirts sold	$1 670
Cost of food items sold	3 990
Cost of surprise bag items sold	500
Cost of office supplies used	300

Authorization: *MG*

SESSION DATE — JULY 31, 2012

Cheque Copy #174   **Dated July 31/12**

To Quiq Kopy, $941 in full payment of account. Reference invoices #QK-5306, QK-2252 and previous balance owing.

Cheque Copy #175   **Dated July 31/12**

To Bell Canada, $239 in full payment of account. Reference invoice #BC-10116 and cheque #167.

Cheque Copy #176   **Dated July 31/12**

To Snack City, $900 in full payment of account. Reference invoice #SC-1005.

Memo #4   **Dated July 31/12**

From Manager: Issue cheque #177 for $500 to transfer funds to Cash on Hand to purchase postage for mailing charitable donation receipts.

Bank Debit Memo #TDCT-3881   **Dated July 31/12**

From TD-Canada Trust, $21.50 in bank charges for cheques and statement preparation. Create new Group account 5010 Bank Charges.

Memo #5   **Dated July 31/12**

From Event Manager: Apply for HST rebate of $1 300.05. Record 50% of HST Paid on Purchases as HST Refund Receivable, and 50% as the Non-refundable HST expense. Create new Group account 1190 HST Refund Receivable. (Refer to Accounting Procedures on page 70.)

Funds Raised Form #FR-12-11   **Dated July 31/12**

Received $92 300 from sponsors for pledges previously recorded. Amount deposited in bank account. (Credit 1180 Donations Receivable.)

SESSION DATE – AUGUST 31, 2012

☑ **Funds Received Form FR-12-12**   **Dated August 31/12**

102   Received $18 400 from sponsors for pledges previously recorded. Amount deposited in bank account.

☐ **Cash Purchase Invoice #CP-2**   **Dated August 31/12**

From Canada Post, $500 plus $65 HST for postage to mail receipts. Invoice total $565. Paid from Cash on Hand.

☐ **Memo #6**   **Dated August 31/12**

From Event Manager: Deposit $287.90, balance of Cash on Hand to bank.

☐ **Bank Debit Memo #TDCT-5218**   **Dated August 31/12**

From TD-Canada Trust, withdraw $15 400 from chequing account to repay loan for $15 000 plus $400 interest. Create new Group account 5100 Interest Expense.

SESSION DATE – SEPTEMBER 30, 2012

☑
102

Toss for Tots

North Toronto
PO Box 42665
Toronto, ON M5N 3A8

M E M O   #7

Date: September 30, 2012
From: Marcie Gilcrest
Re: Final account adjustments required to clear inventory
       of supplies (donated)

Cost of all remaining t-shirts donated to shelters	$110
Cost of all remaining food items donated to shelters	210
Cost of craft and office supplies not needed and donated to Campus Day Care Centre	280

Authorization: *MG*

☐ **Cash Purchase Invoice #BC-32423**   **Dated September 30/12**

From Bell Canada, $120 plus $15.60 HST for telephone service for two months. Invoice total $135.60 paid in full by cheque #178.

☑ **Memo #8**   **Dated September 30/12**

102   All accounts for the event are settled so the books can be closed. Make a backup of the data files. Start a new fiscal period to close the books. (See Keystrokes following the next source document.)

☑ **Memo #9**   **Dated September 30/12**

105   Received cheque #488129 for $1 300.05 from the Receiver General for HST rebate. We closed the books before making the entry.

KEYSTROKES FOR CLOSING

Ending a Fiscal Period

Simply Accounting warns you as you approach the end of a fiscal period because important end of period adjusting entries are usually required.

When you change the session date to August 31, you will see the following warning:

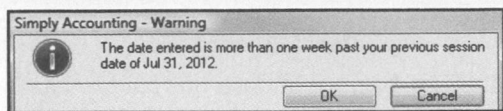

Normally a business would advance the session date by a shorter period so the warning helps you to avoid entering the wrong session date.

Click   OK to confirm that you entered the date you intended.

You will see another warning that Simply Accounting displays about one month before the end of the fiscal period:

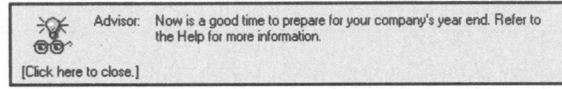

 Close   the **Advisor** and **continue** with the **transactions** for August 31.

Closing Adjusting Entries

When you advance the session date further to a date very close to the end of the fiscal period, September 30 in this case, you see this year-end warning again.

Close   the **Advisor window**.

The required adjusting entries are listed with the source documents for September 30 — for Toss for Tots, they are the adjustments for remaining supplies. For other businesses, adjusting entries include depreciation entries, inventory adjustments, adjustments for prepaid expenses that have expired, accrued wages and so on. Most adjusting entries do not have an external source document that reminds you to complete them, and most of them are General Journal entries.

 Continue with the transactions for September 30.

Starting a New Fiscal Period

Starting a new fiscal period is not a reversible step, so you should prepare a complete set of financial reports and make a backup of the data set.

Print   all the **financial reports** for Toss for Tots for September 30, 2012.

Back up your **data files** with a label to indicate it is the year-end copy.

There are two methods for beginning a new fiscal year. The first is the method we have been using to change the session date.

Choose the **Maintenance menu** and **click Change Session Date** or **click** 🗓, the Change Date icon beside Session Date.

The first date of the new fiscal period is always on the drop-down list of dates in the Session Date window. The program will not accept any dates later than October 1, 2012.

Type October 1, 2012 or choose this date from the date field list or Calendar icon.

Click **OK**. Because this step is not reversible, you will see a warning:

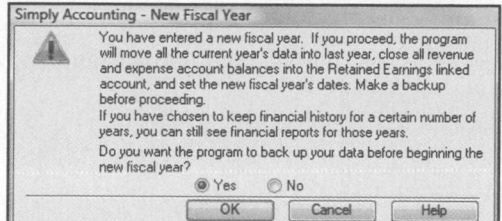

The expense and revenue amounts will be transferred to the capital account but historical data will be saved in the data file.

Read the **warning** carefully.

The warning describes the changes about to take place in the data set. All revenue and expense accounts are reset to zero at the start of the new fiscal year. Their balances are closed out to the linked *Accumulated Surplus (Retained Earnings)* account, and the linked *Net Income (Current Earnings)* account is reset to zero to begin a new income statement. All previous year entries that are not cleared are stored as data for the previous year. The program also updates the fiscal date for the company by one year. The new fiscal end date becomes the final date allowed as a session date.

At this stage you can choose to back up the data files, continue with the date change or cancel the date change by clicking No.

Click **Cancel** to return to the Session Date window and then **click Cancel** again to close the Change Session Date screen. We will use the second menu option to change to a new fiscal year.

Choose the **Maintenance menu** and **click Start New Year**.

You may see a screen asking whether you want to start a new fiscal or calendar year:

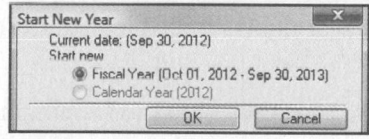

NOTES
The new calendar year prior to the new fiscal year has already passed so this selection is dimmed.

The default will be the period that starts next. Make your choice and click OK to continue. Start New Fiscal Year is correctly selected.

Click **OK** to continue.

You will see a warning similar to the one on the previous page:

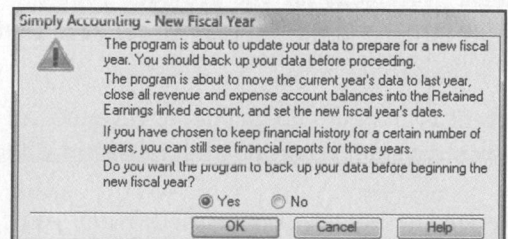

The default setting is to make a backup before continuing. If you have not yet made a backup, do so now. If you do not want to begin a new year, you can click Cancel and the old dates will remain in effect.

Click **No** because you have already backed up your files.

Click **OK** to begin the new fiscal period.

You will see a confirmation that the new year has been started:

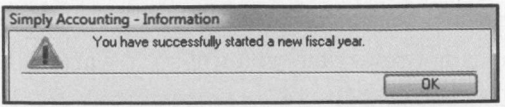

Click **OK** to close the message. You will now see another warning:

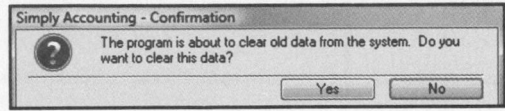

NOTES

If you choose to clear old data, the program will clear the information you selected for the periods you entered in the Automatically Clear Data screen. See Chapter 15, page 609.

We describe how to clear data from company files in Chapter 15.

You have the option of retaining the old data or clearing it. Journal entries from the previous year are never cleared and Income Statement and Balance Sheet details for the previous year are also retained.

Click **Yes** because Toss for Tots has no other data. If in doubt, choose No.

Another message now appears:

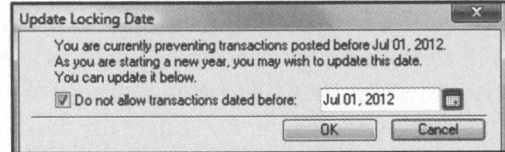

You must now change the earliest date that you will allow transactions for. We should not allow any transactions to the previous fiscal period so that the historical records cannot be altered in error.

Drag through **Jul 01, 2012**, the date entered.

Type 10/01

Click **OK** to continue. Close the message about payroll updates if it appears.

When you have more than one fiscal period, most financial reports offer comparisons with the previous year as an option. Journal reports and other reports are available for both periods — the Report On Fiscal Year field is available with Current Year and Previous Year options in a drop-down list.

Print the **Comparative Trial Balance** and **Balance Sheet** for September 30 and October 1.

Notice the changes in the capital accounts on the Balance Sheet. The *Net Income* balance for September 30 has been added to the *Accumulated Surplus* account to create the October 1 balance in the *Accumulated Surplus* account.

Print the **Comparative Income Statement for the previous year** (Oct. 1, 2011, to Sep. 30, 2012) and the **current fiscal year to date** (Oct. 1, 2012, to Oct. 1, 2012).

The Income Statement for the current year shows no income or revenue. All accounts have a zero balance because you have not recorded any transactions for the new fiscal year.

The files are now ready for transactions in the new fiscal period. When you check the Company Information, the fiscal dates are updated and you will see the additional information about last year's dates.

Choose the **Setup menu** and **click Settings**, or **click** the **Settings icon** 🗑️.

Click **Company** if necessary and then **click Information** to see the changes:

⚠️ **WARNING!**

If you have cleared paid invoices, these details will be unavailable for reports. Comparative Income Statements and Balance Sheets are always available for the two fiscal periods.

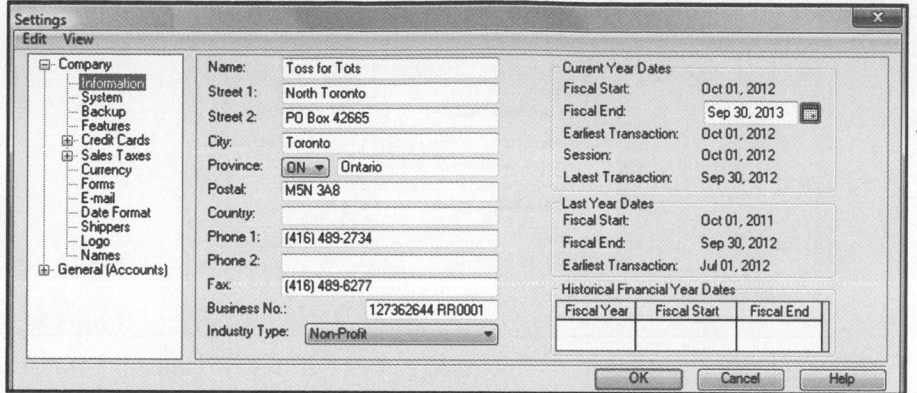

NOTES
The program assumes a fiscal year of one year, so the fiscal end will be advanced by 12 months.

NOTES
After you start a new fiscal period, you cannot change the fiscal start date.

The new Fiscal Start is October 1, 2012, and the new Fiscal End is September 30, 2013. Simply Accounting automatically updates the Fiscal End by 12 months but you can edit this date if the fiscal period is shorter. In fact, this is the only date that you can edit after you have made journal entries to a data file. The Earliest Transaction Date has also been updated to October 1, 2012. The dates for the previous fiscal period are provided for reference.

Click   Cancel to close the Company Information window.

Entering Transactions for an Earlier Fiscal Period

Sometimes not all the information required is available before the books are closed for the fiscal period. However, it may be necessary to close the books (start a new fiscal period) so that transactions in the new year may be entered. The details of the adjusting entries may be calculated by an accountant who does not have the information until after a business has started entering transactions for a new year. Simply Accounting allows you to post transactions to the previous year so that the financial statements for both the previous year and the current year will be correct.

Enter   Memo #9, the HST rebate receipt, with the **September 30** date, after starting the new fiscal period.

When you post the entry, you will see the following message:

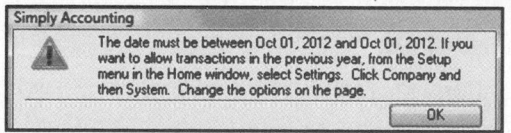

Before the program allows the entry, we must change the System Settings. We indicated that transactions earlier than Oct. 1, 2012, should not be allowed.

Click   OK to close the message. **Close** the **journal** to discard the entry. **Click Yes** to confirm that you want to discard the entry.

Choose the **Setup menu** and **click Settings** or **click** the **Settings icon**.

Click   Company if necessary and then **click System**.

This will access the settings field we need:

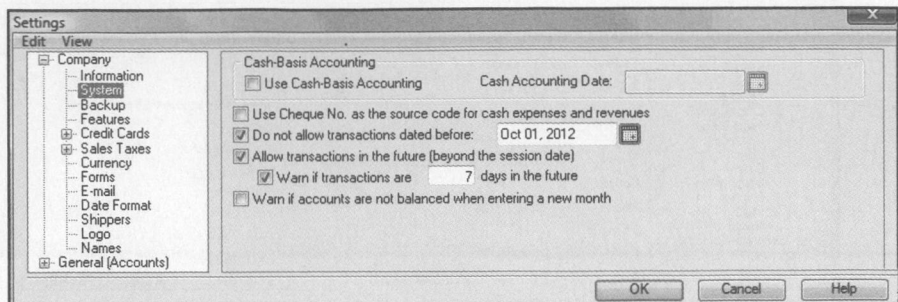

This is the same settings screen we saw earlier but now we must allow transactions in the previous period.

Click   **Do Not Allow Transactions Dated Before** to **remove** the ✓.

Click   **OK**.

Enter   the **transaction** again. **Review** and then **post** it. This time you will see a different warning:

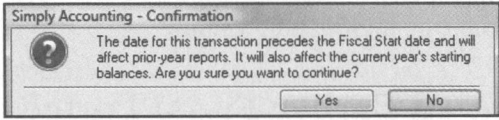

NOTES
The warnings in Simply Accounting make it difficult to post to the wrong year by mistake.

Because the transaction date is in a previous month or period, you are advised that prior period reports may be affected by the transaction. The warning gives you a chance to correct the date if it was incorrect. But we want to proceed. After completing the transaction, we will change the System Settings option again to avoid mistakenly posting to the previous year.

Click   **Yes** to continue with posting.

Close   the **General Journal**.

Click   the **Settings icon** or **choose** the **Setup menu**, then **choose** **Settings** and **click Company** and **System**.

Click   **Do Not Allow Transactions Dated Before** to **add** the ✓.

Enter   **Oct 1** as the date and **click OK**.

Finish   your **session** by closing the files for Toss for Tots.

R E V I E W

The Student DVD with Data Files includes Review Questions and Supplementary Cases for this chapter.

OBJECTIVES

After completing this chapter, you should be able to

- **open** the General and Payables journals
- **enter** supplier- or vendor-related purchase transactions
- **enter** supplier-related payment transactions
- **enter** partial payments to suppliers
- **enter** payments to suppliers with early payment discounts
- **enter** cash purchase transactions
- **enter** sales taxes in the General Journal
- **create** shortcuts in the Home window
- **store** recurring purchase transactions
- **add** new supplier accounts
- **edit** supplier accounts
- **edit** and **review** transactions in the journals
- **recall**, **use** and **edit** stored purchase transactions
- **adjust** and **reverse** purchase invoices and payments after posting
- **understand** Payables Ledger linked accounts
- **display** and **print** payables transactions and reports
- **graph** payables reports

COMPANY INFORMATION

Company Profile

Chai Tea Room, located in Fredericton, New Brunswick, is owned by Sarah Quinte. Originally, Quinte wanted to name her business Quintessentials but after an extended tour of the Far East, where she acquired a taste for exotic blends of tea, she chose the name Chai instead. Canadians are becoming more familiar with the name Chai, an East Indian word for tea that is often used for spiced Indian tea.

The downtown tea room, near the New Brunswick Parliament House, Art Gallery and other historic sites, with its scenic lookout over the Saint John River

NOTES
Chai Tea Room
125 King St.
Fredericton, NB E3B 2P4
Tel 1: (506) 454-6111
Tel 2: (800) 454-6000
Fax: (506) 454-6990
Business No.: 186 522 333

and railroad walking bridge, is very popular with professional women. Adjacent to a women's fitness and recreational centre, the tea room provides a comfortable atmosphere for customers to discuss finance, careers or social or political issues after working out. The tea room boasts refinements such as a fireplace, comfortable living-room-style cushioned sofas and chairs and very personal care and service from the owner and staff.

Chai Tea Room, essentially a tea room serving specialty teas from all around the world, also provides light lunches and superb desserts. Coffees and other beverages — both alcoholic and non-alcoholic — are available too. Quinte sells gift sets as well, packaged variety teas and tea service sets consisting of teacups, teaspoons, a teapot and a tea cozy. The tea service set items can also be purchased separately.

Sarah Quinte manages the day-to-day activities of the store. An assistant manager and kitchen staff handle business during her absence. The payroll is managed by the bank for a small fee. She has set up accounts with regular vendors or suppliers, such as the suppliers of food and beverages as well as the utility companies. Some of her suppliers offer discounts for early payment. Cleaning and maintenance of the premises is done professionally once a week by Sunbury Cleaning; they wash and wax floors and steam clean the carpets and furniture. They also clean and check all equipment and complete minor repairs. On a day-to-day basis, the tea room staff do the regular cleaning.

Chai Tea Room does not pay HST (sales tax) on its food purchases, but its other purchases are subject to HST. Food consumed in restaurants is subject to HST, so HST at 13 percent is charged to customers on all food products consumed in the tea room and on the gift sets.

Quinte currently manages all the accounting records for the tea room and has just finished converting the manual records to Simply Accounting using the following:

- Chart of Accounts
- Post-Closing Trial Balance
- Supplier Information
- Accounting Procedures

NOTES

HST, Harmonized Sales Tax, is charged instead of GST and PST in New Brunswick. HST at 13 percent includes both GST at 5 percent and PST at 8 percent. Refer to Accounting Procedures and Chapter 2 for further details.

CHART OF POSTABLE ACCOUNTS

CHAI TEA ROOM

ASSETS
- 1080 Cash in Bank
- 1300 Beverage Inventory
- 1320 Beer, Wine and Liquor
- 1340 Food Inventory
- 1360 Gift Set Inventory
- 1500 Cash Register and Computer
- 1520 Cutlery and Dishes
- 1540 Furniture and Fixtures
- 1560 Equipment
- 1580 Tea Room Premises ▶

▶LIABILITIES
- 2100 Bank Loan
- 2200 Accounts Payable
- 2650 HST Charged on Sales
- 2670 HST Paid on Purchases
- 2850 Mortgage Payable

EQUITY
- 3100 S. Quinte, Capital
- 3150 S. Quinte, Drawings
- 3600 Net Income ▶

▶REVENUE
- 4100 Customer Service and Sales

EXPENSE
- 5020 Advertising and Promotion
- 5040 Bank Charges
- 5060 Cleaning and Maintenance
- 5080 Cost of Goods Sold
- 5090 Purchase Discounts
- 5100 General Expense
- 5120 Hydro Expense ▶

▶5140 Interest Expense
- 5160 Licences and Permits
- 5180 Payroll Services
- 5220 Telephone Expense
- 5240 Wages

NOTES: The Chart of Accounts includes only postable accounts and the Net Income or Current Earnings account. Simply Accounting uses the Net Income account for the Income Statement to calculate the difference between revenue and expenses before closing the books.

POST-CLOSING TRIAL BALANCE

CHAI TEA ROOM

August 1, 2012		Debits	Credits
1080	Cash in Bank	$ 11 155	
1300	Beverage Inventory	1 500	
1320	Beer, Wine and Liquor	2 500	
1340	Food Inventory	500	
1360	Gift Set Inventory	4 000	
1500	Cash Register and Computer	5 000	
1520	Cutlery and Dishes	5 000	
1540	Furniture and Fixtures	15 000	
1560	Equipment	25 000	
1580	Tea Room Premises	150 000	
2100	Bank Loan		$ 12 000
2200	Accounts Payable		2 945
2650	HST Charged on Sales		4 845
2670	HST Paid on Purchases	345	
2850	Mortgage Payable		120 000
3100	S. Quinte, Capital		80 210
		$220 000	$220 000

SUPPLIER INFORMATION

CHAI TEA ROOM

Supplier Name (Contact)	Address	Phone No. Fax No.	E-mail Web Site	Terms Tax ID
Atlantic Tea Company (Boise Chai)	20 Oceanview Dr. Halifax, NS B3K 2L2	Tel 1: (902) 777-2346 Tel 2: (888) 337-4599	bchai@atcc.com www.atcc.com	net 10 288 411 755
Bathurst Food Supplies (C. Ricotte)	56 Cheddar St. Oromocto, NB E2V 1M8	Tel: (506) 544-6292 Fax: (506) 544-5217	cricotte@bfoods.com www.bfoods.com	1/10, n/30 385 345 865
Fundy Gift House (Red Rose)	71 Ridge Way Hopewell Cape, NB E0A 1Y0	Tel: (506) 499-3481 Fax: (506) 499-3482	rrose@fundygifts.com www.fundygifts.com	net 30 124 653 779
Minto Beverages (Earl Gray)	910 Lemone Ave. Bathurst, NB E2A 4X3	Tel 1: (506) 622-3188 Tel 2: (800) 622-2881	eg@mintobev.com www.mintobev.com	net 30 901 200 862
Moncton Kitchenwares (Tiff Flaun)	4 Pottery Rd. Moncton, NB E1C 8J6	Tel: (506) 721-5121 Fax: (506) 721-5522	tflaun@monctonkitchens.com www.monctonkitchens.com	1/10, n/30 567 321 447
NB Gas (N. Bridge)	355 Pipeline Road Fredericton, NB E3A 5B1	Tel: (506) 454-8110	nbridge@naturalgas.com www.naturalgas.com	net 7
NB Hydro (N. Ergie)	83 Water Street Fredericton, NB E3B 2M6	Tel: (506) 455-5120	n.ergie@nbhydro.nb.ca www.nbhydro.nb.ca	net 7
NB Liquor Control Board (Darke Beere)	4 Spirits Rd. Fredericton, NB E3B 1C5	Tel: (506) 456-1182	dbeere@lcb.gov.nb.ca www.lcb.gov.nb.ca	net 1
NB Tel (Les Chatter)	2 Communicate Rd. Fredericton, NB E3A 2K4	Tel: (506) 456-2355	chatter@nbtel.ca www.nbtel.ca	net 7
Sunbury Cleaning Company (Dee Tergent)	49 Scrub St. Gagetown, NB E0G 1V0	Tel: (506) 454-6611 Fax: (506) 454-3216	dtergent@sunburyclean.com www.sunburyclean.com	1/30, n/60 481 532 556
Vermont Coffee Wholesalers (Java Jean)	60 Columbia Lane Saint John, NB E2M 6R9	Tel 1: (506) 366-1551 Tel 2: (877) 366-1500	java@vermontcoffee.com www.vermontcoffee.com	net 1 345 667 211

OUTSTANDING SUPPLIER INVOICES					
CHAI TEA ROOM					
Supplier Name	Terms	Date	Inv/Chq No.	Amount	Total
Bathurst Food Supplies	1/10, n/30	Jul. 26/12	BF-1044	$ 800	$ 800
Fundy Gift House	n/30	Jul. 6/12	FG-361	$ 920	$ 920
Moncton Kitchenwares	1/10 n/30	Jul. 25/12	MK-1341	$1 725	
		Jul. 25/12	Chq #167	500	
			Balance owing		$1 225
			Grand Total		$2 945

Accounting Procedures

The Harmonized Sales Tax (Provincial Sales Tax and Goods and Services Tax)

In New Brunswick, federal and provincial taxes are replaced by the Harmonized Sales Tax or HST, a single tax at the rate of 13 percent. The HST is applied to most goods and services. Like the GST, HST may be included in the price or added at the time of the sale. Chai Tea Room uses the regular method for calculating and remitting the HST. All items sold in the tea room have HST added to them. At the end of each quarter, the HST liability to the Receiver General is reduced by any HST paid to suppliers on purchases. Beverage and food supplies are zero rated for HST purposes. Chai's *HST Owing (Refund)* subgroup total account shows the amount of HST that is to be remitted to the Receiver General for Canada on the last day of each quarter. (For details please read Chapter 2 on the GST and HST.)

Open-Invoice Accounting for Payables

The open-invoice method of accounting for invoices allows a business to keep track of each individual invoice and partial payment made against the invoice. This is in contrast to methods that keep track only of the outstanding balance by combining all invoice balances owed to a supplier. Simply Accounting uses the open-invoice method. Fully paid invoices can be cleared (removed) periodically; outstanding invoices cannot be cleared.

Discounts

When discounts for early payment are offered by suppliers, Chai takes advantage of them by paying invoices before the discount period ends. When the payment terms are set up correctly for the supplier and invoice, and dates are entered correctly, discounts are calculated automatically by Simply Accounting and credited to *Purchase Discounts*, a contra-expense account that has a credit balance and reduces overall expenses.

Purchase of Inventory Items and Cost of Goods Sold

Inventory items purchased are recorded in the appropriate inventory or supplies asset account. Periodically, the food inventory on hand is counted to determine the value of items remaining and the cost price of inventory and food sold. The manager then issues a memo to reduce the inventory or supplies asset account and to charge the cost price to the corresponding expense account. For example, at the end of each month, the *Beverage Inventory* asset account (*1300*) is reduced (credited) and the *Cost of Goods Sold* expense account (*5080*) is increased (debited) by the cost price of the amount sold.

INSTRUCTIONS

1. **Enter** the **source documents for August** in Simply Accounting using the Chart of Accounts, Trial Balance, Supplier Information and Accounting Procedures for Chai Tea Room. The procedures for entering each new type of transaction for this application are outlined step by step in the Keystrokes section following the source documents. These transactions have a ✓ in the check box, and below the box is the page number where the related keystrokes begin.

2. **Print** the **reports and graphs** indicated on the printing form below after you have completed your entries. Instructions for reports begin on page 146.

REPORTS

Accounts
- [ ] Chart of Accounts
- [ ] Account List
- [ ] General Journal Entries

Financials
- [✓] Comparative Balance Sheet dates: Aug. 1 and Aug. 31 with difference in percentage
- [✓] Income Statement from Aug. 1 to Aug. 31
- [✓] Trial Balance date: Aug. 31
- [ ] All Journal Entries
- [✓] General Ledger accounts: 1340 4100 5080 from Aug. 1 to Aug. 31

Banking
- [ ] Cheque Log Report

Payables
- [ ] Supplier List
- [✓] Supplier Aged Detail for all suppliers Aug. 31
- [ ] Aged Overdue Payables
- [✓] Purchase Journal Entries: Aug. 1 to Aug. 31
- [✓] Payment Journal Entries: Aug. 1 to Aug. 31

Mailing Labels
- [ ] Labels

Management Reports
- [ ] Ledger

GRAPHS
- [ ] Payables by Aging Period
- [✓] Payables by Supplier
- [ ] Revenues by Account
- [ ] Expenses by Account
- [✓] Expenses and Net Profit as % of Revenue

SOURCE DOCUMENTS

SESSION DATE – AUGUST 7, 2012

- [✓] **Purchase Invoice #FG-642** _Purchase J_ _Pay Later_   **Dated Aug. 1/12**

  116   From Fundy Gift House, $800 plus $104 HST for eight tea service sets. Invoice total, $904. Terms: net 30.

- [✓] **Purchase Invoice #BF-1243** _Purchase J_ _Pay Later_   **Dated Aug. 1/12**

  121   From Bathurst Food Supplies, $800 for pastries, breads, condiments and other foods. There is no HST on food products. Terms: 1/10, n/30. Store as a weekly recurring entry.

- [✓] **Cheque Copy #171** _Payment J_ 958417 _Pay invoice by cheque_   **Dated Aug. 2/12**

  122   To Fundy Gift House, $700 in payment of account. Reference invoice #FG-361.

- [✓] **Cash Purchase Invoice #Fton-08** _Payment Journal → Make other Pmt → by cheque_   **Dated Aug. 2/12**

  125   From City Treasurer (use Quick Add for the new supplier), $250 for August licensing fees. Paid by cheque #172.

- [✓] **Cash Purchase Invoice #ACA-3492** _Purchase J_ _cheque_   **Dated Aug. 3/12**

  128   From All Campus Ads (add a complete record for the new supplier), $200 plus $26 HST for advertising brochures. Terms: cash on receipt. Invoice total $226 paid in full by cheque #173.

NOTES
All Campus Ads
- [✓] (contact Pierre Fullovit)
128   447 Slick St.
Fredericton, NB   E3B 8J5
Tel: (506) 564-8907
E-mail: pfullovit@acads.ca
Terms: net 1
Expense account: 5020
Tax code: H - HST @ 13%

☑ **Memo #13**   **Dated Aug. 4/12**

133   From Owner: Adjust invoice #FG-642. The order received from Fundy Gift House was for 10 tea service sets for $900 plus $117 HST. The corrected invoice total is $1 017.

Pay Invoice by cheque.

☑ **Cheque Copy #174**   **Dated Aug. 4/12**

135   To Bathurst Food Supplies, $792 in payment of account, including $8 discount for early payment. Reference invoice #BF-1044.

Invoice by cheque

☑ **Cash Purchase Invoice #BT-100**   **Dated Aug. 7/12**

137   From Bette Tomailik (choose Continue for the new supplier), $25 as compensation to cover cost of dry cleaning for wine spilled by waiter. Issue cheque #175. Charge to General Expense account. No tax is applied on this transaction.

☐ **Purchase Invoice #SC-701**   **Dated Aug. 7/12**

From Sunbury Cleaning Company, $250 plus $32.50 HST for weekly cleaning of store premises. Purchase invoice total $282.50. Terms: 1/30, n/60. Store as a weekly recurring transaction.

☑ **Cash Sales Receipt #34**   **Dated Aug. 7/12**

138   From tea room customers (tapes #5001–5380), $7 600 plus $988 HST for tea room sales and services. Total receipts $8 588 deposited in bank. Add a shortcut for the General Journal

SESSION DATE – AUGUST 14, 2012

☑ **Purchase Invoice #BF-2100**   **Dated Aug. 8/12**

140   From Bathurst Food Supplies, $800 (no HST) for pastries, breads, condiments and other foods. Terms: 1/10, n/30. Recall stored entry.

☑ **Memo #14**   **Dated Aug. 9/12**

142   From Owner: Edit the supplier record for NB Gas to include the default expense account. Create a new Group account 5110 Heating Expense.

P.J. Make other pmt by cheque

☐ **Cash Purchase Invoice #NBG-559932**   **Dated Aug. 9/12**

From NB Gas, $200 plus $26 HST for monthly supply of natural gas on equal billing method. Invoice total $226 paid in full by cheque #176. Because equal billing applies, store as a monthly recurring entry.

☑ **Memo #15**   **Dated Aug. 9/12**

143   From Owner: Adjust cheque #171 to Fundy Gift House. The cheque amount was $600 in partial payment of invoice #FG-361.

☐ **Cash Purchase Invoice #NBH-45321**   **Dated Aug. 9/12**

From NB Hydro, $120 plus $15.60 HST for one month of hydro service. Invoice total $135.60 paid in full by cheque #177.

☐ **Cheque Copy #178**   **Dated Aug. 10/12**

To Bathurst Food Supplies, $792 in payment of account, including $8 discount for early payment. Reference invoice #BF-1243.

☐ **Cash Purchase Invoice #SK-6110**   **Dated Aug. 12/12**

From Moncton Kitchenwares, $180 plus $23.40 HST for pots, pans and kitchen utensils. Invoice total $203.40 paid in full by cheque #179.

⚠ WARNING!
Remember to change the payment method for the Sunbury Cleaners invoice to Pay Later.

📄 NOTES
Use the General Journal for sales in this application.

⚠ WARNING!
Remember to delete the discount taken amount for the second invoice.

☑ **Memo #16**   **Dated Aug. 12/12**

144 Cash Purchase Invoice #SK-6110 was entered for an incorrect supplier. The purchase was from Sweeney's Kitchenwares, a new supplier. Reverse the original entry and then enter the correct purchase (use Full Add for the new supplier) for $180 plus $23.40 HST for pots, pans and kitchen utensils. Invoice total $203.40 paid in full by cheque #180.

NOTES

Sweeney's Kitchenwares
(contact Tracey Potts)
44 Panning Ave.
Grand Sault, NB E3Y 1E1
Tel: (800) 566-7521
Web: www.sweeneys.com
Terms: net 1
Expense account: 1560
Tax code: H - HST @ 13%

MINTO BEVERAGES
www.mintobev.com

910 Lemone Ave.
Bathurst, NB E2A 4X3
Phone: (506) 622-3188   Toll free: (800) 622-2881

Invoice:	MB-6111
Delivery Date:	Aug. 14, 2012
Sold to:	Chai Tea Room 125 King St. Fredericton, NB E3B 2P4 (506) 454-6111

Date	Description	Tax Code	Amount
Aug 14/12	Bottled spring water (20 cases)	1	200.00
Aug 14/12	Natural fruit beverages (10 cases)	1	400.00

Thank you.

Signature

Sarah Prentie

| Payment Terms:
Net 30 days | HST | 0.00 |
| Business No.: 901 200 862 | TOTAL | 600.00 |

Purchase Invoice #SC-1219   **Dated Aug. 14/12**

From Sunbury Cleaning Company, $250 plus $32.50 HST for weekly cleaning of store premises. Purchase invoice total $282.50. Terms: 1/30, n/60. Recall stored transaction.

Bank Debit Memo #AT-53186   **Dated Aug. 14/12**

From Atlantic Trust, withdrawals from bank account for bi-weekly payroll:

Wages, including payroll taxes	$3 200.00
Payroll services	40.00
HST Paid on Purchases (payroll services)	5.20

Cash Sales Receipt #35   **Dated Aug. 14/12**

From tea room customers (tapes #5381–5750), $7 400 plus $962 HST for tea room sales and services. Total receipts $8 362 deposited in bank.

SESSION DATE — AUGUST 21, 2012

Purchase Invoice #BF-2987   **Dated Aug. 15/12**

From Bathurst Food Supplies, $800 for pastries, breads, condiments and other foods. Terms: 1/10, n/30. Recall stored entry.

NOTES

Use the General Journal for the payroll transaction in this application.

Remember to enter the sales tax code for the purchase.

Cash Purchase Invoice

NBTel

2 Communicate Rd.
Fredericton, NB
E3A 2K4
www.nbtel.ca
chatter@nbtel.ca

Account Inquiries: (506) 456-2355

Account Number
506-454-6111

Account Address

Chai Tea Room
125 King St.
Fredericton, NB E3B 2P4

Billing Date: August 18, 2012

ACCOUNT SUMMARY

Current Charges	
Monthly Services (July 13—August 12)	60.00
Equipment Rentals	24.00
Chargeable Messages	16.00
HST (93436 8699)	13.00
Total Current Charges	113.00
Previous Charges	
Amount of last bill	93.00
Payment Received July 19 — thank you	93.00
Adjustments	0.00
Balance Forward	0.00

Paid in full by cheque #181
Sarah Prentis 08/18/12

Invoice: NBT 557121	PLEASE PAY THIS AMOUNT UPON RECEIPT ➡	$113.00

Cheque Copy #182 Dated Aug. 18/12

To Bathurst Food Supplies, $792 in payment of account, including $8 discount for early payment. Reference invoice #BF-2100.

Cash Purchase Invoice #VCW-345 Dated Aug. 19/12

From Vermont Coffee Wholesalers, $400 for specialty coffees. Invoice paid in full by cheque #183.

Cash Purchase Invoice #NBLCB-776 Dated Aug. 19/12

From NB Liquor Control Board, $1 600 including HST and other taxes for beer, wine and liquor. Terms: COD. Invoice paid in full by cheque #184.

☑ **Purchase Invoice #SC-1790** Dated Aug. 21/12

145 From Sunbury Cleaning Company, $300 plus $39 HST for weekly cleaning of store premises. Purchase invoice total $339. Terms: 1/30, n/60. Recall and edit the stored transaction. Store the changed entry.

Cash Sales Receipt #36 Dated Aug. 21/12

From tea room customers (tapes #5751–6149), $7 750 plus $1 007.50 HST for tea room sales and services. Total receipts $8 757.50 deposited in bank.

SESSION DATE — AUGUST 28, 2012

Purchase Invoice #BF-3778 Dated Aug. 22/12

From Bathurst Food Supplies, $800 for pastries, breads, condiments and other foods. Terms: 1/10, n/30. Recall the stored entry.

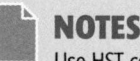

NOTES
Use HST code HI, taxes included, for purchases from the NB Liquor Control Board. This is the default tax code setting for this supplier.

```
 ┌───────────────────────────────────────────────────────────────────────────┐
 │  CHAI TEA          Chai Tea Room          Atlantic Trust                    │
 │  ROOM              123 King Street        55 Freedom Ave.     No: 185       │
 │                    Fredericton, NB E3B 2P4  Fredericton, NB E3C 6S0         │
 │                    (506) 454-1611                                           │
 │                                                                             │
 │                                        Date  2 0 1 2 0 8 2 4                │
 │                                              Y Y Y Y M M D D                │
 │                                                                             │
 │  Pay ──── Seven hundred ninety-two dollars ──── 00  $  792.00              │
 │                                                                             │
 │         ┌                              ┐                                    │
 │  TO THE   Bathurst Food Supplies                                           │
 │  ORDER    56 Cheddar St.                          Sarah Quinte             │
 │  OF       Oromocto, NB E2V 1M8          PER                                 │
 │         └                              ┘                                    │
 │                                                                             │
 │               ⑈──21292─⑈60385 185                                          │
 └───────────────────────────────────────────────────────────────────────────┘
```

Re: pay invoice #BF-2987 $792.00   No: 185
    Includes $8 discount   Aug 24, 2012

Purchase Invoice #ATC-3468   **Dated Aug. 27/12**

From Atlantic Tea Co., $500 for a variety of herbal, black and green teas as specified on order form. Terms: net 10 days.

Cash Purchase Invoice #Party   **Dated Aug. 28/12**

From The Little Party Shop (choose Continue), $30 plus $3.90 HST for party favours and decorations to decorate tea room for special event (General Expense). Invoice total $33.90 paid in full by cheque #186.

Purchase Invoice #SC-2987   **Dated Aug. 28/12**

From Sunbury Cleaning Company, $300 plus $39 HST for weekly cleaning of store premises. Purchase invoice total $339. Terms: 1/30, n/60. Recall stored transaction.

Bank Debit Memo #AT-99553   **Dated Aug. 28/12**

From Atlantic Trust, withdrawals from bank account for bi-weekly payroll:
    Wages, including payroll taxes $3 200.00
    Salaries   8 000.00
    Payroll services   70.00
    HST Paid on Purchases (payroll services)   9.10
Create new Group account 5250 Salaries.

Cash Sales Receipt #37   **Dated Aug. 28/12**

From tea room customers (#6150–6499), $7 250 plus $942.50 HST for tea room sales and services. Total receipts $8 192.50 deposited in bank.

SESSION DATE – AUGUST 31, 2012

Purchase Invoice #BF-4633   **Dated Aug. 29/12**

From Bathurst Food Supplies, $850 for pastries, breads, condiments and other foods. Terms: 1/10, n/30. Recall and edit the stored entry. Store changed entry.

Purchase Invoice #MK-8995   **Dated Aug. 31/12**

From Moncton Kitchenwares, $600 plus $78 HST for new gas burners for tea room kitchen. Invoice total $678. Terms: 1/10, n/30.

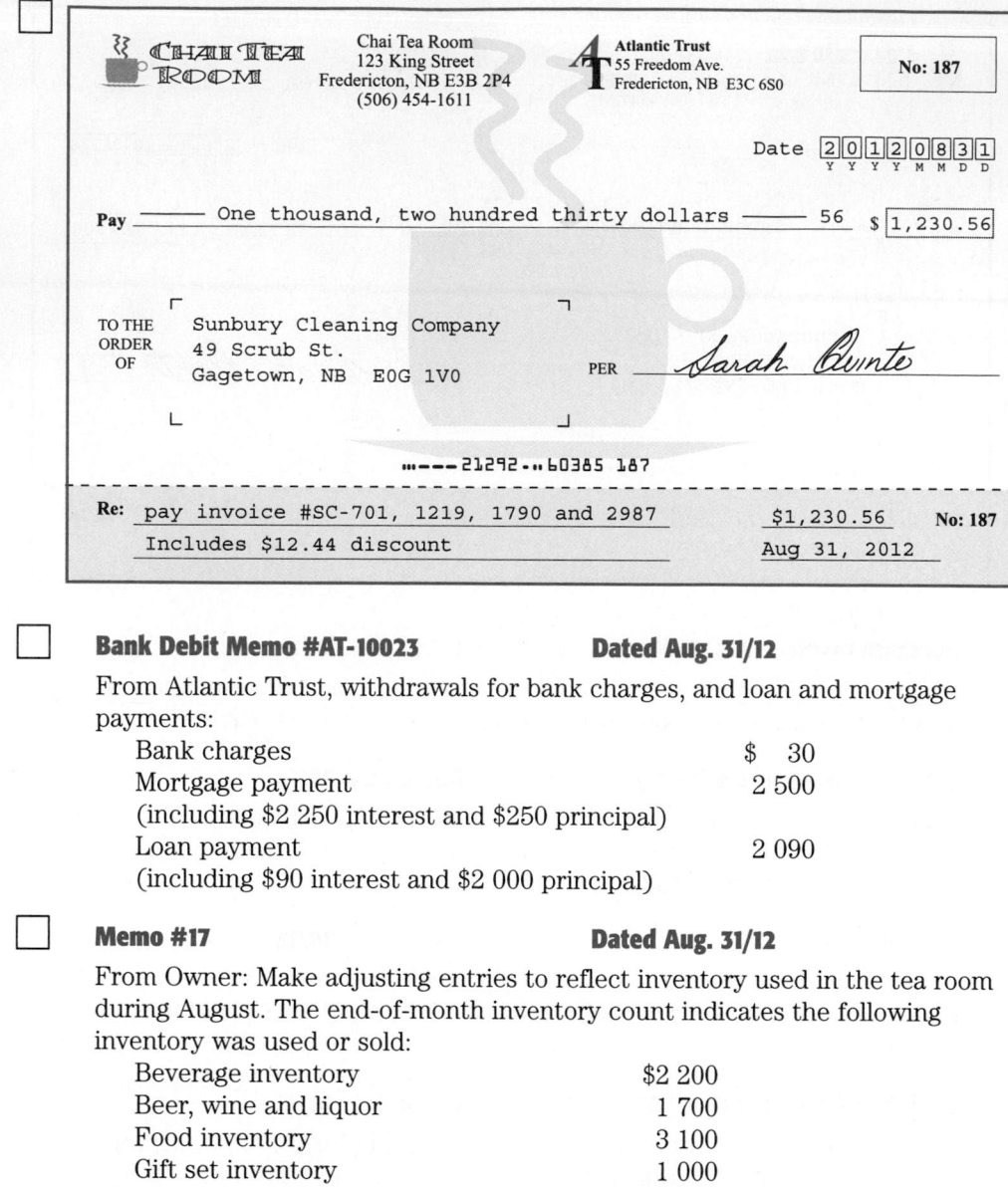

Chai Tea Room
123 King Street
Fredericton, NB E3B 2P4
(506) 454-1611

Atlantic Trust
55 Freedom Ave.
Fredericton, NB E3C 6S0

No: 187

Date 2 0 1 2 0 8 3 1
       Y Y Y Y M M D D

Pay ———— One thousand, two hundred thirty dollars ———— 56 $ 1,230.56

TO THE ORDER OF

Sunbury Cleaning Company
49 Scrub St.
Gagetown, NB   E0G 1V0

PER   *Sarah Quinte*

⑈———21292—⑈60385 187

Re: pay invoice #SC-701, 1219, 1790 and 2987 $1,230.56   No: 187
     Includes $12.44 discount   Aug 31, 2012

Bank Debit Memo #AT-10023   **Dated Aug. 31/12**

From Atlantic Trust, withdrawals for bank charges, and loan and mortgage payments:

Bank charges	$ 30
Mortgage payment	2 500
(including $2 250 interest and $250 principal)	
Loan payment	2 090
(including $90 interest and $2 000 principal)	

Memo #17   **Dated Aug. 31/12**

From Owner: Make adjusting entries to reflect inventory used in the tea room during August. The end-of-month inventory count indicates the following inventory was used or sold:

Beverage inventory	$2 200
Beer, wine and liquor	1 700
Food inventory	3 100
Gift set inventory	1 000

All used inventory is charged to Cost of Goods Sold.

KEYSTROKES

Opening Data Files

Open   SimData10\Chai\chai to access the data files for Chai Tea Room. Refer to page 7 if you need assistance with opening data files.

You are prompted to enter the session date, which is August 7, 2012, for the first group of transactions in this application.

Type   Aug 7 12

Click   OK to enter the first session date for this application.

The Payables module appears. This is the default page for Chai Tea Room.

NOTES

If you are working from backup files, restore SimData10\chai1.CAB to SimData10\Chai\chai. You should create the new folder. Refer to Chapter 1, page 20, if you need assistance with restoring files.

Accounting for Purchases

All supplier-related transactions can be entered from the Payables module window. Purchases from suppliers are entered in the Purchases Journal, accessed from the Invoices icon as shown here:

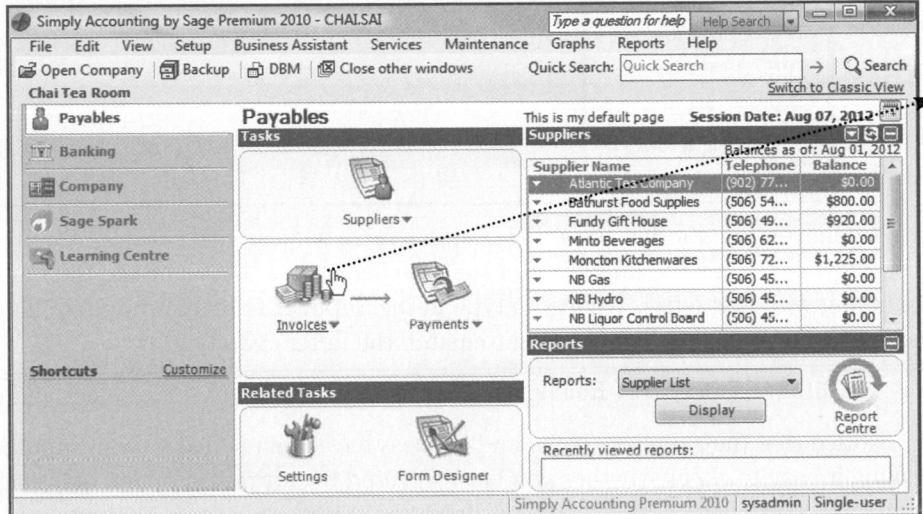

The first transaction is a normal purchase invoice.

Click   the **Invoices icon** to open the Purchases Journal input form:

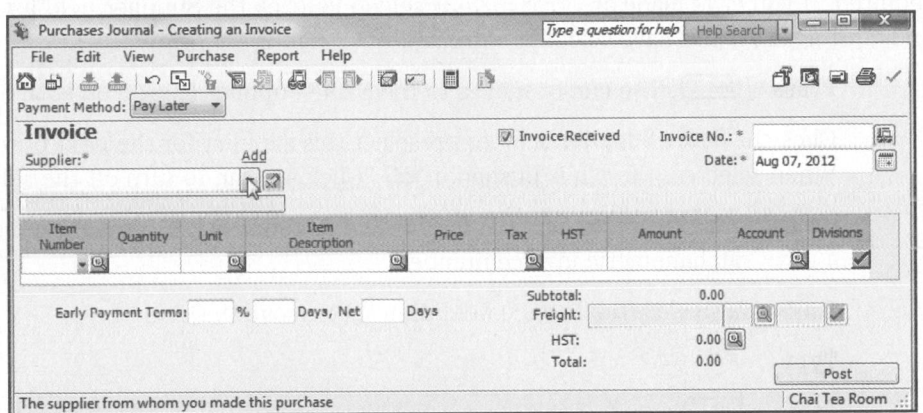

Move the mouse pointer across the various tool buttons and input fields and observe the status bar messages.

Creating An Invoice is indicated in the title bar and the option to Pay Later is correct because this is a credit purchase. Payment methods include cheque, cash and credit cards (when these are set up).

Most tool buttons should already be familiar. Notice that the Calculator button appears again in the tool bar. Several tool buttons have been added to the Purchases Journal window: Look Up An Invoice, Look Up Previous and Next Invoice, Track Shipments, Printer Settings, Print Preview, E-mail and Print. Each tool will be discussed when used. The column for projects is named Divisions for the food and beverage industry.

Click   the **Supplier** (or Vendor) **field list arrow**.

NOTES

Access to the Receivables, Payroll, Inventory and Division ledgers is hidden because these ledgers are not set up or ready to use.

PRO VERSION

pro The term Vendors will replace Suppliers for all icon labels and fields. Purchase Invoices is the label for the Purchases Journal icon.

Click the Purchase Invoices icon to open the journal.

CLASSIC VIEW

In the Classic view Home window, click the Purchases icon

to open the Purchases Journal. Invoice will be selected as the transaction type.

PRO VERSION

pro Projects replaces Divisions as the column heading .

The Refresh Lists tool applies to multi-user mode and does not appear in the Pro version.

NOTES

When the other features are not hidden, you will see a pull-down menu for Transaction types that includes quotes and purchase orders.

When payment is by cheque, a drop-down list of bank accounts is available. These topics are covered in later chapters.

The list of suppliers is expanded:

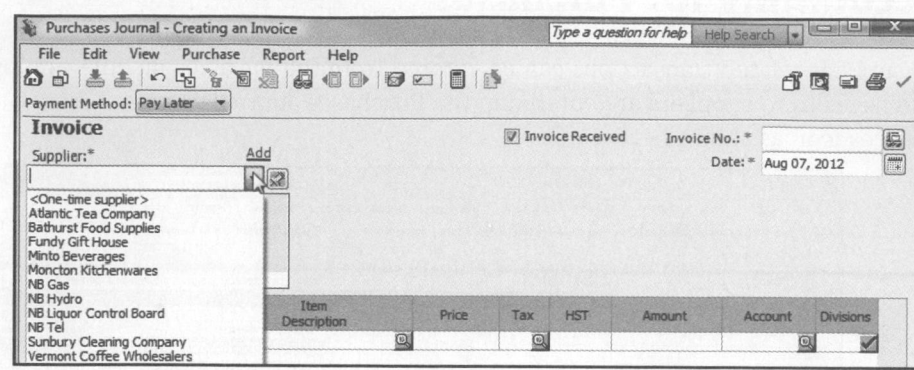

Whenever you see this arrow ▾ beside a field, you can make a selection from a drop-down list. Type the first letter of the supplier's name to advance to the names beginning with that letter. When you type in the Supplier field, the program fills in a name from the supplier list by trying to match the letters you type.

Click   **Fundy Gift House**, the supplier for this purchase, to select and enter it.

Notice that the supplier's name and address have been added to your input form, making it easy to check whether you have selected the correct supplier. Many other details have also been added by default from the supplier's record. The tax code and the account number usually stay the same for a supplier so they are set up as defaults. The payment terms for the supplier are also included. Any of these details can be edited if required. If you have made an error in your selection, click the Supplier field list arrow and start again. If you have selected correctly,

Press   ⬚tab⬚. The cursor moves to the Same Supplier (pin) icon 📌.

Click the **Same Supplier** icon to preselect this supplier for the next purchase. When selected, the pin is pushed in 📌. Click it again to turn off the selection.

Press   ⬚tab⬚ again to move to the Invoice field where you should type the alphanumeric invoice number.

You can also click the Invoice field directly to move the cursor.

Type   FG-642

Press   ⬚tab⬚ to select the Invoice Lookup icon.

Press   ⬚tab⬚ again to advance to the Date field.

Enter the date the transaction took place, August 1, 2012. The session date appears by default, in long (text) format according to the settings for the company file. It is highlighted, ready to be accepted or changed. You need to change the date.

Type   aug 1 12

Many of the invoice fields (Item Number, Quantity, Unit, Item Description and Price) pertain mainly to inventory items. Because we are not using the Inventory Ledger for this application, you can skip the inventory-related fields. Any information you type in these fields does not appear in the journal report.

You can click the Item Description field and type a description. Or add the quantity (8) in the Quantity field and the unit price in the Price field.

Click   the **Item Description field**.

Type   tea service sets

To select a different tax code, or to see the codes set up and available,

Click   the **Tax field List icon** 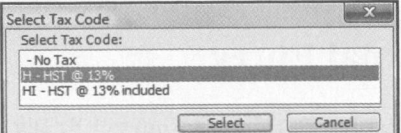 to see the tax codes for Chai Tea Room:

The selected tax code is H, that is, HST is charged on the purchase at 13 percent, and the tax is not included in the price. You can select a different code if needed, but in this case, the tax code is correct.

Click   **Cancel** so that the selection remains unchanged.

Click   the **first line of the Amount field**, where you will enter the total amount for this purchase.

Type   800

Press   ⌧tab .

The cursor moves to the Account field. The Account field for this purchase refers to the debit part of the journal entry, normally the acquisition of an asset or the incurring of an expense. It could also be used to decrease a liability or to decrease equity if the purchase were made for the owner's personal use. When you work in the subsidiary Payables journal, Simply Accounting will automatically credit your *Accounts Payable* control account in the General Ledger for the purchase. In fact, you cannot access *Accounts Payable* directly when the Payables Ledger is set up and linked.

In this example, the business has acquired an asset, and the correct account, *Gift Set Inventory,* is selected as the default for this supplier.

To select a different account, click the List icon for the Account field, double click the Account field or press ⌧enter to show the Select Account screen. You can also add a new account from the Select Account screen.

Press   ⌧tab to advance the cursor to the next invoice line. You can now enter additional purchases from this supplier if there are any.

Simply Accounting uses the tax code to calculate and enter the tax amount automatically in the HST field when you enter the amount for the purchase.

Your screen should now resemble the following:

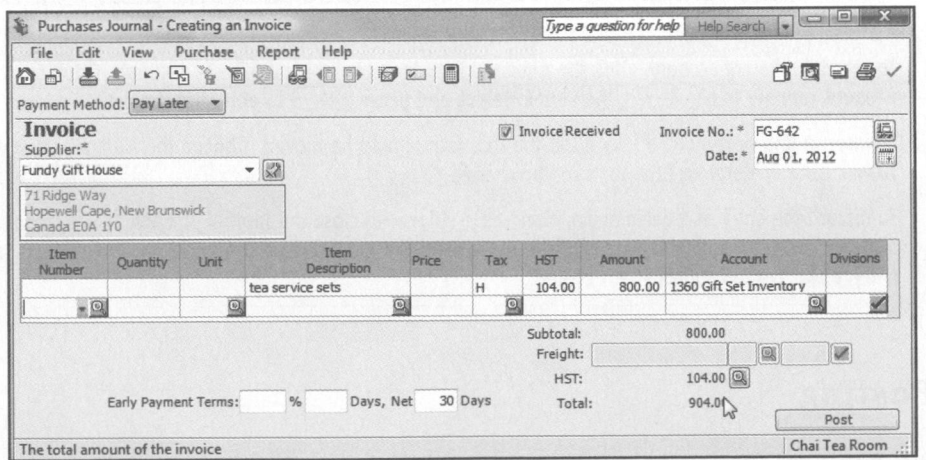

The payment terms have been set up as defaults for this supplier and are entered automatically. They can be edited if needed for specific purchases, but in this case they are correct. There is no discount and full payment is due in 30 days. The subtotal (amount owing before taxes) and the total amount are calculated and added automatically, so the entries for this transaction are complete and you are ready to review the transaction.

Reviewing the Purchases Journal Entry

NOTES
Pressing ⌃ctrl + J will also display the journal entry.

Choose the **Report menu** and **click Display Purchases Journal Entry**:

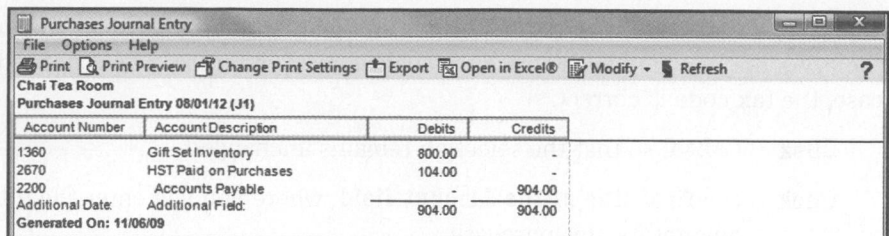

By reviewing the journal entry, you can check for mistakes. Note that the Simply Accounting program automatically updates the *Accounts Payable* control account because the Payables and General Ledgers are linked or fully integrated. Even though you did not enter account *2200*, Simply Accounting uses it because it is defined as the linked account to which all purchases should be credited. *HST Paid on Purchases*, the linked tax account, is also automatically updated. Using the Purchases Journal instead of the General Journal to enter purchases is faster because you need to enter only half the journal entry. The program provides a credit directly to the account of the selected supplier, and prevents you from choosing an incorrect payables account. The automatic selection of tax codes and accounts makes the transaction even simpler to enter.

NOTES
Other linked accounts for the Payables Ledger include a bank account, a freight expense account and a purchase discounts account. Each linked account will be explained when it is used in this workbook.

Close   the **display** to return to the Purchases Journal input screen.

CORRECTING THE PURCHASES JOURNAL ENTRY BEFORE POSTING

Move to the field that has the error. **Press** ⌐tab⌐ to move forward through the fields or **press** ⌐shift⌐ and ⌐tab⌐ together to move back to a previous field. This will highlight the field information so you can change it. **Type the correct information and press** ⌐tab⌐ to enter it.

You can also use the mouse to **point** to a field and **drag through the incorrect information** to highlight it. **Type the correct information and press** ⌐tab⌐ to enter it.

If the supplier is incorrect, reselect from the supplier list by **clicking the Supplier field list arrow**. **Click the name of the correct supplier.**

Click an incorrect amount to highlight it. Then **type the correct amount and press** ⌐tab⌐ to enter the change.

To select a different account, **click the Account List icon** to display the list of accounts. **Click the correct account number to highlight it**, then **click Select and press** ⌐tab⌐ to enter the change.

To insert a line or remove a line, **click the line** that should be moved. **Choose the Edit menu and click Insert Line or Remove Line** to make the change.

To discard the entry and begin again, **click** ☒ (Close) to close the Journal or **click** ↺ (Undo) on the tool bar to open a blank journal window. When Simply Accounting asks whether you want to discard the entry, **click Yes** to confirm your decision.

NOTES
To correct a Purchases Journal entry after posting, refer to page 133 and Appendix C.

Posting

When you are certain that you have entered all the information correctly, you must post the transaction to save it.

NOTES
You can press ⌐alt⌐ + P to post the journal entry.

Click   the **Post button** [Post] or **choose** the **Purchase menu** and **click Post** to save your transaction.

Click   **OK** to confirm successful posting.

A new blank Purchases Journal form appears on the screen.

Storing a Recurring Journal Entry

The second transaction is the recurring purchase of food inventory. Businesses often have transactions that are repeated regularly. For example, loan payments, bank charges and rent payments usually occur on the same day each month; supplies may be ordered daily or weekly; insurance payments may occur less frequently but nonetheless regularly. Chai Tea Room has food supplies delivered weekly. By storing an entry, and indicating the frequency, it can be recalled when it is needed without re-entering all the information.

The Purchases Journal should still be open with payment method and date correct from the previous entry.

Choose   **Bathurst Food Supplies** from the supplier list, or

Click   the **Supplier field** and **type**   B

Press   (tab) **twice** to move to the Invoice field.

Type   BF-1243

Enter   a **description** for the purchase.

The tax code is correct; no tax is charged on the purchase of food. The payment terms and account are also correct by default.

Click   the **Amount field**, **type** 800 and **press** (tab) to complete the transaction.

Choose   the **Report menu** and **click Display Purchases Journal Entry** to review the entry.

Close   the **display** and **make corrections** if necessary.

Click   the **Store tool** ⬇ on the tool bar (or **choose** the **Purchase menu** and **click Store**) to open the following Store Recurring Transaction screen:

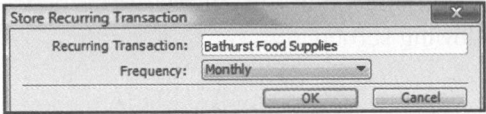

Simply Accounting enters the supplier and Monthly as the default name and frequency for the entry. The name is highlighted, so it can be changed by typing another descriptive name. Be sure to use one that you will recognize easily as belonging to this entry. The default frequency is incorrect since the food items are purchased weekly.

Click   **Monthly** to display the list of choices for the recurring frequency:

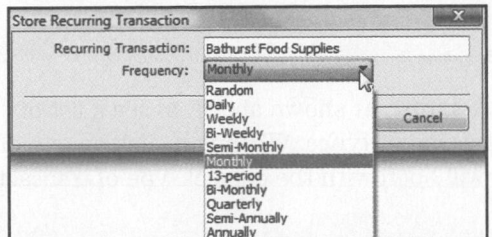

The frequency options are Random (for irregular purchases), Daily, Weekly, Bi-Weekly, Semi-Monthly, Monthly, 13-Period, Bi-Monthly, Quarterly, Semi-Annually and Annually.

NOTES
Typing the first letter of a supplier name in the Supplier field will add the first supplier name beginning with that letter. Since Bathurst Foods is the first supplier name starting with "B," it will be entered.

NOTES
The procedure for storing entries is the same for all journals when the option is available. Choose Store, assign a name to the entry, then choose a frequency and click OK to save it.

NOTES
The recurring frequency options are: Daily, Weekly (52 times per year), Bi-Weekly (26 times per year or every two weeks), Semi-Monthly (24 times per year), Monthly (12 times per year), 13-Period (13 times per year or every four weeks), Bi-Monthly (six times per year or every two months), Quarterly (four times per year or every three months), Semi-Annually (twice per year or every six months), Annually (once per year) and Random (irregular intervals using the session date when the entry is recalled).

Click   **Weekly**.

Simply Accounting will advance the default journal date when you recall the stored entry according to the frequency selected. The session date is entered if the Random frequency is chosen.

Click   **OK** to return to the Purchases Journal window.

Notice that 🔼 (the **Recall tool**) is now darkened and can be selected because you have stored a journal entry. The journal title bar label has also changed. It now shows Using Recurring Bathurst Food Supplies.

CORRECTING A STORED JOURNAL ENTRY

If you notice an error in the stored journal entry before posting, you must first **correct** the **journal entry** in the Purchases Journal window, then **click Store**. When asked to confirm that you want to overwrite or replace the previous version, **click Yes**.

If you edit the journal entry after storing it, Simply Accounting will warn you that the entry has changed. **Click Yes** to proceed.

Posting

When you are sure that you have entered all the information correctly, and you have stored the entry, you must post the transaction to save it.

Click   the **Post button** [Post] or **choose** the **Purchase menu** and **click Post** to save your transaction. **Click OK** to confirm successful posting.

A new blank Purchases Journal form appears on the screen. The Recall tool is now available so we can recall the purchase we stored. Our next transaction is a payment, however, not a purchase.

Close   the **Purchases Journal window** to return to the Payables window.

Accounting for Payments

Payments are made from the Payments Journal icon in the journals Tasks pane indicated by the hand pointer in the following screen:

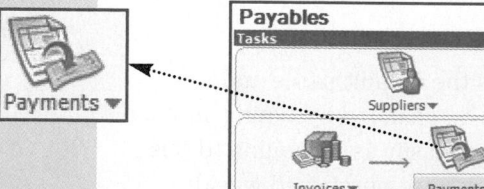

CLASSIC VIEW
From the Classic view Home window, click the Payments icon to open the Payments Journal. Pay Invoices will be selected as the default type of transaction.

PRO VERSION
Choose Pay Purchase Invoices from the shortcuts list to open the Payments Journal.

Click   the **Payments icon list arrow**, as shown above, to see a list of shortcuts for different payment types. When you click on one of these shortcuts, the journal will open with the correct type of transaction preselected.

Click   **Pay Invoices** to open the Payments Journal:

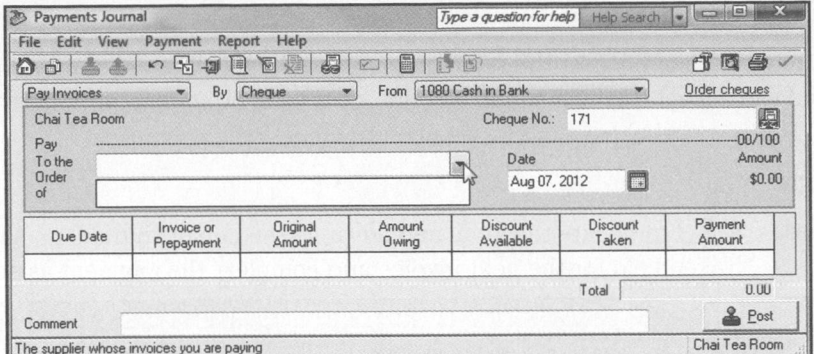

Pay Invoices is selected as the type of payment in the Pay field because we made this selection in the Home window. Pay Invoices is also the default transaction type when you click the Payments icon. Cheque appears as the method of payment in the By field and *1080 Cash in Bank* is the account the payment is made from. These defaults are correct.

Click   the **To The Order Of** (Supplier) **field list arrow** to see the familiar list of suppliers displayed in alphabetical order.

Click   **Fundy Gift House** (or **type** F) to choose and enter the supplier to whom the payment is made.

The journal input form is updated with the supplier's name, address and outstanding invoice(s), making it easy to see whether you have selected correctly. The updated journal is shown here:

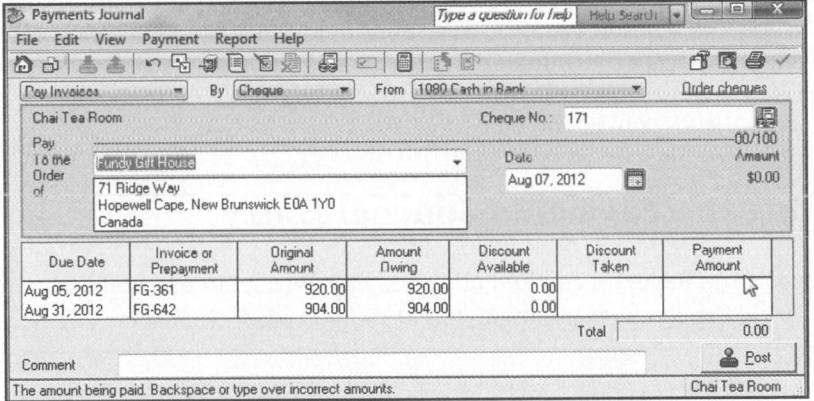

If you need to change the supplier, click the Supplier field list arrow again to select from the supplier list. The cheque number is entered in the Number field. The next cheque number appears according to the settings for the company. It is correct, so you can accept it. Normally the cheque number should be correct. It can be edited, if necessary, for reversing or correcting entries. When you have selected the correct supplier,

Click   the **Calendar icon** 📅 for the Date field.

Click   **2** in the August section. **Press** ⌨tab .

The year will also be added correctly when you type the month and day in the Payments Journal Date field.

The cursor moves to the Due Date field. All outstanding invoices, including both the amount of the original invoice and the balance owing for the selected supplier, are listed on the screen.

Press   ⌨tab to advance to the Discount Taken field. Since there is no discount, the field is blank and you can skip it.

PRO VERSION

pro The Refresh tools do not appear in the Pro version. Pay Purchase Invoices appears as the transaction type.

NOTES

When more than one bank account is set up, you can select the bank from the drop-down list beside From. In Chapter 11, you will use these upper fields to work with multiple bank accounts.

NOTES

You can type F in the Supplier field to enter Fundy Gift House because this is the only supplier beginning with "F."

NOTES

From the Pay drop-down list, you can select the other kinds of transactions for this journal, or you can choose the transaction type from the Payments icon shortcuts list in the Payables module window.

NOTES

Click 📄 (the Include Fully Paid Invoices tool) to display all paid and unpaid invoices for the selected supplier.

NOTES

The Lookup icon 🔍 appears beside the cheque number so you can look up previous payments.

Press (tab) .

The amount outstanding for the selected invoice is highlighted as the payment amount. You can accept the highlighted amount, or type another amount for partial payments. This is a partial payment so we need to change the amount.

Type 700

Press (tab) to update the Total and advance the cursor to the Discount Taken field for the next invoice and complete the payment as shown:

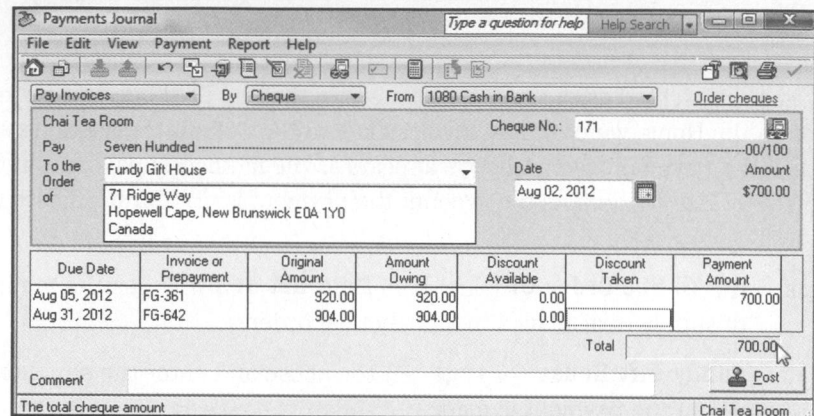

Notice that the upper cheque portion of the form is also complete. Notice too that there is no field for account numbers in the Payments Journal. You need to enter only the amount of the payment on the appropriate invoice line.

As you pay invoices in the subsidiary Payments Journal, you do not enter any accounts. Simply Accounting chooses the default linked accounts defined for the Payables Ledger to create the journal entry.

The entries for this transaction are complete, so you are ready to review and post your transaction.

Reviewing the Payments Journal Entry

Choose the **Report menu** and **click Display Payments Journal Entry** to display the transaction you have entered:

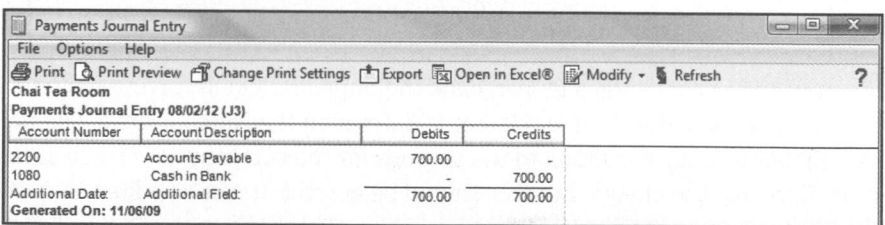

You can see that the Simply Accounting program automatically creates a related journal entry when you complete a Payments Journal entry. The program updates *Accounts Payable* and *Cash in Bank* because the Payables and General Ledgers are fully linked. *Cash in Bank* has been defined as the default Payables linked account to which payments are credited. The payment is also recorded to the supplier's account to reduce the balance owing.

Close the **display** to return to the Payments Journal input screen.

You can also print the cheque but you should make corrections first, if necessary.

CORRECTING THE PAYMENTS JOURNAL ENTRY BEFORE POSTING

Move to the field that has the error. Press (tab) to move forward through the fields or press (shift) and (tab) together to move back to a previous field. This will highlight the field information so you can change it. Type the **correct information** and press (tab) to enter it.

You can also use the mouse to **point** to a field and **drag through** the **incorrect information** to highlight it. **Type** the **correct information** and **press** (tab) to enter it.

If the supplier is incorrect, **click** to undo the entry or **reselect** from the **Supplier** list by **clicking** the **Supplier list arrow**. Click the name of the **correct supplier**. You will be asked to confirm that you want to discard the current transaction. **Click Yes** to discard the incorrect supplier entry and display the outstanding invoices for the correct supplier. **Re-enter** the **payment** information for this supplier.

If you print cheques, you should do so before posting the Payment. Be sure that the information is correct and that you have selected the correct printer and forms for printing cheques (see Chapter 4, page 85). You can check the printer settings by clicking the Change The Default Printer Settings tool in the journal. Turn on the printer and click the Print tool.

Posting

When you are certain that you have entered all the information correctly, you must post the transaction to save it.

> **Click** the **Post button** (or **choose** the **Payment menu** and **click Post**) to save your transaction and then **click OK** to confirm.

Entering Cash Purchases

The licence fees statement on August 2 is to be paid immediately on receipt of the invoice. Instead of recording the purchase and payment separately, you can record the payment with the purchase in the Payments Journal. This transaction also involves a company that is not listed as a supplier, so you must add the City Treasurer to the supplier list in order to record the transaction.

Suppliers can be added directly from the Payables Ledger or from the supplier field in the Purchases Journal or the Payments Journal. We will add the new supplier from the Payments Journal. The Payments Journal should still be open.

The date and the cheque number are correct. The date is unchanged from the previous Payments Journal transaction. The next available cheque number is entered by default, and the bank account is selected for the payment. Cheque numbers are updated in sequence for both payment journal entries and cash purchases.

> **Click** Pay Invoices to see the options for payment transactions:

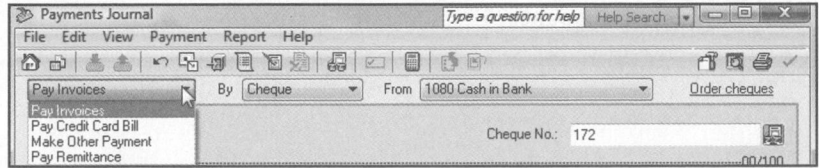

> **Click** Make Other Payment from the drop-down list.

If you have closed the Payments Journal, you can open the form for cash purchases from the Home window. Click the Payments icon list arrow and click **Pay Expenses** (see page 122). In this case, you must enter August 2 as the date.

NOTES
You can correct payment amounts after posting by clicking the Adjust Payment tool. Select the payment to adjust, just as you select a purchase invoice or General Journal entry for editing. Make the correction and post the revised payment.
To correct a payment after posting, refer to page 143 and to the section on NSF cheques on page 184.

NOTES
When the batch printing option is selected in the settings for Forms, you can print cheques in batches after posting them. The Print Batches tool will be added to the tool bar. Batch printing is covered in Chapter 14.

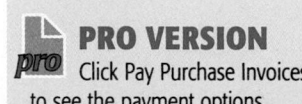
PRO VERSION
Click Pay Purchase Invoices to see the payment options.

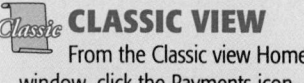
CLASSIC VIEW
From the Classic view Home window, click the Payments icon

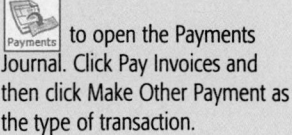
to open the Payments Journal. Click Pay Invoices and then click Make Other Payment as the type of transaction.

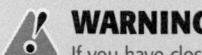
Journal input fields are added to the payment form:

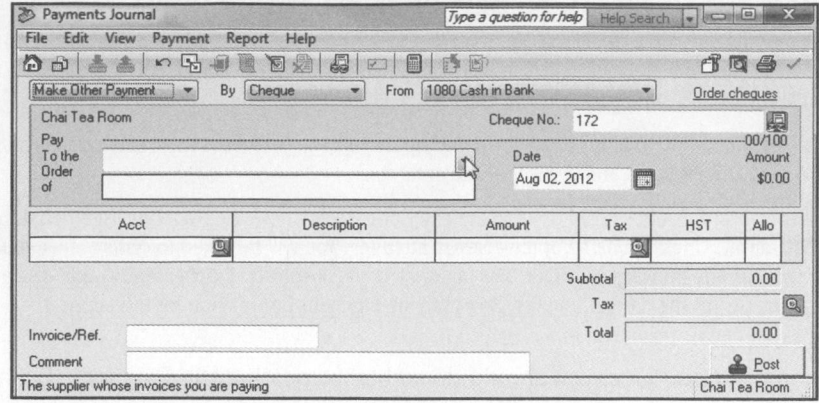

Click   the **To The Order Of (Supplier) field** to move the cursor.

Type   City Treasurer   and then **press** ⌨tab to display the message:

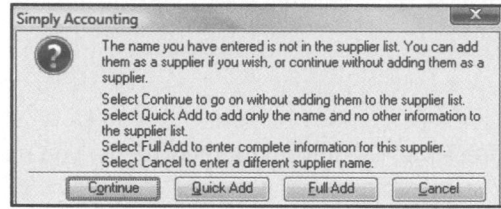

The program recognizes that the name is new and gives you four options. **Continue** will add the name to the journal and the journal report and apply the default settings for the ledger. This option will not create a supplier record or include the name in the supplier list. **Quick Add** will create a partial record with only the supplier's name and will apply the default settings for the ledger. **Full Add** will open a new ledger record for the supplier and you can add complete details. **Cancel** will return you to the journal. You can then type or choose another name if the one you typed was incorrect.

If you are making a cash purchase and you will not be making additional purchases from this supplier, you can choose **One-time Supplier** from the Supplier list. Type the supplier's name and address in the text box area below the To The Order Of field. The default settings for the ledger will apply to the invoice, but you can change them if needed. The transaction will be included in the GST/HST report but the supplier's name will not appear in supplier lists or in the journal reports.

We want to add a partial record for the new supplier.

Click   **Quick Add** to return to the Payments Journal.

The supplier's name is added to the journal. Because an account is not set up for the supplier, you must enter the asset or expense account that is debited for the transaction.

Click   the **Account field List icon** 🔍 to see the Select Account list.

Click   **Suggested Accounts** to modify the list as shown:

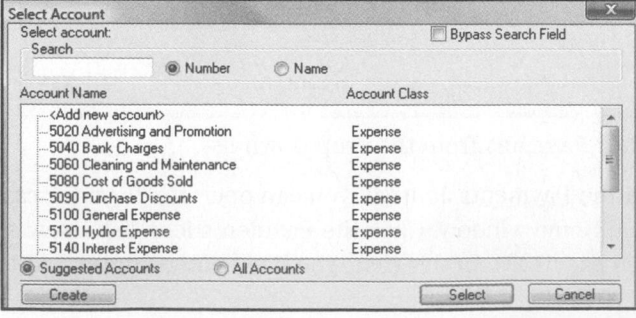

The list now shows only the expense accounts, the ones used most often for purchases. This list is easier to work with because it is shorter. When you enter sales in the Sales Journal, the suggested accounts will list only revenue accounts.

Scroll down   and **click 5160 Licences and Permits**.

Click   **Select** to add the account and advance to the Description field.

Type   August licensing fees

Press   (tab) to advance to the Amount field.

Type   250 **Press** (tab).

Since no tax is charged on the fees, the default entry of No Tax is correct.

Click   the **Invoice/Ref. field**.

Type   Fton-08 **Press** (tab) to advance to the Comment field.

The comment will become part of the journal record so you should include it.

Type   Fton-08, August licensing fees

The subtotal and total amounts are entered automatically. Your completed payment form should now look like the one shown here, and you are ready to review it:

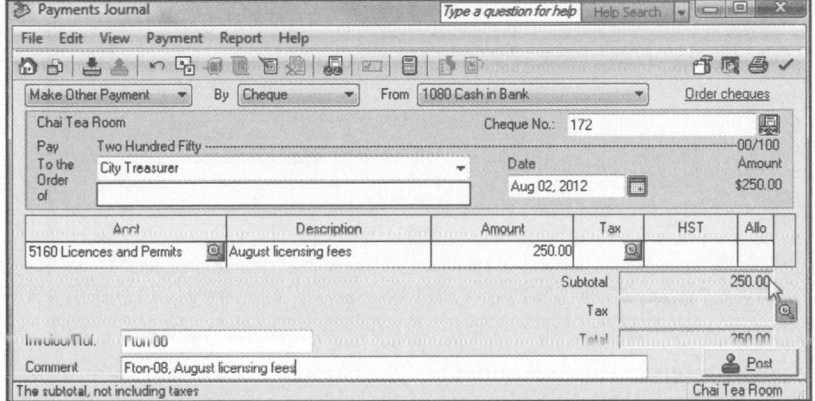

Choose the **Report menu** and **click Display Payments Journal Entry**. Your display should look like the following:

Account Number	Account Description	Debits	Credits
5160	Licences and Permits	250.00	-
1080	Cash in Bank	-	250.00
Additional Date:	Additional Field:	250.00	250.00

Payments Journal Entry — Chai Tea Room — Payments Journal Entry 08/02/12 (J4) — Generated On: 11/06/09

Notice that the program has automatically credited *Cash in Bank*, the Payables linked bank account, for the cash purchase instead of *Accounts Payable*.

Close   the **display** when you have finished.

Make   any **corrections** necessary. Double click an incorrect entry and type the correct details.

Click   the **Post button** [Post] to save the **entry** when you are certain that it is correct. **Click OK**.

Close   the **Payments Journal**.

NOTES
You can use keyboard shortcuts to copy text. Click the text you want to copy, press (ctrl) + C. Then click the field you want the text copied to and press (ctrl) + V.

NOTES
When we tested the keystrokes, the Invoice/Ref. field contents were not included in journal reports and the Comment was included. Therefore, we repeat the invoice number in the Comment field to be sure that it will be included in the journal reports.

Adding a New Supplier Record

Cash purchases and new suppliers may be recorded in the Payments Journal or the Purchases Journal. We will record the next cash purchase in the Purchases Journal after we add a full record for the supplier. You can create a new supplier record on the fly, as in the previous transaction, by choosing Full Add, or you can open the Payables Ledger for a new supplier record from the Add Supplier option in the Suppliers shortcuts list. For this transaction, we will use the ledger option.

Click the **Suppliers icon shortcuts list arrow** as shown:

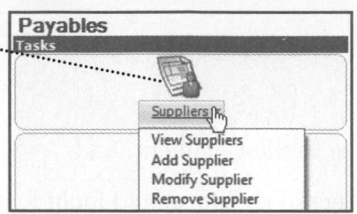

Click **Add Supplier** to open the Payables Ledger input form:

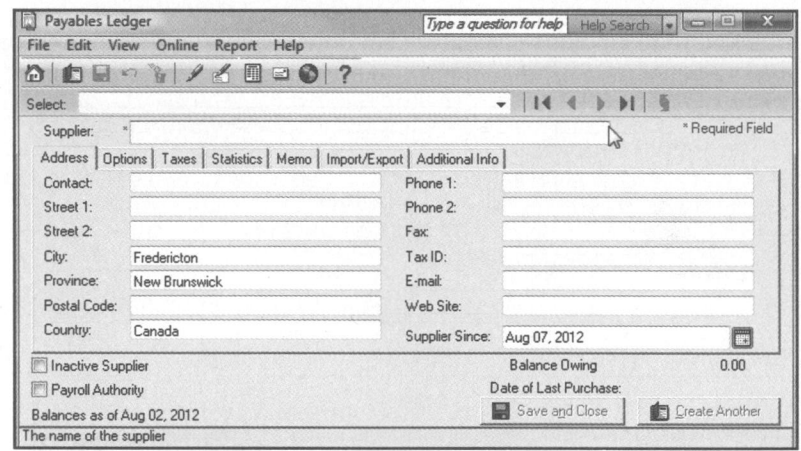

**PRO VERSION**
Click Add Vendor in the Vendors shortcuts list.

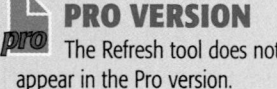**CLASSIC VIEW**
From the Classic view Home window, click the Suppliers icon to open the Suppliers window. Then click the Create tool, or choose the File menu and click Create, or press ctrl + N. Close the Suppliers window after saving the new record.

PRO VERSION
The Refresh tool does not appear in the Pro version.

NOTES
If you are missing any information for a supplier, you can leave the field blank and enter the details later by editing the record. See page 142.
Although the extra fields are not required, entering the details in the ledger record will speed up journal entry when you choose the supplier.

You are ready to enter the new supplier. The Supplier Address tab information screen appears first. Note that required fields have an * beside them as they do in the General Ledger. The supplier name is the only required field. As soon as you begin to type in the field, the * is removed.

Type All Campus Ads **Press** tab .

The cursor advances to the Contact field, where you enter the name of Chai Tea Room's contact person at All Campus Ads. This field can also be used to enter a third address line if two street lines are insufficient. This field or any other may be left blank by pressing tab .

Type Pierre Fullovit

Press tab . The cursor moves to the Street 1 field.

Type 447 Slick St.

The Street 2 field can be used for a second address line, if there is one. By default, the program has entered the name of the city, province and country from the Payables Ledger Address settings. You can accept the defaults because they are correct.

If the supplier is in a different city, province or country, type the correct information before continuing. Press tab to advance to a field and highlight the contents to prepare it for editing.

Click the **Postal Code field** to move the cursor.

When you enter a Canadian postal code, you do not need to use capital letters or to leave a space within the postal code. The program makes these adjustments for you.

Type   e3b8j5

Press   (tab).

Notice that the format of the postal code has been corrected automatically. The cursor moves to the Country field and the entry is correct.

Press   (tab). The cursor moves to the Phone 1 field.

You do not need to insert a dash, space or bracket when you enter a telephone number. Telephone and fax numbers may be entered with or without the area code.

Type   5065648907

Press   (tab).

The format for the telephone number has been corrected automatically. The cursor advances to the Phone 2 field for the supplier's second phone number. We do not have additional phone or fax numbers at this time. They can be added later when they are obtained. The Tax ID number refers to the business federal tax or GST registration number. Adding e-mail and Web site information allows you to send purchase orders by e-mail and connect to the supplier's Web site directly from Simply Accounting. Type e-mail and Web addresses just as you enter them in your Internet program.

Click   the **E-mail field**.

Type   pfullovit@acads.ca

The date in the Supplier Since field is the session date or the date of the earliest transaction you enter for this supplier in Simply Accounting. You can enter a different date if this is appropriate. The Date Of Last Purchase is added automatically by the program, based on the transactions you enter for the supplier.

Press   (tab) **twice** to advance to the Supplier Since date field.

Type   Aug 3

The last two options concern the supplier's status. You can make a supplier inactive and remove the name from the selection lists and reports. Suppliers that you will not use again can be made inactive.

You can also designate the supplier as a Payroll Authority so that the supplier can be selected for payroll remittances.

Click   the **Options tab** to open the next supplier information screen:

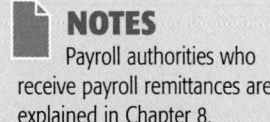

NOTES
Payroll authorities who receive payroll remittances are explained in Chapter 8.

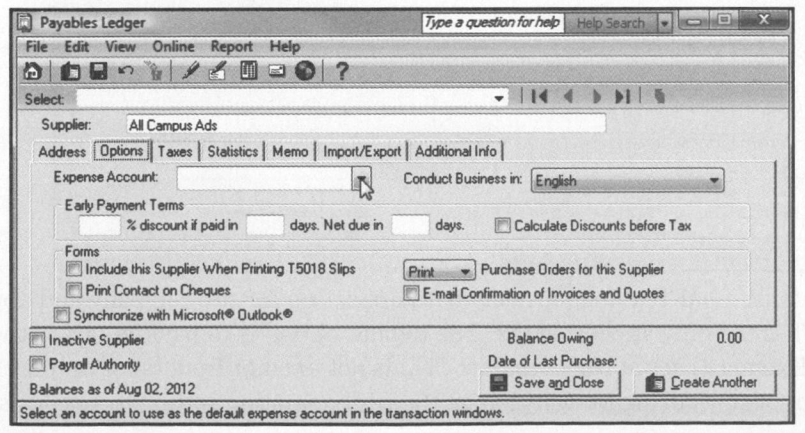

NOTES

Any account can be used as the default expense account, including capital accounts. This allows you to set up the owner as a supplier and link the transactions to the Drawings account.

NOTES

If you need to create a new account for this supplier, type the new account number in the Expense Account field and press `tab`. Click Add to confirm that you want to create the account. The Add An Account wizard will open.

NOTES

Typing 0 (zero) in the Net Days field will leave the payment terms fields on the invoice blank. Therefore, we enter net 1 (one) when payment is due immediately.

PRO VERSION

pro The option to Synchronize With Microsoft Outlook is not available in the Pro version.

WARNING!

The tax exempt option Yes should be selected only if all purchases from the supplier are tax exempt because this setting prevents taxes from being calculated on any purchases from the supplier.

The Options screen has several important fields. In the first part of the Options screen, you can choose the default account and preferred language (English or French) for the supplier. Forms you send to that supplier will be in the selected language, although your own screens will not change. You can also enter a default account for the supplier. Although the field is named Expense Account — usually an expense or asset account is the default — you may select any postable account. If you usually buy the same kinds of goods from a supplier, entering a default account saves time and prevents errors when completing journal entries. All Campus Ads provides promotional materials.

Click the **Expense Account list arrow** to see the accounts available.

Scroll down and **click 5020 Advertising and Promotion**.

In the Early Payment Terms section of the ledger, you can enter the discount for early settlement of accounts and the term for full payment. Discounts may be calculated on the amount before taxes or on the full invoice (after-tax) amount. Three fields are used to enter the discount. The first shows the discount rate as a percentage and the second holds the number of days over which the discount remains valid. In the final field, enter the number of days in which net payment is due. According to the source document, immediate payment is expected.

Click the **Net Due In ___ Days field** (Early Payment Terms section).

Type 1

The next fields appear as check boxes. There are no discounts from this supplier. Leave the check box for Calculate Discounts Before Tax blank.

Include This Supplier When Printing T5018 Slips applies to amounts paid to subcontractors for construction services and does not apply to Chai Tea Room. Selecting Print Contact On Cheques will add the name of the contact person to the cheque written to the supplier. If the Contact field contains address information, check this box; otherwise, leave it unchecked.

The next option allows you to choose Print or E-mail Purchase Orders For This Supplier as the default setting, but you can change the selection for individual purchase orders if necessary. If you choose to e-mail the orders, you should check the E-mail Confirmation Of Purchase Invoices And Quotes option by clicking it.

If you want to synchronize lists in Simply Accounting with Microsoft Outlook, click the Synchronize With Microsoft Outlook check box.

The next input screen defines the tax options for this supplier.

Click the **Taxes tab** to open the screen:

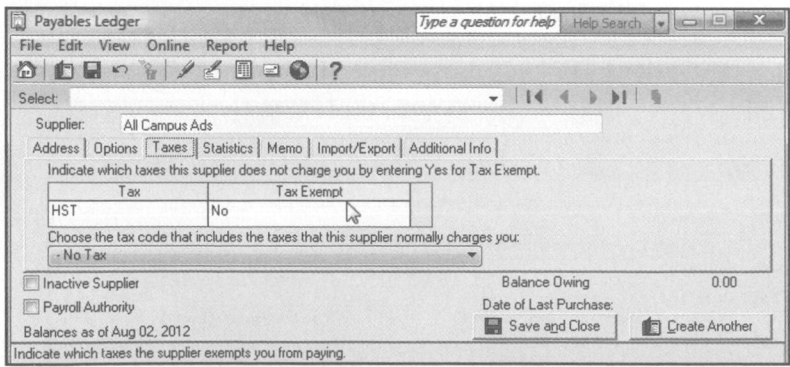

All the taxes Chai Tea Room usually pays are set up for the company and appear on the list. HST is the only applicable tax. The default option is to pay the tax — the option under Tax Exempt is set at No — that is, Chai is not exempt from taxes on purchases from this supplier. Clicking No will change the tax exemption setting to Yes. This change would be appropriate for suppliers, such as the Receiver General, that do not supply goods or services. Refer to Chapter 2 for further information about taxes and discounts.

To enter a default tax code for purchases from the supplier, we can choose a code from the drop-down list in the next field. The default setting, No Tax, is incorrect.

> **Click**   **No Tax** to see the codes available:

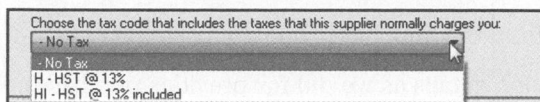

Three codes are defined for Chai Tea Room: **No Tax** for suppliers, such as Bathurst Foods, who do not charge any tax; **H** for suppliers of normal taxable goods or services when HST is not included in the price; and **HI** for suppliers of taxable goods such as gasoline or liquor when the tax is included in the purchase price.

All Campus Ads charges HST but does not include it in the price.

> **Click**   **H - HST @ 13%**.

The remaining input screens are not needed; they will be introduced in a later application. The **Statistics** tab screen stores cumulative historical purchases and payments, the **Memo** tab screen allows you to add messages to the Daily Business Manager and the **Import/Export** tab allows you to specify corresponding inventory item codes for your business and your suppliers. The **Additional Info** tab screen has other supplier information fields that can be customized for the company.

Check your work carefully before saving the information because the options you select will affect the invoices directly.

CORRECTING A NEW SUPPLIER ACCOUNT

Move to the field that has the error by **pressing** `tab` to move forward through the fields or **pressing** `shift` and `tab` together to move back to a previous field. **Type** the **correct information.**

You can also highlight the incorrect information by dragging the cursor through it. You can now type the correct information.

After a field has been corrected, **press** `tab` to enter the correction.

To open a different tab screen, **click** the **tab** you want.

When you are certain that all the information is correct,

> **Click**   **Save And Close**  to save the supplier information and return to the Home window.

Entering Vendor Records from the Purchases Journal

Click the Invoices icon to open the journal and click the Suppliers field.

Type the new supplier's name in the Supplier field. Click the Add link (just above the Supplier field) to open a ledger record at the Address tab screen.

Or press `tab` after typing the name. The program recognizes the name as new:

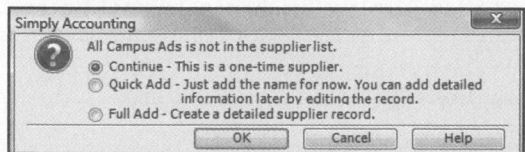

Click Full Add to open a Payables Ledger record at the Address tab screen.

The new supplier name will be entered as you typed it in the Supplier field. Enter all the details for the supplier as described above.

NOTES
When the tax exempt settings are No, you can change the tax codes in the journals and the tax calculations will be correct. If the tax exempt settings are Yes, you can change the codes but no taxes will be calculated.

NOTES
The Daily Business Manager is covered in Chapter 11 and the Import/Export options are explained in Appendix J on the Student DVD.

PRO VERSION
pro Click the Purchase Invoices icon.

CLASSIC VIEW
From the Classic view Home window, click the Purchases icon to open the Purchases Journal.

NOTES
If you click Add before typing the name, add the name when the ledger record opens.

Click the Save And Close button to return to the invoice. The supplier's address, tax code and expense account will be added to the invoice form.

Entering Cash Purchases in the Purchases Journal

Open   the **Purchases Journal**.

Choose **All Campus Ads** from the Supplier drop-down list. **Press** (tab).

We can now enter the transaction details as we did for previous purchases. We need to change the payment method because this is a cash purchase.

Click   **Pay Later** in the Paid By field to see the payment options:

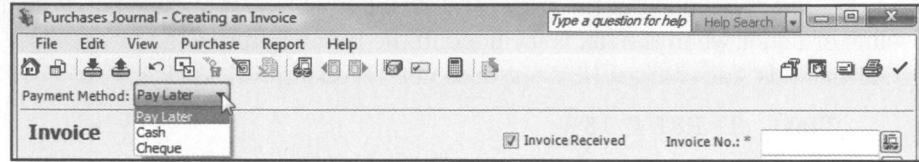

The payment options are the same as those in the Payments Journal for Other Payments, with the addition of Pay Later.

Click   **Cheque**.

A cheque number field is added to the invoice with the next cheque number in the upper right-hand corner of the journal. The cheque number is updated automatically. The account number and payment terms are added from the supplier record information we entered. You need to add the invoice number, transaction date and amount.

Click   the **Invoice field** and **type** ACA-3492

Click   the **Calendar icon** and **choose** August 3.

Click   the **Amount field**.

Type   200 **Press** (tab). You can add a description to complete the invoice:

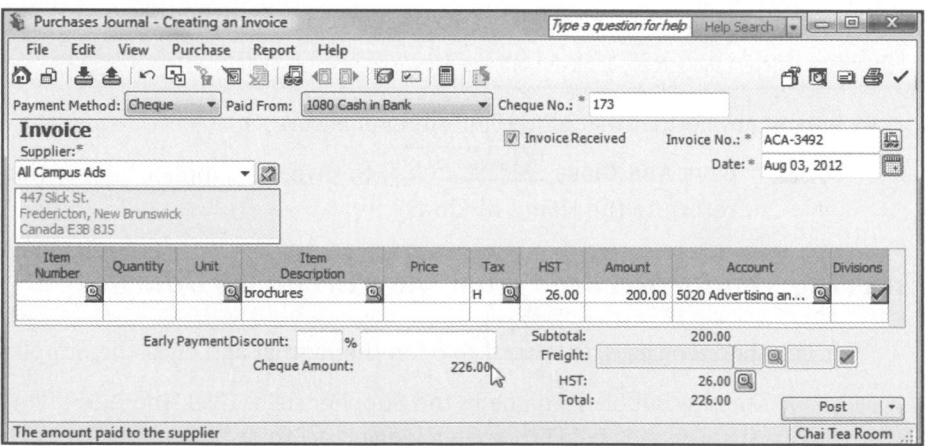

You should review the journal entry before posting it.

Choose the **Report menu** and **click** **Display Purchases Journal Entry**:

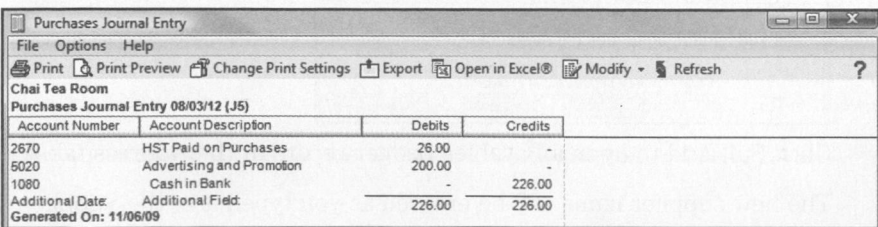

This journal entry is the same as the one from the Payments Journal when we chose Make Other Payment. *Cash in Bank* is credited instead of *Accounts Payable*. The supplier record is updated for the transaction by including both an invoice and a payment for the same date.

Close   the **display**.

Check   the **invoice** for errors and **make corrections** just as you would for regular purchases. When the information is correct,

Click   **Post** ⬚ Post ⬚ to save the transaction. **Click OK**.

Adjusting a Posted Invoice

In the same way that you can correct or adjust a previously posted entry in the General Journal, you can edit a Purchases Journal invoice after posting. Simply Accounting will create the necessary reversing entry when you post the revised invoice.

The Purchases Journal should still be open.

Click   the **Adjust Invoice tool** ⬚ or **choose** the **Purchase menu** and **click Adjust Invoice** to open the Search Purchase Invoices screen:

<table>
<tr><td>NOTES</td></tr>
</table>

You can also press ⬚ctrl⬚ + A to open the Adjust An Invoice window from any journal. See Appendix B for a list of keyboard shortcuts.

<table>
<tr><td>NOTES</td></tr>
</table>

From the Home window, click the Invoices shortcuts list arrow and click Adjust Invoice.

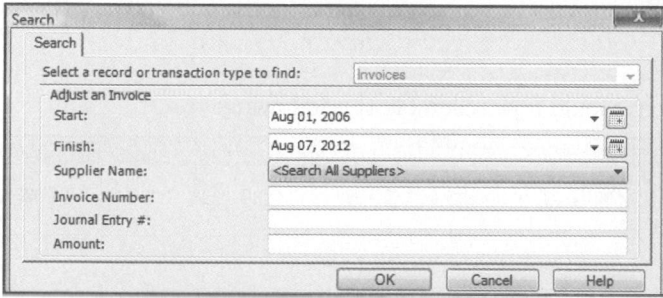

This is similar to the Search screen for the General Journal, but you have the additional option of searching for invoices by the name of the supplier. The program enters default start and finish dates. These dates can be edited like any other date fields or you can choose dates from the calendars. The default dates include all transactions for the journal, so we can accept them.

We will search all invoices by accepting the default to Search All Suppliers.

If you know the invoice or journal entry number, you can enter it in the Invoice Number or Journal Entry # field and click OK to select the invoice directly.

Click   **OK** to see the requested list of Purchases Journal invoices:

Date	Supplier	Invoice #	Journal Entry #	Original Amt
Aug 03, 2012	All Campus Ads	ACA-3492	5	226.00
Aug 01, 2012	Bathurst Food Supplies	B-1243	2	800.00
Aug 01, 2012	Fundy Gift House	FG-642	1	904.00

Invoices are presented in order with the most recent one listed first and selected. The invoice that we need is Journal Entry #1, FG-642. You can change the order of the listed transactions by selecting from the **View Invoices By** drop-down list. You can list in order by date, supplier, invoice number, journal entry number or amount. And you can reverse the order of any list by clicking the ⬚ Z...A↓ ⬚ button.

Click   **FG-642**. (Click anywhere on the line to highlight the invoice.)

<table>
<tr><td>NOTES</td></tr>
</table>

Notice that cash purchases entered in the Payments Journal are not included in this list. You can adjust these transactions from the Payments Journal after you select Make Other Payment (see page 135).

Click   **Select** or **double click** the **entry** to recall the selected transaction:

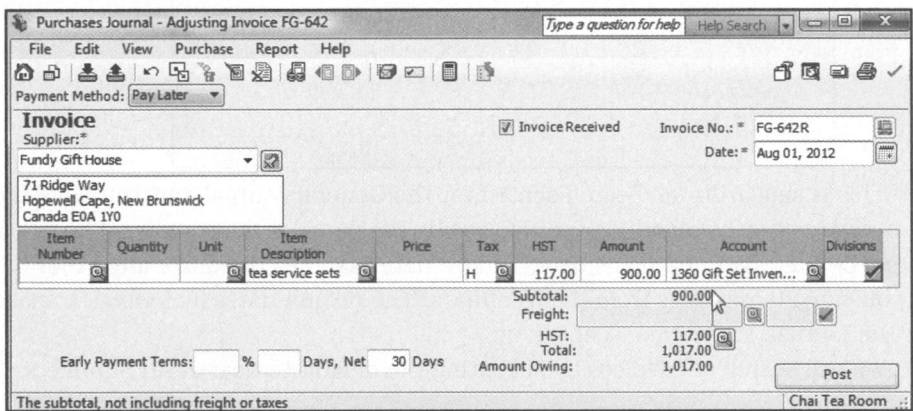

All fields are available for editing. We need to edit the amount.

Click   **800.00** in the Amount field.

Type   900

Press   `tab` to update the tax amount and totals.

You can add -R to the invoice number if you want to indicate that this is the revised invoice.

Your completed entry should now resemble the following:

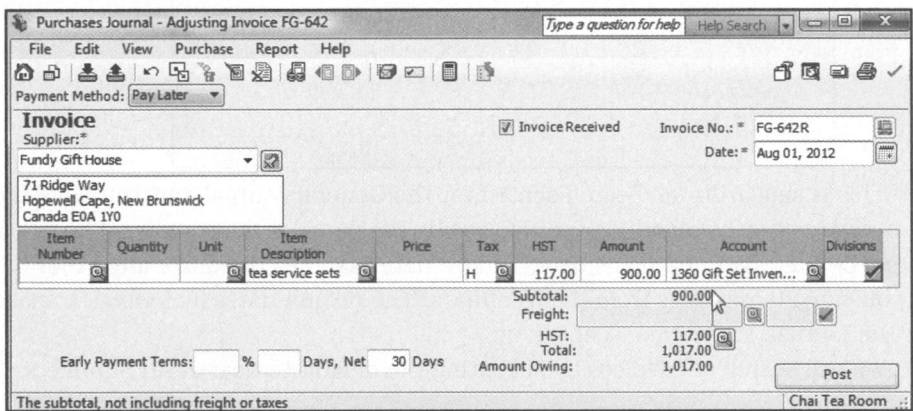

If you change the supplier, you will see a warning:

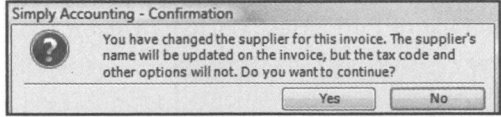

NOTES
When you change the supplier, the default settings for the previously selected supplier will still be used. Check your entry carefully before posting.
    To change the supplier, it is easier and safer to reverse the invoice and then enter it correctly. Refer to page 144.

Before posting the revised transaction, review it for accuracy.

Choose the **Report menu** and **click Display Purchases Journal Entry**:

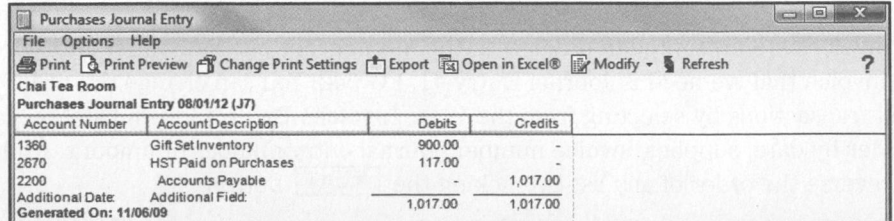

Although only one journal entry is shown, three entries are connected with this transaction — J1, the first one that was incorrect, J6, the second one created by Simply Accounting to reverse the incorrect entry and J7, the final correct one you see displayed.

All use the original posting date unless you change the date for the adjustment. The previous transaction we posted was entry #5 (see page 132).

> **Close** the **report display** when you have finished and **make** additional **corrections** if necessary.

> **Click** the Post button ⬚ Post ⬚, **click** OK and **close** the Purchases Journal.

NOTES
If you edit the date, the correcting entry will be posted with the revised date. To see all three entries in the journal report, Corrections must be selected (see page 149).

CORRECTING CASH PURCHASES AND PAYMENTS FROM THE PAYMENTS JOURNAL

Purchases entered as Other Payments in the Payments Journal do not appear on the Search Purchase Invoices list from the Purchases Journal. You can, however, adjust these other payments from the Payments Journal as follows:

- Click the Home window **Payments icon shortcuts list arrow** ⬚Payments▾⬚, and **click Adjust Payment**.
- **Select** your search parameters: the **date range, supplier** or **cheque number**. Click OK.
- Click the **cheque/invoice** you want to adjust. All cheques used to pay invoices and cash purchases will appear on this list.
- **Double click** the **entry** or **click Select** to open the cheque.
- **Make** the **corrections. Review** your **entry** and post the revised transaction.
- If the **Payments Journal** is already open, **click Make Other Payment** from the transaction list if you want to adjust a cash purchase payment.
- **Click Pay Invoices** from the transaction list if you want to adjust a cheque used to pay invoices.
- Click the **Adjust Payment** or **Adjust Other Payment tool** ⬚ or choose the **Payment** menu and **click Adjust Payment** or **Adjust Other Payment**.
- **Select** your search parameters. **Click OK** to open the list of cheques. Your list will include either payment or cash purchase (other payment) cheques, depending on the type of transaction you started from.
- **Make** the **corrections. Review** your **entry** and post the revised transaction.

Refer to page 143 for detailed instructions on correcting a payment cheque.

Entering Discounts for Early Payments

Entering discounts for early payments is very much like entering regular payments. The discounts show up automatically when the invoices and dates are correct.

> **Click** the **Payments icon** ⬚Payments▾⬚ to open the Payments Journal.

> **Choose** Bathurst Food Supplies from the list to display the outstanding invoices:

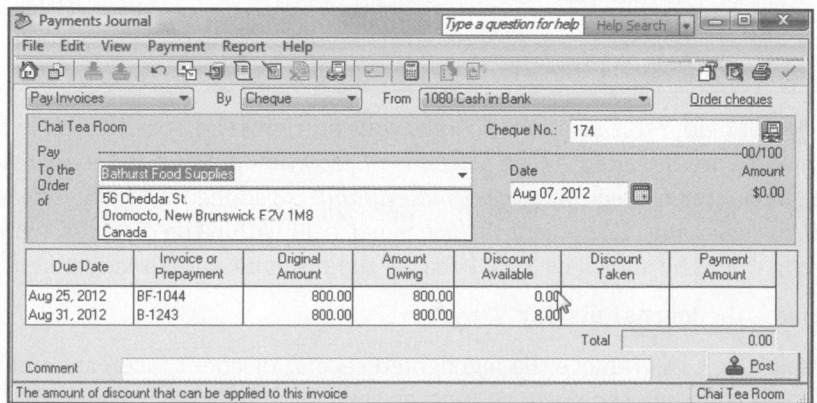

NOTES
The Payments Journal shows the due date for the invoice, the net 30 date that is 30 days after the invoice date of July 26 for invoice #BF-1044.

Initially, no discount is available for invoice #BF-1044 because the session date is beyond the discount period, that is, more than 10 days past the July 26 invoice date.

The discount shows for the second invoice because the session date lies within its 10-day discount period.

> **Enter** **August 4** as the date of the payment. **Press** (tab).

Both discounts are now available because the payment date falls within the 10-day discount period:

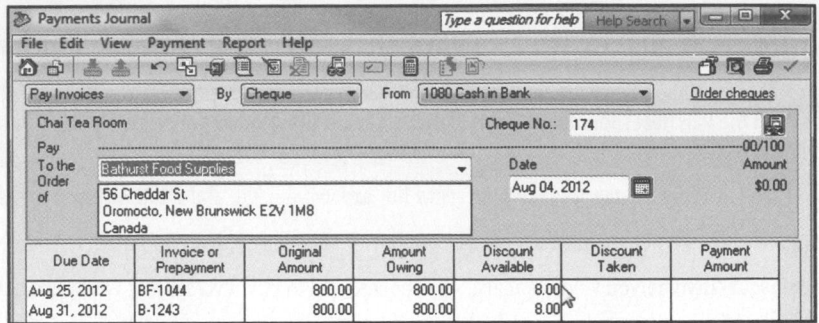

> **Press** (tab) **twice** to advance to the Discount Taken field and enter the amount.

> **Press** (tab) to advance to the Payment Amount field and accept the amount.

Notice that the discount has been subtracted from the invoice amount.

> **Press** (tab) to accept the amount in the Payment Amount field and update the total and the cheque portion of the journal as shown:

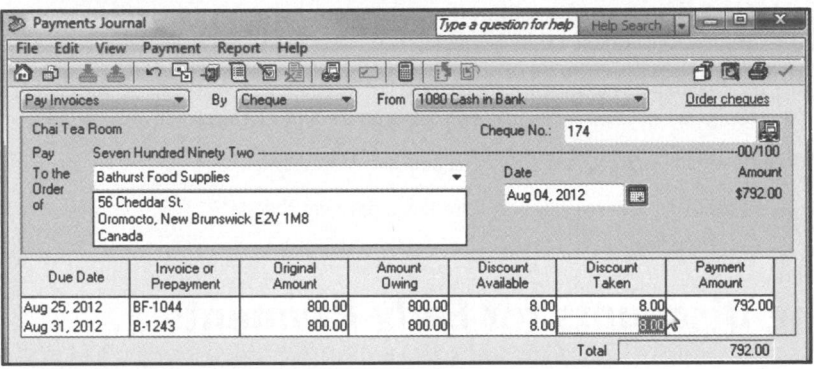

At this stage, a discount amount is entered for the second invoice, but this invoice is not being paid. Therefore you must delete this entry to avoid adding it to the invoice.

> **Press** (ctrl) + **J** to see the payment as you have it entered so far:

Chai Tea Room			
Payments Journal Entry 08/04/12 (J8)			
Account Number	Account Description	Debits	Credits
2200	Accounts Payable	808.00	-
1080	Cash in Bank	-	792.00
5090	Purchase Discounts	-	16.00
Additional Date:	Additional Field:	808.00	808.00

If you do not delete this second discount, your entry will be posted as shown. Both discount amounts are included — the *Purchase Discounts* amount is $16 instead of $8. The cheque amount is correct, but *Accounts Payable* is reduced by $808 instead of $800, the invoice amount. If the next invoice is not paid within the discount period, its balance owing would be shown as $792 because the discount was already taken.

> **Close** the **journal display**.

> **Press** (del) to remove the highlighted second discount taken amount and complete the payment form as shown:

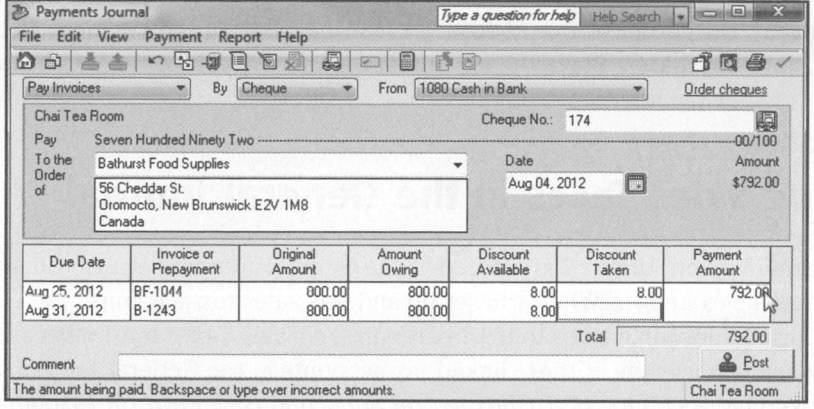

NOTES

If a second discount is not displayed, you can skip the step of deleting the discount amount. Notice that the status bar message advises you how to enter or change the amounts.

Choose the **Report menu** and **click Display Payments Journal Entry** to review the transaction before posting:

Account Number	Account Description	Debits	Credits
2200	Accounts Payable	800.00	-
1080	Cash in Bank	-	792.00
5090	Purchase Discounts	-	8.00
Additional Date:	Additional Field:	800.00	800.00

Payments Journal Entry
Chai Tea Room
Payments Journal Entry 08/04/12 (J8)

In the related journal entry, the program has now updated the General Ledger *Accounts Payable* control account for the full amount of the invoice and reduced the balance owing to the supplier by the same amount. The amount taken from *Cash in Bank* is the actual amount of the payment, taking the single discount amount into consideration. The discount amount is automatically debited to the linked *Purchase Discounts* account. *Purchase Discounts* is a contra-expense account. It has a credit balance, so it reduces total expense and increases income.

Close the **display** to return to the Payments Journal input screen and **correct** your **work** if necessary. (Refer to page 125 for assistance.)

Post the **transaction. Click OK. Close** the **Payments Journal**.

Using Continue to Enter New Suppliers

Sometimes you may want to include the name of a supplier in the journal record without creating a supplier record. In these situations, you can use the Continue feature. For the cheque to Tomailik, a cash purchase, we will use this approach.

Click the **Invoices icon** 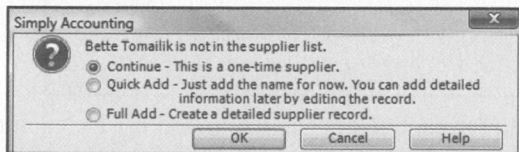 to open the Purchases Journal.

Click the **Supplier field** and **type** Bette Tomailik

Press (tab) to open the message about a new supplier name:

> **Simply Accounting**
>
> Bette Tomailik is not in the supplier list.
> ● Continue - This is a one-time supplier.
> ○ Quick Add - Just add the name for now. You can add detailed information later by editing the record.
> ○ Full Add - Create a detailed supplier record.
>
> [OK] [Cancel] [Help]

Click **Continue** and **OK** to return to the journal. **Press** (tab). Cash is the default payment method when you choose Continue.

Choose **Cheque** as the Payment Method and then **enter** the **remaining details** of the cash purchase as usual. **Review** and **post** the **transaction**.

NOTES

For one-time suppliers, you can type the supplier's name in the Address field. The supplier's name will not be included in journal reports.

NOTES

Pay Later is not an option when you choose Continue or One-time Supplier. Only immediate payment is allowed — Cash and Cheque.

NOTES

When you choose Continue for a new supplier in the Make Other Payment journal, the name is not added to the journal entry.

Enter the **purchase** from **Sunbury Cleaning**. **Change** the Payment Method to **Pay Later**. **Store** the **entry**, **post** it and then **close** the **Purchases Journal**.

Entering Sales Taxes in the General Journal

The sales summary on August 7 is entered in the General Journal because Chai does not use the Receivables Ledger. When you set up and link sales tax accounts, you can add General Journal sales tax entries to the tax reports. A Sales Taxes button becomes available when you use one of these linked tax accounts in the General Journal. Chai has two linked tax accounts, *HST Charged on Sales* and *HST Paid on Purchases*.

The General Journal is accessed from the Company module window that we used in the previous two chapters.

> To open the Company module window, click Company in the list of modules in the upper left-hand Modules pane. Click the General Journal icon.

Instead, we will create a shortcut to open the General Journal.

CLASSIC VIEW Users who are familiar with earlier versions of Simply Accounting may prefer to work from the Classic view. You can access all journals and ledgers from a single Home window.

Creating Shortcuts

Click **Customize** in the Shortcuts pane below the modules as shown:

The Customize Shortcuts window opens:

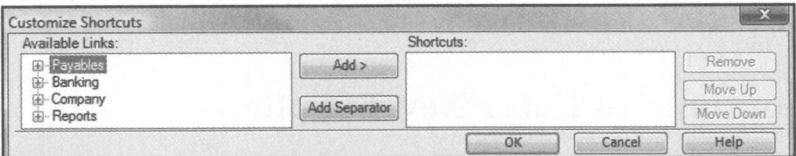

Click the ⊞ beside **Company** to expand the list of Company tasks:

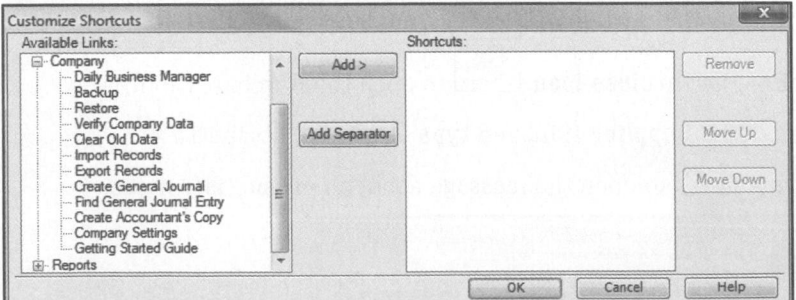

You can create up to 10 shortcuts for each user. The expanded list for each module shows the items for which you can create shortcuts. Once you create it, you can click the name in the Shortcuts pane to access that journal or task directly.

Click **Create General Journal** in the list of Company tasks.

Click **Add>** to move this task to the Shortcuts box as shown:

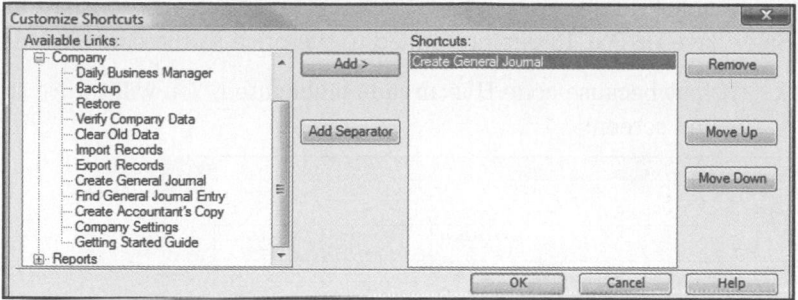

> **NOTES**
> You can remove a shortcut if it is not needed. Just click Customize in the Home window. Click the shortcut in the Shortcuts pane and click Remove and OK.

Click   **OK** to return to the Home window.

Create General Journal now appears in the Home window Shortcuts pane as shown:

Click   **Create General Journal** in the Shortcuts pane. The General Journal opens immediately. This shortcut will be available in all module Home windows.

Enter   the **Source** and **Comment** for the sale. The session date is correct.

Choose   **Cash in Bank** as the account to be debited and **type** 8588 as the amount. **Enter** an appropriate **Comment** for the account.

Choose   **HST Charged on Sales** as the account. Advance to the credit column.

Type   988 as the amount to be credited. **Press** (tab). Your screen should now resemble the one shown here:

> **NOTES**
> Follow the keystroke instructions for the General Journal from the Missoni Marbleworks application starting on page 10.

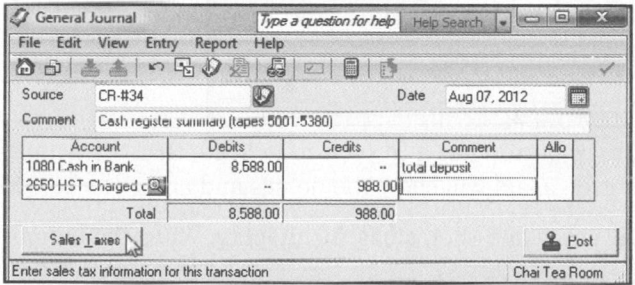

The Sales Taxes button became available as soon as you entered the tax amount.

Click   the **Sales Taxes button** to open the tax detail screen:

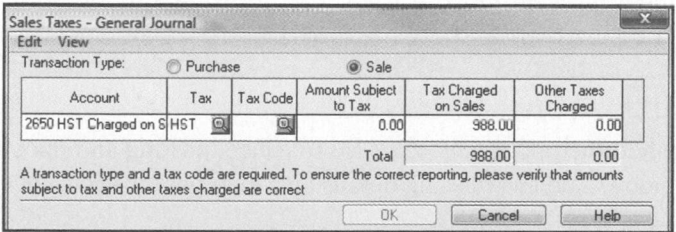

Because you entered *HST Charged on Sales* as the account, the transaction is recognized as a sale. You can change the transaction type if it is not correct. The account and tax amount are already entered on the form. We need to add the tax code.

Click   the **List icon** [icon] in the Tax Code field to open the tax code list:

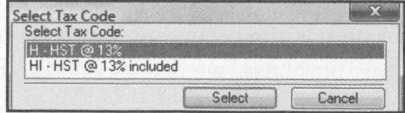

NOTES
When you enter HST Paid on Purchases as the account, Purchase will be selected as the default transaction type because this account is linked to the Payables module.

This is the same list that we saw in the Purchases and Payments journals in the tax code fields. Sales have HST at 13 percent added to the price so the correct code is H.

Click **Select** because code H is already highlighted. You will return to the tax detail screen:

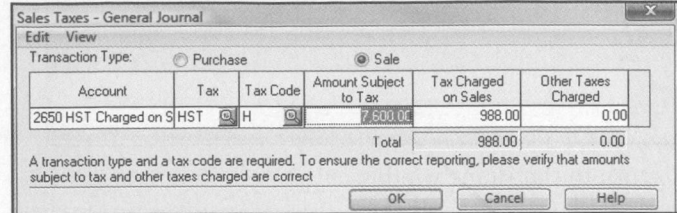

Because the tax amount was already entered, the sales amount — the Amount Subject To Tax — is calculated as soon as you select the tax code. The sales amount is correct so we can continue. If the amount is not correct because there are other taxes included, you can edit the default amount and enter an amount for Other Taxes Charged.

Click **OK**.

Enter a **Comment** for the tax line and then add the final account line — **choose** account **4100**, accept the amount and **add** an appropriate **comment** to complete your journal entry as shown here:

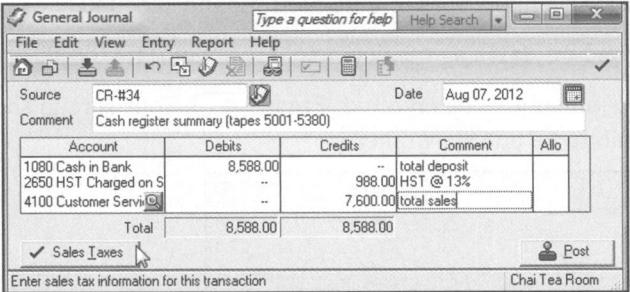

Notice that the Sales Taxes button has a ✓ on it to indicate that tax details have been added. Clicking the button again will show the details and allow you to edit them.

Review the **journal entry** and then **close** the **display**. When the entry is correct,

Click the **Post** button ![Post]. **Click** OK.

If you forgot to enter the tax codes for *HST Charged on Sales*, you will see the warning message to confirm you do not want to add tax details:

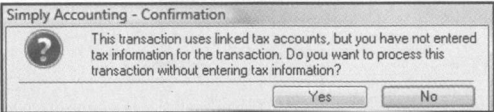

If you forgot to add the tax details, click No to cancel posting and open the Sales Taxes window. Add the missing details and then post the journal entry.

Close the **General Journal** to return to the Home window.

Advance the **session date** to **August 14**. **Back up** your **data file** when prompted.

Recalling a Stored Entry

The first journal entry for the August 14 session date is the recurring purchase from Bathurst Food Supplies. Since we have stored this purchase, we do not need to re-enter all the information.

Click   the **Invoices icon** to open the Journal.

Click   the **Recall tool** in the tool bar (or **choose** the **Purchase menu** and **click Recall**) to display the Recall Recurring Transaction dialogue box as shown here:

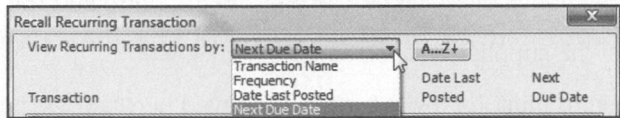

NOTES
You can press `ctrl` + R to recall a stored entry.

The stored entries are listed in order according to the next date that they will be repeated. If you want, you can display the stored entries in a different order.

Click   the **View Recurring Transactions By list arrow** to see the options:

You can choose to view the stored entries in order by Transaction Name (which is the supplier's name if you did not change the default), by Frequency (how often the transaction is repeated), by the Date Last Posted or by the Next Due Date. If you have a large number of stored entries, it may be easier to find the one you need with a different order. You can also reverse the order for any of the order selections with the A...Z+ button. Since we have only two stored entries, the default order, Next Due Date, placed the one we want first. Do not change the default.

From the Recall Stored Entry dialogue box, you can remove an entry that is incorrect or no longer needed. Click an entry to select it. Click Remove and then click Yes to confirm that you want to delete the entry. (See page 447.)

Bathurst Food Supplies, the name of the entry we want to use, should be selected because it is the recurring entry that is due next.

Click   **Bathurst Food Supplies** if it is not already selected.

Click   **Select** or **press** `enter` to return to the Purchases Journal.

The entry we stored is displayed just as we entered it the first time, except that the date has been changed to one week past the previous posting date, as needed, and the Invoice field is blank so we can enter the new invoice number. Remember that Simply Accounting does not accept duplicate invoice numbers.

Click   the **Invoice field** to move the cursor.

Type   BF-2100

The entry is now complete. You should review it before posting.

Choose the **Report menu** and **click Display Purchases Journal Entry**.

Close the **display** when finished and **make** any necessary **corrections**.

Click the **Post button** Post . **Click OK** and then **close** the **journal**.

Editing Supplier Information

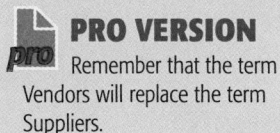

The Home window Suppliers pane has the option to hide or display account phone numbers and balances. For security purposes, you may want to hide these details.

Click the ⊡ button above the Suppliers list to see the options:

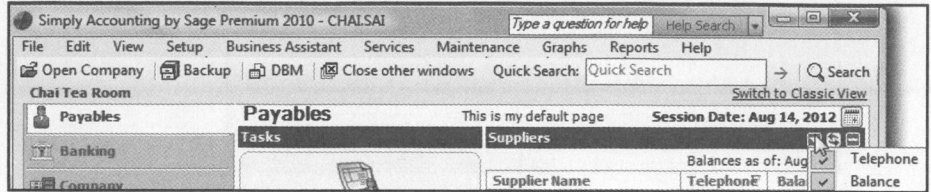

Checkmarks indicate that the information is displayed.

To hide the additional details, click the ⊡ button and click the detail you want to hide. To restore the detail, click the button and the option to add the ✓.

To refresh or update the supplier balance amounts, click ⟳.

Sometimes a supplier record must be revised after it is saved because the initial information has changed or because information that was not available initially is now known. We need to edit the record for NB Gas to add the default expense account.

Supplier records are accessed from the Suppliers icon shortcuts list, the Suppliers list or the Suppliers window. Modify Supplier, as shown in the drop-down shortcuts list with the Suppliers icon, is one starting point for the edit. The other is the supplier's name in the list of suppliers on the right:

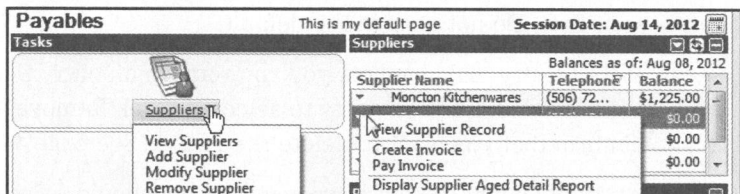

Click   NB Gas in the Suppliers list to open the Address tab information screen. Or, you can

Click   the **Suppliers shortcuts list arrow** and **click Modify Supplier** to open the Search Suppliers window:

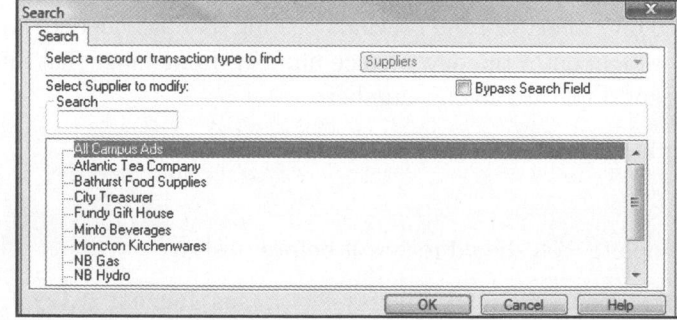

Each supplier on record is listed on the Search Suppliers selection window. Suppliers is entered as the search area. Notice that Bette Tomailik is not listed.

Double click   NB Gas to open the Address tab information screen.

Click   the **Options tab** to access the Expense Account field:

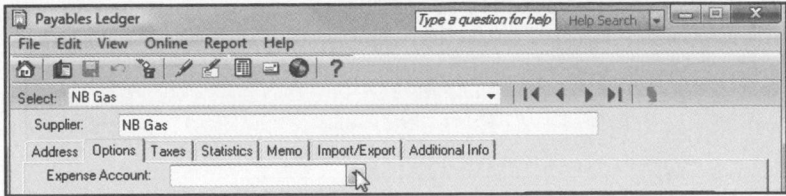

> **NOTES**
> Remember that although the field is named Expense Account, you can choose any postable account as the default for the supplier. You can also select a different account in the journal if necessary.

Click   the **Expense Account field**.

You can choose an account from the list provided by the list arrow, type the account number or add a new account. We need to create an account.

Type   5110 **Press** (tab) and then **click Add** to start the Add Account wizard. **Enter Heating Expense** as the account name and accept the remaining default settings. **Click Finish** to return to the Ledger.

Click   **Save And Close** ⊞Save and Close to close the Payables Ledger (supplier record) window to return to the Payables module window.

Click   **Pay Expenses** from the Payments icon shortcuts list to open the Payments Journal.

Enter   the **cash purchase from NB Gas**; the account will appear automatically.

Adjusting a Posted Payment

Just as you can correct a purchase invoice after posting, you can correct a cheque that has been posted.

Choose   **Pay Invoices** from the Payments transaction list.

Click   the **Adjust Payment tool** 🔲 or **choose** the **Payment menu** and **click Adjust Payment** to open the Search screen for Adjust Payments:

> **NOTES**
> Pressing (ctrl) + A will also open the Search window to begin the adjusting procedure.

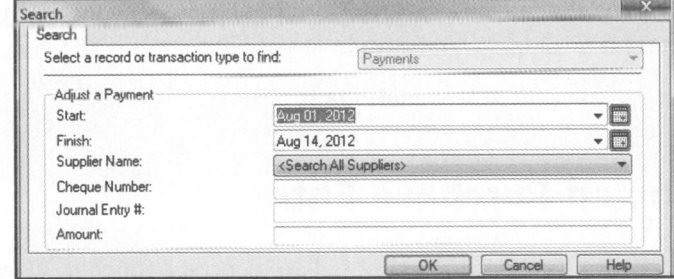

> **NOTES**
> When you choose Adjust Payment from the Home window Payments icon shortcuts list, you will see the list of all cheques, those used to pay invoices and those for other payments.

Again we see the familiar Search window for the selected journal.

Click   **OK** to see the list of cheques already posted for this date range:

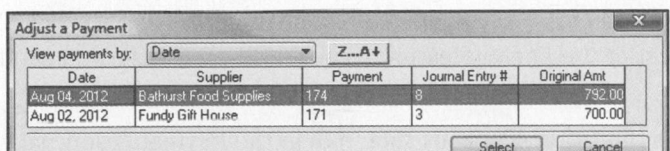

Only the two cheques used to pay invoices are listed because we started from the Pay Invoices window. When you start from the Make Other Payment window, you will see only the cash purchase payment transactions. When you begin from the Home window Payments icon drop-down shortcuts list, both Other Payment and Pay Invoice transactions will be listed.

Double click Fundy Gift House to see the cheque we posted:

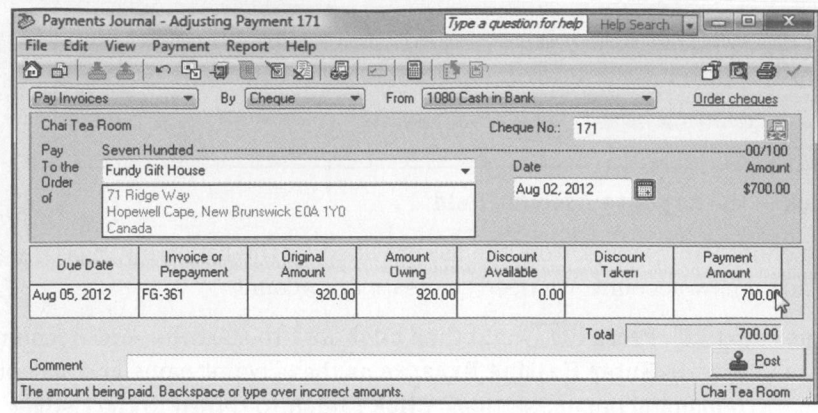

The cheque appears as it was completed. You can edit all the details.

Click   700.00 in the Payment Amount field.

Type   600

Click   the **Comment field**.

Type   previous chq amount incorrectly entered

Check   your **work** carefully. **Click Post** to save the changes:

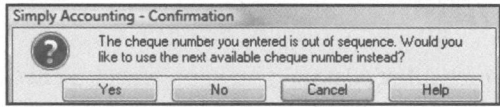

A message about the cheque number being out of sequence appears because we have already used this cheque number. The cheque number is correct so we should continue without changing it.

Click   No to accept the number and continue.

Simply Accounting will create an entry that reverses the original payment, and the original entry is also saved for a complete audit trail.

Enter   the next group of three **transactions**.

Reversing a Posted Purchase Entry

The cash purchase for Moncton Kitchenwares selected an incorrect supplier. We will reverse this entry rather than adjust it because other details may also be incorrect. Any journal that has an Adjust option also has the option to reverse an entry.

The journal you used to enter the purchase should still be open, either the Payments Journal with Make Other Payment selected or the Purchases Journal. You can also use either the Adjust or the Lookup feature to begin. In each case, you can follow the steps below.

Click   the **Lookup Other Payment tool** in the Payments Journal with Make Other Payment selected, or the **Lookup An Invoice tool** in the Purchases Journal. Or

Click   the **Adjust Other Payment (Adjust An Invoice) tool** to open the Search screen.

Click   OK to see the list of cheques (or purchases) already posted.

Double click Moncton Kitchenwares to see the cash purchase.

The Reverse tool 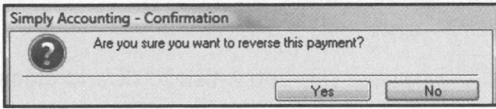 in the tool bar is now available.

Click   the **Reverse tool** 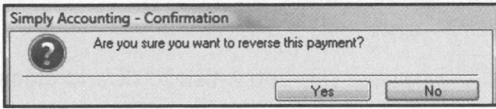, or **choose** the **Payment** (or **Purchase**) **menu** and **click Reverse Other Payment** (or **Invoice**) to see the confirmation:

Click   Yes to confirm.

Simply Accounting will create the entry that reverses the original one automatically. You can see both the original and the reversing entry in the journal report when you choose Show Corrections.

Enter   the transaction, choosing the correct supplier this time.

When you change the supplier for a cash purchase transaction you will see the message stating that the supplier name will be changed (the remaining information on the invoice will be unchanged):

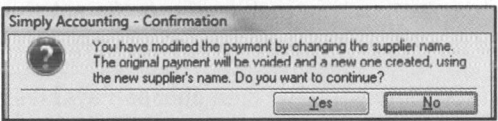

> **NOTES**
> The Receipts Journal Report in Chapter 6, page 185, shows the two entries that result when you reverse a transaction.

 Enter   the next group of **journal transactions** up to August 21.

Changing a Stored Entry

The first entry on August 21 is the weekly purchase from Sunbury Cleaning Supplies. The amount of the purchase has changed, however, and we need to update the stored entry. If the change is for a single purchase and will not be repeated, edit the entry after recalling it but do not store the entry again.

Click   the **Invoices icon** in the Payables window to open the Journal.

Click   the **Recall tool** on the tool bar, or **choose** the **Purchase menu** and **click Recall** to display the Recall Recurring Transaction dialogue box.

Double click Sunbury Cleaning Supplies, the entry we want to use to display the purchase entry with the new date.

Click   the **Invoice field** so you can add the invoice number.

Type   SC-1790

Click   **250.00**, the Amount, to highlight it so that you can edit it. Double click if necessary to select the amount.

Type   300

Press   (tab) to enter the change.

Review the **journal entry** as usual to make sure that it is correct before proceeding.

Click   the **Store button**, or **choose** the **Purchase menu** and **click Store**.

Click   **OK** to accept the name and frequency without changes.

The following warning appears:

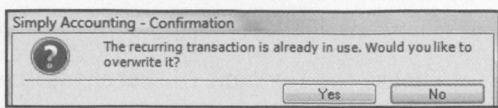

Click   **Yes** to confirm that you want to replace the previous stored version and return to the Purchases Journal.

Click   the **Post button** [Post] to save the entry. **Click OK** and **close** the **Journal**.

 Enter   the **remaining journal transactions** for August.

Displaying Supplier Reports

Like General Ledger reports, supplier-related reports can be displayed and printed from multiple starting points, including the Suppliers window.

 **PRO VERSION**
The term Vendor will replace Supplier in all report names and report fields.
   Grouped Supplier Lists are not available.

Click   the **Suppliers icon** [Suppliers▾] to open the Suppliers window. The Reports menu in this window now lists only supplier reports. **Select** the **report** you want from this list to open the report options window.

Choose   the **Reports menu** in the Home window, then **choose Payables** and **click** the **report** you want in order to see its options window.

NOTES
The Supplier Purchases Report deals mainly with inventory. It will be introduced in a later application.

Click   the **Reports list arrow** in the Reports pane to see the list of supplier reports:

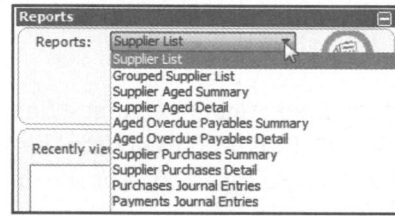

We will work from the Report Centre again so that we can see the report samples, descriptions and options.

NOTES
The Report Centre can also be accessed from the Reports menu.

Reporting from the Report Centre

**CLASSIC VIEW**
Click the Report Centre icon in the My Business column or open the Report Centre from the Reports menu.

Click   the **Report Centre icon** [Report Centre] in the Home window.

Click   **Payables** in the Select A Report Type list to open the list of available supplier reports:

PRO VERSION
Forecast & Analysis reports are not available in the Pro version.

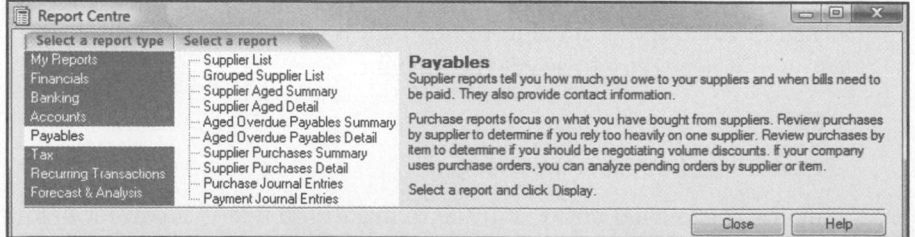

You should see a general description of the Payables module reports.

Displaying Supplier Lists

Click **Supplier List** in the Select A Report list to see the sample report and description.

Click **Modify This Report** to see the report options:

In any Home window, you can choose the Reports menu, then choose Lists and click Suppliers to see the report options.

To select supplier details, you can choose the supplier record fields from the Report Columns screen. You can include suppliers marked as inactive if you want.

Click **OK** to see the report.

Close the **display** when you have finished viewing the report.

You will return to the starting point for the report.

Displaying Supplier Aged Reports

You can display Supplier Aged reports at any time.

Click **Supplier Aged Summary** in the Select A Report list to see the sample report and description.

Click **Modify This Report** to see the report options:

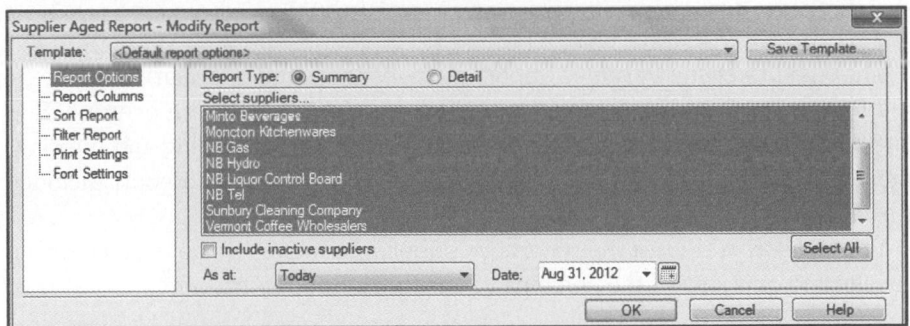

Or, from any Home window, choose the Reports menu, then choose Payables and click Supplier Aged to see this report options window.

If you chose either One-Time Supplier or Continue for Bette Tomailik, she will not be included by name in the list of suppliers for reports and graphs. If you used Quick Add, her name will be included.

The **Summary** option provides the total balance owing to each supplier. It displays an alphabetic list of suppliers with outstanding total balances organized into aged columns. By default, the program selects this option.

Select the **Detail** option if you want to see individual outstanding invoices and payments made to suppliers. This more descriptive report is also aged. Management can use it to make payment decisions. With the Detail option, you can also add supplier payment terms by clicking Include Terms.

You can sort and filter the reports by supplier name or balance owing (or by aging period for the summary report. You can select or omit any columns to customize reports.

CLASSIC VIEW
From the Home window, right-click the Suppliers icon
. (Clicking the left mouse button will open the ledger.) The Display tool label changes to the name of the report for the selected icon.
Click the Display tool on the tool bar.

NOTES
You can drill down to the Supplier Aged Detail Report from the Supplier List.

NOTES
The Grouped Supplier List is similar to the Supplier List, but you can group the suppliers by a number of criteria, such as their city.

WARNING!
You must enter the year in all report option window date fields. The default year is taken from your computer system. This may be incorrect for your data file and will produce an error message. You can enter two digits for the year.

NOTES
The Supplier Aged Summary and Detail reports are both available directly from the Report Centre.

NOTES
From the Supplier Aged Detail Report, you can drill down to look up invoices and supplier ledgers. From the Summary Report, you can drill down to the Detail Report.

Click	Detail if you want the Detail Report.
Click	the **name** or **press** and **hold** ⎡ctrl⎤ and **click** the **names** in the Suppliers list to select the suppliers you want in the report. **Click Select All** to include all suppliers or to remove all when all are selected.
Enter	the **date** you want for the report (including the year) or accept the session date given by default. After you have indicated all the options,
Click	OK to see the report.
Close	the **displayed report** when you have finished.

Displaying Aged Overdue Payables Reports

You can display Aged Overdue Payables reports at any time.

Click	**Aged Overdue Payables Summary** in the Select A Report list to see the sample report and description.
Click	**Modify This Report** to see the report options:

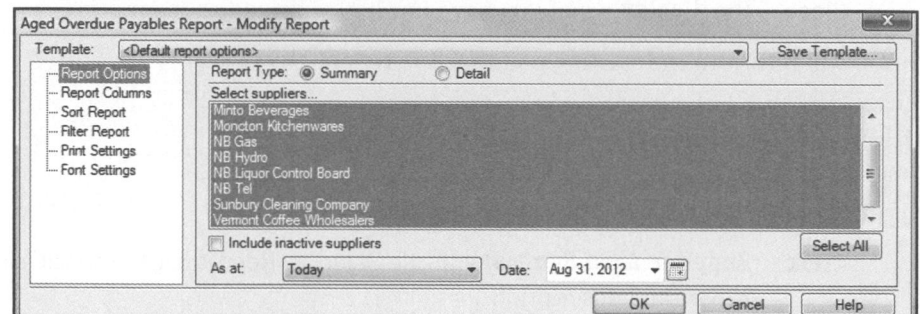

From the Home window, choose the Reports menu, then choose Payables and click Aged Overdue Payables to see the report options.

The Aged Overdue Payables Report includes the same information as the Supplier Aged Report but it adds a column for the invoice amounts that are overdue. Supplier name and balance owing may be selected as the criteria for sorting and filtering. The Summary Report shows totals for each supplier while the Detail Report includes details for each invoice.

You can sort and filter the reports by supplier name or by the balance owing. You can select or omit any of the columns to customize the report.

Choose	Summary or Detail.
Press	and **hold** ⎡ctrl⎤ and then **click** the **names** in the Suppliers list to select the suppliers that you want to see in the report. **Click Select All** to include all suppliers or to remove all when all are selected.
Enter	the **date** you want for the report (including the year), or accept the session date given by default. After you have indicated all the options,
Click	OK to see the report. One invoice from Moncton Kitchenwares and the balance on the first invoice from Fundy Gift House are overdue.
Close	the **displayed report** when you have finished.

Displaying the Purchases Journal

Click   **Purchase Journal Entries** in the Select A Report list to see the sample report and description.

Click   **Modify This Report** to see the report options:

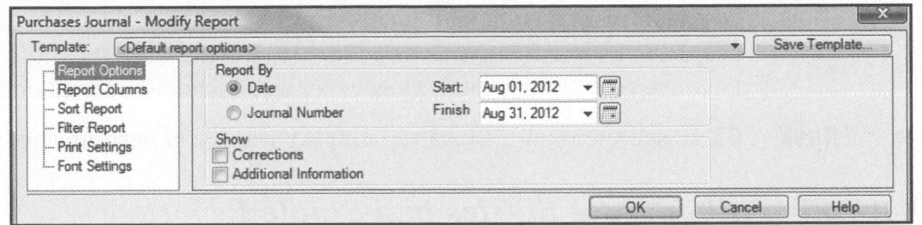

Or, choose the Reports menu, then choose Journal Entries and click Purchases.

Entries for the Purchases Journal can be selected by posting date or by journal entry number. By default, the Date option is selected, and the first transaction date and session date are the default dates for the report. All journal reports may be sorted and filtered by date, journal number, source or comment. You can choose the account name, number, debits and credits columns to customize the report column settings. Correcting or adjusting entries may be included or omitted from the report.

Type   the **beginning date** for the transactions you want (including the year).

Press   ⌨ *tab* ⌨ **twice**.

Type   the **ending date** for your transaction period (including the year).

Click   **Corrections** so that adjusting and reversing entries are included.

Click   **OK** to see the report.

Close   the **display** when you have finished.

Displaying the Payments Journal

Click   **Payment Journal Entries** in the Select A Report list to see the sample report and description.

Click   **Modify This Report** to see the report options:

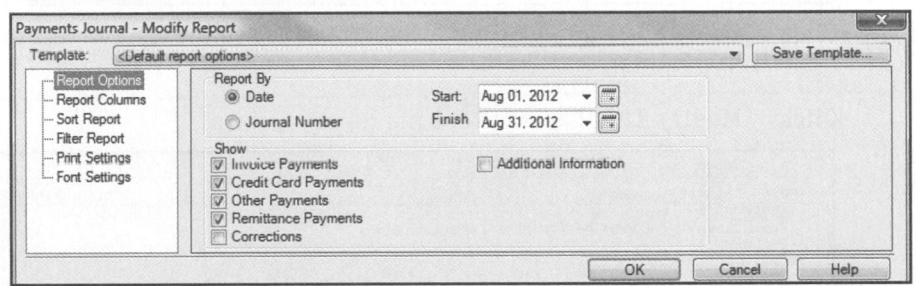

Or, choose the Reports menu, then choose Journal Entries and click Payments to see the report options.

For the Payments Journal, like other journal reports, you can select the transactions by posting date — the default setting — or by journal entry number. In addition, you can choose the type of payment for the report — invoice payments, credit card payments, other payments (cash purchases) and remittance payments. All types are selected initially and clicking any one will remove it from the report. Corrections or adjustments may be included or omitted. Clicking will change your selections.

 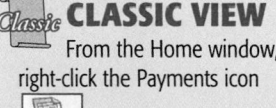

Type	the **beginning date** for the transactions you want (including the year).
Press	`tab` **twice**.
Type	the **ending date** for your transaction period (including the year).
Click	**Corrections**.
Click	**Credit Card Payments** and **Remittance Payments** because we did not use these transaction types. Only Invoice Payments and Other Payments, the transaction types we entered, should be included.
Click	**OK** to see the report. **Close** the **display** when you have finished.

Displaying All Journal Entries in a Single Report

To view the entries for all journals in a single report from a Home window, choose the Reports menu, then choose Journal Entries and click All.

From the Report Centre, click Financials in the Select A Report Type list and then click All Journal Entries in the Select A Report list. Click Display or choose Modify This Report if you want to change the default options.

Displaying Cheque Log Reports

If you regularly print cheques through Simply Accounting from the Payables journals or the Payroll journals, you can display and print a summary of these printed cheques in the Cheque Log Report.

Click	**Banking** in the Select A Report Type list to see the general description of banking reports and the list of available reports:

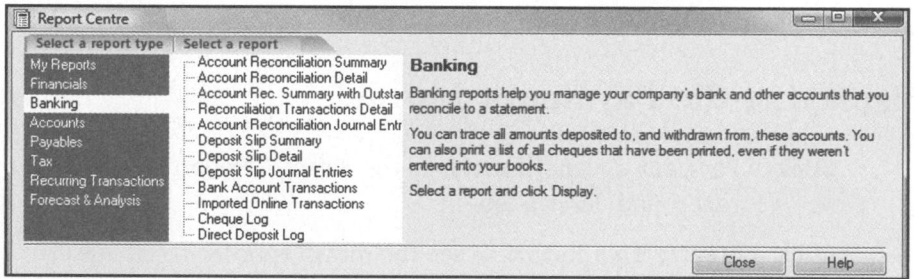

Click	**Cheque Log** in the Select A Report list to see the sample report and description.
Click	**Modify This Report** to see the report options:

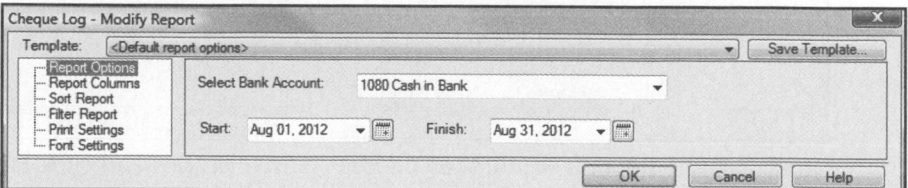

From any Home window, choose the Reports menu, then choose Banking and click Cheque Log to open the report options window.

The report will include details for all cheques that you entered including whether or not the journal entry was posted and the number of times the cheque was printed. If you do not print cheques through the program, these payments are listed with a 0 (zero) for the number of times printed. Adjusted cheques are identified as Reversed.

To customize the report, you can choose any of the column headings to sort or filter the report and you can choose to include or omit any of these columns.

Choose the **bank account** from the Select Bank Account drop-down list.

Enter the **Start** and **Finish dates** for the report (including the year).

Click **OK** to see the report.

Close the **display** when you have finished.

Recurring Transactions Report

If you have stored transactions, you can generate a report of these transactions.

Click **Recurring Transactions** in the Select A Report Type list to see the general description of the report type and the list of available reports:

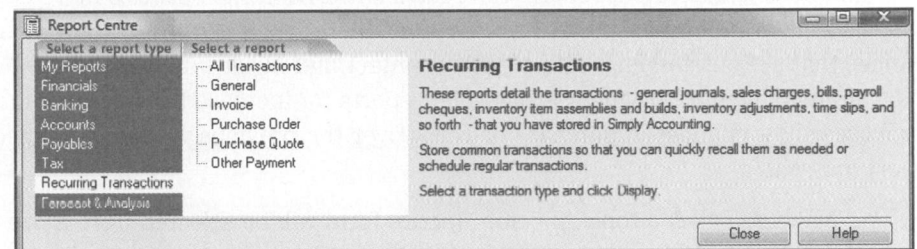

NOTES
Journals for hidden modules are not listed. When you use them and they allow recurring entries, they will be added to this list.

The list now shows the different types of transactions that can be stored.

Click **All Transactions** in the Select A Report list to see the sample report and description.

Click **Modify This Report** to see the report options:

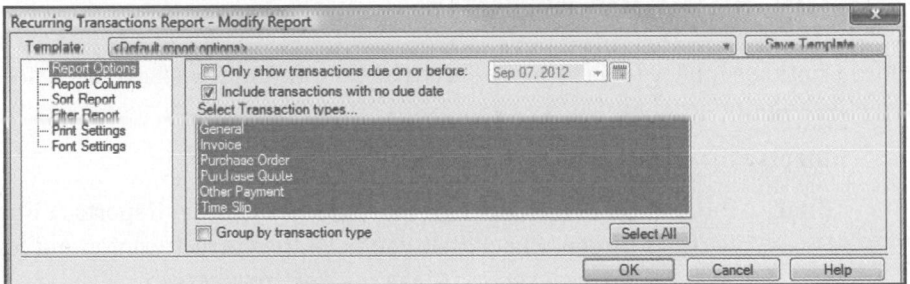

Again, the list shows the different types of transactions that can be stored and all are selected initially. Transactions without due dates are also included by default. You can restrict the report to include only those entries that are due within a specific time period by selecting **Only Show Transactions Due On Or Before**. The default date for this option is one week past the session date, but you can enter any date you want (including the year). You can **Group** the report **By Transaction Type**, or accept the default to show entries in order by the due date.

You can sort and filter this report by type of transaction, description, frequency, the date the entry was last processed or posted or by the due date.

NOTES
When you choose Random as the frequency for recurring transactions, they do not include a due date.

Choose the **options** you want and **click OK**.

Close the **Report Centre** when you have finished.

CLASSIC VIEW
You can also access Management Reports from the Advice tool in the Home window (see page 17).

NOTES

In the management report for overdue payments, negative numbers indicate the number of days until payment is due (current invoices) and positive numbers show the number of days that the payment is overdue.

⚠ **WARNING!**

Always check that the file location for the Form used for the report is correct for your program setup. The file should be in the Forms folder, a subfolder of your Simply Accounting Premium 2010 folder.

⚠ **WARNING!**

You cannot display labels, so you should check the printer settings first.

NOTES

For practice, you can print the labels on plain paper.

Displaying Management Reports

Management reports are available for each ledger. They can be displayed only from the Home window.

> **Choose** the **Reports menu**, then **choose Management Reports** and **click Payables** to open the report options window:

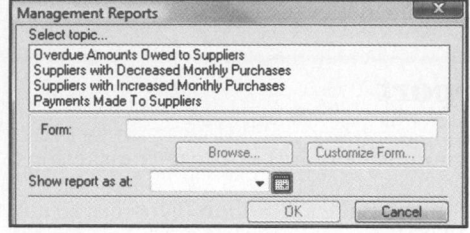

Sometimes management reports can reveal patterns in the business more clearly than the regular financial reports. For example, the report for overdue accounts lists invoices that are outstanding, with supplier contact and invoice details and the number of days remaining until payment is due. The reports for increased or decreased monthly purchases show changes in purchase patterns over the previous year that an aged detail report may not.

> When you click a topic, the appropriate form will be selected from those installed with the program. Unless you have the programs required to customize forms, accept the default. If appropriate, enter a date for the report.

> **Click**   **OK** to see the report. **Print** the **report** and then **close** the **display**.

Printing Supplier Reports

Before printing supplier reports, make sure that the print options have been set correctly. To print a report,

> **Display** the **report** you want to print.

> **Click**   the **Change Print Settings tool** 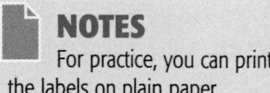 to open the Reports & Forms Settings screen. Check that you have the correct printer and form files selected for your report. **Close** the **Settings screen**.

> **Click**   the **Print tool** 🖨 or **choose** the **File menu** and **click Print**.

Printing Mailing Labels

To print labels, you should first make sure that the print options have been set correctly and that your printer is turned on and has the correct labels paper. To set the program to use your printing labels,

> Choose the Setup menu in the Home window and click Reports & Forms.
> Click Labels in the list under Reports. Choose your printer.
> Enter the appropriate margins, size and number across the page for your labels.
> Click OK to return to the Home window.

> **Choose** the **Reports menu** in the Home window, then **choose Mailing Labels** and **click Suppliers**:

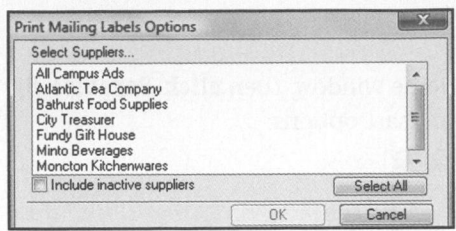

Press   and **hold** ⌷ctrl⌷ and then **click** the **names** of the suppliers for whom you want labels, or **click Select All** to include all suppliers.

Click   **OK** to print the labels.

Graphing Supplier Reports

Payables by Aging Period Charts

Choose the **Graphs menu** in the Home window, then **click Payables By Aging Period** to display the date entry screen:

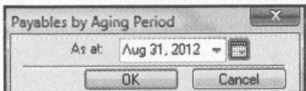

Type   the **date** for the graph or accept the default session date.

Click   **OK** to display the pie chart:

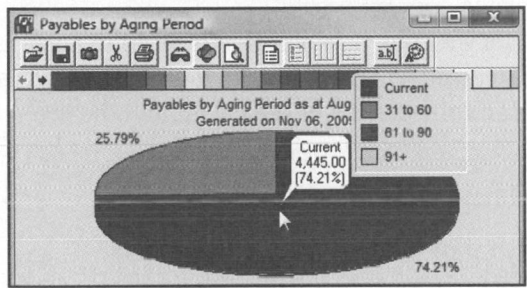

Your graph provides a quick visual reference of amounts due to all suppliers combined in each of the aging periods selected in the company setup options. Most of the payments due are current but about 25 percent are overdue (over 31 days) — the amounts owing to Moncton Kitchenwares and Fundy Gift House.

Double click a portion of a graph to see the aging period, the dollar amount and the percentage of the total. Double click the legend to make it larger and add the aging periods if they are not included already. Double click the expanded legend to reduce it.

Close   the **graph** when you have finished.

NOTES
The tool bar options, and the control of the colour and the legend, are the same for all graphs. Refer to page 63 for a review of these features.

Payables by Supplier Charts

Choose the Graphs menu in the Home window, then **click Payables By Supplier** to display the pie chart options:

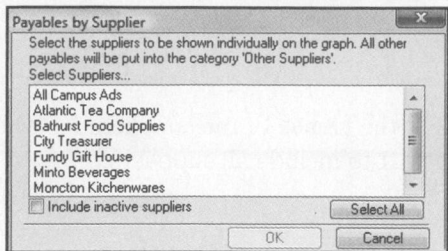

Press and **hold** `ctrl` and then **click** the **names** of the suppliers to include in your pie chart, or **click Select All** to include all the suppliers.

Click OK to display the pie chart:

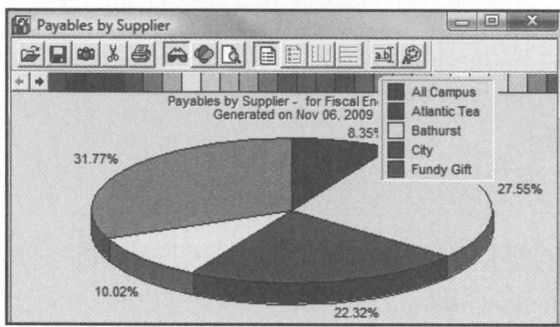

The graph shows the proportion of the total payables that is owed to each selected supplier. Amounts for suppliers not selected will be combined into a single category labelled Other. The tool bar options, and the control of the colour and the legend, are the same as for the other graphs.

Close the **graph** when you have finished.

Close the **data file** to finish your Simply Accounting session.

R E V I E W

The Student DVD with Data Files includes Review Questions and Supplementary Cases for this chapter.

CHAPTER SIX

AirCare Services

OBJECTIVES

After completing this chapter, you should be able to

- **enter** transactions in the General, Payables and Receivables journals
- **enter** and **post** cash, credit card and account sale transactions
- **enter** and **post** customer payment transactions
- **customize** journals and **preview** invoices
- **enter** transactions including GST and PST
- **store** and **recall** recurring entries
- **enter** customer discounts and partial payments
- **add** and **edit** customer accounts
- **reverse** receipts to enter NSF cheques from customers
- **edit** and **review** customer-related transactions
- **create** shortcuts for General and Payables transactions
- **display**, **print** and **graph** customer reports
- **understand** linked accounts for the Receivables Ledger

COMPANY INFORMATION

Company Profile

NOTES
Air Care Services
100 Belair Avenue, Unit 25
Winnipeg, MB R3T 0S3
Tel 1: (204) 456-1299
Tel 2: (888) 455-7194
Fax: (204) 456-3188
Business No.: 533 766 455

Air Care Services, located in Winnipeg, Manitoba, has been operating successfully for the past five years under the ownership and management of Simon Arturro. The company's range of services, related to heating equipment and air-conditioning units, draws on Arturro's experience with electrical, plumbing and chimney work. He has two occasional assistants.

Revenue comes from four sources: installation, repairs, service contracts and subcontracting. Air Care installs air-conditioning, gas fireplaces and heating equipment of all kinds. Because of recent increase in demand, Arturro became certified to install solar heating panels. Installation work may include adding air-filtration and air-cleaning units to existing heating systems and installing gas fireplaces in private homes, offices and funeral homes. Upgrades for furnaces and fireplaces often require replacing chimney liners and installing direct venting.

Product manufacturers pay Air Care for repairing equipment under warranty, and individual customers rely on Air Care for other repairs. Arturro also sells service contracts. And finally, Arturro handles installation subcontracts for large contractors.

Some customers — homeowners, owners of office buildings and companies that sell heating equipment and air conditioners — have accounts with Air Care and receive a 1 percent discount if they pay within 10 days. They are asked to settle their accounts in 30 days, paying by cash or by cheque. PST and GST apply to all service work completed by Air Care.

Accounts have been set up with a local hardware store, suppliers of chimney liners and parts for furnaces and air conditioners, and other regular suppliers.

After remitting all taxes before the end of April 2012, Arturro converted the accounts for Air Care using the following information:

- Chart of Accounts
- Post-Closing Trial Balance
- Supplier Information
- Customer Information
- Accounting Procedures

CHART OF POSTABLE ACCOUNTS

AIR CARE SERVICES

ASSETS
1080 Cash in Bank
1100 Credit Card Bank Account
1200 Accounts Receivable
1300 Air Conditioning Parts
1320 Furnace Parts
1340 Office Supplies
1420 Cash Register
1440 Computer System
1460 Service Equipment ▶

▶1480 Tools
1500 Van
1550 Shop

LIABILITIES
2100 Bank Loan
2200 Accounts Payable
2640 PST Payable
2650 GST Charged on Services
2670 GST Paid on Purchases ▶

▶2850 Mortgage Payable

EQUITY
3560 S. Arturro, Capital
3600 Net Income

REVENUE
4100 Installation Revenue
4120 Repairs Revenue
4140 Service Contract Revenue
4180 Sales Discounts ▶

▶**EXPENSE**
5100 Advertising and Promotion
5120 Bank Charges & Card Fees
5140 Interest Expense
5160 Hydro Expense
5180 Payroll Service Charges
5200 Purchase Discounts
5220 Telephone Expense
5240 Vehicle Expenses
5300 Wages

NOTES: The Chart of Accounts includes only postable accounts and the Net Income or Current Earnings account.

POST-CLOSING TRIAL BALANCE

AIR CARE SERVICES

April 30, 2012		Debits	Credits
1080	Cash in Bank	$ 14 660	
1100	Credit Card Bank Account	1 000	
1200	Accounts Receivable	4 140	
1300	Air Conditioning Parts	1 200	
1320	Furnace Parts	600	
1340	Office Supplies	400	
1420	Cash Register	500	
1440	Computer System	2 500	
1460	Service Equipment	10 000	
1480	Tools	3 000	
1500	Van	25 000	
1550	Shop	100 000	
2100	Bank Loan		$ 10 000
2200	Accounts Payable		4 200
2850	Mortgage Payable		80 000
3560	S. Arturro, Capital		68 800
		$163 000	$163 000

SUPPLIER INFORMATION

AIR CARE SERVICES

Supplier Name (Contact)	Address	Phone No. Fax No.	E-mail Web Site	Terms Tax ID
Beausejour Chimney Products (Janine Beausejour)	50 Fireplace Rd. Winnipeg, Manitoba R3F 2T2	Tel: (204) 476-5282 Fax: (204) 476-5110	jb@beausejour.com www.beausejour.com	1/15, n/30 444 276 534
Brandon Hardware (Nutley Bolter)	72 Hammer St. Winnipeg, Manitoba R4P 1B8	Tel: (204) 369-0808 Fax: (204) 369-6222	nbolter@yahoo.com	net 15 385 416 822
Killarney Solar Equipment (Kieper Warme)	91 Radiation St. Winnipeg, Manitoba R1B 4F4	Tel: (204) 363-0210 Fax: (204) 363-2000	kwarme@heatexchange.com	1/5, n/30 571 277 631
Manitoba Hydro (Kira Strong)	1 Power Station Rd. Winnipeg, Manitoba R6G 2C1	Tel: (204) 479-2999	kira.strong@mnhydro.man.ca www.mnhydro.man.ca	net 1
Manitoba Telephone (Sotto Voce)	4 Speakers Corners Winnipeg, Manitoba R1E 2K2	Tel: (204) 361-3255	www.manitobatel.ca	net 1
Starbuck Advertising Agency (Pam Fletts)	300 Flyer St. Winnipeg, Manitoba R3V 6S3	Tel: (204) 361-1727 Fax: (204) 361-8229	pfletts@saa.com www.saa.com	net 1 610 728 365
Steinbach Airconditioning Inc. (Ezra Steinbach)	2 Ventilate St. Winnipeg, Manitoba R2H 9J9	Tel: (204) 475-6432 Fax: (204) 475-8600	esteinb@steinair.com www.steinair.com	1/10, n/30 177 235 441
UPS Delivery (Bea Carrier)	8 Freight St. Winnipeg, Manitoba R3A 7B2	Tel 1: (204) 479-1UPS (1877) Tel 2: (800) 477-1UPS Fax: (204) 477-6000	www.ups.com	net 1 522 534 677
Willow Garage (Axel Rodd)	699 Willow St. Winnipeg, Manitoba R2P 1B3	Tel: (204) 368-6444 Fax: (204) 368-6000	axel@wefixcars.com www.wefixcars.com	net 30 129 732 010

OUTSTANDING SUPPLIER INVOICES

AIR CARE SERVICES

Supplier Name	Terms	Date	Invoice No.	Amount	Total
Beausejour Chimney Products	1/15, n/30	Apr. 21/12	B-894	$1 600	$1 600
Steinbach Airconditioning Inc.	1/10, n/30	Apr. 27/12	SA-2141	$1 500	$1 500
Willow Garage	net 30	Apr. 10/12	W-1142	$1 100	$1 100
			Grand Total		$4 200

CUSTOMER INFORMATION

AIR CARE SERVICES

Customer Name (Contact)	Address	Phone No. Fax No.	E-mail Web Site	Terms Credit Limit
Brandon School Board (Ed Ducate)	49 Trainer St. Winnipeg, Manitoba R3P 2T5	Tel 1: (204) 466-5000 Tel 2: (204) 466-1123 Fax: (204) 466-2000	Ed.D@bsb.com www.bsb.com	1/10, n/30 $2 500
Grande Pointe Towers (Sophie Grande)	77 LaPointe Cr. Winnipeg, Manitoba R2G 4D1	Tel: (204) 322-7500 Fax: (204) 322-7436	sgrande@GPTowers.com www.GPTowers.com	1/10, n/30 $3 000
Midwestern Funeral Home (N. Mourning)	8 Quiet St. Winnipeg, Manitoba R7B 1E1	Tel: (204) 763-WAKE (9253) Fax: (204) 762-9301	nm@midwestfh.com www.midwestfh.com	C.O.D. (net 1) $2 000

Customer Name (Contact)	Address	Phone No. Fax No.	E-mail Web Site	Terms Credit Limit
Oak Bluff Banquet Hall (Ann Oakley)	4 Celebration Ave. Winnipeg, Manitoba R8V 3H7	Tel: (204) 622-7391 Fax: (204) 622-7900	annie@OBBH.com www.OBBH.com	1/10, n/30 $5 000
Selkirk Furnaces Inc. (Elsa Selkirk)	588 Heater St. Winnipeg, Manitoba R3T 8N1	Tel: (204) 368-4575 Fax: (204) 368-2198	elsas@selkirk.com www.selkirk.com	1/10, n/30 $5 000

OUTSTANDING CUSTOMER INVOICES

AIR CARE SERVICES

Customer Name	Terms	Date	Inv/Chq No.	Amount	Total
Grande Pointe Towers	1/10, n/30	Apr. 25/12	A-696	$1 380	
		Apr. 25/12	Chq #3166	700	
		Apr. 26/12	A-698	700	
			Balance owing		$1 380
Oak Bluff Banquet Hall	1/10, n/30	Apr. 28/12	A-700	$1 140	
		Apr. 30/12	A-702	1 620	
			Balance owing		$2 760
			Grand Total		$4 140

Accounting Procedures

Open-Invoice Accounting for Receivables

The open-invoice method of accounting for invoices issued by a business allows the business to keep track of each individual invoice and of any partial payments made against it. In contrast, other methods keep track only of the outstanding balance by combining all invoice balances owed by a customer. Simply Accounting uses the open-invoice method. Fully paid invoices can be removed (cleared) periodically.

Discounts for Early Payments

Air Care offers discounts to some regular customers if they pay their accounts within 10 days. Full payment is expected in 30 days. Customers who pay by cheque or by credit card do not receive discounts. No discounts are allowed on partial payments.

Some suppliers with whom Air Care has accounts set up also offer discounts for early payments.

NSF Cheques

If a cheque is deposited from an account that does not have enough money to cover it, the bank may return it to the depositor as NSF (non-sufficient funds). The NSF cheque from a customer requires a reversing entry in the Receipts Journal. Simply Accounting can complete these reversals automatically. (See Keystrokes, page 184.) In most companies, the accounting department notifies the customer who wrote the NSF cheque to explain that the debt remains unpaid. Many companies charge an additional fee to the customer to recover their bank charges for the NSF cheque. A separate sales invoice should be prepared for the additional charge. NSF cheques to suppliers are handled in the same way, through reversing entries in the Payments Journal.

Taxes (GST and PST)

Air Care Services is a contracting service business using the regular method of calculating GST. GST, at the rate of 5 percent, charged and collected from customers will be recorded as a liability in *GST Charged on Services*. GST paid to suppliers will be recorded in *GST Paid on Purchases* as a decrease in tax liability. The balance owing, the difference between the GST charged and GST paid, or the request for a refund will be remitted to the Receiver General for Canada quarterly.

Air Care charges customers 7 percent PST on all sales and pays PST on some goods. Air Care is exempt from PST for purchases of items that are sold or used in service work because the customer pays PST on these products.

Cash and Credit Card Sales of Services

Cash and credit card transactions are a normal occurrence in most businesses. Simply Accounting has Paid By options to handle these transactions. When you choose the correct Paid By method, the program will debit *Cash in Bank* or *Credit Card Bank Account* instead of the *Accounts Receivable* control account. (See Keystrokes, page 177 and page 187.)

INSTRUCTIONS

1. **Record entries for the source documents** in Simply Accounting using all the information provided for Air Care Services. The procedures for entering each new type of transaction in this application are outlined step by step in the Keystrokes section following the source documents. These transactions are indicated with a ✓ in the completion box beside the source document. The page on which the relevant keystrokes begin is printed immediately below the check box.

2. **Print** the **reports and graphs** indicated on the following printing form after you have finished making your entries. Instructions for reports begin on page 191.

REPORTS

Accounts
- ☐ Chart of Accounts
- ☐ Account List
- ☐ General Journal Entries

Financials
- ☑ Balance Sheet: May 31
- ☑ Income Statement from May 1 to May 31
- ☑ Trial Balance date: May 31
- ☑ All Journal Entries: May 1 to May 31
- ☑ General Ledger accounts: 1300 4120 4140 from May 1 to May 31
- ☐ Statement of Cash Flows
- ☑ Cash Flow Projection Detail Report for account 1080 for 30 days

Taxes
- ☑ GST Report May 31
- ☑ PST Report May 31

Banking
- ☐ Cheque Log Report

Payables
- ☐ Supplier List
- ☐ Supplier Aged
- ☐ Aged Overdue Payables
- ☐ Purchase Journal Entries
- ☐ Payment Journal Entries

Receivables
- ☐ Customer List
- ☑ Customer Aged Detail for all customers
- ☐ Aged Overdue Receivables
- ☑ Sales Journal Entries: May 1 to May 31
- ☑ Receipt Journal Entries: May 1 to May 31
- ☐ Customer Statements

Mailing Labels
- ☐ Labels

Management Reports
- ☐ Ledger

GRAPHS
- ☐ Payables by Aging Period
- ☐ Payables by Supplier
- ☐ Receivables by Aging Period
- ☐ Receivables by Customer
- ☑ Sales vs Receivables
- ☑ Receivables Due vs Payables Due
- ☑ Revenues by Account
- ☐ Expenses by Account
- ☑ Expenses and Net Profit as % of Revenue

setup / petty / Company / forms / 9584

SOURCE DOCUMENTS

SESSION DATE — MAY 8, 2012

☑ **Sales Invoice #A-710** *S.J., Pay later* **Dated May 1/12**

166 To Selkirk Furnaces Inc., $800 plus $40 GST and $56 PST for subcontracting work on apartment air-conditioning system. Invoice total, $896. Terms: 1/10, n/30. Create new Group account 4160 Subcontracting Revenue. Customize the sales invoice by removing the columns that are not used by Air Care Services.

☑ **Cash Receipt #20** *R.J.* **Dated May 2/12**

173 From Grande Pointe Towers, cheque #3499 for $866.20, including $666.20 in full payment of invoice #A-696 and $200 in partial payment of invoice #A-698, including $13.80 discount for early payment. Customize the journal by changing the tabbing order.

☑ **Cash Sales Invoice #A-711** *S.J. → cheque* **Dated May 3/12**

177 To Midwestern Funeral Home, $900 plus $45 GST and $63 PST for installation of air-conditioning equipment. Terms: Cash on completion of work. Received cheque #395 for $1 008 in full payment.

☑ **Sales Invoice #A-712** *S.J., Pay later* **Dated May 3/12**

179 To Hazel Estates (use Full Add for the new customer), $1 600 plus $80 GST and $112 PST for installation of new furnace equipment. Invoice total $1 792. Terms: 1/10, n/30.

Adjust receipt → Include Fully paid bills / deposit

☑ **Bank Debit Memo #14321** **Dated May 4/12**

184 From Flatlands Credit Union, cheque #3499 for $866.20 from Grand Pointe Towers has been returned because of non-sufficient funds. Reverse the payment and notify the customer of the outstanding charges.

☑ **Memo #1** **Dated May 5/12**

186 From Owner: Edit the ledger record for Grande Pointe Towers to change the payment terms to net 1. Certified cheques will be requested in the future. Edit the records for all other customers to set the credit limit at $4 000.

☑ **Credit Card Sales Invoice #A-713** **Dated May 5/12**

187 Sales Summary *set up an CC sale A/c*
To various one-time customers *posted at one-time customer as textbook*

Repairs Revenue	$ 600
Service Contract Revenue	800
GST charged	70
PST charged	98
Total deposited to credit card bank account	$1 568

Adjust a Bill   don't change the date

☑ **Memo #2** **Dated May 5/12**

189 From Owner: The work done for Hazel Estates included $800 plus $40 GST and $56 PST for repairs to the heating system. The revised and correct invoice total is $2 688. Adjust the posted entry (reference invoice #A-712).

☑ **Memo #3** **Dated May 5/12**

190 Create shortcuts for tasks and transactions in other modules.

☐ **Cheque Copy #101** **Dated May 5/12**

To Beausejour Chimney Products, $1 584 in payment of account, including $16 discount for early payment. Reference invoice #B-894.

NOTES

☑ Hazel Estates
(contact Joelle Beausoleil)
179 488 Sunshine St., Ste 1200
West St. Paul, MB R4G 5H3
Tel 1: (204) 367-7611
Tel 2: (877) 367-9000
Fax: (204) 369-2191
E-mail: JB@hazelestates.com
Web: www.hazelestates.com
Terms: 1/10, n/30
Revenue account: 4100
Tax code: GP
Credit limit: $4 000

NOTES

Choose One-Time Customer and enter Sales Summary in the Address field.
Use tax code GP for the Cash Sales.
If you want, you can store the credit card sale as a weekly transaction. When you recall it, you can edit the amounts and accounts. Refer to page 187.

☐ **Purchase Invoice #W-1993**   **Dated May 6/12**

From Willow Garage, $60 for gasoline, including taxes (use tax code IN) for weekly fill-up of van. Store the transaction as a weekly recurring entry. Terms: net 30.

☐ **Purchase Invoice #SA-2309**   **Dated May 6/12**

From Steinbach Airconditioning, $400 plus $20 GST. Invoice total $420 for air-conditioning parts, filters, coils, etc. Terms: 1/10, n/30. Store as a bi-weekly recurring transaction.

☐ **Sales Invoice #A-714**   **Dated May 7/12**

To Brandon School Board, $500 plus $25 GST and $35 PST for installation of new pipes on school furnace. Invoice total $560. Terms: 1/10, n/30.

☐ **Cheque Copy #102**   **Dated May 7/12**

To Steinbach Airconditioning, $1 485 in payment of account, including $15 discount for early payment. Reference invoice #SA-2141.

☐ **Cheque Copy #103**   **Dated May 8/12**

To Willow Garage, $1 100 in payment of account. Reference invoice #W-1142.

☐ **Purchase Invoice #BH-42001**   **Dated May 8/12**

From Brandon Hardware, $500 plus $25 GST and $35 PST for new ladders and tools. Invoice total $560. Terms: net 15.

☐ **Sales Invoice #A-715**   **Dated May 8/12**

To Vinod Residence (use Full Add for the new customer), $400 plus $20 GST and $28 PST for repairs. Invoice total $448. Terms: 1/10, n/30.

SESSION DATE – MAY 15, 2012

☐ **Bank Credit Memo #21432**   **Dated May 9/12**

From Flatlands Credit Union, $3 000 loan for new service equipment approved and deposited to bank account. Principal of six-month loan and interest at 6.5 percent to be paid in full at the end of six months.

☐ **Cash Receipt #21**   **Dated May 9/12**

From Oak Bluff Banquet Hall, cheque #2995 for $1 900, including $1 140 in full payment of invoice #A-700 and $760 in partial payment of invoice #A-702.

☐ **Sales Invoice #A-716**   **Dated May 9/12**

To Selkirk Furnaces Inc., $1 200 plus $60 GST and $84 PST for subcontracting work. Invoice total $1 344. Terms: 1/10, n/30.

☐ **Cash Receipt #22**   **Dated May 10/12**

From Selkirk Furnaces Inc., cheque #533 for $887.04 in payment of account, including $8.96 discount for early payment. Reference invoice #A-710.

☐ **Cash Receipt #23**   **Dated May 11/12**

From Hazel Estates, cheque #230 for $2 661.12 in full payment of account, including $26.88 discount for early payment. Reference invoice #A-712.

☐ **Cash Receipt #24**   **Dated May 12/12**

From Vinod Residence, cheque #432 for $443.52 in payment of account, including $4.48 discount for early payment. Reference invoice #A-715.

WARNING!
Do not include the discount for the second invoice in the payment to Steinbach.

NOTES
☐ Vinod Residence (contact Viran Vinod)
56 House St.
Winnipeg, MB R2P 8K1
Tel: (204) 761-8114
E-mail: v.vinod@interlog.com
Terms: 1/10, n/30
Revenue account: 4120
Tax code: GP
Credit limit: $2 000

WARNING!
Do not include the discount for the second invoice in the receipt from Oak Bluffs Banquet Hall.

NOTES
Remember to change the amounts if you recall the sales summary.

☑ **Credit Card Sales Invoice #A-717**   **Dated May 12/12**

191   Sales Summary
        To various one-time customers
        Repairs Revenue $ 500
        Service Contracts   600
        GST charged   55
        PST charged   77
        Total deposited to credit card bank account $1 232

☐ **Purchase Invoice #W-2356**   **Dated May 13/12**

From Willow Garage, $60 for gasoline, including taxes (use tax code IN) for weekly fill-up of van. Terms: net 30 days. Recall stored entry.

Pmt J →make other paymt →by cheque

☐ **Cash Purchase Invoice #UPS-3467**   **Dated May 15/12**

From UPS Delivery, $60 for special delivery of air-conditioner parts plus $3 GST. Invoice total $63. Issued cheque #104 in full payment. Create new Group account 5130 Delivery Expenses. Edit the supplier record to add the new expense account as the default expense account.

NOTES
Click the View Suppliers shortcut to open the Suppliers window. Double click UPS Delivery to open the ledger record. Refer to page 142 if you need help with editing a supplier record.

☐ **Cash Receipt #25**   **Dated May 15/12**

From Grande Pointe Towers, certified cheque #3682 for $1 380 in payment of account. Reference invoices #A-696 and A-698.

SESSION DATE — MAY 22, 2012

☐

AirCare Services
www.aircare.com

100 Belair Avenue, Unit 25
Winnipeg, MB R3T 0S3
Phone: (204) 456-1299   Toll free: (888) 455-7194   Fax: (204) 456-3188

	Invoice:	A-718
Date:	May 18, 2012
Sold to:	Oak Bluff Banquet Hall (Ann Oakley) 4 Celebration Ave. Winnipeg, MB R8V 3H7

Description	Tax Code	Amount
Air-conditioning installation	GP	2 000.00
Repairs to solar panels	GP	1 000.00

Authorization to exceed credit limit: Simon Antunova

We guarantee our work.

Payment Terms: 1/10, net 30	Customer Initials AO	GST	150.00
GST #533 766 455		PST	210.00
		TOTAL	3 360.00

☐ **Bank Debit Memo #37191**   **Dated May 18/12**

From Flatlands Credit Union, cheque #432 for $443.52 from Vinod Residence has been returned because of non-sufficient funds. Reverse the payment and notify the customer of the outstanding charges.   *show correction*

☐ **Memo #4**   **Dated May 18/12**

Edit the ledger record for Vinod Residence to set the credit limit to zero and terms to net 1. The customer will be placed on cash-only terms.

☐ **Cash Receipt #26**   **Dated May 19/12**

From Selkirk Furnaces Inc., cheque #586 for $1 330.56 in payment of account, including $13.44 discount for early payment. Reference invoice #A-716.

☐

AirCare Services
www.aircare.com

Invoice:	A-719
Date:	May 19, 2012
Sold to:	Sales Summary

100 Belair Avenue, Unit 25
Winnipeg, MB R3T 0S3
Phone: (204) 456 1299   Toll free: (888) 455-7194   Fax: (204) 456-3188

Description	Tax Code	Amount
Repairs	GP	600.00
Service Contracts	GP	400.00

Deposited to credit card bank account
May 19/12

Thank you.

Payment Terms: Credit Card	Customer Initials	GST	50.00
		PST	70.00
Business No.: 533 766 455		TOTAL	1 120.00

NOTES
Remember to change the amount if you recall the sales summary.

☐ **Purchase Invoice #W-2893**   **Dated May 20/12**

From Willow Garage, $75 for gasoline, including taxes for weekly fill-up of van. Terms: net 30 days. Recall the stored entry, edit the amount and save the changed entry.

☐ **Purchase Invoice #SA-2579**   **Dated May 20/12**

From Steinbach Airconditioning, $400 plus $20 GST for air-conditioning parts and filters, etc. Invoice total $420. Terms: 1/10, n/30. Recall stored entry.

☐ **Cheque Copy #105**   **Dated May 21/12**

To Brandon Hardware, $560 in payment of account. Reference invoice #BH-42001.

☐ **Cash Purchase Invoice #SAA-1098**   **Dated May 21/12**

From Starbuck Advertising Agency, $1 100 plus $55 GST and $77 PST for brochures and flyers. Invoice total, $1 232. Paid by cheque #106.

Vinod Residence
56 House St.
Winnipeg, MB R2P 8K1

No: 432

Date 2 0 1 2 0 5 2 2
Y Y Y Y M M D D

Pay to the order of Air Care Services $ 448.00

———————— Four hundred forty-eight dollars ———————— 00/100 **Dollars**

F **Flatlands Credit Union**
389 Prairie Blvd.
Winnipeg MB R2P 1B6

Vivian Vinod
Signature

⑈⸺⸺ 92999 ⸺⸺ ⑈ 16883 432

- -

Re: pay invoice #A-715 $448.00   No: 432
CERTIFIED Cheque replaces NSF cheque (receipt #27)   May 22, 2012

NOTES
Staples Business Depot
Expense account: 1340
Tax code: GP
Leave the remaining fields blank.

Cash Purchase Invoice #BD-4821   **Dated May 22/12**

From Staples Business Depot (use Full Add for the new supplier), $140 plus $7.00 GST and $9.80 PST for stationery and office supplies. Invoice total, $156.80. Paid by cheque #107.

Sales Invoice #A-720   **Dated May 22/12**

To Grande Pointe Towers, $2 400 plus $120 GST and $168 PST for installation of new solar heating panel. Invoice total, $2 688. Terms: net 1.

Cash Purchase Invoice #MH-44371   **Dated May 22/12**

From Manitoba Hydro, $400 plus $20 GST for two months of hydro service. Invoice total, $420. Paid by cheque #108.

SESSION DATE — MAY 31, 2012

Purchase Invoice #KE-679   **Dated May 24/12**

From Killarney Solar Equipment, $3 000 plus $150 GST and $210 PST for new service equipment. Invoice total, $3 360. Terms: 1/5, n/30.

Cash Purchase Invoice #BD-6113   **Dated May 25/12**

From Staples Business Depot, $40 plus $2.00 GST and $2.80 PST for stationery and other office supplies. Invoice total, $44.80. Paid by cheque #109.

Cash Purchase Invoice #MT-36128   **Dated May 25/12**

From Manitoba Telephone, $130 plus $6.50 GST and $9.10 PST for telephone and Internet service. Invoice total, $145.60. Paid by cheque #110.

NOTES
When you use Quick Add, you can type the address in the Shipping Address field so that it will appear on the printed invoice. The new customer's name appears in the Customer and Shipping Address fields.

Sales Invoice #A-721   **Dated May 26/12**

To Felicia Mountbatten (use Quick Add for the new customer), $1 600 plus $80 GST and $112 PST for installation services. Invoice total $1 792. Terms: net 1.

Sales Invoice #A-722   **Dated May 26/12**

To Midwestern Funeral Home, $1 000 plus $50 GST and $70 PST for repair work on solar heating system. Invoice total $1 120. Terms: 1/10, n/30. Remember to edit the terms for the invoice.

Grande Pointe Towers
77 LaPointe Cr.
Winnipeg, MB R2G 4D1
Tel: (204) 322-7500

F **Flatlands Credit Union**
389 Prairie Blvd.
Winnipeg MN R2P 1B6

No: 4543

Date [2][0][1][2][0][5][2][6]
Y Y Y Y M M D D

Pay — Two thousand six hundred eighty-eight dollars — 00 $ 2,688.00

TO THE
ORDER
OF

Air Care Services
100 Belair Ave. Unit 25
Winnipeg, MB R3T 0S3

PER *Sophie Grande*

⑈⠀⠀92999⠀⠀46771 4543

Re: pay invoice #A-720 $2,688.00   No: 4543
  (receipt #28)   May 26, 2012

Credit Card Sales Invoice #A-723   Dated May 26/12

Sales Summary
To various one-time customers

Repairs Revenue	$400
Installation Revenue	400
GST charged	40
PST charged	56
Total deposited to credit card bank account	$896

NOTES
Remember to change the account as well as the amounts if you recall the sales summary.

Cheque Copy #111   Dated May 28/12

To Killarney Solar Equipment, $3 326.40 in payment of account, including $33.60 discount for early payment. Reference invoice #KE-679.

Bank Debit Memo #55131   Dated May 30/12

From Flatlands Credit Union, pre-authorized monthly payroll for employees

Wages and payroll expenses	$4 000
Payroll services fee	100
GST paid on payroll service	5
Total withdrawal	$4 105

NOTES
Enter the payroll transaction in the General Journal.
Remember to add the sales tax details for GST Paid on Purchases.

Memo #5   Dated May 31/12

From Owner: Create three new Group expense accounts for supplies used during the month: 5125 Air Conditioning Parts Used
      5135 Furnace Parts Used
      5165 Office Supplies Used

Enter adjustments for supplies used: Air Conditioning Parts	$600
Furnace Parts	350
Office Supplies	200

Bank Debit Memo #56159   Dated May 31/12

From Flatlands Credit Union, pre-authorized withdrawals for service charges, mortgage and loan payments

Bank charges, including NSF cheques	$ 80
Interest expense	900
Loan principal repayment	1 000
Mortgage principal repayment	200

KEYSTROKES

Opening Data Files

NOTES
If you are using backup files, restore SimData10\aircare1.CAB to SimData10\Aircare\aircare. Refer to the instructions for restoring data files in Chapter 1, page 20, if you need assistance.

Open   the data file **SimData10\Aircare\aircare** to access the data files for Air Care Services.

Type   May 8 2012 to enter the first session date.

Click   **OK** to see the following warning statement:

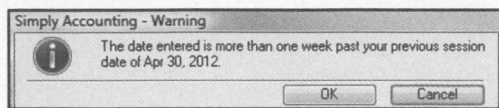

This warning appears whenever you advance the session date by more than one week. Normally a business would update its accounting records more frequently. If you have entered the correct date,

Click   **OK** to accept the date entered and display the Home window.

The Payroll, Inventory and Project ledger names do not appear in the Modules pane list. These ledgers are hidden because they are not set up.

Accounting for Sales

Sales are entered in the Sales Journal indicated by the Bills icon in the Receivables module Home window:

Bills ▼

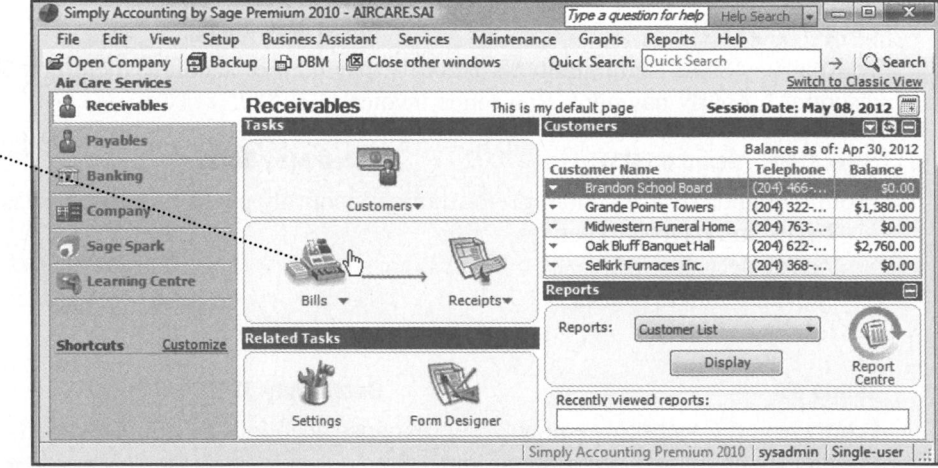

You can enter sales from the Bills icon in the Receivables window. The Bills label is used for Construction/Contracting companies. For other company types, the label for this icon may be Sales, Invoices, Sales Invoices, Customer Invoices, Client Invoices, Statements or Charges. The icon itself does not change.

Click   the **Bills icon** to open the Sales Journal input form:

PRO VERSION
pro Icon labels are the same for all company types.
Click the Sales Invoices icon

 to open the Sales Journal. In the Pro Classic view, this icon is labelled Sales.

CLASSIC VIEW
Click the Sales icon

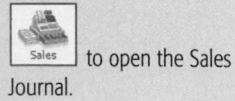 to open the Sales Journal.

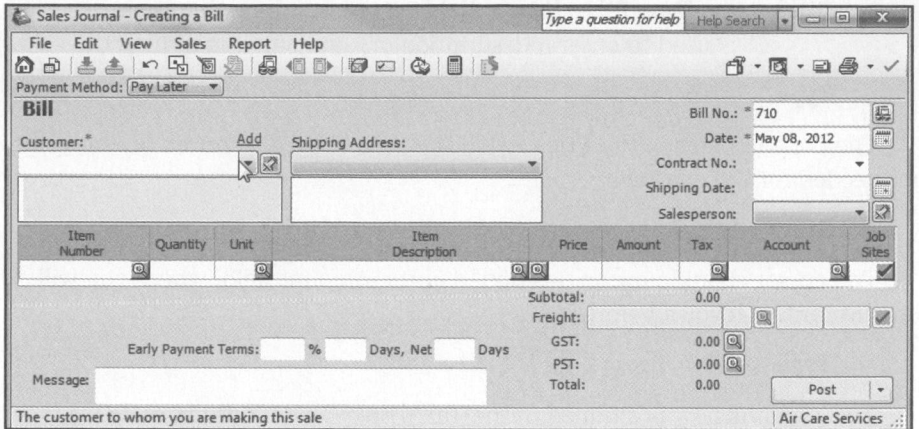

Most tool bar buttons in the Sales Journal are familiar from other journals — Home window, Daily Business Manager, Store, Recall, Undo, Customize Journal, Calculator and Allocate. Print and E-mail buttons allow you to print or e-mail the invoice before posting to provide a customer or store copy of the sales invoice. You can also use tool buttons to preview an invoice, change print settings and to adjust or reverse a posted invoice. The tools for Invoice Lookup, Additional Information, Track Shipments and Add Time Slip Activities will be explained in later applications

Pay Later is correctly selected as the payment option for this regular sale.

> **Click** the **Customer field list arrow** to obtain the list of customers as shown on the following screen:

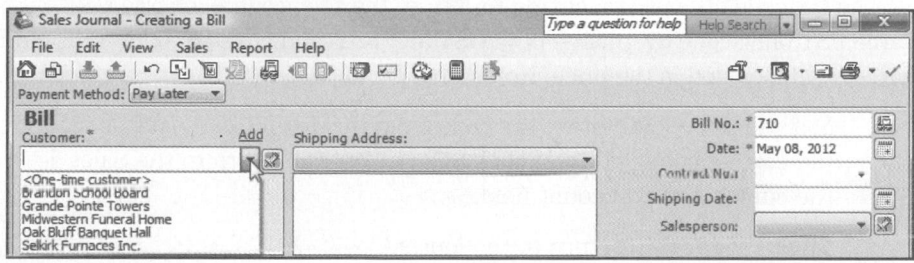

> **Click** **Selkirk Furnaces Inc.**, the customer in the first source document, to select and enter it.

Notice that the customer's name and address have been added to your input form. If you have made an error in your selection, click the customer list arrow and start again. By default, the Customer and the Shipping Address fields are completed from the customer's ledger record. You can edit the shipping address if necessary. If you have selected the correct customer, you can skip over the shipping information.

The invoice number (Bill No. field), 710, the numeric portion, is entered and correct. It is updated automatically by the program. The payment terms and tax code for the customer have also been entered. When a default revenue account is entered in the customer's record, it will also be included on the invoice form.

The session date appears by default so you need to change it. Enter the date on which the transaction took place, May 1, 2012.

> **Click** the **Date field Calendar icon** 🗓.

> **Click** **1**

If you want, you can enter a quantity (one for the service, in this case) and a price per unit in the Price field and let the program calculate the amount by multiplying the two together. You can use this method if you are selling more than one item that is not an inventory item.

NOTES
You can also press (tab) repeatedly to move to any field you need.

NOTES
Entering a negative amount in the Amount field will generate a debit entry for the sale with a credit to Accounts Receivable.

NOTES
PST is usually charged on services, such as repairs, that are applied to goods that are themselves taxable for PST.

NOTES
When you select a tax code from the selection list, the cursor advances to the next invoice field. When you choose Cancel, the cursor does not move to the next field.

NOTES
You can choose any postable account as the default revenue account for customers just as you can use any account as the default expense account for suppliers.

NOTES
Because Add An Account is already selected, pressing (enter) will choose it.

Click   the **Item Description field** on the first line. The Item Description field is used to enter a description or comment concerning the sale.

Type   subcontracting - apartment building **Press** (tab).

The cursor is now in the Price field. The Price field also refers to unit prices; it is not needed for the contract.

Press   (tab).

The cursor should now be positioned in the Amount field, where you will enter the amount for this invoice before taxes.

Type   800 **Press** (tab).

The cursor is now positioned in the Tax field. The default tax code for the customer, GP, is entered from the customer record details in the data files and it is correct. Customers pay both GST and PST on services. The invoice subtotal and total have been updated.

Press   (enter) to see the tax code descriptions set up for Air Care Services:

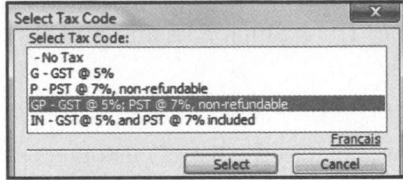

The tax code options are: charge **No Tax** on the sale; code **G**, charge GST only; code **P**, charge PST only; code **GP**, charge both GST and PST; and code **IN**, both GST and PST are charged and included in the price. Notice that PST is described as non-refundable.

You can select a different tax code from this list if the default is incorrect. Click the correct code and then click Select. You will return to the Sales Journal with the cursor in the Account field.

Click   **Cancel** to return to the journal.

Press   (tab) to advance to the Account field.

The Account field in a sales invoice refers to the credit portion of the journal entry, usually a revenue account. Again, you cannot access *Accounts Receivable*, the linked account, directly. The software will automatically debit the *Accounts Receivable* control account in the General Ledger when you enter positive amounts.

You may set up a default revenue account for customers, just as you set up default expense accounts for suppliers. Because Air Care customers use more than one revenue account, we have not entered default accounts for them. In the Account field, you can choose an account from the list of accounts or create a new account, just like any other account field. We need to create a new revenue account for this sale.

Type   4160 **Press** (enter).

Press   (enter) to open the Add An Account wizard (Add An Account is selected).

Press   (tab).

Type   Subcontracting Revenue as the **account name** and **accept** the remaining **defaults**. **Click Finish** to return to the journal.

The account number is added to the journal.

Press   (tab) to advance the cursor to line 2 in the Item field, ready for additional sale items if necessary.

The Message field can be used in two ways: you can set up a default comment for the business that appears on all invoices, or you can enter a comment at the time of the sale. You can add to or change a default comment if you want. We will add a comment.

Click the **Message field**.

Type We guarantee our work.

The payment terms have been set up as defaults for customers as 1 percent discount in 10 days with net payment due in 30 days. You can change terms for individual customers or sales invoices.

Click the **List icon beside the GST** or the **PST amount field** to see the detailed summary of taxes included in the sale:

Total Tax Summary	
View	
Tax amounts that are not included in the price can be changed as needed.	
Invoice Subtotal: $800.00 (includes freight)	
Tax	**Amount**
GST	40.00
PST	56.00
Total Taxes:	96.00
OK	Cancel

Close the **Tax Summary window** to return to the invoice.

The transaction is now complete, and your invoice should resemble the following:

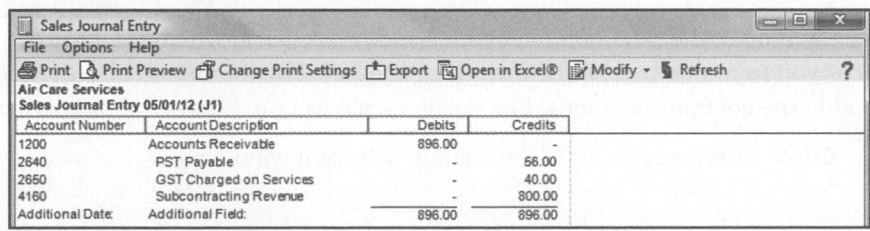

Before storing, posting or printing a sales journal entry, review it carefully.

Reviewing the Sales Journal Entry

Choose the **Report menu** and **click Display Sales Journal Entry** to display the transaction:

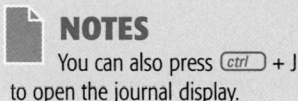

Account Number	Account Description	Debits	Credits
1200	Accounts Receivable	896.00	-
2640	PST Payable	-	56.00
2650	GST Charged on Services	-	40.00
4160	Subcontracting Revenue	-	800.00
Additional Date:	Additional Field:	896.00	896.00

Review the **journal entry** to check for mistakes.

You can see that *Accounts Receivable*, the control account, has been updated automatically by the Simply Accounting program because the Receivables and General

NOTES
Payment terms can be modified for individual customers in the Receivables Ledger. You can also edit the terms for individual sales in the Sales Journal.

NOTES
If necessary, such as for rounding errors, you can edit the tax amounts on the Tax Summary screen.

NOTES
You can also press ⌃ctrl + J to open the journal display.

ledgers are fully integrated. All credit sales are debited to *Accounts Receivable*, the default linked account for the Receivables Ledger. *GST Charged on Services* has also been updated correctly because of the tax code you entered and because *GST Charged on Services* was defined as the GST linked account for sales. Similarly, *PST Payable* is defined as the linked account for PST collected from customers and it too is updated correctly because of the tax code. You did not need to enter any of these accounts directly in the Sales Journal. The balance owing by this customer is also directly updated as a result of the Sales Journal entry.

Close the **display** to return to the Sales Journal input screen.

CORRECTING THE SALES JOURNAL ENTRY BEFORE POSTING

Move to the field that has the error. **Press** ⬚tab⬚ to move forward through the fields or **press** ⬚shift⬚ and ⬚tab⬚ together to move back to a previous field. This will highlight the field information so you can change it. **Type** the **correct information** and **press** ⬚tab⬚ to enter it.

You can also use the mouse to **point** to a field and **drag** through the **incorrect information** to highlight it. **Type** the **correct information** and **press** ⬚tab⬚ to enter it.

If the customer is incorrect, **reselect** from the **Customer** list by **clicking** the **Customer list arrow**. **Click** the name of the **correct customer**.

Click an **incorrect amount** or description to highlight it. Then **type** the **correct information** and **press** ⬚tab⬚ to enter the change.

To correct an account number or tax code, **click** the **Account List icon** to display the selection list. **Click** the **correct entry** to highlight it, then **click Select** and **press** ⬚tab⬚ to enter the change.

To insert a line or remove a line, **click** the **line** that you need to move. **Choose** the **Edit menu** and **click Insert Line** and **type** the new line or **click Remove Line** to delete a line.

To discard the entry and begin again, **click** ⬚X⬚ **(Close)** to close the journal or **click** ⬚↺⬚ **(Undo)** on the tool bar to open a blank journal window. When Simply Accounting asks whether you want to discard the entry, **click Yes** to confirm your decision.

Customizing the Sales Invoice

The sales invoice includes a number of fields/columns that we do not need. Before saving the invoice, we will customize it to remove the unnecessary columns.

Click the **Customize Journal tool** ⬚🔳⬚ or **choose** the **View menu** and **click Customize Journal** to open the Settings options for Sales Invoices:

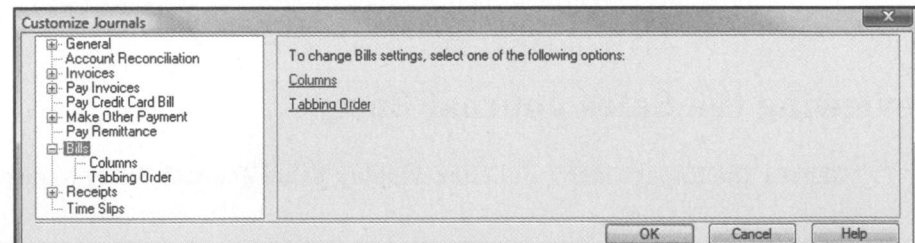

We can modify the selection of columns and the order in which the tab key advances you from one part of the invoice to another. For the Bills (Sales Invoices), we will modify the column selections. For Receipts, we will modify the tabbing order.

Click **Columns** to open the column selection window:

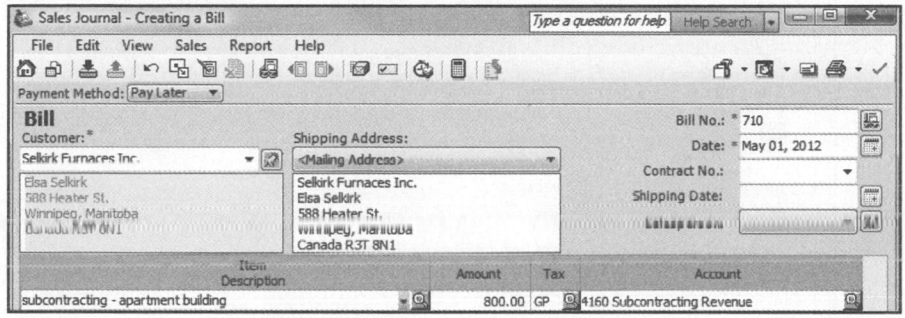

The Premium version has three predefined invoice styles for different business types built in. Each style displays a different combination of columns. The Standard Style, the default, includes all columns. The Standard and Retail styles include columns for inventory and orders while the Professional style does not. The Tax Code, Account, Description and Job Site columns are common to all styles.

We can remove or hide most of the fields to match the Professional Style (refer to sidebar Warning). The columns we can remove are listed under the For Standard Style, Do Not Show These Columns heading. We can remove additional columns by clicking check boxes to add ✓s. The Form Options button accesses printer setup options for the forms. Modifying printed forms is covered in Appendix G on the Student DVD.

Click   the **check boxes** for **Item Number**, **Quantity Shipped**, **Price**, **Unit** and **Job Site**.

Click   **OK** to return to the modified journal:

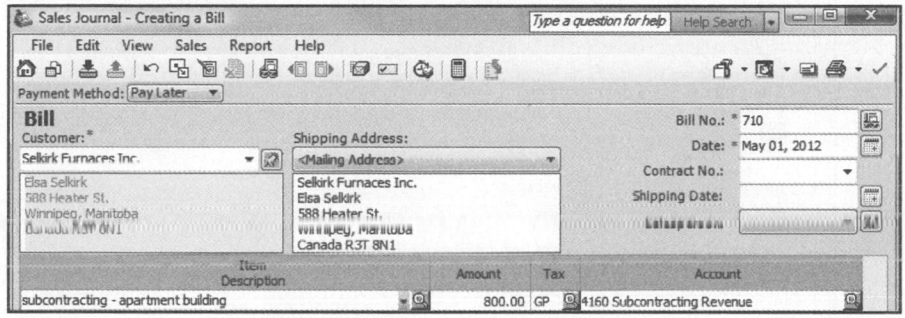

You can adjust the column spacing by dragging the column headings to change the size of columns and display all the information in all fields.

Point to the column heading margin. When the arrow changes to ◄══► (a double-headed arrow), drag the margin to its new location or size. Dragging the right column margin to the left until it overlaps the next column will remove that column. You can restore missing columns from the Customize Journal window.

Now when we press the (tab) key for the invoice details, the cursor will advance to the next field, and it will be one we use for the sale.

Previewing Invoices

Before printing and posting the invoice, you can preview it from the Preview tool 🔲 . You can preview the invoice or, if you have the packing slip details, you can preview the packing slip (an invoice with shipping and item details and without prices.

Click   the **list arrow** beside the Preview tool 🔲 to see these options:

NOTES
Customizing the journal does not change the printed invoice. Refer to Appendix G on the Student DVD to learn how to customize printed invoices and other forms.

Click **Print Preview For Bill** to see a copy of your bill:

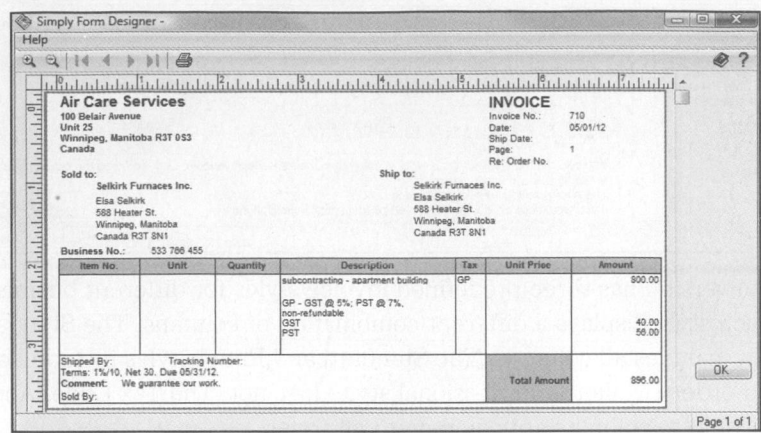

If your print forms are not correct for previewing, you will see this error message:

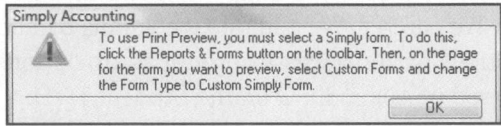

Click OK to return to the invoice. Click 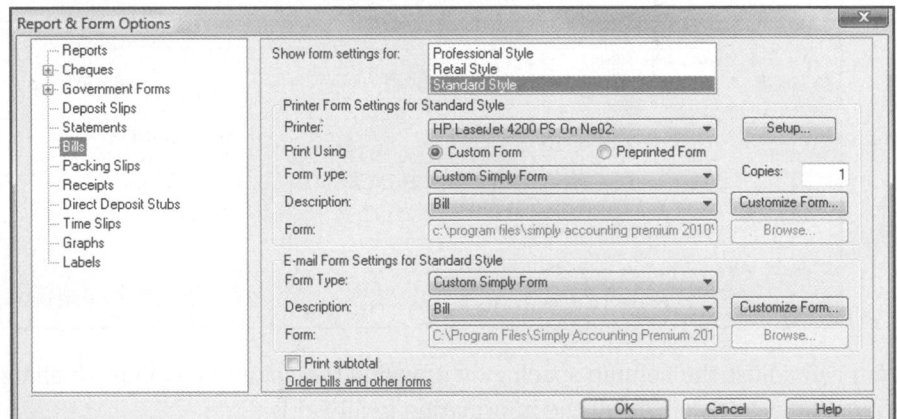 Change The Default Printer Settings tool to open the forms settings screen for customer invoices or bills:

WARNING!
The file locations in the Form fields (for Printer and E-mail) must be correct for your setup or you will receive an error message. If you select a generic Description (Bill or Invoice) the form reference will be dimmed and you will not have an error message.

You must choose Custom Form as the Print Using option and Custom Simply Form as the Form Type. Click OK. You should now be able to preview the invoice.

Click **OK** to close the preview. You can now print the invoice if you want.

Posting

When you are certain that you have entered the transaction correctly, you must post it. Notice that the Post button has a list arrow with two options:

NOTES
If invoices are posted as a batch or when you are learning the program, you should use Post as the default selection.
Batch printing of invoices and other forms is covered in Chapter 14.

If you regularly print invoices when you enter them, as for point-of-sale transactions, you can click Print & Post on this button (add a ✓). Printing and posting will become the default selection and the button label changes to reflect this choice:

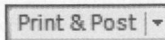

Previewing invoices is always recommended before printing. Because we do not want to print all invoices, we will accept the initial default setting to Post.

Click   the **Post button** . **Click OK** to confirm successful posting. A new blank Sales Journal form appears on the screen.

Close   the **Sales Journal** because the next transaction is a receipt.

Notice that the balance for Selkirk Furnaces in the Customers list has been updated.

Accounting for Receipts

Receipts from customers are entered in much the same way as payments to suppliers. After you choose the customer, outstanding invoices appear automatically and you can enter the payment amounts without entering any accounts. Air Care offers early payment discounts as an incentive to customers to pay their accounts promptly.

Receipts are entered in the Receipts Journal indicated by the hand pointer:

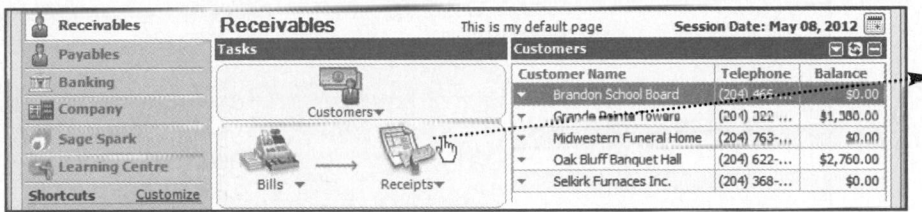

Click   the **Receipts icon** to open the Receipts Journal:

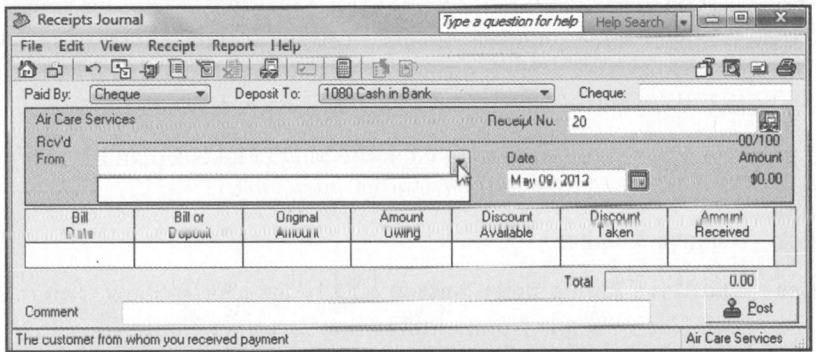

As with the Sales Invoice, you can customize the journal.

Click   the **Customize Journal tool** 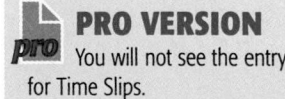 or **choose** the **View menu** and **click Customize Journal**:

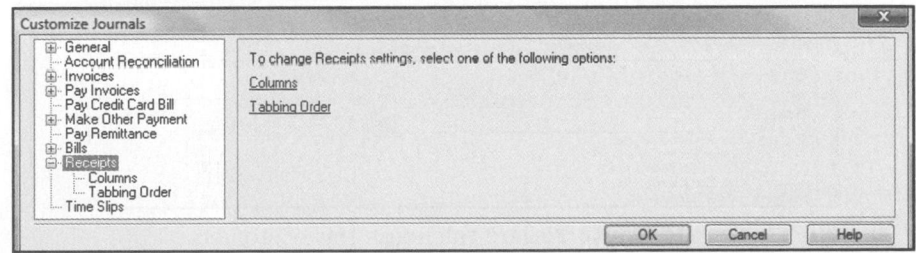

Click   **Columns** to open the customization options for columns.

When they are not needed, you can remove the Invoice Date and the two Discount columns. Air Care offers customer discounts so we must include these columns.

Click **Tabbing Order** to continue:

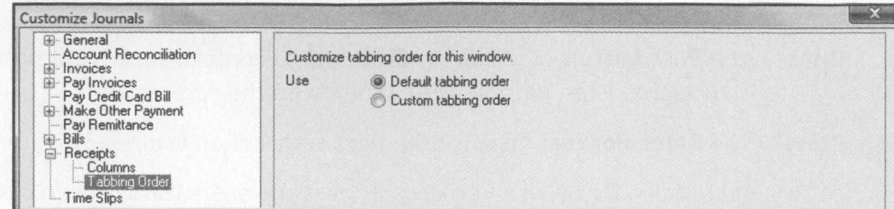

You can choose the default tabbing order or you can change the order. We will change the order so that after choosing the customer, the cursor will move to the cheque number field. This field is in the upper right-hand corner. With the default tabbing order, the cursor reaches this field last, making it easy to forget to enter the number.

Click **Custom Tabbing Order** to continue:

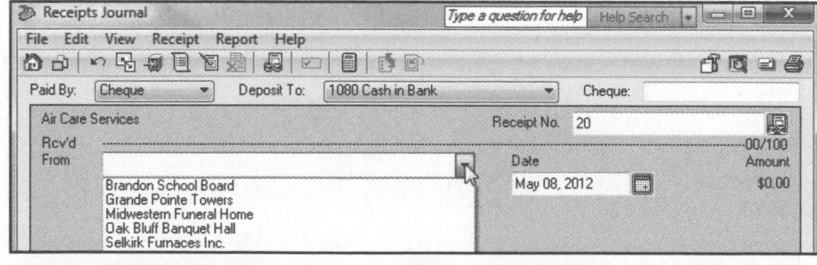

Notice that Cheque Number appears before Customer Name. However, when you open the Receipts Journal, the cursor starts in the Customer Name field, so the Cheque Number field is last. We want the next field to be the Cheque Number.

To move a field, select it and then click the Move Fields Up and Down arrows beside the list until you have the order you want.

Click **Cheque Number**.

Click the **Move Fields Down button** ▼ beside the Tabbing Order list. This will place Cheque Number after the Customer Name.

Click **OK** to return to the form.

Click the **Customer (Rcv'd From) list arrow** to display the Customer list:

> **NOTES**
> You can customize the order further by making the date field follow the cheque number, and so on, until the customer address fields are last.
> You can also choose to remove the Address fields from the tabbing order entirely. To access the address in that case, you can click the field.

Receipts Journal			
File Edit View Receipt Report Help			
Paid By: Cheque ▼ Deposit To: 1080 Cash in Bank ▼		Cheque:	
Air Care Services		Receipt No. 20	
Rcv'd From			-00/100
		Date	Amount
Brandon School Board		May 08, 2012	$0.00
Grande Pointe Towers			
Midwestern Funeral Home			
Oak Bluff Banquet Hall			
Selkirk Furnaces Inc.			

Click **Grande Pointe Towers** to choose this customer:

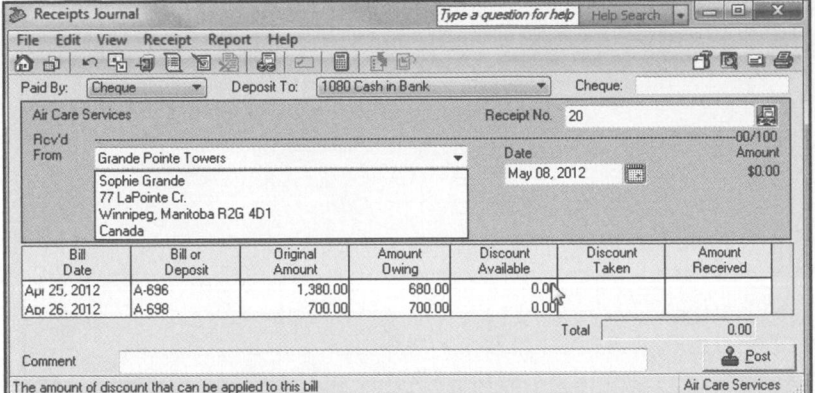

The customer's name and address have been added to your input form, together with all outstanding invoices for the customer. Notice that no discount appears in the Discount Available fields because the session date is past the 10-day discount period.

As with payments to suppliers, you cannot enter account numbers in the Receipts Journal. You need to enter only the amount paid on the appropriate invoice line. The program automatically creates the journal entry.

Air Care has a single bank account so it is correctly selected in the Deposit To field. If you have chosen the wrong customer, display the list again and click the correct customer. If you have selected correctly,

Press (tab) to move to the **Cheque field**.

Type 3499

The Receipt No. field records the receipt number that increases automatically. From the Lookup icon beside the Receipt No. field, you can look up previously posted receipts. We need to replace the session date with the date for this transaction.

Choose May 2 from the Date field pop-up calendar. **Press** (tab) to move the cursor to the Bill Date field. The discounts are now available:

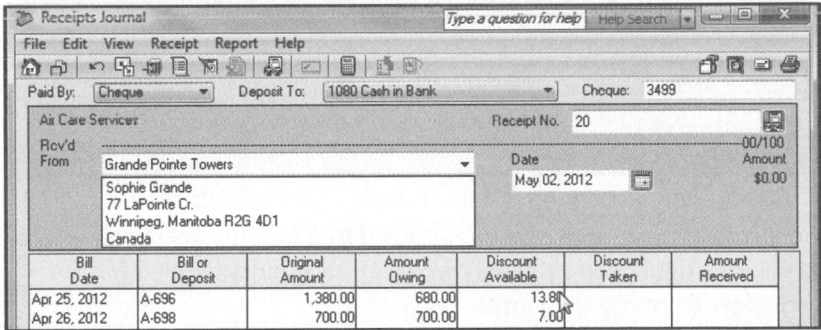

Notice that the discount is 1 percent of the original amount, not the amount owing. Until the discount period has passed, the full discount remains available.

Press (tab) to advance to the Discount Taken field.

Discount amounts can be changed or deleted. We will accept this discount.

Press (tab) to advance to the Amount Received field.

By default, the amount owing on the first invoice is shown and highlighted. All outstanding invoices are listed on the screen. For this invoice, the full amount is being paid so you can accept the default. Notice that the discount has been subtracted from the amount received.

Press (tab) to accept the amount in the Amount Received field.

NOTES
Simply Accounting allows you to set up more than one bank account. When more than one bank account is set up, choose the account from the Deposit To drop-down list.

NOTES
You can use the Lookup button to review a receipt, or to reverse it (see page 184).

NOTES
The year is added correctly in the Receipts Journal when you type the month and day.

PRO VERSION
pro The cursor advances to the column labelled Invoice Date.

NOTES
For other company types, the Bill Date column may be labelled Statement Date, Invoice Date and so on.

NOTES
You can accept a highlighted amount, or type an exact amount for a partial payment.

The cursor will advance to the Discount Taken field for the next invoice:

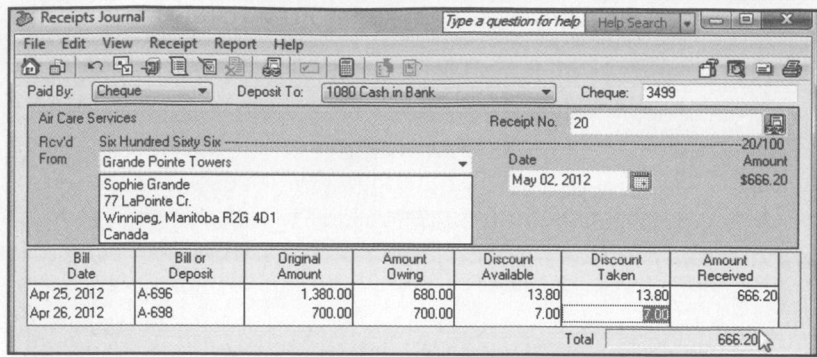

WARNING!
When an invoice or discount amount is highlighted and it is not being included, press (del) to remove the amount from the total, and press (tab) to update the total.

Refer to the Payment transaction on page 136 to see the error from not removing the second discount. Even though the cheque total appears correct on the screen, the posted entry will be incorrect.

Because the payment for this invoice is only a partial payment, we need to remove the discount.

Press (del) to remove the discount for the second invoice.

Press (tab) to advance to the Amount Received field.

This time the full invoice amount is entered because the discount has been changed to zero. However, the full amount is not being paid, so we must edit the amount. To replace the highlighted default amount,

Type 200

Press (tab) to enter the new amount and complete the invoice as shown:

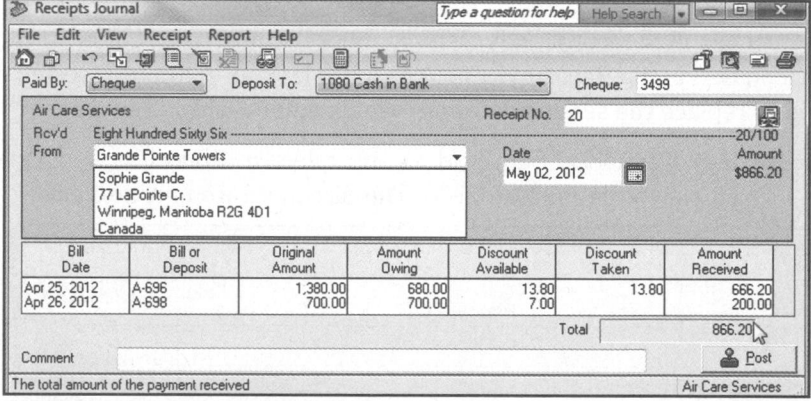

Notice that the upper cheque portion of the form has also been completed. In making Receipts Journal entries, you do not need to enter any accounts because Simply Accounting chooses the linked bank and receivable accounts defined for the Receivables Ledger to create the journal entry.

You have made all the entries for this transaction, so you are ready to review before posting your transaction.

Reviewing the Receipts Journal Entry

Choose the **Report menu** and **click Display Receipts Journal Entry**:

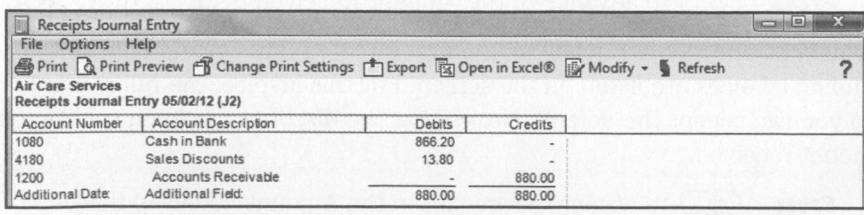

Here you can see the related journal entry created for the Receipts Journal transaction. The Simply Accounting program updates the General Ledger *Accounts Receivable* control account and *Cash in Bank* because the Receivables and General ledgers are fully integrated. *Cash in Bank* is defined as the default linked bank account for the Receivables Ledger as well as for the Payables Ledger because Air Care has only one bank account. *Accounts Receivable* and the customer's balance owing are reduced by the full amount of the payment plus the amount of the discount taken ($880). The discount amount is automatically debited to the linked *Sales Discounts* account. *Sales Discounts* is a contra-revenue account. It has a debit balance and reduces total revenue.

Close   the **display** to return to the Receipts Journal input screen.

CORRECTING THE RECEIPTS JOURNAL ENTRY BEFORE POSTING

Move to the field with the error. **Press** `tab` to move forward or `shift` and `tab` together to move back to a previous field. This will highlight the field contents. **Type** the **correct information** and **press** `tab` to enter it.

You can also use the mouse to **point** to a field and **drag** through the **incorrect information** to highlight it. **Type** the **correct information** and **press** `tab` to enter it.

If the customer is incorrect, **reselect** from the **Customer** list by **clicking** the **Customer list arrow**. **Click** the name of the correct **customer**. To confirm that you want to discard the current transaction, **click Yes** to display the outstanding invoices for the correct customer. **Type** the **correct** receipt **information**.

You can also discard the entry. **Click** ☒ or ↺ and then **click Yes** to confirm.

Posting

When you are certain that you have entered all the information correctly, you must post the transaction to save it.

Click   the **Post button** ![Post] or **choose** the **Receipt menu** and **click Post** to save your transaction. **Click OK.**

Close   the **Receipts Journal**.

Entering Cash Sales

To enter the cash sale on May 3,

Click   the **Bills icon** ![Bills] to open the Sales Journal. Notice that the invoice number (Bill No.) has been updated to 711.

Click   the **Payment Method list arrow** to view the payment options — Pay Later, Cash, Cheque and Credit Card:

PRO VERSION
Click the Sales Invoices icon ![Sales Invoices] to open the Sales Journal.

NOTES

When you choose Cash, as the payment method, the cheque number field is not included.

Click   **Cheque** as the method of payment to modify the invoice screen.

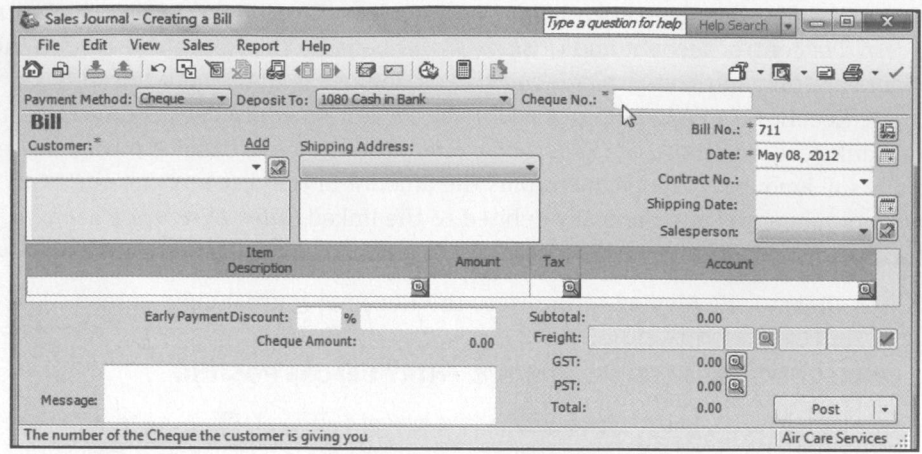

As shown here, when you choose Cheque as the method of payment, a cheque number field is added in the upper right-hand corner of the invoice so that you can add the customer's cheque number. The Deposit To bank account field is also added. In the payment terms section, the Net Days field has been removed and a Cheque Amount field has been added.

Press   ⌨tab **twice** to advance to the Cheque number field.

Type   395 **Press** ⌨tab to advance to the Customer field.

Type   M

NOTES

Remember to add the year when you type the date in the Sales Journal.

Midwestern Funeral Home is added to the Customer field because it is the first customer entry beginning with M. The rest of the name is still highlighted in case you want to continue typing another name.

Enter   **May 3** in the Date field as the transaction date.

Enter   a **description. Press** ⌨tab to advance to the Amount field. **Type**   900

Double click the **Account field**.

Notice that the cheque amount below the terms field has been updated.

Click   **Suggested Accounts** below the account list to modify the list:

NOTES

When you open the Purchases Journal, the list of suggested accounts will show only the Expense accounts. You will need to choose All Accounts to include Asset accounts in the list.

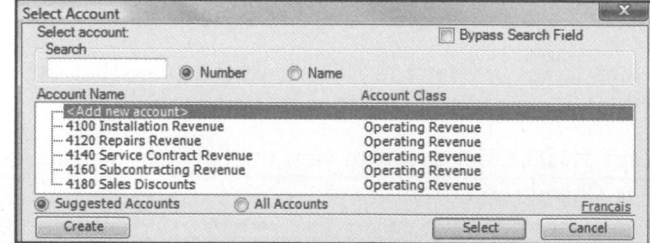

The list of suggested accounts now includes only Revenue accounts because we are in the Sales Journal. This shorter list makes it easier to select the correct account. For purchases, only expense accounts will be listed. You can switch back to the complete account list at any time by selecting **All Accounts**. The Suggested Accounts button remains selected when we close the journal until we change the selection again.

Click   **4100 Installation Revenue. Press** ⌨enter .

Click   the **Message field. Type**   Thank you to complete the sales entry:

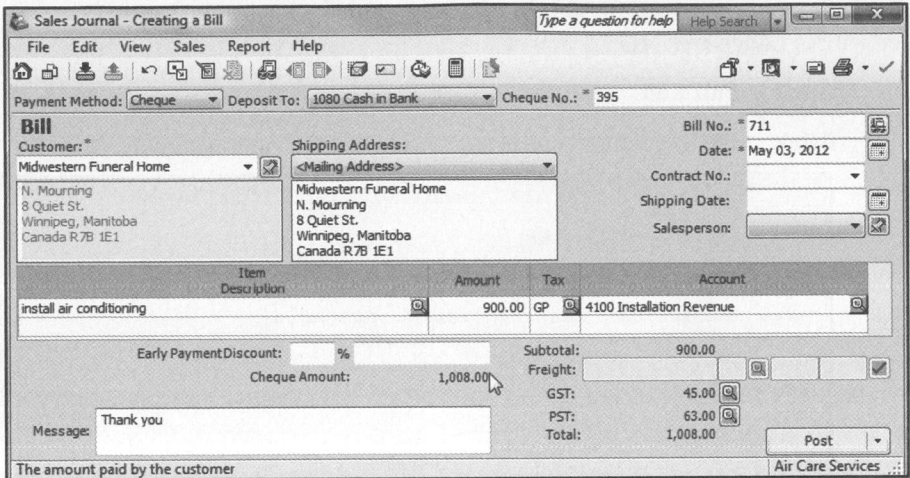

As usual, you should review the entry.

Choose the **Report menu** and **click Display Sales Journal Entry**:

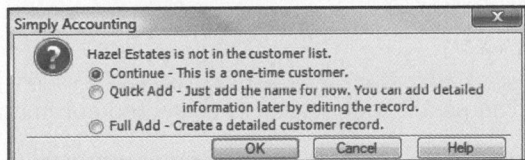

Notice that *Cash in Bank* is debited automatically instead of *Accounts Receivable* because we selected Cheque as the method of payment.

Close   the **display** when you have finished. **Make corrections** if necessary.

Click   **Post** [Post ▾] to save the entry. **Click OK**. Leave the journal open.

Adding a New Customer

The next sale is to a new customer who should be added to your files. We will add the customer directly from the Sales Journal.

Click   the **Payment Method field** and **choose Pay Later**. The date is correct.

Click   the **Customer field**.

Type   Hazel Estates

Press   (tab) to display the warning that you have typed a name that is not on the list and the option to add a ledger record:

The options are the same as for new suppliers. If you typed an incorrect name, click **Cancel** to return to the journal and start again. If you typed the name correctly, you can choose to add the customer's name only — **Quick Add** — or to add a full customer record with the **Full Add** option. If you need to change any defaults, you must choose the Full Add option. You can still skip customer fields that you do not need. The remaining option, **Continue**, will add the customer's name to the journal entry but will

NOTES

If you need to change the payment terms, revenue account or tax options for a new customer, you must choose Full Add to enter these fields in the ledger. You can also edit the journal information.

You can use the Full Add option and create an incomplete customer record. For example, you can enter the customer's name, tax code, payment terms, revenue account and credit limit and then add the remaining details later.

not create a ledger record for the customer or add the customer to the other Receivables Ledger reports.

> **Click**   **Full Add**.
>
> **Click**   **OK** to open the customer's Address information screen:

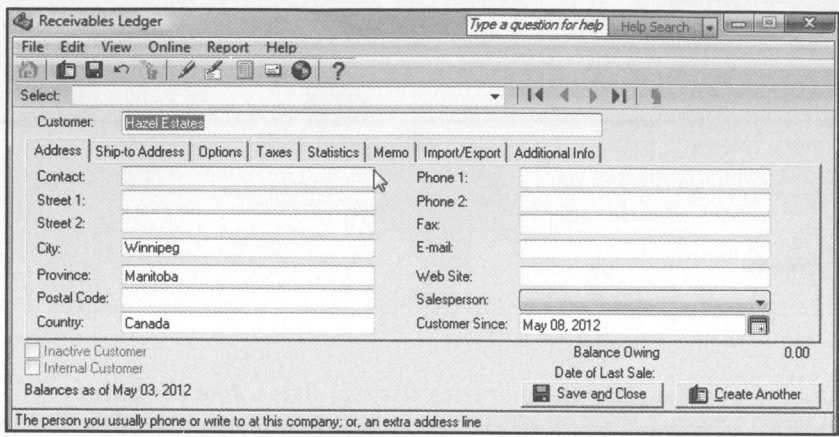

Clicking Add above the Customer field opens this ledger form directly from the journal at the Address tab screen.

You are ready to enter your new customer. The Customer field is completed with the new name highlighted for editing if necessary. The Customer name is the only required field for new customer records. Because it is already entered, the * reminder symbol for required fields has been removed.

The field we need next is the Contact field. Enter the name of the particular individual Air Care normally deals with.

> **Click**   the **Contact field**.
>
> **Type**   Joelle Beausoleil
>
> **Press**   (tab) to move the cursor to the Street 1 field.
>
> **Type**   488 Sunshine St. **Press** (tab).
>
> **Type**   Suite 1200 **Press** (tab) to move to and select the City field.

Notice that the city, province and country in which Air Care is located have been entered by default from the Address Settings. The province is correct but you must change the city.

> **Type**   West St. Paul
>
> **Click**   the **Postal Code field**.

You do not need to use capital letters or to leave a space within Canadian postal codes. The program will make these adjustments.

> **Type**   r4g5h3
>
> **Click**   the **Phone 1 field**. The postal code format is corrected automatically.

You do not need to add spaces, dashes or brackets for telephone numbers. Telephone and fax numbers may be entered with or without the area code.

> **Type**   2043677611 **Press** (tab).
>
> **Type**   8773679000 **Press** (tab) to move to the Fax field.
>
> **Type**   2043692191 **Press** (tab) to advance to the E-mail field.

Notice that the format for telephone and fax numbers is corrected automatically.

E-mail and Web addresses are typed exactly as you would type them in your regular Internet and e-mail access programs. You can also add these details later when you actually want to use them. When you click the Web or E-mail buttons, you will be prompted to enter the addresses if they are not part of the customer's record already.

> **Type** JB@hazelestates.com **Press** (tab).
>
> **Type** www.hazelestates.com

When salespersons are set up, you can choose the name of the regular sales contact person for a customer from the drop-down list in the **Salesperson** field. Air Care does not have salespersons set up. Salespersons are covered in Chapter 9.

Hazel Estates is completing its first sale on May 3 but the session date is entered as the default date in the **Customer Since** field.

> **Choose May 3** from the Customer Since field calendar icon.

The **Internal Customer** option applies when one department supplies services to another and charges for these services. The option is available when time and billing is used. If the customer no longer buys from the company, but you still want to keep the record on file, mark the customer as **Inactive**. The **Balance Owing** and **Date Of Last Sale** will be entered automatically by the program based on the customer's transactions.

> **Click** the **Ship-to Address tab**.
>
> **Click** the **Address Name list arrow** to see the predefined names:

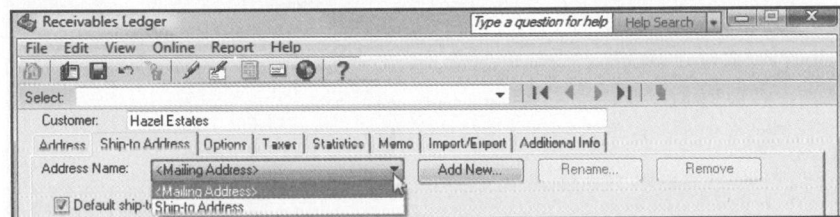

You can enter multiple customer addresses, and apply your own labels for these addresses. For example, you may have separate summer and winter addresses for residential customers or different store locations for wholesale customers. The billing address may be different from the location where a service is provided or products are delivered. The mailing address is provided as the default ship-to address, as indicated by the ✓ for Default Ship-to Address and its entry in the Address Name field. The address information is dimmed because you cannot remove the mailing address on this screen. You can enter complete address and contact information for the shipping address, add new address labels and information for them, edit the labels and remove address names and labels that are not needed.

To enter information for an address name, click the name from the drop-down list.

> **Click** **Ship-to Address** to open the address fields for editing:

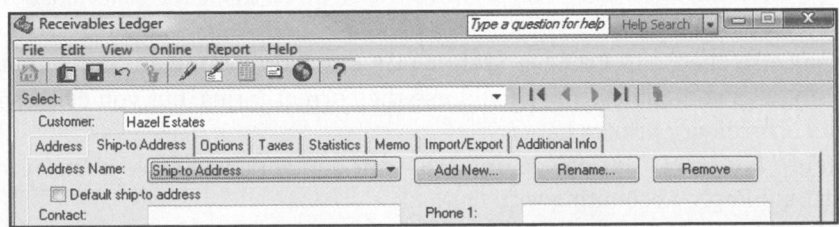

All the fields are now open for editing. You can make any address the Default Ship-to Address by clicking the check box when this label's information is displayed.

 PRO VERSION

pro Only one additional address can be entered in the Pro version – the shipping address. You cannot edit the name of this second address. If the mailing address is different from the shipping address, click the Same as Mailing Address check box to remove the ✓ and open the address fields for editing.

The shipping address is the same as the mailing address for this customer, so we can remove the ship-to address name for this customer.

Click   **Remove** to see the confirmation warning message:

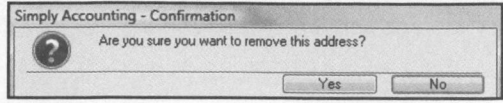

Click   **Yes** to confirm the removal.

Click   **Add New** to open the name field to add a new address:

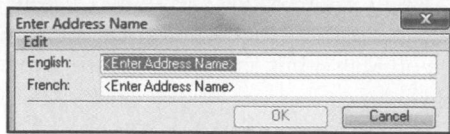

Type a new name and then click OK to have the new name appear in the drop-down list. Then you can select it to add the address details.

Click   **Cancel** to return to the Ship-to Address tab screen.

Click   the **Options tab**:

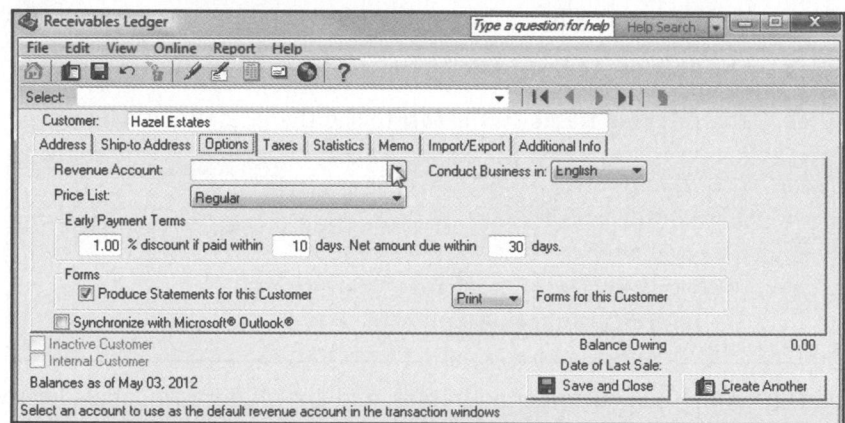

The first option is to add a default revenue account for the customer.

Click   the **Revenue Account list arrow**.

Click   **4100**.

The Options tab screen contains payment terms details. The **Price List** — Regular, Preferred or Web Price — refers to the prices customers pay for inventory items and will be introduced in Chapter 10. For Air Care, all customers pay Regular prices. You can select French or English as the customer's preferred **language for conducting business**. Sales invoices and other forms you prepare for customers will be printed in the language you select here. Your own program screens will not change.

The payment terms for Hazel Estates are the same as those for other customers and are entered by default.

You may also choose to **Produce Statements For This Customer**, and you may print or e-mail invoices and quotes. You should use the correct forms, but you can also print statements on ordinary printer paper.

If you use **Microsoft Outlook** to organize your contacts, you can synchronize the address list in Simply Accounting with Outlook.

You can change the Options tab settings at any time.

Click   the **Taxes tab**:

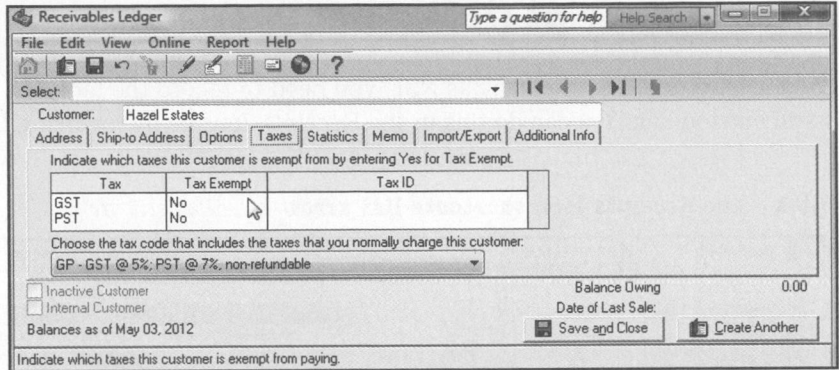

The customer is correctly described as not **Tax Exempt** for PST and GST by default, allowing accurate tax calculations for sales transactions to be included in Tax reports. The default tax code taken from the ledger settings is also correct.

> **Click**   **GP - GST @5%; PST @7%, non-refundable** to see the codes available.

> **Click**   the **Statistics tab** to open the next screen we need:

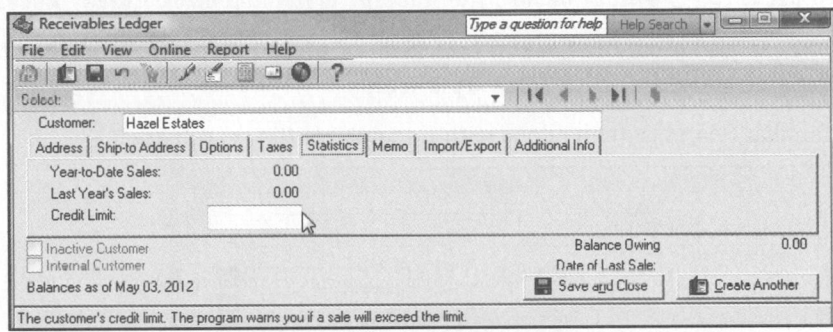

The Statistics screen has a summary of the sales to the customer for the current year and previous year. These fields are updated from sales transactions.

In the **Credit Limit** field, you can enter the customer's credit limit to help minimize bad debts. When a customer exceeds the credit limit, the program will warn you before you can post the sale. You can accept the over-the-limit sale, or ask for a deposit to avoid exceeding the credit limit. Customers should be notified of credit policy changes. Customers who have previously defaulted on making their payments can be placed on a cash-only basis by setting their credit limits at zero. Air Care is analyzing customer payment trends at present and will set the limit at $4 000 on a trial basis.

> **Click**   the **Credit Limit field** to position the cursor and **type** 4 0 0 0

Saving a New Customer Account

The remaining tab screens are not required. They serve the same purpose as they do for suppliers. When you are certain that all the information is correct, you must save the newly created customer account and add it to the current list.

> **Click**   **Save And Close** ⊞ Save and Close to save the new customer information.

You will return to the Sales Journal. Notice that the tax code, revenue account and payment terms are added. Any of these fields can be edited for an individual invoice.

> **Enter**   the **sale** for the new customer by following the procedures outlined earlier.
>
> **Review** the **journal entry**. **Close** the **display** and **make corrections**.
>
> **Click**   **Post** [Post ▾] . **Click OK** and then **close** the **Sales Journal**.

Reversing a Receipt (NSF Cheques)

When a cheque is returned by the bank as NSF, you need to record the fact that the invoice is still outstanding. You can do this in the Receipts Journal by reversing the cheque.

Click the **Receipts icon shortcuts list arrow** as shown:

NOTES

The Lookup and Adjust tools both open the Search window. The Reverse tool and menu option are available from the journal windows provided by both.

Find Receipt in the Receipts icon shortcuts list also opens the Search window.

From Lookup and Find Receipt, the search parameters will show Receipt Lookup as the heading.

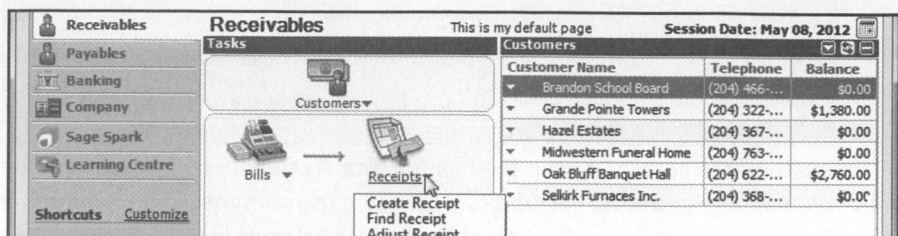

Click **Adjust Receipt**.

When the Receipts Journal is open, you can click the **Adjust Receipt tool**, or **press** ⌃ctrl + **A**, or **choose** the **Receipt menu** and **click Adjust Receipt**.

You can also **click** the **Lookup tool**, or **press** ⌃ctrl + **L**, or **choose** the **Receipt menu** and **click Look Up Receipt**.

The familiar Search screen opens with Receipts as the search area:

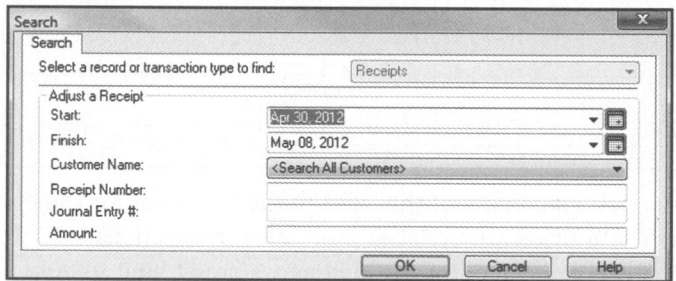

Click **OK** to see all the receipts we have entered:

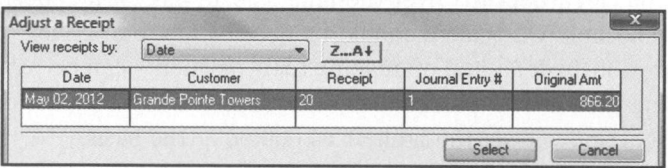

The single cheque from Grande Pointe Towers we have entered is selected.

Press ⏎enter or **click Select** to open the cheque we entered:

NOTES

If you recorded a receipt incorrectly, and do not need to reverse it, you can choose the Adjust Receipt tool to access the posted receipt and make the correction, just as you do for sales (page 189) or for payments (page 143).

NOTES

If you started from the Lookup window, click the Adjust Receipt tool to open the fields for editing.

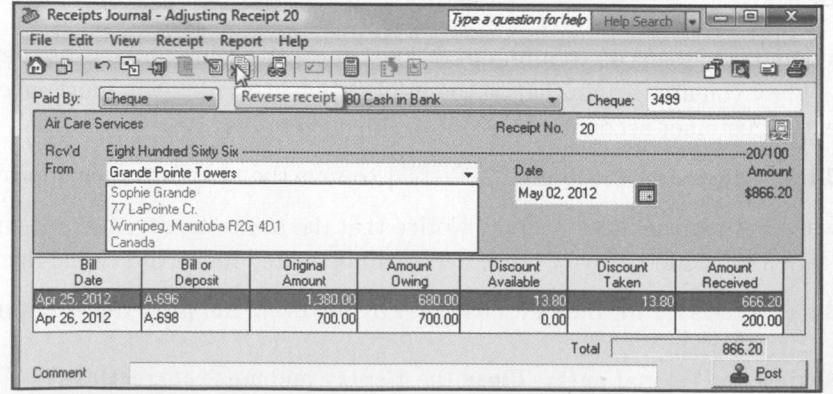

At this stage you can adjust the cheque by editing incorrectly entered information, just as you can edit a purchase invoice or payment cheque.

We need to reverse the cheque because it has been returned as NSF.

Click   the **Reverse Receipt tool** or **choose** the **Receipt menu** and **click Reverse Receipt** to see the confirmation message:

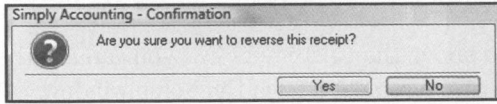

Click   **Yes** to confirm the reversal. **Click OK** when Simply Accounting confirms the successful reversal. A blank Receipts Journal form opens.

We will look at the journal report generated by reversing this receipt.

Minimize   the **Receipts Journal** to return to the Home window.

Choose   the **Reports menu**, then **choose Journal Entries** and **click Receipts** to open the report options window:

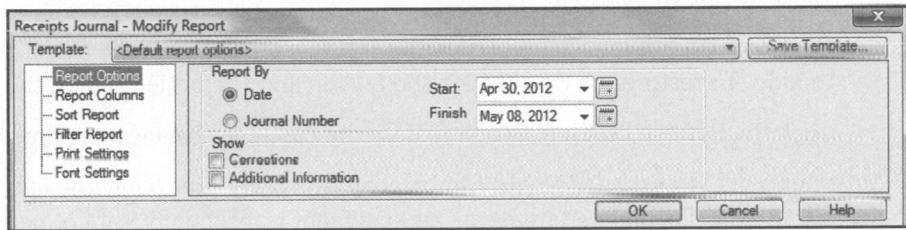

By default, corrections are not included in reports. In order to see adjustments, we must include them. The remaining defaults are correct.

Click   **Corrections** under the Show heading.

Click   **OK** to display the two journal entries:

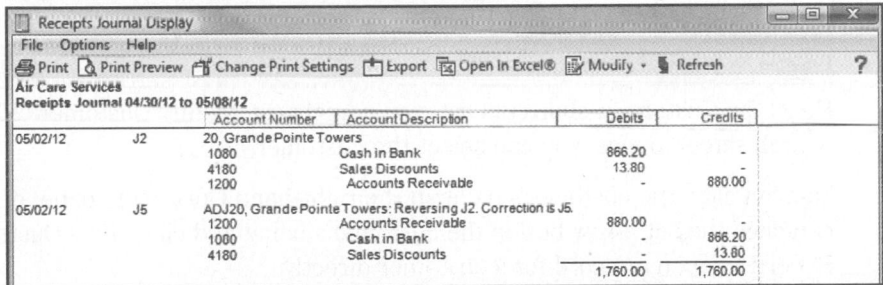

You can see that the two entries cancel each other — all amounts were reversed, including the discount. The debits to *Cash in Bank* and *Sales Discounts* were entered as credits in the reversing entry, and the credit to *Accounts Receivable* was entered as a debit. Simply Accounting created the reversing entry automatically when we reversed the receipt, adding ADJ to the receipt number so that you can link the two transactions.

When you adjust a receipt and post the corrected entry, Simply Accounting will create the intermediate reversing entry automatically. Three entries result — the original incorrect one, the reversing entry and the final corrected version, just as they do when you make adjustments in the General, Purchases and Payments journals. You can see the complete audit trail by including Corrections in the Journal Reports.

Close   the **display** when you have finished.

Restore the **Receipts Journal**.

Choose Grande Pointe Towers from the Customer list.

Both invoices have been fully restored. When the replacement payment is received, you can enter it in the usual way.

Close   the **Receipts Journal**.

NOTES
In Chapter 15, you will see that you cannot reverse the receipt if the cheque is not deposited directly to the bank account when you enter the receipt (that is, the bank deposit is recorded later as a separate transaction). Instead, you must enter a negative receipt.

NOTES
If you change the customer for a receipt, Simply Accounting will reverse the original receipt when you click Yes to confirm this action.

CLASSIC VIEW
From the Home window, right-click the Receipts icon . Click the Display tool to see the Receipts Journal report options.

NOTES
You can also click the Report Centre icon. Then click Receivables, Receipts Journal Entries and Modify This Report.

WARNING!
If you display the Journal Report from the Home window Reports pane list of reports, you will use the default settings, which do not show corrections. You will see the message that there is no data because there are no other Receipts Journal entries.

Editing Customer Information

You can change customer information and you can change the way the home window displays Customers pane details, just as you can modify the Suppliers pane.

When you click the 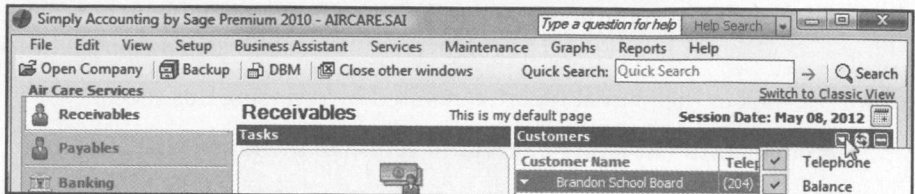 button above the Customers list, you can see that the telephone and balance owing can be removed from the home window.

The ✓ indicates that information is displayed. When the computer is in a public area, you should hide the extra information.

To hide the additional details, click the 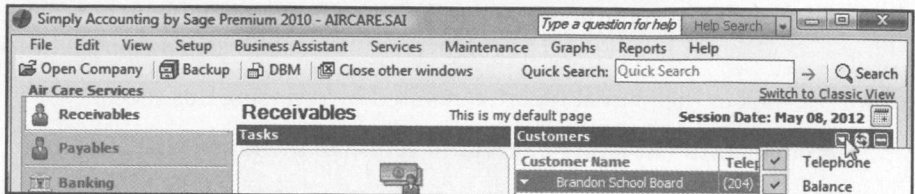 button and click the detail you want to hide. To restore the detail, click the button and the option to add the ✓.

Click the Refresh lists tool to update the customer balance amounts.

Most fields in the customer record can be changed at any time. Only the current balance owing, which is updated from sale and payment transactions, cannot be changed.

Click the **Customers icon shortcuts list arrow** as shown:

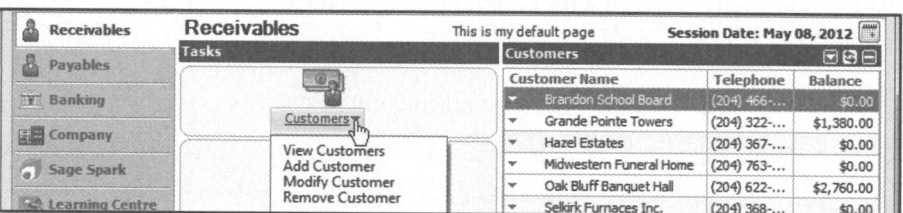

From the Customers shortcuts list, you can choose Modify Customer. When the Search screen opens, you can select the customer.

You can click the customer's name in the right-hand Customers pane, or you can click the list arrow beside the customer's name and click View Customer Record to open a record for a customer directly.

We will use a third option — to work from the Customers window.

Click the **Customers icon** to open the Customers window:

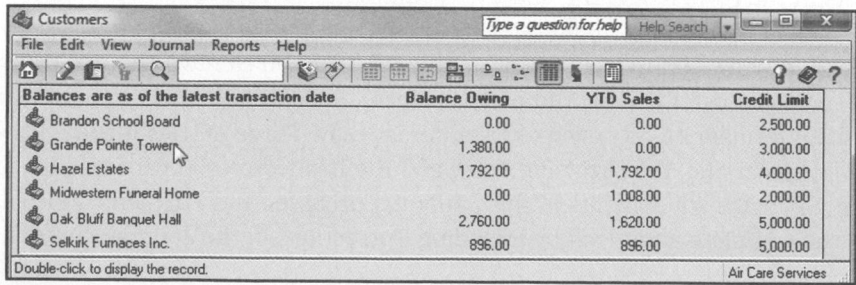

Click **Grande Pointe Towers** to select it.

Click the **Edit tool** or **choose** the **File menu** and **click Open**.

The Receivables Ledger record for Grande Pointe Towers opens at the Address screen. We need to modify the Terms, which appear on the Options tab.

Click the **Options tab** to access the payment terms information:

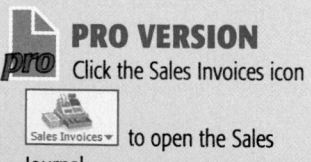
PRO VERSION
Click the Sales Invoices icon
to open the Sales Journal.

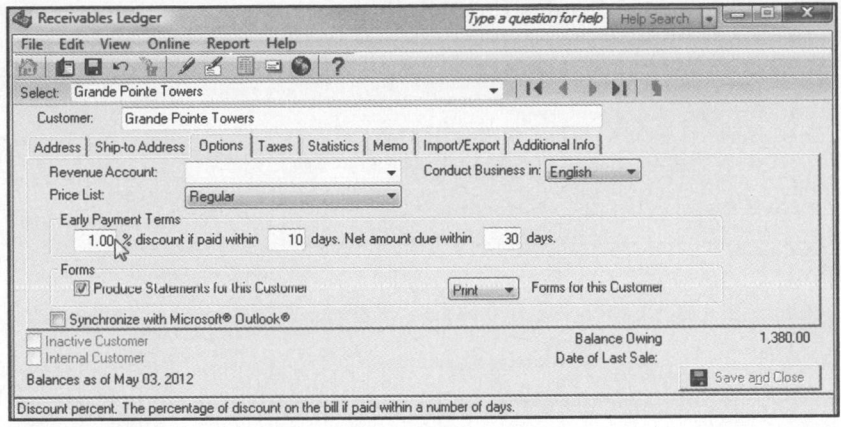

Click   **1.00** in the % Discount field of the Early Payment Terms section.

Press   ⌈del⌉ to remove the entry. **Press** ⌈tab⌉ to advance to the Days field.

Press   ⌈del⌉. **Press** ⌈tab⌉ to advance to the Net Days field.

Type   1

To modify other customer records, click Next ▶ or Previous ◀ to move to a different record or choose the customer you need from the Select drop-down list.

Click   the **Statistics tab** to change credit limits for the remaining customers.

Close   the **Receivables Ledger** and **close** the **Customers window**. You can now continue with the journal entries.

Entering Credit Card Sales

Most businesses accept credit cards from customers in lieu of cash and cheques. Customers expect this convenience, and although businesses benefit by avoiding NSF cheques, they do incur a cost for this service. Credit card companies charge the business a transaction fee: a percentage of each sale is withheld by the card company.

Credit card sales are entered like other sales, by selecting the correct payment method and then entering the invoice details.

Click   the **Bills icon** 🖳.

Click   the **Payment Method list arrow** and **click Credit Card** to modify the invoice.

As for cash sales, the Net Days field for early payment discounts is removed and a Credit Card Amount is added. There is no cheque number field for credit cards.

Choose One-Time Customer from the Customer drop-down list.

Type   Sales Summary in the Mailing Address text box.

Enter   **May 5** as the transaction date.

Click   the **Item Description field** and **type** the **description** for the first sale item.

Press   ⌈tab⌉ and **type** 600

Press   ⌈tab⌉ **twice** and **enter 4120** as the account.

NOTES
Typing zero (0) in the Net Days field will leave the field blank in the ledger and the journal.

NOTES
The transaction fee varies from one card company to another, as well as from one retail customer to another. Stores that have a larger volume of credit card sales usually pay lower transaction fees.

Enter the **second invoice line details** for the service contract revenue work to complete the invoice as shown:

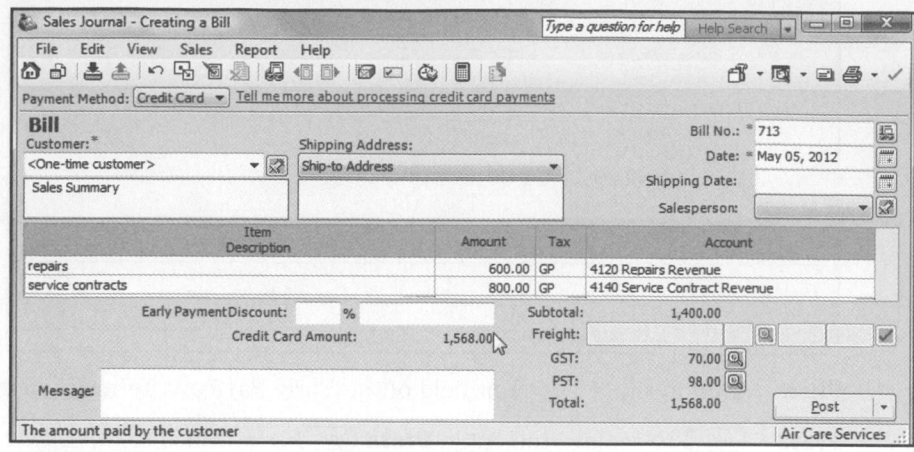

As usual, we will review the journal entry before posting.

Choose the **Report menu** and **click Display Sales Journal Entry**:

Account Number	Account Description	Debits	Credits
1100	Credit Card Bank Account	1,528.80	-
5120	Bank Charges & Card Fees	39.20	-
2640	PST Payable	-	98.00
2650	GST Charged on Services	-	70.00
4120	Repairs Revenue	-	600.00
4140	Service Contract Revenue	-	800.00
Additional Date:	Additional Field:	1,568.00	1,568.00

This entry differs somewhat from the standard cash sale entry. Instead of *Cash in Bank*, the linked *Credit Card Bank Account* is debited for the amount of the deposit, but this is less than the total amount of the sale. The deposit is reduced by the transaction fee that is charged to the linked expense account *Bank Charges & Card Fees*. In this case, the credit card company withholds 2.5 percent of each transaction as the fee for using the card. This fee includes the cost to the credit card company for assuming the risk of non-payment from customers.

Close the **display** and **make corrections** to the invoice if necessary.

Before posting the transaction, we will store it so that we will not need to re-enter all the details the next time we enter the sales summary transaction.

Storing a Recurring Sales Entry

Completing and storing a recurring entry in the Sales Journal is similar to storing a General or Purchases Journal entry.

Click the **Store tool** 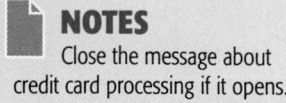 or **choose** the **Sales menu** and **click Store**.

The familiar Store Recurring Transaction window appears with the customer name as the entry name, and the default frequency, Monthly, selected. If you want, you can change the entry name to Sales Summary.

Click **Monthly** to display the frequency options. **Click Weekly** as the frequency.

Click **OK** to save the entry and return to the Sales Journal. The Recall button will be available.

Click **Post** Post ▾ to save the journal entry. **Click OK**.

Adjusting a Posted Sales Journal Entry

If you discover an error in a Sales Journal entry after posting it, you can adjust or correct the posted transaction in the same way that you can adjust a purchase invoice after posting. You can edit any field in the invoice except the customer. If you need to change the customer, you can open the Adjust (or Lookup) window and click the Reverse tool, just as you do for purchases or receipts.

The entry for Hazel Estates was missing the second invoice line to record the revenue from repair work. The Sales Journal should still be open.

Click the **Adjust Bill tool** 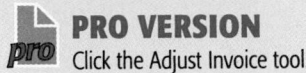 to open the Search window:

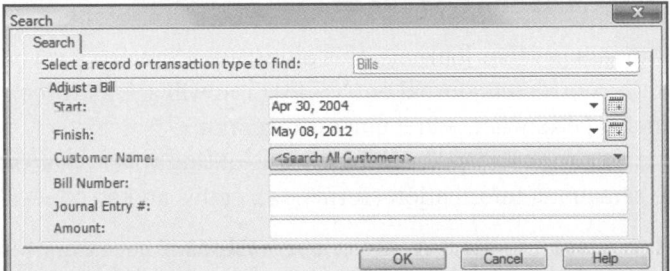

The default date and customer selections will include all invoices.

Click **OK** to open the Select Entry to Adjust screen:

View bills by:	Date	▼	Z...A+		
Date	Customer	Bill #	Journal Entry #	Original Amt	
May 05, 2012	<One-time customer>	713	6	1,568.00	
May 03, 2012	Hazel Estates	712	4	1,792.00	
May 03, 2012	Midwestern Funeral Home	711	3	1,008.00	
May 01, 2012	Selkirk Furnaces Inc.	710	1	896.00	

All Sales Journal entries for the selected customers and within the selected date range are listed. You can **view** the list of transactions in order by date, the default selection, customer, invoice number, journal entry number or amount. For each view, you can switch between descending and ascending order with the Z...A+ button.

Journal Entry #4 for Hazel Estates is the one we need to edit.

Click **Hazel Estates**.

To choose an invoice for adjusting, you can click on any part of the line for that invoice to highlight it, then click Select or you can double click the entry to open the journal immediately.

Click **Select** to open the invoice. It is ready for editing:

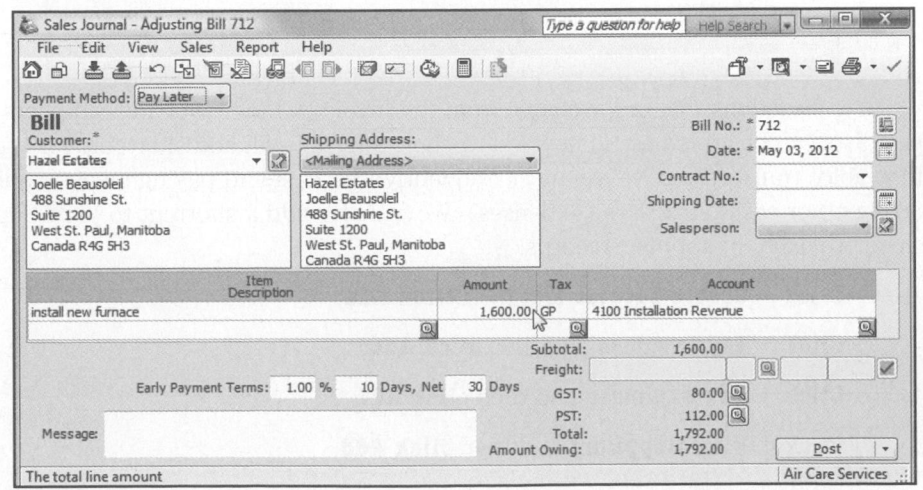

PRO VERSION

pro Click the Adjust Invoice tool.

NOTES
Just as you can choose a specific supplier for purchase invoice adjustments, you can choose a specific customer and click OK to see a reduced list of invoices for the selected customer. You can also enter a specific invoice number and click OK to access the invoice directly.

NOTES
If the invoice has already been paid, the program will ask if you want to create a credit note for the customer — a negative invoice. The default source for this invoice will be CN plus the original invoice number, e.g., CN-712, but you can enter a different reference number if you want.
This credit amount can be applied (paid) to other outstanding invoices for the customer.

Click	the **Item Description field** on the second line, below the first description.
Type	repair work **Press** (tab) to advance to the Amount field.
Type	800 **Press** (tab).

The tax code GP should be entered. You can select or change the code if needed. Click the Tax code List icon to open the Tax Code screen. Double click GP.

Click	the **Account field List icon** [icon].
Double click	**4120 Repairs Revenue**.
Click	the **Message field** and **type** Revised invoice

As with other adjustments in other journals, this adjustment creates a reversing entry (J7) in addition to the corrected journal entry (J8). You will see all three transactions in the journal reports when you include Corrections.

If you change the customer for an invoice, Simply Accounting warns that the name will be changed, but the remaining information (terms, tax codes and so on) will not.

Review	the **entry**. **Close** the **display**. **Make corrections** if necessary.
Post	the **transaction** and then **close** the **Sales Journal**.

Adding Shortcuts for Other Transactions

Just as we added a shortcut for General Journal entries in Chapter 5, we can add shortcuts for the Payables journals and tasks we will use for Air Care. Refer to page 138 if you need help.

Click	**Customize** beside Shortcuts.
Click	the [+] **beside Company** to expand the list.
Click	**Create General Journal** and then **click Add**.
Click	the [+] **beside Payables** to expand this list as shown:

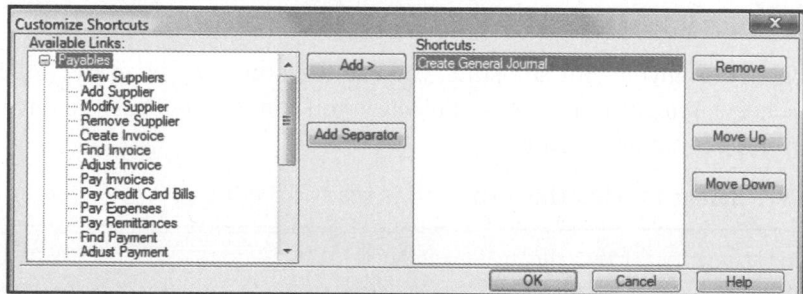

All transactions that are available from the Invoices, Payments and Suppliers drop-down lists can be added as Home window shortcuts. We will add shortcuts for the types of Payables transactions we use most frequently: creating and paying invoices and making other cash purchases (expenses). We will also add a shortcut to View Suppliers so that we can edit supplier records.

Click	**Create Invoice** and then **click Add**.
Click	**Pay Invoices** and then **click Add**.
Click	**Pay Expenses** and then **click Add**.
Click	**View Suppliers** and then **click Add**.

NOTES
You can add more shortcuts if you want. The maximum number is 10 for each user.

Click   **OK** to return to the Home window with your shortcuts added:

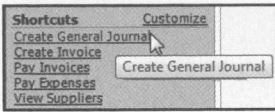

These five tasks/windows are now available from any module Home window by clicking the shortcut.

   Enter the **remaining transactions** and then **restore** the **Home window**.

Recalling a Stored Sales Entry

Click   the **Bills** (Sales or Sales Invoices) **icon** to open the Sales Journal.

Click   the **Recall tool** or **choose** the **Sales menu** and **click Recall** to display the Recall Recurring Transaction window.

Click   the **transaction** you want to use. **Click Select** to display a copy of the entry previously posted.

Edit   the **amounts** or the **accounts** as needed.

The default date is entered according to the frequency selected. The payment method is still selected as Credit Card. The invoice number is updated automatically so the entry is complete.

Review the **entry** to be certain that it is correct.

Click   the **Post button** to save the entry.

If you have made any changes to the entry, Simply Accounting may warn that posting the entry may affect the next due date. This warning will appear if you have made any changes to the entry before posting, although the message mentions only the date.

Click   **Yes** to accept the change and post. **Click OK** to confirm posting.

Displaying Customer Reports

Customer reports can be accessed any time from the Home or the Customers window, or from the Report Centre.

Click the Customers icon to open the Customers window.

NOTES
Management reports and graphs are not available from the Customers window or from the Report Centre. You can access these from the Home window.

The Reports menu now contains only customer reports. You can select the report you want from this list and follow the instructions below to choose report options. You can also obtain all customer reports from the Home window Reports menu.

In the Receivables module Home window, the Reports pane includes all the customer reports in the drop-down list. Opening the reports from this list will display them immediately with the default settings. This report list is shown here:

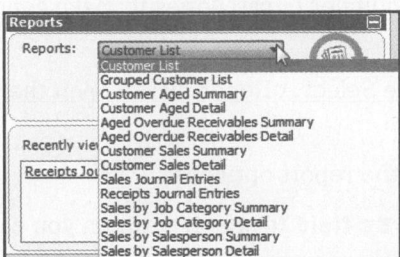

We will continue to work from the Report Centre, so we can see the sample reports, descriptions and report options.

Click the **Report Centre icon** in the Home window.

The Receivables reports are listed because we started from the Receivables window. The sample and description for Customer List, the first report, is displayed.

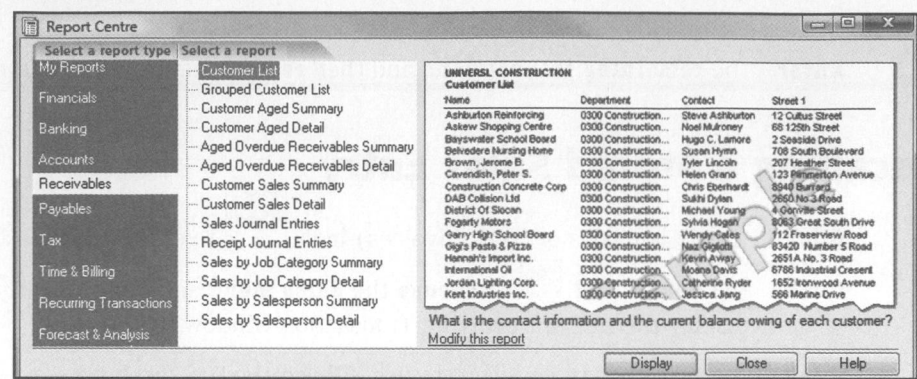

If you click Receivables on the Select A Report Type list, you will see the general description for Receivables reports.

Displaying Customer Lists

Click **Customer List** in the Select A Report list if necessary to open the sample report.

Click **Modify This Report** to open the report options:

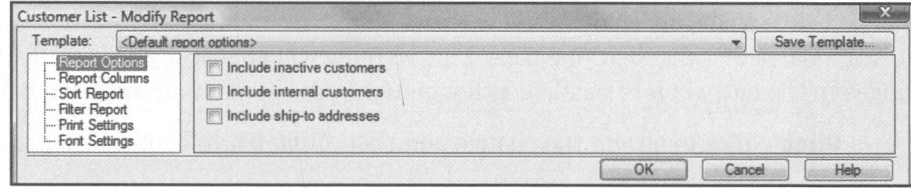

Or, choose the Reports menu, then choose Lists and Customers to see the options.

You can include or omit inactive and internal customers, and shipping addresses. You can sort and filter Customer Lists by any of the fields selected for the report. You can select customer record fields by customizing the Report Columns. You can also sort the columns directly in the report. For example, if you want to list customers in order according to the amount they owe, with the largest balance reported first, click the Balance column heading to sort the report by balance. Then click the heading again to reverse the order.

Click **OK**. **Close** the **display** when you have finished viewing it.

Displaying Grouped Customer Lists

You can also organize your customer list by a number of categories to make contacting customers more efficient.

Click **Grouped Customer List** in the Select A Report list to open the sample report and its description.

Click **Modify This Report** to open the report options.

Click the **list arrow for the Group By field** to see the criteria you can use to sort your report:

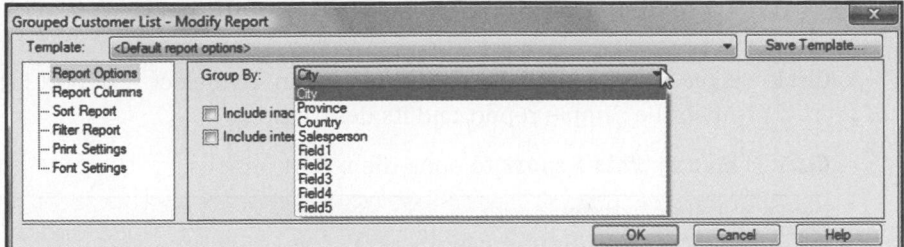

Choose the **grouping criterion** you want. Click OK to display the report.

Close the **display** when you have finished viewing it.

Displaying Customer Aged Reports

Click **Customer Aged Summary** in the Select A Report list to open the sample report and its description.

Click **Modify This Report** to open the report options:

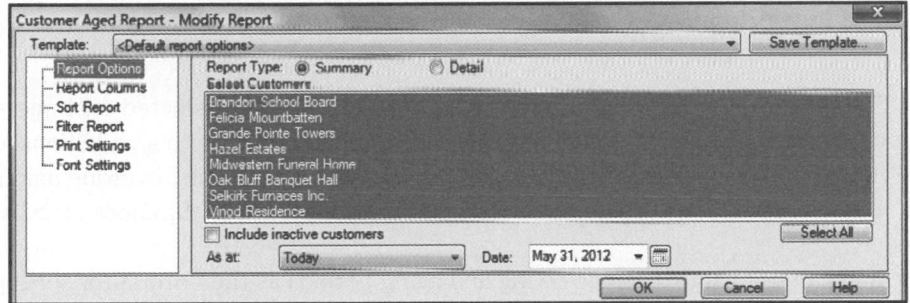

Or, choose the Reports menu, then choose Receivables and Customer Aged.

New customers you entered using Quick Add will appear on the list of customers in the report options windows. Sales for one-time customers and customers for whom you chose the Continue option will not appear because these cash transactions did not create an entry for Accounts Receivable.

The **Summary** option will display an alphabetic list of the selected customers with outstanding total balances owing, organized into the aging periods columns set up for the company. The **Detail** option shows all the invoices and payments made by customers and the balance owing. This more descriptive report is also aged and can be used to make credit decisions. You can add payment terms to the Detail Report.

You can customize the Customer Aged and Aged Overdue reports (that is, choose columns, sort and filter) by name, balance owing and aging periods.

Click **Detail** to include details for individual transactions.

Enter the **date** for the report (including the year), or accept the default session date.

Press and **hold** `ctrl` and **click** the appropriate **names** in the customer list. **Click Select All** to include all customers, or remove them when they are all selected.

After you have indicated the options you want,

Click **OK** to see the report. **Close** the **displayed report** when finished.

⚠ WARNING!
You must enter the year in all report options window date fields. The default year is taken from your computer system. This may be incorrect for your data file and will produce an error message. You can enter two digits for the year.

📄 NOTES
You can drill down to look up invoices and to the Customer Ledger from the Customer Aged Report. From the Summary Report, you can drill down to the Detail Report.

📄 NOTES
The Customer Aged and Aged Overdue Detail Reports are also available directly from the Select A Report list for Receivables in the Report Centre.

📄 NOTES
You can drill down to look up invoices and to the Customer Aged Report from the Aged Overdue Receivables Report. From the Summary Report, you can drill down to the Detail Report.

Displaying Aged Overdue Receivables Reports

Click   **Aged Overdue Receivables Summary** in the Select A Report list to open the sample report and its description.

Click   **Modify This Report** to open the report options:

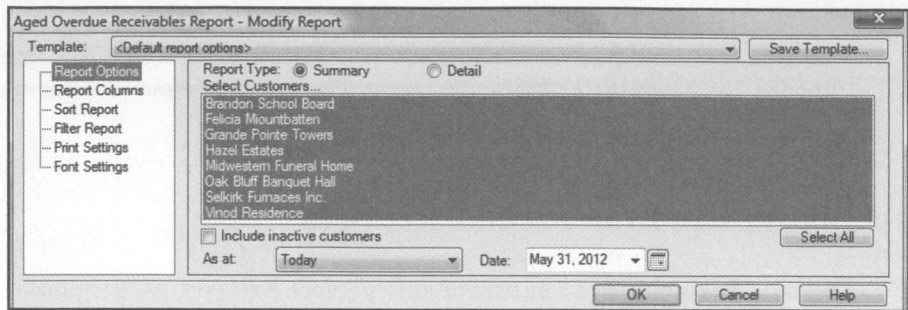

From the Home window, choose the Reports menu, then choose Receivables and click Aged Overdue Receivables to see the options.

Enter   the **date** for the report including the year, or accept the default session date.

The **Summary** option will display an alphabetic list of the selected customers with outstanding total balances owing, organized into aging periods, with an additional column for the overdue amount. Individual invoices, due dates, payments, overdue amounts and the balance owing for the selected customers are added when you choose the **Detail** Report.

You can use name, balance owing and aging periods as the criteria for sorting and filtering the Aged Overdue Receivables reports and for choosing columns.

Click   **Detail** if you want to include the invoice details.

Enter   the **date** for the report (including the year), or accept the default session date.

Press   and **hold** `ctrl` and **click** the appropriate **names** in the customer list. **Click Select All** to include all customers, or remove them all.

Click   **OK** to see the report. **Close** the **displayed report** when finished.

Displaying the Customer Sales Report

Click   **Customer Sales Summary** in the Select A Report list to open the sample report and its description.

Click   **Modify This Report** to open the report options:

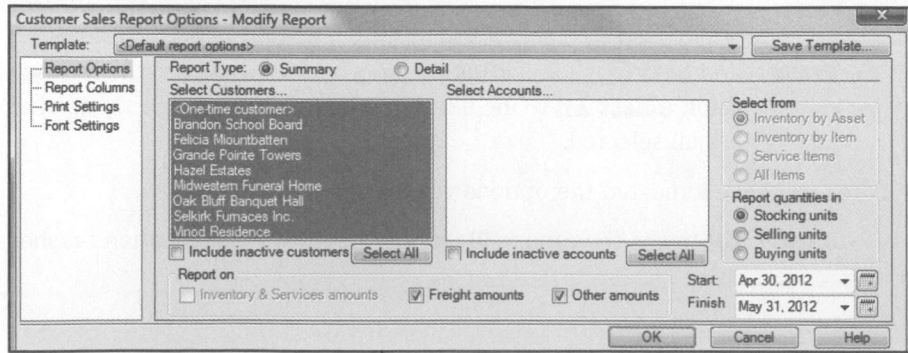

From the Home window, choose the Reports menu, then choose Receivables and click Customer Sales to see the options.

In this report, you can display the total number of transactions and the total sales for each customer (in the **Summary** Report) or the individual sales invoice amounts (in the **Detail** Report). The Detail Report also includes journal details (date, source, journal entry number and revenue amounts) for each transaction. Only the Other Amounts and Freight amounts are available when the inventory module is not set up. When inventory items are set up, you can display the sales for these items as well. This report will be discussed further when inventory is introduced in Chapter 10. The earliest transaction and session date provide the default date range.

You can select the customers to include and the date range for the report.

Press   and **hold** ⟨ctrl⟩ and **click** the appropriate **names** in the customer list. **Click Select All** to include all customers, or remove the entire selection.

Enter   the **Start** and **Finish dates** for the report (including the year).

Click   **OK** to see the report. **Close** the **displayed report** when finished.

Displaying the Sales Journal

Click   **Sales Journal Entries** in the Select A Report list to open the sample.

Click   **Modify This Report** to open the report options:

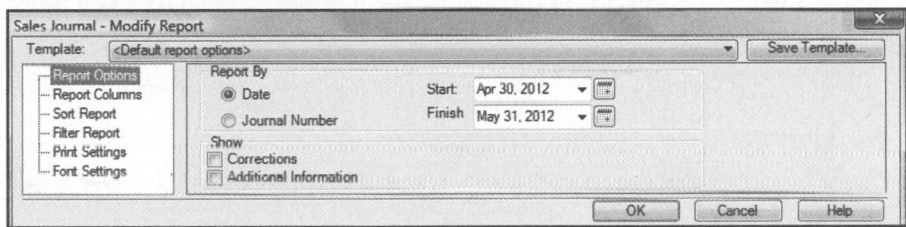

From the Home window, choose the Reports menu, then choose Journal Entries and click Sales to see the report options.

You can select Sales Journal entries by posting date or by journal entry number. We use the default setting, By Date, for all reports in this workbook, so leave the selection unchanged. You can include corrections (adjusting and reversing entries) or omit them.

You can sort and filter journal reports by Date, Journal No., Source and Comment. You can choose account, description, debits and credits columns for the reports.

Enter   the **beginning date** for the journal transactions you want (including the year). Or choose a date from the list arrow selections.

Press   ⟨tab⟩ **twice**. **Enter** the **ending date** for the transaction period (including the year).

Click   **Corrections** to provide a complete audit trail.

Click   **OK** to view the report. **Close** the **display** when you have finished.

Displaying the Receipts Journal

The Receipts Journal was covered earlier in this chapter. Refer to page 185.

CLASSIC VIEW
From the Home window, right-click the Sales icon

. Click the Display tool

. Sales and Receipts Journal reports are also available from the Select Report list when you click the Display tool button if no icon is selected in the Home window.

NOTES
You can drill down to an invoice, to the Customer Aged Report and to the General Ledger Report from the Sales and the Receipts Journal reports.

NOTES
To include all journal entries in a single report, choose the Reports menu, then choose Journals and click All. Enter May 1 12 and May 31 12 in the Start and Finish date fields if these are not the default entries.

From the Report Centre, you can choose Financials and then All Journal Entries to include all transactions in a single report.

Displaying Tax Reports

The next three reports are general financial reports that include customer information. Because they are accessed from the Report Centre, they are included before the final customer reports and graphs that are accessed from the Home window Reports menu.

Tax reports show the taxable purchases and sales with and without tax amounts included, the taxes paid or charged on each transaction and the totals.

Click **Tax** in the Select A Report Type list to open the list of tax reports:

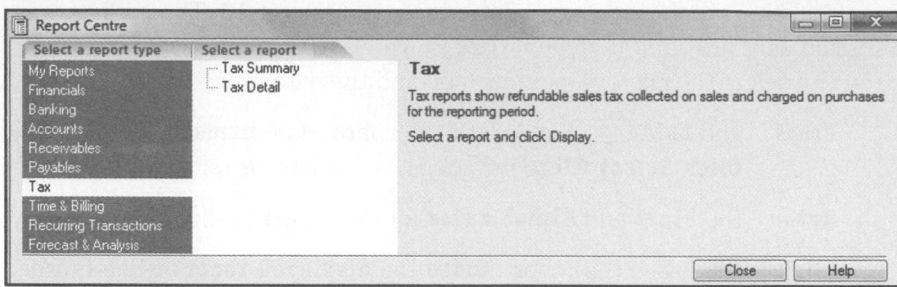

Click **Tax Summary** to display a sample report and description.

Click **Modify This Report** to display the Tax Report options window:

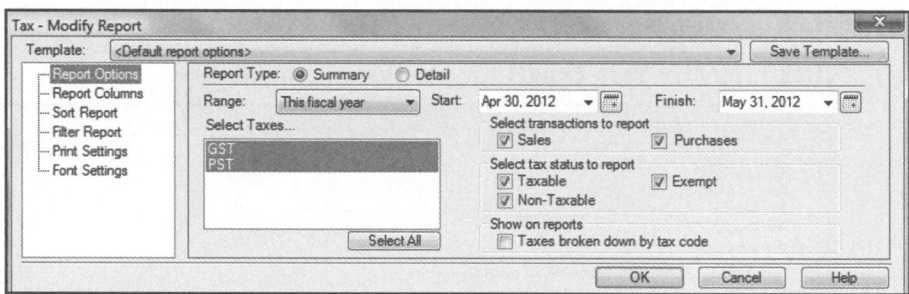

> **NOTES**
> You can sort and filter tax reports by name, invoice number, date, taxable purchases/sales excluding or including taxes, taxes paid/charged, other taxes paid/charged and total purchases/sales including taxes.

From the Home window, choose the Reports menu and click Tax to display the Tax Report options window.

All taxes that were defined for the company and included the option to report on them are listed in the Select Taxes field.

The earliest transaction and the session date are entered as the default date range for the report. You can include either sales or purchase transactions that include tax or both. Both purchases and sales are reported by default for all taxes. In addition, the report can include taxable, exempt and non-taxable transactions. By default all are selected. You can also organize the report by tax codes.

The **Summary** Report has only the totals for each category selected while the **Detail** Report lists individual transactions for each category. You can include the total tax amounts for each tax code as well.

Click **Detail** to select the more detailed level for the report.

Enter or **choose** the **dates** for which you want the report to start and finish (including the year).

Click a **tax name** in the Select Tax list to change the selection and then **click Select All** to report on all the taxes listed.

Click the **transactions** (Purchases or Sales) to remove a ✓ or to add one if it is not there to include the transaction in the report.

Click a **transaction tax status** (Taxable, Exempt or Non-Taxable) to remove a ✓ or to add one if it is not there.

Once you have selected the options you want,

Click   OK to view the report. **Close** the **display** when you have finished.

Displaying Cash Flow Reports

Displaying the Statement of Cash Flows

The Statement of Cash Flows summarizes sources (income, investments, etc.) and uses of cash (purchase of assets, etc.) and changes in liabilities during the designated period.

Click   Financials in the Select A Report Type list to open the list of reports:

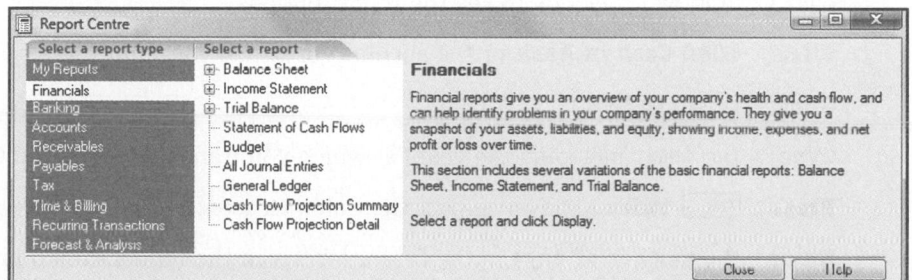

Click   Statement of Cash Flows to display a sample report and description.

Click   Modify This Report to display the Modify Report window:

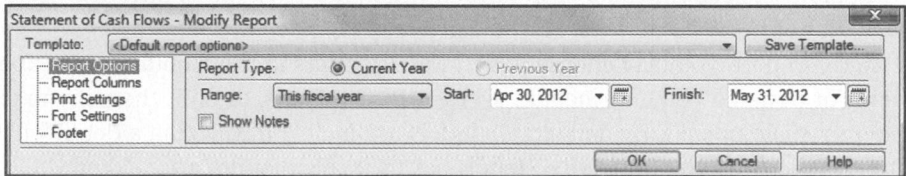

From the Home window, choose the Reports menu, then choose Financials and click Statement Of Cash Flows to see the report options.

Enter the **Start** and **Finish dates** for the report (including the year). The fiscal start and session dates are the defaults.

Click   OK to view the report.

By organizing the transactions involving cash, net changes in cash positions, as well as changes in liabilities, the statement allows the owner to judge how efficiently cash is being used for the business. The owner can also see potential problems resulting from increases in liabilities or decreases in the collection of receivables.

Close the **display** when you have finished.

Displaying Cash Flow Projection Reports

Cash Flow Projection reports predict the flow of cash in and out of an account — usually a bank account — over a specific future period based on current information.

Click   Cash Flow Projection Summary to display a sample report and description.

NOTES
You cannot sort or filter the Statement of Cash Flows or the Cash Flow Projection Report, but you can choose report columns.

Click **Modify This Report** to display the Modify Report window:

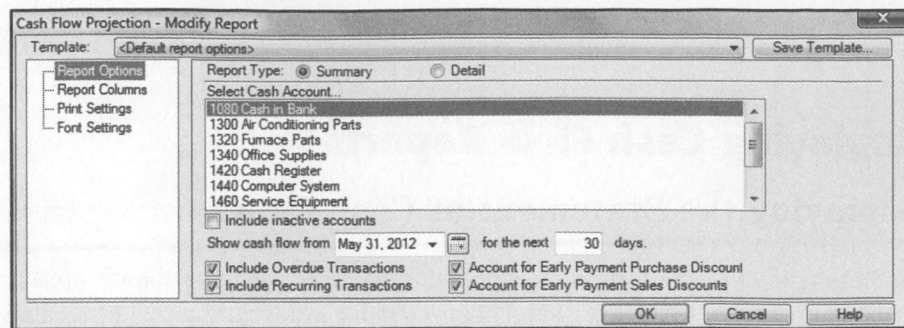

From the Home window, choose the Reports menu, then choose Financials and click Cash Flow Projection to see the report options.

Click **1080 Cash in Bank** or the account for which you want the report.

Click the **Date field**.

Type the **date** (including the year) at which you want the projection to start.

Press ⟨tab⟩ **twice** to advance past the Calendar icon.

Enter the **number of days** in the future for which the report should project the cash flow.

Usually, you will include only the number of days for which you have reasonable information, such as the number of days in which net payment is due. The session date and 30 days are useful periods, so you can accept the defaults.

In the report, you may choose to include discounts in the amounts you expect to receive or pay, and you may include overdue transactions, or omit them if you expect them to remain unpaid. By default, all details are included. Clicking a detail will remove it from the report. The Projection Report assumes all amounts are paid on the invoice due date.

The report projects the account balance based on receivables and payables due and recurring transactions coming due within the time frame specified. The **Summary** Report shows the totals for the specified report period while the **Detail** Report shows, by date, the individual transactions that are expected.

Select the **additional categories** for which you want details.

Click **Detail** to include individual transactions.

Click **OK** to view the report.

Close the **display**. **Close** the **Report Centre** to return to the Home window.

Displaying Management Reports

Management reports are displayed from the Home window Reports menu.

Choose the **Reports menu**, then **choose Management Reports** and **click Receivables** to see the reports and options:

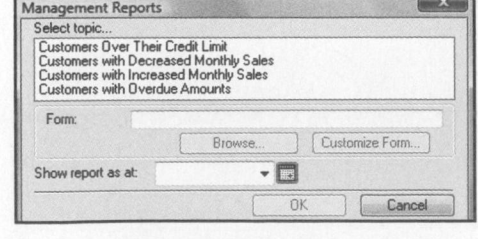

You can produce four different reports for the Receivables Ledger: a list of all customers who have exceeded their credit limits, sales amounts for customers who have decreased their purchases since the previous year, amounts for customers who have increased purchases and customers with overdue payments. The Overdue Amounts Report is helpful for making a list of customers to remind about settling their accounts because it includes customer contact details.

Click   the **topic** for the report.

The program will add a date, if appropriate, and a form for the report. Change the date if you need to, but leave the default report form unless you have the programs required to modify these forms.

Click   **OK** to display the report and print it if you want. **Close** the **display**.

Printing Customer Reports

Display the **report**.

Click   the **Change Print Settings tool** 🖷 to check that you have the correct printer selected. **Click OK** to return to the report.

Click   the **Print tool** 🖶 or **choose** the **File menu** in the report window, and then **click Print**.

Close   the **display** when you have finished.

Printing Customer Statements

You can e-mail all customer statements or print them, or you can choose e-mail and print on a customer-by-customer basis according to the setting (preference) in the customer's ledger record.

Choose   the **Reports menu** in the Home window, then **choose Receivables** and **click Customer Statements**.

You will see the following customer list with statement options:

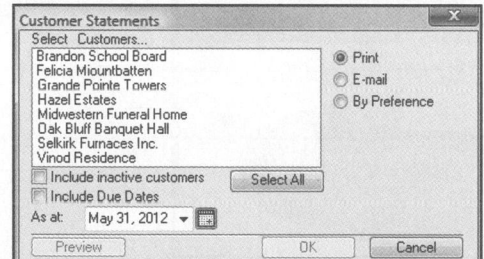

You should preview statements before printing them.

Press   and **hold** ⌷ctrl⌷ and **click** the **customers** for whom you want to print statements, or **click Select All** to include all customers.

Enter   the **date** (including the year) for the statements.

Click   **Include Due Dates** if you want to add the payment due dates for invoices, and **click Preview**.

Click   **OK** to close the preview and return to the options screen.

Click   **OK** again to print the statements.

WARNING!
If a form appears in the Form field, check that its location is correct for your program installation. It should be located in the Forms folder, in your Simply Accounting Premium 2010 folder.

NOTES
One customer account is currently overdue by more than 30 days. Two more customers have passed the 10-day discount window.

NOTES
Refer to Chapter 4, page 85, for details on setting up printers for different forms, reports and labels.

WARNING!
Be sure your printer is set up with the correct forms before you begin because statements are printed immediately when you click OK after selecting your options.

NOTES
You can customize customer statements but not mailing labels.
Customizing statements is similar to customizing invoices. Refer to Appendix G on the Student DVD for assistance with previewing and customizing forms.

NOTES
To preview statements, you must select Custom Simply Form. Choose the Setup menu and click Reports & Forms. Click Statements. Choose Custom Form and then Custom Simply Form. If you also want to customize the statements, choose User Defined Form in the Printed Form Description field. Click the Customize button to open the Simply Form Designer. Save the new form when finished.

Printing Customer Mailing Labels

You should turn on the printer, insert labels paper and set the program for printing labels before choosing the options for the labels because printing begins immediately.

Choose the Setup menu in the Home window and click Reports & Forms. Click Labels. Enter the details for the labels. Click OK.

Choose the **Reports menu** in the Home window, then **choose Mailing Labels** and **click Customers** to see the following options:

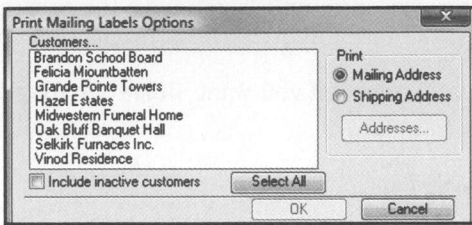

You can print labels for business mailing addresses, for shipping addresses or for any address list you created.

Press and **hold** ⌨ctrl⌨ and **click** the **customers** for whom you want to print the labels, or **click Select All** to include all customers. **Click OK**.

Graphing Customer Reports

Receivables by Aging Period Graph

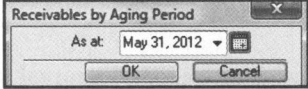

Choose the **Graphs menu** in the Home window and **click Receivables By Aging Period** to see the options screen:

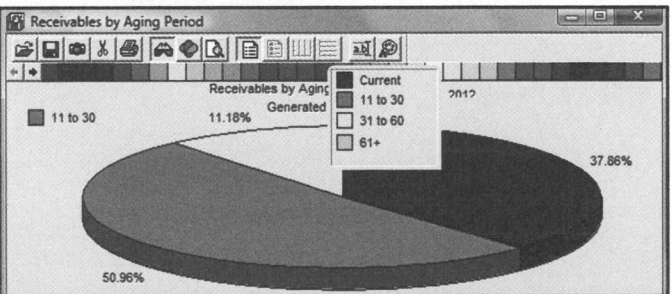

Enter a **date** for the graph and **click OK**.

The pie chart shows the total receivables divided according to the aging intervals set up in the company defaults. The chart is the customer equivalent of the Payables By Aging Period graph and shows the timeliness of account collections. You have the same tool bar options and colour and legend control choices that you have for the other graphs. Refer to page 63 for a review of these features if you need further assistance.

Double click a portion of a graph to see the aging period, the dollar amount and the percentage of the total. Double click the legend to make it larger. Double click the expanded legend to reduce it.

Close the **graph** when you have finished.

Receivables by Customer Graph

Choose the **Graphs menu** in the Home window and **click Receivables By Customer** to see the following options:

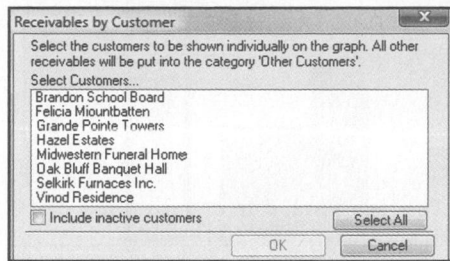

Press and **hold** ⌈ctrl⌉ and **click** the individual **customers** you want on the chart, or **click Select All** to include all customers.

Click **OK** to see the pie chart graph:

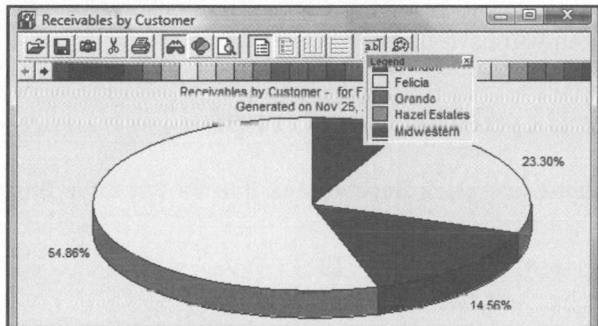

The amount owed by each customer, represented by different colours in the pie chart, is shown as a proportion of the total receivables. The options for displaying, editing, printing and exporting the graph are the same for all graphs.

Double click a portion of a graph to see the customer, the dollar amount and the percentage of the total. Double click the legend to make it large and add the customer names. Double click the expanded legend to reduce it.

Close the **graph** when you have finished.

Sales vs Receivables Graph

Choose the **Graphs menu** and **click Sales Vs Receivables** to see the options:

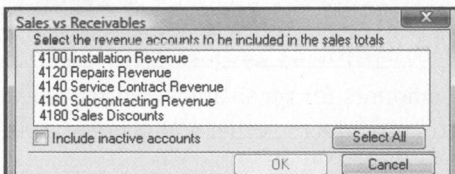

Press and **hold** ⌈ctrl⌉ and **click** the **revenue accounts** that you want in the graph. **Click Select All** to include all revenue accounts.

NOTES

The sales for April show as zero because we have not entered any transactions for April. The April receivables balance was the historical amount outstanding when we set up the data file.

NOTES

Although this is not a pie chart, you have the same options for exporting, copying, changing the display and so on that you do for other graphs.

Click   OK to display the following bar chart for the end of May:

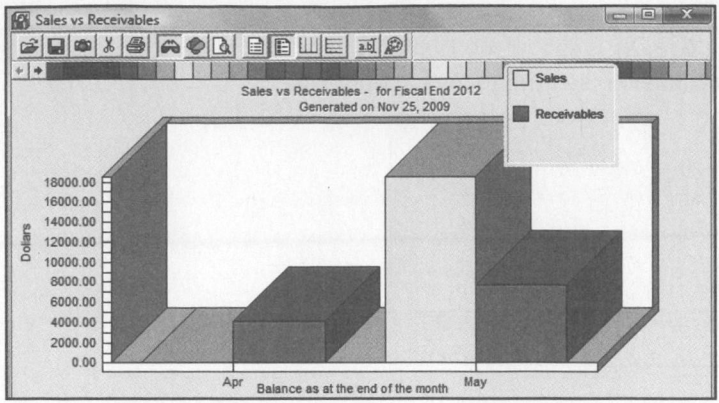

The graph indicates cash flow by showing the amount of sales not yet collected.

Double click a portion of the chart to see the period, the category (Sales or Receivables) and the dollar amount.

Close   the **graph** when you have finished.

Receivables Due vs Payables Due Graph

Choose the **Graphs menu** and **click Receivables Due Vs Payables Due**:

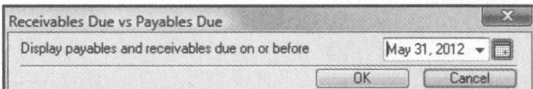

All receivables and payables due by the date displayed will be included. The session date is the default.

Enter   the **date** that you want for the graph. **Click OK** to display the bar chart:

NOTES

For the Receivables Due vs Payables Due bar chart, you have the same options for exporting, copying, changing the display and so on that you do for other graphs.

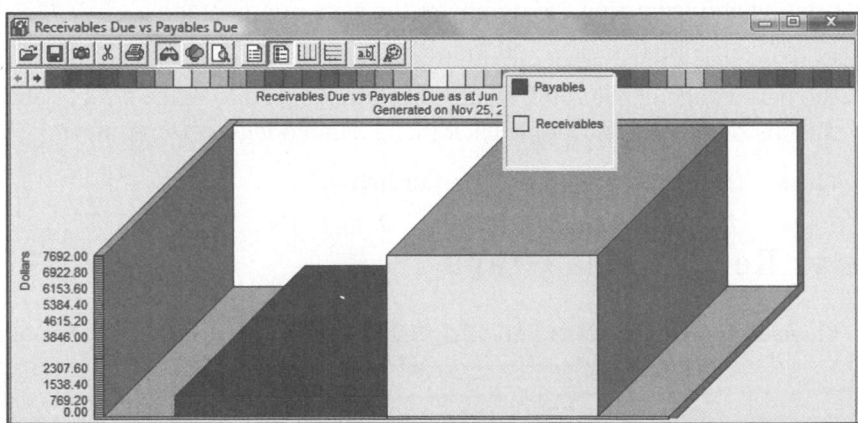

The graph shows the total amounts for receivables and payables due by June 30, 30 days beyond the session date, providing another indicator of cash flow.

NOTES

We entered June 30 as the date for this chart because no payments were due by May 31.

Double click a portion of the graph to see the period, the category (Payables or Receivables) and the dollar amount.

Close   the **graph** when you have finished.

R E V I E W

The Student DVD with Data Files includes Review Questions and Supplementary Cases for this chapter.

CHAPTER SEVEN

DorfmannDesign

OBJECTIVES

- **plan** and **design** an accounting system for a small business
- **prepare** procedures for converting from a manual system
- **understand** the objectives of a computerized system
- **create** company files
- **create** and **understand** linked accounts
- **set up** accounts in the General, Payables and Receivables ledgers
- **enter** historical information for suppliers and clients
- **correct** historical transactions after recording them
- **set up** credit cards for receipts and payments
- **set up** sales taxes and tax codes
- **finish** entering history after entering journal transactions
- **enter** postdated transactions

COMPANY INFORMATION

Company Profile

NOTES
Dorfmann Design
17 Tapestry Lane
Calgary, AB T3B 4U2
Tel: (403) 683-9145
Fax: (403) 685-8210
Business No.: 233 281 244

Dorfmann Design, owned by Desiree Dorfmann, has operated successfully in Calgary, Alberta, for several years. As a master of space management, Dorfmann is invited to take on many different work assignments. She has designed boutiques in department stores, cosmetic counters and coffee bars; office space in banks; offices for professionals; countertop display areas in stores; shelving for display items, books or journals; and classroom and auditorium arrangements in colleges, universities and schools. She is frequently asked to convert unpleasant or unused spaces into attractive, inviting places by maximizing the usable space and making it open and comfortable while respecting the need for privacy. Sometimes she combines rich, textured fabrics in classical designs with sleek and modern materials to enhance an office or sales area. The end result always attracts attention.

Some clients ask only for her consultation, preferring to do the work themselves. For those clients she generates reports on how to maximize the use of space, or how to create attractive environments that encourage clients to buy. Most clients employ her because they understand the value of good design.

Dorfmann has accounts set up with her regular suppliers, some of whom offer discounts for early payment on a before-tax basis. These suppliers provide office and computer supplies, specialized design software and materials for building scale models. She also has a maintenance contract with a local cleaning company. All purchases are subject to 5 percent GST.

Most of Dorfmann's clients are in the Calgary region. She is negotiating with businesses in Wyoming, but so far none of these leads has led to confirmed contracts. Canadian clients pay 5 percent GST on all services provided and are offered an after-tax discount of 1 percent if they pay within five days. Overdue accounts are subject to interest charges at the rate of 1.5 percent after 30 days.

On March 31, she gathered the following business information to convert her accounting records to Simply Accounting:

- Business Information
- Chart of Accounts
- Income Statement
- Balance Sheet
- Trial Balance
- Supplier Information
- Client Information
- Accounting Procedures

BUSINESS INFORMATION

DORFMANN DESIGN

COMPANY INFORMATION
Address: 17 Tapestry Lane
            Calgary, Alberta T3B 4U2
Phone: (403) 683-9145
Fax: (403) 685-8210
Business No.: 233 281 244 RT0001
Fiscal Start: Jan. 1, 2012
Fiscal End: June 30, 2012
Earliest Transaction: March 31, 2012
Company Type: Service

REPORTS & FORMS
Choose settings for your printer and forms

USER PREFERENCES
Options
Use Accounting Terms
Automatically Save Changes to Records
Show List Buttons
Calculate Record Balances in Home Window
      by Session Date
View Settings
Hide: Inventory & Services, Employees &
      Payroll, Project, Time & Billing
Daily Business Manager: turn off
Checklists: turn off
Show Session Date at Startup
Transaction Confirmation: turned on

COMPANY SETTINGS
System
Allow Future Transactions
      Warn if more than 7 days in future
Warn if Accounts Not Balanced
Backup
Backup Weekly
Turn off scheduled backup
Features
Do not use orders, quotes, packing slips &
      projects
Use both French and English
Credit Card Information
Card Accepted: Visa
Discount Fee: 2.9%
Expense Account: 5020
Asset Account: 1070
Card Accepted: MasterCard
Discount Fee: 2.7%
Expense Account: 5020
Asset Account: 1080
Card Used: Visa
Payable Account: 2160
Expense Account: 5020
Sales Taxes
Taxes: GST 5%
Code: G - GST @ 5%
Date Format: Use long dates on the screen
Logo: SimData10\Setup\logos\dorfmann.bmp

Forms Settings (Next Number)
Sales Invoices   No. 44
Receipts   No. 25

GENERAL SETTINGS: No changes

PAYABLES SETTINGS
Address: Calgary, Alberta, Canada
Options
Aging Periods: 15, 30, 45 days
Discounts before Tax: Yes

RECEIVABLES SETTINGS
Address: Calgary, Alberta, Canada
Options
Aging Periods: 5, 15, 30 days
Interest Charges: 1.5% after 30 days
Statements Include Invoices for 31 days
New Client Tax Code: G
Discounts
Payment Terms: 1/5, n/15 after tax
Discounts before Tax: No
Line Discounts: No
Comments
Sales Invoice: Interest @ 1.5% per month
      charged on accounts over 30 days.

BANK ACCOUNTS: NEXT CHEQUE NO.
Bank: Chequing   65

CHART OF ACCOUNTS

DORFMANN DESIGN

ASSETS
- 1000 CURRENT ASSETS [H]
- 1010 Test Balance Account
- 1060 Bank: Chequing [A]
- 1070 Bank: Visa [A]
- 1080 Bank: MasterCard [A]
- 1100 Net Bank [S]
- 1200 Accounts Receivable
- 1210 Prepaid Insurance
- 1220 Model Parts Inventory
- 1230 Computer Supplies
- 1240 Office Supplies
- 1250 Software
- 1290 TOTAL CURRENT ASSETS [T]

- 1400 OFFICE & EQUIPMENT [H]
- 1410 Computer Equipment
- 1420 Design Equipment
- 1430 Furniture & Fixtures ▶
- ▶1440 Motor Vehicle
- 1450 Office Condominium
- 1490 TOTAL OFFICE & EQUIPMENT [T]

LIABILITIES
- 2000 CURRENT LIABILITIES [H]
- 2100 Bank Loan
- 2160 Credit Card Payable
- 2200 Accounts Payable
- 2650 GST Charged on Services [A]
- 2670 GST Paid on Purchases [A]
- 2750 GST Owing (Refund) [S]
- 2790 TOTAL CURRENT LIABILITIES [T]

- 2800 LONG TERM LIABILITIES [H]
- 2850 Mortgage Payable
- 2890 TOTAL LONG TERM LIABILITIES [T] ▶

▶EQUITY
- 3000 OWNER'S EQUITY [H]
- 3560 D. Dorfmann, Capital
- 3650 Current Earnings [X]
- 3690 UPDATED CAPITAL [T]

REVENUE
- 4000 GENERAL REVENUE [H]
- 4020 Revenue from Design
- 4040 Revenue from Consulting
- 4060 Sales Discounts
- 4100 Interest Revenue
- 4290 TOTAL REVENUE [T]

EXPENSE
- 5000 OPERATING EXPENSES [H]
- 5010 Bank Charges
- 5020 Credit Card Fees
- 5040 Purchase Discounts ▶

- ▶5050 Delivery Expenses
- 5060 Hydro Expense
- 5070 Maintenance Services
- 5100 Model Parts Used
- 5110 Computer Supplies Used
- 5120 Office Supplies Used
- 5150 Insurance Expense
- 5160 Telephone Expense
- 5200 Loan Interest Expense
- 5210 Mortgage Interest Expense
- 5990 TOTAL OPERATING EXPENSES [T]

NOTES: The Chart of Accounts includes all accounts. Account types are marked for all subgroup Accounts [A], Subgroup totals [S], Heading accounts [H], Total accounts [T] and the type X account. All other unmarked accounts are postable Group accounts.

INCOME STATEMENT

DORFMANN DESIGN

January 1 to March 31, 2012

Revenue

4000	GENERAL REVENUE	
4020	Revenue from Design	$38 000
4040	Revenue from Consulting	7 400
4060	Sales Discounts	–400
4100	Interest Revenue	371
4290	TOTAL REVENUE	$45 371
	TOTAL REVENUE	$45 371 ▶

▶ Expenses

5000	OPERATING EXPENSES	
5010	Bank Charges	$ 225
5020	Credit Card Fees	590
5040	Purchase Discounts	–300
5050	Delivery Expenses	180
5060	Hydro Expense	750
5070	Maintenance Services	1 391
5100	Model Parts Used	1 600
5110	Computer Supplies Used	1 200
5120	Office Supplies Used	1 150
5150	Insurance Expense	600
5160	Telephone Expense	400
5200	Loan Interest Expense	625
5210	Mortgage Interest Expense	6 000
5990	TOTAL OPERATING EXPENSES	$ 14 411
	TOTAL EXPENSE	$ 14 411
	NET INCOME (LOSS)	$30 960

BALANCE SHEET

DORFMANN DESIGN

March 31, 2012

Assets				Liabilities			
1000	CURRENT ASSETS			2000	CURRENT LIABILITIES		
1060	Bank: Chequing	$ 29 211		2100	Bank Loan		$ 25 000
1070	Bank: Visa	1 950		2160	Credit Card Payable		1 010
1080	Bank: MasterCard	1 060		2200	Accounts Payable		9 174
1100	Net Bank		$ 32 221	2650	GST Charged on Services	$1 530	
1200	Accounts Receivable		3 860	2670	GST Paid on Purchases	−840	
1210	Prepaid Insurance		1 800	2750	GST Owing (Refund)		690
1220	Model Parts Inventory		4 000	2790	TOTAL CURRENT LIABILITIES		$ 35 874
1230	Computer Supplies		1 500				
1240	Office Supplies		1 000	2800	LONG TERM LIABILITIES		
1250	Software		2 000	2850	Mortgage Payable		75 000
1290	TOTAL CURRENT ASSETS		$ 46 381	2890	TOTAL LONG TERM LIABILITIES		$ 75 000
				TOTAL LIABILITIES			$ 110 874
1400	OFFICE & EQUIPMENT						
1410	Computer Equipment		12 000	Equity			
1420	Design Equipment		8 000	3000	OWNER'S EQUITY		
1430	Furniture & Fixtures		4 000	3560	D. Dorfmann, Capital		$ 78 547
1440	Motor Vehicle		50 000	3650	Current Earnings		30 960
1450	Office Condominium		100 000	3690	UPDATED CAPITAL		$ 109 507
1490	TOTAL OFFICE & EQUIPMENT		$174 000	TOTAL EQUITY			$ 109 507
TOTAL ASSETS			$220 381 ▶	LIABILITIES AND EQUITY			$220 381

TRIAL BALANCE

DORFMANN DESIGN

March 31, 2012

		Debit	Credit				Debit	Credit
1060	Bank: Chequing	$ 29 211		▶	3560	D. Dorfmann, Capital		78 547
1070	Bank: Visa	1 950			4020	Revenue from Design		38 000
1080	Bank: MasterCard	1 060			4040	Revenue from Consulting		7 400
1200	Accounts Receivable	3 860			4060	Sales Discounts	400	
1210	Prepaid Insurance	1 800			4100	Interest Revenue		371
1220	Model Parts Inventory	4 000			5010	Bank Charges	225	
1230	Computer Supplies	1 500			5020	Credit Card Fees	590	
1240	Office Supplies	1 000			5040	Purchase Discounts		300
1250	Software	2 000			5050	Delivery Expenses	180	
1410	Computer Equipment	12 000			5060	Hydro Expense	750	
1420	Design Equipment	8 000			5070	Maintenance Services	1 391	
1430	Furniture & Fixtures	4 000			5100	Model Parts Used	1 600	
1440	Motor Vehicle	50 000			5110	Computer Supplies Used	1 200	
1450	Office Condominium	100 000			5120	Office Supplies Used	1 150	
2100	Bank Loan		$ 25 000		5150	Insurance Expense	600	
2160	Credit Card Payable		1 010		5160	Telephone Expense	400	
2200	Accounts Payable		9 174		5200	Loan Interest Expense	625	
2650	GST Charged on Services		1 530		5210	Mortgage Interest Expense	6 000	
2670	GST Paid on Purchases	840					$236 332	$236 332
2850	Mortgage Payable		75 000 ▶					

SUPPLIER INFORMATION

DORFMANN DESIGN

Supplier Name (Contact)	Address	Phone No. Fax No.	E-mail Web Site Tax ID	Terms Account	YTD Expenses (YTD Payments) Tax Code
Alberta Energy Corp. (Con Edison)	50 Watts Rd. Suite 800 Calgary, Alberta T3G 5K8	Tel 1: (403) 755-6000 Tel 2: (403) 755-3997 Fax: (403) 754-7201	accounts@aeg.ca www.aeg.ca 459 021 643	net 10 5060	$802 ($802) G
Designers Den (Art Masters)	166 Blackfoot Trail Calgary, Alberta T3P 5P4	Tel: (403) 459-3917 Fax: (403) 459-6200	artm@artful.com www.artful.com 562 553 400	2/10, n/30 (before tax) 1420	G
DesignMaster Software (Dee Collage)	233 Crowchild Trail Mississauga, Ontario L4F 2B5	Tel: (905) 566-3754 Fax: (905) 566-5623	deecoll@dms.com www.dms.com 465 377 299	1/5, n/30 (before tax) 1250	G
Maintenance & More (Rehab Major)	51 Bragg Creek Rd. Calgary, Alberta T3C 4N3	Tel: (403) 762-7622 Fax: (403) 762-9888	RMajor@mandm.com www.mandm.com 712 300 807	net 15 5070	$1 155 ($1 155) G
Models to Scale (Bill Derr)	649 4th Street Calgary, Alberta T4P 5D6	Tel: (403) 477-5997 Fax: (403) 478-8103	billd@models.com www.models.com 923 488 561	2/10, n/30 (before tax)	G
Purolator Delivery (Cam Carter)	598 Bow River Rd. Calgary, Alberta T4T 2M1	Tel 1: (403) 458-2144 Tel 2: (888) 458-2144	www.purolator.com 822 012 906	net 1 5050	$193 ($193) G
Receiver General for Canada	Sudbury Tax Services Office PO Box 20004 Sudbury, Ontario P3A 6B4	Tel 1: (800) 561-7761 Tel 2: (800) 959-2221	www.cra-arc.gc.ca	net 1 2650	($790) No tax
Staples Business Depot (Joel)	60 Richmond Rd. Calgary, Alberta T4G 2T2	Tel: (403) 761-6288 Fax: (403) 769-5532	joel@businessdep.com www.businessdep.com	net 10 1240	$1 890 ($1 890) G
Western Bell (Sal Fone)	74 Sounder Ave. Calgary, Alberta T5L 4G2	Tel 1: (403) 755-3255 Tel 2: (403) 755-5721	accounts@bell.ca www.bell.ca 492 304 590	net 1 5160	$630 ($630) G

OUTSTANDING SUPPLIER INVOICES

DORFMANN DESIGN

Supplier Name	Terms	Date	Inv/Chq No.	Amount	Tax	Total
Designers Den	2/10, n/30 (before tax)	Mar. 26/12 Mar. 26/12	DD-4502 Chq 62	$2 500	$125	$2 625 2 180
	2/10, n/30 (before tax)	Mar. 28/12	DD-4630 Balance owing	500	25	525 $ 970
DesignMaster Software	1/5, n/30 (before tax)	Mar. 13/12	DMS-234	$1 900	95	$1 995
Maintenance & More	net 15 net 15	Mar. 24/12 Mar. 31/12	MM-211 MM-242 Balance owing	$105 105		$105 105 $210
Models to Scale	2/10, n/30 (before tax)	Mar. 25/12 Mar. 25/12	MS-376 Chq 59	$4 000	$200	$4 200 2 000
	2/10, n/30 (before tax)	Mar. 28/12	MS-453 Balance owing	2 000	100	2 100 $4 300
			Grand Total			$7 475

CLIENT INFORMATION

DORFMANN DESIGN

Client Name (Contact)	Address	Phone No. Fax No.	E-mail Web Site	Terms Revenue Acct Tax Code	YTD Sales (Credit Limit) Client Since
Alberta Heritage Bank (A. Spender)	306 Revenue Road Fourth Floor Okotoks, Alberta T0L 1T3	Tel 1: (403) 744-5900 Tel 2: (403) 744-6345 Fax: (403) 744-5821	spender@heritagebank.com www.heritagebank.com	1/5, n/15 (after tax) 4020 G	$3 150 ($5 000) Jan. 1/12
Banff Condominiums (R.T. House)	99 Main Street Banff, Alberta T0L 0C0	Tel: (403) 764-3884 Fax: (403) 764-3917	rthouse@banffcondos.ca www.banffcondos.ca	1/5, n/15 (after tax) 4020 G	($5 000) Jan. 1/12
Calgary Arms Hotel (Enda Lodge)	601 Regiment Road Calgary, Alberta T4G 5H4	Tel 1: (403) 622-4456 Tel 2: (877) 623-9100 Fax: (403) 622-5188	enda@calgarms.com www.calgarms.com	1/5, n/15 (after tax) 4020 G	$7 770 ($5 000) Apr. 1/09
Calgary District School Board (Seconde Grader)	88 Learnex Avenue 8th Floor Calgary, Alberta T3C 4B6	Tel 1: (403) 788-3000 Tel 2: (403) 788-7107 Fax: (403) 788-3327	sg@cdsb.ca www.cdsb.ca	1/5, n/15 (after tax) 4020 G	$8 400 ($5 000) Jul. 1/05
Glitter Jewellers (Di Monde)	60 Ruby Street Calgary, Alberta T4C 2G6	Tel: (403) 745-6181 Fax: (403) 745-6297	di@glitter.com www.glitter.com	1/5, n/15 (after tax) 4020 G	$5 250 ($5 000) Apr. 1/09
Lougheed, Klein & Assoc - Lawyers (Bill Bigger)	121 Advocate Ave. Suite 300 Calgary, Alberta T4D 2P7	Tel 1: (403) 398-4190 Tel 2: (403) 377-2534 Fax: (403) 377-3799	bbigger@LKlawyers.com www.LKlawyers.com	1/5, n/15 (after tax) 4020 G	$10 500 ($5 000) Jul. 1/07
Passions Dept Store (Mann E. Kinn)	44 Highlife Ave. Bragg Creek, Alberta T0L 0K0	Tel: (403) 762-8662 Fax: (403) 763-9115	www.passions.com	1/5, n/15 (after tax) 4020 G	$6 300 ($5 000) Jan. 1/06

OUTSTANDING CLIENT INVOICES

DORFMANN DESIGN

Client Name	Terms	Date	Inv/Chq No.	Amount	Total
Alberta Heritage Bank	1/5, n/15 (after tax)	Mar. 23/12	38	$3 150	
		Mar. 23/12	Chq 6754	1 400	
			Balance owing		$1 750
Banff Condominiums	1/5, n/15 (after tax)	Mar. 28/12	39	$2 100	
		Mar. 28/12	Chq 4388	1 040	
	1/5, n/15 (after tax)	Mar. 31/12	41	1 050	
			Balance owing		$2 110
				Grand Total	$3 860

Accounting Procedures

Open-Invoice Accounting for Payables and Receivables

The open-invoice method of accounting for invoices allows the business to keep track of each individual invoice and any partial payments made against it. This method is in contrast to methods that only keep track of the outstanding balance by combining all invoice balances owed to a supplier or by a client. Simply Accounting uses the

NOTES
Provincial sales taxes are not levied in Alberta.
Most bank services and other financial institution services are exempt from GST collection.

open-invoice method. When invoices are fully paid, they should be removed periodically after statements are received from the supplier or sent to the clients.

The Goods and Services Tax: Remittances

Dorfmann uses the regular method for GST remittances. GST collected from clients is recorded as a liability in *GST Charged on Services*. GST paid to suppliers is recorded in *GST Paid on Purchases* as a decrease in the liability. The balance, or request for refund, is remitted to the Receiver General for Canada by the last day of the month for the previous quarter.

Sales of Services

Accounts are set up for several clients. Other clients pay for their purchases immediately by cash, cheque or credit card. Separate bank accounts are set up for credit card deposits. You can enter transactions for cash and credit card clients by choosing One-Time Client/Customer and typing the name of the client in the Address field or by typing the client's name in the Name field and choosing the Quick Add or Continue option.

For cash sales, the program will debit *Bank: Chequing* (or *Bank: Visa* or *MasterCard* for credit card payments) instead of the *Accounts Receivable* control account.

Purchases

Most regular suppliers have given Dorfmann credit terms, including some discounts for early payment. Some purchases are accompanied by immediate payment, usually by cheque or credit card. Cheque payments are preferred because the cancelled cheques become part of the business records. Enter the cash transaction for purchases from new suppliers in the Payments Journal as an Other Payment. Choose the appropriate Payment Method; choose One-Time Supplier from the Supplier list; type the supplier's name in the Address field. You can also type the name in the Supplier field and choose Quick Add or Continue.

For cash purchases paid by cash or cheque, the program will credit *Bank: Chequing* instead of the *Accounts Payable* control account. For credit card purchases, *Credit Card Payable* is credited. All other accounts for this transaction will be appropriately debited and credited.

Discounts

Dorfmann Design offers a 1 percent discount to account clients if they settle their accounts within five days. Full payment is requested within 15 days. These payment terms are set up as defaults. When the receipt is entered, if the discount is still available, the program will show the amount of the discount and the net amount owing automatically. Discounts are not allowed on partial payments or on cash purchases paid by cheque or credit card. All client sales discounts are calculated on after-tax amounts.

Some suppliers also offer discounts, calculated on the amounts before taxes, for early settlement of accounts. Again, when the terms are entered for the supplier and full payment is made before the discount period expires, the program will display the pretax discount as available and automatically calculate a net balance owing. Payment terms vary from supplier to supplier.

INSTRUCTIONS

1. **Set up** the **company accounts** using the Business Information, Chart of Accounts, Balance Sheet, Income Statement, Trial Balance and Supplier and Client Information provided for March 31, 2012. Detailed instructions to assist you in setting up the company accounts follow.

2. If you prefer to enter the source documents before setting up the data files, you can restore the dorfman1.CAB file in the SETUP folder (inside the SimData10 folder). In this way, you will become familiar with the account structure, and the setup may be easier to complete.

3. **Enter** the **transactions** beginning on page 254 in Simply Accounting using the Chart of Accounts, Supplier Information, Client Information and Accounting Procedures.

4. **Print** the **reports and graphs** indicated on the following printing form after you have completed your entries:

REPORTS

Accounts
- [ ] Chart of Accounts
- [ ] Account List
- [ ] General Journal Entries

Financials
- [✓] Comparative Balance Sheet: April 1 and April 30, difference in percentage
- [✓] Income Statement: January 1 to April 30
- [✓] Trial Balance: April 30
- [✓] All Journal Entries: April 1 to June 15
- [✓] General Ledger accounts: 1060 4020 4040 from April 1 to April 30
- [✓] Cash Flow Projection Detail Report for account 1060 for 30 days
- [ ] Statement of Cash Flows

Tax
- [✓] GST Report April 1 to April 30

Banking
- [ ] Cheque Log Report

Payables
- [ ] Supplier List
- [ ] Supplier Aged
- [ ] Aged Overdue Payables
- [ ] Expense Journal Entries
- [ ] Payment Journal Entries

Receivables
- [ ] Client List
- [ ] Client Aged
- [ ] Aged Overdue Receivables
- [ ] Revenues Journal Entries
- [ ] Receipt Journal Entries
- [ ] Client Statements

Mailing Labels
- [ ] Labels

Management Reports
- [ ] Ledger

GRAPHS
- [ ] Payables by Aging Period
- [ ] Payables by Supplier
- [ ] Receivables by Aging Period
- [ ] Receivables by Client
- [ ] Sales vs Receivables
- [ ] Receivables Due vs Payables Due
- [ ] Revenues by Account
- [ ] Expenses by Account
- [✓] Expenses and Net Profit as % of Revenue

KEYSTROKES FOR SETUP

Creating Company Files

For Dorfmann Design, we will create the company files from scratch rather than use one of the starter files. Once we create the files and define the defaults, we will add the accounts, define linked accounts for the General, Payables and Receivables ledgers and create supplier and client records.

Start   the **Simply Accounting program**.

You should see the Simply Accounting, Select Company window:

Click   **Create A New Company**. **Click OK**.

You will see the Setup wizard introduction screen:

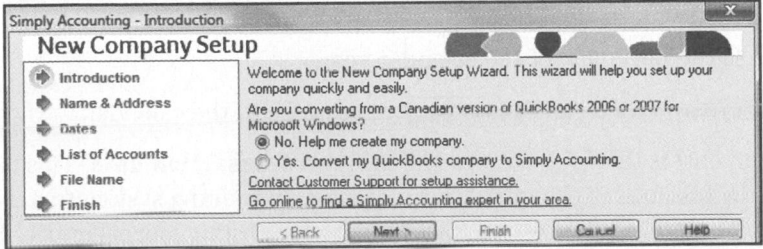

This screen introduces the Setup wizard and some support options.

Click   **Next** to continue:

You must now enter company information for the business. The cursor is in the Name field. Alberta and its two-letter abbreviation — the first entry in the province list — are entered as defaults. Use the Business Information on page 204 to enter the company name and address details.

Type	Dorfmann Design **Press** ⟨tab⟩ to enter the name.
Type	17 Tapestry Lane **Press** ⟨tab⟩ to enter the street address.
Press	⟨tab⟩ to skip the Street 2 field.
Type	Calgary and **click** the **Postal Code field**.
Type	t3b4u2 **Press** ⟨tab⟩ to enter the postal code.
Type	Canada **Press** ⟨tab⟩ to enter the country.
Type	4036839145 **Press** ⟨tab⟩ to enter the phone number.
Press	⟨tab⟩ to skip the Phone 2 field and move to the Fax field.
Type	4036858210

NOTES
Another setup option is to convert data files that were created with the QuickBooks program to Simply Accounting data files.

NOTES
Remember that you can personalize the data file by adding your own name to the company name.

NOTES

We will set the date format with the Company settings. The initial date format for your new file is determined by your computer system settings, so your screen may show DD-MM-YYYY or MM-DD-YYYY. The author's computer had DD-MM-YYYY as the setting so this format is shown for dates.

The Calendar icon shows the current month for your computer system. It is easier to type in the dates than it is to scroll through several months to find the one you need.

Typing the date in text format ensures that you will enter it correctly. You should type a four-digit year the first time you enter a date in the year 2000 or later to be certain that the year will be 2012 and not 1912.

NOTES

To find out if you need to enter four digits for the year, try typing a date such as 6-5-12.

NOTES

The Earliest Transaction date is also the initial date before which you do not allow transactions.

Click   **Next** to open the company fiscal dates screen:

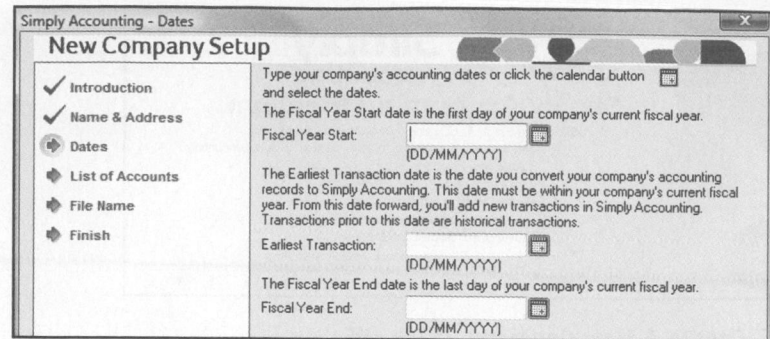

These company fiscal dates are like the ones you entered for Toss for Tots (Chapter 4) as part of the Company Information setup. The cursor is in the Fiscal Year Start field. This is the date on which the business begins its fiscal year. For Dorfmann Design, the fiscal start date is the beginning of the calendar year.

Type   jan 1 2012 **Press** (tab) to advance to the calendar.

The program enters the fiscal start as the **earliest transaction date**. This is the date on which the business is changing from a manual accounting system to a computerized accounting system — the earliest date for posting journal entries and the latest date for historical information. Dorfmann is converting her records on March 31.

Press   (tab) to advance to the Earliest Transaction date field.

Type   mar 31 2012

Press   (tab) **twice** to advance to the Fiscal Year End field — the date Dorfmann Design ends its fiscal period. The end of the year is the default fiscal end date. Dorfmann Design's fiscal period is six months.

Type   jun 30 2012 **Click Next** to continue:

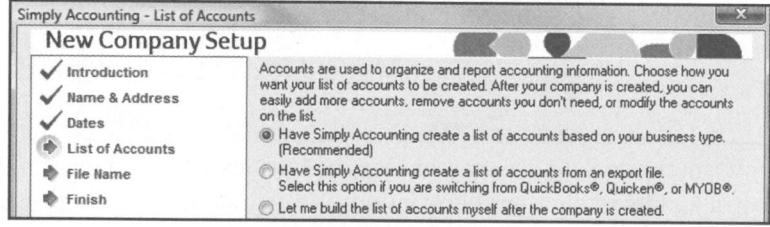

You can let Simply Accounting create a set of accounts that are suitable for the business type you selected, start from scratch to create the data files or copy data from another program. The set of accounts created by the program will included many accounts not required for Dorfmann Design. Because our setup is relatively small and we want to show all the stages of the setup, we will start from scratch. This approach allows us to show all the options available for each stage.

Click   **Let Me Build The List Of Accounts Myself After The Company Is Created**:

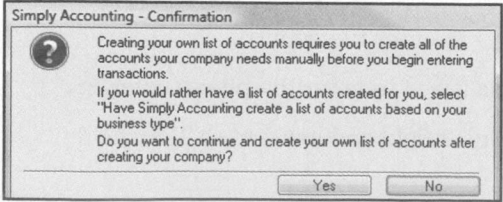

This message confirms your selection to create all the accounts on your own.

Click **Yes** to continue to the industry type selection list:

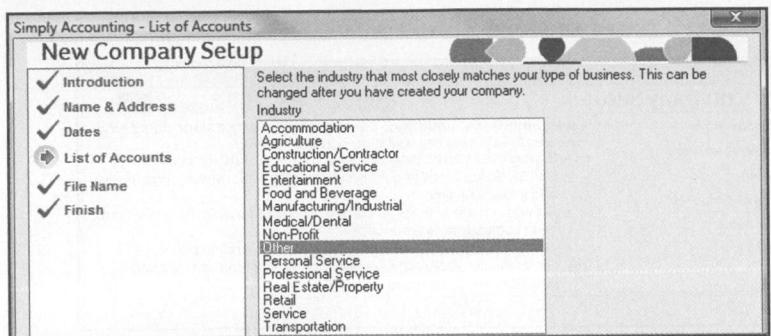

PRO VERSION

pro Remember that icon labels are the same for all company types — Customer and Vendor are the terms used throughout the Receivables and Payables modules respectively.

At this stage you should choose the type of business that best describes your company. This selection will determine some of the default settings and icon labels. You can scroll down the list to see the various types. Dorfmann Design is a service business.

Click **Service** as the Industry type.

Click **Next** to open the File Name screen:

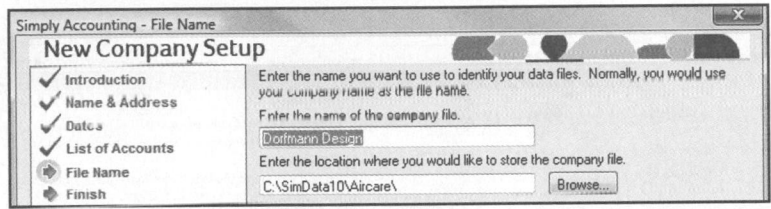

Now you must choose a file name and folder to store the new data set. The company name is entered as the default name for the data file, and it is selected.

Type dorfmann

Press (tab) to advance to the location field.

The last folder you used will be the default selection — that is, Aircare, if you last worked with the Air Care Services data set. Change folders if necessary to access the one with your other data files. If you have already created the folder you want to use,

Click **Browse** to open the Browse For Folder screen to select a folder. Otherwise,

Drag through Aircare\ in the folder name or the last folder in the location field.

Type Dorfmann\ to replace Aircare or the last folder in the location.

Click **Next** to see the confirmation message:

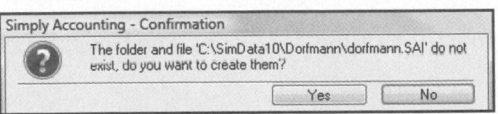

NOTES
Simply Accounting will automatically add the correct file extension. You do not need to type it when you are creating a new data set.

Simply Accounting advises that you have named a new folder and asks if you want to create it.

Click **Yes** to create the new folder and file:

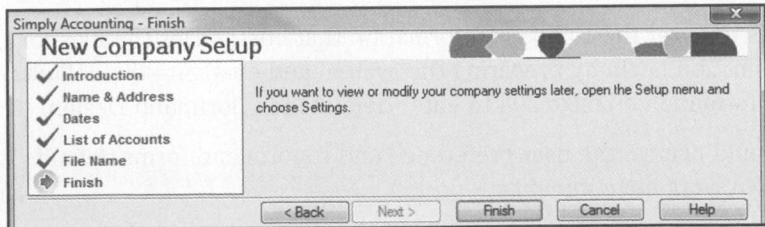

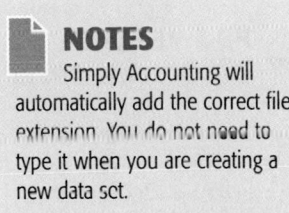

This screen reminds you that you can change this information from the Setup menu.

Click   Finish to see the final Setup screen:

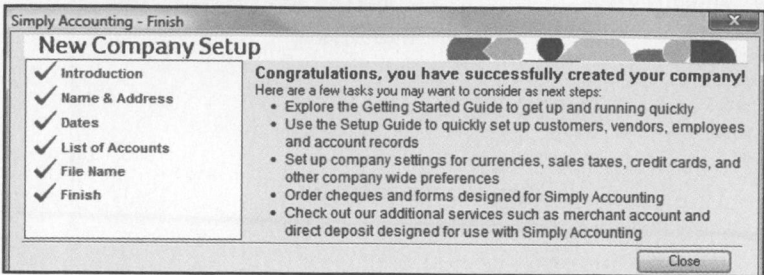

Click   Close to complete the file creation stage.

Click   Show This Window On Startup to remove the ✓ so that the Getting Started Guide window will not open each time you start the program.

Click   Close to display the Receivables module Home window:

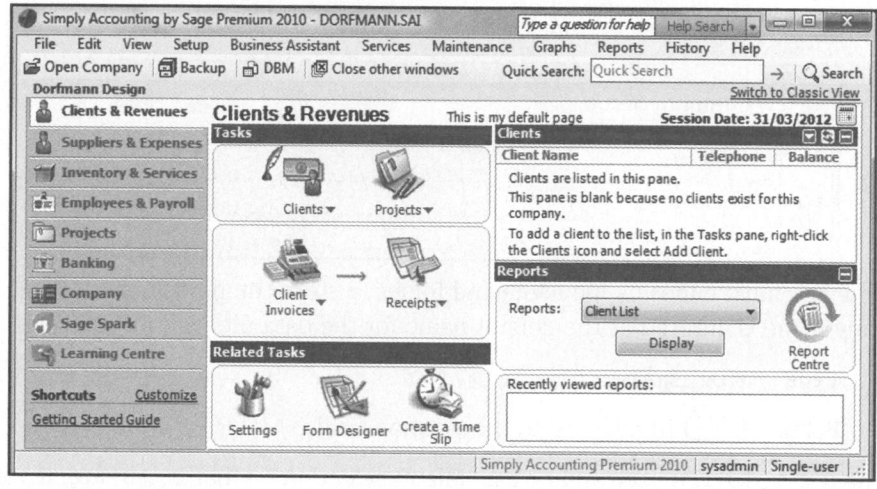

The Home window is now open with the name Dorfmann in the title bar. One shortcut, for the Getting Started Guide Welcome screen, is added by default. However, non-accounting terms are selected, so the module names are different from the ones in previous applications. Clients & Revenues replaces Receivables and Suppliers & Expenses replaces Payables. We will change these terms as part of the setup.

The Clients ledger icon has the open history quill pen icon [icon] because the ledgers are still open for entering historical information. No ledgers are hidden.

Display the **Chart of Accounts** for the Current Year.

The only account provided by default is the type X account, the General Ledger linked account, *Current Earnings*.

Close the **Chart of Accounts**.

Preparing the System

The next step is to enter the company information that customizes the files for Dorfmann Design. You begin by preparing the system and changing the defaults. Use the Business Information on page 204 to enter defaults for Dorfmann Design.

You should change the user preference and reports and forms defaults to suit your own work environment.

Changing User Preferences

Choose the **Setup menu**, then **click User Preferences**.

If you are working in multi-user mode, decide whether you want to refresh lists automatically so that changes other users make affect your file immediately. The option to Show List Buttons is already selected.

Choose Use Accounting Terms so that your on-screen terms will match the ones used in this workbook.

Choose Automatically Save Changes To Supplier, Client And Other Records.

Choose Calculate Record Balances In The Home Window By Session Date, instead of the default — balances based on the latest transactions.

Click View.

Click Inventory & Services, **Employees & Payroll**, **Project** and **Time & Billing** to hide the unused modules and features.

Click After Changing Session Date to remove the ✓ for **Daily Business Manager** and **Checklists**.

Choose Show Change Session Date At Startup.

Click Transaction Confirmation. **Confirm** that the **Confirmation Message Box** is checked to activate this option.

Click OK to save the preference changes and return to the Home window.

You should now see the familiar accounting term labels for the modules. At this stage your Home window should look like the following, with hidden modules removed:

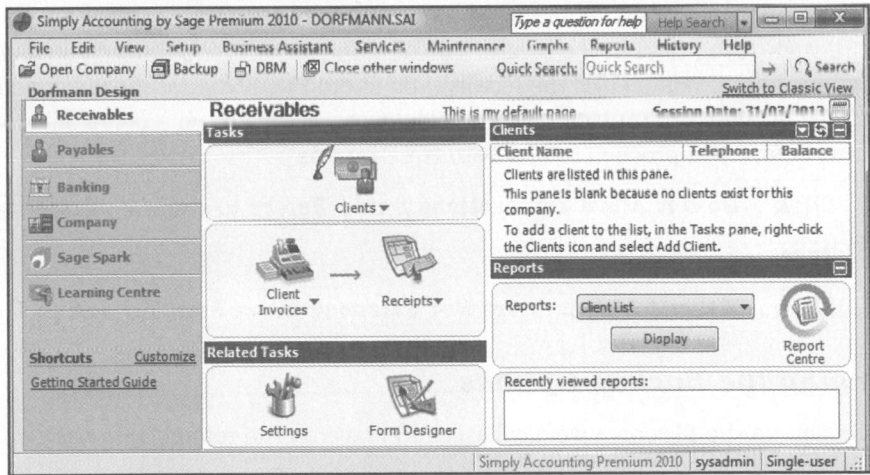

Changing Default Settings

Many of the next steps for setting up company defaults and entering General Ledger accounts can be completed directly from the Company module Home window. We will start from that point.

Click Company in the Modules list to change the Home window.

You should now see the company window that we used for Missoni Marbleworks and Toss for Tots. You can open the Company Settings screen from the Settings icon, and you are able to create ledger accounts by clicking on the Chart of Accounts icon.

If you need help entering company settings, refer to page 75.

PRO VERSION

The Automatically Refresh Lists option does not apply for the single-user Pro version.

NOTES

When you automatically save changes to records, you will not be prompted to save information each time you close a ledger after making a change.

When you display record balances by the session date, you can automatically refresh these amounts or refresh them yourself by clicking the Refresh tool.

PRO VERSION

The Time & Billing module is not available in Pro so you do not need to hide it.

NOTES

The option to show inventory lists does not apply to Dorfmann. You can remove this checkmark if you want.

NOTES

The session date is still set at the default format, based on your computer system settings. We will change this when we customize the other Company Settings (Date Format options).

WARNING!

You cannot complete many of the setup steps in multi-user mode.

Changing Company Information

Click the **Settings icon** ⚙ in the Related Tasks pane.

Click **Information** to display the Company Information screen.

From any Home window, you can also choose the Setup menu, then click Settings, Company and Information.

Most of the fields on this screen are complete from the information we entered to create the company files. You can edit the information if you made a mistake. We still need to add the business number.

Notice that the earliest transaction date appears as the session date on the Company Information screen. If there are any postdated transactions in the file, the Latest Transaction Date will be later than the session date.

You can return to the Company Information screen at any time to make changes. The program will set up defaults for the session date based on this information.

Click the **Business Number field**.

Type 233 281 244 RT0001

Changing System Defaults

Click **System** in the list of company options on the left.

Most of the default System Settings are correct. Dorfmann uses the accrual basis of accounting, so Use Cash-Basis Accounting should be unchecked. The option to Use Cheque No. as the source code can remain selected because Dorfmann uses cheques and may later choose to use account reconciliation.

Initially, we will not allow any transactions before March 31, the earliest transaction date. We want to allow posting to future transactions but receive a warning if the dates are more than seven days in the future. The defaults are correct. Since you can enter transactions before completing the history, you should activate the warning about unbalanced accounts to prevent mistakes. The warning makes you aware of errors or omissions before you proceed too far with transactions.

Click **Do Not Allow Transactions Dated Before** to add a ✓. **Press** tab .

Type 3-31-12

Click **Warn If Accounts Are Not Balanced When Entering A New Month**.

Changing the Backup Options

We will back up the files on a weekly basis and leave on the reminder to back up each time we close the data file.

Click **Backup** in the list on the left.

Choose **Weekly** as the frequency for Backup Reminders.

Click **Automatically Back Up This File** to remove the ✓.

Changing the Features Selections

Customizing the icons and features that appear can simplify journal entries.

Click **Features** in the list on the left.

Click **Packing Slips For Clients** and **My Company Does Business in English and French** to change the status.

CLASSIC VIEW

The Setup tool 🔧 is available. Clicking it when a ledger icon is selected will display the settings for that ledger.

If you click the Setup tool when no ledger or journal icon is selected, you must select a ledger from the list.

NOTES

The RT extension for the business number indicates the area of the business for reporting purposes to Canada Revenue Agency. For example, payroll has a different extension than income tax.

NOTES

If you click the calendar for the prior transactions field, you will see that the program does not allow you to choose a date before March. Entering a date prior to March 31 will generate an error with the advice that the date must be between March 31 and June 30.

NOTES

If you choose to back up your file automatically, leave the option checked and choose the backup frequency and the backup file location.

PRO VERSION

Packing slips are not available in the Pro version.

This removes the unused features and makes bilingual data entry and forms available. Since we need to choose linked accounts when we set up credit cards and sales taxes, we will create accounts before entering these settings. Since Dorfmann does not use other currencies, we can skip this setup screen.

Changing Forms Default Settings

Click   **Forms** to display the Settings for Forms:

NOTES
Form Numbers for features in the modules that are not used are hidden. For Payroll, the Direct Deposit Stubs are numbered, and for Time & Billing, the time slips are numbered. Form Number fields for unused features are dimmed.

The Forms screen allows us to set up the automatic numbering sequences for business forms and to include warnings if the number you entered is a duplicate or out of sequence. You can set up the numbering sequence for all business forms that are generated internally or within the company.

Forms for features that Dorfmann does not use are dimmed. The remaining one, for client deposits, we will leave blank. Cheque and bank deposit sequence numbers are added separately in the reports and forms settings for each bank account. (See page 223.)

Click   the **Invoices Next Form Number field**.

Type   44

Click   the **Receipts Next Form Number field**.

Type   25

The column checklists on the Forms Settings screen allow you to **verify sequence numbers** and add reminders if you print invoices, quotes, purchase orders and so forth. Verifying sequence numbers will warn you if you skip or duplicate a number and give you a chance to make a correction if necessary before posting. Choosing to **confirm** will set up the program to remind you to print or e-mail the form if you try to post before printing since posting removes the form from the screen. You should add the confirmation if you print or e-mail these forms regularly.

NOTES
The additional options in the columns also apply to Cheques, even though we do not have sequence numbers for them on the Forms Settings screen. These should be set correctly for your own setup.

The third column allows you to add the **company address** to various forms. If you use preprinted forms that already include the address, remove the checkmarks to avoid double printing this information. If you have generic blank forms, leave the checkmarks so that the address is included. The next column refers to **batch printing**. If you want to print the forms on the list in batches (for example, print all the invoices for the day at the end of each day) you should check this option. The final column allows the program to check for duplicate invoice and receipt numbers. We should check for these duplicates as well.

Click   the **check box for Invoices** and the **check box for Receipts** in the Check For Duplicates column.

Click to add a ✓ to any check box and click again to remove a ✓.

NOTES
Batch printing is covered in Chapter 14.

Entering Default Comments for E-mail

The next step is to add a default message to e-mail communications.

Click   **E-mail** in the list of Company options to open the next Settings screen:

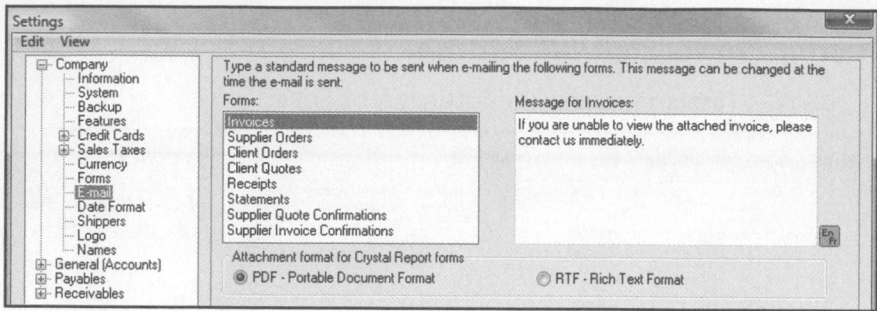

The left-hand list box contains the forms that you can e-mail to suppliers or clients. The right-hand box contains the message that will be added to the selected e-mails. You could add the company phone and fax numbers to the message so that the client or supplier can contact you more easily. You can also select PDF or RTF as the format for the file you e-mail to your clients and suppliers. You do not need to change the default messages for Dorfmann.

Click a form to select it and then type a message in the box beside it.

Entering Defaults for Date Formats

The default date formats use the short form on-screen. We want to use the long form so that the date will always be clear. Sunday is correct as the first day of the week.

Click   **Date Format** in the list of Company options:

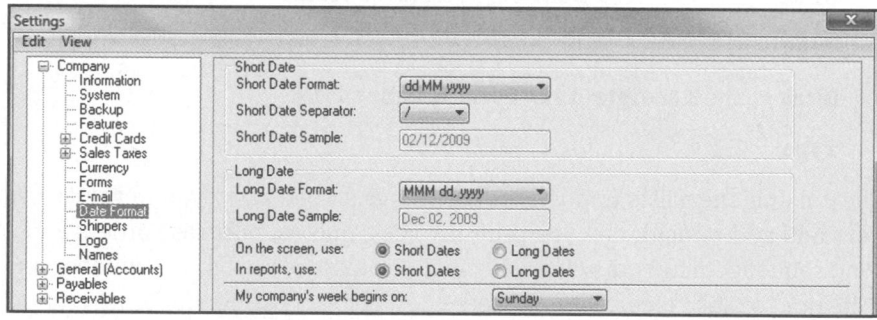

Click   **Long Dates** beside On The Screen, Use to change the selection. **Choose MM dd yyyy** from the Short Date Format drop-down list if necessary.

Adding a Company Logo

We still need to add the company logo. The logo is located in the SimData10\Setup\ Logos folder (or the folder you chose) where you installed the other data files.

Click   **Logo** in the list on the left:

> ⚠️ **WARNING!**
> If your screen shows dd MM yyyy as the Short Date Format, you must change this to match the date formats used in the text. Select MM dd yyyy from the Short Date Format drop-down list.

> **Click**   **Browse. Click Computer** in the left pane. **Double click C:**, **SimData10**,
> **Setup**, **Logos** and then **click dorfmann**.
>
> **Click**   the **Open button** to add the image and file name as shown:

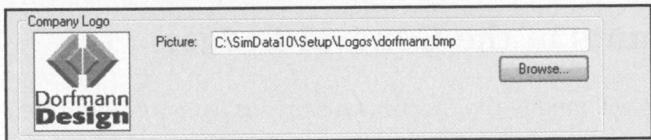

> **Check**   the **information** you have just entered and **make** any necessary
> **corrections**, including corrections to the fiscal dates.
>
> **Click**   **OK** to save the new information and return to the Home window.

Changing the Printer Defaults

> **Choose**   the **Setup menu** and **click Reports & Forms**.

The printer setting options for reports are given. Notice that the defaults include adding the computer system (calendar) date to reports and information about whether the report is filtered. You can check to see if the report fits on the page to improve the appearance of your printed reports, and you can change Reports & Forms settings any time. When the settings are correct,

> **Click**   **OK** to save the new information, or click Cancel if you have not made
> any changes, and return to the Home window.

Preparing the Ledgers

Before entering the remaining settings, we will create the Chart of Accounts because many of the settings require us to enter default or linked accounts.

The next stage in setting up an accounting system involves preparing each ledger beginning with the General Ledger. This stage involves the following steps:

1. organizing all accounting reports and records (this step has been completed)
2. modifying the *Current Earnings* account
3. creating new accounts
4. setting up credit cards, taxes and other features
5. defining linked accounts for the ledgers
6. entering supplier and client information
7. adding historical account balances, invoices and payments

Preparing the General Ledger

Accounts are organized by section, including Assets, Liabilities, Equity, Revenue and Expense. **Account type** — such as **Heading** (H), **Subgroup total** (S), **Total** (T), **subgroup Account** (A), **Group account** (G) and **Current Earnings** (X) — is a method of classifying and organizing accounts within a section or subsection of a report.

The accounts follow the same pattern described previously:

- 1000–1999   Assets
- 2000–2999   Liabilities
- 3000–3999   Equity
- 4000–4999   Revenue
- 5000–5999   Expense

Use the Chart of Accounts, Income Statement and Balance Sheet on pages 205–206 to enter all the accounts you need to create. Remember to include all group headings, totals and subgroup totals in addition to the postable group and subgroup accounts.

Modifying Accounts in the General Ledger

The following keystrokes will modify the *Current Earnings* account in the General Ledger to match the account number defined in the Chart of Accounts.

In the Home window,

Click   the **Chart Of Accounts icon** in the Accountant's Tasks pane to open the Accounts window.

The accounts should be displayed in Type view — in numerical order, with names, account types and balances. There is only one predefined account.

Double click   3600 Current Earnings to display its ledger form.

You can also open the ledger by clicking the account to select it. Then click the Edit tool button or choose the Edit menu and click Edit.

Press   (tab) to select the Account number field.

Type   3650

The account types are dimmed because the *Current Earnings* account type must remain as type X. Only the account number and account name can be edited. You cannot enter a balance because the program automatically calculates the amount as the net difference between the total revenue and expense account balances for the fiscal period.

Click   Save And Close [Save and Close].

Close the Accounts window to return to the Home window unless you want to continue to the next step, which also involves working in the General Ledger.

Creating New Accounts in the General Ledger

We will enter account balances as a separate step so that you can enter all balances in a single session. This may help you avoid leaving the data file with an incorrect Trial Balance.

Open   the **Accounts window** or any **account ledger window**, if necessary.

Click   the **Create tool** in the Accounts window or **choose** the **File menu** and **click Create**.

Enter   **account information** for all accounts from the Chart of Accounts on page 205. Remember, you cannot use duplicate account numbers.

Type   the **account number** and **press** (tab).

Type   the **account name** or title.

Click   the **account Type** for the account.

If this is a postable account, indicate whether you want to omit the account from financial statements if its balance is zero. You do not need to change the default setting for Allow Project Allocations. The option will be checked when you enter 4000- and 5000-level accounts.

Skip   the **Opening Balance field** for now. We will enter all account balances in the next stage.

NOTES
If necessary, change the view by choosing the Accounts window View menu and clicking Type.

NOTES
You can also close the ledger window directly to save the changes. If you did not choose to save changes automatically (page 215), you will be asked if you want to save the changes and if you want to always save changes without asking. Choose to save changes without asking.

NOTES
Pressing (ctrl) + N will also open a new ledger record form.

NOTES
Refer to page 93 for assistance with creating new account records and page 95 for assistance with entering historical account balances.

NOTES
The project allocation option will not apply until you choose to use projects. The default settings will then be appropriate.

When all the information is entered correctly, you must save your account.

Click   **Create Another** [Create Another] to save the new account and advance to a new blank ledger account window.

Create   the **remaining accounts** from the Chart of Accounts.

Click   **Save And Close** [Save and Close] to close the General Ledger account window after entering the last account.

Display or **print** your updated **Chart of Accounts** to check for account type errors as well as incorrect numbers and misspelled names. **Make corrections**.

Click   the **Check The Validity Of Accounts tool** [✓] for descriptions of errors in account type. **Make** the **corrections** required.

Check   the **validity** again and repeat the process until you see the message that the accounts are in logical order.

Entering Opening Account Balances

The opening historical balances for Dorfmann Design can be found in the Trial Balance dated March 31, 2012, on page 206. Headings, totals and subgroup totals — the non-postable accounts — have no balances and the Balance field is removed.

> Use the *Test Balance Account* for any adjustments that would leave the Trial Balance in a forced balance position before you are finished or if one of the remaining balances is incorrect. After entering all balances, the *Test Balance Account* should have a zero balance, and you can remove it.

The Accounts window should be open.

Open   the **General Ledger** account information window for the first account that has a balance, **1080 Bank: Chequing**.

Click   the **Opening Balance field** to highlight its contents.

Type   the **balance**.

Balances for accounts that decrease the total in a group or section (i.e., *GST Paid on Purchases*, *Sales Discounts* and *Purchase Discounts*) must be entered as negative numbers. The balances for these accounts have a (–) minus sign in the Balance Sheet or Income Statement.

Correct the **information** if necessary by repeating the above steps.

Click   the **Next button** [▶] in the Ledger window to advance to the next account ledger record.

Enter   the **remaining account balances** as indicated in the Trial Balance by repeating the above procedures.

Close   the **General Ledger window** to return to the Accounts window. You can check your work from the Trial Balance.

Choose the **Reports menu** and **click Trial Balance** to display the Trial Balance. **Print** the **report**.

Close   the **display**. **Correct** the account **balances** if necessary. Open the Ledger window, click the amount and type the correction.

Close   the **Accounts window** if you want to save your work and finish your session.

WARNING!
Remember that Net Bank and GST Owing (Refund) are subgroup totals, following the subgroup bank and GST accounts respectively.

NOTES
To remove the Test Balance Account, click its icon or name in the Accounts window and click the Remove tool or choose the File menu and click Remove. Check that you have selected the right account. Click Yes to confirm that you want to remove the account.
    If the Test Account balance is not zero, you cannot remove the account.

Entering the Account Class: Bank Accounts

Before setting up the Payables and Receivables ledgers, we must change the account class for bank accounts and some other accounts. **Account class** is another way of organizing accounts into related groups. Each section may be divided into various classes. For example, assets may be subdivided into bank accounts, credit card accounts, receivables, inventory and so on. When you create a new account, the program assigns a default class (Asset, Liability, Equity, Operating Revenue or Cost of Goods Sold) according to the first digit of the account number. For most accounts, you can accept this setting and the program will prompt you to change the class for special purpose accounts as needed. Bank accounts are not automatically reassigned by the program. You should also change the class for expense accounts by choosing either Expense or Operating Expense as the account class. Dorfmann does not sell merchandise and has no Cost of Goods Sold accounts.

Chequing bank accounts have additional information that must be entered in the ledger and therefore require that you change the class. You cannot select bank accounts for payments and receipts unless the **Bank** or **Cash class** is assigned. Bank class accounts must also be defined as such before you can select them as the default linked accounts for the Payables, Receivables and Payroll ledgers. The chequing account *Bank: Chequing* must be defined as a Bank class account.

> **Click**   the **Chart of Accounts icon**.

> **Double click**   **1060 Bank: Chequing** to open its ledger window.

> **Click**   the **Class Options tab** to see the current class setting — Asset:

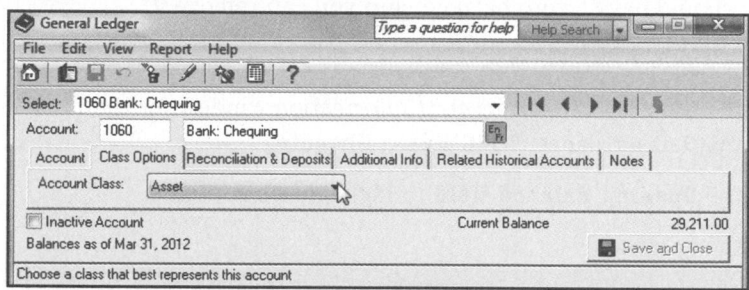

> **Click**   the **Account Class list arrow** to see the asset account class options.

> **Click**   **Bank** from the list to open the bank-related fields:

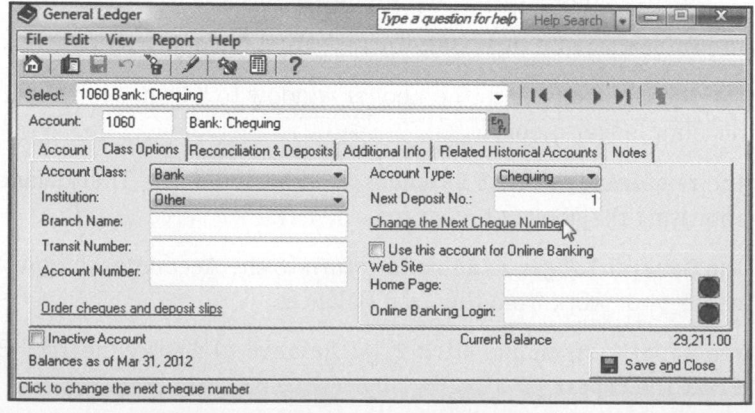

This screen allows you to define the type of bank account, and Chequing, the default, is correct. You can also enter a starting number for the deposit slip sequence and identify the bank for online banking access. We are not using deposit slips in this exercise, so you can skip this field. When different currencies are used, the currency for the bank account is also identified on the Class Options tab screen.

Click   **Change The Next Cheque Number** to open the cheque Form settings:

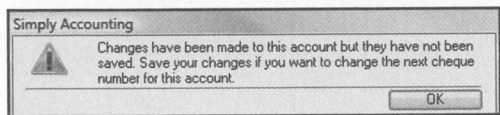

Before entering the cheque number, we need to save the account class change.

Click   **OK** to return to the ledger window.

Click   the **Save tool** 🖫 or **choose** the **File menu** and **click Save**.

Click   **Change The Next Cheque Number** to open the cheque Form settings:

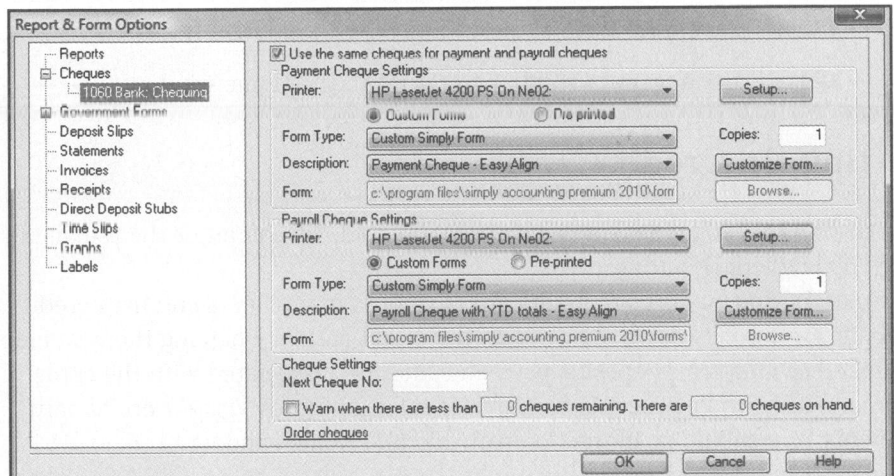

We need to enter only the cheque number. We do not need to change the printer settings for the cheques.

Click   the **Next Cheque No. field** near the bottom of the form.

Type   65

Click   **OK** to return to the account ledger window at the Class Options tab..

Defining the Class for Credit Card Accounts

Although credit card accounts are bank accounts, they are used as credit card linked accounts and are assigned the Credit Card class. Before setting up the cards with their linked accounts, we must change the account class for the accounts we need. We will change the linked asset accounts to the Credit Card Receivable class and the payable account to the Credit Card Payable class. If you also write cheques from or deposit client cash or cheques to these accounts, you should use the Bank class so they will be available in the bank account fields in the journals.

Click   the **Next button** ▶ to advance to account 1070 Bank: Visa.

Choose   **Credit Card Receivable** from the Account Class list to change the class.

Click   the **Next button** ▶ to open the ledger for 1080 Bank: MasterCard.

Choose   **Credit Card Receivable** from the Account Class list.

Click   the **Select field list arrow** to see the list of accounts.

Click   **2160 Credit Card Payable** to open this account ledger.

Choose   **Credit Card Payable** from the Account Class list.

Defining the Class for Expense Accounts

Expense accounts are defined as Cost of Goods Sold by default when you create them from the General Ledger new account window. These account classes should be changed unless they refer to inventory cost accounts. When you create expense accounts from an Account field using the Add An Account wizard, the default account class is Operating Expense, so you do not need to change it.

To create the Gross Margin Income Statement Report, you must correctly separate the Cost of Goods Sold accounts from other expenses.

Choose account 5010 from the Select Account list to open the ledger.

Choose Operating Expense (or Expense) from the Account Class list.

Click the Next button ▶. **Change** the class for all Group expense accounts.

Click Save and Close to close the Ledger window.

Close the Accounts window to return to the Home window.

Setting Up Credit Cards

Now that all the ledger accounts have been created, we can enter the remaining company and ledger settings.

Since Dorfmann accepts credit card payments from clients and uses credit cards in payment for purchases, we must set up the credit cards by naming them and identifying the linked accounts for deposits, payments and fees associated with the cards. Dorfmann accepts Visa and MasterCard for sales, and uses Visa for credit card payments. You should be in the Company module Home window.

Entering the Credit Cards

Click the Settings icon [Settings] to open the Company Settings options list.

Click Credit Cards (**click Company** first if necessary):

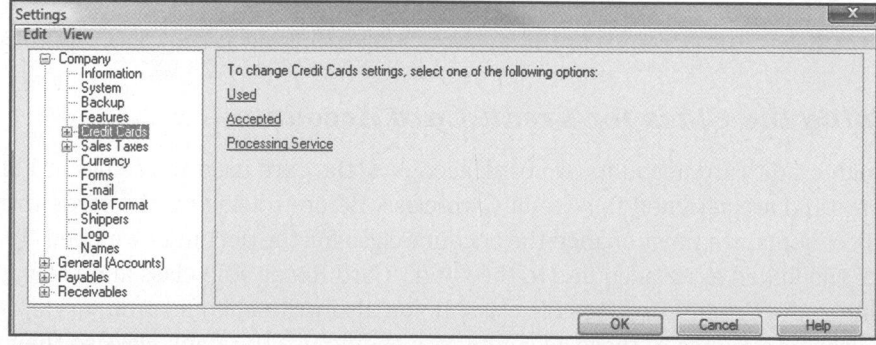

You can set up Credit Cards Used to make purchases from suppliers and Credit Cards Accepted from clients in payment.

Click Used to open the screen for the cards that the business uses:

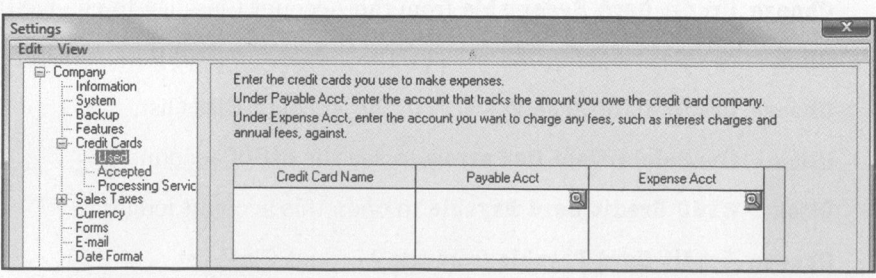

Each card named on this screen will appear in the Purchases Journal in the Payment Method list. There is no discount fee associated with individual purchases, although there may be an annual or monthly fee attached to the card. Each card is listed on a separate line with its associated linked accounts.

Click   the **Credit Card Name field**.

Type   Visa **Press** (tab).

The cursor moves to the **Payable Acct** field. This account is the liability account that records the balance owing to the card company.

Click   the **Account List icon** 🔍 to see the list of available accounts.

Click   **2160**, the liability account for the card.

Click   **Select** to add the account and move to the Expense Acct field.

The **Expense Account** records any monthly or annual fees paid to the card company for the privilege of using the card and interest charges on cash advances or overdue amounts. Not all cards have user fees, but all cards charge interest on cash advances and balances not paid by the due date. These additional fees are added to this linked expense account when you pay credit cards in the Payments Journal (Chapter 12). Dorfmann uses one expense account for all credit card–related expenses.

Click   the **Account List icon** 🔍 to see the account list.

Double click **5020**.

Cards accepted in payment from clients are set up in the same way. The business may use and accept the same cards or different cards.

Click   **Accepted** in the Company list under Credit Cards.

The cards clients can use to make payments are entered on this screen:

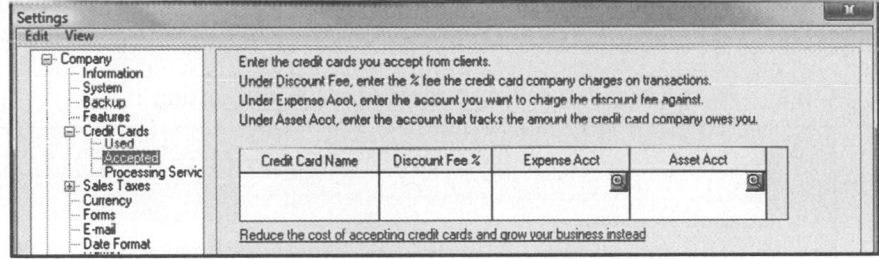

All the cards you name here will appear in the Paid By list for Sales Invoices. Each card accepted should be listed on a separate line.

Click   the **Credit Card Name field**.

Type   Visa **Press** (tab).

The cursor advances to the **Discount Fee %** field. The discount fee is the amount that the card company withholds as a merchant transaction fee for use of the card. This expense is withheld from the total invoice amount that the card company deposits to the business bank account for each sale. Fees vary from one credit card company to another and also for the type of business. For example, high-volume businesses pay a lower percentage than businesses with a smaller volume of sales.

Type   2.9 **Press** (tab).

The cursor advances to the **Expense Account** field. This is the linked account that will be debited automatically for the discount fee for a credit card sale. The expense amount or fee is the total invoice amount times the discount fee percentage.

WARNING!
You must choose either a Credit Card or Bank class account as the linked asset account for cards accepted. Although other accounts are displayed, choosing them will give you an error message.

Click   the **Account List icon**  to see the accounts available for linking.

Click   **5020** to choose the account.

Click   **Select** to add the account to the Card Information screen.

The cursor is in the **Asset Account** field, the linked account for deposits from the card company. Normally a bank account is set up for credit card deposits.

Click   the **Account List icon** to see the list of accounts available for linking.

Click   **1070 Bank: Visa** to choose the account.

Click   **Select** to add the account and advance to the second line.

Enter   **MasterCard** in the Name field and **2.7** in the Discount Fee % field. **Choose** Expense Account **5020** and Asset Account **1080**.

You can enter information for additional credit cards the same way.

NOTES
Return to the section Defining the Class for Credit Card Accounts (page 223) if you need assistance with this step.

If you did not change the account class correctly, you will see the following warning message about incorrect account classes:

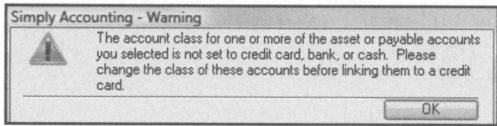

Click OK. Click Cancel to close the Credit Card Information window. Make the necessary account class changes and re-enter the credit card details.

Setting Up Sales Taxes

Setting up sales taxes before entering supplier and client records will allow us to choose default tax codes for clients and suppliers for automatic entry in journals.

Click   **Sales Taxes** to see the options for sales tax settings:

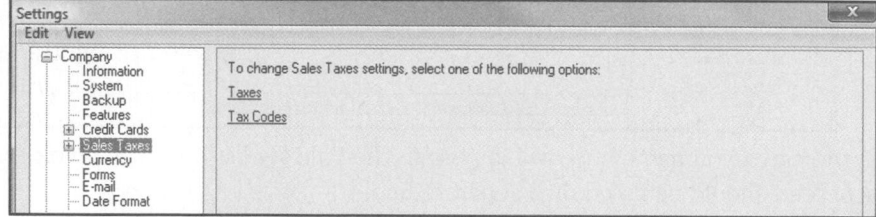

To set up sales taxes, we must identify the taxes that are charged and paid, and then define the codes that will be displayed in the journals.

Click   **Taxes**:

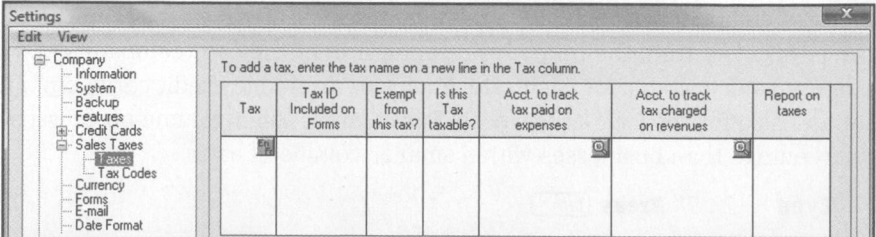

NOTES
Other taxes and tax codes can be added later if needed. The details for each tax and code can be modified if the tax legislation changes.

Simply Accounting has no preset tax information. You can customize the taxes to suit any business by entering all the taxes applied and paid by a business and by creating as many tax codes as needed to account for all the possible combinations of taxes. Taxes can be added later or edited if needed. For Dorfmann, the only tax that applies is the GST.

Click the **Tax field** or **press** (tab) so you can enter the name of the tax.

Type GST **Press** (tab) to advance to the Tax ID field.

If the tax number should be included on invoices, you can enter it in this field. For GST, this is the business number. For PST, it is the provincial registration number that indicates the supplier is licensed to charge PST. GST numbers are normally included on forms because GST is refundable. PST numbers are not normally included on invoices.

Type 233 281 244 **Press** (tab).

The cursor moves to the **Exempt From This Tax?** column. Choose Yes only if your business — Dorfmann in this case — does not pay the tax. Dorfmann Design pays GST, so the default selection No is correct. The next field, **Is This Tax Taxable?** asks if another tax includes this tax in its base calculation. For example, in Quebec and Prince Edward Island, PST is charged on GST so the GST in those provinces is taxable. For Alberta, where Dorfmann is located, the correct answer is No.

The next two fields define the linked accounts that **track the taxes paid** and the **taxes charged**. The taxes paid account records the total of the amounts entered in the GST field in the Purchases Journal whenever a purchase is made. Although you may choose an asset or a liability account, we use liability accounts because there is normally a balance owing to the Receiver General. If the tax is not refundable, such as PST paid, you should leave the account field for tracking taxes paid blank.

Click the **List icon for Acct. To Track Tax Paid On Expenses**.

Double click 2670 GST Paid on Purchases.

The cursor advances to the field for the Account To Track Tax Charged On Revenues. This account records the total of the amounts entered in the GST field in the Sales Journal whenever a sale is made. You may use an asset or a liability account.

Choose 2650 GST Charged on Services from the List icon ▣ list of accounts.

The cursor advances to the **Report On Taxes** field. To generate tax reports from Simply Accounting, you should choose Yes. The Yes and No entries on the tax screens act as toggle switches. Clicking will change the entry from one to the other, and you can change these entries at any time.

Click **No** to change the default entry to Yes.

Click **Tax Codes** to open the next information screen:

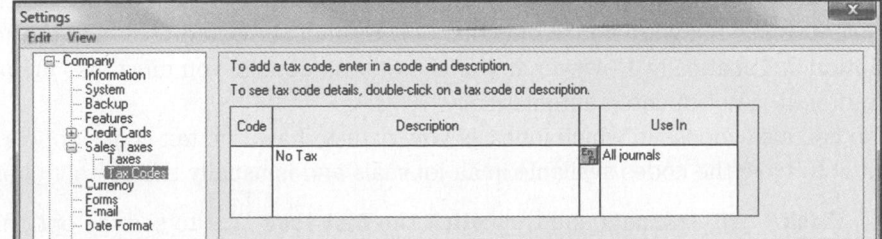

On this screen, you can create the tax codes required for all the different rates and combinations of taxes that apply to a business. No codes are entered initially so the only entry is the blank code when **No Tax** is applied.

Click the **Code column** below the blank on the first line.

Type G **Press** (tab) to move to the Description field.

NOTES
PST registration is required for businesses that charge PST on sales and do not pay PST on purchases of merchandise that they sell to clients (only the final client pays PST).

NOTES
Sales tax amounts entered in the General Journal are also tracked in these linked accounts.

NOTES

If at any time the tax regulations change, you can return to this screen and change the settings. For example, in 2004, B.C. decreased the PST rate from 7.5 percent to 7 percent and in 2010, it applied the 12 percent HST to replace the separate GST and PST. The federal government has changed the GST rate twice in recent years. To make these changes in the data files, just edit the Rate in the Tax Code Details screen and the Description in the Tax Code screen. The description is not automatically updated when you change the tax rate.

NOTES

For charities that get 50 percent of the GST they pay refunded, you can set up two taxes: one for the refundable portion and one for the non-refundable portion, one at 2.4999 percent and one at 2.5001 percent. Then create a tax code that uses both the 2.4999 percent refundable tax and the 2.5001 percent non-refundable tax. (The extra decimals will ensure that you avoid rounding errors resulting in overclaiming refunds.) For the non-refundable tax, you do not need to track taxes paid. They will then be added to the asset or expense portion of the entry, just like non-refundable PST.

NOTES

Charities that do not charge GST but are eligible for GST refunds may choose to show tax codes only in the Purchases Journal.

Press   (enter) or **double click** to open the Tax Code Details screen:

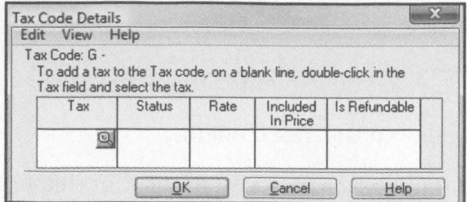

On this screen, you define how the tax is calculated and reported.

Click   the **Tax field List icon** to see the list of taxes entered:

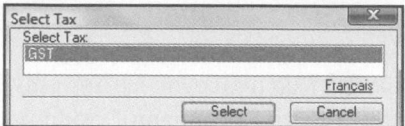

Because only one tax was entered on the taxes list, only one is listed here. At this stage, you are asked to choose the taxes that should be applied (charged or paid) when this code is used in a journal entry.

Click   **Select**, because GST is already selected, and return to the Details.

Defaults are entered for the remaining fields. The tax **Status** is Taxable and this is correct — tax is calculated and charged. Other status options and their explanations can be viewed by clicking the List icon. The Non-taxable Status is used for items that are not taxed but for which the amounts are still included in reports to the Receiver General. Similarly, the Exempt Status is used for items that are exempt from the tax but the amounts are still included in the tax reports filed. For example, although food is zero rated (no tax is charged), suppliers may still claim a GST refund and must report their sales amounts.

The remaining fields are straightforward. **Rate** is the percentage rate for the tax. Taxes may be **included** in the sales and purchase prices or not included. If some suppliers include the tax and others do not, create two separate tax codes. And finally, is the tax **refundable** — that is, are the taxes paid on purchases refunded? GST is not included for any of Dorfmann's suppliers' or clients' prices and GST is refundable. Non-refundable taxes are automatically added to the asset or expense amount for the purchase.

Click   the **Rate field**.

Type   5

Click   **No** in the Is Refundable column to change the entry to Yes.

Click   **OK** to return to the Tax Codes screen for additional codes.

The description GST @ 5% appears beside the code G. You can edit the description if you want. If the tax were not refundable, non-refundable would be added to the description automatically. However, if you change the details, you must also update the description. It is not updated automatically.

You can also choose in which journals you want to have the tax codes appear. The default is to have the codes available in all journals and is usually the correct choice.

Click   **All Journals** and then **click** the **List icon** to see the options:

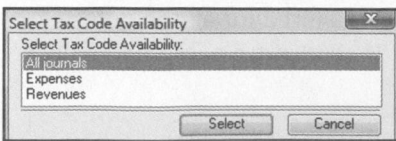

You can choose to have the tax codes available for all revenues, all expenses, or for all transactions (Purchases Journal, Sales Journal and General Journal).

Click   **Cancel** or **Select** to return to the Tax Codes screen because the default selection is correct.

Click   the ⬜ **beside Company** to reduce the Settings list.

Linked Accounts

Linked accounts are accounts in the General Ledger that are affected by changes that result from entries in journals for the other ledgers. We have seen some of these linked accounts at work in journal entries in previous chapters. For example, an entry to record a credit sale in the Sales Journal will cause automatic changes in several General Ledger accounts. In the General Ledger, the *Accounts Receivable* [+], *Revenue from Sales* [+], *GST Charged on Services* [+] and *PST Payable* [+] accounts will all be affected by the sale. The type of change, increase [+] or decrease [–], is indicated in the brackets. The program must know which account numbers are to be used for posting journal entries in any of the journals. Often you do not enter account numbers for linked accounts in the journals. It is this interconnection of account numbers and information between ledgers that makes Simply Accounting fully integrated.

Since only *Current Earnings*, the General linked account for Current Earnings, is defined, we must identify the remaining linked accounts for the General, Payables and Receivables ledgers. Dorfmann does not use the Payroll or Inventory ledgers and you do not need to define linked accounts for them. Linked accounts are entered from the Settings screens for the ledgers, so we will enter them with other default ledger settings.

Changing Ledger Settings and Linked Accounts

Changing General Ledger Settings and Linked Accounts

Click   **General (Accounts)** in the list on the left:

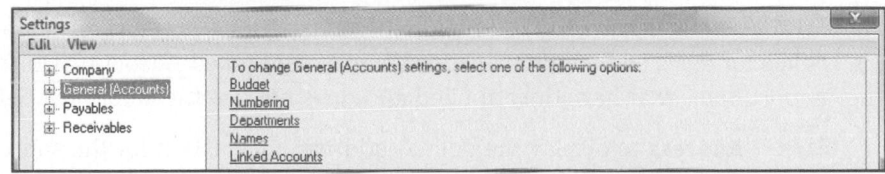

The General Ledger settings are correct for Dorfmann Design. The budget feature, departmental accounting and expanded account numbers are not used.

We need to add linked accounts.

Defining the General Linked Accounts

Click   **Linked Accounts** to display the General Linked Accounts window:

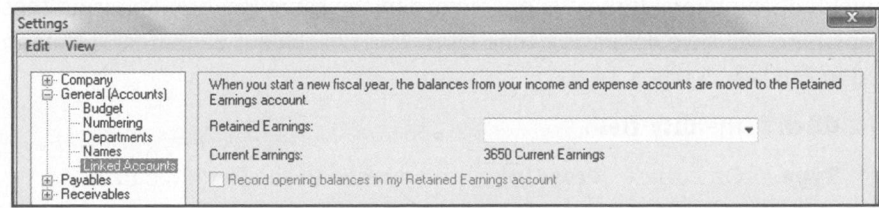

Press   (tab) to place the cursor in the Retained Earnings field.

The Retained Earnings account is the capital (equity) account to which expense and revenue accounts are closed at the end of the fiscal period. You must choose a capital (3000 range) account.

Click   the **list arrow** beside the field. All postable capital accounts are listed.

 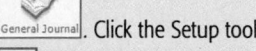

Click   **3560 D. Dorfmann, Capital**.

You can also type account numbers directly in the linked account fields. Then press (tab) to complete the entry and advance to the next field. If you type a new account number, you can create the new account.

The Current Earnings account is predefined — the single type X account is always used. This linked setup cannot be changed, although you can modify the account number and account name.

The final option, to Record Opening Balances In My Retained Earnings Account, will automatically use the Retained Earnings linked account for amounts that will balance the Trial Balance when you close the ledger. To use this option, you must enter the linked accounts before adding the historical account opening balances. We have already added the opening balances. Instead of showing the select account window from which we selected *Test Balance* (see page 95), choosing this option will display the following message when you have a discrepancy:

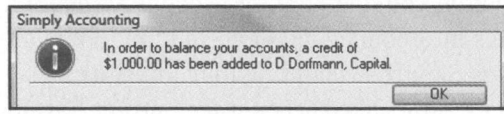

Click OK to confirm and to update the Retained Earnings opening balance.

Payables Default Settings

Click   **Payables** in the list on the left to expand the options list:

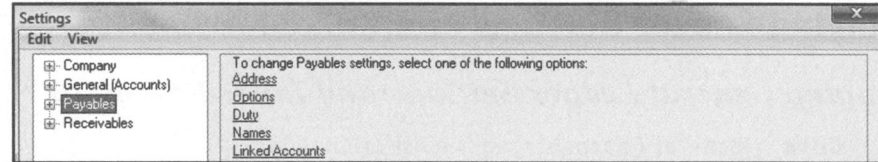

The Payables Ledger has address settings, general options, settings for imports (Duty), Names for icons and additional ledger fields, and Linked Accounts. Dorfmann does not import items that have duty applied and does not use the additional fields.

Click   **Address** to display the default address information for the suppliers:

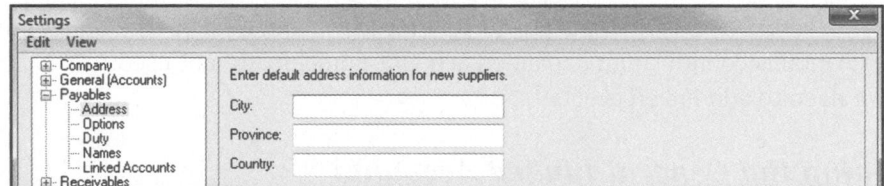

The information you enter here will be used in the ledger records as the defaults when you add suppliers. If most suppliers are in the same location, entering these locations here will save data entry time later. Most of the suppliers for Dorfmann are located in Calgary, Alberta.

Click   the **City field**.

Type   Calgary **Press** (tab) to advance to the Province field.

Type   Alberta **Press** (tab) to advance to the Country field.

Type   Canada

Click   **Options** to display the default settings for the Payables Ledger:

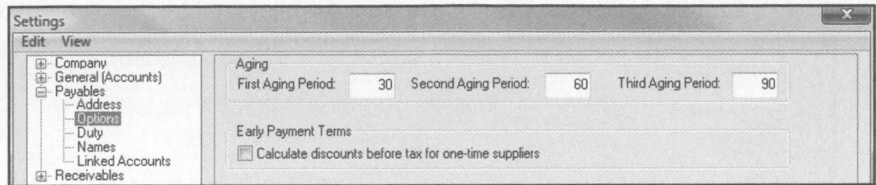

The option for the aging of accounts in the Payables Ledger is preset at 30, 60 and 90 days. We will change these options for Dorfmann to reflect the payment and discount terms most commonly used by Dorfmann's suppliers.

Double click 30 in the First Aging Period field.

Type 15 **Press** (tab) to advance to the Second Aging Period field.

Type 30 **Press** (tab) to advance to the Third Aging Period field.

Type 45

The second option determines how discounts are calculated. If the discount is taken only on pretax subtotals, the discount is calculated before taxes. If the discount is applied to the entire invoice amount, including taxes, the discount is not calculated before taxes. Dorfmann's suppliers calculate discounts before taxes so you must change the setting.

Click   Calculate Discounts Before Tax For One-Time Suppliers.

Changing Payables Terminology

Simply Accounting has a set of default terms that it uses, based on the type of company you define. These are the terms we saw that changed for different company types in previous chapters. If you want, you can modify the default selections.

Click   Names under Payables to display the Names and Terminology window:

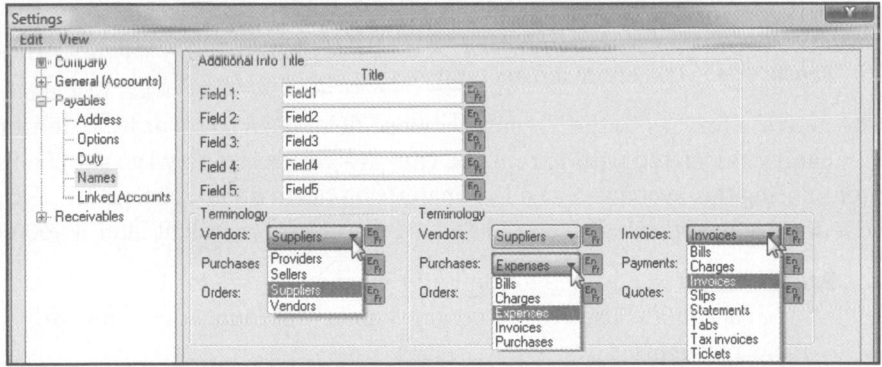

The Names window includes fields for five Additional Information names for the Payables Ledger. These will appear on the Additional Information tab screen for ledger records and you have the option to include them in journal windows.

The second part of the screen has the terms used for icons and fields throughout the program. The drop-down lists for the three names you can change — the names for Vendors, Purchases and Invoices — are shown together in the screen above. You cannot modify the Payments label. The names you select will apply to icons, fields and reports.

If you want to use different names, click the field for the name you want and select a different name from the drop-down list.

Defining the Payables Linked Accounts

We will enter the Payables Ledger linked accounts next.

Click   Linked Accounts under Payables to display the Linked Accounts window:

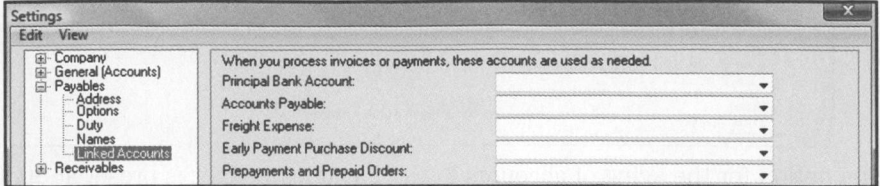

We need to identify the default General Ledger bank account used to make payments to suppliers. This is an essential linked account; it is required before you can finish the history for the company data file. Cash transactions in the Payments Journal will be posted to the bank account you select in the journal window. All Bank and Cash class accounts are available in the journals, and the principal linked account defined here will be selected as the default.

You can see the accounts available for linking by clicking the drop-down list arrow for any linked account field. Only Bank class (or Cash) accounts may be used in the bank fields. That is why we needed to define the Bank class accounts first.

When additional currencies are used, fields will be available for linked bank accounts for those currencies as well. Because we have not set up foreign currencies, their linked bank account fields are omitted. The chequing account is Dorfmann's principal bank account for supplier transactions.

Click   the **Principal Bank Account field list arrow**.

Click   **1060 Bank: Chequing** and **press** (tab).

The cursor advances to the Accounts Payable field. This control account is also required and is used to record the amounts owing to suppliers whenever a credit (Pay Later) Purchases Journal entry is completed. The balance in this account reflects the total owing to all suppliers. You must use a liability account in this field.

Select   **2200 Accounts Payable** from the Account list.

Press   (tab) to enter the account number.

The cursor advances to the Freight Expense field, used to record the delivery or freight charges associated with purchases. Only freight charged by the supplier should be entered using this account. Since Dorfmann's suppliers do not charge for delivery, you should leave this field blank. You can add a linked account for freight later if you need it.

Press   (tab) to advance to the Early Payment Purchase Discount field. This account is used to record any supplier discounts taken for early payments.

Choose   **5040 Purchase Discounts** from the drop-down list.

Press   (tab) to advance to the Prepayments And Prepaid Orders field.

Dorfmann's suppliers do not request prepayments at this time, but you cannot leave this field blank.

Choose   **2200 Accounts Payable** from the drop-down list.

Check the linked accounts carefully. To delete a linked account, click it to highlight it and press (del). You must complete this step of deleting the linked account before you can remove the account in the General Ledger from the Accounts window.

To select a different account, highlight the one that is incorrect and type the correct number, or select an account from the drop-down list.

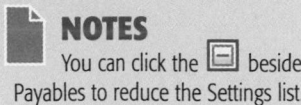

Receivables Default Settings

Click **Receivables** to display the Receivables Ledger choices:

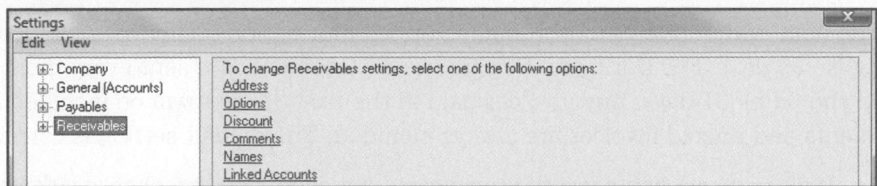

The Receivables Ledger has address, general (Options), Discount and Comments settings, and Names for icons and additional ledger fields and Linked Accounts.

Click **Address** to display the default address information for the Clients:

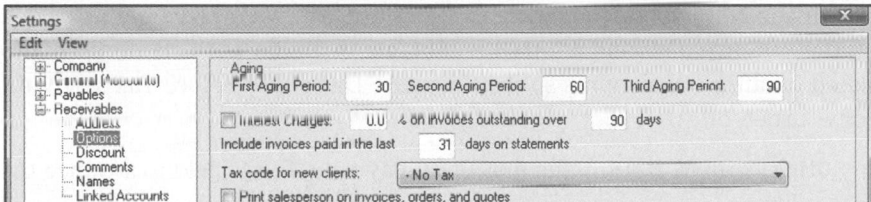

Just as you entered default address information for suppliers, the information you enter here will be used in the ledger records as the defaults when you add clients. Most of Dorfmann's clients are also located in Calgary.

Click the **City field**. **Type** Calgary **Press** (tab).

Type Alberta **Press** (tab) to advance to the Country field.

Type Canada

Click **Options** to display the default settings for the Receivables Ledger:

Dorfmann Design offers a 1 percent discount if clients pay within five days and expects full payment within 15 days. After 30 days, clients are charged 1.5 percent interest per month on the overdue accounts. Therefore, the aging periods 5, 15 and 30 days will be used, and we must change the default settings.

Double click **30** in the First Aging Period field.

Type 5 **Press** (tab) to advance to the Second Aging Period field.

Type 15 **Press** (tab) to advance to the Third Aging Period field.

Type 30

Click **Interest Charges** to add a ✓ and select this feature.

When interest charges are applied on overdue invoices, Simply Accounting calculates interest charges and prints them on the client statements and management reports. However, the program does not create an invoice for the interest. You must create a Sales Journal entry for the amount of interest charged.

Press (tab) to advance to and select the contents of the Interest Rate field.

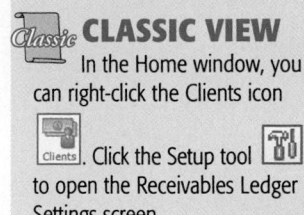

CLASSIC VIEW
In the Home window, you can right-click the Clients icon

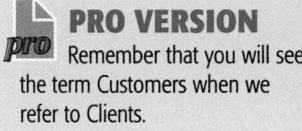

. Click the Setup tool to open the Receivables Ledger Settings screen.

PRO VERSION
Remember that you will see the term Customers when we refer to Clients.

NOTES
You can use the statements to find the interest amount that you will enter on the invoice.

Type 1.5 **Press** (tab) to advance to and select the Days field for editing.

Type 30

The next option relates to printing historical information on invoices. The maximum setting is 999 days. For Dorfmann Design, client statements are sent every month so the period should be 31 days. Any invoices paid in the past 31 days will be included in the statements and unpaid invoices are always included. The default setting is correct.

If all or most clients use the same sales tax code, you can choose a **default tax code** that will be entered when you create new clients or when you choose One-time Client or Quick Add in a sales invoice.

Click the **Tax Code For New Clients list arrow**.

Click **G GST @ 5%** as the default tax code.

When salespersons are set up, you can **print** the name of the **salesperson** on invoices, orders and quotes. Dorfmann does not have sales staff.

Entering Discount Settings

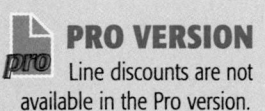
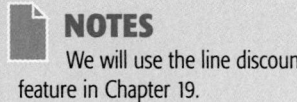
Next we must enter the payment terms for account clients.

Click **Discount** in the list under Receivables on the left:

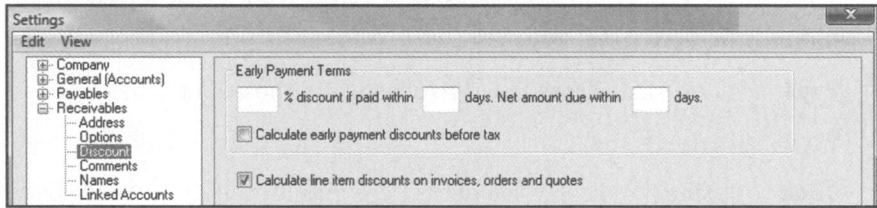

For all account clients, the payment terms are: 1 percent discount if the account is paid in the first five days and net payment is due in 15 days. All client discounts are calculated on after-tax amounts so the Calculate Discounts Before Tax selection is correctly turned off.

Click the **% field** in the first Early Payment Terms field to advance the cursor.

Type 1.0 **Press** (tab) to advance to the Days field.

Type 5 **Press** (tab) to advance to the Net Days field.

Type 15

Simply Accounting adds the payment terms you just entered as a default for all clients. Individual client records or invoices can still be modified if needed.

Dorfmann does not use the remaining discount option — to apply discounts to individual lines on an invoice. A % Discount column will be added to the invoice form.

Click **Calculate Line Item Discounts on Invoices, Orders And Quotes** to remove the ✓. You will see a warning:

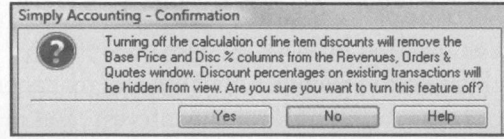

Click **Yes** to confirm the removal of line discounts.

Entering Default Comments

Simply Accounting allows you to add a default comment to the Message field on all client forms. You can change the default message any time you want, and you can edit it for a particular form when you are completing the invoice, quote or order confirmation.

Click   **Comments** under Receivables to open the screen for default comments:

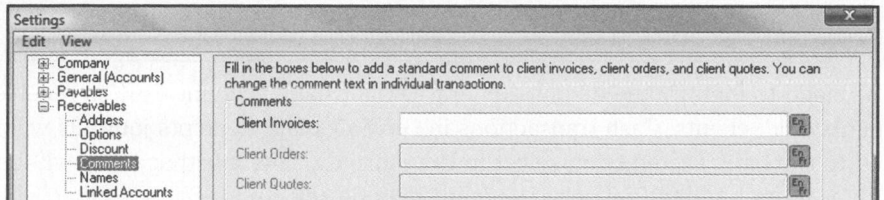

We want to add a comment that will appear on every client invoice. The comment may include payment terms, company motto, notice of an upcoming sale or a warning about interest charges.

Click   the **Client (Sales) Invoices field** to move the cursor.

Type   `Interest at 1.5% per month charged on accounts`
       `over 30 days.`

You can enter the same comment for all sales forms (invoices, orders and quotes), or you can add a unique comment for each. The comment fields for quotes and orders are dimmed because Dorfmann does not use these features.

Changing Receivables Terminology

The terms for the Receivables Ledger can also be customized.

Click   **Names** under Receivables to display the Names and Terminology window:

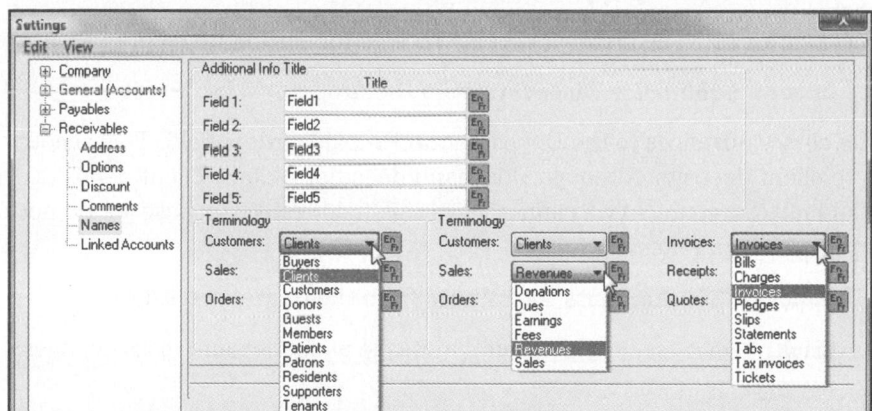

For Receivables, you can also name five additional fields to appear in ledger records and, if you choose, in journal windows.

The second part of the screen shows the industry-specific terms used. The drop-down lists for the names you can change — Customers, Sales and Invoices — are shown together in the screen above. You cannot modify the Receipts label. The names you select will apply to icons, fields and reports.

If you want to use different names, click the field for the name you want and select a different name from the drop-down list.

Defining the Receivables Linked Accounts

The Receivables Ledger linked accounts parallel those for the Payables Ledger.

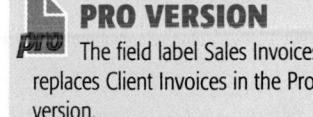

PRO VERSION
The field label Sales Invoices replaces Client Invoices in the Pro version.

PRO VERSION
The Names screen includes only the Additional Information fields. You cannot change the terminology in the Pro version.

CLASSIC VIEW

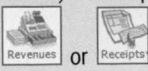

In the Home window, you can right-click the Revenues (Sales Journal) or Receipts Journal icon

Click the Setup tool to open the Receivables Linked Accounts screen.

NOTES

The linked accounts for Principal Bank, Accounts Receivable and Deposits are all essential linked accounts.

NOTES

When additional currencies are used, fields will be available for linked bank accounts for them as well. You can choose a separate linked account for each currency, or you may use the Canadian dollar account for more than one currency. Because we have not set up foreign currencies, their linked bank account fields are omitted.

NOTES

You must choose Yes to confirm the account class changes and to continue. If you choose No, you will return to the Linked Accounts screen.

Click   Linked Accounts under Receivables:

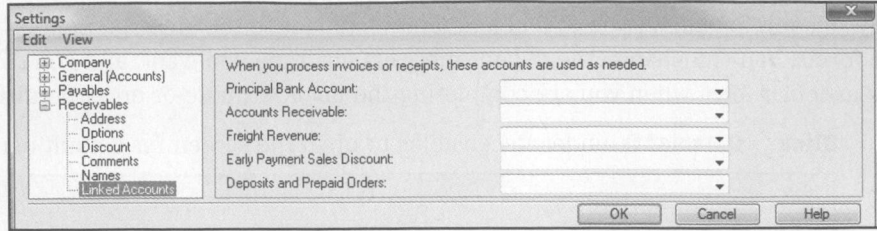

We need to identify the default General Ledger bank account used to receive payments from clients. Cash transactions in the Sales and Receipts journals will be posted to the bank account you select in the journals. The linked account will be the default account but any Bank class account may be selected.

Dorfmann uses *Bank Account: Chequing* as the principal bank account for client transactions. Although most linked accounts may be used only once, one bank account can be linked to the Payables, Receivables and Payroll ledgers.

Click   the **Principal Bank Account field list arrow**.

Click   **1060 Bank: Chequing** and **press** tab .

The cursor advances to the Accounts Receivable field. This control account records the amounts owed to Dorfmann by clients whenever a credit (Pay Later) Sales Journal entry is completed. The balance in this account reflects and must match the total owed by all clients. You must use an asset account in this field.

Select   1200 Accounts Receivable from the drop-down list.

Dorfmann does not collect freight revenue because it does not charge for deliveries. Leave the Freight Revenue field blank.

Click   the **Early Payment Discount field list arrow**.

This field records the discounts clients receive for early settlement of their accounts.

Choose   4060 Sales Discounts from the drop-down list. **Press** tab .

The cursor advances to the Deposits And Prepaid Orders field. This account is linked to client deposits. Although Dorfmann does not request client deposits, this is an essential linked account so we cannot leave this field blank. Because we do not use it, we can use *Accounts Receivable*.

Choose   1200 Accounts Receivable from the drop-down list.

Click   **OK** to see the program's message about account class changes:

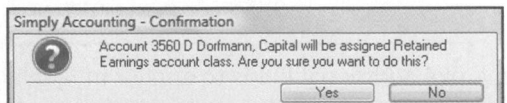

Many linked accounts must have a specific account class to be used as linked accounts. Normally, you can accept the account class definitions and changes assigned by the program. The exception is the Bank class accounts, which you must define before you can use them as linked bank accounts.

Click   **Yes** to accept the change and save the linked account setting. You will see a second confirmation message for account 2200:

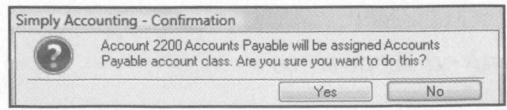

Click   **Yes** to accept the class change and save the linked accounts.

You will see the final message about the account class change for account 1200:

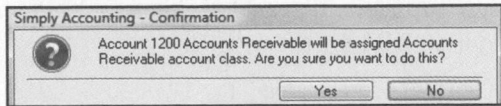

Click   **Yes** to accept the change and return to the Home window.

Entering Suppliers in the Payables Ledger

Use the Supplier Information for Dorfmann Design on page 207 to enter supplier details and historical invoices. The following keystrokes will enter the information for Alberta Energy Corp., the first supplier on Dorfmann Design's list.

You can open the ledger screen from the Payables module window Suppliers icon or from its shortcuts list. First we must open the Payables module window.

Click   **Payables** in the Modules pane to open the window we need.

Click   the **Suppliers shortcuts list arrow** as shown and **choose View Suppliers**:

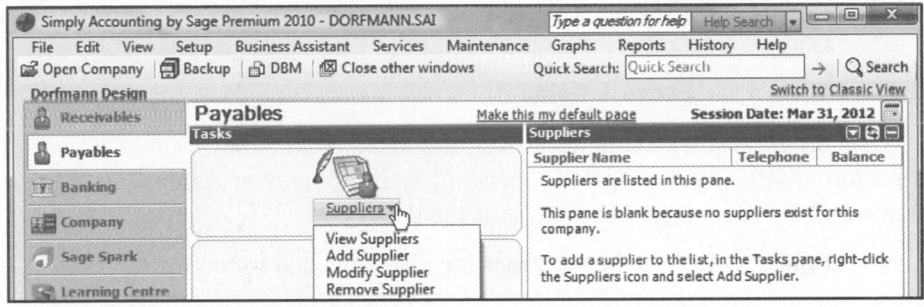

Or, **click** the **Suppliers icon** in the window:

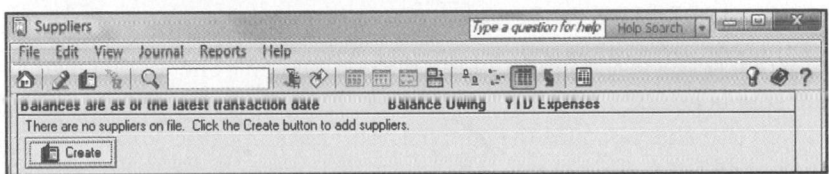

The Suppliers window is empty because no suppliers are on file. Once we add the supplier accounts, this window will contain a listing for each supplier that you can use to access the supplier's ledger record. The suppliers may be displayed in icon form or by name with balances and year-to-date amounts. The default is the listing by name.

Click   the **Create button** or the **Create tool** in the Suppliers window, or **choose** the **File menu** and **click Create**:

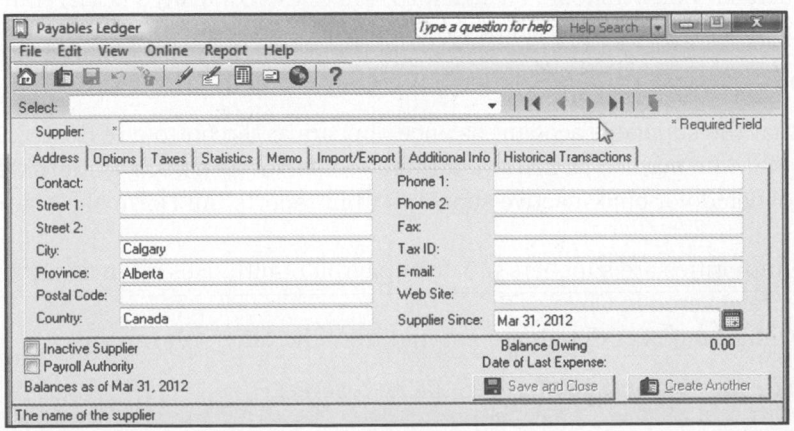

The supplier Address tab screen opens. Most of the Supplier input screens should be familiar from entering records for new suppliers in previous chapters. The cursor is in the Supplier name field, the only required field for the record.

> **Type**   `Alberta Energy Corp.` **Press** (tab).

The cursor advances to the Contact field. Here you should enter the name of the person (or department) at Alberta Energy Corp. with whom Dorfmann Design will be dealing. This information enables a company to make inquiries more professionally and effectively. For a small business, the owner's name may appear in this field.

> **Type**   `Con Edison` **Press** (tab) to advance to the Street 1 field.
>
> **Type**   `50 Watts Rd.` **Press** (tab) to move to the Street 2 field.
>
> **Type**   `Suite 800`

The program uses the Payables Address Settings as the defaults for City, Province and Country fields. In this case, they are correct.

> **Click**   the **Postal Code field**.
>
> **Type**   `t3g5k8`
>
> **Click**   the **Phone 1 field**.

The program corrects the format of the postal code. (Only Canadian postal codes are reformatted — those with the specific letter and number sequence.) You can enter phone and fax numbers with or without the area code.

> **Type**   `4037556000` **Press** (tab) to advance to the Phone 2 field.
>
> **Type**   `4037553997` **Press** (tab) to advance to the Fax field.
>
> **Type**   `4037547201` **Press** (tab) to advance to the Tax ID field.

The program corrects the format of the phone numbers. The Tax ID field allows you to enter the supplier's tax ID or business number. The following two fields contain the e-mail and Web site addresses for the supplier. Enter them just as you would type them in your Internet and e-mail programs.

> **Type**   `459 021 643` **Press** (tab).
>
> **Type**   `accounts@aeg.ca` **Press** (tab).
>
> **Type**   `www.aeg.ca` **Press** (tab).

The cursor moves to the Supplier Since field. The program has entered the session date as the default, but we should change it to reflect the company's actual transaction history. All suppliers have been used by Dorfmann since she started her business in 2002.

> **Type**   `July 1 2002`

Notice that the supplier's account balance appears at the bottom of the ledger. A supplier may also be marked as Inactive if there are currently no transactions. You have the option to include or omit inactive suppliers from reports. All Dorfmann's suppliers are active.

Payroll Authorities are suppliers to whom payroll remittances are made. Payroll remittances are covered in Chapter 8.

The remaining supplier details are entered from the other tab screens.

> **Click**   the **Options tab** to open the next screen:

NOTES

You may skip any of the address tab fields, except the name, if the information is missing for the supplier. Just click the next field for which you have information to move the cursor. To edit any field, drag to highlight the contents and type the correct information.

NOTES

Remember that the postal code sequence for Canada is letter, number, letter, number, letter and number.

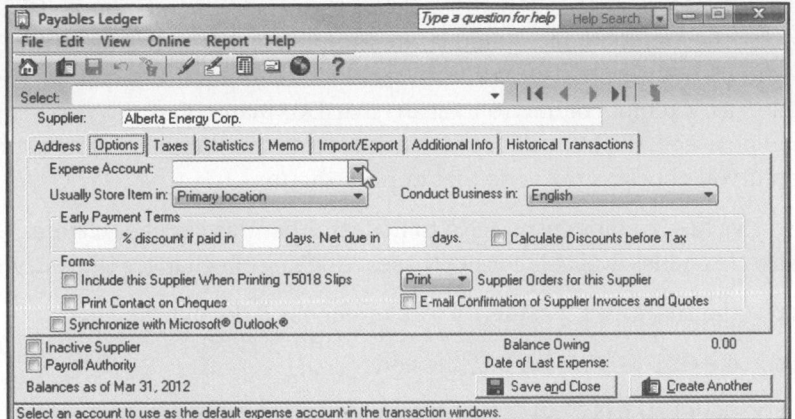

The supplier's name appears at the top of each tab screen for reference. We want to enter the default expense account so that it will automatically appear in journal entries.

Click   the **Expense Account list arrow**. All postable accounts are listed.

Click   **5060 Hydro Expense** (you will need to scroll down first).

When you use multiple currencies and inventory locations, they are also linked to vendors on the Options tab screen.

Regardless of the language you use to work in Simply Accounting, you can choose a language for the supplier so that all Simply Accounting forms you send to this supplier will be in the language selected on the Options tab screen.

If the supplier offers a discount for early payment or has a term for the net amount, enter these details in this screen. There is no discount, so start in the third Terms field.

Click   the **Net Due In ____ Days field**.

Type   10

Skip the Discount Before (or after) Tax option because there is no discount.

Do not turn on the option to Print Contact On Cheques because the Contact field does not contain address information.

If you e-mail purchase orders to a supplier, choose this option from the drop-down list to replace the default option to print purchase orders. Click E-mail Confirmation if you e-mail purchase orders to be certain that the order is received. Even if you choose Print as the default, you can still e-mail the order from the Purchases Journal.

Click   the **Taxes tab** to access the next input screen:

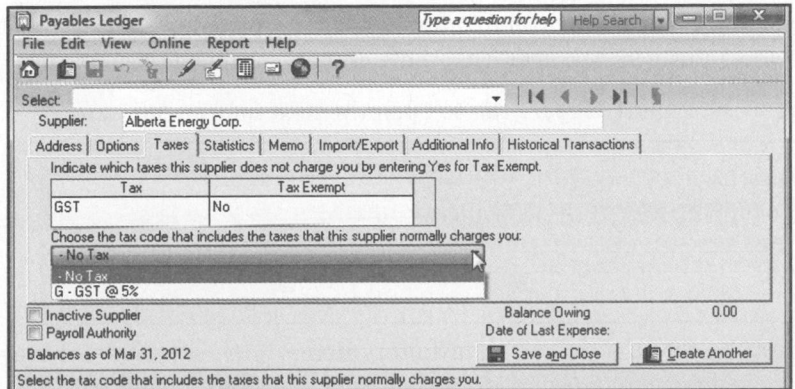

This screen allows you to indicate which taxes the supplier normally charges and the default tax code for journal entries. The codes are available from the drop-down list as shown in the screen above.

PRO VERSION

pro You will not see the Usually Store Item In Location field.

NOTES

T5018 slips are submitted to CRA by construction companies when they make payments to subcontractors.

Multiple inventory locations are used in Chapter 18.

NOTES

If you have not yet created the account you want to use as the default account, type the new account number in the Expense Account field and press (*tab*) to start the Add An Account wizard. Choose Add when asked if you want to create the account.

NOTES

Remember that all supplier discounts are calculated on before-tax amounts.

NOTES

For suppliers who request payment on receipt, enter 1 in the Net Days field. When you enter zero in the Net Days field, the Terms fields remain blank and invoices will not show as overdue. Payment terms may be changed in the journal for individual invoices.

NOTES

When PST applies, businesses that sell inventory at the retail level do not pay PST on the inventory they purchase for resale. Thus they are exempt from paying PST. If, however, the supplier charges for shipping — and shipping charges are subject to PST charges — you must choose No in the Exempt column for PST so that taxes can be calculated correctly for the shipping charges.

All suppliers for Dorfmann Design, except the Receiver General, charge GST so the correct entry for the Tax Exempt column is No. Suppliers such as the Receiver General for Canada, who do not supply goods or services eligible for input tax credits, should have Yes in the Tax Exempt column to indicate that Dorfmann does not pay tax to them. If you choose Yes, the tax will not be calculated in the Purchases Journal for that supplier, even if you choose a tax code that applies the tax.

Leave the Tax Exempt entry as No to indicate that this supplier charges GST and to make tax codes available for purchases. Clicking No changes the entry to Yes.

Click   the **list arrow beside No Tax** to choose a default tax code.

Click   **G - GST @ 5%** to select the code.

Click   the **Statistics tab** to open the next information screen:

PRO VERSION
Purchases replaces Expenses in the field names for Statistics.

NOTES
When the supplier uses a foreign currency, the statistics summary information is presented for both currencies.

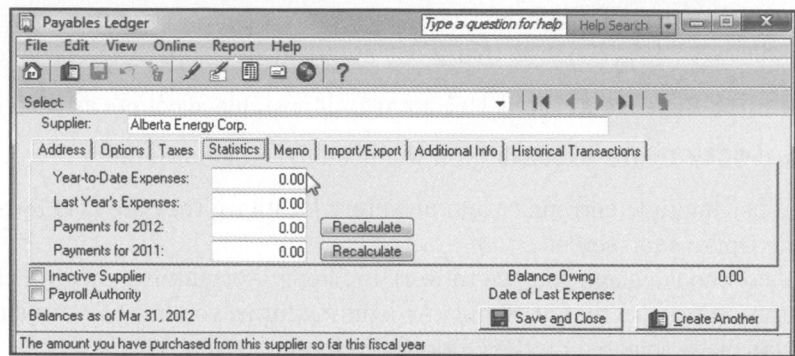

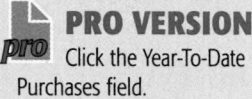
PRO VERSION
Click the Year-To-Date Purchases field.

The Statistics fields record the historical purchase and payment totals for two years and are updated automatically from journal entries.

Click   the **Year-To-Date Expenses field**.

Type   802

Click   **the Payments For 2012 field**.

Type   802

Click   the **Memo tab** to advance to the next screen:

NOTES
The message in the memo may be up to 255 characters in length.

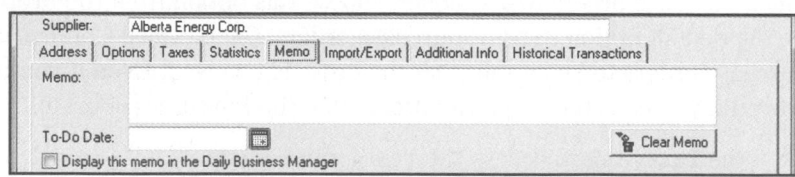

NOTES
The Daily Business Manager is used in Chapter 11.
    The Import/Export feature is described in Appendix J on the Student DVD.

The Memo tab screen allows you to enter a message related to the supplier that is added to the Daily Business Manager lists, the automatic reminder system.

Click   the **Import/Export tab** to open the next information screen:

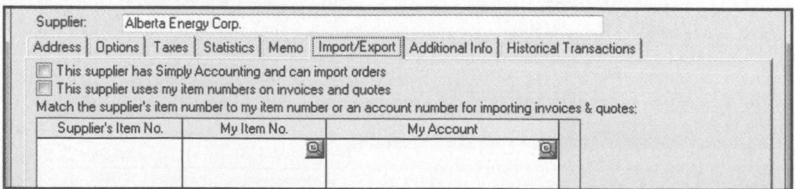

The Import/Export screen refers to inventory items. If the supplier also uses Simply Accounting, you can match the supplier's inventory item codes to your own for electronic transfers of information.

Click   the **Additional Info tab**:

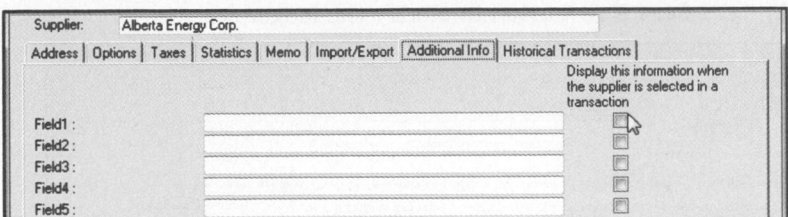

NOTES
The field names on this tab screen are taken from the Names settings for the ledger.

We will customize Payroll Ledger records by adding fields in Chapter 9.

You can customize the records for any ledger by adding up to five fields. The customized names you added from the Names Settings option for the ledger will appear on this Additional Info screen. This additional information can be included in journal transaction windows and in Supplier List reports. Dorfmann Design does not use any additional fields and there are no outstanding invoices for Alberta Energy Corp. so we are ready to check the supplier details.

> **Correct** any **errors** by returning to the field with the mistake. **Highlight** the **errors**, **enter** the **correct information** and then save the record.

> **Click** **Create Another** [Create Another] to save the supplier information and display a blank New Supplier screen.

> **Click** the **Address tab** to prepare for entering the next supplier record.

When you return to the Suppliers window, you will see that Simply Accounting has created a Supplier icon and listing for Alberta Energy Corp. The default view for suppliers is to list them alphabetically by name with the balance owing and year-to-date purchases.

The Create button has been removed. The Create tool is still available.

WARNING!
Remember to click Calculate Discounts Before Tax for all suppliers who offer discounts.

NOTES
You can also display suppliers by icon. Choose the Icon tool or choose the View menu and click Icon. Supplier icons may be moved to a different position by dragging. New suppliers are added to the end of the display, regardless of order. To restore the alphabetic order for icons, choose the View menu and then Re-sort Icons.

Entering Historical Supplier Information

You can enter all the historical invoices and payments for the fiscal year to date, but you must enter all outstanding invoices and partial payments toward them. Designers Den has outstanding invoices so we must enter historical transaction details. The following keystrokes will enter the historical information from page 207 for Designers Den. You should have a blank Payables Ledger Address tab window on-screen.

> **Create** a new **record for Designers Den** by repeating the steps above.

> **Finish** entering the **Address, Options, Taxes and Statistics details**, remembering to **click Calculate Discounts Before Tax**.

You can also enter these details for all suppliers and then open the ledger to add historical information by clicking the Historical Transactions tab. Open the ledger for any supplier by double clicking the supplier's name in the Suppliers window.

> **Click** the **Historical Transactions tab**:

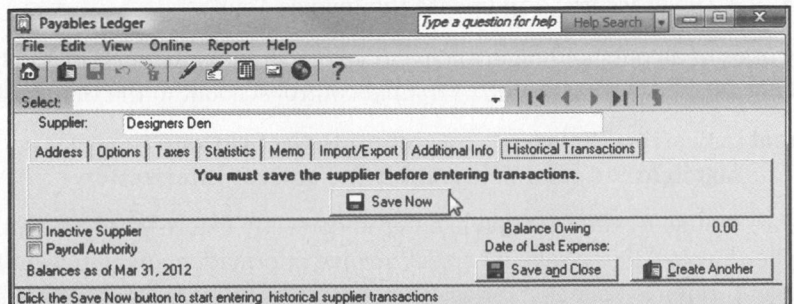

NOTES
If you have already created the record, you will not see the Save Now option on the Historical Transactions tab screen. Instead, you will see the next screen asking you to choose Invoices or Payments.

You must save or create the supplier record before adding historical invoices.

Click the **Save Now button** to modify the ledger screen:

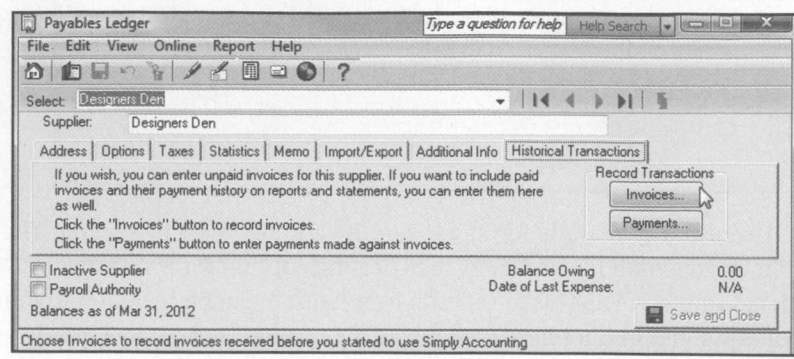

The Create Another button has been removed and the Save And Close button is dimmed. The screen now has two new buttons: Invoices and Payments. You should select Invoices to record outstanding invoices and Payments to record prior payments that you want to keep on record after entering invoices.

Click the **Invoices button** to see the following input screen:

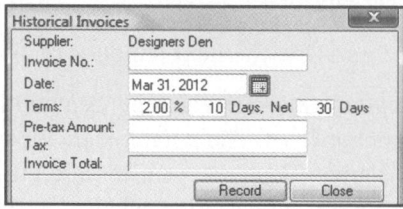

The cursor is in the Invoice No. field so you can enter the first invoice number.

Type DD-4502 **Press** (tab) to advance to the Date field.

Enter the invoice date to replace the default earliest transaction date. The invoice date must not be later than the earliest transaction date — the date of the first journal transaction after the historical data in the setup.

Type 03-26-12

The Terms are entered from the Supplier record and are correct, although they can be edited if necessary. You should enter the amount for the first invoice. The amount is divided into pretax and tax amounts so that Simply Accounting can correctly calculate the discount on the before-tax amount. When the option to calculate discounts before tax is not selected, a single amount field appears on the invoice for the full amount of the invoice with taxes included.

Click the **Pre-tax Amount field** to advance the cursor.

Type 2500 **Press** (tab) to advance to the Tax amount field.

Type 125 **Press** (tab) to update the Invoice Total.

The totals of all outstanding invoice and payment amounts must match the opening balance in the *Accounts Payable* control account in the General Ledger.

Correct any **errors. Press** (tab) to return to the field with the error and **highlight** the **error**. Then **enter** the **correct information**.

Be sure that all the information is entered correctly before you save your supplier invoice. If you save incorrect invoice information and you want to change it, refer to page 252 for assistance.

Click **Record** to save the information and to display another blank invoice for this supplier.

Enter   invoice DD-4630 (not the payment, Chq #62) for Designers Den by repeating the steps above.

When you have recorded all outstanding invoices for a supplier,

Click   Close to return to the ledger.

The two invoices have been added to the Balance Owing field at the bottom of the ledger screen. Now you can enter historical payment information for this supplier.

Click   the Payments button to display the payments form:

All outstanding invoices that you entered are displayed. Notice that the discount amounts are 2 percent of the pretax amounts. Entering historical payments is very much like entering current payments in the Payments Journal. You should make separate payment entries for each cheque.

Click the Number field if necessary to move the cursor to the cheque number field.

Type   62   Press (tab) to advance to the Date field.

Enter the cheque date for the first payment toward invoice #DD-4502 to replace the default earliest transaction date.

Type   3-26

Click   the Amount Paid column on the line for Invoice #DD-4502.

Because the full amount is not being paid, the discount does not apply. The full amount of the discount will remain available until the 10 days have passed. If the balance is paid within that time, the full discount will be taken.

The full invoice amount, displayed as the default, is highlighted so you can edit it.

Type   2180   Press (tab). **Press** (del) to delete the Disc. Taken amount.

Check   the information carefully and **make corrections** before you proceed.

Click   Record to save the information and display another payment form for this supplier in case there are additional payments to record.

The amount owing for invoice DD-4502 has been updated to include the payment you entered but the full discount amount remains available.

Repeat these procedures to enter any other payments to this supplier.

When you have recorded all outstanding payments to a supplier,

Click   Close to return to the supplier information form.

When you click the Statistics tab, you will see that the invoices and payment you entered have been included to increase the totals for 2012.

Click   the Create tool 🔲 **or press** (ctrl) **+ N** to enter the next supplier.

Click   the Address tab to prepare for entering the next supplier record.

NOTES
The View menu has the option to refresh the invoices from information added by other users. It applies only to the multi-user mode and is not available in the Pro version.

NOTES
The discount amounts based on pre-tax amounts are $50 (2 percent of $2 500) and $10 (2 percent of $500).

NOTES
Clicking the Amount Paid field directly ensures the discount amount is not entered.

⚠ WARNING!
If an amount appears in the Disc. Taken field, delete it before recording the payment.

NOTES
Even though the historical invoices and payments were entered correctly, you will notice that there is an outstanding historical difference. This is addressed on page 252.

PRO VERSION
Customer replaces Client on all Receivables Ledger screens.

NOTES
If you choose not to view the Customers icon window from the Home window Setup menu (User Preferences, View), you will see this Receivables Ledger window immediately when you click the Clients icon.

Enter the **remaining suppliers** and historical transactions on page 207. After entering the last supplier record,

Click **Save And Close** [💾 Save and Close] to close the Supplier Ledger. **Close** the **Suppliers window** to return to the Home window.

Display or **print** your **Supplier List** to check the address details.

Display or **print** a **Supplier Aged Detail Report**. Include terms and historical differences to check the historical transactions.

Entering Clients in the Receivables Ledger

Use the Client Information chart for Dorfmann Design on page 208 to complete this step. The following keystrokes will enter the information for Alberta Heritage Bank, the first client on the list for Dorfmann Design. You should open the Receivables window.

Click **Receivables** in the Modules pane list to open the window we need.

Click the **Clients icon** [Clients ▾] to display the Clients (Customers) window. The Clients window is empty because there are no clients on file yet.

Click the **Create button** [Create] or **tool** [🗐] in the Clients window, or **choose** the **File menu** and **click Create**.

You will open the Receivables Ledger new customer Address tab screen:

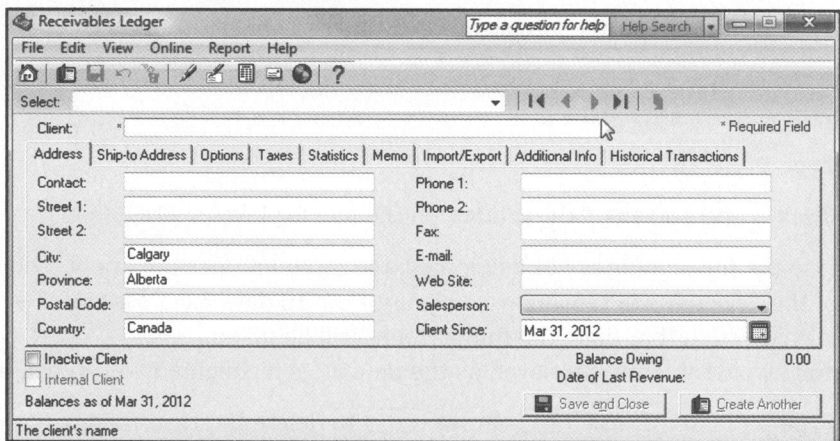

The client information screen opens at the Address tab screen. The cursor is in the Client field, the only required field. The default Province and Country entered from the Receivables Address settings are correct, but we need to change the city name.

You may skip any of the address tab fields if information is missing. Just click the next field for which you have information to move the cursor.

Type Alberta Heritage Bank **Press** (tab).

Dorfmann's primary contact about a sale should be entered in the Contact field.

Type A. Spender **Press** (tab) to advance to the Street 1 field.

Type 306 Revenue Road **Press** (tab) to move to the Street 2 field.

Type Fourth Floor **Press** (tab) to advance to the City field. We need to replace the default entry.

Type Okotoks

Click the **Postal Code field**.

Type   t0l1t3

Click   the **Phone 1 field**. The postal code format is corrected.

Type   4037445900 **Press** (tab). The format is corrected automatically.

Type   4037446345 **Press** (tab).

Type   4037445821 **Press** (tab) to advance to the E-mail field.

Type   spender@heritagebank.com **Press** (tab) to move to the Web Site field.

Type   www.heritagebank.com

Press   (tab) **twice** to move to the Client Since date field.

Type   Jan 1 12

The current balance is noted at the bottom of the Ledger window. Like suppliers and accounts, clients may be marked as inactive and omitted from reports if they have not bought merchandise or services for some time.

Click   the **Ship-To Address tab**:

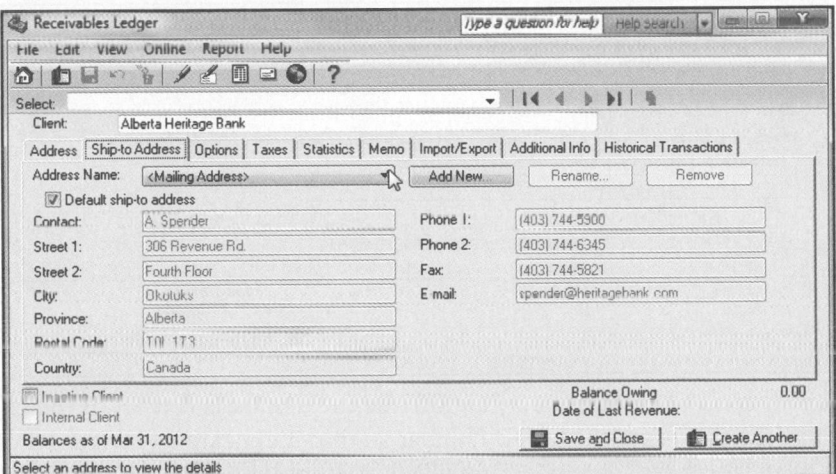

The Ship-to Address screen allows you to enter multiple addresses for clients who want merchandise to be shipped to different addresses. You can apply labels to each address. The default setting is to use the mailing address as the shipping address.

Click   the **Options tab** to see the payment and invoice options for the client:

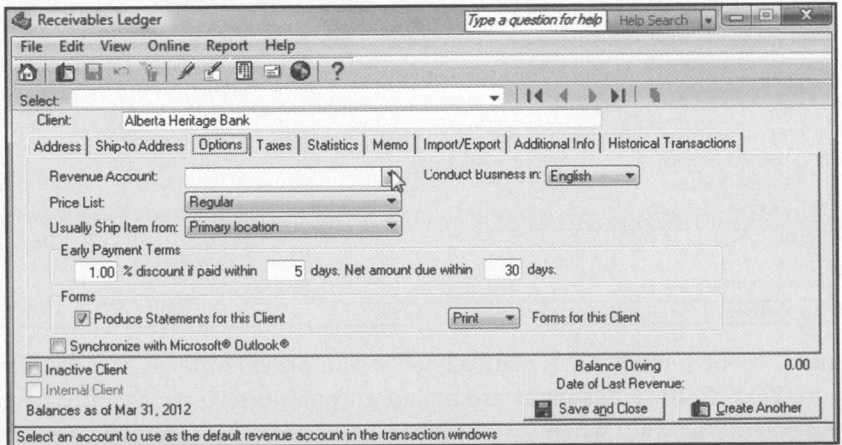

All the default settings are correct. You can select English or French as the client's language — all forms you send to the client will be prepared in the selected language.

NOTES
Remember that the postal code sequence for Canada is letter, number, letter, number, letter and number.

NOTES
The Internal Clients option works with the Time & Billing feature and is used to identify other departments within the company who use your services. The time and cost for these internal services can be tracked. Time and billing is covered in Chapter 18.

PRO VERSION
pro The option to define Internal Customers/Clients does not appear in the Pro version.

PRO VERSION
pro The Pro version does not allow multiple addresses. Only one mailing and one shipping address can be entered. Click Same As Mailing Address to remove the ✓ and open the address fields.

NOTES
As soon as you choose another address in the Address Name field, the address fields will open.

PRO VERSION
pro You will not see the options for inventory location (Usually Ship Item From) or Synchronize With Microsoft Outlook.

NOTES
The option to calculate discounts before or after tax is selected for the Receivables Ledger as a whole (see page 234). You cannot change the setting for individual clients.

The Price List field applies to inventory and services prices that can be set at different rates for different clients. Dorfmann supplies customized services and does not use the Inventory module. The payment terms are entered automatically from the Receivables Settings. Terms can be edited if necessary for individual clients and invoices in the Sales Journal. Dorfmann charges interest on overdue accounts so we need to be able to produce statements.

When a business sells inventory from more than one location, you can link a customer to one of these locations. The customer's currency is also defined on the Options tab screen when a business uses more than one currency.

You need to add only a default revenue account for the client. Although there are two revenue accounts that apply to clients, most clients use Dorfmann's design services, so we can choose this as the default. Remember that you can choose a different account in the Sales Journal for any invoice. You may prefer to omit the default Revenue Account so that you do not use an incorrect revenue account in the Sales Journal.

> **Click**   the **Revenue Account field list arrow**.
>
> **Click**   **4020 Revenue from Design**.
>
> **Click**   the **Taxes tab**:

NOTES

The PST number for retailers identifies that they can collect PST from their clients and be exempted from paying the tax on purchases of the items they sell.

NOTES

You can change the default tax code for individual clients if necessary by choosing a different code from the Tax Code list. You can also change the code for individual invoices or amounts on the invoice.

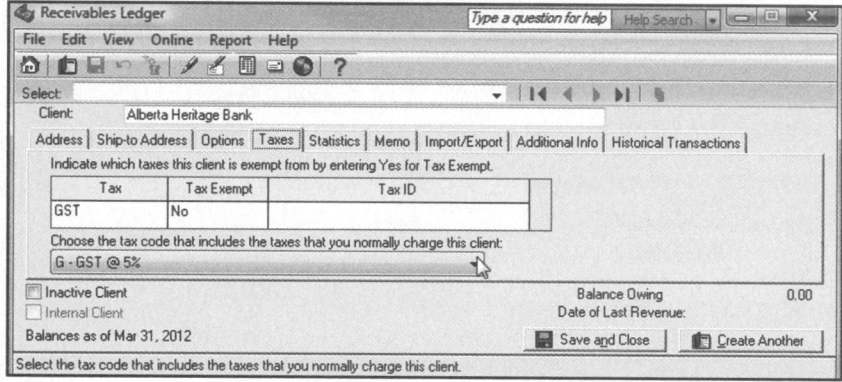

The client is not exempt from paying GST so the default is correct. If the client does not pay the tax, enter the tax ID number so that it appears on invoices. For example, retail stores do not pay PST on inventory that they will sell. They must have a tax number to permit the exemption. Some clients are also exempt from GST payments. Taxes will be calculated only if the client is marked as not tax exempt. The default tax code, G - GST @ 5%, should be entered.

> **Click**   the **Statistics tab** to view the next set of client details:

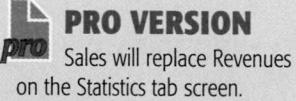 **PRO VERSION**

Sales will replace Revenues on the Statistics tab screen.

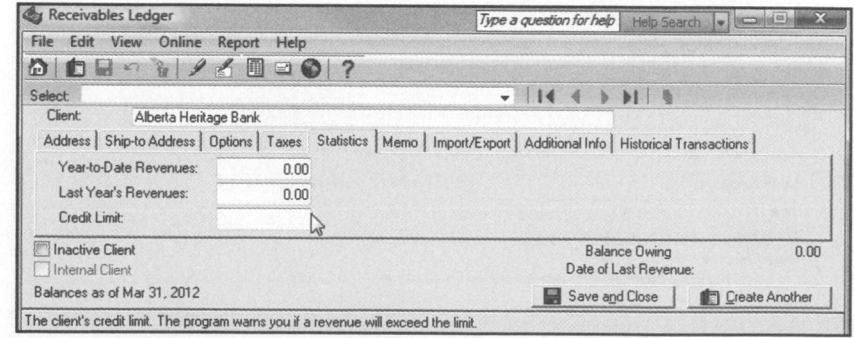

Balances will be included automatically once you provide the outstanding invoice information. **Year-To-Date Revenues** are updated from journal entries, but you can add a historical balance as well. When you have two years of data, there will be an amount for last year's sales too. Records for foreign clients will have sales summary amounts and balances in both currencies.

The **Credit Limit** is the amount that the client can purchase on account before payments are required. If the client goes beyond this credit limit, the program will issue a warning when you attempt to post the invoice.

Click   the **Year-To-Date Revenues field**.

Type   3150 **Press** (tab) **twice** to advance to the Credit Limit field.

Type   5000

The **Memo tab** screen for clients is just like the Memo tab screen for suppliers. It allows you to enter messages related to the client. If you enter a reminder date, the program will display the message in the Daily Business Manager on the date you provide.

If the client also uses Simply Accounting, you can match the client's inventory codes to your own on the **Import/Export tab** screen to allow for electronic data transfers.

The **Additional Info tab** screen allows you to enter details for the custom-defined fields you created for clients, similar to the Additional Info tab fields for suppliers.

> **Correct errors** by returning to the field with the error. **Click** the appropriate **tab**, **highlight** the **error** and **enter** the **correct information**. You can correct address and options details any time.

If there are no historical invoices, proceed to the final step of saving the client record (page 249). Click Create Another [Create Another] and then click the Address tab to prepare for entering the next client.

NOTES
The Daily Business Manager is covered in Chapter 11.

Entering Historical Client Information

As for suppliers, you can enter all historical invoices and payments for the year to date, but you must enter outstanding invoice amounts. The following keystrokes will enter historical information for Alberta Heritage Bank from page 208.

Click   the **Historical Transactions tab**:

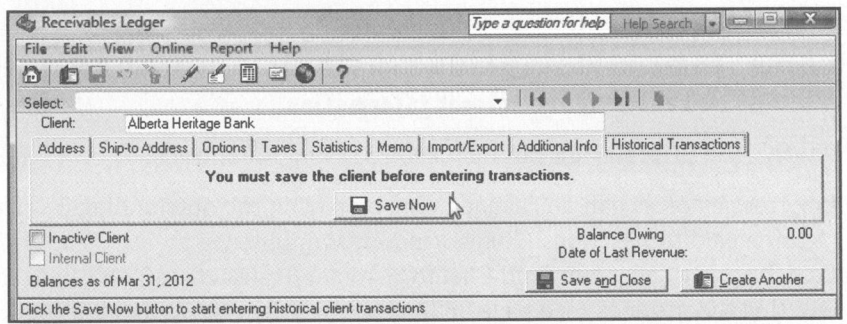

You must save or create the client record before adding historical invoices.

Click   the **Save Now button** to access the invoice and payment buttons:

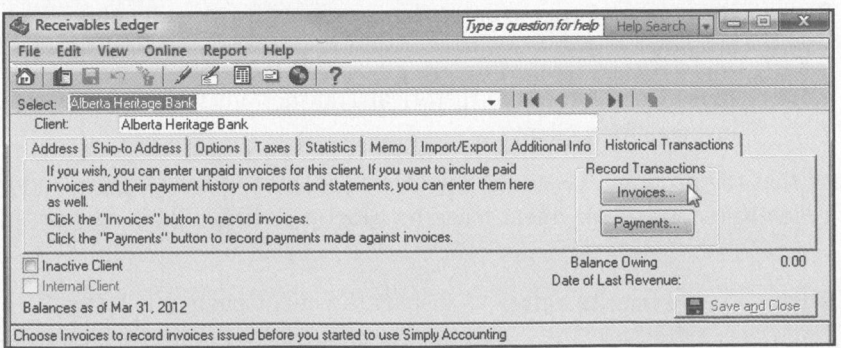

NOTES
If you have already saved (created) the record, you will not see the Save Now option on the Historical Transactions tab screen. Instead, you will see the next screen asking you to choose Invoices or Payments.

Again, the Create Another button has been removed and the Save And Close button is dimmed because you have already saved the record.

If you prefer, you can enter address, options and credit limit details for all clients before adding historical invoices and payments from the Historical Transactions tab screen. You can open a client ledger record by double clicking the client's name in the Clients window. Then click the Historical Transactions tab.

Just as in the Payables Ledger, you enter invoices and payments separately. You can use the Payments option to record any payments against previous invoices that you want to keep on record. The totals of all outstanding invoices, after payments, must match the opening balance in the *Accounts Receivable* control account in the General Ledger.

Click   the **Invoices button** to display the following input form:

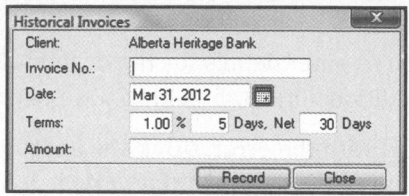

There is a single Amount field because client discounts are calculated on after-tax amounts. When discounts are calculated before tax, there is an additional input field so that the sale and the tax amounts can be entered separately as we saw in the Payables Historical Invoices screen. The earliest transaction date is the default invoice date. The cursor is in the Invoice No. field so you can enter the first invoice number.

Type   38 **Press** (*tab*) to advance to the Date field.

Type   mar 23

Because the payment terms are correctly entered, we can skip them. Discounts are calculated after taxes so only the single after-tax amount is needed.

Click   the **Amount field**.

Type   3150

Correct   **errors** by returning to the field with the error, **highlighting** the **error** and **entering** the **correct information**.

Check   the **information** carefully before saving the invoice.

Incorrect invoices can be changed only by paying the outstanding invoices, clearing paid transactions (Home window, Maintenance menu, Clear Data, Clear Paid Transactions, Clear Paid Client/Customer Transactions) and then re-entering the invoices (see page 252).

Click   **Record** to save the invoice and to display a new blank invoice form for this client.

Repeat   these **procedures** to enter the remaining invoices for this client, if there are any.

Click   **Close** to return to the Historical Transactions window after entering all invoices for a client.

Notice that the program has added the client's balance to the Ledger window. You are now ready to record the payment made by Alberta Heritage Bank against this invoice.

Click   the **Payments button** to display the client payments form:

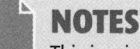

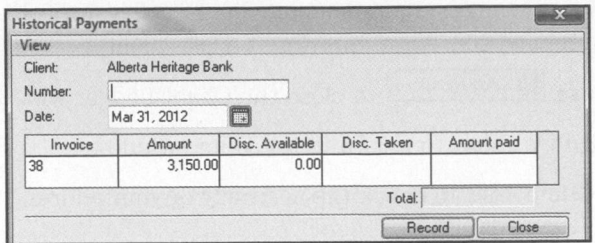

All outstanding invoices that you entered are displayed. Entering historical client payments is much like entering current receipts in the Receipts Journal. As usual, the earliest transaction date is the default. The default March 31 transaction date is more than five days after the invoice date so no discount is available.

> Click the Number field to move the cursor to the cheque number field if necessary.

> **Type**   6754 **Press** (tab) to advance to the Date field.

> **Type**   03-23

The discount is now available. Discounts can be taken only when the full payment is made before the due date, so we must skip the Discount fields. The full discount remains available until the discount period has ended.

> **Click**   the Amount Paid column on the line for invoice #38.

The full invoice amount is displayed as the default and highlighted so you can edit it.

> **Type**   1400 **Press** (tab).

> **Check**   your **information** carefully before you proceed and **make corrections** if necessary.

> **Click**   **Record** to save the information and to display another payment form for this client in case there are additional payments to record.

Notice that the full discount remains available after the payment — its amount is not reduced although the balance owing has been reduced.

> Repeat these procedures to enter other payments by this client if there are any.

When you have recorded all outstanding payments by a client,

> **Click**   **Close** to return to the client information form.

Notice that the balance owing in the ledger has been updated to include the payment entry just completed.

> **Click**   the **Address tab** to prepare for entering the next client.

> **Click**   the **Create tool** to open another new client input screen.

Saving the Client Record

When all the information is entered correctly, you must save the client information. If you have not added historical information,

> **Click**   **Create Another** [Create Another] to save the information and advance to the next new client input screen.

> **Click**   the **Address tab** to prepare for entering the next client.

Simply Accounting created a listing for Alberta Heritage Bank in the Clients window.

WARNING!
If an amount appears in the Disc. Taken field, delete it before recording the payment.

Repeat these **procedures** to enter the remaining clients and historical transactions on page 208. After entering the last client,

Click   **Save And Close** to close the Client Ledger window.

Close   the **Clients icon window** to return to the Home window.

Display or **print** the **Client List** to check the accuracy of your address information.

Display or **print** a **Client Aged Detail Report** including terms and historical differences to check the historical information.

Preparing for Journal Entries

The last stage in setting up the accounting system involves closing off the historical entries. This step indicates that all historical data have been entered and cannot be changed. You can proceed with journalizing before finishing the history, but you must complete this step before beginning a new fiscal period. Finishing history involves changing the status of each ledger from an open to a finished history state. In the open history state the ledgers are not integrated, so you can add or change historical information in one ledger without affecting any other ledger. It is easier to correct mistakes.

Making a Backup of the Company Files

To make a backup of the not-finished files, you can use Save A Copy from the File menu or use the Backup command. Both methods allow you to keep working in your original working data file.

Choose the **File menu** and **click Backup** or **click** the **Backup tool** :

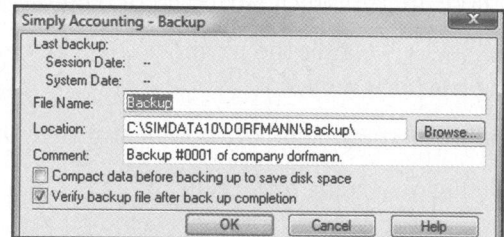

On this backup screen, you should enter the name and location of the new backup.

Click Browse.

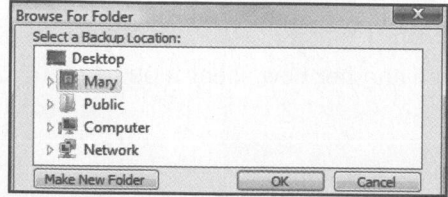

Click   **Computer**, then **click C:**. **Scroll down** and **click SimData10** to locate and select the SimData10 folder that contains your other data files.

Click   the **Make New Folder button** and **type** NF-DORF to replace New Folder — the selected name. **Click OK** to return to the Backup screen.

Double click **Backup** in the File Name field. **Type** nf-dorf

Click   **OK** to begin backing up the data file.

The "NF" designates files as not finished or open to distinguish them from the ones you will work with to enter journal transactions. Continue by following the backup instructions on-screen. You can use another name and location for your backup if you want. This will create a backup copy of the files for Dorfmann Design.

Click   OK when the backup is complete.

Working with Unfinished History

Simply Accounting allows you to enter current journal transactions before the history is finished and balanced. In this way, you can keep the journal records current and enter the historical details later when there is time available to do so, or the setup may be completed later by a different individual.

There are, however, a number of elements that you must complete before you can make journal entries. You must create the General Ledger accounts and define the essential linked accounts before you can use the journals. You must enter historical client and supplier invoices before you can enter payments for them, and invoices must have the correct payment terms and dates.

You do not need to enter General Ledger opening account balances. These balances may be added later in the Opening Balance field on the Account tab screen. The General Ledger also shows the current balance that changes as you post new journal entries. However, without the opening balances, the current balance is not correct and you cannot get accurate reports. The Trial Balance and the Accounts window display only current balances, making it more difficult to trace the correct historical amounts.

Some errors may be corrected at any time. For example, after entering journal transactions and after finishing the history, you can correct account, supplier and client names and address details, but you cannot change historical amounts because their dates precede the earliest transaction date.

From a control point of view, it is preferable to enter all historical information first so that you do not confuse the historical and current data or work with accounts that are not correct in some way. You cannot change account numbers after the accounts are used in journal entries so some corrections may be difficult to make later. After you start journalizing, the balances for *Accounts Receivable* and *Accounts Payable* reflect all the entries made to date. There may be mistakes in current journal entries as well as in the history, making it more difficult to find the historical errors later.

There are a number of checks that you can perform to increase the accuracy of your work. You should compare your reports carefully with the charts given at the beginning of this application and make corrections. Pay particular attention to correct account numbers and historical invoices. Printing Supplier and Client Aged Detail reports with historical differences can reveal errors in invoices or payments. The Accounts window has an option to check the validity of accounts from the Edit menu or the tool button. The Home window Maintenance menu has an option to check data integrity that looks for differences in balances between the subsidiary ledgers and the corresponding General Ledger control accounts. All these checks help point to mistakes that should be corrected before proceeding.

Both the Data Integrity check and the error summary when we attempt to finish the history will show that the supplier history is not correct — the A/P Balance does not match the Unpaid Invoices amount. This error will prevent us from finishing the history.

WARNING!
Read this section carefully before proceeding.

NOTES
You can create new accounts "on the fly" while making journal entries by using the Add An Account wizard. You will also be prompted to add the essential linked accounts when you try to open the journals. Some linked accounts, such as Sales Discounts, are not essential and you can access the journals without them. However, the journal entry will not be correct without the linked account, so there are some accounts that you must create before you can use the journals.

NOTES
If you printed the Supplier Aged Detail Report with historical difference, you would also see that the supplier history was not correct.

WARNING!
Make sure that the Test Account balance is zero. An error in this amount will not prevent you from finishing the history.

NOTES
Notice that the unused, hidden ledgers are balanced. If you view these ledgers and finish the history, you will be unable to add historical information for them later.
If you finish the history when the unused ledgers are hidden, they remain in the unfinished state and you can add historical information later. (See Chapter 9.)

Choose the **Maintenance menu** and **click Check Data Integrity**:

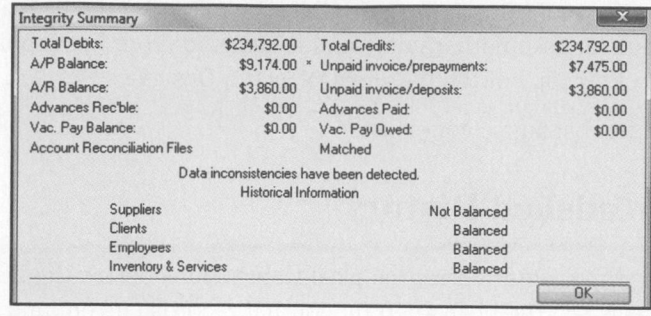

Click **OK** to return to the Home window.

Choose the **History menu** and **click Finish Entering History**:

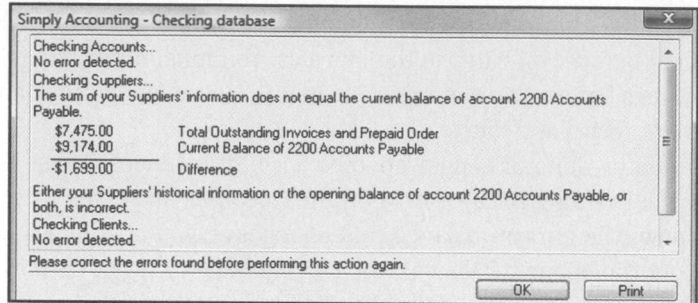

When all your essential linked accounts are defined and all historical amounts balance, you will see the warning that this step cannot be reversed, as in Chapter 4, page 96. Otherwise, Simply Accounting warns you about errors that prevent you from finishing the history. For example, the accounts may be out of order if a subgroup total is missing after a set of subgroup accounts, or the Receivables Ledger balances may not equal the *Accounts Receivable* control account balance. If you have omitted an essential linked account, that information will also be included on this screen.

In this case, we see the message that the Suppliers or Accounts Payable history is not balanced, the same information we had in the Data Integrity Check. Since the Trial Balance is correct, we may be missing a historical Payables Ledger invoice.

Click **Print** to print the message for reference to help you correct mistakes.

Click **OK** to return to the Home window.

We can proceed with entering the source documents. When the missing invoice surfaces, we can enter it and finish the history. You can proceed with journal entries until you start the next fiscal period. At that point, you must finish the history.

Correcting Historical Invoices

In reviewing all the records for the year to date, Dorfmann discovered part of the discrepancy between the *Accounts Payable* balance and the supplier ledger balances. Invoice #DD-4630 from Designers Den was incorrectly entered. The correct amount was $1 500 plus $75 tax, not $500 and $25. We will correct this error before making journal entries. The first step is to pay the invoices already entered.

Click **Payables** in the Home window Modules pane list.

Click **Designers Den** in the Suppliers list pane to open the ledger.

Click the **Historical Transactions tab**.

Click   **Payments** to open the Historical Payments form:

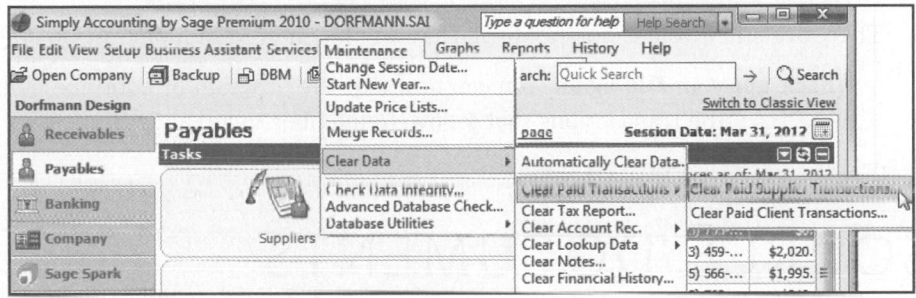

Type   55 in the Number field.

Type   3–28 in the Date field.

Click   the **Amount Paid column for Invoice DD-4502**.

Click   the **Amount Paid column for Invoice DD-4630** and **press** (tab) to update the total.

Click   **Record** and then **click Close**.

Close   the **supplier ledger record**.

The next step is to clear the paid transactions for Designers Den so that these invoices and payments will be removed from the records.

Choose   the **Maintenance menu** and then **choose Clear Data** and **Clear Paid Transactions**. **Click Clear Paid Supplier Transactions** as shown:

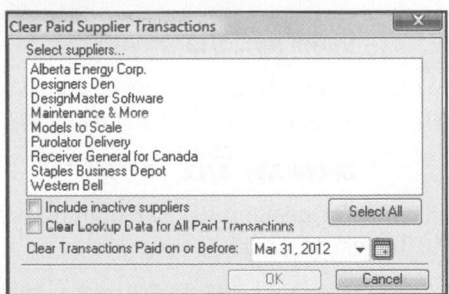

You will see the list of suppliers:

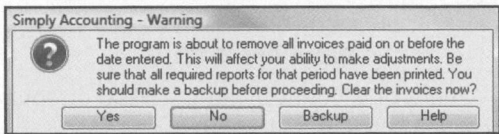

Click   **Designers Den** to select the supplier.

Accept   the **default date** and the other **settings** and **click OK**:

Simply Accounting - Warning

> The program is about to remove all invoices paid on or before the date entered. This will affect your ability to make adjustments. Be sure that all required reports for that period have been printed. You should make a backup before proceeding. Clear the invoices now?

Yes   No   Backup   Help

Click   **Yes** to confirm that you want to clear the data.

Click   **Designers Den** in the Home window Suppliers list pane.

Click   the **Statistics tab**.

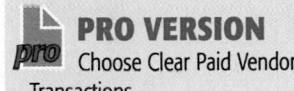

Delete the **year-to-date** expense and payment **amounts** to restore the balance amounts to zero. **Click** the **Save tool** 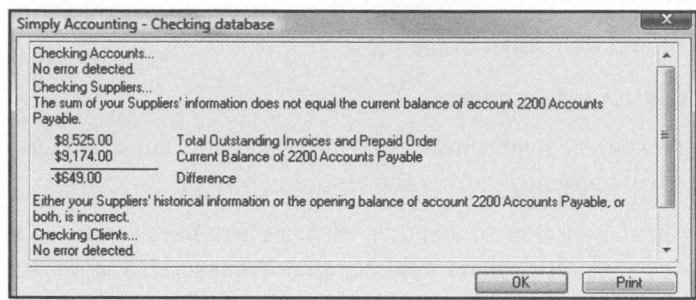.

Click the **Historical Transactions tab**.

Enter the **correct invoices** and **payments** shown below:

Supplier Name	Terms	Date	Inv/Chq No.	Amount	Tax	Total
Designers Den	2/10, n/30 (before tax)	Mar. 26/12	DD-4502	$2 500	$125	$2 625
		Mar. 26/12	Chq 62			2 180
	2/10, n/30 (before tax)	Mar. 28/12	DD-4630	1 500	75	1 575
			Balance Owing			$2 020

Close the **supplier ledger record**.

When we change the session date to April 7, Simply Accounting will show a warning because we are entering a new month and we turned on the warning:

There are still invoices outstanding. They will be entered in Memo #7 on May 1.

Back up your **file** again. You can now exit the program or continue by entering the transactions that follow. Remember to advance the session date.

SOURCE DOCUMENTS

SESSION DATE – APRIL 7, 2012

☐ **Memo #1**   **Dated Apr. 1/12**

Create shortcuts for General Journal entries, purchase invoices, other payments, invoice payments, the journals used in this chapter.

☐ **Sales Invoice #44**   **Dated Apr. 4/12**

To Glitter Jewellers, $2 000 plus $100 GST for designing a "welcoming" space for shopping. Sales invoice total, $2 100. Terms: 1/5, n/15.

☐ **Cash Receipt #25**   **Dated Apr. 4/12**

From Alberta Heritage Bank, cheque #7110 for $1 750 in full payment of account. Reference invoice #38. Customize the tabbing order so that Cheque Number follows the client (refer to pages 173–174).

☐ **Cheque Copy #65**   **Dated Apr. 4/12**

To Models to Scale, $4 180 in payment of account including $120 discount for early payment. Reference invoices #MS-376 and MS-453.

☐ **Cheque Copy #66**   **Dated Apr. 4/12**

To Designers Den, $1 940 in payment of account including $80 discount for early payment. Reference invoices #DD-4502 and DD-4630.

NOTES

You will see this reminder again when you advance the session date to May 1.

NOTES

Create shortcuts for General Journal entries (Company module) and for purchase invoices, other payments and invoice payments (Payables module). Refer to pages 138 and 190 if you need assistance with creating these shortcuts.

WARNING!

Be sure to select the correct revenue account for sales. You may need to change the default selection.

☐ **Purchase Invoice #DMS-596**   **Dated Apr. 5/12**

From DesignMaster Software, $750 plus $37.50 GST for new design software. Purchase invoice total, $787.50. Change the payment terms to net 30 days.

☐ **Purchase Invoice #SBD-643**   **Dated Apr. 5/12**

From Staples Business Depot, $200 for office supplies and $300 for computer supplies, plus $25 GST. Purchase invoice total, $525. Terms: net 10 days.

☐ **Cash Receipt #26**   **Dated Apr. 7/12**

From Glitter Jewellers, cheque #342 for $2 079 in full payment of account including $21 discount for early payment. Reference sales invoice #44.

☐

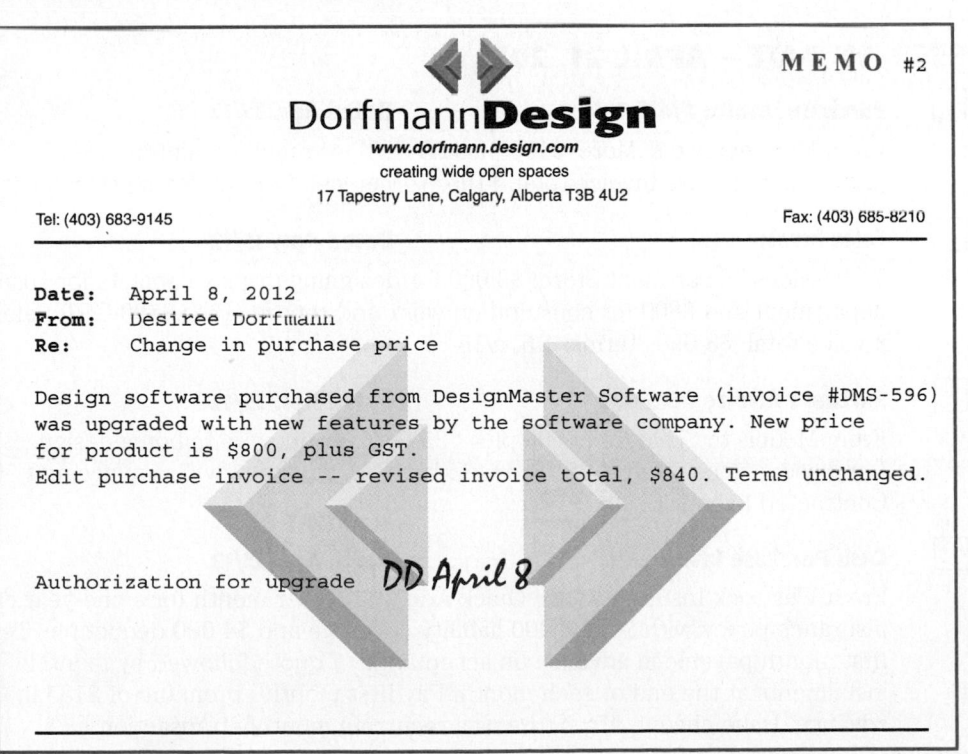

DorfmannDesign	MT Midwestern Trust 2596 Eighth Avenue Calgary AB T1D 1P3	**No: 067**

17 Tapestry Lane
Calgary, Alberta
T3B 4U2
(403) 683-9145

Date 2 0 1 2 0 4 0 7
Y Y Y Y M M D D

Pay ——— Two hundred and ten dollars ——— 00 $ 210.00

TO THE ORDER OF
Maintenance & More
51 Bragg Creek Rd.
Calgary, Alberta T3C 4N3

PER *Desiree Dorfmann*

⑈⑈···⑈044 21876···133774-067

Re: Pay invoices #MM-211 & MM-242 $210.00 **No: 067**
April 7, 2012

SESSION DATE – APRIL 14, 2012

☐

MEMO #2

DorfmannDesign
www.dorfmann.design.com
creating wide open spaces
17 Tapestry Lane, Calgary, Alberta T3B 4U2

Tel: (403) 683-9145   Fax: (403) 685-8210

Date: April 8, 2012
From: Desiree Dorfmann
Re: Change in purchase price

Design software purchased from DesignMaster Software (invoice #DMS-596) was upgraded with new features by the software company. New price for product is $800, plus GST.
Edit purchase invoice -- revised invoice total, $840. Terms unchanged.

Authorization for upgrade   *DD April 8*

☐ **Visa Purchase Invoice #P-61142**   **Dated Apr. 8/12**

From Purolator Delivery, $30 plus $1.50 GST for delivery charges for express shipment of designs and reports. Purchase invoice total, $31.50 charged to Visa credit card.

☐ **Purchase Invoice #MM-263**   **Dated Apr. 8/12**

From Maintenance & More, $100 plus $5 GST for regular maintenance of premises. Purchase invoice total, $105. Terms: net 15 days. Store as a weekly recurring entry.

☐ **Memo #3**   **Dated Apr. 10/12**

From Owner: Withdrew $250 from the business to pay for daughter's birthday presents. Issued cheque #68. Use Full Add for the Owner's supplier record. Create new Group account 3580 Dorfmann, Drawings.

☐ **Memo #4**   **Dated Apr. 10/12**

From Owner: A model of store interior was accidentally dropped and destroyed. It was worth $400 in model parts. Charge to new Group account 5025 Damaged Model Parts.

☐ **Purchase Invoice #DD-6431**   **Dated Apr. 11/12**

From Designers Den, $800 for Artograph vertical projector and $450 for tracer projector, plus $62.50 GST paid. Purchase invoice $1 312.50. Terms: 2/10, n/30.

☐ **Bank Debit Memo #642067**   **Dated Apr. 13/12**

From Midwestern Trust, $1 500 for reduction of bank loan principal. Since this is a fixed payment, store it as a recurring monthly entry. Interest on the loan was $200. The bank withdrew $1 700 from the chequing account.

☐ **Cheque Copy #69**   **Dated Apr. 14/12**

To Staples Business Depot, $525 in full payment of account. Reference invoice #SBD-643.

SESSION DATE – APRIL 21, 2012

☐ **Purchase Invoice #MM-314**   **Dated Apr. 15/12**

From Maintenance & More, $100 plus $5 GST for regular maintenance of premises. Purchase invoice total, $105. Terms: net 15 days. Recall stored entry.

☐ **Sales Invoice #45**   **Dated Apr. 15/12**

To Passions Department Store, $3 000 for designing display cabinets for cosmetic department and $800 for consultation work and reports, plus $190 GST. Sales invoice total, $3 990. Terms: 1/5, n/15.

☐ **Purchase Invoice #MS-850**   **Dated Apr. 15/12**

From Models to Scale Co., $500 plus $25 GST for outsourcing on a design. Purchase invoice total, $525. Terms: 2/10, n/30. Create new Group account 5015 Contracted Labour Costs.

☐ **Cash Purchase Invoice #WI-6913**   **Dated Apr. 15/12**

From Westrock Insurance (use Quick Add), $185 per month for a one-year car insurance policy with $2 000 000 liability coverage and $4 000 deductible. Terms: first month payable in advance on acceptance of quote followed by monthly instalments at the end of each month. Pay first month's premium of $185 in advance. Issue cheque #70. Store as a recurring monthly transaction.

NOTES

Although the owner's withdrawal is a cash purchase, you should create a supplier record for the owner because she will make further withdrawals. Leave the address tab fields blank. Enter Yes in the Tax Exempt column and enter 3580 Dorfmann, Drawings as the default expense account. Record the withdrawal as a cash purchase in the Payments Journal or the Purchases Journal.

NOTES

Use Full Add for the new suppliers if you want to add the default expense account (Insurance Expense). GST is not charged on insurance so you do not need to add a tax code.

Memo #5   **Dated Apr. 15/12**

Recall the stored entry for car insurance from Westrock Insurance to pay next month's premium of $185. Issue cheque #71 postdated for May 15. After posting, recall the entry again to pay the premium due June 15 with cheque #72. Choose Yes to confirm that the future date is correct.

Dorfmann Design	**Invoice:** 46
17 Tapestry Lane	**Date:** April 15, 2012
Calgary, Alberta	**Sold to:** Calgary District School Board
T3B 4U2	88 Learnex Avenue 8th Floor
	Calgary, AB T3C 4B6
	Phone: (403) 788-3000

Service Provided	Amount
Consultation and reports on redesign	
To refurbish atrium at Board's central office	1 200.00

Payment: 1/5, n/15	1.5% interest on accounts over 30 days	**GST** 60.00
GST #233 281 244	Customer Initials *SG*	**Invoice Total** 1 260.00

creating wide open spaces   www.dorfmann.design.com
Tel: (403) 683-9145   Toll free: (888) 455-7194   Fax: (403) 685-0210

Cheque Copy #73   **Dated Apr. 16/12**

To DesignMaster Software, $1 995 in payment of account. Reference invoice #DM-234.

Cash Receipt #27   **Dated Apr. 18/12**

From Calgary District School Board, cheque #1437 for $1 247.40 in full payment of account including $12.60 early payment discount. Reference sales invoice #46.

Sales Invoice #47   **Dated Apr. 18/12**

To Banff Condominiums, $2 500 for designing foyer with water fountain for condominium complex and $800 for consultation work and reports, plus $165 GST. Sales invoice total, $3 465. Terms: 1/5, n/15. Reports and designs to be shipped by Purolator Delivery. Allow client to exceed credit limit.

Sales Invoice #48   **Dated Apr. 18/12**

To Lougheed, Klein and Associates, $800 plus $40 GST for consultation on future design work on law office building. Sales invoice total, $840. Terms: 1/5, n/15.

Cheque Copy #74   **Dated Apr. 20/12**

To Designers Den, $1 287.50 in payment of account including $25 discount for early payment. Reference invoice #DD-6431.

Purchase Invoice #DD-6898   **Dated Apr. 20/12**

From Designers Den, $1 200 plus $60 GST for new Designtek aluminum drawing table. Purchase invoice total $1 260. Terms: 2/10, n/30.

□

DorfmannDesign		
17 Tapestry Lane		
Calgary, Alberta		
T3B 4U2		

Invoice: 49

Date: April 20, 2012

Sold to: Alliance Party Headquarters

Phone:

Service Provided	Amount
Consultation fee (for New Customer) Re: Redesign and refurbish party headquarters	500.00

Payment: Visa		GST	25.00
GST #233 281 244	Customer Initials *RK*	Invoice Total	525.00

creating wide open spaces

www. dorfmann.design.com

Tel: (403) 683-9145   Toll free: (888) 455-7194   Fax: (403) 685-8210

□ **Cash Receipt #28**   **Dated Apr. 21/12**

From Lougheed, Klein and Associates, cheque #444 for $831.60 in full payment of account including $8.40 discount for early payment. Reference sales invoice #48.

□ **Cheque Copy #75**   **Dated Apr. 21/12**

To Maintenance & More, $210 in payment of account. Reference invoices #MM-263 and MM-314.

SESSION DATE – APRIL 30, 2012

□ **Purchase Invoice #MM-399**   **Dated Apr. 22/12**

From Maintenance & More, $120 plus $6 GST for regular maintenance of premises. Purchase invoice total, $126. Terms: net 15 days. Recall and edit the stored entry to enter the increased price. Store the entry to save the changes.

□ **Sales Invoice #50**   **Dated Apr. 27/12**

To Calgary Arms Hotel, $3 200 for design work and $800 consultation fee, plus $200 GST charged. Sales invoice total, $4 200. Terms: 1/5, n/15.

□ **Cash Receipt #29**   **Dated Apr. 28/12**

From Passions Department Store, cheque #614 for $3 990 in full payment of account. Reference sales invoice #45.

□ **Cash Purchase Invoice #WB-669943**   **Dated Apr. 28/12**

From Western Bell, $125 plus $6.25 GST for telephone services. Purchase invoice total, $131.25. Issue cheque #76 in full payment.

□ **Cash Purchase Invoice #AE-43214**   **Dated Apr. 28/12**

From Alberta Energy Corp., $120 plus $6 GST for hydro services. Purchase invoice total, $126. Issue cheque #77 in full payment.

☐ **Visa Purchase Invoice #P-70431**   **Dated Apr. 28/12**

From Purolator Delivery, $30 plus $1.50 GST for delivery charges for sending reports to Banff Condominiums. Purchase invoice total, $31.50. Full amount charged to Visa credit card.

☐ **Purchase Invoice #MM-464**   **Dated Apr. 29/12**

From Maintenance & More, $120 plus $6 GST for regular maintenance. Purchase invoice total, $126. Terms: net 15 days. Recall the stored entry.

☐ **Memo #6**   **Dated Apr. 30/12**

From Owner: Prepare adjusting entries for the following

Model Parts used	$450
Computer Supplies used	240
Office Supplies used	220
Prepaid Insurance expired	208

☐ **Bank Debit Memo #643214**   **Dated Apr. 30/12**

From Midwestern Trust, $30 for monthly bank service charges and $1 320 for monthly mortgage payment withdrawn from chequing account. The mortgage payment includes $1 200 for interest and $120 for reduction of principal.

SESSION DATE – MAY 1, 2012

☐ **Memo #7**   **Dated May 1/12**

From Owner: Received monthly statements showing missing historical information. The statement from Staples Business Depot included an overdue amount of $166 from invoice #SBD-201 dated March 24, 2012. The statement from Models to Scale included an overdue amount of $460 plus $23 GST from invoice #MS-287 dated March 14, 2012.

Add the historical invoices for these two transactions in the supplier ledger records as historical transactions. Refer to page 241. You can open the Payables module window or add a Payables shortcut to modify supplier to access the records for these suppliers.

Pay these two invoices in the Payments Journal as current transactions dated May 1 using cheques #78 and #79.

☐ **Memo #8**   **Dated May 1/12**

Check the data integrity (Maintenance menu) after entering the historical invoices. Make a backup copy of the data files and finish entering the history. Choose the History menu in the Home window and click Finish Entering History.

☐ **Memo #9**   **Dated May 1/12**

From Owner: Print or preview client statements. Two invoices for Banff Condominiums are overdue. Complete sales invoice #51 for Banff Condominiums for $31.65, the interest charges on the overdue amount. Terms: net 15 days. Use the No Tax code for the interest charges and choose Interest Revenue as the account. Remember to remove the discount.

⚠ **WARNING!**
You must enter these outstanding invoices as historical invoices and the payments as current payments or you will be unable to finish the history.

R E V I E W

The Student DVD with Data Files includes Review Questions and Supplementary Cases for this chapter.

CHAPTER EIGHT

HELENA'S ACADEMY

After completing this chapter, you should be able to

OBJECTIVES

- **open** the Payroll Journal
- **enter** employee-related payroll transactions
- **understand** automatic payroll deductions
- **understand** Payroll Ledger linked accounts
- **edit** and **review** payroll transactions
- **adjust** Payroll Journal invoices after posting
- **enter** employee benefits and entitlements
- **complete** payroll runs for a group of employees
- **release** vacation pay to employees
- **remit** payroll taxes
- **display** and **print** payroll reports
- **prepare** record of employment and T4 slips

COMPANY INFORMATION

Company Profile

NOTES
Helena's Academy
250 Satchel Lane
Edmonton, AB T7F 3B2
Tel: (780) 633-8201
Fax: (780) 633-8396
Business No.: 188 255 345

Helena's Academy was opened in Edmonton, Alberta, in 2002 by Helena Teutor as a small private junior elementary school. The school has maintained its small size in order to offer individualized programming with high academic standards for students with artistic interests and abilities. Helena works as principal and also teaches the upper grades. Two other teachers handle the kindergarten and junior primary grades. Although all teachers have a background in fine arts and are trained music teachers, an additional half-time art and music specialist rotates among all the classes. A full-time office administrator, caretaker and classroom assistant make up the rest of the staff. The classroom assistant also runs the after-school program.

Parents pay tuition fees in two instalments, one before the start of the school year in August and the second at the beginning of January. They pay additional fees to participate in the after-school programs. Three teachers offer private half-hour weekly music lessons that parents also pay for separately.

All classes are split-grade classes, an arrangement required by the small school enrolment, but desired because of the opportunities for students to help each other. Older students in each class, even in kindergarten, are expected to help their younger classmates. All parents are also required to volunteer in the classroom and library, and the kindergarten parents provide the healthy daily snacks for the kindergarten classes. The volunteer expectations are viewed favourably by the families at the school because they enable parents to understand and reinforce the learning philosophy of the school.

The school closes for the month of July each year, but all teachers and staff return to work in August to plan their programs for the coming year. The caretaker uses this month before students return to catch up on repairs and maintenance.

Individual client accounts are not set up for this exercise and all regular tuition fees have been paid. Fees for the after-school program and private lessons are paid on the first of each month. No taxes are charged on any of the school's fees, and as an educational institution providing only tax-exempt services, the academy is not eligible for GST refunds on the taxes it pays. The school has accounts set up with a few regular suppliers and some of these offer discounts.

On October 1, 2012, Helena's Academy converted its accounts, using the following information:

- Chart of Accounts
- Trial Balance
- Supplier Information
- Client Information
- Employee Profiles and Information Sheet
- Accounting Procedures

CHART OF POSTABLE ACCOUNTS

HELENA'S ACADEMY

ASSETS
- 1080 Bank: Chequing Account
- 1090 Bank: Savings Account
- 1100 Investments: Restricted Use Funds
- 1200 Fees Receivable
- 1240 Advances Receivable
- 1260 Prepaid Taxes
- 1280 Office Supplies
- 1300 Arts Supplies
- 1320 Library Material
- 1340 Textbooks
- 1520 Classroom Computers
- 1540 Office Equipment
- 1560 Furniture
- 1580 School Vehicle
- 1620 School Premises ▶

▶LIABILITIES
- 2100 Bank Loan
- 2200 Accounts Payable
- 2300 Vacation Payable
- 2310 EI Payable
- 2320 CPP Payable
- 2330 Income Tax Payable
- 2400 RRSP Payable
- 2410 Family Support Payable
- 2430 Medical Payable - Employee
- 2440 Medical Payable - Employer
- 2460 WCB Payable
- 2920 Mortgage Payable

EQUITY
- 3560 Academy, Invested Capital
- 3580 Retained Surplus
- 3600 Net Income ▶

▶REVENUE
- 4020 Revenue from School Fees
- 4040 Revenue from Lessons
- 4060 Revenue from Programs
- 4100 Revenue from Interest

EXPENSE
- 5020 Purchase Discounts
- 5040 Bank Charges
- 5060 Hydro Expenses
- 5080 Insurance Expense
- 5100 Office Supplies Used
- 5110 Textbook Expenses
- 5120 Art Supplies Used
- 5140 Interest Expense
- 5180 Promotional Expenses
- 5190 Property Taxes
- 5200 Telephone Expenses ▶

▶
- 5210 Vehicle Expenses
- 5250 Wages: Teaching Staff
- 5260 Wages: Support Staff
- 5280 Wages: Music Lessons
- 5310 EI Expense
- 5320 CPP Expense
- 5330 WCB Expense
- 5380 Tuition Fees Expense
- 5400 Medical Premium Expense

NOTES: The Chart of Accounts includes only postable accounts and Net Income.

TRIAL BALANCE

HELENA'S ACADEMY

October 1, 2012

		Debits	Credits				Debits	Credits
1080	Bank: Chequing Account	$ 90 000.00		▶ 3560	Academy, Invested Capital			540 000.00
1090	Bank: Savings Account	160 000.00		3580	Retained Surplus			57 604.02
1100	Investments: Restricted			4020	Revenue from School Fees			680 000.00
	Use Funds	540 000.00		4040	Revenue from Lessons			500.00
1260	Prepaid Taxes	2 700.00		4060	Revenue from Programs			3 000.00
1280	Office Supplies	4 100.00		4100	Revenue from Interest			2 150.00
1300	Arts Supplies	3 850.00		5040	Bank Charges		66.00	
1320	Library Material	14 500.00		5060	Hydro Expenses		1 220.00	
1340	Textbooks	5 300.00		5080	Insurance Expense		3 680.00	
1520	Classroom Computers	6 800.00		5100	Office Supplies Used		240.00	
1540	Office Equipment	4 900.00		5110	Textbook Expenses		800.00	
1560	Furniture	16 000.00		5120	Art Supplies Used		280.00	
1580	School Vehicle	23 000.00		5140	Interest Expense		4 600.00	
1620	School Premises	840 000.00		5180	Promotional Expenses		2 800.00	
2100	Bank Loan		$ 65 000.00	5190	Property Taxes		1 800.00	
2200	Accounts Payable		1 880.00	5200	Telephone Expenses		350.00	
2300	Vacation Payable		2 320.50	5210	Vehicle Expenses		600.00	
2310	EI Payable		948.58	5250	Wages: Teaching Staff		31 838.00	
2320	CPP Payable		2 044.60	5260	Wages: Support Staff		16 917.60	
2330	Income Tax Payable		3 841.06	5280	Wages: Music Lessons		750.00	
2400	RRSP Payable		300.00	5310	EI Expense		1 095.93	
2410	Family Support Payable		1 000.00	5320	CPP Expense		2 033.31	
2430	Medical Payable - Employee		187.00	5330	WCB Expense		504.87	
2440	Medical Payable - Employer		187.00	5380	Tuition Fees Expense		180.00	
2460	WCB Payable		299.95	5400	Medical Premium Expense		357.00	
2920	Mortgage Payable		420 000.00 ▶				$1 781 262.71	$1 781 262.71

SUPPLIER INFORMATION

HELENA'S ACADEMY

Supplier Name (Contact)	Address	Phone No. Fax No.	E-mail Web Site	Terms Tax ID
Aspen Life Financial (A.M. Weller)	280 Wellness Blvd. Edmonton, AB T6G 2B7	Tel: (780) 37-7164 Fax: (780) 327-8109	www.aspenlife.com	net 1
Alberta Workers' Compensation Board	55 Payout Cr. Edmonton, AB T5J 2S5	Tel: (780) 498-3999 Fax: (780) 498-7999	www.wcb.ab.ca	net 1
Energy Supply Services (N.U. Cleer)	690 Service Ave. Edmonton, AB T6T 4G4	Tel: (780) 456-3293 Fax: (780) 456-1229	nucleer@ess.ca www.ess.ca	net 1
Loomis Art Supplies (Dee Ziner)	64 Canvas St. Edmonton, AB T5Z 2S4	Tel: (780) 462-1706 Fax: (780) 452-1700	dz@loomis.com www.loomis.com	1/10, n/30 186 519 184
Maintenance Enforcement Program (Al I. Mony)	43 Brownlee St. Edmonton, AB T5J 3W7	Tel: (780) 422-5555 Fax: (780) 401-7575	alberta.mep@gov.ab.ca www.justice.gov.ab.ca/mep	net 1
Receiver General for Canada	56 Heron Rd. Ottawa, Ontario K3A 6B4	Tel 1: (800) 561-7761 Tel 2: (800) 959-2221	www.cra-arc.gc.ca	net 1
Rocky Mountain Trust (Rocky)	59 High St. Edmonton, AB T4P 1M3	Tel: (780) 388-1825 Fax: (780) 388-2663	www.rockymtntrust.ca	net 1
Telus Alberta (Toks Lotts)	499 Cellular Rd. Edmonton, AB T8F 2B5	Tel: (780) 348-5999	www.telus.com	net 1

OUTSTANDING SUPPLIER INVOICES

HELENA'S ACADEMY

Supplier Name	Terms	Date	Invoice No.	Amount	Total
Loomis Art Supplies	1/10, n/30	Sep. 29/12	LT-438	$1 880	$1 880

CLIENT INFORMATION

HELENA'S ACADEMY

Client Name	Address
Parents of Students	Edmonton

(individual client records are not set up for this application)

EMPLOYEE INFORMATION SHEET

HELENA'S ACADEMY

	Helena Teutor	Marina Booker	Lars Teicher	Arte Tiste	Neela Nerture	Morty Filer	Jerome Handie
Position	Principal	Teacher	Teacher	Specialist	Assistant	Office Admin	Caretaker
Social Insurance No.	699 344 578	277 639 118	403 401 599	513 288 191	129 495 768	374 588 127	813 402 302
Address	21 Socratic Blvd. Edmonton, AB T5H 2L2	49 Dewey Pl. Edmonton, AB T6K 4K2	15 Practicurn St. Edmonton, AB T5B 4C1	2 Creative Way Edmonton, AB T6H 1X3	93 Formula Cr. Edmonton, AB T5E 2L2	10 Basics Lane Edmonton, AB T5A 4K2	4 Repairal Cr. Edmonton, AB T5B 4C1
Telephone	(780) 466-7736	(780) 436-9015	(780) 463-4870	(780) 429-5656	(780) 488-8554	(780) 440-3301	(780) 461-1328
Date of Birth (mm-dd-yy)	7-28-78	9-14-81	10-5-82	7-18-79	5-19-77	4-3-74	3-3-71
Federal (Alberta) Tax Exemption – TD1							
Basic Personal	$10 382 (16 825)	$10 382 (16 825)	$10 382 (16 825)	$10 382 (16 825)	$10 382 (16 825)	$10 382 (16 825)	$10 382 (16 825)
Spouse	–	$10 382 (16 825)	–	$10 382 (16 825)	$10 382 (16 825)	$10 382 (16 825)	–
Other	–	$1 460 (1 684)	–	$4 223 (9 739)	–	$3 720 (4 168)	–
Total Exemptions	$10 382 (16 825)	$22 224 (35 334)	$10 382 (16 825)	$24 987 (43 389)	$20 764 (33 650)	$24 484 (37 818)	$10 382 (16 825)
Employee Earnings							
Regular Wage Rate	–	–	–	$30.00	$18.00	$20.00	$20.00
Overtime Wage Rate	–	–	–	–	$27.00	$30.00	$30.00
Regular Salary	$5 000	$4 200	$3 800	–	–	–	–
Pay Period	monthly	monthly	monthly	semi-monthly	semi-monthly	semi-monthly	semi-monthly
Hours per Period	160	160	160	40	82.5	82.5	82.5
Lessons (#/period)	–	$25.00 (16)	$25.00 (12)	$25.00 (22)	–	–	–
Vacation	4 weeks	4 weeks	4 weeks	6% retained	6% retained	6% retained	6% retained
Vacation Pay Owed	–	–	–	$1 152.00	$345.60	398.40	424.50
WCB Rate	0.89	0.89	0.89	0.89	1.15	0.89	2.44
Employee Deductions							
Medical	$22.00	$44.00	$22.00	$22.00	$22.00	$22.00	$11.00
RRSP	$100.00	$50	$50	–	$25.00	–	$25.00
Family Support	–	–	$500.00	–	–	–	$250.00
Additional Tax				$200.00			
EI, CPP & Income Tax	Calculations built into Simply Accounting program						
Direct Deposit	No	Yes	Yes	No	Yes	No	Yes

NOTES: Medical premiums are deducted every pay period. The amounts are adjusted for the monthly rates.

Employee Profiles and TD1 Information

Employee Benefits and Entitlements   All employees are entitled to 10 days per year as sick leave. If the days are not needed, employees can carry these days forward to a new year, to a maximum of 90 days. Currently, all employees have some unused sick leave days accrued from previous years. Most employees take their vacations in July when the school is closed, with salaried employees receiving their regular salary and the full-time hourly workers receiving the retained vacation pay at the end of June with their regular paycheque. Vacation pay cannot be accumulated or carried forward beyond the calendar year. Tiste has not yet collected any vacation pay this year.

In keeping with the educational goals, the Academy encourages all employees to continue their education by paying 50 percent of the tuition fees for college or university programs. Booker and Filer are currently taking courses and receiving the tuition fee benefit. A second benefit applies to all employees — the Academy pays 50 percent of the medical premiums for an extended health care insurance plan. Both benefits are taxable income for the employee and expenses for Helena's Academy.

Music Lessons   Booker, Teicher and Tiste give private music lessons at lunchtime and after school. Parents pay the school $30 per half-hour lesson and the school pays the teachers. These fees are set up on a "piece rate" basis at $25 per lesson and added to each paycheque.

Employer Expenses   In addition to the expenses for the tuition fees and medical premium benefits, Helena's Academy pays the compulsory CPP, EI and WCB.

Helena Teutor   As the principal and founder of the school, Teutor frequently speaks to parent groups in order to promote the school. She also teaches the senior class of grade 4, 5 and 6 students and hires new staff when needed. She is married and has no children. Since her husband is also fully employed, she uses the single federal and provincial tax claim and medical premium amounts. At the end of each month, she receives her salary of $5 000 per month by cheque. She makes monthly contributions to her RRSP plan as well.

Marina Booker   is the regular teacher for the primary class of grade 1, 2 and 3 students. She supplements her monthly salary of $4 200 with income from private music lessons offered through the school. She earns $25 for each half-hour lesson taught in the previous month. Booker is married and claims the basic and spousal amounts for income tax purposes. She also has a claim for her RRSP contributions and her tuition fees of $900 for a four-month university course and the $140 per month federal ($196 provincial) education deduction for the part-time course. She pays medical premiums at the family rate. Her pay is deposited directly to her bank account every month.

Lars Teicher   teaches the two junior and senior kindergarten classes. He too supplements his monthly salary of $3 800 with income from private music lessons at $25 per lesson. Teicher is separated from his wife and is required to make family support payments. For this, $500 is deducted from each paycheque. As a single employee, he claims only the basic federal and provincial amounts for income tax purposes, but he does have an additional deduction for his RRSP contributions. He also pays the single rate towards the provincial medical plan. He too has his paycheque deposited directly to his bank account.

Arte Tiste   is the half-time art teacher who works four hours in the school every afternoon, dividing his time among the three classes but concentrating on the senior class. He spends the mornings painting in his home art studio. Although he is single, he can claim the spousal equivalent plus caregiver amounts because he looks after his infirm brother. These claims significantly reduce the income tax he pays on his wages of

$30 per hour. He teaches music lessons after school at the per-lesson rate of $25. His medical premium is deducted from his semi-monthly paycheque at the family rate to cover himself and his brother. His 6 percent vacation pay is retained. Instead of receiving his vacation pay in June like the other hourly workers, Tiste takes his vacation pay sometime in the fall to pay for his December travels. Because Tiste has additional income from the sale of his paintings, he has elected to pay additional federal taxes in each pay period instead of making extra quarterly tax remittances on this extra income. Tiste is paid by cheque twice each month.

Neela Nerture works full-time in the school as a classroom assistant and also runs the after-school program for children who require daycare. She divides her time among the three classes as needed by the teachers and program schedules. Nerture is married and fully supports her child and her husband while he is finishing his studies. Therefore, she pays the family medical premiums and has the basic and spousal claim amounts for income taxes. She is paid twice a month at the hourly rate of $18 per hour. When she works more than 7.5 hours in a day, she earns $27 per hour for the extra time. This time is sometimes required for extended daycare and can be charged back to the parents. This extra charge encourages parents to pick up their children on time. On top of her pay, she earns 6 percent vacation pay that is retained until the end of June. Nerture has her paycheques deposited directly to her bank account.

Morty Filer runs the school office, handling the routine phone calls to and from parents, arranging lessons, scheduling parent volunteers, collecting fees and doing the bookkeeping. For these duties he earns $20 per hour for the first 7.5 hours each day in each half-month pay period and is paid by cheque. For additional hours, he earns $30 per hour. The 6 percent vacation pay he earns on his regular and overtime wages is retained until the end of June. Filer supports his wife and claims both the basic and spousal federal and provincial amounts for tax purposes. His medical premium is at the family rate. He has an additional claim for his university tuition of $2 600 and the $140 per month federal education deduction ($196 provincial) for the eight-month school year.

Jerome Handie is the caretaker for the school and grounds. He works year-round, except for his vacation time in July, cleaning the school's rooms and providing general maintenance. During August, he paints the classrooms and steam-cleans all carpets. From each semi-monthly paycheque that is deposited to his bank account, $250 is withheld to support his ex-wife and two children. He claims only the basic federal and provincial amounts for tax purposes, and the single medical premium. He also makes contributions to his RRSP program with regular payroll deductions. His hourly pay rate is $20 for the first 7.5 hours per day and $30 per hour for any additional time. His vacation pay is calculated and retained at the rate of 6 percent.

Accounting Procedures

Taxes: GST and PST

As an educational institution that offers only tax-exempt services, Helena's Academy is not eligible for any refunds on the GST it pays for products and services. Therefore, no sales taxes are set up in this application and the prices in the source documents include all taxes. Provincial sales tax is not charged in Alberta.

Discounts

Some suppliers offer discounts on after-tax purchase amounts. These discount terms are set up in the supplier records so that Simply Accounting will automatically calculate the discount when full payment is made within the discount period. No discounts are offered on school fees.

NOTES
Because hourly employees are paid twice a month, the pay period may include 10 or 11 days. The number of regular hours is therefore either 75 or 82.5 hours, based on working 7.5 hours per day.

NOTES
The Academy pays $1 300 of Filer's tuition at the rate of $130 per pay period for five months (10 pay periods).

NOTES
The sales tax amounts are included with the asset or expense portion of the purchase.

Direct Payroll Deposits

The Academy allows employees to have their regular pay deposited directly to their bank accounts or to be paid by cheque. Four employees have selected direct payroll deposits.

Payroll Remittances

Some suppliers are identified as payroll authorities with the following remittances: EI, CPP and income tax are remitted to the Receiver General for Canada; medical premiums are remitted to Aspen Life Financial; Workers' Compensation Board premiums are remitted to Aspen Life Financial; RRSP contributions are remitted to Rocky Mountain Trust; family support payments are remitted to Maintenance Enforcement Program. All payments are remitted monthly for the pay period ending the previous month.

Tuition fees are reimbursed directly to the employee on their regular payroll cheques.

INSTRUCTIONS

PRO VERSION

pro In the Pro version, Customer replaces the term Client, Vendor replaces the term Supplier, Sales Invoices replaces the icon label Statements and Sales Journal replaces the term Fees Journal.

1. **Enter** the **transactions** in Simply Accounting using the Chart of Accounts and Supplier, Client and Employee Information. The procedures for entering new transactions for this application are outlined step by step in the Keystrokes section following the source documents. These transactions have a ✓ in the check box, and the page number where the keystrokes begin appears immediately below the check box.

2. **Print** the **reports and graphs** marked on the following printing form after you have finished making your entries. Keystrokes for payroll reports begin on page 299.

REPORTS

Accounts
- ☐ Chart of Accounts
- ☐ Account List
- ☐ General Journal Entries

Financials
- ☑ Balance Sheet: Dec. 31
- ☑ Income Statement: Aug. 1 to Dec. 31
- ☑ Trial Balance date: Dec. 31
- ☑ All Journal Entries: Oct. 1 to Dec. 31
- ☑ General Ledger accounts: Oct. 1 to Dec. 31
  5250 5260 5280
- ☐ Statement of Cash Flows
- ☑ Cash Flow Projection Detail Report:
  for 1080 for next 30 days

Banking
- ☐ Cheque Log Report

Payables
- ☐ Supplier List
- ☐ Supplier Aged

- ☐ Aged Overdue Payables
- ☐ Purchase Journal Entries
- ☐ Payment Journal Entries

Receivables
- ☐ Client List
- ☐ Client Aged
- ☐ Aged Overdue Receivables
- ☐ Fees Journal Entries
- ☐ Receipt Journal Entries
- ☐ Client Statements

Employees & Payroll
- ☐ Employee List
- ☑ Summary for all employees
- ☐ Deductions & Expenses
- ☑ Remittances Summary Report:
  for all payroll authorities Dec. 31
- ☑ Payroll Journal Entries: Oct. 1 to Dec. 31
- ☑ T4 Slip for Tiste
- ☑ Record of Employment for Tiste

Mailing Labels
- ☐ Labels

Management Reports
- ☐ Ledger

GRAPHS
- ☐ Payables by Aging Period
- ☐ Payables by Supplier
- ☐ Receivables by Aging Period
- ☐ Receivables by Client
- ☐ Fees vs Receivables
- ☐ Receivables Due vs Payables Due
- ☐ Revenues by Account
- ☐ Expenses by Account
- ☐ Expenses and Net Profit as % of Revenue

SOURCE DOCUMENTS

SESSION DATE – OCTOBER 15, 2012

☐ **Cash Sales Invoice #1036**   **Dated Oct. 1/12**

To parents of students, $3 200, total monthly fees for after-school programs and $2 130, total monthly fees for individual music lessons. Deposited $5 330 to chequing account.

☐ **Cash Purchase Invoice #GL-38827**   **Dated Oct. 2/12**

From Global Liability Inc. (use Full Add for new supplier), $1 800 for monthly premium on a one-year insurance policy for school and staff. Paid by cheque #211. Store as a recurring monthly entry.

☐ **Cheque Copy #212**   **Dated Oct. 5/12**

To Loomis Art Supplies, $1 861.20 in payment of account, including $18.80 discount for early payment. Reference invoice #LT-438.

EMPLOYEE TIME SUMMARY SHEET #19

(Dated October 15, 2012, for the pay period ending October 15, 2012)

Name of Employee	Regular Hours	Overtime Hours	Lessons	Tuition	Advance (Repaid)	Sick Days	Direct Deposit
☑ Filer, Morty	82.5	4	–	$130	$200	–	No
273							
☑ Handie, Jerome	82.5	2	–	–	–	1	Yes
278							
☐ Nerture, Neela	82.5	–	–	–	–	–	Yes
☑ Tiste, Arte	44.0	–	20	–	–	–	No
280							

a. Using Employee Time Summary Sheet #19 and the Employee Information Sheet, complete payroll for weekly paid employees. Handie has taken one sick day.

b. Issue $200 advance to Morty Filer and recover $50 from each of the following four paycheques.

c. Issue cheques #213 and #214 and Direct Deposit (DD) slips #55 and #56.

SESSION DATE – OCTOBER 31, 2012

☑ **Memo #1**   *Adjust paycheque & Re-calculate*   **Dated Oct. 17/12**

281   From Manager: Morty Filer returned his paycheque for adjustment. He worked 6 hours of overtime during the week but was paid for only 4 hours. Adjust his paycheque and re-issue cheque #213 to make the correction.

☑ **Memo #2**   **Dated Oct. 17/12**

284   Tiste has booked his vacation and will receive his retained vacation pay to pay for the holiday. Release the accrued retained vacation pay for Arte Tiste and issue cheque #215.

☑ **Memo #3**   **Dated Oct. 17/12**

287   Make payroll remittances for the pay period ending October 1.
     Receiver General for Canada: EI, CPP and income tax
     Aspen Life Financial: Medical premiums from employee and employer
     Alberta Workers' Compensation Board: WCB
     Rocky Mountain Trust: RRSP
     Maintenance Enforcement Program: Family support payments
Issue cheques #216 to #220.

NOTES
Keystroke instructions begin on page 273.
You should create shortcuts for the non-payroll transactions.

NOTES
For the educational service company, the Customers icon is labelled Clients, Sales Invoices are labelled as Statements and Sales or Revenues are renamed Fees.

NOTES
Global Liability Inc.
Terms: net 1
Expense account: 5080

NOTES
The pay period for hourly paid employees included 11 days and 7.5 hours per day.

☐ **Cash Purchase Invoice #ESS-4689**   **Dated Oct. 18/12**

From Energy Supply Services, $610 including taxes for heat and hydro on equal monthly billing plan. Store as a recurring monthly entry. Paid by cheque #221.

☐ **Cash Purchase #TA-113368**   **Dated Oct. 20/12**

From Telus Alberta, $220 including all taxes for one month of telephone services. Invoice total paid in full with cheque #222.

EMPLOYEE TIME SUMMARY SHEET #20

(Dated October 31, 2012, for the pay period ending October 31, 2012)

Name of Employee	Regular Hours	Overtime Hours	Lessons	Tuition	Advance (Repaid)	Sick Days	Direct Deposit
✓ Filer, Morty	82.5	2	–	$130.00	($50)	–	No
✓ Handie, Jerome	82.5	2	–	–	–	–	Yes
✓ Nerture, Neela	82.5	–	–	–	–	–	Yes
✓ Tiste, Arte	44.0	–	22	–	$100	–	No
✓ Booker, Marina	160	–	16	$45.00		1	Yes
✓ Teicher, Lars	160	–	12				Yes
✓ Teutor, Helena	160	–	–				No

291

a. Using Employee Time Summary Sheet #20 and the Employee Information Sheet, complete payroll for all employees.
b. Recover $50 advanced to Morty Filer.
c. Issue $100 advance to Tiste and recover $25 from each of the next four paycheques.
d. Issue cheques #223, #224 and #225 and DD slips #57, #58, #59 and #60.

NOTES
The pay period for hourly paid employees included 11 days.

☐ **Bank Debit Memo #277581**   **Dated Oct. 31/12**

From Scholar Heights Bank, $4 025 was withdrawn from chequing account for the following pre-authorized transactions:

Bank Charges	$ 25
Interest on Bank Loan	320
Reduction of Principal on Bank Loan	880
Interest on Mortgage	2 500
Reduction of Principal on Mortgage	300

Store as a recurring monthly entry.

☐ **Bank Credit Memo #467116**   **Dated Oct. 31/12**

From Scholar Heights Bank, $1 890 interest on investments and bank account was deposited to chequing account. Store as a recurring monthly entry.

☐ **Memo #4**   **Dated Oct. 31/12**

Complete end-of-month adjusting entries for the following:

Office supplies used	$180
Art supplies used	335
Textbooks used	85
Prepaid property taxes	900

You can store this as a recurring monthly entry if you want.

SESSION DATE – NOVEMBER 15, 2012

NOTES
You will see an Advisor message about preparing for year-end.

☐ **Cash Sales Invoice #1037**   **Dated Nov. 1/12**

To parents of students, $3 200 total monthly fees for after-school programs, and $2 280 total monthly fees for individual music lessons. Deposited $5 480 to chequing account.

☐ **Cash Purchase Invoice #GL-38827-B**   **Dated Nov. 2/12**

To Global Liability Inc., $1 800 for monthly insurance premium as stated on policy #GL-38827. Paid by cheque #226. Recall stored entry.

☐ **Cash Purchase Invoice #ES-1446**   **Dated Nov. 15/12**

From Engine Services (use Quick Add), $220 including taxes for gasoline, tire repairs, oil change and lubrication on school vehicle. Invoice total paid in full with cheque #227.

☐

HELENA'S ACADEMY

art 2

Aim higher!

Employee Time Summary Sheet
Business No.: 188 255 345 RT 0003

#21
Cheque Date: November 15, 2012   Last day of pay period end: November 15, 2012

Employee SIN	M. Filer 374 588 127	J. Handie 813 402 302	N. Nerture 129 495 760	A. Tiste 513 288 191	H. Teutor 699 344 578	M. Booker 277 639 118	L. Teicher 403 401 599
Nov 1-2	15.0	17.0	15.0	8			
Nov 5-9	37.5	37.5	37.5	20			
Nov 12-15	30.0	32.0	30.0	16			

Reg. hrs	82.5	82.5	82.5	44			
Overtime	--	4	--	--			
Lessons	--	--	--	22			
Tuition	130.00	--	--	--			
Advance	-50.00	--	--	-25.00			
Sick leave	--	--	1	--			
Chq/DD #	Chq 228	DD61	DD62	Chq 229			

Payroll Prepared by: Morty Filer Nov 15/12

SESSION DATE – NOVEMBER 30, 2012

☐ **Memo #5**   **Dated Nov. 17/12**

Make payroll remittances for the pay period ending October 31.
Receiver General for Canada: CPP, EI and income tax
Aspen Life Financial: Medical premiums from employee and employer
Alberta Workers' Compensation Board: WCB
Rocky Mountain Trust: RRSP
Maintenance Enforcement Program: Family support payments
Issue cheques #230 to #234.

☐ **Cash Purchase Invoice #ESS-5568**   **Dated Nov. 18/12**

From Energy Supply Services, $610 including taxes for heat and hydro on equal monthly billing plan. Recall stored entry. Paid by cheque #235.

☐ **Cash Purchase #TA-193245**   **Dated Nov. 20/12**

From Telus Alberta, $165 including all taxes for one month of telephone services. Invoice total paid in full with cheque #236.

NOTES
Type –50 in the Advance Amount field for Filer and –25 for Tiste to recover these amounts.

NOTES
The pay period for hourly paid employees included 11 days.

NOTES
You will see the message that the date precedes the current period because October 31 is in the previous month. You can click Yes to confirm that this is correct or you can enter November 1 as the ending date for the pay period.

NOTES
Type –50 in the Advance Amount field for Filer and –25 for Tiste to recover these amounts.

NOTES
The pay period for hourly paid employees included 11 days. They were paid for 4 days in the week of Nov. 12 on Nov. 15, leaving one day for this pay period.

Aim higher!

HELENA'S ACADEMY

Employee Time Summary Sheet
Business No.: 188 255 345 RT 0003

#22
Cheque Date: November 30, 2012   Last day of pay period end: November 30, 2012

Employee SIN	M. Filer 374 588 127	J. Handie 813 402 302	N. Nerture 129 495 768	A. Tiste 513 288 191	H. Teutor 699 344 578	M. Booker 277 639 118	L. Teicher 403 401 599
Nov 1-2	pd	pd	pd	pd	➤➤	➤➤	➤➤
Nov 5-9	pd	pd	pd	pd	➤➤	➤➤	➤➤
Nov 12-16	7.5	7.5	9.5	4	➤➤	➤➤	➤➤
Nov 19-23	37.5	39.5	41.5	20	➤➤	➤➤	➤➤
Nov 26-30	37.5	37.5	37.5	20	➤➤	➤➤	➤➤
Reg. hrs	82.5	82.5	82.5	44	160	160	160
Overtime	--	2	6	--	--	--	--
Lessons	--	--	--	22	--	16	12
Tuition	130.00	--	--	--		45.00	
Advance	-50.00	--	--	-25.00			
Sick leave	--	--	1	--			
Chq/DD #	Chq 237	DD64	DD65	Chq 239	Chq 238	DD63	DD66

Payroll Prepared by: Morty Filer Nov 30/12

Bank Debit Memo #422344   Dated Nov. 30/12

From Scholar Heights Bank, $4 025 was withdrawn from chequing account for the following pre-authorized transactions:

Bank Charges	$ 25
Interest on Bank Loan	320
Reduction of Principal on Bank Loan	880
Interest on Mortgage	2 500
Reduction of Principal on Mortgage	300

Recall stored entry.

Bank Credit Memo #64567   Dated Nov. 30/12

From Scholar Heights Bank, $1 890 interest on investments and bank account was deposited to chequing account. Recall stored entry.

Memo #6   Dated Nov. 30/12

Complete end-of-month adjusting entries for the following:

Office supplies used	$275
Art supplies used	180
Textbooks used	110
Prepaid property taxes	900

SESSION DATE – DECEMBER 15, 2012

Cash Sales Invoice #1038   Dated Dec. 1/12

To parents of students, $2 400 total monthly fees for after-school programs, and $1 580 total monthly fees for individual music lessons. Deposited $3 980 to chequing account.

NOTES
When you advance the session date to December 15, you will see the year-end Advisor message. This includes a message about renewing your payroll plan to receive tax table updates. Tax tables are updated by the federal government every six months.

☐ **Cash Purchase Invoice #GL-38827-C**   **Dated Dec. 2/12**

To Global Liability Inc., $1 800 for monthly insurance premium as stated on policy #GL-38827. Paid by cheque #240. Recall stored entry.

☐

Aim higher!

Employee Time Summary Sheet
Business No.: 188 255 345 RT 0003

#23
Cheque Date: December 15, 2012   Last day of pay period end: December 15, 2012

Employee SIN	M. Filer 374 588 127	J. Handie 813 402 302	N. Nerture 129 495 768	A. Tiste 513 288 191	H. Teutor 699 344 578	M. Booker 277 639 118	L. Teicher 403 401 599
Dec 3-7	37.5	38.5	37.5	20			
Dec 10-14	37.5	38.5	41.5	20			

Reg. hrs	75	75	75	40			
Overtime	--	2	5	--			
Lessons	--	--	--	22			
Tuition	130.00	--	--	--			
Advance	-50.00	--	--	-25.00			
Sick leave	--	--	--	--			
Chq/DD #	Chq 241	DD67	DD68	Chq 242			

Payroll Prepared by: Morty Filer Dec 15/12

NOTES
Type –50 in the Advance Amount field for Filer and –25 for Tiste to recover these amounts.

⚠ **WARNING!**
Remember to change the number of regular hours from 82.5 to 75 for Income (Regular Hours) and Entitlements. This pay period included 10 days for hourly paid employees.

SESSION DATE – DECEMBER 31, 2012

☐

Aim higher!

M E M O   #7

From the desk of Morty Filer
Dated: Dec. 17, 2012

RE: Payroll remittances
Made payroll remittances for the pay period ending November 30 to

        Receiver General for Canada for EI, CPP and
          income tax cheque #243
        Aspen Life Financial for medical premiums
          from employee and employer cheque #244
        Alberta Workers' Compensation Board for WCB cheque #245
        Rocky Mountain Trust for RRSP cheque #246
        Maintenance Enforcement Program for
          Family support payments cheque #247

Payments submitted   *Dec 17 Morty Filer*

NOTES
You will see the message that the date precedes the current period because November 30 is in the previous month. You can click Yes to confirm that this is correct or you can enter December 1 as the ending date for the pay period.

✓ **Memo #8** *adjust existing paycheque & recalculate tax* **Dated Dec. 17/12**

296   Adjust the Dec. 15 paycheque for Tiste — he is leaving and should have the full advance recovered from his paycheque. (Increase the advance recovered to $50.) Create an additional paycheque #248 to release his accrued vacation pay. *uncheck 'retain' & delete all field except (vacation paid)*

☐ **Cash Purchase Invoice #ESS-7889** **Dated Dec. 18/12**

From Energy Supply Services, $610 including taxes for heat and hydro on equal monthly billing plan. Recall stored entry. Paid by cheque #249.

☐ **Cash Purchase #TA-266778** **Dated Dec. 20/12**

From Telus Alberta, $170 including all taxes for one month of telephone services. Invoice total paid in full with cheque #250.

EMPLOYEE TIME SUMMARY SHEET #24

(Dated December 31, 2012, for the pay period ending December 31, 2012)

Name of Employee	Regular Hours	Overtime Hours	Lessons	Tuition	Advance (Repaid)	Sick Days	Direct Deposit
☐ Filer, Morty	75	–	–	$130.00	–	–	No
☐ Handie, Jerome	75	4	–	–	–	–	Yes
☐ Nerture, Neela	75	–	–	–	–	1	Yes
☐ Booker, Marina	160	–	10	$45.00			Yes
☐ Teicher, Lars	160	–	8		$200		Yes
☐ Teutor, Helena	160	–	–				No

a. Using Employee Time Summary Sheet #2 and the Employee Information Sheet, complete payroll for all employees. Hourly paid employees are paid for their regular hours during the Christmas holiday break.

c. Issue $200 advance to Teicher and recover $50 from each of the next four paycheques.

d. Issue cheques #251 and #252 and DD slips #69, #70, #71 and #72.

☐ **Bank Credit Memo #69886** **Dated Dec. 31/12**

From Scholar Heights Bank, $1 890 interest on investments and bank account was deposited to chequing account. Recall stored entry.

☐ **Bank Debit Memo #532281** **Dated Dec. 31/12**

From Scholar Heights Bank, $4 025 was withdrawn from chequing account for the following pre-authorized transactions:

Bank Charges	$ 25
Interest on Bank Loan	320
Reduction of Principal on Bank Loan	880
Interest on Mortgage	2 500
Reduction of Principal on Mortgage	300

Recall stored entry.

☐ **Memo #9** **Dated Dec. 31/12**

Complete end-of-month adjusting entries for the following:

Office supplies used	$230
Art supplies used	250
Textbooks used	150
Prepaid property taxes	900

☐ **Memo #10** **Dated Dec. 31/12**

Transfer $30 000 from the savings account to the chequing account.

✓ **Memo #11** **Dated Dec. 31/12**

297   Prepare a Record of Employment and T4 slip for Tiste.

KEYSTROKES

Entering Payroll Transactions

Payroll transactions may be entered in the Payroll Journal or in the Payroll Run Journal. We will show both methods. If you are preparing paycheques for more than one employee, the Payroll Run Journal is usually faster. For this application, we made the Employees & Payroll module the Home window.

> **Open**   **SimData10\Helena\helena.SAI** for Helena's Academy. **Enter October 15** as the session date.
>
> **Create**   **shortcuts** for **Create General Journal** (Company), **Create Statement** (Reccivables) and **Pay Expenses** (Payables). **Enter** the **cash sale** and the **cash purchase** and **payment transactions**.

Individual paycheques are entered in the Payroll Journal indicated by the pointer on the Paycheques icon on the following screen:

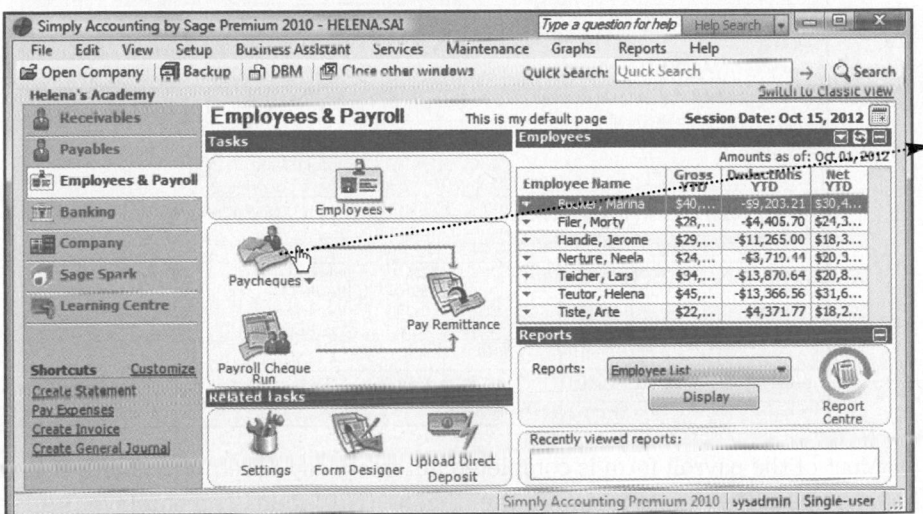

> **Click**   the **Paycheques icon** to open and display the Payroll Journal:

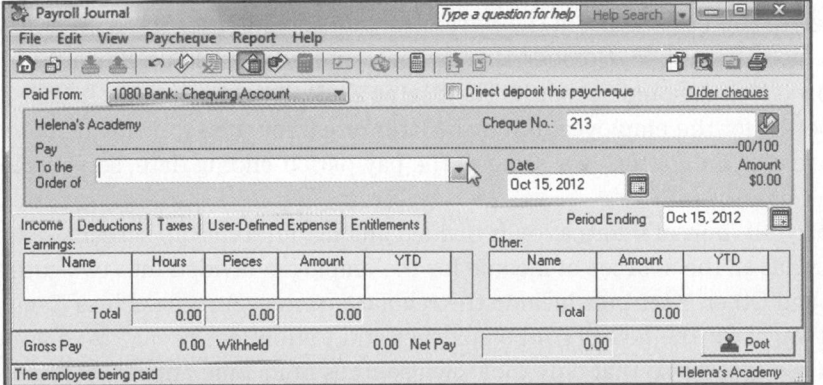

Three tool buttons on the tool bar relate specifically to the Payroll Journal: Calculate Taxes Automatically, Enter Taxes Manually and Recalculate Taxes. The Time Slips tool is used to add information from time slips for the employee and will be covered in Chapter 18. The remaining tools — Home window, Daily Business Manager, Store, Recall, Undo, Adjust Cheque, Reverse Cheque, Enter Additional Information, Windows Calculator, Refresh and Print — are the same as those found in other journals.

NOTES
Remember that you must have a valid payroll ID code from Sage Software to use the payroll features. The Student version does not require a payroll ID.
Choose the Business Services menu in the Home window and click Simply CARE Service for more information.

NOTES
If you are using the backup files, restore helena1.CAB to SimData10\Helena\helena.

NOTES
If you choose not to create shortcuts, you can change modules each time you need to access a journal in a different module.

NOTES
Close the message about HR Manager. HR Manager is introduced in Appendix M.

PRO VERSION
pro The Refresh and Time Slips tools do not appear in the Pro version.

You can also change report form options and preview the paycheque before printing. Adjust Cheque is the Payroll equivalent of the Adjust tool in other Journals.

The cursor is in the Employee (To The Order Of) field.

Click   the **To The Order Of (Employee) field arrow** to see the employee list:

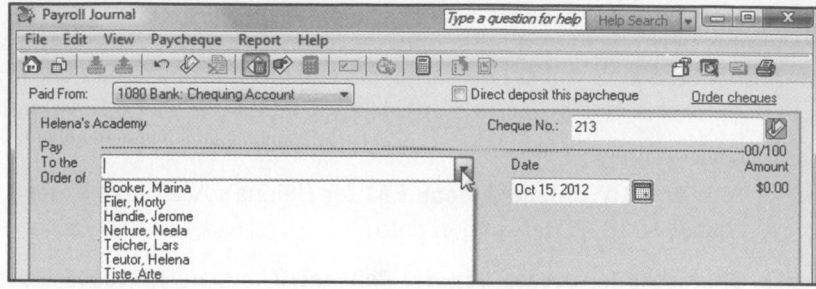

Click   **Filer, Morty** to select this employee and add his name to the form. If you have not chosen correctly, return to the employee list and select again.

Press   `tab`   to add the payroll details for the selected employee:

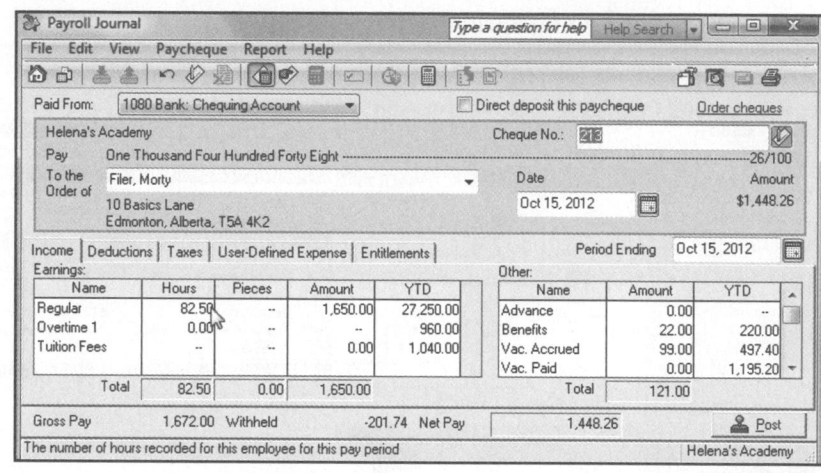

Most of the payroll form is completed automatically based on the ledger details for the employee. The cursor is now in the Cheque (No.) field. The employee's address has been added. The cheque number, 213, should be correct because we have set up automatic numbering. If the number is incorrect, you can change it.

There are two date fields. In the **Date** field, you should enter the date of payment. As usual, the session date, October 15, has been entered by default. Since this session date is correct, you should accept it. The **Period Ending** field refers to the last day of the pay period for the employee. It may be later or earlier than the cheque date. In this case, the session date is also the same as the pay period ending date, so you can accept the default date again.

The Payroll Journal information is divided among different tab screens. The Income tab screen has all the sources of income for the employee divided into two categories: Earnings and Other. **Earnings** include the regular income sources such as Regular and Overtime wages for the hourly paid employees and tuition fees repaid. We have set up the employee records so that only their own sources of income appear on the form. **Other** has all the other sources of income, including payroll advances, taxable benefits and vacation pay accrued and paid out. Year-to-date amounts are added for all fields.

The **Regular Hours** field contains the number of hours an employee has worked for the regular pay rate during the pay period. You can edit the default entry. The **Overtime** field contains the number of overtime hours an employee has worked during the pay period. No default number of overtime hours is entered because the time varies from week to week. If there are different overtime rates, you can set up a second overtime field and rate. For example, employees may be paid more for overtime work on Sundays or holidays than in the evenings. You can define 20 different sources of income.

The **Gross Pay** amount (the pay rate times number of hours worked) is calculated and added to the bottom portion of the journal window. The total amount **Withheld** for taxes and other deductions and the **Net Pay** also appear at the bottom of the journal.

For salaried employees, the Salary field will replace the Regular and Overtime fields and salary amounts are entered automatically from the employee record.

Click   the **Taxes tab**. Tax amounts are calculated automatically:

Income	Deductions	Taxes	User-Defined Expense	Entitlements		Period Ending	Oct 15, 2012	
CPP/QPP		75.55		QPIP				
EI		28.55						
Tax		75.64						
Tax (Que)								

Because we have chosen to let the program complete the tax calculations, the tax fields are not available for editing.

If you need to edit the tax amounts, click the **Enter Taxes Manually tool** to open the tax fields for editing.

Click   the **Income tab** to continue with the payroll entry.

Click   the **Overtime 1 Hours field** to continue.

Type   4 **Press** (tab).

Notice that the Gross Pay and Vacation pay are updated to include the additional pay. Notice, too, that the upper cheque portion of your Input Form window is updated continually as you add information. Year-to-date (YTD) amounts are also updated continually as you add information.

If amounts are not updated, click the **Calculate Taxes Automatically tool** on the tool bar. The option to enter taxes manually may be selected, an option that allows you to edit tax amounts but will not update these amounts automatically.

The cursor has advanced to the **Tuition Fees** Amount field. Helena's Academy pays 50 percent of eligible tuition fees and the amount refunded to employees — a taxable benefit — is entered in this income field. Because the amount is paid directly to the employee, and it is taxable, it is set up as an income amount. Filer is currently taking a course and will receive $130 per pay period as the refund for his tuition until the entire amount has been repaid.

Type   130 **Press** (tab) to enter the Amount paid for tuition fees.

The cursor now moves to the Advance field in the Other income column. The **Advance Amount** field is used to enter amounts advanced to an employee in addition to his or her normal pay from wages or salary. Advances are approved by management for emergencies or other personal reasons. An advance offered to an employee is shown as a positive amount. An advance recovered is indicated as a negative amount in this same field. An advance of $200 for Morty Filer has been approved. Advance amounts owing will appear in the YTD column for Advance.

Press   (tab) again if necessary to move to the Amount field for Advances.

Type   200 **Press** (tab).

The cheque portion of the journal and the gross pay are updated again. Advances do not affect the tax amounts or vacation pay.

The **Benefits** field under Other Earnings is used to enter the total amount of taxable benefits a business offers to its employees, such as health insurance or dental plans

NOTES
If sales commissions are paid to employees, they must be calculated separately and added manually.

NOTES
To verify that tax amounts have also changed, click the Taxes tab. Click the Income tab again to continue with the payroll entry, and click the Tuition Fees Amount field to position the cursor.

NOTES
The tuition fee benefit could also be set up in the employee ledger so that it is added automatically until the entire amount is paid. Then you would remove it from the ledger. Instead, we will edit the amount in the journal.

NOTES
By dividing the tuition fee benefit among several pay periods, the income tax burden will also be spread out over several paycheques.

NOTES
Medical benefits are not paid in cash to the employee. They are added to gross pay to determine income tax and then subtracted again to determine the net pay.
    You can see the tax implications of benefits by deleting the amount and then re-entering it while observing the changes in gross pay and amounts withheld.

NOTES
If the User-Defined Expense amount is omitted from the record, it can be entered in the paycheques journal as needed.

NOTES
Salaried employees receive their regular pay during their vacations instead of receiving vacation pay. They receive vacation days as an entitlement.

NOTES
If the amount of a deduction is incorrect, and it is not a one-time change, you should edit the employee record in the Payroll Ledger. The next time you open the Payroll Journal for the employee, the edited amount will be entered.

when the payments are made to a third party. Half of Filer's medical premium is paid by Helena's Academy. Benefit amounts are included in the pretax total income to arrive at the amount of income tax and then subtracted again to determine the net pay amount.

Click   the **User-Defined Expense tab**:

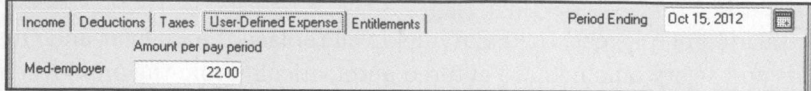

The employer contribution to medical premiums (an employer expense) is also set up as an automatic entry that appears on the User-Defined Expense tab screen.

Click   the **Income tab** to continue.

Simply Accounting automatically calculates an amount in the **Vac. Accrued Amount** field and displays it as a default. Filer's default amount is calculated at the vacation pay rate of 6 percent and will be retained by the business (*Vacation Payable* account) until he takes a vacation in July or leaves the employ of the business. Therefore, the Vacation Paid Amount on this cheque is zero. (See the Employee Information Sheet on page 263 for each employee's vacation pay rate.) The Vacation Paid amount in the YTD (Year-To-Date) column shows the amount of vacation pay that has been paid to the employee already this year.

The total accumulated vacation pay owing (withheld since vacation pay was last paid and including this pay) shows as the YTD amount for the Vac. Accrued. This amount appears in the **Vac. Paid** field when you release the accumulated vacation pay retained for an employee. The amount retained and available for release appears as a default when you turn off the option to retain vacation in the Employee Ledger. (See page 285.)

Click   the **Deductions tab**:

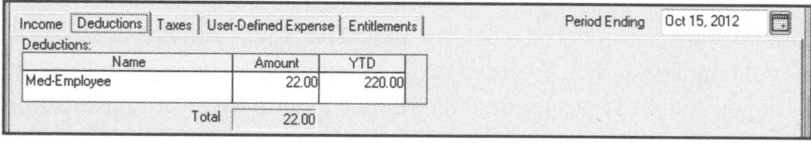

The **Deductions tab screen** has the employee medical deduction entered automatically from the amounts stored in the ledger record. For other employees, the RRSP contributions and/or family support payments also appear on this screen. These amounts can be edited.

We will use the Entitlements tab screen for Handie's payroll entry.

Click   the **Income tab** again to see the complete payroll form:

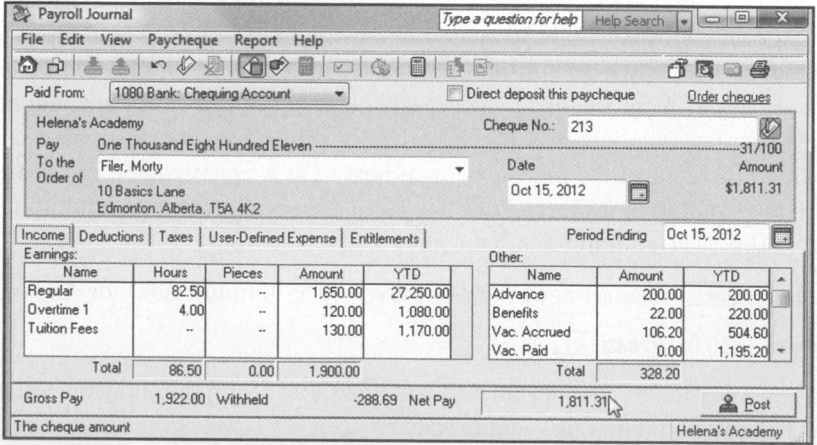

When you have entered all the information, you should review the completed transaction before posting.

Reviewing the Payroll Journal Transaction

Choose the **Report menu** and **click Display Payroll Journal Entry**. The transaction you have just completed appears as follows:

Helena's Academy			
Payroll Journal Entry 10/15/2012 (J4)			
Account Number	Account Description	Debits	Credits
1240	Advances Receivable	200.00	-
5260	Wages: Support Staff	1,876.20	-
5310	EI Expense	42.87	-
5320	CPP Expense	87.92	-
5330	WCB Expense	17.12	-
5380	Tuition Fees Expense	130.00	-
5400	Medical Premium Expense	22.00	-
1080	Bank: Chequing Account	-	1,811.31
2300	Vacation Payable	-	106.20
2310	EI Payable	-	73.49
2320	CPP Payable	-	175.84
2330	Income Tax Payable	-	148.15
2430	Medical Payable - Employee	-	22.00
2440	Medical Payable - Employer	-	22.00
2460	WCB Payable	-	17.12
Additional Date:	Additional Field:	2,376.11	2,376.11

Notice that all the relevant wage expense accounts have been debited. The hourly wages and tuition fee benefit are tracked in separate wage expense accounts. In addition, all the wage-related liability accounts and *Bank: Chequing Account* have been updated automatically because the Payroll Ledger is linked to the General Ledger. All accounts in the journal entry have been defined as linked accounts for the Payroll Ledger so you do not enter any account numbers directly.

Simply Accounting uses the Canada Revenue Agency tax formulas to calculate the deduction amounts for CPP, EI and income tax. These formulas are updated every six months. The remaining deductions are determined from Employee Ledger entries when different rates apply to different employees (WCB, vacation pay rate and Medical), or from Payroll Ledger settings when the same rate applies to all employees (EI factor of 1.4). These rates can be modified for individual employees in their ledger records.

Payroll expense accounts reflect the employer's share of payroll tax obligations. The liabilities reflect the amounts that the owner must remit to the appropriate agencies and include both the employer's share of these tax liabilities and the employee's share (deductions withheld). For example, CPP contributions by the employee are matched by the employer. Therefore, the *CPP Expense* (employer's share) is one-half of the *CPP Payable* amount (employee plus employer's share). WCB is paid entirely by the employer, so the expense amount is the same as the liability amount. Medical contributions by employer and employee are equal but they are represented in different accounts — the employer's share is shown in expense and payable accounts, *Medical Premium Expense* and *Medical Payable - Employer*, while the employee's share appears only in the payable account, *Medical Payable - Employee*. For EI, the employer's share is 1.4 times the employee's share. Vacation pay is part of the Wages expense. The tuition benefit is entered as a debit to *Tuition Fees Expense*.

Close the **display** to return to the Payroll Journal input screen.

CORRECTING THE PAYROLL JOURNAL ENTRY BEFORE POSTING

Move the cursor to the field that contains the error. If you need to change screens to access the field you want, **click** the appropriate **tab**. **Press** (tab) to move forward through the fields or **press** (shift) and (tab) together to move back to a previous field. This will highlight the field information so that you can change it. **Type** the **correct information** and **press** (tab) to enter it.

You can also use the mouse to **point** to a field and **drag** through the **incorrect information** to highlight it. You can highlight a single number or letter or the entire field. **Type** the **correct information** and **press** (tab) to enter it.

Click an **incorrect amount** to highlight it. **Type** the **correct amount** and **press** (tab).

You can discard the entry by **clicking** ☒ (Close) or ↺ (Undo) or by returning to the Employee list and **clicking** a **different employee** name. **Click** the name of the **correct employee** and **press** (tab). When prompted, confirm that you want to discard the incorrect entry. **Click Yes**, and start again.

NOTES

If you are using a later version of the Simply Accounting program than 2010 Release A, your tax amounts and amount withheld may be different from those shown because different tax tables are used. Your Gross Pay and Vacation amounts should always be the same as the ones we show.

The tax tables for version 2010 Release A cover the period from January to December in 2009, as indicated in the confirmation note on the following page. The rates in the 2010 tax tables may be different.

NOTES

Separate linked wage accounts are set up for the wages of teaching staff and for support staff and for music lesson wages. Vacation pay can also be linked to a separate account if you want to track this amount separately from other wage expenses.

NOTES

Both the employer's and the employee's share of the medical premiums are payable to Aspen Life Financial.

The province of Alberta recently eliminated the personal medical premiums for the provincial health plan.

NOTES

If you see an error message about a missing file or form when you preview the cheque, click OK. In the Journal, click the Change The Default Printer Settings tool to access the form settings. Choose Custom Forms and Custom Simply Form. In the Description fields, choose the generic forms Payment Cheque for payments and Payroll Cheque With YTD Payments for paycheques. If you are previewing direct deposit stubs, choose Direct Deposit Stubs as the description. The file location reference should be dimmed. Click OK.

You should now be able to preview the payment.

NOTES

A real business should work only with the current payroll tax tables. Sage Software provides payroll updates every six months when you sign up for the payroll update service. We cannot change the source dates in the text after publishing, and using fixed dates and program (tax table) versions assures that you can obtain the same results we show.

You cannot update payroll tax tables in the Student version.

NOTES

Payroll Journal entries may be stored as recurring entries before posting. Follow the same steps as you do for recurring sales or purchases.

NOTES

We have turned on the option to confirm successful posting of transactions, so you should click OK each time you see this message.

You can preview the paycheque before printing it if you want. You can also modify the reports and forms settings from the journal. Tool buttons are included for both these functions. You must have selected Custom Forms and Custom Simply Form as the Form Type in the Reports and Forms settings screen to preview the cheque. The default form locations should be dimmed; otherwise, they may refer to incorrect file locations because these settings are saved with the data file that was created with different default settings.

Click   the **Print Preview tool** . (See margin Notes.)

You will see a warning about payroll formulas:

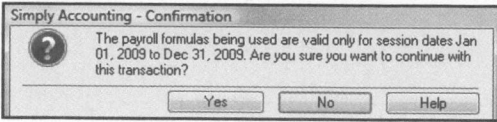

The caution is displayed whenever the dates of the transaction are different from the dates of the tax tables in your Simply Accounting program.

Click   **Yes** to continue to the preview. At this point, you have not yet posted the transaction, so you can still make changes if needed.

The preview shows the cheque and cheque stub with payroll summary details.

Click   **OK** to close the preview when finished to return to the journal.

Posting

When all the information in your journal entry is correct,

Click   **Post** to see the caution about dates and tax tables again.

Click   **Yes** to continue. **Click OK**. A blank Payroll Journal input screen appears.

Entering Payroll Entitlements

Choose Handie, Jerome from the employee list. **Press** `tab` :

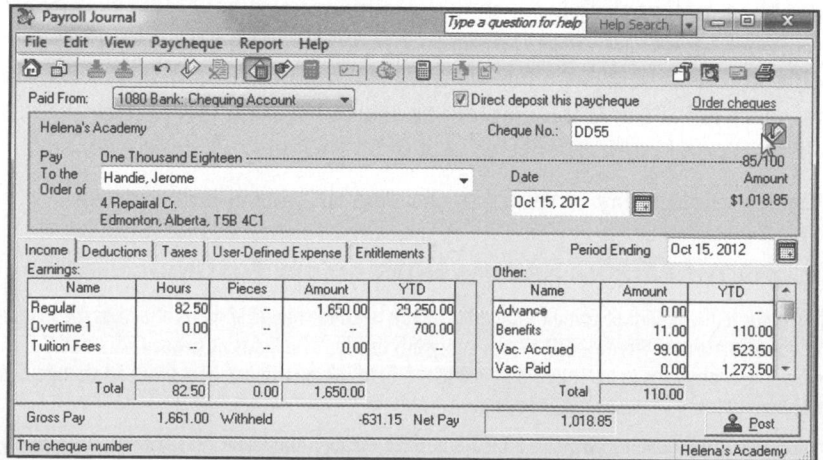

Handie's payroll details are added to the form. You will notice that instead of a cheque number, the entry DD55 appears on the form because the check box for Direct Deposit This Paycheque is selected. Handie has chosen to have his pay deposited directly to his bank account. The bank account deposit details are added to the employee's ledger record.

Handie has overtime hours for this pay period.

Click   **0.00** in the **Hours field** beside Overtime 1.

Type   2

Click   the **Deductions tab** to open these fields.

Handie has two deductions in addition to the medical premium: one for his RRSP contribution and one for his family support payment.

Jerome Handie has taken a sick leave day during the two-week period. We add this information on the Entitlements tab screen.

Click   the **Entitlements tab** to open these fields:

Income	Deductions	Taxes	User-Defined Expense	Entitlements		Period Ending	Oct 15, 2012	

The number of hours worked in this pay period: 82.50

	Days Earned	Days Released
Vacation		
Sick Leave	0.52	

Two entitlements are defined for Helena's Academy: vacation days (for salaried employees only) and sick leave days for all full-time employees. The amounts entered in the Days Earned fields show only the number of days earned for this pay period — two weeks. Sick leave is accrued at the rate of 5 percent per hour worked. The total number of days accrued from prior work periods will be recorded and updated in the ledger record. If the number of days released exceeds the number of days accrued, you will see a warning message that asks you if a negative balance is allowed.

Handie has taken one day of sick leave in this pay period.

Click   the **Days Released column beside Sick Leave**.

Type   1 **Press** (tab) to save the entry and update the form:

Income	Deductions	Taxes	User-Defined Expense	Entitlements		Period Ending	Oct 15, 2012	

The number of hours worked in this pay period: 82.50

	Days Earned	Days Released
Vacation		
Sick Leave	0.52	1.00

Gross Pay	1,721.00	Withheld	-649.15	Net Pay	1,060.85	🧑 Post

The number of days released for Sick Leave during the pay period   Helena's Academy

Entitlements do not affect gross pay, net pay or taxes. You are now ready to review the journal entry.

Choose the **Report menu** and **click Display Payroll Journal Entry**:

Helena's Academy
Payroll Journal Entry 10/15/2012 (J5)

Account Number	Account Description	Debits	Credits
5260	Wages: Support Staff	1,812.60	-
5310	EI Expense	41.41	-
5320	CPP Expense	77.97	-
5330	WCB Expense	41.99	-
5400	Medical Premium Expense	11.00	-
1080	Bank: Chequing Account	-	1,060.85
2300	Vacation Payable	-	102.60
2310	EI Payable	-	70.99
2320	CPP Payable	-	155.94
2330	Income Tax Payable	-	255.60
2400	RRSP Payable	-	25.00
2410	Family Support Payable	-	250.00
2430	Medical Payable - Employee	-	11.00
2440	Medical Payable - Employer	-	11.00
2460	WCB Payable	-	41.99
Additional Date:	Additional Field:	1,984.97	1,984.97

This entry is similar to the previous one, with the additional payable entries for RRSP and family support. Entitlements taken do not appear in the payroll journal entry, but the days accrued are recorded on the cheque stub and in the employee's ledger record.

Close   the **journal entry display** to return to the journal.

Make   **corrections** to the journal entry if necessary.

Click   **Post** 🧑 Post to save your work.

Click   **Yes** to bypass the warning about payroll dates. **Click** the **Income tab**.

Select   Nerture, Neela for the next payroll transaction. **Press** `tab`.

Nerture has no additional income, deductions or entitlements, so you can accept all the default amounts.

Click   Post `Post` . **Click Yes** to bypass the warning about payroll dates.

Select   Tiste, Arte for the next payroll transaction. **Press** `tab` to add his default payroll amounts:

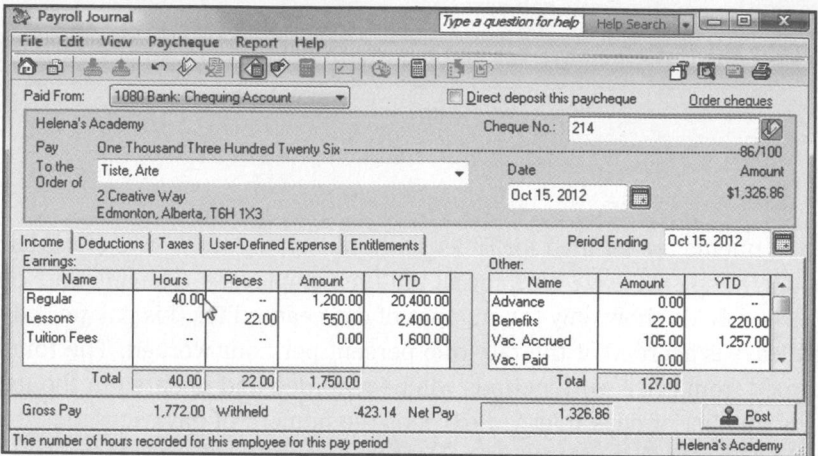

Tiste has 40 entered as the regular number of hours per period. Because this half month has 11 days and he works 4 hours per day, we need to change the hours. Tiste does not receive overtime pay.

Click   40.00 in the Hours field for Regular.

Type   44 Press `tab` to update the gross pay and taxes.

Lesson rates and a default number of lessons per period are entered for teachers in their ledger records. Simply Accounting calculates the total dollar amount by multiplying the per lesson piece rate times the number of lessons. You can define a different rate for each employee. If different rates are paid for different kinds of work, you can define additional piece rate fields. Tiste has given 20 individual lessons in the past two weeks, so we need to change the default entry, 22.00. This amount should be highlighted.

Type   20 Press `tab` to enter the Amount for lessons and complete the entry as shown:

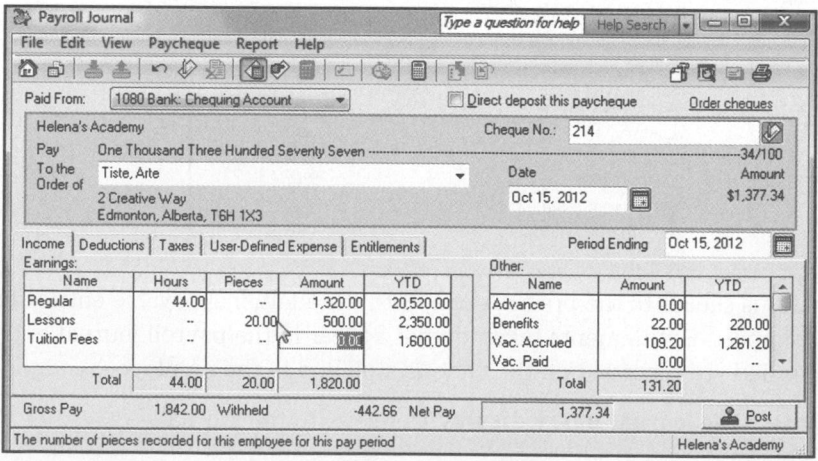

Press   ** `ctrl` **+ J to open the journal entry display:

Helena's Academy
Payroll Journal Entry 10/15/2012 (J24)

Account Number	Account Description	Debits	Credits
5250	Wages: Teaching Staff	1,929.20	-
5310	EI Expense	44.09	-
5320	CPP Expense	83.96	-
5330	WCB Expense	16.40	-
5400	Medical Premium Expense	22.00	-
1080	Bank: Chequing Account	-	1,377.34
2300	Vacation Payable	-	109.20
2310	EI Payable	-	75.58
2320	CPP Payable	-	167.92
2330	Income Tax Payable	-	305.21
2430	Medical Payable - Employee	-	22.00
2440	Medical Payable - Employer	-	22.00
2460	WCB Payable	-	16.40
Additional Date:	Additional Field:	2,095.65	2,095.65

Again, we see a similar journal entry. For each employee, you can define one overall linked income account, or you can choose the default linked accounts for each income. For Tiste, a teacher, we have linked his hourly wages to *Wages: Teaching Staff* rather than to the *Wages: Support Staff* account used for other hourly employees. Therefore, his wages for lessons are included with the expense for teaching wages. For salaried teachers, lesson wages are linked to a separate expense account.

Close   the **display** when finished and make corrections if necessary.

Post   the **entry** and **click Yes** to bypass the warning about payroll formulas.

Close   the **Payroll Journal window** to return to the Home window. **Advance the session date** to October 31.

Adjusting Payroll Entries

On October 17, Filer returned his paycheque because he worked six hours of overtime instead of the four he was paid for. Simply Accounting does not require reversing and correcting entries for these situations. Instead, you can complete a paycheque adjustment in the Payroll Journal, just as you do in the other journals. You can access the Adjust Journal screen in different ways.

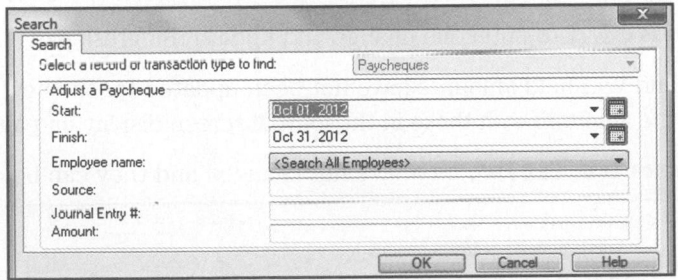

Click   the **Paycheques icon shortcuts list arrow** and **click Adjust Paycheque**. Or,

Click   the **Paycheques icon** to open the Payroll Journal.

Click   the **Adjust Paycheque tool** or **choose** the **Paycheque menu** and **click Adjust Cheque**.

Both methods will open the familiar Search window:

Search

Search

Select a record or transaction type to find: Paycheques

Adjust a Paycheque
Start: Oct 01, 2012
Finish: Oct 31, 2012
Employee name: <Search All Employees>
Source:
Journal Entry #:
Amount:

OK   Cancel   Help

Paycheques is selected as the search area.

You can select beginning and ending dates to create the list. You can also enter the source (cheque or direct deposit number) or journal entry number and click OK to access the paycheque immediately.

The default dates are the earliest transaction date and the session date for the data file. We can accept the default dates to have all payroll transactions listed.

📄 **NOTES**

Your journal entry numbers may be different if you have made other correcting or adjusting entries.

Click **OK** to access the list of posted payroll entries:

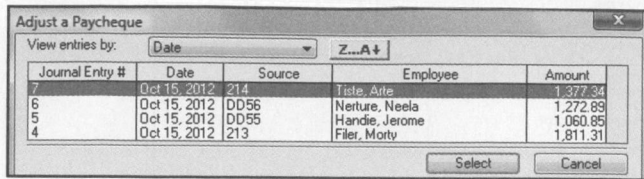

Click **Journal Entry #4 Filer, Morty** to select Filer's journal entry.

Click **Select** to display the entry that was posted.

First, Simply Accounting reminds you about recalculating taxes:

> 💡 Advisor: Remember to recalculate taxes if you changed the employee's income, or any income information in the employee record since processing the original transaction.
> [Click here to close.] You can use the button on the toolbar to recalculate taxes.

The program is advising you that the tax recalculation will not be automatic if you change an amount on the payroll entry.

Click the **Advisor icon** to close the warning and display the journal:

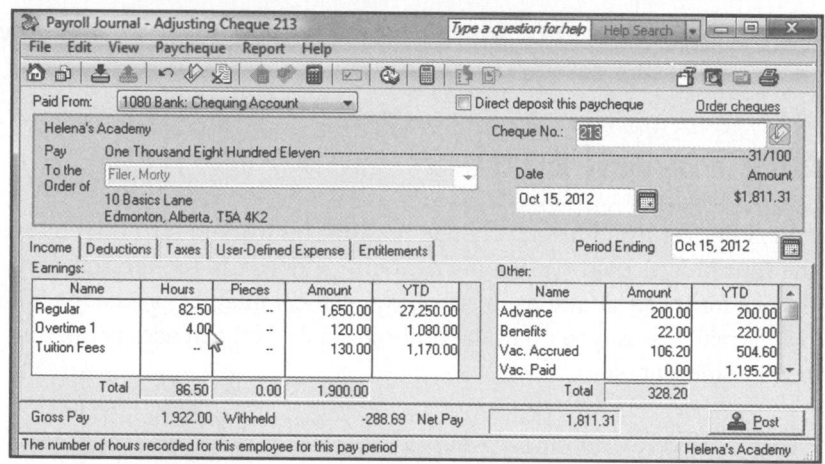

📄 **NOTES**

If you need to change the employee or to reverse a cheque for other reasons, you can reverse the payroll transaction. See page 283.

This is a duplicate of the payroll entry. All the fields can be edited with the exception of the employee name. If you want, you may change the date for the new cheque to October 17. The reversing entry will retain the original posting date. The cheque number is highlighted because normally you would prepare a new cheque. However, Filer has returned the cheque so we can use the same number. We need to change the number of overtime hours.

Click **4.00** in the **Hours column for Overtime 1** to select the current entry.

Type 6 **Press** ⟨tab⟩ to enter the change and update the gross pay.

The Vacation pay and Withheld amounts have not been updated for the new amount of gross pay. Compare the amounts with those in the journal screen display on page 276.

📄 **NOTES**

The total amount Withheld is still $288.89 and the Vacation Accrued is still $106.20.

Click the **Taxes tab**. Tax amounts have not changed and they can be edited:

Income	Deductions	Taxes	User-Defined Expense	Entitlements		Period Ending	Oct 15, 2012
CPP/QPP		87.92		QPIP			
EI		30.62					
Tax		148.15					
Tax (Que)							
Gross Pay	1,982.00	Withheld	-288.69	Net Pay	1,871.31		Post

The amount of income tax deducted from this paycheque — Helena's Academy

WARNING!
Do not confuse the Recalculate Taxes tool with the Windows Calculator tool. The Calculator tool is the last one on the left side of the tool bar before the Refresh tools.

Click   the **Recalculate Taxes button** 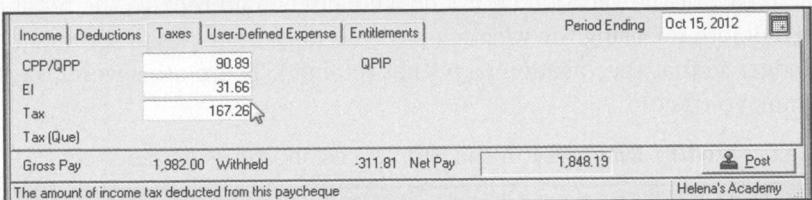 on the Payroll Journal tool bar or **choose** the **Paycheque menu** and **click Recalculate Taxes**:

Income	Deductions	Taxes	User-Defined Expense	Entitlements			Period Ending	Oct 15, 2012	
CPP/QPP		90.89		QPIP					
EI		31.66							
Tax		167.26							
Tax (Que)									
Gross Pay	1,982.00	Withheld	-311.81	Net Pay		1,848.19		👤 Post	

The amount of income tax deducted from this paycheque   Helena's Academy

All the tax deduction and vacation pay amounts are updated for the extra overtime hours worked.

Click   the **Income tab** to see that the Vacation amount has increased from $106.20 to $109.80.

Review the Payroll Journal **entry. Close** the **display** when you have finished. **Make corrections** if necessary.

Click   the **Post button** 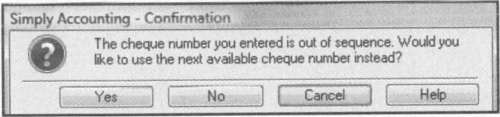 to save the adjustment.

Simply Accounting displays the following warning when you do not change the cheque number:

> **Simply Accounting - Confirmation**
> ❓ The cheque number you entered is out of sequence. Would you like to use the next available cheque number instead?
> [Yes] [No] [Cancel] [Help]

NOTES
When you review the adjusted entry, you will see that the entry is J9. The reversing entry that you do not see at this stage is J8.

Read the question in the warning carefully. To change the cheque number to the next number in the automatic sequence, click Yes. In this case, you can use the duplicate cheque number because Filer returned the original cheque.

Click   **No** to continue. **Click OK** to confirm posting.

Close   the **Payroll Journal** to return to the Home window.

When you display the Payroll Journal and include corrections, you will see three journal entries for Filer: the original entry, the reversing adjusting entry and the final correct entry.

NOTES
The program provides a warning about the cheque sequence because we selected to verify number sequences in the Forms Settings window (see page 217).

All three journal entries are posted with the original date, unless you changed it.

Reversing a Paycheque

You should reverse an entry to correct it when you have selected the wrong employee, or because you need to delete it. The Reverse tool performs this in a single step.

Click the Adjust Paycheque tool 🖊 or press *ctrl* + A.

Define your search parameters and click OK to access the list of posted entries.

Double click the entry you want to reverse to open the journal entry.

Click the Reverse Paycheque tool 🗒 or choose the Paycheque menu and click Reverse Paycheque.

NOTES
The procedure for reversing a transaction is the same in all journals when the option is available.

Click Yes to confirm that the entry will be reversed.

Simply Accounting saves both the original and the reversing entry. When you show corrections for journal reports, you have a complete audit trail.

Releasing Vacation Pay

Tiste needs to pay for the vacation he has booked and should receive the retained vacation pay. Before releasing the vacation pay, you must change the setting in the employee ledger so that the vacation pay is not retained. There are several ways to open the employee record.

Click **Modify Employee** in the Employees shortcuts list as shown:

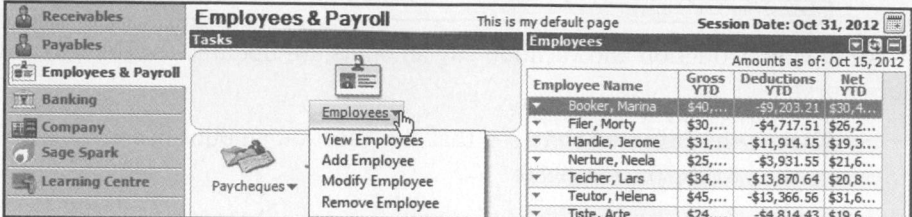

The Search window for employees will open for you to select the employee:

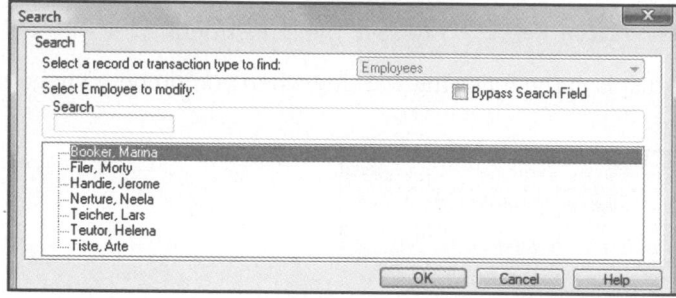

Click **Cancel**. (Double clicking an employee name opens the record.)

Click the **Employees icon** to open the Employees window:

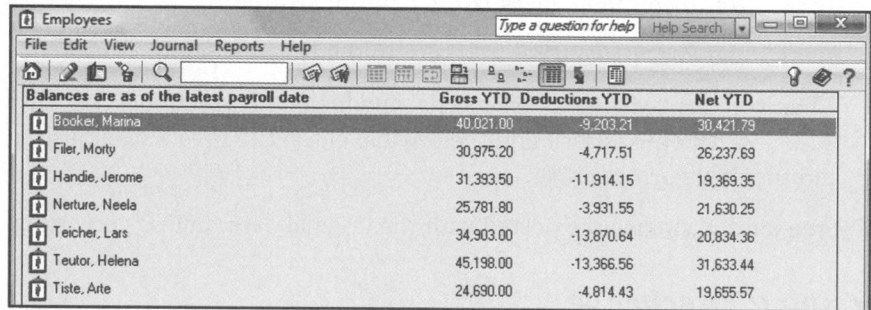

Double click the listing for **Arte Tiste**.

However, the most direct way to open the record is from the the Home window Employees pane list: click Tiste, Arte or click the shortcuts list arrow beside his name and choose View Employee Record as shown:

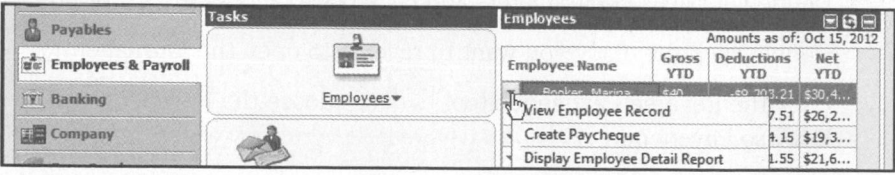

The ledger record opens with the Personal tab screen:

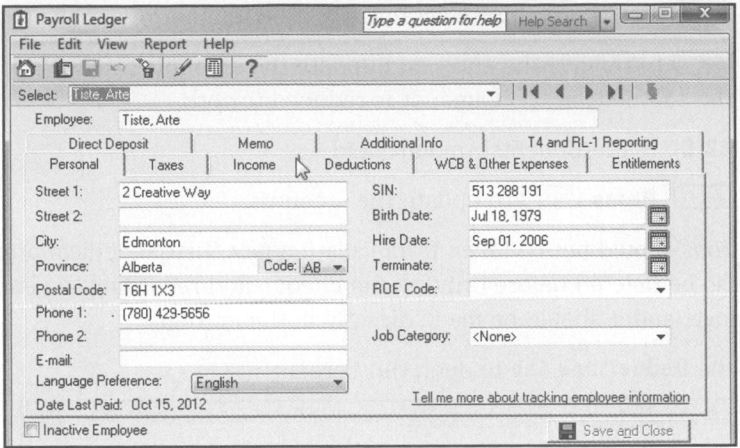

Click the **Income tab** to access the vacation pay settings:

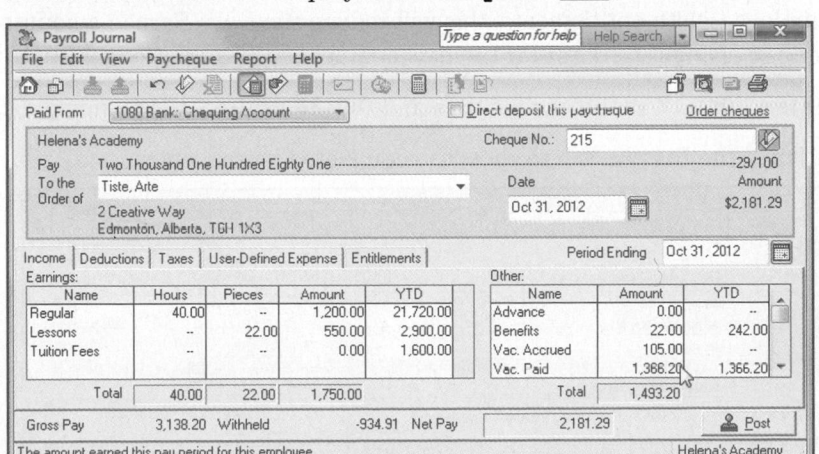

NOTES
The ✓s in the Use column show which items will appear in the journal for this employee. There is no ✓ for Overtime 1, so Overtime does not appear in the Income column for Tiste (see the Payroll Journal screen for Tiste on this page).

Click **Retain Vacation** near the bottom of the screen to remove the ✓.

Close the **Ledger window** to return to your starting point. Close the Employees window if it is open.

Click the **Paycheques icon** .

Choose **Tiste** from the employee list and **press** ⌨ tab to continue:

NOTES
In the Employees window, if Tiste is selected, you can click the Payroll Journal icon or choose the Type menu and click Payroll Journal to access the journal with Tiste already selected.

The accumulated vacation pay now appears in the Vac. Paid Amount field. However, amounts also appear for regular wages and benefits so we must edit the default entries. No regular hours should be included and benefits do not apply to vacation pay.

Click **40.00** in the Regular Hours field. (Double click if the entire amount is not selected.)

NOTES
The Vac. Accrued amount ($105.00) is the vacation pay on the wages for this pay period and is included in the Vac. Paid amount.
When you remove the regular hours and number of lessons, the accrued vacation is reduced to zero and the vacation paid is also reduced by $105.00.

> **Press** (del). **Press** (tab) to select entry for the number of lessons (Pieces).
>
> **Press** (del) to remove the entry and update the amounts again. Notice that the accrued vacation amount is reduced to zero.
>
> **Click** **22.00** in the Benefits Amount field.
>
> **Press** (del). **Press** (tab) to update the amounts.

Since deductions should not be taken from vacation pay, Tiste's medical premium amount should also be deleted before printing the cheque and recording the entry. This is a one-time change, and it should be made directly in the journal.

> **Click** the **Deductions tab** to open this screen:

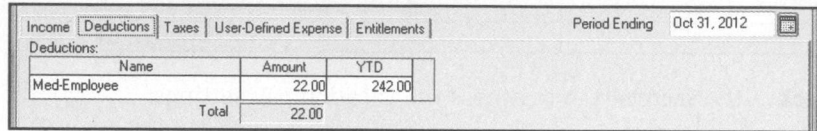

> **Click** the **Med-Employee Amount field entry** to select it.
>
> **Press** (del) to remove the amount. **Press** (tab) to update the net pay. The Taxes tab screen opens.
>
> **Click** the **User-Defined Expense tab**:

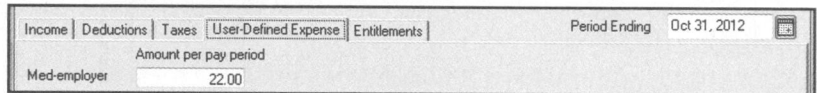

> **Click** the **Med-employer Amount field entry** to select it.
>
> **Press** (del) to remove the amount. **Press** (tab) to update the journal and open the Entitlements tab screen:

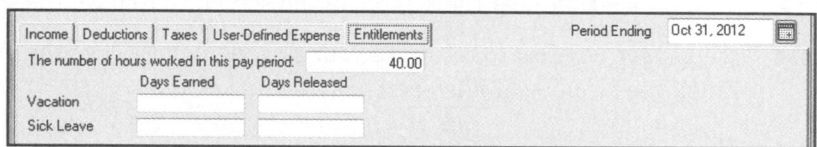

> **Click** **40.00** in the Number Of Hours field. **Press** (del) to remove the entry.

For employees with entitlements, this will reduce the Days Earned amounts to zero. We still need to change the dates for the paycheque.

> **Enter** **Oct 17** as the cheque date and **Oct 15** as the Period Ending date.
>
> **Click** the **Income tab** to show the completed journal entry:

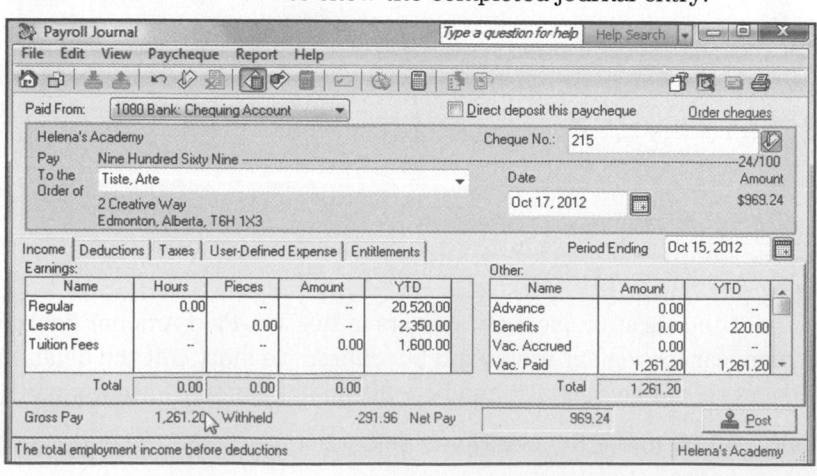

You should review the journal entry before posting.

Choose the **Report menu** and **click Display Payroll Journal Entry**:

Helena's Academy				
Payroll Journal Entry 10/17/2012 (J10)				
Account Number	Account Description	Debits	Credits	
2300	Vacation Payable	1,261.20	-	
5310	EI Expense	30.55	-	
5320	CPP Expense	55.21	-	
5330	WCB Expense	11.22	-	
1080	Bank: Chequing Account	-	969.24	
2310	EI Payable	-	52.37	
2320	CPP Payable	-	110.42	
2330	Income Tax Payable	-	214.93	
2460	WCB Payable	-	11.22	
Additional Date:	Additional Field:	1,358.18	1,358.18	

The released vacation pay shows as a debit (decrease) to *Vacation Payable*. Payroll taxes are charged on the vacation pay, as they are charged on other wages, because they have not yet been paid on this income, that is, on retained vacation pay. The employer's expense for vacation pay, a debit to the wages expense account, was recognized when the original paycheque was prepared. At that time Vacation Payable was credited to create the liability.

Close the **display** to return to the journal and **make corrections** if necessary.

Click **Post** . **Click Yes** to skip the payroll formula warning.

Close the **Payroll Journal**.

Open the **Ledger** for **Tiste** and **click** the **Income tab**.

Click **Retain Vacation** so that his future paycheques will be entered correctly with vacation pay retained.

Close the **Ledger window** and the **Employees window** if it is open to return to the Home window.

Making Payroll Tax Remittances

Simply Accounting tracks payroll remittances when the suppliers are designated as payroll authorities and the taxes are linked to these suppliers.

You cannot adjust these remittances once they are posted; therefore, you should make a backup copy of your data file before making the payments.

Back up your **data file**.

Taxes are remitted from the Payments Journal. You can open this journal from the Payables module Payments Journal, or from its shortcuts list arrow or from the Employees & Payroll module. We will demonstrate the access from the Payroll window first.

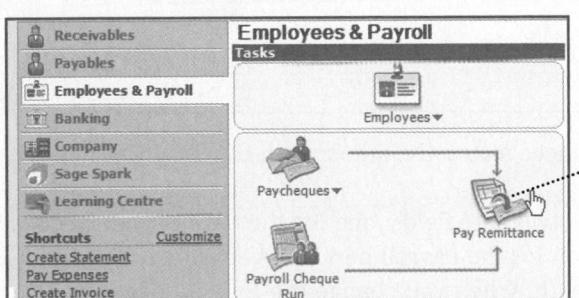

Click the **Pay Remittance icon** to open the Payments Journal form we need.

WARNING!
Remember to turn the Retain setting back on.

WARNING!
Because you cannot adjust payroll remittances once they are posted, you should back up your data file before making the payments. Corrections must be entered as Adjustments in the Payments Journal Pay Remittance form, but it may be difficult to sort out the exact amounts that you need to enter for the correction.

Pay Remittance

NOTES
The Pay Remittance icon has no shortcuts list.

Classic **CLASSIC VIEW**
Click the Payments icon to open the Payments Journal. Then select Pay Remittance from the Pay transaction list to open the journal form we need.

Click   the **Pay To The Order Of list arrow** to see the payroll authorities:

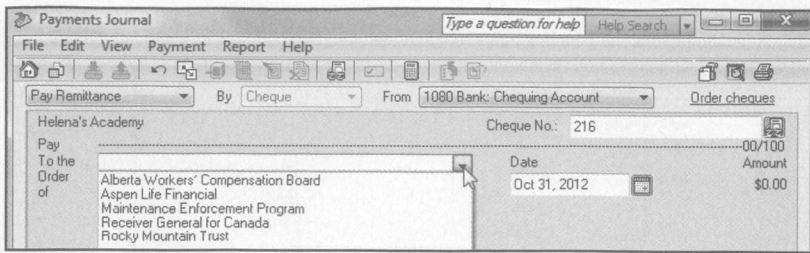

Notice that the Adjust tool button is dimmed and unavailable.

Five suppliers who collect payroll deductions and taxes have been identified as payroll authorities in the supplier records so their names appear on the list of suppliers.

The first remittance will be to the Receiver General for EI, CPP and income tax.

Click   **Receiver General for Canada** to select the supplier.

The Payments Journal is updated with the taxes collected for this supplier:

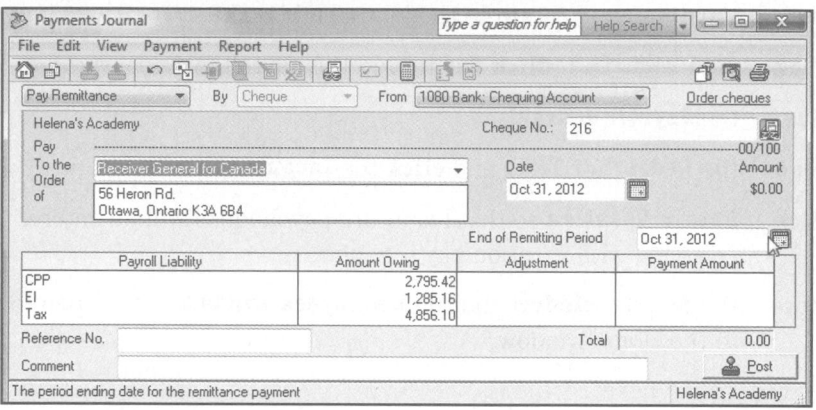

NOTES
Your tax amounts may be different if your program uses later payroll tax tables.
Accept the default amounts in your data file, unless you know that you have made an error in the paycheque.

These amounts include only the taxes entered through Payroll Journal entries and any opening balance adjustments. If taxes were not remitted immediately before the files were converted to Simply Accounting, the payroll tax liability accounts will have outstanding balances. For Helena's Academy, these opening balances were entered as part of the Payroll Ledger setup. These amounts are shown here:

NOTES
In Chapter 9, we show how to enter these opening balances as Payroll Ledger settings. To view this screen, click the Settings icon, then click Payroll and Remittance.
The Medical liability has two entries, one for the employee's share and one for the employer's share.

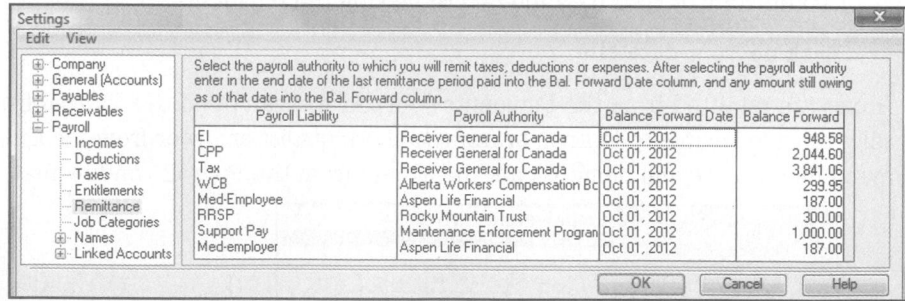

You can see that these balances match the amounts in the Trial Balance for October 1 on page 262.

The Remittance journal has two date fields: one for the date of the cheque and a second below the cheque section for the payroll period covered by the remittance. The session date is the default for both. When you change the **End Of Remitting Period date**, the amounts will be updated to show the General Ledger amounts at that date. Remittances are usually due one month after the pay period they cover, so we are paying the taxes that were withheld to the end of September.

The Adjustment field should be used for any tax expenses that are not already included in the payable account balances. A positive entry will increase the tax expense and the total amount submitted. Negative adjustment amounts will decrease the tax expense amount and the total amount submitted.

Enter **Oct 17** as the date of the cheque. **Press** `tab` **twice**.

Enter **October 1** in the End Of Remitting Period date field and **press** `tab` to update the amounts owing:

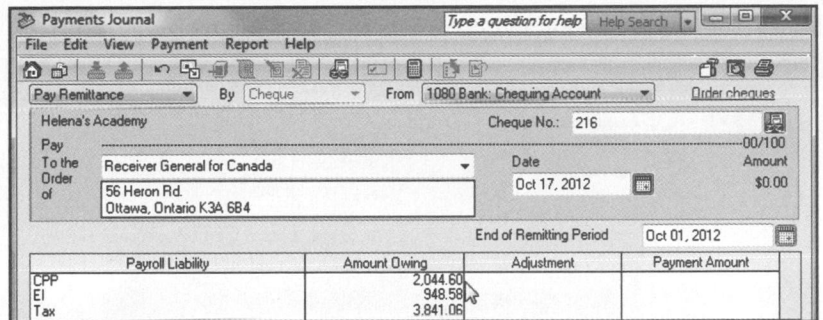

> **NOTES**
> Because the earliest transaction date allowed is October 1, we cannot enter September 30 as the date for the end of the remitting period. The amounts for October 1 are the same as the amounts for September 30.

Notice that all the tax amounts have been reduced to match the opening balance amounts. The full amount is being paid for each tax.

Click the **Payment Amount column for CPP** to enter the amount owing as the payment amount.

Press ⬇ to enter the payment amount for EI.

Press ⬇ to enter the payment amount for Tax.

Press `tab` to accept the final payment, update the cheque amount and advance to the Reference field.

Type Memo 3A **Press** `tab` to advance to the comment field.

Type Memo 3A, Payroll Tax remittance for September to complete the form:

> **NOTES**
> The Reference No. is not added to the journal so we repeat it in the Comment, just as we did for Other Payment entries in this journal.

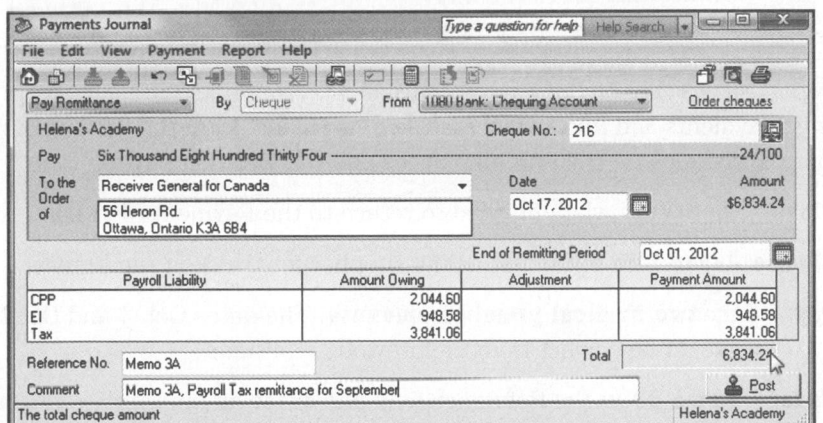

We can now review the journal entry.

Choose the **Report menu** and **click Display Payments Journal Entry**:

> **NOTES**
> Amounts entered in the Adjustment field do not affect the liability account balances.

Helena's Academy			
Payments Journal Entry 10/17/2012 (J11)			
Account Number	Account Description	Debits	Credits
2310	EI Payable	948.58	-
2320	CPP Payable	2,044.60	-
2330	Income Tax Payable	3,841.06	-
1080	Bank: Chequing Account		6,834.24
Additional Date:	Additional Field:	6,834.24	6,834.24

The three liability accounts have been debited to reduce the liability, and the bank account is credited. If you had entered adjustments, those amounts would be debited (for positive adjustments) to the corresponding tax expense account.

From the journal Report menu you can also display the Remittance Report, the same report that you get from the Home window Reports menu or Report Centre. If you display this report before posting the payment, the payment amount will still be zero.

Close   the **display** when finished. **Make corrections** if necessary.

Post   the **payment**.

Choose   the **Report menu** and **click Display Remittance Report**:

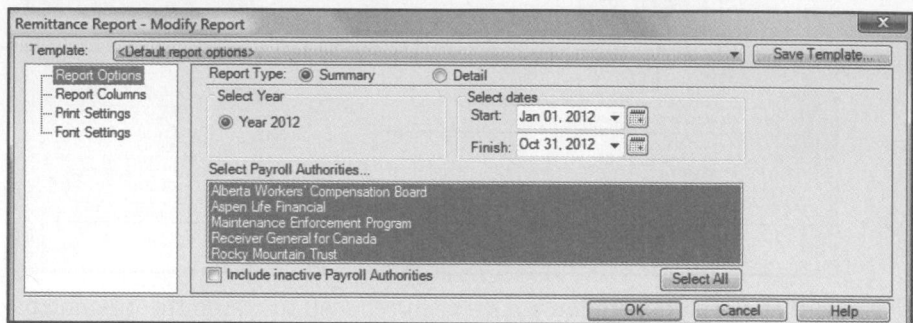

You can display a **Summary Report** with total amounts for each tax, or a **Detail Report** with a line entry for each tax for each payroll transaction in the report period. You can prepare the report for one or more payroll authorities, and you can choose a remittance period for the report. We can accept the default dates — we want the report for October — but only one remittance was posted so we will view the Summary Report for the Receiver General to see the remittance we just completed.

Click   **Receiver General For Canada** and then **click OK** to see the report:

Helena's Academy
Remittances Summary 01/01/2012 to 10/31/2012

Payable	Amount	Adjustments	Payments	Balance	No. Of Employees
Receiver General for Canada					
CPP	750.82	0.00	-2,044.60	750.82	4
EI	336.58	0.00	-948.58	336.58	4
Tax*	1,015.04	0.00	-3,841.06	1,015.04	4
	2,102.44	0.00	-6,834.24	2,102.44	4
* The gross (taxable) payroll amount for all employees for this period is $8,313.20					
	2,102.44	0.00	-6,834.24	2,102.44	4

This report includes only remittance payments that have been made using the 'Pay Remittance' feature in the Payments Journal

The report shows the total of Payroll Journal entry amounts for each tax, adjustments, payments and final balances. The new balances are the total amounts for the October paycheques for the four employees and the vacation pay for Tiste.

Close   the **report** when finished to return to the Payments Journal.

Choose Aspen Life Financial as the supplier for the next remittance.

Pay   the **two Medical premium amounts**. The dates Oct. 1 and Oct 17 should be correct from the previous remittance.

Enter   **Memo 3B** in the Reference field and **enter** an appropriate **comment**.

Review and then **post** the **payment**.

Choose Alberta Workers' Compensation Board as the supplier.

Pay   the **WCB amount**.

Enter   **Memo 3C** in the Reference field and **enter** an appropriate **comment**.

Review and then **post** the **payment**.

Choose Rocky Mountain Trust as the supplier for the next remittance.

Pay   the **RRSP contributions** withheld.

Enter   **Memo 3D** in the Reference field and **enter** an appropriate **comment**.

Review and then **post** the **payment**. Leave the journal open.

Choose **Maintenance Enforcement Program** as the supplier.

Pay   the **Family Support payments** withheld.

Enter   **Memo 3E** in the Reference field and **enter** an appropriate **comment**.

Review and then **post** the **payment**. **Close** the **Payments Journal**.

Entering Remittances from the Payables Module Window

Click Payables in the Modules pane list to open the Payables window. Click the Payments icon shortcuts list arrow:

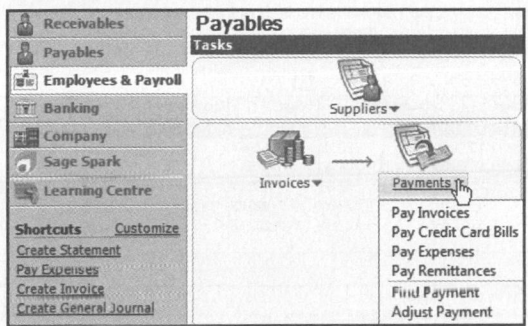

The shortcuts include Pay Remittances. Click Pay Remittances to modify the Payments Journal.

You can also click the Payments icon  to open the Payments Journal. Once the Journal is open, click Pay Invoices to see the payment types:

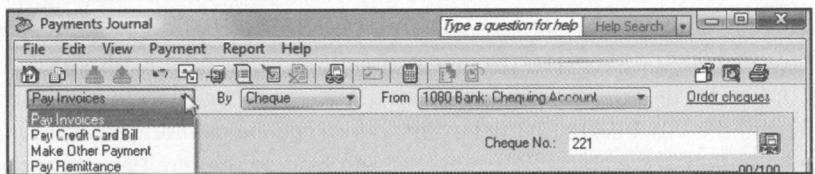

Click Pay Remittance to modify the Payments Journal. Choose the payroll authority and continue with the remittance entry as outlined above.

Enter   the **next two cash purchase transactions** and then close the journal.

Completing a Payroll Cheque Run

When several employees are paid at the same time, you can complete a payroll cheque run to prepare all the cheques and journal entries in a single transaction.

Click   **Employees & Payroll** in the Modules list.

All employees are being paid on October 31, so we will pay them from the Payroll Run Journal, shown with the pointer in the following screen:

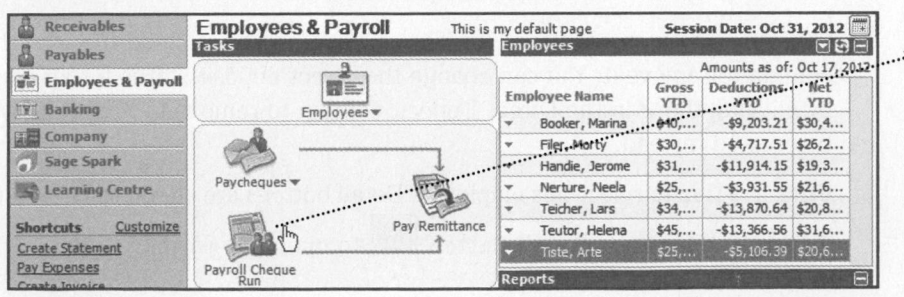

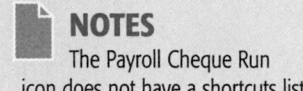

Notice that the details in the Home window Employees list have been updated. You can hide these year-to-date details for employees as you do for vendors and customers from the Employees list pane arrow button:

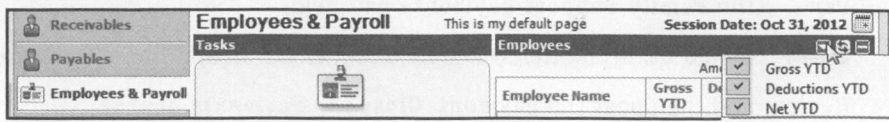

Click the **Payroll Cheque Run** icon to open the Payroll Run Journal:

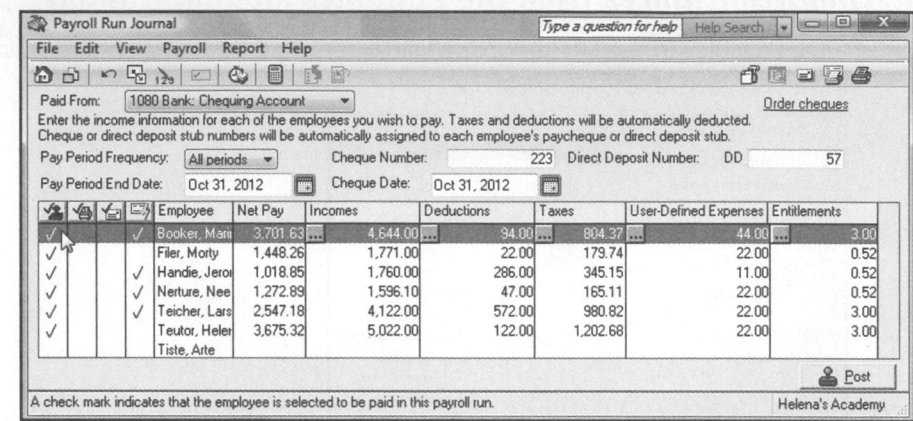

From this screen, you can pay all employees with a single transaction, and you can enter or edit any details that you can enter or edit in the Payroll Journal. Employees are listed in alphabetic order and checkmarks indicate who will be paid in this payroll run and who has selected direct deposits instead of cheques.

Initially, all employees have a ✓ in the **Post column** except Tiste because he received a cheque since the last paycheque date of October 15. The program selects all employees for inclusion if their pay cycle has ended because the default **Pay Period Frequency** option is All Periods. You can select a single pay period frequency for the cheque run from the Pay Period Frequency list or you can choose All Periods to include more than one period. If we chose 24 (semi-monthly pay) as the Pay Period Frequency, only the four hourly paid employees would be marked with a ✓ in the Post column.

The form also includes deposit information in the **Direct Deposit column**. A ✓ in this column indicates that the paycheque will be deposited to the employee's bank account. Both the next Cheque and Direct Deposit Numbers are on the form.

The pay period end date and initial cheque and deposit numbers can all be edited if necessary. You cannot change the cheque date

The columns mirror the tabs in the Payroll Journal and contain total amounts for all fields in that tab screen, using the default ledger entries. If you do not need to change any details, you can post the transaction directly. To change some of the details, you can access the individual fields for a column heading by selecting an employee and clicking the **Detail button** beside an amount.

Click the **Post column** **beside Tiste** to select the employee and add a ✓ and his default paycheque amounts.

You can remove an employee from the payroll run by clicking the ✓ in the Post column to remove it. You can change the direct deposit status for an employee by clicking the ✓ in the Direct Deposit column to remove it. A cheque will then be created instead.

Click **Filer** to select this employee. Detail buttons are added to his amounts.

Click the **Incomes Detail button** to open the Earnings fields:

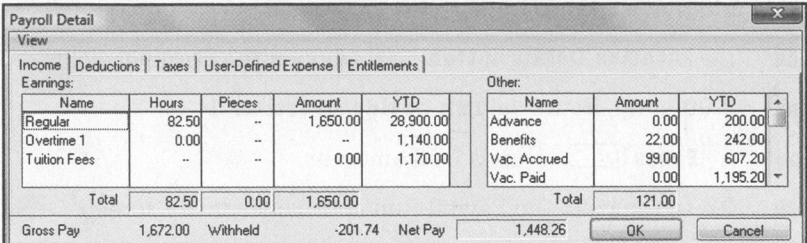

This screen is just like Filer's Income tab screen in the Payroll Journal as shown on page 274, and we can enter or edit all the amounts in the same way as in that journal. For Filer, we need to add the overtime hours, tuition fee amount and the advances repayment. All these details are entered in the Income tab Detail screen.

Click   0.00 in the **Hours column beside Overtime 1**.

Type   2

Press   (tab) to select the Tuition Fees amount.

Type   130

Press   (tab) **twice** to select the Advance amount.

By default, –200.00, the entire amount owing, is entered. Filer is repaying $50 each pay period so we must change the amount.

Type   –50

Click   the **Deductions tab**:

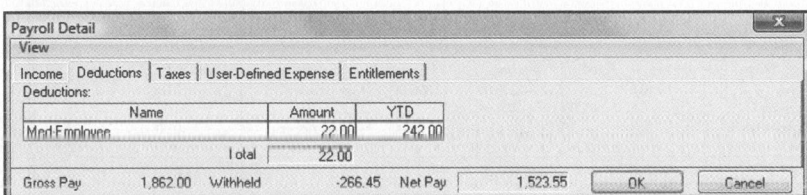

We do not need to change these amounts, but you can see that the deduction amounts are available for editing.

Click   the **Taxes tab**:

Income	Deductions	Taxes	User-Defined Expense	Entitlements
CPP/QPP		84.95		QPIP
EI		29.58		
Tax		129.92		
Tax (Que)				

Gross Pay   1,862.00   Withheld   –266.45   Net Pay   1,523.55   [OK] [Cancel]

Taxes cannot be edited in the Payroll Run Journal. If you need to change tax amounts, you must use the Payroll Journal and choose to calculate taxes manually.

Click   the **User-Defined Expense tab**:

	Amount per pay period
Med-employer	22.00

Gross Pay   1,862.00   Withheld   –266.45   Net Pay   1,523.55   [OK] [Cancel]

The employer's expense for the medical premium is included here and can be edited if required. Entitlements can also be edited (see page 294).

Click   **OK** to return to the Payroll Run Journal summary screen.

Click   **Handie** to prepare for entering his additional details.

We need to add the overtime hours.

Click   the **Incomes Detail button** to open the Earnings fields.

Click   **0.00** in the **Hours column beside Overtime 1**.

Type   2 **Press** *tab* to update all amounts.

Click   **OK** to return to the Payroll Run Journal summary screen.

No changes are needed for Nerture's pay, so we can enter the information for Tiste next. We need to change the number of regular hours and include the advance. The default entry for number of lessons is correct.

Click   **Tiste** to prepare for entering his additional details.

Click   the **Incomes Detail button** to open the Earnings fields.

Click   **40.00** in the **Hours column beside Regular**.

Type   44

Click   **0.00** beside Advance in the Amount column.

Type   100 **Press** *tab* to update all amounts.

Click   **OK** to return to the Payroll Run Journal summary screen.

Click   **Booker** to prepare for entering the additional details for her.

Click   the **Incomes Detail button** to open her Earnings fields:

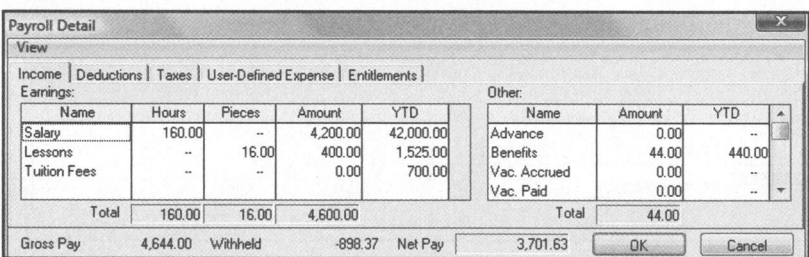

Booker is a salaried employee who also teaches music lessons after school. Her regular salary is entered as the default but the amount can be edited if necessary. We need to add her tuition fees benefit and enter one day of sick leave.

Click   **0.00** in the Tuition Fees Amount column.

Type   45 **Press** *tab* to update all amounts.

Click   the **Entitlements tab** to open the entitlements fields:

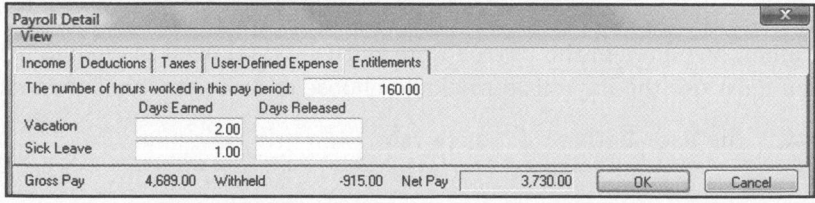

Once again, the fields we see are the same as those in the Payroll Journal Entitlements tab screen (see page 279).

Click   the **Days Released field beside Sick Leave**.

Type   1

Click   **OK** to return to the Payroll Run Journal summary screen.

NOTES
You can access the Entitlements Detail screen from the Payroll Run Journal by clicking the Details button for the employee in the Entitlements column.

NOTES
Remember that the entry for Days Earned reflects only the amount earned for this pay period based on the number of hours worked in this pay period.

No changes are required for Teicher or Teutor's salaried paycheques, so the transaction is complete and should look like the one we show here:

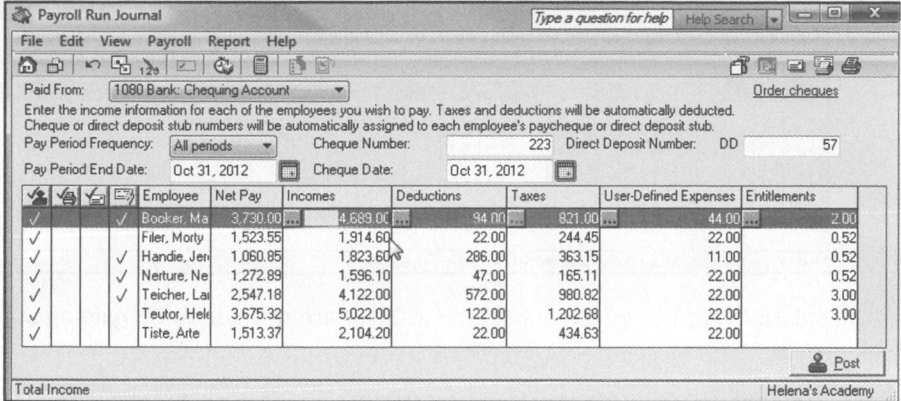

You are now ready to review the journal entry.

Choose the **Report menu** and **click Display Payroll Run Journal Entry** to review the journal entry.

There are seven journal entries, one for each employee in the payroll run.

Close the **display** when finished.

You cannot preview a paycheque from the Payroll Run Journal. You can modify the reports and forms setting from the journal by using the tool button.

Turn on your **printer**.

Choose the **Report menu** and **click Print Payroll Cheque Run Summary** to provide a printed record of the payroll run transactions paid by cheque or **click Print Direct Deposit Stub Summary** to provide a printed record of the payroll run transactions paid by direct deposit. You cannot display these summaries.

Click Post ![Post] to save the transaction. **Click Yes** to bypass the warning about payroll formula dates.

The confirmation message advises that seven journal entries were posted. The Payroll Run Journal remains open with the direct deposit and cheque numbers updated after the payroll run cheques and direct deposits as shown:

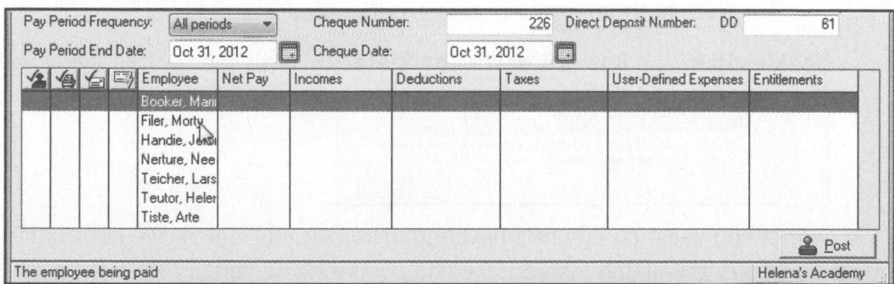

No employees are selected because they have all been paid. There are no ✓ in the Post column.

Close the **Journal** to return to the Home window.

NOTES
You will see this screen after you change the session date to November 15.

When you open the Payroll Run Journal for the November 15 pay period, the four hourly paid employees will be selected, as shown:

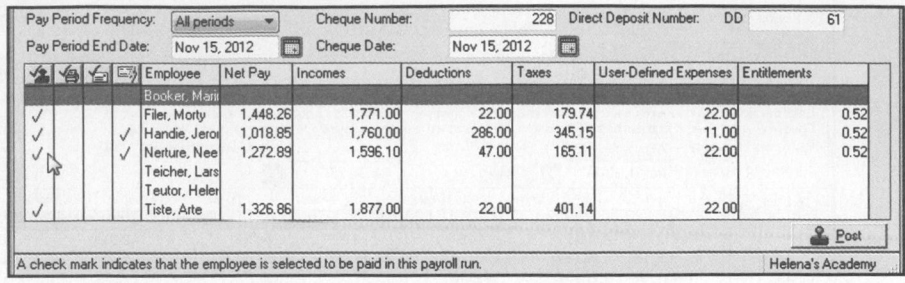

The salaried employees are not selected. They are not due to be paid again until November 30.

 Continue entering **transactions** up to the payroll adjustment for Dec. 17.

Adjusting a Payroll Run Entry

We can adjust a Payroll Run Journal entry from the Payroll Journal, just as we edited the transaction for Filer. Tiste has handed in his resignation and should repay the remainder of the amount he received as an advance. He should also receive his final vacation pay.

First, we will change his retained vacation pay option as we did before. Refer to page 284 if you need assistance.

Click   **Tiste, Arte** in the Employees List pane in the Home window to open his ledger record.

Click   the **Income tab**.

Click   the ✓ **for Retain Vacation** to change the setting.

Close   the **ledger record**.

Click   the **Paycheques icon** .

Click   the **Adjust Paycheque tool** or **press** ⎉ **ctrl** + **A**.

Click   **OK** to see the list of posted payroll entries. Notice that all the entries from both payroll journals are included.

Double click   the **Dec. 15 entry for Tiste**. You will see the following warning:

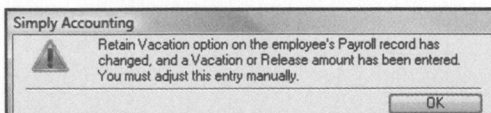

We cannot add vacation pay as a paycheque adjustment unless we enter all the amounts and taxes manually. Instead, we will prepare a separate paycheque for the vacation pay amount.

Click   **OK** to close the message. **Close** the **Paycheques Journal**.

Click   **Tiste, Arte** in the Employees List pane of the Home window to open his ledger record. **Click** the **Income tab**. **Click Retain Vacation** to change the option again so that his vacation pay is retained.

Close   the **ledger record**.

NOTES
You do not need to close the Paycheques Journal to open the ledger window, but you cannot edit the ledger for Tiste while he is selected in the journal.

Click   the **Paycheques icon** to open the Payroll Journal.

Click   the **Adjust Paycheque tool**, or **choose** **Adjust Paycheque** from the Paycheques icon shortcuts list.

Click   **OK** to access the list of posted payroll entries.

Double click the **Dec. 15 entry for Tiste**.

Click   the **Advisor icon** to close the warning and display the Payroll Journal:

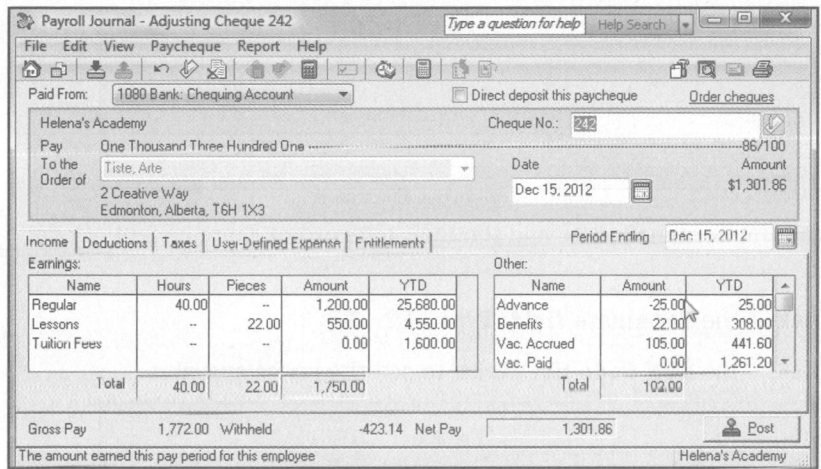

Click   **-25** in the **Amount field for Advance** to select the current entry.

Type   **-50** **Press** tab to enter the change and update the gross pay. The YTD amount for Advance is reduced to zero.

Click   the **Recalculate Taxes tool** on the Payroll Journal tool bar or **choose** the **Paycheque menu** and **click Recalculate Taxes**.

Review the Payroll Journal **entry**. **Close** the **display** when you have finished. **Make corrections** if necessary.

Click   the **Post button** to save the adjustment.

Click   **No** to bypass the cheque number warning.

Change the **Retain Vacation** settings for Tiste so you can issue the vacation pay.

Release the **remaining accrued vacation for Tiste**. Remember to delete all amounts that do not apply. Refer to page 285.

Close   the **Paycheques Journal**. **Enter** the **remaining transactions**.

Terminating an Employee

When an employee leaves the company, his or her ledger record should be updated with the date of termination and the reason for leaving. Then a record of employment can be issued that indicates the number of hours worked and the total income. This form is used to determine eligibility for employment insurance.

Tiste will be going back to school full time in January and he has received his last paycheque, so we should modify his record. We will work from the Employees window, so that we can also print reports.

Click   the **Employees icon** to open the Employees window.

NOTES
The tax amounts do not change this time because advances are not taxed. However, if you do not click Recalculate Taxes, you will be warned to do so because you have changed the entry.

NOTES
From the Report Centre, you can print only the reports that you can display. For reports that are only printed, you must start from the Employees window or from the Reports menu.

Double click Tiste, Arte to open his ledger record at the Address tab screen:

We need the Terminate date and the ROE (Record of Employment) Code fields on this screen.

Click   the **Terminate field. Type** 12 15

Click   the **ROE Code list arrow** to see the codes available:

Click   C - Return To School.

Click   Save And Close to open the following message:

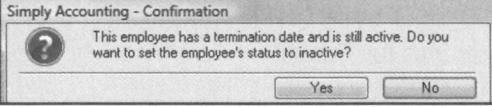

Normally, an employee's status is changed to inactive when he or she has left the company. In this way, the employee's name will no longer appear in the employee lists in the journals. Data for the individual can still be included in any reports by including inactive employees.

Click   Yes to change the status and close the ledger.

We will now be able to print a record of employment for Tiste. We will print this report from the Employees window.

Printing Payroll Reports

You can access payroll reports from the Reports menu in the Employees window and from the Home window. In addition, most payroll reports can also be accessed from the Report Centre. Some payroll reports cannot be displayed; they are printed directly.

Printing Record of Employment Reports

The Record of Employment Report provides information about employees who have terminated their employment to determine their eligibility for Employment Insurance benefits. The report includes the length of employment, the earnings, the total number of hours worked and the reason (code) for the termination. You can print the report only for employees who have been terminated, and you must have the correct preprinted forms. You should still be in the Employees window.

Choose the **Reports menu**, and **click Print Record Of Employment**:

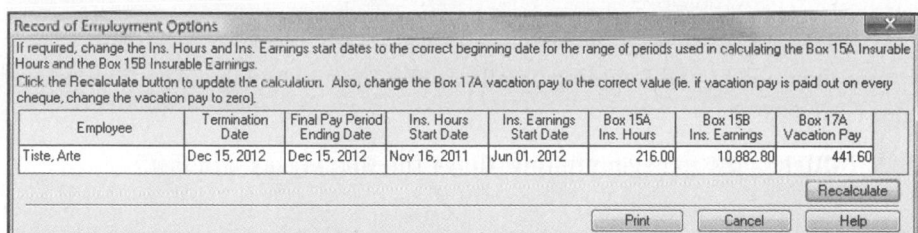

From the Home window, choose the Reports menu, then choose Payroll and click Print Record Of Employment.

Tiste is the only employee listed in this option window because he is the only one with a termination date. The date range includes the fiscal year to date. If you have data for a different time period, you can change these dates and then click Display to update the list of employees. For this report, you need to provide the name and telephone number to contact about the company payroll.

Click   **Tiste, Arte** to select the employee for the report.

If there are more employees with termination dates, you can click Select All to create reports for all the listed employees.

Click   the **Payroll Contact Person field**. **Type** `Morty Filer`

Click   **OK** to continue:

Employee	Termination Date	Final Pay Period Ending Date	Ins. Hours Start Date	Ins. Earnings Start Date	Box 15A Ins. Hours	Box 15B Ins. Earnings	Box 17A Vacation Pay
Tiste, Arte	Dec 15, 2012	Dec 15, 2012	Nov 16, 2011	Jun 01, 2012	216.00	10,882.80	441.60

You now have the summary details for the selected employee. They include only the amounts entered in the payroll journals; they do not include the year-to-date opening balance amounts. You can edit the fields in this window. If you have payroll data for a longer period, you can enter those dates and recalculate the amounts. However, only the three months of payroll data we entered in Simply Accounting are tracked in this form, so we must update the details.

The year-to-date insurable earnings amount is tracked in the employee ledger on the T4 and RL-1 Reporting tab screen as shown here:

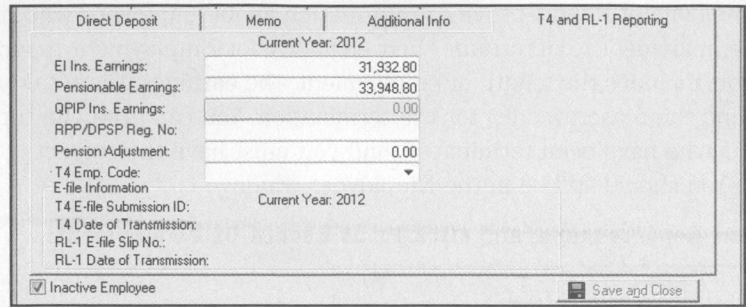

NOTES
You cannot view the employee's ledger record while the Record of Employment report or its options window is open.

We can see that Tiste has $31 932.80 in EI insurable earnings this year. He has also worked additional hours before October — 20 hours per week for 34 weeks, or 680 hours, so his total number of hours is 896 (680 + 216). And finally, he has received all his vacation pay, so this amount should be changed to zero. You can also edit the start dates for EI insurable hours and earnings.

Enter   **Jan 1** in the Ins. Hours Start Date field and also in the Ins. Earnings Start Date field.

Click   **216.00** in the Box 15A Ins. Hours field.

Type   896

Press   (tab) to select the Ins. Earnings amount.

Type   31932.80

Press   (tab) to select the Vacation Pay amount.

Press   (del). Check your entries.

Click   **Print** to see an additional warning:

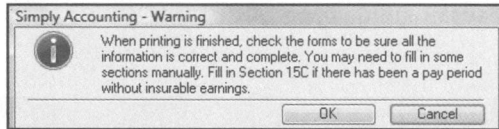

NOTES
For practice, you can print on plain paper, but you will not see any labels for the details on the report.

You may need to add missing details on the form manually if the final printed form is not complete.

Click   **OK** to begin printing. **Close** the **Employees window**.

Printing T4s

NOTES
You cannot access the T4 Slips from the Report Centre.

T4 Slips and Relevé 1 Slips are also not available for display but they be can be printed. Relevé 1 slips are used only in Quebec, and the Print Relevé 1 Slips Report options screen will list only employees for whom Quebec is the province of taxation. Relevé 1 options are similar to those for T4 slips. You can print T4 slips, which are compulsory for employees filing income tax returns, using either the tax statement forms from Canada Revenue Agency (CRA) or plain paper. You should retain payroll information for employees who leave during the year so that you can prepare T4 slips to mail to them.

Before printing T4s, you should check your printer and forms selections.

Choose the **Setup menu**, then **choose Reports & Forms** and **click Government Forms** and **click Federal Payroll** to display the following options:

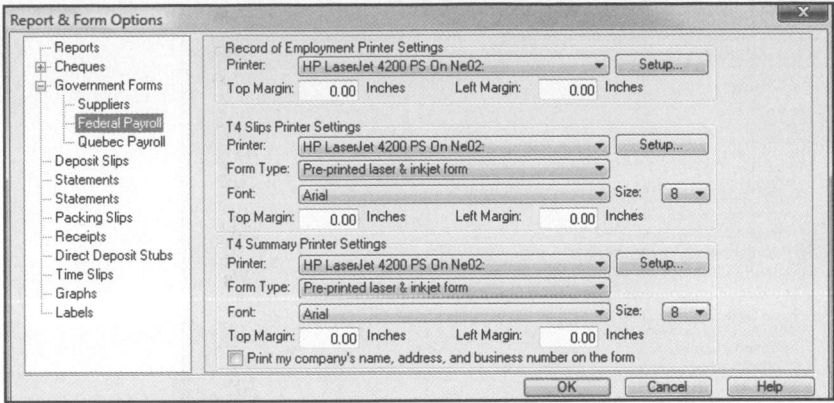

Select **Plain Paper** as the Form Type for T4 Slips and T4 Summary.

Click **OK** to save the selections and return to the Home window.

Choose the **Reports menu**, then **choose Payroll** and **click Print T4 Slips and Summary** (or Print Relevé 1 Slips) to display the following options:

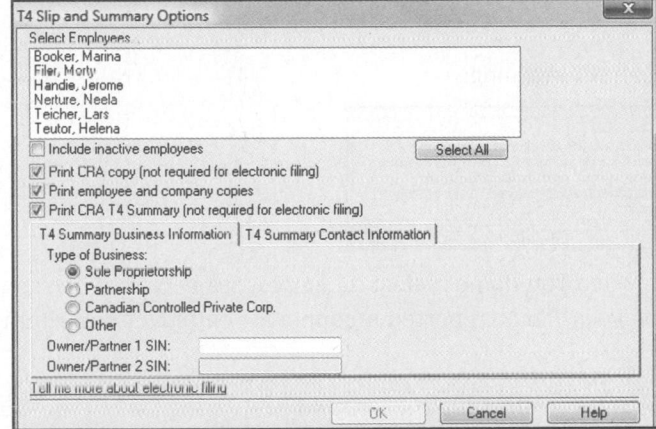

NOTES
You can also print 14s and Summary from the Employees window. Choose the Reports menu and click Print T4s and Summary to open the options window.

You need to select the employees in order to prepare their T4 slips. Inactive employees are not listed by default. You can print copies of the T4s for the employees and the company, or for Canada Revenue Agency (CRA). You can also print the summary for CRA. All are selected as the default.

To submit the report, you must also include the type of business, the social insurance numbers (SIN) of the owners/partners, the name of the person who can be contacted about the form and the phone number and position of that individual.

NOTES
The social insurance number (SIN) must be a valid number and you cannot leave the field blank.

Click **Include Inactive Employees** to add Tiste to the list.

Click **Tiste, Arte**.

Press and hold (ctrl) and click the names of the employees for whom you want the report printed or click Select All to prepare T4s for all employees.

Select the **Type Of Business**. **Click** the **Type** that applies: sole proprietorship, partnership or private company. For these types,

Enter the **Social Insurance Number** of the owners or partners. You can enter Teutor's Social Insurance Number (from page 263) as the owner's SIN.

On the second tab screen, you must enter the contact details for the person completing the forms.

Click the **T4 Summary Contact Information tab** to open the contact fields:

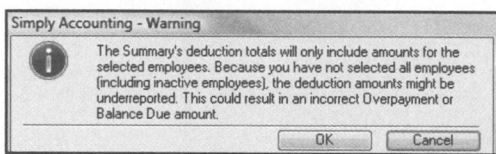

Enter the **contact details** for the person completing the forms: name, phone number and position in the company. You can use Morty Filer's name and Social Insurance Number (see page 263).

Click **OK** to open the warning:

Simply Accounting - Warning

The Summary's deduction totals will only include amounts for the selected employees. Because you have not selected all employees (including inactive employees), the deduction amounts might be underreported. This could result in an incorrect Overpayment or Balance Due amount.

The warning appears when you do not select all employees because the remittance amounts apply to all employees. Thus, reported amounts for employer contributions may be incorrect.

Click **OK** to open the T4 Box Options screen:

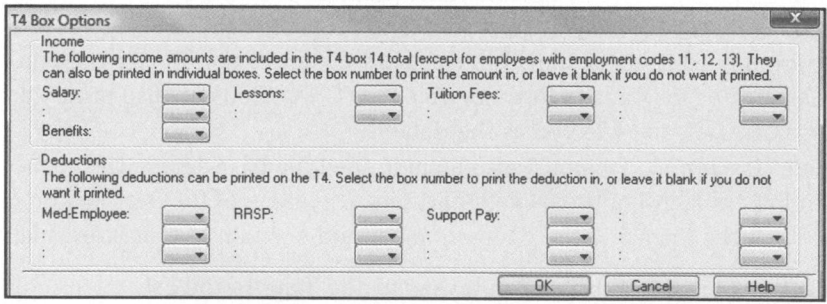

Each box on the T4 slip is numbered and can be designated for a specific deduction or income. You can choose a form box number for these amounts if they are related to income tax and should be included on the T4s. Each item has a list of box numbers that you can select. Income and tax items that are standard for T4s are not listed because their boxes are already assigned. If you do not change the box selections, the income amounts are all combined and the deductions listed are not reported. You can check with CRA to see what each box number is used for. The defaults are correct for Tiste.

Choose appropriate **box numbers** for the items that should appear on the T4.

Click **OK** to begin printing. After the T4s are printed, the T4 Summary report is displayed:

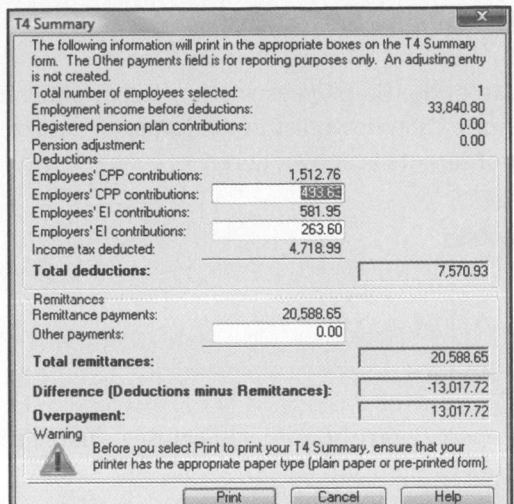

NOTES
Total income includes vacation pay paid and benefits.
    Employee year-to-date historical amounts are entered in the ledger record when you set up the payroll module. However, year-to-date employer amounts are not included as part of the setup, so these amounts may be incomplete.
    If you have entered all payroll transactions for the entire year, the amounts on the summary should be correct.

These amounts do not include the year-to-date remittances made before Simply Accounting was used for payroll. The remittance amounts shown are those for all employees for three months. The employee contribution amounts are the year-to-date totals for the individual, and the employer contribution amounts are those related to this employee for three months. The employer contribution and remittance year-to-date totals are not included in the payroll history when you do not set up the program at the start of the calendar year. You should edit the amounts.

Click   Print when the amounts are correct to continue.

After printing, you should see a summary of the items printed:

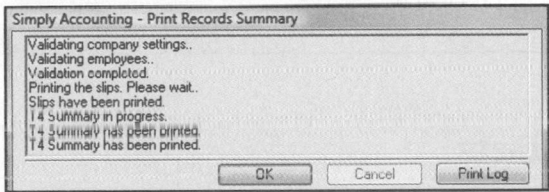

Click   Print Log to print the report printing summary or **click OK** to close the summary.

Printing Employee Mailing Labels

We will continue with the payroll reports that are not available from the Report Centre. You can print labels for employees (like labels for suppliers and clients).

Set up the **printer** for printing labels (Setup menu, Reports and Forms, Labels) before starting.

Choose the **Reports menu**, then **choose Mailing Labels** and **click Employees** to display the list of employee names:

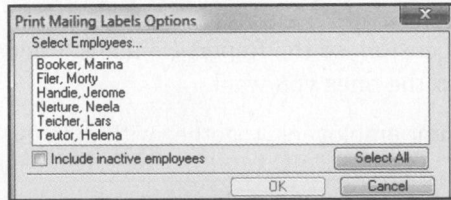

NOTES
You cannot display mailing labels.
    You can include or omit inactive employees.

Press and **hold** ctrl and **click** the employees' **names** or **click Select All**.
    Click OK to start printing.

Displaying Payroll Reports

Most payroll reports can be accessed from the Employees window Reports menu, the Home window Reports menu, the Reports drop-down list in the Reports pane or the Report Centre. The Reports pane list of reports is shown here:

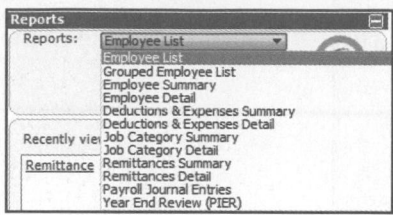

As usual, we will work from the Report Centre so that you can see sample reports and the report description and purpose.

Click   the **Report Centre icon** in the Reports pane.

Click   **Employees & Payroll** in the Select A Report Type list to see the list of payroll reports with the employee list described:

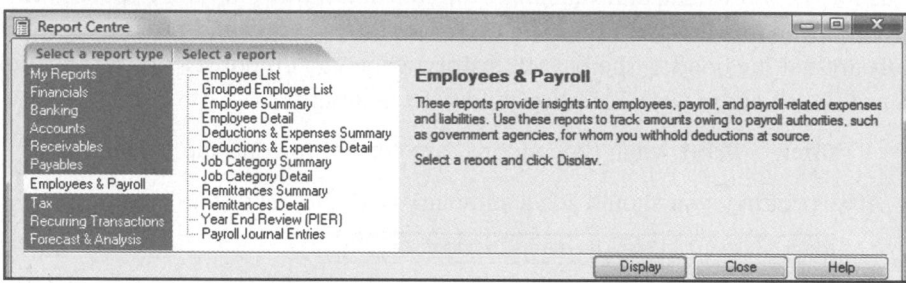

Displaying Employee Lists

Lists of employees are available, just like lists for other ledgers.

Click   **Employee List** in the Select A Report list.

Click   **Modify This Report** to see the report options:

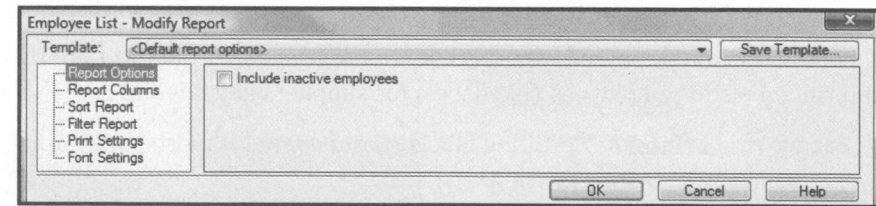

Or choose the Reports menu, then choose Lists and click Employees to see the report options.

To select employee fields, you can customize the Report Columns. Choose Custom Report Columns and select the ones you want.

The report will display a list of all current employees, together with data for all the details you chose.

Close   the **display** when you have finished.

Displaying Employee Reports

Click **Employee Summary** in the Select A Report list.

Click **Modify This Report** to see the report options:

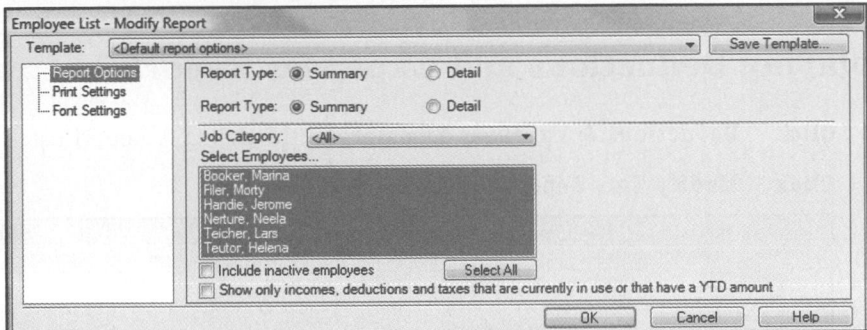

Or, choose the Reports menu, then choose Payroll and click Employee.

The **Summary** report has accumulated totals for each selected employee for all incomes, deductions and payments, which are updated each pay period. Summary reports are available only for the session date.

You can include or omit inactive employees from the report. You can also omit details that have no amounts or have not been used.

If you use job categories, you can prepare a report for a specific category by choosing it from the drop-down list of categories.

You cannot customize the Employee Summary Report. You can use the **Detail** Report to see individual amounts for each paycheque. To prepare a report for specific deductions or payments, you can customize the column selection for the Detail Report.

Click **Include Inactive Employees** if you want to report on them as well.

Press and **hold** `ctrl` and **click** the **employees** you want in the report, or **click Select All** to include all employees in the report.

Click **Detail** to include individual transaction details.

Click **Report Columns** in the left-hand pane.

Click **Custom Report Column Settings** to see the information that is included by default and the details that you can add to the report:

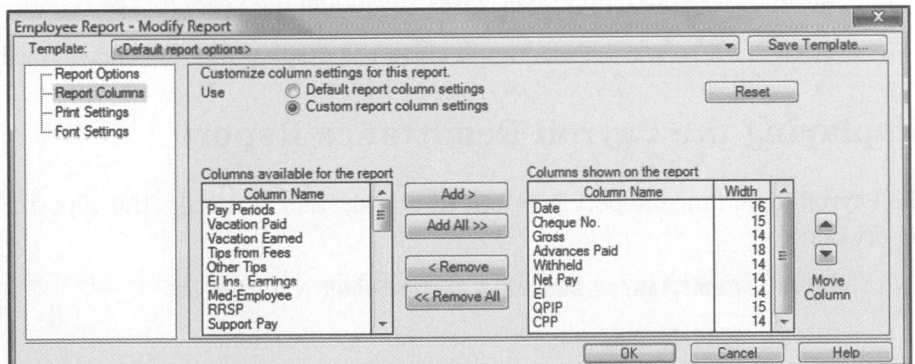

Select the **columns** you want to include or remove and **click OK** to save your new column selections and return to the Report Options screen.

The amount for each detail you choose will be listed for each payroll period in the selected date range for the selected employees, together with the totals for the period selected. The earliest transaction and session dates are the defaults for the Detail Report.

Enter the **beginning date** (including the year) for the report you want in the Start field.

Enter the **ending date** (including the year) for the report in the Finish field.

Click **OK** to see the report. **Close** the **display** when you have finished.

Displaying Deductions and Expenses Reports

Click **Deductions & Expenses Summary** in the Select A Report list.

Click **Modify This Report** to see the report options:

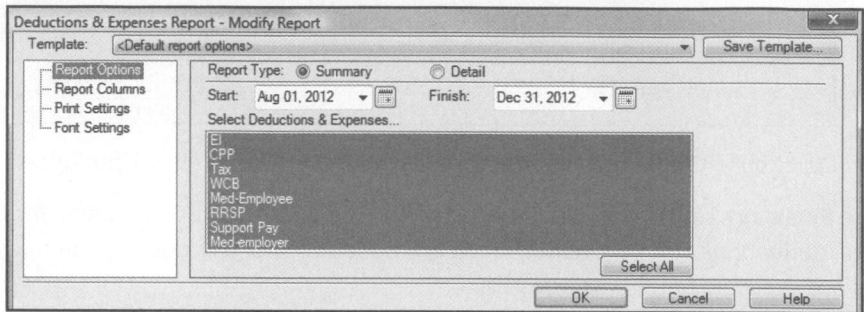

From the Home window, choose the Reports menu, then choose Payroll and click Deductions & Expenses.

This report provides details for all payroll deductions and expenses. Only amounts entered in the Payroll journals in Simply Accounting will be included in this report. Prior balance amounts for the year-to-date will not be shown. The **Summary Report** shows the total amounts and the number of employees the deduction or expense applied to for each payroll item in the selected date range. The **Detail Report** shows individual entries for each selected item, including the date, cheque or deposit number, employee, job category, amount, period totals and number of employees.

You can customize the report by selecting the columns you want to include.

Select the details you want in the report and the date range for the report. The earliest transaction and session dates are the default selections.

Press and **hold** ⌐ctrl⌐ and **click** the **deductions** and **expenses** you want in the report, or **click Select All** to include all details in the report.

Enter the **Start** and **Finish dates** (including the year) for the report.

Click **OK** to see the report and **close** the **display** when you have finished.

Displaying the Payroll Remittance Report

The Payroll Remittance Report is described on page 290. To access this report from the Report Centre,

Click **Remittances Summary** in the Select A Report list.

Click **Modify This Report** to see the report options.

Displaying the Payroll Journal

The Payroll Journal Report includes all transactions from the Payroll Journal and the Payroll Run Journal.

Click **Payroll Journal Entries** in the Select A Report list.

CLASSIC VIEW
From the Home window, right-click either the Paycheques or the Payroll Cheque Run icon

Paycheques or Payroll Cheque Run.

Then click the Display tool

to open the Modify Report window for the Payroll Journal Report.

Click   Modify This Report to see the report options:

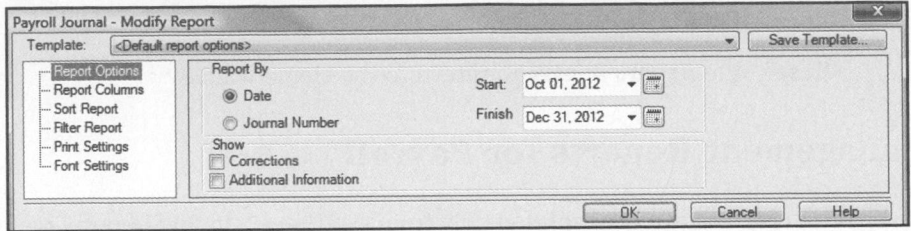

Or, choose the Reports menu, then choose Journal Entries and click Payroll to display the Options window.

The usual sort and filter journal options are available for the Payroll Journal Report. By default, the Date option we use for selecting transactions is the default. Your earliest transaction and latest session dates appear as the default Start and Finish dates.

Type   the **beginning** and **ending dates** (including the year) for the report.

Click   Corrections to include the original and reversing entries for the paycheques you adjusted or reversed.

Click   OK. Close the **display** when you have finished.

Displaying Year End Review (PIER) Reports

Click   Year End Review (PIER) in the Select A Report list.

Click   Modify This Report to see the report options:

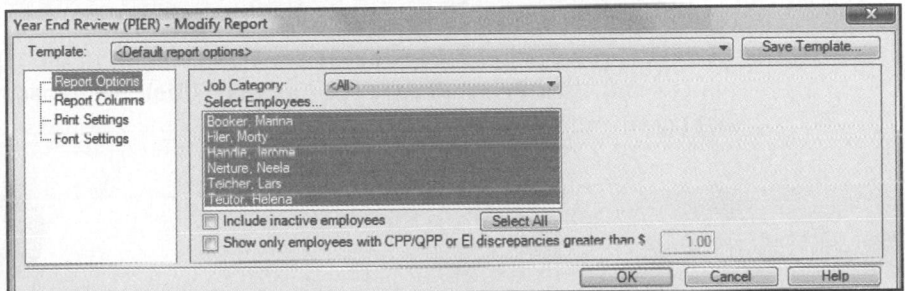

From the Home window, choose the Reports menu, then choose Payroll and click Year End Review (PIER) to display the report options.

The PIER (Pensionable and Insurable Earnings Review) report shows the total amounts contributed in the year to date for EI and CPP. Based on the Insurable Earnings amount for each employee (also in the report), the program determines whether the employee has contributed the correct amounts, and displays the amount of under- or overcontributions. You can define the minimum discrepancy that should be included and then show the report only for those employees who have a discrepancy of this amount or more. The default amount is $1.00.

You can modify this report by selecting the report columns, removing any of the default information or adding the amounts for expected EI and CPP deductions and the number of paycheques and pay periods.

You cannot sort or filter the report.

Click   Include Inactive Employees to add these employees to the list.

Click   the **name** of the employee you want the report for, **press** and **hold** `ctrl` and **click additional names**, or **click Select All** to include all employees in the report.

Click   **OK** to display the report.

Close   the **display** when you have finished.

Close   the **Report Centre** to return to the Home window.

Management Reports for Payroll

Management reports can be displayed only from the Home window Reports menu.

Choose the **Reports menu**, then **choose Management Reports** and **click Payroll**:

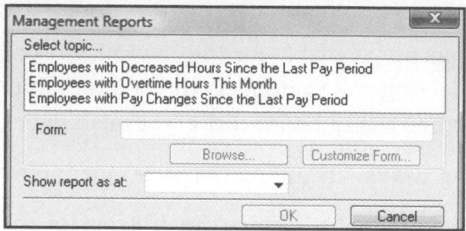

Click   the **topic** you want to see. For the report on Employees With Overtime Hours This Month,

Choose a **month** from the list for Show Report As At. Choose a form, if appropriate.

Click   **OK** to see the report. **Close** the **display** when you have finished.

Printing Other Payroll Reports

Display the **report** you want to print. **Choose** the **File menu** from the report window and **click Print**. **Choose** your **printer**. **Click OK**. **Close** the **display** when finished.

REVIEW

The Student DVD with Data Files includes Review Questions and Supplementary Cases for this chapter.

CHAPTER NINE

Lime Light Laundry
Laundry Services • Pickup & Deliver

OBJECTIVES

After completing this chapter, you should be able to

- **add** the Payroll Ledger to a company data file
- **enter** Payroll Ledger settings
- **enter** Payroll Ledger linked accounts
- **define** payroll authorities
- **create** employee ledger records
- **enter** employee historical information
- **set up** payroll remittances
- **set up** taxes for income, benefits and deductions
- **create** job categories
- **assign** employees to job categories
- **enter** salespersons on invoices
- **display** and **print** job category and salesperson reports

COMPANY INFORMATION

Company Profile

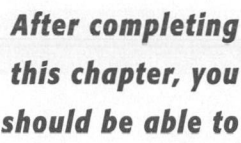

NOTES
Lime Light Laundry
25 Snow White Lane
Vancouver, BC V8G 3B2
Tel: (604) 633-8201
Fax: (604) 633-8396
Business No.: 324 732 911

Lime Light Laundry started in Vancouver, British Columbia, in 1994 with a single employee assisting the owner, Charles Chaplin. They provided laundry services to one hotel as a regular client and to a few individual clients. Now Lime Light provides complete laundry services for a number of large hotels in the Vancouver area and has seven full-time employees. Chaplin himself is no longer involved in daily business operations, and the laundry serves only hotels and no individual clients. Chaplin's goal as an entrepreneur is business growth. In fact, two employees have recently been hired. Chaplin is negotiating new contracts with a major hotel chain and considering expansion into adjacent premises that are for sale.

Lime Light's business success has enabled it to establish favourable account terms with regular suppliers, including some discounts for early payments. The discount terms for clients also encourage timely payment of accounts. All discounts are calculated on after-tax amounts. Because there are no individual

PRO VERSION

The terms Vendor and Customer will replace Supplier and Client. Sales and Purchases replace the terms Revenues and Expenses in the program for journals and reports.

clients, only hotels, Lime Light does not accept credit card payments. Similarly, most regular suppliers do not accept credit cards and Chaplin does not use them in his business.

All laundry services provided by Lime Light are subject to 12 percent HST. Lime Light also pays the 12 percent HST on non-exempt purchases.

On January 31, 2012, Chaplin closed his books so he could begin using the payroll feature in Simply Accounting. The following information summarizes his data:

- Chart of Accounts
- Post-Closing Trial Balance
- Supplier Information
- Client Information
- Employee Profiles and Information Sheet
- Accounting Procedures

CHART OF POSTABLE ACCOUNTS

LIME LIGHT LAUNDRY

ASSETS
- 1080 Cash in Bank
- 1200 Accounts Receivable
- 1240 Advances Receivable
- 1260 Prepaid Insurance
- 1280 Cleaning Supplies
- 1320 Packaging Supplies
- 1520 Computer System
- 1540 Delivery Vehicle
- 1560 Laundry and Cleaning Equipment
- 1580 Pressing Equipment
- 1600 Railings and Belts
- 1620 Laundry Premises ▶

▶LIABILITIES
- 2100 Bank Loan
- 2200 Accounts Payable
- 2250 Accrued Wages
- 2300 Vacation Payable
- 2310 EI Payable
- 2320 CPP Payable
- 2330 Income Tax Payable
- 2400 MSP Payable - Employee
- 2410 RRSP Payable
- 2420 Travel Allowances Payable
- 2430 Tuition Fees Payable
- 2440 MSP Payable - Employer
- 2460 WCB Payable
- 2650 HST Charged on Services ▶

- ▶2670 HST Paid on Purchases
- 2920 Mortgage Payable

EQUITY
- 3560 C. Chaplin, Capital
- 3600 Current Earnings

REVENUE
- 4020 Revenue from Services
- 4040 Sales Discounts

EXPENSE
- 5020 Advertising Expenses
- 5040 Bank Charges
- 5060 Hydro Expenses
- 5080 Insurance Expense ▶

- ▶5100 Cleaning Supplies Used
- 5140 Packaging Supplies Used
- 5150 Purchase Discounts
- 5160 Telephone Expenses
- 5180 Vehicle Expenses
- 5300 Wages: General
- 5305 Wages: Cleaning Staff
- 5310 EI Expense
- 5320 CPP Expense
- 5330 WCB Expense
- 5340 Commissions
- 5350 Piece Rate Bonuses
- 5360 Travel Allowances
- 5380 Tuition Fees Expense
- 5400 MSP Premium Expense

NOTES: The Chart of Accounts includes only postable accounts and Current Earnings.

POST-CLOSING TRIAL BALANCE

LIME LIGHT LAUNDRY

February 1, 2012

		Debits	Credits				Debits	Credits
1080	Cash in Bank	$ 52 640.30		▶	2250	Accrued Wages		1 150.00
1200	Accounts Receivable	4 592.00			2300	Vacation Payable		1 098.00
1240	Advances Receivable	200.00			2310	EI Payable		1 022.80
1260	Prepaid Insurance	2 200.00			2320	CPP Payable		2 090.94
1280	Cleaning Supplies	2 000.00			2330	Income Tax Payable		3 054.53
1320	Packaging Supplies	1 200.00			2400	MSP Payable - Employee		296.28
1520	Computer System	3 800.00			2410	RRSP Payable		200.00
1540	Delivery Vehicle	35 000.00			2430	Tuition Fees Payable	325.00	
1560	Laundry and Cleaning Equipment	15 000.00			2440	MSP Payable - Employer		296.28
1580	Pressing Equipment	25 000.00			2460	WCB Payable		678.97
1600	Railings and Belts	10 000.00			2650	HST Charged on Services		4 765.00
1620	Laundry Premises	250 000.00			2670	HST Paid on Purchases	1 415.00	
2100	Bank Loan		$12 000.00		2920	Mortgage Payable		200 000.00
2200	Accounts Payable		5 040.00 ▶		3560	C. Chaplin, Capital		171 659.50
							$403 372.30	$403 372.30

SUPPLIER INFORMATION

LIME LIGHT LAUNDRY

Supplier Name (Contact)	Address	Phone No. Fax No.	E-mail Web Site	Terms Tax ID
BC Energy Group (Sol R. Heater)	33 Windmill Rd. Vancouver, BC V8K 3C3	Tel: (604) 388-1298	srh@bceg.ca www.bceg.ca	net 1
BC Minister of Finance (M.T. Handed)	7 Fiscal Way Victoria, BC V8V 2K4	Tel: (250) 887-3488 Fax: (250) 887-8109	www.fin.gov.bc.ca	net 1
BC Telephone (Kommue Nicate)	91 Cellular Way Vancouver, BC V8G 8B5	Tel: (604) 348-2355	www.bell.ca	net 1
BC Workers' Compensation Board (N. Jured)	55 Accidental Cr. Victoria, BC V8W 3X6	Tel: (250) 887-7199 Fax: (250) 887-9211	www.worksafebc.com	net 1
Ferndale Paper Products (T. Issue)	43 Ferndale Ave. Vancouver, BC V8F 2S6	Tel: (604) 466-3929 Fax: (604) 466-3935	tissue@ferndalepaper.com www.ferndalepaper.com	1/10, n/30 (after tax) 445 668 714
Langley Service Centre (Otto Fixer)	64 Mechanic St. Langley, BC V2Z 2S4	Tel: (604) 556-7106 Fax: (604) 556-7188	otto@lss.com www.lss.com	net 1 672 910 186
Pacific Laundry Suppliers (Al Washindon)	29 Spotless Dr. Vancouver, BC V8K 1N6	Tel: (604) 782-1618 Fax: (604) 781-5127	aw@pacificlaundry.com www.pacificlaundry.com	net 30 129 554 377
Receiver General for Canada	PO Box 20004 Sudbury, Ontario P3A 6B4	Tel 1: (800) 561-7761 Tel 2: (800) 959-2221	www.cra-arc.gc.ca	net 1
Richmond Equipment Co. (N.U. Dryer)	78 Richmond St. Richmond, BC V7C 3V2	Tel: (604) 699-3601 Fax: (604) 699-1577	Dryer@REC.com www.REC.com	1/10, n/30 (after tax) 366 455 281
Surrey Printers (H.P.L. Jett)	690 Surrey Ave. Surrey, BC V3H 6T1	Tel: (604) 286-9193 Fax: (604) 286-9100	jett@surreyprinters.com www.surreyprinters.com	net 1 125 481 262
Victoria Trust (Victoria Royale)	59 Queen St. Vancouver, BC V8U 1M6	Tel: (604) 388-1825 Fax: (604) 388-2663	www.victoriatrust.ca	net 1

OUTSTANDING SUPPLIER INVOICES

LIME LIGHT LAUNDRY

Supplier Name	Terms	Date	Invoice No.	Amount	Total
Ferndale Paper Products	1/10, n/30	Jan. 29/12	FP-901	$560	$560
Pacific Laundry Suppliers	net 30	Jan. 3/12	PL-644	$1 120	$1 120
Richmond Equipment Co.	1/10, n/30	Jan. 27/12	RE-4111	$3 360	$3 360
			Grand Total		$5 040

CLIENT INFORMATION

LIME LIGHT LAUNDRY

Client Name (Contact)	Address	Phone No. Fax No.	E-mail Web Site	Terms Credit Limit
Capilano Centre Hotel (Lotte Reste)	3 Stopover Cr. North Vancouver, BC V7H 5D3	Tel 1: (604) 587-2563 Tel 2: (888) 587-3882	lreste@cch.com www.cch.com	1/15, n/30 (after tax) $5 000
Coquitlam Motel (B. & B. Roadside)	56 Sliepers Rd. Vancouver, BC V8K 6F3	Tel 1: (604) 366-7155 Tel 2: (800) 366-9175	bbr@coquitlammotel.com www.coquitlammotel.com	1/15, n/30 (after tax) $5 000

CLIENT INFORMATION CONTINUED

Client Name (Contact)	Address	Phone No. Fax No.	E-mail Web Site	Terms Credit Limit
Delta Hotel (A. Good-Knight)	86 Holiday St. Richmond, BC V7R 4D9	Tel: (604) 782-5431 Fax: (604) 781-7528	goodknight@deltahotel.com www.deltahotel.com	1/15, n/30 (after tax) $5 000
Kingsway Inn (Abel Traveller)	77 Roomie Dr. Vancouver, BC V8E 2W2	Tel: (604) 566-7188 Fax: (604) 565-4281	at@kingsway.com www.kingsway.com	1/15, n/30 (after tax) $5 000
Port Moody Resort (Kat Napper)	425 Vacation Ave. Port Moody, BC V3H 4S3	Tel: (604) 369-5826 Fax: (604) 369-7993	knapper@pmresort.com www.pmresort.com	1/15, n/30 (after tax) $5 000

OUTSTANDING CLIENT INVOICES

LIME LIGHT LAUNDRY

Client Name	Terms	Date	Invoice No.	Amount	Total
Delta Hotel	1/15, n/30	Jan. 28/12	69	$3 136	$3 136
Kingsway Inn	1/15, n/30	Jan. 30/12	72	$1 456	$1 456
			Grand Total		$4 592

EMPLOYEE INFORMATION SHEET

LIME LIGHT LAUNDRY

	Clyne Fretton	Mouver Durtee	Soffte Landings	Iean Sissler	Claire Brumes	S. Pott Tran	Cryper Houseman
Position	Senior Cleaner	Cleaner	Senior Presser	Presser	Manager	Delivery	Maintenance
Social Insurance No.	218 738 631	552 846 826	422 946 541	931 771 620	726 911 134	638 912 634	822 546 859
Address	21 Spotter St. Vancouver, BC V3K 4K2	34 Wash Ave. Vancouver, BC V9B 4C1	92 Flat St. Vancouver, BC V8U 1X3	63 Iron Blvd., #2 Vancouver, BC V7N 2L2	11 Sweeper St. Vancouver, BC V7N 2L2	2 Kerry St. Richmond, BC V8K 4K2	4 Fixall Cr. Vancouver, BC V9B 4C1
Telephone	(604) 693-7595	(604) 381-8138	(604) 488-6353	(604) 389-2291	(604) 829-6291	(604) 693-7995	(604) 381-2238
Date of Birth (mm-dd-yy)	8-15-81	11-3-78	8-6-68	7-31-75	7-31-75	8-15-81	11-3-78
Date of Hire (mm-dd-yy)	2-7-06	12-4-11	4-6-06	11-6-11	1-1-07	8-5-07	6-6-03
Federal (BC) Tax Exemption – TD1							
Basic Personal	$10 382 (11 000)	$10 382 (11 000)	$10 382 (11 000)	$10 382 (11 000)	$10 382 (11 000)	$10 382 (11 000)	$10 382 (11 000)
Spouse	$10 382 (9 653)	–	$10 382 (9 653)	–	–	$10 382 (9 653)	$10 382 (9 653)
Other		–	$10 669 (8 338)	$1 970 (1 330)	–	–	–
Total Exemptions	$20 764 (20 653)	$10 382 (11 000)	$31 433 (28 991)	$12 352 (12 330)	$10 382 (11 000)	$20 764 (20 653)	$20 764 (20 653)
Additional Fed Taxes	$100	–	–	–	–	–	–
Employee Taxes							
Historical Income tax	$398.92	$375.68	$172.72	$328.64	$869.49	$423.90	$485.18
Historical EI	$68.97	$48.40	$52.29	$47.00	$82.34	$59.84	$67.32
Historical CPP	$164.75	$116.01	$127.27	$117.28	$206.18	$147.54	$166.44
Deduct EI; EI Rate	Yes; 1.4	Yes; 1.4	Yes; 1.4	Yes; 1.4	Yes; 1.4	Yes; 1.4	Yes; 1.4
Deduct CPP	Yes	Yes	Yes	Yes	Yes	Yes	Yes
Employee Income							
Advances: Hist Amt	$200.00	(use) ✓	(use) ✓	(use) ✓	(use) ✓	(use) ✓	(use) ✓
Benefits Per Period	$23.54	$ 6.58	$23.54	$ 6.58	$57.00	$26.31	$57.00
Benefits: Hist Amt	$47.08	$26.32	$47.08	$126.32	$57.00	$52.62	$57.00
Vacation Pay Owed	$564.98	$170.06	$295.76	$67.20	–	–	–
Vacation Paid	–	–	–	–	–	–	–

▶

EMPLOYEE INFORMATION SHEET CONTINUED

	Clyne Fretton	Mouver Durtee	Soffte Landings	Iean Sissler	Claire Brumes	S. Pott Tran	Cryper Houseman
Employee Income Continued							
Regular Wage Rate	$18.00	$14.00	$16.00	$14.00	(do not use)	(do not use)	(do not use)
(Hours per Period)	(80 hours)	(40 hours)	(80 hours)	(40 hours)	–	–	–
Reg. Wages: Hist Amt	$2 880.00	$2 240.00	$2 560.00	$2 240.00	–	–	–
Overtime 1 Rate	$27.00	$21.00	$24.00	$21.00	(do not use)	(do not use)	(do not use)
Overtime 1: Hist Amt	$54.00	$168.00	$48.00	$84.00	–	–	–
Salary	(do not use)	(do not use)	(do not use)	(do not use)	$4 000.00	$1 600.00	$3 600.00
(Hours Per Period)	–	–	–	–	(150 hours)	(80 hours)	(150 hours)
Salary: Hist Amt		—	–	–	$4 000	$3 200	$3 600
Commission	(do not use)	(do not use)	(do not use)	(do not use)	1% net sales	(do not use)	(do not use)
Commission: Hist Amt	–	–	–	–	$390.00	–	–
Piece Rate/Set	$0.10	$0.10	$0.10	$0.10	(do not use)	(do not use)	(do not use)
Piece Rate: Hist Amt	$189.00	$180.00	$188.00	$190.00	–	–	–
Pay Periods	26 (bi-weekly)	52 (weekly)	26 (bi-weekly)	52 (weekly)	12 (monthly)	26 (bi-weekly)	12 (monthly)
Vacation Rate	6% retained	4% retained	6% retained	4% retained	0% (3 weeks)	0% (3 weeks)	0% (3 weeks)
Record Wage Exp in	Linked Accts	Linked Accts	Linked Accts	Linked Accts	Linked Accts	Linked Accts	Linked Accts
Employee Deductions							
RRSP	(use) ✔	(use) ✔	(use) ✔	$25.00	$50.00	(use) ✔	$50.00
RRSP: Hist Amt	–	–	–	$100.00	$50.00		$50.00
MSP-Employee	$23.54	$6.58	$23.54	$6.58	$57.00	$26.31	$57.00
MSP-Hist Amt	$47.08	$26.32	$47.08	$26.32	$57.00	$52.62	$57.00
WCB and Other Expenses							
WCB Rate	3.02	3.02	3.02	3.02	3.02	5.00	3.02
Travel Allow	–	–	–	–	$300.00	–	–
Travel Allow: Hist Amt	–	–	–	–	$300.00	–	–
Tuition Fee	–	–	–	$25.00	–	–	–
Tuition Fee: Hist Amt	–	–	–	$100.00	–	–	–
MSP-Employer	$23.54	$6.58	$23.54	$6.58	$57.00	$26.31	$57.00
MSP-Employer: Hist Amt	$47.08	$26.32	$47.08	$26.32	$57.00	$52.62	$57.00
Entitlements: Rate, Maximum Days, Clear? (Historical Amount)							
Vacation: Rate: Max	–	–	–	–	8%, 25 days	8%, 25 days	8%, 25 days
Clear? (Days Accrued)	–	–	–	–	No (10 days)	No (5 days)	No (15 days)
Sick Leave: Rate: Max	5%, 20 days	5%, 20 days	5%, 20 days	5%, 20 days	5%, 20 days	5%, 20 days	5%, 20 days
Clear? (Days Accrued)	No (7 days)	No (5 days)	No (9 days)	No (8 days)	No (8 days)	No (8 days)	No (10 days)
Personal Days: Rate: Max	2.5%, 10 days	2.5%, 10 days	2.5%, 10 days	2.5%, 10 days	2.5%, 10 days	2.5%, 10 days	2.5%, 10 days
Clear? (Days Accrued)	No (3 days)	No (4 days)	No (1 day)	No (2 days)	No (3 days)	No (2 days)	No (2 days)
Direct Deposit							
Yes/No	Yes	No	No	Yes	Yes	No	Yes
Bank, Transit No.	300, 49921	–	–	180, 06722	103, 30099	–	285, 12084
Account No.	2883912	–	–	4556221	2009123	–	2399012
Percent	100%	–	–	100%	100%	–	100%
Additional Information							
Emergency Contact	Aidan Fretton	Alex Durtee	Petra Landings	Kierin Safta	Jay Brumes	Sima Tran	Pedro Perez
Contact Number	(604) 497-1469	(604) 477-4573	(604) 488-6353	(604) 364-1892	(604) 899-2197	(604) 693-7995	(604) 447-5602
T4 and RL-1 Reporting							
EI Insurable Earnings	$3 123.00	$2 588.00	$2 796.00	$2 514.00	$4 390.00	$3 200.00	$3 600.00
Pensionable Earnings	$3 170.08	$2 614.32	$2 843.08	$2 640.32	$4 447.00	$3 252.62	$3 657.00
Withheld	$679.72	$566.41	$399.36	$619.24	$1 265.01	$683.90	$825.94
Net Pay	$2 643.28	$2 021.59	$2 396.64	$1 894.76	$3 124.99	$2 516.10	$2 774.06

EI, CPP & Income Tax Calculations built into Simply Accounting program

NOTES: Medical (MSP) premiums are deducted every pay period. The amounts are adjusted for the monthly rates.

Employee Profiles and TD1 Information

Employee Benefits and Entitlements   All employees are entitled to 10 days per year as sick leave and five days' leave for personal reasons. If the days are not needed, employees can carry these days forward to a new year, to a maximum of 20 and 10 days respectively. Currently, all employees have some unused sick leave and personal leave days accrued from the previous year. Salaried employees are allowed to carry forward two of their three weeks' vacation entitlement. That is, they are allowed to accumulate a maximum of 25 unused vacation days at any one time.

To encourage personal development, Lime Light offers to pay 50 percent of the tuition fees for any employee enrolled in college or university programs. Currently, only Iean Sissler is taking courses and receiving the tuition fee benefit. This benefit for Sissler is considered an expense for Lime Light Laundry. A second benefit applies to all employees — Lime Light Laundry pays 50 percent of the medical premiums.

Piece Rate Bonuses   Lime Light Laundry pays the cleaning staff — the cleaners and pressers — a piece rate bonus of 10 cents per sheet set in excess of the first 500 sets each week. This bonus is added to each paycheque.

Employer Expenses   Lime Light Laundry currently has three employer payroll expenses beyond the compulsory CPP, EI and WCB: 50 percent of the employee's medical premiums for the BC Medical Services Plan (MSP), 50 percent of eligible tuition fees and a travel allowance for Brumes as compensation for using her car for business travel.

Claire Brumes   As the manager of the laundry, Brumes negotiates deals with clients, schedules work, hires new staff and discusses problems with the owner, who does not participate in the day-to-day affairs of the business. She is married and has no children. Since her husband is also fully employed, she uses the single federal and provincial tax claim amounts but she pays the family medical premiums. At the end of each month, her salary of $4 000 per month plus a commission of 1 percent of revenue from services, net of taxes, is deposited to her account. She is recorded as salesperson for all sales for the purpose of calculating her commission. In addition, she receives $300 per month in a separate cheque as a travel allowance to cover the expense of her regular client visits and business promotion. This amount is an employer expense, not an employee benefit. She makes monthly contributions to her RRSP plan as well. In lieu of vacation pay, she is entitled to take three weeks of paid vacation each year.

Clyne Fretton   As the senior cleaner, Fretton performs regular laundry duties, such as cleaning the incoming bed sheets and table linens. She has several years of experience with Lime Light and is helping to train Durtee, the junior cleaner who was recently hired. Her regular pay of $18 per hour is supplemented by the piece rate bonus and by overtime wages at the rate of $27 per hour when she works more than 40 hours per week. In addition, she receives vacation pay at the rate of 6 percent of her total wages, equivalent to about three weeks of pay, but this amount is retained until she chooses to take a vacation. Because she is married and fully supports her husband, she claims a spousal amount for income tax purposes and she also pays medical premiums at the family rate. To offset the tax from her additional income, she chooses to have an additional $100 in taxes withheld each month. She has received an advance of $200 which she will repay over the next four pay periods. She has her pay deposited directly to her bank account every two weeks.

Mouver Durtee   is the second and junior cleaner. For sharing all the cleaning duties with Fretton, he earns $14 per hour, $21 per hour overtime when he works more than 40 hours in a week and the piece rate bonus. He is paid weekly by cheque and his 4 percent vacation pay is retained. As a single self-supporting person, Durtee claims the basic single amount for income tax and pays single medical premiums.

Soffte Landings   is the senior presser. She operates the clothes pressing equipment, assisted by Sissler. Landings is single but supports her invalid aged mother so she is able to claim the spousal equivalent TD1 amount, the caregiver amounts and her mother's age amount. These claims significantly reduce the income tax she pays on her wages of $16 per hour, $24 for overtime hours and her piece rate bonus. Her medical premium is deducted from her bi-weekly paycheque at the family rate to cover herself and her mother. Her 6 percent vacation pay is retained.

Iean Sissler   assists Landings with operating the equipment to press the laundry. She is single with no dependants, so she pays single medical premiums and has only the basic single TD1 claim amounts, plus her tuition of $850 and the education allowances ($140 per month federal and $60 provincial). From her weekly deposited pay, she contributes $50 to an RRSP program. Her pay, at $14 per hour and $21 for overtime hours with 4 percent vacation pay, is less than Landings' pay because she has less experience. She also receives the piece rate bonus. Sissler is enrolled in a business program at the local community college. She pays 50 percent of her tuition herself and Lime Light Laundry pays an equal amount. This taxable benefit, entered on Sissler's paycheque at the rate of $25 per week, has already been paid for one month.

S. Pott Tran   Tran's main responsibility with Lime Light is delivery. He picks up the dirty laundry from hotels throughout the city and drops off the clean linens. Tran is married and fully supports his wife and one child, so he pays the family medical premiums and has the basic and spousal claim amounts for income taxes. He is paid his bi-weekly salary of $1 600 by cheque, and he can take three weeks of vacation yearly.

Cryper Houseman   is responsible for general maintenance at Lime Light — he keeps the machines running and cleans the premises. As a single parent who supports two children, he can claim the spousal amount for income tax purposes. He has worked for Lime Light since the business started. At the end of each month, Houseman has his monthly salary of $3 600 deposited to his bank account. He also makes contributions to his RRSP program with regular payroll deductions. As a salaried employee, he is entitled to take three weeks of paid vacation per year.

Accounting Procedures

Taxes: HST and PST

The provincial and federal sales taxes are harmonized in British Columbia at the single rate of 12 percent HST. Of this, 5 percent is the federal and 7 percent is the provincial portion. Lime Light Laundry uses the regular method for remitting the HST. It records the HST collected from clients as a liability in *HST Charged on Services*. HST paid to suppliers is recorded in *HST Paid on Purchases* as a decrease in the liability to Canada Revenue Agency. The HST quarterly refund or remittance is calculated automatically in the *HST Owing (Refund)* subgroup total account. Lime Light files for a refund or remits the balance owing to the Receiver General for Canada by the last day of the month for the previous quarter. All services provided and all purchases made by Lime Light Laundry are subject to the 12 percent HST.

Tax codes are set up in the defaults for the company so that Simply Accounting will automatically calculate the tax when it is paid.

Discounts

All clients are offered a discount of 1 percent on the after-tax amount of the sale if they pay their accounts in full within 15 days. Full payment is requested in 30 days. Discount terms are set up as the default in the client records. Some suppliers also offer discounts on after-tax purchase amounts. These discount terms are set up in the supplier records so that Simply Accounting will automatically calculate the discount when full payment is made within the discount period.

Direct Payroll Deposits

Chaplin allows employees to have their regular pay deposited directly to their bank accounts or to be paid by cheque. Four employees have selected direct payroll deposits.

Payroll Remittances

Four suppliers are identified as payroll authorities with the following remittances: EI, CPP and income tax are remitted to the Receiver General for Canada; medical premiums are remitted to the BC Minister of Finance; Workers' Compensation Board premiums are remitted to the BC Workers' Compensation Board; and RRSP contributions are remitted to Victoria Trust.

NOTES
If you want to enter the source documents before attempting the payroll setup, or if you do not want to complete the payroll setup, you can restore the backup file SimData10\Setup\ lime-pay1.CAB.

INSTRUCTIONS

1. **Set up** the **Payroll Ledger** using the employee information, employee profiles and TD1 information. Detailed keystroke instructions for setting up payroll follow.

2. **Enter** the **transactions** in Simply Accounting using the Chart of Accounts and Supplier, Client and Employee Information. Source documents begin on page 343 following the payroll setup instructions.

2. **Print** the **reports and graphs** marked on the following printing form after you have finished making your entries.

REPORTS

Accounts
- [ ] Chart of Accounts
- [ ] Account List
- [ ] General Journal Entries

Financials
- [✓] Comparative Balance Sheet: Feb. 1 and Feb. 28 with difference in percentage
- [✓] Income Statement: Feb. 1 to Feb. 28
- [✓] Trial Balance date: Feb. 28
- [✓] All Journal Entries: Feb. 1 to Feb. 28
- [✓] General Ledger accounts: Feb. 1 to Feb. 28 4020 5300 5305 5350
- [ ] Statement of Cash Flows
- [✓] Cash Flow Projection Detail Report: for 1080 for next 30 days

Tax
- [ ] HST Report

Banking
- [ ] Cheque Log Report

Payables
- [ ] Supplier List
- [ ] Supplier Aged
- [ ] Aged Overdue Payables
- [ ] Expense Journal Entries
- [ ] Payment Journal Entries

Receivables
- [ ] Client List
- [ ] Client Aged
- [ ] Aged Overdue Receivables
- [ ] Revenues Journal Entries
- [ ] Receipt Journal Entries
- [✓] Revenues by Salesperson Feb. 1 to Feb. 28
- [ ] Revenues by Job Category
- [ ] Client Statements

Employees & Payroll
- [ ] Employee List
- [ ] Summary
- [ ] Deductions & Expense
- [ ] Job Category

- [ ] Remittances
- [✓] Payroll Journal Entries: Feb. 1 to Feb. 28
- [ ] T4 Slips
- [ ] Record of Employment

Mailing Labels
- [ ] Labels

Management Reports
- [ ] Ledger

GRAPHS

- [ ] Payables by Aging Period
- [ ] Payables by Supplier
- [ ] Receivables by Aging Period
- [ ] Receivables by Client
- [ ] Revenues vs Receivables
- [ ] Receivables Due vs Payables Due
- [ ] Revenues by Account
- [ ] Expenses by Account
- [✓] Expenses and Net Profit as % of Revenue

PAYROLL SETUP KEYSTROKES

Adding the Payroll Module

Open   **SimData10\Limelite\limelite** to access the data file for **Lime Light**.
Accept Feb. 1 as the **session date**.

The Payroll module is hidden because it was not used. Before we can set it up, we need to unhide it. We will then work from this module to enter settings and employees.

Choose the **Setup menu** and **click User Preferences** to open the Options screen.

Click   **View** to access the screen we need:

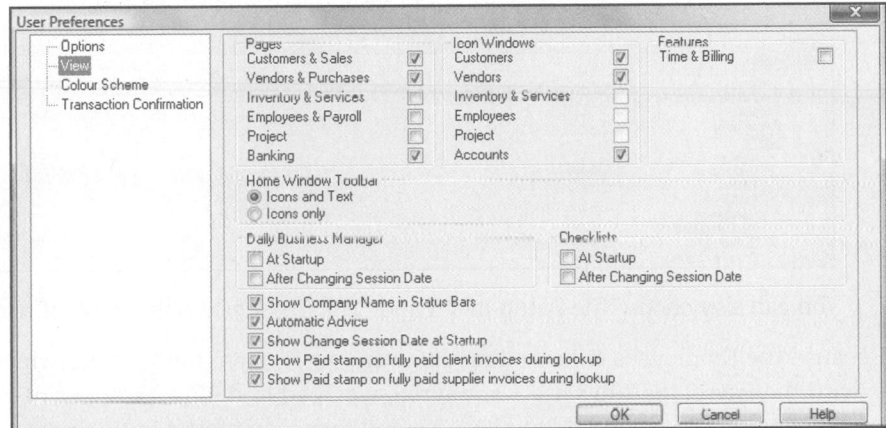

Click   the **Pages check box for Employees & Payroll** to add ✓s.

Click   **OK** to save the settings and return to the Home window.

Click   **Employees & Payroll** in the Modules pane list:

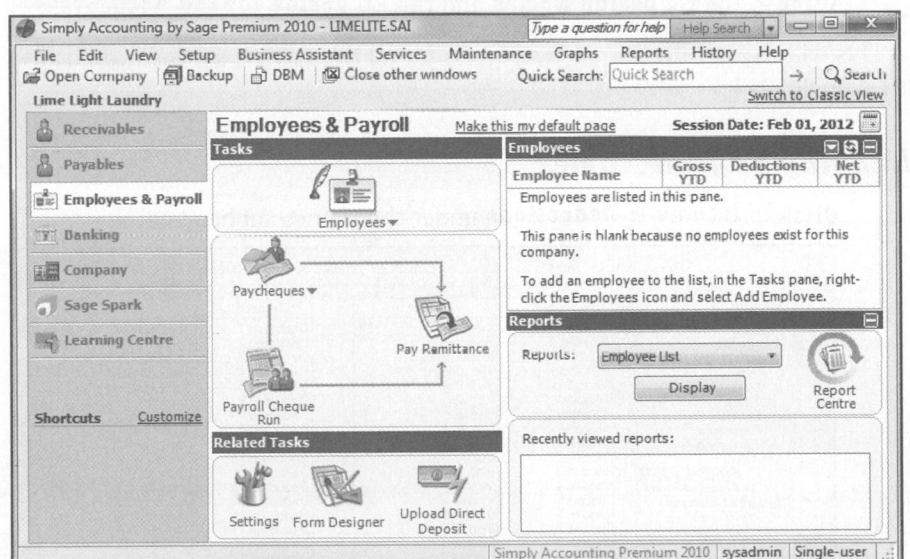

The Payroll ledger and its icons have been added. The Employees icon has the not finished symbol to indicate that the module history is not finished. If you try to finish the Payroll history now, you will see an error message about several missing linked accounts.

From the Employees & Payroll window we can enter ledger settings and records.

NOTES
Remember that you must have a valid Payroll ID code from Sage Software in order to use the payroll features for non-student versions of the program.
Choose the Business Services menu and click Simply CARE Services for more information.

NOTES
If you are using the backup installation set or the Pro version, restore SimData10\limelite1.CAB to SimData10\Limelite\limelite to open the data file for Lime Light.

CLASSIC VIEW
The User Preferences View screen has two columns: one for Modules that includes Time & Billing and one for the Icon Windows.

NOTES
Clicking the Pages check box will add the ✓s for viewing both the Module and Icon Windows. Then you can remove the ✓ for the Icon Window if you want.

NOTES
You can make Employees & Payroll your default homepage while you are completing the payroll setup. When you close the file and re-open it, you will open this page to continue the setup.

Setting Up the Payroll Ledger

Before you can enter payroll journal transactions, you must set up the payroll module. This involves the same steps as setting up other ledgers:

1. Change the settings for the ledger.
2. Create employee ledger records.
3. Add historical employee data.
4. Back up the data file and finish the history.

Changing Payroll Ledger Settings

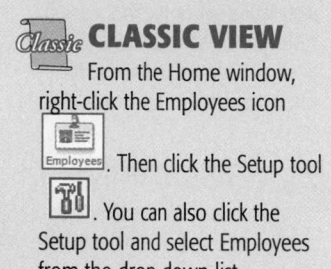

CLASSIC VIEW

From the Home window, right-click the Employees icon

. Then click the Setup tool

. You can also click the Setup tool and select Employees from the drop-down list.

Click   the **Settings icon** to open the Payroll Settings screen:

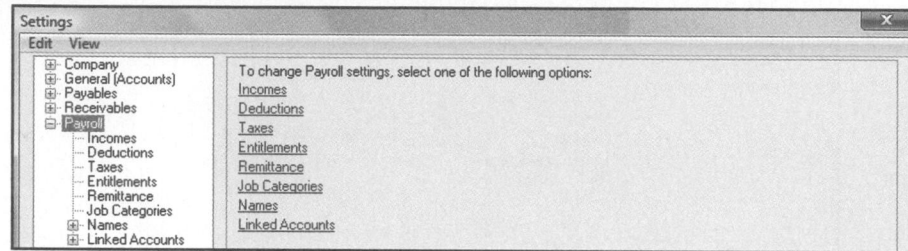

You can also choose the Setup menu and click Settings. Click Payroll if necessary.

Because the Employees & Payroll module window is open, the Settings window opens with the Payroll Settings list. For payroll, we need to define the types of income paid to employees, the payroll deductions, payroll taxes, employee entitlements, remittances, job categories, names for income, deductions and additional fields and linked accounts for all these functions. We will begin by entering names and deleting the ones we do not need. The reduced list will be easier to work with.

NOTES

In any module window, click the Settings icon and then click Payroll to open the Payroll Settings screen.

Click   the ⊞ beside **Names** and the ⊞ beside **Linked Accounts**.

NOTES

By modifying the names first, only the ones we need to set up will appear on later screens.

This will expand the list, so that labels for all the Payroll settings will be available with a single click.

Changing Payroll Names

NOTES

You can enter names for any of these fields later if you need to add more incomes or deductions.

Click   **Income & Deductions** under the Names subheading:

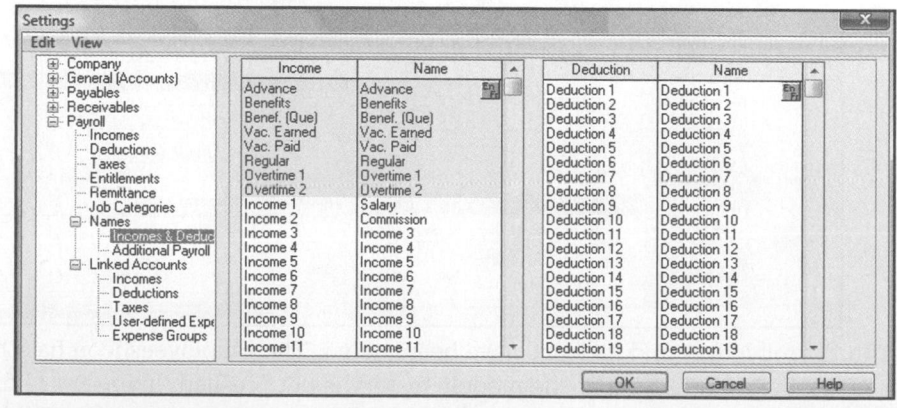

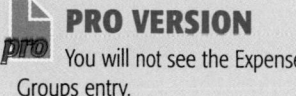

PRO VERSION

You will not see the Expense Groups entry.

NOTES

Lime Light Laundry does not use Expense Groups (under Linked Accounts).

The first screen we need to modify has all the names for incomes and deductions used. Many of the standard income types are mandatory and cannot be changed. These fields are shown on a shaded background. Some of the other default names are also correct so you do not need to redefine them. You can leave Income 1 and Income 2, labelled "Salary" and "Commission," unchanged because Lime Light Laundry has salaried employees and pays a sales commission to Brumes. There is allowance for 20 different kinds of income in addition to the compulsory fields and 20 different payroll deductions. Each income and deduction label may have up to 12 characters.

Lime Light uses an additional income field for the piece rate bonus that is based on the number of sets of bedding the employees launder. The travel allowance for Brumes will be set up as a user-defined expense. The remaining income fields are not used.

Lime Light also has two payroll deductions at this time: RRSP, the Registered Retirement Savings Plan, and the employee share of provincial medical plan premiums (MSP-Employee). The remaining deduction fields are not used.

> **Click**   **Income 3 in the Name column** to highlight the contents.
>
> **Type**   Piece Rate **Press** (tab) to advance to the Income 4 field.

Click the **En/Fr language icon** to open the extra fields if you want to enter labels or names in both French and English.

> **Press**   (del). **Press** (tab) to advance to the Income 5 field.
>
> **Press**   (del) to remove the entry. **Press** (tab) to select the next field.
>
> **Delete**   the **remaining Income names** until they are all removed.
>
> **Press**   (tab) **twice** after deleting Income 20 to select Deduction 1 in the Name column.
>
> **Type**   RRSP **Press** (tab) to advance to the second deduction Name field.
>
> **Type**   MSP-Employee **Press** (tab) to highlight the next field.
>
> **Press**   (del). You can delete the remaining Deduction fields because Lime Light Laundry does not have other payroll deductions.
>
> **Press**   (tab) to select the next field. **Delete** the **remaining deductions**.
>
> **Click**   **Additional Payroll** under the Names subheading:

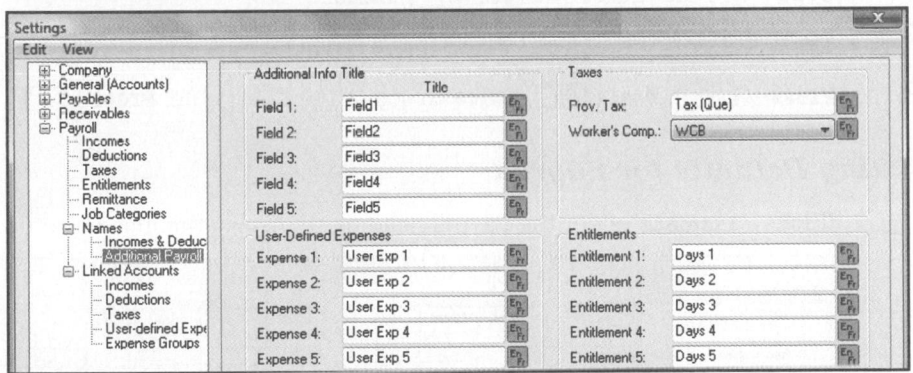

The Prov. Tax field is used for Quebec payroll taxes. Since we will not choose Quebec as the employees' province of taxation, the program will automatically skip the related payroll fields. WCB (Workers' Compensation Board) is entered as the name for Workers' Compensation because we selected British Columbia as the business province.

We can also name the additional ledger fields, the additional payroll expenses for Lime Light and the entitlements for employees. Lime Light pays 50 percent of the employees' provincial health care plan medical premiums and eligible tuition fees. It also pays a travel allowance to Brumes and offers sick leave and personal leave days for all employees as well as vacation days for salaried employees. First, we will name the ledger fields. We will use these fields to store the name and phone number of each employee's emergency contact.

> **Double click**   **Field1** or **press** (tab).

NOTES
We are not setting up travel allowances as income because separate cheques are issued for this. If it were set up as an income (reimbursement), it would be added to the paycheque as non-taxable income.

NOTES
If clicking does not highlight the field contents, drag through an entry to select it. Double clicking will select only one word, either Income or 3.

WARNING!
If you later change the province in the Company Information screen, the WCB name entered will not change automatically. You must enter the correction manually by choosing from the drop-down list.

Type   Emergency Contact

Press   (tab) **twice** to skip the language label icon and highlight the next field.

Type   Contact Number

Press   (tab) **twice. Press** (del) to delete the name for Field 3.

Delete   the **names** for Field 4 and Field 5.

Benefits and expenses can be handled in different ways.

The medical premium payment is a taxable benefit for employees. It is also entered as a user-defined expense because the premiums are paid to a third party rather than to the employee. Tuition, the other taxable benefit and user-defined expense, is also paid to a third party — the educational institution. Benefits paid directly to the employee on the payroll cheque should be set up as income. Reimbursements for expenses may be entered as non-taxable income or as user-defined expenses. If we repay the expenses on the payroll cheque, we define them as reimbursements — an income type that is not taxable — and link them to an expense account. If we enter them as user-defined expenses, we create both a linked payable and expense account and issue a separate payment to the employee. Brumes' travel allowance is set up as a user-defined expense.

> ### NOTES
> For Lime Light Laundry, we use the generic Benefits field to enter all employee benefits.

> ### NOTES
> In Chapter 16, we create Travel Expenses as an income (reimbursement type) that is added to the paycheque. Here it is a user-defined expense and we issue separate cheques to the employee for them.

> ### NOTES
> You can use up to 12 characters for User-Defined Expense and Entitlement names including spaces – that is why we omitted the space for the Personal Days entitlement name.

Drag through   **User Exp 1**, the Expense 1 field, to highlight the contents.

Type   Travel Allow **Press** (tab) **twice** to select the next expense name.

Type   Tuition Fees **Press** (tab) **twice**.

Type   MSP-Employer **Press** (tab) **twice**.

Press   (del). **Press** (tab) **twice** to select the final expense. **Press** (del).

Drag through   **Days 1**, the Entitlement 1 field, to highlight the contents.

Type   Vacation **Press** (tab) **twice** to select the next entitlement name.

Type   Sick Leave **Press** (tab) **twice**.

Type   PersonalDays **Press** (tab) **twice**.

Press   (del). **Press** (tab) **twice** to select the final name. **Press** (del).

Setting Defaults for Payroll

Click   **Incomes** under the Payroll heading to display the income setup:

Income	Type	Unit of Measure	Calc. Tax	Calc. Tax (Que)	Calc. EI	Calc. Ins. Hours	Calc. CPP/QPP	Calc. EHT	Calc. QHSF	Calc. Vac.	Calc. QPIP
Advance	System	Period									
Benefits	System	Period	✓				✓	✓			
Benef. (Que)	System	Period		✓			✓		✓	✓	
Vac. Earned	System	Period									
Vac. Paid	System	Period	✓	✓	✓		✓	✓	✓		✓
Regular	urly Rate	Hour	✓	✓	✓	✓	✓	✓	✓	✓	✓
Overtime 1	Hourly Rate	Hour	✓	✓	✓	✓	✓	✓	✓	✓	✓
Overtime 2	Hourly Rate	Hour	✓	✓	✓	✓	✓	✓	✓	✓	✓
Salary	Income	Period	✓	✓	✓	✓	✓	✓	✓	✓	✓
Commission	Income	Period	✓	✓	✓	✓	✓	✓	✓	✓	✓
Piece Rate	Income	Period	✓	✓	✓	✓	✓	✓	✓	✓	✓

At this stage, we will change the tax settings for Incomes and Deductions.

We will first modify this screen by hiding the columns that do not apply to British Columbia so that only the columns we need are on-screen at the same time.

Point to   the **right column heading margin for Calc. Tax (Que.)** until the pointer changes to a two-sided arrow [↔].

Drag the **margin to the left** until the column is hidden.

Point to the **right column heading margin for Calc. QHSF** until the pointer changes to a two-sided arrow. **Drag** the **margin to the left** until the column is hidden.

Point to the **right column heading margin for Calc. QPIP** until the pointer changes to a two-sided arrow. **Drag** the **margin to the left**.

Point to the **right column heading margin for Calc. EHT** until the pointer changes to a two-sided arrow. **Drag** the **margin to the left**.

Notice that only the income names you did not delete (page 319) appear on this screen. For each type of income you must indicate what taxes are applied and whether vacation pay is calculated on the income. Most of the information is correct. Regular and overtime hours are paid on an hourly basis, while salary and commissions are paid at designated income amounts per period. All taxes apply to these types of income in British Columbia so these default settings are correct. Vacation pay, however, is paid only to the hourly paid employees, so some of these checkmarks should be removed. In addition, we should designate the type of income for Piece Rate, the income we added, and the taxes that apply to it. Choosing the type of income will change the defaults that are applied.

Click **Piece Rate** to place the cursor on the correct line.

Press (tab) to move to the Type column. A List icon is added.

Click the **List icon** 🔍 to see the types we can select:

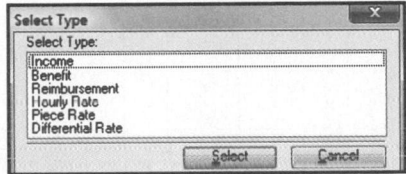

By default, all new income entries are assigned to the Income type. This assignment is correct for Salary. Taxable benefits paid directly to the employee instead of a third party should also be classified as Income. The Benefit type is used only for items such as medical or life insurance premiums that the employer pays directly to a third party on behalf of the employee. The monetary value of the premiums is added as a benefit to the employee's gross wages to determine taxes but is not added to the net pay. The employee does not receive the actual dollar amount. If a benefit is added to net pay, it should be classified as an Income.

Reimbursements are not taxable — the employee is being repaid for company-related expenditures. The **Piece Rate** type calculates pay based on the number of units. **Differential Rates** apply to different hourly rates paid at different times and are not used by Lime Light.

Click **Piece Rate** to select this type for Piece Rate.

Click **Select** to add the Type to the Settings screen. **Press** (tab).

The cursor advances to the Unit of Measure field and the entry has changed to Item. The amount paid to employees is based on the number of sheet sets laundered. Notice that the Insurable Hours checkmark was removed when we changed the type.

Type Sets

We need to modify the other Insurable Hours settings. The number of hours worked determines eligibility for Employment Insurance benefits. Regular, overtime and salary paid hours are entered but commissions are not — no time can be reasonably attached

---

NOTES

When you close and re-open the Payroll Settings screen, the hidden and resized columns will be restored — the column changes you made are not saved.

QHSF is the provincial health services plan for Quebec.

QPIP (Quebec Parental Insurance Plan) provides parental leave benefits to EI insurable employees. Both employers and employees pay into the plan.

EHT (Employer Health Tax) applies only in Ontario.

NOTES

An alternative approach for tuition fees is to set them up as a taxable income (on which vacation pay is not calculated) and add the amount to the employee's paycheque. You would use this method when the employee pays the tuition and is repaid (as in Helena's Academy, Chapter 8, and Flabuless Fitness, Chapter 16). Tuition is not a reimbursement type of income because it is taxable.

NOTES

When you select Reimbursement as the type, all taxes are removed because this type of payment is not taxable.

to commissions so they are not counted. The checkmark for it should be removed. The ✓ for Piece Rate was automatically removed when we changed the income type.

> **Click**   **Commission** to select this income line.
>
> **Press**   (tab) **repeatedly** until the cursor is in the **Calc. Ins. Hours field**.
>
> **Click**   to remove the ✓, or **press** the **space bar**.

We also need to modify the entries for vacation pay. In British Columbia, vacation pay is calculated on all performance-based wages. This includes the regular wages, overtime wages and piece rate pay. We need to remove the remaining ✓s. Salaried workers receive paid time off rather than a percentage of their wages as vacation pay. We do not need to remove the ✓ for Overtime 2. If it is used later, vacation pay will be calculated on it as well.

> **Click**   **Salary** in the Income column.
>
> **Press**   (tab) **repeatedly** until the cursor is in the **Calc. Vac. column**.
>
> **Click**   to remove the ✓, or **press** the **space bar**.
>
> **Press**   (↓) to place the cursor in the **Calc. Vac. field for Commission**.
>
> **Click**   to remove the ✓, or **press** the **space bar**.

The completed Settings screen is shown below:

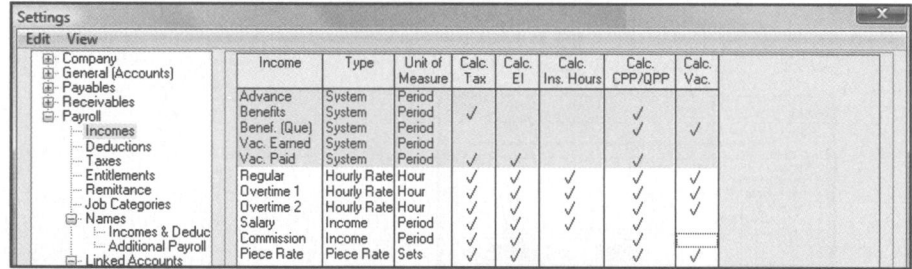

> **Click**   **Deductions** under the Payroll heading:

You can hide the columns you do not need — those for Quebec taxes and EHT.

Only the two deduction names you entered earlier appear on this screen. You can calculate deductions as a percentage of the gross pay or as a fixed amount. Some deductions, like union dues, are usually calculated as a percentage of income. The Amount settings are correct for Lime Light Laundry.

All deductions are set by default to be calculated after all taxes (Deduct After Tax is checked). For MSP-Employee, this is correct — it is subtracted from income after income tax and other payroll taxes have been deducted. However, RRSP contributions qualify as tax deductions and will be subtracted from gross income before income tax is calculated, but not before EI, CPP and so on, so you must change only this setting.

> **Click**   the **Deduct After Tax column** for RRSP to remove only the one ✓ and change the setting to before tax.

The remaining settings are correct. RRSP is deducted after the other payroll taxes and vacation pay because these deductions are based on gross wages.

NOTES

Vacation pay is also paid for statutory holidays. Lime Light pays workers their regular pay for these days, as if they had worked. For occasional workers, this pay may be calculated as a percentage of wages.

In Quebec, vacation pay is also paid on benefits.

NOTES

Vacation pay is calculated on all wages. This calculation includes the piece rate pay — number of sheet sets — because it is a performance-based wage or income. Vacation pay is not applied to benefits.

The regulations governing vacation pay are set provincially.

NOTES

You can modify the Deductions screen as you modified the Incomes Settings screen so that only the columns you need are on-screen. You can remove the Deduct After Tax (Que.), EHT, QHSF and QPIP columns.

Click   **Taxes** under the Payroll heading:

This next group of fields refers to the rate at which employer tax obligations are calculated. The factor for Employment Insurance (**EI Factor**) is correct at 1.4. The employer's contribution is set at 1.4 times the employee's contribution. In the next field, you can set the employer's rate for **WCB** (Workers' Compensation Board) premiums. On this screen, you can enter 3.02, the rate that applies to most Lime Light employees. You can modify rates for individual employees in the ledger records, as we will do for Tran.

The next field, **EHT Factor**, shows the percentage of payroll costs that the employer contributes to the provincial health plan in Ontario. The rate is based on the total payroll costs per year. It does not apply to BC employees.

The **QHSF Factor** (Quebec Health Services Fund) applies to payroll in Quebec, so we do not need to enter it. QHSF is similar to EHT.

Click   the **WCB Rate field**.

Type   3.02

The Quebec tax fields will not be available when we select British Columbia as the province for employees.

Click   **Entitlements** under the Payroll heading:

On this screen you can enter the rules for entitlements that apply to all or most employees. When we enter the rules here, they will be added to each employee's record. You can change entitlement amounts for individual employees in their ledger records.

Entitlements may be given directly or may be linked to the number of hours worked. For example, usually employees are not entitled to take vacation time until they have worked for a certain period of time. Or they may not be allowed to take paid sick leave immediately after being hired. You can use the **Track Using % Hours Worked** to determine how quickly vacation or sick days accumulate. For example, 5 percent of hours worked yields about one day per month. Thus, you would enter 5 percent if the employee is entitled to 12 days of leave per year. You can also indicate the **Maximum** number of **Days** per year that an employee can take or accumulate. And finally, you must indicate whether the unused days are **cleared at the end of a year** or can be carried forward. If the days earned, but not used, at the end of a year are carried forward, then the Maximum will still place a limit on the number of days available. When the maximum number of days has been reached, no additional days will accrue — the entry in the Days Earned field on the Entitlements tab screen will be zero — until the employee takes time off and the days accrued drops below the maximum again. The number of days of entitlement is based on an eight-hour day, but this can be changed.

NOTES
The WCB rate is based on the injury history and risk factors for the job and for the industry. Tran's rate is higher than the others' because his work — driving a delivery truck — is considered more dangerous.

NOTES
EHT in Ontario applies if the total payroll is greater than $400 000.
QHSF is used for Village Galleries in Chapter 14.

NOTES
You can also apply entitlements as a fixed amount per year by omitting the tracking percentage, entering a maximum and then entering the balance for the employee in the ledger.

Lime Light Laundry gives salaried workers three weeks of vacation (tracked at 8 percent) and allows a maximum of 25 days. Sick leave at 10 days per year is earned at the rate of 5 percent to the maximum of 20 days. Personal leave days (5 days) accrue at the rate of 2.5 percent for a maximum of 10 days. None are cleared at year-end.

Lime Light Laundry allows two weeks of vacation time and sick leave and one week of personal days to be carried over to the following year.

> **Click**   the **Track Using % Hours Worked field for Vacation**.
>
> **Type**   8 **Press** (tab) to advance to the Maximum Days field.
>
> **Type**   25 **Press** (tab).
>
> **Click**   the **Track Using % Hours Worked field for Sick Leave**.
>
> **Type**   5 **Press** (tab) to advance to the Maximum Days field.
>
> **Type**   20 **Press** (tab).
>
> **Click**   the **Track Using % Hours Worked field for PersonalDays**.
>
> **Type**   2.5 **Press** (tab) to advance to the Maximum Days field.
>
> **Type**   10 **Press** (tab).

Until we modify the supplier records and create the employee records, we will not have all the information we need to set up Remittances and Job Categories. Therefore, we will add Payroll Remittance and Job Category settings later.

Identifying the Payroll Linked Accounts

There are many linked accounts for payroll because each type of income, tax, deduction and expense that is used must be linked to a General Ledger account. You do not need to create any of these accounts; they are already in the Chart of Accounts. The following income linked accounts are used by Lime Light Laundry for the Payroll Ledger.

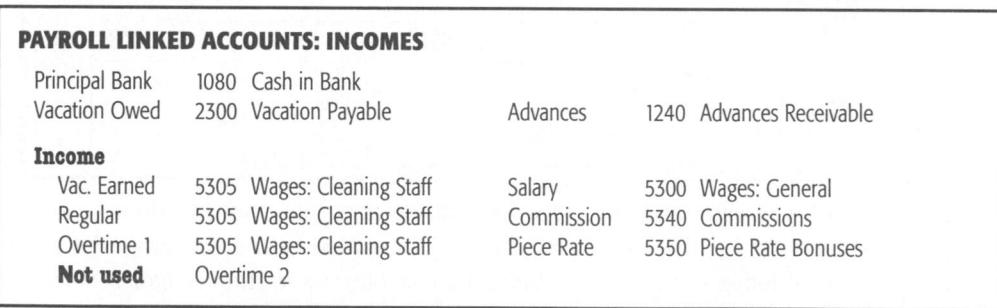

PAYROLL LINKED ACCOUNTS: INCOMES

Principal Bank	1080	Cash in Bank			
Vacation Owed	2300	Vacation Payable	Advances	1240	Advances Receivable
Income					
Vac. Earned	5305	Wages: Cleaning Staff	Salary	5300	Wages: General
Regular	5305	Wages: Cleaning Staff	Commission	5340	Commissions
Overtime 1	5305	Wages: Cleaning Staff	Piece Rate	5350	Piece Rate Bonuses
Not used		Overtime 2			

> **Click**   **Incomes** under the Linked Accounts subheading:

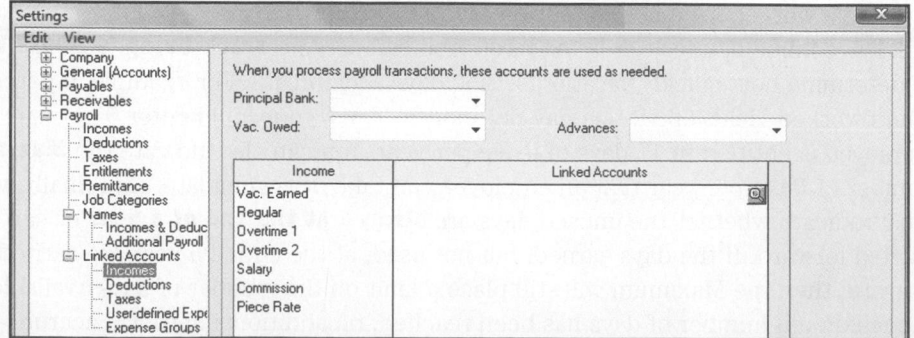

The linked accounts for all types of income appear together on this first screen. You must identify a wage account for each type of employee payment used by the company, even if the same account is used for all of them. Once the Payroll bank account is

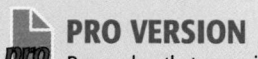

identified as the same one used for Payables, the program will apply a single sequence of cheque numbers for all cheques prepared from the Payables and Payroll journals.

Accounts you can use for more than one link will be available in the drop-down list. Otherwise, once an account is selected as a linked account, it is removed from the list.

To enter accounts, you can **type** the **account number** or **select** the **account** from the drop-down list and **press** (tab) to advance to the next linked account field, just as you did to enter the linked accounts for Dorfmann.

Choose 1080 Cash in Bank for the Principal Bank field.

Choose 2300 Vacation Payable for the Vacation field.

Choose 1240 Advances Receivable for the Advances field.

Choose 5305 Wages: Cleaning Staff for Vacation Earned, Regular and Overtime 1.

Choose 5300 Wages: General for Salary.

Choose 5340 Commissions for Commission.

Choose 5350 Piece Rate Bonuses for Piece Rate.

The following linked accounts are used for payroll deductions:

PAYROLL LINKED ACCOUNTS: DEDUCTIONS			
RRSP	2410 RRSP Payable	MSP-Employee	2400 MSP Payable - Employee

Click Deductions under Linked Accounts to see the next set of accounts:

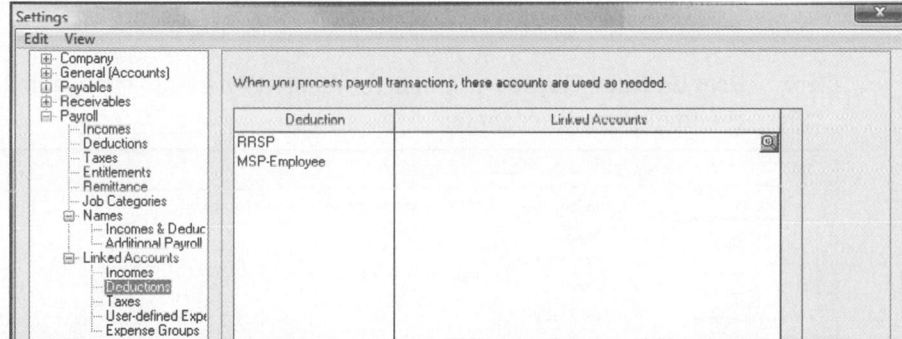

The names here are the ones you entered in the Names: Incomes & Deductions screen. If you deleted a name, it will not appear here.

Enter the **linked accounts** for **RRSP** and **MSP-Employee** from the chart above.

The following linked accounts are used for payroll taxes:

PAYROLL LINKED ACCOUNTS: TAXES					
Payables			**Expenses**		
EI	2310	EI Payable	EI	5310	EI Expense
CPP	2320	CPP Payable	CPP	5320	CPP Expense
Tax	2330	Income Tax Payable	WCB	5330	WCB Expense
WCB	2460	WCB Payable			
Not used	EHT, Tax (Que.), QPP, QHSF, QPIP		**Not used**	EHT, QPP, QHSF, QPIP	

NOTES
The deleted income and deduction names do not appear on the screens for linked accounts. Deleting the unused names also simplifies the data entry for linked accounts.

NOTES
You can add accounts from the Linked Accounts windows. Type a new number, press (enter) and choose to add the account.

Click   **Taxes** under Linked Accounts to see the next set of linked accounts:

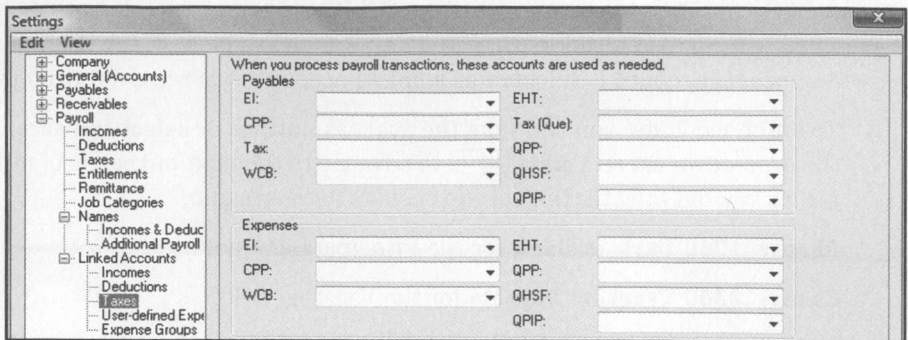

When the employer pays the tax, linked payable and expense accounts are needed. Only the employee pays the income tax, so only the payable linked account is needed. This tax does not create an employer expense. For EI and CPP, employee contributions are added to those of the employer to calculate the total amount payable.

Enter   the **linked payables accounts** for **EI**, **CPP**, **Tax** and **WCB** in the Payables section and the **linked expense accounts** for **EI**, **CPP** and **WCB** in the Expenses section from the chart on the previous page.

The following linked accounts are used for the user-defined expenses:

PAYROLL LINKED ACCOUNTS: USER-DEFINED EXPENSES					
Payables			**Expenses**		
Travel Allow	2420	Travel Allowances Payable	Travel Allow	5360	Travel Allowances
Tuition Fees	2430	Tuition Fees Payable	Tuition Fees	5380	Tuition Fees Expense
MSP-Employer	2440	MSP Payable - Employer	MSP-Employer	5400	MSP Premium Expense

Click   **User-Defined Expenses** under the Linked Accounts subheading to see the final Payroll accounts:

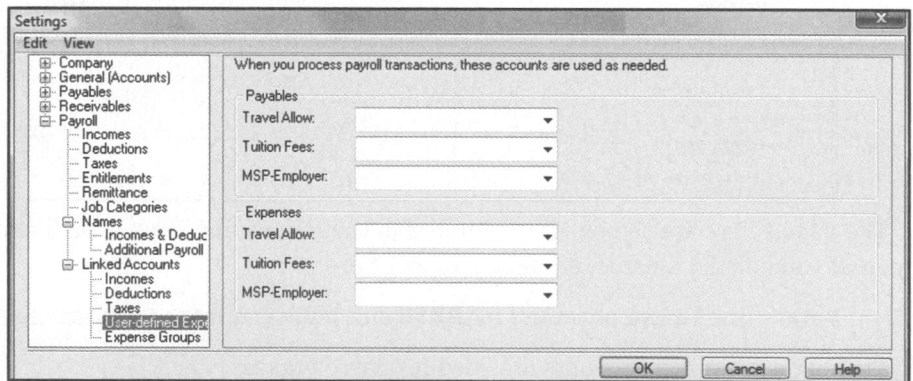

Enter   the **linked payable accounts** for **Travel Allow**, **Tuition Fees** and **MSP-Employer** from the chart above on this page.

Enter   the **linked expense accounts** for **Travel Allow**, **Tuition Fees** and **MSP-Employer** from the chart above on this page.

Check   the **linked** payroll **accounts** against the charts on pages 324–326 before proceeding. **Click** each **heading** under Linked Accounts to see the different screens.

Click   **OK** to save the Settings changes and return to the Payroll Home window:

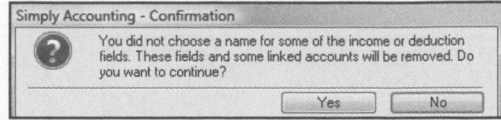

Because we deleted some income and deduction names, we are being warned that any accounts linked to these deleted fields will also be removed. We can proceed.

Click   **Yes** to open a second confirmation message:

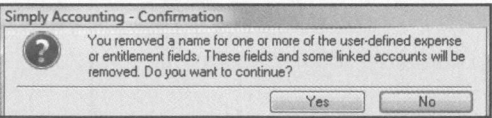

Again, we are warned because of the additional field names we deleted.

Click   **Yes** to continue and return to the Payroll Home window.

Entering Employee Ledger Records

Use the Lime Light Laundry Employee Information Sheet, Employee Profiles and Additional Payroll Information on pages 312 315 to create the employee records and add historical information.

We will enter the information for Lime Light Laundry employee Clyne Fretton.

Click   the **Employees icon** in the Home window.

The Employees icon window opens:

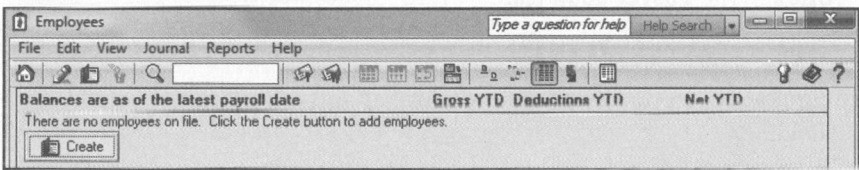

The Employees icon window is blank because no employees are on file at this stage.

Click   the **Create button** or **choose** the **File menu** and **click Create**.

You can also choose Add Employee from the Employees icon shortcuts list, as shown below, to bypass the Employees window and open the new employee ledger window:

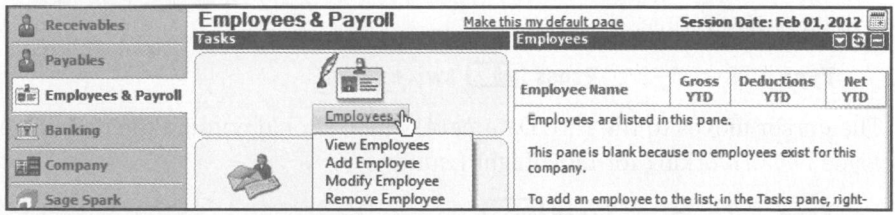

Entering Personal Details

The Payroll Ledger new employee information form will open so you can begin to enter the employee record. There are several required fields in the employee ledger records because this information links to government income tax tables and rules.

The opening page holds the personal details for the employee that you can change at any time.

NOTES

If you skip the Employees icon window (Setup menu, User Preferences, View screen) you will see the Payroll Ledger window immediately when you click the Employees icon.

You will also skip the Employees window if you use the Add Employee shortcut.

NOTES

The Set Field Names tool in the ledger window will open the Payroll Settings Additional Names screen.

NOTES

As in other ledgers, required fields that you cannot leave blank are marked with *.

On the Address tab screen, the employee name and the date of birth are essential. All other fields can be completed later.

NOTES

The program will allow you to omit the Social Insurance Number but you must enter the employee's date of birth. The SIN can be added later. The date of birth is required because it determines whether CPP will be deducted.

NOTES

The termination date and reason for leaving a job will determine the employee's eligibility to collect Employment Insurance. Refer to page 297.

You will see the Personal information tab screen:

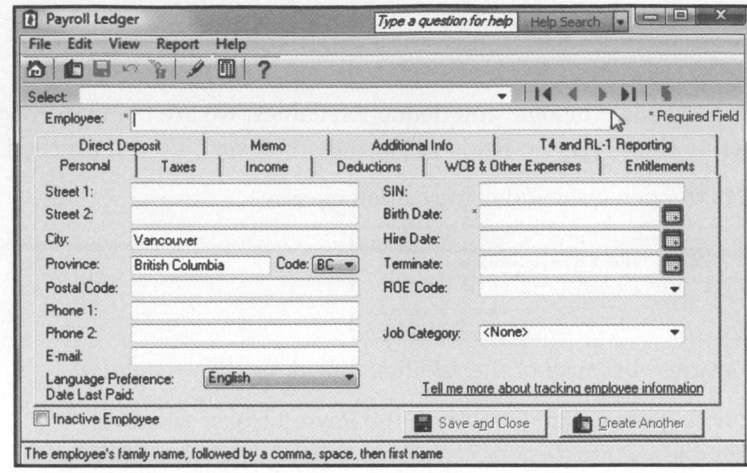

The Payroll Ledger has a large number of tabs for the different kinds of payroll information. The cursor is in the Employee field, ready for you to enter information. If you enter the surname first, your employee lists will be in correct alphabetic order.

Type   Fretton, Clyne **Press** (tab).

The cursor advances to the Street 1 field.

Type   21 Spotter St.

The default city, province and province code, those for the business, are correct.

Click   the **Postal Code field**.

Type   v3k4k2 **Press** (tab).

The program corrects the postal code format and advances the cursor to the Phone 1 field.

Type   6046937595 **Press** (tab) to see the corrected phone number format.

The default **Language Preference** is correctly set as English.

Click   the **Social Insurance Number (SIN) field**. You must use a valid SIN.

Type   218738631 **Press** (tab).

The cursor advances to the Birth Date field. Enter the month, day and year using any accepted date format.

Type   8-15-81 **Press** (tab) **twice**.

The cursor moves to the Hire Date field, which should contain the date when the employee began working for Lime Light Laundry.

Type   2-7-06 **Press** (tab).

The next two fields will be used when the employee leaves the job — the date of termination and the reason for leaving that you can select from the drop-down list. The final option designates employees as active or inactive. All employees at Lime Light Laundry are active, so the default selection is correct.

Job Categories are used to identify salespersons who can be linked to specific sales so that their sales revenue is tracked and used to calculate commissions. The employee's Job Category can be selected here if categories are already set up, or you can place employees in categories when you create the categories. We will create categories later and assign employees to them at that stage.

When you use Simply Accounting to pay employees, the Date Last Paid will be entered automatically by the program.

The remaining details for the employee are entered on the other tab screens.

Entering Tax Information

Click   the **Taxes tab** to advance to the next set of employee details:

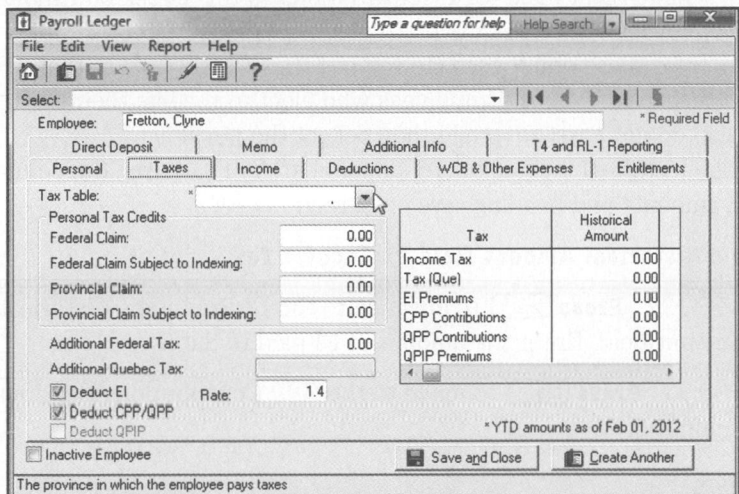

This screen allows you to enter income tax–related information for an employee, including the historical amounts for the year to date.

> **Click**   the **Tax Table list arrow**. A list of provinces and territories appears on the screen. This is a required field.

> **Click**   **British Columbia**, the province of taxation for Lime Light Laundry for income tax purposes

> **Press**   (*tab*) to advance to the **Federal Claim** field, which holds the total claim for personal tax credits.

> **Type**   20764 **Press** (*tab*) to advance to the next field.

The **Federal Claim Subject To Indexing** is the amount of personal claim minus pension and tuition/education amounts.

> For **Sissler**, enter **10382** in this field.

> **Type**   20764 **Press** (*tab*) to advance to the Provincial Claim field.

Provincial personal income taxes are not linked to the rates for federal income taxes so separate **provincial claim** amounts are needed.

> **Type**   20653 **Press** (*tab*).

> **Type**   20653 **Press** (*tab*) to enter the Provincial Claim Amount Subject To Indexing.

> For **Sissler**, enter **11000** in this field.

The cursor advances to the **Additional Federal Tax** field.

When an employee has chosen to have additional federal income tax deducted from each paycheque, you enter the amount of the deduction in the **Additional Fed. Tax** field. Employees might make this choice if they receive regular additional income from which no tax is deducted. By making this choice, they avoid paying a large amount of tax at the end of the year and possible interest penalties. Fretton is the only employee with other income who chooses to have additional taxes withheld.

> **Type** 100

If an employee is insurable by EI, you must leave the box for **Deduct EI** checked. The default EI contribution factor, 1.4, for Lime Light Laundry is correct. We entered it in the Payroll Taxes Settings window (page 323).

All employees at Lime Light make CPP contributions so this check box should remain selected. Employees under 18 or over 70 years of age do not contribute to CPP, so clicking the option for these employees (to remove the ✓) will ensure that CPP is not deducted from their paycheques. Employees who elect to receive their CPP payments earlier also do not pay CPP while they collect the pension.

We will enter the historical income tax amounts next. You can drag the column margins so that all amounts and headings are on-screen.

> **Click** the **Historical Amount field** for **Income Tax**.
>
> **Type** 398.92 **Press** (tab) to advance to the EI Premiums Historical Amount field. Enter the amount of EI paid to date.
>
> **Type** 68.97 **Press** (tab) to move to the CPP Contributions Historical Amount field.
>
> **Type** 164.75

Entering Income Amounts

We defined all the types of income for Lime Light Laundry when we set up Names (see page 318). All the details you need to complete the Income tab chart are on pages 312–313. The following list summarizes the types of income used by each employee. Not all will be used on all paycheques.

- Advance and Benefits: all employees (see Notes)
- Vac. Owed and Vac. Paid: all hourly paid employees (see Notes)
- Regular: four hourly paid employees — Fretton, Durtee, Landings, Sissler
- Overtime 1: four hourly paid employees — Fretton, Durtee, Landings, Sissler
- Piece Rate: four hourly paid employees — Fretton, Durtee, Landings, Sissler
- Salary: three salaried employees — Brumes, Tran, Houseman
- Commission: Brumes

> **Click** the **Income tab** to open the next screen of employee details:

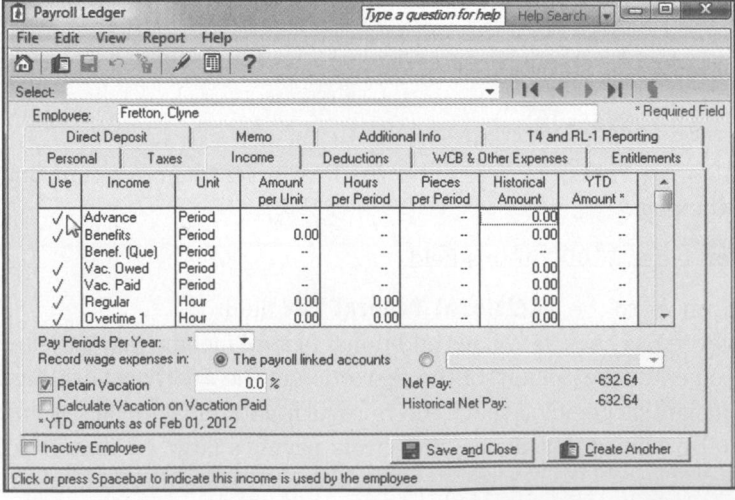

NOTES
These historical details are needed because there are yearly maximum amounts for CPP and EI contributions. Totals for optional deductions are also retained in the employee record.

NOTES
The program skips the Quebec tax fields because British Columbia was selected as the province of taxation and no linked accounts were entered for the Quebec taxes.

NOTES
In the chart on pages 312–313, the incomes that are used by an employee have a ✓ or an amount in the employee's column.

NOTES
Checkmarks are added by default for all incomes, deductions and expenses that have linked accounts entered for them.
The checkmarks for Advance, Benefits, Vacation Owed and Vacation Paid cannot be removed.

WARNING!
Enter employee historical payroll details carefully. You will be unable to edit these fields after finishing the history or after making Payroll Journal entries for the employee.
They must also be correct because they are used to create T4s for tax reporting.

On the Income chart you can indicate the types of income that each employee receives (the **Use** column), the usual rate of pay for that type of income (**Amount Per Unit**), the usual number of hours worked (**Hours Per Period**), the usual number of units for a piece rate pay base (**Pieces Per Period**) and the amounts received this year before the earliest transaction date or the date used for the first paycheque (**Historical Amount**). The **Year-To-Date (YTD) Amount** is added automatically by the program based on the historical amounts you enter and the paycheques entered in the program.

Checkmarks should be entered in the Use column so that the fields are available in the payroll journals, even if they will not be used on all paycheques.

We need to add the historical advances, benefits and vacation amounts for Fretton. Fretton has $200 in advances not yet repaid, and she has not received all the vacation pay she has earned. The total of the advance and vacation owed amounts for all employees must match the opening General Ledger balances for the corresponding linked accounts.

No employees have received vacation pay this year. If they have, you enter the amount in the **Vac. Paid** field. Vacation pay not yet received is entered in the **Vac. Owed** field. Any advances paid to the employees and not yet repaid are recorded in the **Advance Historical Amount** field. There is no record of advance amounts recovered.

Click   the **Historical Amount column beside Advance** to move the cursor.

Type   200 **Press** ⌜tab⌟ to move to the Benefits Amount Per Unit column.

The provincial medical premiums paid by the employer are employee benefits.

Type   23.54 **Press** ⌜tab⌟ to move to the Historical Amount for Benefits.

Type   47.08 **Press** ⌜tab⌟ to advance to the Vac. Owed Historical Amount.

Type   564.98 **Press** ⌜tab⌟ to advance to the Historical Vac. Paid Amount.

Press   ⌜tab⌟ again to advance to the **Use column for Regular**.

Press   ⌜tab⌟ to advance to the Amount Per Unit field where we need to enter the regular hourly wage rate.

Type   18

Press   ⌜tab⌟ to advance to the Hours Per Period field.

Bi-weekly paid employees usually work 80 hours per period. You can change the amount in the Payroll journals. Salaried workers normally work 150 hours each month.

Type   80 **Press** ⌜tab⌟ to advance to the Historical Amount field.

Historical income and deduction amounts for the year to date are necessary so that taxes and deductions can be calculated correctly and T4 statements will be accurate.

Type   2880 **Press** ⌜tab⌟.

The amount is entered automatically in the YTD column and the cursor advances to the Use column for Overtime 1.

Press   ⌜tab⌟ so you can enter the overtime hourly rate.

Type   27

Press   ⌜tab⌟ **twice** to advance to the Historical Amount field. There is no regular number of overtime hours.

Type   54 **Press** ⌜tab⌟ to advance to the Overtime 2 Use column.

The next three income types do not apply to Fretton so they should not be checked. The next income that applies is Piece Rate, the piece rate method of pay. We need to enter the rate or amount per unit (set) and the historical amount. There is no fixed amount per unit or period for Piece Rate.

If no linked account is entered for an income, the Use column will be blank.

Click   the **Use column beside Salary** to remove the ✓.

Click   the **Use column beside Commission** to remove the ✓.

Click   **Piece Rate** in the Income column to select the line. **Press** ⸨tab⸩.

Type   0.10 to enter the amount received for each set. **Press** ⸨tab⸩ **twice**.

Type   189 to enter the historical amount.

For **Tran** and **Houseman**, click the Use column for Regular, Overtime 1, Commission and Piece Rate to remove the ✓. Enter the monthly salary and press ⸨tab⸩. Enter 150 as the number of hours worked in the pay period for Houseman and 80 for Tran. Press ⸨tab⸩ and enter the historical amount. You cannot remove the ✓ for Vac. Owed and Vac. Paid, even if they are not used.

For **Brumes**, repeat these steps but leave Commission checked and enter $390 as the historical amount.

Pay Periods Per Year refers to the number of times the employee is paid, or the pay cycle. This is a required field. Fretton is paid every two weeks, 26 times per year.

Click   the **list arrow** beside the field **for Pay Periods Per Year**:

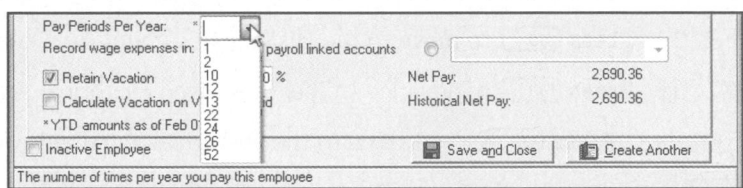

Click   **26**.

Retaining Vacation pay is normal for full-time hourly paid employees. Part-time and casual workers often receive their vacation pay with each paycheque because their work schedule is irregular. You will turn the option to retain vacation off when an employee receives the vacation pay, either when taking a vacation or when leaving the company (see page 284). If the employee is salaried and does not receive vacation pay, the option should also be turned off. For employees who receive vacation pay, leave the option to Retain Vacation checked and type the vacation pay rate in the % field.

Double click the **% field beside Retain Vacation**.

Type   6

For **Brumes**, **Tran** and **Houseman**, click Retain Vacation to remove the ✓.

Employee wages may be linked to the default expense account or to another expense account that you can select from the drop-down list. Wage expenses for all Lime Light Laundry employees are linked to the default accounts entered on pages 324–325.

Entering Payroll Deduction Amounts

The next step is to enter current and historical details for deductions, just as we did for income. You must indicate which deductions apply to the employee (Use column), the amount normally deducted and the historical amount — the amount deducted to date this year.

Click   the **Deductions tab** to open the screen for payroll deductions:

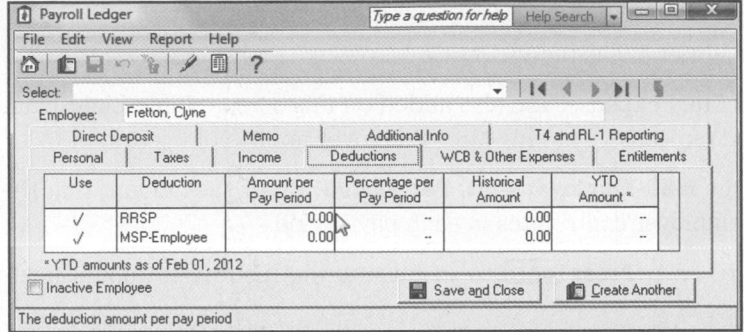

Both deductions are selected in the Use column (a ✓ is entered).

By entering deductions here, they will be included automatically on the Payroll Journal input forms. Otherwise, you must enter them manually in the Journal for each pay period. Not all employees make RRSP contributions at this time, but they have done so in the past, so we will leave this field available. When you enter the amounts here, the deductions are made automatically, but changes can still be made in the journals. You should make permanent changes by editing the employee ledger record. Fretton does not currently have RRSP contributions withheld from her pay.

> If you choose to calculate deductions as a percentage of gross pay in the Payroll Settings, the Percentage Per Pay Period fields will be available.

Click   **MSP-Employee** in the Deduction column to select the line.

Press   (tab). You should enter the amount that is withheld in each pay period.

Type   23.54 **Press** (tab) to advance to the Historical Amount field.

Type   47.08 **Press** (tab) to update the YTD Amount.

The remaining deductions are not used by Lime Light Laundry. The names were deleted so they do not appear on the chart.

Entering WCB and Other Expenses

In other provinces, the tab label will be changed to match the name used for WCB in that province. Ontario uses the name WSIB — Workplace Safety and Insurance Board — instead of WCB, so the tab label will be WSIB & Other Expenses for businesses in Ontario.

Click   the **WCB & Other Expenses tab**:

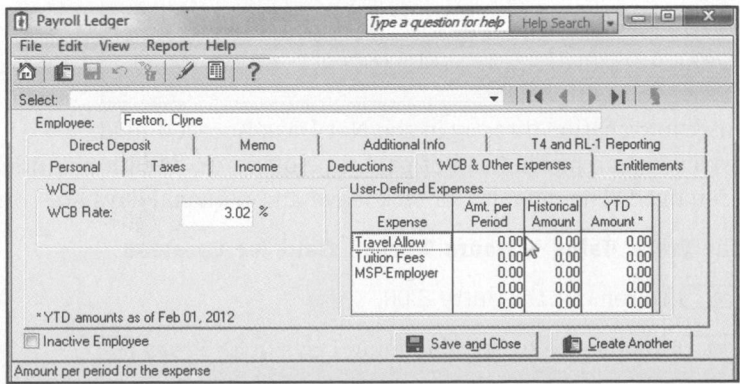

The user-defined expenses we created in the Additional Payroll Names screen (page 319) and the default WCB rate (page 323) are entered on this screen. The default

WCB rate is entered from our setup information, but you can enter a different rate for an individual employee in this field. The rate is correct for Fretton.

For **Tran**, enter 5.0 as the WCB rate.

Other user-defined expenses are also added on this screen. Lime Light Laundry has three user-defined expenses, but only MSP-Employer applies to Fretton now.

> **Click**   the **MSP-Employer Amt. Per Period**. Enter the amount that the employer contributes in each pay period.
>
> **Type**   23.54   **Press** (tab) to advance to the Historical Amount field.
>
> **Type**   47.08

For **Sissler**, enter **25** as the Tuition Fees Amt. Per Period and **100** as the Historical Amount.

For **Brumes**, enter **300** as the Travel Allow Amt. Per Period and **300** as the Historical Amount.

The remaining expenses are not used by Lime Light Laundry.

Entering Entitlements

We entered the default rates and amounts for entitlements as Payroll Settings (page 323), but they can be modified in the ledger records for individual employees.

We must also enter the historical information for entitlements. This historical number will include any days carried forward from the previous periods. The number of days accrued cannot be greater than the maximum number of days defined for the entitlement for an employee. The number of Net Days Accrued, the amount unused and available for carrying forward, is updated automatically from the historical information and current payroll journal entries.

> **Click**   the **Entitlements tab**:

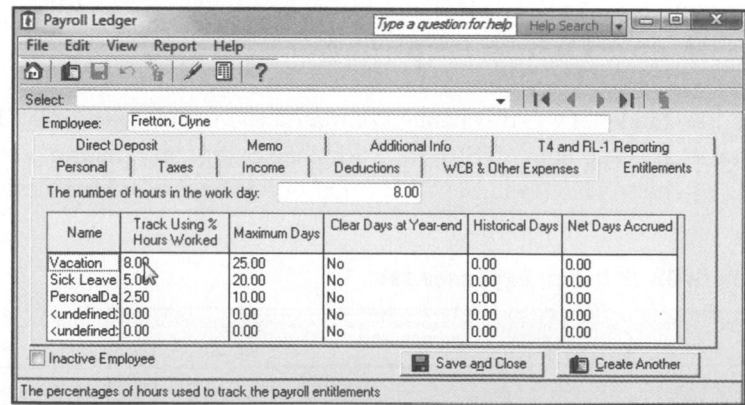

You cannot enter information directly in the Net Days Accrued field.

Fretton receives vacation pay instead of paid time off so the vacation entitlements details should be removed. The defaults for sick leave and personal days are correct.

> **Click**   the **Track Using % Hours Worked field for Vacation**.
>
> **Press**   (del) to remove the entry 8.00.
>
> **Press**   (tab) to advance to the Maximum Days field. **Press** (del).
>
> **Click**   the **Historical Days field for Sick Leave**.
>
> **Type**   7

Press   ↓ to advance to the Historical Days field for PersonalDays. The number of days is added to the Net Days Accrued.

Type   3 **Press** (tab) to enter the amount.

For Brumes, Tran and Houseman, the default entries for tracking and maximum days are correct, but you must enter the Historical Days for each entitlement.

Entering Direct Deposit Information

Click   the **Direct Deposit tab:**

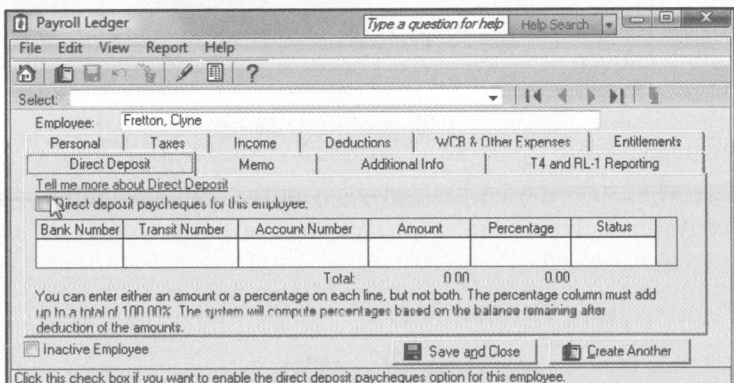

Four employees have elected to have their paycheques deposited directly to their bank accounts. On this screen, we need to enter the bank account details. For each employee who has elected the Direct Deposit option, you must turn on the selection in the Direct Deposit Paycheques For This Employee check box. Then you must add the three-digit **Bank Number**, five-digit **Transit Number**, the bank **Account Number** and finally the amount that is deposited, or the percentage of the cheque. Fretton has chosen the direct deposit option for 100 percent of her net pay.

Click   the **Direct Deposit Paycheques For This Employee check box** to add a ✓.

Click   the **Bank Number field.**

Type   300 **Press** (tab) to advance to the Transit Number field.

Type   49921 **Press** (tab) to advance to the Account Number field.

Type   2883912 **Press** (tab) **twice** to advance to the Percentage field.

Type   100

Click   the **Memo tab:**

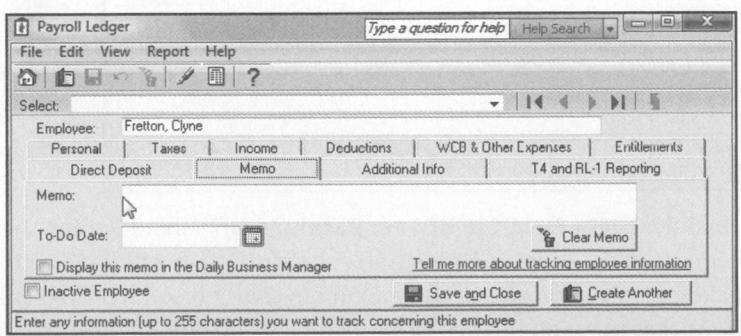

The Memo tab will not be used at this time. You could enter a note with a reminder date to appear in the Daily Business Manager, for example, a reminder to issue vacation paycheques on a specific date or to recover advances.

NOTES

If employees take days before the sufficient number of hours worked have been accrued, the program will warn you. Then you can allow the entry for entitlements or not. This permission is similar to allowing clients to exceed their credit limits.

NOTES

All banks in Canada are assigned a three-digit bank number and each branch has a unique five-digit transit number. Account numbers may vary from five to twelve digits.

NOTES

The paycheque deposit may be split among more than one bank account by entering different percentages for the accounts.

To delete bank account details, change the employee's Direct Deposit Status to Inactive and then delete the bank information. Click the check box for Direct Deposit Paycheques to remove the ✓. Then reset the employee's status to Active.

NOTES

The Daily Business Manager is covered in Chapter 11.

Entering Additional Information

Lime Light Laundry enters emergency contacts for each employee.

Click   the **Additional Info tab** to access the additional fields:

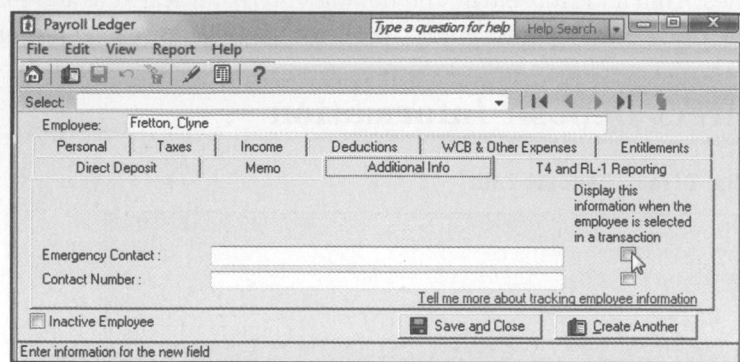

You can indicate whether you want to display any of the additional information when the employee is selected in a transaction. We do not need to display the contact information in the Payroll Journal.

Click   the **Emergency Contact field**.

Type   Aidan Fretton **Press** ⟨tab⟩ **twice**.

Type   (604) 497-1469 to enter the contact's phone number.

Entering T4 and RL-1 Reporting Amounts

The next information screen allows you to enter the year-to-date EI insurable and pensionable earnings. By adding the historical amounts, the T4 slips prepared for income taxes at the end of the year and the record of employment termination reports will also be correct.

Click   the **T4 and RL-1 Reporting tab** to open the final screen:

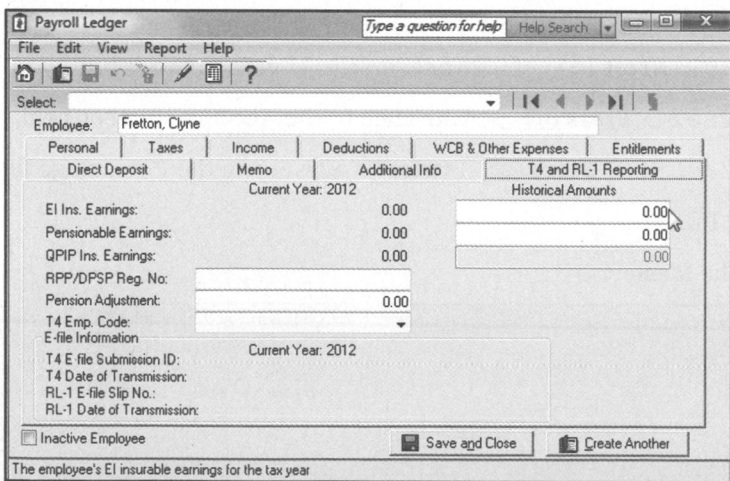

In the **Historical Amounts field for EI Ins. Earnings**, you should enter the total earned income received to date that is EI insurable. The program will update this total every time you make payroll entries until the maximum salary on which EI is calculated has been reached. At that time, no further EI premiums will be deducted.

Pensionable Earnings — the total of all income plus benefits — are also tracked by the program. This amount determines the total income that is eligible for Canada Pension Plan. The Pension Adjustment amount is used when the employee has a workplace pension program that will affect the allowable contributions for personal registered pension plans and will be linked with the Canada Pension Plan. Workplace pension income is reduced when the employee also has income from the Canada Pension Plan. Since Lime Light Laundry has no company pension plan, the Pension Adjustment amount is zero and no pension plan registration number is needed.

The T4 Employee Code applies to a small number of job types that have special income tax rules.

> **Double click** the **Historical Amounts field for EI Ins. Earnings**.
>
> **Type**   3123
>
> **Double click** the **Historical Amounts field for Pensionable Earnings field**.
>
> **Type**   3170.08
>
> **Correct** any employee information **errors** by returning to the field with the error. **Highlight** the **error** and **enter** the **correct information**. **Click each tab** in turn so that you can check all the information.

When all the information is entered correctly, you must save the employee record.

> **Click**   **Create Another** to save the record and to open a new blank employee information form.
>
> **Click**   the **Personal tab** so that you can enter address information.
>
> **Repeat** these procedures to **enter** other employee **records** using the information on pages 312–315.
>
> **Click**   **Save And Close** Save and Close after entering the last record to save the record and close the Payroll Ledger.
>
> **Do not finish** the **history** if you are prompted to do so at this stage.

Only the *Advances Receivable* and *Vacation Payable* amounts must match before you can finish the history. Other amounts that are not verified may be incorrect and you will be unable to change them after finishing the history.

> **Close**   the **Employees window** to return to the Home window.
>
> **Display** or **print** the **Employee List** and the **Employee Summary Report** to check the accuracy of your work.

Setting Up Payroll Remittances

Because we have entered all payroll settings and all suppliers, we can enter the final settings — for payroll remittances and job categories. Entering remittance settings involves three steps: identifying the suppliers who receive payroll remittance amounts, linking the suppliers to the taxes or deductions they receive, and entering opening dates and balances. First, we should designate the suppliers that are payroll authorities.

Identifying Payroll Authorities

The chart on the following page identifies the payroll authorities and the balances owing as at February 1. Balances are those shown in the Trial Balance on page 310.

⚠ WARNING!
When you close the payroll ledger after entering the last hourly employee, or after all employees, you may see the message that the payroll history is balanced, asking if you want to finish the history now. Choose No. Do not finish the history until you have printed your reports to check all the historical and current amounts.

📄 NOTES
If you started from the Add Employee shortcut, you will return directly to the Payroll Home window.

PAYROLL AUTHORITIES

Supplier	Payroll Liability	Balance Date	Balance Forward
BC Minister of Finance	MSP-Employee	Feb. 1, 2012	296.28
	MSP-Employer	Feb. 1, 2012	296.28
BC Workers' Compensation Board	WCB	Feb. 1, 2012	678.97
Receiver General for Canada	EI	Feb. 1, 2012	1 022.80
	CPP	Feb. 1, 2012	2 090.94
	Tax	Feb. 1, 2012	3 054.53
Victoria Trust	RRSP	Feb. 1, 2012	200.00

Click   **Payables** in the Modules pane list.

Click   **BC Minister of Finance** in the Suppliers pane list in the Payables window to open this supplier's record:

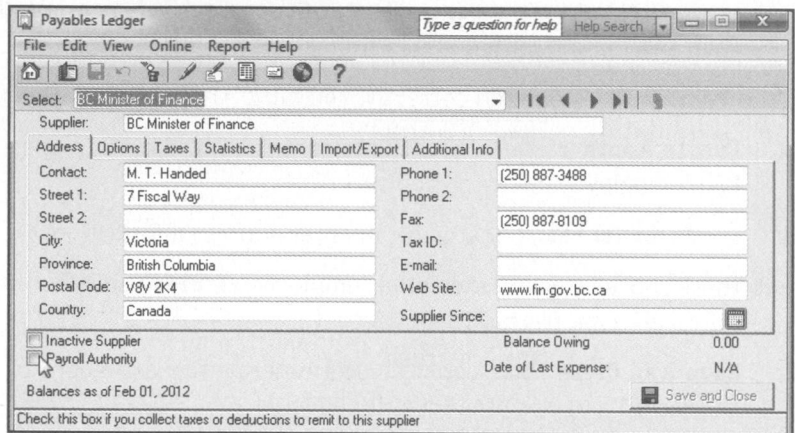

Click   **Payroll Authority** to add the ✓ and change the supplier's payroll status.

Click   the **Next Supplier tool** ▶ **twice** to access the record for the BC Workers' Compensation Board, the next payroll authority. Or,

Click   the **Select list arrow** and **click BC Workers' Compensation Board**.

Click   **Payroll Authority** to add the ✓ and change the supplier's payroll status.

Repeat   these **steps** for the remaining payroll authorities: **Receiver General for Canada** and **Victoria Trust**.

Close   the **Payables Ledger** to return to the Payables Home window.

Linking Remittances to Suppliers

Click   the **Settings icon** [Settings] to open the Payables Settings screen.

Click   **Payroll** and then **click Remittance** to open the screen we need:

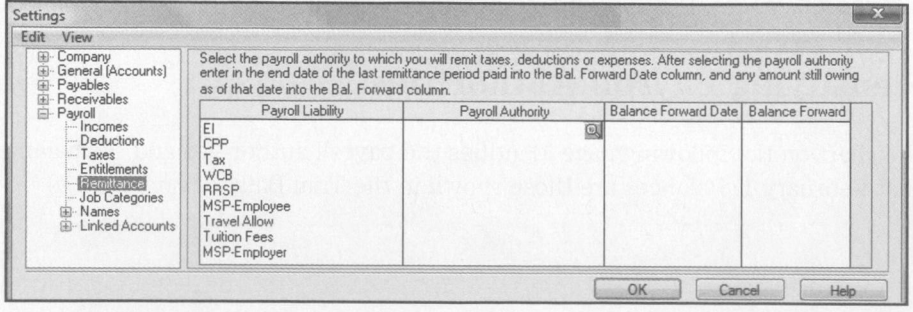

All the payroll items that are linked to liability (remittance) accounts are listed: taxes, deductions and user-defined expenses. For each liability, we can select a supplier and enter the balance forward date and amount.

Click   the **List icon**  in the Payroll Authority column on the line for EI to see the list of suppliers we marked as Payroll Authorities:

Click   **Receiver General for Canada**.

Click   **Select** or **press** (enter) to return to the Remittance Settings screen.

The Receiver General for Canada appears beside EI. The cursor advances to the Balance Forward Date field for EI. We need to enter the balances owing at the time we are converting the data to Simply Accounting and the pay period covered by those amounts. These balances are in the Trial Balance on page 310 and the chart on page 338. The effective date is February 1 for all liabilities.

Type   Feb 1 **Press** (tab) to advance to the Balance Forward field.

Type   1022.80 **Press** (tab) to advance to the Payroll Authority field for CPP.

Enter   the remaining **Payroll Authorities**, **dates** and **balances** from page 338.

<aside>
NOTES
You can also double click the supplier's name to add it to the Settings screen.
If you type the first few letters of the name and then press (tab), the Select Supplier list will have the supplier you need selected. Press (enter) to add the name to the Settings screen.
</aside>

Entering Job Categories

Job categories can be used to identify salespersons and to organize reports.

Click   **Job Categories**:

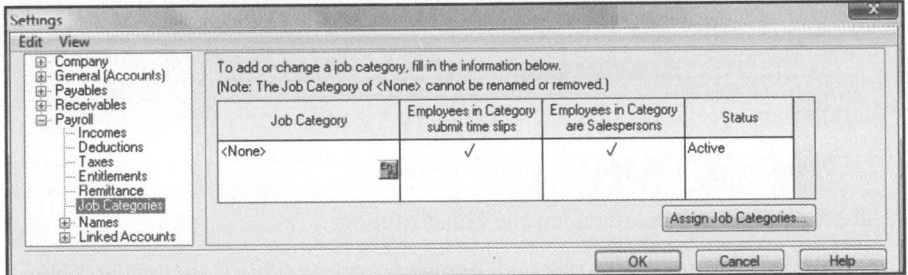

On the Job Categories screen, you enter the names of the categories and indicate whether the employees in each category submit time slips and whether they are salespersons. Categories may be active or inactive. We need a new category called Sales.

Notice that if you do not create categories, the employees in the default selection <None> are salespersons so they can be selected in the Sales Journal.

Click   the **Job Category field below <None>**.

Type   Sales **Press** (tab) to add checkmarks to the next two columns and set the status to Active.

Click   the **Job Category field below Sales**.

Type   Other **Press** (tab) to add the checkmarks.

<aside>
PRO VERSION
The column for Submit Time Slips is not available in the Pro version. It applies to Time & Billing, a Premium feature.
</aside>

The Other category does not apply to sales or time slips so we need to change the settings. Employees in the Other category will not appear in the Salesperson field on sales invoices. We should remove the ✓s for them.

Click   the ✓ in the column Employees In Category Submit Time Slips.

Click   the ✓ in the column Employees In Category Are Salespersons.

Click   **Sales** in the Job Category list.

Click   **Assign Job Categories** to change the screen:

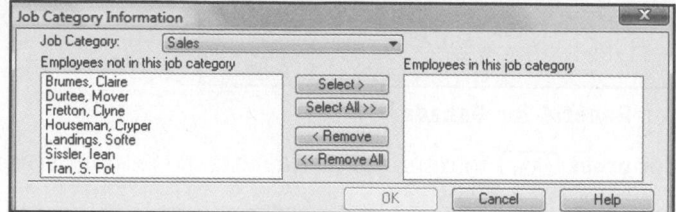

The screen is updated with employee names. Initially all are Employees Not In This Job Category.

You can add employee names to the category by choosing an employee and clicking **Select** or by choosing **Select All**. Once employees are in a category (the column on the right), you can remove them by selecting an employee and clicking **Remove** or clicking **Remove All** to move all names at the same time.

Click   **Brumes** and then **click Select** to place her in the Sales category:

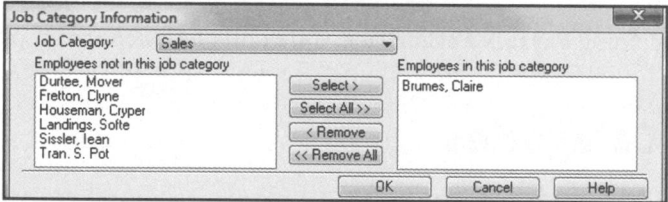

Choose   **Other** from the Job Category drop-down list:

Notice that <None> is one of the category list choices.

Press   `tab` to add the employee names.

All employees are listed as Not In This Category.

Click   **Select All** to place all names on the In This Category list. Now we need to remove Brumes' name from this list.

Click   **Brumes** and then **click Remove** to remove her from the Other category:

Click   **OK** to save the information and return to the Settings screen.

Changing Payroll Form Settings

Before closing the setting screens, we still need to enter the form number to set up the automatic numbering of direct deposit slips.

Click   **Company** and then **click Forms** to see the number setup screen:

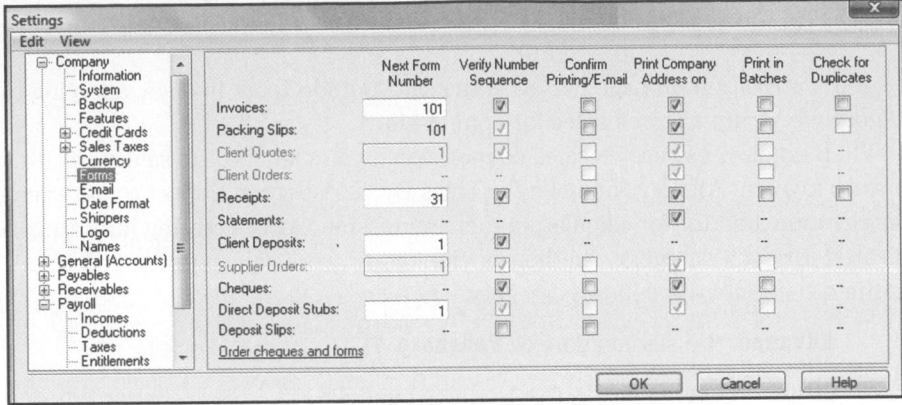

Click the **Direct Deposit Stubs Next Form Number field**.

Type 48

Click the **Check For Duplicates check boxes** if these are not yet checked.

Click **OK** to save the change and return to the Home window.

Finishing Payroll History

Once the setup is complete, we can back up the data file and finish the payroll history. Like the other modules, you can use the payroll journals before finishing the history. However, the automatic payroll calculation feature will be turned off. Therefore, we should finish the history first. We can also check the data integrity as we did for Dorfmann to see if there are any data inconsistencies that we need to correct.

> **Choose** the **Maintenance menu** and **click Check Data Integrity**.

Two control accounts are used for the Payroll Ledger. The *Advances Receivable* General Ledger account balance must equal the advances paid (the total of all historical employee amounts) and the *Vacation Payable* balance must equal the total of all vacation owed amounts in the ledgers. Employees Historical Information should be Balanced.

> **Click** **OK** to close the Data Integrity window.

If corrections are necessary, compare your amounts with the ones on pages 312–313 and modify the employee ledger records.

Once we finish the history, we cannot change any historical amounts. Therefore, we should prepare a backup first.

> **Back up** the **data file**. Refer to page 250 if necessary.

> **Choose** the **History menu** and **click Enter Historical Information** and **Payroll** as shown:

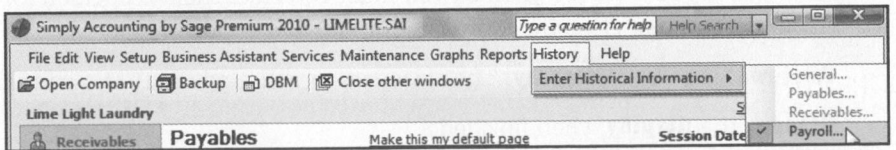

When we added the Payroll module, the History menu became available again, but only for this module — the other module names are dimmed because the history for them is finished. When you finish the Payroll history, the Home window has all modules in the finished history state. You are now ready to enter transactions.

Adding Salespersons to Sales Invoices

The first transaction on page 343 adds the salesperson to an invoice, applying the job category we set up to track sales for commissions.

When employees receive sales commissions, you can add the salesperson's name to the sales invoice. You can then use the Sales By Salesperson Report to determine the sales revenue amount for calculating the commission. After creating job categories, we indicated for each category whether its employees were salespersons and then identified the employees in the category.

Advance the session date to **February 7**.

Click   **Receivables** in the Modules pane list.

Click   the **Client Invoices icon** to open the Revenues (Sales) Journal.

Choose   **Capilano Centre Hotel** as the client.

Enter   **Feb 2, 2012** as the invoice date.

Enter   a **description** for the sale.

Enter   **2900** as the invoice amount.

Click   the **Salesperson list arrow** to see the list of salespersons as shown:

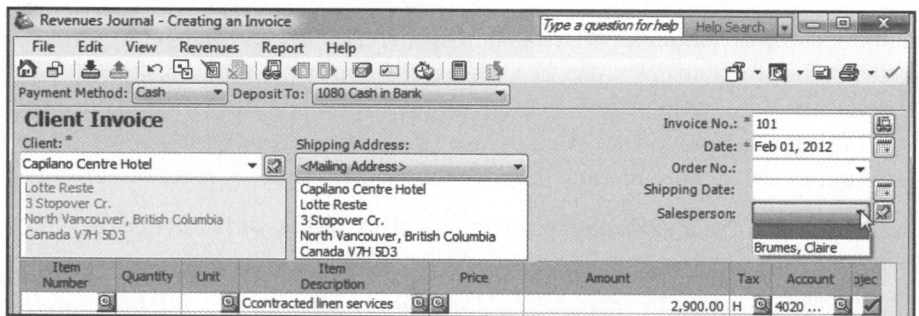

Brumes is the only employee responsible for sales at Lime Light Laundry, so she is the only employee we placed in the Sales job category. Therefore, Brumes is the only name listed. All other employees are in the second category labelled "Other," which does not have any salespersons.

Click   **Brumes** to add her name to the invoice.

Click   the **Use The Same Salesperson pin icon** 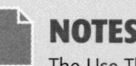.

This will lock in the salesperson's name on the invoice form until we close the journal. The pin has changed position  — it now looks like it has been pushed in:

Salesperson: | Brumes, Claire

NOTES

The Use The Same Salesperson pin icon is the same as the Use The Same Client Next Time tool and it works the same way.

If you leave the journal open in the background, the salesperson remains selected. If you close the journal, you must re-select the salesperson for each invoice. You must close the journal before advancing the session date.

Review the **journal display**. The salesperson is not added to the journal report.

Close   the **display** when finished.

Check   your **work** and **make corrections** if necessary.

Store   the **transaction** to recur **weekly**. Brumes will be entered as the salesperson in the stored transaction.

Post   the **invoice** and **minimize** (or close) the **Sales Journal**.

Adding Salespersons to Client Records

Because Brumes is the only salesperson, we can add her name to all client records.

Click   **Capilano Centre Hotel** in the Clients pane list of clients to open the ledger.

Click   the **Salesperson field list arrow** as shown:

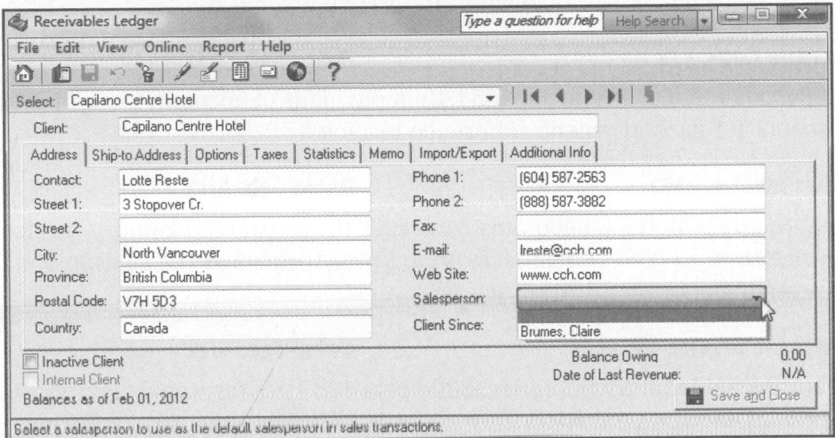

Click   **Brumes** to add her name.

Click   the **Next Record tool** ▶ to open the next client's record.

Choose   **Brumes** for this client and the remaining ones.

Click   **Save And Close** to return to the Home window.

When you open the sales journal and choose any client on record, Brumes will be entered automatically in the Salesperson field. However, when you add a new client in the Sales Journal, you must remember to choose the salesperson.

     Continue with the **transactions** for February.

SOURCE DOCUMENTS

SESSION DATE – FEBRUARY 7, 2012

☑ **Sales Invoice #101**   **Dated Feb. 2/12**

342   To Capilano Centre Hotel, $2 900 plus $348 HST for weekly contracted linen laundry service. Invoice total $3 248. Terms: 1/15, n/30. Enter Brumes as the salesperson. Store as a recurring weekly transaction.

☐ **Memo #1**   **Dated Feb. 2/12**

Add shortcuts for Create General Journal (Company), Create Supplier Invoice and Pay Supplier Invoices (Payables), Payroll Cheque Run and Create Paycheque (Employees & Payroll).

☐ **Cash Purchase Invoice #LS-504**   **Dated Feb. 2/12**

From Langley Service Centre, $400 plus $48 HST for maintenance service and repairs to delivery truck. Invoice total $448. Paid by cheque #74.

NOTES
If you use Full Add for new clients, you can add the salesperson to the new ledger record. When you use Quick Add or Continue, you must add the salesperson in the journal.

NOTES
Enter Brumes as the salesperson for all sales, either in the journal (see page 342) or by adding her to the client records (see page 343).

PRO VERSION
Purchase will replace Supplier for the shortcut labels.

NOTES
You can Pay Remittances and Make Other Payments from the Pay Supplier Invoices transaction drop-down list. You can adjust paycheques from the Payroll Journal.

Purchase Invoice #FP-1297   **Dated Feb. 2/12**

From Ferndale Paper Products, $200 plus $24 HST for bags and wrapping paper for clean laundry. Invoice total $224. Terms: 1/10, n/30. Store as a bi-weekly recurring entry.

Cash Receipt #31   **Dated Feb. 3/12**

From Delta Hotel, cheque #4123 for $3 104.64 in payment of account, including $31.36 discount for early payment. Reference invoice #69.

Cheque Copy #75   **Dated Feb. 5/12**

To Ferndale Paper Products, $554.40 in payment of account, including $5.60 discount for early payment. Reference invoice #FP-901.

Sales Invoice #102   **Dated Feb. 6/12**

To Coquitlam Motel, $3 400 plus $408 HST for contracted laundry services. Invoice total $3 808. Terms: 1/15, n/30. Enter Brumes as the salesperson. Store as a recurring bi-weekly transaction.

Purchase Invoice #PL-903   **Dated Feb. 6/12**

From Pacific Laundry Suppliers, $300 plus $36 HST for weekly supply of cleaning products. Invoice total $336. Terms: net 30. Store as a weekly recurring transaction.

WARNING!
Remember not to include the discount for the second invoice in payments and receipts.

NOTES
You can use the Paycheques or the Payroll Cheque Run Journal to complete the payroll transactions.

WARNING!
Remember to edit the Benefit amount for Sissler so that the tuition amount is included — type 31.58 in the Benefits Amount field.
Or, you can edit her ledger record and enter 31.58 as the Amount Per Unit for Benefits.

Lime Light Laundry
Laundry Services • Pickup & Deliver

Lime Light Laundry
Employee Time Summary Sheet #5

Cheque Date: Feb 7, 2012   Pay period end: Feb 7, 2012

Employee SIN	M. Durtee 552 846 826	I. Sissler 931 771 620	C. Fretton 218 738 631	S. Landings 422 946 541	S. Pott Tran 638 912 634	C. Houseman 822 546 859	C. Brumes 726 911 134
Week 1	40	40					
Regular hrs	40	40					
Overtime hrs	2	—					
#sheet sets	480	395					
Benefits	6.58	31.58					
Advance	100.00*	—					
Sick leave days	—	—					
Personal days	—	1**					
Chq/DD #	Chq 76	DD48					

* to be repaid at $25 per pay
** personal day to enroll in university course

Completed by: *Brumes* 2/7/12

Cash Purchase Invoice #SP-2991   **Dated Feb. 7/12**

From Surrey Printers, $600 plus $72 HST for copying and mailing advertising brochures outlining new prices to clients. Invoice total $672 paid in full with cheque #77.

Cheque Copy #78   **Dated Feb. 7/12**

To Pacific Laundry Suppliers, $1 120 in partial payment of account. Reference invoice #PL-644.

☐ **Sales Invoice #103**   **Dated Feb. 7/12**

To Port Moody Resort, $2 600 plus $312 HST for contracted laundry services for two weeks. Invoice total $2 912. Terms: 1/15, n/30. Enter Brumes as the salesperson. Store as a recurring bi-weekly transaction.

SESSION DATE – FEBRUARY 14, 2012

☐
![lime light laundry — Laundry Services • Pickup & Deliver]

Memo #2
From Manager's Desk

Dated Feb. 8/12
Corrected Feb 7 paycheque for Mouver Durtee to include
6 hours of overtime.
He was paid for only 2 hours.
Re-issued cheque #76 -- original cheque returned

Claire Brumes

☐ **Sales Invoice #104**   **Dated Feb. 9/12**

To Capilano Centre Hotel, $2 900 plus $348 HST for weekly contracted linen laundry service. Invoice total $3 248. Terms: 1/15, n/30. Recall stored transaction.

☐ **Cheque Copy #79**   **Dated Feb. 12/12**

To Richmond Equipment, $3 360 in payment of invoice #RE-4111.

☐ **Cash Receipt #32**   **Dated Feb. 13/12**

From Capilano Centre Hotel, cheque #2314 for $3 215.52 in partial payment of account, including $32.48 discount for early payment. Reference invoice #101.

☐ **Purchase Invoice #PL-1213**   **Dated Feb. 13/12**

From Pacific Laundry Suppliers, $300 plus $36 HST for weekly supply of cleaning products. Invoice total $336. Terms: net 30. Recall stored transaction.

☐ **Sales Invoice #105**   **Dated Feb. 13/12**

To Kingsley Inn (use Full Add for the new client), $2 800 plus $336 HST for new contract for daily laundry service with bi-weekly invoices. Invoice total $3 136. Terms: 1/15, n/30. Brumes is the salesperson. Store as recurring bi-weekly entry.

☐ **Sales Invoice #106**   **Dated Feb. 13/12**

To Delta Hotel, $2 900 plus $348 HST for bi-weekly invoice for contracted laundry services. Invoice total $3 248. Terms: 1/15, n/30. Enter Brumes as the salesperson. Store as a bi-weekly recurring transaction.

NOTES

Brumes will be entered as the salesperson in the stored transaction.
    Allow clients to exceed the credit limit.

NOTES
Kingsley Inn
(contact Rume Kingsley)
302 Sandman Dr.
Vancouver, BC V8H 1P1
Tel: (604) 259-1881
Fax: (604) 259-1893
Terms: 1/15, n/30
Revenue account: 4020
Tax code: H - HST @ 12%
Credit limit: $5 000
Salesperson: Brumes

NOTES
Type –25 in the Advance Amount field for Durtee and –50 for Fretton to recover the advances.
Type 31.58 in the Benefits Amount field for Sissler.

Lime Light Laundry

Laundry Services * Pickup & Deliver

Lime Light Laundry
Employee Time Summary Sheet #6

Cheque Date: Feb 14, 2012   Pay period end: Feb 14, 2012

Employee SIN	M. Durtee 552 846 826	I. Sissler 931 771 620	C. Fretton 218 738 631	S. Landings 422 946 541	S. Pott Tran 638 912 634	C. Houseman 822 546 859	C. Brumes 726 911 134
Week 1	pd	pd	40	40	40		
Week 2	40	40	40	42	40		
Regular hrs	40	40	80	80			
Overtime hrs	–	–	–	2			
#sheet sets	370	470	860	950			
Benefits	6.58	31.58	23.54	23.54	26.31		
Advance	–25.00	200.00*	–50.00	–	–		
Sick leave days	1	–	1	–	–		
Personal days	–	–	–	–	–		
Chq/DD #	Chq 80	DD50	DD49	Chq 81	Chq 82		

* to be repaid at $50 per pay

Completed by: *Brumes* 2/14/12

Cash Purchase Invoice #BCEG-78522   **Dated Feb. 14/12**

From BC Energy Group, $600 plus $72 HST for one month of hydro services. Invoice total $672 due within five days to avoid interest penalty. Paid in full with cheque #83.

Cash Purchase #BCT-11229   **Dated Feb. 14/12**

From BC Telephone, $100 plus $12 HST for one month of telephone services. Invoice total $112. Paid in full with cheque #84.

SESSION DATE – FEBRUARY 21, 2012

Purchase Invoice #FP-2635   **Dated Feb. 16/12**

From Ferndale Paper Products, $200 plus $24 HST for wrapping paper and bags. Invoice total $224. Terms: 1/10, n/30. Recall stored entry.

Sales Invoice #107   **Dated Feb. 16/12**

To Capilano Centre Hotel, $2 900 plus $348 HST for weekly contracted linen laundry service. Invoice total $3 248. Terms: 1/15, n/30. Recall stored transaction.

Cash Receipt #33   **Dated Feb. 18/12**

From Port Moody Resort, cheque #5120 for $2 882.88 in payment of account, including $29.12 discount for early payment. Reference invoice #103.

Cash Receipt #34   **Dated Feb. 18/12**

From Capilano Centre Hotel, cheque #2692 for $3 215.52 in partial payment of account, including $32.48 discount for early payment. Reference invoice #104.

☐ **Purchase Invoice #PL-1634**   **Dated Feb. 20/12**

From Pacific Laundry Suppliers, $300 plus $36 HST for weekly supply of cleaning products. Invoice total $336. Terms: net 30. Recall stored entry.

☐ **Sales Invoice #108**   **Dated Feb. 20/12**

To Coquitlam Motel, $3 400 plus $408 HST for contracted bi-weekly laundry services. Invoice total $3 808. Terms: 1/15, n/30. Recall stored transaction. Allow client to exceed credit limit.

☐ **Cash Sales Invoice #109**   **Dated Feb. 20/12**

To Burnaby Private Hospital (use Quick Add), $1 200 plus $144 HST for emergency linen and laundry service. Invoice total $1 344. Terms: C.O.D. Received cheque #561 for $1 344 in full payment. There is no discount.

NOTES
Use Quick Add for new cash clients. Remember to enter Brumes as the salesperson.

NOTES
Type –25 in the Advance Amount field for Durtee and –50 for Sissler to recover these amounts.
Type 31.58 in the Benefits Amount field for Sissler.

EMPLOYEE TIME SUMMARY SHEET #7

(pay period ending February 21, 2012)

Name of Employee	Regular Hours	Overtime Hours	Piece Rate Quantity	Benefits	Advance (Repaid)	Sick Days	Personal Days	Direct Deposit
☐ Durtee, Mouver	40	2	440	$ 6.58	–$25	1	–	No
☐ Sissler, Iean	40	2	520	$31.58	–$50	–	–	Yes

a. Using Employee Time Summary Sheet #7 and the Employee Information Sheet, complete payroll for the weekly paid employees. Use the Payroll Journal or the Payroll Run Journal.
b. Recover $25 advanced to Mouver Durtee and recover $50 advanced to Iean Sissler.
c. Issue cheque #05 and DD slip #51.

☐ **Sales Invoice #110**   **Dated Feb. 21/12**

To Port Moody Resort, $2 600 plus $312 HST for contracted laundry services for two weeks. Invoice total $2 912. Terms: 1/15, n/30. Recall stored transaction.

☐ **Cash Receipt #35**   **Dated Feb. 21/12**

From Delta Hotel, cheque #4439 for $3 215.52 in payment of account, including $32.48 discount for early payment. Reference invoice #106.

☐ **Purchase Invoice #RE-6998**   **Dated Feb. 21/12**

From Richmond Equipment, $2 000 plus $240 HST for new presser. Invoice total $2 240. Terms: 1/10, n/30.

SESSION DATE – FEBRUARY 28, 2012

☐ **Sales Invoice #111**   **Dated Feb. 23/12**

To Capilano Centre Hotel, $2 900 plus $348 HST for weekly laundry service. Invoice total $3 248. Terms: 1/15, n/30. Recall stored entry.

☐ **Cash Receipt #36**   **Dated Feb. 25/12**

From Capilano Centre Hotel, cheque #2974 for $3 215.52 in payment of account, including $32.48 discount for early payment. Reference invoice #107.

☐ **Cash Receipt #37**   **Dated Feb. 25/12**

From Kingsley Inn, cheque #439 for $1 966 in partial payment of account. Reference invoice #105.

☐ **Cash Receipt #38**   **Dated Feb. 25/12**

From Coquitlam Motel, cheque #276 for $3 808 in payment of account. Reference invoice #102.

Cheque Copy #86   **Dated Feb. 26/12**

To Ferndale Paper Products, cheque #86 for $445.76 in payment of account, including $2.24 discount for early payment. Reference invoices #FP-1297 and #FP-2635.

Purchase Invoice #PL-2098   **Dated Feb. 27/12**

From Pacific Laundry Suppliers, for $300 plus $36 HST for weekly supply of cleaning products. Invoice total $336. Terms: net 30. Recall stored entry.

Sales Invoice #112   **Dated Feb. 27/12**

To Delta Hotel, sales invoice #112 for $2 900 plus $348 HST for bi-weekly invoice for linen service. Invoice total $3 248. Terms: 1/15, n/30. Recall stored entry.

Sales Invoice #113   **Dated Feb. 27/12**

To Kingsley Inn, sales invoice #113 for $2 800 plus $336 HST for bi-weekly billing for laundry service. Invoice total $3 136. Terms: 1/15, n/30. Recall stored entry.

Memo #3   **Dated Feb. 28/12**

From Manager: Receipt #37 from Kingsley Inn for $1 966 was entered incorrectly. On Feb. 25, cheque #439 for $3 104.64 was received from Kingsley Inn in full payment of invoice #105, including $31.36 for early payment. Adjust the original receipt to make the correction.

> **NOTES**
> Use the Adjust Receipt tool to correct the receipt. Simply Accounting will automatically make the reversing entry. Delete the original Payment Amount. You will need to enter the amount of discount taken manually. It may be easier to reverse the receipt (refer to page 283) and then enter the client's payment correctly.
> When you reverse the receipt, the new receipt number will be updated to #39.

> **NOTES**
> Type –25 in the Advance Amount field for Durtee and –50 for Sissler and Fretton to recover these amounts.
> Type 31.58 in the Benefits Amount field for Sissler.

EMPLOYEE TIME SUMMARY SHEET #8

(pay period ending February 28, 2012)

Name of Employee	Regular Hours	Overtime Hours	Piece Rate Quantity	Benefits	Advance (Repaid)	Sick Days	Personal Days	Direct Deposit
Durtee, Mouver	40	–	510	$ 6.58	–$25	–	–	No
Sissler, Iean	40	2	510	31.58	–$50	–	–	Yes
Fretton, Clyne	80	2	1 030	23.54	–$50	–	–	Yes
Landings, Soffte	80	–	930	23.54		1	–	No
Tran, S. Pott	80	–		26.31		–	–	No

a. Using Employee Time Summary Sheet #8 and the Employee Information Sheet, complete payroll for all employees. Use the Payroll Journal or the Payroll Run Journal.
b. Recover $25 advanced to Mouver Durtee, $50 from Clyne Fretton and $50 advanced to Iean Sissler.
c. Issue cheques #87, #88 and #89, and DD #52 and #53.

SESSION DATE – FEBRUARY 29, 2012

Memo #4   **Dated Feb. 29/12**

Complete an adjusting entry for one month of prepaid insurance expired. The one-year insurance policy was purchased on December 31, 2011, for $2 400.

Bank Debit Memo #532281   **Dated Feb. 29/12**

From Mountain Heights Bank, $2 045 was withdrawn from the chequing account for the following pre-authorized transactions:

Bank Charges	$ 45
Interest on Bank Loan	120
Reduction of Principal on Bank Loan	880
Interest on Mortgage	750
Reduction of Principal on Mortgage	250

Create new Group account: 5110 Interest Expense

☐ **Memo #5**   **Dated Feb. 29/12**

Complete month-end adjusting entries for supplies used in February.

Cleaning supplies used	$680
Packaging supplies used	350

☐ **Memo #6**   **Dated Feb. 29/12**

Pay Brumes and Houseman their monthly salary. Issue deposit slips #54 and #55. Claire Brumes earned a sales commission of $258 for the month of February and took five days' vacation (use the Vacation Days Released field, Entitlements tab).

☐

lime light Laundry
Laundry Services • Pickup & Deliver

Memo #7
From Manager's Desk

Dated Feb. 29/12
Paid Claire Brumes' travel allowance for February 2012.
Issued cheque #90 for $300 to Brumes as other payment in Payments
Journal.(Added Brumes as vendor and used Travel Allowances
Payable account.)

Claire Brumes

> **NOTES**
> The travel allowance for Brumes is set up in her ledger record so that the amount is included automatically as an employer expense that debits Travel Allowance Expenses and credits Travel Allowances Payable just as tuition fees were set up for Sissler. You do not need to enter the expense separately.
> This is not a taxable benefit.
> In Chapter 16, we set up travel expenses as non-taxable reimbursement income.

☐ **Memo #8**   **Dated Feb. 29/12**

Clyne Fretton is taking some vacation time. Clyne asked to receive her vacation pay by cheque. Release her retained vacation pay and issue cheque #91. Refer to page 284.

☑ **Memo #9**   **Dated Feb. 29/12**

350 Adjust the paycheque for Brumes. She has returned her deposit pay stub because her earned commission was incorrect. Use the Revenues By Salesperson Report to verify that the correct amount was $362, not $258.

☐ **Memo #10**   **Dated Feb. 29/12**

Using the payroll remittance option, remit the following payroll taxes for the pay period ending February 29, including the balance owing from January:
To Receiver General: EI Payable, CPP Payable and Income Tax Payable
To BC Minister of Finance: MSP Payable - Employee and MSP Payable - Employer
To BC Workers' Compensation Board: WCB Payable
To Victoria Trust: RRSP Payable
Issue cheques #92 through #95 in payment.

☐ **Memo #11**   **Dated Feb. 29/12**

Complete an adjusting entry to reverse the year-end accrued wages entry for $1 150. (Debit 2250 Accrued Wages and credit 5305 Wages: Cleaning Staff.)

Displaying Salesperson Reports

Two reports become available when we add salespersons to journal entries.

Displaying the Sales by Salesperson Report

Click   the **Report Centre icon**   in the Home window.

Click   **Receivables** to open the list of client reports that you can display from the Report Centre.

Click   **Revenues By Salesperson Summary** in the Select A Report list.

Click   **Modify This Report** to open the report options:

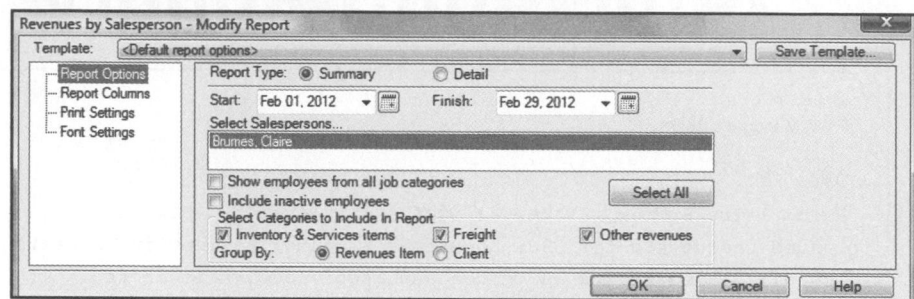

Or, choose the Reports menu, then choose Receivables and click Revenues By Salesperson to open the report options screen.

Brumes is the only employee designated as a salesperson so only her name appears on the list, and she is already selected. You have the option to show all employees, but we do not need them all — we want Brumes' February sales data. The default dates for Start and Finish cover the period we want. You can group the sales information by client or by sales item. You can also include information for freight and other non-inventory sales. For Lime Light, we need to show only the Other sales because inventory and freight do not apply. You can also show the report in detail with a line item for each sale, or in summary form with totals only for each item or client.

You can exclude amounts that do not apply. Click Freight and Inventory & Services Items to remove the ✓s.

Click   **OK** to see the report.

The total sales revenue for January was $36 200, so Brumes' commission amount should be changed to $362.

Close   the displayed **report**.

Displaying the Sales by Job Category Report

This next report is similar except that it combines the information for all employees in each category. Because we have only one person in the Sales category, reporting by this category should give us the same information as the Revenues By Salesperson Report. The list of Receivables reports should still be open in the report centre.

Click   **Revenues By Job Category Summary** in the Select A Report list.

Click   **Modify This Report** to open the report options:

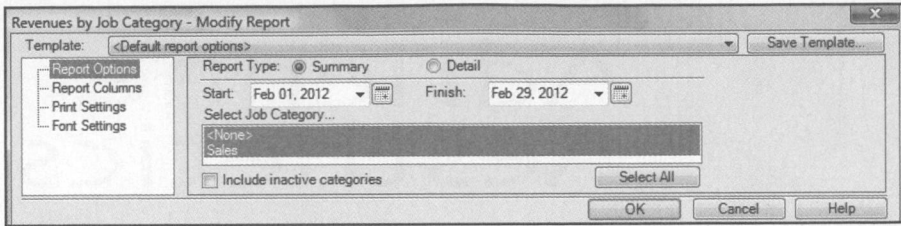

Or, choose the Reports menu, then choose Receivables and click Revenues By Job Categories to open the report options screen.

Again the default dates give us the report for the month we need. Categories that do not have salespersons in them are not included in this report. You can create a Detail Report with a listing for each individual invoice or a Summary Report that provides the total for each selected category.

Click   **Sales** to select only this category.

Click   **OK** to see the total sales for all persons in the Sales category.

Close   the **report** when finished. **Close** the **Report Centre**.

 Enter   the **remaining transactions for Feb. 29** to complete the application.

R E V I E W

The Student DVD with Data Files includes Review Questions and Supplementary Cases for this chapter.

CHAPTER TEN

Adrienne Aesthetics

OBJECTIVES

*After completing
this chapter, you
should be able to*

- **enter** inventory-related purchase transactions
- **enter** inventory-related sale transactions of goods and services
- **make** inventory adjustments
- **assemble** new inventory items from other inventory
- **enter** returns on sales and purchases
- **enter** sales to preferred customers
- **enter** freight on purchases
- **understand** the integration of the Inventory Ledger with the Payables, Receivables and General ledgers
- **create** new inventory items
- **display** and **print** inventory reports

COMPANY INFORMATION

Company Profile

NOTES
Adrienne Aesthetics
20 Portage Ave. E.
Winnipeg, MB R3C 4R1
Tel 1: (204) 722-9876
Tel 2: (204) 722-8701
Fax: (204) 722-8000
Business No.: 567 643 778

Adrienne Aesthetics Beauty Salon and Spa is located in the heart of downtown Winnipeg, near the government buildings and the financial and entertainment districts. Adrienne Aesthetics caters to professional women and the well-to-do clientele of the local business community.

Regular products for sale include high-quality cosmetic and beauty products but the salon also provides a variety of services and consultation for clients. For Valentine's Day, the salon offers special packages, which have been popular gifts.

Adrienne Kosh, the owner, is active in the day-to-day sales and management of the salon, assisted by two employees who provide all the services. All are trained cosmeticians. Among the repeat customers, Adrienne serves a local television show and a film studio. All customers rely on the honest and professional advice and service provided by the staff. The on-site service is also appreciated by the regular customers who receive a 2 percent discount for settling their accounts within five days. Full payment is requested in 30 days. Preferred price list customers receive an additional discount of about 10 percent off the regular prices and are eligible for the early payment discount for 15 days. Adrienne has accounts with most of her regular suppliers, including beauty product manufacturers.

At the end of January, Adrienne converted all her business records to Simply Accounting using the following information:

- Chart of Postable Accounts
- Post-Closing Trial Balance
- Supplier Information
- Customer Information
- Employee Profiles and TD1 Information
- Inventory Information
- Accounting Procedures

CHART OF POSTABLE ACCOUNTS

ADRIENNE AESTHETICS

ASSETS
Current Assets
1080 Bank Account: Chequing
1090 Bank Account: Credit Cards
1150 Investments
1200 Accounts Receivable
1250 Clinical Supplies
1260 Packaging Supplies
1270 Prepaid Insurance
1280 Towels and Capes

Inventory Assets
1310 Creams and Lotions
1320 Face Care Products
1330 Sun Care Products
1380 Miscellaneous Inventory Products

Fixed Assets
1420 Cash Register
1440 Computer Equipment ▶

▶1480 Display Cabinets
1500 Clinical Equipment
1520 Aesthetics Salon

LIABILITIES
Current Liabilities
2100 Bank Loan
2200 Accounts Payable
2220 Credit Card Payable
2300 EI Payable
2310 CPP Payable
2320 Income Tax Payable
2400 Group Insurance Payable
2420 WCB Payable
2640 RST Payable
2650 GST Charged on Sales
2670 GST Paid on Purchases

Long Term Liabilities
2940 Mortgage Payable ▶

▶EQUITY
Equity
3560 Share Capital
3600 Current Earnings

REVENUE
Revenue
4020 Revenue from Sales
4030 Sales Allowances and Discounts
4040 Revenue from Services
4050 Sales Returns
4080 Freight Revenue
4100 Sales Tax Compensation

EXPENSE
Operating Expenses
5020 Advertising & Promotion
5030 Bank Charges
5040 Credit Card Fees
5060 Cost of Goods Sold ▶

▶5065 Cost of Services
5070 Variance Costs
5080 Item Assembly Costs
5090 Purchases Returns
5100 Inventory Losses
5200 Freight Expense
5220 Interest Expense
5240 Hydro Expense
5250 Telephone Expense

Payroll Expenses
5300 Salaries
5310 EI Expense
5320 CPP Expense
5330 WCB Expense

NOTES: The Chart of Accounts includes only postable accounts and Current Earnings.

POST-CLOSING TRIAL BALANCE

ADRIENNE AESTHETICS

February 1, 2012

		Debits	Credits				Debits	Credits
1080	Bank Account: Chequing	$51 625.92		▶ 1520	Aesthetics Salon		100 000.00	
1090	Bank Account: Credit Cards	2 100.00		2100	Bank Loan			$ 5 000.00
1150	Investments	90 000.00		2200	Accounts Payable			3 150.00
1200	Accounts Receivable	4 095.00		2220	Credit Card Payable			255.00
1250	Clinical Supplies	600.00		2300	EI Payable			270.00
1260	Packaging Supplies	700.00		2310	CPP Payable			481.26
1270	Prepaid Insurance	2 200.00		2320	Income Tax Payable			2 605.26
1280	Towels and Capes	1 200.00		2400	Group Insurance Payable			30.00
1310	Creams and Lotions	2 660.00		2420	WCB Payable			284.40
1320	Face Care Products	5 810.00		2640	RST Payable			2 400.00
1330	Sun Care Products	5 240.00		2650	GST Charged on Sales			2 100.00
1420	Cash Register	1 500.00		2670	GST Paid on Purchases		875.00	
1440	Computer Equipment	2 500.00		2940	Mortgage Payable			80 000.00
1480	Display Cabinets	4 500.00		3560	Share Capital			187 430.00
1500	Clinical Equipment	8 400.00 ▶					$284 005.92	$284 005.92

SUPPLIER INFORMATION

ADRIENNE AESTHETICS

Supplier Name (Contact)	Address	Phone No. Fax No.	E-mail Web Site	Terms Tax ID
Acqua Viva Cosmetics (Tomi Hillfinger)	466 Ralf Loren Dr. Montreal, Quebec H3B 4C4	Tel: (888) 448-7274 Fax: (514) 447-3726	thill@acquaviva.com www.acquaviva.com	net 10 438 456 120
Biotech Laboratories (Avivah Rubenstein)	75 Klinique St. Markham, Ontario L3K 1P1	Tel: (800) 466-2991 Fax: (905) 471-2494	avivah@biotech.com www.biotech.com	net 10 297 382 266
Derma Laboratories (Masc Karah)	34 Makeover Way Mississauga, Ontario L8H 7V1	Tel: (877) 374-8107 Fax: (905) 722-5491	mk@skindeep.com www.skindeep.com	net 5 178 629 718
Esthetica Inc. (Ellis Arden)	61 Pumice Rd. Winnipeg, Manitoba R2P 2R1	Tel: (204) 556-4997 Fax: (204) 558-1900	ea@superficial.com www.superficial.com	net 30 364 139 617
Grand Life Insurance				net 1
Manitoba Bell (Annie Heard)	82 Wireless Alley Winnipeg, Manitoba R3B 5R9	Tel: (204) 781-2355	heard@bell.ca www.bell.ca	net 1
Receiver General for Canada				net 1
Sun Lab Products, Inc. (Maxine Factor)	59 Botox Cr. Regina, Saskatchewan S4F 3M8	Tel: (306) 620-5388 Fax: (306) 621-7392	maxine@sunlab.com www.sunlab.com	net 15 724 527 455
Winnipeg Hydro (Kohl Genrater)	77 Voltage St. Winnipeg, Manitoba R2B 3N7	Tel: (204) 785-9113	www.winnhydro.ca	net 1
Workers' Compensation Board				net 1

OUTSTANDING SUPPLIER INVOICES

ADRIENNE AESTHETICS

Supplier Name	Terms	Date	Invoice No.	Pretax Amount	Tax	Total
Esthetica Inc.	net 30	Jan. 8/12	EI-641	$3 000.00	$150.00	$3 150.00

CUSTOMER INFORMATION

ADRIENNE AESTHETICS

Customer Name (Contact)	Address	Phone No. Fax No.	E-mail Web Site	Terms Credit Limit
Ariandanos Residence (Arianne Ariandanos)	29 Revlon Blvd. Winnipeg, Manitoba R2P 2M2	Tel: (204) 762-8664	arianne@radiantway.com www.radiantway.com	2/5, n/30 $1 500
Botelli & Giroux, Lawyers (Gina Botelli)	30 Court St. Winnipeg, Manitoba R3R 1C7	Tel: (204) 699-2911 Fax: (204) 697-2735	gina@botelli.giroux.com www.botelli.giroux.com	2/5, n/30 $1 500
Boutique Fashions (Leontyne Coutumier)	85 Haute Couture Ave. Dauphin, Manitoba R7N 5F9	Tel: (204) 622-1711 Fax: (204) 623-8118	leontyne@lookpretty.com www.lookpretty.com	2/5, n/30 $3 000
Lavender Estates (Katherine Harris)	9 Lavender Ct. Winnipeg, Manitoba R2X 3J6	Tel: (204) 782-7300 Fax: (204) 782-8190	harris@lavender.com www.lavender.com	2/5, n/30 $3 000
*Red River TV (CWTV) (Celeb Brittie)	17 Broadcast Ave. Winnipeg, Manitoba R3B 7F3	Tel: (204) 784-6000 Fax: (204) 784-5234	celebrit@redriverstars.com www.redriverstars.com	2/15, n/30 $4 000
*The Forks Film Corporation (Francine Despardieu)	6 Gilroy St. Winnipeg, Manitoba R3C 2M2	Tel: (204) 787-1226	fdes@forksfilm.com www.forksfilm.com	2/15, n/30 $3 000

NOTES: The asterisk (*) indicates preferred price list customers. A record is also set up for Cash Customers.

OUTSTANDING CUSTOMER INVOICES

ADRIENNE AESTHETICS

Customer Name	Terms	Date	Invoice No.	Pretax Amount	Tax	Total
*Red River TV (CWTV)	2/15, n/30	Jan. 24/12	AA-16	$1 750.00	$87.50	$1 837.50
*The Forks Film Corporation	2/15, n/30	Jan. 20/12	AA-11	$2 150.00	$107.50	$2 257.50
			Grand Total			$4 095.00

EMPLOYEE INFORMATION SHEET

ADRIENNE AESTHETICS

	Blossom, Lysis	Hydra, Collagen
Position	Beautician	Beautician
Social Insurance No.	459 562 344	562 391 888
Address	522 Colvin Cline Ct., #22 Winnipeg, Manitoba R2B 2L8	71 Lipogone St. Winnipeg, Manitoba R3V 5F2
Telephone	(204) 729-1991	(204) 753-7994
Date of Birth (mm-dd-yy)	02-02-70	02-14-73
Federal (Manitoba) Tax Exemption - TD1 Total Exemptions	$10 382 (8 134)	$10 382 (8 134)
Employee Earnings Regular Salary Commission	$2 000 bi-weekly (75 hours) 2% (sales less returns)	$2 000 bi-weekly (75 hours) 2% (sales less returns)
WSIB Rate	2.37	2.37
Employee Deductions Group Insurance EI, CPP & Income Tax	$12 Calculations built into Simply Accounting program	$12

Employee Profiles and TD1 Information

Lysis Blossom and **Collagen Hydra** both assist with sales in the salon and provide the services to customers. Blossom specializes in facials, pedicures and massages while Hydra handles the waxing and electrolysis services. Both are salaried employees who receive their $2 000 bi-weekly pay by cheque and contribute $12 each period to a group insurance plan. Blossom and Hydra are single and self-supporting with no dependants and no other deductions, so they have the basic claim amounts for income tax. Instead of vacation pay, they take three weeks of vacation with regular pay each year. Neither has received any payroll advances.

Both employees are listed as salespersons. They receive a sales commission of 2 percent of their net sales (sales less returns) with each paycheque. Their names are entered as salespersons on invoices so that the commissions can be tracked for the Sales by Salesperson Report.

INVENTORY INFORMATION

ADRIENNE AESTHETICS

Code	Description	Min Stock	Selling Price Reg	(Pref)	Unit	Qty on Hand	Total (Cost)	Taxes
Creams and Lotions (asset account 1310)								
CL01	Cleansing Lotion 225 ml	2	$15	($13)	tube	20	$ 120	GST & RST
CL02	Cleansing Milk 225 ml	2	25	(22)	tube	20	240	GST & RST
CL03	Eye Contour Smoothing Cream 30 ml	2	35	(32)	jar	20	320	GST & RST
CL04	Eye Contour Smoothing Gel 30 ml	2	40	(36)	jar	20	360	GST & RST
CL05	Masks: herb 100 ml	2	40	(36)	jar	20	360	GST & RST
CL06	Masks: sea 100 ml	2	35	(32)	jar	20	320	GST & RST
CL07	Night Cream 200 ml	2	45	(41)	jar	20	420	GST & RST
CL08	Protection Cream: dbl action 60 ml	2	25	(22)	tube	20	240	GST & RST
CL09	Protection Cream: moisturizer 60 ml	2	30	(27)	tube	20	280	GST & RST
	Total Creams and Lotions						$ 2 660	
Face Care Products (asset account 1320)								
FC01	Blush 8 g	3	10	(9)	each	30	$ 120	GST & RST
FC02	Concealer 15 ml	3	20	(18)	tube	30	240	GST & RST
FC03	Epidermal Cleanser: face+ 300 ml	3	60	(55)	jar	30	750	GST & RST
FC04	Epidermal Cleanser: phytogel 300 ml	3	50	(45)	jar	30	660	GST & RST
FC05	Eye Shadow duo-pack	3	15	(13)	pair	30	120	GST & RST
FC06	Foundation 35 ml	3	25	(22)	jar	30	360	GST & RST
FC07	Lipstick 5 g	20	15	(13)	tube	400	2 400	GST & RST
FC08	Kohl Pencil	10	15	(13)	each	60	180	GST & RST
FC09	Mascara 9 ml	12	10	(9)	tube	80	320	GST & RST
FC10	Powder: loose 15 g	3	20	(18)	jar	30	240	GST & RST
FC11	Powder: pressed 15 g	3	30	(27)	each	30	420	GST & RST
	Total Face Care Products						$ 5 810	
Sun Care Products (asset account 1330)								
SC01	Sun Care Cream SPF#15 125 ml	4	30	(27)	tube	40	560	GST & RST
SC02	Sun Care Cream SPF#30 125 ml	4	45	(41)	tube	40	840	GST & RST
SC03	Sun Tan Milk SPF#4 200 ml	4	40	(36)	jar	40	720	GST & RST
SC04	Sun Tan Milk SPF#15 200 ml	4	50	(45)	jar	40	840	GST & RST
SC05	UV #15 Total Cream 125 ml	4	50	(45)	tube	40	880	GST & RST
SC06	UV #30 Total Cream 125 ml	4	75	(68)	tube	40	1 400	GST & RST
	Total Sun Care Products						$ 5 240	
	Total Inventory						$13 710	
Aesthetic Services								
AS01	Bridal Makeup/Styling		$ 70	($63)	job			GST, no RST
AS02	Cellulite Treatment		80	(72)	job			GST, no RST
AS03	Electrolysis: 45 min treatment		60	(54)	session			GST, no RST
AS04	Electrolysis: 60 min treatment		75	(68)	session			GST, no RST
AS05	European Deep Cleansing Facial		60	(54)	job			GST, no RST
AS06	Hydroptimate Treatment		120	(108)	job			GST, no RST
AS07	Makeup		40	(36)	job			GST, no RST
AS08	Massage: Swedish		75	(68)	job			GST, no RST
AS09	Promotional Pkg: spa treatment		100	(90)	job			GST, no RST
AS10	Package: Super 5 spa treatments		600	(540)	series			GST, no RST
AS11	Package: Deluxe 5 spa treatments		800	(720)	series			GST, no RST
AS12	Skin Treatment		100	(90)	job			GST, no RST
AS13	Manicure/Pedicure		25	(22)	job			GST, no RST
AS14	Waxing: full leg		50	(45)	job			GST, no RST
AS15	Waxing: half leg or bikini		20	(18)	job			GST, no RST

NOTES: All inventory products use the same linked Revenue, COGS and Variance accounts: 4020 Revenue from Sales, 5060 Cost of Goods Sold and 5070 Variance Costs. Linked asset accounts are shown in the inventory list with the heading line for each inventory group.
All Services are linked to 4040 Revenue from Services for revenue and to the expense account 5065 Cost of Services.

Accounting Procedures

The Goods and Services Tax (GST): Remittances

Adrienne Aesthetics uses the regular method for remittance of the Goods and Services Tax. GST collected is recorded as a liability in *GST Charged on Sales*. GST paid, recorded in *GST Paid on Purchases,* decreases the liability. The salon files its return with the Canada Revenue Agency (CRA) quarterly, either requesting a refund or remitting the balance owing.

Retail (Provincial) Sales Tax (RST)

Retail Sales Tax of 7 percent is applied to all cash and credit sales of goods in Manitoba. Customers do not pay RST on the services provided by Adrienne Aesthetics. RST on goods is remitted quarterly to the Minister of Finance.

RST at the rate of 7 percent is also paid on purchases that are not inventory items for resale. Since RST paid is not refundable, it is charged to the asset or expense account associated with the purchase, not to a separate account.

NOTES
We use the term Retail Sales Tax (RST) for Provincial Sales Tax (PST) in this chapter. Refer to Chapter 2 for further information about GST and RST remittances.

Sales Invoices

Adrienne allows customers to pay on account, or by cash, cheque or credit card. The keystrokes for cash and credit card inventory transactions are similar to those for account sales, except for the method of payment. The program will automatically debit the appropriate bank account instead of *Accounts Receivable.*

Source documents for cash and credit card sales are presented as weekly summaries to avoid a large number of small revenue transactions. A Cash Customer record is set up for tracking these sales.

You can print and e-mail sales invoices through the program. Before posting the Sales Journal transaction, preview the invoice. Then click the Print button or the E-mail button.

NOTES
We apply the term cash sales and purchases to payments by cash and by cheque.

NOTES
Printing of invoices will begin immediately, so be sure you have selected the correct printer and forms before you begin.
Remember that to preview invoices, you should select Custom Form and Custom Simply Form on the Reports & Forms Settings screen for Invoices.

Credit Card Sales and Purchases

Adrienne has set up its accounts for credit card sales and purchase transactions.

Freight Expenses and Charges

When a business purchases inventory items, the cost of any freight that cannot be directly allocated to a specific item must be charged to *Freight Expense*. This amount is regarded as an expense rather than a charge to an inventory asset account. Freight or delivery charges to customers are allocated to *Freight Revenue*.

NOTES
Freight charges for goods that are exempt from RST do not usually have RST applied to them in Manitoba.

Discounts

To encourage customers to settle their accounts early, Adrienne Aesthetics offers its account customers a 2 percent discount on before-tax amounts if they pay their accounts within five days. For preferred customers, the discount period is 15 days. Discounts are calculated automatically when the payment terms are set up and the customer is eligible for the discount. There are no discounts on cash or credit card sales.

In addition, some customers have preferred price list status that entitles them to reduced prices. Regular and preferred prices are set up in the Inventory Ledger so the prices are entered automatically.

Valentine's Day Packages

Each February, Adrienne Aesthetics offers special promotional gift packages that include a variety of popular beauty products and services. When assembled, these packages require some special packaging materials such as boxes, wrappings, foils and ribbons, which incur additional costs.

Returns

Returned goods are a normal part of retail businesses. Customers may not be satisfied with the product for a number of reasons. Adrienne Aesthetics provides full refunds on unopened items returned within 14 days. Some items such as lipstick cannot be returned for hygienic reasons. Returned items are debited to the contra-revenue account, *Sales Returns*, so that the returns can be tracked. Refer to page 387.

Returns on purchases also occur for a variety of reasons; for example, the goods may be damaged or the wrong items may have been shipped. Refer to page 388.

INSTRUCTIONS

1. **Record entries** for the source documents in Simply Accounting using the Chart of Accounts, Trial Balance, and Supplier, Customer, Employee and Inventory Information provided. The procedures for entering each new type of transaction are outlined step by step in the Keystrokes section that follows the source documents. These transactions have a ✓ in the check box, and the page number where the keystrokes begin is printed below the check box.

2. **Print** the **reports** indicated on the following printing forms after finishing your entries. Instructions for printing inventory reports begin on page 389.

REPORTS

Accounts
- ☐ Chart of Accounts
- ☐ Account List
- ☐ General Journal Entries

Financial
- ✓ Balance Sheet date: Feb. 14
- ✓ Income Statement: Feb. 1 to Feb. 14
- ✓ Trial Balance date: Feb. 14
- ✓ All Journal Journal Entries: Feb. 1 to Feb. 14
- ✓ General Ledger accounts: 1310 1320 1330 4020 4040 from Feb. 1 to Feb. 14
- ☐ Statement of Cash Flows
- ☐ Cash Flow Projection Detail Report
- ✓ Gross Margin Income Statement: Feb. 1 to Feb. 14

Tax
- ☐ Report on

Banking
- ☐ Cheque Log Report

Payables
- ☐ Supplier List

- ☐ Supplier Aged
- ☐ Aged Overdue Payables
- ☐ Purchase Journal Entries
- ☐ Payment Journal Entries
- ☐ Supplier Purchases

Receivables
- ☐ Customer List
- ☐ Customer Aged
- ☐ Aged Overdue Receivables
- ☐ Sales Journal Entries
- ☐ Receipt Journal Entries
- ☐ Customer Sales
- ✓ Sales by Salesperson: Feb. 1 to Feb. 14
- ☐ Customer Statements

Payroll & Employees
- ☐ Employee List
- ✓ Summary: All employees
- ☐ Deductions & Expenses
- ☐ Remittances
- ☐ Payroll Journal Entries
- ☐ T4 Slips
- ☐ Record of Employment

Inventory & Services
- ☐ Inventory & Services List
- ✓ Summary
- ☐ Quantity
- ☐ Inventory Statistics
- ✓ Sales Summary for all Services: from Feb. 1 to Feb. 14
- ✓ Transaction Summary for FC07 Lipstick, all journals: Feb. 1 to Feb. 14
- ☐ Price Lists
- ✓ Item Assembly Journal Entries: Feb. 1 to Feb. 14
- ✓ Adjustments Journal Entries: Feb. 1 to Feb. 14

Mailing Labels
- ☐ Labels

Forecast & Analysis
- ☐ Forecast
- ☐ Customer Analysis
- ☐ Product Analysis
- ☐ Sales Synopsis

Management Reports
- ☐ Ledger

SOURCE DOCUMENTS

SESSION DATE – FEBRUARY 7, 2012

☑ **Sales Invoice #20**   Dated Feb. 1/12

366   Sold by Hydra to Boutique Fashions

8	CL04	Eye Contour Smoothing Gel 30 ml	$40 /jar
8	FC02	Concealer 15 ml	20 /tube
4	FC03	Epidermal Cleanser: face+ 300 ml	60 /jar
4	FC04	Epidermal Cleanser: phytogel 300 ml	50 /jar
8	FC05	Eye Shadow duo-pack	15 /pair
5	AS02	Cellulite Treatment	80 /job
8	AS07	Makeup	40 /job
		Goods and Services Tax	5%
		Retail Sales Tax	7%

Terms: 2/5, n/30.

☐ **Cash Receipt #11**   Dated Feb. 1/12

From The Forks Film Corporation, cheque #6732 for $2 214.50 in payment of account including $43 discount for early payment. Reference invoice #AA-11.

☑ **Purchase Invoice #AC-1124**   Dated Feb. 1/12

370   From Acqua Viva Cosmetics

5	SC03	Sun Tan Milk SPF#4 200 ml	$ 90.00
5	SC04	Sun Tan Milk SPF#15 200 ml	105.00
		Freight	10.00
		GST Paid	10.25
	Invoice Total		$215.25

Terms: net 10 days.

☑ **Memo #1**   Dated Feb. 2/12

373   From Owner: Adjust inventory records for Eye Contour Smoothing Gel, item CL04. One jar was dropped and broken. Charge to Inventory Losses.

☑ **Memo #2**   Dated Feb. 3/12

376   From Owner: Two new inventory items are required for special Valentine's Day gift packages. Create new asset Group account 1350 Gift Packages. Create two new inventory records.

Number Description	Min.	Reg (Pref) Selling Price	/Unit	Picture
VP01 Valentine Gift: super pkg	1	$100 (95)	/pkg	VP01.bmp
VP02 Valentine Gift: deluxe pkg	1	$150 (140)	/pkg	VP02.bmp
Linked accounts:	Asset 1350			
	Revenue 4020			
	Expense 5060			
	Variance not required			

NOTES
Notice that only inventory items appear on the list for adjustments because service items do not have quantities in stock.

NOTES
The image files (VP01.bmp and VP02.bmp) were installed in the SimData10\Setup\Logos folder when you installed your other data files.

NOTES
Do not forget to save the item assembly as a recurring transaction with Random as the period.

☑ **Item Assembly #ItA-1**   **Dated Feb. 3/12**

382   Assemble 10 VP01 Valentine Gift: super packages. Transfer 10 of each component item as follows:

10	CL01	Cleansing Lotion 225 ml	$ 6 each tube
10	CL07	Night Cream 200 ml	21 each jar
10	FC01	Blush 8 g	4 each
10	FC07	Lipstick 5 g	6 each tube
10	SC01	Sun Care Cream SPF#15 125 ml	14 each tube

Additional Costs $50

Assembled Items:
    10 VP01   Valentine Gift: super pkg $56 each pkg

NOTES
You will see the Advisor message that one or more inventory items has dropped below the reorder point. Read and then close the message.

☐ **Item Assembly #ItA-2**   **Dated Feb. 3/12**

Assemble 10 VP02 Valentine Deluxe Gift Packages. Transfer 10 of each component item as follows:

10	CL02	Cleansing Milk 225 ml	$12 each tube
10	CL07	Night Cream 200 ml	21 each jar
10	FC07	Lipstick 5 g	6 each tube
10	FC11	Powder: pressed 15 g	14 each
10	SC06	UV #30 Total Cream 125 ml	35 each tube

Additional Costs $50

Assembled Items:
    10 VP02 Valentine Gift: deluxe pkg $93 each pkg

Save the item assembly as a recurring transaction.

☐ **Memo #3**   **Dated Feb. 3/12**

From Owner: Adjust purchase invoice #AC-1124 from Acqua Viva Cosmetics. Change the quantity for both items to 10. The unit cost price and freight are unchanged. The revised invoice total is $420.

☑ **Sales Invoice #21**   **Dated Feb. 4/12**

386   Sold by Hydra to Red River TV (CWTV) preferred customer

5	CL03	Eye Contour Smoothing Cream 30 ml	$ 32.00 /jar
5	CL05	Masks: herb 100 ml	36.00 /jar
5	FC02	Concealer 15 ml	18.00 /tube
5	AS06	Hydroptimate Treatment	108.00 /job
5	AS07	Makeup	36.00 /job
		Goods and Services Tax	5%
		Retail Sales Tax	7%

Terms: 2/15, n/30.

NOTES
To change a purchase price, click the number in the Amount field to select it. Type the new total amount to replace it, and press (tab) to update the unit price and totals.

☐ **Purchase Invoice #DL-518**   **Dated Feb. 4/12**

From Derma Laboratories

10	CL01	Cleansing Lotion 225 ml	$ 60.00
10	CL02	Cleansing Milk 225 ml	120.00
20	CL07	Night Cream 200 ml	440.00
		Freight	20.00
		GST Paid	32.00
		Invoice Total	$672.00

Terms: net 5 days. Note price increase for CL07.

⚠ **WARNING!**
Do not include the discount for the second invoice in the amount received from Red River TV.

☐ **Cash Receipt #12**   **Dated Feb. 5/12**

From Red River TV (CWTV), cheque #29975 for $1 802.50 in payment of account, including $35 discount taken. Reference invoice #AA-16.

SUN LAB PRODUCTS, INC.
59 Botox Cr. Regina, SK S4F 3M8
Tel: (306) 620-5388 Fax: (306) 621-7392
www.sunlab.com

To:
Customer: **Adrienne Aesthetics**
Address: 20 Portage Ave. E.
Winnipeg, MB R3C 4R1
Reg # 29977336

Invoice #: SL-4100
GST # 724 527 455

Feb. 5, 2012

qty	code	item	total
10	SC01	Sun Care Cream SPF#15 125 ml @ $14	140.00
15	SC06	UV #30 Total Cream 125 ml @ $35	525.00
		Freight	10.00
		GST	33.75
		Invoice Total	708.75

Terms: n/15 *MF*

INVOICE # 22
Adrienne Aesthetics
20 Portage Ave. E.
Winnipeg, MB R3C 4R1
567 643 778

Sold to: Visa Sales Summary
Address: One-time Cash Customers

Salesperson: Blossom

Date: Feb. 6/12

QTY	CODE	DESCRIPTION	PRICE/UNIT	TAX CODE	TOTAL
5	CL08	Protection Cream: dbl action 60 ml	25 /tube	1	125.00
3	FC05	Eye Shadow duo-pack	15 /pair	1	45.00
5	FC10	Powder: loose 15 g	20 /jar	1	100.00
3	SC05	UV #15 Total Cream 125 ml	50 /tube	1	150.00
2	AS08	Massage: Swedish	75 /job	2	150.00
4	AS13	Manicure/Pedicure	25 /job	2	100.00
4	AS14	Waxing: full leg	50 /job	2	200.00
2	VP02	Valentine Gift: deluxe pkg	150 /pkg	1	300.00

Direct deposit to Visa account *LB*

Terms: Visa	GST 5%	58.50
	RST 7%	50.40
	Total	1 278.90

Tel 1: (204) 722-9876   or   (204) 722-8701   Fax: (204) 722-8000
www.adrienneaesthetics.com
look good, feel good

NOTES
Choose Cash Customers for
the Visa and MasterCard sales
summaries.

☐ **MasterCard Sales Summary Invoice #23**   **Dated Feb. 6/12**

Sold by Blossom to various one-time Cash Customers

20	FC08	Kohl Pencil	$ 15 each	$	300.00
10	FC09	Mascara 9 ml	10 /tube		100.00
2	SC03	Sun Tan Milk SPF#4 200 ml	40 /jar		80.00
2	AS12	Skin Treatment	100 /job		200.00
4	AS15	Waxing: half leg or bikini	20 /job		80.00
3	VP02	Valentine Gift: deluxe pkg	150 /pkg		450.00
		Goods and Services Tax	5%		60.50
		Retail Sales Tax	7%		65.10
		Total paid by MasterCard			$1 335.60

☐ **Cheque Copy #205**   **Dated Feb. 6/12**

To Derma Laboratories, $672 in full payment of account. Reference invoice #DL-518.

☐ **Cheque Copy #206**   **Dated Feb. 6/12**

To Esthetica Inc., $3 150 in full payment of account. Reference invoice #EI-641.

☐ **Item Assembly #ItA-3**   **Dated Feb. 7/12**

NOTES
If you recall the stored item assembly transaction, change the total amount for the Assembled Items to $470. Notice that the assembly component price for CL07 is updated from $21 to $22 automatically for the new costs. (See Item Assembly #ItA-2 on page 360.)

Assemble five VP02 Valentine Deluxe Gift Packages. Transfer five of each item as follows:

5	CL02	Cleansing Milk 225 ml	$12	each tube
5	CL07	Night Cream 200 ml	22	each jar
5	FC07	Lipstick 5 g	6	each tube
5	FC11	Powder: pressed 15 g	14	each
5	SC06	UV #30 Total Cream 125 ml	35	each tube
Additional Costs			$25	

Assembled Items:

5	VP02	Valentine Gift: deluxe pkg	$94	each pkg

☐ **Cash Sales Summary Invoice #24**   **Dated Feb. 7/12**

NOTES
Choose Cash Customers for the cash sales summary.

Sold by Hydra to various one-time Cash Customers

2	CL04	Eye Contour Smoothing Gel 30 ml	$ 40 /jar	$	80.00
5	CL06	Masks: sea 100 ml	35 /jar		175.00
15	FC07	Lipstick 5 g	15 /tube		225.00
3	SC02	Sun Care Cream SPF#30 125 ml	45 /tube		135.00
2	AS01	Bridal Makeup/Styling	70 /job		140.00
5	AS03	Electrolysis: 45 min treatment	60 /session		300.00
2	AS06	Hydroptimate Treatment	120 /job		240.00
2	VP01	Valentine Gift: super pkg	100 /pkg		200.00
		Goods and Services Tax	5%		74.75
		Retail Sales Tax	7%		57.05
		Total cash received			$1 626.80

SESSION DATE – FEBRUARY 14, 2012

☐ **Purchase Invoice #BL-669**   **Dated Feb. 8/12**

From Biotech Laboratories

5	FC10	Powder: loose 15 g	$	40.00
15	FC11	Powder: pressed 15 g		210.00
		Freight		10.00
		GST Paid		13.00
		Invoice Total		$273.00

Terms: net 10 days.

☐ **Cheque Copy #207**   **Dated Feb. 8/12**

To Sun Lab Products, $708.75 in full payment of account. Reference invoice #SL-4100.

☐

Adrienne Aesthetics

INVOICE # 25
Adrienne Aesthetics
20 Portage Ave. E.
Winnipeg, MB R3C 4R1
567 643 778

Sold to: The Forks Film Corp.
Address: 6 Gilroy St.
              Winnipeg, MB R3C 2M2
ATTN: Francine Despardieu

Salesperson: Blossom   **Date:**   Feb. 8/12

QTY	CODE	DESCRIPTION	PRICE/UNIT	TAX CODE	TOTAL
4	CL05	Masks: herb 100 ml	36 /jar**	1	144.00
4	CL06	Masks: sea 100 ml	32 /jar	1	128.00
8	FC03	Epidermal Cleanser: face+ 300 ml	55 /jar	1	440.00
8	FC04	Epidermal Cleanser: phytogel 300 ml	45 /jar	1	360.00
3	FC06	Foundation 35 ml	22 /jar	1	66.00
5	SC06	UV #30 Total Cream 125 ml	68 /tube	1	340.00

** preferred customer discounts applied LB

Terms: 2/15, n/30	GST 5%	73.90
	RST 7%	103.46
	Invoice Total	**1,655.36**

Tel 1: (204) 722-9876   or   (204) 722-8701   Fax: (204) 722-8000
www.adrienneaesthetics.com
look good, feel good

☑ **Visa Sales Return #22-R**   **Dated Feb. 8/12**

387   Returned to Blossom by Cash Customer

–1 CL08	Protection Cream: dbl action 60 ml	$25.00
–1 SC05	UV #15 Total Cream 125 ml	50.00
	Goods and Services Tax	3.75
	Retail Sales Tax	5.25
	Total credited to Visa account	$84.00

☑ **Purchase Return #BL-669R**   **Dated Feb. 8/12**

388   Return to Biotech Laboratories because package safety seal was broken.

–5 FC10	Powder: loose 15 g	$40.00
	GST Paid	2.00
	Total Credit	$42.00

Terms: net 60 days.

☐ **Purchase Invoice #EI-933**   **Dated Feb. 9/12**

From Esthetica Inc.

	Manicure and pedicure preparation products	$ 90.00
5	FC02 Concealer 15 ml	45.00
5	CL03 Eye Contour Smoothing Cream 30 ml	65.00
5	CL04 Eye Contour Smoothing Gel 30 ml	95.00
	Freight	20.00
	GST Paid	15.75
	Invoice Total	$330.75

Terms: net 30 days. Note the price increases.

NOTES
Remember to edit the purchase prices by changing the numbers in the Amount field.
Use account 1380 Miscellaneous Inventory Products for the manicure and pedicure products.

☐ **Cheque Copy #208**   **Dated Feb. 9/12**

To Acqua Viva Cosmetics, $420 in full payment of account. Reference invoice #AC-1124.

☐

Adrienne Aesthetics

INVOICE # 26   **Sold to:** Lavender Estates
Adrienne Aesthetics   **Address:** 9 Lavender Ct.
20 Portage Ave. E.   Winnipeg, MB R2X 3J6
Winnipeg, MB R3C 4R1   **ATTN:** Katherine Harris
567 643 778

Salesperson: Blossom   **Date:**   Feb. 10/12

QTY	CODE	DESCRIPTION	PRICE/UNIT	TAX CODE	TOTAL
3	CL09	Protection Cream: moisturizer 60 ml	30 /tube	1	90.00
3	SC04	Sun Tan Milk SPF#15 200 ml	50 /jar	1	150.00
2	AS11	Package: Deluxe 5 spa treatments	800 /series	2	1,600.00
2	VP02	Valentine Gift: deluxe pkg	150 /pkg	1	300.00

LB

Terms: 2/5, n/30	GST 5%	107.00
	RST 7%	37.80
	Invoice Total	**2,284.80**

Tel 1: (204) 722-9876   or   (204) 722-8701   Fax: (204) 722-8000
www.adrienneaesthetics.com
look good, feel good

☐ **Sales Invoice #27**   **Dated Feb. 11/12**

Sold by Hydra to Botelli & Giroux, Lawyers

3	AS09	Promotional Pkg: spa treatment	$100 /job
3	VP01	Valentine Gift: super pkg	100 /pkg
3	VP02	Valentine Gift: deluxe pkg	150 /pkg
		Goods and Services Tax	5%
		Retail Sales Tax	7%

Terms: 2/5, n/30.

☐ **Cash Purchase Invoice #VP-125**   **Dated Feb. 11/12**

From Vista Promotions (use Quick Add for the new supplier), $200 plus $10 GST and $14 RST for business cards and flyers for promotion. Purchase invoice total $224 paid by cheque #209.

☐ **Purchase Invoice #EI-1303**   **Dated Feb. 12/12**

From Esthetica Inc.

		Manicure and pedicure preparation products	$ 90.00
5	CL05	Masks: herb 100 ml	80.00
5	CL06	Masks: sea 100 ml	90.00
5	FC03	Epidermal Cleanser: face+ 300 ml	125.00
5	FC04	Epidermal Cleanser: phytogel 300 ml	110.00
		Freight	20.00
		GST Paid	25.75
		Invoice Total	$540.75

Terms: net 30 days.

Cash Purchase Invoice #WH-42455   **Dated Feb. 13/12**

From Winnipeg Hydro, $200 plus $10 GST for hydro services. Purchase invoice total $210 paid by cheque #210.

Cash Purchase Invoice #MB-16721   **Dated Feb. 13/12**

From Manitoba Bell, $80 plus $4.00 GST and $5.60 RST for telephone services. Purchase invoice total $89.60 paid by cheque #211.

Sales Invoice #28   **Dated Feb. 13/12**

Sold by Blossom to Ariandanos Residence

1	AS01	Bridal Makeup/Styling	$ 70 /job
1	AS04	Electrolysis: 60 min treatment	75 /session
1	AS05	European Deep Cleansing Facial	60 /job
1	AS06	Hydroptimate Treatment	120 /job
1	AS12	Skin Treatment	100 /job
		Goods and Services Tax	5%

Terms: 2/5, n/30.

Visa Sales Summary Invoice #29   **Dated Feb. 13/12**

Sold by Hydra to various one-time Cash Customers

3	CL02	Cleansing Milk 225 ml	$ 25 /tube	$ 75.00
2	CL07	Night Cream 200 ml	45 /jar	90.00
5	AS09	Promotional Pkg: spa treatment	100 /job	500.00
2	VP01	Valentine Gift: super pkg	100 /pkg	200.00
1	VP02	Valentine Gift: deluxe pkg	150 /pkg	150.00
		Goods and Services Tax	5%	50.75
		Retail Sales Tax	7%	36.05
		Total paid by Visa		$1 101.80

MasterCard Sales Summary Invoice #30   **Dated Feb. 13/12**

Sold by Blossom to various one-time Cash Customers

2	CL01	Cleansing Lotion 225 ml	$ 15 /tube	$ 30.00
2	CL02	Cleansing Milk 225 ml	25 /tube	50.00
1	AS05	European Deep Cleansing Facial	60 /job	60.00
2	AS11	Package: Deluxe 5 spa treatments	800 /series	1 600.00
2	VP01	Valentine Gift: super pkg	100 /pkg	200.00
		Goods and Services Tax	5%	97.00
		Retail Sales Tax	7%	19.60
		Total paid by MasterCard		$2 056.60

Cash Sales Summary Invoice #31   **Dated Feb. 14/12**

Sold by Hydra to various one-time Cash Customers

1	CL06	Masks: sea 100 ml	$ 35 /jar	$ 35.00
2	FC01	Blush 8 g	10 each	20.00
2	AS01	Bridal Makeup/Styling	70 /job	140.00
3	AS10	Package: Super 5 spa treatments	600 /series	1 800.00
2	VP02	Valentine Gift: deluxe pkg	150 /pkg	300.00
		Goods and Services Tax	5%	114.75
		Retail Sales Tax	7%	24.85
		Total cash received		$2 434.60

Cash Receipt #13   **Dated Feb. 14/12**

From The Forks Film Corporation, cheque #8091 for $1 625.80 in payment of account including $29.56 discount for early payment. Reference invoice #25.

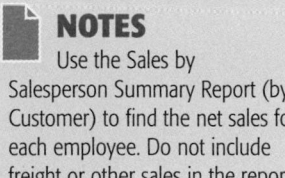

NOTES
Use the Sales by Salesperson Summary Report (by Customer) to find the net sales for each employee. Do not include freight or other sales in the report.

NOTES
If you are working from backups, restore the backup file SimData10\adrienne1.CAB to SimData10\Adrienne\adrienne.
Refer to to the instructions in Chapter 1, page 20, if you need assistance with restoring files from backups.

NOTES
We have selected Retail as the type of industry for Adrienne Aesthetics because they sell inventory items.

CLASSIC VIEW
Click the Sales icon to open the Sales Journal.

PRO VERSION
The invoice does not include Order No. or Shipping Date fields.

☐   **Memo #4**   **Dated Feb. 14/12**

From Owner: Complete payroll run to pay salaried employees Blossom and Hydra. Issue cheques #212 and #213. Add the 2 percent sales commissions based on the net sales for each employee from Feb. 1 to Feb. 14.

KEYSTROKES

Accounting for Inventory Sales

The first transaction involves the sale of inventory items. Many of the steps are identical to those you used for sales in previous applications. You will be using the inventory database and all the Sales Invoice fields to complete this transaction.

Open   **SimData10\Adrienne\adrienne** to access the data files for Adrienne Aesthetics.

Type   2 7 12 or **choose Feb. 7** from the calendar and **click OK**.

This will enter the session date February 7, 2012. The familiar Receivables module window appears. Inventory & Services has been added to the Modules pane list. Inventory sales are entered in the Sales Journal.

Click   the **Sales Invoices icon** [icon] to open the familiar Sales Journal:

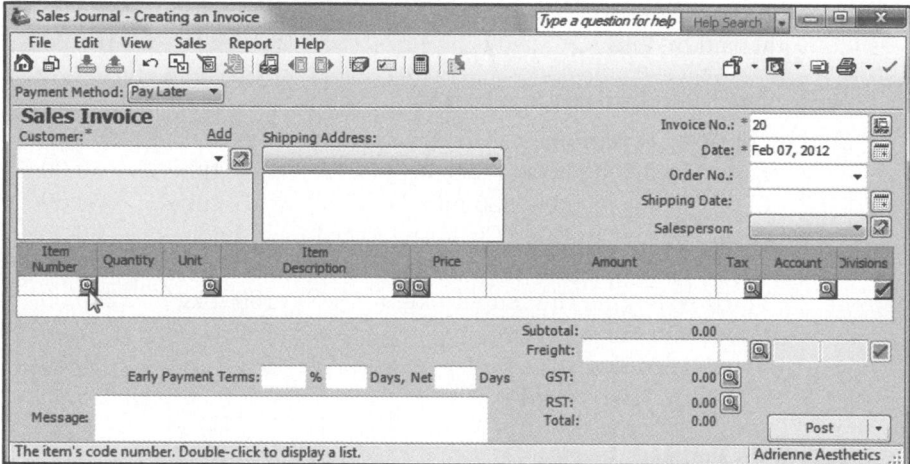

The Sales Journal looks the same as in earlier data files, except for the Sales Journal we customized for Air Care Services in Chapter 6. All the invoice fields are used when we sell inventory. Pay Later is correctly selected as the payment method.

Click   the **Customer field list arrow** to display the list of customers.

Click   **Boutique Fashions** to enter the customer's name and address on the form. If you selected an incorrect customer, return to the customer list and select again.

You can skip the Shipping Address fields — the default information is correct. The Invoice number is correct because the numeric invoice sequence has been set up in the defaults. If necessary, you can edit the invoice number. The Order No. is not used for invoices. The payment terms, tax code and revenue account are also added from the customer's default settings and can be edited if necessary.

Click   the **Date field Calendar icon** ▦ to advance the cursor. The default session date is incorrect.

Click   **1** on the February calendar.

Click   the **Salesperson field** and **choose Hydra** as the salesperson.

One line is used for each inventory item or service sold by the business. A separate line would also be used for non-inventory sales and to enter returns and allowances made.

Click   the **Item Number field List icon** 🔍, or **press** (enter) or **double click** the **field** to access the inventory list:

Select Inventory/Service				

Select inventory/service: ☐ Bypass Search Field
Search
[_____]   ● Number   ○ Description

Item Number	Type	Qty on Hand	Item Description
<Add new inventory/service>			
AS01	Service	--	Bridal Makeup/Styling
AS02	Service	--	Cellulite Treatment
AS03	Service	--	Electrolysis: 45 min treatment
AS04	Service	--	Electrolysis: 60 min treatment
AS05	Service	--	European Deep Cleansing Facial
AS06	Service	--	Hydroptimate Treatment
AS07	Service	--	Makeup
AS08	Service	--	Massage: Swedish
AS09	Service	--	Promotional Pkg: spa treatment
AS10	Service	--	Package: Super 5 spa treatments
AS11	Service	--	Package: Deluxe 5 spa treatments
AS12	Service	--	Skin Treatment

Francais

Create   Select   Cancel

Notice that you can add new inventory items from the Select Inventory/Service screen. The inventory items are listed in order by number or code, but you can change the order and sort by description or name. Sorting inventory items by number or description is also an option in the Inventory Settings. For inventory items, the quantities available are also included in this display for reference.

The cursor is in the Search field. We will bypass the search field so that future references to this list will place the cursor in the list rather than in the Search field.

Click   **Bypass Search Field** so that the next time the cursor will start in the item list.

Click   ▼ to scroll down the list. **Click** in the **list** and **type**   c   if you want to advance the list to the codes beginning with C.

Click   **CL04 Eye Contour Smoothing Gel 30 ml** from the list.

Click   **Select** to add the inventory item to your form. If you have made an incorrect selection, return to the Item Number field and reselect from the inventory list.

You can also type the code number in the Item Number field and press (tab), but you must match the case of the code number in the ledger.

The cursor moves to the Quantity field. Notice that the program adds information in each field automatically, based on the inventory record information. All the information except quantity and amount is added by default as soon as you enter the inventory item number. If you select a preferred customer, the default price is the preferred customer price instead of the regular selling price (see the screen on page 386).

You should enter the number of units of this item sold in the Quantity field.

Type   8   **Press** (tab).

If your company settings do not allow inventory levels to go below zero, the program prevents you from continuing when you enter a quantity greater than the available stock.

NOTES
Remember that you must include the year when you type the date in the Sales Journal.

NOTES
Inventory codes are case sensitive – you must type CL04 in the journal (match the upper-case Cl in the item code) to enter the item directly in the journal. To use the list of items, you can type a lower-case c to advance to the C-items

NOTES
If you want to search for items by description, you can type the first letter in the Item Description field to see the item list beginning with the letter you typed and sorted alphabetically by description.

NOTES
Inventory items can be oversold, but you must change the Inventory Ledger settings to allow the quantity on hand to go below zero. This setting is explained in the setup for Flabuless Fitness (Chapter 16).
No quantities are shown for services because they are not held in stock.

You will see this warning if the quantity you enter is greater than the available stock:

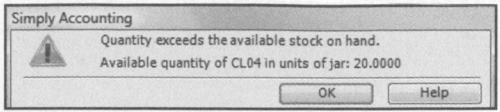

Click **OK** to return to the journal so you can reduce the quantity.

Since the remaining default information is correct, you do not need to change it. The default tax code — GP — is the code entered for the customer because the customer pays both GST at 5 percent and RST at 7 percent. Services have been set up in the Inventory Ledger so that by default RST is not applied.

The program automatically calculates an amount based on the selling price per unit. This figure appears in the Amount field.

The default revenue account for the item appears but can be accepted or changed. You would change the account for returns and allowances or unusual entries. Accept the default revenue account for this sale.

You can select another tax code from the Tax Code list if necessary. You can also edit the price to change the selling price for a particular item or customer. To change the account, click the Account field List icon [icon], press *enter* or double click in the Account field to obtain a list of accounts.

Press *tab* **repeatedly** to advance to the next invoice line and update the first line because all the default record information is correct.

Or you can click the Item Number field on the second line, or the third line, if the item description wraps around to the second invoice line.

Type f

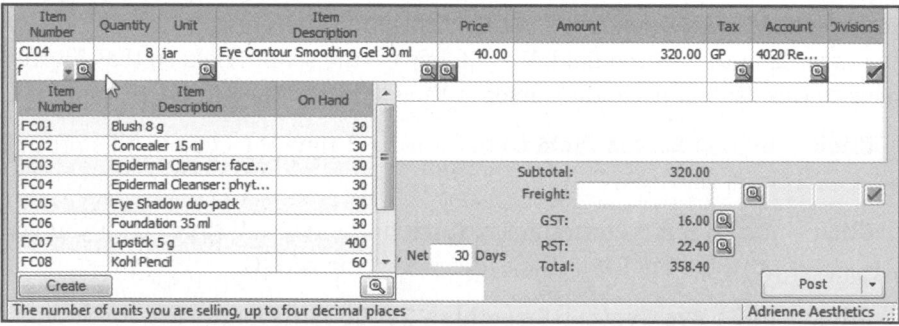

The list arrow in the Item Number field provides a drop-down item list. Click to select an item from this list. When you type f, the first letter or number of the code, in the Item Number field the inventory item drop-down list shows all items starting with F. The inventory list is also available when you type in the Item Description field, but it is sorted by description instead of by item number.

Click **FC02** and **press** *tab* to advance to the Quantity field. **Type** 8

Press *tab* in the Account field to add a new invoice line in the viewing space of the journal when you reach the last invoice line of the journal.

Enter the **remaining sale items** using the steps above for the first item.

As you complete each line and advance to the next, the totals and tax amounts at the bottom of the form are updated to include the last item entered.

GP is entered as the tax code for the service items, but only GST is added to the invoice total. We will confirm this when we review the journal entry.

To include more invoice lines on your screen, drag the lower frame of the Sales Journal window or maximize the window.

There are no freight charges for these items, so your invoice is complete after you enter the final service item for the customer. It should look like the one shown here:

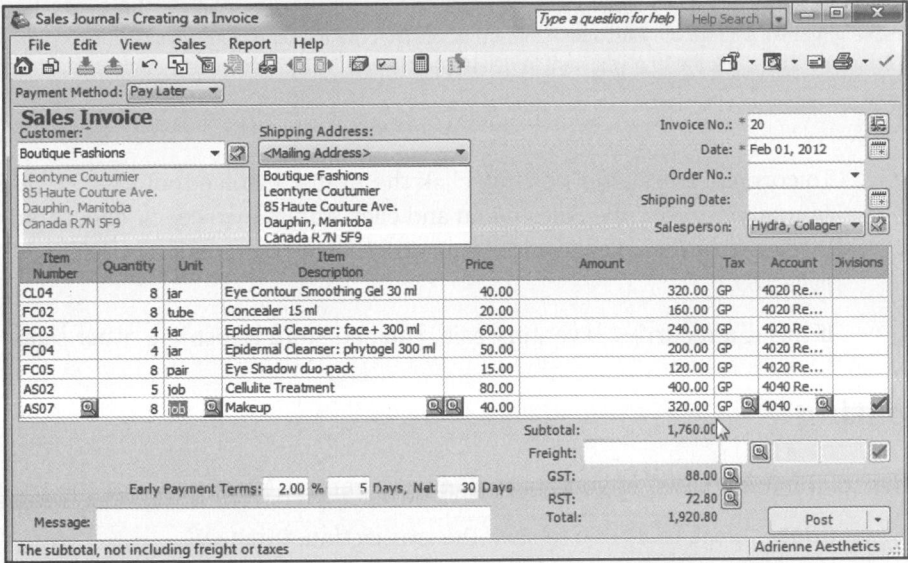

You should review the journal entry before posting it.

Reviewing the Inventory Sales Journal Transaction

Choose the **Report menu** and **click Display Sales Journal Entry**:

Adrienne Aesthetics
Sales Journal Entry 02/01/2012 (J1)

Account Number	Account Description	Debits	Credits
1200	Accounts Receivable	1,920.80	-
5060	Cost of Goods Sold	428.00	-
1310	Creams and Lotions	-	144.00
1320	Face Care Products	-	284.00
2640	RST Payable	-	72.80
2650	GST Charged on Sales	-	88.00
4020	Revenue from Sales	-	1,040.00
4040	Revenue from Services	-	720.00
Additional Date:	Additional Field:	2,348.80	2,348.80

From the tax amounts, you can see that RST is charged only on the *Revenue from Sales* amount — 7% × $1 040 = $72.80 — while GST is charged on both sales and services — 5% × ($1 040 + $720) = $88. Both taxes are calculated correctly because of the tax exemptions assigned in the Inventory Ledger records.

Notice that all relevant accounts have been updated automatically because the Inventory and Receivables ledgers are linked to the General Ledger. Therefore, the linked asset, revenue and expense accounts defined for each inventory item have been debited or credited as required. In addition, the linked Receivables accounts we saw earlier are used — *RST Payable*, *GST Charged on Sales* and *Accounts Receivable*. The inventory database and customer record are also updated.

Adrienne Aesthetics uses the average cost method to determine the cost of goods sold. If the stock for an inventory item was purchased at different times and prices, the average of these prices would be used as the cost of goods sold.

Close the **display** to return to the journal input screen.

CORRECTING THE INVENTORY SALES ENTRY BEFORE POSTING

To **correct** an **item** on the inventory line, **click** the **incorrect field** to move the cursor and highlight the field contents. **Press** _enter_ to display the list of inventory items, tax codes or accounts. **Click** the **correct selection** to highlight it, then **click Select**, or for the remaining fields, **type** the **correct information**. **Press** _tab_ to enter the change.

If you **change** the **inventory** item, you must **re-enter** the **quantity sold** in the Quantity field and **press** _tab_. The totals will be updated correctly if you follow this procedure.

...continued

NOTES
Pressing _ctrl_ + J will also open the journal display.

WARNING!
You should always check that the taxes are correct. To be certain that the taxes will be correctly applied, you can change the tax code for the service items to G. This method is required in Chapter 16, where separate tax rates apply to the sale of inventory and of books.

NOTES
Adrienne uses a single cost of goods sold account for all inventory items.
In the Premium version you can choose the first-in, first-out method of costing.

To correct errors after posting, click the Adjust Invoice tool  in the Sales Journal or choose the Sales menu and click Adjust Invoice. Or choose Adjust Invoice from the Sales Invoices icon drop-down shortcuts list. (Refer to page 189.)

If this is a recurring inventory sale, you can store it just like other sales.

Posting

When all the information in your journal entry is correct, you must post the transaction.

> **Click**   **Post** `Post ▾` to save the transaction. **Click OK**.
>
> **Close**   the **Sales Journal** to exit to the Home window.
>
> **Enter**   the **sales receipt** as the next transaction.
>
> **Create**   **shortcuts** for transactions in other modules (Create Purchase Invoice, Pay Purchase Invoices, Create General Journal and Payroll Cheque Run.)

Accounting for Inventory Purchases

The third transaction involves the purchase of inventory items. Inventory purchases are entered in the Purchases Journal, and many of the steps are the same as those for other credit purchases. Now the inventory database will provide the additional information.

> **Click**   **Create Purchase Invoice** in the Shortcuts pane to display the familiar Purchases Journal input form window:

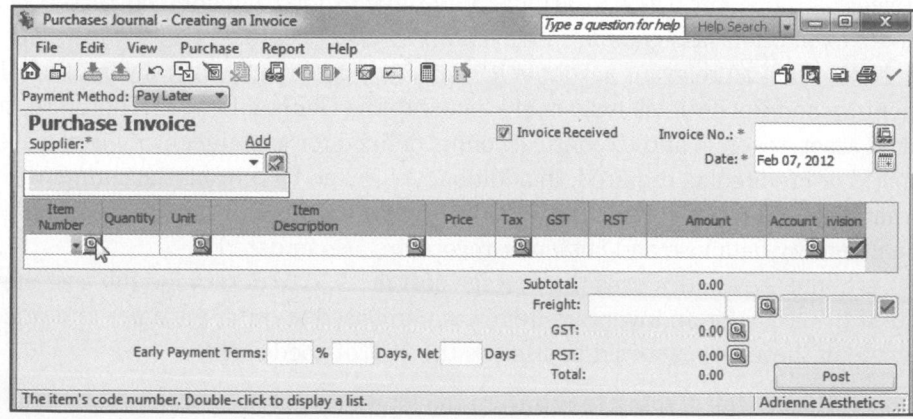

Pay Later is correctly selected as the method of payment.

> **Click**   the **Purchased From field list arrow** to display the list of suppliers.
>
> **Click**   **Acqua Viva Cosmetics** from the list to add it to your input form.

Check your selection. If you chose an incorrect supplier, select again from the supplier list. If you selected correctly, proceed by entering the invoice number.

> **Click**   the **Invoice No. field**.

WARNING!

If you adjust a posted invoice to correct for selecting the wrong customer, the customer options, such as payment terms or tax codes, are not updated and may be incorrect. For these errors, you should reverse the entry.

NOTES

Transaction confirmation is turned on, so you should click OK when you post or record each transaction.

NOTES

You can add a shortcut for Pay Expenses if you want.

NOTES

If you did not create shortcuts, click Payables in the Modules pane list to open the Payables window. Then click the Purchase Invoices icon to open the journal.

CLASSIC VIEW

Click the Purchases Journal icon `Purchases` to open the journal.

Type   AC-1124 **Press** (tab) **twice**.

The cursor advances to the Date field, where you should enter the invoice date.

Type   Feb 1 12

Press   (tab) **twice** to advance the cursor to the Item Number field. **Press** (tab) **once** if you choose the date from the Date field calendar.

Press   (enter) or **click** the **List icon** 🔍 to see the list of inventory items.

Notice that you can add new inventory from the Select Inventory/Service window.

Scroll down   and **click SC03 Sun Tan Milk SPF#4 200 ml** from the list to highlight it.

Press   (enter). If you have made an incorrect selection, return to the Item Number field and select again.

You can also click the list arrow, to see the entire inventory item list, or a partial list if you type the first letter of the item code, just as you did in the Sales Journal. Press (tab) to move to the next field.

The cursor advances to the Quantity field. The Item Description field should now show the name, Sun Tan Milk SPF#4 200 ml. The default price is the most recent purchase price. Now enter the quantity for this item.

Type   5 **Press** (tab).

The cursor advances to the Unit field. The Unit and Description are correct based on Inventory Ledger records.

The Price field records the unit price paid for the purchase of the inventory items. This amount should not include any GST paid that can be used as an input tax credit. The default information, based on previous purchases, is correct so do not change it.

The correct tax code — code G — is entered by default from the supplier record. Adrienne pays only GST on purchases of inventory items that will be resold.

If a price is incorrect because it has changed, you can edit the default amount. If a tax code is incorrect, you can change it by selecting from the tax code list.

When purchasing new inventory, no price is recorded. You should enter the quantity and, in the Amount field, enter the total purchase amount. Press (tab) to advance the cursor. Simply Accounting will calculate the price per unit.

Press   (tab) **repeatedly** to advance to the next line, with the cursor blinking in the Item Number field again, or **click** the **Item Number field** in the next line.

Notice that the cursor skips the RST amount field because the supplier tax code does not include RST. The Account field was also skipped over, because you cannot change the entry for inventory purchases. The Asset account for the inventory purchase is defined in the Inventory Ledger as the linked account for purchases and sales. To change the account, you must edit the Inventory Ledger record. The default account for the supplier does not apply to the inventory purchase.

Enter   **the second item** from the source document, using the same steps that you used to record the first item.

⚠ WARNING!
Remember that you need to add the year when you type the date in the Purchases Journal.

📄 NOTES
If you want to search for items by description, you can type the first letter in the Item Description field to see the item list beginning with the letter you typed and sorted alphabetically by description.

📄 NOTES
RST is not paid on items that are purchased for resale because the store is not the final customer.

Your journal looks like the following when you are ready to enter the freight charge:

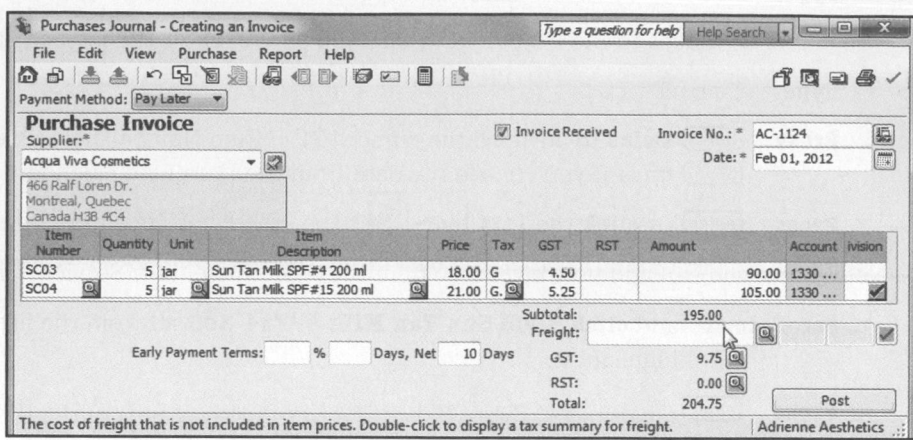

The Freight fields are used to enter any freight charges that cannot be allocated to the purchase of a specific item and to enter the taxes paid on the freight charges. There are four Freight fields: the base amount of the freight charge, tax code, GST amount and, finally, the RST amount. Because GST is paid on freight you must enter a tax code if the supplier charges freight.

Click   the **first Freight field**, the amount field, below the Subtotal.

Type   10   **Press** (tab).

The tax code for the supplier, code G, should be entered by default.

If the tax code for freight is not entered automatically, press (enter) to see the familiar list of tax codes. Click G and then click Select.

You do not need to enter amounts for the taxes on freight; they are calculated as soon as you enter the amount of freight charged and the tax code.

Simply Accounting calculates the amount of GST (and RST if it is paid) and updates all the totals. Your input form is complete and should appear as follows:

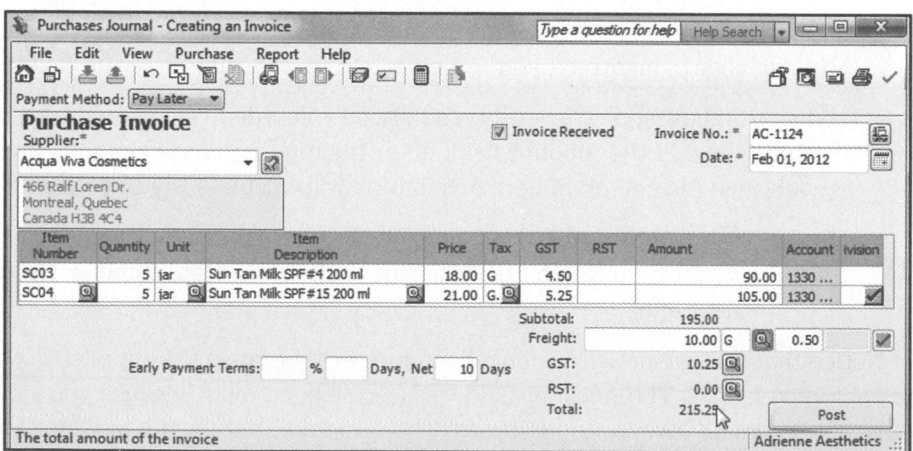

The Subtotal includes all items purchased but does not include freight or taxes.

Reviewing the Inventory Purchase Transaction

Choose the **Report menu** and **click Display Purchases Journal Entry**:

| Adrienne Aesthetics | | | |
| Purchases Journal Entry 02/01/2012 (J3) | | | |
Account Number	Account Description	Debits	Credits
1330	Sun Care Products	195.00	-
2670	GST Paid on Purchases	10.25	-
5200	Freight Expense	10.00	-
2200	Accounts Payable	-	215.25
Additional Date:	Additional Field:	215.25	215.25

NOTES
RST is not charged on freight in Manitoba when it is applied to an RST-exempt purchase. The correct tax code for freight is code G - GST @ 5%.

NOTES
Pressing (ctrl) + J will also open the journal display.

Simply Accounting has automatically updated all accounts relevant to this transaction. The appropriate inventory asset account (*Sun Care Products*), *Accounts Payable, GST Paid on Purchases* and *Freight Expense* have been updated as required because the ledgers are linked. The inventory database and the supplier record are also updated.

Close   the **display** to return to the Purchases Journal input screen.

CORRECTING THE INVENTORY PURCHASES JOURNAL ENTRY

If the inventory item is incorrect, **reselect** from the **inventory** list by **pressing** (enter) while in this field. **Click Select** to add the item to your form. **Type** the **quantity** purchased and **press** (tab) to update the totals.

Account numbers cannot be changed for inventory items on the purchase invoice. They must be edited in the Inventory Ledger.

To **insert** a new **line,** if you have forgotten a complete line of the invoice, **click** the **line below** the one you have forgotten. **Choose** the **Edit menu** and **click Insert Line** to add a blank invoice line to your form. To **remove** a complete **line, click** the **line** you want to delete, **choose** the **Edit menu** and **click Remove Line.**

For assistance with correcting other invoice details, refer to page 120.

To correct an inventory purchase after posting, use the **Adjust Invoice tool** or **choose** the **Purchase Menu** and **click Adjust Invoice.** Refer to page 133. If you selected the wrong supplier, you can reverse the purchase transaction (page 144).

Posting

When all the information in your journal entry is correct, you must post the transaction.

Click   **Post** [Post] . **Close** the **Purchases Journal**.

The Inventory Module

Click   **Inventory & Services** in the Modules pane list:

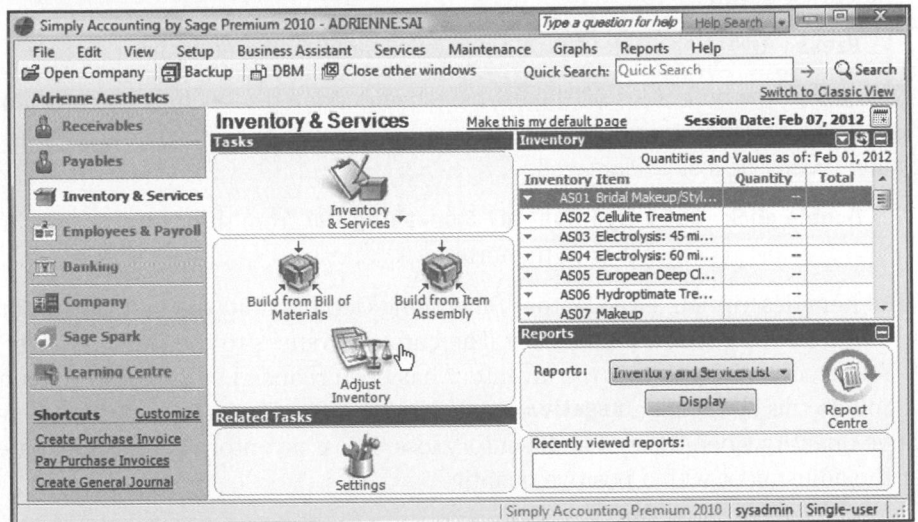

The Inventory module has icons for the ledger records and for journal entries. Records are listed in the Inventory Item list pane as they are for other modules so you can access them directly. The Reports pane includes all inventory reports in the Reports list.

NOTES
If this is a recurring purchase, you can store it, just like other recurring purchases.

WARNING!
If you adjust a posted invoice to correct for selecting the wrong supplier, the supplier options, such as payment terms and tax codes, are not updated and may be incorrect. For these errors, you should reverse the entry.

NOTES
Remember that you will see the transaction confirmation message each time you post. We will not repeat the instructions to click OK for this message.

PRO VERSION
The Inventory module in the Pro version does not include the the Build From Bill Of Materials icon.

You will see only two journal icons: Build From Item Assembly and Adjust Inventory.

Making Inventory Adjustments

Sometimes inventory is lost, stolen or damaged and adjusting entries are required to reflect the expenses. These inventory adjustments are made in the Inventory Adjustments Journal in the Inventory & Services window. This journal is also used to record lost inventory that is recovered and inventory that is used by the business instead of being sold to customers.

Click the **Adjust Inventory icon** 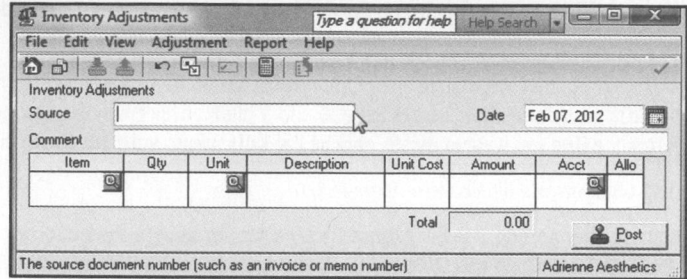, the one with the hand pointer in the previous Home window screen, to open the blank Adjustments Journal:

The cursor is in the Source field. The source for an adjustment will normally be a memo from a manager or owner.

Type Memo 1 **Press** (tab).

The cursor is in the Date field, with the session date entered and highlighted.

Type 02-02 **Press** (tab) **twice**.

The cursor is now in the Comment field, where you can enter a brief explanation for this transaction.

Type Jar dropped and broken **Press** (tab).

The cursor advances to the Item field.

Press (enter) or **click** 🔍 to display the familiar inventory list.

Notice that the quantities on the list have been updated to include the previous sale and purchase. Services are not included in the list because they have no quantities in stock and cannot be lost or damaged.

Double click CL04 Eye Contour Smoothing Gel from the list to select it and enter it onto the form.

The item description, Eye Contour Smoothing Gel, the unit, the unit cost and the account have been added automatically. The cursor advances to the Quantity (Qty) field. You need to indicate that the inventory has been reduced because of the damaged item. You do this by typing a **negative** number in the field. Remember always to enter a negative quantity when there is an inventory loss. If lost inventory is recovered later, enter the adjustment with a positive quantity.

Type -1 **Press** (tab).

The cursor advances to the Unit field. The rest of the journal line is completed automatically. In the Amount field, a negative amount, reflecting the inventory loss, automatically appears as a default based on the average cost. In the Account field, *Inventory Losses*, the default linked account for inventory losses appears for this entry. This is the correct account.

If you need to choose another account, press (enter) to display the list of accounts and select the account as usual. You can also edit the unit cost or

amount if you know that the price of the unit was different from the default price, the average of all inventory in stock. You can store and recall Adjustments Journal entries just as you do entries in other journals.

Your entry is complete as shown and you are ready to review it:

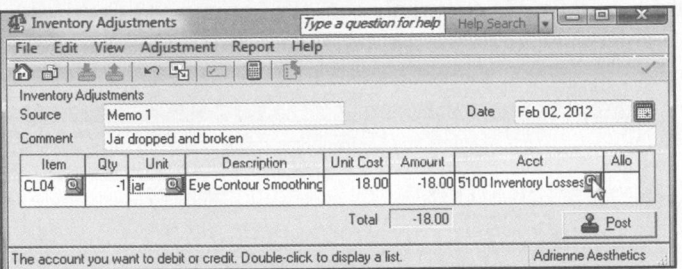

Reviewing the Adjustments Journal Entry

Choose the **Report menu** and **click Display Inventory Adjustments Journal Entry** to display the transaction you have entered as shown here:

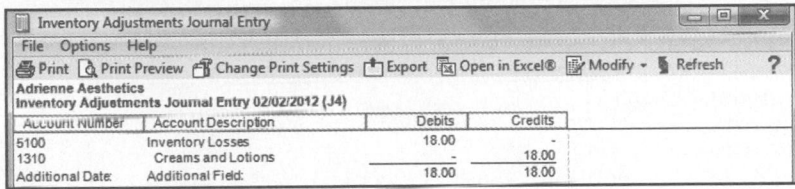

You can see that Simply Accounting has automatically updated all relevant accounts for this transaction. The appropriate inventory asset defined for this inventory item, *Creams and Lotions*, and the inventory database have been reduced to reflect the loss at the average cost price. *Inventory Losses*, the Inventory linked expense account that was defined for inventory losses or adjustments, has been debited or increased.

Close the **display** to return to the Adjustments Journal input screen.

CORRECTING THE ADJUSTMENTS JOURNAL ENTRY

Move to the field that has the error. **Press** (tab) to move forward or **press** (shift) and (tab) together to move back to a previous field. This will highlight the field information so you can change it. **Type** the **correct information** and **press** (tab) to enter it.

You can also use the mouse to **point** to a field and **drag** through the **incorrect information** to highlight it. **Type** the **correct information** and **press** (tab) to enter it.

If the inventory item is incorrect, **reselect** from the **inventory** list by **pressing** (enter) while in this field. **Click Select** to add it to the form. **Type** the **quantity** and **press** (tab). After changing any information on an inventory item line, **press** (tab) to update the totals.

To start over, **click**  or (or **choose** the **Edit menu** and **click Undo Entry**). **Click Yes** when asked to confirm that you want to discard the transaction.

Posting

When all the information in your journal entry is correct, you must save the transaction.

Click **Post** [Post] .

Close the **Adjustments Journal** to return to the Inventory window. The next keystroke transaction creates and assembles new inventory items.

NOTES
The Allo (allocation) field for project allocations is not used by Adrienne Aesthetics. We will discuss it in a later application.

NOTES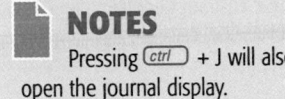
Pressing (ctrl) + J will also open the journal display.

NOTES
The second Inventory Ledger linked account is used for item assembly costs in the Item Assembly Journal. Item assembly is introduced in the next transaction.

WARNING!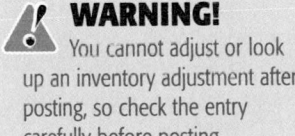
You cannot adjust or look up an inventory adjustment after posting, so check the entry carefully before posting.

Adding a New Inventory Item

Before entering the item assembly transaction, we will create the necessary new inventory items. Refer to Memo #2 (page 359) for the inventory item details. Inventory items can be added from any inventory item field in a journal, from the Inventory & Services icon (that opens the Inventory & Services window), or from the icon shortcuts list as shown:

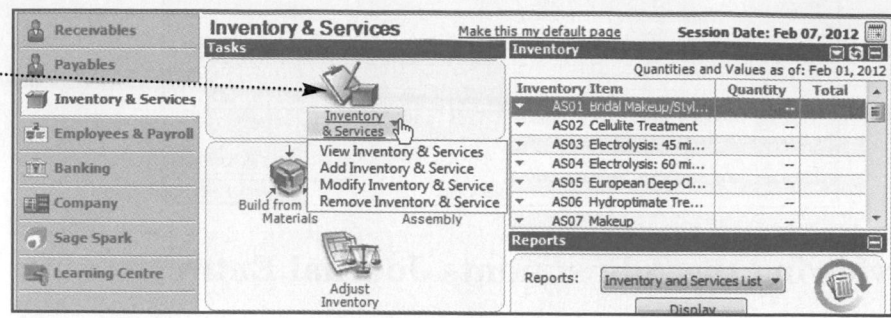

NOTES
You can hide the Quantity and Total inventory details in the Inventory list pane just as you can hide customer and supplier details. For services, these fields are blank.

Click   the **Inventory & Services icon** to open the Inventory & Services window:

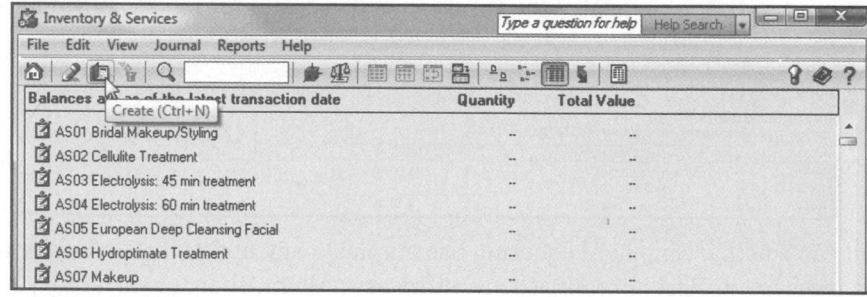

NOTES
You can add inventory items from any journal inventory field when the selection list is available, that is, in the Sales and Purchases journals and the two inventory journals, Adjustments and Item Assembly. Click the List icon in the Item field to open the selection list. Click Add New Inventory/Service and press (enter) to open the Inventory Ledger window.

This window is like the Accounts, Suppliers, Customers and Employees windows in other modules and it lists all inventory items and services. If you chose the Add Inventory shortcut, you will open a new ledger record directly and skip this Inventory & Services window.

Click   the **Create tool** , **choose** the **File menu** and **click Create**, or **press** (ctrl) + **N** to open the the Inventory Ledger:

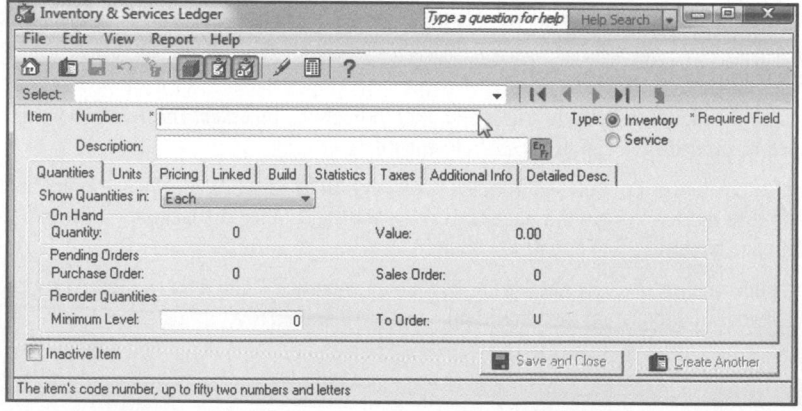

PRO VERSION
pro The Pro version does not have the Build tab. It applies to the Build From Bill Of Materials option in the Bill of Materials & Item Assembly Journal. This feature is not available in the Pro version.

PRO VERSION
pro The Time & Billing function is not available in the Pro version. The Pro version has only two Show tools — one for inventory items and one for service items. The Refresh tool is also not on the Pro version tool bar.

The Inventory & Services Ledger record has many of the tools that are available in other ledgers, including the Refresh tool. The Show tool icons allow you to limit the Select field list to inventory items, services or activities (for time and billing). If all three tools are selected, the list includes all three kinds of items. All Show tools are selected for Adrienne Aesthetics, so all records are included in the Select list.

You can enter both inventory and service items in the Inventory Ledger. When you enter a service item, you can designate it as an activity with time and billing information attached. Activities are available for the time and billing features and for selection as internal services — services that are provided by one department to another within the company and can be tracked as expenses. The Time & Billing function will be covered in Chapter 18.

The gift packages are inventory, so as a result the type selection is correct and the fields we need are included. The Quantities tab information is displayed because it is the first tab screen. As usual, required fields are marked with *.

The setup option we selected for inventory sorts the items by code or number.

Therefore, the Item Number field is the first item field. When you choose to sort by description, the longer Description field will come first. (See Chapter 16, page 655.)

From the source document information, you must enter the item code and description. The first Item field contains the code or number of the inventory item — the only required field on this screen; the second Item field contains the description or item name.

Click   the **Item Number field**.

Type   VP01 **Press** ⟨tab⟩ to advance to the Item Description field.

Type   Valentine Gift: super pkg

Click   the **Minimum Level field** in the Reorder Quantities section.

Here you must enter the stock level at which you want to reorder the item in question, or in this case, assemble more packages. When you print inventory reports, items that have fallen below the minimum level will be flagged.

Type   1

The Quantity On Hand, Value, and Order fields are updated from journal entries. Before the Inventory Ledger history is finished, you can add this information as historical data.

Click   the **Units tab**:

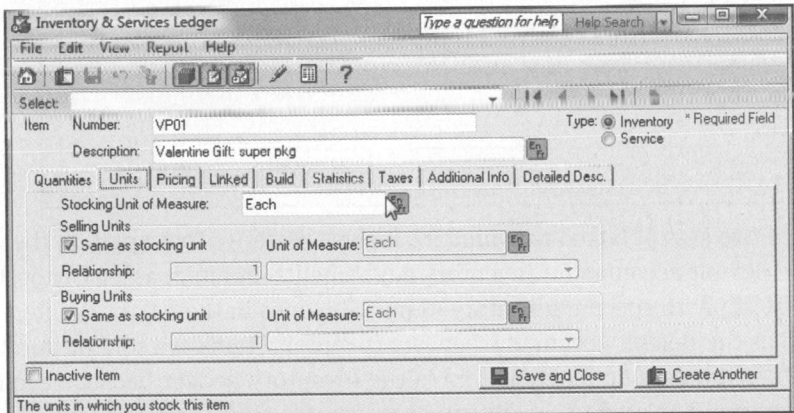

Units show the way in which goods are stored, bought and sold (e.g., by the dozen, by the tonne or by the item). These units may be different if, for example, merchandise is purchased in bulk packages and sold in individual units. When a store buys or stocks inventory in different units from those it sells, you also enter the relationship between the sets of units, for example, 12 units per carton.

Adrienne Aesthetics measures all units the same way so only one entry is needed.

Double click Each in the Stocking Unit Of Measure field.

Type   pkg

NOTES
As in other ledgers and journals, the Refresh tool applies when you work in multi-user mode. Clicking the tool will update the record with changes made by other users who are accessing the data file at the same time.

Click   the **Pricing tab**:

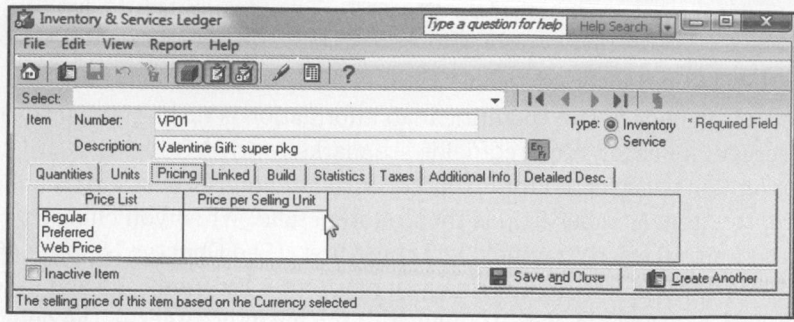

Each item may be assigned a regular price, a selling price for preferred customers and a Web price. Adrienne Aesthetics has two customers with preferred customer status. Regular, preferred and Web selling prices can also be entered in foreign currencies when other currencies are used.

Click   the **Price Per Selling Unit column** beside Regular.

Type   100

Press   ⎡tab⎤ to advance to the Price Per Selling Unit field for preferred prices.

The regular price is entered as the default Preferred and Web Price.

Type   95

Click   the **Linked tab** to access the linked accounts for the inventory item:

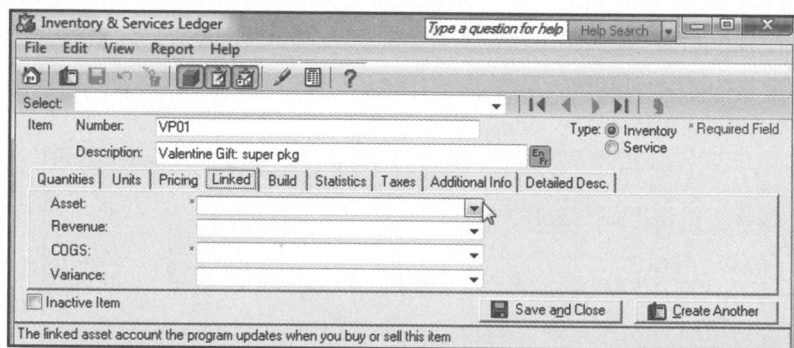

There are two sets of linked accounts for inventory: those that apply to the entire ledger — the default accounts for inventory adjustments and item assembly costs — and those that apply to specific inventory items. The ones in the ledger are item specific and are used as the default accounts whenever inventory items are sold or purchased. Linked accounts are defined for each item in the Inventory Ledger because each inventory item can be related to separate asset, revenue, expense and variance accounts.

In the **Asset** field, you must enter the number of the linked asset account affected by purchases and sales of this item. A list of accounts is available from the drop-down list arrow in the Asset field. Only asset accounts are available in the list for the Asset field. Because the account does not yet exist, we cannot choose it from the account list for the field, so we will create it here. The linked asset account is a required field.

Click   the **Asset field**.

Type   1350 Gift Packages **Press** ⎡tab⎤.

You will see the screen that allows you to create the new account:

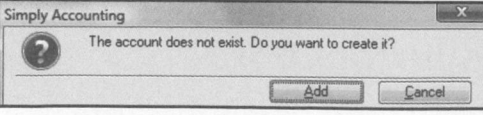

Click   **Add** to proceed to the Add An Account wizard. **Click Next** to continue.

Accept the **remaining** account **settings** and **finish** creating the account.

After you click Finish, you will see another message advising you of an account class change for the linked account:

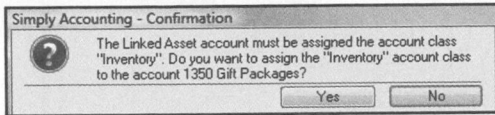

Click   **Yes** to accept the change. Clicking No will return you to the Linked Accounts screen so you can select a different account.

In the **Revenue** field, you must enter the linked revenue account that will be credited when this inventory item is sold. You can type the account number or select from the list. Only revenue accounts are available for the Revenue field.

Click   the **Revenue field list arrow** to see the revenue accounts available.

Click   **4020 Revenue from Sales** to enter it on your form.

Click   the **C.O.G.S. field list arrow** (Cost of Goods Sold expense) to see the expense accounts available.

In the **C.O.G.S.** field, you must enter the linked expense account that will be debited when this inventory item is sold. Only expense accounts are available for the C.O.G.S. field and the Variance field. Adrienne uses the single *Cost of Goods Sold* account for all inventory items. The linked C.O.G.S. account is also required.

Click   **5060 Cost of Goods Sold** from the list.

The **Variance** field contains the linked variance expense account used when the inventory sold is on order, before the goods are in stock. At the time of the sale, *Cost of Goods Sold* is debited for the average cost of the inventory on hand, based on previous purchases. When the goods are received, the actual purchase price may be different from this historical average cost. The price difference is charged to the variance account. Adrienne Aesthetics does not allow inventory to be oversold so you can leave the Variance account field blank.

Click   the **Build tab**:

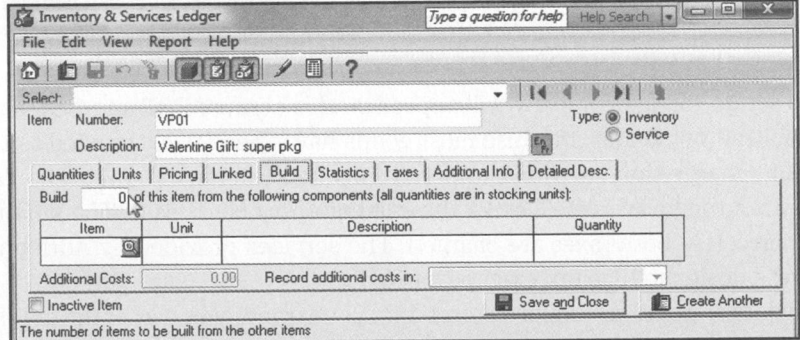

On the Build tab screen, you enter the inventory components that are needed to make the item. You identify the number of items you are building at one time and the required component items. This process is similar to the one found in the Components section of the Item Assembly Journal (see page 382). When it is time to build the item (in the Bill of Materials & Item Assembly Journal), you indicate how many items you are building — the Assembled Items section of the Item Assembly — and the rest of the details are taken from the Build screen of the ledger record. We will use the Build feature in Chapter 18.

NOTES
If necessary, you can create new linked revenue and expense accounts in the same way you created the new asset account.

NOTES
The linked revenue account is not a required account — you can choose an account in the Sales Journal when you sell inventory. The linked asset and C.O.G.S accounts are required — you cannot choose these accounts in the journals.

WARNING!
Check the linked account numbers carefully. If they are incorrect, corresponding journal entries will be posted incorrectly. If you discover the error when you are reviewing the journal entry, you should delete the journal entry line and then edit the Inventory Ledger record before posting.

NOTES
Variance accounts are used in the Truman Tires application in Chapter 13.

PRO VERSION
pro Click the Statistics tab at this stage.
The Pro version does not have a Build tab because this screen applies to Build From Bill Of Materials, a function not available in the Pro version.

NOTES
You can define multiple levels of building — one item may be made from other items that in turn are made from multiple inventory items.

Click the **Statistics tab**:

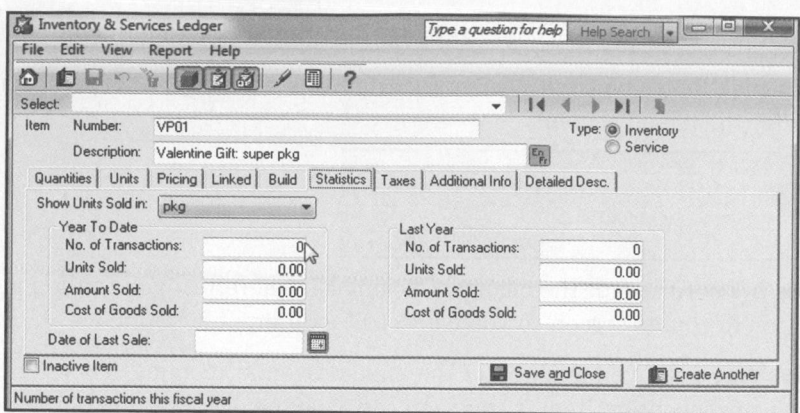

This screen applies to historical data. Since this is a new inventory item, there are no previous sales, and you should leave all entries at zero. The **Date Of Last Sale** shows the most recent date that this item was sold. The **Year To Date** section refers to historical information for the current fiscal period, and the **Last Year** fields apply to the previous year. Inventory Statistics are added to inventory tracking reports.

The **No. (number) Of Transactions** refers to the total number of times the item was sold. For example, if one customer bought the item on three separate dates, there would be three transactions. If four customers bought the item on one day, there would be four transactions. If one customer bought four of the same item at one time, there would be one transaction. The **Units Sold** counts the total number of items that were sold on all occasions to all customers in the relevant period. In the **Amount Sold** field you would enter the total sale price of all items sold in the period, and in the **Cost Of Goods Sold** field, you would enter the total purchase price of all items sold.

Click the **Taxes tab**:

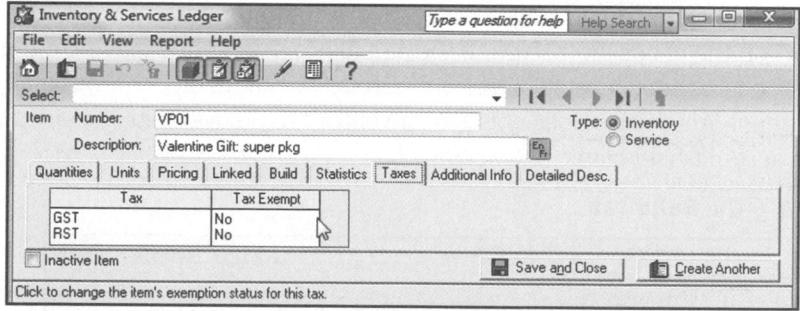

All taxes set up for the company will appear on this screen. RST and GST may be charged or omitted by default. Because most goods have these taxes applied to the sale, the default is to charge them — No is entered in the Tax Exempt column. The **Tax Exempt** entry is a toggle switch. Clicking the current entry changes it. The default settings are correct — both taxes are charged. The services provided by Adrienne Aesthetics were designated as tax exempt for RST.

When inventory items are imported and duty is charged, you can enter the duty rate on this screen as well.

The **Additional Info** tab allows for custom-defined information fields relating to the item, just like the Additional Info tabs in other ledgers. It is not used by Adrienne.

Click the **Detailed Desc. tab**:

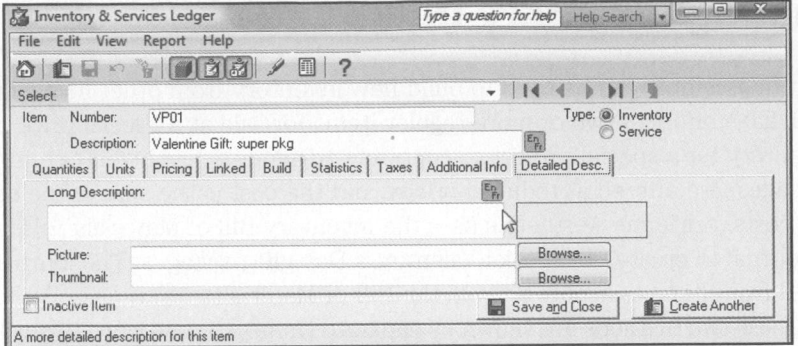

NOTES
When you first click Browse, the default location may be Documents and Settings. Because we do not know how you have organized your files and folders, we continue to use C:\SimData10 as the location for all the files for this text. This allows us to give clear file path instructions.

On this screen you can enter a detailed description of the inventory item and the name of a file where an image of the item is stored. The bitmap file for this item is located in the Setup\Logos folder in the SimData10 folder that has your other data files.

Click   **Browse** beside the Picture field to open the file location window.

Locate and **open** the **SimData10 folder**.

Double click **Setup** and then **double click** **Logos** to open these folders.

Double click **VP01** (or **VP01.bmp**) to add the image and file name:

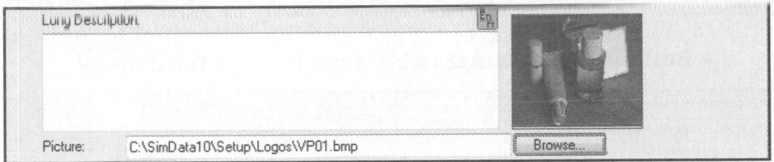

CORRECTING THE INVENTORY ITEM BEFORE CREATING THE RECORD

Correct the information if necessary by **clicking** the field that contains the **error**. **Click** the appropriate **tab** to change information screens if necessary. **Highlight** the **error** and **type** the **correct information**. **Press** (*tab*) to enter the correction.

When all the information is correct, you must save your information.

Click   **Create Another** [Create Another] to save the new record. The ledger remains open so you can add the second new item.

Click   the **Quantities tab**.

Enter   all the details for item **VP02** from page 359.

Click   **Save And Close** [Save and Close] to save the new record. Both items are added to your ledger list of inventory items.

Close   the **Inventory & Services window** to return to the Home window.

EDITING AN INVENTORY ITEM AFTER CREATING THE RECORD

You cannot edit an Inventory Ledger record while you are using the item in a journal. You must first **delete** the **journal line containing the item**. **Click** the **journal line**, **choose** the **Edit menu** and **click Remove Line**. Then **click** the journal's **Home window tool** [home icon] to return to the Home window. **Click Inventory & Services** in the Modules pane list. **Click** the name of the **inventory item** that you need to change in the Inventory pane Item list to open the item's record. **Click** the **tab** you need. **Highlight** the **information** that is incorrect, and then **type** the **correct information**. **Close** the **Ledger window**. **Click** the **Home window journal icon you need** (or the task bar icon/button for the journal) to return to the journal.

Assembling Inventory Items

Inventory item assembly can be used to build new inventory from other inventory items, to create package offers of two or more regular items for sale at a special price or to reserve inventory for a special project or contract. Adrienne's new inventory items, the special packages, are offered at reduced prices, and the cost is the sum of the original component costs. Adrienne Aesthetics uses the inventory Bill of Materials & Item Assembly Journal to create the special Valentine's Day gift packages. The journal can be used to build from Item Assembly or from the Bill of Materials.

The journal's two methods are shown by separate Home window icons. We will use the Item Assembly approach:

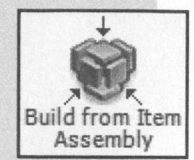

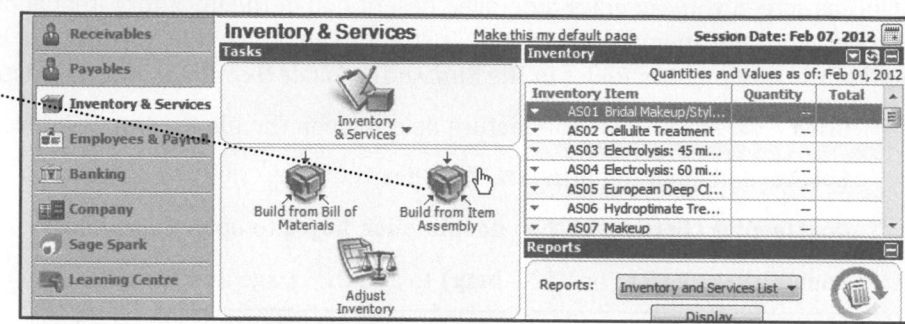

Click   the **Build From Item Assembly icon** to open the Journal:

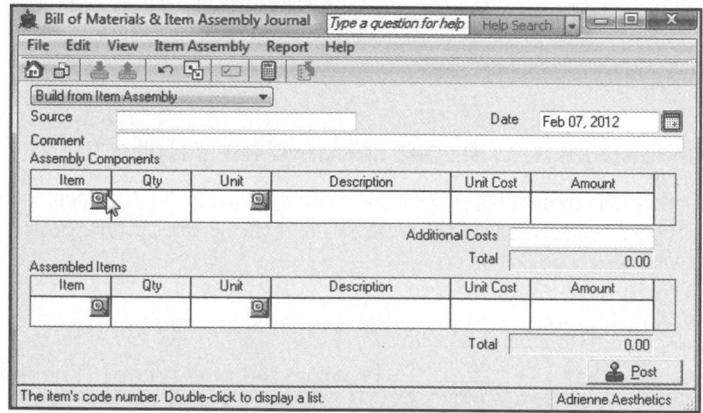

There are two ways to assemble items in the Premium version of Simply Accounting: Item Assembly or Build From The Bill Of Materials defined in the ledger on the Build tab screen (see page 379). The build method will be covered in Chapter 18. We will use the Item Assembly method now. You can access both methods from the Build drop-down list in the journal as shown:

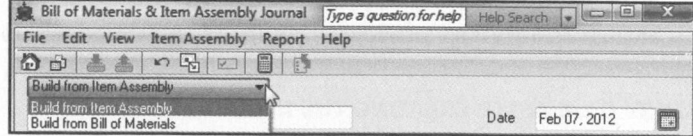

When you build items from the bill of materials, the journal has only the assembled items part — the components information is drawn from the ledger record.

We are using the item assembly method, so you do not need to modify the journal.

Press   `tab` to place the cursor in the Source field, where you should enter the reference or form number.

Type   ItA-1

Press   `tab` to advance to the Date field. Enter the date of the transfer.

PRO VERSION

In the Pro version, only the Item Assembly approach is available.

**CLASSIC VIEW**

Click the Bill of Materials & Item Assembly icon

to open the journal.

NOTES

We will use Item Assembly Journal to refer to the Bill of Materials & Item Assembly Journal.

PRO VERSION

The drop-down list is not available. The cursor will be in the Source field.

CLASSIC VIEW

Click Build From Item Assembly in the Build drop-down list if necessary to open the journal form we need.

Type   02-03

Press   (tab) **twice** to advance to the Comment field.

Type   Assemble super gift packages

Press   (tab) to advance to the first line in the Item field.

You are in the **Assembly Components** section. This first section refers to the items that are being removed from inventory, the "from" part of the transfer or assembly. These items will form the gift package.

Press   (enter) or **click** the **List icon** [icon] to display the familiar inventory selection list.

Notice that you can add new inventory items from the Select Inventory list in the Item Assembly Journal. Services are not on this list because they cannot be assembled.

Click   **CLO1 Cleansing Lotion 225 ml** to select the first item needed.

Click   **Select** to add the item to the item assembly form and advance to the Quantity (Qty) field. You must enter the quantity.

Type   10 **Press** (tab) to advance the cursor to the Unit field and to update the amount.

The unit cost is correct but it can be edited if you know it is incorrect.

Drag   the **lower frame of the journal window** to have more input lines on the screen and see your entire entry on the screen at once.

Click   the **next line** in the Item column.

Select   the next **inventory item** to be transferred, **enter** the **quantity** and then continue to **enter** the **remaining inventory** for the package.

At this stage, your screen should look like the one shown here:

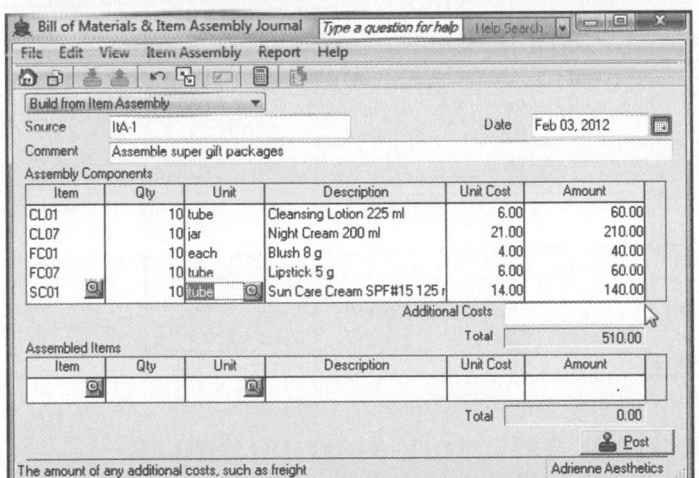

The middle part of the item assembly form contains two fields, Additional Costs and Total. **Additional costs** may come from shipping or packaging involved with assembling, moving or transferring the inventory. Services involved in the package may also be entered as additional costs. The extra costs for all items transferred should be entered into the Additional Costs field. The **Total** is calculated automatically by Simply Accounting to include the individual costs of all items transferred — the assembly components — plus any additional costs. Adrienne Aesthetics has additional costs of $50 ($5 per package) for wrapping materials and gift boxes.

Click   the **Additional Costs field**.

NOTES
You do not need to add the year when you type the date in the Item Assembly Journal.

NOTES
You could also add the new inventory items, the gift packages, and the new asset account, 1350 Gift Packages, directly from the journal while entering the assembly transaction.

NOTES
The unit cost may be different when the cost of transferred items is lower than the default because older stock is being transferred and it was purchased at a lower price. If you change the unit cost, press (tab) to update the amount.

> **Type**   50   **Press** (tab) to update the total.

The cursor advances to the first line in the Item column of the **Assembled Items** section. This section refers to the new or reserved inventory, the item being assembled or the "to" part of the transfer.

> **Press**   (enter) or **click** the **List icon** 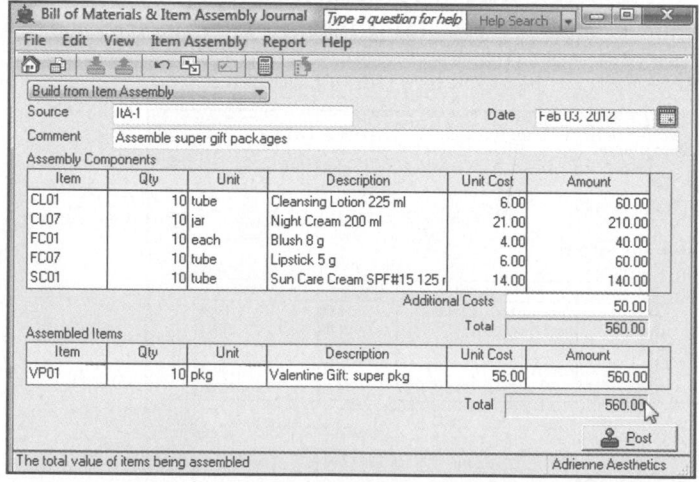 to display the familiar inventory selection list.

> **Click**   **VP01 Valentine Gift: super pkg** to select the item we created.

> **Click**   **Select** or **press** (enter) to add the item to the item assembly form and advance to the Quantity (Qty) field.

> **Type**   10

The unit cost of the assembled items is the total cost of the assembly components, plus additional costs, divided by the quantity or number of units assembled. When a single type of item is assembled and the quantity is greater than one, it is simpler to enter the quantity and the amount (the Total in the assembly components portion in the top half of the form) and let Simply Accounting calculate the unit cost. You can also enter the individual item cost in the Unit Cost field and allow the program to calculate the Amount (Qty times Unit Cost). We will enter the total from the upper portion of the journal.

> **Click**   the **Amount field**.

> **Type**   560   **Press** (tab) to enter the cost and update the unit cost and total.

The totals in the two parts of the assembly form should be the same. If they are not, you will be unable to post the entry.

Your completed form should now resemble the following:

NOTES
Because the two totals must be the same, enter the total cost and allow the program to determine the unit cost to ensure this balance.

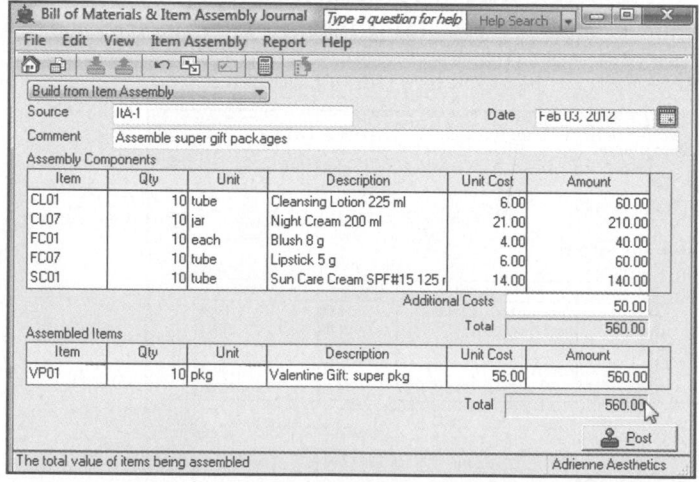

Reviewing the Item Assembly Journal Entry

PRO VERSION
pro In the Pro version, you will choose the Report menu and then click Display Item Assembly Journal Entry to see the transaction.

> **Choose** the **Report menu**, then **click Display Bill Of Materials & Item Assembly Journal Entry** to display the transaction you have entered:

NOTES
Pressing (ctrl) + J will also open the journal display.

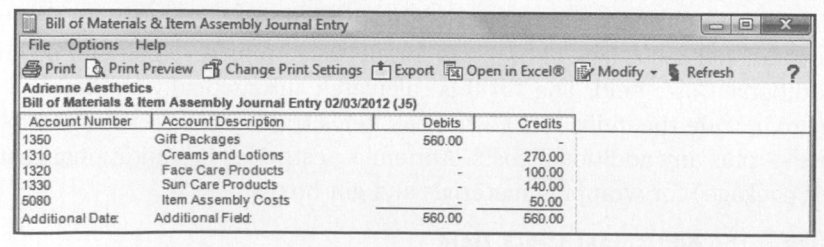

Notice that Simply Accounting has moved the inventory items from their original asset accounts (credit entries) to the newly created inventory account (debit entry). When you display inventory selection lists or quantity reports, you will see that the quantities for all items involved have been updated. The necessary items are taken out of their regular individual item inventory account and transferred to the new account. Thus the quantities of the original items are reduced because they have been transferred to the new account. Additional Costs are assigned to *Item Assembly Costs*, the linked account defined for these costs. This is a contra-expense account — the credit expense entry is added to the inventory value of the assembled inventory asset.

Close   the **display** to return to the Item Assembly Journal input screen.

CORRECTING THE ITEM ASSEMBLY JOURNAL ENTRY

Move to the field that has the error. **Press** (tab) to move forward through the fields or **press** (shift) and (tab) together to move back to a previous field. This will highlight the field information so you can change it. **Type** the **correct information** and **press** (tab) to enter it. You must advance the cursor to the next field to enter a change.

You can also use the mouse to **point** to a field and **drag** through the **incorrect information** to highlight it. **Type** the **correct information** and **press** (tab) to enter it.

If an inventory item is incorrect, **press** (enter) while the cursor is in the Item field to **display** the appropriate **list. Double click** the **correct inventory item. Re-enter** the **quantity** and **press** (tab) to update the totals.

Because the item assembly is a complex transaction, it is very easy to make a mistake, so check your work carefully. You may also want to store the original entry. If you discover later that you have made an error, you can recall the entry and add a minus sign to each quantity and to the Additional Costs amount to create a reversing entry.

Click   the **Store button** ⬇ to display the familiar Store Recurring
            Transaction screen:

Because this is not a regular recurring transaction, we will use the Random frequency. Choosing the Random frequency for recurring entries enters the session date as the default transaction date when you recall the journal entry.

Click   **Monthly** to display the Frequency options.

Click   **Random** to select this frequency.

Click   **OK** to save the entry and return to the Item Assembly Journal. Notice
            that the Recall button is now active.

Posting

Click   **Post** when you are certain that all the information is correct.

Enter   the next **assembly transaction**. When you post it, you will see the
            message about low inventory:

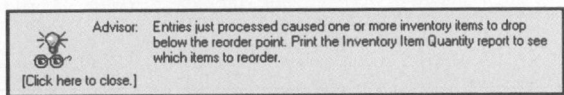

Click   the **Advisor message** to close it.

Close   the **Journal** to return to the Inventory & Services module window.

Click	**Receivables** in the Modules pane list to restore this window.
Add	**shortcuts** for **Item Assembly** and **Inventory Adjustments** from the Inventory & Services list in the Customize Shortcuts window.
Enter	the **purchase invoice adjustment**. (Open the journal and click the Adjust tool.)

Selling to Preferred Customers

NOTES
Customers may also be identified as using Web prices or another user-defined price list.

Simply Accounting allows you to record multiple inventory prices and to identify customers by the prices they will pay (preferred or regular). Sales for both groups of customers are entered the same way since the program automatically enters the correct price depending on the customer selected. Red River TV is a preferred customer — Preferred is entered as the Price List on the customer's Options tab screen.

Click	the **Sales Invoices icon** to open the Sales Journal.

Pay Later is the correct selection for this sale to Red River TV. The Invoice number is also correct by default.

Choose	**Red River TV (CWTV)** from the customer list.
Type	Feb 4 12 in the Date field.
Choose	**Hydra** as the salesperson in the Salesperson field.
Double click	the **Item Number field** to see the inventory list.
Scroll down	and then **double click CL03 Eye Contour Smoothing Cream 30 ml** to add it and advance to the Quantity field.

This adds the first item sold to the customer at the preferred customer price of $32.00 instead of $35.00, the regular price.

Type	5 **Press** (tab).
Enter	the **remaining items** sold to this customer to complete the journal entry as shown:

WARNING!
If the Price List is not selected in the customer's record, you must manually change all the prices in the journal. You cannot choose the price list in the journal.

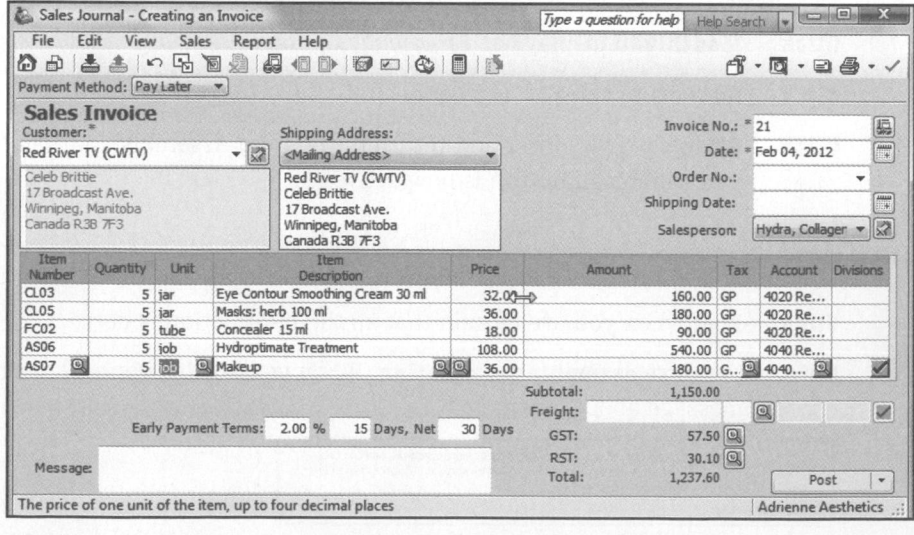

You should review the entry as usual.

Choose the **Report menu** and **click Display Sales Journal Entry**:

Adrienne Aesthetics Sales Journal Entry 02/04/2012 (J9)			
Account Number	Account Description	Debits	Credits
1200	Accounts Receivable	1,237.60	-
5060	Cost of Goods Sold	210.00	-
1310	Creams and Lotions	-	170.00
1320	Face Care Products	-	40.00
2640	RST Payable	-	30.10
2650	GST Charged on Sales	-	57.50
4020	Revenue from Sales	-	430.00
4040	Revenue from Services	-	720.00
Additional Date:	Additional Field:	1,447.60	1,447.60

This entry is the same as a regular non-discounted sale. Revenue is reduced because of the change in selling price but this change is not recorded as a discount.

Close the **display** when finished and **make corrections** if necessary.

Post the **entry** and **close** the **Sales Journal**.

Continue with the **journal entries** up to the sales return on February 8.

Entering Sales Returns

Customers may return purchases for many different reasons. For example, the size, colour or quality may have been other than expected. Stores have different policies with respect to accepting and refunding returns. Most stores place reasonable time limits on the period in which they will give refunds. Some stores offer credit only and some charge a handling fee on goods returned. Adrienne Aesthetics will provide full refunds for purchases within two weeks of the sale if the items have not been opened. Sales returns are entered in the Sales Journal and are very similar to sales, but the quantity is entered with a minus sign — a negative quantity is sold. Different accounts may be used.

Open the **Sales Journal** if it is not open from the previous transactions.

The return must use the same customer and payment method as the original sale.

Choose Visa from the Payment Method list.

Choose Cash Customers from the Customer list.

You should use a different invoice number so that the return can be differentiated from a normal sale.

Click the **Invoice No. field** and **type** 22-R

Enter **Feb. 8** in the Date field if this is not the date shown already.

Enter **Blossom** as the salesperson.

Click the **Item Number field** and **type** C to see the inventory list.

Click **CL08 Protection Cream: dbl action 60 ml** to enter it and **press** ⎡tab⎤ to move the cursor to the Quantity field.

This adds the first item returned by the customer at the regular price.

Type -1 **Press** ⎡tab⎤.

Notice that a positive amount appears in the Price field and a negative amount is added to the Amount field — a positive price times the negative quantity. We should also change the default account so that returns can be tracked separately.

Click the **Account field List icon** 🔍 and **choose 4050 Sales Returns**.

Enter the **second item** returned by this customer.

NOTES
Most stores have separate forms for returns with their own separate number sequences.

NOTES
The salesperson should be entered for sales returns because commissions are calculated on total sales less returns.

Your finished journal entry should look like the following one:

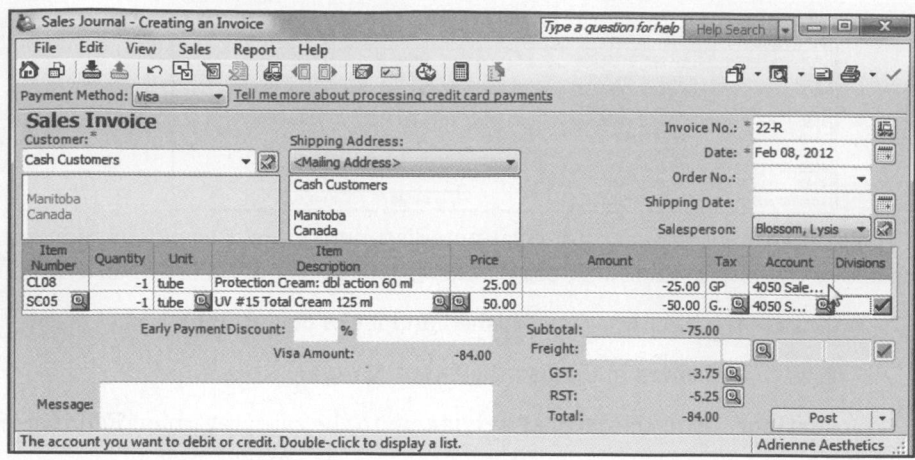

Choose the **Report menu** and **click Display Sales Journal Entry** to review it:

Adrienne Aesthetics
Sales Journal Entry 02/08/2012 (J22)

Account Number	Account Description	Debits	Credits
1310	Creams and Lotions	12.00	-
1330	Sun Care Products	22.00	-
2640	RST Payable	5.25	-
2650	GST Charged on Sales	3.75	-
4050	Sales Returns	75.00	-
1090	Bank Account: Credit Cards	-	81.69
5040	Credit Card Fees	-	2.31
5060	Cost of Goods Sold	-	34.00
Additional Date:	Additional Field:	118.00	118.00

NOTES
When you reverse an invoice that has been paid from the Adjust Invoice journal window, Simply Accounting will create a credit note for the customer and assign a number (cn#) for reference.

Notice that the entry is the reversal of a regular sale. The two asset accounts are debited because inventory is added back. *Sales Returns* — a contra-revenue account — is debited, and *Bank Account: Credit Cards* is credited because money has been returned to the customer's credit card account. Similarly, *RST Payable* and *GST Charged on Sales* are debited because the tax liabilities have decreased and finally, the expense accounts, *Credit Card Fees* and *Cost of Goods Sold* are credited because these expenses have gone down.

If the sale was a Pay Later invoice, the sales return entry will add a negative invoice amount to the Receipts Journal for the customer — a credit balance is created.

Close the **display** when finished to return to the journal. **Make corrections** if necessary.

In the Comment field, you could add the reason for the return. The customer's name and address could be added to the Ship To field or the Comment field.

Post the **entry** and **close** the **Sales Journal**.

Entering Purchase Returns

Purchase returns are entered in the same way as sales returns — by adding a minus sign to the quantity so that all the amounts become negative. The supplier and payment method must be the same as the original purchase.

Open the **Purchases Journal**. Pay Later is correct.

Choose Biotech Laboratories as the supplier.

Enter BL-669R as the invoice number and **Feb. 8** as the date.

Choose FC10 Powder: loose 15 g from the inventory selection list and advance to the Quantity field.

Type −5 (the quantity with a minus sign).

You cannot change the default asset account for inventory purchases or returns.

Change the **payment terms** to **net 60** so that the credit does not show as overdue.

Review the **journal entry** to see that it is a reversed purchase entry.

The inventory asset account, *Face Care Products*, and *Accounts Payable* have decreased. *GST Paid on Purchases* has been credited to restore the tax liability.

Close the **display**. **Make corrections** if needed and **post** the **transaction**.

Enter the **remaining transactions**.

Displaying Inventory Reports

Most inventory reports can be displayed from the Reports menu in the Inventory & Services window, from the Home window Reports menu, from the Inventory & Services module window Reports pane drop-down list and from the Report Centre. We will access the reports from the Report Centre.

Click the **Report Centre icon** in any window.

Click **Inventory & Services** to open the list of inventory reports:

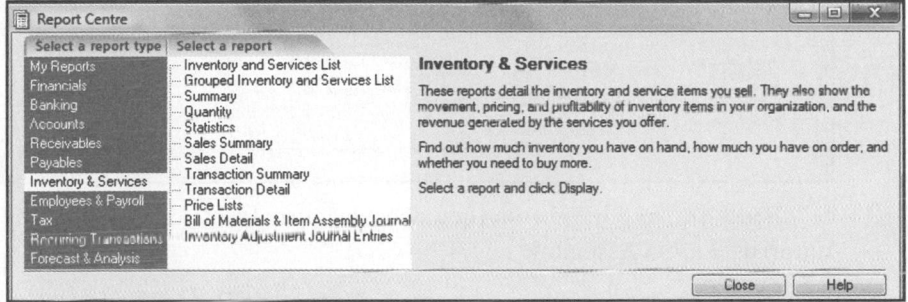

Displaying Inventory Lists

Click **Inventory And Services List. Click Modify This Report**:

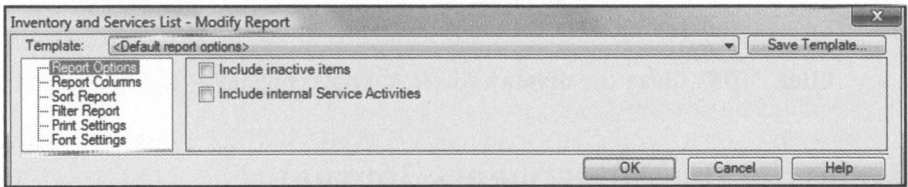

Or, you can choose the Reports menu and choose Lists; then click Inventory & Services to see the report options.

To select the fields for the report, choose Report Columns.

Click **OK** to see the list. **Close** the **display** when you have finished.

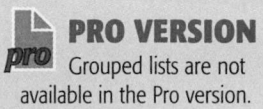

PRO VERSION
Grouped lists are not available in the Pro version.

NOTES
You can drill down to the Inventory Transaction Detail Report from the Inventory List and from the Grouped Inventory List.

WARNING!
When you type dates in the inventory report options date fields, you must include the year.

PRO VERSION
In the Report Centre list, click Item Assembly Journal Entries. Or, choose the Report menu, then choose Journal Entries and click Item Assembly.

CLASSIC VIEW
Right-click the Bill of Materials & Item Assembly icon

Click the Display tool 🔲.

NOTES
Additional Information for journal entries is covered in Chapter 11.

NOTES
You can drill down to the General Ledger reports from the Item Assembly Journal and from the Adjustments Journal.

CLASSIC VIEW
Right-click the Inventory Adjustments icon

Click the Display tool 🔲.

Displaying Grouped Inventory Lists

Click   **Grouped Inventory And Services List**. **Click Modify This Report**.

Click   **Type** in the Group By field:

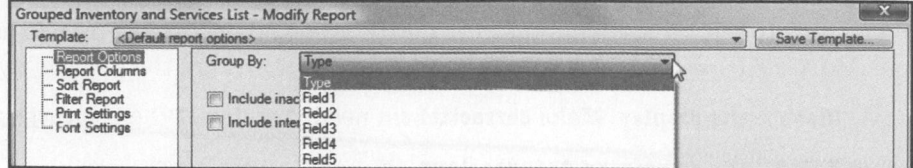

From this list, choose the way you want to sort the list. You can organize by Type (inventory and services are separated) or by any of the additional information fields you created for the ledger. To select the fields for the report, choose Report Columns.

Click   **OK** to see the list. **Close** the **display** when you have finished.

Displaying the Item Assembly Journal

Click   **Bill Of Materials & Item Assembly Journal Entries** to see the report sample and description.

Click   **Modify This Report** to open the report options window:

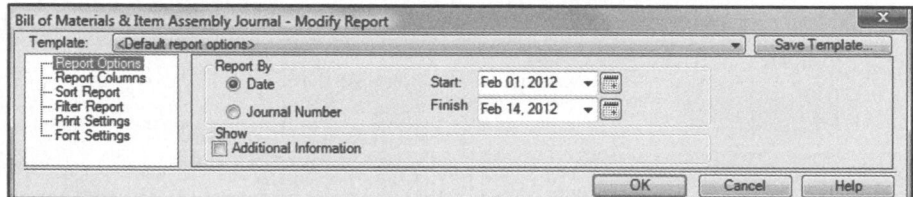

Or, choose the Reports menu, then choose Journal Entries and click Bill of Materials & Item Assembly.

As usual, the earliest transaction date, session date and Report By Date options are provided by default. The sorting, filtering and column options are the same for all journal reports.

Enter   the **beginning date** for the report you want (including the year).

Press   (tab) (**twice** if you type the date).

Enter   the **ending date** for the report (including the year).

Click   **OK**. **Close** the **display** when you have finished.

Displaying the Adjustments Journal

Click   **Inventory Adjustment Journal Entries** to see the sample.

Click   **Modify This Report** to open the report options window:

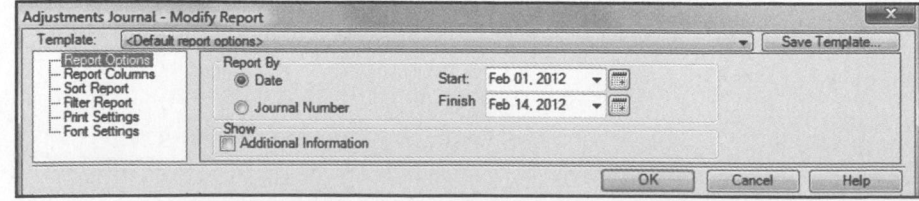

Or, you can choose the Reports menu, then choose Journal Entries and click Inventory Adjustments.

As usual, the earliest transaction date, session date and Report By Date options are provided by default.

Enter   the **beginning date** for the report you want (including the year).

Press   (tab) (**twice** if you type the date).

Enter   the **ending date** for the report (including the year).

Click   **OK**. **Close** the **display** when you have finished.

Displaying Inventory Summary Reports

Click   **Summary** from the Select A Report list to see the sample.

Click   **Modify This Report** to open the report options window:

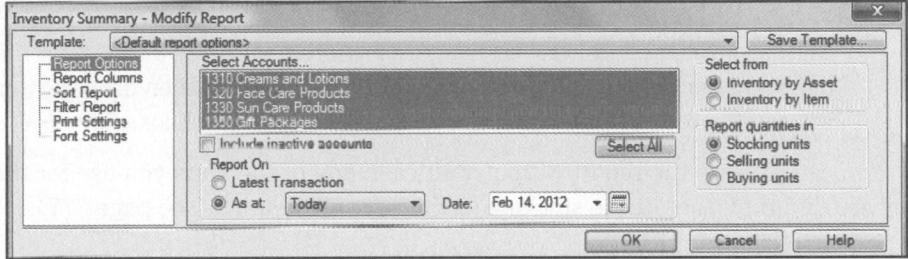

You can also choose the Reports menu, then choose Inventory & Services and click Summary to display the report options.

Selecting **Inventory By Asset** will provide information for all inventory items in the asset group(s) chosen. The **Inventory By Item** option will provide information for all the items selected. When you click Inventory By Item, the Select box lists all inventory items. Services are not included because there is no quantity or cost information for them.

Click a single asset or item to change selections or provide a report for that item only. To select multiple items, press and hold (ctrl) and then click the items you want in the report. To obtain information for all items, choose Select All.

The **Summary** Report lists the quantity on hand, the unit cost of the inventory and the total value or cost of inventory on hand for the items requested. The total value of the inventory in an asset group is also provided when you select one asset group. You can view the Summary Report for the Latest Transaction Date, or for another date that you enter in the **As At** Date field.

You can prepare the report with quantities in any of the units you use for the item if these are different, that is, the stocking, buying or selling units (see page 377).

Choose   the **options** you need for your report.

Press   and **hold** (ctrl) and **click** the **items** or **assets** you want included.

Click   **OK**. **Close** the **display** when you have finished.

Displaying Inventory Quantity Reports

The Inventory Quantity Report provides current information about the quantity on hand, the minimum stock levels and outstanding purchase and sales orders. The report also displays the order quantity needed to restore the minimum level when an item has fallen below the minimum level.

NOTES
You can customize Summary reports by selecting any of the columns usually included in the report. You can sort and filter by item or description.

NOTES
You can drill down to the Inventory Transaction Report from the Inventory Summary or Quantity reports.

NOTES
Select All acts as a toggle switch. When all items are selected, clicking Select All will remove all selections. When one or a few items are selected, clicking Select All will select all the entries on the list.

NOTES
When you display the report with the Latest Transaction option, it includes the profit (either the markup or margin) for each item.

NOTES
You can customize Quantity Reports by selecting any of the columns usually included in the report. You can sort and filter by most of the columns usually included in the report.

Click   **Quantity** from the Select A Report list. **Click Modify This Report**:

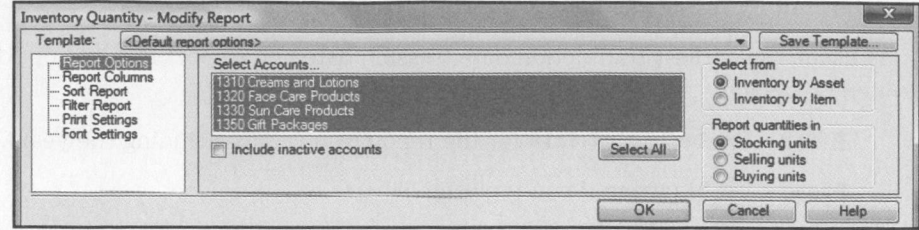

Or, choose the Reports menu, then choose Inventory & Services and click Quantity to display the report options.

You can select the items for the report in the same way as you did for the Inventory Summary Report. Selecting **Inventory By Asset** will provide information for all inventory items in the asset group(s) chosen. The **Inventory By Item** option will provide information for all the items selected. When you click Inventory By Item, the Select Accounts box lists all inventory items. Services are not included in the Quantity Report because there is no quantity or cost information for them.

Click a single asset or item to change selections or provide a report for that item only. To select multiple items, press and hold ctrl and then click the items you want in the report. To obtain information for all items, choose Select All.

You can prepare the report with quantities in any of the units you use for the item if they are different, that is, the stocking, buying or selling units (see page 377).

Choose the **options** you need for your report.

Press and **hold** ctrl and **click** the **names** of all the items or asset groups you want to include in the report.

Click   **OK** and **close** the **display** when you have finished.

Displaying Inventory Price Lists

NOTES
You cannot sort or filter the Price List Report but you can select or omit the Item and Description columns.

The different inventory prices — regular, preferred, Web and customized prices — are not available in the other inventory reports, but you can see all of these prices together on the Price Lists Report.

NOTES
If you have created other price lists or use additional currencies, they will be listed in the Modify Report screen and you can include them in the report.
If you use other currencies, you can also add the price lists in these currencies and then group your lists by currency or by price list.

Click   **Price Lists** from the Select A Report list. **Click Modify This Report**:

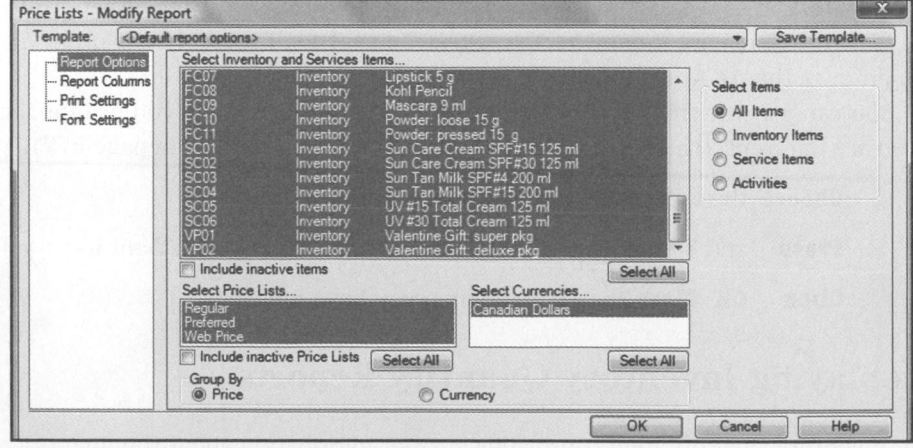

You can also choose the Reports menu, then choose Inventory & Services and click Price Lists to display the report options.

You can choose the item or items that you want on the price list by selecting them from the list, just as you select items for other inventory reports. You can include Regular, Preferred, Web prices and any customized price lists you created.

Click   the **Price List** you want to report on.

Click   **OK** to see the price lists and **close** the **display** when you have finished.

Displaying Inventory Tracking Reports

Several reports provide information about the turnover of inventory products. These reports show whether items are selling well and are profitable and how the sales are distributed over time and customers.

Inventory Statistics Reports

Click   **Statistics** from the Select A Report list. **Click Modify This Report**:

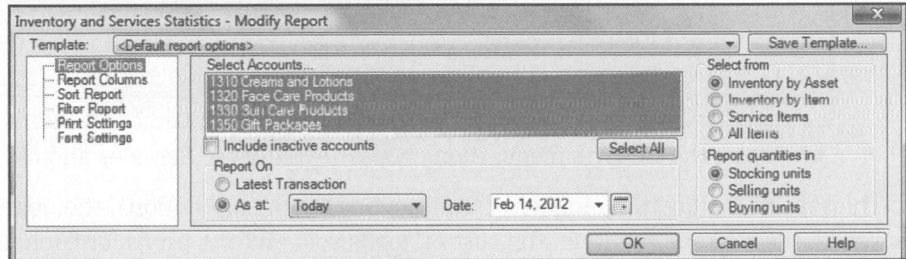

Or, choose the Reports menu, then choose Inventory & Services and click Statistics to display the report options.

The Statistics Report summarizes transactions for the year to date and the previous year, the same historical information that is contained in the Inventory Ledger record (see page 000). For example, the report can show whether a large volume of sales resulted from a single sale for a large quantity or from a large number of smaller sales.

You can prepare the report for the session date (**Latest Transaction**) or for another date (**As At Date**). When you choose As At, the Date field is available. The report will show the statistics you request as at the date you enter.

The report shows: the **Number Of Transactions** (the number of separate sales invoices that included the inventory item); **Units Sold** (the total number of individual items of a kind that were sold in the period); the **Amount Sold** (the total sale price for all items sold); and the **Cost Of Goods Sold** (the total purchase cost of all the items that were sold). The average cost method is used to calculate the cost of goods sold for Adrienne Aesthetics.

Press and hold ⟨ctrl⟩ and click one or more asset groups to include them in the report, or click Select All to include all asset groups in the report. Selecting an asset group will include all the inventory items in that group in the report. To select multiple assets or items, press ⟨ctrl⟩ and then click the items you want.

Click **Inventory By Item** to list individual inventory items. Select one or more items for the report, or click Select All to include all inventory items. Click **Service Items** to list individual services. Press ⟨ctrl⟩ and hold and click services to include them, or click Select All to include all services. Click **All Items** to include both individual inventory items and individual services in the report. Press ⟨ctrl⟩ and hold and click the items and services to include them in the report, or click Select All to include all items and services.

NOTES
For Inventory Statistics Reports, you can sort and filter by most of the columns usually included in the report.
You can customize Statistics Reports by selecting any of the columns usually included in the report.

NOTES
You can drill down to the Inventory Sales Report from the Inventory Statistics Report.

NOTES
When you display the report with the Latest Transaction option, it includes the statistics for the previous year as well.

NOTES
You can also choose the FIFO (first in, first out) method of determining inventory costs. You make this choice in the Inventory Settings screen. This method is not available for the Pro version.

NOTES
Remember that Select All acts as a toggle switch — when all items are already selected, clicking Select All clears the selection. Clicking Select All when no items are selected, or when one or more items (but not all items) are selected, will select all items.

The list of items will expand according to your selection, and you can choose single or multiple items for inclusion. **Quantities** can be reported in any of the units on record — the units for stocking the inventory, for buying and for selling — if these are different.

> **Choose** the **items** you want in the report.
>
> **Choose** the **date** for the report (Latest Transaction or As At Date). **Enter** a **date** in the Date field (including the year) if you chose the As At option.
>
> **Click** **OK** to display the report. **Close** the **display** when you have finished.

Inventory Sales Reports

> **Click** **Sales Summary** from the Select A Report list. **Click Modify This Report**:

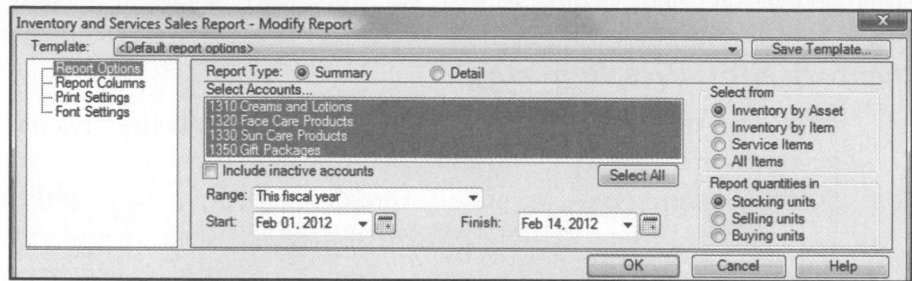

Or, choose the Reports menu, then choose Inventory & Services and click Sales.

The reports include the number of transactions (Summary option), the quantity of items sold, the revenue per item, the cost of goods sold and the profit for each item. Non-inventory sales are not included. The **Summary** option, selected by default, shows the total for each detail for the selected inventory items organized by item. The **Detail** option provides the same information listed by individual journal entry, including the source document numbers and journal entry numbers. Click Detail to add these details.

As usual, you can choose to report on inventory items, services or both. To report only on all services, click **Service Items** and then Select All. Click **All Items** to include both inventory and services. The list of items will expand accordingly, and you can choose single or multiple items for inclusion. Select All at this stage will provide a report on all inventory and service items.

Again, **quantities** may be reported in stocking, buying or selling units.

> **Type** the report's **starting** and **ending dates** (including the year) in the Start and Finish fields, or choose from the Range drop-down list.
>
> **Choose** the **items** to include in the report.
>
> **Choose** the **Summary** or **Detail** option.
>
> **Click** **OK**. **Close** the **display** when you have finished.

Inventory Transaction Reports

The Transaction Report summarizes inventory activity according to the journal used to record the transaction.

The report includes details on the number of transactions (Summary option only), the **Quantity In** (increases to inventory from purchases, sales returns, recovery of lost items or assembled items) and **Out** (decreases in inventory from sales, purchase returns, losses and adjustments or assembly components used) and the **Amount In** and **Out** (cost price) for each item chosen in each of the selected journals.

> **Click** **Transaction Summary**. **Click Modify This Report**:

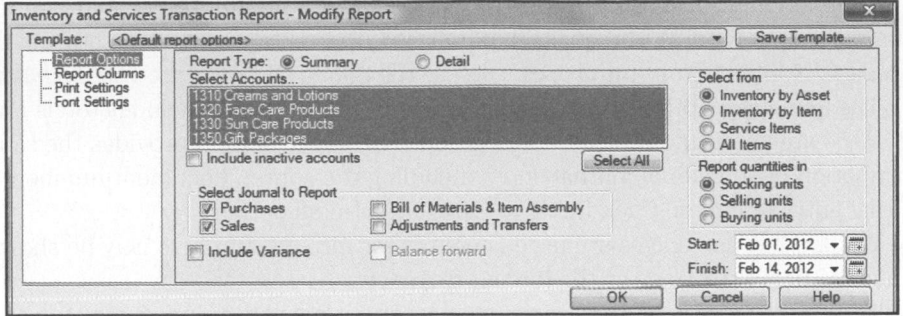

PRO VERSION
pro Item Assembly is the Journal name in the Pro version instead of Bill of Materials & Item Assembly, and Adjustments replaces Adjustments and Transfers.

Or, choose the Reports menu, then choose Inventory & Services and click Transaction to display the report options.

The **Summary** option, the default, includes totals for the selected inventory items organized by item. The **Detail** option provides the same information listed by individual journal entry, including the source document numbers and journal entry numbers.

As in the Sales Report, you can prepare a report for one or more asset groups, one or more inventory items, one or more service items or a combination of services and items (All Items). Clicking the appropriate entry in the Select From list will expand the item list accordingly.

Quantities may be reported in stocking, buying or selling units. Variances can also be added to the report when they are used.

You can choose to show the Balance Forward and include opening balances or to Include Variance and add cost variances for each item.

> **Click**   **Detail** to include individual transaction details.
>
> **Type**   the **starting and ending dates** for the report (including the year) in the Start and Finish fields. By default, the earliest transaction and session date appear.
>
> **Click**   the **journals** to include in the report.
>
> **Click**   **OK. Close** the **display** when you have finished.

NOTES
You can drill down to the Transaction Detail Report from the Transaction Summary Report. You can display the Inventory Ledger and Journal Report from the Transaction Detail Report. You can also look up invoices from the Detail Report.

Supplier Purchases Reports

The next two reports combine inventory information with supplier or customer details to show how purchases are spread among suppliers and how sales are divided among customers. The Supplier Purchases and Customer Sales reports also allow you to include information for non-inventory purchases or sales.

> **Click**   **Payables** in the Select A Report Type list.
>
> **Click**   **Supplier Purchases Summary. Click Modify This Report**:

PRO VERSION
pro This report is named the Vendor Purchases Report.

NOTES
You cannot sort or filter the Supplier Purchases Report, but you can select the columns you want in the report.

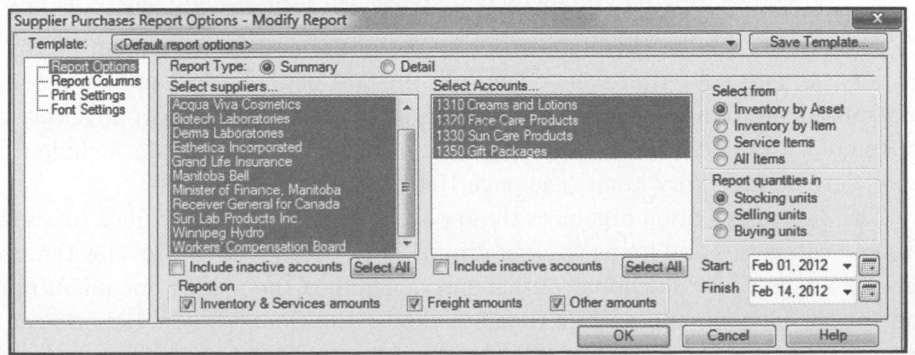

Or, choose the Reports menu and choose Payables and click Supplier Purchases.

NOTES
You can drill down to the Inventory Purchases Detail Report from the Purchases Summary Report. You can look up invoices or display the Supplier Aged and Purchases Journal Report from the Purchases Detail Report.

The Supplier Purchases report includes details on the number of transactions (Summary option only), the quantity purchased, the unit cost and the total cost of the purchase. Non-inventory purchases, such as telephone services, are listed as **Other**.

The **Summary** option organizes the report by supplier and includes totals for the selected categories and items or asset group. The **Detail** option provides the same information by individual journal entry, including the source document numbers and journal entry numbers. Click Detail to choose the Detail option.

When other currencies are used, amounts for foreign suppliers may be shown in either the home currency or the foreign currency.

The selection of inventory, services or asset groups is the same as for the other inventory reports. Reports can be prepared for either stocking, buying or selling units if these are different.

All items and suppliers are selected initially.

> **Click**   a **supplier name** or item to begin a new selection.
>
> **Enter**   the **starting** and **ending dates** for the report (including the year) in the Start and Finish fields.

Click a purchase category — Inventory & Services, non-inventory (Other Amounts) and Freight Amounts — to remove the ✓ and deselect it for the selected supplier and item transactions. Click it again to select it.

> **Click**   **OK**. **Close** the **display** when you have finished.

Customer Sales Reports

The Customer Sales Report provides the same details as the Inventory Sales Report, but the Customer Sales Report has the details organized by customer as well as by item. Customer Sales reports also have the option to include non-inventory sales.

> **Click**   **Receivables** in the Select A Report Type list.
>
> **Click**   **Customer Sales Summary**. **Click Modify This Report**:

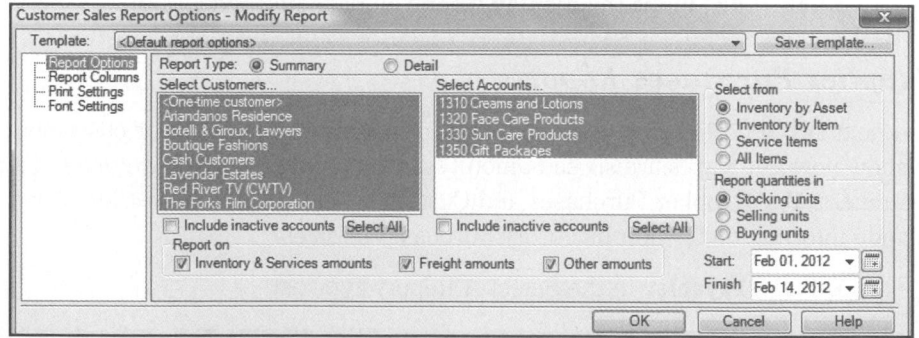

Or, choose the Reports menu and choose Receivables and click Customer Sales.

The report includes the number of transactions (Summary option only), the quantity of items sold, the revenue per item, the cost of goods sold and the profit on each sale transaction. Non-inventory sales, such as sales allowances or non-inventory services, are listed as **Other Amounts**. In Chapter 6, only the customer list was included because there were no inventory items (see page 194).

The **Summary** option organizes the report by customer and includes totals for the selected categories and items or asset groups. The **Detail** option provides the same information listed by individual journal entry, including the source document numbers and journal entry numbers. Click Detail to choose the Detail option. Reports can be prepared for stocking, buying or selling units if these are different. All customers and items are selected initially.

Select   **assets**, **inventory** or **services**, **customers**, **dates** and **categories** as you do for Supplier Purchases reports.

Click   **OK**. **Close** the **display** when you have finished.

Gross Margin Income Statement

This financial report becomes relevant when a business sells inventory. The report shows the income after inventory costs have been deducted from revenue and before operating expenses are included. This report is available from the Financials report types list.

Click   **Financials** in the Select A Report Type list.

Click   the for **Income Statement** to expand the list.

Click   **Gross Margin - Standard (under Income Statement)**.

Click   **Modify This Report** to open the report options window:

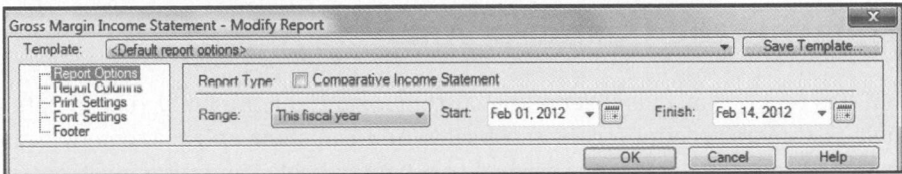

Or, choose the Reports menu, then choose Financial and click Gross Margin Income Statement to display the report options.

The report will include different income amounts: gross margin (revenue minus cost of goods sold, before taking into account the other operating expenses), income from operations (operating expenses are deducted from the gross margin) and net income (non-operating revenue and expenses are entered).

The options for this Income Statement are the same as for regular Income Statements, including the option to generate a Comparative Income Statement.

Type   the **starting** and **ending dates** for the report (including the year) in the Start and Finish fields.

Click   **OK**. **Close** the **display** when you have finished.

Displaying Forecast & Analysis Reports

This group of reports provides more detailed information about performance and trends.

Click   **Forecast & Analysis** in the Select A Report Type list:

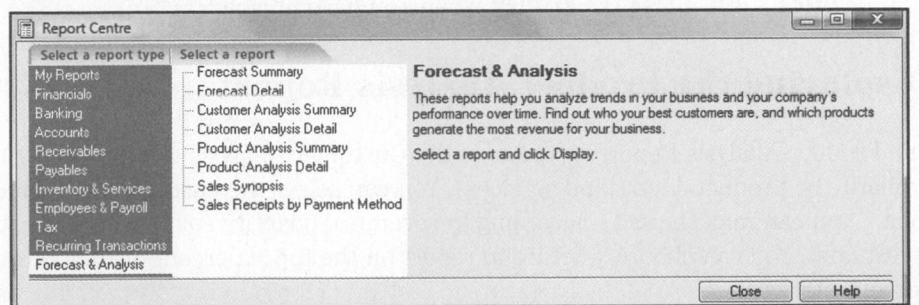

⚠️ **WARNING!**
You must assign the correct account classes to expense accounts to generate the Gross Margin Income Statement. Cost of Goods Sold accounts must be correctly identified and separated from other types of expenses.

📄 **NOTES**
Refer to page 55 for details on the Comparative Income Statement.

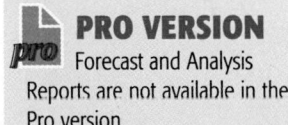 **PRO VERSION**
Forecast and Analysis Reports are not available in the Pro version.

Displaying the Forecast Report

The report will provide monthly forecasts for revenues and expenses, based on the same month in the previous year. This report requires data for more than one year, so you will be unable to view this report for Adrienne Aesthetics data.

Click   Forecast Summary and then **click Modify This Report:**

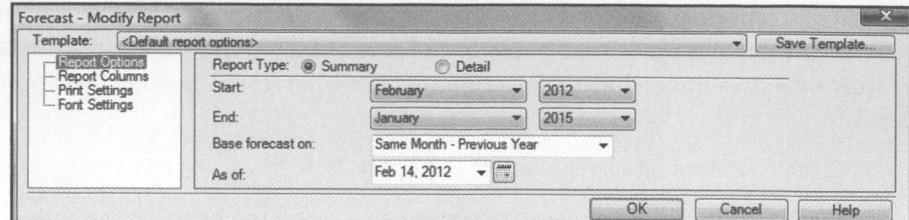

Choose the **months** for which you want the forecast and the date for the report.

Click   OK. Close the **display** when you have finished.

Displaying the Customer Analysis Report

From this report, you can observe the customer sales for the fiscal year to date to see which customers account for the most sales. You can show only customers in the top or bottom x percent, rank them according to revenue, profit, quantity or return on investment (ROI), and you can select the items you want to report on.

Click   Customer Analysis and then **click Modify This Report:**

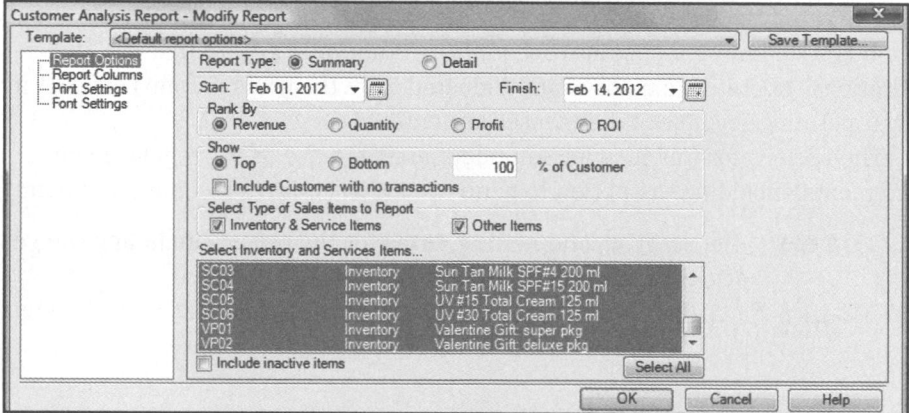

Detail Reports shows individual journal entries while the summary has total amounts.

Choose the **reporting period**, **ranking criteria**, **percentage** and **items**.

Click   OK. Close the **display** when you have finished.

Displaying the Product Analysis Report

The Product Analysis Report is similar to the Customer Analysis Report but organized primarily by product (items and services). You can select the customers to include. Again, you can rank the sales according to revenues, quantity sold, profit and return on investment. You can choose whether to report on the top x percent or the bottom x percent of items.

Click   Product Analysis and then **click Modify This Report**:

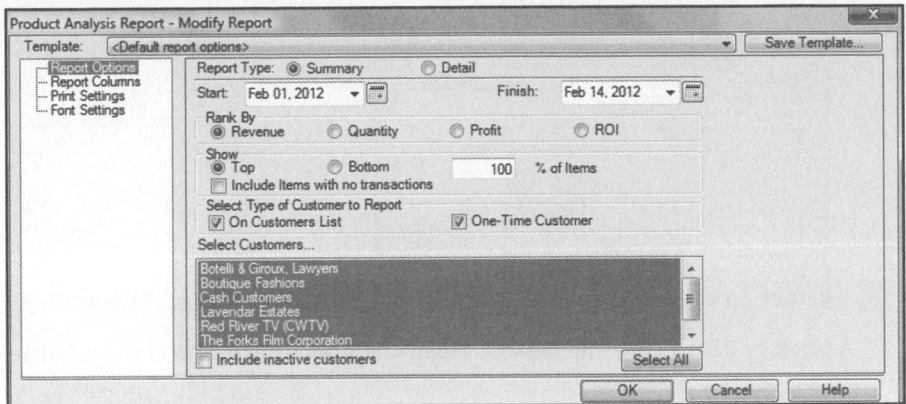

Choose the **reporting period**, **ranking criteria**, **percentage** and **customers**.

Click   OK. **Close** the **display** when you have finished.

> **NOTES**
> In the Product Analysis Report, ROI (return on investment) is measured as the profit divided by the average inventory value.

Displaying the Sales Synopsis Report

The Sales Synopsis Report summarizes sales and receipts. The report includes the items sold, gross sales per item and the methods of payment used.

Click   Sales Synopsis and then **click Modify This Report**:

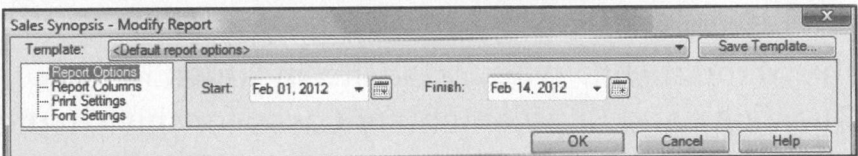

Choose the **reporting period**. Customize the report columns to select details.

Click   OK. **Close** the **display** when you have finished.

Displaying Sales Receipts by Payment Method Reports

The final forecast and analysis report summarizes the sales according the the customer payment methods, that is, by cash, credit card or on account (pay later).

Click   Sales Receipts by Payment Method and then **click Modify This Report**:

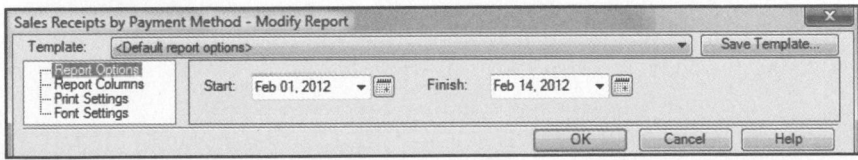

Choose the **reporting period**. Customize the report columns to select details.

Click   OK. **Close** the **display** when you have finished. **Close** the **Report Centre**.

Displaying Inventory Management Reports

> **NOTES**
> You cannot access Management Reports from the Report Centre.

The management reports for the Inventory Ledger focus on potential problem items, inventory items with low markup or items that are not profitable.

NOTES
Adrienne currently has no products that meet the Inventory Management Reports' criteria so there will be no data included in these reports.

Choose the **Reports menu**, then **choose Management Reports** and **click Inventory & Services**:

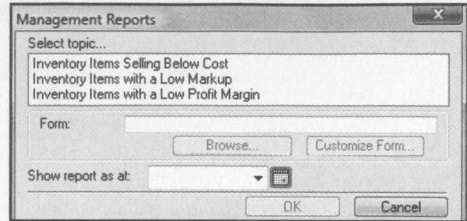

Select a **report** from the list and choose the report form if necessary.

Click **OK** to view the report. **Close** the **display** when you have finished.

Printing Inventory Reports

To print inventory reports, **display** the **report** you want.

Click the **Reports & Forms Settings tool** to check your printer settings.

Choose the **File menu** and **click Print**. **Close** the **display** when finished.

REVIEW

The Student DVD with Data Files includes Review Questions and Supplementary Cases for this chapter.

CHAPTER ELEVEN

Andersson Chiropractic Clinic

OBJECTIVES

- **track** additional information for receipts, sales and purchases
- **place** and **fill** supplier orders and quotes
- **enter** and **fill** sales quotes and orders
- **convert** sales and purchase quotes to orders
- **adjust** orders and quotes
- **enter** debit card sale transactions
- **make** payments and deposits using multiple bank accounts and a line of credit
- **enter** deposits from customers and prepayments to suppliers
- **enter** deposits and prepayments on orders
- **delete** stored transactions
- **remove** quotes
- **enter** transactions from the Daily Business Manager

After completing this chapter, you should be able to

COMPANY INFORMATION

Company Profile

NOTES
Andersson Chiropractic Clinic
4500 Rae St.
Regina, SK S4S 3B4
Tel 1: (306) 577-1900
Tel 2: (306) 577-2199
Fax: (306) 577-1925
Business No.: 459 556 291

Andersson Chiropractic Clinic is a private clinic owned by Maria Andersson, who practises her profession in Regina, Saskatchewan. This is her second year in private practice after graduating with D.C. (Doctor of Chiropractic) and D.Ac. (Doctor of Acupuncture) degrees. She used some bank loans and her line of credit to consolidate her student loans and set up the clinic.

Andersson specializes in sports injuries and has some sports teams as clients. To treat patients, she uses chiropractic treatments and adjustments for back pain, and physiotherapy, massage, ultrasound, laser treatments, electrical stimulation and acupuncture for other joint and soft tissue injuries. Individual regular patients usually come two or three times per week, although some come daily. These patients settle their accounts bi-weekly. Sports teams have contracts and are billed monthly. Contract customers are offered a discount if they settle their accounts within 10 days. Cash, cheques and debit cards are accepted in payment.

A single assistant in the clinic divides her time between reception, administration and some basic treatments such as laser and ultrasound under the chiropractor's supervision. Andersson designates the precise area to be treated and the time and intensity settings for the equipment.

The office space that Andersson rents has a reception area and four treatment rooms with tables. The monthly rent includes heat but not hydro or telephone. One of the four treatment rooms doubles as Andersson's office and another room has the potential to accommodate a whirlpool. She is considering adding a whirlpool for hydrotherapy and deep water massage treatments because some sports injuries respond well to hydrotherapy.

For new sports team contracts, Andersson prepares sales quotes. When new customers accept a contract, they pay a deposit that is applied to the first month's payment.

Andersson has two bank accounts and a line of credit she uses to pay her bills. The limit on her line of credit is $50 000, and she has already borrowed $15 000 against it. A third bank account is used exclusively for debit card transactions.

Accounts for regular suppliers of treatment equipment, linens, laundry services, office maintenance and so on, are set up. Some of these suppliers also offer discounts for early payments and some require Andersson to make prepayments with purchase orders.

No taxes are charged for medical treatment and supplies. Because GST is not charged to customers the business is not eligible for a GST refund. Therefore tax amounts are not tracked — they are included with the expense or asset amounts. Andersson pays both PST and GST for other goods and services.

To convert her accounting records to Simply Accounting on October 1, 2012, she used the following information:

- Chart of Accounts
- Trial Balance
- Supplier Information
- Patient/Customer Information
- Accounting Procedures

CHART OF POSTABLE ACCOUNTS

ANDERSSON CHIROPRACTIC CLINIC

ASSETS
1060 Bank: Regina Chequing
1080 Bank: Eastside Chequing
1100 Bank: Interac
1200 Accounts Receivable
1220 Prepaid Insurance
1240 Prepaid Subscriptions
1280 Purchase Prepayments
1300 Linen Supplies
1320 Office Supplies
1340 Other Supplies
1420 Computer Equipment
1430 Accum Deprec: Computers
1450 Treatment Equipment
1460 Accum Deprec: Equipment
1520 Office Furniture ▶

▶1530 Accum Deprec: Furniture
1550 Treatment Tables
1560 Accum Deprec: Tables
1580 Vehicle
1590 Accum Deprec: Vehicle

LIABILITIES
2100 Loans Payable
2200 Accounts Payable
2250 Prepaid Sales and Deposits
2300 Line of Credit Payable

EQUITY
3400 M.A. Capital
3450 M.A. Drawings
3600 Net Income ▶

▶**REVENUE**
4100 Revenue from Services
4150 Sales Discounts
4200 Interest Income

EXPENSE
5010 Bank Charges and Interac Fees
5030 Purchase Discounts
5050 Office Supplies Used
5060 Other Supplies Used
5080 Subscriptions and Books
5090 Insurance Expense
5100 Interest Expense
5110 Freight Expense
5120 Clinic Maintenance ▶

▶5140 Laundry Services
5150 Professional Dues
5180 Depreciation Expenses
5200 Hydro Expense
5240 Telephone Expense
5260 Rent
5300 Vehicle Expenses
5500 Wages Expense
5520 Payroll Services

NOTES: The Chart of Accounts includes only postable accounts and the Net Income or Current Earnings account.

TRIAL BALANCE

ANDERSSON CHIROPRACTIC CLINIC

September 30, 2012

		Debits	Credits				Debits	Credits
1060	Bank: Regina Chequing	$33 530		▶	3450	M.A. Drawings	18 000	
1080	Bank: Eastside Chequing	19 100			4100	Revenue from Services		114 000
1100	Bank: Interac	3 430			4150	Sales Discounts	140	
1200	Accounts Receivable	12 500			4200	Interest Income		160
1220	Prepaid Insurance	1 600			5010	Bank Charges and Interac Fees	390	
1240	Prepaid Subscriptions	480			5030	Purchase Discounts		210
1300	Linen Supplies	1 300			5050	Office Supplies Used	350	
1320	Office Supplies	270			5060	Other Supplies Used	1 130	
1340	Other Supplies	530			5080	Subscriptions and Books	2 400	
1420	Computer Equipment	4 200			5090	Insurance Expense	8 000	
1430	Accum Deprec: Computers		$ 1 050		5100	Interest Expense	2 500	
1450	Treatment Equipment	12 600			5110	Freight Expense	120	
1460	Accum Deprec: Equipment		2 100		5120	Clinic Maintenance	2 100	
1520	Office Furniture	9 600			5140	Laundry Services	1 800	
1530	Accum Deprec: Furniture		800		5150	Professional Dues	495	
1550	Treatment Tables	8 400			5180	Depreciation Expenses	10 850	
1560	Accum Deprec: Tables		1 400		5200	Hydro Expense	1 200	
1580	Vehicle	22 000			5240	Telephone Expense	1 100	
1590	Accum Deprec: Vehicle		5 500		5260	Rent	23 000	
2100	Loans Payable		45 000		5300	Vehicle Expenses	1 300	
2200	Accounts Payable		7 290		5500	Wages Expense	21 000	
2300	Line of Credit Payable		15 000		5520	Payroll Services	450	
3400	M.A. Capital		33 355 ▶				$225 865	$225 865

SUPPLIER INFORMATION

ANDERSSON CHIROPRACTIC CLINIC

Supplier Name (Contact)	Address	Phone No. Fax No.	E-mail Web Site	Terms
Canadian Chiropractic Association (O. Fisshal)	33 Backer Road Toronto, Ontario M4T 5B2	Tel 1: (416) 488-3713 Tel 2: (888) 488-3713	www.cca.ca	net 10
Cleanol and Laundry Services (Bessie Sweeps)	19 Duster Road Regina, Saskatchewan S4R 4L4	Tel: (306) 398-0908 Fax: (306) 398-8211	bsweeps@cls.com www.cls.com	net 30
Grasslands Fuel				net 1 (cash)
Medical Linen Supplies (Oll Whyte)	500 Agar St. Saskatoon, Saskatchewan S7L 6B9	Tel: (306) 662-6192 Fax: (306) 662-4399	owhyte@medsupplies.com www.medsupplies.com	2/10, n/30
OnLine Books			www.onlinebooks.com	net 1 (cheque)
Prairie Power Corp. (M. Jouls)	48 Powers Bay Regina, Saskatchewan S4X 1N2	Tel: (306) 395-1125	www.prairiepower.ca	net 1
Pro Suites Inc. (Kendra Walls)	19 Tenant Cr. Regina, Saskatchewan S4N 2B1	Tel: (306) 396-6646 Fax: (306) 396-5397	walls@prosuites.com www.prosuites.com	net 1 (first of month)
Sonartek Ltd. (T. Waver)	390 Retallack St. Regina, Saskatchewan S4R 3N3	Tel: (306) 579-7923 Fax: (306) 579-8003	twaver@sonartek.com www.sonartek.com	2/15, n/30
The Papery				net 15
Thera-Tables Inc. (Li Flatte)	60 Flatlands Cr. Saskatoon, Saskatchewan S7K 5B1	Tel: (306) 662-6486 Fax: (306) 662-7910	www.theratables.com	2/5, n/30
Western Communications (V. Du Parler)	99 Listener St. Regina, Saskatchewan S4R 5C9	Tel: (306) 395-5533	www.westcom.ca	net 1

OUTSTANDING SUPPLIER INVOICES

ANDERSSON CHIROPRACTIC CLINIC

Supplier Name	Terms	Date	Invoice No.	Amount	Total
Cleanol and Laundry Services	net 30	Sep. 14/12	CLS-2419	$90	
	net 30	Sep. 28/12	CLS-2683	90	
			Balance owing		$180
Medical Linen Supplies	2/10, n/30	Sep. 26/12	MLS-102		$690
Sonartek Ltd.	2/15, n/30	Sep. 22/12	SL-3456		$6 420
			Grand Total		$7 290

PATIENT INFORMATION

ANDERSSON CHIROPRACTIC CLINIC

Patient Name (Contact)	Address	Phone No. Fax No.	E-mail Web Site	Terms Credit Limit
Albert Blackfoot	16 Prairie Bay Regina, Saskatchewan S4N 6V3	Tel: (306) 582-1919	ablackfoot@shaw.ca	net 15 $500
Canadian Royals (K. Player)	1910 Buckingham St. Regina, Saskatchewan S4S 2P3	Tel: (306) 578-4567 Fax: (306) 578-7382	kplayer@canroyals.com www.canroyals.com	1/10, n/30 $5 000
Interplay Ballet School (S. Lightly)	2755 Flamenco St. Regina, Saskatchewan S4V 8C1	Tel: (306) 396-6190 Fax: (306) 396-8186	lightly@lighterthanair.com www.lighterthanair.com	1/10, n/30 $5 000
Roughrider Argos (B. Ball)	2935 Fowler St. Regina, Saskatchewan S4V 1N5	Tel: (306) 399-8000 Fax: (306) 399-8115	www.proball.com/ra	1/10, n/30 $5 000
Suzanne Lejeune	301 Pasqua St. Regina, Saskatchewan S4R 4M8	Tel: (306) 573-6296	slejeune@hotmail.com	net 15 $500

OUTSTANDING PATIENT INVOICES

ANDERSSON CHIROPRACTIC CLINIC

Patient Name	Terms	Date	Invoice No.	Amount	Total
Canadian Royals	1/10, n/30	Sep. 29/12	#638	$4 500	$4 500
Interplay Ballet School	1/10, n/30	Sep. 26/12	#632	$3 100	$3 100
Roughrider Argos	1/10, n/30	Sep. 29/12	#639	$4 900	$4 900
			Grand Total		$12 500

Accounting Procedures

Taxes

Since medical services are not taxable, patients do not pay GST or PST on the treatments and GST paid is not refundable. Therefore, no taxes have been set up in the data files, and no tax options are available in the journal Tax fields. Andersson pays provincial tax at the rate of 5 percent and GST at 5 percent on normal purchases — medical equipment is not taxed. All prices are shown with taxes included but taxes are not recorded separately — they are included with the expense or asset part of purchases.

Cash and Debit Card Sales

Andersson's individual patients frequently pay by Interac or debit card. Sales invoice amounts are deposited directly to the linked bank account. For this service, Andersson pays a small fee to the bank for each transaction, as well as a monthly rental fee for the terminal. These fees are deducted from the account periodically and are not deducted from deposits for individual transactions. Rather than create a large number of small invoices, debit card transactions are summarized every two weeks.

Payroll

Andersson's assistant is paid a monthly salary through arrangements with the bank. In lieu of a salary, Andersson draws $2 500 per month.

Discounts

Customers (sports teams) who have contracts with Andersson are offered a 1 percent discount if they pay their accounts in full within 10 days. Full payment is requested within 30 days. Individual patients are asked to pay their accounts every two weeks. Some suppliers also offer discounts for early payments.

All discount terms are set up in the customer and supplier records.

Deposits

When sports team managers sign new contracts for regular monthly billing for treating the team members, they pay a deposit to Andersson. Similarly, some suppliers ask for a deposit or prepayment when Andersson places a large order.

Revenue and Expense Accounts

The customer records for Andersson Chiropractic Clinic are set up with *Revenue from Services* as the default account. For suppliers, the account most often associated with purchases for a supplier has been entered as the default for that supplier.

Bank Accounts and Line of Credit

Andersson has two chequing accounts for deposits and payments. A third bank account is used for all Interac or debit card payments.

Andersson also uses her line of credit when making payments by cheque. At the end of each month Andersson makes a payment for the interest owing on the line of credit used. When she has the funds, she also pays down the principal owing.

All cheque numbers are updated automatically when the correct account is selected.

INSTRUCTIONS

1. **Record entries for the source documents** in Simply Accounting using the Chart of Accounts, Supplier Information, Patient Information and Accounting Procedures for Andersson Chiropractic Clinic. The procedures for entering each new type of transaction in this application are outlined step by step in the Keystrokes section following the source documents. These transactions are indicated with a ✓ in the completion box beside the source document. The page on which the relevant keystrokes begin is printed immediately below the check box.

2. **Print** the **reports and graphs** indicated on the following printing form after you have finished making your entries.

NOTES
The terms Patient and Customer will be used interchangeably in this chapter. Simply Accounting applies the label Patient for Customer in medical companies. For sports teams, we will use the term Customer unless the program displays the term Patient on the screen.

NOTES
All discounts are calculated on the full invoice amounts. For purchases, these amounts include taxes.

NOTES
The line of credit is set up as a liability account (the money is owed to the bank), but the Bank class is applied so that the account can be selected in journals to write cheques and deposit receipts. The amount of credit available does not appear on the Balance Sheet or Trial Balance. It is usually added as a Note to the financial statements.

REPORTS

Accounts
- [ ] Chart of Accounts
- [ ] Account List
- [ ] General Journal Entries

Financials
- [✓] Comparative Balance Sheet: amounts only for Oct. 31, 2012, and Nov. 30, 2012
- [✓] Income Statement from Dec. 1, 2011, to Nov. 30, 2012
- [✓] Comparative Trial Balance: amounts only for Nov. 30 and Dec. 1, 2012
- [✓] All Journal Entries: Oct. 1 to Nov. 30
- [ ] General Ledger
- [✓] Statement of Cash Flows from Oct. 1 to Nov. 30
- [✓] Cash Flow Projection Detail Report for accounts 1060 and 1080 for 30 days

Taxes
- [ ] Tax

Banking
- [ ] Cheque Log Report

Payables
- [ ] Supplier List
- [✓] Supplier Aged Detail for all suppliers
- [ ] Aged Overdue Payables
- [ ] Expenses Journal Entries
- [ ] Payments Journal Entries
- [✓] Pending Supplier Orders as at Jan. 15, 2013

Receivables
- [ ] Patient List
- [✓] Patient Aged Detail for all customers
- [ ] Aged Overdue Receivables
- [ ] Patient Statements
- [ ] Fees Journal Entries
- [ ] Receipts Journal Entries
- [✓] Pending Patient Orders as at Jan. 15, 2013

Mailing Labels
- [ ] Labels

Management Reports
- [ ] Ledger

GRAPHS
- [ ] Payables by Aging Period
- [ ] Payables by Supplier
- [ ] Receivables by Aging Period
- [ ] Receivables by Patient
- [✓] Fees vs Receivables
- [✓] Receivables Due vs Payables Due
- [ ] Revenues by Account
- [ ] Expenses by Account
- [✓] Expenses and Net Profit as % of Revenue

PRO VERSION

In the Pro version, the terms Purchases and Vendors will replace Expenses and Suppliers.

Sales, Customer and Invoice will replace Fees, Patient and Statement.

WARNING!

Two bank accounts and the line of credit are available for receipts and payments. Before posting a transaction, check carefully that you have selected the right account.

SOURCE DOCUMENTS

SESSION DATE – OCTOBER 7, 2012

[✓] **Purchase Quote #TT-44**   **Dated October 1, 2012**

415   Delivery date October 10, 2012

From Thera-Tables Inc., $4 000 including taxes for custom-built adjustable height treatment table with drop ends. Terms: 2/5, n/30. Deposit of 10 percent required on accepting quote.

[ ] **Purchase Quote #MT-511**   **Dated October 1, 2012**

Delivery date October 20, 2012

From Medi-Tables (use Quick Add for the new supplier), $4 550 including all taxes for custom-built treatment table. Terms: net 20. Deposit of 20 percent required on accepting quote.

[✓] **Purchase Order #TT-44**   **Dated October 2, 2012**

417   Delivery date October 10, 2012

To Thera-Tables Inc., $4 000 including taxes for custom-built treatment table. Terms: 2/5, n/30. Convert quote #TT-44 to purchase order #TT-44.

[✓] **Cheque Copy #567**   **Dated October 3, 2012**

419   To Thera-Tables Inc., $400 from Regina Chequing account as prepayment in acceptance of quote #TT-44 and to confirm order #TT-44.

[✓] **Cheque Copy #103**   **Dated October 3, 2012**

421   To Sonartek Ltd., $6 291.60 from the line of credit in payment of account including $128.40 discount for early payment. Reference invoice #SL-3456.

☐ **Cash Purchase R2012-10**   **Dated October 3, 2012**

To Pro Suites Inc., cheque #121 for $2 300 to pay rent for October. Store the transaction as a monthly recurring entry. Pay from Eastside Chequing account.

☐ **Cheque Copy #568**   **Dated October 4, 2012**

To Medical Linen Supplies, $676.20 from Regina Chequing account in payment of account including $13.80 discount for early payment. Reference invoice #MLS-102.

☑ **Cash Receipt #58**   **Dated October 4, 2012**

422   From Interplay Ballet, cheque #447 for $3 069 in payment of account including $31 discount for early payment. Reference invoice #632. Deposited to Eastside Chequing account.

☑ **Sales Quote #51**   **Dated October 4, 2012**

422   Starting date October 15, 2012
To Giant Raptors (use Full Add for the new customer), a local basketball team, $3 500 per month for unlimited chiropractic services during the regular six-month training and playing season. Andersson will attend or be on call for all home games. If the team enters the playoffs, the contract may be extended for $1 200 per week. Terms: 1/10, n/30. A deposit of $2 000 will be required on acceptance of the contract. Enter 6 as the number ordered.

☑ **Memo #1**   **Dated October 5, 2012**

424   After some negotiations with the Giant Raptors, Andersson agreed to reduce the contract price to $3 300 per month for the playing season. Playoff games will be billed at $1 100 per week. Adjust the sales quote to change the price.

☑ **Sales Order #51** Convert quote to Order   **Dated October 5, 2012**

425   Starting date October 15, 2012
The Giant Raptors have accepted the modified sales quote #51. Convert the quote to a sales order. All terms and dates are unchanged from the revised quote for $3 300 per month.

☑ **Cash Receipt #59**   **Dated October 6, 2012**

426   From the Giant Raptors, cheque #838 for $2 000 as deposit #14 to confirm sales order #51. Deposited to Regina Chequing account.

SESSION DATE – OCTOBER 14, 2012

☐ **Cash Receipt #60**   **Dated October 8, 2012**

From Roughrider Argos, cheque #1122 for $4 851 in payment of account including $49 discount for early payment. Reference sales invoice #639. Deposited to Eastside Chequing account.

☐ **Cash Receipt #61**   **Dated October 8, 2012**

From Canadian Royals, cheque #3822 for $4 455 in payment of account including $45 discount for early payment. Reference sales invoice #638. Deposited to Regina Chequing account.

☑ **Purchase Order #44 and Cheque #104**   **Dated October 9, 2012**

428   Delivery date October 19, 2012
From Sonartek Ltd., $6 000 including taxes for ultrasound machine with multiple frequencies and interchangeable wands. Terms: 2/15, n/30. Deposit of $1 500 paid with cheque #104 from Line of Credit Payable account to confirm order.

NOTES
Each month, the sales invoice for Giant Raptors will be entered as partially filling the order.

NOTES
Giant Raptors
(contact Rex Saurus)
550 Tyrannus Dr.,
Regina, SK S4R 5T1
Tel 1: (306) 398-8753
Tel 2: (306) 398-5339
Fax: (306) 398-5339
F-mail: rex@raptors.com
Web: www.raptors.com
Terms: 1/10, n/30
Revenue account: 4100
Credit limit: $5 000

Convert order to Invoice

☑ **Purchase Invoice #TT-4599**   **Dated October 10, 2012**

430 From Thera-Tables Inc., to fill purchase order #TT-44 for $4 000 including taxes for custom-built treatment table. Terms: 2/5, n/30.

☑ **Sales Invoice #649**   **Dated October 10, 2012**

432 To Giant Raptors, to fill the first month of the contract on sales order #51 for $3 300. Terms: 1/10, n/30.

☑ **Cash Receipt #62**   **Dated October 13, 2012**

433 From the Giant Raptors, cheque #939 for $1 267 in full payment of account including $33 discount for early payment. Reference sales invoice #649 and deposit #14. Deposited to Eastside Chequing account.

☐

Quote:	52		
Date:	Oct 13, 2012		
Starting date:	Oct 25, 2012		
Customer:	Veronica Kain		
	Veronica Kain School of Dance		
	35 Lady Slipper Rd.		
Address:	Regina, SK S3V 4H7		
Phone No:	(306) 376-3218		

Andersson Chiropractic Clinic
www.betterbacks.com

4500 Rae St.
Regina, SK S4S 3B4
Tel 1: (306) 577-1900
Tel 2: (306) 577-2199   Fax: (306) 577-1925

QUOTE

Treatment description	Amount
Chiropractic services for the school year (Sep-Jun) Monthly contract rate $1 000 deposit when contract accepted Contract may be extended for summer months	2 500.00

Terms: 1/10, n/30

Signed: *Maria Andersson* | Customer Initials: *VK* | **TOTAL** | 2 500.00

☑ **Sales Order #52 and Deposit #15**   **Dated October 14, 2012**

435 Starting date October 25, 2012
From Veronica Kain School of Dance, acceptance of quote #52. Convert the quote to a sales order leaving all terms and amounts unchanged. Received cheque #865 for $1 000 as deposit #15 to confirm sales order #52. Deposited to Eastside Chequing account.

☑ **Debit Card Sales Summary Invoice #650**   **Dated October 14, 2012**

436 To various one-time patients, $260 for initial assessments for new patients and $450 for follow-up treatment sessions. Total amount deposited in Interac bank account, $710. Store as a recurring bi-weekly transaction.

☐ **Cheque Copy #122**   **Dated October 14, 2012**

To Cleanol and Laundry Services, $90 from Eastside Chequing account in payment of account. Reference invoice #CLS-2419.

☐ **Cheque Copy #123**   **Dated October 14, 2012**

To Thera-Tables Inc., $3 520 from Eastside Chequing account in full payment of account including $80 discount for early payment. Reference invoice #TT-4599 and cheque #567. Remember to "pay" the prepayment.

☐ **Purchase Invoice #CLS-3926**   **Dated October 14, 2012**

From Cleanol and Laundry Services, $90 for contracted twice weekly laundry service. Terms: net 30. Store the transaction as a bi-weekly recurring entry.

SESSION DATE – OCTOBER 21, 2012

☑ **Purchase Invoice #SL-4622**   Convert order to Invoice , Pay Later   **Dated October 17, 2012**

437   From Sonartek Ltd., to fill purchase order #44, $6 000 including taxes for multi-frequency ultrasound machine. Terms: 2/15, n/30.

☐ **Cash Purchase GF-2641**   **Dated October 18, 2012**

From Grasslands Fuel, $62 for gasoline for business vehicle. Invoice total $62 paid in full by cheque #569 from Regina Chequing account. Store as a bi-weekly recurring entry.

☐ **Cash Sales Invoice #651**   **Dated October 20, 2012**

To Albert Blackfoot, $315 for seven treatment sessions. Invoice total paid in full by cheque #426 and deposited to Regina Chequing account. Store as a monthly recurring entry.

SESSION DATE – OCTOBER 31, 2012

pay Later

☑ **Sales Invoice #652**   Convert order to Statement   **Dated October 25, 2012**

439   To Veronica Kain School of Dance, to fill sales order #52, $2 500 for contracted services for one month. Terms: 1/10, n/30. Store as a recurring monthly entry

☐ **Sales Invoice #653**   **Dated October 25, 2012**

To Interplay Ballet School, $2 500 for contracted services for one month. Terms: 1/10, n/30. Store transaction as a recurring monthly entry.

☐ **Purchase Invoice #CLS-4723**   **Dated October 28, 2012**

From Cleanol and Laundry Services, $90 for contracted laundry service. Terms: net 30. Recall stored transaction.

☐ **Cash Purchase Invoice #WC-83825**   **Dated October 28, 2012**

From Western Communications, $125 including taxes for one month of telephone and Internet service. Invoice total paid by cheque #124 from Eastside Chequing account. Store as a monthly recurring entry.

☐ **Sales Invoice #654**   **Dated October 28, 2012**

To Canadian Royals, $4 500 for contracted services for one month. Terms: 1/10, n/30. Store transaction as a recurring monthly entry.

☐ **Sales Invoice #655**   **Dated October 28, 2012**

To Roughrider Argos, $4 900 for contracted services for one month. Terms: 1/10, n/30. Store transaction as a recurring monthly entry.

NOTES
You may need to scroll down to see the line for the prepayment amount.

NOTES
When you advance the session date to Oct. 31, you will see an advice statement that it is time to prepare for year-end. Read and then close the Advisor statement to proceed

NOTES
Recall the stored transaction but do not store the changed transaction. When you post the transaction, you will see the message that the transaction has changed and the next posting date will be updated. Click Yes to continue. Refer to page 191.

Sales Invoice:	656	
Date:	Oct 28, 2012	

Andersson Chiropractic Clinic
www.betterbacks.com

Customer:	Debit card sales summary	4500 Rae St.
Address:		Regina, SK S4S 3B4
		Tel 1: (306) 577-1900
Phone No:		Tel 2: (306) 577-2199 Fax: (306) 577-1925

Treatment description	Amount
Initial assessments	130.00
Follow-up treatments	630.00

Terms: paid by Interac

Direct deposit to Interac account

Signed: *Maria Andersson*

Customer Initials:	**INVOICE TOTAL**	760.00

Cash Receipt #63   **Dated October 29, 2012**

From Interplay Ballet, cheque #501 for $2 475 in payment of account including $25 discount for early payment. Reference sales invoice #653. Deposited to Regina Chequing account.

Cheque Copy #570   **Dated October 29, 2012**

To Cleanol and Laundry Services, $180 from Regina Chequing account in payment of account. Reference invoices #CLS-2683 and #CLS-3926.

Bank Debit Memo #477211   **Dated October 29, 2012**

From Eastside Trust, $2 100 for monthly payroll and $45 payroll service fee withdrawn from chequing account. Store payroll transaction as a monthly recurring entry.

☑ **Cash Receipt #64**   **Dated October 29, 2012**

440   From Veronica Kain School of Dance, cheque #878 for $1 475 in payment of account including $25 discount for early payment. Reference sales invoice #652. Deposited to Regina Chequing account.

Purchase Quote #45   **Dated October 29, 2012**

Starting date November 1, 2012
From Cleanol and Laundry Services, $210 every two weeks to increase service from twice per week to daily laundry service. Terms: net 30.

Purchase Quote #FS-644   **Dated October 29, 2012**

Starting date November 1, 2012
From Fresh Spaces (use Quick Add for the new supplier), $125 per week for daily laundry service. Terms: net 30.

PO#:   45
Date: Oct 29, 2012
Starting date: Nov 1, 2012

**Andersson
Chiropractic Clinic**
www.betterbacks.com

Ordered from: Cleanol and Laundry Services
Address: 19 Duster Road
              Regina, SK S4R 4L4
Phone No: (306) 398-0908
Fax No:
Contact: Bessie Sweeps

4500 Rae St.
Regina, SK S4S 3B4
Tel 1: (306) 577-1900
Tel 2: (306) 577-2199   Fax: (306) 577-1925

P U R C H A S E   O R D E R

Order description	Amount
Contract for daily laundry service bi-weekly rate including GST terms: net 30 days	210.00
Ref: quote #45	

Order Total	210.00
Deposit	——
Balance Owing	210.00

Authorization: *Maria Andersson*

Memo #2   **Dated October 31, 2012**

Transfer $1 060 from the Regina Trust Chequing account to pay down the line of credit. This amount includes $60 for one month of interest on the amount of credit used. Store as a monthly recurring entry. (Use the General Journal.)

NOTES
To transfer the funds, you should debit the Line of Credit Payable and Interest Expense accounts and credit the bank account.

SESSION DATE – NOVEMBER 7, 2012

☑ **Memo #3**   **Dated November 1, 2012**

441   Review memos and enter the next transactions from the Daily Business Manager.

☑ **Cheque Copy #571**   **Dated November 1, 2012**

442   To Sonartek Ltd., $4 380 from Regina Chequing account in full payment of account including $120 discount for early payment. Reference purchase invoice #SL-4622 and cheque #104 (prepayment).

☑ **Cash Purchase Invoice #GF-3677**   **Dated November 1, 2012**

444   From Grasslands Fuel, $62 for gasoline for business vehicle. Invoice total paid in full from Regina Chequing account by cheque #572. Recall stored entry.

☑ **Cash Purchase R2012-11**   **Dated November 3, 2012**

444   To Pro Suites Inc., cheque #125 for $2 300 from Eastside Chequing account to pay rent for November. Recall stored entry.

☑ **Cash Receipt #65**   **Dated November 5, 2012**

445   From Canadian Royals, cheque #4011 for $4 455 in payment of account including $45 discount for early payment. Reference sales invoice #654. Deposited to Regina Chequing account.

WARNING!
We observed some inconsistencies in the dates for recurring entries in the Daily Business Manager, so check your transactions carefully if you use this approach.

✓ **Cash Receipt #66**   **Dated November 7, 2012**

446   From Roughrider Argos, cheque #1636 for $4 851 in payment of account
including $49 discount for early payment. Reference sales invoice #655.
Deposited to Regina Chequing account.

NOTES
Use Full Add for the new
supplier.
☐ Web: www.gbw.com
Expense acct: 1480
Whirlpool (Create new account.)
Use the source document
for the remaining supplier details.

PO#: 46	
Date: Nov 7, 2012	**Andersson**
Starting date: Dec 28, 2012	**Chiropractic Clinic**
	www.betterbacks.com
Ordered from: Get Better Whirlpools	
Address: 35 Eddy Circle	4500 Rae St.
Saskatoon, SK S7K 6E3	Regina, SK S4S 3B4
Phone No: (306) 665-7210 or	Tel 1: (306) 577-1900
(877) 699-1270	Tel 2: (306) 577-2199 Fax: (306) 577-1925
Fax No: (306) 663-6281	
Contact: Ira Spinner	PURCHASE ORDER

Order description	Amount
therapeutic whirlpool (Model WP-299X) including GST and PST terms: net 20 days	24 000.00
Deposit: $2 000 paid by cheque #573 (Regina Chequing Account)	

Authorization: *Maria Andersson*	
Order Total	24 000.00
Deposit	2 000.00
Balance Owing	22 000.00

SESSION DATE – NOVEMBER 14, 2012

✓ **Sales Invoice #657**   **Dated November 9, 2012**

446   To Giant Raptors, to fill one month of the contract in sales order #51 for $3 300.
Terms: 1/10, n/30.

✓ **Purchase Invoice #CLS-6543**   **Dated November 11, 2012**

447   From Cleanol and Laundry Services, to fill purchase order #45, $210 for
contracted daily laundry service. Terms: net 30. Store as a bi-weekly recurring
entry. (Remove the old stored entry then store the new one.)

☐ **Debit Card Sales Summary Invoice #658**   **Dated November 11, 2012**

To various one-time patients, $260 for initial assessments and $450 for follow-up
treatment sessions. Total amount deposited in Interac bank account, $710. Enter
the stored transaction from the Daily Business Manager. (Advance the calendar
date selection in the Daily Business Manager if you do not see the transaction
listed.)

☐ **Cash Purchase Invoice #TP-1188**   **Dated November 12, 2012**

From The Papery, $230 for paper supplies for treatment rooms and $60 for office
supplies. Invoice total $290 paid in full from Eastside Chequing account by
cheque #126.

SESSION DATE – NOVEMBER 21, 2012

☐ **Cash Receipt #67**   **Dated November 18, 2012**

From the Giant Raptors, cheque #1334 for $3 267 in full payment of account including $33 discount for early payment. Reference sales invoice #657. Deposited to Eastside Chequing account.

☐ **Purchase Order #47**   **Dated November 19, 2012**

Starting date January 1, 2013
From HydraTub Care (use Full Add for new supplier), $200 per month, including taxes for one-year service contract. The contract includes weekly maintenance of whirlpool and repairs. Parts required for repairs will be billed separately. Terms: net 20. Remember to enter 2013 as the year for the starting date.

☐ **Purchase Quote #SU-5532**   **Dated November 19, 2012**

Starting date December 1, 2012
From Space Unlimited (use Quick Add), $2 250 per month for rent of office space for the next 12 months. Rent does not include heat or hydro. Terms: net 1. Rent payment is due on the first of each month. Security deposit of one month's rent required in advance. Postdated cheques will be accepted.

☐ **Purchase Quote #48**   **Dated November 19, 2012**

Starting date December 1, 2012
From Pro Suites Inc., $2 350 per month for rent of office space for the next 12 months. Rent includes heat but does not include hydro. Rent payment is due on the first of each month. A series of postdated cheques will be accepted.

☐ **Purchase Order #48**   **Dated November 20, 2012**

Starting date December 1, 2012
From Pro Suites Inc., $2 350 per month for rent of office space for the next 12 months. Convert purchase quote #48 to a purchase order.

SESSION DATE – NOVEMBER 28, 2012

☐ **Debit Card Sales Summary Invoice #659**   **Dated November 25, 2012**

To various one-time customers, $260 for initial assessments and $630 for follow-up treatment sessions. Total amount deposited in Interac bank account, $890. Recall the stored transaction and edit the amounts.

☐ **Purchase Invoice #CLS-8210**   **Dated November 25, 2012**

From Cleanol and Laundry Services, $210 for contracted laundry service. Terms: net 30. Recall the stored transaction.

☑ **Sales Invoices #660**   **Dated November 25, 2012**

448   Enter the recurring sale to Interplay Ballet School, $2 500 for contracted services for one month, directly from the Daily Business Manager. Terms: 1/10, n/30.

☐ **Sales Invoices #661**   **Dated November 25, 2012**

To Veronica Kain School of Dance, $2 500 for contracted services for one month. Terms: 1/10, n/30. Recall the stored transaction.

☐ **Sales Invoices #662**   **Dated November 28, 2012**

To Canadian Royals, $4 500 for contracted services for one month. Terms: 1/10, n/30. Recall the stored transaction.

NOTES
HydraTub Care
550 Splash St.
Regina, SK S4T 7H5
Tel: (306) 578-2996
Terms: net 20
Expense acct: 5220 (Create a new Group account: 5220 Whirlpool Maintenance.)

NOTES
The year-end Advisor appears when you advance the session date. Read the message and close the Advisor.

NOTES
Enter the recurring transactions from the Daily Business Manager.

☐ **Sales Invoices #663**   **Dated November 28, 2012**

To Roughrider Argos, $4 900 for contracted services for one month. Terms: 1/10, n/30. Recall the stored transaction.

☐ **Cash Purchase Invoice #WC-122022**   **Dated November 28, 2012**

From Western Communications, $125 including taxes for telephone and Internet service. Invoice total paid from Eastside Chequing account by cheque #127. Recall the stored transaction.

☑ **Cheque Copy #128**   **Dated November 28, 2012**

449 To Cleanol and Laundry Services, $300 from Eastside Chequing account in payment of account. Reference invoices #CLS-4723 and CLS-6543.

SESSION DATE – NOVEMBER 30, 2012

☐ **Cash Receipt #68**   **Dated November 29, 2012**

From Interplay Ballet, cheque #553 for $2 475 in payment of account including $25 discount for early payment. Reference invoice #660. Deposited to Eastside Chequing account.

☐ **Bank Debit Memo #747721**   **Dated November 29, 2012**

From Eastside Trust, $2 100 for monthly payroll and $45 payroll service fee withdrawn from chequing account 1080. Recall the stored transaction.

☐ **Memo #4**   **Dated November 30, 2012**

Transfer $1 060 from the Regina Trust Chequing account to pay down the line of credit. This amount includes $60 for one month of interest on the amount of credit used. Recall the stored transaction.

☐ **Cash Purchase Invoice #PPC-76511**   **Dated November 30, 2012**

From Prairie Power Corp., $380 including taxes for two months of hydro service. Invoice total paid from Regina Chequing account by cheque #574.

☐ **Bank Debit Memo #747937**   **Dated November 30, 2012**

From Eastside Trust, pre-authorized withdrawals from chequing account:
  For bi-monthly loan repayment, $1 370 principal and $230 interest
  For bank service charges and debit card fees, $108

☐ **Bank Debit Memo #120022**   **Dated November 30, 2012**

From Regina Trust, $36 withdrawn from account for service charges.

☐ **Memo #5**   **Dated November 30, 2012**

From Manager: Record the accumulated depreciation for the two-month period for all fixed assets as follows:

Computer Equipment	$ 230
Treatment Equipment	420
Office Furniture	160
Treatment Tables	280
Vehicle	1 100

☐ **Memo #6**   **Dated November 30, 2012**

From Manager: Record the adjusting entries for supplies used in the previous two months:

Office Supplies	$105
Paper and Other Supplies	260

☐ **Cheque Copy #129 & Memo #7**   **Dated November 30, 2012**

To M. Andersson (use Quick Add), $5 000 from Eastside Chequing account for drawings to cover personal expenses.

☐ **Memo #8**   **Dated November 30, 2012**

From Manager: Close out the M.A. Drawings account by transferring the balance to M.A. Capital.

☑ **Memo #9**   **Dated November 30, 2012**

450   From Manager: Three purchase quotes that are on file are no longer valid. Remove quote #MT-511 from Medi-Tables, quote #FS-644 from Fresh Spaces and quote #SU-5532 from Space Unlimited.
Remove the recurring transactions for Grasslands Fuel (cash purchase) and Albert Blackfoot (sale) because they will no longer be used.

☐ **Memo #10**   **Dated November 30, 2012**

From Manager: Print all financial reports. Back up the data files and start a new fiscal period on December 1, 2012.

KEYSTROKES

Opening Data Files

Open   **SimData10\Anderson\anderson** to access the data files for Andersson. **Enter Oct 7, 2012** as the Session date.

Entering a Purchase Quote

On October 1, Andersson received two quotes for a treatment table that will be delivered later in the month. A quote usually provides a guaranteed price for some work or products. The offer is often limited to a stated time period. If the business chooses to accept the offer, the quote may be filled as a purchase for immediate delivery or converted to a purchase order for future delivery. When the goods are received, or the work is completed, the quote is filled and the purchase is completed. Supplier quotes are entered and filled in the Expenses or Purchases Journal.

Click   **Payables** in the Modules pane list. Icons are added for quotes and orders.

Click   the **Supplier Quotes icon** shown in the following screen:

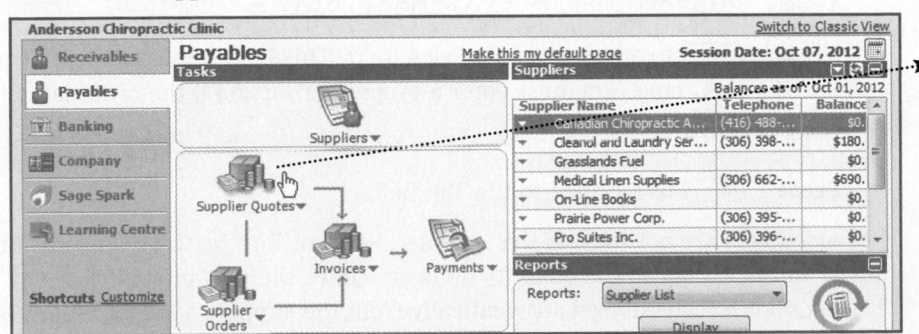

> **NOTES**
> Enter the drawings cheque as an Other Payment in the Payments Journal. You can add a memo number as the source if you want.

> **NOTES**
> To close the Drawings account, credit Drawings and debit Capital. You can find the amount in the Trial Balance, Balance Sheet or General Ledger.

> **NOTES**
> Refer to page 102 for assistance with starting a new fiscal period if needed.

> **NOTES**
> If you are using backups, restore SimData10\anderson1.CAB to SimData10\Anderson\anderson to open the data files for Andersson. Refer to Chapter 1, page 20, if you need assistance.

> **NOTES**
> The Payroll, Inventory and Project modules are not included in the Modules pane — they are hidden because these ledgers are not used and are not set up.

> **PRO VERSION**
> *pro* Purchase replaces the term Supplier. Purchase Quotes, Purchase Orders and Purchase Invoices are used as the Home window icon labels.
> Click the Purchase Quotes icon to open the journal.

> **CLASSIC VIEW**
> *pro* Click the Expenses, Orders & Quotes icon to open the journal. Choose Quote from the journal's Transaction drop-down list.

The Expenses Journal – Creating A Quote window opens:

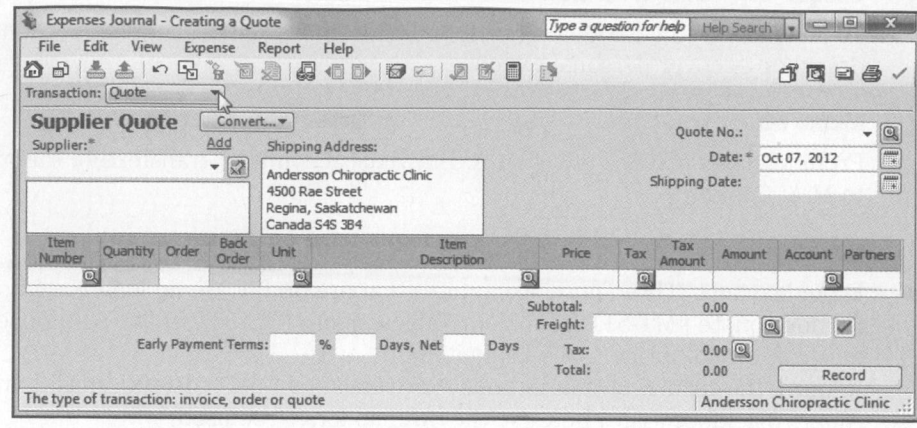

Quote is selected in the Transaction field.

Click   the **Supplier field** and **select Thera-Tables Inc.**

Click   the **Date field** to advance the cursor and skip the address fields.

Type   10-1-12   (Remember to add the year when you type in a date.)

Press   (tab) **twice** to advance to the Order No. field.

Type   TT-44

Press   (tab) **twice** to advance to the Shipping Date field.

This is the date on which the order is to be received or the work is to be completed. Sometimes, instead of shipping date, we use the term delivery date for services or starting date for a contract because these terms are more appropriate for quotes and orders for services.

Type   10-10-12

The Item Number field refers to the code for inventory items. The Quantity (quantity received with this purchase) field will remain blank because this is not a purchase and no goods are received. However, you must enter the number of units that are ordered. You cannot leave the Order field blank. One table is being ordered.

Click   the **Order field**.

Type   1

Press   (tab) to advance to the Unit field that also applies to inventory.

Press   (tab) to advance to the Item Description field.

Type   custom-built treatment table

Press   (tab) to advance to the Price field. This field refers to the unit price of the items. You must enter a price in order to fill the order later.

Type   4000

Press   (tab) to advance to the Tax field.

Because taxes are not used in this data set, we can skip the tax fields. The amount is entered automatically as the quantity on order times the unit price.

The account is also entered automatically from the supplier's ledger record, so the quote is complete as shown:

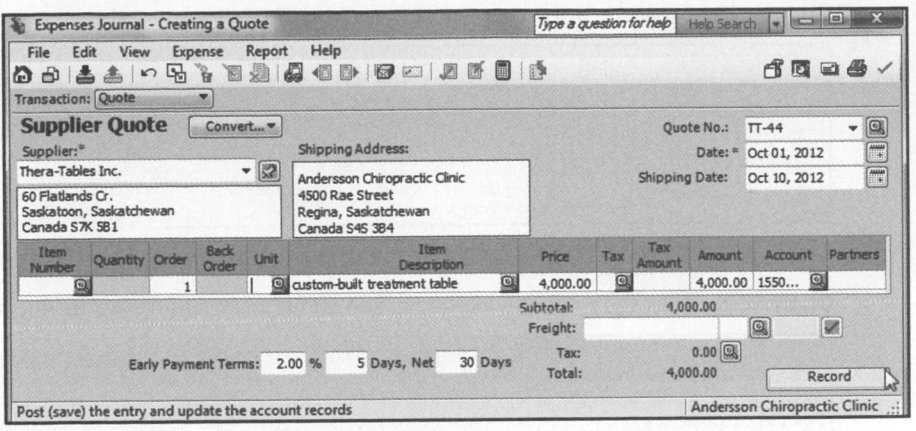

Check your **work** carefully and **make** any **corrections** necessary just as you do for other Purchases Journal entries.

If you try to display the Journal entry, you will see that there is no journal entry associated with the quote. The related journal entry will be completed when the quote is filled and the purchase is completed. When you are sure that the entry is correct,

Click the **Record button** 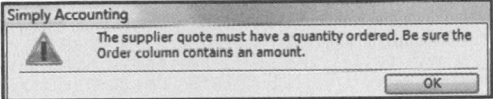 or **choose** the **Expense menu** and **click Record** to save your transaction.

If you forgot to enter the quantity ordered, you will see the following warning:

Click OK and enter the quantity in the Order field and try again to record.

Enter the **second purchase quote** from a new supplier. Remember to add the account number and payment terms to the quote.

Placing a Purchase Order from a Quote

Sometimes purchase orders are entered without a quote and sometimes they are converted from a purchase quote. Entering a purchase order directly, without the quote, is the same as entering a purchase quote except that you choose Order as the type of transaction instead of Quote.

The purchase order to Thera-Tables Inc. is a quote converted to an order. The Expenses Journal should still be open and Quote is selected as the Transaction type.

Click the **Quote No. field list arrow** as shown:

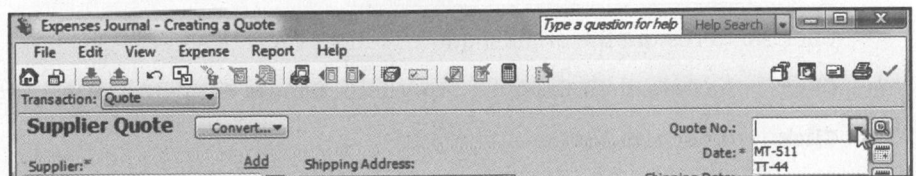

The drop-down list includes all unfilled purchase quotes and purchase orders. The two quotes entered above are listed.

Click **TT-44** to select it.

Press (tab) to select the quote and place it on-screen.

You can change the order to a quote in different ways.

NOTES
Refer to page 120 if you need help correcting the entry.

NOTES
The Post button label changes to Record for quotes and orders because no journal entry is posted.
You should click OK to confirm successful posting or recording of transactions. We will not repeat this instruction for every transaction.

NOTES
Notice that Continue is not an option when you add a new supplier for a quote.

NOTES
We will use the terms purchase order and supplier order interchangeably, unless the term appears in the Simply Accounting screen.

Click the **Convert list arrow** to see conversion options as shown:

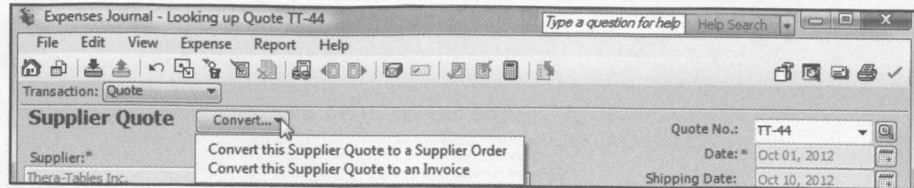

You can convert the quote to an order or directly to an invoice from this menu. Or,

Click the **Transaction list arrow** to see the transaction types as shown:

Click **Convert This Supplier Quote To A Supplier Order** from the Convert drop-down list, or

Click **Order** from the Transaction type drop-down list.

The quote screen changes to an order. Order No. replaces Quote No. as the field label:

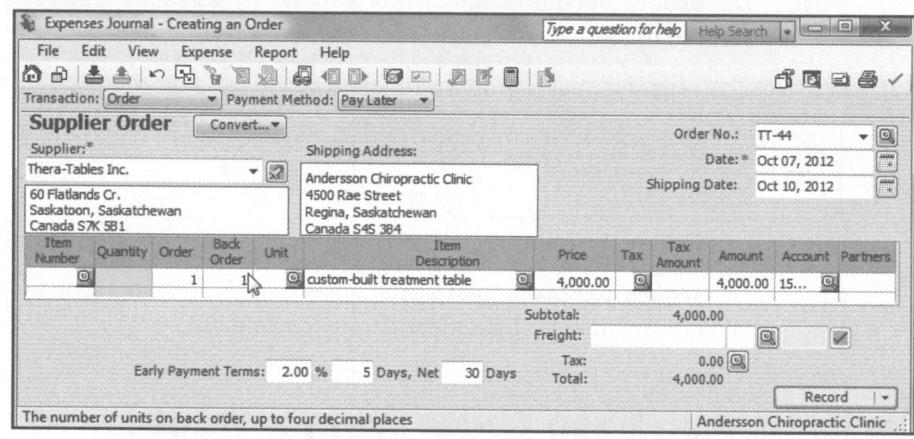

Notice that the purchase order includes a Payment Method field. You can enter prepayments with the order. We show this method of entering prepayments on page 428.

The Order quantity has been copied to the Back Order field.

The session date is entered on the revised form so we need to change it. If you try to change the quote number, you will see the warning (see margin note):

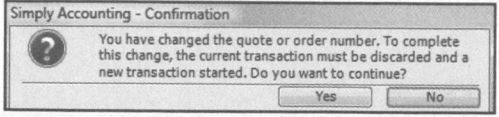

Click No to restore the original quote number.

Click the **Date field Calendar icon** 📅. **Choose October 2. Press** (tab).

Click the **Record button** ⎡ Record ▾ ⎤.

The Record button now includes the option to print on its drop-down list. Print & Record may be selected as the default, just like the Post & Print option for Sales.

The program displays the warning message:

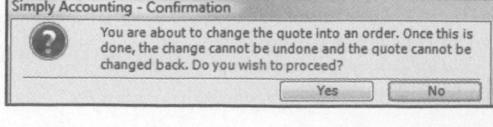

PRO VERSION

Click Convert This Purchase Quote To A Purchase Order from the Convert drop-down list.

NOTES

To change the number of a purchase order to match the number sequence on preprinted forms, you should
- Recall the quote
- Choose the Adjust Quote tool (adjust purchase quotes in the same way as sales quotes — see page 424)
- Change the quote number
- Record the revised quote
- Recall the quote
- Convert the quote to an order by choosing Order from the Transaction list or by choosing Convert to an Order from the Convert drop-down list
- Record the purchase order
- Confirm the conversion
- Check that the order sequence number is correct and update the next order number if necessary

Since we want to convert the quote to an order, we can proceed. The order will replace the quote.

Click   Yes.

Purchase order numbers are updated automatically by the program, just like sales invoice and cheque numbers. (Alpha-numeric numbers are not updated.) If the number for the quote that you are converting is larger than the next purchase order sequence number, a second warning will appear when you record the order because the number is out of sequence. Simply Accounting will ask if you want to update your sequence starting number:

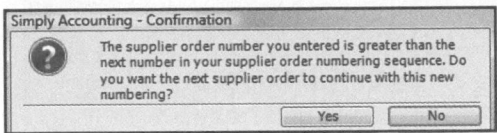

This does not apply to the alphanumeric number we used.

Click Yes if you want to reset the numbering sequence for future purchase orders. Click No to avoid resetting the automatic sequence to the higher number. When you choose No, the higher purchase order number will still be recorded, and later skipped, but the automatic counter will not be changed.

Close   the **Supplier Order window**.

Making a Prepayment to a Supplier

Businesses frequently request a deposit — down payment or prepayment — when an order is placed, especially for customized orders. Deposits may be refundable or not. A deposit may be used to pay for materials that are ordered specifically for a project; it may ensure that the purchaser will follow through with the order or it may provide the supplier with some revenue if the order is cancelled and part of the deposit is not refundable.

Prepayments can be made in the Payments Journal or in the Supplier Order Journal window. If the prepayment accompanies the order, you should enter it on the Order form. This prepayment is made later, so we will enter it in the Payments Journal.

Click   the **Payments icon** [Payments] to open the Payments Journal.

Click   the **Enter Supplier Prepayments tool** or **choose** the **Payment menu** and **click Enter Prepayments**.

This tool button/menu option acts as a switch that opens the fields for deposits:

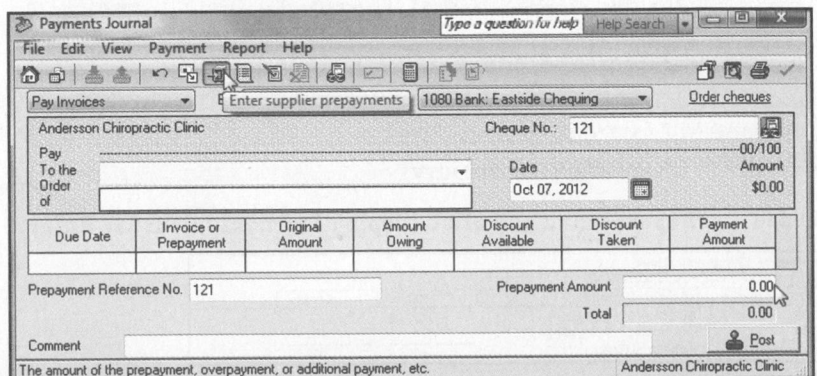

You can leave this tool selected, so that the optional fields will always be available.

NOTES
The higher order number will be skipped in the automatic numbering sequence when you reach it if you choose not to reset the number sequence.

NOTES
Entering a prepayment on the Supplier Order form is shown on page 428.

PRO VERSION
Click the Enter Vendor Prepayments tool.

Two new fields are added to the journal: one for the prepayment reference number and one for the amount. The reference number is the next cheque number in sequence for the selected bank account and is updated automatically by the program. The rest of the journal is the same as before, but the invoice payment lines are not used. Outstanding invoices, if there are any, will be included in the journal.

When the payment is made by cheque, the From field has the list of bank accounts you can choose. The default bank account and cheque number for this payment are not correct. We must change them.

Click the **From field list arrow** to see the list of available bank accounts:

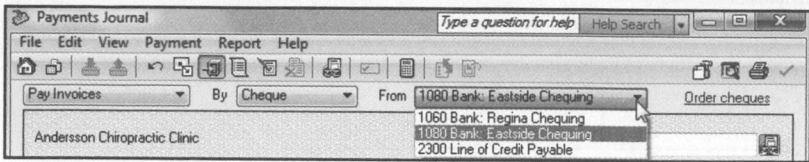

Click **Bank: Regina Chequing**.

When you select a different bank account, the cheque number is updated for the new account. Each bank account has its own cheque number sequence, and these numbers are updated as you make payments from each account.

Choose **Thera-Tables Inc.** as the supplier from the drop-down list.

Enter **October 3** as the date of the cheque.

Click the **Prepayment Amount field**.

Type 400

Click the **Comment field**. Advancing the cursor updates the Total.

Type Prepayment for order #TT-44

If an outstanding invoice is paid with the same cheque, enter the invoice payment in the usual way in addition to the deposit amount.

The entry is complete and the journal looks like the one shown here:

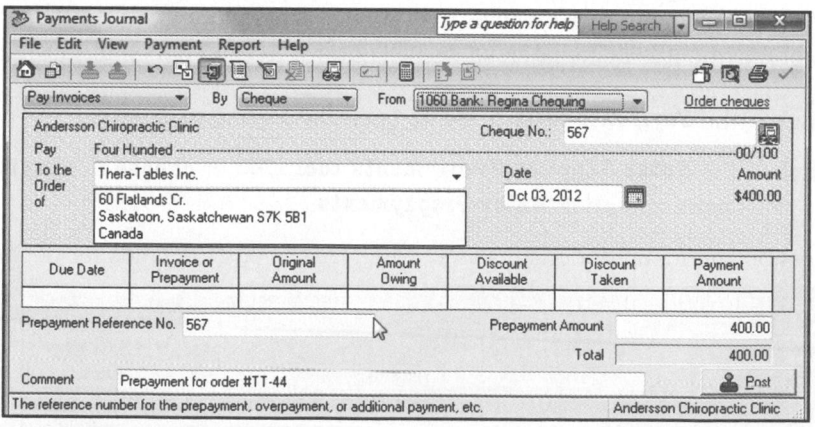

You are ready to review the journal entry.

Choose the **Report menu** and **click Display Payments Journal Entry**:

Andersson Chiropractic Clinic Payments Journal Entry 10/03/12 (J1)			
Account Number	Account Description	Debits	Credits
1280	Purchase Prepayments	400.00	-
1060	Bank: Regina Chequing	-	400.00
Additional Date:	Additional Field:	400.00	400.00

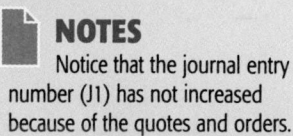

NOTES
Notice that the journal entry number (J1) has not increased because of the quotes and orders.

As for other payments, the bank account is credited. However, the prepayment creates an asset until the order is filled, so *Purchase Prepayments*, the linked contra-asset account, is debited — the supplier owes something to us. If there is no previous balance owing to the supplier, the prepayment creates a debit balance for the account. After the purchase, when you pay the supplier, the prepayment will be displayed in red under the heading "Prepayments" and you "pay" it by accepting the amount, just as you do to pay the invoice itself.

Close   the **display** when you have finished and **make corrections** to the journal entry if necessary.

Click   **Post** Post to save the transaction.

Click   the **Enter Supplier Prepayments tool** again to close the prepayment fields if you want to close these optional fields.

Entering Payments from a Line of Credit

Choose   **Sonartek** from the Supplier list to enter the next payment.

This payment is made from Andersson's line of credit. However, *Bank: Regina Chequing* is still selected as the bank account in the From field.

Click   the **From list arrow** to select a different account as shown:

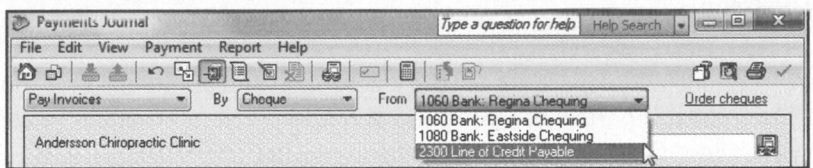

The line of credit is a liability account that operates like a bank account, but it has a credit balance. By defining it as a Bank class account, it can be used to write cheques in the Payments Journal.

Choose   **Line of Credit Payable** to select this account and to update the cheque number for the new account.

Enter   the cheque **date**, the **discount** amount and the **payment amount**.

Press   ⌨ctrl + **J** to open the journal display:

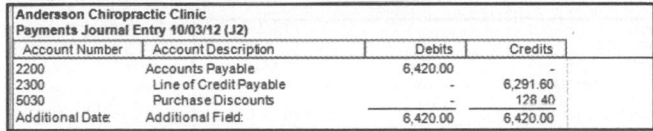

The only difference between this entry and the earlier payment entries is the use of *Line of Credit Payable* as the account that is credited. This increases the business liability — more money has been borrowed against the line of credit available.

Close   the **journal display. Check** your transaction **details** carefully.

Post   the **payment** when you are certain the details are correct.

Choose   **Make Other Payment** from the transaction drop-down list.

Enter   the **cash purchase** from Pro Suites (store the transaction) and the **payment** to Medical Linen Supplies on October 4 (Pay Invoices). Remember to change the selected bank account. **Close** the **Payments Journal**.

NOTES
For corrections to deposits or prepayments after posting, use the Adjust tool or refer to Appendix C. They can also be reversed, just like receipts. (See page 184.)

NOTES
The Credit Card account class is assigned to Bank: Interac so it does not appear with the list of banks.
The Bank account class is available for all Balance Sheet accounts from the Options tab in the General Ledger. Account classes were introduced in Chapter 7, page 222.

NOTES
You can click the Invoice/Prepayment field and press ⌨tab to accept the discount and payment amounts.

PRO VERSION
Choose Pay Purchase Invoices from the transaction list to pay the invoice.

Entering Additional Information for Transactions

The tool bar in journals has an icon for the option of adding information to a journal report. This Additional Information tool allows tracking of one additional date and one other field for transactions in all journals. Andersson has chosen to enter the number of the invoice paid as additional information so it will be included in journal reports.

Click **Receivables** in the Modules pane list.

Click the **Receipts icon** 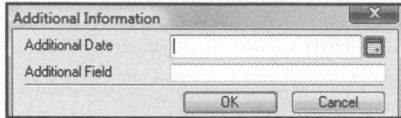 to open the Receipts Journal.

Customize the **tabbing order** for the journal so that the cheque number follows the customer and the address fields will be last. Refer to page 173.

Choose Interplay Ballet. The default bank account is correct.

Enter the **cheque number**, **date**, **discount** and **amount received**.

Click the **Enter Additional Information tool** ✓ or **choose** the **Receipt menu** and **click Enter Additional Information**:

Additional Information		
Additional Date		
Additional Field		
	OK	Cancel

You can enter one additional date for the transaction and additional text. Both will be available for journal reports when you show the Additional Information (page 452). You can rename these fields as part of the company setup.

Click the **Additional Field** text box.

Type `Ref: inv #632`

Click **OK** to return to the journal.

Adding the additional details does not change the appearance of the journal. You are ready to review the transaction before posting it.

Choose the **Report menu** and **click Display Receipts Journal Entry** to display the transaction you have entered as follows:

Andersson Chiropractic Clinic			
Receipts Journal Entry 10/04/12 (J5)			
Account Number	Account Description	Debits	Credits
1080	Bank: Eastside Chequing	3,069.00	-
4150	Sales Discounts	31.00	-
1200	Accounts Receivable	-	3,100.00
Additional Date:	Additional Field: Ref: inv #632	3,100.00	3,100.00

In addition to the usual debit and credit details, the invoice number entered as additional information is included in the display so that you can check it as well.

Close the **display** to return to the Receipts Journal input screen and **correct** your **work** if necessary. (Refer to page 177 for assistance.)

Click Post 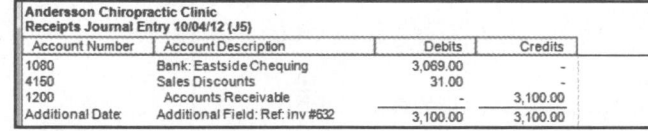.

Close the **Receipts Journal** to return to the Home window.

Entering a Sales (Patient) Quote

Sales quotes are like purchase quotes. They offer a customer a guaranteed price for a limited time for merchandise or for work to be completed. The customer may choose to accept or reject the offer.

Quotes are entered from the Patient Quotes icon shown in the Enhanced view Receivables window:

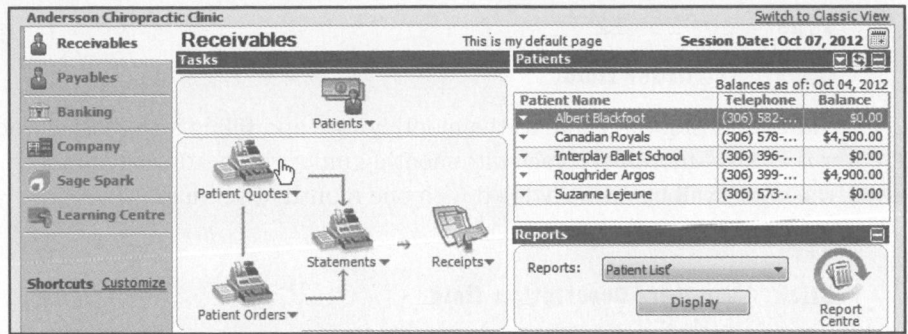

Separate icons are added for orders and quotes, just as they are for the suppliers.

Click   the **Patient Quotes icon**  to open the Fees Journal.

The invoice screen changes to the form for a patient quote:

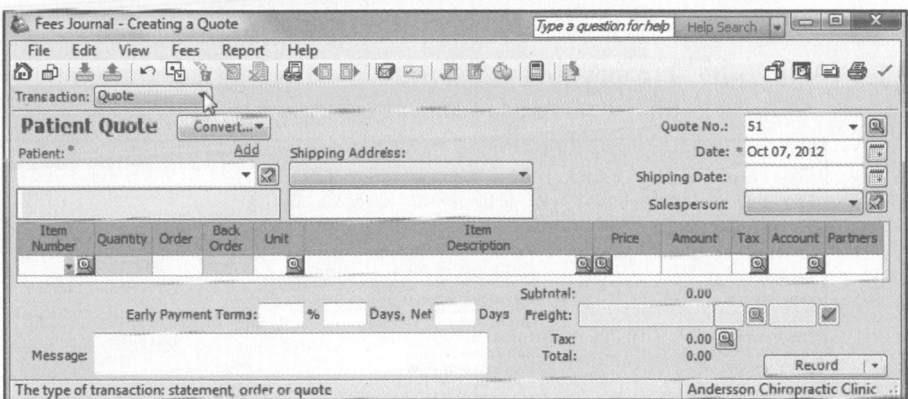

The quote is completed in much the same way as the sales invoice. However, you must enter a quantity in the Order field, just as you did for purchase quotes and orders. The quote number is entered and updated automatically from the defaults for the Receivables Ledger.

Additional fields are not available for quotes and orders. The tool is dimmed.

Click   the **Patient field**.

Type   Giant Raptors **Click** the **Add link** above the Patient field to open the ledger directly.

If you type the new name and press ⌜tab⌟ you will notice that Continue is not an option for a quote. You must create at least a partial ledger record.

Patient Name (Contact)	Address	Phone No. Fax No.	E-mail Web Site	Revenue Account	Terms Credit Limit
Giant Raptors (Rex Saurus)	550 Tyrannus Dr. Regina, Saskatchewan S4R 5T1	Tel 1: (306) 398-8753 Tel 2: (306) 398-5339 Fax: (306) 398-5339	rex@raptors.com www.raptors.com	4100	1/10, n/30 (change default terms) $5 000

Click   **Save And Close** 🖫 Save and Close after entering all the customer details.

You will return to the quote screen with the account and payment terms added.

Drag through the **date in the Date field**.

Type   10 4 12

NOTES
For services such as those provided by Andersson, the term Shipping Date is not appropriate. In the source documents, we use Starting Date instead.

Click   the **Shipping Date field** to move the cursor because the shipping address and quote number are correct.

Type   10 15 12

Click   the **Order field**.

Instead of entering the quote as the monthly rate and filling it in the first month, we will enter it as a six-month contract with monthly unit prices. After each month of service, the quote will be partially filled with one month of service.

Type   6

Click   the **Item Description field**.

Type   6 months of treatment

Press   ⸤tab⸥ to move to the Price field. You must complete the Price field.

Type   3500

Press   ⸤tab⸥ to advance to the Amount field. The program enters the amount correctly as the quantity times the price.

Press   ⸤tab⸥ to move to the Tax field. The Tax field is not used and the account is entered so the quote is complete:

WARNING!
If you do not enter a price in the Price field, you cannot fill the quote or order. When you choose this option, the form will remain incomplete.

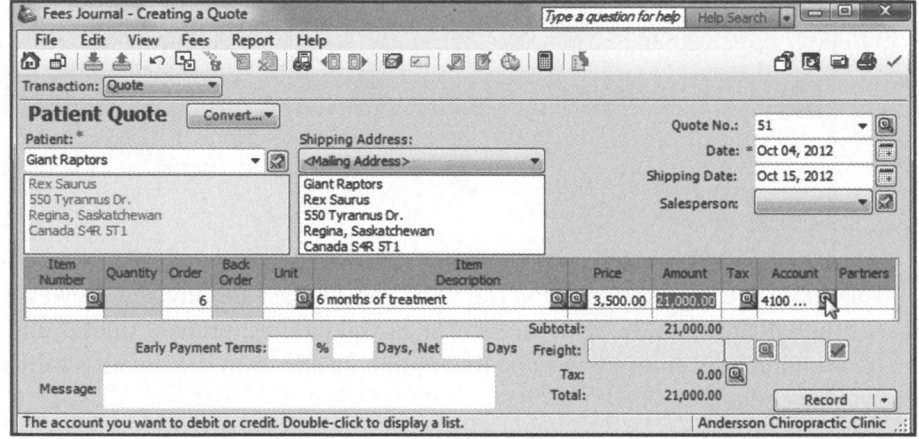

Check   the **quote** carefully and **correct mistakes** just as you do in sales invoices. Refer to page 170 for assistance if needed.

There is no journal entry to display. When a quote is filled by making a sale, the journal entry will be created.

Click   **Record** [Record |▼] to save the quote.

Leave   the **Fees Journal open** to adjust the quote.

NOTES
You can choose Print & Record or Record as the default action for the quote by selecting your preference from the Record button drop-down list.

Adjusting a Sales Quote

Sometimes a quote contains an error or must be changed if prices are renegotiated. You can adjust sales and purchase quotes and orders after recording them just as you can adjust sales and purchase invoices after posting.

The Fees Journal – Creating A Quote screen should still be open.

Click   the **Quote No. field list arrow** to see the list of quotes on file.

Click   **51** to select the quote you just entered.

WARNING!
If Quote is not selected as the Transaction type, you will convert the quote to a sales order, or fill the quote when you bring the quote on to the screen.

Press `tab` to add the quote to the screen:

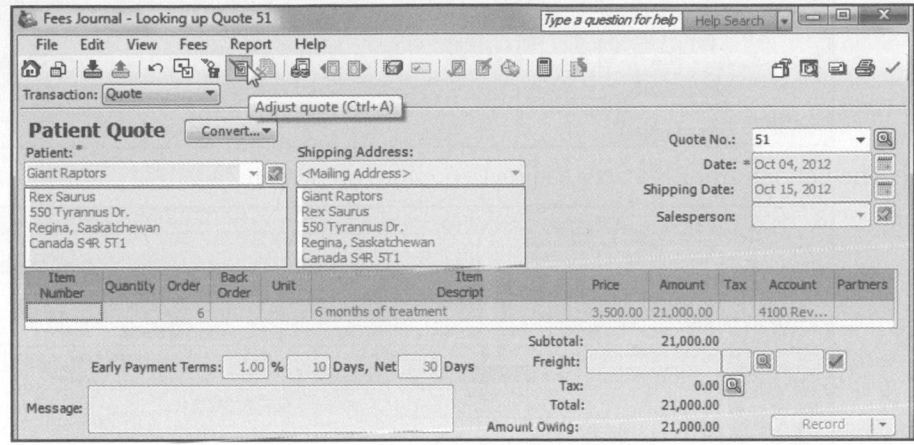

At this stage, you cannot edit the quote.

Click the **Adjust Quote tool** or **choose** the **Fees menu** and **click Adjust Quote** to open the fields for editing.

Adjusting Quote 51 replaces Looking Up Quote 51 in the title bar.

Click **3,500.00** in the Price field.

Type 3300 **Press** `tab` to update the subtotal and total amount to $19 800.

Drag through the **date in the Date field**.

Type 10-5-12 to enter the date for the revised quote.

Click the **Message field** and **type** Revised quote

Check your **work** carefully.

Click **Record** to save the revised quote. Keep the journal open.

Converting a Sales Quote to a Sales Order

Sales quotes can be converted to orders just as purchase quotes can be converted to purchase orders.

The Fees Journal should be open with Quote selected as the transaction type.

Click the **Quote No.** field drop-down list.

Click **51**, the quote number we want, and **press** `tab` to recall the quote.

There are different ways to convert the quote to an order, as there were for supplier quotes.

Click **Convert This Patient Quote To A Patient Order** from the Convert drop-down list as shown:

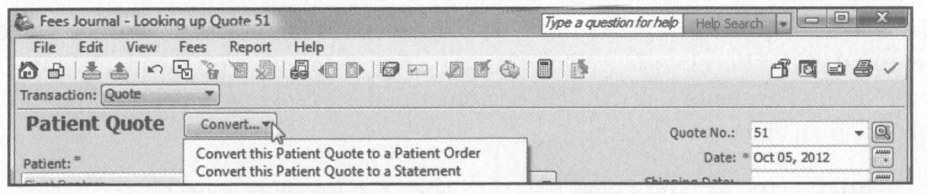

> **NOTES**
> To view and adjust orders and quotes, you do not need to use the lookup or search features we used to adjust purchase and sales invoices after posting. Orders and quotes are available directly from the Order/Quote No. field.

> **NOTES**
> Pressing `ctrl` + A will open the quote fields for editing. In other journals, pressing `ctrl` + A opens the Adjust An Invoice Search window.

> **NOTES**
> All fields in a quote can be edited, except the name and address details. To change the name, you must remove the quote and re-enter it for the correct customer. However, you cannot use the same quote number twice.

> **PRO VERSION**
> *pro* Choose Convert This Sales Quote To A Sales Order from the Convert drop-down list or choose Order in the Transaction field.
> The term Invoice will replace Statement in the Transaction list.

Or, **click Quote** in the Transaction field and then **click Order** as shown:

The patient order replaces the revised quote on-screen:

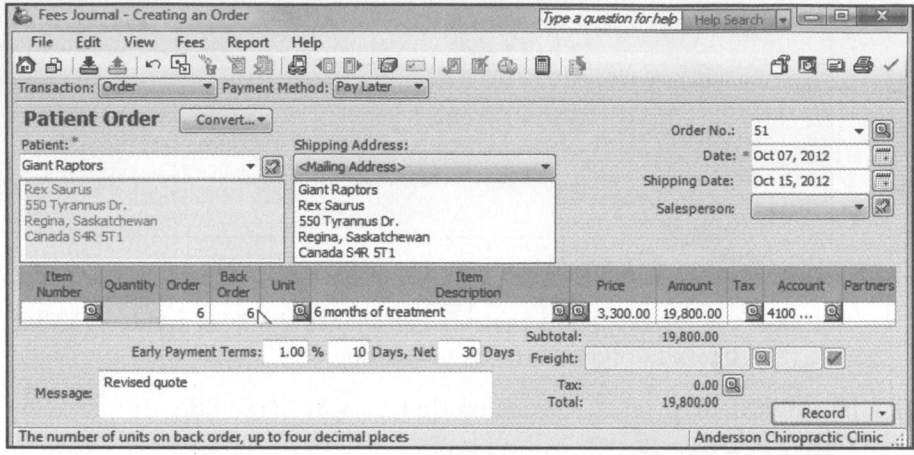

You can also choose Order from the Transaction list first, or click the Home window Patient Orders icon, then choose #51 from the Order/(Quote) No. drop-down list. Press (tab) to place the quote on-screen as an order.

The order quantity — 6 — has been added to the Back Order field.

> **Enter**   **Oct 5-12** as the order date to replace the session date.

> **Check**   all the **details** carefully because there is no journal entry to review.

All other details should be correct for the order because they have not changed. The order can be edited at this stage if needed. We will revise the comment.

> **Click**   the **Message field. Type** Order based on revised quote

> **Click**   **Record** Record ▾ to save the sales order and see the warning:

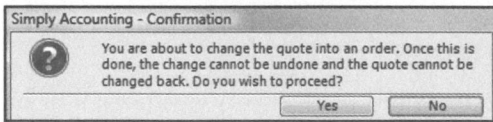

Since we want to change the quote to an order, we should proceed.

> **Click**   **Yes**.

> **Close**   the **Fees Journal** so that you can enter the customer's deposit.

Entering Customer Deposits

(page 435).

Andersson also requests deposits from her customers when they place orders. Deposits are entered in the Receipts Journal in the same way as supplier prepayments are entered in the Payments Journal. The customer deposit tool opens fields for a reference number and an amount.

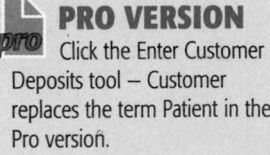
> **Click**   the **Receipts icon** [Receipts▾] to open the Receipts Journal.

> **Click**   the **Enter Patient Deposits tool** [icon] or **choose** the **Receipt menu** and **click Enter Deposits**.

This tool button/menu option acts as a switch that opens the fields for deposits:

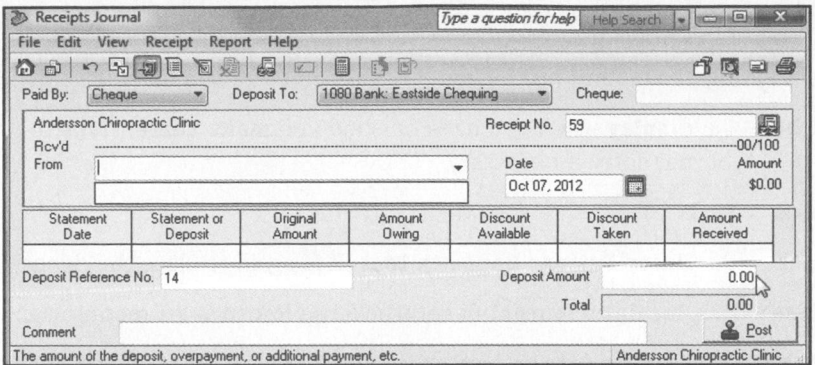

The two new fields added to the journal for the reference number and for the amount serve the same purpose as they do for supplier prepayments. The reference number is the deposit number and is updated automatically by the program. The invoice lines are not used for the deposit. Outstanding invoices, if there are any, will be included in the journal. If they are being paid with the same customer cheque, enter the receipt in the usual way in addition to the deposit amount.

The receipt number is updated and correct, but we need to change the bank account.

Choose **Giant Raptors** from the Rcv'd From drop-down list.

Click the **Cheque field**.

Type 838

Enter **October 6** as the date of the cheque.

Click the **Deposit To list arrow** to see the list of bank accounts:

Just as we can pay from any of the accounts that we identify as Bank class accounts, we can deposit to any bank account.

Choose **Bank: Regina Chequing** to change the account selection.

Click the **Deposit Amount field** at the bottom of the journal.

Type 2000 **Press** (tab).

Click the **Enter Additional Information tool** [icon], or **choose** the **Receipt menu** and **click Enter Additional Information**.

Click the **Additional Field** text box.

Type Deposit for SO #51

Click **OK** to return to the journal so you can review the transaction.

Choose the **Report menu** and **click Display Receipts Journal Entry**:

Andersson Chiropractic Clinic			
Receipts Journal Entry 10/06/12 (J6)			
Account Number	Account Description	Debits	Credits
1060	Bank: Regina Chequing	2,000.00	-
2250	Prepaid Sales and Deposits	-	2,000.00
Additional Date:	Additional Field: Deposit for SO #51	2,000.00	2,000.00

As for other receipts, the bank account is debited. The account credited is *Prepaid Sales and Deposits*, a contra-liability account linked to the customer deposits field. If the customer has no previous outstanding balance, the deposit creates a credit entry for

NOTES
If you modified the tabbing order, pressing tab after selecting the customer will place the cursor in the Cheque field.

NOTES
The Credit Card account class is assigned to Bank: Interac; it does not appear with the list of banks.

Line of Credit Payable has been defined as a Bank class account. Therefore, it appears on the list of bank accounts.

Cash class accounts will also appear on this list. We will use the Cash class in Chapter 15.

the account. Until the sale is completed, the deposit creates a liability — we owe the customer this amount until the order is filled. After the sale, when the customer pays the invoice, the deposit will be displayed in red under the heading "Deposits" and it is "paid" by accepting its amount, just as you enter receipts for the invoice itself.

Close the **display** when you have finished and **make corrections** to the journal entry if necessary.

Click **Post** 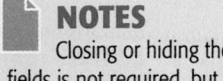 to save the transaction.

Click the **Enter Patient Deposits tool** 🔲 again to close the deposit fields.

Close the **Receipts Journal** to return to the Receivables module window.

Change the **session date** and **enter** the **next two receipts**. Remember to **change** the selected **bank account** when necessary.

Placing a Purchase Order with Prepayment

Placing a purchase order directly without the quote is similar to entering a purchase quote. For this order, a prepayment is included so we will enter it directly on the order.

Click **Payables** in the Modules pane list to open the Payables window.

Click the **Supplier Orders icon**  to open the Expenses Journal with Order selected as the transaction type.

The Order No. is entered automatically (Forms Settings), and it will be incremented automatically because purchase orders are generated within your business.

Choose **Sonartek Ltd.** from the supplier list.

Enter **Oct 9 12** as the order date. (Add the year if you type the date).

Enter **Oct 19 12** (including the year) as the shipping date.

Click the **Order field**.

Type **1 Press** (tab).

The program automatically completes the Back Order field with the quantity on order. The entire order quantity is considered as backordered.

Click the **Item Description field**.

Type ultrasound machine **Press** (tab) to move to the Price field.

Type 6000 **Press** (tab).

If the account number is not entered by default, or if it is incorrect for this order, choose the correct account from the Account field selection list.

We will now enter the prepayment details.

Click the **Payment Method field list arrow** to see the payment options:

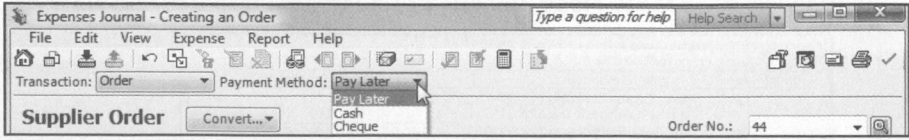

The options are the same as they are for other payments.

Click **Cheque** to open the Paid From bank account field. *Bank: Eastside Chequing*, the default bank account, is entered.

Click   the **Paid From list arrow** to see the familiar list of Bank class accounts:

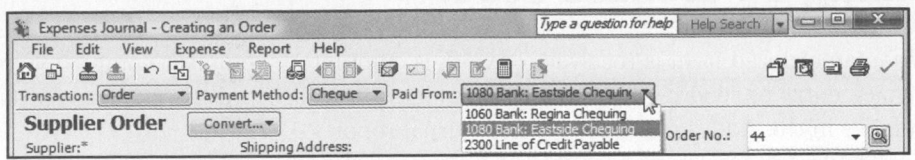

Choose Line of Credit Payable to open the cheque number field with the next cheque number for this account.

A Prepayment Applied field has also been added below the invoice lines on the order form. By default the entire order amount is entered so we need to change it. $1 500 is being paid at this time.

Double click the **Prepayment Applied field** to select the default amount.

Type   1500 **Press** (tab) to complete the order form as shown:

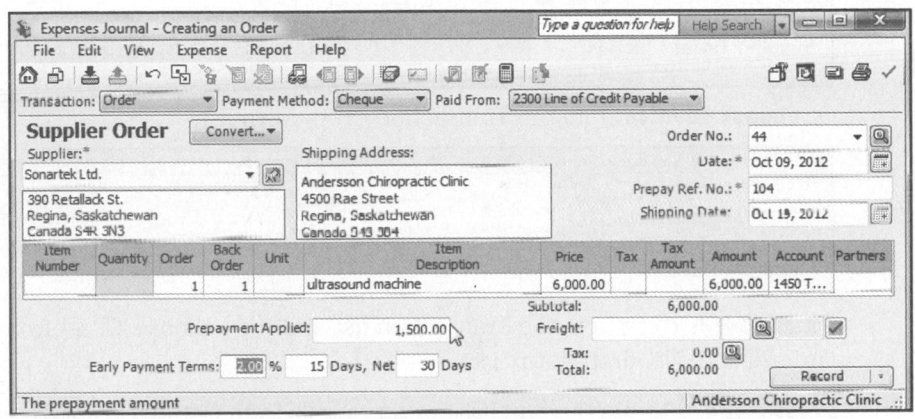

Check   the **order** details carefully.

Because we have now actually entered a transaction that affects our account balances, there is a journal entry to review for the order.

Choose the **Report menu** and **click Display Expenses Journal Entry**:

Andersson Chiropractic Clinic			
Expenses Journal Entry 10/09/12 (J9)			
Account Number	Account Description	Debits	Credits
1280	Purchase Prepayments	1,500.00	-
2300	Line of Credit Payable	-	1,500.00
Additional Date:	Additional Field:	1,500.00	1,500.00

This prepayment journal entry is the same as the one we made earlier from the Payments Journal (page 420). Only the bank account used is different.

Close   the **journal display** to return to the order.

Make   **corrections** if necessary. **Click Record** [Record │▾] to save the order. Leave the journal open for the next transaction.

Entering a Sales Order

Sales orders are entered in the same way as sales quotes, except that you start with the Patient or Sales Order form instead of the Patient or Sales Quote form.

Click Receivables in the Modules pane and click the Patient Orders icon. Then choose the customer and complete the order details. The Order field cannot be left blank. Sales order numbers are generated by the customer; they are not entered or updated by the program. Enter the customer's sales order number.

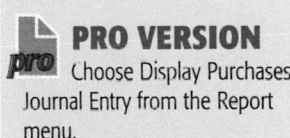

PRO VERSION

Choose Display Purchases Journal Entry from the Report menu.

NOTES

You can choose Print & Record as the default action for the supplier order by making this selection from the Record button's drop-down list.

CLASSIC VIEW

Click the Fees, Orders & Quotes icon [Fees, Orders & Quotes] to open the journal, and choose Order from the journal's Transaction drop-down list.

Filling a Purchase Order

When an ordered item is received, or work is completed, you must complete a purchase invoice entry to record the transaction. Andersson will record the purchase order number in the Additional Field for the journal reports.

The Expenses Journal should still be open with Order selected as the Transaction type. Again, there are different ways to turn the order into an invoice.

> **Choose** **TT-44** from the Order No. field drop-down list and **press** (tab) to recall the order.
>
> **Choose** **Convert This Supplier Order To An Invoice** from the Convert drop-down list:

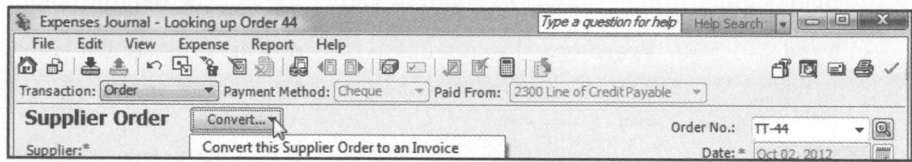

Or **choose Invoice** from the Transaction drop-down list:

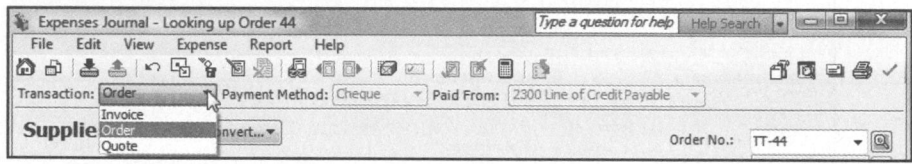

Or, choose Invoice from the Transaction list and then choose TT-44 from the Order/Quote No. drop-down list.

> **Press** (tab) to see the purchase order details from October 2 entered on the invoice:

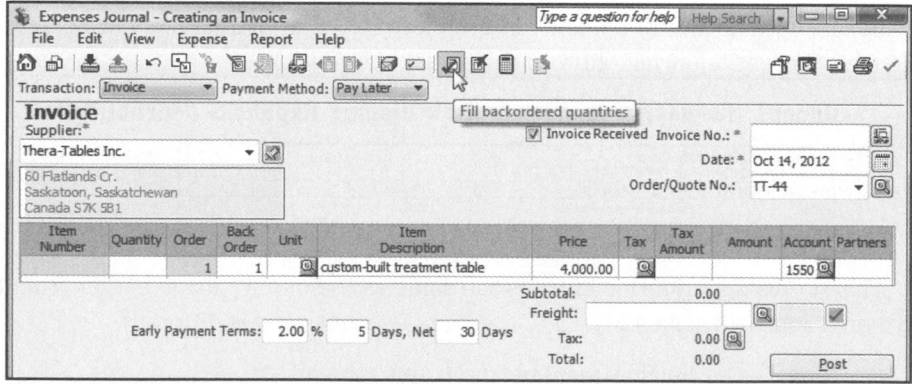

The default selection in the Payment Method field has changed to Pay Later and is correct because this is a credit purchase.

> **Click** the **Invoice field**. **Type** TT-4599
>
> **Press** (tab) **twice** to advance to the Date field.
>
> **Type** 10-10-12

The invoice is still incomplete because the quantity displays as backordered and the invoice amount is zero. We need to "fill" the order.

> **Click** the **Fill Backordered Quantities tool**  in the tool bar or **choose** the **Expense menu** and **click Fill Supplier Order**.

If you did not enter the price for the order, you must edit the invoice to add the missing details. Your invoice should now look like the one that follows:

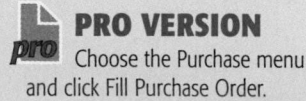

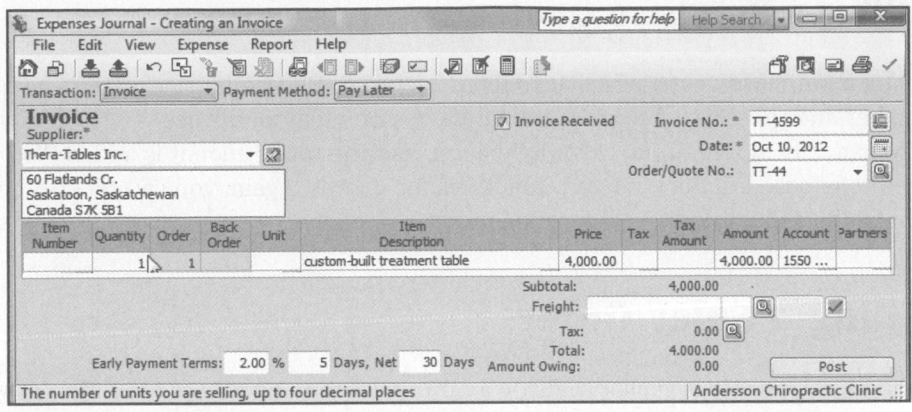

The Back Order quantity has been moved to the Quantity column to reflect the completion of the order. Notice that the prepayment made in the Payments Journal does not show on the invoice and that the full amount is invoiced. When the prepayment is added to the order form, it does appear on the invoice (page 438).

> **Click**   the **Enter Additional Information tool** 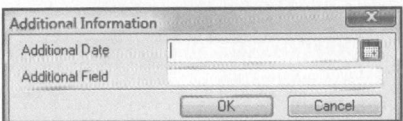 or **choose** the **Expense menu** and **click Enter Additional Information**:

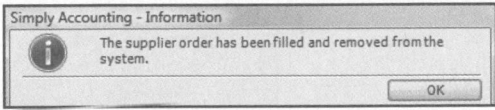

This data entry screen is the same for all journals.

> **Click**   the **Additional Field** text box.
>
> **Type**   `Ref: fill P.O. #TT-44`
>
> **Click**   **OK** to return to the journal.
>
> **Check**   the **entry** carefully to be sure that it is correct.
>
> **Choose**   the **Report menu** and **click Display Expenses Journal Entry**.

You can see that this is a normal journal entry with the order number as additional information. Prepayment amounts are not included.

> **Close**   the **display**. When the information is correct,
>
> **Click**   the **Post button** [Post] or **choose** the **Expense menu** and **click Post** to see the following message:

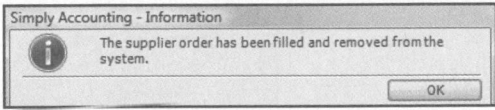

Filled orders and quotes are not saved, but their numbers cannot be used again.

> **Click**   **OK** to display a new Expenses Journal invoice form.
>
> **Close**   the **Expenses Journal**.
>
> **Click**   **Receivables** in the Modules pane list to open the Receivables window for the next group of transactions.

NOTES
If the order is partially filled, the backordered quantity will be reduced as in the sales order on page 433.

PRO VERSION
Choose the Purchase menu and click Enter Additional Information.

NOTES
To fill the quote, you can also start with the quote on-screen. Then choose Invoice from the Transaction drop-down list or Convert This Purchase Quote To An Invoice from the Convert drop-down list.

PRO VERSION
pro Click the Sales Orders icon to open the Sales Journal. You will see Sales Journal – Creating An Order in the journal's title bar.
Choose Convert This Sales Order To A Sales Invoice from the Convert drop-down list.

NOTES
Statement replaces the term Invoice for a Medical company. Fees Journal replaces Sales Journal.

NOTES
Only one conversion option is possible from the order screen, that is, changing the order to an invoice.

 NOTES
If you customized the columns for the Quote form, they will be restored for the Order. In the Premium version, you can customize Quote, Order and Invoice forms differently.

PRO VERSION
pro If you customized the columns for the Quote form, you will see the same changes applied on the Order and Invoice forms. You cannot customize them differently.

Filling a Purchase Quote

Filling a purchase quote is similar to filling an order. Choose Invoice, select the quote number and press (tab) to place the quote on-screen as an invoice. The quantity automatically moves to the Quantity column and the total Amount is added. You do not need to choose Fill Backordered Quantities for quotes. Again, you can record the quote number as an additional field for the journal.

Filling a Sales Order

Filling a sales order is similar to filling a purchase order, and there are different ways to do this.

Click the **Patient Orders icon** [Patient Orders] to open the Fees Journal.

Click the **Order No. list arrow** to see the available orders.

Click **51**. Press (tab) to display the original sales order on the screen.

Click **Convert This Patient Order To A Statement** from the Convert drop-down list as shown:

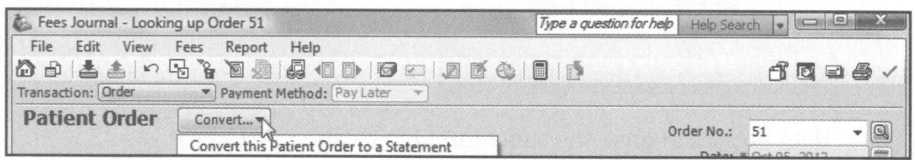

Or, **click Statement** from the Transaction drop-down list as shown:

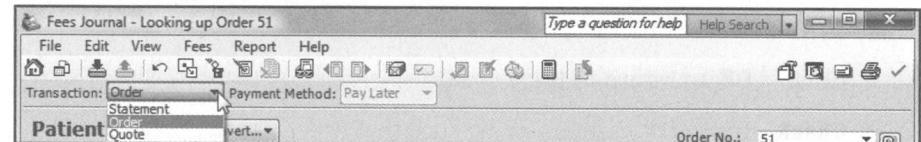

Or, choose the Statements icon from the Receivables module Home window. Then choose #51 from the Order/Quote field drop-down list and press (tab).

Each of these three approaches will replace the order with an invoice as shown:

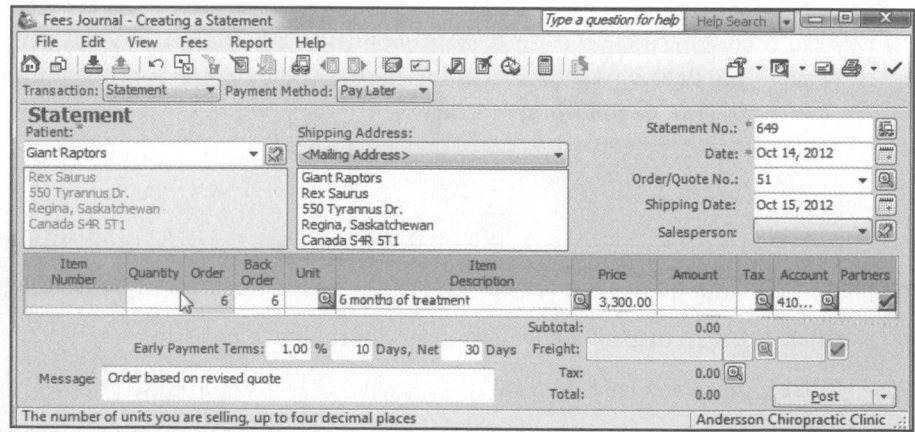

Sometimes only part of the order is received and the order is not completely filled at once, as in this case.

Pay Later should be selected as the payment option for the Statement transaction.

Enter **October 10** as the transaction date.

Click the **Quantity field**. Only one month is being billed at this time.

Type   1 **Press** (tab) to update the invoice as shown:

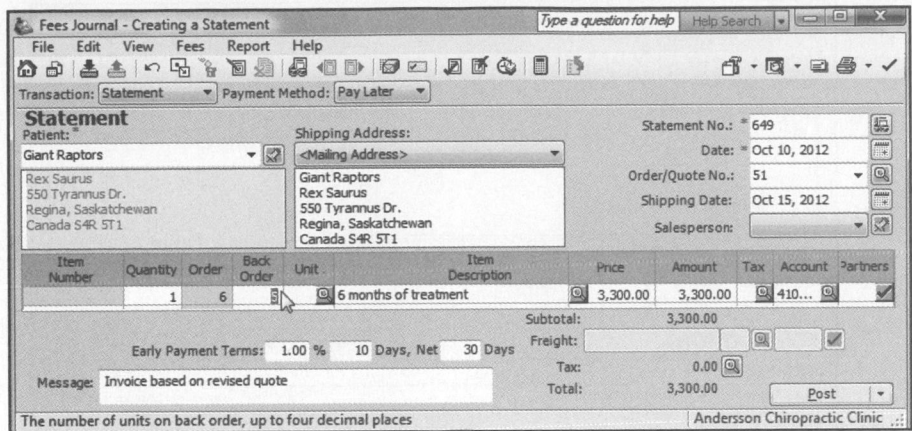

The Amount entered is the fee for one month of service and the Back Order quantity is reduced to five. When the sixth and final month is completed, the order will be filled and removed.

Click   the **Enter Additional Information tool** ☑ or **choose** the **Fees menu** and **click Enter Additional Information**.

Click   the **Additional Field** text box.

Type   Ref: S.O. #51

Click   **OK** to return to the journal. We should also modify the comment.

Click   the **Message field**.

Type   Invoice based on revised quote

Review the **journal entry** and **check** your **work** carefully.

Choose the **Report menu** and **click Display Fees Journal Entry**.

Close   the **display** to return to the invoice. **Make corrections** if necessary.

Click   **Post** Post ▾ to record the invoice. The order is not filled, so you do not see the message that the order will be removed.

Close   the **Fees Journal**.

Filling a Sales Quote

Filling a sales quote is similar to filling an order. Choose Statement (or Invoice), select the quote number and press (tab) to place the quote on-screen as an invoice. The quantity automatically moves to the Quantity column and the total Amount is added. You do not need to choose Fill Backordered Quantities for quotes.

Entering Receipts on Accounts with Deposits

The next receipt pays the balance of an account for a customer who has made a deposit.

Click   the **Receipts icon** Receipts▾ to open the Receipts Journal.

NOTES

If necessary, drag the lower frame of the journal to include the deposit on the screen or maximize the window.

Choose **Giant Raptors** from the Received From customer drop-down list:

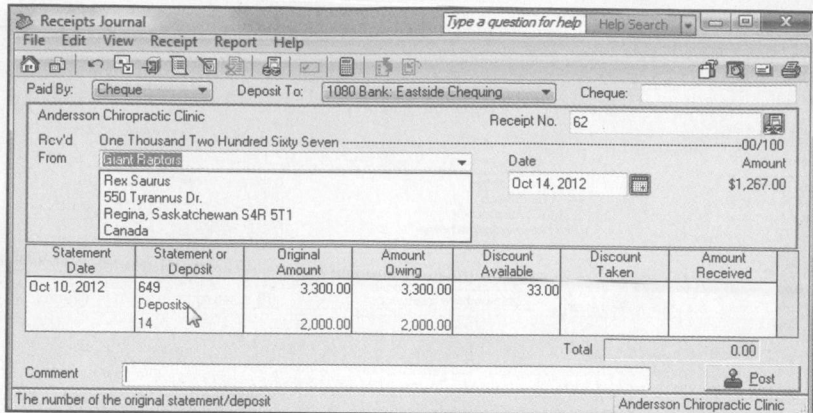

Customer deposits are displayed in red below the outstanding invoices. The colour indicates that they are negative invoices that reduce the balance owing. The invoice line shows with the full amount owing and the full discount amount available.

Enter **939** as the Cheque number field and **enter** **Oct 13** in the Date field.

Click the **Discount Taken field** for invoice #649 to accept the discount.

Press ⌐tab⌐ to accept the Amount Received.

Press ⌐tab⌐ **twice** to accept the Deposit amount and update the receipt.

Enter the **invoice number** as additional information.

The discount and deposit are subtracted from the full invoice amount so that the total amount now matches the cheque amount as shown in the completed receipt:

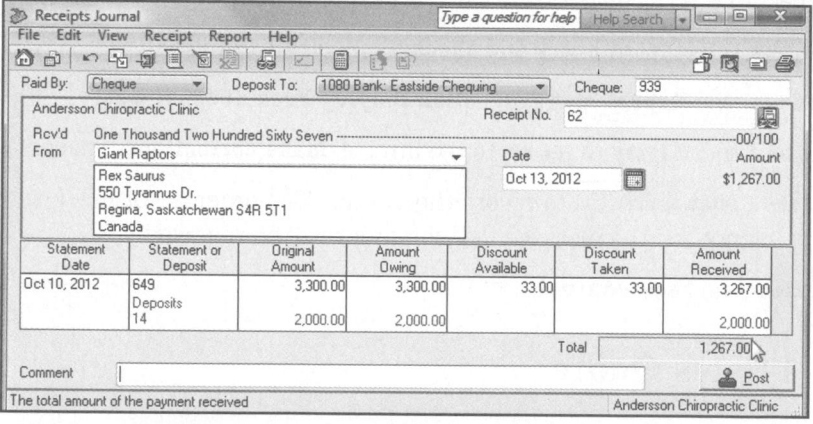

Choose the **Report menu** and **click** **Display Receipts Journal Entry**:

Andersson Chiropractic Clinic			
Receipts Journal Entry 10/13/12 (J12)			
Account Number	Account Description	Debits	Credits
1080	Bank: Eastside Chequing	1,267.00	-
2250	Prepaid Sales and Deposits	2,000.00	-
4150	Sales Discounts	33.00	-
1200	Accounts Receivable	-	3,300.00
Additional Date:	Additional Field: Ref: inv #649 & dep...	3,300.00	3,300.00

NOTES

The initial deposit creates a liability. The customer has paid us and we have not provided anything yet. When the order is filled, the liability is removed, so the Accounts Receivable balance debit is offset by the initial liability. When the customer pays the invoice for the balance owing, the initial credit entry must be removed from the record.

Accounts Receivable has been credited for the full invoice amount to clear the invoice. The *Sales Discounts* contra-revenue account has been debited to record the reduction to sales revenue. The *Prepaid Sales and Deposits* contra-liability account has been debited for the full deposit amount to clear its credit balance, and the bank account is debited for the amount of the cheque.

Close the **journal display window**. **Make** **corrections** if necessary. **Post** the **receipt** and then **close** the **Receipts Journal**.

 Enter **sales quote #52** for the new customer.

Entering Deposits with Sales Orders

Just as you can enter prepayments to suppliers in the Supplier Order window, you can enter customer deposits on the Patient Order form. When the deposit accompanies the order, this method is recommended.

The Fees Journal should still be open with Quote selected as the transaction type.

Choose 52 from the Quote No. field list and **press** `tab`.

Choose Order as the transaction type or **choose Convert This Patient Quote to a Patient Order** from the Convert list to convert the quote to an order.

Click the **Payment Method list arrow** to see the payment options:

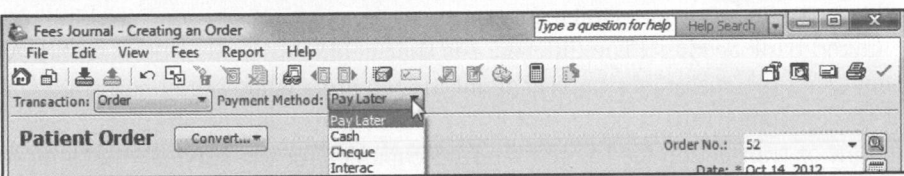

The same customer payment types are available here as in the Receipts Journal.

PRO VERSION
Your screen's title bar will show Sales Journal – Creating An Order.

Click Cheque in the Payment Method list to open the extra payment fields:

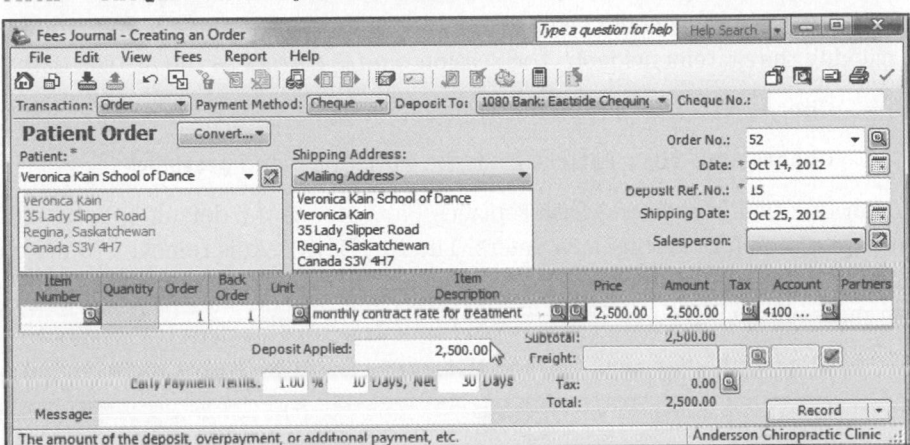

PRO VERSION
Choose Order from the Transaction list in the Sales Journal.

The default bank account is selected for the Deposit To field at the top of the order form. A Cheque number field has also been added to the top of the form and a Deposit Applied amount field has been added to the bottom of the order form, as it is for cash sales. The Deposit Reference Number field with the next deposit number has also been added.

The session date and bank account are correct so we can add the payment details.

Click the **Cheque No. field**.

Type 865

Double click the **Deposit Applied field**. The full amount of the order is entered as the default amount and we need to change it.

Type 1000

Press `tab` to update and complete the form.

Choose the **Report menu** and **click Display Fees Journal Entry**:

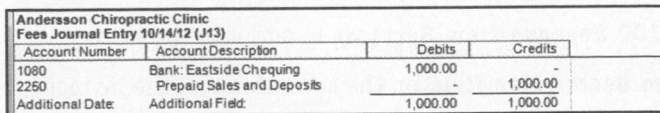

Andersson Chiropractic Clinic			
Fees Journal Entry 10/14/12 (J13)			
Account Number	Account Description	Debits	Credits
1080	Bank: Eastside Chequing	1,000.00	-
2250	Prepaid Sales and Deposits	-	1,000.00
Additional Date:	Additional Field:	1,000.00	1,000.00

PRO VERSION
Choose the Report menu and click Display Sales Journal Entry.

You can see that this journal entry is identical to the journal entry for deposits entered in the Receipts Journal (page 427). Only the bank account is different. The prepayment or deposit with the sales order creates a journal entry although the sales order itself does not.

Close   the **display** and **click Record** Record ⏷ to save the transaction.

Click   **Yes** to confirm that you are changing the quote to an order.

Entering Debit Card Sale Transactions

Customers pay for purchases using cash, cheques, credit cards or debit cards. Debit and credit card purchases are similar for a store — the payment is deposited immediately to the linked bank account. The difference is that debit card transactions withdraw the money from the customer's bank account immediately while credit cards advance a loan that the customer repays on receipt of the credit card bill. The store pays a percentage discount or transaction fee to credit card companies for the service. For debit card transactions, the store pays a flat fee for each transaction. Both involve a setup fee and a monthly rental charge for the terminal that communicates electronically with the card-issuing company. Andersson uses the name Interac for all debit card transactions.

The Fees Journal should be open from the previous transaction. If it is not, open it by clicking the Statements icon. The session date is correct as the invoice date.

Choose Statement from the Transaction list.

Choose One-Time Patient from the Patient list and **press** ⟨tab⟩.

For one-time customers, Cash replaces Pay Later as the default option — Pay Later is not an option for one-time customers. The Net Days field is removed to match the immediate payment option and the default bank account is selected. The terms for new customers offer no discount so the discount fields are blank.

Click   the **Payment Method list arrow** as shown to see the payment options:

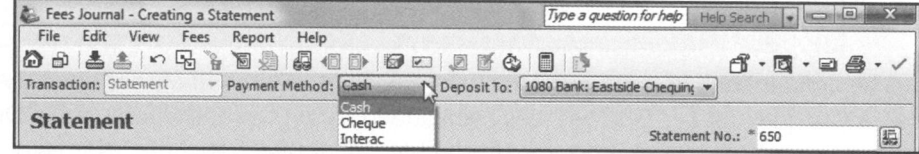

Click   Interac as the method of payment to modify the invoice.

There is no bank account field or cheque number field as there is when the payment is made by cheque. Interac is linked automatically to a dedicated bank account as part of the company file setup, just like credit cards. Interac Amount replaces Cash Amount as the label for the amount received.

Type   Debit Card Sales Summary (in the Address field).

Complete   the rest of the **invoice** in the same way as account or cash sales.

Click   the **Item Description field** and **type** initial assessments

Click   the **Amount field** and **type** 260

Click   the **List icon** 🔍 in the Account field to display the Account list.

Double click 4100 Revenue from Services to add it to the invoice.

Click   the **Item Description field** on the second line of the invoice.

Type   follow-up treatments

 **NOTES**
Fees for debit cards can be lower than credit card fees because the risk of non-payment is eliminated. Debit card payments require the customer's bank balance to cover the amount before the payments are approved.

PRO VERSION
Choose Invoice from the Transaction list. Choose One-Time Customer from the Customer list.

NOTES
Pay Later is not an option for one-time customers so the Cash Amount (amount received) field is added automatically.

PRO VERSION
You will see Sales Journal – Creating An Invoice in the journal's title bar.

Click   the **Amount field** and **type**   450

Click   the **List icon** [icon] in the Account field and **double click 4100 Revenue from Services** to complete the invoice:

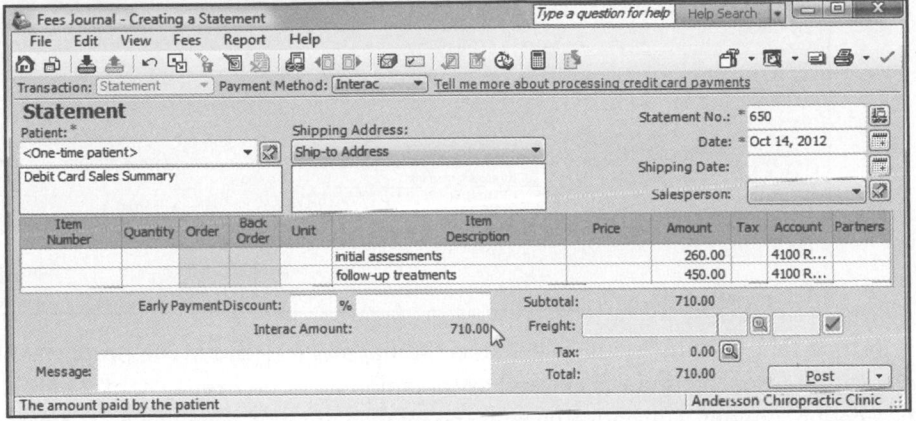

Choose the **Report menu** and **click Display Fees Journal Entry** to review the entry before posting:

	Andersson Chiropractic Clinic Fees Journal Entry 10/14/12 (J14)		
Account Number	Account Description	Debits	Credits
1100	Bank: Interac	710.00	-
4100	Revenue from Services	-	710.00
Additional Date:	Additional Field:	710.00	710.00

Notice the new linked account for this transaction. The debit card account — *Bank: Interac* — replaces the usual bank account for other cash sales and *Accounts Receivable* for account sales. Unlike credit card sales, no additional fees are charged.

Close   the **display** to return to the Fees Journal input screen.

Make   **corrections** if necessary, referring to page 170 for assistance.

We can store the entry and use it to enter the debit card summaries every second week. When you recall the transaction, you can edit the amounts. You will not need to save the changes and store the transaction again.

Click   the **Store tool** [icon] to save the transaction for repeated entries.

Choose Biweekly as the frequency and **click OK** to save the stored entry.

Click   the **Post button** [Post ▾].

Close   the **Fees Journal. Click Payables** in the Modules pane list.

Enter   the **next three transactions** for October 14 and then **advance** the **session date** to October 21.

Filling Purchase Orders with Prepayments

When a prepayment is added directly to the purchase order, the payment details remain on the invoice when you fill the order.

Click   the **Supplier Orders icon** to open the Expenses Journal.

Choose order #44 from the Order No. field drop-down list and **press** ⒯ab .

Choose Convert This Supplier Order To An Invoice, or **choose Invoice** from the Transaction drop-down list.

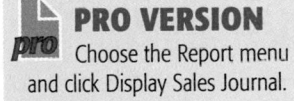

PRO VERSION
Choose the Report menu and click Display Sales Journal.

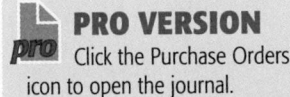

PRO VERSION
Click the Purchase Orders icon to open the journal.

CLASSIC VIEW

Click the Expenses, Orders & Quotes icon.

Choose Order from the Transaction drop-down list.

This will add the order details to the invoice form:

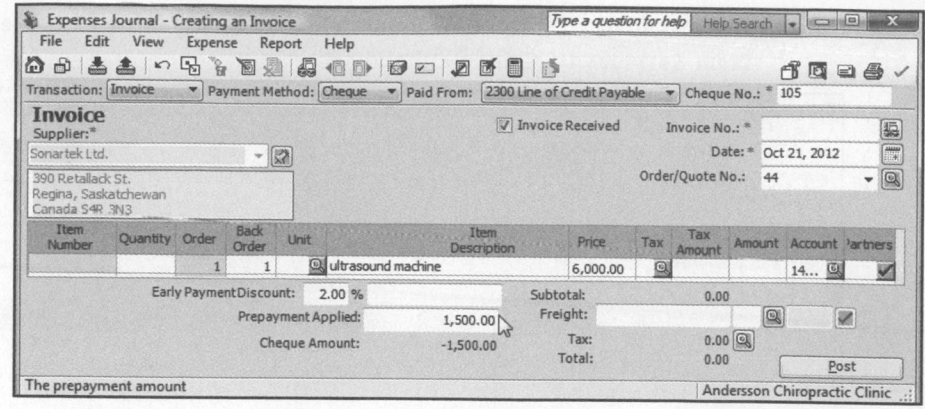

Notice that Cheque is still selected as the Payment Method. The prepayment information from the order is entered as the amount in the **Prepayment Applied** field. The cheque amount is negative because no invoice amount has been added yet.

PRO VERSION

You will choose the Purchase menu and click Fill Purchase Order.

WARNING!

If you do not change the method of payment, the purchase amount owing will be posted to the Line of Credit Payable account (a payment by cheque) instead of to Accounts Payable.

Click the **Fill Backordered Quantities tool** in the tool bar or **choose** the **Expense menu** and **click Fill Supplier Order**.

Now the cheque amount is $4 380.00 — the total invoice amount minus the prepayment and 2 percent discount. This is not a cash purchase, so we need to change the payment method.

Choose Pay Later from the Paid By drop-down list to update the form. The amount owing changes to $4 500 ($6 000 minus the $1 500 prepayment).

Enter the **invoice number** and **purchase date** to complete the form:

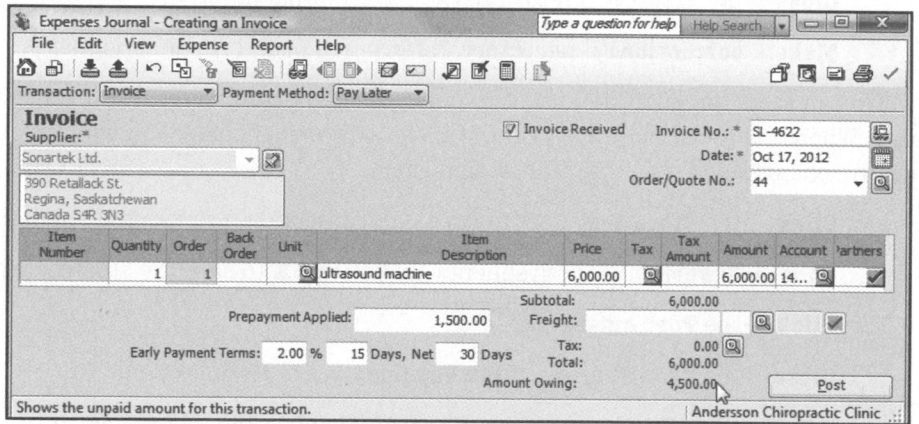

Click the **Additional Information tool**. **Click** the **Additional Information field**.

Type `Ref: fill PO #44` **Click OK** to return to the journal.

Press (ctrl) + **J** to open the journal display:

Andersson Chiropractic Clinic Expenses Journal Entry 10/17/12 (J18)			
Account Number	Account Description	Debits	Credits
1450	Treatment Equipment	6,000.00	-
1280	Purchase Prepayments	-	1,500.00
2200	Accounts Payable	-	4,500.00
Additional Date:	Additional Field: Ref: P.O. #44	6,000.00	6,000.00

The entry is different from the standard journal entry because of the amount for *Purchase Prepayments*. Because the purchase is complete, the credit with the supplier is removed and the prepayment is treated like a partial payment toward the invoice. Thus, *Purchase Prepayments* has been credited to reduce this account's balance to zero. *Treatment Equipment* is debited for the full purchase invoice amount and *Accounts Payable* is credited for the balance owing after the prepayment is subtracted.

When you enter a prepayment in the Payments Journal, Simply Accounting does not know which purchase it is related to, so the prepayment shows later in the Payments Journal for that supplier. It can be applied to any purchase. Entering the prepayment on the order establishes a link to this purchase. When the prepayment is made at the same time as the order, it should be entered on the order. When it is made at a different time, either prior to or later than the order, it should be entered in the Payments Journal.

Close the **Journal display**.

Make **corrections** to the invoice if necessary and then **post** the **purchase**.

Click **OK** to confirm that the order has been filled.

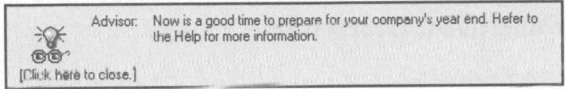 **Enter** the **next two transactions**. **Change** modules as needed.

Filling Sales Orders with Deposits

When you advance the session date to October 31, you will see an Advisor message:

> Advisor: Now is a good time to prepare for your company's year end. Refer to the Help for more information.
>
> [Click here to close.]

Click to close the message about year-end preparation.

Open the **Fees Journal**. Statement should be selected as the transaction.

Select **Sales Order #52** from the Order/Quote No. list and **press** ⟨*tab*⟩ to recall the order as a statement or invoice:

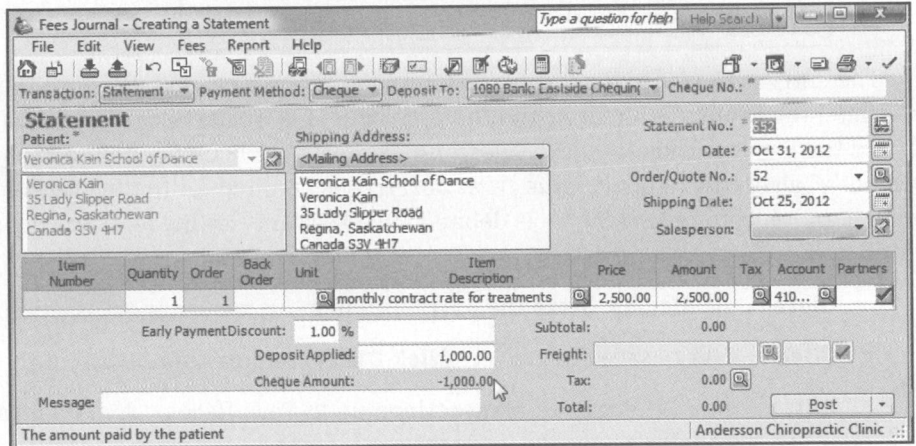

Or, click the Patient Orders icon to open the Order form of the journal. Choose #52 from the Order No. drop-down list and press ⟨*tab*⟩ to recall the order. Then choose Convert This Patient Order To A Statement from the convert drop-down list, or choose Statement from the Transaction drop-down list to change the order to a statement.

Information about the deposit is included in the invoice. Since the deposit was paid by cheque, this is the default payment method, and we need to change it.

Click the **Payment Method list arrow** and **choose** **Pay Later** to modify the form.

Click the **Fill Backordered Quantities tool** 🔲 in the tool bar or **choose** the **Fees menu** and **click Fill Patient Order**.

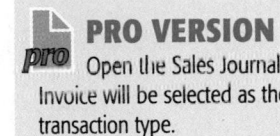
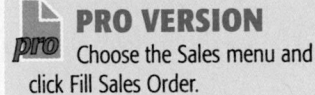

With this step, you will update the amounts and complete the form:

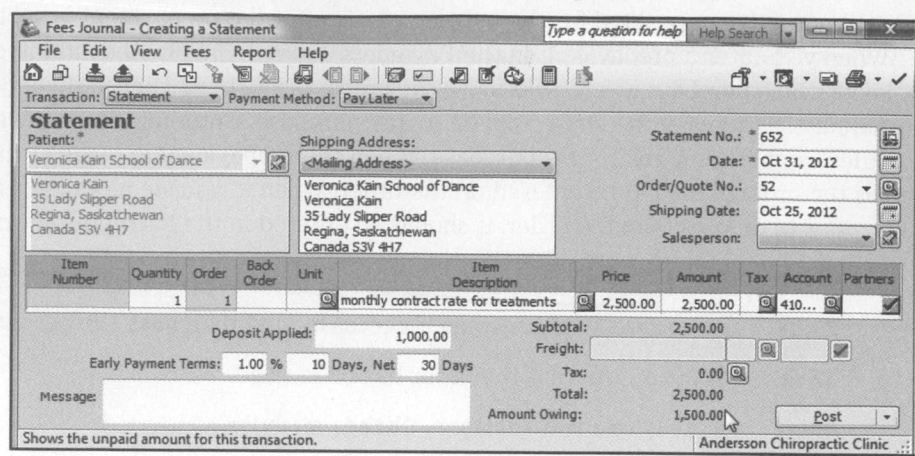

The Cheque Amount field has been removed but the Deposit Applied details remain. The Amount Owing is reduced by the $1 000 deposit.

Enter   **Oct 25** as the date for the sale.

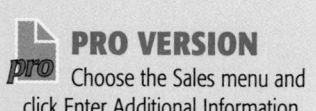

Click   the **Enter Additional Information tool** [✓] or **choose** the **Fees menu** and **click Enter Additional Information**.

Enter   `Ref SO #52 & deposit #15` in the Additional Field.

Click   **OK** to return to the journal.

Choose   the **Report menu** and **click Display Fees Journal Entry**:

Andersson Chiropractic Clinic
Fees Journal Entry 10/25/12 (J21)

Account Number	Account Description	Debits	Credits
1200	Accounts Receivable	1,500.00	-
2250	Prepaid Sales and Deposits	1,000.00	-
4100	Revenue from Services	-	2,500.00
Additional Date:	Additional Field: Ref: SO #52 dep...	2,500.00	2,500.00

The entry is similar to the Expenses Journal entry on page 438. Because the sale is complete, the liability is removed and the prepayment is treated like a partial payment toward the invoice. Thus *Prepaid Sales and Deposits* has been debited to reduce this account's balance to zero, *Revenue from Services* is credited for the full sales invoice amount and *Accounts Receivable* is debited for the balance owing after the deposit is subtracted.

Close   the **display**. **Store** the **entry** as a monthly recurring transaction.

Click   **Post** to save the invoice. **Click OK** to confirm the removal of the order.

Enter   the **next group of transactions** up to Cash Receipt #64. **Change modules** as needed, or **create shortcuts**.

Entering Receipts for Sales with Deposits on Orders

When a customer makes the final payment toward an invoice that had a deposit with the sales order, the journal entry is different from an entry with a separate deposit.

Open   the **Receivables module window**.

Open   the **Receipts Journal** and **select Veronica Kain School of Dance**:

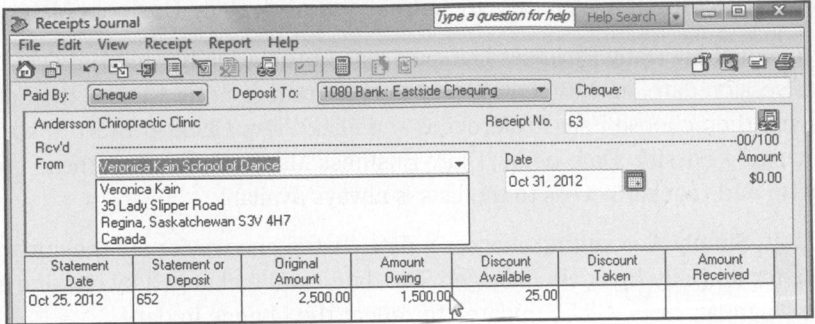

Because the prepayment was cleared at the time of the sale, it does not appear in the Receipts Journal. Instead, the Amount Owing has been reduced so this is a standard receipt entry. The discount is based on the full invoice amount, or 1 percent of $2 500.

Enter the **remaining transaction details** to complete the entry. Remember to change the bank account.

Review the **transaction** and then **post** it.

Enter the **remaining transactions** for the Oct. 31 session date and then **advance** the **session date**. **Change** modules as needed.

Working from the Daily Business Manager

Simply Accounting helps a business monitor its performance and cash flow by generating several of the reports that you have seen so far. It also keeps track of recurring transactions, payments and receipts with the Daily Business Manager lists. These lists offer an additional method of internal control. In addition to these lists, the Daily Business Manager can compile financial performance data for the company.

You should be in the Home window after changing the session date to November 7. You can enter many transactions directly from the Daily Business Manager.

You can open the Daily Business Manager from the Company window Daily Business Manager icon, the Business Assistant menu or the Daily Business Manager tool:

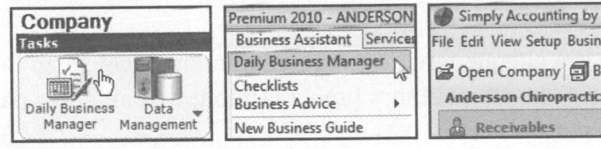

Click the **Daily Business Manager icon**, or **choose** the **Business Assistant menu** and **click Daily Business Manager** or **click** the **DBM tool**:

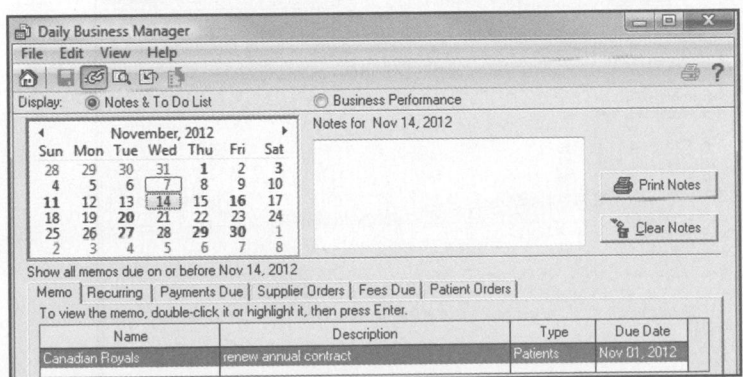

You can also access the Daily Business Manager from any journal by clicking the Daily Business Manager tool icon .

NOTES
In the Company module window, the Daily Business Manager icon is in the upper Tasks pane beside Data Management.

CLASSIC VIEW
Click the Daily Business Manager tool in the tool bar, or click the Daily Business Manager icon in the My Business column.

PRO VERSION
The tabs are labelled Purchase Orders, Sales Due and Sales Orders instead of Supplier Orders, Fees Due and Patient Orders.

NOTES

Refer to page 83 to see the Daily Business Manager Settings on the User Preferences View screen.

Or choose the View menu in any journal and click Daily Business Manager.

You can show Daily Business Manager lists automatically each time you advance the session date, each time you start the program or both. Choose the Setup menu, then choose User Preferences and click View. Click At Startup and After Changing Session Date below Daily Business Manager to select these options. Menu and tool bar access to the lists is always available.

By default, Simply Accounting chooses a date that is one week past the current session date for its Daily Business Manager. The date can be changed by clicking a new date on the calendar. Lists will be updated to reflect the change in date.

Each tab screen includes instructions for accessing journals or selecting an entry.

You can also type notes for a date directly into the Notes box. They will remain on-screen for that date until you choose Clear Notes. You can print these notes and clear them when they are no longer needed.

The Memo tab screen opens with a note for one of the customers about renewing the contract. This memo was entered in the customer's ledger Memo tab screen with a due date and the option to display in the Daily Business Manager.

Double click **Canadian Royals** to open memo in the customer's ledger record:

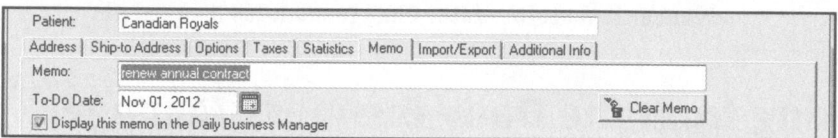

The customer's record opens at the Memo tab screen. You now have the option to remove the memo, if it no longer applies, or to change the date for its appearance in the Daily Business Manager. You can see that we have checked the option to display the memo.

Change the **date** in the To-Do Date field to **Nov. 1, 2013**.

Click **Save And Close** 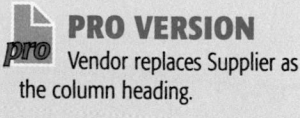 to return to the Daily Business Manager.

Payments Due

The first entry for November is a cheque issued for an outstanding invoice. To be certain that all outstanding invoices are paid in a timely fashion, we can enter payments from the Daily Business Manager.

Click the **Payments Due tab**:

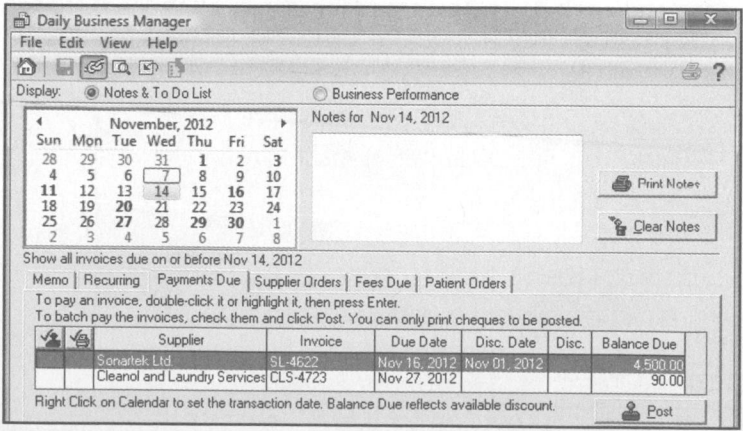

PRO VERSION

pro Vendor replaces Supplier as the column heading.

The list includes payments due and any applicable discounts. To see the payments due in a longer period, and to be sure that all discounts available will be included, you can select a later date on the calendar. You might use this list to plan a payment schedule. We want to be able to take advantage of purchase discounts and we can see only the payments due in the next two weeks.

The list includes the Supplier name, Invoice number, payment Due Date, Discount Date, Discount availability and the Balance Due (owing). The Disc. Date shows when the discount period ends. You can pay the invoices directly from this screen when no changes are needed. You can also open the Payments Journal by double clicking an invoice line or by clicking an invoice and pressing (enter).

If you pay from the Daily Business Manager, the session date is the default, so the discount is no longer available. To change the cheque date, right-click the date you want in the calendar.

Right-click Nov 1 on the calendar. The discount for Sonartek is now available.

In the November calendar section, 1 now has an open box framing it to indicate it will be the transaction posting date. The Disc. column now has a ✓ and the Balance Due for invoice #SL-4622 has been updated to include the discount:

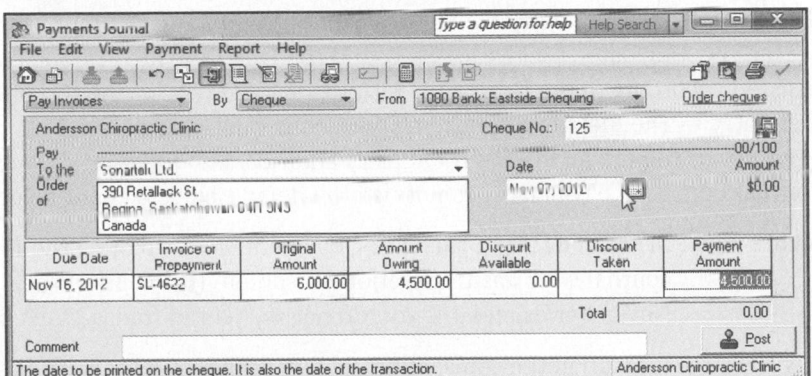

If we post from the Business Manager now, the date and discount will be correct, but the bank account will not. The default amount and bank account will be entered when you pay from the Business Manager and you cannot change these fields. Therefore, we must open the journal to pay the invoice.

Double click the **entry for Sonartek** to open the Payments Journal:

The session date is now entered again as the default, so the full amount owing is entered by default without the discount. We must change both these details. First we will delete the payment amount because it is already selected.

Press (del) to remove the amount.

Enter **Nov 1** as the date for the payment. **Press** (tab) to make the discount available.

Choose **Bank: Regina Chequing** in the From field to update the cheque number.

Click the **Discount Taken field** and then the **Payment Amount field.**

Press (tab) to complete the cheque.

Click the **Post button** 🖰 Post to save the entry.

Close the **Payments Journal** to return to the Daily Business Manager.

The Sonartek Paper Products entry has been removed from the list.

Recurring Transactions Due

The next transaction is the recurring cash purchase.

An advantage to using the Daily Business Manager is that the recurring entries for all journals are listed together. You can open a journal and recall a stored transaction in a single step. You can also post and print sales invoices, individually or in batches, directly from this screen, but you cannot preview them.

> **Right-click Nov 7** on the calendar to reset the session date as the posting date.
>
> **Click** the **Recurring tab**:

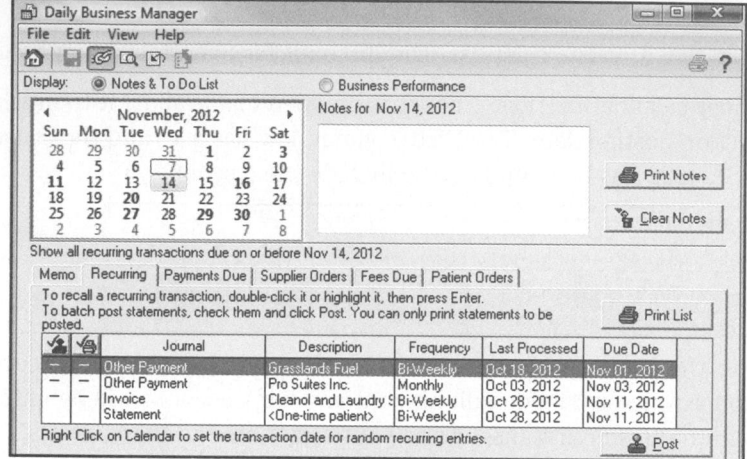

All recurring entries due on or before November 14 (the date marked on the calendar) should be listed (read the Warning margin note), together with the Journal used for the original entry, the entry name (Description) and its recurring Frequency. The most recent posting date (Last Processed) and the Due Date are also included. The entries are listed according to the Due Date, with the earliest date at the top of the list.

The first entry — the fuel purchase from Grasslands Fuel — is due Nov. 1. Recurring purchases require an invoice number as additional information so we need to open the journal first. This payment does not use the default bank account selection.

> **Double click Grasslands Fuel**, the Other Payment entry, to open the Payments Journal with this transaction on-screen. (**Click 30** in the November calendar if you do not see all the transactions listed.)

You may need to scroll up in the transaction section of the journal to see the original entry if this area appears empty.

Bank: Regina Chequing is preselected as the bank account in the From field because we stored the transaction with this selection. This is another advantage to storing a transaction.

> **Enter** **GF-3677** in the Invoice/Ref. field. If you are using the Make Other Payment approach, you should update the Comment as well.
>
> **Post** the **transaction**.
>
> **Close** the **Payments Journal** to return to the Daily Business Manager. The entry for Grasslands Fuel has been removed.
>
> **Double click Pro Suites**, the Other Payment entry, to open the journal.
>
> **Enter** **R2012-11** in the Invoice/Ref. field. Copy this number to the Comment line as well.
>
> **Post** the **transaction. Close** the **Payments Journal**.

⚠️ **WARNING!**

Back up your data file before entering transactions from the Daily Business Manager. We observed some inconsistencies in the transaction dates and entries on the Recurring tab screen. When we advanced the calendar date to November 30, the transactions we needed were included, but the dates were not always correct. Therefore you should check your transactions carefully when you use the Daily Business Manager.

This error in the recurring entry dates has been reported to Sage, and it should be corrected in later releases of the software.

📝 **NOTES**

If you entered the purchases from Grasslands Fuel and Pro Suites in the Expenses Journal, that will be listed as the journal in the Daily Business Manager window and it will open instead of the Payments Journal. In this case, you should enter the transaction in the Expenses Journal.

The instructions here used the Make Other Payment option in the Payments Journal.

📝 **NOTES**

When you open the cash purchase transaction, the transaction detail section may appear blank. Scroll up to see the first line — the recurring transaction information you entered previously.

The Recurring Transactions list has been updated again — the Pro Suites transaction has been removed.

The remaining list items are not due today, so we can proceed to another list in the Daily Business Manager. We want to process some receipts next.

Fees (Sales) Due

Click   the **Fees Due tab** to see the list of Invoices due within the week:

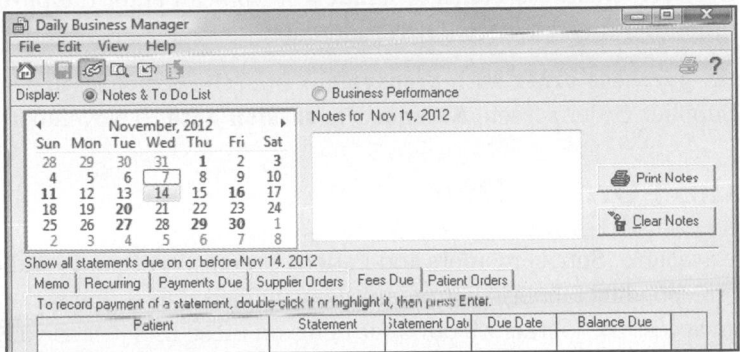

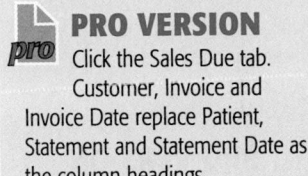

PRO VERSION
Click the Sales Due tab. Customer, Invoice and Invoice Date replace Patient, Statement and Statement Date as the column headings.

The Fees Due list is easy to use as well. It can be used to locate customers with outstanding debts. The list shows the Patient's name, Statement number and Date, payment Due Date and Balance Due (owing) on the due date without the discount. Invoices displayed can be matched against receipts on hand, and you can open the Receipts Journal directly from this window. No invoices are listed because they are not due in the next week. However, most of Andersson's customers take advantage of sales discounts, so we should look at sales due over a longer span than one week. Payments were received from Canadian Royals and Roughrider Argos. These payments are not due until late November, but the customers are paying early to take the discounts.

We cannot post receipts from the Daily Business Manager because customer cheque numbers cannot be added automatically.

Click   **30** on the November calendar to see all sales invoices due this month:

Patient	Statement	Statement Date	Due Date	Balance Due
Canadian Royals	654	Oct 28, 2012	Nov 27, 2012	4,500.00
Roughrider Argos	655	Oct 28, 2012	Nov 27, 2012	4,900.00

The invoices we need now appear on the list so we can enter receipts for them.

To open the journal, you can double click any part of the line for the entry you want or click the line and press (enter).

Double click   the **Canadian Royals** (Invoice #654) to open the Receipts Journal for the selected customer.

Press   (tab) to accept the discount and amount for the first invoice. The amount should appear in the Total field and the upper cheque portion.

Choose Bank: Regina Chequing as the bank account in the Deposit To field.

Add   the customer's **cheque number** (#4011) in the Cheque field.

Change   the **date** of the cheque to November 5. Add the invoice number as additional information.

Display the **journal entry** to review your work. **Close** the **display** and **make corrections** if necessary.

WARNING!
If the discount had expired by November 7, the session date, you would change the date first, as we did for the payment entry. Then delete the default amount and re-enter the discount taken and payment amount.

Click Post ⌷ Post ▾ ⌷ to record the transaction.

Enter the next **receipt** from the Receipts Journal because it is already open. (Deposit cheque #1636 from **Roughrider Argos** on Nov. 7 for the discounted amount to Regina Chequing Account.)

Close the **Receipts Journal** to return to the Daily Business Manager. Both Sales Due entries have been removed.

Close the **Daily Business Manager window** so you can enter the purchase order and then advance the session date.

Enter the **purchase order with prepayment** from the Expenses Journal, Supplier Order screen. **Advance** the **session date** to November 14.

Patient (Sales) Orders Due

Two more lists are available, Supplier Orders and Patient Orders. To see outstanding items, click the corresponding tab. Lists for orders show unfilled orders due within the next week. You can access the journal windows for items on these lists just as you did for payments and fees due. We can enter the sale from order #51 on November 9 from the Daily Business Manager.

Open the **Daily Business Manager window**.

Click the **Patient Orders tab** to see the list:

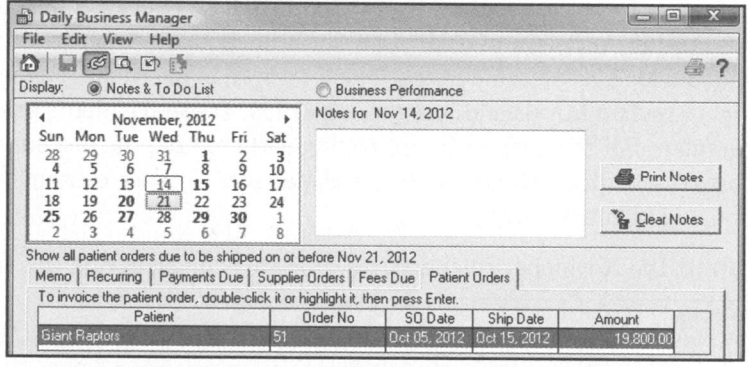

The list displays the patient, order number, order date (SO Date), shipping date and amount. The order we want is listed. You can turn the order into an invoice from the Daily Business Manager by opening the journal with the order on-screen. As usual, double clicking will open the transaction window we need.

Double click **Giant Raptors** (Order #51).

The Fees Journal opens with the order converted to a statement or invoice. Notice that the backordered amount is 5. One month of the contract has been completed.

Enter **Nov 9** in the Date field.

Click the **Quantity field** and **type** 1

Press ⌷tab⌷ to update the amount. The backordered amount changes to 4.

Check your **entry** and when it is correct, **click Post**.

Close the **Fees Journal** to return to the Daily Business Manager. The order remains on the list because it has not been completely filled.

Purchase Orders Due

The next transaction fills the order from Cleanol and Laundry Services.

> **Click** the **Supplier Orders tab** to see the list:

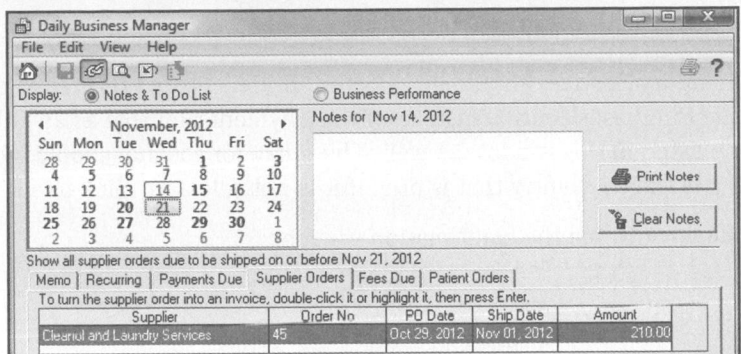

The list displays the supplier, order number, order date, shipping date and amount, making it easy to find orders that you need to track or follow up with the supplier.

Again, we can turn the order from Cleanol and Laundry Services into an invoice from the Daily Business Manager by opening the journal with the order on-screen.

> **Press** (enter) to open the journal entry — Cleanol and Laundry Services is already selected.

> **Enter** **CLS-6543** as the invoice number.

> **Enter** **Nov 11** as the invoice date.

> **Click** the **Fill Backordered Quantities tool** 🔁 .

> **Enter** the **order number** as additional information.

> **Do not post** the **transaction** yet because we want to store it.

Removing Recurring Transactions

Sometimes a recurring transaction is no longer required, or it needs to be replaced. If you try to store the new purchase invoice from Cleanol and Laundry Services before removing the old entry, Simply Accounting will not allow you to continue because the name duplicates the entry on file.

> **Click** the **Store tool** 📥 . **Choose Biweekly** as the frequency for the transaction and **click OK**.

You will see the Duplicate Entry warning:

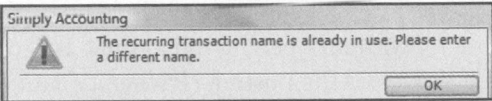

> **Click** **OK** to return to the Store Recurring Transaction screen.

> **Click** **Cancel** to return to the journal. We need to remove the old stored transaction first.

PRO VERSION

pro Click the Purchase Orders tab. Vendor replaces Supplier as the column heading.

Click the **Recall tool** 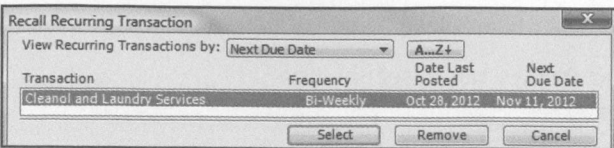 to open the Recall Recurring Transaction list:

Cleanol and Laundry Services should be selected. If you entered the rental payment to Pro Suites in the Purchases Journal instead of the Payments Journal as an Other Payment, it will be listed in this window as well. The entry for Cleanol should still be selected because it is the next entry that is due. If it is not selected, click to select it.

Click **Remove** to see the confirmation warning:

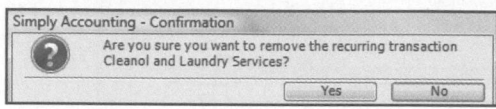

Click **Yes** to confirm the removal if you have selected the correct entry.

Click **Cancel** if the Recall Transaction window is still open. (See Notes.)

Click the **Store tool** .

Choose **Biweekly** as the frequency for the new recurring invoice. **Click OK**.

Post the **purchase transaction**.

Click **OK** to confirm that the filled order has been removed.

Close the **Expenses Journal** to return to the Daily Business Manager. The order is no longer listed.

Enter the next **recurring cash sale** and then **close** the **Daily Business Manager**. **Enter** the **next of group of transactions**, including the **recurring purchase from Cleanol and Laundry Services** on November 25.

Posting Directly from the Daily Business Manager

All the Daily Business Manager transactions we have shown so far have been posted after opening the journals. Cheques (payments) and recurring sales invoices can also be posted directly from the Daily Business Manager, if you can accept the default information, that is, the bank account used. The cheque to Cleanol can be posted directly without opening the journal because it uses the default account.

Posting Sales Directly

We will post the next recurring sale directly without opening the journal. It is due on November 25 so we must change the date. We set the posting (Payment) date on the November calendar, not December.

Although you can post several sales invoices at the same time, we will not do so because the dates were not consistently correct. However, we do want to demonstrate the method.

The Daily Business Manager Recurring tab window should be open. If not,

Open the **Daily Business Manager** and **click** the **Recurring tab**.

If you need to print the invoices, click the Print column beside the invoice.

NOTES
If you have only one recurring transaction, the window closes after you remove it. If there are more transactions, the window stays open and you must click Cancel to close it.

NOTES
When you advance the session date to November 28, you will see the Advisor year-end message.

WARNING!
When you post directly from the Daily Business Manager, you cannot review the journal entry or make other changes.

Click   the **left arrow**  at the top of the December calendar to access the November calendar.

Right-click **25** in the November calendar to select this as the posting date.

Click   (left-click) **28** to reset the session date.

Click   the **Post column** 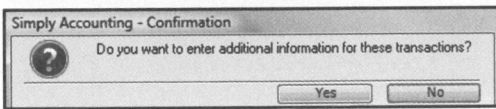 (the first column) **beside** the sale for **Interplay Ballet** to add a ✓.

Click   Post .

A message appears asking if there is additional information to enter before posting:

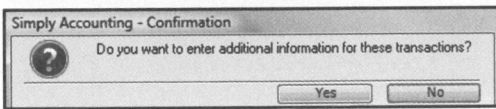

If you want to add details, click Yes to open the Additional Information screen. This screen will not open the journal itself for any other changes. There are no details to add to the Sales Journal entry. We can continue.

Click   **No** to see a message naming the invoices that are currently being processed. When posting is completed, you will see the confirmation:

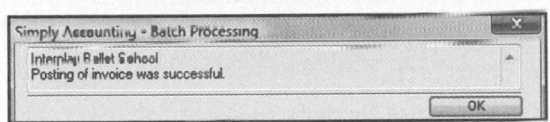

All the invoices that were processed will be listed.

Click   **OK** to return to the list of recurring entries. The sale we posted has been removed.

If the entry did not post successfully, check the journal report for the transaction. If it is not included, open the Sales Journal to enter the transaction.

Close   the **Daily Business Manager**. **Enter** the next **four recurring transactions**. If you enter these from the Daily Business Manager, open the journals and review each journal entry to be certain they will be posted correctly.

Posting Payment Directly

Open   the **Daily Business Manager** if necessary.

Click   the **Payments Due tab**. The cheque is posted on the session date.

Click   the **Post column** 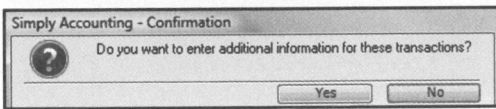 beside Inv #CLS-4723 and CLS-6543 (Cleanol and Laundry Services) to add two ✓.

Click   Post .

You will be asked if you want to enter additional information for the cheque.

Click   **Yes** to open the additional information window or **click No** to continue.

After a brief period, you will see the successful posting confirmation:

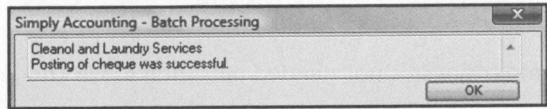

Click   **OK**.

NOTES
If you have set the dates correctly, November 25 on the calendar should have an open box framing it and November 28 will appear in a solid coloured box.

WARNING!
Remember that when you pay from the Daily Business Manager, the default amount and bank account are selected. You cannot change them.

NOTES

As indicated on the screen, the cash balance is the total for all cash and bank accounts. Thus, the balance for Line of Credit Payable is included but the balance for Bank: Interac is not.

The balance for Line of Credit Payable appears to be added to the other two bank account balances.

Business Performance

Before closing the Business Manager, we will look at the key performance indicators.

Click   **Business Performance**:

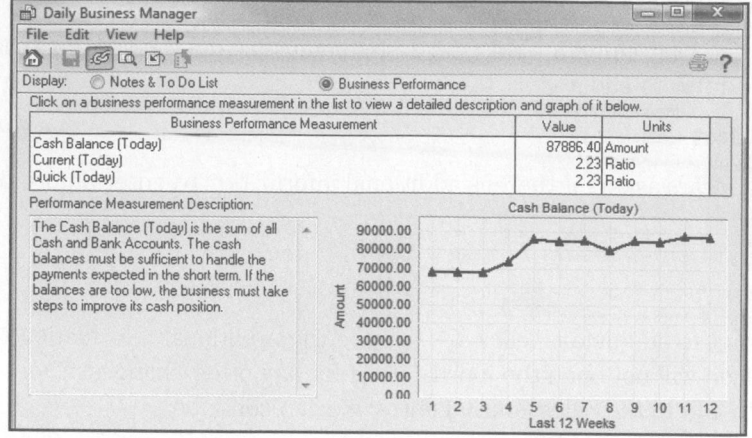

Performance information includes the current bank account balance, the current ratio and the quick ratio at the session date. The information is provided numerically and graphically. Detailed descriptions explain the indicators and guidelines for these financials. Clicking an indicator will display the results.

Click   **Notes & To Do List** to restore the lists.

Click   ⊠ to close the Daily Business Manager and return to the Home window.

Advance the **session date** to November 30.

Enter   the **remaining transactions** for November 30, including memo #8.

Removing Quotes and Orders

Quotes and orders that will not be filled should be removed so that they are not confused with active quotes and orders. To remove purchase quotes,

PRO VERSION

Click the Purchase Invoices icon to open the Purchases Journal.

In the Quote transaction window, choose the Purchase menu and click Remove Purchase Quote Or Purchase Order.

Click   the **Invoices icon** in the Payables module window or **click** the **Create Invoice shortcut** if you added one to open the Expenses Journal.

Choose **Quote** from the Transaction list.

Choose   **quote #MT-511** and **press** (tab) to place the quote on-screen.

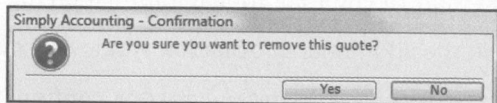

Click   the **Remove tool**

NOTES

If you start from the Home window Quotes icon, the menu option is Remove Patient/Supplier Quote. If you start from the Home window Orders icon, the menu option is Remove Patient/Supplier Order.

Or, **choose** the **Expense menu** and **click Remove Supplier Quote Or Supplier Order** to see the usual warning message:

> Simply Accounting - Confirmation
>
> ?   Are you sure you want to remove this quote?
>
> [Yes]   [No]

Click   **Yes** to confirm.

Remove the **other two quotes** that are not needed and then **close** the **journal**.

To remove purchase orders, open the Expenses (Purchases) Journal. Choose Supplier Order from the Transaction list. Choose the order number and press `tab` to put the order on-screen.

Click the Remove Supplier Order tool or choose the Expense menu and click Remove Supplier Quote or Supplier Order. Click Yes to confirm deletion.

To remove sales quotes or sales orders, open the Fees (Sales) Journal. Choose Quote (or Patient Order) as the transaction and then select the Quote or Order No. from the list. Press `tab` to bring the quote or order onto the screen.

Click the Remove Patient Quote (or Patient Order) tool or choose the Fees menu and click Remove Patient Quote or Patient Order. Click Yes to confirm.

Print   **all relevant financial reports**. **Make** a **backup** and then **start** a **new fiscal period**.

Displaying Reports

Displaying Pending Supplier (Purchase) Orders

Any purchase orders that are not yet filled can be displayed in a report. You can also use this report to check for orders that are delayed or should be removed.

Open   the **Report Centre**. **Click Payables** in the Select A Type Of Report list.

Click   **Pending Supplier Orders Summary by Supplier** and **click Modify This Report**:

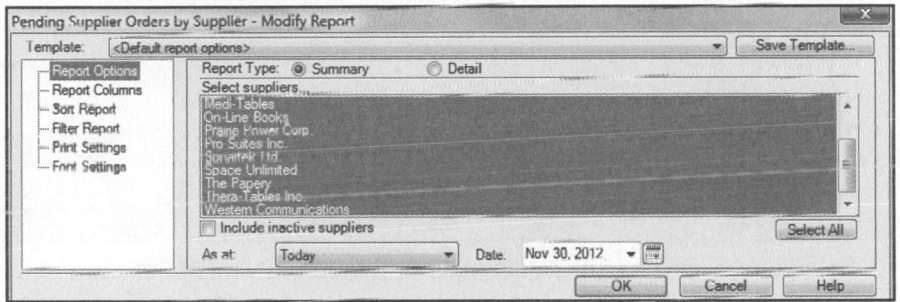

Press   and **hold** `ctrl` and **click** the appropriate **names** in the supplier list.

Enter   **Dec. 31, 2012** as the date for the report.

Click   **OK** to view the report.

All orders due in the next month should be included in the report. The purchase order with HydraTub Care is not included because its starting date is January 1.

Click   the **Modify Report tool** .

Display the **report** again using January 15, 2013, as the date to see all outstanding orders. **Close** the **display** when you have finished.

Displaying Pending Patient (Sales) Orders

Any sales orders that are not yet filled can be displayed in the Pending Sales Orders Report. You can also use this report to check for orders that should be removed.

Click   **Receivables** in the Select A Type Of Report list.

PRO VERSION
The labels/terms Purchase Journal, Purchase menu and Purchase Order will be used.
The labels/terms Sales Journal, Sales menu and Sales Order will be used.

PRO VERSION
The report is named Pending Purchase Orders By Vendor.

NOTES
From the Home window, choose the Reports menu, then choose Payables and Pending Supplier Orders and click By Supplier to see the report options.

NOTES
From the Pending Orders reports, you can drill down to the Supplier/Patient Aged Report and to the order form.
If you drill down to the order, you can fill the order directly by choosing Invoice as the type of transaction and then filling the order as usual. Confirm your intention to change the order to an invoice.

NOTES
The Pending Supplier/Patient Orders reports can be sorted and filtered by Order No., Order Date, Ship Date and Amount.

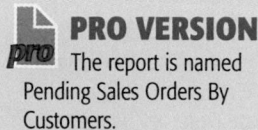
Click   Pending Patient Orders Summary by Patient to open the sample.

Click   Modify This Report to open the report options window:

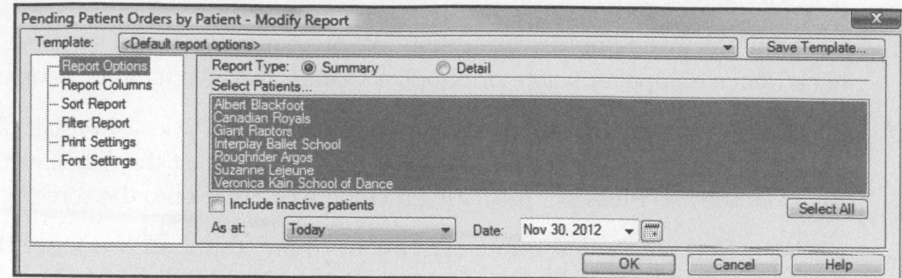

Press   and hold (ctrl) and **click** the appropriate **names** in the customer list.

Enter   Dec 31, 2012 as the report date to see orders for the next month.

Click   OK to view the report. One sales order is listed, the partially filled order for the Giant Raptors' contract.

Close   the **display** when you have finished.

Displaying Journal Reports

When you choose to include additional fields in the journal entries, you can also include these details in the journal reports.

Click   Financials in the Select A Type Of Report list.

Click   All Journal Entries and **click Modify This Report**:

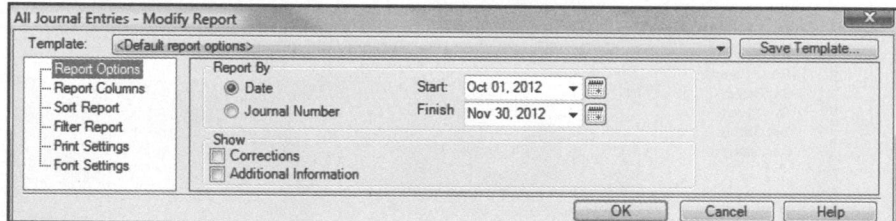

A check box is used for the Additional Information. If you do not want to include these details in the report, you can leave the check box blank.

Click   Additional Information to add a ✓.

Click   Corrections.

Enter   the **Start date** and **Finish dates** for the report (including the year).

Click   OK to see the Journal Report.

Close   the **display** when you have finished.

Close   the **Report Centre**.

NOTES
You can also choose the
Reports menu, then choose
Receivables and Pending Patient
Orders and click By Patient to view
the report options.

NOTES
You can also choose the
Reports menu, then choose
Journal Entries and click All to see
the report options.

R E V I E W

The Student DVD with Data Files includes Review Questions and Supplementary Cases for this chapter.

OBJECTIVES

After completing this chapter, you should be able to

- **make** payments toward credit card accounts
- **make** GST, HST and PST remittances
- **apply** sales taxes to interprovincial sales
- **enter** sales and receipts for foreign customers
- **enter** purchases and payments for foreign suppliers
- **access** supplier or customer Web sites
- **e-mail** invoices to customers
- **look up** invoices after posting them
- **track** shipments to customers
- **transfer** funds between different currency bank accounts
- **monitor** business routines with Checklists
- **create** an Accountant's Copy of data for adjustments
- **import** Accountant's Copy journal entries

COMPANY INFORMATION

Company Profile

> **NOTES**
> Maple Leaf Rags Inc.
> 2642 Coldstream Avenue
> Summerside, PE C1N 2X2
> Tel 1: (902) 63M-USIC
> Tel 2: (888) 63M-USIC
> Fax: (902) 633-4888
> Business No.: 128 488 632
> Rag is a style of music set in ragtime. Many of Scott Joplin's tunes, including "Maple Leaf Rag," are examples of ragtime music.

Maple Leaf Rags Inc. is a privately held corporation operated by Jaz Bands. Bands recently relocated his small home office from Victoria, British Columbia, to Summerside, Prince Edward Island. While studying fine arts at Concordia University, Bands worked part time in local music stores. Customers frequently asked about Canadian performing artists in general and were sometimes frustrated that they had to look in every department to find a variety of types of music by Canadians. After completing an MBA at Queen's University, and based on his knowledge of and contacts in the music industry and some careful business research, Bands opened his own business, Maple Leaf Rags Inc., a store specializing in Canadian recording artists. He also sells the book that he wrote and published — *A Guide to Canadian Music*.

Maple Leaf Rags Inc. sells CDs by Canadian artists over the Internet to individuals. It also sells to music stores throughout Canada and the United States, usually to American stores that serve a large Canadian resident and tourist clientele. These stores rely on Bands as a convenient source of Canadian artists' recordings, including native and ethnic music produced by A.B. Original Sounds, which is Bands' recording company. Bands hopes to expand the business to other countries where pockets of Canadian populations can be found, such as countries with Canadian Armed Forces bases. His recent book has also been popular with these customers.

Bands is fortunate to be able to rely on the advice of his friend Dave Manga, whose Outset Media board-game business distributes its products in a similar way to Maple Leaf Rags. His friend also shares information about suppliers who might be able to provide some of Bands' supplies.

Maple Leaf Rags has expanded rapidly, though Bands is still able to operate out of his own home because the demands for inventory storage space are small. He pays himself rent for use of his home office space.

Bands buys CDs from various recording studios. He buys CD masters from A.B. Original Sounds, and suppliers across Canada copy and package the CDs for his company at competitive prices. He has accounts set up for all his regular suppliers, many of whom offer discounts for early payments. Bands also has set up accounts for his wholesale customers, with discounts for early payment.

At the end of each fiscal year, Bands creates a copy of the data files for the accountant, who checks the accuracy of the accounting records and adds the outstanding adjusting entries.

Bands converted his accounting records to Simply Accounting after completing a brief course at the community college. The following company information summarizes the conversion after the first nine months of the current fiscal period:

- Chart of Accounts
- Trial Balance
- Supplier Information
- Customer Information
- Accounting Procedures

CHART OF POSTABLE ACCOUNTS

MAPLE LEAF RAGS INC.

ASSETS
1020	Bank: Savings Account
1040	Bank: Chequing Account
1060	Bank: Visa
1080	Bank: MasterCard
1140	Bank: USD
1200	Accounts Receivable
1240	Purchase Prepayments
1280	Office Supplies
1300	CD Inventory
1340	Book Inventory
1380	Prepaid Expenses
1410	Computers
1420	Accum Deprec: Computers
1450	Furniture & Equipment
1480	Accum Deprec: Furn & Equip ▶

▶1500	Automobile
1520	Accum Deprec: Automobile

LIABILITIES
2100	Bank Loan
2180	Prepaid Sales and Deposits
2200	Accounts Payable
2250	Amex Payable
2260	Visa Payable
2460	PST Payable
2650	GST Charged on Sales
2660	HST Charged on Sales
2670	GST Paid on Purchases
2680	HST Paid on Purchases
2850	Long Term Loan ▶

▶EQUITY
3560	Common Stock
3600	Retained Earnings
3800	Current Earnings

REVENUE
4100	Revenue from CD Sales
4140	Revenue from Book Sales
4180	Sales Discounts
4200	Freight Revenue
4250	Interest Revenue
4280	Sales Tax Compensation
4300	Exchange Rate Differences

EXPENSE
5100	Advertising & Publicity
5150	Bank Charges & Card Fees ▶

▶5200	Depreciation Expense
5220	Freight & Shipping Expenses
5260	Purchase Discounts
5280	Interest Expense
5300	Internet & Web Site Expenses
5320	Storage Expense
5340	Cost of Books Sold
5360	CD Assembly Materials Costs
5380	Cost of CDs Sold
5400	Office Rent
5500	Office Supplies Used
5520	Research Expenses
5560	Telephone Expenses
5580	Travel Expenses

NOTES: The Chart of Accounts includes only postable accounts and the Net Income or Current Earnings account.

TRIAL BALANCE

MAPLE LEAF RAGS INC.

June 30, 2012		Debits	Credits				Debits	Credits
1020	Bank: Savings Account	$ 76 675		▶ 2850	Long Term Loan			60 000
1040	Bank: Chequing Account	41 000		3560	Common Stock			160 000
1060	Bank: Visa	1 800		3600	Retained Earnings			22 014
1080	Bank: MasterCard	2 350		4100	Revenue from CD Sales			389 000
1140	Bank: USD ($705 USD)	760		4140	Revenue from Book Sales			61 000
1200	Accounts Receivable	67 200		4180	Sales Discounts		6 840	
1280	Office Supplies	600		4200	Freight Revenue			5 460
1300	CD Inventory	180 350		4250	Interest Revenue			2 150
1340	Book Inventory	44 840		4280	Sales Tax Compensation			45
1380	Prepaid Expenses	3 900		5100	Advertising & Publicity		18 800	
1410	Computers	8 200		5150	Bank Charges & Card Fees		1 980	
1420	Accum Deprec: Computers		$ 1 100	5220	Freight & Shipping Expenses		4 810	
1450	Furniture & Equipment	9 100		5260	Purchase Discounts			850
1480	Accum Deprec: Furn & Equip		1 500	5280	Interest Expense		9 960	
1500	Automobile	16 800		5300	Internet & Web Site Expenses		540	
1520	Accum Deprec: Automobile		9 800	5340	Cost of Books Sold		32 400	
2100	Bank Loan		12 000	5360	CD Assembly Materials Costs		1 800	
2200	Accounts Payable		1 607	5380	Cost of CDs Sold		188 250	
2250	Amex Payable		390	5400	Office Rent		7 200	
2260	Visa Payable		860	5500	Office Supplies Used		800	
2460	PST Payable		450	5520	Research Expenses		1 200	
2650	GST Charged on Sales		1 450	5560	Telephone Expenses		905	
2660	HST Charged on Sales		3 634	5580	Travel Expenses		1 950	
2670	GST Paid on Purchases	500					$733 310	$733 310
2680	HST Paid on Purchases	1 800		▶				

SUPPLIER INFORMATION

MAPLE LEAF RAGS INC.

Supplier Name (Contact)	Address	Phone No. Fax No.	E-mail Web Site	Terms Tax ID
A.B. Original Sounds (Marie Raven)	380 Abbey Rd. Vancouver, BC V3P 5N6	Tel: (604) 882-6252 Fax: (604) 882-1100		1/10, n/30 (before tax) 129 646 733
Atlantic Tel (Manny Voyses)	45 Nexus Ave. Summerside, PE C1N 3D1	Tel: (902) 679-1011 Fax: (902) 679-1000	www.bell.ca	n/1
Federal Express (DayLee Runner)	59 Effex Road Summerside, PE C1N 6X2	Tel: (800) 488-9000 Fax: (902) 488-1230	www.fedex.com	n/1
Grandeur Graphics (Kathy Grandeur)	26 Drawing Way Halifax, NS B5T 3D1	Tel: (902) 665-3998 Fax: (902) 665-3900	www.wedesignit.com	2/20, n/30 (before tax) 459 112 341
Let 'm Know (Jabber Jaws Lowder)	599 Broadcast Rd. Summerside, PE C1N 7J8	Tel: (902) 604-6040 Fax: (902) 604-4660	www.wetellit.com	2/20, n/30 (before tax) 453 925 376
Miles 'R on Us (N. Gins)	522 Drivers St. Winnipeg, MB R3F 5E3	Tel: (800) 592-5239 Fax: (204) 591-4929		n/1
Minister of Finance			www.TaxandLand.pe.ca	n/1
Purolator (Speedy Carriere)	46 Shipping Mews Summerside, PE C1N 6S2	Tel: (800) 355-7447 Fax: (902) 355-7000	www.purolator.com	n/1
Receiver General for Canada	Summerside Tax Centre Summerside, PE C1N 6L2	Tel: (902) 821-8186	www.cra-arc.gc.ca	n/1
Wrap It (Able Boxer)	80 Cubit Road Richmond Hill, ON L5R 6B2	Tel: (905) 881-7739 Fax: (905) 881-7000		1/5, n/30 (before tax) 634 529 125

OUTSTANDING SUPPLIER INVOICES

MAPLE LEAF RAGS INC.

Supplier Name	Terms	Date	Invoice No.	Amount	Tax	Total
Grandeur Graphics	2/20, n/30 (before tax)	6/28/12	GG-1304	$ 400	$ 52	$ 452
Let 'm Know	2/20, n/30 (before tax)	6/29/12	LK-692	$1 000	$155	$1 155
			Grand Total			$1 607

CUSTOMER INFORMATION

MAPLE LEAF RAGS INC.

Customer Name (Contact)	Address	Phone No. Fax No.	E-mail Web Site	Terms Credit Limit
Canadian Sounds (X. Pats)	46 Ontario St. Tampa, Florida 33607 USA	Tel: (813) 930-4589 Fax: (813) 930-7330	XPats@cansounds.com www.cansounds.com	3/30, n/60 (before tax) $20 000 USD
CDN Music (Michelle Strings)	230 Nightingale Pl. Scarborough, ON M2R 9K4	Tel: (416) 288-6189 Fax: (416) 288-6000	mstrings@upbeat.com www.cdn.music.ca	3/30, n/60 (before tax) $20 000
Entertainment House (Rob Blinde)	101 Booker St. Toronto, ON M4F 3J8	Tel: (416) 484-9123 Fax: (416) 488-8182	www.ent.house.com	3/30, n/60 (before tax) $150 000
It's All Canadian (Leaf Mapleston)	39 Federation Ave. Victoria, BC V8W 7T7	Tel: (250) 598-1123 Fax: (250) 598-1000	www.canstuff.com	3/30, n/60 (before tax) $20 000
Music Music Music (M. Porter)	10 Red Rock Canyon Sedona, Arizona 86336 USA	Tel: (520) 678-4523 Fax: (520) 678-4500	mporter@music3.com www.music3.com	3/30, n/60 (before tax) $10 000 USD
Total Music (Goode Sounds)	93 Waterside Rd. Fredericton, NB E3B 4F4	Tel: (506) 455-7746 Fax: (506) 455-7000	goode@totalmusic.com www.totalmusic.com	3/30, n/60 (before tax) $50 000
Treble & Bass (Bea Flatte)	399 Chord Blvd. Summerside, PE C1N 5T6	Tel: (902) 557-5438 Fax: (902) 557-5550	bflatte@t&b.com www.t&b.com	3/30, n/60 (before tax) $30 000
Web Store Customers				Prepaid by Credit Card

OUTSTANDING CUSTOMER INVOICES

MAPLE LEAF RAGS INC.

Customer Name	Terms	Date	Invoice No.	Amount	Tax	Total
CDN Music	3/30, n/60 (before tax)	6/25/12	591	$ 4 500	$ 225	$ 4 725
Entertainment House	3/30, n/60 (before tax)	1/4/12	233	$56 000	$2 800	$58 800
It's All Canadian	3/30, n/60 (before tax)	6/6/12	589	$ 3 500	$ 175	$ 3 675
			Grand Total			$67 200

Accounting Procedures

GST

Maple Leaf Rags Inc. uses the regular method of calculating GST. The GST charged and collected from customers is recorded as a liability in *GST Charged on Sales*. Customers in New Brunswick, Newfoundland and Labrador and Ontario pay HST at the rate of 13 percent instead of GST, and customers in British Columbia pay HST at 12 percent. These HST amounts are recorded in *HST Charged on Sales*. In the remaining provinces and territories, customers pay the 5 percent GST on all their purchases. Bands has set up both GST and HST as taxes with appropriate codes. GST paid to suppliers is recorded in *GST Paid on Purchases* (or *HST Paid on Purchases*) as a decrease in tax liability. The balance owing is the difference between the GST plus HST charged and GST plus HST paid. Customers who buy books pay only GST at the rate of 5 percent on their purchases — books are exempt for PST and HST in all provinces.

Cash Sales of Services

Cash transactions for Bands are limited to credit card sales since most of his business is with wholesale customers who have accounts. He has merchant Visa and MasterCard arrangements with two financial institutions. Maple Leaf Rags pays a percentage of each sale directly to the credit card companies (the fee is withheld from the sale amount). To simplify the transaction entries, we provide summaries of these credit card sales as if they were to a single customer called Web Store Customers.

Bands uses a Visa gold card and an American Express card for some business purchases and pays annual user fees for these cards.

Discounts

Discounts are calculated automatically by the program when the discount terms are entered as part of the invoices. If the payments are made before the discount term has expired, the discount appears in the Payments and Receipts journals automatically. All discounts are calculated on before-tax amounts. Bands offers a 3 percent discount to wholesale customers to encourage them to pay their accounts on time. Web store customers pay by credit card and do not receive discounts.

Some suppliers offer before-tax discounts to Maple Leaf Rags as well. These discount terms are set up in the supplier and customer records.

PST

PST, also called Revenue Tax, is charged at the rate of 10 percent on the base price of goods plus GST in Prince Edward Island. Wholesale customers do not pay PST on merchandise they buy for resale. Thus, when Bands sells directly to stores, he charges only GST. He does not charge PST to stores because they are not the final consumers of the product. Individual customers and retail stores in PEI pay GST and PST on the purchase of CDs but only GST on books. Customers in other provinces pay GST at 5 percent or HST at 13 percent (12 percent in BC). When Maple Leaf Rags makes the PST remittance, it reduces the amount of the remittance by 3.0 percent, the amount of the sales tax compensation.

Freight

Customers who order through the Internet pay a shipping rate of $5 for the first CD or book and $2 for each additional item. Wholesale customers pay the actual shipping costs. GST is charged on freight in Prince Edward Island. Bands has accounts set up with his three regular shippers so that he can track shipments online. Their Web site addresses are included in the shipping setup data.

Sales Orders and Deposits

When a customer places a sales order, Bands requests a deposit as confirmation of the order. Deposits are entered on the Sales Order form (see page 435) or in the Receipts Journal (see page 426).

Foreign Customers and Suppliers

Customers outside Canada do not pay GST, HST or PST on goods imported from Canada. Therefore, sales outside the country do not have taxes applied to them. These customers also do not pay any taxes on their shipping charges.

Purchases from suppliers outside of Canada are subject to GST when the goods are used in Canada. No import duties are charged on goods coming from the United States.

NOTES
For Maple Leaf Rags' retail business type, the terms Customer and Supplier are used. Sales and Purchases are used as icon labels, in journal names and in reports.

PRO VERSION
pro Vendors will replace Suppliers for icon, field and report names.

INSTRUCTIONS

1. **Record entries for the source documents** in Simply Accounting using the Chart of Accounts, Supplier Information, Customer Information and Accounting Procedures for Maple Leaf Rags. The procedures for entering each new type of transaction in this application are outlined step by step in the Keystrokes section following the source documents. These transactions are indicated with a ✓ in the completion box beside the source document. The number for the page on which the relevant keystrokes begin is printed immediately below the check box.

    Change module windows as needed, or create shortcuts for journals in other modules.

2. **Print the reports for the end of the fiscal period** suggested by the Simply Accounting checklists after you have finished making your entries. Refer to the Keystrokes section, page 491. If you have started a new fiscal period, choose **Previous Year** to see the reports you need.

SOURCE DOCUMENTS

SESSION DATE — JULY 15, 2012

☑   **Visa Credit Card Sales Invoice #593**   **Dated July 2/12**

467   To various Web Store customers, for CDs sold during previous three months

CD sales to PEI customers	$ 500 plus 5% GST and 10% PST
CD sales to BC customers	700 plus 12% HST
CD sales to other HST customers	2 400 plus 13% HST
CD sales to other GST customers	900 plus 5% GST
Book sales	3 000 plus 5% GST
Shipping	680 plus 5% GST

(Shipped by Purolator #PCU773XT)
Invoice total $8 882.50. Paid by Visa.

NOTES
Remember to select the correct credit card name.
You do not need to enter shipping information for the remaining Web store sales.

☐ **MasterCard Credit Card Sales Invoice #594   Dated July 2/12**

To various Web Store customers, for CDs sold during previous three months

CD sales to PEI customers	$ 400	plus 5% GST and 10% PST
CD sales to BC customers	680	plus 12% HST
CD sales to other HST customers	1 980	plus 13% HST
CD sales to other GST customers	920	plus 5% GST
Book sales	2 700	plus 5% GST
Shipping	630	plus 5% GST

Invoice total $7 923.50. Paid by MasterCard.

☐ **Visa Purchase Invoice #MR-1699   Dated July 2/12**

To Miles 'R on Us, $520 plus 5% GST and 7% PST for two-week car rental while attending Trade Show in Winnipeg. Invoice total $582.40. Paid by Visa.

☑ **Cheque #761   Dated July 2/12**

470   To Visa, $723.50 in payment of credit card account, including $609 for purchases charged from May 16 to June 15, $105 for annual renewal fee and $9.50 in interest charges on the unpaid balance from a previous statement.

☑ **Memo #43   Dated July 3/12**

473   From J. Bands: Access the Web site for Canada Revenue Agency to see whether any recent announcements about GST affect the business.

☑ **Memo #44   Dated July 5/12**

475   From J. Bands: Refer to June 30 General Ledger balances to remit GST and HST to the Receiver General. Issue cheque #762 for $2 784 from Chequing Account.

☑ **Memo #45   Dated July 5/12**

477   From J. Bands: Refer to the June 30 General Ledger balance to remit PST Payable to the Minister of Finance. Reduce the payment by the sales tax compensation of 3.0% of the balance owing. Issue cheque #763 for $436.50 from Chequing Account.

☑ **Sales Invoice #595   Dated July 5/12**

478   To Canadian Sounds, $2 190 USD for CDs and $300 USD for books. Shipped by Federal Express (#F19YTR563) for $140. Invoice total $2 630 USD. Terms 3/30, n/60. The exchange rate is 1.078.

☐ **Cash Receipt #125   Dated July 5/12**

From It's All Canadian, cheque #884 for $3 570 in payment of account including $105 discount taken for early payment. Reference invoice #589.

☐ **Sales Order #TB-04 & Deposit #14   Dated July 5/12**

Shipping date July 10/12
From Treble & Bass, $10 300 plus 5% GST for CDs and $900 for books. Enter one (1) as the order quantity for each invoice line. Shipping by Purolator for $120 plus GST. Invoice total $11 886. Terms 3/30, n/60. Received cheque #911 for $2 000 as deposit #14 to confirm the order. Refer to page 435.

☐ **Sales Invoice #596   Dated July 10/12**

To Treble & Bass, to fill sales order #TB-04, $10 300 for CDs and $900 for books plus 5% GST. Shipped by Purolator (#PCU899XT) for $120 plus GST. Invoice total $11 886. Terms 3/30, n/60. Enter the shipper so you can track the shipment.

NOTES
Because the car rental is purchased and used in Manitoba, the Manitoba Provincial Sales Tax rate applies. Use tax code TM (GST plus Manitoba PST).

NOTES
You can use the Additional Field for the invoice number.
Use the bank account 1040 for receipts from Canadian customers.

NOTES
Wholesale customers who will be selling the product to their own customers do not pay PST.
Remember to add the year in the Shipping Date field.

⚠ WARNING!
Remember to change the payment method to Pay Later for invoice #596. Cheque remains selected from the Sales Order. Refer to page 439. The balance owing is $9 886.

☐   **Sales Invoice #597**   **Dated July 11/12**

To Music Music Music, $1 630 USD for CDs plus $450 USD for books. Shipped by Federal Express (#F27CGB786) for $110. Invoice total $2 190 USD. Terms 3/30, n/60. The exchange rate is 1.081.

☑   **Cash Receipt #126**   **Dated July 15/12**

480   From Canadian Sounds, cheque #2397 for $2 551.10 USD in payment of account less $78.90 discount for early payment. Reference invoice #595. The exchange rate for July 15 is 1.082.

☑   **Memo #46**   **Dated July 15/12**

481   From J. Bands: Treble & Bass called to inform you that they have not received their shipment of CDs. Look up invoice #596, e-mail a copy of the invoice to the customer and check the delivery status.

SESSION DATE — JULY 31, 2012

☑   **Purchase Invoice #DA-722**   **Dated July 16/12**

485   From Design Anything (use Full Add for new USD supplier), $3 200 plus 5% GST for design of labels and CD case inserts for new CDs. Invoice total $3 360 USD. Terms: net 30. The exchange rate is 1.0825.

☐   **Cheque Copy #764**   **Dated July 16/12**

To Amex, $335 in payment of credit card account, including $290 for purchases charged from May 25 to June 25 and $45 for annual renewal fee.

☐   **Cheque Copy #765**   **Dated July 18/12**

To Grandeur Graphics, $444 in full payment of account, including $8 discount for early payment. Reference invoice #GG-1304.

☐   **Cheque Copy #766**   **Dated July 18/12**

To Let 'm Know, $1 135 in full payment of account, including $20 discount for early payment. Reference invoice #LK-692.

☐   **Cash Receipt #127**   **Dated July 20/12**

From CDN Music, cheque #28563 for $4 590 in payment of account including $135 discount taken for early payment. Reference invoice #591.

☑   **Cheque Copy #284**   **Dated July 30/12**

487   To Design Anything, $3 360 USD in full payment of account. Reference invoice #DA-722. The exchange rate is 1.084.

☑   **Memo #47**   **Dated July 30/12**

488   From J. Bands, transfer $1 000 USD from Bank: Chequing Account to Bank: USD. The exchange rate is 1.084.

☐   **Purchase Order #204 & Cheque #767**   **Dated July 31/12**

Shipping date Aug. 15/12
To A.B. Original Sounds, $50 000 plus 12% HST for master copies of new CDs. Invoice total $56 000. Enter 1 as the order quantity. Terms: 1/10, n/30. Use CD Assembly Materials Costs account.
Paid $10 000 as prepayment on order with cheque #767.

NOTES
Use Full Add so you can enter the correct currency.
☐ Design Anything
(contact Joy Pikchur)
900 Park St., Unit 5
Seattle, Washington 98195
USA
Tel: (800) 639-8710
Fax: (206) 755-8852
Currency: USD
Terms: net 30
Expense account: 5360
Tax code: G

NOTES
Remember that you need to include the year for the shipping date field.

Purchase Order #205 & Cheque #768   **Dated July 31/12**

Shipping date Aug. 15/12

To Super Dupers (use Full Add for the new supplier), $7 000 for duplicating CDs, labels and case inserts plus $8 000 for reprinting books plus 13% HST. Invoice total $16 950. Terms: 1/10, n/30.

Paid $4 000 as prepayment on order with cheque #768.

Maple Leaf Rags

www.mapleleafrags.com

2642 Coldstream Avenue
Summerside, PE C1N 2X2
Tel 1: (902) 63M-USIC
Tel 2: (888) 63M-USIC   Fax: (902) 633-4888

PO#:	206
Date:	July 31, 2012
Shipping date:	Aug 15, 2012
Ordered from:	Wrap It
Address:	80 Cubit Road
	Richmond Hill, ON L5R 6B2
Phone No:	(905) 881-7739
Fax No:	(905) 881-7000
Contact:	Able Boxer

PURCHASE ORDER

Order description	Amount
Provide CD cases add labels and inserts terms: 1/5, n/30	6 300.00
	Freight (Canada Post) 120.00
	GST --
	HST 834.60
	Order Total 7 254.60
Deposit: chq #769 for $2 000	**Deposit** 2 000.00
Approved by: *Jaz Bands*	**Balance Owing** 5 254.60

NOTES

Super Dupers
777 Copiers Ave.
Richmond Hill, ON L4T 6V2
Terms: 1/10, n/30 after tax
Tax code: H (The supplier is located in Ontario.)
Use CD Assembly Materials Costs and Book Inventory accounts for the purchase.

Purchase Invoice #LK-2303   **Dated July 31/12**

From Let 'm Know, $1 500 plus 5% GST and 10% PST for series of ads to run for the next five months (prepaid expense). Invoice total $1 732.50. Terms: 2/20, n/30.

NOTES

Change the default account to Prepaid Expenses for the invoice from Let 'm Know.

Cash Purchase Invoice #AT-6632   **Dated July 31/12**

From Atlantic Tel, $165 plus 5% GST and 10% PST for telephone services for two months. Invoice total $190.58. Terms: payment on receipt of invoice. Paid by cheque #770.

Cash Purchase Invoice #PE-49006   **Dated July 31/12**

From Purolator, $1 400 plus 5% GST for shipping services used from May 25 to July 25. Invoice total $1 470. Terms: payment on receipt of invoice. Paid by cheque #771.

Visa Purchase Invoice #PC-34992   **Dated July 31/12**

From Petro-Canada (use Quick Add), $50 plus 5% GST and 10% PST for gasoline for business use. Invoice total $57.75 paid by Visa.

NOTES

Use Quick Add for the new supplier. Include gasoline costs with Travel Expenses. Use tax code GP — GST and PST apply.

SESSION DATE — AUGUST 15, 2012

Cheque Copy #772   **Dated Aug. 2/12**

To Visa, $833.40 in payment of balance shown on Visa account statement for purchases before July 15, 2012.

☐ **Cash Receipt #128** **Dated Aug. 7/12**

From Music Music Music, cheque #8531 for $2 124.30 USD in payment of account less $65.70 discount for early payment. Reference invoice #597. The exchange rate for Aug. 7 is 1.077. Deposit to Bank: USD account.

☐ **Cheque Copy #773** **Dated Aug. 8/12**

To Let 'm Know, $1 702.50 in full payment of account, including $30 discount for early payment. Reference invoice #LK-2303.

☐ **Cash Receipt #129** **Dated Aug. 9/12**

From Treble & Bass, cheque #1144 for $9 546.40 in payment of account including $339.60 discount taken for early payment. Reference invoice #596 and deposit #14. Deposit to Bank: Chequing Account.

☐ **Sales Invoice #598** **Dated Aug. 9/12**

To Total Music, $4 000 plus 13% HST for CDs. Shipping charges $210 plus HST. Invoice total $4 757.30. Terms 3/30, n/60.

☐ **Sales Order #FA-05** **Dated Aug. 9/12**

Shipping date Aug. 22/12

To Fiddler & Associates (use Full Add for the new customer), $24 000 for CDs and $9 000 for books plus 5% GST — items purchased by major music store chains. Shipping charges $200 plus GST. Invoice total $34 860. Terms 3/30, n/60.

NOTES

Fiddler & Associates
(contact Ken Fiddler)
50 Rue des Bagatelles
Montreal, QC H4S 9B3
Tel: (514) 487-2936
Fax: (514) 488-1500
E-mail: kfiddler@istar.ca
Terms: 3/30, n/60
Revenue account: 4100
Tax code: G - GST @ 5%
Credit limit: $70 000

☐

Maple Leaf Rags

No: 774

2642 Coldstream Avenue
Summerside, PE C1N 2X2

Date ☐2☐0☐1☐2☐0☐8☐1☐0
     Y Y Y Y M M D D

Pay to the order of   Amex $ 100.00

——— One hundred dollars ———   00 /100 **Dollars**

GT Gables Trust
3598 Anne Avenue
Summerside, PE C1N 1K1

Jaz Bands

⑄—⌐— 029 17643 ⑄ 988652 774

- -

Re: pay Amex bill for June 26-July 25 purchases

$100.00 **No: 774**
Aug. 10, 2012

☐ **Cash Receipt #130** **Dated Aug. 11/12**

From Fiddler & Associates, cheque #502 for $5 000 as down payment, deposit #15, to confirm sales order #FA-05.

☐ **Purchase Invoice #CA-7998** **Dated Aug. 12/12**

To Cars for All (use Quick Add for new supplier), $20 000 plus 5% GST and 10% PST for new automobile less $5 000 as a trade-in allowance on old car. Invoice total $17 325. The entry to write off the old car will be made by the accountant at year-end.

☐ **Purchase Invoice #ABO-8823** **Dated Aug. 13/12**

From A.B. Original Sounds, to fill purchase order #204, $50 000 plus 12% HST for CD masters. Invoice total $56 000. Terms: 1/10, n/30. (Balance owing is $46 000.)

⚠ **WARNING!**
Remember to change the payment method to Pay Later for invoices that fill purchase orders with prepayments.

SESSION DATE — AUGUST 31, 2012

☐ **Purchase Invoice #SD-9124**   **Dated Aug. 18/12**

From Super Dupers, to fill purchase order #205, $7 000 for duplicating CDs, labels and case inserts plus $8 000 for reprinting books plus 13% HST. Invoice total $16 950. Terms: 1/10, n/30. Terms: 1/10, n/30. (Balance owing is $12 950.)

☐ **Purchase Invoice #WI-3719**   **Dated Aug. 18/12**

From Wrap It, to fill purchase order #206, $6 300 plus 13% HST to prepare CDs for sale. Shipped by Canada Post (#75 553 789 249) for $120 plus 13% HST. Invoice total $7 254.60. Terms: 1/5, n/30. (Balance owing is $5 254.60.)

☐ **Memo #48**   **Dated Aug. 20/12**

From J. Bands: Owner invests $50 000 personal capital to finance production of new inventory. Amount deposited to Bank: Savings Account and credited to Common Stock.

☐ **Sales Invoice #599**   **Dated Aug. 21/12**

To Fiddler & Associates, to fill sales order #FA-05, $24 000 for CDs and $9 000 for books plus 5% GST — items purchased by major music store chains. Shipping charges $200 plus GST. Invoice total $34 860. Terms 3/30, n/60.

☐ **Cheque Copy #775**   **Dated Aug. 23/12**

To A.B. Original Sounds, $45 500 in full payment of account, including $500 discount for early payment. Reference invoice #ABO-8823 and prepayment by cheque #767.

☐ **Cheque Copy #776**   **Dated Aug. 23/12**

To Wrap It, $5 190.40 in full payment of account, including $64.20 discount for early payment. Reference invoice #WI-3719 and prepayment by cheque #769.

☐ **Cheque Copy #777**   **Dated Aug. 23/12**

To Super Dupers, $12 780.50 in full payment of account, with the $169.50 discount for early payment. Reference invoice #SD-9124 and prepayment by cheque #768.

☐ **Memo #49**   **Dated Aug. 23/12**

From J. Bands: Transfer $60 000 CAD from Bank: Savings Account to Bank: Chequing Account to cover cheques because the chequing account is overdrawn.

☐ **Purchase Invoice #JH-0875**   **Dated Aug. 23/12**

To J. Henry & Associates (use Quick Add), $1 500 plus $75 GST for legal fees to recover money owed by Entertainment House. Invoice total $1 575. Terms: net 30. Create new Group account 5240 Legal Fees.

☐ **Visa Purchase Invoice #PC-49986**   **Dated Aug. 30/12**

From Petro-Canada, $50 plus 5% GST and 10% PST for gasoline for business use. Invoice total $57.75 paid by Visa.

SESSION DATE — SEPTEMBER 15, 2012

☐ **Memo #50**   **Dated Sep. 2/12**

When his Visa bill arrived, Bands realized that he had entered the purchase from Cars for All as a Pay Later invoice instead of a Visa payment. Adjust invoice #CA-7998 from Cars for All. Change the method of payment to Visa.

NOTES
When you advance the session date to Aug. 31, you should see an Advisor message that it is time to prepare for year-end. Read and then close the advisory statement to proceed.

NOTES
Close the Advisor warnings about the overdrawn chequing account. The funds transfer in memo #49 will cover the cheques.

NOTES
If you do not change the date for the purchase invoice adjustment, you will see a warning that the transaction date precedes the session date because the transaction was dated in a previous month. Click Yes to proceed.

☐ **Cheque Copy #778**   **Dated Sep. 2/12**

To Visa, $17 382.75 in payment of account for purchases from July 16 to August 15, 2012.

☐ **Sales Invoice #600**   **Dated Sep. 5/12**

To Canadian Sounds, $4 500 USD for CDs and $750 for books. Shipped by Federal Express (#F36FYT863) for $170. Invoice total $5 420 USD. Terms 3/30, n/60. The exchange rate is 1.076.

☐ **Cash Receipt #131**   **Dated Sep. 5/12**

From Total Music, cheque #2491 for $4 631 in payment of account including $126.30 discount taken for early payment. Reference invoice #598. Deposit to Bank: Chequing Account.

☐

Maple Leaf Rags		
www.mapleleafrags.com		

2642 Coldstream Avenue
Summerside, PE C1N 2X2
Tel 1: (902) 63M-USIC
Tel 2: (888) 63M-USIC   Fax: (902) 633-4888
GST # 128 488 632

I N V O I C E

Sales Invoice:	#601
Date:	September 10, 2012
Customer:	Music Music Music
Address:	10 Red Rock Canyon
	Sedona, Arizona 86336 USA
Phone No:	(520) 678-4523
Fax No:	
Contact:	M. Porter

Item description	Amount
150 CDs	1 500.00 USD
25 Books	750.00 USD
Freight	140.00 USD
GST	—
PST	—
HST	—
Invoice Total	2 390.00 USD

Shipped by: Federal Express

Payment: 3/30, n/60
Exchange rate for Sep 10 was 1.078 — *JB*

Sold by: *Jaz Bands*

SESSION DATE — SEPTEMBER 29, 2012

☐ **Cash Receipt #132**   **Dated Sep. 18/12**

From Fiddler & Associates, cheque #574 for $28 864 in payment of account including $996 discount taken for early payment. Reference invoice #599 and deposit #15. Deposit to Bank: Chequing Account.

☐ **Visa Purchase Invoice #PC-59128**   **Dated Sep. 29/12**

From Petro-Canada, $50 plus 5% GST and 10% PST for gasoline for business use. Invoice total $57.75 paid by Visa.

NOTES

When you advance the session date to Sep. 29, you may see an Advisor message about the year-end adjustments required. Read and then close the advisory statement to proceed.

Maple Leaf Rags

www.mapleleafrags.com

2642 Coldstream Avenue
Summerside, PE C1N 2X2
Tel 1: (902) 63M-USIC
Tel 2: (888) 63M-USIC   Fax: (902) 633-4888
GST # 128 488 632

Sales Invoice: #602
Date: September 29, 2012

Customer: Web Store customers
Address:

Phone No:
Fax No:
Contact:

I N V O I C E

Description	Amount
Sales summary for 3 months	
CDs sold to PEI customers (add GST and PST)	400.00
CDs sold to BC province customers (add 12% HST)	300.00
CDs sold to customers in other HST provinces (add 13% HST)	1 600.00
CDs sold to customers in other GST provinces (add 5% GST)	1 100.00
Books sold in all provinces (add 5% GST)	1 800.00

	Amount
Freight (add GST)	450.00
GST	187.50
PST	42.00
HST	244.00
Invoice Total	6 123.50

Shipped by: Purolator

Payment: Visa
Direct deposit to Visa bank account *JB*

MasterCard Credit Card Sales Invoice #603   Dated Sep. 29/12

To various Web Store customers, for CDs sold during previous three months

CD sales to PEI customers	$1 200 plus 5% GST and 10% PST
CD sales to BC customers	1 400 plus 12% HST
CD sales to other HST customers	600 plus 13% HST
CD sales to other GST customers	600 plus 5% GST
Book sales	3 000 plus 5% GST
Shipping	590 plus 5% GST

Invoice total $8 031.50. Paid by MasterCard.

Cash Purchase Invoice #AT-9810   Dated Sep. 29/12

From Atlantic Tel, $180 plus 5% GST and 10% PST for telephone services for two months. Invoice total $207.90. Terms: payment on receipt of invoice. Paid by cheque #779.

Cash Purchase Invoice #PE-62331   Dated Sep. 29/12

From Purolator, $1 200 plus 5% GST for shipping services. Invoice total $1 260. Terms: payment on receipt of invoice. Paid by cheque #780.

Cash Purchase Invoice #FE-46678   Dated Sep. 29/12

From Federal Express, $2 100 plus 5% GST for shipping services. Invoice total $2 205. Terms: payment on receipt of invoice. Paid by cheque #781.

SESSION DATE — SEPTEMBER 30, 2012

☐ **Memo #51**   **Dated Sep. 30/12**

From J. Bands: Refer to the Sep. 30 General Ledger balance to remit PST Payable to the Minister of Finance. Reduce the $262.50 payment by $7.88, the sales tax compensation of 3.0% of the balance owing. Issue cheque #782 for $254.62 from Bank: Chequing Account.

☐ **Memo #52**   **Dated Sep. 30/12**

From J. Bands: Prepare for closing the books by completing adjusting entries for prepaid expenses and supplies used:

Office Supplies	$ 280
Prepaid Internet Expenses (3 months)	135
Prepaid Rent (3 months of 6)	2 400
Prepaid Advertising (2 months of 5)	663

☐ **Memo #53**   **Dated Sep. 30/12**

From J. Bands: Complete an adjusting entry for goods sold during the quarter
CDs $36 500   (Debit Cost of CDs Sold and credit CD Inventory)
Books $12 600   (Debit Cost of Books Sold and credit Book Inventory)

☐ **Memo #54**   **Dated Sep. 30/12**

From J. Bands: Complete an adjusting entry to transfer $68 564 in completed CDs from production and assembly to CDs inventory. Debit CD Inventory and credit CD Assembly Materials Costs.

☐ **Memo #55**   **Dated Sep. 30/12**

From J. Bands: Received debit memo from Western Trust regarding pre-authorized withdrawals from Bank: Chequing Account for quarterly interest payments on loans. Complete adjusting entries for interest paid during the quarter:

On bank loan	$ 200
On long term loan	4 000

☐ **Memo #56**   **Dated Sep. 30/12**

From J. Bands: The following transfers of funds were completed.
$15 000 from Bank: Chequing Account to Bank: Savings Account
$12 000 from Bank: Visa to Bank: Savings Account
$12 000 from Bank: MasterCard to Bank: Savings Account

☐ **Memo #57**   **Dated Sep. 30/12**

From J. Bands: Record Interest Revenue as follows:

Bank: Savings Account	$300
Bank: Chequing Account	70

☑ **Memo #58**   **Dated Sep. 30/12**

490 From J. Bands: Create an Accountant's Copy of the data files so the accountant can review the accounting entries and add the final adjustments for depreciation and the trade-in on the automobiles.

☑ **Memo #59**   **Dated Sep. 30/12**

491 From J. Bands: Review the year-end checklists. Print all reports for the fiscal period ended. Back up the data files. Check data integrity. Advance the session date to October 1, the first day of the next fiscal period.

☑ **Memo #60**   **Dated Oct. 1/12**

492 From J. Bands: Import the adjusting entries completed by the accountant.

NOTES
Bands pays only interest on the loans. Both amounts are deducted from the Bank: Chequing Account.

NOTES
To use the Transfer Funds Journal for the first transfer, you must enter the transfer from each account as a separate transaction. To complete the funds transfer entry as a single journal entry, you must use the General Journal.

KEYSTROKES

Opening Data Files

Open **SimData10\Maple\maple** to access the data files.

Enter **July 15, 2012** as the session date for this application.

Click **OK** and then **click OK** to bypass the session date warning.

Session dates are advanced two weeks at a time for Maple Leaf Rags, and the backup frequency is set at two-week intervals. The Receivables Home window opens.

Tracking Sales

Businesses that ship goods to customers usually have accounts set up with shipping companies so they can track shipments.

Click the **Sales Invoices icon** 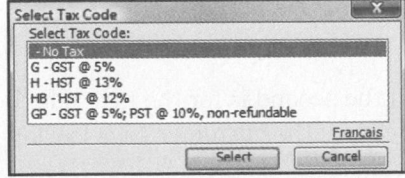 to open the Sales Journal.

Choose Web Store Customers from the Customer list. Leave the transaction type as Invoice.

Web store purchases are usually paid by credit card.

Click the **Paid By list arrow**:

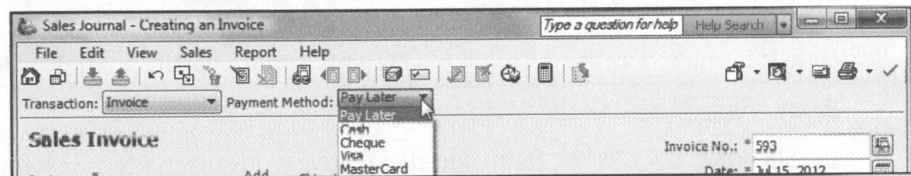

Internet customers have been set up without discounts so the discount fields are blank. Two credit cards are set up for the methods of payment accepted.

Click **Visa** as the method of payment.

Type July 2 12 (as the transaction date).

Click the **Item Description field** and **type** CD sales - PEI

Click the **Amount field** and **type** 500

Press (tab) to advance to the Tax field and **press** (enter) to see the tax codes:

```
Select Tax Code                        x
  Select Tax Code:
  - No Tax
  G - GST @ 5%
  H - HST @ 13%
  HB - HST @ 12%
  GP - GST @ 5%; PST @ 10%, non-refundable
                              Francais
        Select          Cancel
```

We have created tax codes to accommodate interprovincial sales to customers who pay HST (**code H** or **HB** for BC customers) and to customers in other provinces who do not pay PST or HST (**code G**). The first sale is to PEI customers, so the **code GP** is used — the GST rate is 5 percent and the PST rate is 10 percent (on the sales price plus GST).

Click **GP - GST @ 5%, PST @ 10%, non-refundable**.

Click **Select** to return to the sales invoice and advance to the Account field. Account 4100 is correctly entered as the default revenue account.

PRO VERSION
pro Restore the backup file SimData10\maple1.CAB to SimData10\Maple\maple.SAI. Refer to Chapter 1, page 20, if you need assistance with restoring backup files.

NOTES
Payroll, Inventory and Project do not appear in the Modules pane list because these ledgers are not set up.

NOTES
Remember that you need to add the year when you type the date in the Sales Journal.

NOTES
We have used the tax name PST for provincial sales tax in PEI and PO for the provincial sales tax in other provinces. Two additional codes apply only to purchases — TM for Manitoba (GST @ 5%, PO @ 7%) and TS for Saskatchewan (GST@5%, PO @5%).

Goods and services consumed in a province are subject to the PST for that province. Goods shipped to other provinces are exempt from the PST, but not from HST.

Click the **Item Description field** on the second invoice line.

Type CD sales - BC

Click the **Amount field** and **type** 700 **Press** (tab).

The tax code GP is entered as the default from the previous invoice line. PST is charged only to PEI customers. Customers in BC pay 12 percent HST, so code HB is needed.

Press (enter) or **click** the **List icon** to see the Tax Code list.

Double click HB - HST @ 12% to add the code and advance to the Account field. The default account is entered only for the first invoice line.

Type 4100 **Click** the **Item Description field** on the next invoice line.

Type CD sales to other provinces - HST

Click the **Amount field** and **type** 2400 **Press** (tab).

Tax code HB is now entered as the default from the previous line. The HST rate at 13 percent applies to these sales.

Press (enter) or **click** the **List icon** to see the Tax Code list.

Double click H - HST @ 13% to add the code and advance to the Account field.

Type 4100 **Click** the **Item Description field** on the next invoice line.

Type CD sales to other provinces - GST

Click the **Amount field** and **type** 900 **Press** (tab).

Tax code H is entered as the default, but GST at 5 percent applies to these sales.

Press (enter) or **click** the **List icon** to see the Tax Code list.

Double click G - GST @ 5% to add the code and advance to the Account field.

Type 4100 **Click** the **Item Description field** on the next invoice line.

Type Book sales

Click the **Amount field** and **type** 3000 **Press** (tab).

Tax code G, the new default, is correct for the sale of books in all provinces.

Click the Account field. **Type** 4140

There are two freight fields in the Sales Journal, directly below the subtotal amount:

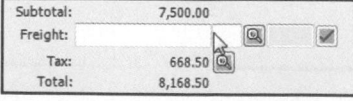

The first field is for the freight amount and the second is for the tax code. Because taxes are paid on freight you must enter a tax code if the customer pays freight. In Prince Edward Island, only GST applies to freight.

Click the **first Freight field**.

Type 680 **Press** (tab) to advance to the tax code field for Freight.

Code G is required and is correct from the previous invoice line. The tax amount is calculated as soon as you enter the amount of freight charged and the tax code. This amount is added to the Tax total.

We will now enter the shipping information so that the shipments can be traced if they are not delivered within the expected time. To track a shipment, you must have the tracking number for the package. To arrange for tracking shipments online, a business must have an account with the shipper and a PIN (personal identification number) to access the account. When an invoice for these shipments is received from the shipper, it will be entered as a purchase to record the expense to Maple Leaf Rags.

NOTES
Pressing (ctrl) + K will also open the Track Shipments screen from the journal.

Click   the **Track Shipments tool** or **choose** the **Sales menu** and **click Track Shipments** to open the shipping data entry window:

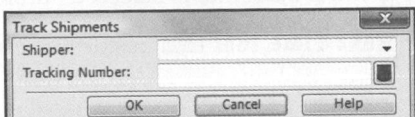

Click   the **Shipper field list arrow** to see the list of shippers:

Click   **Purolator**.

Press   (tab) to advance to the Tracking Number field.

Type   PCU773XT

Click   **OK** to return to the completed invoice. The tracking details do not appear on the invoice form.

All taxes are combined on the invoice as a single entry in the Tax field. To see the breakdown of individual taxes paid by the customer,

Click   the **List icon** beside the Tax field to see the detailed list:

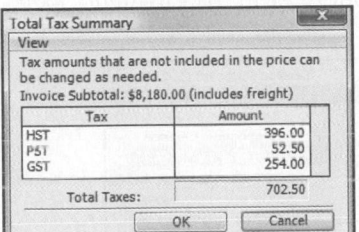

NOTES
Tax amounts may be incorrect because rounded off amounts are added together. If the tax is calculated for each line, the total may be different from the tax calculated on a single subtotal amount.

Individual amounts are shown for the three taxes applied to the sale. You can edit these tax amounts if they are incorrect.

Click   **OK** to return to the Sales Journal.

Before posting the entry, you should review it.

Choose the **Report menu** and **click Display Sales Journal Entry**:

Maple Leaf Rags Inc.			
Sales Journal Entry 07/02/12 (J1)			
Account Number	Account Description	Debits	Credits
1060	Bank: Visa	8,571.61	-
5150	Bank Charges & Card Fees	310.89	-
2460	PST Payable	-	52.50
2650	GST Charged on Sales	-	254.00
2660	HST Charged on Sales	-	396.00
4100	Revenue from CD Sales	-	4,500.00
4140	Revenue from Book Sales	-	3,000.00
4200	Freight Revenue	-	680.00
Additional Date:	Additional Field:	8,882.50	8,882.50

Several linked accounts are used for this transaction. The credit card account — *Bank: Visa* — is debited for the total invoice amount minus the transaction discount fees withheld by the credit card company. These fees are debited to the linked fees expense account — *Bank Charges & Card Fees*. Both the *GST* and *HST Charged on Sales* accounts are credited to show the increase in the tax liability to the Receiver General. PST collected from customers is credited to the *PST Payable* account to show the increased liability to the Minister of Finance for PEI. Freight charged to customers is credited automatically to the linked *Freight Revenue* account.

Close   the **display** to return to the Sales Journal input screen. **Make corrections** if necessary, referring to page 170 for assistance.

Click   **Store** 📥 and **choose Random** as the frequency. **Add Visa** to the description.

The next two transactions are also summary sales to Web Store customers. We can choose to use the same customer next time so that the customer is selected automatically.

Click   the **Use The Same Customer Next Time tool** 📌 beside the customer name.

The Use The Same Customer Next Time tool 📌 has changed shape to indicate it is selected. Clicking the tool again will turn off the selection.

Click   the **Post button** [Post ▾]. We will not include the reminder to click OK each time you see the successful posting message.

Enter   the next credit card **sale** and the Visa car rental **purchase**. **Change modules** as needed or **create** the **shortcuts** required to complete transactions. You will need shortcuts to enter purchases, payments and General Journal transactions.

Entering Credit Card Bill Payments

Click   **Payables** in the Modules pane to open this Home window, if necessary.

Credit card payments are entered in the Payments Journal. You can access the bill payment window from the Pay Credit Card Bills shortcut in the Payments icon drop-down shortcuts list as shown:

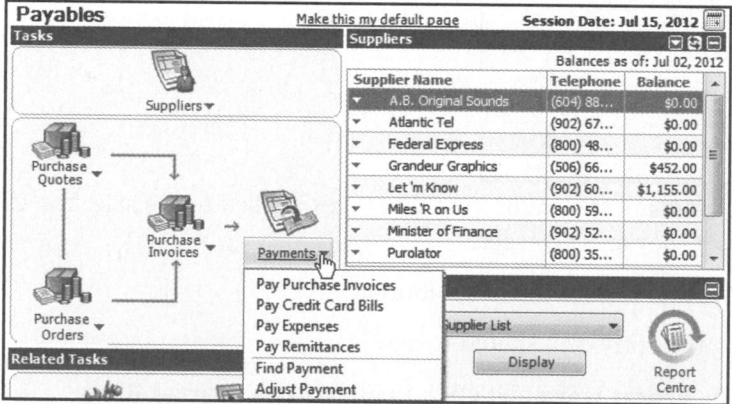

Click   **Pay Credit Card Bills** in the Payments icon shortcuts list:

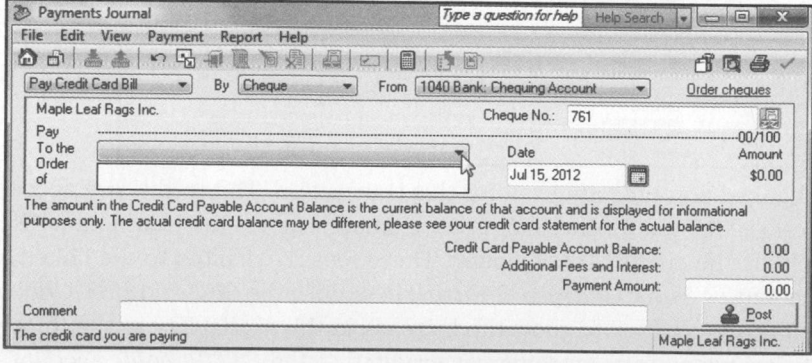

Pay Credit Card Bill is selected as the transaction type in the Pay field. The Pay list in the journal allows you to choose between paying suppliers, paying credit card bills, making cash purchases (other payments) and making payroll remittances. You can make these choices from the Pay field drop-down list.

To access the form you need, you can also click the Payments icon and select Pay Credit Card Bill from the transaction (Pay) drop-down list as shown:

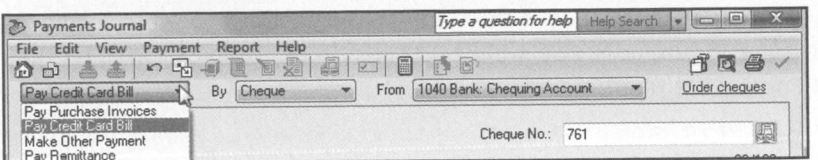

The **By** field (method of payment) has the same options as other journals — payment by cash, cheque or any of the credit cards set up. The **From** field allows you to select a bank account from which to pay because more than one bank account is defined as a Bank class account. The default payment is by cheque. The bank account and the cheque number — the next one in the sequence for this account — are correct. The From list has three bank accounts. The default account is correct for this payment.

> **Click** the **To The Order Of field list arrow** to access the list of credit cards Maple Leaf Rags has set up for purchases:

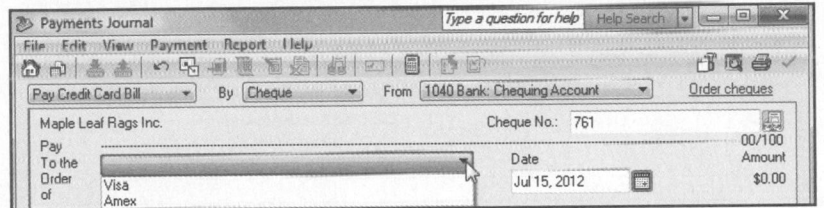

Credit card accounts are set up for Visa and Amex (American Express).

> **Click** **Visa** to update the journal with the Visa account information:

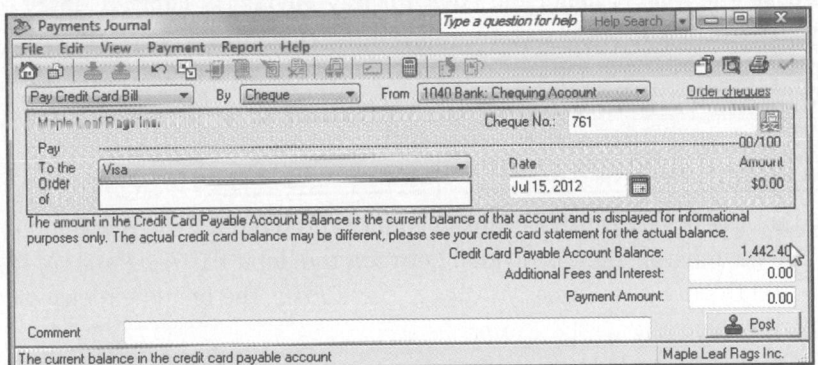

The Account Balance shows the accumulation of all unpaid purchases to date according to the General Ledger *Visa Payable* account balance. This amount is not usually the same as the balance that appears on the credit card statement. Purchases after the statement date will not appear on the statement, and interest charges or renewal fees are not included in the General Ledger account balance.

> **Drag through** the **date in the Date field**.
>
> **Type** Jul 2
>
> **Click** the **Additional Fees And Interest field**.

This field is used to record interest charges on previous unpaid amounts as well as other fees associated with the use of the card. These amounts usually appear on the statement. You must add these amounts together and enter the total in the Additional Fees And Interest field. Maple Leaf Rags owes $105 for the annual card renewal fee and $9.50 in accumulated interest for a total of $114.50.

NOTES
When a partial payment is made to a credit card bill, the payment is applied first to interest and additional fees before reducing the outstanding balance from current purchases.

Type   114.50 **Press** (tab) to advance to the Payment Amount field.

In this field you should enter the total amount of the cheque that is written in payment, including interest, fees and purchases. This will match the balance owing on the statement if the full amount is being paid, or some other amount if this is a partial payment. The remaining balance in the General Ledger *Visa Payable* account reflects current charges or purchases that will be included in the balance owing on the next statement and paid at that time.

Type   723.50

Press   (tab) to update the journal and complete the cheque amount in the upper portion of the journal.

You can add a comment to the journal entry in the Comment field.

The journal is now complete and should look like the following:

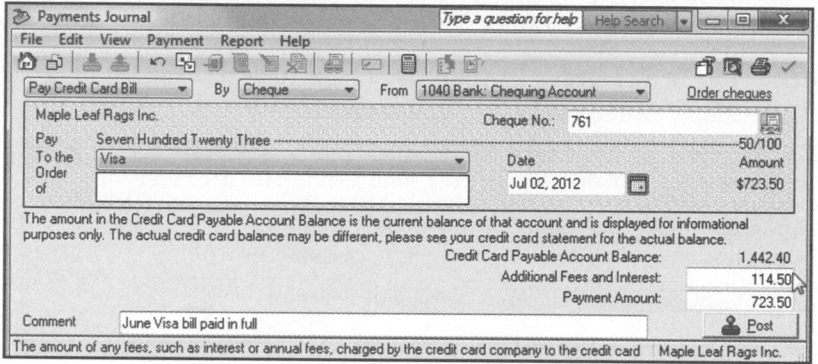

You should review the journal entry before proceeding.

Choose the **Report menu** and **click Display Payments Journal Entry** to display the transaction:

Maple Leaf Rags Inc. Payments Journal Entry 07/02/12 (J4)			
Account Number	Account Description	Debits	Credits
2260	Visa Payable	609.00	-
5150	Bank Charges & Card Fees	114.50	-
1040	Bank: Chequing Account	-	723.50
Additional Date:	Additional Field:	723.50	723.50

Notice that the linked Payables bank account is credited for the full amount of the payment. The payment amount is divided between the debit to *Visa Payable* to reduce the liability and the debit to *Bank Charges & Card Fees*, the linked expense account for credit card expenses.

Close the **display** when you have finished reviewing it to return to the Payments Journal.

NOTES
Remember that you will click OK after posting because transaction confirmation is activated.

Make **corrections** by reselecting from a drop-down list or by highlighting an incorrect entry and typing the correct amount. Press (tab) after changing an amount to update the totals.

Click the **Post button** [Post]. A message appears about the cheque number:

NOTES
This message appears only for credit card bill payments.

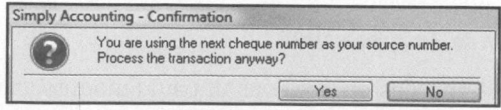

Click **Yes** to continue processing the payment.

Close the **Payments Journal** to return to the Payables window.

Accessing a Supplier's Web Site

Before making the GST remittance, we will search the Canada Revenue Agency Web site to see whether there are any recent tax changes that affect this business.

There are a number of ways to access a supplier record. Because the principles are the same for finding records in all ledgers, we will illustrate different methods.

> **Click**   **Receiver General** in the Suppliers pane list in the Payables module window to open the record directly. **Close** the **ledger record**.

You can type text in the Search field or use the Search tool (or Search menu option).

> **Click**   the **Quick Search field** in the upper-right section of the Home window.

> **Type**   `rec` and **click** ⟶ (click the arrow, not the Search tool):

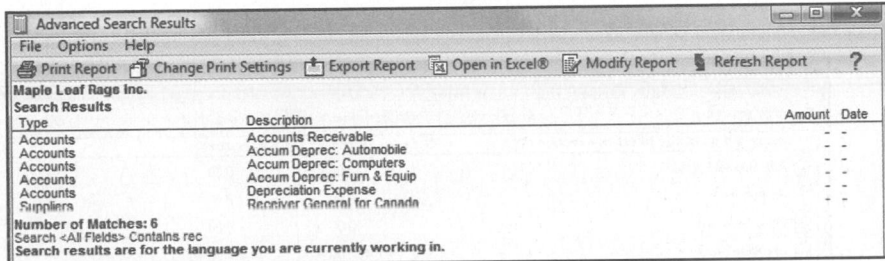

Several account names include this text as well as the supplier record we want.

> **Double click** the supplier **Receiver General for Canada** to open the record. **Close** the **ledger record** and **Search window**.

> **Click**   the **Search tool** 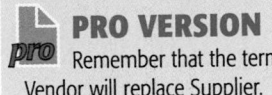, or **choose** the **Edit menu** and **click Search** or **press** ⟨ctrl⟩ + **F** to begin:

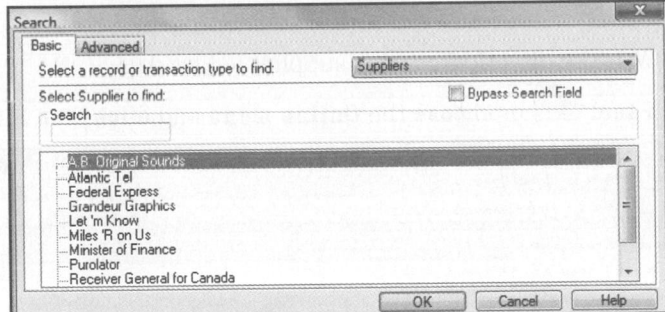

The Search window opens. The default list depends on your starting point. In any Search window, you can select the search area from the Select A Record Or Transaction Type To Find drop-down list as shown:

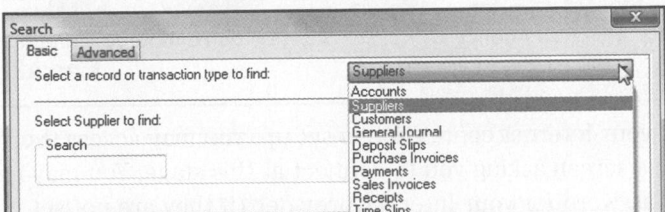

Clicking Suppliers will display the list of suppliers. Click the Search field and type R to advance to that part of the list. Receiver General for Canada will be selected because it is the first record beginning with R.

> **Double click** **Receiver General** to open the record. **Close** the **ledger record**.

Another option is to start from the Suppliers icon shortcuts list.

Choose **Modify Supplier** from the Suppliers (Payables window) drop-down shortcuts list to open the Search window:

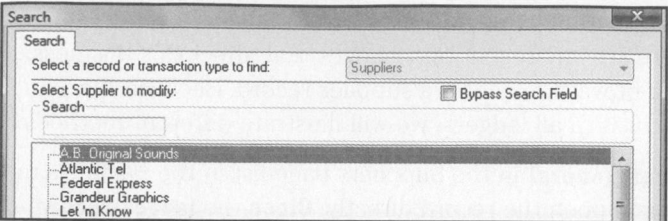

This Search screen looks the same, but Select Supplier To **Modify** replaces Find.

Double click **Receiver General** to open the record. **Close** the **ledger record**.

You can also access the record from the Suppliers window.

Click   the **Suppliers icon** to open the Suppliers window:

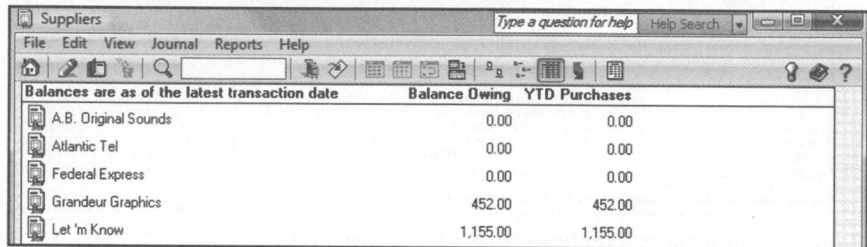

All suppliers are listed with their balances and total year-to-date purchases.

Double click **Receiver General for Canada** to open the supplier's ledger:

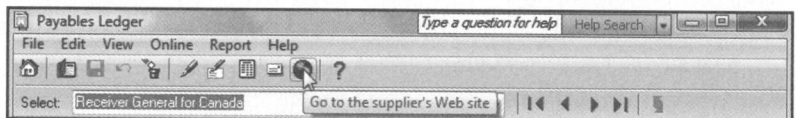

You can access the Web site directly from this supplier ledger page.

Click   the **Web tool** or **choose** the **Online menu** and **click Web Site**:

Depending on how your Internet connection is set up, you may access the Web site directly or you may see a screen asking you to connect at this stage. You may need to enter the user ID and password for your Internet provider (if they are not set up to be saved and allow automatic connection). Again, your setup may be different.

You should see the home page for the Canada Revenue Agency.

Choose your language preference.

Click   the **Forms And Publications** option.

Click   the **Listed By Document Type** option.

You should see a list of types of publications. Several types of GST publications are listed. Select one to list the items for that type.

You can also click Search, enter "GST publications" in the Search For field and click the Search button.

Close your **Internet connection** when you have found the information you need or when you have finished. You will return to the supplier's ledger.

Close the **Ledger window**. **Close** the **Suppliers window** if it is open.

Tax Remittances

Tax remittances are entered in the Purchases Journal as non-taxable purchase invoices with payment by cheque, or as Other Payments in the Payments Journal. There are two parts to a GST remittance — accounting for the GST (and HST) collected from customers and accounting for the GST (and HST) paid for purchases. The first is owed to the Receiver General while the second part — the input tax credit — is refunded or used to reduce the amount owing. Refer to Chapter 2 for further details. The GST Report can be used to help prepare the GST return, but the ledger account balances for the date of the filing period should be used as a final check in case there are opening balance amounts that were not entered in the journals. For Maple Leaf Rags, the opening or historical balance is needed. These amounts were not entered through journal transactions so we cannot use the GST or the PST Report.

PST remittances also have two parts — accounting for the PST collected from customers and reducing the tax remitted by the sales tax compensation for filing the return on time. Again, you can refer to the PST Report to help you.

Display or **print** the **General Ledger Report** for the following tax accounts for June 30, 2012, to see the amounts you must enter. (See page 57 if you need assistance.)

- 2460 PST Payable
- 2650 GST Charged on Sales
- 2660 HST Charged on Sales
- 2670 GST Paid on Purchases
- 2680 HST Paid on Purchases

The General Ledger balances you need are the GST and PST amounts in the Trial Balance on page 455. You can also display or print the Trial Balance or Balance Sheet for June 30 to see the amounts for the tax accounts.

Making GST Remittances

Choose **Pay Expenses** from the Payments icon shortcuts list.

Choose **Receiver General for Canada** as the supplier.

Choose **July 5** from the pop-up calendar as the transaction date.

Click the **Account field List icon** 🔍 to display the account list.

Choose **2650 GST Charged on Sales** to advance to the Description field.

Type Debiting GST Charged on Sales

Press ⟨tab⟩ to advance to the Amount field. **Type** 1450

No Tax is correctly selected as the default tax code.

NOTES
The Pay Remittances shortcut for the Payments icon is used only to remit payroll taxes.

NOTES
Tax amounts that you enter on the Sales Taxes screen in the General Journal are included in the tax reports.

CLASSIC VIEW
Click the Payments icon to open the journal and select Make Other Payment from the Pay drop-down list.

NOTES

If the Payments Journal is already open, choose Make Other Payment from the Pay transactions drop-down list.

NOTES

No default account was entered for the Receiver General because four different accounts are required.

Click   the **Account field List icon** 🔍 on the next journal line.

Choose 2660 HST Charged on Sales and advance to the Description field.

Type   Debiting HST Charged on Sales

Press (tab) to advance to the Amount field. **Type** 3634

Click   the **Account field List icon** 🔍 on the next journal line.

Choose 2670 GST Paid on Purchases. In the Description field,

Type   Crediting GST Paid

Press (tab) to advance to the Amount field.

Type   −500 (Use a **minus sign** or hyphen. The minus sign is necessary to create a credit for the liability account.)

Click   the **Account field List icon** 🔍 on the next journal line.

Choose 2680 HST Paid on Purchases. In the Description field,

Type   Crediting HST Paid

Press (tab) to advance to the Amount field.

Type   −1800

Click   the **Invoice/Ref. field**.

Type   Memo 44 **Press** (tab).

Type   Memo 44, GST/HST remittance for June

This completes your entry as shown here:

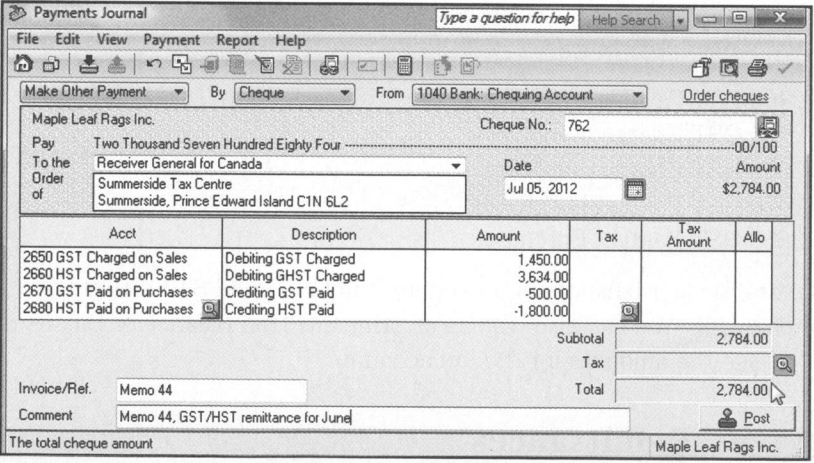

A review of the journal entry will help to clarify the transaction.

Choose the **Report menu** and **click Display Payments Journal Entry**:

Maple Leaf Rags Inc.
Payments Journal Entry 07/05/12 (J5)

Account Number	Account Description	Debits	Credits
2650	GST Charged on Sales	1,450.00	-
2660	HST Charged on Sales	3,634.00	-
1040	Bank: Chequing Account	-	2,784.00
2670	GST Paid on Purchases	-	500.00
2680	HST Paid on Purchases	-	1,800.00
Additional Date:	Additional Field:	5,084.00	5,084.00

Normally, a positive amount will create a debit entry in the Payments Journal for an expense or an asset purchase. *GST/HST Charged on Sales* are GST payable accounts with a credit balance. Therefore, entering a positive amount will reduce the GST payable balance by debiting the accounts, as we did for the GST and HST collected from customers. The negative entries or credits for the refundable *GST Paid on Purchases* and *HST Paid on Purchases* will offset the debit balance in the ledger for these contra-liability accounts and will reduce the total amount that is paid to the Receiver General. The net cheque amount is credited to the bank account.

Close the **display** window when you have finished. **Make corrections** if necessary.

Click Post 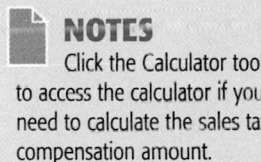. You are now ready to make the PST remittance.

Making PST Remittances

You should still be in the Payments Journal with Make Other Payment selected as the type of transaction.

Choose **Minister of Finance** as the supplier. Accept the default bank account.

Accept **July 5** as the date and **accept** the default **account**, *2460 PST Payable*.

Click the **Description field**.

Type Debiting PST Payable

Press (tab) to move the cursor to the Amount field. **Type** 450

You are now ready to enter the revenue from sales tax compensation, 3.0 percent of the *PST Payable* amount.

Click the **Account field List icon** 🔍 on the second journal line.

Choose **4280 Sales Tax Compensation**. The cursor advances to the Description field.

Type Sales Tax Compensation **Press** (tab).

Type -13.50 (Use a **minus sign**. The minus sign will reduce the total amount that is paid to the Minister of Finance.)

Click the **Invoice/Ref. number field.**

Type Memo 45 **Press** (tab) to advance to the Comment field.

Type Memo 45, PST remittance for June

Choose the **Report menu** and **click Display Payments Journal Entry**:

Maple Leaf Rags Inc.			
Payments Journal Entry 07/05/12 (J6)			
Account Number	Account Description	Debits	Credits
2460	PST Payable	450.00	-
1040	Bank: Chequing Account	-	436.50
4280	Sales Tax Compensation	-	13.50
Additional Date:	Additional Field:	450.00	450.00

The full *PST Payable* amount is debited to reduce the entire liability by crediting the bank account for the amount of the cheque and the *Sales Tax Compensation* revenue account for the amount of the tax reduction.

Close the **display** when you have finished. **Make corrections** if needed.

Click Post 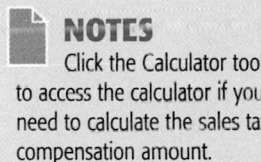. **Close** the **Payments Journal**.

NOTES
Click the Calculator tool to access the calculator if you need to calculate the sales tax compensation amount.

Entering Sales to Foreign Customers

Click   **Receivables** in the Modules pane list to open the Receivables window.

Click   the **Sales Invoices icon**  to open the Sales Journal. Invoice and Pay Later, the default selections, are correct.

Choose Canadian Sounds from the Customer drop-down list:

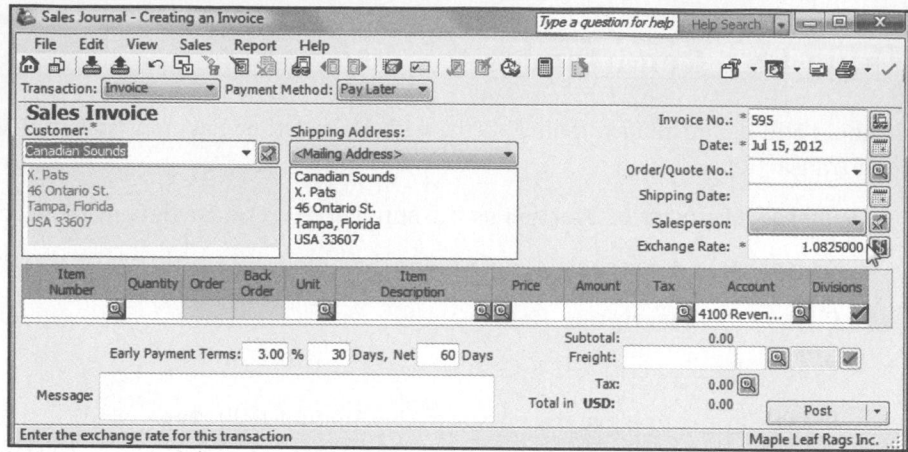

The invoice is modified for the foreign customer. A field for the exchange rate appears below the Date, and the Total is expressed in USD (United States dollars) rather than in Canadian dollars. An exchange rate button provides a list of exchange rates already entered for various dates. There is no rate for July 5.

Choose July 5 from the Date field calendar.

The Exchange Rate screen opens because the exchange rate on record is more than one day old and no rate has been recorded for this date:

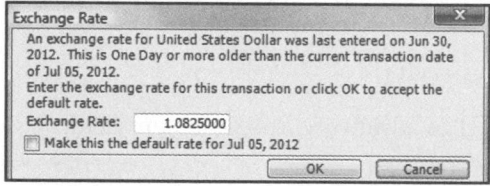

The Exchange Rate setting for the company file warns when the exchange rate on record is more than one day old so that an incorrect old rate is not accepted in error. The most recent exchange rate is entered and selected for editing. You can also edit the exchange rate directly in the journal screen just as you enter information in other fields.

Type   1.078

Click   **Make This The Default Rate For Jul 05, 2012**.

Click   **OK** to return to the Sales Journal.

Click   the **Item Description field**. **Type** CDs

Click   the **Amount field**. **Type** 2190   The default revenue account is correct.

Click   the **Item Description field** on the next invoice line. **Type** books

Click   the **Amount field**. **Type** 300

Click   the **Account field List icon** and **select** account **4140**.

Exported goods are not taxable because they are "consumed" outside of Canada. The No Tax code (blank) is entered as the default and it is correct.

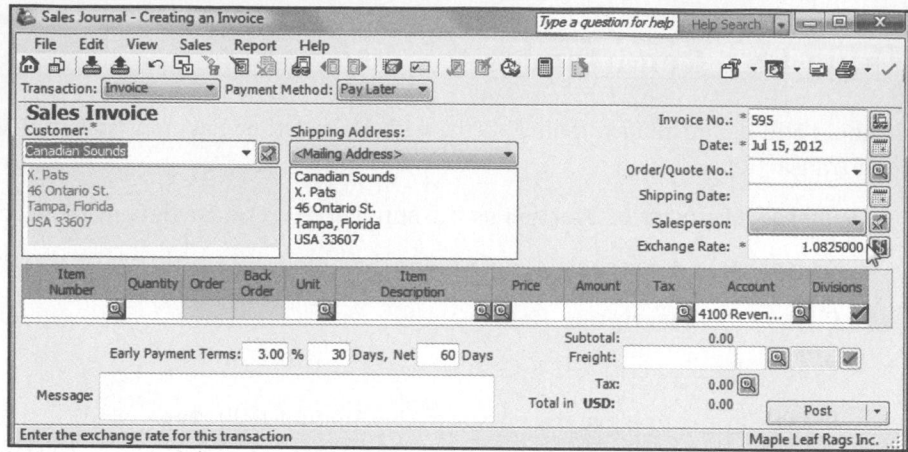

WARNING!
If you click the Date field before clicking the calendar, the Exchange Rate screen pops up with July 15 (the session date) as the date for which you are entering the rate. Then when you enter the transaction date, the Exchange Rate screen pops up again.

If you click the calendar first, the Exchange Rate screen will not open until after you choose the date.

Click   the **Freight field**.

Type   140 **Press** (tab) to update the amounts.

No taxes are applied to freight on exported goods.

Click   the **Track Shipments tool** 📧.

Choose **Federal Express** as the shipper from the Shipped By list.

Press   (tab) to advance to the Tracking Number field.

Type   F19YTR563

Click   **OK** to return to the Sales Journal.

Your completed journal entry, ready for review, should look like the one shown:

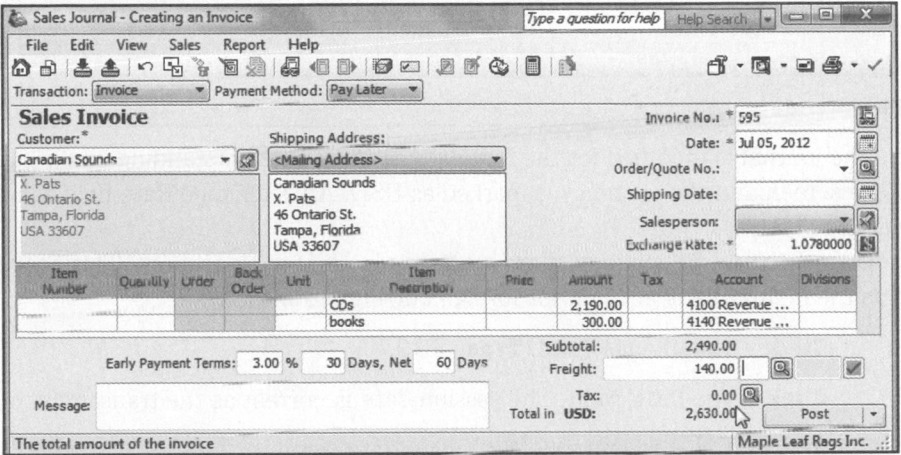

Choose the **Report menu** and **click Display Sales Journal Entry**:

Maple Leaf Rags Inc.				
Sales Journal Entry 07/06/12 (JT)				
Account Number	Account Description	Foreign Amount	Debits	Credits
1200	Accounts Receivable	US$2,630.00	2,835.14	-
4100	Revenue from CD Sales	US$2,190.00	-	2,360.82
4140	Revenue from Book Sales	US$300.00	-	323.40
4200	Freight Revenue	US$140.00	-	150.92
1 United States Dollar equals 1.0780000 Canadian Dollars			2,835.14	2,835.14

Although the journal itself shows the amounts only in US dollars, the journal entry has both the Canadian amounts and the US amounts as well as the exchange rate applied to the transaction. The remainder of the entry is the same as it would be for sales to Canadian customers.

Close   the **display** when finished and **make corrections** if necessary.

Click   Post [Post ▾] to save the transaction. **Close** the **Sales Journal**.

Enter   the **next group of transactions** up to the receipt from Canadian Sounds.

Entering Foreign Customer Receipts

Click   the **Receipts icon** to open the Receipts Journal.

Choose Canadian Sounds from the customer list:

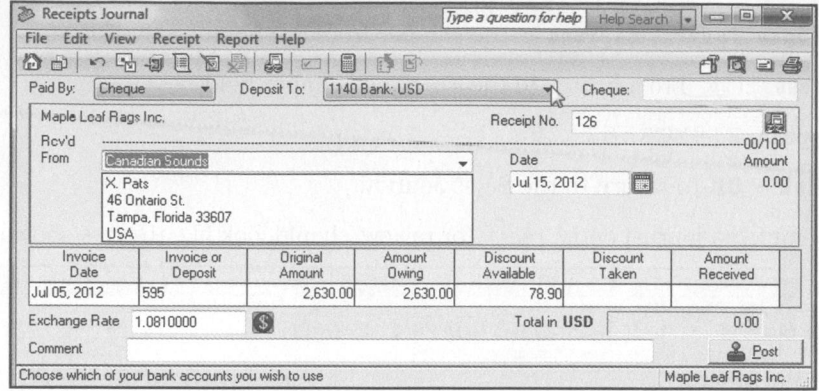

The journal is modified for the foreign customer. The outstanding invoice appears on the screen and the currency is marked as USD. An Exchange Rate field also becomes available.

Deposits from US customers are made to the USD bank account. This account is set up as the default bank account for foreign currency transactions.

Click   the **Cheque field**. **Type**   2397

Click   the **Date field**. The session date is correct as the transaction date.

Press   *tab*   to open the Exchange Rate screen.

If the rate has not changed, you can accept it by clicking Make This The Default Rate For Jul 15, 2012 and click OK.

Again, because the last exchange rate we entered was for July 10, the rate is out of date, and we must enter a new one. The previous rate is highlighted.

Type   1.082

Click   **Make This The Default Rate For Jul 15, 2012**.

Click   **OK** to return to the Receipts Journal. The cursor is on the calendar icon.

Click   the **Discount Taken field**.

Press   *tab*   to accept the discount because the full invoice is being paid. The cursor advances to the Amount Received field.

Press   *tab*   to accept the amount and update the cheque portion of the form.

Click   the **Enter Additional Information tool** ☑ .

The Total and cheque amount fields are updated in the background journal window.

Click   the **Additional Field text box** to move the cursor.

Type   Ref: inv #595

Click   **OK** to return to the completed journal entry:

Receipts Journal		Type a question for help	Help Search					

File Edit View Receipt Report Help

Paid By: Cheque   Deposit To: 1140 Bank: USD   Cheque: 2397

Maple Leaf Rags Inc.   Receipt No. 126

Rcv'd Two Thousand Five Hundred Fifty One ---------------------------------- 10/100

From Canadian Sounds   Date   Amount

X. Pats
46 Ontario St.
Tampa, Florida 33607
USA   Jul 15, 2012   2,551.10

Invoice Date	Invoice or Deposit	Original Amount	Amount Owing	Discount Available	Discount Taken	Amount Received
Jul 05, 2012	595	2,630.00	2,630.00	78.90	78.90	2,551.10

Exchange Rate 1.0820000   Total in **USD**   2,551.10

Comment   Post

Enter the exchange rate for this transaction   Maple Leaf Rags Inc.

You should review the journal entry.

Choose the **Report menu** and **click Display Receipts Journal Entry**:

Maple Leaf Rags Inc.
Receipts Journal Entry 07/15/12 (J12)

Account Number	Account Description	Foreign A...	Debits	Credits
1140	Bank: USD	US$2,551.10	2,760.29	-
4180	Sales Discounts	US$78.90	85.37	-
1200	Accounts Receivable	US$2,630.00	-	2,835.14
4300	Exchange Rate Differences		-	10.52
	1 United States Dollar equals 1.0820000 Canadian Dollars		2,845.66	2,845.66
Additional Date:	Additional Field: Ref: inv #595			

In addition to the usual linked accounts for receipts, an entry for *Exchange Rate Differences* appears. Because the exchange rate was lower on the day of the sale, the date the revenue was recorded, than on the day of the receipt, there has been a credit to the account. Maple Leaf Rags has gained money on the delay in payment — more Canadian dollars are received for the same US dollar amount than when the exchange rate is lower. When the rate decreases, there is a loss. As for foreign customer sales, amounts are given in both currencies along with the exchange rate.

Close   the **display** to return to the journal and **make corrections** if necessary.

Click   **Post**   Post   to save the transaction.

Close   the **Receipts Journal**.

Looking Up Invoices to Track Shipments

Lookup provides an exact copy of the posted invoice that you can store, print or e-mail if you have forgotten to do so before posting. This feature can be useful if a customer has an inquiry about a purchase or needs a copy of the invoice. Once a sales or purchase invoice is posted with details about the shipping company, you can look up the invoice to track the shipment to see when delivery is expected. You can use the Find Invoice approach or the Search feature (see Notes).

Choose **Find Invoice** from the Sales Invoices shortcuts list as shown:

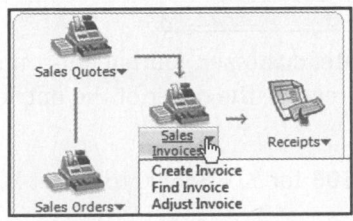

NOTES
The gain/loss situation is reversed for payments to foreign suppliers. When the rate increases, the purchased goods cost more and money is lost. A decrease in exchange rate creates a gain.

NOTES
You can also type Treble in the Search field and click —>.
The result will list the record for the customer and the sales invoice. Double click the sales invoice entry to open the Lookup screen for this transaction.
The Next and Previous tools will not be available because this sales invoice is the only one that meets the criterion.

You will open the Search dialogue window:

If the Sales Journal is open, you can click the Look Up An Invoice tool on the tool bar or beside the Invoice field, or choose the Sales menu and click Look Up Invoice, to open this Search window.

The Lookup screen options are like those for adjusting an invoice. You can search through all invoices for the fiscal year to date (or for the previous year if you have not cleared the transactions and lookup data) or enter a narrower range of dates; you can search through invoices for all customers or for a specific customer; or you can search for a specific invoice number. Your search strategy will depend on how much information you have before you begin the search and how many invoices there are altogether.

The default displayed Start date may be the start of the fiscal period, the calendar date or the date you created the company files. The Finish date is the most recent session date. You can change these dates to narrow the search, just as you would edit any other date fields, or you can choose dates from the drop-down list or calendar. We want to include all invoices in the search, beginning with the earliest transaction date in the data file.

Click   the **Start date. Type** 7 1 12

The Customer Name option allows you to Search All Customers, the default setting, or a specific customer's invoices. You can also look up the invoices for one-time customers.

To display the list of customers, click the Customer Name field or its drop-down list arrow and click the name you need to select a specific customer.

If you know the invoice number, enter it in the Invoice Number field and click OK.

In this case we will look at all invoices by choosing the default to Search All Customers.

Click   **OK** to display the list of invoices that meet the search conditions of date and customers:

You can sort the list by order of posting date, customer, journal entry number, invoice number and amount. You can also reverse the order of the entries in the list by clicking the **Z...A+** button.

Click   **Treble & Bass, Invoice Number 596** for $11 886.00 to select it. Click anywhere on the line.

Click   **Select** to display the requested invoice as follows:

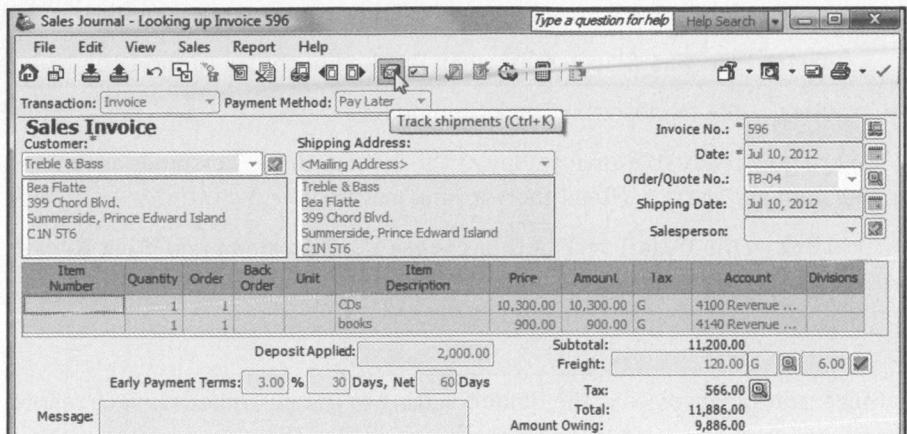

Notice that this is an exact copy of the original invoice, except that you cannot edit or post it. You can, however, store, e-mail or print it. Although you cannot adjust an invoice from the Lookup window directly, the Adjust Invoice tool is available. When you click Adjust Invoice, the journal screen changes to the Adjust Invoice form. You can use the Lookup method to locate the invoice you need to adjust. You can also reverse a transaction directly from the Lookup screen.

If you have selected the wrong invoice, or if you want to view other invoices from this one, you can access them from any Lookup window. If there are no invoices in one or both directions, the corresponding button or tools will be dimmed.

Click Look Up Next Invoice ⬛ or Look Up Previous Invoice ⬛ or choose Previous or Next Invoice from the Sales menu to display other invoices. You can browse through the invoices in this way until you find the one you need. You should practise viewing other invoices by clicking the Look Up Next and Previous Invoice tools.

Click   the **Track Shipments tool** ⬛ or **choose** the **Sales menu** and **click Track Shipments** to see the shipping details for the sale.

If you need to add or edit the shipping information, click Cancel to close the tracking details window. Click the Adjust Invoice tool in the journal and then Track Shipments.

Click   the Web icon ⬛ to close the shipping details screen and continue:

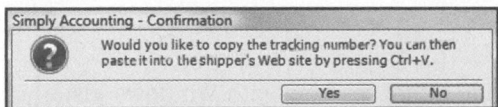

If you have set up a shipping account and have entered the actual number, you can choose Yes and save the number for entering on the Web site tracking page. However, we do not have an account with Purolator.

Click   **No** to continue to the Internet connection.

Your screen at this stage will depend on your Internet setup — you may connect and access the Web site directly, or you may need to enter your account and password first.

Continue as you would for your usual Internet connection.

You will access the Web site for Purolator.

WARNING!
You must have a valid form file reference in the Reports & Forms Settings for E-mail (Invoice forms). If you have used different computers for your data file, the default form reference may be incorrect. If you see an error message about an invalid form, close the e-mail message. In the Sales Journal, click the Change Form Options For Invoices tool. Choose the generic entry Invoices in the Description field for Invoices and for E-mail.

NOTES
The E-mail feature in Simply Accounting works best when Microsoft Outlook Express is set up as your default e-mail program.
If you are using a program other than Outlook Express as your default e-mail program, you may be asked to choose a profile and enter the settings before you can e-mail the invoice.
The free online billing program (Billing Boss) can also be used to send the invoice. Billing Boss is described in Appendix L on the Student DVD.

NOTES
When we tested the e-mail function again with Microsoft Outlook 2007, the Yes and No buttons were replaced with Allow and Deny. You should click Allow.

Enter   the **Tracking Number/PIN** in the Track Shipments pane, **click GO** and follow the instructions provided to continue tracking the shipment.

Close   the **Web Site screen** when finished to return to the Lookup screen.

Click   **OK** to close the Track Shipments screen.

We are now ready to e-mail a copy of the invoice to the customer as notice of the shipping date and carrier. (Read the Warning margin note.)

Click   the **E-mail tool** or **choose** the **File menu** and **click E-mail**.

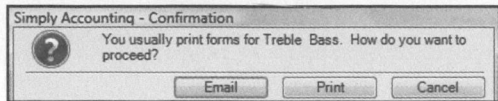

Since printing invoices is the default setting in the customer's ledger record, you are asked if you want to continue, just in case you clicked the wrong button.

Click   **E-mail** to continue to the E-mail Information screen:

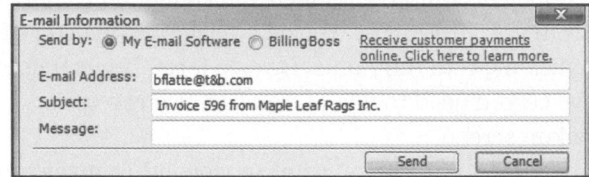

If there is no e-mail address in the ledger record, you can enter it here. You could also edit the default ledger record entry if needed. The E-mail Address field should be selected. You can replace it with your own address to test the e-mail feature.

Type   (Type your own e-mail address in this field, or that of a classmate.)

You can add a message in the Message field about the shipment tracking details to inform the customer of the expected delivery date.

Click   **Send**.

You will see another advisory screen asking whether you want to update the e-mail address in the ledger record.

Click   **Yes** to proceed.

At this stage, your screens will depend on your e-mail and Internet setups. You should be connected to your Internet provider. Depending on the e-mail program you are using, you may see a message that the program is trying to send a message:

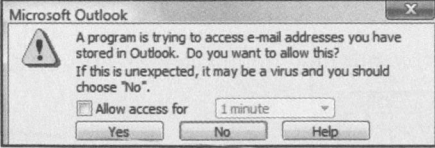

Click   **Yes**. You may see an additional warning with Windows Vista:

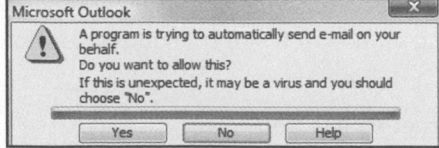

You may have to enter your ID and password before your e-mail program starts.

Close   your **e-mail** and **Internet connections** to return to the Sales Journal – Invoice Lookup window.

Close   the **Lookup window** to return to the Receivables window.

Looking Up and Tracking Purchases

You can look up purchase invoices in the same way as you look up sales invoices. You can look up purchase invoices from the Purchases Journal and from the Payments Journal.

> Open the Purchases or Payments Journal, click Look Up An Invoice , decide whether you want to restrict the search dates or suppliers and click OK. Choose an invoice from the displayed list and click Select. If you know the invoice number, you can enter it directly, and click OK to display the requested invoice.
>
> From the Payments Journal, choose Make Other Payment then click  (Look Up An Invoice) to see cash invoices posted in the Purchases Journal.

Once you look up a purchase invoice, you can track shipments and look up other invoices in the same way as you do for sales. You can also adjust the invoice. Tracking is not available for cash purchases entered as Other Payments in the Payments Journal.

NOTES
You can also look up Purchases Journal invoices from the Payments Journal, Pay Purchase Invoices screen.

Entering Purchases from Foreign Suppliers

Purchases from foreign suppliers are entered in much the same way as purchases from other suppliers. Once you choose a supplier who uses a different currency, the Purchases Journal changes to add the appropriate fields.

Advance the **session date** to July 31. **Back up** your data set.

Open the **Payables module window**.

Click the **Purchase Invoices icon** [Purchase Invoices ▾] to open the Purchases Journal. Invoice and Pay Later are correctly selected.

Click the **Supplier field**. **Type** Design Anything

WARNING!
You must choose Full Add for the new supplier so that you can choose USD as the currency.

Entering a Foreign Supplier Record

Click the **Add link** above the Supplier field to open the Payables Ledger supplier input screen.

Type the supplier address details from the source documents (page 460).

Enter **July 16** as the date for the Supplier Since field.

Click the **Options tab**. Notice the additional field for currency.

Choose 5360 CD Assembly Materials Costs as the default expense account.

Click the **Currency list arrow** as shown:

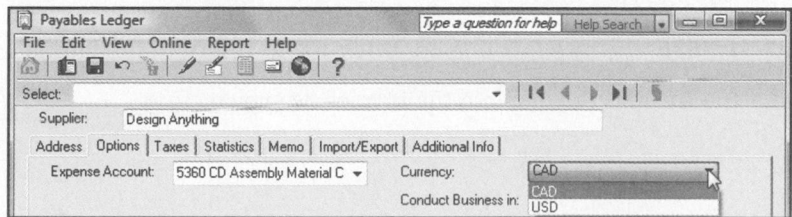

Choose USD. A Balance Owing in USD amount is added to the record.

Enter **net 30 days** as the payment terms.

Click the **Taxes tab** to see the default settings.

Click the **Tax Code list arrow** to see the options:

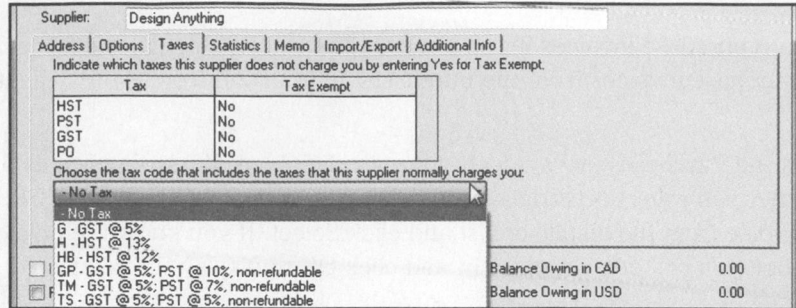

Maple Leaf Rags is not exempt from paying taxes on purchases from Design Anything, and that is the default selection. All tax codes will be available. Most purchases from US suppliers are subject to GST so we should choose G - GST @ 5% as the default tax code. Maple pays GST on imported goods.

Click Code **G - GST @ 5%**.

Click **Save And Close** to return to the modified invoice:

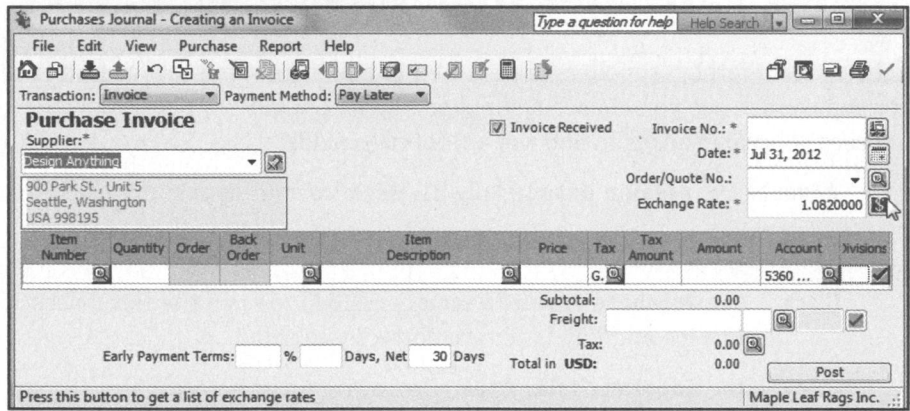

The invoice currency is now shown as USD and exchange rate fields are added. The default terms, expense account and tax code are also on the invoice.

Enter the **Invoice number** and **Date**. **Do not press** tab. If the Exchange Rate update screen opens, click Cancel.

Click the **Exchange Rate tool**, to open the list of rates we have already used so that we can choose from this list:

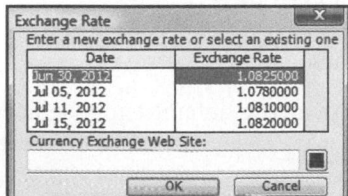

Click **1.0825**, the rate for June 30. **Click OK** to return to the journal.

Enter the **Amount** to complete the invoice as shown:

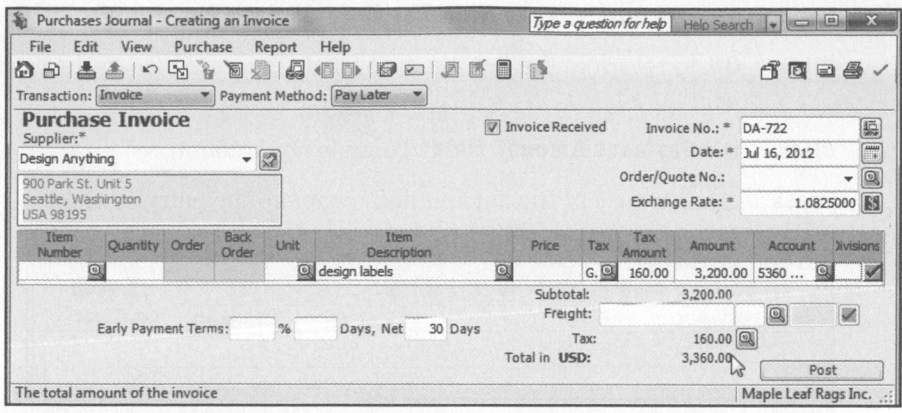

Choose the **Report menu** and **click Display Purchases Journal Entry** to review the entry:

Maple Leaf Rags Inc. Purchases Journal Entry 07/16/12 (J13)				
Account Number	Account Description	Foreign A...	Debits	Credits
2670	GST Paid on Purchases	US$160.00	173.20	-
5360	CD Assembly Material Costs	US$3,200.00	3,464.00	-
2200	Accounts Payable	US$3,360.00	-	3,637.20
1 United States Dollar equals 1.0825000 Canadian Dollars			3,637.20	3,637.20

The only difference between this and other purchase entries is the addition of the USD currency amounts and exchange rate.

Close the **display** to return to the journal and **make corrections** if necessary.

Click **Post** [Post] . **Close** the **Purchases Journal**.

Return to the source documents and **enter** the **next group of transactions**, until Cheque #284. **Change module windows** as needed or use your shortcuts.

Entering Payments to Foreign Suppliers

Click the **Payments icon** [Payments] or use the shortcut to open the Payments Journal.

Choose Design Anything from the Supplier list to modify the journal:

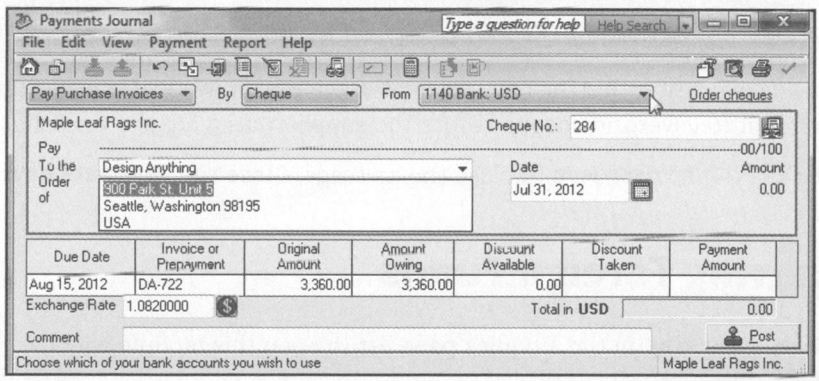

The outstanding invoice appears on the screen and the currency is marked as USD. An Exchange Rate field also becomes available.

Payments to US suppliers are made from the USD bank account. This account is set up as the default bank account for foreign currency transactions. The cheque number is the next in sequence for this account.

Click the **Calendar icon** [ ] and **choose July 30** as the transaction date.

The Exchange Rate screen should open automatically — the rate is out of date.

Type   1.084 **Click Make This The Default Rate For Jul 30, 2012**.

Click   **OK** to return to the Payments Journal. The cursor is on the calendar icon.

Click   the **Payment Amount field**. There is no discount.

Press   `tab` to accept the amount and complete the entry as shown:

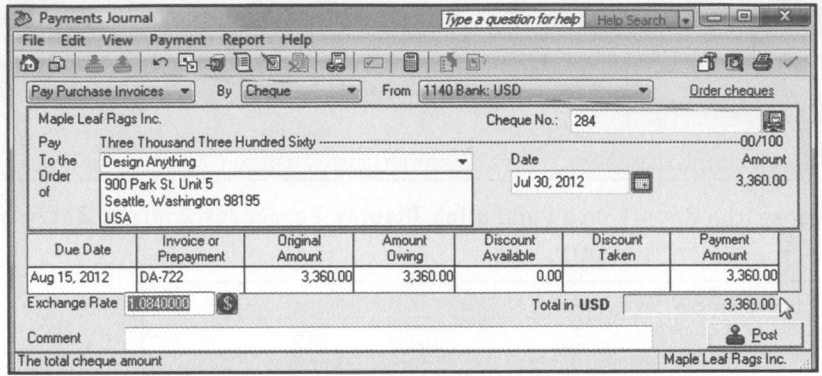

Press   `ctrl` + **J** so you can review the journal entry:

Account Number	Account Description	Foreign A...	Debits	Credits
2200	Accounts Payable	US$3,360.00	3,637.20	-
4300	Exchange Rate Differences		5.04	
1140	Bank: USD	US$3,360.00	-	3,642.24
1 United States Dollar equals 1.0840000 Canadian Dollars			3,642.24	3,642.24

A debit entry for *Exchange Rate Differences* appears because the exchange rate was lower on the day of the purchase, the date the purchase was recorded, than on the day of the payment. However, because this is a payment, Maple Leaf Rags has lost on the payment delay as shown by the debit entry for a revenue account — more Canadian dollars are needed to pay the same US dollar amount. As for other foreign currency transactions, amounts are given in both currencies, and the exchange rate is included.

Close   the **display** to return to the journal. **Make corrections** if necessary.

Click   **Post** [Post] to see this message:

Advisor: Your chequing account is overdrawn. See the Advice topic "Managing Your Cash Flow" for suggestions.
[Click here to close.]

The message indicates that the bank account is overdrawn. We will transfer funds to the USD account to cover the cheque before the supplier has a chance to cash it.

Click   the **Advisor icon** to close the message. **Close** the **Payments Journal**.

Transferring Foreign Funds

Click   **Banking** in the Modules pane list to open this module window:

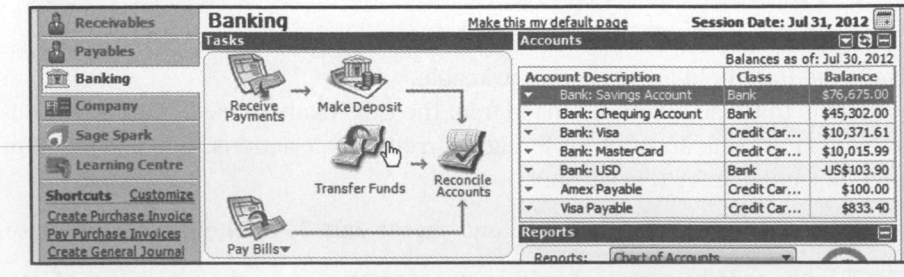

Transfer Funds

Classic **CLASSIC VIEW**
    The Transfer Funds Journal is not available in the Classic view.

The Banking module window has no ledger icons although it does allow direct access to the ledger records for all accounts involved in making or receiving payments (cash, bank and credit card class accounts). Three journal icons — Make Deposit, Transfer Funds, Reconcile Accounts — are for bank account transactions. The Receive Payments and Pay Bills icons open the Receipts and Payments journals and are duplicated from Receivables and Payables modules.

We use the Transfer Funds Journal to move money from one bank account to another.

Click   the **Transfer Funds icon** to open the journal we need:

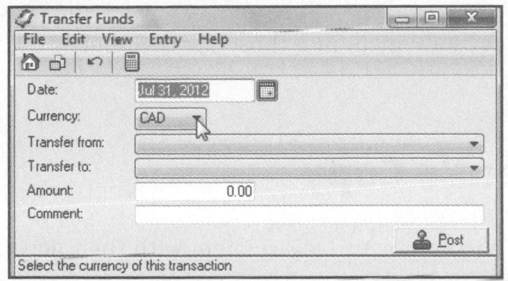

Type   July 30 (as the Date).

Click   the **Currency list arrow** to see the currency options as shown:

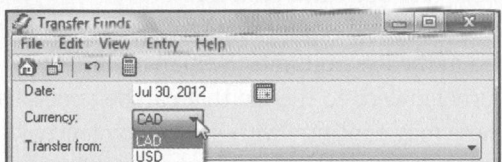

Both currencies are available for Transfer Funds transactions.

Click   **USD**. The exchange rate is entered correctly for this date.

Click   the **Transfer From list arrow** to see the list of available accounts:

Choose 1040 Bank: Chequing Account in the Account field. **Press** (tab).

Click   the **Transfer To list arrow** to see the same list of available accounts.

Choose 1140 Bank: USD and **press** (tab) to advance to the Amount field.

Type   1000 **Press** (tab) to advance to the comment field.

Type   Transfer funds to cover cheque to complete the entry:

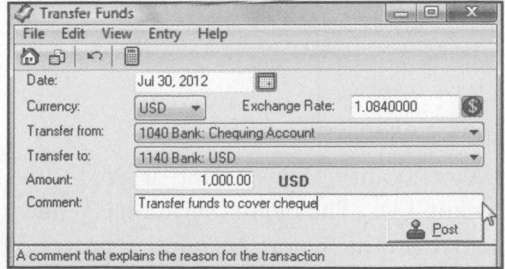

Check your transaction carefully. You cannot display the journal entry before posting. To make corrections after posting, adjust or reverse the transfer in the General Journal.

When you display the Journal Entries Report, the transfer is entered as a typical debit and credit entry, with the exchange rate added and amounts given in both currencies as for other foreign currency transactions.

Click   Post **Post** to save the transaction.

Close   the **Transfer Funds Journal**. The Baking Home window balances are updated.

Enter   the **remaining transactions**, including those for September 30, up to memo #58.

Creating an Accountant's Copy

Many businesses rely on professional accountants to assist them with their accounting. The accountants will check the data entered by the business for errors and make corrections. They also may add the adjusting entries required at the end of a fiscal period to bring the books up to date and to prepare for filing tax returns. The business then begins the new year with a complete and accurate data file.

Simply Accounting allows a data file to be saved as an accountant's copy. This backup data file can only be restored and opened in the Accountants' Edition of Simply Accounting. The accountant can add journal entries to the file that can be added back to the original business data file. The business may continue with day-to-day journal entry and even start a new fiscal period while the accountant is preparing the additional entries.

You can create an accountant's copy from the File menu or from the Company window Accountant's Tasks pane Accountant's Copy icon shortcuts.

Click   **Company** in the Modules pane list to open that module window.

Choose   the **File menu**, then **choose Accountant's Copy** and **click Create Accountant's Copy** or **choose Create Accountant's Copy** from the Accountant's Copy icon shortcuts drop-down list as shown:

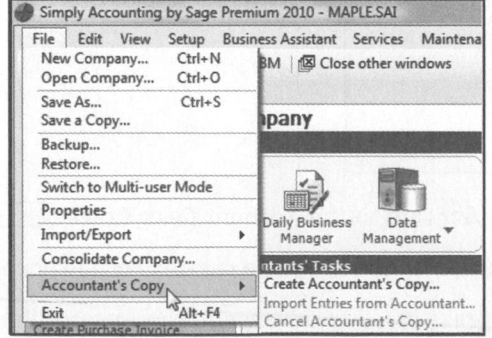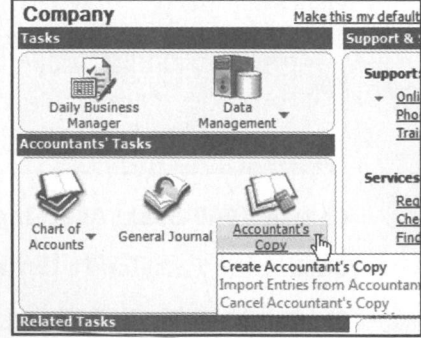

You will be asked to choose a location for the new backup file:

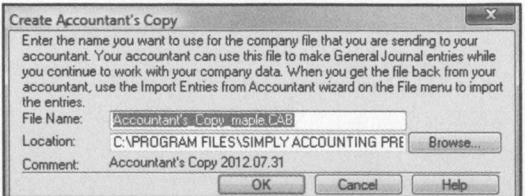

The default name for the file adds Accountant's_Copy_ to the original name so it will not be confused with your other backup files. The default location is a new ACCOUNTANT folder inside the Data folder (in the Simply Accounting program folder).

To choose another folder, click Browse and click the folder you want to use. Enter a different name for the file if you want.

Click   OK to begin making the specialized backup.

When the copy is complete, you will see the following information window:

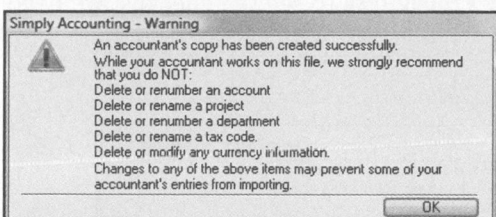

Read this message carefully as it warns what changes you can and cannot make to your working file while the accountant is working with the accountant's copy of your file.

Click   OK to return to your data file.

Monitoring Routine Activities

The end of September is the end of Bands' fiscal year. There are a number of steps to complete before beginning the new year. Simply Accounting provides assistance with these steps in its checklists.

Choose the **Business Assistant menu** and **click Checklists** to see the lists available:

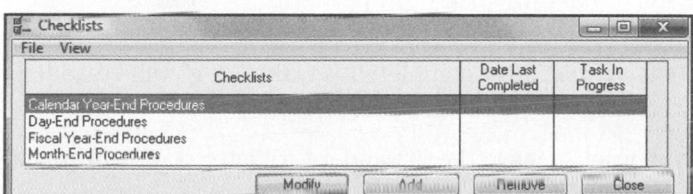

Checklists are available for different periods — end of a fiscal period, end of a business day, end of a month and end of a calendar year for payroll.

You can also create your own checklists, add procedures to one of the predefined checklists and print the checklists for reference.

Before checking the fiscal year-end procedures, we will add a reminder to the daily tasks checklist.

Click   Day-End Procedures and then **click Modify** to open the list:

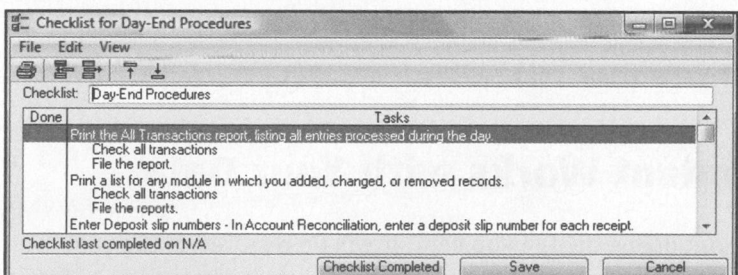

Each checklist can be customized for a company by using the tool buttons or the Edit menu items to insert tasks, delete them or rearrange them.

Click the **Insert Item tool** 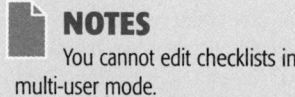 or **choose** the **Edit menu** and **click Insert** to add a blank line at the top of the task list.

CLASSIC VIEW
Click ▣ (the Checklists tool) to open the Checklists window.

NOTES
You cannot edit checklists in multi-user mode.

Press   (tab) to advance to the Tasks field.

Type   Check bank balances for possible overdrafts

Click   **Save** to return to the Checklists window.

Double click   Fiscal Year-End Procedures to see the checklist we need:

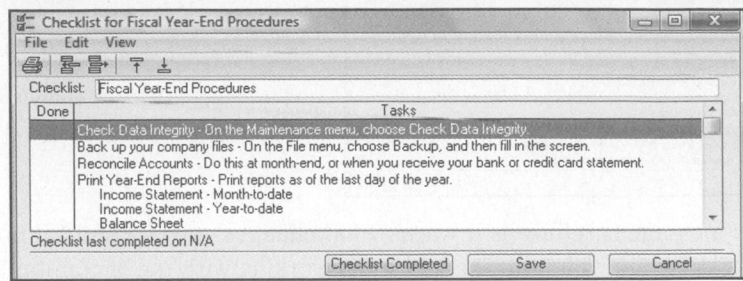

Maple Leaf Rags does not use the budgeting feature of the program so we can remove these tasks from the checklist.

Scroll down and **click Print Budget Reports**.

Click   the **Remove Item tool** or **choose** the **Edit menu** and **click Remove**.

Click   **Yes** to confirm that you want to continue with the deletion.

Click   the **Print tool** to print the checklist for reference.

Back up the **data files** and **print reports**. These are the most important elements on this list. Do not print reports for Payroll, Inventory or Projects. You can remove these reports from the list if you want.

Click   the **Done column** after completing a task — a ✓ will be added to the Done column.

Click Save if you want to leave the list and return later. A ✓ will appear in the Task In Progress column on the Checklists screen.

Complete all the **tasks** listed, except printing the reports for the modules that are not used. After finishing all the tasks,

Click   **Checklist Completed**. The session date will be added to the Date Last Completed column on the Checklists screen.

Open the remaining checklists to see the tasks to be completed at the end of each month and at the end of a calendar year. Print these lists for reference.

Click   **Close** to leave the Checklists window when you have finished.

Start   the **new fiscal year** on October 1, 2012.

The Accountant Works with Your Data

When the accountant opens the file you sent, it will be restored in the same version of Simply Accounting that you used. Only the General Journal, the one used for adjusting entries, is available to the accountant. The following two screens show your data file as it will open for the accountant using the special Accountants' Edition version of Simply Accounting.

NOTES
Reconciling Accounts will be explained in Chapter 15 and Budgeting is covered in Chapter 14.

NOTES
In Chapter 15, we describe how to clear data from company files.

NOTES
Refer to page 102 for assistance with starting a new fiscal period.

NOTES
The accountant works with a special version of the program — the Accountants' Edition. This program must be used to restore the Accountant's Copy backup file you created.
The Accountants' Edition allows full access to regular data files created in any version (Pro, Premium, First Step and Enterprise). The Accountant's Copy data file, however, restricts access to the General Journal.

The Classic view Home window in the Accountants' Edition file is shown here:

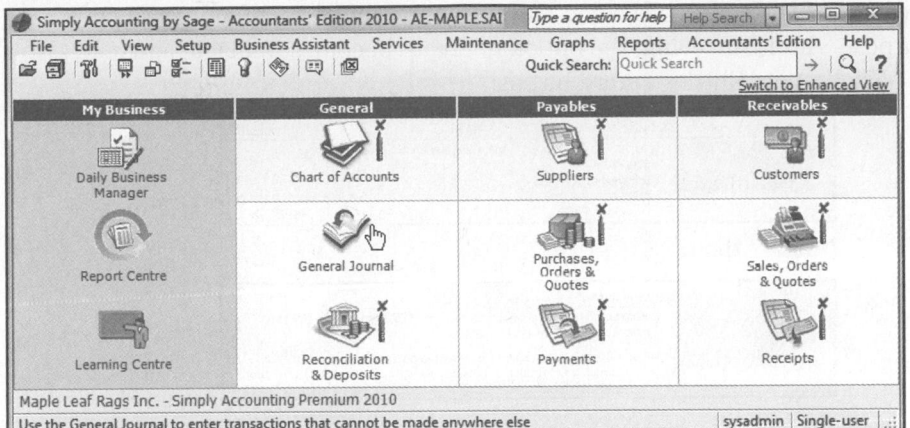

NOTES
You will not see this screen or the next one in your own version of Simply Accounting. We show these screens for reference only.

The No Edit symbol 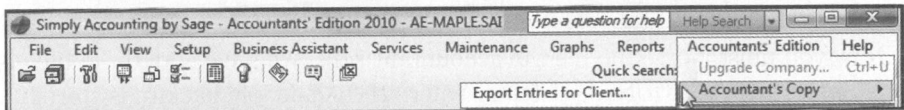 appears with all the ledger and journal icons except for the General Journal. The accountant can view, but not change, the information in the other journals and ledgers.

After adding the required adjustments, the accountant exports the new journal entries to a text file. This option is available from the Accountants' Edition menu by choosing Accountant's Copy and then Export Entries for Client as shown:

NOTES
We show the Classic view Home window so that you can see the restrictions (the No Edit symbols).

The exported text file of journal entries is sent back to you, the client.

Importing the Accountant's Journal Entries

When you receive the file from the accountant, you must import the journal entries to add them to your working file.

Restore the data file **SimData10\ACCOUNTANT\AE-maple1.CAB** for this step.

Choose the **File menu**, then **choose Accountant's Copy** and **click Import Entries from Accountant**. Or **choose Import Entries from Accountant** from the Accountant's Copy icon shortcuts list:

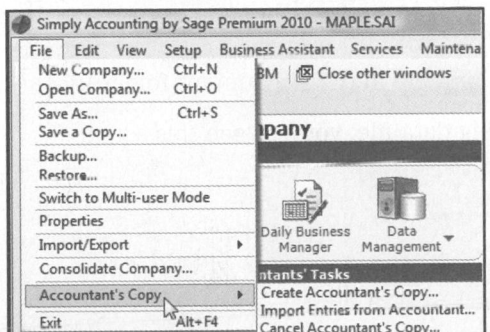

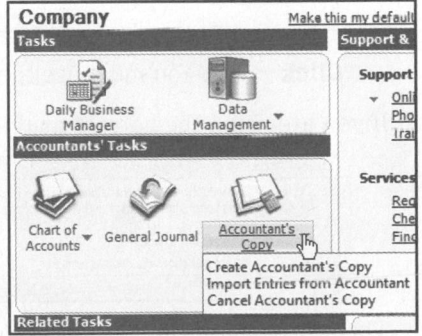

⚠ **WARNING!**
You must use the special file we created for this part of the exercise because it matches the imported entries.
You must use the same file for creating the accountant's copy and importing the accountant's entries. You will not be able to import the accountant's entries to your own working file.

Both the file menu options and the shortcuts list for Accountant's Tasks in the Company module window have changed. Once you create an accountant's copy, the other submenu options become available. The program stores the information that there is an outstanding accountant's copy for the file so you can import the journal entries later. This menu option remains available until the entries have been imported. You cannot create another accountant's copy while there is one outstanding. If you discover an error after you create the accountant's copy, you can cancel that version and then create a new accountant's copy. The option to Cancel Accountant's Copy is used for this purpose. After cancelling, the option to create becomes available again.

The Import Entries wizard begins:

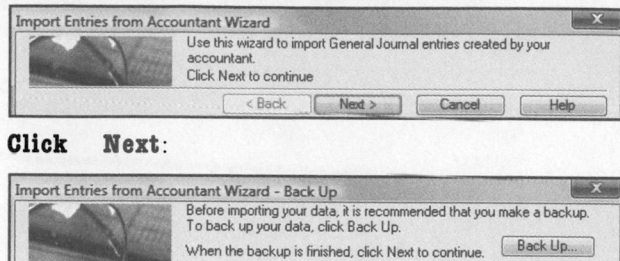

Click **Next**:

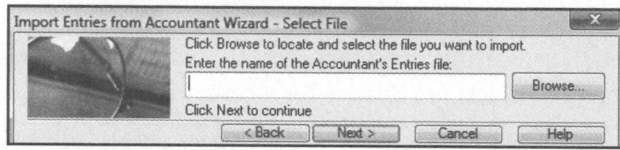

You are asked to make a backup before proceeding. Since the step of importing entries cannot be reversed, you should back up the data file first.

> **Click** **Backup** and follow the steps for creating a backup of the data file. **Click Next** to continue:

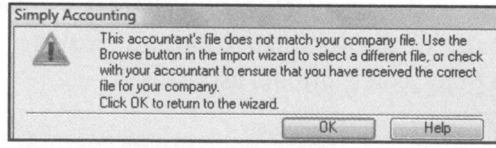

NOTES
The procedure for importing entries from the accountant is similar to importing other General Journal entries. Refer to Appendix J.

Now you must locate the file the accountant sent. We have added the file you need to the SimData10\ACCOUNTANT folder where the AE-Maple backup is stored.

> **Click** **Browse**.
>
> **Locate** **SimData10\ACCOUNTANT\Accountant's_Entries_maple-AE.TXT** and **click** to select it.
>
> **Click** **Open** and then **click Next**.

NOTES
The file you need is Accountant's_Entries_maple-AE.TXT. It is located in the SimData10\ACCOUNTANT folder.

If you try to import the journal entries to your own Maple Leaf Rags data file, or any other file that is different from the one used to create the accountant's copy, you will see the following error message:

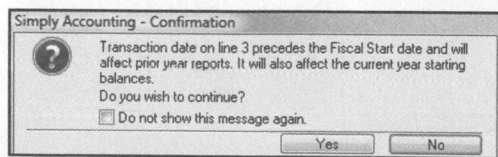

> **Click** **OK**. You must use the data file in the Accountant folder for this step.

If you are using the correct matching data file, you will see this screen:

NOTES
If your system settings do not allow transactions in the previous year, you must first change this setting. Refer to page 105.

This warning appears because the entries are dated in the previous fiscal year. We want to accept the dates the accountant used because they are correct and the entries should be added to the financial reports for the previous year. We have already changed the settings for this file to allow transactions dated before October 1. Simply Accounting still provides this warning whenever you are posting to a previous month. We need to allow all these entries and do not want the message to appear for each one.

> **Click** **Do Not Show This Message Again**.

Click   Yes:

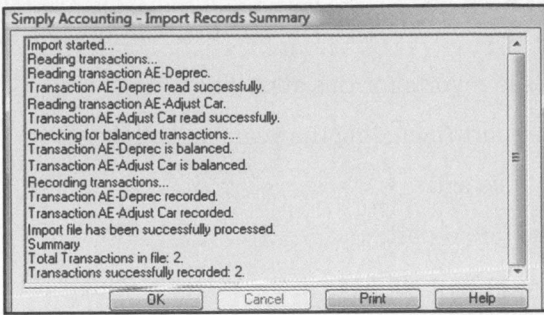

This summary of the imported transactions shows the entries added to your file.

Click   OK:

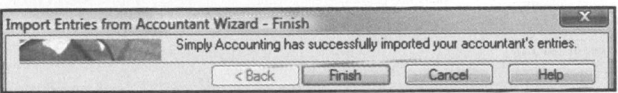

Click   Finish. The process is now complete.

The General Journal report for September 30 will include the accountant's entries:

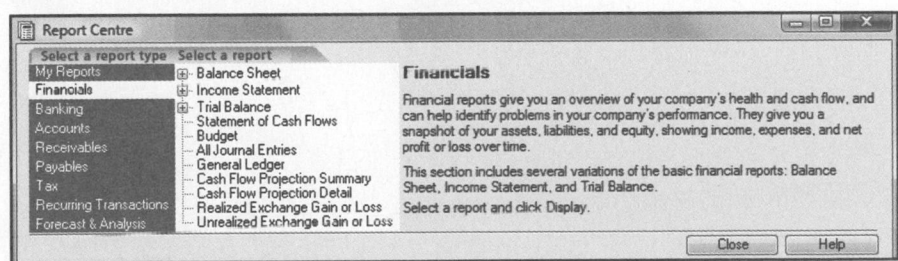

The journal entry numbers are marked *** with a note that they were created outside the regular file by the accountant. The numbers may be out of sequence if you have added transactions while the accountant was working with the file.

Displaying Exchange Rate Reports

When a business has foreign currency transactions, Simply Accounting will generate reports related to exchange rate gains and losses.

Open   the **Report Centre** and **click Financials**:

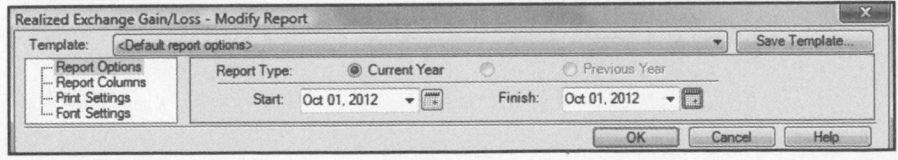

Click   Realized Exchange Gain or Loss. Click Modify This Report:

> **NOTES**
> For this report, we selected the journal options Previous Year and Show Only Entries Posted After Year End. The All Journal Entries Report for the previous year will include these two transactions at the end.

This first exchange rate report includes the gains or losses already realized or recorded because the payment has been made or received and the exchange rate difference is known.

Click   **Previous Year** to see reports for this application.

Enter   the **dates** for the report (including the year) and **click OK**.

Close   the **display** when finished.

To access the second exchange rate report,

Click   **Unrealized Exchange Gain or Loss** in the Select A Report list.

Click   **Modify This Report**:

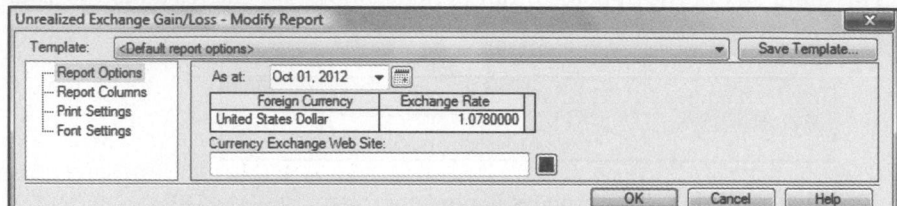

The second report includes the gains or losses that have not yet been realized or recorded — the payment has not been made but the exchange rate is known to have changed since the purchase or sale. When the payment is made or received, the actual gain may be different if the rate has changed again.

The report also revalues existing account balances and previous payments and receipts for the new exchange rate.

Enter   the **date** for the report (including the year) and an **Exchange Rate** for that date. **Click OK**.

Close   the **display** when finished. **Close** the **Report Centre**.

R E V I E W

The Student DVD with Data Files includes Review Questions and Supplementary Cases for this chapter, including a case with stock transactions that can be completed in the General Journal.

OBJECTIVES

After completing this chapter, you should be able to

- **enter** transactions in all journals
- **allocate** revenues and expenses in the General, Sales, Purchases, Payroll and Inventory journals
- **create** new divisions
- **change** the Division Ledger name
- **enter** import duty on purchases from foreign suppliers
- **make** import duty remittances
- **enter** purchases with cost variances
- **display** and **print** transactions with division details
- **display** and **print** division reports

COMPANY INFORMATION

Company Profile

NOTES
Truman Tires
600 Westminster St.
London, ON N6P 3B1
Tel: (519) 729-3733
Fax: (519) 729-7301
Business No.: 230 192 821

Truman Tires, located in London, Ontario, sells tires and wheels for all types of passenger cars, including taxis and service fleets for other businesses. Tyrone Truman completed an auto mechanics program at the local community college and then worked for an auto repair shop in Windsor for several years. He studied business administration part time to prepare him for starting his own business, which he now has operated for several years.

Although he sells all kinds of tires, throughout the year most people buy all-season radial tires. In December, the month in this application, Truman Tires sells mainly winter tires. All tire sales include free installation. The service centre, with its four service bays, also provides a limited range of services for automobiles, including oil changes, brake repairs and replacements, shocks replacements and wheel alignments. Four employees work on the cars while a manager and assistant manager handle all customer contacts and schedule appointments.

Truman Tires has a number of regular suppliers of inventory and other parts and supplies. Truman has accounts with most of these suppliers and some offer discounts for early payment. Some of the tires and wheels are imported from Japan and Truman pays import duties on these items.

Regular customers also have accounts with Truman Tires and are offered a 2 percent discount if they settle their accounts within 10 days. Some customers receive additional discounts through the preferred pricing schedule for all inventory sales and services.

In preparation for expanding his business, Tyrone Truman has decided to apply project costing for his two divisions, Sales and Service. He hopes to determine which aspect of the company is more profitable.

At the end of November 2012, Truman remitted all the company payroll taxes and deductions and closed his books. To convert his accounting records to Simply Accounting, he used the following:

- Chart of Accounts
- Post-Closing Trial Balance
- Supplier Information
- Customer Information
- Employee Information
- Employee Profiles and TD1 Information
- Inventory Information
- Division Information
- Accounting Procedures

PRO VERSION
The term Vendors will be used instead of Suppliers throughout the program.

CHART OF ACCOUNTS

TRUMAN TIRES

ASSETS
Current Assets
1050 Bank: Chequing CAD
1060 Bank: Foreign Currency
1070 Bank: Visa
1080 Bank: MasterCard
1090 Bank: Interac
1200 Accounts Receivable
1220 Purchase Prepayments
1240 Brakes & Shocks Parts
1250 Supplies: Garage
1260 Supplies: Office

Inventory Assets
1360 Wheels
1380 Wheel Nuts & Locks
1400 Winter Tires

Plant & Equipment
1650 Cash Register
1660 Computer Equipment
1670 Garage Equipment
1680 Machinery & Tools
1690 Shop & Garage Bays ►

►1700 Tow Truck
1710 Yard

LIABILITIES
Current Liabilities
2100 Bank Loan
2150 Prepaid Sales and Deposits
2200 Accounts Payable
2220 Import Duty Payable
2250 Credit Card Payable
2300 Vacation Payable
2310 EI Payable
2320 CPP Payable
2330 Income Tax Payable
2390 EHT Payable
2400 CSB Payable
2410 Union Dues
2460 WSIB Payable
2650 HST Charged on Sales
2670 HST Paid on Purchases

Long Term Liabilities
2850 Mortgage Payable ►

EQUITY
Owner's Equity
3560 T. Truman, Capital
3580 T. Truman, Drawings
3600 Net Income

REVENUE
Revenue
4020 Revenue from Sales
4040 Revenue from Services
4100 Other Revenue
4150 Sales Discounts

EXPENSE
Operating Expenses
5020 Advertising & Promotion
5030 Bank Charges
5035 Exchange Rate Differences
5040 Credit Card Fees
5045 Assembly Costs
5050 Cost of Goods Sold
5055 Variance Costs ►

►5060 Cost of Services
5065 Freight Expense
5070 Hydro Expense
5080 Interest Expense - Loan
5090 Interest Expense - Mortgage
5100 Inventory Adjustment
5110 Tool Rentals
5120 Inventory Parts Used
5130 Purchase Discounts
5140 Repairs & Maintenance
5150 Telephone Expense

Payroll Expenses
5300 Management Wages
5310 General Wages
5320 Piece Rate Wage Expense
5330 Commissions and Bonuses
5410 EI Expense
5420 CPP Expense
5430 WSIB Expense
5460 EHT Expense

NOTES: The Chart of Accounts includes only postable accounts and Net Income. WSIB (Workplace Safety and Insurance Board) is the name for WCB (Workers' Compensation Board) in Ontario.

POST-CLOSING TRIAL BALANCE

TRUMAN TIRES

November 30, 2012

		Debits	Credits				Debits	Credits
1050	Bank: Chequing CAD	$20 765		▶	1670	Garage Equipment	75 000	
1060	Bank: Foreign Currency (¥182 000)	2 000			1680	Machinery & Tools	25 000	
1070	Bank: Visa	8 000			1690	Shop & Garage Bays	175 000	
1080	Bank: MasterCard	5 000			1700	Tow Truck	40 000	
1090	Bank: Interac	2 500			1710	Yard	25 000	
1200	Accounts Receivable	4 181			2100	Bank Loan		$ 12 000
1240	Brakes & Shocks Parts	6 800			2200	Accounts Payable		6 048
1250	Supplies: Garage	2 400			2250	Credit Card Payable		235
1260	Supplies: Office	600			2300	Vacation Payable		6 943
1360	Wheels	9 136			2650	HST Charged on Sales		6 300
1380	Wheel Nuts & Locks	738			2670	HST Paid on Purchases	2 960	
1400	Winter Tires	15 480			2850	Mortgage Payable		140 000
1650	Cash Register	2 500			3560	T. Truman, Capital		254 034
1660	Computer Equipment	2 500 ▶					$425 560	$425 560

SUPPLIER INFORMATION

TRUMAN TIRES

Supplier Name (Contact)	Address	Phone No. Fax No.	E-mail Web Site	Terms Tax ID
Bell Canada (Louis Gossip)	100 Ring Road London, Ontario N5W 2M3	Tel: (519) 387-2355	www.bell.ca	n/10
CAW Union				n/30
Equity Life				n/30
Gulf Oil Company (Petro Crewd)	30 Refinery Cr. London, Ontario N4R 6F1	Tel: (519) 641-6277	pc@gulfoil.com www.gulfoil.com	n/30
London Hydro (Les Current)	755 Ohm Blvd. London, Ontario N6C 1P9	Tel: (519) 649-8100	lesc@londonhydro.on.ca www.londonhydro.on.ca	n/10
London Tool Rentals (Roto Tiller)	239 Pneumatics Rd. London, Ontario N5X 2S4	Tel: (519) 633-7102 Fax: (519) 635-8191	roto@getitfromus.com www.getitfromus.com	n/20 325 622 934
Minister of Finance	Box 620, 33 King St. W Oshawa, Ontario L1H 8H5	Tel: (905) 443- 8200	www.gov.on.ca/fin	n/30
MoTech Auto Parts (Moe Torrs)	2 Revving Parkway Windsor, Ontario N7T 7C2	Tel: (519) 722-1973 Fax: (519) 725-3664	moe@motech.com www.motech.com	2/10, n/30 (after tax) 163 482 977
Receiver General for Canada	PO Box 20004, Station A Sudbury, Ontario P3A 6B4	Tel: (705) 821-8186	www.cra-arc.gc.ca	n/30
Snowmaster Tire Company (I.C. Winters)	86 Sleet St. Tokyo, Japan 162 0829	Tel: (81-3) 5249 7331 Fax: (81-3) 5261 6492	icw@snowmaster.com www.snowmaster.com	net 15
Sylverado Wheels (Roy Rimmer)	100 Round Rd., Unit 2 Tokyo, Japan 100-7227	Tel: (81-3) 3643 8459 Fax: (81-3) 3663 5188	royrimmer@sylverado.com www.sylverado.com	n/30
TuffArm Shocks (Sally Shockley)	489 Spring St. Toronto, Ontario M4Z 3G3	Tel: (416) 699-2019 Fax: (416) 699-3854	Sal@tuffarm.shocks.com www.tuffarm.shocks.com	n/30 263 495 687
Western Hydraulic Repairs (Otto Raizer)	109 Lift St. London, Ontario N6F 8A5	Tel: (519) 645-6722 Fax: (519) 646-1145	o_raizer@whydraulics.com www.whydraulics.com	n/30 466 345 291
Workplace Safety & Insurance Board				n/30

OUTSTANDING SUPPLIER INVOICES

TRUMAN TIRES

Supplier Name	Terms	Date	Invoice No.	Amount CAD	Amount JPY
MoTech Auto Parts	2/10, n/30 (after tax)	Nov. 27/12	MT-1142	$678	
Snowmaster Tire Company	net 15	Nov. 26/12	ST-842	$2 544	¥231 273
Sylverado Wheels	n/30	Nov. 10/12	SW-724	$1 696	¥154 182
TuffArm Shocks	n/30	Nov. 4/12	TS-699	$1 130	
		Grand Total		$6 048	

CUSTOMER INFORMATION

TRUMAN TIRES

Customer Name (Contact)	Address	Phone No. Fax No.	E-mail Web Site	Terms Credit Limit
*Airport Taxi Service (Jett Plane)	100 Runway Rd. London, Ontario N5G 3J7	Tel: (519) 643-6182 Fax: (519) 645-1772	jett@gofly.com www.gofly.com	2/10, n/30 $4 000
Cash Customers				n/1
City Cab Company (Able Driver)	890 Transport St. London, Ontario N5W 1B3	Tel: (519) 641-7999 Fax: (519) 641-2539	driver@wetakeyou.com www.wetakeyou.com	2/10, n/30 $4 000
*London Car Leasing (Nick Borrow)	44 Fleet St. London, Ontario N6T 7V2	Tel: (519) 788-2538 Fax: (519) 789-3264	borrow@whybuy.com www.whybuy.com	2/10, n/30 $4 000
Lovely U Cosmetics (N.O. Blemish)	450 Phare Skinn Cr. London, Ontario N6B 3H3	Tel: (519) 782-4477 Fax: (519) 781-4372	blemish@lovelyU.com www.lovelyU.com	2/10, n/30 $4 000
*Polly Maid Services (Polly Mayden)	92 Scouring St. London, Ontario N6T 2K6	Tel: (519) 648-3645 Fax: (519) 648-2774	polly@pollymaid.com www.pollymaid.com	2/10, n/30 $4 000
Pronto Pizza & Delivery (Wayte Nott)	52 Marguerite St. London, Ontario N5B 2R5	Tel: (519) 784-7287 Fax: (519) 785-8220	waytenott@pronto.com www.pronto.com	2/10, n/30 $4 000

NOTES: Preferred price list customers are marked with an asterisk (*) beside their names. All discounts are after tax.

OUTSTANDING CUSTOMER INVOICES

TRUMAN TIRES

Customer Name	Terms	Date	Invoice No.	Amount	Total
City Cab Company	2/10, n/30 (after tax)	Nov. 26/12	120	$1 808	$1 808
Lovely U Cosmetics	2/10, n/30 (after tax)	Nov. 24/12	116	$1 356	$1 356
Polly Maid Services	2/10, n/30 (after tax)	Nov. 29/12	124	$1 017	$1 017
		Grand Total			$4 181

EMPLOYEE INFORMATION SHEET

TRUMAN TIRES

	Trish Tridon	Joy Fram	Shockley Monroe	Karlby Holley	Troy Niehoff	Albert C. Delco
Position	Manager	Asst Manager	Auto Worker	Auto Worker	Auto Worker	Auto Worker
Social Insurance No.	464 375 286	572 351 559	398 577 619	821 887 114	618 524 664	404 535 601
Address	59 Pond Mills Rd. London, Ontario N5Z 3X3	8 Rington Cres. London, Ontario N6J 1Y7	36 Artisans Cres. London, Ontario N5V 4S3	44 Lockyer St. London, Ontario N6C 3E5	98 Novello Ave. London, Ontario N6J 2A5	18 Ravenglass Cres. London, Ontario N6G 4K1
Telephone	(519) 645-6238	(519) 738-5188	(519) 784-7195	(519) 648-1916	(519) 641-6773	(519) 788-2826
Date of Birth (mm-dd-yy)	09-28-68	02-03-80	05-21-79	08-08-77	05-28-75	08-19-81
Federal (Ontario) Tax Exemption - TD1						
Basic Personal	$10 382 (8 943)	$10 382 (8 943)	$10 382 (8 943)	$10 382 (8 943)	$10 382 (8 943)	$10 382 (8 943)
Spouse	$10 382 (7 594)	–	–	–	$10 382 (7 594)	–
Other	–	–	–	$7 720 (7 828)	–	–
Total Exemptions	$20 764 (16 537)	$10 382 (8 943)	$10 382 (8 943)	$18 102 (16 791)	$20 764 (16 537)	$10 382 (8 943)
Employee Earnings						
Regular Wage Rate	–	–	$16.00	$16.00	$16.00	$16.00
Overtime Wage Rate	–	–	$24.00	$24.00	$24.00	$24.00
Regular Salary	$3 500/mo	$2 500/mo	–	–	–	–
Pay Period	monthly	monthly	bi-weekly	bi-weekly	bi-weekly	bi-weekly
Hours per Period	150	150	80	80	80	80
Piece Rate	–	–	$10/job	$10/job	$5/job	$5/job
Commission	1% (Sales – Returns)	–	–	–	–	–
Vacation	4 weeks	3 weeks	4% retained	4% retained	4% retained	4% retained
Vacation Pay Owed	–	–	$1 793	$1 486	$1 811	$1 853
WSIB Rate	3.40	3.40	3.40	3.40	3.40	3.40
Employee Deductions						
CSB	$200	$100	$50	$50	–	–
Union Dues	–	–	1%	1%	1%	1%
EI, CPP & Income Tax	Calculations built into Simply Accounting program.					

Employee Profiles and TD1 Information

All Employees   All employees are allowed 10 days per year for illness and five for personal reasons. All employees have their paycheques deposited directly into their bank accounts. There are no other company benefits. All payroll remittances are due at the end of each month.

Trish Tridon   As the manager at Truman Tires, Tridon supervises the other employees, resolves customer problems and assists with sales. Her salary of $3 500 per month is supplemented by a commission of 1 percent of sales, less returns. Tridon is entered as the salesperson on all sales invoices to calculate the commission. She is paid at the end of each month and is allowed four weeks of vacation with pay. Tridon is married with two children under 12, and claims the basic and spousal tax claim amounts. She has $200 deducted from each paycheque to buy Canada Savings Bonds.

Joy Fram   As assistant manager, Fram helps Tridon with all her duties and also manages the accounting records for the business. She is paid a monthly salary of $2 500 and is allowed three weeks of vacation with pay. She has only the basic tax claim amount because she is single and self-supporting. She has chosen to buy Canada Savings Bonds by having $100 deducted from each paycheque.

Hourly Paid Employees   The four hourly paid employees — Monroe, Holley, Niehoff and Delco — share the work of servicing vehicles. Every two weeks, they are paid $16 per hour for the first 40 hours each week and $24 per hour for additional time for performing the full range of services provided by Truman Tires: installing, repairing and rotating tires, brake work, shocks and oil service. However, each hourly employee has one area of specialization and the piece-rate supplement is based on the number of jobs in this area. All receive 4 percent vacation pay that is retained until they take time off. All are union members and pay 1 percent of their wages as union dues.

Shockley Monroe   specializes in brake work. He is single and pays $50 from each paycheque toward the purchase of Canada Savings Bonds.

Karlby Holley   also buys Canada Savings Bonds through payroll deductions. Her specialty is shocks. As a recent graduate, she has $4 000 tuition and eight months of full-time study to increase her basic single tax claim amount.

Troy Niehoff   is married with one child under 12 years of age, so he has the basic and spousal tax claim amounts. He is not enrolled in the Canada Savings Bonds plan. His area of specialization is tire installation and wheel alignment.

Albert C. Delco   is single and does not purchase Canada Savings Bonds through payroll. His area of specialization is oil service and winter preparation.

INVENTORY INFORMATION

TRUMAN TIRES

Code	Description	Min Stock	Selling Price Reg	(Pref)	Unit	Qty on Hand	Total (Cost)	Duty	Taxes
Winter Tires (Linked Accounts: Asset 1400; Revenue: 4020; COGS: 5050; Var: 5055)									
T101	P155/80R14 Tires	4	$ 70	($ 65)	each	20	$ 560	7.0%	HST
T102	P175/70R14 Tires	4	85	(80)	each	20	680	7.0%	HST
T103	P195/75R15 Tires	4	95	(88)	each	20	760	7.0%	HST
T104	P205/75R15 Tires	8	100	(92)	each	28	1 120	7.0%	HST
T105	P185/70R15 Tires	4	105	(96)	each	20	840	7.0%	HST
T106	P195/65R15 Tires	4	110	(100)	each	20	880	7.0%	HST
T107	P185/65R15 Tires	4	115	(105)	each	20	920	7.0%	HST
T108	P185/60R15 Tires	4	120	(110)	each	20	960	7.0%	HST
T109	P195/60R16 Tires	8	125	(115)	each	28	1 400	7.0%	HST
T110	P195/65R16 Tires	8	130	(120)	each	28	1 456	7.0%	HST
T111	P205/65R16 Tires	8	135	(124)	each	28	1 512	7.0%	HST
T112	P205/60R16 Tires	8	140	(127)	each	28	1 568	7.0%	HST
T113	P215/60R16 Tires	8	145	(132)	each	28	1 624	7.0%	HST
T114	P225/60R17 Tires	4	150	(136)	each	20	1 200	7.0%	HST
							$15 480		
Wheels (Linked Accounts: Asset 1360; Revenue: 4020; COGS: 5050; Var: 5055)									
W101	Aluminum R14 Wheels	4	180	(165)	each	16	$1 152	6.0%	HST
W102	Aluminum R15 Wheels	4	195	(187)	each	16	1 248	6.0%	HST
W103	Aluminum R16 Wheels	8	210	(190)	each	20	1 680	6.0%	HST
W104	Aluminum R17 Wheels	4	225	(207)	each	16	1 440	6.0%	HST
W105	Chrome-Steel R14 Wheels	4	70	(65)	each	16	448	6.0%	HST
W106	Chrome-Steel R15 Wheels	4	80	(75)	each	16	512	6.0%	HST
W107	Chrome-Steel R16 Wheels	8	90	(83)	each	20	720	6.0%	HST
W108	Chrome-Steel R17 Wheels	4	100	(92)	each	16	640	6.0%	HST
W109	Steel R14 Wheels	4	40	(38)	each	16	256	6.0%	HST
W110	Steel R15 Wheels	4	45	(42)	each	16	288	6.0%	HST
W111	Steel R16 Wheels	8	50	(46)	each	20	400	6.0%	HST
W112	Steel R17 Wheels	4	55	(50)	each	16	352	6.0%	HST
							$9 136		

▶

INVENTORY INFORMATION

TRUMAN TIRES

Code	Description	Min Stock	Selling Price Reg	(Pref)	Unit	Qty on Hand	Total (Cost)	Duty	Taxes
Wheel Nuts & Locks (Linked Accounts: Asset 1380; Revenue: 4020; COGS: 5050; Var: 5055)									
WN01	Chrome Wheel Nuts	4	$ 10	($ 10)	pkg	24	$ 96	6.0%	HST
WN02	Chrome Wheel Locks	4	25	(23)	pkg	24	240	6.0%	HST
WN03	Nickel/Chrome Wheel Nuts	4	10	(10)	pkg	24	114	6.0%	HST
WN04	Nickel/Chrome Wheel Locks	4	30	(28)	pkg	24	288	6.0%	HST
							$738		
Services (Linked Accounts: Revenue: 4040; COGS: 5060)									
SRV01	Alignment - standard		75	(70)	job				HST
SRV02	Alignment - w caster replacement		130	(120)	job				HST
SRV03	Brake Service - standard pkg		140	(130)	job				HST
SRV04	Brake Service - complete pkg		175	(163)	job				HST
SRV05	Oil Service - standard pkg		30	(28)	job				HST
SRV06	Oil Service - premium pkg		40	(37)	job				HST
SRV07	Shocks - economy gas-charged		100	(92)	job				HST
SRV08	Shocks - premium gas-matic		140	(130)	job				HST
SRV09	Tire Repairs		30	(28)	job				HST
SRV10	Tire Rotation		10	(10)	job				HST
SRV11	Winter Prep. Service		60	(55)	job				HST

Division Information

Truman Tires uses two divisions — one for sales of tires and wheels and their installation and one for services. Fram will set up these divisions at the beginning of December and Tridon will keep track of the percentage of time each employee works in each division. Because these times vary from one vehicle to another, the percentage allocation is included with each source document. Allocation details for other expenses and revenues are also included with the source documents. Amounts for assets, liabilities and equity accounts are not allocated.

Accounting Procedures

The Employer Health Tax (EHT)

The Employer Health Tax (EHT) is paid by employers in Ontario to cover the costs of health care for all eligible residents in the province. The EHT rate depends on the total annual remuneration paid to employees (gross wage expense). Employers with total payroll less than $400 000 are exempt from paying EHT. For those with higher annual payrolls, the EHT rate is 1.95 percent. Simply Accounting will calculate the employer's liability to the Ontario Minister of Finance automatically once the information is set up correctly in the payroll defaults and linked accounts. In Chapter 16, we will show the keystrokes necessary for setting up the EHT information. The EHT can be remitted monthly or annually, depending on the total payroll amount.

Taxes: HST

Truman Tires pays HST on all goods and services that it buys, including the imported products, and charges HST on all sales and services. It uses the regular method for remittance of the Harmonized Sales Tax. HST collected from customers is recorded as a liability in *HST Charged on Sales*. HST paid to suppliers is recorded in *HST Paid on*

NOTES
Although the total payroll for Truman is below the minimum amount at which they must pay the EHT, we have included the tax for teaching purposes.

Purchases as a decrease in liability to Canada Revenue Agency. The report is filed with the Receiver General for Canada by the last day of the month for the previous quarter, either including the balance owing or requesting a refund.

In Ontario, PST is harmonized with GST. The provincial portion of HST is 8 percent.

NSF Cheques

When a bank returns a customer's cheque because there were insufficient funds in the customer's bank account to cover the cheque, the payment must be reversed. If the payment was processed through the Receipts Journal, the reversal should also be processed through the Receipts Journal (see page 184). If the sale was a cash sale, the reversal must be processed through the Sales Journal. Create a customer record for the customer and process a credit (Pay Later) sale for the full amount of the NSF cheque. Enter No Tax in the Tax Code field to show that the amount is non-taxable because taxes for the sale were recorded at the time of the original sale. Enter the amount as a **positive** amount in the Amount field and enter *Bank: Chequing CAD* in the Account field. On a separate invoice line, enter the amount of the handling charge for the NSF cheque in the Amount field with *Other Revenue* in the Account field. Again, the handling charge is non-taxable.

Returns

When customers return merchandise, they are charged a 20 percent handling charge. In the Sales Journal, enter the quantity returned with a **minus** sign at the regular sale price, add the tax code and enter *Sales Returns & Allowances* in the Account field. The amounts will automatically be negative because of the minus sign in the quantity field, so that *Accounts Receivable* will be credited automatically as well. On a separate invoice line, enter the amount withheld — the handling charge — as a positive amount and credit *Other Revenue. Accounts Receivable* will be debited automatically for the amount of the handling charge.

If the original sale was a credit sale, and the account is not yet paid, the return should also be entered as a credit sale so that *Accounts Receivable* will be credited. If the original sale was paid in cash or by credit card, or the account has been paid, the return should be entered as a cash sale or credit card sale so that the appropriate bank account will be credited. (See page 387.)

Reserved Inventory for Divisions

When customers sign a contract, the inventory items needed to complete the work are set aside or reserved by transferring them through the Item Assembly Journal to a designated account. (Refer to page 382.) In this way, these items cannot be sold to other customers because the inventory quantities are already reduced. The minimum stock level for reserved inventory will be zero.

Cash, Credit Card and Debit Card Sales

Cash and credit card transactions for goods and services occur normally in most types of businesses. The Simply Accounting program handles these transactions automatically through the Sales Journal when you choose the appropriate method of payment. Choose Cash Customers from the Customer list, and add the new customer's name in the Ship To or Address fields if this is not a regular customer. If payment is by cheque, a Cheque Number field opens. Truman Tires accepts Visa, MasterCard and Interac debit cards from customers for store sales.

The program will debit the appropriate bank account instead of the *Accounts Receivable* control account. All other accounts for this transaction will be appropriately debited or credited.

NOTES
The Sales Journal entry will credit Bank: Chequing CAD for the full amount of the sale including taxes and debit Accounts Receivable for the customer.

NOTES
If you created a customer record by using Quick Add, or used an existing record (e.g., Cash Customers), you can adjust the sales invoice by changing the method of payment from Cheque to Pay Later. You cannot choose Pay Later as the payment method for one-time customers.

NOTES
We use the term Cash Sales and Purchases for cash and cheque transactions.
You can also enter the name in the Customer field and choose Continue when prompted. The name is then added to the journal report without creating a customer record.

Cash Purchases

Similarly, for cash purchases, choose the supplier from the Supplier list or add the supplier using Quick Add. Cash purchases may be entered in the Payments Journal as Other Payments or in the Purchases Journal. Choose the appropriate method of payment from the Paid By list. For cheque payments, a Cheque Number field opens with the next cheque number entered. Complete the remainder of the cash transaction in the same way you would enter other transactions.

The program will debit *Bank: Chequing CAD* instead of *Accounts Payable*, the control account. All other accounts for the transaction will be appropriately debited or credited.

Freight Expense

When a business purchases inventory items, the cost of any freight that cannot be directly allocated to a specific item must be charged to *Freight Expense*. This amount will be regarded as an expense rather than charged to an inventory asset account.

Printing Invoices, Orders and Quotes

If you want to print the invoices, purchase orders or sales quotes through the program, complete the journal transaction as you would otherwise. Before posting the transaction, preview the invoice. If the invoice is correct, you can print it from the preview window, from the invoice by choosing the File menu and then Print or by clicking the Print tool on the tool bar for the invoice form. Printing will begin immediately, so be sure you have the correct forms for your printer before you begin. If you and the customer or supplier have e-mail, click the E-mail tool to send the invoice or order.

Foreign Purchases

Truman Tires imports some inventory items from companies in Japan. The currency for these transactions is Japanese yen (JPY) and the currency symbol is ¥. Truman Tires pays HST and import duties on these purchases. Duty rates are set up in the Inventory Ledger for the individual items and the amounts are calculated automatically by the program.

INSTRUCTIONS

1. **Record entries** for the source documents for December 2012 in Simply Accounting using the Chart of Accounts, Trial Balance and other information. The procedures for entering each new type of transaction are outlined step by step in the Keystrokes section that follows the source documents. A ✓ in the source document completion check box indicates that keystrokes are provided. The page number immediately below the check box indicates where these specific keystroke instructions begin. Keystroke instructions begin on page 517, after the source documents.

2. **Print** the **reports** and **graphs** indicated on the following printing form after you have finished making your entries.

PRO VERSION

Remember that you will see the term Vendors when we use the term Suppliers.

NOTES

To preview, print or e-mail invoices, you must have the correct forms selected for invoices in the Reports & Forms Settings. You can access these settings from the Sales Journal tool bar.

NOTES

The transactions in this exercise provide a comprehensive practice set. If you want to use it only for review, you can complete the transactions without entering allocations.

REPORTS

Accounts
- [ ] Chart of Accounts
- [ ] Account List
- [ ] General Journal Entries

Financials
- [x] Comparative Balance Sheet: Dec. 1 and Dec. 31, difference in percentage
- [x] Income Statement from Dec. 1 to Dec. 31
- [x] Trial Balance date: Dec. 31
- [x] All Journals Entries: Dec. 1 to Dec. 31 with division allocations and foreign amounts
- [x] General Ledger accounts: 1400 4020 4040 from Dec. 1 to Dec. 31
- [ ] Statement of Cash Flows
- [x] Cash Flow Projection Detail Report for account 1050 for 30 days
- [x] Gross Margin Income Statement from Dec. 1 to Dec. 31

Tax
- [x] Report on HST from Dec. 1 to Dec. 31

Banking
- [ ] Cheque Log Report

Payables
- [ ] Supplier List
- [ ] Supplier Aged
- [ ] Aged Overdue Payables

- [ ] Purchase Journal Entries
- [ ] Payment Journal Entries
- [ ] Supplier Purchases

Receivables
- [ ] Customer List
- [ ] Customer Aged
- [ ] Aged Overdue Receivables
- [ ] Sales Journal Entries
- [ ] Receipt Journal Entries
- [ ] Customer Sales
- [x] Sales by Salesperson
- [ ] Customer Statements

Payroll
- [ ] Employee List
- [x] Employee Summary for all employees
- [ ] Deductions & Expenses
- [ ] Remittance
- [ ] Payroll Journal Entries
- [x] T4 Slips for all employees
- [ ] Record of Employment

Inventory & Services
- [ ] Inventory & Services List
- [ ] Inventory Summary
- [ ] Inventory Quantity
- [ ] Inventory Statistics
- [x] Inventory Sales Summary for Winter Tires from Dec. 1 to Dec. 31

- [x] Inventory Transaction Summary for Wheels, all journals from Dec. 1 to Dec. 31
- [ ] Item Assembly Journal Entries
- [ ] Adjustment Journal Entries
- [ ] Inventory Price Lists

Division
- [ ] Division List
- [x] Division Income Summary: all divisions, all accounts from Dec. 1 to Dec. 31
- [ ] Division Allocation Report

Mailing Labels
- [ ] Labels

Management Reports
- [ ] Ledger

GRAPHS
- [ ] Payables by Aging Period
- [ ] Payables by Supplier
- [ ] Receivables by Aging Period
- [ ] Receivables by Customer
- [ ] Sales vs Receivables
- [ ] Receivables Due vs Payables Due
- [ ] Revenues by Account
- [ ] Expenses by Account
- [x] Expenses and Net Profit as % of Revenue

NOTES
We have used a straight text format for source documents in this chapter.

NOTES
There is no allocation in the Payments or the Receipts journals.

SOURCE DOCUMENTS

SESSION DATE – DECEMBER 7, 2012

- [x] **517** Based on memo #1 from owner on December 1, created two new divisions: Sales Division and Service Division. Both divisions begin Dec. 1, 2012, and are active.

- [x] **520** On December 1, received invoice for specialty tool rental contract from London Tool Rentals. The rental agreement amount was $280 plus $36.40 HST for a total of $316.40. Terms: net 20 days. Charged 20% of the expenses to Sales Division and 80% to Service Division. This was a one-year contract, stored as a monthly recurring entry.

- [ ] Sent cheque #200 for $1 130 to TuffArm Shocks on Dec. 1 to pay invoice #TS-699.

- [ ] On Dec. 2, sent cheque #201 to MoTech Auto Parts, to pay invoice #MT-1142. Cheque for $664.44 included $13.56 discount for early payment.

- [ ] Received cheque #4887 for $1 328.88 on Dec. 2 from Lovely U Cosmetics. Receipt #80 was applied to invoice #116 with early payment discount of $27.12.

☐ Received payment from City Cab Company on Dec. 2. Receipt #81, cheque #855 for $1 771.84 including $36.16 discount was applied to invoice #120.

☑ **524** Recorded invoice #ST-916 from Snowmaster Tire Company for tires and parts on Dec. 2/12. Payment is due in 15 days. The exchange rate on Dec. 2 was 0.0109. Total import duty charged was ¥ 16 580 (CAD $180.73). The freight expense was allocated entirely to the Sales Division.

items purchased		amount	duty rate
	Miscellaneous parts	¥ 50 000	6%
20 T110	P195/65R16 Tires	95 000	7%
20 T111	P205/65R16 Tires	99 000	7%
	Freight	6 500	
	HST Paid	32 565	
	Invoice Total	¥283 065	

NOTES
Edit the purchase amounts. Amounts for Balance Sheet accounts are not allocated so there is no allocation for inventory purchases.
Allocate freight expenses for purchases by clicking the Allocate tool beside the Freight fields.
Remember that HST is charged on freight expenses.

☐ Recorded invoice #SW-876 from Sylverado Wheels for wheels on Dec. 2, 2012, at the exchange rate of 0.0109. Payment is due in 30 days. Total import duty assessed was ¥ 13 200 (CAD $143.88). Freight was charged to the Sales Division.

items purchased		amount	duty rate
20 W103	Aluminum R16 Wheels	¥154 000	6%
20 W107	Chrome-Steel R16 Wheels	66 000	6%
	Freight	5 000	
	HST Paid	29 250	
	Invoice Total	¥254 250	

☑ **527** Tridon made sale #125 to Bruno Scinto on Dec. 4/12. Scinto paid by Visa. 100% of revenue and expenses for inventory items was allocated to Sales Division and for service item to Service Division.

items sold		amount	total
4 T104	P205/75R15 Tires	$100 each	$ 400.00
4 T105	P185/70R15 Tires	105 each	420.00
4 W102	Aluminum R15 Wheels	195 each	780.00
1 SRV06	Oil Service - premium pkg	40 /job	40.00
	Harmonized Sales Tax	13%	213.20
Total paid by Visa #4205 5921 7456 3010			$1 853.20

NOTES
You can add Tridon as the Salesperson in all customer records.
For all cash, credit card or debit card sales, you can type the new customer name and choose Continue or choose Cash Customers and use the Additional Field for the customer name or credit card number.
There is no discount for cash, credit card or debit card sales (Visa, MasterCard and Interac).

☐ Tridon completed MasterCard sale #126 to Alice Ferante on Dec. 4, 2012, and allocated 100% of revenue to Sales Division.

items sold		amount	total
4 T114	P225/60R17 Tires	$150 each	$ 600.00
4 W104	Aluminum R17 Wheels	225 each	900.00
	Harmonized Sales Tax	13%	195.00
Total paid by MasterCard #5901 8223 6558 6201			$1 695.00

☐ Tridon made sale #127 to London Car Leasing on Dec. 6. Terms for the preferred customer were 2/10, n/30. All revenue was allocated to Sales Division.

items sold		amount
12 T101	P155/80R14 Tires	$ 65 each
12 T106	P195/65R15 Tires	100 each
12 W106	Chrome-Steel R15 Wheels	75 each
12 W109	Steel R14 Wheels	38 each
	Harmonized Sales Tax	13%

☐ Recorded Tridon's Sales Summary as sale #128 for one-time Cash Customers on Dec. 7, 2012. Allocated 100% of revenue and expenses for inventory items to Sales Division and for service items to Service Division.

items sold			amount	total
12	T101	P155/80R14 Tires	$ 70 each	$ 840.00
8	T103	P195/75R15 Tires	95 each	760.00
2	W103	Aluminum R16 Wheels	210 each	420.00
6	SRV02	Alignment - w caster replacement	130 /job	780.00
2	SRV03	Brake Service - standard pkg	140 /job	280.00
8	SRV06	Oil Service - premium pkg	40 /job	320.00
3	SRV08	Shocks - premium gas-matic	140 /job	420.00
		Harmonized Sales Tax	13%	496.60
		Total cash received and deposited to bank account		$4 316.60

NOTES
Packages will not be oversold, so the variance account is not required.

☐ Received memo #2 from Owner. Created two new inventory records for winter special packages, both including four tires and wheels and a winter preparation service. One included alignments. A new asset Group account was used for the new items: 1420 Winter-Holiday Tire Packages. The other linked accounts used were Revenue from Sales (account 4020) and Cost of Goods Sold (account 5050). Both items are taxed for HST. Import Duty does not apply.

New item	Description	Min Amt	Selling Price/unit	
			Regular	(Preferred)
WHP1	Tires/Wheels/Winter Pkg	0	$ 900 /pkg	($850)
WHP2	Tires/Wheels/Alignment/Winter Pkg	0	$1 400 /pkg	($1 300)

⚠ WARNING!
The unit costs change continually as new inventory is purchased at different prices.
Accept the default prices for assembly components and copy the total to the assembled items total. The totals for assembly components (including additional costs) and assembled items must be exactly the same.

☐ Used Form ITA-1 dated Dec 7/12 to assemble five WHP1 Tires/Wheels/Winter Pkg. using 20 tires and 20 wheels as follows:

Components			unit cost	total
20	T110	P195/65R16 Tires	$53.4165 each	$1 068.33
20	W107	Chrome-Steel R16 Wheels	37.064 each	741.28
Additional Costs (for services)				$250.00

Assembled items (package)			unit cost	total
5	WHP1	Tires/Wheels/Winter Pkg	$411.922 each	$2 059.61

NOTES
The services are included as additional costs. You cannot assemble the service items with the inventory to create the package because no purchase costs are associated with the services. Accept the default prices for assembly components and copy the total to the assembled items total. There is no allocation in the Item Assembly Journal.

☐ Used Form ITA-2 dated Dec 7/12 to assemble five WHP2 Tires/Wheels/Alignment/Winter Pkg using 20 tires and wheels as follows:

Components			unit cost	total
20	T111	P205/65R16 Tires	$55.555 each	$1 111.10
20	W103	Aluminum R16 Wheels	86.4829 each	1 729.66
Additional Costs				$500.00

Assembled items (package)			unit cost	total
5	WHP2	Tires/Wheels/Alignment/Winter Pkg	$668.152 each	$3 340.76

SESSION DATE — DECEMBER 14, 2012

NOTES
The duty rate does not appear on purchase orders or quotes.

☐ Recorded purchase order #21 from Snowmaster Tire Company on Dec. 8 at the exchange rate of 0.0115. Payment is due 15 days after delivery on Dec 13.

items purchased			amount
16	T101	P155/80R14 Tires	¥ 39 000
16	T103	P195/75R15 Tires	53 000
8	T106	P195/65R15 Tires	31 000
8	T107	P185/65R15 Tires	32 000
		Freight	6 500
		HST	20 995
Invoice Total			¥182 495

☐ Recorded purchase order #22 from Sylverado Wheels on Dec. 8 at the exchange rate of 0.0115. Payment is due 30 days after delivery on Dec 13.

items purchased			amount
16	W106	Chrome-Steel R15 Wheels	¥44 500
8	W109	Steel R14 Wheels	11 100
8	W110	Steel R15 Wheels	12 500
		Freight	5 000
		HST Paid	9 503
Invoice Total			¥82 603

☐ On Dec. 9, deposited receipt #82 from Polly Maid Service, cheque #2189 for $996.66 for invoice #124. A discount of $20.34 for early payment was allowed.

☐ Entered 0.011 as the exchange rate on Dec. 9 to pay invoices.
Paid #ST-842 from Snowmaster Tire Company with cheque #330 for ¥231 273.

☐ Paid #SW-724 from Sylverado Wheels with cheque #331 for ¥154 182 in payment.

☐ Owner authorized bank transfer of ¥400 000 on Memo #3, dated Dec 9/12 to cover cheques written. Money was taken from Chequing account and deposited to Foreign Currency account. The exchange rate for the transfer was 0.011.

☐ Tridon made sale #129 to Pronto Pizza & Delivery on Dec. 11. Terms for the sale were 2/10, n/30. 100% of revenue and expenses for inventory items was allocated to Sales Division and for service items to Service Division.

items sold			amount
12	T108	P185/60R15 Tires	$120 each
12	W106	Chrome-Steel R15 Wheels	80 each
4	SRV03	Brake Service - standard pkg	140 /job
4	SRV07	Shocks - economy gas-charged	100 /job
		Harmonized Sales Tax	13%

☐ Tridon completed sale #130 to Airport Taxi Service on Dec. 13. Terms for the preferred customer were 2/10, n/30. 100% of revenue and expenses for inventory items was allocated to Sales Division and for service items to Service Division.

items sold			amount
8	T103	P195/75R15 Tires	$ 88 each
8	W102	Aluminum R15 Wheels	187 each
8	WN04	Nickel/Chrome Wheel Locks	28 /pkg
6	SRV04	Brake Service - complete pkg	163 /pkg
6	SRV08	Shocks - premium gas-matic	130 /job
		Harmonized Sales Tax	13%

☑ Received all items ordered from Snowmaster Tire Company purchase order #21
529 on Dec. 13/12 with invoice #ST-1141 with payment terms of net 15. Used the exchange rate of 0.012. Total import duty charged was ¥ 10 850 (CAD $130.20). The freight expense was allocated entirely to Sales Division.

items purchased			amount	duty rate
16	T101	P155/80R14 Tires	¥ 39 000	7%
16	T103	P195/75R15 Tires	53 000	7%
8	T106	P195/65R15 Tires	31 000	7%
8	T107	P185/65R15 Tires	32 000	7%
		Freight	6 500	
		HST	20 995	
Invoice Total			¥182 495	

NOTES
Close the Advisor message about the overdrawn account. The transaction, memo #3, will transfer funds to cover the overdraft.

NOTES
Remember to change the currency setting to JPY for the bank transfer.

NOTES
You will see the Advisor message that inventory items have dropped below the re-order point. Close the Advisor message to continue.

NOTES
Allow Airport Taxi Service to exceed the credit limit.

WARNING!
You may need to add the duty rates to the invoice as they might not be added when you fill the order.
The exchange rate from the order will be the default and you will need to change it.

NOTES
You will need to update the exchange rate from the one for the purchase order. You will also need to add the duty rates.

On Dec. 13, all items ordered from Sylverado Wheels on purchase order #22 arrived. Invoice #SW-1024 confirmed payment terms of net 30 days. Used the exchange rate of 0.0120 for the invoice. Total import duty charged was ¥ 4 086 (CAD $49.03). The freight expense was allocated entirely to Sales Division.

items purchased			amount	duty rate
16	W106	Chrome-Steel R15 Wheels	¥44 500	6%
8	W109	Steel R14 Wheels	11 100	6%
8	W110	Steel R15 Wheels	12 500	6%
	Freight		5 000	
	HST Paid		9 503	
Invoice Total			¥82 603	

NOTES
This is a non-inventory sales order. Credit Revenue from Sales.

Tridon received sales order #12-1 on Dec. 13 from Lovely U Cosmetics. Contract required five sets of tires and wheels to be installed on Dec. 21/12. The contract price for the job was $5 100 plus $663 HST. Lovely U Cosmetics provided cheque #9754 for $1 020 as a deposit (#13) for the contract. Terms for the balance of the payment were 2/10, n/30, on completion of installation.

Received payment from London Car Leasing for invoice #127. Cheque #111 for $3 694.29 was deposited on December 13 as receipt #83. Discount of $75.39 was allowed for early payment.

NOTES
Enter 2 as the quantity for the purchases from MoTech Auto Parts and edit the amount if necessary.
The wheel locks and nuts have different buying and selling units. They are purchased in boxes of one dozen packages and sold as individual packages.

Recorded invoice #MT-1521 from MoTech Auto Parts for shipment of wheel nuts received on December 13. Terms for the purchase were 2/10, n/30. The freight amount was allocated to Sales.

items purchased			amount
2 dozen	WN01	Chrome Wheel Nuts	$ 96.00
2 dozen	WN02	Chrome Wheel Locks	240.00
2 dozen	WN03	Nickel/Chrome Wheel Nuts	114.00
2 dozen	WN04	Nickel/Chrome Wheel Locks	288.00
	Freight		20.00
	HST Paid		98.54
Invoice Total			$856.54

✓

530   Dec. 14 memo #4 from Owner requested payment of import duty charged on purchases to date to Receiver General. Wrote cheque #202 for $503.84 to pay duty on invoices #ST-916, ST-1141, SW-876 and SW-1024.

Used Form RIF-1001 dated Dec 14/12 to reserve contract items for Lovely U Cosmetics. Free installation included in contract. All items entered at average cost prices. New inventory record was created for the contract using a new linked inventory asset Group account 1440 Reserved Inventory for Workorders and existing accounts 4020 and 5050 for linked Revenue and COGS. HST is charged on the sale and duty does not apply.

New item	Description		Min Amt	Regular Selling Price
LC1	Lovely U Cosmetics Inventory		0	$5 100/contract
Reserved components			unit cost	total
20	T111	P205/65R16 Tires	$55.555 each	$1 111 10
20	W107	Chrome-Steel R16 Wheels	37.064 each	741.28
20	WN04	Nickel/Chrome Wheel Locks	12 /pkg	240.00
Contract (assembled) item			unit cost	total
1	LC1	Lovely U Cosmetics Inventory	$2 092.38 each	$2 092.38

NOTES
Accept the default costs and enter total assembly components cost for assembled items total cost.

NOTES
Refer to page 424 for assistance with editing the sales order. Editing orders is like editing quotes. Choose Sales Order as the transaction type before choosing the order to adjust. Do not edit the prepayment.

Dec. 14 memo #5 included reminder to edit Sales Order #12-1 from Lovely U Cosmetics. Changed the contract item ordered to the reserved inventory LC1. The quantity ordered (one), price and terms are unchanged.

☐ Recorded Tridon's Sales Summary as sale #131 for one-time Cash Customers on Dec. 14, 2012. The following allocations were applied: 100% of service revenue to Service Division; 95% of revenue for WHP1 to Sales and 5% to Service; 90% of revenue for WHP2 to Sales and 10% to Service.

items sold			amount	total
6	SRV01	Alignment - standard	$ 75 /job	$ 450.00
8	SRV03	Brake Service - standard pkg	140 /job	1 120.00
6	SRV05	Oil Service - standard pkg	30 /job	180.00
7	SRV06	Oil Service - premium pkg	40 /job	280.00
12	SRV11	Winter Prep. Service	60 /job	720.00
1	WHP1	Tires/Wheels/Winter Pkg	900 /pkg	900.00
2	WHP2	Tires/Wheels/Alignment/Winter Pkg	1 400 /pkg	2 800.00
		Harmonized Sales Tax	13%	838.50
	Total cash received and deposited to bank account			$7 288.50

EMPLOYEE TIME SUMMARY SHEET #51   **DATED DEC. 14/12**

(pay period ending December 14, 2012)

Name of Employee	Week 1	Week 2	Regular Hours	Overtime Hours	No. of Piece Rate Jobs	Sick Days	Personal Days
☑ Delco	40	40	80	0	34	1	–
530							
☐ Holley	40	42	80	2	13	–	1
☐ Monroe	42	40	80	2	20	–	–
☐ Niehoff	40	42	80	2	12	–	–

a. Use Employee Time Summary Sheet #51 and the Employee Information Sheet to complete the payroll run for hourly paid employees.

b. Allocate 100% of the payroll expenses to Service for all employees.

c. Issue deposit slips #112 to #115.

SESSION DATE – DECEMBER 21, 2012

☐ Paid invoice #ST-916 from Snowmaster Tire Company with cheque #332 for ¥283 065 on Dec. 16 in payment of account. The exchange rate was 0.01105.

☐ On memo #6 dated Dec 16/12, owner authorized transfer of ¥400 000 to cover cheques written. Money was taken from Chequing account and deposited to Foreign Currency account. The exchange rate for the transfer was 0.01105.

☐ Paid hydro bill with cheque #203 on Dec. 17 for $293.80. The bill from London Hydro, #LH-31421, was for $260 for hydro services plus $33.80 HST. The expense was allocated to Sales — 30% and to Service Division — 70%.

☐ Paid invoice #BC-64261 from Bell Canada for $90 plus $11.70 HST for telephone services. Cheque #204 for $101.70 was sent on Dec. 17. 40% of the expense was charged to Sales and 60% to Service Division.

☐ On December 17, wrote cheque #205 to Western Hydraulic Repairs, for $452 to pay for repairs to the hydraulic lift in service bay and maintenance of other lifts. Repairs on invoice #WH-690 amounted to $400 plus $52 HST. 10% of the expense was allocated to Sales and 90% to Service Division.

☐ Deposited receipt #84 from Pronto Pizza & Delivery on Dec. 19/12. Cheque #399 for $3 720.86 was applied to invoice #129 with $75.94 discount allowed for early payment.

NOTES
If you have difficulty accessing the Allo column, you can click an employee name and then click the Allo tool button.
You can apply the allocation to the entire transaction in the Payroll Cheque Run Journal.

NOTES
Remember that the amounts in the Entitlements fields reflect only the time earned during this pay period. All employees have accrued time from previous periods. These times are recorded in the employee's ledger record.

Recorded Tridon's sale #132 to Daniel BenDavid on Dec. 20. BenDavid paid by MasterCard. Allocations for the sale were applied as follows: 100% of the revenue and expenses for inventory items to Sales Division; 100% of revenue for service items to Service Division; 95% of revenue for WHP1 to Sales and 5% to Service Division; and 90% of revenue for WHP2 to Sales and 10% to Service.

items sold			amount	total
4	WN01	Chrome Wheel Nuts	$ 10 /pkg	$ 40.00
1	SRV04	Brake Service - complete pkg		175.00
5	SRV05	Oil Service - standard pkg	30 /job	150.00
5	SRV06	Oil Service - premium pkg	40 /job	200.00
2	SRV08	Shocks - premium gas-matic		280.00
1	WHP1	Tires/Wheels/Winter Pkg		900.00
1	WHP2	Tires/Wheels/Alignment/Winter Pkg		1 400.00
		Harmonized Sales Tax	13%	408.85
		Total paid by MasterCard #5809 8213 6238 1601		$3 553.85

Cleaning fluids, cleaning cloths and other garage supplies were purchased from Motor Supply Company on Dec. 21 and paid for with cheque #206 for $565. Invoice #MS-40002 provided the details of the sale: the cost of the materials purchased was $500 plus $65 HST.

Daniel BenDavid returned a set of wheel nuts because they were not required. The returned items were recorded as Tridon's sale on form #R-132 on Dec. 21 using account 4130 Sales Returns & Allowances, a new Group revenue account. The handling charge was recorded to Other Revenue and all amounts were allocated to Sales. With the owner's permission, the refund was paid in cash.

items returned			amount	total
–4	WN01	Chrome Wheel Nuts	$10 /pkg	–$40.00
		Handling charge (20% of total sales price)		9.04
		Harmonized Sales Tax	13%	–4.02
		Total cash paid to customer		–$34.98

Sales order #12-1 for Lovely U Cosmetics was filled by Tridon on Dec. 21 and recorded as sale #133. Terms of sale were 2/10, n/30 with $4 743 as the balance owing. Revenue from the sale was allocated entirely to the Sales Division.

items sold			amount
1	LC1	Lovely U Cosmetics Inventory	$5 100
		Harmonized Sales Tax	13%

SESSION DATE – DECEMBER 28, 2012

Tridon made an Interac sale (sale #134) to Cedric Ng on Dec. 22, 2012. 100% of the revenue from the sale of inventory items was allocated to the Sales Division; 100% of revenue for the service item to Service Division and 95% of revenue for WHP1 to Sales and 5% to Service Division.

items sold			amount	total
4	T111	P205/65R16 Tires	$135 each	$ 540.00
4	W103	Aluminum R16 Wheels	210 each	840.00
2	WHP1	Tires/Wheels/Winter Pkg	900	1 800.00
2	SRV03	Brake Service - standard pkg	140	280.00
		Harmonized Sales Tax	13%	449.80
		Total paid in full by debit card #5300 5291 6730 8161		$3 909.80

NOTES

Remember to enter the quantity returned with a minus sign and to change the default account.

Enter Tridon as the salesperson so that her net sales revenue will be calculated correctly for the sales commission.

WARNING!

When filling the sales order, change the method of payment to Pay Later.

Allow the customer to exceed the credit limit.

☐ Received invoice #SW-1159 from Sylverado Wheels with shipment on Dec. 22 with payment terms of net 30 days. Total import duty for the purchase was ¥1 584 (CAD $17.42). The purchase was recorded with an exchange rate of 0.011 and the freight was charged to Sales.

items purchased		amount	duty rate
8	W107 Chrome-Steel R16 Wheels	¥26 400	6%
	Freight	1 000	
	HST Paid	3 562	
	Invoice Total	¥30 962	

☐ Recorded invoice #TS-817 for shocks and parts for service work from TuffArm Shocks on Dec. 22. Cost of the parts was $2 000 plus $260 HST. Invoice total $2 260 is due in 30 days.

☐ Deposited receipt #85, cheque #9902 from Airport Taxi Service, cheque #9902 for $4 631.15 in payment of invoice #130 on Dec. 23. $94.51 discount allowed.

☐ Wrote cheque #207 to MoTech Auto Parts, for $839.41 to pay invoice #MT-1521 on Dec. 23 and take early payment discount of $17.13.

☐ Purchased brake hoses, cables, pads and other brake parts and hardware from MoTech Auto Parts on December 26. Invoice #MT-1894 showed $800 for the parts plus $104 HST. Total amount of $904 due in 30 days; 2% discount if full amount is paid in 10 days.

☐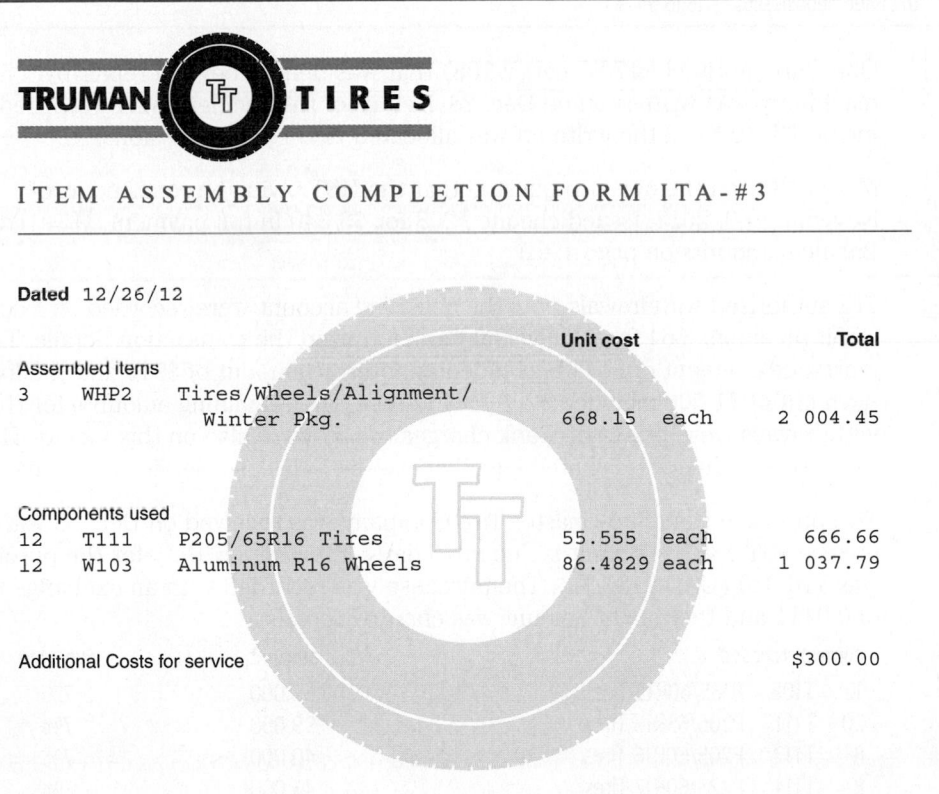

TRUMAN ⓉⓉ TIRES

ITEM ASSEMBLY COMPLETION FORM ITA-#3

Dated 12/26/12

			Unit cost		Total
Assembled items					
3	WHP2	Tires/Wheels/Alignment/ Winter Pkg.	668.15	each	2 004.45
Components used					
12	T111	P205/65R16 Tires	55.555	each	666.66
12	W103	Aluminum R16 Wheels	86.4829	each	1 037.79
Additional Costs for service					$300.00

NOTES
Accept the default prices for assembly components and copy the Total to the assembled items Amount field.

☐ Paid invoice # ST-1141 from Snowmaster Tire Company with cheque #333 for ¥182 495 on Dec. 26. The recorded exchange rate was 0.0112.

NOTES
Allow the customer to exceed the credit limit.

On Dec. 27, 2012, Tridon sold winter packages to City Cab Company (sale #135). The customer's terms are 2/10, n/30. For WHP1, 95% of revenue was allocated to Sales and 5% to Service Division. For WHP2, 90% of revenue for WHP2 to Sales and 10% to Service Division.

items sold			amount
1	WHP1	Tires/Wheels/Winter Pkg	$ 900 /pkg
2	WHP2	Tires/Wheels/Alignment/Winter Pkg	1 400 /pkg
	Harmonized Sales Tax		13%

NOTES
If you have difficulty accessing the Allo column, you can click an employee name and then click the Allo tool button.

EMPLOYEE TIME SUMMARY SHEET #52   **DATED DEC. 28/12**

(pay period ending December 28, 2012)

Name of Employee	Week 1	Week 2	Regular Hours	Overtime Hours	No. of Piece Rate Jobs	Sick Days	Personal Days
Delco	40	42	80	2	10	–	–
Holley	42	40	80	2	5	–	–
Monroe	42	40	80	2	6	1	–
Niehoff	40	44	80	4	5	–	2

a. Use Employee Time Summary Sheet #52 and the Employee Information Sheet to complete the payroll run for hourly paid employees.
b. Add a holiday bonus of $200 to each employee's paycheque. Use the Bonus field for the bonus.
c. Allocate 100% of the payroll expenses to Service for all employees.
d. Issue deposit slips #116 to #119.

One Chrome-Steel R17 Wheel (W108) that was dented beyond repair by machinery was written off on Dec. 28. Details of the accident were recorded in memo #7. 100% of the write-off was allocated to the Sales division.

Memo #8 from the owner requested that the HST owing be remitted as of November 30, 2012. Issued cheque #208 for $3 340 in full payment. (Use Trial Balance amounts on page 499.)

Pre-authorized withdrawals from the chequing account were recorded on Dec. 28. Debit memo #92564 from Universal Bank itemized the transaction details. The mortgage payment of $1 000 included an interest amount of $910 and the loan payment of $1 200 included $200 for interest. The remaining amounts for these withdrawals were principal. Bank charges of $30 were also on this memo. The expense amounts were shared equally between Sales and Service Divisions.

NOTES
You will see another message about Variance Costs not fully allocated.

Tire purchase from Snowmaster Tire Company was received on Dec. 28 with invoice #ST-1383. Payment is due in 15 days. Total import duty for the purchase was ¥16 380 (CAD $181.81). The purchase was recorded with an exchange rate of 0.0111 and the freight amount was charged to Sales.

items purchased			amount	duty rate
12	T108	P185/60R15 Tires	¥ 52 000	7%
20	T111	P205/65R16 Tires	99 000	7%
8	T112	P205/60R16 Tires	40 000	7%
8	T114	P225/60R17 Tires	43 000	7%
	Freight		5 000	
	HST Paid		31 070	
	Invoice Total		¥270 070	

Truman Tires
600 Westminster St., London, ON N6P 3B1
Tel: (519) 729-3733 Fax: (519) 729-7301

Date of sale: Dec. 28/12

To: Summary
One-time cash customers

INVOICE 136

No.	Item		Price	Total	Division*
8	T112	P205/60R16 Tires	140	1 120.00	Sales
4	W101	Aluminum R14 Wheels	180	720.00	Sales
4	W103	Aluminum R16 Wheels	210	840.00	Sales
4	W105	Chrome-Steel R14 Wheels	70	280.00	Sales
4	WN02	Chrome Wheel Locks	25	100.00	Sales
5	SRV01	Alignment - standard	75	375.00	Service
3	SRV03	Brake Service - standard pkg	140	420.00	Service
3	SRV07	Shocks - economy gas-charged	100	300.00	Service

Terms: Cash

* Internal use only	**Salesperson:** Tridon	**HST# 230 192 821**	**13%**	540.15

Total cash deposited to bank 12/28/12 *T Tridon*		**4 695.15**

Truman Tires
600 Westminster St., London, ON N6P 3B1
Tel: (519) 729-3733 Fax: (519) 729-7301

Date of sale: Dec. 28/12

To: Louise Binder
One-time customer

INVOICE 137

No.	Item		Price	Total	Division*
4	T114	P225/60R17 Tires	150	600.00	Sales
4	W104	Aluminum R17 Wheels	225	900.00	Sales
4	WN04	Nickel/Chrome Wheel Locks	30	120.00	Sales
1	SRV08	Shocks - premium gas-matic	140	140.00	Service

Terms: Visa (4515 7827 4563 8900)

* Internal use only	**Salesperson:** Tridon	**HST# 230 192 821**	**13%**	228.80

Total deposited to bank 12/28/12 *T Tridon*		**1 988.80**

SESSION DATE – DECEMBER 31, 2012

☐ Recorded invoice #SW-1419 from Sylverado Wheels on Dec. 29. Payment is due in 30 days. Total import duty for the purchase was ¥19 704 (CAD $226.60). The purchase was recorded with an exchange rate of 0.0115 and the freight amount was charged to Sales.

items purchased			amount	duty rate
8	W102	Aluminum R15 Wheels	¥ 54 200	6%
16	W103	Aluminum R16 Wheels	123 200	6%
8	W104	Aluminum R17 Wheels	62 600	6%
8	W106	Chrome-Steel R15 Wheels	22 400	6%
20	W107	Chrome-Steel R16 Wheels	66 000	6%
		Freight	5 000	
		HST Paid	43 342	
		Invoice Total	¥376 742	

☐

MEMO #9
Date 12/30/2012
From: T. Tridon
To: T. Truman

Paid import duty charged to Receiver General on all outstanding purchases (#SW-1159, ST-1383, SW-1419).

Wrote cheque #209 for $425.83 to pay balance in full.

Trish Tridon

☐ Memo #10 from Owner on Dec. 31 requested a payroll run for Fram and Tridon, salaried employees, with holiday bonus amounts ($300 for Fram and $500 for Tridon) added. Deposit slips #120 and 121 were issued. 50% of Tridon's pay was allocated to Sales and 50% to Service. 60% of Fram's pay was allocated to Sales and 40% to Service.

☐ Also issued cheque #210 to Tridon for $359.40, her sales commission (1% of sales less returns based on Income Statement amounts). Allocated 100% of the commission to Sales. 10% income tax was withheld. (Refer to margin notes.)

☐ Memo #10 also included a reminder to make payroll remittances for the December 31 pay period. Entered Memo #10a, 10b, etc., as the reference.

Issued cheque #211 to Receiver General for Canada for EI, CPP and Income Tax
Issued cheque #212 to Minister of Finance for EHT
Issued cheque #213 to Equity Life for CSB Payable
Issued cheque #214 to CAW Union for Union Dues
Issued cheque #215 to Workplace Safety & Insurance Board for WSIB

NOTES
Use the Bonus field for the bonus amounts.

Issue a separate cheque for Tridon's sales commission. Use the Paycheques Journal so that you can change the tax amounts. Remove the salary hours and amounts. Click the Taxes tab. Choose the Enter Taxes Manually tool to open the tax fields for editing. Enter 35.94 in the Income Tax field. Do not remove the CPP amount. Remove the CSB deduction on the Deductions tab screen and the number of hours worked on the Entitlements tab screen.

The Sales by Salesperson Report includes revenue from services. The sales commission is based only on the sales revenue.

☐ Received credit memo #65925 from Universal Bank on Dec. 31. $215 interest was deposited to chequing account. This entry required a new Group account 4200 Revenue from Interest. 50% of the interest revenue was allocated to Sales and 50% to the Service Division.

☐ Memo #11 from Owner on Dec. 31 reminded that adjusting entries were needed for supplies and parts used. Allocated 90% of the Parts and Garage supplies to Service and 10% to Sales. Allocated 50% of the Office Supplies to Service and 50% to Sales. Inventory counts were used for the following entries:

part/supplies used	amount	new account required
Brakes and Shocks Parts	$4 900	5160 Brakes & Shocks Parts Used
Supplies: Garage	1 820	5170 Supplies Used: Garage
Supplies: Office	430	5180 Supplies Used: Office

KEYSTROKES

Creating New Divisions

Simply Accounting allows allocations for all accounts. Each account ledger record has a check box to allow division allocations for the account (refer to page 94). If this box is checked, the allocation option is available for that account in any journal entry. If it is not checked, you cannot allocate an amount for that account. If you are unable to allocate an amount, check the ledger record for the account you are using to be sure that the option to Allow Division Allocations is selected. Truman Tires will allocate amounts for all revenue and expense accounts. The option to allow allocations is already turned on for all these accounts in your file.

Before entering any transactions with allocations, you should create the divisions.

Open   **SimData10\Truman\truman. Enter Dec 7, 2012** as the session date.

Click   **OK** to enter the session date. The Receivables Home window appears.

Click   **Divisions** in the Modules pane list to change the Home window:

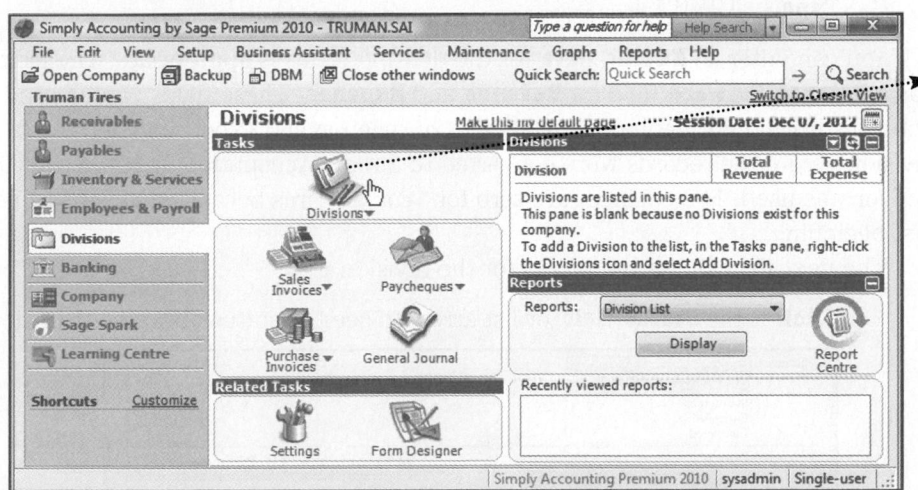

Click   **Make This My Default Page** to keep this as the Home window.

The Divisions module window has access to the Divisions ledger records, as well as to four journals that most often have allocated amounts. Divisions are created from the

NOTES
Allocation for the new revenue and expense accounts should be the default setting.

NOTES
Assign the Expense or Operating Expense account class to the new accounts. Operating Expense is the default when you use the Add Account wizard.

NOTES
For Truman Tires, the option to allow allocations is not selected in the ledger records for Balance Sheet accounts.

PRO VERSION
The ledger record option is to Allow Project Allocations.

NOTES
If you are working with backups, you should restore SimData10\truman1.CAB to SimData10\Truman\truman.

PRO VERSION
Click Projects in the Modules pane list. The ledger is named Projects instead of Divisions. We will change this name on page 520.

NOTES
For the Retail company type, Projects are named Divisions. For other industry types, the term Project, Fund, Job Site, Partner, Crops or Property will be applied. Refer to Appendix B in this text.

NOTES

You can also enter allocations in the Inventory Adjustments Journal, but the Divisions icon is not included in the Inventory module window.

Divisions icon that opens the Division window. The Division window can be also be accessed from the Company, Receivables, Payables and Employees & Payroll modules:

These four modules, as shown above, include the Divisions icon in the Tasks panes. These modules have journals that use allocations.

Click the **Divisions icon** to open the Division window:

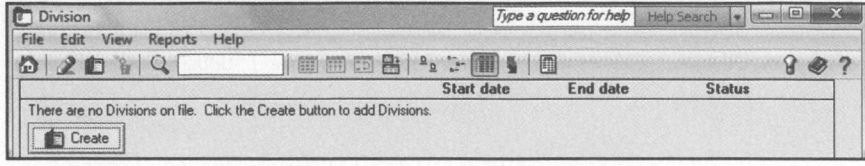

PRO VERSION

Click the Projects icon. You will see Project and Project Ledger as the headings in the Title bar for these screens instead of Division and Division Ledger.

Click **Create**. The new Division Ledger screen appears:

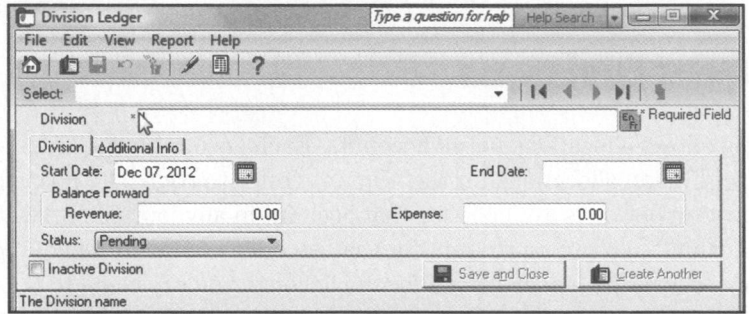

The cursor is in the Division name field, the only required field for the new record. You must enter the name of the first division.

Type Sales Division **Press** (tab) **twice** to skip the language button.

NOTES

You can enter division names in French and English when you choose to use both languages.

The cursor moves to the Start Date field. Enter the date on which you want to begin recording division information, December 1, 2012. The session date appears automatically as the default, ready to be edited. You need to change the date.

Type 12-01

You can enter an **Ending Date** for the division if this is appropriate. The ledger also has a **Balance Forward** field for **Revenue** and **Expense**. These fields can be used to enter historical information — the amount of revenue and expense generated by the division before the records were converted to Simply Accounting or before the Division Ledger was used. The balances are zero for Truman Tires because a new fiscal period is just beginning.

The next field shows the Status for the division.

Click the **Status field** or list arrow to see the status options:

The division may be Pending (not yet started), In Progress or ongoing, Cancelled or Completed. The two divisions at Truman Tires are In Progress or active.

Click **In Progress** from the Status drop-down list.

Click **Create Another** [Create Another] to save the new division.

Enter the **Service Division** division, using the steps described above for the Sales Division, **use Dec 1, 2012** as the starting date and **select In Progress** as the Status.

Click **Save And Close** 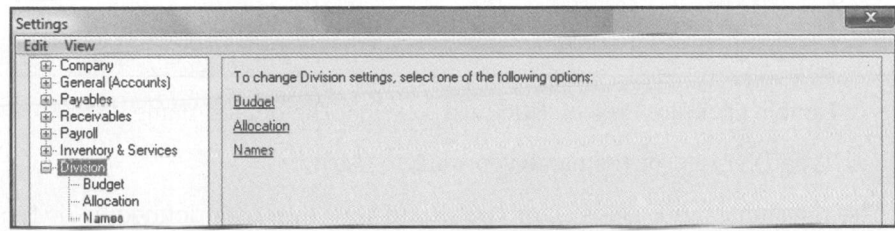 to save the second division.

You will return to the Division window. Notice that Simply Accounting has created a listing for each division including the name, starting and ending dates and status.

Close the **Division window** to return to the module window. The two divisions are added to the Division pane in the module window.

Changing Division Settings

Click the **Settings icon** to display the Settings window as shown:

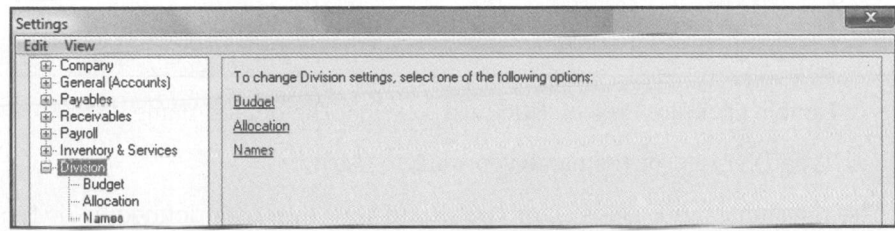

Or choose the Setup menu, then choose Settings. If the Divisions module window is open, the Division Settings screen should open directly.

The Division Ledger has settings for budgeting, allocation and names. Budgeting is covered in Chapter 14. We need to view the setting for allocations.

Click **Allocation** either in the list under Division or in the list on the right:

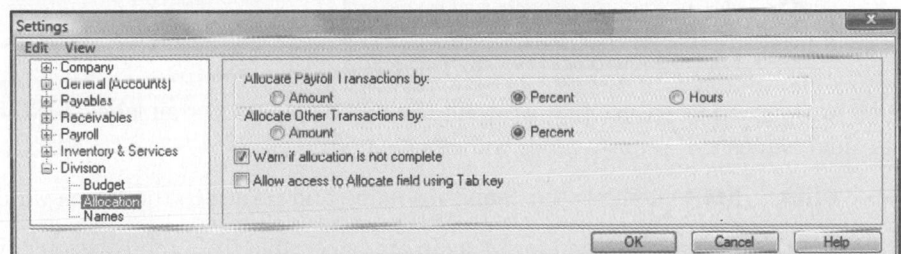

You can enter the allocation in different ways — by Amount, by Percent or by Hours. The option to Allocate By Amount requires you to enter the exact dollar amount for each division. Division work for payroll purposes is often recorded by time spent on the division. This is the third option for payroll allocations.

Simply Accounting includes a warning for incomplete allocations. It is easy to miss an allocation because you must complete the allocation procedure even if 100 percent of the costs are allocated to a single division, and you must allocate each account line in the journals. You will receive the warning if you try to post an entry that has not been fully allocated. If you are using divisions, you should always turn on the warning. The warning should be selected by default.

If this option is not selected, click Warn If Allocation Is Not Complete. The default settings to allocate expenses by percentage are correct.

You can also choose to access Allocate fields in journals with the ⌨tab key. Without this option, you must click the Divisions field to access it or click the Allocate tool to open the Allocation window. Using the ⌨tab key allows you to use the keyboard to enter the transaction and allocation. You can still click the field to move the cursor if you want.

Click **Allow Access To Allocate Field Using Tab Key**.

PRO VERSION

These steps are included so that Pro version users will see the same names as the Premium version users.

NOTES

We are not renaming Divisions as Departments because Simply Accounting has a feature called departmental accounting that is different from division allocation (see Chapter 19).

NOTES

Once the project name is changed by changing the Names setting, the terms will not change automatically when you change the industry type. You must change the name on the Settings screen if you want to use a different term.

Changing Division Names

In any version, you can change the name of the Ledger to Project, Department, Profit Centre, Cost Centre or something that is more appropriate for a business. The new name will replace Division in all windows and reports. Division as the ledger name for Truman Tires' Sales and Service Departments is appropriate.

Pro version users should change the name from Project to Division.

> **Click**   **Names** under the Division heading:

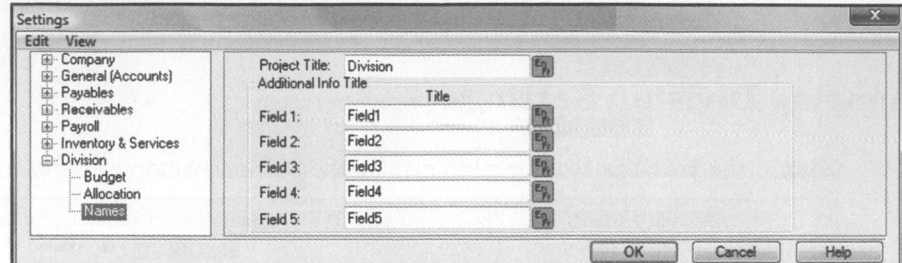

Double click the Project Title field to select the default name.

Type Division (or the name you want to use).

The remaining input fields allow you to add your own user-defined fields for the ledger. The new fields will appear on the Additional Info tab screen. The ledger name can be changed at any time by repeating this step.

> **Click**   **OK** to save the Division settings.

A confirmation message is displayed when you change the name:

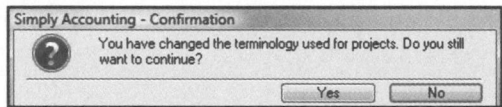

We are warned to ensure that we want the name changed — all labels for the ledger icons, field names and report names will be changed.

> **Click**   **Yes** to confirm the change in name and return to the Home window.

Most of the journals we need for Truman are accessible from the Divisions module window; therefore, we will work from here. We can create shortcuts for the other journals used.

NOTES

All transactions can be completed from these shortcuts and journal windows. For example, other payments and payroll remittances are completed from the Payments Journal. Orders and Quotes are entered from the Sales Invoices or Purchase Invoices windows by selecting from the transactions drop-down list in the journal.

> **Create**   **shortcuts** for **Pay Purchase Invoices** (Payables), **Create Receipt** (Receivables), **Transfer Funds** (Banking), **Item Assembly** and **Inventory Adjustments** (Inventory & Services) and **Payroll Cheque Run** (Employees & Payroll).

Entering Cost Allocations

Costs (or expenses) and revenues are allocated after the regular journal details are added but before the entry is posted. In a journal entry, whenever you use an account for which you have allowed division allocations in the General Ledger, the allocation option is available. For Truman Tires, all revenue and expense accounts allow division allocations.

NOTES

You can allow allocations for Balance Sheet accounts, but we have not done so for Truman Tires.

> **Click**   the **Purchase Invoices icon** ![Purchase Invoices] to open the Purchases Journal.

The journal has not changed with the setup of allocations, and we enter the purchase details the same way.

The first transaction does not involve the purchase of inventory items, so you will not use the inventory database to complete this transaction. Invoice is correct as the transaction type, and Pay Later is the correct payment method.

From the list of suppliers,

Click   London Tool Rentals.

Click the **Invoice No. field**.

Type L-4441 **Press** ⌨tab twice.

The cursor moves to the Date field. Replace the default session date with the transaction date.

Type dec 1 12

The tax code H and the account number 5110 should be added as the default. If they are not, you can add them or edit them as needed.

Enter a **description**.

Click the **Amount field** or press ⌨tab repeatedly to advance the cursor.

Type 280

Press ⌨tab **twice** to enter the amount of the invoice and the tax amounts, and to advance to the Divisions column.

The journal now looks like a regular completed purchase transaction:

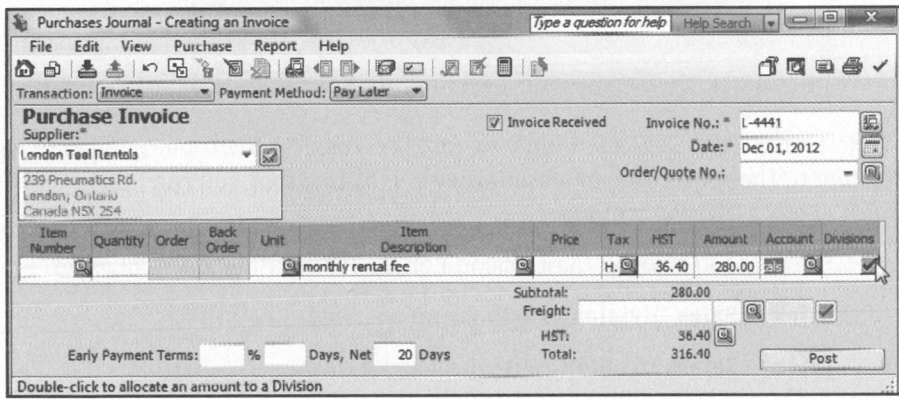

Notice that the Allocate tool 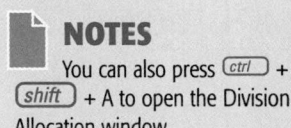 is no longer dimmed. The cursor must be on an invoice line with an account that allows allocation. If the account does not allow allocation or if the cursor has advanced to an invoice line without an account, the Allocate tool and menu option will be dimmed and unavailable.

Click the invoice line for the amount you want to allocate to activate the Allocate option. Only accounts that have selected the option to Allow Division Allocations will activate the Allocate tool.

Click the **Allocate tool** 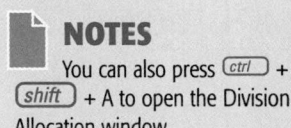 in the tool bar or in the Divisions column, or **double click** the **Divisions column** beside the account or **choose** the **Purchase menu** and **click Allocate**.

NOTES
You can also press ⌨ctrl + ⌨shift + A to open the Division Allocation window.

You will see the Division Allocation window for the Purchases Journal:

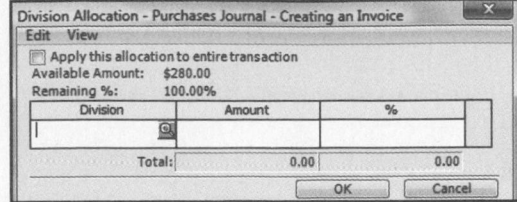

The cursor is in the Division field. The full amount to be allocated, $280 (the base expense amount), is shown at the top for reference together with the proportion remaining to be allocated, 100.00%. Amounts can be allocated by percentage or by actual amount. This choice is made in the Division Settings window shown on page 519. (Choose the Setup menu, click Settings and then click Division and Allocation.) The setting can be changed as needed. Truman Tires uses the Percentage allocation method as indicated in the Division Information.

You must complete the allocation process even if 100 percent of the revenue or expense is assigned to a single division. You must complete the allocation process for each account or invoice line on your input form.

Click the **Division List icon** 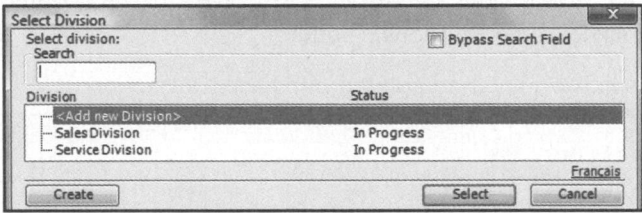 to display the Divisions in alphabetic order:

The first division is Sales, which incurs 20 percent of the total rental expense according to the source document information. Notice that you can add a new division from the Select Division window.

Choose Add to open the Division Ledger for creating a new division.

Click **Sales Division**, the first one we need.

Click **Select** to enter it on your form.

The cursor advances to the Percentage field because we selected this method of allocation. By default the unallocated portion (100%) is indicated in this field and selected for editing.

Type 20 **Press** (tab).

The program calculates the dollar amount for this division automatically based on the percentage entered. The percentage remaining at the top of the input form has been updated to 80.00%. The cursor moves to the next line in the Division field. Now you are ready to enter the amount for the remaining division, 80 percent. You need to repeat the steps above to allocate the remainder of the expense.

Press (enter).

Double click **Service Division**.

The cursor is in the Percentage field again, with 80.00 as the default amount because this was the unallocated percentage remaining. Since this amount is correct, we can accept it.

Press ⟨tab⟩ to enter it and complete the allocation as shown here:

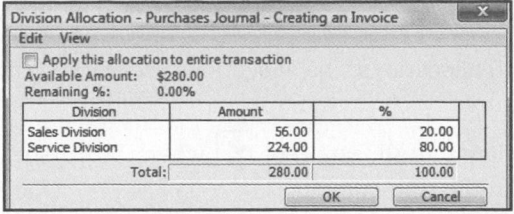

Click **OK** to return to the Purchases Journal.

Your form is now complete as shown, and you are ready to review your work:

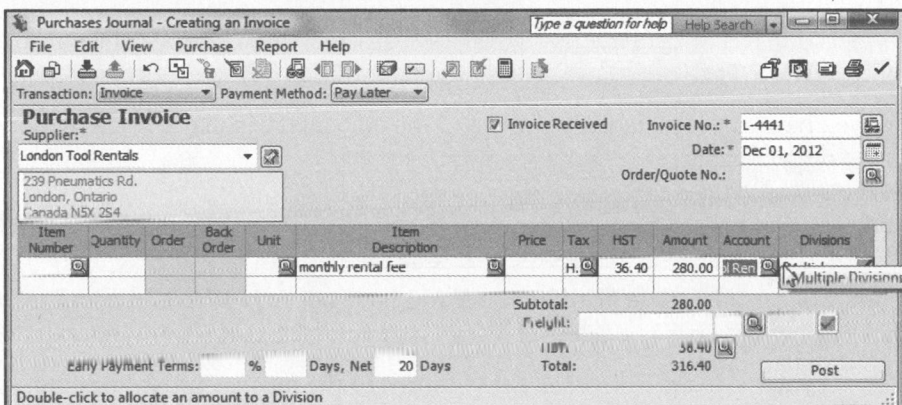

The journal appears unchanged, except for the entry in the Divisions column indicating that the amount has been allocated. The Division name is entered, but because more than one division was used, the entry is Multiple Divisions.

Reviewing the Purchases Journal Allocation

Choose the **Report menu** and **click Display Purchases Journal Entry**:

Truman Tires					
Purchases Journal Entry 12/01/12 (J1)					
Account Number	Account Description	Division	Debits	Credits	Division Amt
2670	HST Paid on Purchases		36.40	-	
5110	Tool Rentals		280.00	-	
		- Sales Division			56.00
		- Service Division			224.00
2200	Accounts Payable		-	316.40	
Additional Date:	Additional Field:		316.40	316.40	

Simply Accounting has automatically updated the *Accounts Payable* control account because the Payables and General ledgers are fully integrated. Notice also that the rental expense has been allocated to the two divisions. Only the amount for the expense account *Tool Rentals* is allocated because the other accounts are Balance Sheet accounts that are not set up to allow allocations.

Close the **display** to return to the Purchases Journal input screen.

CORRECTING THE PURCHASES JOURNAL ENTRY ALLOCATION

Correct the Purchases Journal part of the entry as you would correct any other purchase invoice. Refer to page 120 if you need assistance.

If you have made an error in the allocation, **click** the **Allocate tool** ☑ to return to the Allocation window. **Click** the **line** for the amount being allocated to activate the Allocate tool if necessary. **Click** an **incorrect division** to highlight it. **Press** ⟨enter⟩ to access the Division list. **Click** the **correct division** and **click Select** to enter the change. **Click** an **incorrect percentage** and **type** the **correct information**. **Press** ⟨tab⟩ to save the correction. **Click OK** to return to the Journal window.

Click   the **Store tool** 📥. Accept the supplier name and **choose Monthly** as the frequency. **Click OK** to return to the journal.

When you store a transaction with allocations, the allocations are stored with the other transaction details.

To see the allocation again, click the Allocate tool ☑ when the cursor is on the relevant line or click the ✓ in the Allo column.

Posting

When you are certain that you have entered all the information correctly,

Click   **Post** [Post] to save the entry. **Click OK** to confirm posting.

If you have not allocated 100 percent of the amounts, you may see the warning:

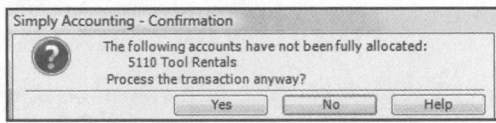

You will see a message like this one if you have not fully allocated a journal amount. If the warning option is not selected (page 519) you may post a transaction incorrectly.

If you made an error, click No to return to the invoice in the Purchases Journal. Click the Allo column beside the account that is not fully allocated to return to the Allocation screen. Make the changes, click OK and then post.

If you do not want to allocate the full amount, or if the account that was not fully allocated was one for which you cannot access the allocation procedure, such as *Variance Costs* (see page 530), you should click Yes to continue.

Close   the **Purchases Journal**. The Division list pane total revenue and expense amounts have been updated with amounts from this transaction. Click the list pane refresh tool 🔄 if necessary to update division amounts.

Enter   the next **two payment** and **two receipt transactions**.

Entering Import Duties

Governments may apply import duties that raise the price of imported goods to encourage the local economy. Duty rates or tariffs vary from one type of item to another, and from one country to another. The duty is collected by Canada Revenue Agency when the goods first enter Canada, before they are released to the buyer.

In Simply Accounting, before you can enter duty amounts with the purchase, you must change the Payables settings to charge and track import duties (see page 644). You must also indicate in the foreign supplier's record (Options tab screen) that duty is applied to purchases from that supplier (see page 659). In the Inventory Ledger records (Taxes tab screen), you can enter the duty applied as a percentage (see page 675), or you can enter the rates in the Purchases Journal. For non-inventory purchases, you must enter the rate directly in the Purchases Journal.

The purchase invoice from Snowmaster Tire Company has import duties applied because Canada does not have a free trade agreement with Japan. The company settings and the Supplier and Inventory Ledger records for Truman Tires are set up to apply duty.

Open   the **Purchases Journal**.

📝 **NOTES**
You should click OK for the successful posting message each time you record or post a transaction. We will not repeat this instruction.

📝 **NOTES**
Later in the chapter, we will see that cost variances are not allocated.
You may want to proceed with an incomplete allocation when part of the amount applies to none of the divisions or it applies to an earlier time period before division recording was started.

📝 **NOTES**
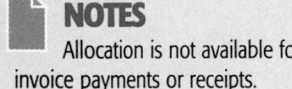
Allocation is not available for invoice payments or receipts.

Choose Snowmaster Tire Company as the supplier and **press** ⌞tab⌟:

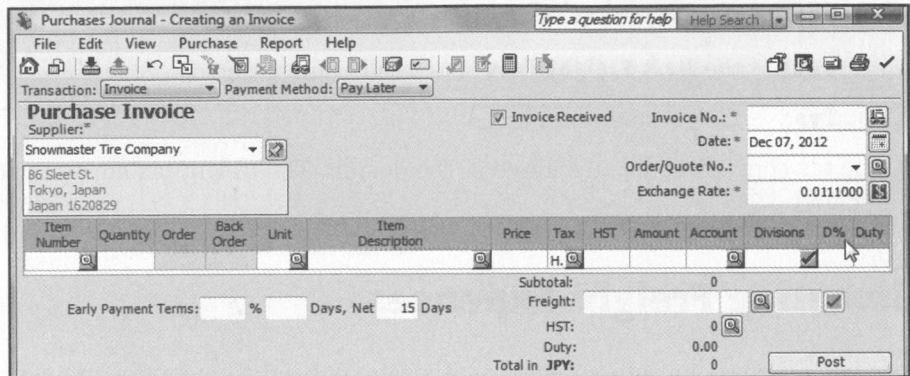

In addition to the Exchange Rate field and the indication that Japanese yen (JPY) is the currency for this supplier, the duty fields are added because we selected a supplier for whom duty applies. The extra fields are used for the duty percentage and for the duty amount. Duty is charged on all items purchased from Snowmaster Tire Company.

Click   the **Invoice field** and **type** ST-916

Enter   **Dec 2-12** in the Date field and **press** ⌞tab⌟ to open the Exchange Rate screen with the most recent rate highlighted.

Type   .0109 **Click Make This The Default Rate For Dec. 2, 2012**.

Click   **OK** to return to the journal.

Click   the **Item Description field**. **Type** miscellaneous parts

Click   the **Amount field**. **Type** 50000 **Press** ⌞tab⌟.

Choose 1240 Brakes & Shocks Parts from the Account list. **Press** ⌞tab⌟ **twice**.

You will advance the cursor to the D% (duty rate) field where you should enter the rate that the government applies to this type of product.

Type   6 **Press** ⌞tab⌟ to enter the duty amount.

Press   ⌞tab⌟ again to advance to the next line in the Item field. You can now add the inventory item purchases.

Double click the **Item Number field** to open the Inventory Selection screen.

Double click **T110** to add this item to the invoice:

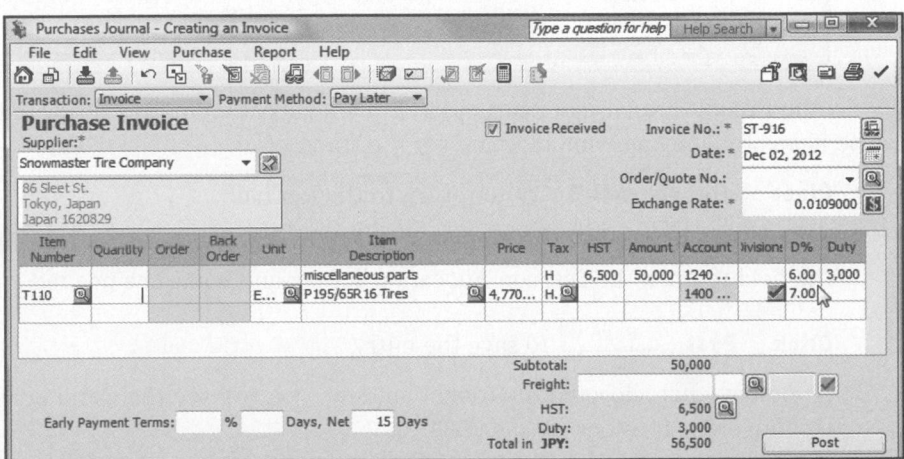

This time the duty rate is added automatically because the rate is recorded in the ledger record for the item.

> **Type** 20 to enter the quantity. **Enter 95000** as the Amount.
>
> **Enter** the **second inventory item** in the same way.
>
> **Click** the **first Freight field**, the freight amount field.
>
> **Type** 6500 and **press** (tab).

The tax code H should be entered as the default. The freight tax amount and total are updated.

Allocating Freight Expenses

When you purchase inventory items, the Allocate tool and menu option are not available because the asset accounts were not set up to allow allocations. However, the freight expense for these purchases can be allocated.

The Freight field **Allocate button** ☑ (to the right of the freight amount field), indicated with the pointer in the following screen, is used for this purpose:

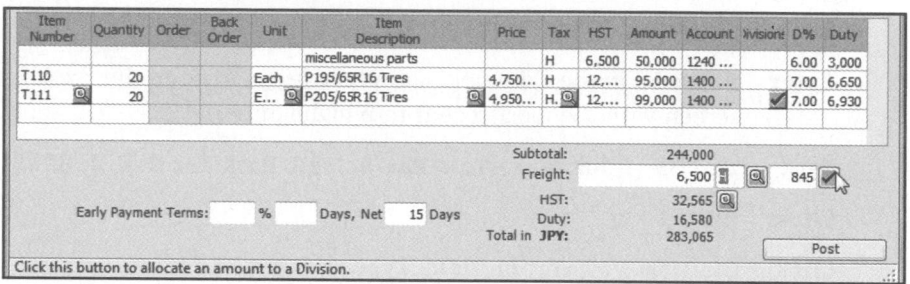

> **Click** the **Allocate button** ☑ to the right of the Freight fields.

The Division Allocation screen opens. It is the same as the one we saw earlier. The Freight amount, ¥6 500, is entered as the amount to be allocated.

> **Choose** the **Sales Division** and **accept** the **amount** and percentage allocation.
>
> **Click** OK to return to the journal. The journal has not changed in appearance.
>
> **Choose** the **Report menu** and **click Display Purchases Journal Entry**:

Account Number	Account Description	Division	Foreign A...	Division Frgn Amt	Debits	Credits	Division Amt
1240	Brakes & Shocks Parts		¥53,000		577.70	-	
1400	Winter Tires		¥207,580		2,262.63	-	
2670	HST Paid on Purchases		¥32,565		354.96	-	
5065	Freight Expense		¥6,500		70.85	-	
		- Sales Division		¥65,000			70.85
2200	Accounts Payable		¥283,065		-	3,085.41	
2220	Import Duty Payable		¥16,580		-	180.73	
1 Japanese Yen equals 0.0109000 Canadian Dollars					3,266.14	3,266.14	

Truman Tires
Purchases Journal Entry 12/07/12 (J6)

Only the Freight Expense amount has a division allocation in the journal entry because it was the only amount allocated for the transaction.

> **Close** the **Journal Entry** to return to the journal.

To correct the freight expense allocation, click the Allocate button ☑ beside the field to open the Division Allocation screen and make the needed changes.

> **Click** Post [Post] to save the entry.

If you have not allocated the freight amount, you will see the warning about incomplete allocations on page 524.

> **Enter** the next **purchase transaction** from Sylverado Wheels.

Allocating in the Sales Journal

Amounts for revenue accounts in the Sales Journal are allocated in the same way as amounts for expense accounts in the Purchases Journal. Each revenue amount in the journal must be allocated completely, but you can assign the same allocation percentages to all accounts in the journal rather than repeating the allocation entry for each invoice line. We will demonstrate this method by showing the steps involved in the Visa sale to Scinto on December 4.

Click   the **Sales icon** to open the Sales Journal.

Enter   **Bruno Scinto** in the Customer field.

Press   `tab`. **Click OK** to accept Continue, the default selection.

Choose **Visa** as the method in the Paid By field.

Enter   **Dec 4 12** as the invoice date.

Choose **Tridon** as the salesperson in the Sold By field.

Click   the **Use The Same Salesperson tool** 📌.

Choose **T104** from the inventory selection list as the first item for the sale. The cursor advances to the Quantity field.

Type   4

Press   `tab` repeatedly to advance to the Divisions column.

Double click the **Divisions column** or **click** ✅ in the Divisions column to open the Division Allocation window.

As long as the cursor is on the invoice line you are allocating, the allocate function is available. Click the Allocate tool button in the tool bar or choose the Sales menu and click Allocate to open the Division Allocation screen.

Choose the **Sales Division** for 100% of the revenue amount.

The allocation screen has a check box for the option Apply This Allocation To Entire Transaction as shown:

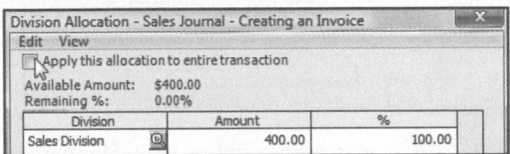

This option allows you to enter the allocation for one amount and let the program apply the same percentages for all other amounts, including freight, automatically. Otherwise you will need to repeat the allocation procedure for each account in the journal.

Click   **Apply This Allocation To Entire Transaction** to open the message about this selection:

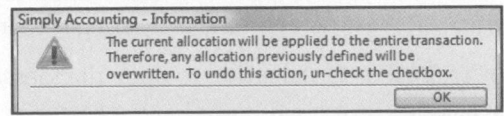

Read   the **message** and then **click OK** to return to the allocation screen.

If you do not want to continue with this selection, click the check box again.

NOTES

You can leave the Sales Journal open in the background while you complete transactions in other journals. The salesperson will remain selected until you change the session date. If you use this approach, ensure that you update the dates and payment methods for each sale.

You can also add Tridon as the salesperson in customer records. Remember to add the salesperson for new customers.

NOTES

You can also press `ctrl` + `shift` + A to open the Division Allocation window.

The Division Allocation screen has changed as shown:

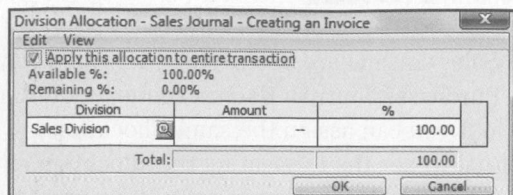

No amounts are entered at this time because the same percentages will be applied and the amounts will be different.

Click   **OK** to save the allocation and return to the journal.

Enter   the **remaining inventory** and **service items** for the sale.

The division name is added to the Divisions column automatically as you complete the invoice:

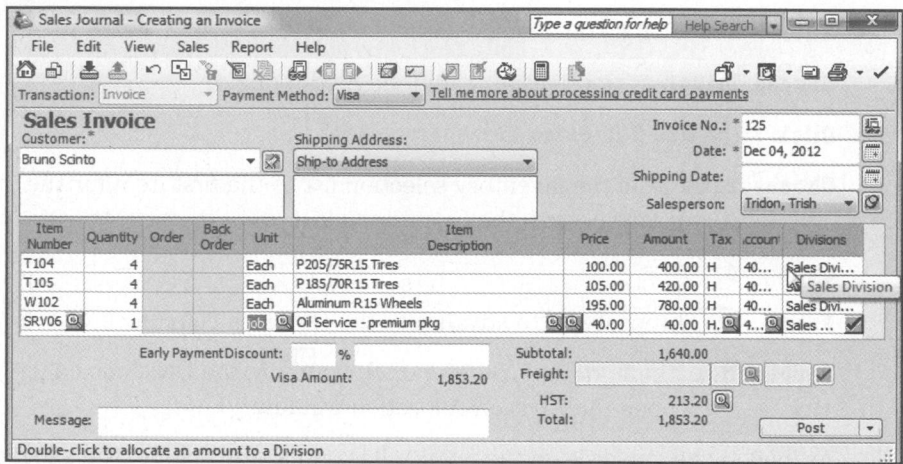

The invoice has been completely allocated, but the allocation is not correct, as you will see when you review the journal entry for the transaction.

Press   `ctrl` + **J** to open the journal display:

Truman Tires					
Sales Journal Entry 12/04/12 (J8)					
Account Number	Account Description	Division	Debits	Credits	Division Amt.
1070	Bank: Visa		1,801.31	-	
5040	Credit Card Fees		51.89	-	
		- Sales Division			51.90
5050	Cost of Goods Sold		640.00	-	
		- Sales Division			640.00
1360	Wheels		-	312.00	
1400	Winter Tires		-	328.00	
2650	HST Charged on Sales		-	213.20	
4020	Revenue from Sales		-	1,600.00	
		- Sales Division			1,600.00
4040	Revenue from Services		-	40.00	
		- Sales Division			40.00
Additional Date:	Additional Field:		2,493.20	2,493.20	

All amounts are allocated to the Sales Division. However, the service revenue should be allocated to the Services Division, so we must change it.

Close   the displayed **report** to return to the journal.

Click   anywhere on the line for **item SRV06**.

Click   the **Allo tool** ☑, **double click Sales** in the Divisions column or **choose** the **Sales menu** and **click Allocate** to open the Allocation screen.

Click   **Apply This Allocation To Entire Transaction** to open the message about this change in selection:

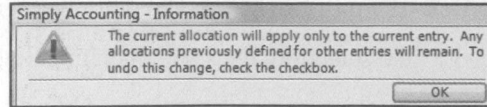

NOTES
After you change this setting, you can change allocations for other amounts individually as well without affecting the remaining allocations.

We can change the allocation for this invoice line without changing any other line.

Click   **OK** to return to the Division Allocation screen.

Click   the **List icon** 🔍 in the Division field to open the list of divisions.

Double click **Service Division** to add it to the Division Allocation screen.

Click   **OK** to save the change. Service has been entered in the Journal.

Choose the **Report menu** and **click Display Sales Journal Entry**:

Account Number	Account Description	Division	Debits	Credits	Division Amt
1070	Bank: Visa		1,801.31	-	
5040	Credit Card Fees		51.89	-	
		- Sales Division			50.63
		- Service Division			1.27
5050	Cost of Goods Sold		640.00	-	
		- Sales Division			640.00
1360	Wheels		-	312.00	
1400	Winter Tires		-	328.00	
2650	HST Charged on Sales		-	213.20	
4020	Revenue from Sales		-	1,600.00	
		- Sales Division			1,600.00
4040	Revenue from Services		-	40.00	
		- Service Division			40.00
Additional Date:	Additional Field:		2,493.20	2,493.20	

Truman Tires — Sales Journal Entry 12/04/12 (J8)

The allocation is now correct. The allocation for *Credit Card Fees* is automatically split in the correct proportion. *Cost of Goods Sold* is also allocated. We can post the entry.

Close   the **Journal Entry** to return to the journal.

Click   **Post** [Post |▾] to save the entry.

↩ **Continue** entering the **transactions** to purchase invoice #ST-1141.

Creating Cost Variances

If items are sold to a customer when the inventory stock is too low to fill the sale completely, the levels in inventory fall below zero and the outstanding items are backordered. The estimated cost of goods for the sale is based on the average cost for the items in stock at the time of the sale. When the items are received, the price may have changed, and the items that fill the rest of the customer's order will have a different cost price from the one recorded for the sale. The difference is the cost variance and is assigned to the linked variance account for the inventory item. The amount of the variance shows in the journal entry for the purchase. Thus two conditions are required for a variance to occur — the inventory is oversold and the cost has changed.

Normally, you do not have to do anything to record a cost variance because the program makes the calculations automatically and assigns the amount to the linked variance account for the inventory item.

After entering the purchase from Snowmaster Tire Company on Dec. 13, display the journal entry. It should match the one shown here:

Account Number	Account Description	Division	Foreign A...	Division Frgn Amt	Debits	Credits	Division Amt
1400	Winter Tires		¥164,751		1,977.01	-	
2670	HST Paid on Purchases		¥20,995		251.94	-	
5055	Variance Costs		¥1,099		13.19	-	
5065	Freight Expense		¥6,500		78.00	-	
		- Sales Division		¥6,500			78.00
2200	Accounts Payable		¥182,495		-	2,189.94	
2220	Import Duty Payable		¥10,850		-	130.20	
1 Japanese Yen equals 0.0120000 Canadian Dollars					2,320.14	2,320.14	

Truman Tires — Purchases Journal Entry 12/13/12 (J20)

There was insufficient stock left for item T101 on Dec. 7 when the cash summary sale was recorded, so the average historic cost for 12 tires, $336, was credited to *Cost of Goods Sold*. Only eight tires were in stock at the time of the sale, with an average cost of $28 ($112 for four tires). When the purchase of item T101 was recorded, the total cost for 16 tires was $500.76, or $125.19 for four tires. The difference, $13.19, between

NOTES
You can also double click the Divisions field, or press [ctrl] + [shift] + A for the selected item to open the Division Allocation screen.

NOTES
When a purchase entry creates a variance and you have not set up the linked account for variances, you will be prompted to select or create a variance account.

NOTES
The calculated price for the four tires includes the import duty at the rate of 7 percent.
The 16 tires cost ¥39 000 (ST-1141 on page 509) plus duty for a total cost of ¥41 730. This amount is multiplied by the exchange rate of 0.0120 for a cost of $500.76 CAD.

the new cost and the cost in the sales transaction for the four out-of-stock tires is the cost variance.

When you post the transaction, you will see the following warning:

> Simply Accounting - Confirmation
> The following accounts have not been fully allocated:
>   5055 Variance Costs
> Process the transaction anyway?
> [Yes]   [No]   [Help]

NOTES
You may also see a message about incomplete allocations resulting from rounding off dollar amounts in currency conversions. In this case, you should check that you have allocated all amounts correctly and then accept the incomplete allocation.

Variance costs cannot be allocated, so you must accept the incomplete allocation.

Click   **Yes** to continue posting the purchase.

Enter   the next group of **transactions** up to memo #4.

Making Import Duty Remittances

Paying the import duty owing on imported merchandise is like paying other taxes. Normally duty must be paid before the package is released by Customs.

Open   the **Payments Journal**. The cheque number, bank account and date are correct.

Choose **Make Other Payment**.

Choose **Receiver General for Canada** as the supplier.

Choose **2220 Import Duty Payable** as the account from the Selection list.

You should record the corresponding purchase invoice numbers in the journal as well.

Type   Duty re ST916, ST1141, SW876, SW1024

Press   (tab) to move to the Amount field.

Type   503.84

Click   the **Invoice/Ref. field** and **type** Memo 4 **Press** (tab).

Type   Memo 4, Import duty remittance

Review the **journal entry**. **Close** the **display**. **Make corrections** if needed and then **post** the **transaction**.

Enter the remaining **transactions** up to Employee Time Sheet Summary #51.

NOTES
You can enter the invoice numbers in the Description field if the entry is very long or in the Comment field if the entry is short.

Allocating in the Payroll and Other Journals

Use the same principles outlined above to allocate revenues and expenses in the General Journal, Adjustments Journal or the Payroll journals to divisions or profit centres. You can change the setup to make allocations by dollar amounts or by percentage (see page 519).

Once you have entered the journal information for an account that allows allocation, the Allocate tool ☑ will be available. You can use it to enter the allocation information.

In the **Paycheques Journal**, click the Allo tool ☑.

To correct allocations, click ☑ to re-open the allocation screen.

In the setup for Payroll allocations, you can choose to allocate expenses according to the number of hours worked on each division (see page 519).

In the **Payroll Cheque Run Journal**, use the Allo column for the employee who is selected from the list. You can allocate for one employee at a time. Click the employee's name. Then click the Allo column or choose the Payroll menu and click Allocate to begin the allocation. You can also apply the same allocation to the entire transaction, just as we did in the Sales Journal.

In the Payroll journals, the total payroll expense, not the net pay, is allocated. This includes employer contributions such as EI, CPP, WSIB/WCB and EHT. When you review the journal entry, you will see that all the payroll-related expenses are divided among the divisions according to the percentages you entered. They are shown under the Division column. You may have to scroll to see all the information.

↺ **Enter** the remaining **transactions**.

Displaying Division Reports

Division reports can be displayed from the Divisions window, from the Division module window Reports pane drop-down list, from the Home window Reports menu and from the Report Centre. We will continue to show reports from the Report Centre.

To print division reports, display the report you want using the instructions that follow. Click the Print tool 🖨 or choose the File menu and click Print.

To display the reports,

Click   the **Report Centre icon** 🗑 in the Home window.

Click   **Division** to open the list of division reports:

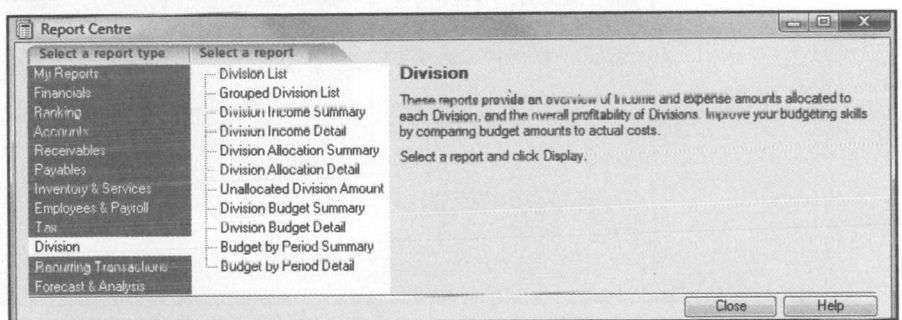

Displaying the Division List

Click   **Division List**. **Click Modify This Report** to open the report options:

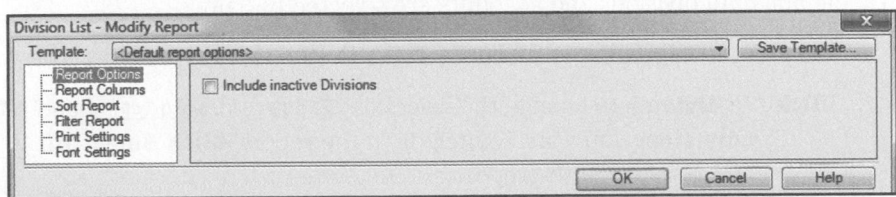

Or, choose the Reports menu, then choose Lists and click Division.

Click Report Columns to customize the fields shown on the report.

Click   **OK**. **Close** the **display** when you have finished viewing the report.

NOTES
The Paycheques Journal does not have a column for allocations, so you must use the tool or the menu approach.

PRO VERSION
pro Remember that if you have not changed the ledger name, you will see Project instead of Division throughout the report menus and options.
For other company types, Division may be replaced by a name that is appropriate for that type of company. Refer to Appendix B in this text.

NOTES
The terms used for other types of industries will replace Division in all report titles and fields.

CLASSIC VIEW
Classic Right-click the Divisions icon  to select it. Click the Display tool  .

NOTES
You can display the Division Allocation Detail Report from the Division List.

Displaying the Grouped Division List

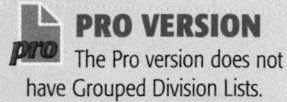

Click **Grouped Division List**. **Click Modify This Report** to see the options.

Click the **Grouped By drop-down list arrow** to see the ways you can organize the report:

You can group the divisions by division status (e.g., pending, in progress and so on), or by any of the additional fields you added for the ledger.

Choose the **criterion** for grouping.

Click **OK**. **Close** the **display** when you have finished viewing the report.

Displaying Division Income Reports

The Division Income Report provides an income statement with revenue, expenses and net income for each division you select for the report.

Click **Division Income Summary**. **Click Modify This Report**:

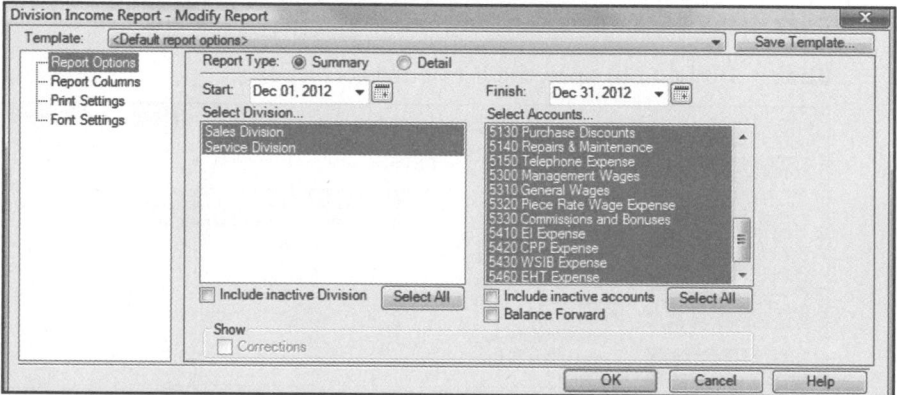

Or, choose the Reports menu, then choose Division and click Income to display the Options window.

NOTES
You can drill down to the Division Income Detail Report from the Division Income Summary Report. You can drill down to the Division Ledger, Journal Report, General Ledger, Invoice Lookup, Customer or Supplier Aged or Employee reports (if applicable) from the Division Income Detail Report.

You can sort and filter Division Income Detail reports by date, comment, source, journal number and amount per transaction. As usual, the fiscal start and session dates are the defaults. All divisions and accounts are selected initially.

Enter the **beginning** and **ending dates** for the report (including the year).

Click a **division** to change the selection. **Press** and **hold** `ctrl` and **click** the **divisions** you want to include in the report. **Click Select All** to include all divisions in the report.

Leave the **Summary** option, the one selected by default, if you want your report to show summary information (i.e., totals) for each account selected for each division. The **Detail** option provides complete journal information for each account for each division selected, including the names of all customers, suppliers and employees, as well as the document's reference number, journal entry number and date. Both options provide a calculation for revenue minus expense.

Next you should select the revenue and expense accounts you want in the report.

Click   an **account** to change the selection. **Press** and **hold** ⎡ctrl⎤ and **click** the **accounts** you want to include in the report or **click Select All** to include them all.

Click   **OK** to display the report. **Close** the **display** when finished.

Displaying Division Allocation Reports

When you allow allocation for Balance Sheet accounts, they are reported in the Division Allocation Report together with Income Statement accounts. The Division Income Report has only revenue and expense accounts.

Click   **Division Allocation Summary**. **Click Modify This Report**:

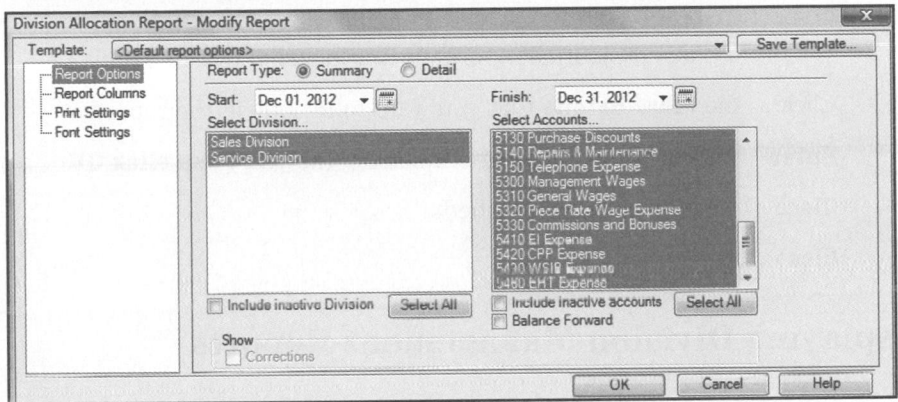

From any Home window, choose the Reports menu, then choose Division and click Allocation to display the Division Allocation Report Options window.

The Division Allocation Report shows the breakdown of amounts for each division by account. It is similar to the Division Income Report, but the total revenue and expense and the net division income are omitted. Instead, a single total for all accounts is provided for each division.

Although the report options look the same as for the Income Report, if you scroll up the list of accounts, you will see that Balance Sheet accounts are included. All reports for which you have allowed allocation will be on the list.

Enter   the **start** and **end dates** for the report (including the year).

Click   a **division** to change the selection. **Press** and **hold** ⎡ctrl⎤ and **click** the **divisions** you want to include in the report or **click Select All**.

Like the Income Report, the Summary option will show totals and the Detail option provides complete journal information for each account for each division.

After you have indicated which options you want, choose the accounts.

Press   and **hold** ⎡ctrl⎤ and **click** the **accounts** you want or **click Select All**.

Click   **OK** to display the report. **Close** the **display** when you have finished.

Adding Division Details to Journal Reports

When you have entered division information in a journal, you can include the allocation details to any journal report.

Click   **Financials** in the Select A Report Type list.

NOTES
You must allow allocations for the Balance Sheet accounts to see all the accounts in this report. Without this change, the Account list will include only the revenue and expense accounts.

NOTES
Drill-down reports from the Allocation Report are the same as the reports from the Division Income Report.

Click   **All Journal Entries**. **Click Modify This Report**:

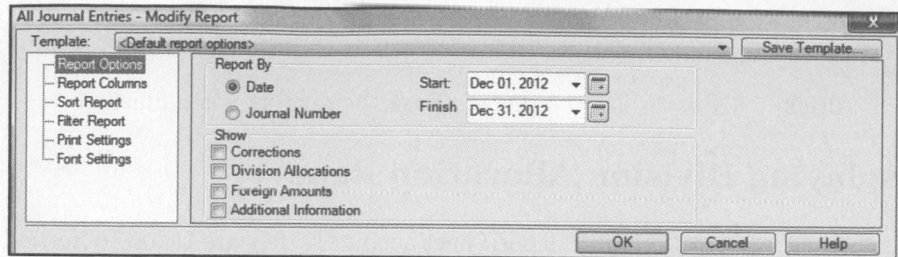

The Journal Report Options window includes a check box for division allocations. For a complete Journal Report, you should also show foreign amounts, corrections and additional information.

Click   **Division Allocations** to include division information in journal reports. By default, journal reports do not include division details.

Click   the **other details** that you want to include in the report.

Enter   the **dates** for the report (including the year) and **click OK**.

Close   the **display** when finished.

Close   the **Report Centre**.

Displaying Division Management Reports

There are management reports for the Division Ledger, just as there are for other ledgers in Simply Accounting. Management Reports can be displayed only from the Home window Reports menu.

Choose   the **Reports menu**, then **choose Management Reports** and **click Division** to see the list of management reports:

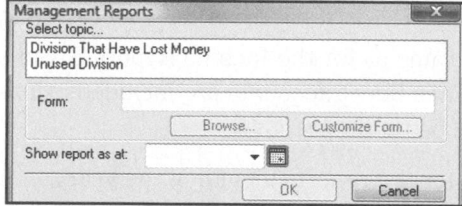

Click   the **topic** for the report. **Click OK** to display the report. **Close** the **display** when you have finished.

CHAPTER FOURTEEN

Village Galleries

OBJECTIVES

After completing this chapter, you should be able to

- **turn on** the budgeting feature in Simply Accounting
- **determine** budgeting periods and amounts
- **allocate** budget amounts to revenue and expense accounts
- **enter** transactions involving Quebec Sales Tax
- **display** and **print** income statements with budget comparisons
- **graph** budget reports
- **analyze** budget reports
- **print** invoices in batches

COMPANY INFORMATION

Company Profile

NOTES
Village Galleries
509 Boul. Rouin
Montreal, QC H3F 5G5
Tel: (514) 529-6391
Fax: (514) 529-7622
Business No.: 236 412 540

Village Galleries, located in Outremont, an upscale area of Montreal, is owned and operated by Renée and Gilles Montand, a husband-and-wife partnership. The small family-run business recently hired one employee, who will earn a commission on sales. She works in the store several days a week but the Montands maintain the regular operation of the business. Renée performs the accounting duties for the business. Other jobs are occasionally subcontracted.

The store, more like a furniture boutique, carries a limited range of high-quality inventory, selling to clients who are selective in their furniture and accessory preferences. Accessories and furniture for living rooms, bedrooms, dining rooms and kitchens comprise the major inventory items in the boutique. The brass furniture pieces are imported from Italy, and some items are high-quality reproductions of antiques made in small Quebec furniture factories by respected artisans. Most of the furniture is made of wood or wood frames covered with fine fabrics. The choice of wood includes mahogany, oak, cherry, ash and, of course, pine. Rich select woods of the highest quality are used to create solid wood pieces, but sometimes expensive veneers are used to complement the designs. In addition, the furniture boutique sells home accessories such as lamps, a small selection of handmade Persian and Oriental rugs made of wool and silk, mirrors and original framed numbered prints imported from Italy.

Most customers are local but, occasionally, customers from abroad who visit Montreal ask for furniture to be shipped to them. Delivery (shipping or freight) is charged on most orders and exported items. Preferred price list customers do not pay for delivery, and they receive discounted inventory prices. All account customers are entitled to a before-tax 2 percent discount if they settle their accounts within 10 days. After 30 days, interest charges accrue at the rate of 1.5 percent per month. Customer deposits from 20 to 25 percent of the total sale are required on all orders. Customers may pay by cheque, cash or credit card.

Some suppliers with whom Village Galleries has accounts require deposits to accompany purchase orders, and some suppliers offer after-tax purchase discounts for early payments. The store has a business credit card account with American Express.

The currency for all foreign transactions, including the purchases from Italy and the sales to European customers, is the euro (€). Foreign prices for inventory are calculated from the exchange rate at the time of sale. No foreign prices are entered in the inventory ledger. Village Galleries pays import duties on the imported furniture but not on original art work such as the numbered prints.

Renée Montand used the following to set up the accounting files for Village Galleries in Simply Accounting:

- Chart of Accounts
- Post-Closing Trial Balance
- Supplier Information
- Customer Information
- Employee Information
- Inventory Information
- Accounting Procedures

CHART OF ACCOUNTS

VILLAGE GALLERIES

ASSETS

Current Assets
1060 Chequing Bank Account
1070 Visa Bank Account
1080 MasterCard Bank Account
1090 Bank Account - Euro
1100 Investment Portfolio
1150 Purchase Prepayments
1200 Accounts Receivable
1220 Office Supplies
1240 Furniture Supplies
1260 Prepaid Insurance

Inventory Assets
1320 Bedroom Furniture
1340 Home Accessories
1360 Kitchen & Dining Room Furniture
1380 Living Room Furniture

Fixed Assets
1420 Cash Register ▶

▶1440 Computer Equipment
1460 Equipment & Tools
1480 Gallery Fixtures
1500 Gallery

LIABILITIES

Current Liabilities
2200 Accounts Payable
2220 Prepaid Sales and Deposits
2250 Credit Card Payable
2260 Import Duty Payable
2330 Income Tax Payable
2350 QPP Payable
2360 Quebec Income Tax Payable
2370 QHSF Payable
2460 CSST Payable
2650 GST Charged on Sales
2670 GST Paid on Purchases
2800 Refundable QST Paid
2810 QST Charged on Sales ▶

▶Long Term Liabilities
2950 Mortgage Payable - Gallery

EQUITY

Owner's Equity
3560 Montand, Capital
3580 Montand, Drawings
3600 Current Earnings

REVENUE
4020 Revenue from Sales
4040 Sales Discount
4060 Freight Revenue
4100 Investment Revenue
4120 Interest Revenue

EXPENSE

Operating Expenses
5020 Advertising & Promotion
5030 Exchange Rate Differences
5040 Bank Charges
5050 Credit Card Fees ▶

▶5060 Cost of Goods Sold
5070 Variance Costs
5080 Furniture Supplies Used
5100 Damaged Inventory
5120 Purchase Discounts
5130 Freight Expense
5140 Delivery Expense
5160 Hydro Expense
5180 Insurance Expense
5190 Mortgage Interest Expense
5200 Office Supplies Used
5220 Telephone Expenses

Payroll Expenses
5300 Commissions
5330 CSST Expense
5340 QPP Expense
5350 QHSF Expense
5380 Subcontractor Fees

NOTES: The Chart of Accounts includes only postable accounts and Current Earnings. QPP (Quebec Pension Plan) replaces CPP in Quebec. QHSF (Quebec Health Services Fund) is an employer-funded provincial health and services tax program.
Linked payable and expense accounts for EI, CPP and QPIP (Quebec Parental Insurance Plan) are also included because they are essential linked accounts, but they are not used in this example.

POST-CLOSING TRIAL BALANCE

VILLAGE GALLERIES

June 30, 2012

		Debits	Credits				Debits	Credits
1060	Chequing Bank Account	$ 51 897.25		▶	1440	Computer Equipment	2 800.00	
1070	Visa Bank Account	5 445.00			1460	Equipment & Tools	1 500.00	
1080	MasterCard Bank Account	3 555.00			1480	Gallery Fixtures	1 000.00	
1090	Bank Account - Euro (€ 1 460)	2 100.00			1500	Gallery	150 000.00	
1100	Investment Portfolio	50 000.00			2200	Accounts Payable		$ 11 395.00
1200	Accounts Receivable	5 643.75			2250	Credit Card Payable		240.00
1220	Office Supplies	400.00			2260	Import Duty Payable		240.00
1240	Furniture Supplies	600.00			2650	GST Charged on Sales		1 680.00
1260	Prepaid Insurance	250.00			2670	GST Paid on Purchases	980.00	
1320	Bedroom Furniture	35 200.00			2800	Refundable QST Paid	90.00	
1340	Home Accessories	30 900.00			2810	QST Charged on Sales		1 926.00
1360	Kitchen & Dining Room Furniture	24 995.00			2950	Mortgage Payable - Gallery		145 000.00
1380	Living Room Furniture	41 925.00			3560	Montand, Capital		250 000.00
1420	Cash Register	1 200.00	▶				$410 481.00	$410 481.00

SUPPLIER INFORMATION

VILLAGE GALLERIES

Supplier Name (Contact)	Address	Phone No. Fax No.	E-mail Web Site	Terms Tax ID
Domo Carvaggio (Arturo Dessini)	8 Via Artistes Forli, 47100 Italy	Tel: (39-0543) 457 882 Fax: (39-0543) 457 113	www.domocarvaggio.com	net 30
Énergie Québec (Marie Nuclaire)	5010 Ave. Atomique Montreal, Quebec H2B 6C9	Tel: (514) 782-6101	www.energie.quebec.ca	net 1
L'Ascension Mobiliers (Suzie LaChaise)	RR #2 Jonquière, Quebec G7S 4L2	Tel: (450) 821-1029 Fax: (450) 822-1927	suzie@lascension.com www.lascension.com	1/5, n/30 (after tax) 322 749 610
Montreal Persia Emporium (Perse Moquette)	40 Rue de Tapis Longueuil, Quebec J4K 2L7	Tel: (450) 288-4334 Fax: (450) 288-8201	moquette@MPE.com www.MPE.com	2/5, n/30 (after tax) 473 540 911
Normandin Meubles (Normand Armoire)	RR #3 Nicolet, Quebec J3T 1H5	Tel: (450) 371-7273 Fax: (450) 371-7229	na@normand.meubles.com www.normand.meubles.com	2/10, n/30 (after tax) 136 492 446
Papineau Delivery (Martin Carnion)	56 Papineau Ave. Outremont, Quebec H1M 3B3	Tel: (514) 690-2810 Fax: (514) 691-7283	martin@papineau.com www.papineau.com	net 10 288 344 566
Receiver General for Canada	Sudbury Tax Services Office PO Box 20004 Sudbury, Ontario P3A 6B4	Tel 1: (800) 561-7761 Tel 2: (800) 959-2221	www.cra-arc.gc.ca	net 1
Staples (Hélène Magazinier)	777 Ave. de Bureau Montreal, Quebec H4K 1V5	Tel: (514) 759-3488 Fax: (514) 758- 3910	www.staples.com	net 15 128 634 772
Telébec (Robert Bavarde)	84 Rue Causerie Montreal, Quebec 113C 7S2	Tel: (514) 488-2355	www.bell.ca	net 1

NOTES: All supplier discounts are calculated on after-tax amounts.

OUTSTANDING SUPPLIER INVOICES

VILLAGE GALLERIES

Supplier Name	Terms	Date	Invoice	Amount CAD	Total
L'Ascension Mobiliers	1/5, n/30 (after tax)	June 29/12	LM-2114	$4 558.00	$4 558.00
Normandin Meubles	2/10, n/30 (after tax)	June 28/12	NM-192	$6 837.00	$6 837.00
			Grand Total		$11 395.00

CUSTOMER INFORMATION

VILLAGE GALLERIES

Customer Name (Contact)	Address	Phone No. Fax No.	E-mail Web Site	Terms Credit Limit
Caisse Metropolitain (Tomas Monaire)	50 Rue Berri Montreal, Quebec H1B 6F4	Tel: (514) 466-2991 Fax: (514) 468-1826	tmonaire@caissemetro.ca www.caissemetro.ca	2/10, n/30 $5 000
Cash Customers				cash or credit card
Deon Estates (Kaline Deon)	600 Rue St. Denis Montreal, Quebec H2K 7C9	Tel: (514) 729-8217 Fax: (514) 729-9283	kaline.deon@istar.com	2/10, n/30 $5 000
*St. Leonard's Homebuilders (Félice Charpentier)	31 Boul. St. Joseph Montreal, Quebec H4N 2M1	Tel: (514) 788-3645 Fax: (514) 787-7114	felice@stleonards.com www.stleonards.com	2/10, n/30 $10 000
*Westmount Primrose Condos (M.T. Sweets)	121 Rue Notre Dame Montreal, Quebec H3K 4G5	Tel: (514) 499-7117 Fax: (514) 498-2889	sweets@wpcondos.com www.wpcondos.com	2/10, n/30 $10 000

NOTES: All customer discounts are calculated on amounts before tax. Customers pay 1.5% interest on accounts over 30 days. Asterisk (*) indicates preferred price list customer.

OUTSTANDING CUSTOMER INVOICES

VILLAGE GALLERIES

Customer Name	Terms	Date	Invoice	Amount	Tax	Total
Deon Estates	2/10, n/30 (before tax)	June 24/12	168	$5 000	$643.75	$5 643.75

NOTES

As an employer, Village Galleries makes contributions to the Quebec Health Services Fund equal to 2.7 percent of the total payroll amount for the provincial health care plan. This amount is entered in the Payroll Settings.

CSST (La Commission de la Santé et de la Sécurité du Travail) is the Workplace Compensation Board agency in Quebec.

Employer and employee deductions for the new Quebec Parental Insurance Plan are not required because Décor is not EI-insurable.

Employee Profile and TD1 Information

Lianne Décor   started working for the boutique on July 1, 2012. Using her interior decorating and design skills, she visits homes for consultations to assess needs and suggest furniture from the store that matches the home style and customer taste. She is paid a commission of 20 percent of her monthly sales and takes four weeks of vacation each year. Décor is single and self-supporting. Her tax claim amounts are $13 382 federal and $12 945 provincial for basic and education amounts. She works for the store part time and supplements her sales commission with her independent business as an interior design consultant.

Other employee details:

SIN:	566 811 014	Address:	45 Rue Collage
Date of birth:	August 26, 1976		Montreal, QC H2G 4R5
CSST (WCB) rate:	2.04	Tel:	(514) 639-9202

INVENTORY INFORMATION

VILLAGE GALLERIES

Code	Description	Unit	Min Qty	Selling Price Reg	(Pref)	Qty on Hand	Total (Cost)	Duty (Taxes)
Bedroom Furniture: Total asset value $35 200 (Linked accounts: Asset 1320; Revenue 4020; COGS 5060; Variance 5070)								
BF-01	Armoire: dark oak	1-pc	0	$3 100	$3 000	2	$4 400	9.5%
BF-02	Armoire: light ash	1-pc	0	3 000	2 900	2	4 000	9.5%
BF-03	Bed: 3 piece oak	set	0	2 000	1 900	2	2 400	9.5%
BF-04	Bed: 5 piece light ash/oak	set	0	3 000	2 900	2	3 600	9.5%
BF-05	Bed: brass/silver	1-pc	0	1 800	1 700	3	3 300	8.0%
BF-06	Chest: cherry	1-pc	0	1 000	950	3	1 800	9.5%
BF-07	Dresser: cashmere, burl-maple	1-pc	0	1 600	1 500	5	4 500	9.5%
BF-08	Dresser: highboy - dark oak	1-pc	0	1 900	1 800	5	5 500	9.5%
BF-09	Wardrobe: light ash	1-pc	0	2 800	2 700	2	3 600	9.5%
BF-10	Wardrobe: pine	1-pc	0	1 750	1 650	2	2 100	9.5%
Home Accessories: Total asset value $30 900 (Linked accounts: Asset 1340; Revenue 4020, COGS 5060; Variance 5070)								
HA-01	Framed Art: prints 45 x 60cm	each	0	200	180	40	4 000	0.0%
HA-02	Framed Art: prints 75 x 100cm	each	0	300	270	30	4 500	0.0%
HA-03	Lamp: floor solid brass	1-pc	0	400	360	10	2 200	7.0%
HA-04	Lamp: table solid brass	1-pc	0	600	550	10	3 500	7.0%
HA-05	Mirror: oval dark oak	1-pc	0	500	450	5	1 500	9.5%
HA-06	Mirror: square ash/mahogany	1-pc	0	550	500	5	1 900	9.5%
HA-07	Rugs: Persian Isfahan 185 x 275cm	each	0	1 250	1 150	10	6 000	n/a
HA-08	Rugs: Persian Kashan 185 x 275cm	each	0	990	950	10	4 500	n/a
HA-09	Rugs: Persian Tabriz 90 x 160cm	each	0	650	600	10	2 800	n/a
Kitchen & Dining Room Furniture: Total asset value $24 995 (Linked accounts: Asset 1360; Revenue 4020; COGS 5060; Variance 5070)								
KD-01	Buffet: oak	1-pc	0	1 750	1 650	2	2 000	9.5%
KD-02	Buffet: cherry	1-pc	0	2 250	2 150	2	2 200	9.5%
KD-03	Chairs: 4 piece cherry	set	0	1 100	1 000	5	3 000	9.5%
KD-04	Chairs: 4 piece oak	set	0	975	950	5	2 375	9.5%
KD-05	China Cabinet: walnut	1-pc	0	2 100	2 000	2	2 100	9.5%
KD-06	China Cabinet: cherry	1-pc	0	850	800	2	800	9.5%
KD-07	Credenza: maple	1-pc	0	1 675	1 575	2	1 950	9.5%
KD-08	Extension Table: oak	1-pc	0	1 825	1 725	2	2 050	9.5%
KD-09	Huntboard: white pine	1-pc	0	725	650	2	850	9.5%
KD-10	Server: fruitwood	1-pc	0	980	950	2	1 000	9.5%
KD-11	Sideboard: cherry	1-pc	0	1 625	1 525	2	1 850	9.5%
KD-12	Table: brass with glass	1-pc	0	1 780	1 680	4	3 520	8.0%
KD-13	Table: ivory lacquer/pine	1-pc	0	625	550	4	1 300	9.5%
Living Room Furniture: Total asset value $41 925 (Linked accounts: Asset 1380; Revenue 4020; COGS 5060; Variance 5070)								
LR-01	Bookcase: oak/walnut solid	1-pc	0	1 150	1 050	3	1 950	9.5%
LR-02	Chair: various patterns cotton	1-pc	0	525	500	10	2 750	9.5%
LR-03	Cocktail Table: cherry	1-pc	0	925	850	5	2 375	9.5%
LR-04	Console Table: oak	1-pc	0	950	900	5	2 500	9.5%
LR-05	Curio Cabinet: walnut/oak	1-pc	0	1 450	1 350	3	2 400	9.5%
LR-06	Desk: mahogany	1-pc	0	1 840	1 740	5	4 400	9.5%
LR-07	End Table: brass with glass	1-pc	0	610	550	5	1 400	8.0%
LR-08	Lamp Table: ash/oak solid	1-pc	0	825	750	5	2 625	9.5%
LR-09	Loveseat: chenille	1-pc	0	1 325	1 225	5	3 625	9.5%
LR-10	Ottoman & Slipcover: grey leather	2-pc	0	380	350	5	1 000	9.5%
LR-11	Recliner & Ottoman: brown leather	2-pc set	0	1 020	950	5	3 100	9.5%
LR-12	Sectional Sofa: charcoal linen	3-pc	0	2 300	2 200	3	4 200	9.5%
LR-17	Settee: light ash	1-pc	0	850	800	3	1 650	9.5%
LR-18	Sofa & Slipcover: celadon	2-pc	0	1 475	1 375	5	4 375	9.5%
LR-19	Swivel Chair & Slipcover: cotton	2-pc	0	640	600	5	1 950	9.5%
LR-20	Wing Chair: pastel	1-pc	0	575	525	5	1 625	9.5%
Total Inventory Value							$133 020	

Accounting Procedures

The Goods and Services Tax (GST): Remittances

Village Galleries uses the regular method for remittance of the Goods and Services Tax. GST collected from customers is recorded as a liability in *GST Charged on Sales*. GST paid to suppliers is recorded in *GST Paid on Purchases* as a decrease in the liability to Canada Revenue Agency. Montand files returns to the Receiver General for Canada by the last day of the month for the previous quarterly period, either requesting a refund or remitting the balance owing.

Quebec Sales Tax (QST)

Provincial sales tax (Quebec Sales Tax or QST) of 7.5 percent is applied to all cash and credit sales of goods and services in the province of Quebec. The Quebec Sales Tax is applied to the amount of the invoice with GST included (i.e., GST is taxable). This is often referred to as a "tax on a tax." The defaults for this application are set so that the program will automatically calculate the QST on the amount with GST included. Accounting examples for sales taxes in different provinces are provided in Chapter 2.

QST owing (*QST Charged on Sales* less *Refundable QST Paid*) must be remitted quarterly to the ministre du Revenu du Québec.

NOTES
In this chapter, insurance is the only item for which QST is not refundable. GST is not applied to insurance. The QST on all telecommunication services in this chapter is refundable.

Refundable and Non-refundable QST

Most business purchases qualify for refundable QST credits to reduce the QST owing in much the same way as the GST owing is calculated. Some exceptions are the QST on insurance and on some telecommunication services. The tax codes for GST and QST included in the ledgers for customers and suppliers, therefore, include both refundable and non-refundable codes as follows:

> G - GST @ 5%
> GQ - GST @ 5%, QST @ 7.5%
> Q - QST @ 7.5%, included, non-refundable

Deposits on Custom Orders

NOTES
Processing the advance in this way ensures that the advance will appear in the correct customer account in the Receivables Ledger. The manual approach, a General Journal entry that debits the bank account and credits Unearned Revenue, a liability account, does not show this link with the customer – the customer's ledger is updated separately.

When customers place a sales order for furniture, they pay an advance of 20 percent to 25 percent of the price. The deposit may be entered in the Receipts Journal or on the Sales Order form. The Accounts Receivable Ledger for the selected customer will be credited for the advance and *Chequing Bank Account* will be debited. When the work is complete, fill the sales order to make a Sales Journal entry for the full amount of the contract, including relevant taxes. When the customer settles the account, mark the invoice amount and the deposit (if you used the Receipts Journal) as paid. The balance in the Receipts Journal should then match the amount of the customer's cheque.

Freight Expenses

When a business purchases inventory items, the cost of freight that cannot be directly allocated to a specific item purchased must be charged to *Freight Expense*. This amount will be regarded as an expense and will not be part of the costs of any inventory asset account.

Printing Sales Invoices

NOTES
Remember that if you want to preview or print invoices, you must select the correct printing form. Click the Change Print Forms tool in the Sales Journal to access the settings.

If you want to print sales invoices through the program, complete the Sales Journal transaction as you would otherwise. Preview the transaction before posting it. You can print from the preview window or from the journal (click Print or choose the File menu and then Print). Printing will begin immediately, so be sure you have selected the correct printer and forms before you begin. To e-mail an invoice, click the E-mail tool.

Foreign Purchases and Import Duty

Goods imported from Italy are subject to GST and to import duties at various rates. These taxes are collected at the time the goods are received and are usually paid directly to the Receiver General. To simplify the transactions in Simply Accounting, we have set up the foreign supplier record so that the supplier collects GST, just like suppliers in Canada.

Import duties are handled separately in the program. Duty is calculated automatically because the rates are entered in the Inventory Ledger records. The amount is credited to the linked *Import Duty Payable* account instead of *Accounts Payable* so the duty is not added to the balance owing to the supplier. The linked asset account is debited.

On receiving the merchandise, the business writes a cheque to the Receiver General to pay the import duties on the purchase. This payment is just like any other tax remittance — enter the duty payable as a positive amount for a cash purchase from the Receiver General and choose *Import Duty Payable* as the account. The amount is the current General Ledger account balance.

INSTRUCTIONS

1. **Set up** the **budget** for Village Galleries on July 1, 2012, using Simply Accounting. Detailed keystroke instructions to assist you begin on page 548 following the source documents.

2. **Enter** the **source documents** for July 2012 in Simply Accounting using the Chart of Accounts, Trial Balance, Supplier, Customer, Payroll and Inventory information provided.

3. **Print** the following **reports** and **graphs**. Instructions for budget reports and graphs begin on page 555.

    *   Balance Sheet as at July 31
    *   Journal Entries for all journals from July 1 to July 31
    *   Inventory Sales Detail Report for Bedroom Furniture
    *   Inventory Quantity Report for all items to check re-order requirements
    *   Income Statement, Budget Report with Difference in Percentage for July 1 to July 31
    *   Sales vs Budget graph for accounts 4020 and 4040
    *   Expenses vs Budget graph for accounts 5060, 5120 and 5300

SOURCE DOCUMENTS

SESSION DATE – JULY 7, 2012

☐   **Memo #1**   **Dated July 2/12**

From Owner: Pay import duties owing to the Receiver General on June 30. Issue cheque #125 for $240 in full payment of duty owing.

Village Galleries

509 Boul. Rouin
Montreal, Quebec
H3F 5G5

Telephone:
(514) 529-6391
Fax:
(514) 529-7622

Date: July 2/12
To be delivered: July 14/12
For: Caisse Metropolitain
(Tomas Monaire)
50 Rue Berri
Montreal, QC H1B 6F4

QUOTE #71

Description	Qty	Price	Total
HA-03 Lamp: floor solid brass	1	400	400.00
HA-09 Rugs: Persian Tabriz 90 x 160cm	1	650	650.00
LR-01 Bookcase: oak/walnut solid	1	1150	1150.00
LR-12 Sectional Sofa: charcoal linen	1	2300	2300.00

Sale Terms: 2/10, n/30	Delivery	N/C
GST # 236 412 540	GST 5.0%	225.00
QST # 3344992	QST 7.5%	354.38
Prices quoted will remain valid for 15 days	Total	5079.38

Memo #2   Dated July 2/12

From Owner: Convert sales quote #71 to sales order #71. All amounts, dates and terms are unchanged.

Purchase Quote #224   Dated July 2/12

Policy Start date July 5/12
From Quebecor Insurance Co. (use Quick Add), $3 600 for a one-year extension of business insurance policy. Terms: first two months' premium required as deposit on acceptance of quote. Balance is payable in 10 equal monthly payments. Enter 1 (one) as the quantity ordered and debit Prepaid Insurance.

Purchase Order #224 & Cheque #126   Dated July 2/12

Convert purchase quote #224 from Quebecor Insurance Co., $3 600 for a one-year extension of business insurance policy, to a purchase order. Issued cheque #126 for $600 as deposit to confirm the order.

Purchase Invoice #QI-7711   Dated July 3/12

From Quebecor Insurance Co., to fill purchase order #224, $3 600 for a one-year extension of business insurance policy. The premium balance is due in 10 equal monthly payments. Change the payment method to Pay Later.

Cash Receipt #43   Dated July 3/12

From Deon Estates, cheque #118 for $5 543.75 in payment of account, including $100 discount for early payment. Reference invoice #168.

Cheque Copy #127   Dated July 4/12

To L'Ascension Mobiliers, $4 512.42 in payment of account, including $45.58 discount for early payment. Reference invoice #LM-2114.

NOTES
You may need to update the cheque number to 127 and then accept the new numbering.

☐ **Sales Invoice #170**   **Dated July 4/12**

To Vasco Cardigos (use Full Add for the new Portuguese customer)

1	BF-02	Armoire: light ash	€2 005.00
1	HA-06	Mirror: square ash/mahogany	365.00
		Shipping	200.00

Terms: net 1
The exchange rate is 1.420.

☐ **Credit Card Purchase Invoice #A-1141**   **Dated July 4/12**

From Antoine's Hardware Store (use Quick Add for the new supplier), $50 plus $2.50 GST and $3.94 QST for computer screen cleaning kit (office supplies). Purchase invoice total $56.44 paid in full by Amex credit card.

☐ **Credit Card Purchase Invoice #PD-211**   **Dated July 5/12**

From Papineau Delivery, $180 plus $9.00 GST and $14.18 QST for contracted delivery of furniture. Purchase invoice total $203.18. Paid in full by Amex.

☐ **Interac Sales Invoice #171**   **Dated July 6/12**

To Catherine Geneve (choose Continue)

1	LR-04	Console Table: oak		$ 950.00
1	LR-05	Curio Cabinet: walnut/oak		1 450.00
		Delivery		100.00
		Goods and Services Tax	5.0%	125.00
		Quebec Sales Tax	7.5%	196.88
		Invoice total		$2 821.88

Paid by debit card #7695 4559 0062 0103.

☐ **Cheque Copy #128**   **Dated July 7/12**

To Normandin Meubles, $6 700.26 in payment of account including $136.74 discount for early payment. Reference invoice #NM 102.

SESSION DATE – JULY 14, 2012

☐ **Memo #3**   **Dated July 8/12**

From Owner: Adjust inventory for one HA-02 Framed Art Print dropped and damaged beyond repair. Charge to Damaged Inventory account.

☐ **MasterCard Sales Invoice #172**   **Dated July 8/12**

To Pierre Boudin

1	HA-07	Rugs: Persian Isfahan 185 x 275cm		$1 250.00
1	KD-07	Credenza: maple		1 675.00
1	LR-02	Chair: various patterns cotton		525.00
		Delivery		100.00
		Goods and Services Tax	5.0%	177.50
		Quebec Sales Tax	7.5%	279.57
		Invoice total		$4 007.07

Paid by MasterCard #5450 5590 0620 1036.

☐ **Credit Card Purchase Invoice #S-34689**   **Dated July 9/12**

From Staples, $150 plus $7.50 GST and $11.81 QST for sales invoice forms and other office supplies. Purchase invoice total $169.31 paid in full by Amex.

NOTES
Edit the sales prices. Prices for foreign transactions are taken from the exchange rate rather than from the Inventory Ledger records.

☐ Vasco Cardigos
Rua Mariella 36
1207 Lisbon, Portugal
Tel: (351-21) 347 6273
Terms: net 1
Currency: EUR
Revenue account: 4020
Tax code: no tax

☐ **Credit Card Purchase Invoice #QA-197**   **Dated July 10/12**

From Quik-Ads (use Quick Add), $200 plus $10.00 GST and $15.75 QST for promotional cards and flyers to advertise home design gallery. Purchase invoice total $225.75 paid in full by Amex credit card.

☐ **Cash Purchase Invoice #EQ-979764**   **Dated July 13/12**

From Énergie Québec, $100 plus $5.00 GST and $7.88 QST for hydro service for one month. Purchase invoice total $112.88 paid in full by cheque #129.

☐ **Cash Sales Invoice #173**   **Dated July 13/12**

To Marie Broussard

1	LR-18 Sofa & Slipcover: celadon		$1 475.00
	Goods and Services Tax	5.0%	73.75
	Quebec Sales Tax	7.5%	116.16
	Invoice total		$1 664.91

Received cheque #339 in full payment. Customer to arrange own delivery.

☐ **Visa Sales Invoice #174**   **Dated July 14/12**

To Allysa Morel

1	KD-10 Server: fruitwood		$ 980.00
1	KD-12 Table: brass with glass		1 780.00
1	LR-09 Loveseat: chenille		1 325.00
	Goods and Services Tax	5.0%	204.25
	Quebec Sales Tax	7.5%	321.70
	Invoice total		$4 610.95

Paid by Visa #4185 4458 6712 8405.

NOTES
Allow the customer to exceed the credit limit.

☐

Village Galleries

509 Boul. Rouin
Montreal, Quebec
H3F 5G5

Telephone: (514) 529-6391
Fax: (514) 529-7622

Date: July 14/12

To: Caisse Metropolitain
(Tomas Monaire)
50 Rue Berri
Montreal, QC H1B 6F4

#175

Description	Qty	Price	Total
HA-03 Lamp: floor solid brass	1	400	400.00
HA-09 Rugs: Persian Tabriz 90 x 160cm	1	650	650.00
LR-01 Bookcase: oak/walnut solid	1	1150	1150.00
LR-12 Sectional Sofa: charcoal linen	1	2300	2300.00

Ref: quote/order #71

GM

Sale Terms: 2/10, n/30	**Delivery**	N/C
GST # 236 412 540	**GST 5.0%**	225.00
QST # 3344992	**QST 7.5%**	354.38
	Sales Total	5079.38

Sales Invoice #176   **Dated July 14/12**

To Marie Broussard (use Quick Add), $50 plus $2.50 GST and $3.94 QST for delivery of sofa. Sales invoice total $56.44. Terms: net 10. (Credit Freight Revenue.)

Credit Card Purchase Invoice #QD-980   **Dated July 14/12**

From Quickie Delivery Service (use Quick Add), $50 plus $2.50 GST and $3.94 QST for emergency delivery of sofa to Marie Broussard. Purchase invoice total $56.44 paid in full by Amex. (Charge to Delivery Expense.)

SESSION DATE – JULY 21, 2012

Village Galleries

Telephone:
(514) 529-6391
Fax:
(514) 529-7622

509 Boul. Rouin
Montreal, Quebec
H3F 5G5

Date: July 16/12
To be delivered: July 20/12
From: St. Leonard's Homebuilders
               (Félice Charpentier)
               31 Boul. St. Joseph
               Montreal, QC H4N 2M1

ORDER #72

Description	Qty	Price	Total
BF-01 Armoire: dark oak	1	3000	3000.00
BF-05 Bed: brass/silver	1	1700	1700.00
HA-08 Rugs: Persian Kashan 185 x 275cm	1	950	950.00
LR-09 Loveseat: chenille	1	1225	1225.00

Telephone order 7/16/12 *GM*

Sale Terms: 2/10, n/30	Delivery	N/C
GST # 236 412 540	GST 5.0%	343.75
QST # 3344992	QST 7.5%	541.41
	Total	7760.16

Purchase Invoice #MPE-664   **Dated July 17/12**

From Montreal Persia Emporium (Create new inventory)

2 HA-10 Rugs: Mashad 170 x 240cm	$1 000.00
2 HA-11 Rugs: Qum silk 80 x 150cm	1 600.00
Goods and Services Tax	130.00
Quebec Sales Tax	204.75
Invoice total	$2 934.75

Terms: 2/5, n/30.

New inventory items   **Prices**

Number	Description	Unit	Min	Reg.	(Pref.)
HA-10	Rugs: Mashad 170 x 240cm	1-pc	1	$ 800	($ 750)
HA-11	Rugs: Qum silk 80 x 150cm	1-pc	1	1 500	(1 400)

Linked Accounts: Asset 1340 **Revenue** 4020 **Cost of Goods Sold** 5060 **Variance** 5070

Taxes: GST exempt No   **QST exempt** No   **Duty Rate** Not applicable

☐ **Credit Card Purchase Invoice #PD-274**   **Dated July 17/12**

From Papineau Delivery, $300 plus $15 GST and $23.63 QST for contracted delivery of furniture. Purchase invoice total $338.63 paid in full by Amex.

☐ **Cash Purchase Invoice #T-55612**   **Dated July 18/12**

From Telébec, $75 plus $3.75 GST and $5.91 QST for telephone service. Purchase invoice total $84.66 paid in full by cheque #130.

☐ **Memo #4**   **Dated July 18/12**

From Owner: Adjust purchase invoice #MPE-664. Montreal Persia Emporium sent a revised invoice for MPE-664 that included a freight charge of $50 plus $2.50 GST and $3.94 QST. New purchase invoice total $2 991.19.

☐ **MasterCard Sales Invoice #177**   **Dated July 20/12**

To Jacques Altain

1	LR-06	Desk: mahogany		$1 840.00
1	LR-11	Recliner & Ottoman: brown leather		1 020.00
		Delivery		100.00
		Goods and Services Tax	5.0%	148.00
		Quebec Sales Tax	7.5%	233.11
		Invoice total		$3 341.11

Paid by MasterCard #5145 0559 0062 3612.

☐

Village Galleries

509 Boul. Rouin
Montreal, Quebec
H3F 5G5

Telephone:
(514) 529-6391
Fax:
(514) 529-7622

Date: July 20/12

To: St. Leonard's Homebuilders
(Félice Charpentier)
31 Boul. St. Joseph
Montreal, QC H4N 2M1

#178

Description	Qty	Price	Total
BF-01 Armoire: dark oak	1	3000	3000.00
BF-05 Bed: brass/silver	1	1700	1700.00
HA-08 Rugs: Persian Kashan 185 x 275cm	1	950	950.00
LR-09 Loveseat: chenille	1	1225	1225.00

Ref: sales order #72 *GM*

Sale Terms: 2/10, n/30	Delivery	N/C
GST # 236 412 540	GST 5.0%	343.75
QST # 3344992	QST 7.5%	541.41
	Total	7760.16

☐ **Credit Card Bill #AM-07020**   **Dated July 20/12**

From American Express (Amex), $894.68 for new purchases before the billing date, July 14, plus $10.50 monthly fee. Total payment required to avoid interest charges is $905.18. Issue cheque #131 for $905.18 to pay Amex balance in full.

☐ **Cheque Copy #132**   **Dated July 21/12**

To Montreal Persia Emporium, $2 931.37 in payment of account including $59.82 discount for early payment. Reference revised invoice #MPE-664.

☐ **Interac Sales Invoice #179**   **Dated July 21/12**

To Julie Marie Delpy

1	LR-20	Wing Chair: pastel		$375.00
		Goods and Services Tax	5.0%	18.75
		Quebec Sales Tax	7.5%	29.53
		Invoice total		$423.28

Paid by debit card #7855 5867 1284 0505.
Edit the selling price. The price was reduced because the chair legs were scratched. Enter "Final sale" as the Comment.

☐ **Cash Receipt #44**   **Dated July 21/12**

From Caisse Metropolitain, cheque #967 for $4 989.38 in payment of account including $90 discount for early payment. Reference invoice #175.

SESSION DATE – JULY 28, 2012

☐ **Sales Invoice #180**   **Dated July 23/12**

To Westmount Primrose Condos (preferred customer)

1	LR-12	Sectional Sofa: charcoal linen	$2 200
2	LR-19	Swivel Chairs & Slipcovers: cotton	600 each
		Goods and Services Tax	5.0%
		Quebec Sales Tax	7.5%

Terms: 2/10, n/30.

☐ **Visa Sales Invoice #181**   **Dated July 27/12**

To Juliette Servais

1	KD-02	Buffet: cherry		$2 250.00
		Delivery		100.00
		Goods and Services Tax	5.0%	117.50
		Quebec Sales Tax	7.5%	185.07
		Invoice total		$2 652.57

Paid by Visa #4150 8671 2840 5052.

☐ **MasterCard Sales Invoice #182**   **Dated July 28/12**

To Pierre Binoche

1	KD-08	Extension Table: oak		$1 825.00
		Delivery		100.00
		Goods and Services Tax	5.0%	96.25
		Quebec Sales Tax	7.5%	151.60
		Invoice total		$2 172.85

Paid by MasterCard #5555 8445 5900 6236.

☐ **Cash Receipt #45**   **Dated July 28/12**

From Marie Broussard, cheque #357 for $56.44 in payment of account. Reference invoice #176.

SESSION DATE – JULY 31, 2012

☐ **Credit Card Purchase Invoice #PD-304**   **Dated July 30/12**

From Papineau Delivery, $400 plus $20 GST and $31.50 QST for contracted delivery of furniture. Purchase invoice total $451.50 paid in full by Amex.

☐ **Bank Debit Memo #643177**   **Dated July 30/12**

From Bank of Montreal, $30 for bank service charges for one month and $1 700 for mortgage payment that included $1 525 interest and $175 principal.

☐ **Bank Credit Memo #46234**   **Dated July 30/12**

From Bank of Montreal, $638 interest earned on investment securities deposited to chequing account.

☐ **Cash Receipt #46**   **Dated July 30/12**

From St. Leonard's Homebuilders, cheque #3199 for $7 622.66 in payment of account including $137.50 discount for early payment. Reference invoice #178.

☐ **Memo #5**   **Dated July 31/12**

From Owner: Issue cheque #133 for $300 to pay the premium for one month toward the Quebecor Insurance Co. account. Reference invoice #QI-7711. Repeat the entry five times to prepare the remaining payments for the year as postdated cheques. Issue cheques #134 to 138, dated August 31, September 30, October 31, November 30 and December 31.

☐ **Memo #6**   **Dated July 31/12**

From Owner: Make adjusting entries for July.

Office Supplies used	$75
Furniture Supplies used	50
Prepaid insurance expired	300

☐ **Memo #7**   **Dated July 31/12**

From Owner: Lianne Décor earned $5 200 in commissions on her share of sales in July. Issue cheque #139 to pay Décor's commissions.

☑ **Memo #8**   **Dated July 31/12**

553   From Owner: Decrease all revenue and expense budget amounts by 10%.

☑ **Memo #9**   **Dated July 31/12**

559   From Owner: Print all sales invoices for July.

KEYSTROKES

Setting Up Budgets

It is important for a business to gauge its performance against some standards. These standards can be provided through comparisons with other companies that are in the same kind of business or by comparing the same company over several time periods. It is common for a business to set goals for the future based on past performance. For example, there may be an expectation that profits will increase by 10 percent over the previous year or that expenses will be reduced because of the introduction of new cost-reduction methods. If a business waits until the end of the year to assess its progress toward its goals, it may be too late to make necessary corrections if things are not proceeding according to plan. Budgets offer a realistic financial plan for the future that can be used to assess performance.

Before analyzing a budget report, you must turn on the option and enter the budget amounts for the relevant accounts.

Turning On the Budgeting Feature

Open   **SimData10\Village\village**. Do not advance the session date until you have finished the budget setup.

Click   the **Settings icon** 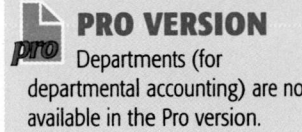. **Click General (Accounts)** to open the General Settings list:

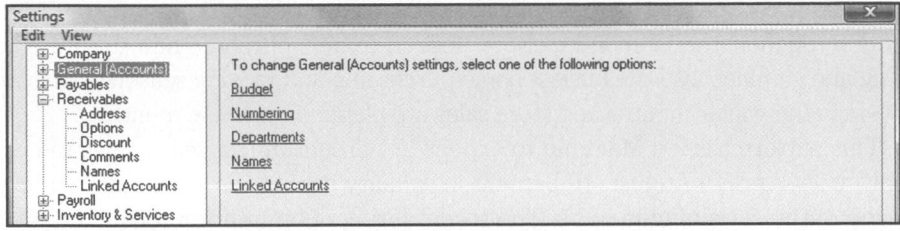

Click   **Budget** to open the budgeting options:

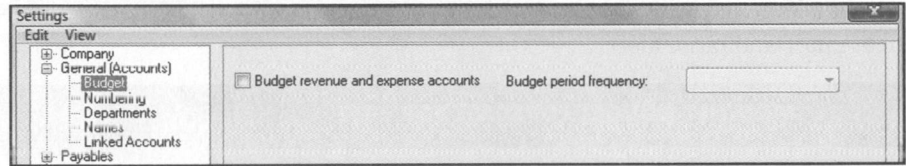

Click   **Budget Revenue And Expense Accounts** to turn on the budget feature.

The first decision after choosing the budgeting feature involves a budget period. Whether a business chooses to budget amounts on a yearly, quarterly or monthly basis depends on the needs and nature of the business. Monthly budget reports will be appropriate if the business cycle of buying and selling is short but not appropriate if long-term projects are involved. The period chosen must provide meaningful feedback about performance. If the periods are too short, there may be insufficient information to judge performance; if the periods are too long, there may be no opportunity to correct problems because they will not be detected soon enough. Village Galleries will use monthly budget periods initially because the Montands want frequent progress reports.

Click   the **Budget Period Frequency field** to see the period options:

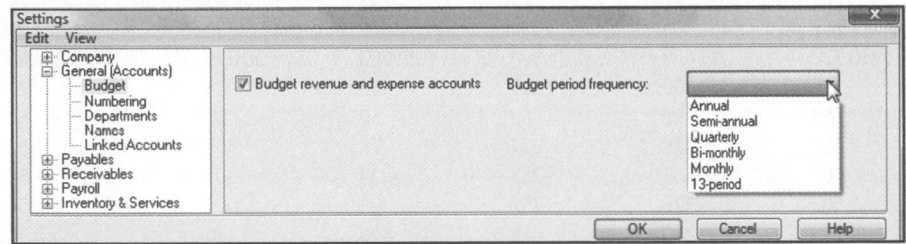

Click   **Monthly**.

Click   **OK** to return to the Home window and save the settings.

Setting a Budget

The next step is to enter the budget amounts for all expense and revenue accounts.

Budgets can be determined in several different ways. The most common methods are zero-based and incremental budgeting. With the zero-based method, a forecast is made for each revenue and expense account based on expectations about specific planned activities and expenditures. Each budget item must be justified. More commonly, last year's budgets and income statements are used as the starting point and a specific percentage change is applied. Thus, a company might expect to improve its

NOTES

If you are working from backups, restore the backup file SimData10\village1.CAB to SimData10\Village\village.

PRO VERSION

pro   Departments (for departmental accounting) are not available in the Pro version.

NOTES

You cannot activate the budget feature in multi-user mode, but you can add and change budget amounts.

performance over last year by 10 percent, either by increasing sales or by decreasing expenses. Planned special events such as annual month-long sales, new customer drives, and peak or slow periods can be built into the changes in budgeted amounts from one period to the next. Whatever method is used, it is important that the budget be realistic.

Renée Montand examined previous income statements and business practices to see where they could make improvements and to get a realistic forecast. The business has been growing by about 10 percent per year. The corresponding expenses, sales discounts, cost of goods sold and so on also increased by about the same amount. Sales are not divided evenly throughout the 12-month period. Most customers purchase new furniture in the spring and summer, also the busiest home purchasing and moving seasons. Sales are slowest in the winter months and store sales are planned for those months.

This pattern has led Montand to expect 12 percent of the year's sales to occur each month from April to August, 10 percent in January during the store sales and 5 percent in each of the remaining months. The recent hiring of an interior consultant should also boost sales over last year's results.

Renée Montand's detailed budget forecast is presented in the following item-by-item budget chart and rationale:

MONTHLY BUDGET FORECAST FOR 2012

VILLAGE GALLERIES

Account	Jul–Aug	Sep–Dec	Jan	Feb–Mar	Apr–Jun	Total for 12 months
REVENUE						
Revenue from Sales	$50 454	$21 023	$42 042	$21 023	$50 454	$420 450
Sales Discount	−504	−210	−420	−210	−504	−4 200
Freight Revenue	1 010	420	830	420	1 010	8 400
Investment Revenue	638	638	638	638	638	7 656
Interest Revenue	22	22	22	22	22	264
TOTAL REVENUE	$51 620	$21 893	$43 112	$21 893	$51 620	$432 570
EXPENSES						
Advertising & Promotion	$ 288	$ 120	$ 240	$ 120	$ 288	$ 2 400
Exchange Rate Differences	0	0	0	0	0	0
Bank Charges	29	12	23	12	29	240
Credit Card Fees	252	105	210	105	252	2 100
Cost of Goods Sold	30 720	12 800	25 600	12 800	30 720	256 000
Variance Costs	144	60	120	60	144	1 200
Furniture Supplies Used	50	50	50	50	50	600
Damaged Inventory	307	128	257	128	307	2 560
Purchase Discounts	−307	−128	−257	−128	−307	−2 560
Freight Expense	307	128	257	128	307	2 560
Delivery Expense	1 010	420	830	420	1 010	8 400
Hydro Expense	90	90	90	90	90	1 080
Insurance Expense	300	300	300	300	300	3 600
Mortgage Interest Expense	1 270	1 270	1 270	1 270	1 270	15 240
Office Supplies Used	65	65	65	65	65	780
Telephone Expenses	80	80	80	80	80	960
Commissions	3 000	1 250	2 500	1 250	3 000	25 000
CSST Expense	61	26	49	26	61	510
QPP Expense	125	52	103	52	125	1 040
QHSF Expense	144	60	120	60	144	1 200
Subcontractor Fees	600	250	500	250	600	5 000
TOTAL EXPENSES	$38 535	$17 138	$32 407	$17 138	$38 535	$327 910
NET INCOME	$13 085	$ 4 755	$10 705	$ 4 755	$13 085	$104 660

BUDGET RATIONALE FOR 2012

VILLAGE GALLERIES

Estimates used to create budget forecasts

Revenue from Sales: increase by 10% over previous year. January, 10% of annual sales; February and March 5%; April, May, June, July and August, 12%; September, October, November and December, 5% each

Sales Discount: expect about 1% of sales on average; most sales are not discounted

Freight Revenue: this has averaged around 2% of sales; most customers request delivery

Interest and Investment Revenue: constant monthly income; same as previous year

Cost of Goods Sold: 60% of net sales (based on markup)

Variance Costs: estimated from price variations in previous years

Damaged Inventory: 1% of Cost of Goods Sold

Purchase Discounts: average 1% of Cost of Goods Sold

Delivery: same amount as Freight Revenue

Freight Expense: average at about 1% of sales

Insurance and Mortgage Interest: same amount each month; small decrease from previous year

Furniture Supplies Used: for maintaining store inventory; constant amount each month

Commissions: estimate, will pay 20% of direct contributions to sales

EI, CPP and QPIP: these do not apply; do not choose Budget This Account

QPP, CSST (WCB) and QHSF: straight percentage of commissions (QPP replaces CPP for Quebec)

Subcontractors' Fees: estimated additional assistance needed for peak periods

Bank Charges & Credit Card Fees: increase over last year for increased credit card usage

Exchange Rate Differences: zero — these are expected to cancel each other over time

Other Expenses: constant each month; no change over last year

Entering Budget Amounts in the General Ledger

Click **Company** in the Modules pane list to change windows.

Click the **Chart of Accounts shortcuts list arrow** and **click Modify Account** to open the Search window. Accounts is selected as the record type:

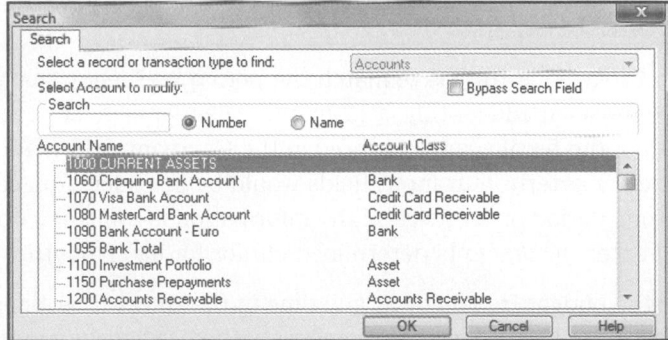

Click the **Search field**.

Type 4 to advance the cursor and **scroll down** the list to see the 4000-level Revenue accounts.

Click **4020 Revenue from Sales** to highlight the first postable revenue account.

NOTES
You can also click the Chart of Accounts icon and then double click the account to open the ledger record.

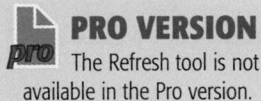

NOTES
Budgeting applies only to the postable revenue and expense accounts on the Income Statement. Budget reports are Income Statement reports.

Click   **OK** to open the Account Ledger window as shown:

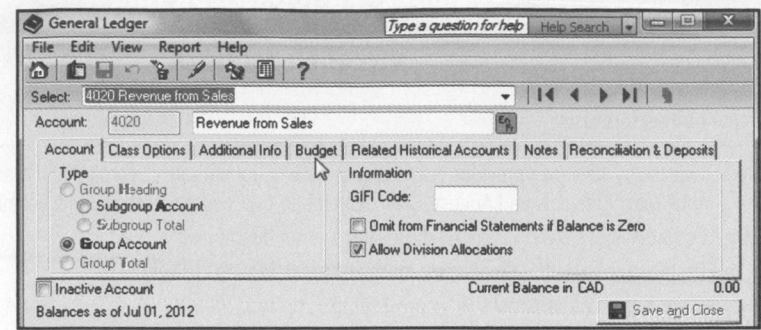

Because we turned on the Budgeting feature in the General Settings window, the Budget tab has been added. This tab will appear only for Income Statement accounts.

Click   the **Budget tab** to open the budget activation window as shown:

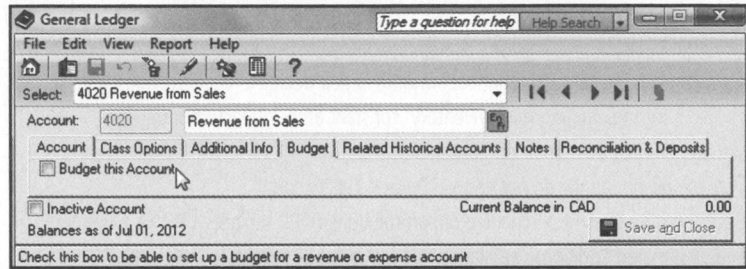

Click   **Budget This Account** to open the Budget amount fields as shown:

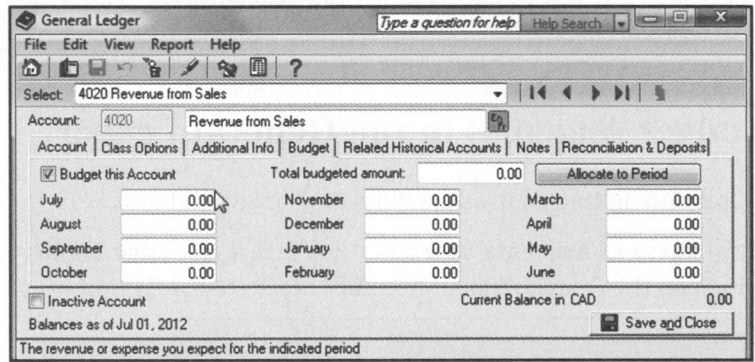

The budget periods displayed at this stage match the period frequency selected in the setup stage. Because we selected Monthly, a 12-month calendar is given, beginning with July, the first month of the fiscal year as entered in the Company Information window. If we had selected Quarterly, four input fields would be provided. You can enter the budget amounts for one period or for more, if the information is available. For Village Galleries, we will enter the amounts determined earlier for each month.

You can change the budget frequency at any time in the General Settings Budget option window. The program will reallocate the previously budgeted amounts proportionately for the new periods after warning you that this will be done and giving you a chance to confirm that you want to proceed.

Refer to the chart on page 550 for budget amounts.

For each revenue and expense, you can add or omit budget amounts. Including budget details for all accounts will, of course, provide the most meaningful budget reports.

Click   the **July field** to select the amount.

Type   50454 **Press** tab .

The cursor advances to the August field and highlights the entry for editing.

> **Enter** the **amounts** for the **remaining 11 months** according to the budget
> forecast on page 550 by **typing** the **amount** and **pressing** (tab) to move
> to the next month.

You can use the **Copy** and **Paste** commands (Edit menu) to copy amounts from
one field to another and save some data entry time.

The **Total Budgeted Amount** is updated continually as you enter amounts for each
period. When you enter individual monthly amounts, use the Total Budgeted Amount to
check your work. It should equal the budget amount for 12 months.

When you have entered the amounts for each month,

> **Click** the **Next button** to advance to the next revenue account in the
> budget tab screen.

> **Enter** budget information for the **remaining** revenue and expense **accounts**
> by following the steps outlined above. Use the amounts determined for
> each account in the chart on page 550

Remember to enter **negative** budget amounts for accounts that decrease the
total in a Group or Section (e.g., *Sales Discount*).

For some accounts, when the budget amounts for each month are equal, you can
use a shortcut to enter the amounts. For example, for *4100 Investment Revenue*,

> **Click** the **Total Budgeted Amount field**.

> **Type** 7 6 5 6 **Click Allocate To Period** to divide the amount evenly among all
> budget periods (638 is entered for each month, 7 656/12).

After entering the budget amounts for all accounts,

> **Close** the **account's General Ledger window**.

> **Display** or **print** the **Budget Report** for July to June to check your amounts
> (see page 556).

> **Enter** the **source documents** for July.

Updating Budgets

Changing Budget Amounts

Budget amounts can be updated if needed based on feedback from earlier budget
reports. They should not, of course, be changed without good reason.

If you discover that your budget forecasts are incorrect, you can update the
amounts for each account individually by repeating the process described above for
entering initial budget amounts. Or you can globally update all amounts by a fixed
percentage. To update the amounts globally,

> **Choose** the **Maintenance menu** in the Home window and **click Update Budget**
> **Amounts** to see the Update Budget window:

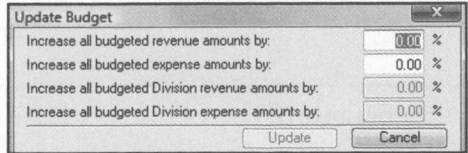

You can change the budgets for revenue and expense accounts separately. You can
change division revenue and expense amounts by a different percentage.

Type the percentage change that you want to apply. Type a negative number for decreases. Click Update to apply the change. The screen that follows will ask you to confirm that you want to update the budget.

Click Yes to apply the changes and return to the Home window.

When you review the account's budget information in the account ledger, you will see that the change has been applied.

Changing Budget Frequencies

You can also change the budget frequency. This change is made in the General Ledger Settings screen. For example, to change the period from monthly to quarterly, choose the Setup menu, then click Settings. Click General (Accounts) and Budget. Then choose Quarterly from the Budget Period Frequency drop-down list and click OK.

When you have a quarterly budget with different amounts for each quarter and you change the frequency to monthly, each month will have the same budget amount — the total for the four quarters divided by 12. You must edit the amounts if they are incorrect.

For example, a quarterly budget of $1 000, $3 000, $2 000 and $6 000 for the four quarters becomes $1 000 each month if the frequency is changed to monthly ($12 000/12).

Before applying the new budget settings, Simply Accounting generates the following warning each time you change a budget frequency:

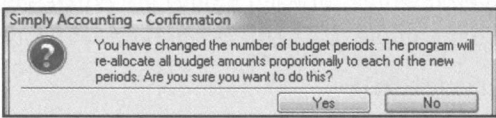

The statement warns that previous budget amounts will be reallocated evenly among the new number of periods. If you change a monthly budget to quarterly, each quarter will have the same budget amount. You can accept or cancel the change.

Adding Budget Amounts to Divisions

If you are using division allocations, you can also enter budget amounts for each division. You must first turn on the budgeting feature and then choose a budget period or frequency. The following steps will illustrate this procedure.

Click the Settings icon and click Division to open the Division Settings:

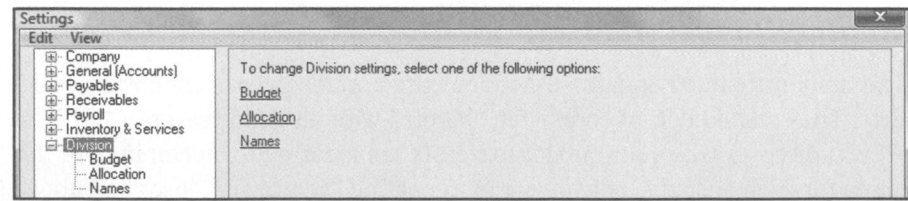

Click Budget to see the division activation screen:

These options are like the General Ledger options.

Click Budget Division.

Choose a frequency from the Budget Period Frequency drop-down list.

NOTES
If you change the frequency to quarterly, the budget amount you entered for Revenue from Sales will become $105 112.50 for each quarter — the total budget for the year or 12 months will be divided by 4 ($420 450/4).

NOTES
If you want to see the next group of screens or to enter budget amounts for divisions, you must first view the module (Setup menu, User Preferences, View option; click the check box for Division).

PRO VERSION
Click Project instead of Division. The module label does not change when you select a different company type.

Click OK to save the settings.

Click the Divisions icon to open the Divisions window.

Create the divisions if you have not already done so.

The Division Ledger window includes a Budget tab.

Click the Budget tab to open the budget activation window:

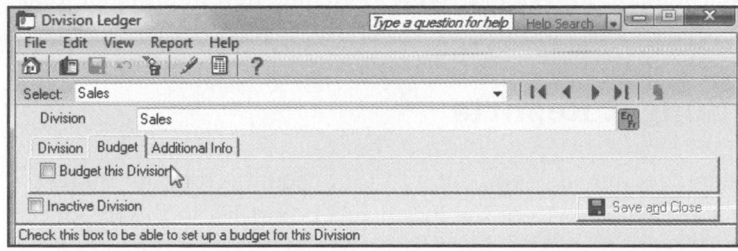

Click Budget This Division to open the budget amount fields. Quarterly periods have been selected for this illustration:

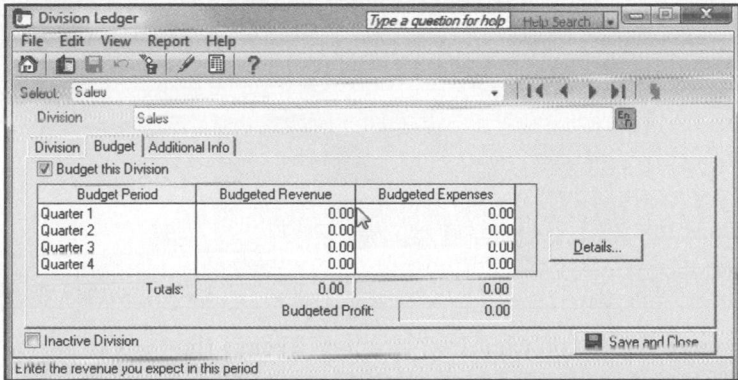

Enter the budgeted Revenue and Expense amounts for each period for this division.

Click Details to enter division budget amounts for individual accounts:

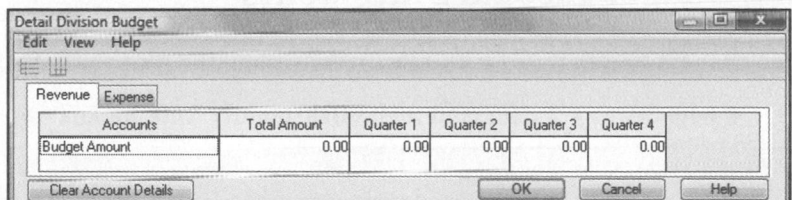

On line one, enter the total revenue or expense amounts and amounts for each period. The Select list button will become available. Then enter these details for individual accounts. Click OK to save the details and return to the ledger record. Open the ledger for the next division, and enter the budget amounts.

Close the ledger when you have finished and enter the allocations as usual in the journals. Division budget reports will be available.

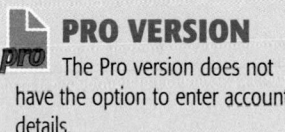

PRO VERSION
The Pro version does not have the option to enter account details.

Budget Reports

Effective use of budget reports involves more than merely observing whether budgeted targets were met or not. Sometimes more information is gained when targets are not met, because the differences can lead to important questions:

- Were the targets realistic? What items were not on target and why?

- If performance exceeds the targets, how can we repeat the success?
- If performance did not meet the targets, were there factors that we failed to anticipate?
- Should we revise future budgets based on the new information?

The problem-solving cycle is set in motion. Even an Income Statement that is on target should be reviewed carefully. There may be room for improvement if the budget was a conservative estimate. Or, you may want to include new information that will affect future performance and was unknown when the budget was drawn up.

Displaying Budget Reports

You can check the budget amounts you entered for accounts from the Budget Report. Budget reports are available from the Financials report list in the Report Centre.

Open the **Report Centre** and **click Financials** in the Select A Report Type list.

Click **Budget** and then **click Modify This Report**:

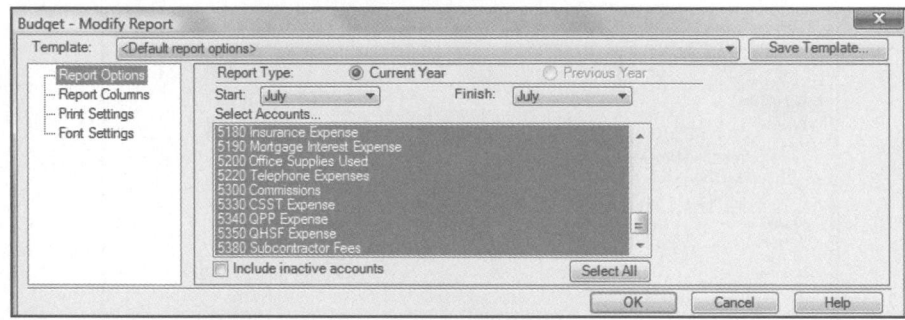

Select the **accounts** you want in the report. **Choose** the **budget periods** in the Start and Finish fields and **click OK** to see the amounts.

Close the **display** when you have finished.

Displaying Budget Income Statements

Click the ⊞ beside **Income Statement** to expand the list.

Click **Comparative 2 Period** and then **click Modify This Report**:

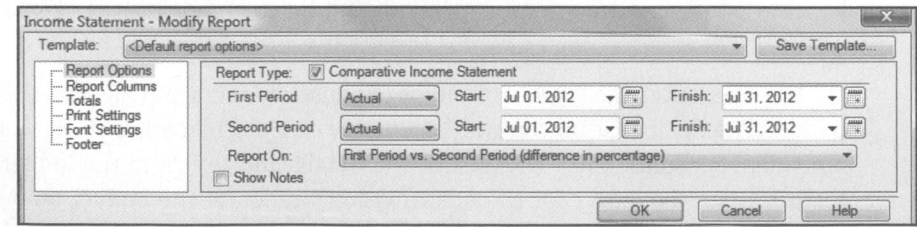

Click **Actual** in the First Period field to see the budget-related option:

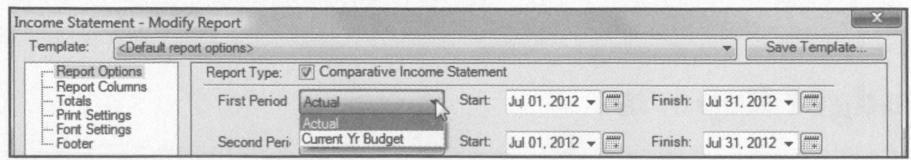

Click **Current Yr Budget** to change the option.

Budget income statements compare budget to actual amounts.

The **Report On** options are the same as the options for regular comparative income statements, but now the Second Period refers to budget amounts. Three types of reports are available. The first, **First Period Vs. Second Period (Amounts Only)**, lists the amounts that were budgeted for the revenue and expense accounts for the period indicated and the revenues and expenses actually obtained for the same period. The second, **First Period Vs. Second Period (Difference In Percentage)**, gives these two amounts as well as the percentage that the actual amount is above or below the budgeted amount. The third option, **First Period Vs. Second Period (Difference In Amounts)** provides budget and actual as base amounts, plus the difference between them as a dollar amount.

For the dollar difference and the percentage difference reports, a positive difference means that the budget was exceeded, a negative difference indicates that the results came in under budget. Remember that for revenues, a positive difference means results were better than expected, but for expenses, a positive difference means that results were poorer than expected (expenses were higher than budgeted). Cost of goods sold will increase directly with sales, so positive differences can mean either improved sales or higher costs, or both.

> **Click**   the **budget report** you want. **Close** the **display** when finished.

> When you add budget details for divisions, you can also create **division budget reports**. Choose the Reports menu, then choose Division and click Budget. Choose the Report Type, dates and divisions and click OK.

Printing Budget Reports

> **Display** the **report** you want to print. **Click** the **Print button**  or **choose** the **File menu** in the report window and **click Print**.

> **Close**   the **displayed report** when you have finished. **Close** the **Report Centre**.

Graphing Budget Reports

When the Budgeting option is activated and set up, two budget-related graphs are added to the Graphs menu: Sales vs Budget and Expenses vs Budget. Graphs are available only from the Home window.

Sales vs Budget Graphs

> **Choose**   the **Graphs menu** in the Home window and **click Sales Vs Budget** to display the set of revenue accounts:

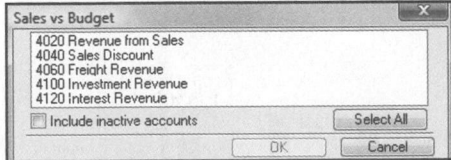

> **Press**   and **hold** `ctrl` and **click** the **accounts** you want to include in the graph or **click Select All**.

NOTES
Remember to check your printer selection before you print reports.

Click **OK** to display the graph as a bar chart:

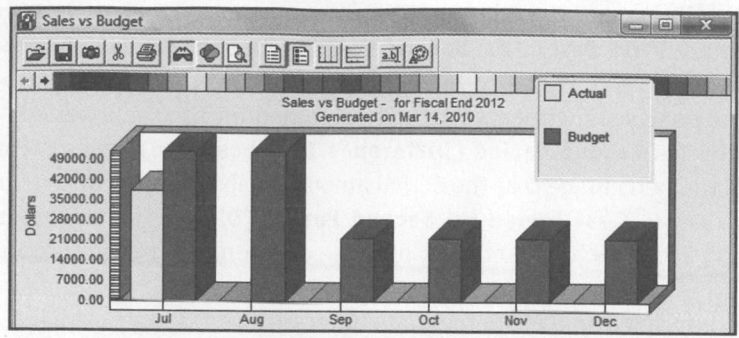

The options for displaying, editing, printing and copying budget graphs, and so on, are the same as those for other graphs.

The displayed graph includes all revenue accounts **before** the 10 percent budget decrease at the end of July. The amounts for the selected revenue accounts are added together in the single bar labelled Actual. The other bar represents the budgeted amount for the same accounts together. Revenue was much lower than expected, indicating a decline in performance. Budget amounts are shown for the remaining months of the fiscal period. There are no actual sales amounts after July.

Close the **displayed graph** when you have finished.

Expenses vs Budget Graphs

Choose the **Graphs menu** in the Home window and **click Expenses Vs Budget** to display the set of expense accounts:

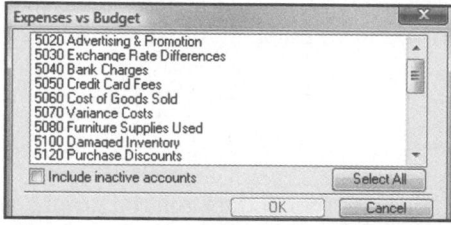

Press and **hold** ⌨ctrl and **click** the **accounts** you want to include in the graph or **click Select All**.

Click **OK** to display the bar chart:

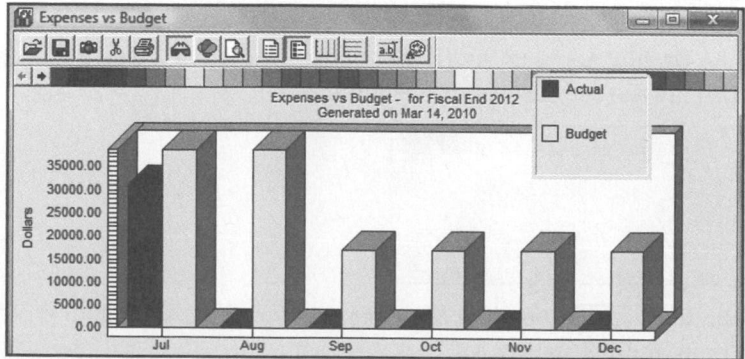

The displayed graph includes all expense accounts at the end of July, before changing the budget amounts. The amounts for the selected expense accounts are added together in the bar labelled Actual. The second bar represents the budgeted amount for the same accounts. The graph shows that expenses were also lower than expected. This result supports the trend in the revenue graph for decreased sales because cost of goods sold, the largest expense, is directly proportional to sales. Net income for July was also significantly below the budget forecast. Budget amounts are shown for the remaining months of the fiscal period. There are no actual expense amounts after July.

Close   the **displayed graph** when you have finished.

Printing in Batches

In addition to printing invoices, orders, quotes and cheques at the time of a transaction, you can print them in batches at the end of a period, such as the end of a business day. Batch printing makes it easier to share printers. Any forms that can be printed individually can be printed in batches. First you need to allow batch printing for the data file.

Choose   the **Setup menu** and **click Settings**.

Click   **Company** and then **click Forms** to open the Settings screen for Forms:

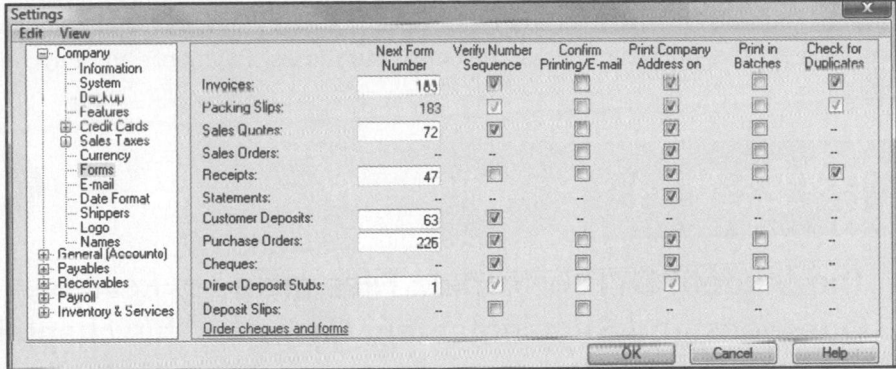

Click   the **Print In Batches check box for Invoices**, the first form listed.

Click   the **check box for the other forms** that you want to be able to print in batches.

Click   **OK** to save the changes.

Now, the Reports menu in the Home window has a Print Batches menu option.

Choose   the **Reports menu** then **choose Print Batches** and **click Sales Invoices** to see the printing options:

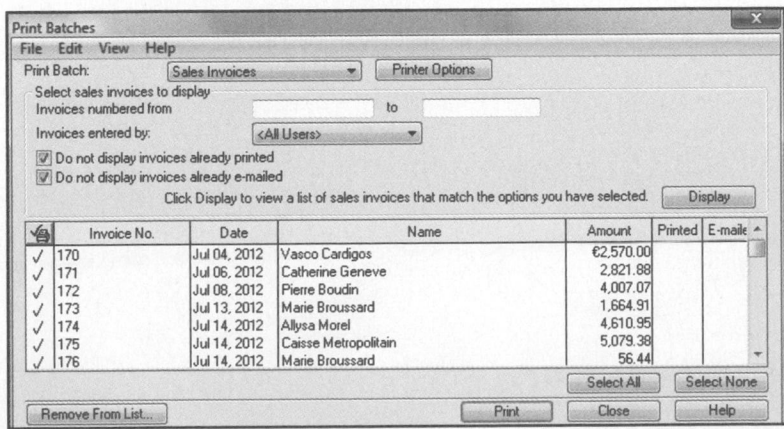

From this screen, you can choose other forms to print in batches. These are available from the **Print Batch** drop-down list. If some invoices have already been

NOTES
To set up for printing in batches, you must work in single-user mode.

NOTES
To print the invoices, you must choose Custom Form and Custom Simply Form in the Reports & Forms settings on the Invoices screen. Choose Invoice in the Description field for invoices and e-mail.

NOTES
Remember that you can customize the invoices before printing them. Refer to Appendix G on the Student DVD.
You cannot preview the invoices from the Print Batches window.

Printed or **E-mailed**, you can remove them from the display by clicking the appropriate check boxes. You can choose a **range of Invoice Numbers** or a specific **User** as selection criteria. After making these selections, click **Display** to show only the requested invoices. Initially all invoices are selected for printing as indicated by the ✓ in the Print column. Clicking **Select None** will remove all the ✓s and clicking **Select All** will select all listed invoices. You can also select invoices individually by clicking Select None and then clicking the invoices you want to print.

Choose the **invoices** you want to print so that only those invoices have a ✓.

Click **Print**. Printing begins immediately, so be sure that you have loaded the forms you need (or use plain paper for practice).

Click **Close** or select another form from the Print Batch list to print other forms.

Printing in Batches from Journals

When you allow batch printing from the Forms Settings screen, you can print these forms in batches directly from the related journal.

All the journals that have a Print tool will have a **Print Batches tool** added to the tool bar for this purpose, that is, the Sales, Purchases, Payments and Paycheques journals.

R E V I E W

The Student DVD with Data Files includes Review Questions and Supplementary Cases for this chapter.

CHAPTER FIFTEEN

Tesses Tresses

OBJECTIVES

After completing this chapter, you should be able to

- **prepare** bank deposit slips
- **print** Transaction Reports for bank accounts
- **compare** bank statements with Transaction Reports
- **turn on** the account reconciliation feature
- **create** new linked accounts for reconciliation
- **set up** the account reconciliation information
- **reconcile** the bank account statement with the General Ledger
- **display** and **print** account reconciliation reports
- **clear** paid invoices and **remove** accounts

COMPANY INFORMATION

Company Profile

NOTES
Tesses Tresses
55 Salon Rd.
Charlottetown, PE C1A 6D3
Tel: (902) 729-6211
Fax: (902) 728-4821
Business No.: 136 422 374

Tesses Tresses, a hair salon in Charlottetown, Prince Edward Island, is a family business owned by Tess Dubois, her husband, Ian, and her daughter, Felicia. All three had both professional and business management training to prepare them for running the salon. Together they provide a full range of hair care services to clients, most of whom return regularly. Unlike many salons where the price depends on the stylist and client, Tesses Tresses charges one price for each service regardless of client gender or stylist. They also sell a limited range of high-quality hair care products.

The salon building that they own includes two apartments that are rented to students. These tenants provided postdated cheques for three months at the beginning of January.

Instead of hiring a maintenance, cleaning and laundry company to take care of the premises, the Dubois family share this responsibility to reduce expenses. Cleaning is required almost continually to meet hygiene standards for health and safety.

The salon's regular suppliers provide inventory products including those used in the salon for regular client services; office supplies; cleaning supplies for the salon; linens such as towels, capes and gowns; and hairdressing equipment.

Supplier records are set up for all of these suppliers as well as for utility service companies and government agencies to which Tesses Tresses remits taxes. The salon pays GST on all purchases and PST on taxable goods and services except inventory.

Although most clients are one-time clients who pay by cash and credit card, some repeat clients have accounts and are entitled to a 2 percent discount if they pay within five days. Net payment is due in 15 days. The cash clients do not receive a discount. A record called Cash Customers is set up for the weekly summaries of cash and credit card sales. Clients pay both GST at 5 percent and PST at the rate of 10 percent on merchandise they buy from the salon and GST only on all services. The PST in Prince Edward Island is calculated on the base price of goods plus GST. The tax rates and codes are entered into client and inventory records, so the program automatically calculates taxes.

Tesses Tresses also provides hair styling services to local theatre companies, cutting and styling hair for cast members before performances, re-styling throughout the show for cast character changes and styling wigs. These evening commitments do not conflict with the usual daytime salon business hours. The theatre companies pay preferred prices at about 20 percent off regular prices in addition to the discount for early payment.

At the beginning of February, some unfilled purchase orders will provide the inventory for the additional purchases anticipated for Valentine's Day.

The accounting records for Tesses Tresses were converted to Simply Accounting at the beginning of January, and the transactions for January have been completed. The files are ready for January bank account transactions (deposits and account reconciliation) and February transactions. The current accounting records include:

- Chart of Accounts
- Trial Balance as at January 31, 2012
- Supplier Information
- Client Information
- Inventory Information
- Accounting Procedures

CHART OF ACCOUNTS

TESSES TRESSES

ASSETS
- 1030 Undeposited Cash and Cheques
- 1060 Bank: Chequing Account
- 1080 Bank: Credit Cards
- 1200 Accounts Receivable
- 1240 Prepaid Insurance
- 1260 Prepaid Subscriptions
- 1300 Towels and Capes
- 1320 Office Supplies
- 1340 Washroom & Cleaning Supplies
- 1360 Salon Supplies
- 1420 Hair Care Products ▶

- ▶1520 Computer and Cash Register
- 1540 Furniture and Fixtures
- 1560 Salon Equipment
- 1580 Salon and Building

LIABILITIES
- 2100 Bank Loan
- 2150 Credit Card Payable
- 2200 Accounts Payable
- 2640 PST Payable
- 2750 GST Charged on Sales
- 2760 GST Paid on Purchases
- 2850 Mortgage Payable ▶

▶EQUITY
- 3100 TT Capital
- 3150 TT Drawings
- 3600 Net Income

REVENUE
- 4100 Revenue from Sales
- 4120 Revenue from Services
- 4140 Rental Income
- 4160 Sales Discounts
- 4200 Sales Tax Compensation
- 4220 Interest Revenue
- 4240 Other Revenue ▶

▶EXPENSE
- 5020 Advertising and Promotion
- 5040 Bank Charges
- 5060 Credit Card Fees
- 5080 Cost of Services
- 5180 Inventory Losses
- 5200 Cost of Goods Sold
- 5220 Purchase Discounts
- 5240 Insurance Expense
- 5260 Subscriptions Expense
- 5300 Supplies Used
- 5320 Utilities
- 5340 Interest Expense

NOTES: The Chart of Accounts includes only postable accounts and Net Income.

TRIAL BALANCE

TESSES TRESSES

January 31, 2012

		Debits	Credits				Debits	Credits
1030	Undeposited Cash and Cheques	$ 13 677.19		▶	2750	GST Charged on Sales		1 079.40
1060	Bank: Chequing Account	33 463.35			2760	GST Paid on Purchases	172.90	
1080	Bank: Credit Cards	7 958.63			2850	Mortgage Payable		149 750.00
1200	Accounts Receivable	21.00			3100	TT Capital		101 749.00
1240	Prepaid Insurance	750.00			4100	Revenue from Sales		4 699.00
1260	Prepaid Subscriptions	270.00			4120	Revenue from Services		16 889.00
1300	Towels and Capes	530.00			4140	Rental Income		945.00
1320	Office Supplies	130.00			4160	Sales Discounts	52.04	
1340	Washroom & Cleaning Supplies	572.35			4200	Sales Tax Compensation		62.70
1360	Salon Supplies	255.00			5060	Credit Card Fees	298.55	
1420	Hair Care Products	1 567.50			5200	Cost of Goods Sold	1 860.50	
1520	Computer and Cash Register	4 200.00			5220	Purchase Discounts		57.08
1540	Furniture and Fixtures	7 600.00			5240	Insurance Expense	150.00	
1560	Salon Equipment	4 684.80			5260	Subscriptions Expense	30.00	
1580	Salon and Building	220 000.00			5300	Supplies Used	840.00	
2100	Bank Loan		$23 520.00		5320	Utilities	300.50	
2150	Credit Card Payable		80.85		5340	Interest Expense	1 370.00	
2200	Accounts Payable		1 428.00				$300 753.51	$300 753.51
2640	PST Payable		493.48 ▶					

SUPPLIER INFORMATION

TESSES TRESSES

Supplier Name (Contact)	Address	Phone No. Fax No.	E-mail Web Site	Terms Tax ID
Air Pro (Curly Locks)	390 Brows Lane Charlottetown, PE C1A 6M3	Tel: (902) 722-0217 Fax: (902) 723-8100	curly@airpro.com www.airpro.com	net 15 137 456 199
All U Need	Maypoint Plaza #64 Charlottetown, PE C1E 1E2	Tel: (902) 728-4314	www.alluneed.com	net 1 382 732 162
Atlantic Power Corp.	16 Lektrik Rd. Charlottetown, PE C1C 6G1	Tel: (902) 726-1615	www.apc.ca	net 1
Charlottetown City Treasurer	78 Fitzroy St. Charlottetown, PE C1A 1R5	Tel: (902) 725-9173	www.charlottetown.ca/fin	net 1
Eastern Tel (I.D. Caller)	36 Nassau St. Charlottetown, PE C1A 7V9	Tel: (902) 723-2355	www.bell.ca	net 1
Fine Brushes (Harry Bristle)	13 Ave. Costey Dorval, QC H9S 4C7	Tel: (514) 457-1826 Fax: (514) 457-1883	bristle@finebrushes.com www.finebrushes.com	net 20 188 462 457
Lookin' Good (N. Vayne)	18 Vivanle Cr. Summerside, PE C1N 6C4	Tel: (902) 829-4763 Fax: (902) 829-7392	vayne@lookingood.com www.lookingood.com	net 10 192 721 214
Pro-Line Inc. (Awl Fluff)	190 Rue Mutchmore Hull, QC J8Y 3S9	Tel: (819) 658-7227 Fax: (819) 658-7192	awl.fluff@proline.com www.proline.com	2/10, n/30 (after tax) 621 372 611
Provincial Treasurer	95 Rochford St., PO Box 2000 Charlottetown, PE C1A 7N8	Tel: (902) 368-4070 Fax: (902) 368-6164	www.gov.pe.ca/pt	net 1
Receiver General for Canada	Summerside Tax Centre Summerside, PE C1N 6L2	Tel: (902) 821-8186	www.cca-arc.gc.ca	net 1
Seaside Papers (Fyne Pulp)	40 Harbour View Dr. Charlottetown, PE C1A 7A8	Tel: (902) 720-1623 Fax: (902) 720-1639	pulp@seasidepapers.com www.seasidepapers.com	net 1 810 721 011

▶

SUPPLIER INFORMATION CONTINUED

Supplier Name (Contact)	Address	Phone No. Fax No.	E-mail Web Site	Terms Tax ID
Sharp Scissors (S. Cutter)	22 Bellevue Ave. Summerside, PE C1N 2C7	Tel: (902) 923-1995 Fax: (902) 923-1726	cutter@sharp.com www.sharp.com	net 10 138 221 100
Zines Inc. (Buetee Tipps)	344 Lepage Ave. Summerside, PE C1N 3E6	Tel: (902) 553- 6291 Fax: (902) 553-7155	tipps@zines.com www.zines.com	net 10 205 602 301

OUTSTANDING SUPPLIER INVOICES

TESSES TRESSES

Supplier Name	Terms	Date	Inv/Chq No.	Amount	Discount	Total
Fine Brushes	net 20	Dec. 20/11	FB-4321	$330.00		$330.00
		Jan. 09/12	CHQ 411	330.00		330.00
	net 20	Jan. 17/12	FB-6219	504.00		504.00
			Balance owing			$504.00
Pro-Line Inc.	2/10, n/30	Dec. 28/11	PL-1002	$ 945.00		$ 945.00
		Jan. 4/12	CHQ 410	926.10	$18.90	945.00
	2/10, n/30	Jan. 4/12	PL-1012	1 908.90		1 908.90
		Jan. 14/12	CHQ 413	1 870.72	38.18	1 908.90
Sharp Scissors	net 10	Jan. 24/12	SS-432	$924.00		$924.00
			Grand Total			$1 428.00

NOTES: Cash and Credit Card Purchases are not included in the chart of supplier invoices.

CLIENT INFORMATION

TESSES TRESSES

Client Name (Contact)	Address	Phone No. Fax No.	E-mail Web Site	Terms Credit Limit
Atta Schule (tenant)		Tel: (902) 724-2996	atta.schule@undergrad.upei.ca	first of month
Brioche Bridal Party (Bonnie Brioche)	75 Marital Way Charlottetown, PE C1E 4A2	Tel: (902) 723-1194 Fax: (902) 726-1921	brioche@weddingbells.com	2/5, n/15 $1 000
Cash Customers				cash/credit card
Conn Seted	14 Hi Brow St. Charlottetown, PE C1E 3X1	Tel: (902) 723-0099	conn.seted@aol.com	net 15 $1 000
Irma Vannitee	77 Makeover Cr. Charlottetown, PE C1B 1J5	Tel: (902) 726-7715	irma.van@skindeep.com	2/5, n/15 $1 000
*On Stage Theatre Company (Marvelle Stage)	100 Marquee Blvd. Charlottetown, PE C1A 2M1	Tel: (902) 727-8201 Fax: (902) 727-0663	marvelle@onstage.com www.onstage.com	2/5, n/15 $2 000
Proud Family	98 Proud St. Charlottetown, PE C1B 3C1	Tel: (902) 721-1113	theprouds@shaw.ca	net 15 $1 000
Stu Dents (tenant)		Tel: (902) 724-7103	stu.dents@undergrad.upei.ca	first of month
*Twilight Theatre (Ona Roll)	55 Footlights Dr. Charlottetown, PE C1B 6V2	Tel: (902) 728-4661 Fax: (902) 724-1556	ona.roll@twilight.com www.twilight.com	2/5, n/15 $2 000

NOTES: All client discounts are calculated on after-tax amounts.
* Indicates preferred customer.

OUTSTANDING CLIENT INVOICES

TESSES TRESSES

Client Name	Terms	Date	Inv/Chq No.	Amount	Discount	Total
Atta Schule	rent payment	Jan. 2/12	CHQ 415			$395.00
	rent payment	Feb. 1/12	CHQ 416 (postdated rent payment)			395.00
	rent payment	Mar. 1/12	CHQ 417 (postdated rent payment)			395.00
Brioche Bridal Party	2/5, n/15	Jan. 9/12	468	$119.39		$119.39
		Jan. 14/12	CHQ 206	$117.00	$2.39	119.39
Conn Seted	net 15	Jan. 24/12	477			$42.00
		Jan. 29/12	CHQ 238			42.00
Irma Vannitee	2/5, n/15	Dec. 28/11	452	$120.00		$120.00
		Jan. 2/12	CHQ 46	117.60	$2.40	120.00
	2/5, n/15	Jan. 2/12	464	89.36		89.36
		Jan. 7/12	CHQ 918	87.57	1.79	89.36
	2/5, n/15	Jan. 4/12	467	124.01		124.01
		Jan. 17/12	CHQ CC-61	124.01		124.01
	2/5, n/15	Jan. 16/12	471	66.05		66.05
		Jan. 20/12	CHQ 74	64.73	1.32	66.05
	2/5, n/15	Jan. 27/12	478	21.00		21.00
			Balance owing			$21.00
On Stage Theatre Company	2/5, n/15	Dec. 29/11	455	$250.00		$250.00
		Jan. 3/12	CHQ 382	245.00	$ 5.00	250.00
	2/5, n/15	Jan. 20/12	474	873.60		873.60
		Jan. 24/12	CHQ 429	856.13	17.47	873.60
	2/5, n/15	Jan. 28/12	479	873.60		873.60
		Jan. 31/12	CHQ 498	856.13	17.47	873.60
Stu Dents	rent payment	Jan. 2/12	CHQ 161			$550.00
	rent payment	Feb. 1/12	CHQ 162 (postdated rent payment)			550.00
	rent payment	Mar. 1/12	CHQ 163 (postdated rent payment)			550.00
Twilight Theatre	2/5, n/15	Dec. 28/11	453	$210.00		$210.00
		Jan. 2/12	CHQ 5121	205.80	$4.20	210.00
			Grand Total			$21.00

INVENTORY ITEM INFORMATION

TESSES TRESSES

Item Code	Item Description	Unit	Min Qty	Selling Price Reg	(Pref)	Qty on Hand	Total (Cost)
Hair Products: Total asset value $1 886.50 (Asset account: 1420, Revenue account: 4100, Expense account: 5200)							
BRS1	Hair Brush: natural bristle	each	2	$28	(24)	16	$ 192.00
BRS2	Hair Brush: styling	each	2	24	(21)	28	224.00
CN1	Pro-Line Conditioner: 150 ml	bottle	3	26	(22)	14	154.00
CN2	Pro-Line Hot Oil Treatment 75 ml	tube	3	29	(25)	33	313.50
FRZ1	Pro-Line Defrizzer: cream 100 ml	jar	3	14	(12)	29	174.00
GEL1	Pro-Line Spray Gel: shaper 150 ml	can	5	22	(18)	21	189.00
SHM1	Pro-Line Shampoo: 225 ml	bottle	5	21	(17)	17	153.00
SPR1	Pro-Line Hair Spray: gentle 150 ml	can	5	17	(14)	28	168.00
							$1 567.50

NOTES: Brushes are purchased and sold individually. All other hair care products are purchased in cartons of 12 units and sold in individual units.

	INVENTORY INFORMATION CONTINUED: SERVICES						
Code	Description	Unit	Regular Price	(Preferred)	PST	GST
Salon Services (Revenue account: 4120, Expense account: 5080)						
SRV1	Colour	each	$ 45	($36)	No PST	Yes
SRV2	Conditioning Treatment	each	20	(16)	No PST	Yes
SRV3	Cut and Style	each	40	(32)	No PST	Yes
SRV4	Highlights	each	100	(80)	No PST	Yes
SRV5	Perm	each	80	(64)	No PST	Yes
SRV6	Wash and Style	each	20	(16)	No PST	Yes
SRV7	Wig Wash, Set and Style	each	30	(24)	No PST	Yes

Accounting Procedures

Taxes

GST at 5 percent is charged on all goods and services sold by the salon. Tesses Tresses remits the GST owing — *GST Charged on Sales* less *GST Paid on Purchases* — to the Receiver General by the last day of each month for the previous month.

PST at 10 percent for Prince Edward Island is charged on all inventory items sold by the salon. PST is calculated on the sale price plus the GST Charged (i.e., GST is taxable). Personal services, such as those provided by the salon, are exempt from PST. The inventory ledger records contain this information so that the correct taxes will be applied automatically. When PST is remitted, 3 percent of the PST collected is withheld as sales tax compensation, to an annual maximum compensation of $500.

Sales Summaries

Most salon sales are to one-time clients who do not have accounts. These sales are summarized weekly according to payment — by cash or by credit card — and entered for the client named Cash Customers. By choosing Cash Customers as the client for these sales, the default tax codes and terms should be correct.

Receipts and Bank Deposits

Cash and cheques received in payment are held for weekly deposits. Upon receipt, they are debited to the *Undeposited Cash and Cheques*.

NSF Cheques

If a cheque is deposited from an account that does not have enough money to cover it, the bank returns it to the depositor as NSF (non-sufficient funds). To record the NSF cheque, enter a negative receipt in the Receipts Journal. Select *Bank: Chequing Account* as the Deposit To account. Turn on the option to Include Fully Paid Invoices and enter a negative payment amount. Enter the bank debit number as the receipt and add NSF to the original cheque number in the Cheque field. If a discount was taken for early payment, reverse this amount as well. Then enter a Sales Journal invoice for the amount of the handling charge. Refer to page 601 and A–30 if you need more help.

Cost of Supplies

Instead of buying separate salon supplies for regular client services, Tesses Tresses uses its inventory stock of shampoos, conditioners, gels and so on. Inventory Adjustment entries are completed to make these transfers at cost from the inventory asset account to the supplies account.

⚠️ **WARNING!**
You need to enter a negative receipt for these NSF cheques. You cannot reverse the receipt because different accounts are involved. The original receipt was deposited to Undeposited Cash and Cheques, but the NSF cheque credits the Bank: Chequing Account, after the deposit was entered.

NOTES
The store is liable for the PST on the cost of these transferred inventory items – the store sells the merchandise to itself at cost.

INSTRUCTIONS

1. **Enter** the **deposit slips** and **set up** and **complete** the **account reconciliation** for January using the Chart of Accounts, Trial Balance, Supplier, Client and Inventory information provided and using the keystrokes that start on page 580 as a guide. The journal transactions for January have been completed for you.

2. **Enter** the **source documents** for February, including the account reconciliation.

3. **Print** the **reports** indicated on the chart below after completing your entries.

NOTES

If you want to complete only the deposit and reconciliation transactions for this chapter, complete the bank deposits and reconciliations for January 31 and then restore the Bank\tess1.cab file to complete the reconciliation transactions for February 28.

REPORTS

Accounts
- [ ] Chart of Accounts
- [ ] Account List
- [ ] General Journal Entries

Financials
- [✓] Comparative Balance Sheet dates: Feb. 1 and Feb. 28 with difference in percentage
- [✓] Income Statement from Jan. 1 to Feb. 28
- [✓] Trial Balance date: Feb. 28
- [✓] All Journals Entries: Feb. 1 to Feb. 28
- [✓] General Ledger: for accounts 1060 and 1080 from Jan. 1 to Feb. 28
- [ ] Statement of Cash Flows
- [✓] Cash Flow Projection Detail Report for account 1060 for 30 days
- [ ] Gross Margin Income Statement

Tax
- [ ] Report on

Banking
- [✓] Account Reconciliation Summary Report: for 1060 and 1080 from Jan. 1 to Feb. 28
- [ ] Bank Transaction Report
- [ ] Reconciliation Transaction Report
- [✓] Deposit Slip Detail Report for account 1060 from Jan. 1 to Feb. 28

- [✓] Account Reconciliation Journal Entries: Jan. 1 to Feb. 28
- [✓] Deposit Slip Journal Entries: Jan. 1 to Feb. 28
- [ ] Cheque Log Report

Payables
- [ ] Supplier List
- [ ] Supplier Aged
- [ ] Aged Overdue Payables
- [ ] Expense Journal Entries
- [ ] Payment Journal Entries
- [ ] Supplier Expenses

Receivables
- [ ] Client List
- [ ] Client Aged
- [ ] Aged Overdue Receivables
- [ ] Revenues Journal Entries
- [ ] Receipt Journal Entries
- [ ] Client Revenues
- [ ] Revenues by Salesperson
- [ ] Client Statements

Inventory & Services
- [ ] Inventory & Services List
- [ ] Inventory Summary
- [ ] Inventory Quantity

- [✓] Inventory Statistics: all items and all details
- [ ] Inventory Sales Summary
- [ ] Inventory Transaction Summary
- [ ] Item Assembly Journal Entries
- [ ] Adjustment Journal Entries
- [ ] Inventory Price Lists

Mailing Labels
- [ ] Labels

Management Reports
- [ ] Ledger

GRAPHS
- [ ] Payables by Aging Period
- [ ] Payables by Supplier
- [ ] Receivables by Aging Period
- [ ] Receivables by Client
- [ ] Sales vs Receivables
- [ ] Receivables Due vs Payables Due
- [ ] Revenues by Account
- [ ] Expenses by Account
- [ ] Expenses and Net Profit as % of Revenue

SOURCE DOCUMENTS

SESSION DATE – JANUARY 31, 2012

- [✓] **Memo #7**   **Dated Jan. 31/12**

580   Use the following deposit information slips to prepare deposit slips #1 to #5. All amounts were deposited to Bank: Chequing Account.

DEPOSIT SLIP # 1   JANUARY 7, 2012

Date	Cheque #	Client	Amount
Jan 2	46	Irma Vannitee	$ 117.60
Jan 2	5121	Twilight Theatre	205.80
Jan 2	161	Stu Dents	550.00
Jan 2	415	Atta Schule	395.00
Jan 3	382	On Stage Theatre Company	245.00
Jan 7	918	Irma Vannitee	87.57
		Total Cheques	$1 600.97
		Cash	$2 170.04

(Consisting of 7 × $10; 35 × $20; 10 × $50; 9 × $100; Coin $0.04)

Total Deposit $3 771.01

NOTES
For all deposits, choosing January 1 from the drop-down list in the On Or After field will show all cheques not yet deposited.

DEPOSIT SLIP # 2   JANUARY 14, 2012

Date	Cheque #	Client	Amount
Jan 9	61	Irma Vannitee	$121.53
Jan 14	206	Brioche Bridal Party	117.00
		Total Cheques	$238.53
		Cash	$1 733.34

(Consisting of 6 × $5; 10 × $10; 10 × $20; 8 × $50; 10 × $100; Coin $3.34)

Total Deposit $1 971.87

DEPOSIT SLIP # 3   JANUARY 21, 2012

Date	Cheque #	Client	Amount
Jan 17	CC-61	Irma Vannitee	$124.01
Jan 20	74	Irma Vannitee	64.73
		Total Cheques	$188.74
		Cash	$1 961.30

(Consisting of 6 × $5; 7 × $10; 18 × $20; 12 × $50; 9 × $100; Coin $1.30)

Total Deposit $2 150.04

DEPOSIT SLIP # 4   JANUARY 28, 2012

Date	Cheque #	Client	Amount
Jan 24	429	On Stage Theatre Company	$856.13
		Total Cheques	$856.13
		Cash	$1 750.14

(Consisting of 20 × $5; 15 × $10; 20 × $20; 8 × $50; 7 × $100; Coin $0.14)

Total Deposit $2 606.27

DEPOSIT SLIP # 5   JANUARY 31, 2012

Date	Cheque #	Client	Amount
Jan 29	238	Conn Seted	$ 42.00
Jan 31	498	On Stage Theatre Company	856.13
		Total Cheques	$898.13
		Cash	$2 279.87

(Consisting of 9 × $5; 12 × $10; 18 × $20; 13 × $50; 11 × $100; Coin $4.87)

Total Deposit $3 178.00

✓ **Memo #8**   **Dated Jan. 31/12**

587   Set up account reconciliation for Bank: Chequing Account and Bank: Credit Cards.

✓ **Memo #9**   **Dated Jan. 31/12**

590   Use the following bank statement to reconcile Bank: Chequing Account.

		SAVERS TRUST			

321 Queen St., Charlottetown, PE C1A 6D3   www.saverstrust.com

Tesses Tresses
55 Salon Road   ACCOUNT STATEMENT
Charlottetown, PE C1A 6D3   CHEQUING

Transit / Account No   Statement period
0290   003 433 38-2   Jan 1, 2012 to Jan 31, 2012

Date	Note #	Description	Deposits	Withdrawals	Balance
		Balance Fwd			37,238.00
2 Jan	1	Deposit	1,177.00		38,415.00
7 Jan		Cheque #410		926.10	37,488.90
7 Jan	2	Deposit	3,771.01		41,259.91
9 Jan		Cheque #411		330.00	40,929.91
14 Jan	2	Deposit	1,971.07		42,901.78
14 Jan		Cheque #412		199.50	42,702.28
14 Jan		Cheque #413		1,870.72	40,831.56
14 Jan		Transfer 0290 004 123 22-8	5,000.00		45,831.56
15 Jan		NSF Cheque #61		121.53	45,710.03
15 Jan	3	Service Charge – NSF cheque		30.00	45,680.03
17 Jan		Cheque #414		1,830.00	43,850.03
20 Jan		Cheque #415		115.50	43,734.53
21 Jan	2	Deposit	2,150.04		45,884.57
27 Jan		Cheque #416		431.00	45,453.57
27 Jan	5	Scheduled payment: loan		600.00	44,853.57
27 Jan	5	Scheduled payment: mortgage		1,500.00	43,353.57
28 Jan	2	Deposit	2,606.27		45,959.84
31 Jan	3	Service Charges		23.50	45,936.34
31 Jan	4	Interest	52.25		45,988.59
31 Jan		Closing balance			45,988.59

Total Deposits   # 7 $16,728.44
Total Withdrawals   # 12 $7,977.85

✓ **Memo #10**   **Dated Jan. 31/12**

600   Use the bank statement on the following page to reconcile Bank: Credit Cards.
There is one outstanding prior transaction:
Sales invoice #457 dated Dec. 31, 2011, deposited to Cash Sales for $230.

SAVERS TRUST				

321 Queen St., Charlottetown, PE C1A 6D3　　　　www.saverstrust.com

Tesses Tresses
55 Salon Road
Charlottetown, PE C1A 6D3

ACCOUNT STATEMENT
CREDIT CARD

Transit / Account No
0290　004 123 22-8

Statement period
Jan 1, 2012 to Jan 31, 2012

Date	Description	Deposits	Withdrawals	Balance
	Balance Fwd			1,970.00
2 Jan	Deposit	230.00		2,200.00
2 Jan	Deposit	2,094.39		4,294.39
9 Jan	Deposit	2,350.31		6,644.70
14 Jan	Transfer to 0290 003 433 38-2		5,000.00	1,644.70
16 Jan	Deposit	2,234.67		3,879.37
23 Jan	Deposit	2,135.77		6,015.14
30 Jan	Deposit	1,943.49		7,958.63
31 Jan	Service Charges		11.50	7,947.13
31 Jan	Interest	6.50		7,953.63
31 Jan	Closing balance			7,953.63
Total Deposits	# 7	$10,995.13		
Total Withdrawals	# 2	$5,011.50		

SESSION DATE – FEBRUARY 7, 2012

☐ **Cheque Copy #418**　　　　　　**Dated Feb. 2/12**

To Sharp Scissors, $924.00 in payment of account. Reference invoice #SS-432.

☐ **Sales Invoice #482**　　　　　　**Dated Feb. 2/12**

To Irma Vannitee
1	BRS1	Hair Brush: natural bristle	$28
1	CN2	Pro-Line Hot Oil Treatment 75 ml	29
1	SRV3	Cut and Style	40
1	SRV5	Perm	80
	GST		5%
	PST		10%

Terms: 2/5, n/15.

☐ **Purchase Invoice #PL-1988**　　　**Dated Feb. 4/12**

From Pro-Line Inc., to fill purchase order #52
2	CN1	Pro-Line Conditioner: 150 ml	$ 264.00
2	CN2	Pro-Line Hot Oil Treatment 75 ml	228.00
2	GEL1	Pro-Line Spray Gel: shaper 150 ml	216.00
2	FRZ1	Pro-Line Defrizzer: cream 100 ml	144.00
2	SHM1	Pro-Line Shampoo: 225 ml	216.00
2	SPR1	Pro-Line Hair Spray: gentle 150 ml	144.00
	GST	5%	60.60
Invoice total			$1 272.60

Terms: 2/10, n/30.

☐ **Cash Purchase Invoice #CCT-12-2**　　**Dated Feb. 4/12**

From Charlottetown City Treasurer, $220 plus $11 GST for water and sewage treatment for three months. Purchase invoice total $231 paid by cheque #419 (Utilities account).

☐ **Sales Invoice #483**   **Dated Feb. 4/12**

To Conn Seted

1	FRZ1	Pro-Line Defrizzer: cream 100 ml	$14
1	GEL1	Pro-Line Spray Gel: shaper 150 ml	22
1	SRV1	Colour	45
1	SRV3	Cut and Style	40
	GST		5%
	PST		10%

Terms: net 15.

☐ **Sales Invoice #484**   **Dated Feb. 5/12**

To Twilight Theatre to partially fill sales order #102

6	SRV3	Cut and Style	$32 each
18	SRV6	Wash and Style	16 each
	GST		5%

Terms: 2/5, n/15.

☐ **Cash Purchase Invoice CCT-299392**   **Dated Feb. 6/12**

From Charlottetown City Treasurer, $4 800 for annual property tax assessment, payable in three equal instalments of $1 600. First instalment is due on receipt of invoice. Remaining two instalments are due May 6 and August 6. Issue cheques #420, 421 and 422 dated Feb. 6, May 6 and August 6 in payment of account. Create new Group account 5380 Property Taxes. Store as a quarterly recurring entry and recall for postdated series.

☐ **Credit Card Sales Invoice #485**   **Dated Feb. 6/12**

Sales Summary for credit card sales (to Cash Customers)

4	BRS1	Hair Brush: natural bristle	$ 28 each	$ 112.00
6	CN1	Pro-Line Conditioner: 150 ml	26 /bottle	156.00
3	FRZ1	Pro-Line Defrizzer: cream 100 ml	14 /jar	42.00
3	GEL1	Pro-Line Spray Gel: shaper 150 ml	22 /can	66.00
8	SIIM1	Pro-Line Shampoo: 225 ml	21 /bottle	168.00
26	SRV3	Cut and Style	40 each	1 040.00
5	SRV4	Highlights	100 each	500.00
6	SRV6	Wash and Style	20 each	120.00
	GST		5%	110.20
	PST		10%	57.12
	Invoice total paid by credit cards			$2 371.32

Deposited to credit card bank account.

☐ **Credit Card Purchase Invoice #AUN-344**   **Dated Feb. 7/12**

From All U Need department store, $300 plus $15.00 GST and $31.50 PST for 100 white hand towels for use in the salon. Purchase invoice total $346.50 paid in full by credit card. Change the default account entry.

☐ **Cash Sales Invoice #486**   **Dated Feb. 7/12**

Sales Summary for cash sales (to Cash Customers)

4	BRS2	Hair Brush: styling	$24 each	$ 96.00
3	CN2	Pro-Line Hot Oil Treatment 75 ml	29 /tube	87.00
5	GEL1	Pro-Line Spray Gel: shaper 150 ml	22 /can	110.00
5	SPR1	Pro-Line Hair Spray: gentle 150 ml	17 /can	85.00
2	SRV1	Colour	45 each	90.00
16	SRV3	Cut and Style	40 each	640.00
	GST		5%	55.40
	PST		10%	39.70
	Invoice total paid by cash			$1 203.10

Deposited to Undeposited Cash and Cheques.

NOTES

Sales Invoice #484 provides services for four theatre performances for six cast members. Do not fill the order. Enter the numbers in the quantity field. The remainder of the order is filled later.

DEPOSIT SLIP # 6			FEB. 7, 2012
Date	Cheque #	Client	Amount
Feb 1	416	Atta Schule	$395.00
Feb 1	162	Stu Dents	550.00
		Total Cheques	$945.00
Feb 7		Cash	$1 203.10
		(Consisting of 4 × $5; 10 × $10; 4 × $20; 4 × $50; 8 × $100; Coin $3.10)	
		Total Deposit	$2 148.10

SESSION DATE – FEBRUARY 14, 2012

Cash Purchase Invoice #AP-63322   **Dated Feb. 8/12**

From Atlantic Power Corp., $220 plus $11 GST for hydro services for one month. Purchase invoice total $231 paid by cheque #423.

Sales Invoice #487   **Dated Feb. 8/12**

To Brioche Bridal Party to partially fill sales order #101
    3 SRV3 Cut and Style $40 each
        GST   5%
Terms: 2/5, n/15.

Sales Invoice #488   **Dated Feb. 9/12**

To Irma Vannitee
    1 SRV6 Wash and Style $20
        GST   5%
Terms: 2/5, n/15. Store as a weekly recurring entry.

Credit Card Purchase Invoice #Z-6775   **Dated Feb. 10/12**

From Zines Inc., $110 plus $5.50 GST and $11.55 PST to renew subscriptions for one year to hair and fashion magazines. Purchase invoice total $127.05 paid in full by credit card (Prepaid Subscriptions account).

Cash Receipt #144   **Dated Feb. 10/12**

From Irma Vannitee, cheque #93 for $233.42 in payment of account including $0.42 discount for early payment. Reference sales invoices #478, 482 and 488.

Purchase Order #55   **Dated Feb. 10/12**

Delivery date Feb. 22/12
From Air Pro, $300 for two large hair dryers and $50 for two small hair dryers plus $17.50 GST and $36.75 PST. Purchase invoice total $404.25. Terms: net 15.

Purchase Invoice #FB-27731   **Dated Feb. 10/12**

From Fine Brushes, to fill purchase order #53
To Fine Brushes (stocking up for Valentine's gifts)
    30 BRS1 Hair Brush: natural bristle   360.00
    20 BRS2 Hair Brush: styling   160.00
        GST 5%   26.00
    Invoice total $546.00
Terms: net 20.

Cheque Copy #424   **Dated Feb. 10/12**

To Pro-Line Inc., $1 247.15 in full payment of account including $25.45 discount for early payment. Reference invoice #PL-1988.

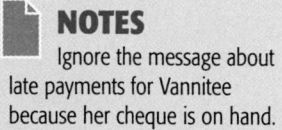

NOTES
Ignore the message about late payments for Vannitee because her cheque is on hand.

Sales Invoice #489   **Dated Feb. 10/12**

To Proud Family

2	BRS1	Hair Brush: natural bristle	$ 28 each
2	BRS2	Hair Brush: styling	24 each
2	SHM1	Pro-Line Shampoo: 225 ml	21 each
4	SRV3	Cut and Style	40 each
1	SRV4	Highlights	100
1	SRV5	Perm	80
	GST		5%
	PST		10%

Terms: net 15.

Credit Card Sales Invoice #490   **Dated Feb. 13/12**

Sales Summary for credit card sales (to Cash Customers)

8	BRS1	Hair Brush: natural bristle	$28 each	$ 224.00
6	BRS2	Hair Brush: styling	24 each	144.00
8	CN1	Pro-Line Conditioner: 150 ml	26 /bottle	208.00
8	SHM1	Pro-Line Shampoo: 225 ml	21 /bottle	168.00
30	SRV3	Cut and Style	40 each	1 200.00
7	SRV4	Highlights	100 each	700.00
3	SRV5	Perm	80 each	240.00
4	SRV6	Wash and Style	20 each	80.00
	GST		5%	148.20
	PST		10%	78.12
	Invoice total paid by credit cards			$3 190.32

Deposited to credit card bank account.

Purchase Order #56   **Dated Feb. 13/12**

Delivery date Feb. 21/12
From Pro-Line Inc.

1	CN1	Pro-Line Conditioner: 150 ml	$132.00
1	GEL1	Pro-Line Spray Gel: shaper 150 ml	108.00
2	SHM1	Pro-Line Shampoo: 225 ml	216.00
1	SPR1	Pro-Line Hair Spray: gentle 150 ml	72.00
	GST	5%	26.40
	Invoice total		$554.40

Terms: 2/12, n/30.

Cash Sales Invoice #491   **Dated Feb. 14/12**

Sales Summary for cash sales (to Cash Customers)

6	BRS2	Hair Brush: styling	$24 each	$ 144.00
8	GEL1	Pro-Line Spray Gel: shaper 150 ml	22 /can	176.00
3	FRZ1	Pro-Line Defrizzer: cream 100 ml	14 /jar	42.00
7	SPR1	Pro-Line Hair Spray: gentle 150 ml	17 /can	119.00
6	SRV1	Colour	45 each	270.00
24	SRV3	Cut and Style	40 each	960.00
1	SRV4	Highlights:	100 each	100.00
	GST		5%	90.55
	PST		10%	50.51
	Invoice total paid by cash			$1 952.06

Deposited to Undeposited Cash and Cheques.

Purchase Invoice #SS-555   **Dated Feb. 14/12**

From Sharp Scissors, to fill purchase order #54, $600 plus $30 GST and $63 PST
for professional high-grade stainless steel stylist scissors. Purchase invoice total
$693. Terms: net 10.

```
┌─────────────────────────────────────────────────────────────────────────┐
│ □ DEPOSIT SLIP # 7                                    FEBRUARY 14, 2012   │
│                                                                           │
│   Date    Cheque #  Client                         Amount                 │
│   ──────────────────────────────────────────────────────────────────     │
│   Feb 10    93      Irma Vannitee                   $233.42               │
│                     Total Cheques                   $233.42               │
│                                                                           │
│                     Cash                          $1 952.06               │
│                     (Consisting of 6 × $5;  7 × $10;  15 × $20;  13 × $50; │
│                      9 × $100;  Coin $2.06)                                │
│                     Total Deposit                 $2 185.48               │
└─────────────────────────────────────────────────────────────────────────┘
```

SESSION DATE – FEBRUARY 21, 2012

□ **Sales Invoice #492**   **Dated Feb. 16/12**

To Irma Vannitee

1	SRV6	Wash and Style	$20
	GST		5%

Terms: 2/5, n/15. Recall stored transaction.

□ **Memo #11**   **Dated Feb. 16/12**

From Owners: Transfer $10 000 from credit card account to chequing account.

□ **Memo #12**   **Dated Feb. 17/12**

From Owners: Pay GST owing to the Receiver General for the period ending January 31, 2012.

□ **Cash Purchase Invoice #ET-4588**   **Dated Feb. 17/12**

From Eastern Tel, $110 plus $5.50 GST and $11.55 PST for telephone service. Purchase invoice total $127.05 paid in full by cheque #426.

□ **Sales Quote #103**   **Dated Feb. 19/12**

First performance date Mar. 1/12
To On Stage Theatre Company (for 12 theatre performances for three cast members) at preferred customer prices

3	SRV3	Cut and Style	$32 each
36	SRV6	Wash and Style	16 each
9	SRV7	Wig Wash, Set and Style	24 each
	GST		5%

Terms: 2/5, n/15.

□ **Cash Receipt #145**   **Dated Feb. 19/12**

From Conn Seted, cheque #269 for $130.83 in payment of account. Reference invoice #483.

□ **Cash Receipt #146**   **Dated Feb. 20/12**

From Twilight Theatre, cheque #5635 for $504 in payment of account. Reference invoice #484.

□ **Credit Card Purchase Invoice #SP-399**   **Dated Feb. 20/12**

From Seaside Papers, $200 plus $10 GST and $21 PST for office supplies for salon. Purchase invoice total $231 paid in full by credit card.

□ **Credit Card Purchase Invoice #AUN-478**   **Dated Feb. 20/12**

From All U Need department store, $90 plus $4.50 GST and $9.45 PST for cleaning supplies. Purchase invoice total $103.95 paid in full by credit card.

NOTES

You can use the Tax Report for GST for January to obtain the GST amounts for the remittance, or you can refer to the General Ledger Report for the two GST accounts.

☐ **Purchase Invoice #AP-7111**   **Dated Feb. 20/12**

From Air Pro, to fill purchase order #55, $350 plus $17.50 and $36.75 PST for two bonnet-style hair dryers and two handheld hair dryers. Purchase invoice total $404.25. Terms: net 15.

☐ **Purchase Invoice #PL-3488**   **Dated Feb. 20/12**

From Pro-Line Inc., to fill purchase order #56

1	CN1	Pro-Line Conditioner: 150 ml	$132.00
1	GEL1	Pro-Line Spray Gel: shaper 150 ml	108.00
2	SHM1	Pro-Line Shampoo: 225 ml	216.00
1	SPR1	Pro-Line Hair Spray: gentle 150 ml	72.00
	GST	5%	26.40
	Invoice total		$554.40

Terms: 2/10, n/30.

☐ **Cash Receipt #147**   **Dated Feb. 20/12**

From Brioche Bridal Party, cheque #986 for $126 in payment of account. Reference invoice #487.

☐ **Credit Card Sales Invoice #493**   **Dated Feb. 20/12**

Sales Summary for credit card sales (to Cash Customers)

3	BRS1	Hair Brush: natural bristle	$28 each	$ 84.00
2	CN2	Pro-Line Hot Oil Treatment 75 ml	29 /tube	58.00
2	FRZ1	Pro-Line Defrizzer: cream 100 ml	14 /jar	28.00
4	SHM1	Pro-Line Shampoo: 225 ml	21 /bottle	84.00
6	SRV1	Colour	45 each	270.00
16	SRV3	Cut and Style	40 each	640.00
	GST		5%	58.20
	PST		10%	26.67
	Invoice total paid by credit cards			$1 248.87

Deposited to credit card bank account.

☐ **Purchase Order #57**   **Dated Feb. 21/12**

Shipping date Mar. 3/12
From Lookin' Good, $400 plus $20 GST and $42 PST for 25 polyester and nylon water-resistant monogrammed capes for salon client use. Unit price is $16. Purchase invoice total $462. Terms: net 10.

☐ **Cash Sales Invoice #494**   **Dated Feb. 21/12**

Sales Summary for cash sales (to Cash Customers)

5	BRS2	Hair Brush: styling	24 each	$ 120.00
4	CN1	Pro-Line Conditioner: 150 ml	26 /bottle	104.00
6	GEL1	Pro-Line Spray Gel: shaper 150 ml	22 /can	132.00
7	SPR1	Pro-Line Hair Spray: gentle 150 ml	17 /can	119.00
3	SRV1	Colour	45 each	135.00
22	SRV3	Cut and Style	40 each	880.00
10	SRV6	Wash and Style	20 each	200.00
	GST		5%	84.50
	PST		10%	49.88
	Invoice total paid by cash			$1 824.38

Deposited to Undeposited Cash and Cheques.

☐ **Cheque Copy #427**   **Dated Feb. 21/12**

To Sharp Scissors, $693 in payment of account. Reference invoice #SS-555.

```
┌─────────────────────────────────────────────────────────────────────────────┐
│  DEPOSIT SLIP #8                                      Date: Feb 21, 2012      │
│  Tesses Tresses                                                               │
│  55 Salon Rd.                                                                 │
│  Charlottetown PE  C1A 6D3                                                    │
│                                                                              │
│  Account No:  0290 3433382                                                    │
│                                                                              │
│  Cheques                                                          Amount     │
│  ┌──────────────────────────────────────┐  ┌──────┬──────┬───────────┐      │
│  │ 269   Conn Seted         130.83      │  │  8   │ × 5  │   40   00  │      │
│  │ 5635  Twilight Theatre   504.00      │  │ 17   │ × 10 │  170   00  │      │
│  │ 986   Brioche Bridal Party 126.00    │  │ 28   │ × 20 │  560   00  │      │
│  │                                      │  │  5   │ × 50 │  250   00  │      │
│  │                                      │  │  8   │ × 100│  800   00  │      │
│  └──────────────────────────────────────┘  │      │ coin │    4   38  │      │
│                                             ├──────┴──────┼───────────┤      │
│                              Total cash     │             │ 1824   38 │      │
│                              Total cheque   │             │  760   83 │      │
│                              Subtotal       │             │ 2585   21 │      │
│                              Cash received  │             │           │      │
│                              Net Deposit    │             │ 2585   21 │      │
│                                                                              │
│  Signature  Tess Dubois                                                       │
│                                                                              │
│                                 02/21/12     PW                              │
└─────────────────────────────────────────────────────────────────────────────┘
```

SESSION DATE – FEBRUARY 29, 2012

Sales Invoice #495   **Dated Feb. 23/12**

To Irma Vannitee

1	SRV6 Wash and Style	$20
	GST	5%

Terms: 2/5, n/15. Recall stored transaction.

Sales Invoice #496   **Dated Feb. 23/12**

To Brioche Bridal Party to fill remainder of sales order #101

5	SRV6 Wash and Style	$20 each
	GST	5%

Terms: 2/5, n/15.

Credit Card Bill Payment #2-12   **Dated Feb. 24/12**

From credit card company, $554.40 for purchases made before Feb. 11 and $24 annual card fee. Total payment due to avoid interest penalty $578.40. Issued cheque #428 for $578.40 in full payment.

☑ **Bank Debit Memo #983321**   **Dated Feb. 25/12**

601

From Savers Trust Co., cheque #986 from Brioche Bridal Party was returned because of insufficient funds. The cheque amount, $126, was withdrawn from the chequing account. (You cannot reverse this receipt because it was deposited to Undeposited Cash and Cheques and withdrawn from Bank: Chequing Account after the deposit slip entry.)

⚠ WARNING!
Do not reverse the receipt to record this NSF cheque. You must change the Deposit To account. Refer to page 601.

☐ **Memo #13**   **Dated Feb. 25/12**

Prepare sales invoice #497 for $30 to charge Brioche Bridal Party for the NSF fee. Credit Other Revenue. Terms: net 15. (Do not charge tax or allow discount.)

☐ **Sales Invoice #498**   **Dated Feb. 25/12**

To Conn Seted

1	CN1	Pro-Line Conditioner: 150 ml	$ 26
2	SHM1	Pro-Line Shampoo: 225 ml	21 each
1	SRV4	Highlights	100
	GST		5%
	PST		10%

Terms: net 15.

☐ **Cash Receipt #148**   **Dated Feb. 27/12**

From Brioche Bridal Party, certified cheque #RBC7333 for $156 in payment of account. Reference invoices #487 and 497 and bank debit memo #983321.

☐ **Credit Card Sales Invoice #499**   **Dated Feb. 27/12**

Sales Summary for credit card sales (to Cash Customers)

6	BRS2	Hair Brush: styling	$24 each	$ 144.00
6	CN1	Pro-Line Conditioner: 150 ml	26 /bottle	156.00
3	FRZ1	Pro-Line Defrizzer: cream 100 ml	14 /jar	42.00
8	SPR1	Pro-Line Hair Spray: gentle 150 ml	17 /can	136.00
3	SRV1	Colour	45 each	135.00
26	SRV3	Cut and Style	40 each	1 040.00
2	SRV5	Perm	80 each	160.00
2	SRV6	Wash and Style	20 each	40.00
	GST		5%	92.65
	PST		10%	50.19
	Invoice total paid by credit cards			$1 995.84

Deposited to credit card bank account.

☐ **Sales Invoice #500**   **Dated Feb. 27/12**

To Twilight Theatre to fill the remainder of sales order #102 (for five nights of theatre performances for four cast members) at preferred customer prices

4	SRV3	Cut and Style	$32 each
16	SRV6	Wash and Style	16 each
4	SRV7	Wig Wash, Set and Style	24 each
	GST		5%

Terms: 2/5, n/15.

☐ **Cash Sales Invoice #501**   **Dated Feb. 28/12**

Valentine's Day sales did not meet expectations, so at the end of the month, all hair brushes were sold at discounted prices. Edit the selling price for BRS1 and BRS2.

Sales Summary for cash sales (to Cash Customers)

20	BRS1	Hair Brush: natural bristle	$18 each	$ 360.00
10	BRS2	Hair Brush: styling	14 each	140.00
28	SRV3	Cut and Style	40 each	1 120.00
4	SRV6	Wash and Style	20 each	80.00
	GST		5%	85.00
	PST		10%	52.50
	Invoice total paid by cash			$1 837.50

Deposited to Undeposited Cash and Cheques.

DEPOSIT SLIP #9   Date: Feb 28, 2012
Tesses Tresses
55 Salon Rd.
Charlottetown PE C1A 6D3

Account No: 0290 3433382

Cheques				Amount	
RBC-7333 Brioche Bridal Party 156.00	5	× 5	25	00
	21	× 10	210	00
	10	× 20	200	00
	12	× 50	600	00
	8	× 100	800	00
		coin	2	50
	Total cash		1837	50
	Total cheque		156	00
	Subtotal		1993	50
	Cash received			
	Net Deposit		1993	50

Signature *Tess Dubois*

02/28/12   PW

Memo #14   Dated Feb. 28/12

Enter the adjustments for expired prepaid expenses. $150 of the prepaid
insurance and $40 of the subscriptions have expired.

Memo #15   Dated Feb. 28/12

Enter adjustments for supplies used: Office Supplies $ 60
                                           Salon Supplies   285
                          Washroom & Cleaning Supplies   75

Memo #16   Dated Feb. 28/12

From Owners: The following items were transferred from inventory for use in the
salon. Transfer all items at cost to Salon Supplies.
- 6 CN1 Pro-Line Conditioner: 150 ml
- 3 CN2 Pro-Line Hot Oil Treatment 75 ml
- 4 GEL1 Pro-Line Spray Gel: shaper 150 ml
- 8 SHM1 Pro-Line Shampoo: 225 ml
- 6 SPR1 Pro-Line Hair Spray: gentle 150 ml

Bank Debit Memo #10012   Dated Feb. 28/12

From Savers Trust Co. pre-authorized withdrawals

	Interest	Principal	Total
Mortgage	$1 240	$260	$1 500
Loan	115	485	600

Memo #17   Dated Feb. 28/12

Use the following bank statements to reconcile the bank and credit card accounts
for February.

NOTES
Use the Inventory
Adjustments Journal to transfer the
inventory to the supplies account.
Enter **negative** quantities and
change the default Inventory
Losses account to Salon Supplies
for all items. Refer to Accounting
Procedures, page 566.

SAVERS TRUST

321 Queen St., Charlottetown, PE C1A 6D3   www.saverstrust.com

Tesses Tresses
55 Salon Road   ACCOUNT STATEMENT
Charlottetown, PE C1A 6D3   CHEQUING

Transit / Account No   Statement period
0290   003 433 38-2   Feb 1, 2012 to Feb 28, 2012

Date	Deposit #	Description	Deposits	Withdrawals	Balance
		Balance Fwd			45,988.59
1 Feb	5	Deposit	3,178.00		49,166.59
2 Feb		Cheque #417		2,027.30	47,139.29
5 Feb		Cheque #418		924.00	46,215.29
5 Feb		Cheque #419		231.00	45,984.29
7 Feb	6	Deposit	2,148.10		48,132.39
8 Feb		Cheque #420		1,600.00	46,532.39
10 Feb		Cheque #423		231.00	46,301.39
14 Feb	7	Deposit	2,185.48		48,486.87
16 Feb		Cheque #424		1,247.15	47,239.72
18 Feb		Transfer funds from 004 123 22-8	10,000.00		57,239.72
19 Feb		Cheque #426		127.05	57,112.67
21 Feb	8	Deposit	2,585.21		59,697.88
21 Feb		Cheque #425		906.50	58,791.38
25 Feb		NSF Cheque #986		126.00	58,665.38
25 Feb		Service Charge - NSF cheque		30.00	58,635.38
26 Feb		Cheque #427		693.00	57,942.38
28 Feb		Scheduled loan payment		600.00	57,342.38
28 Feb		Scheduled mortgage payment		1,500.00	55,842.38
28 Feb		Service Charges - chequing acct		23.50	55,818.88
28 Feb		Interest	57.75		55,876.63
28 Feb		Closing balance			55,876.63

Total Deposits   # 6 $20,149.54
Total Withdrawals   # 14 $10,266.50

SAVERS TRUST

321 Queen St., Charlottetown, PE C1A 6D3   www.saverstrust.com

Tesses Tresses
55 Salon Road   ACCOUNT STATEMENT
Charlottetown, PE C1A 6D3   CREDIT CARD

Transit / Account No   Statement period
0290   004 123 22-8   Feb 1, 2012 to Feb 28, 2012

Date	Description	Deposits	Withdrawals	Balance
	Balance Fwd			7,953.63
6 Feb	Deposit	2,307.29		10,260.92
13 Feb	Deposit	3,104.18		13,365.10
18 Feb	Transfer funds to 003 433 38-2		10,000.00	3,365.10
20 Feb	Deposit	1,215.15		4,580.25
28 Feb	Service charges		11.50	4,568.75
28 Feb	Interest	8.25		4,577.00
28 Feb	Closing balance			4,577.00

Total Deposits   # 4 $6,634.87
Total Withdrawals   # 2 $10,011.50

NOTES
The backup data file **Bank\tess1** has all the journal entries completed except the bank reconciliation for February. If you prefer, you can use this file to complete the bank reconciliation for February.

NOTES
Enter Feb 28 as the Statement and Reconciliation dates.

NOTES
You do not need to add linked accounts or prior transactions. Enter the statement ending balance and then mark journal entries as cleared (keystrokes on page 594) to complete the reconciliation.
Enter Feb 28 as the Statement End and Reconciliation dates.
There are four deposit slips for group deposits.
The loan and mortgage payments were entered together: 1 500 + 600 = 2 100.
Remember to change the status of the NSF cheque from Brioche Bridal Party for $126 (in deposit slip #8) to NSF and the status of its reversing entry to Adjustment.
At the end of February, a cheque for $578.40 and one deposit for $1 993.50 are outstanding.

NOTES
Enter Feb 28 as the Statement and Reconciliation dates.

Memo #18   **Dated Feb. 29/12**

604   Back up the data files. Clear journal entries and paid transactions that are no longer needed using January 31 as the date for clearing. Do not clear data for February.

KEYSTROKES

Entering Bank Deposit Slips

 NOTES
    If you are working from backups, you should restore SimData10\tess1.CAB to SimData10\Tess\tess.

Previously, we recorded receipts directly as deposits to the linked bank accounts. In this chapter, we show the procedure for recording receipts and deposits separately. The deposits for the cash and cheques received in January have not yet been recorded.

> **Open**   **SimData10\Tess\tess. Accept January 31** as the session date.
>
> **Click**   **Banking** in the Modules pane list.

Deposits are made using the Make Deposit icon marked with the pointer:

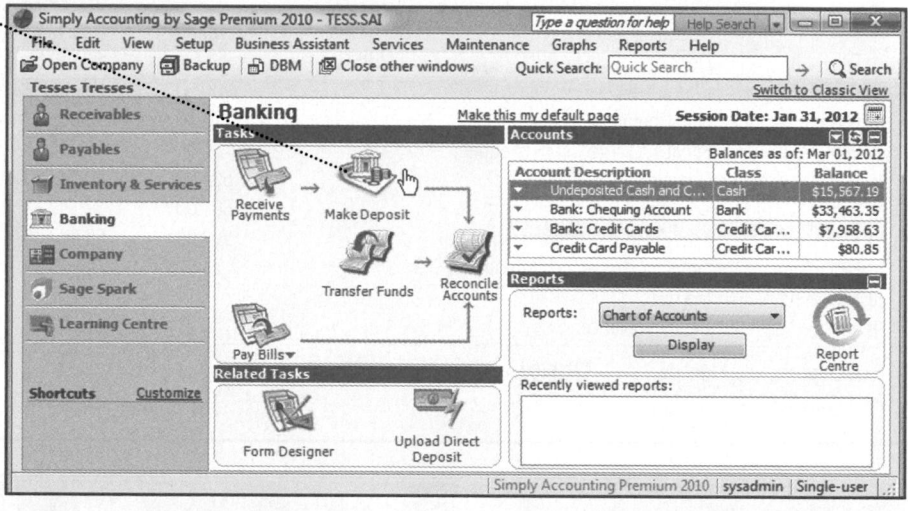

NOTES
    Home window ledger record balances for Tesses Tresses are shown as at March 1, the latest transaction date (for the postdated rent cheques).
    Remember that Make Other Payment is the default type of transaction from the Pay Bills icon in the Banking module window.

WARNING!
    You cannot adjust deposit slips or account reconciliation after posting, except with General Journal entries. Back up your data files before beginning the banking transactions.

CLASSIC VIEW
    Click the Reconciliation & Deposits icon  to open the journal and choose Deposit Slip from the Transaction drop-down list.

> **Click**   the **Make Deposit icon** to open the Reconciliation & Deposits journal:

The journal is named Reconciliation & Deposits because both types of transactions are entered here. You can choose from the Transaction drop-down list to change the type. Deposit Slip is selected in the Transaction field because we selected this Home window icon.

The deposit transaction has two parts: the Deposit To component that we see here and the Deposit From portion. All cash and cheques were debited to *Undeposited Cash and Cheques*, a Cash class clearing account that is the default account for all receipts. Now we need to transfer these receipts to the *Bank: Chequing Account* as deposits.

First we choose the bank account receiving the deposit.

Click   the **Account list arrow** as shown:

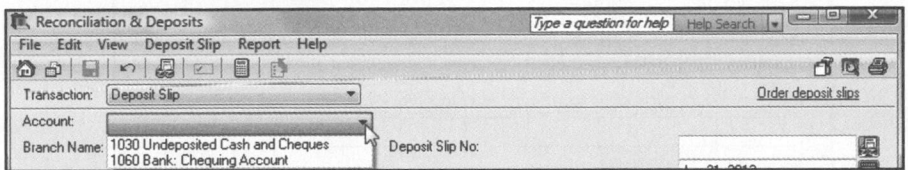

Both banking accounts are listed: *Undeposited Cash and Cheques* (the default linked Receivables Cash class account) and the Bank class *Bank: Chequing Account*. We must select *Bank: Chequing Account*, the account that is receiving the deposit.

Click   **Bank: Chequing Account**.

The deposit slip number is entered and will be updated automatically like the other forms in Simply Accounting.

Tesses Tresses makes weekly deposits to the bank account of all cash and cheques received during the week. We need to enter the date of the first deposit.

Enter   **January 7, 2012** in the Date field for the first deposit.

Next, we must select the outstanding cheques and cash that will be deposited. The Deposit Slip has cheques on the left and cash on the right. There are separate Select buttons for these two types of currency. We will add the cheques first by using the Select button in the centre of the journal, above the field for listing the cheques.

The Select button we need is shown with the arrow pointer on it:

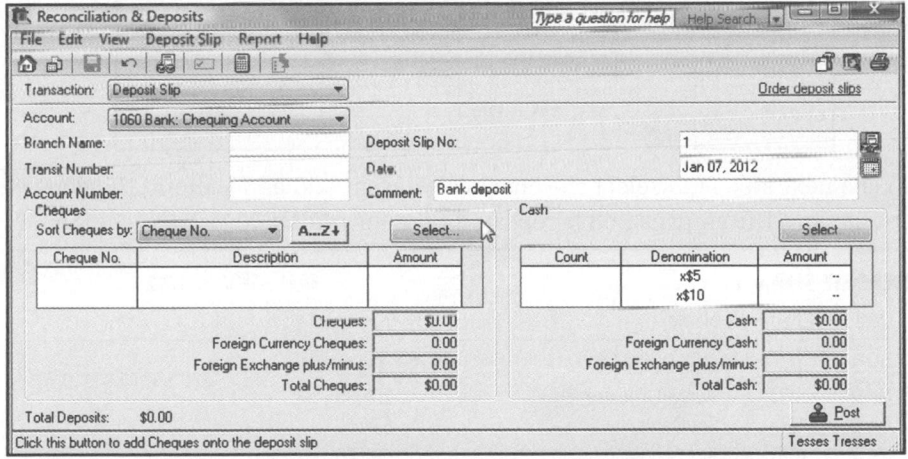

You can drag the column heading margins to change column sizes if you are unable to see all the information. Or you can maximize the journal.

Click   the **Select button** for Cheques to open the list of outstanding cheques:

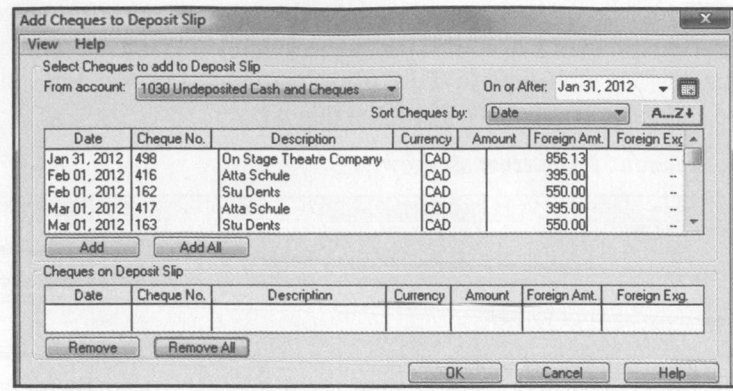

The first banking account, *Undeposited Cash and Cheques*, is selected as the default From Account and this is the one we want. Cheques are listed by date in ascending order, but you can choose a different order from the Sort Cheques By drop-down list. Cheques may also be sorted by any of the column headings for the list of cheques (cheque number, currency, amount, description, foreign amount or foreign exchange amount). You can use the A...Z↓ button to sort in descending order.

The session date, January 31, is entered in the On Or After date field, so only the cheques for January 31 and the postdated rent cheques are listed. We need to show all cheques that are dated on or after January 1, so this is the date we should enter.

Click   the **On Or After field Calendar icon** and **click Jan 1** as the date to list all the outstanding cheques:

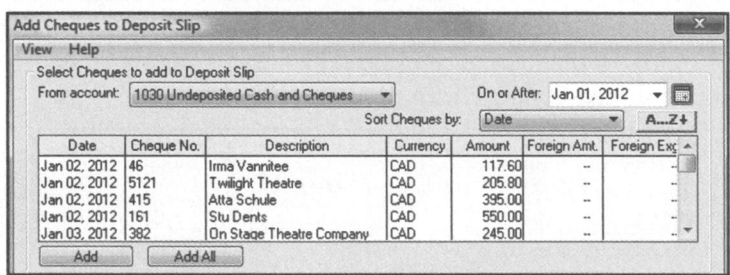

The next step is to select the cheques we want and add them to the deposit. Deposit slip #1 from page 568 is repeated here for reference:

DEPOSIT SLIP # 1			**JANUARY 7, 2012**
Date	Cheque #	Name	Amount
Jan 2	46	Irma Vannitee	$ 117.60
Jan 2	5121	Twilight Theatre	205.80
Jan 2	161	Stu Dents	550.00
Jan 2	415	Atta Schule	395.00
Jan 3	382	On Stage Theatre Company	245.00
Jan 7	918	Irma Vannitee	87.57
		Total Cheques	$1 600.97
		Cash	$2 170.04
		(Consisting of 7 × $10; 35 × $20; 10 × $50; 9 × $100; Coin $0.04)	
		Total Deposit	$3 771.01

We should select the six cheques that are dated on or before January 7, cheques from Vannitee, Twilight Theatre, Stu Dents, Atta Schule and On Stage Theatre Company.

Click to select a single cheque. To select multiple cheques, press and hold (ctrl) and click each cheque you want. To select several cheques in a row, click the first cheque you want, then press (shift) and click the last cheque you need.

NOTES

Once the list is in descending order, the order button label changes to Z...A↓. Clicking this button again restores the list to ascending order.

NOTES

You can also choose Jan 1 from the On Or After date field drop-down list. You can choose this date for all deposit slip transactions in this chapter if you want.

Click   **cheque number 46 from Irma Vannitee**, the first cheque on the list.

Click   the **down scroll arrow** ▼ until you see cheque #918 from Vannitee.

Press   (*shift*) and **click cheque number 918**.

All six cheques should now be selected. We should add them to the list of Cheques On Deposit Slip in the lower half of the form.

Click   the **Add button** to place the selected six cheques on the deposit slip:

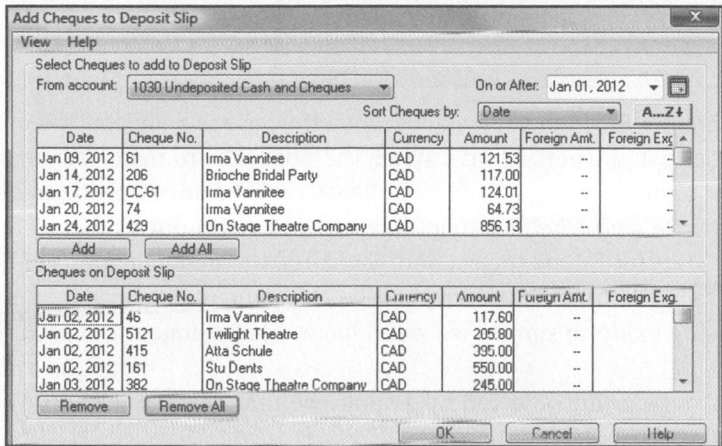

You can also add the cheques one at a time. Click a cheque and then click the Add button to move the cheque. Then click the next cheque and click Add. Repeat until all the cheques you want are in the Cheques On Deposit Slip list. If all cheques are deposited together, you can click Add All.

To change a selection, click a cheque in the Cheques On Deposit Slip list and click Remove. To start again, click Remove All to clear the list.

Click   **OK** to return to the updated Reconciliation & Deposits Journal:

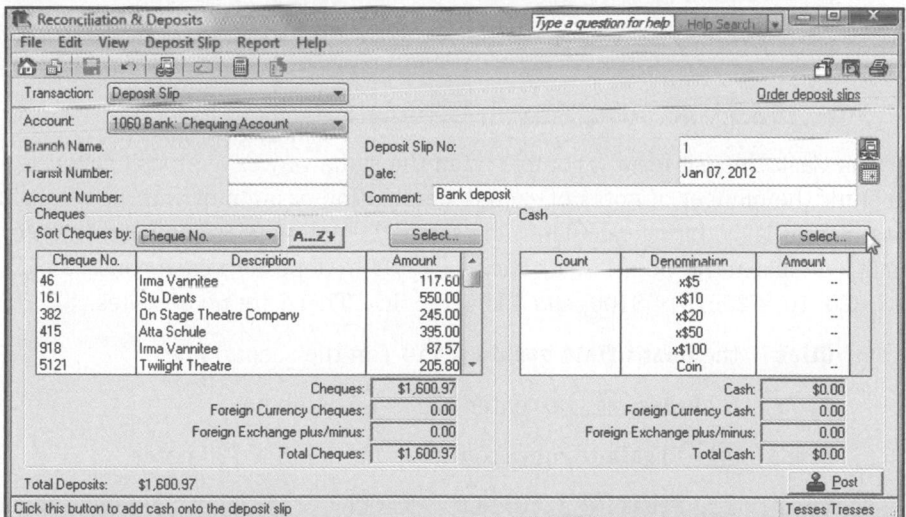

NOTES
The cheques on the deposit slip are sorted by cheque number. You can reverse the order (A...Z↓ button) or sort the cheques by description or amount by making the selection from the Sort Cheques By drop-down list.

The total of the cheques should match the amount on the Deposit Slip source document. If it does not, click the Select button again to correct the cheque selection. If a cheque amount is incorrect, close the journal without saving the changes and correct the original receipt transaction.

The next step is to add the cash portion of the deposit. Tesses Tresses has one cash sale summary amount to deposit, $2 170.04.

Click the **Select button** for Cash to open the deposit form for cash:

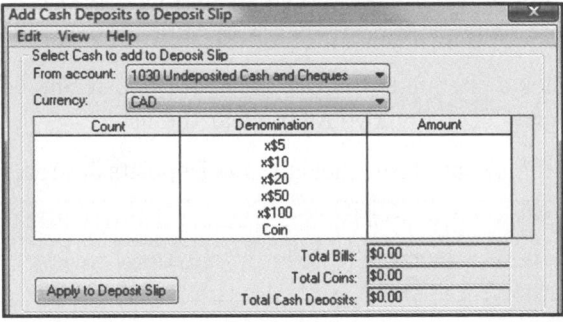

Cash receipts are not listed individually because they are usually combined in the store and held in the cash drawers or safe. When the deposits are made, some cash may be kept in the store to make change for future clients. This balance may be transferred from *Undeposited Cash and Cheques* to a *Cash on Hand* account by completing a General Journal or Transfer Funds transaction. Similarly, the denominations of notes and coins that are received from clients may not be the same as the ones that are deposited. To keep the exercise simple, we will deposit the full amount of cash received each week.

Since there isn't an account selected by default, we first need to select the account that we are depositing from.

Choose Undeposited Cash and Cheques from the From Account drop-down list to modify the deposit form:

The Cash Deposit form is completed in the same way as a deposit slip at the bank. You enter the number of notes of each denomination or amount and the total amount of coins. Simply Accounting calculates and totals the amounts as soon as you enter the number of bills in the Count field. The $2 170.04 in deposited cash consists of 7 × $10; 35 × $20; 10 × $50; 9 × $100; and $0.04 in coins. There are no $5 notes.

Click the **Count field beside ×$10** (on the second line).

Type 7 **Press** ⟨tab⟩ to enter $70 as the Amount.

Press ⟨tab⟩ **again** to move to the Count field for $20 notes.

Type 35 **Press** ⟨tab⟩ **twice** to advance to the Count field for $50 notes.

Type 10 **Press** ⟨tab⟩ **twice** to advance to the Count field for $100 notes.

Type 9 **Press** ⟨tab⟩ **twice** to advance to the Count field for coins.

The amount for coins is entered as a total amount in the Amount field. You cannot type in the Count field for Coin.

Press ⟨tab⟩ to advance to the Amount field for coins.

Type .04 (You must enter the decimal.)

NOTES
Instead of pressing ⟨tab⟩ twice, you can press ⟨↓⟩ to move the cursor to the next Count line on the form.
Instead of entering the count for each denomination, you can enter the amount and Simply Accounting will enter the corresponding count.

Press (tab) to update the total as shown:

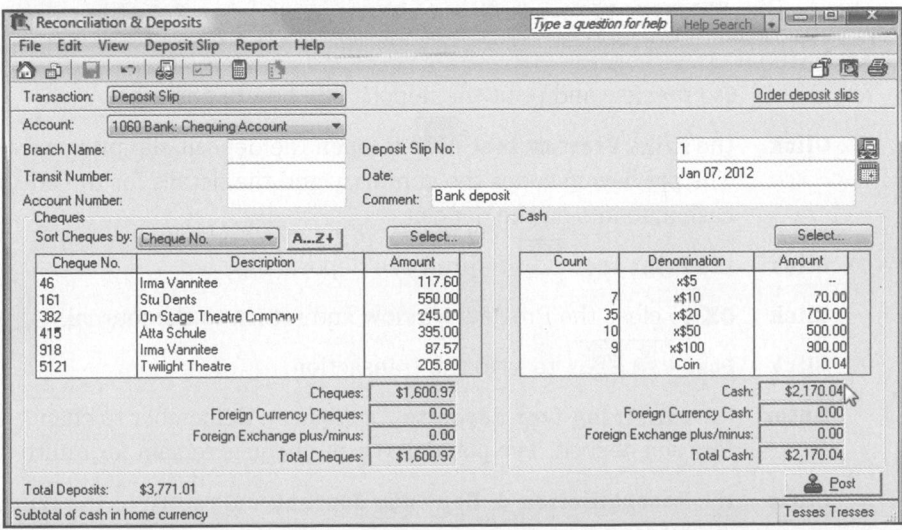

The total amounts for bills and coins remain separated, and the total for the cash deposit is calculated.

The next step is to apply the amount to the deposit slip.

Click the **Apply To Deposit Slip button** to update the form:

The total cash deposit amount is added to the Cash On Deposit Slip section. The currency for the amount is also included.

> To make changes, edit an amount in the Count field and press (tab). Click Apply To Deposit Slip to update the Cash On Deposit Slip.

We are now ready to add this deposit information to the journal form.

Click **OK** to return to the Reconciliation & Deposits journal:

The form is complete. We can accept the default comment "Bank deposit" or change it. The comment will become part of the journal record.

NOTES
Tesses Tresses does not have any foreign currency transactions.

Reviewing the Deposit Slip Entry

Before posting, we should review the journal entry created by the deposit.

Choose the **Report menu** and **click Display Deposit Slip Journal Entry**:

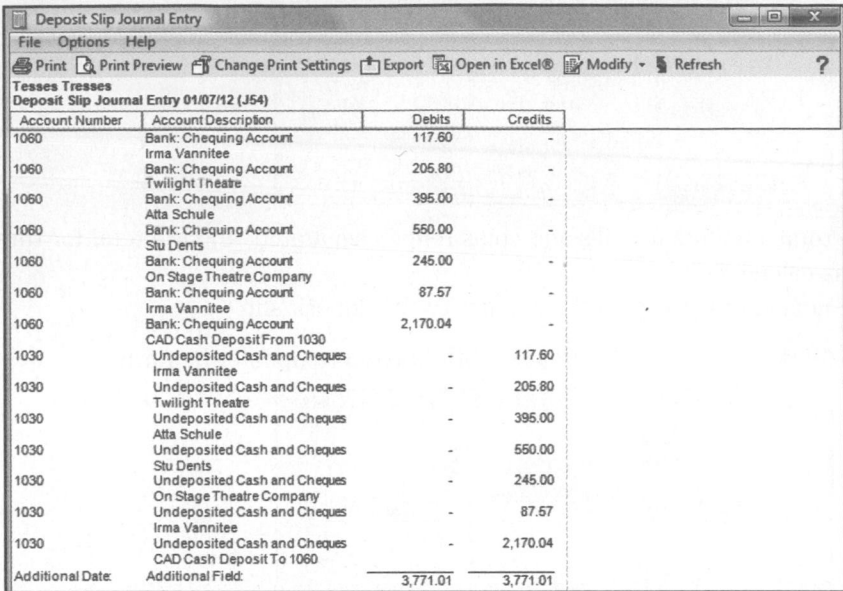

In the journal, each cheque and cash amount is listed separately. The payer for each cheque is also included. Each deposit item is shown as a debit to the *Bank: Chequing Account* and a credit to *Undeposited Cash and Cheques*. This detailed reporting makes it easier to find mistakes if any have been made.

Close the **Journal Entry Display** to return to the journal.

Check your **work** and **make corrections** if necessary.

CORRECTING THE DEPOSIT SLIP JOURNAL ENTRY

To change the cheque part of the deposit, **click** the **Select button** for the Cheque part of the journal. To change a selection, **click** a **cheque** in the Cheques On Deposit Slip list and **click Remove**. To start again, **click Remove All** to clear the list. **Click Cancel** to close the Cheques Deposit form without saving changes.

If you need to make changes to the Cash part of the deposit, **click** the **Select button** on the Cash side of the Journal. **Click** the **incorrect amount** in the Count field and **type** the **correct amount**. Press (tab) to update the total. **Click Apply To Deposit Slip** to update the deposit amount that will be recorded. **Click Cancel** to close the Cash Deposit form without saving changes.

You should also preview and print the deposit slip before posting it.

Click the **Print Preview tool** to open the deposit slip preview window. The preview includes the summary and the details for the cheques and cash amounts on the deposit.

Click the **Print tool** to print the deposit slip.

Click **OK** to close the Preview window and return to the journal.

Click **Post** to save the transaction.

Enter the **remaining four deposits** for January. Remember to change the date for each deposit. The postdated rent cheques remain for future deposits.

Close the **Reconciliation & Deposits Journal** and return to the Banking module window.

We are now ready to set up the bank accounts for reconciliation.

Account Reconciliation

For any bank account, the timing of monthly statements is usually not perfectly matched with the accounting entries of the corresponding transactions. Usually some of the cheques written do not appear on the statement, and interest earned on the account or bank charges are not yet recorded because they may be unknown until receipt of the statement. Thus the balance of the bank statement usually does not match the General Ledger balance for the bank account. The process of identifying the differences to achieve a match is the process of account reconciliation.

You can apply account reconciliation to any Balance Sheet account for which you have regular statements, including credit card payable accounts. For each account you want to reconcile, you must complete the setup procedure.

The keystrokes that follow will set up account reconciliation for *Bank: Chequing Account* for Tesses Tresses.

Turning On the Account Reconciliation Feature

Before completing the reconciliation procedure, the General Ledger accounts that will be reconciled must be identified and modified. For the next stage, you will also need a report of all bank account transactions to compare with the bank statement. We will continue to work from the Banking module window to modify the account.

> **Click**   **1060 Bank: Chequing Account** in the Banking module Home window Accounts list.

The ledger record for the bank account opens at the Account tab screen:

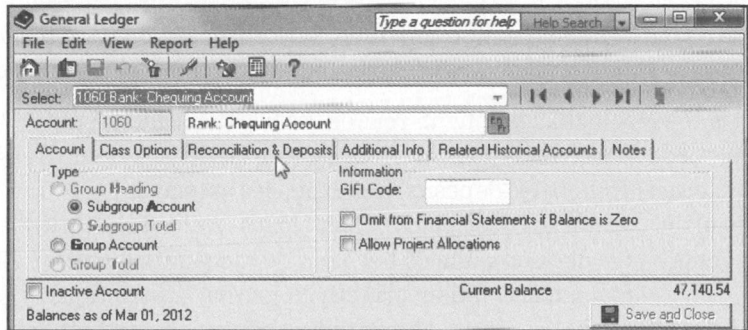

All Balance Sheet accounts have a Reconciliation & Deposits tab. You can reconcile any account for which you have regular statements. Usually these are the bank accounts or credit card accounts.

> **Click**   the **Reconciliation & Deposits tab**:

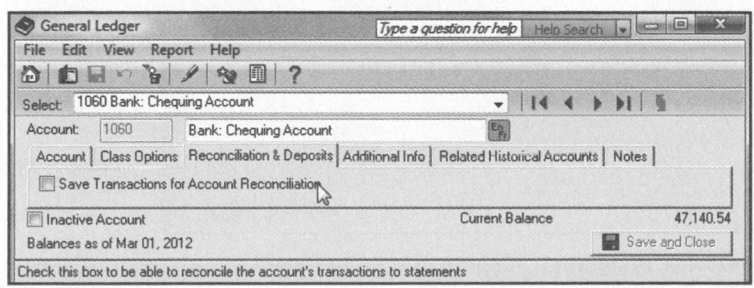

NOTES
Online bank reconciliation is explained in Appendix K on the Student DVD. The Web site for this text is set up for online reconciliation so you can try this feature of the program.

Click   **Save Transactions For Account Reconciliation** to display the Set Up button shown in the following screen:

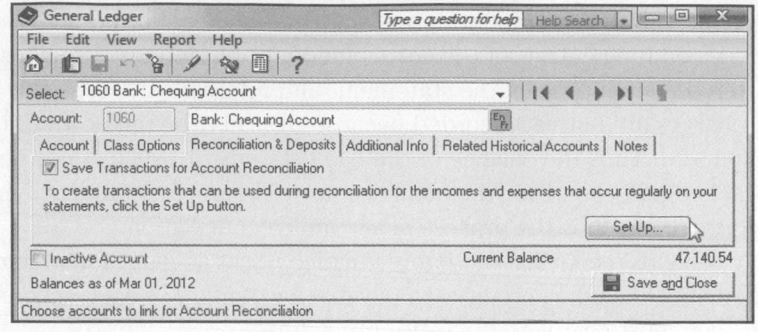

Naming and Linking Reconciliation Accounts

Most bank statements include monthly bank charges, loan or mortgage payments and interest on deposits. That is, there are usually some regular sources of income and expense. Normally the only source document for these bank account transactions is the bank statement. To use Simply Accounting's account reconciliation feature, you must first create the accounts that link to these regular bank account transactions. When you examine the January Bank Statement for Tesses Tresses on page 569, you can see that there is an interest deposit and a withdrawal for service charges. The salon already has accounts for both of these items. In addition, you will need an account to enter adjustments related to the reconciliation. The exact role of these accounts will become clearer as we proceed with the account reconciliation setup.

You can save your work and exit at any time. Any changes you have made will be saved and you can continue from where you left off when you are ready.

The next step is to name bank statement–related transactions and identify the appropriate General Ledger accounts that link to these transactions. Tesses Tresses has income (interest received) from bank deposits and expenses associated with the bank account, such as bank charges or interest paid on bank loans. A third account will be needed for adjustments — small discrepancies between the accounting entries and the bank statements, such as amounts entered incorrectly in journal transactions.

You can edit these names and accounts at any time, and you can add other sources of income or expense later if they are needed.

Click   **Set Up** to display the following Linked Accounts screen:

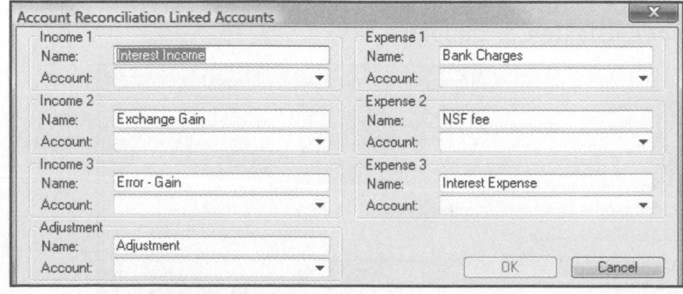

On this Account Reconciliation Linked Accounts form, you can identify up to three regular sources of income, three types of expenses and one adjustment account for each account you want to reconcile.

The name fields on this form cannot be left blank. You can leave the default names or enter "n/a" for "not applicable" if they are not needed.

The first Income Name field is highlighted, ready for editing. The only source of income for this account that is not accounted for elsewhere is interest income. This name is already entered so we can accept it.

Click   the **list arrow for the Income 1 Account field** to list the revenue accounts that are available.

Click   **4220 Interest Revenue**. **Press** (tab) to advance to the second Income field.

This field and the third Income field are not needed, so we will indicate that they are not applicable.

Type   n/a

Press   (tab) **twice** to skip the Account field and advance to the third Income field. **Type** n/a to indicate that it too is not applicable.

Leave the default name for adjustments unchanged.

Click   the **Adjustment Account field list arrow**.

Either an expense or a revenue account can be used for adjustments. Tesses Tresses will create an expense account for this purpose.

Type   5050 Reconciliation Adjustments

Press   (tab). **Click Add** to start the Add An Account wizard.

Accept the **remaining defaults** and **click Finish** to add the account to the Linked Accounts form. **Press** (tab) to advance the cursor.

The first Expense 1 Name field is highlighted. The salon has one automatic bank account–related expense, bank charges. NSF fee, the second expense, is also used but we do not expect this to be a regular expense. These names are already entered as the default, so we can accept them. Tesses Tresses uses the same account for both expenses.

Click   the **Account field list arrow for Expense 1** to display the list of expense accounts.

Select **5040 Bank Charges** for this expense account.

Click   the **Account field list arrow for Expense 2**.

Select **5040 Bank Charges** for this expense account.

Press   (tab) to advance to the third Expense field.

Type   n/a to indicate that it is not needed.

Check   your **work** carefully. When you are certain that all the names and accounts are correct,

Click   **OK** to save the new information. The Set Up button remains available because you can add and change linked accounts.

While the General Ledger is still open, we will set up the linked accounts for *Bank: Credit Cards*.

Click   the **Next Account button** [▶] to open the ledger we need.

Click   the **Reconciliation & Deposits tab** if necessary.

Click   **Save Transactions For Account Reconciliation**.

Click **Set Up**.

Choose **4220** as the linked account for Interest Income.

Choose **5050** as the linked account for Adjustment. **Press** (tab) to advance to the Expense 1 Name field.

Type Card Fees **Press** (tab).

Choose **5060** as the linked account for Card Fees.

Click **OK** to save the reconciliation accounts.

Close the **Ledger window** to return to the Banking module window.

Reconciling the Bank Statement

Comparing the Bank Statement and Transaction Report

We are now ready to compare the Bank Transaction Report with the bank statement. The Bank Account Transaction Report will show all transactions for the account, similar to the General Ledger Report.

Choose the **Reports menu**, then **choose Banking** and **click Bank Account Transactions Report**. The Modify Report window opens:

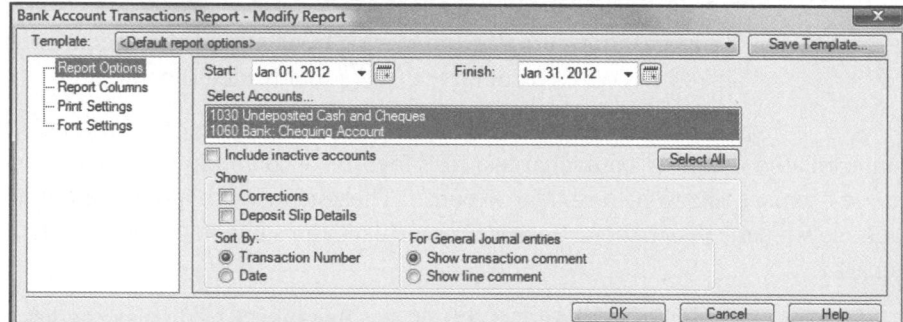

Only Bank and Cash class accounts are listed because the report is available only for bank accounts. The credit card bank account is not shown because it is classified as a Credit Card Receivable account. In order to reconcile the credit card account, you can display or print the General Ledger Report for the period covering the bank statement.

For bank account reports, you can include corrections and deposit slip details or omit them. By default both items are omitted from the report. Since it is easier to work from a report that most closely matches the bank statement, you should omit corrections for this step. The deposit slip details do not appear on the bank statement, but they can be viewed or omitted in the Transactions Report. Because they can help us locate errors, we will include them at this stage.

You can report by date or transaction number and include transaction or line comments.

Click **1060 Bank: Chequing Account** to select the account.

The default report dates are correct. In an ongoing business, include the date of the oldest outstanding item from your previous bank statement up to the date of the most recent statement.

Click **Deposit Slip Details** to add the ✓.

Click **OK** to view the report:

```
┌─────────────────────────────────────────────────────────────────────────────┐
│ 🗋 Bank Account Transactions Report                              □ X          │
│ File  Options  Help                                                           │
│ 🖨 Print  🔍 Print Preview  🖶 Change Print Settings  📤 Export  📊 Open in Excel®  📝 Modify ▾  ⟳ Refresh │
│ Tesses Tresses                                                                │
│ Bank Account Transactions Report 01/01/12 to 01/31/12                         │
│ Sorted by: Transaction Number                                                 │
```

Date	Comment	Source #	JE#	Debits	Credits	Balance
1060	**Bank: Chequing Account**					38,415.00 Dr
01/04/12	Pro-Line Inc.	410	J14	-	926.10	37,488.90 Dr
01/09/12	Fine Brushes	411	J17	-	330.00	37,158.90 Dr
01/10/12	Atlantic Power Corp.: AP-57321, hyd...	412	J22	-	199.50	36,959.40 Dr
01/14/12	Pro-Line Inc.	413	J24	-	1,870.72	35,088.68 Dr
01/14/12	Memo 1	FundsTransfer	J25	5,000.00	-	40,088.68 Dr
01/14/12	Receiver General for Canada: Memo...	414	J26	-	1,830.00	38,258.68 Dr
01/15/12	Irma Vannitee	DM-61899	J27	-	121.53	38,137.15 Dr
01/18/12	Eastern Tel: ET-4003, telephone ser...	415	J34	-	115.50	38,021.65 Dr
01/24/12	Credit Card	416	J42	-	431.00	37,590.65 Dr
01/27/12	Savers Trust - preauthorized withdra...	DM-792218	J44	-	2,100.00	35,490.65 Dr
01/31/12	Provincial Treasurer: Memo 6, PST r...	417	J53	-	2,027.30	33,463.35 Dr
01/07/12	Bank deposit	1	J54	117.60	-	33,580.95 Dr
01/07/12	Bank deposit	1	J54	205.80	-	33,786.75 Dr
01/07/12	Bank deposit	1	J54	395.00	-	34,181.75 Dr
01/07/12	Bank deposit	1	J54	550.00	-	34,731.75 Dr
01/07/12	Bank deposit	1	J54	245.00	-	34,976.75 Dr
01/07/12	Bank deposit	1	J54	87.57	-	35,064.32 Dr
01/07/12	Bank deposit	1	J54	2,170.04	-	37,234.36 Dr
01/14/12	Bank deposit	2	J55	121.53	-	37,355.89 Dr
01/14/12	Bank deposit	2	J55	117.00	-	37,472.89 Dr
01/14/12	Bank deposit	2	J55	1,733.34	-	39,206.23 Dr
01/21/12	Bank deposit	3	J56	124.01	-	39,330.24 Dr
01/21/12	Bank deposit	3	J56	64.73	-	39,394.97 Dr
01/21/12	Bank deposit	3	J56	1,961.30	-	41,356.27 Dr
01/28/12	Bank deposit	4	J57	856.13	-	42,212.40 Dr
01/28/12	Bank deposit	4	J57	1,750.14	-	43,962.54 Dr
01/31/12	Bank deposit	5	J58	42.00	-	44,004.54 Dr
01/31/12	Bank deposit	5	J58	856.13	-	44,860.67 Dr
01/31/12	Bank deposit	5	J58	2,279.87	-	47,140.54 Dr
				18,677.19	9,951.65	

The transactions part of the January bank statement is repeated on the following page for comparison with the Transaction Report above.

	Note #				
		Balance Fwd			37,238.00
2 Jan	1	Deposit	1,177.00		38,415.00
7 Jan		Cheque #410		926.10	37,488.90
7 Jan	2	Deposit	3,771.01		41,259.91
9 Jan		Cheque #411		330.00	40,929.91
14 Jan	2	Deposit	1,971.87		42,901.78
14 Jan		Cheque #412		199.50	42,702.28
14 Jan		Cheque #413		1,870.72	40,831.56
14 Jan		Transfer 0290 004 123 22-8	5,000.00		45,031.56
15 Jan		NSF Cheque #61		121.53	45,710.03
15 Jan	3	Service Charge – NSF cheque		30.00	45,680.03
17 Jan		Cheque #414		1,830.00	43,850.03
20 Jan		Cheque #415		115.50	43,734.53
21 Jan	2	Deposit	2,150.04		45,884.57
27 Jan		Cheque #416		431.00	45,453.57
27 Jan	5	Scheduled payment: loan		600.00	44,853.57
27 Jan	5	Scheduled payment: mortgage		1,500.00	43,353.57
28 Jan	2	Deposit	2,606.27		45,959.84
31 Jan	3	Service Charges		23.50	45,936.34
31 Jan	4	Interest	52.25		45,988.59

When you compare the statement with the Transaction Report, you will notice the following differences. (The numbers below correspond to the numbers in the margin notes and the bank statement Note # column.)

1   One deposit on January 2 appears on the bank statement and not in the Bank Transaction Report because the deposit was entered late in December.
2   Four deposits on the bank statement were multiple deposits entered on deposit slips and do not match any single entry in the Transactions Report.
3   Monthly bank charges of $23.50 and NSF charges of $30.00 have not been recorded in the Transactions Report.
4   Interest of $52.25 received on the deposit account does not appear in the Transactions Report.
5   A single General Journal entry combined the loan and mortgage payments.

PRO VERSION
pro Remember that the General Ledger Report will show the deposit slip total amounts instead of details.

NOTES
You may want to print the Transaction Report with and without deposit slip details to compare with the bank statement that has only the total deposit amounts.

NOTES
These numbers correspond to the Note # column of the statement.
1 Deposit recorded in December
2 Deposit Slips: total amounts from deposit slips
3 Service charges
4 Interest received
5 Scheduled loan payments $2 100 (1 500 + 600)

In addition,

- Deposit slip #5 for $3 178.00 and cheque #417 for $2 027.30 in the Report are not listed on the bank statement, and the order of transactions is different.

All these items must be accounted for in order to have the bank statement match the bank balance in the account's General Ledger or on the Balance Sheet.

Reconciling the Account

After entering the linked accounts, you can begin the reconciliation. The account reconciliation procedure consists of the following steps to update the General Ledger.

1. Record the opening and ending balances from the bank statement for the account.
2. Add outstanding transactions from prior periods that were not resolved in the previous bank statement.
3. Identify all the deposits and withdrawals that have been processed by the bank.
4. Complete journal entries for any transactions for which the bank statement is the source document.

The result should be a match between the bank balances in the two statements. All these steps are completed in the Account Reconciliation Journal.

The Banking module window should still be open.

Click   the **Reconcile Accounts icon** shown with the hand pointer:

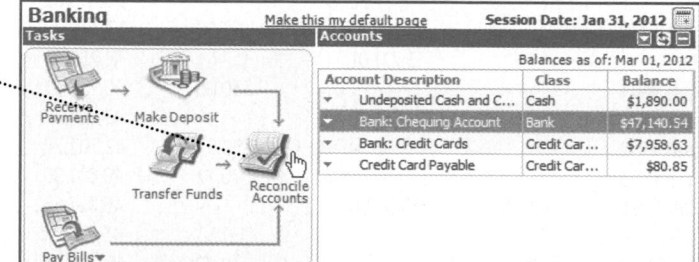

Account record balances in the Home window are shown at the latest transaction date, March 1, the date of the post-dated rent cheques. These cheques account for the balance in the *Undeposited Cash and Cheques* account.

The Reconciliation Journal opens:

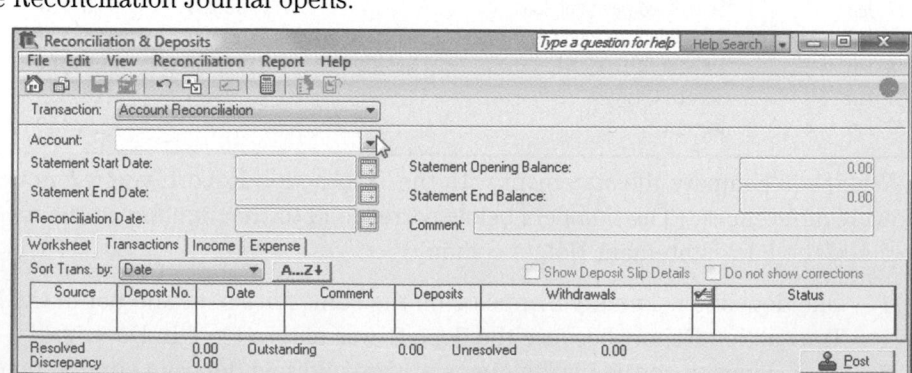

Click   the **Account field list arrow** to display the available accounts for reconciliation. The list displays the bank and credit card accounts that we set up for account reconciliation.

Select   **1060 Bank: Chequing Account** to display the reconciliation information for this bank account:

CLASSIC VIEW

Click the Reconciliation &

Deposits icon [Reconciliation & Deposits] to open the journal and choose Account Reconciliation from the Transaction drop-down list if necessary.

NOTES

There is no allocation option in the Account Reconciliation Journal but additional fields are available, as they are in the other journals.

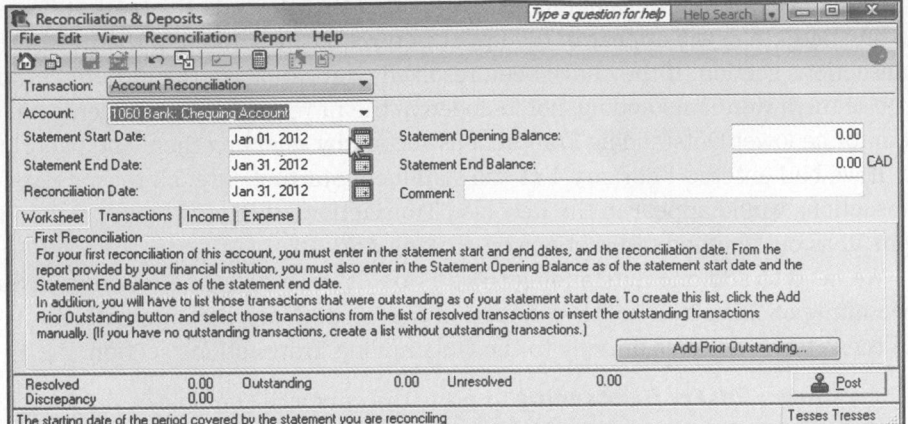

NOTES
Read the instructions on the screen about the first reconciliation before proceeding. It advises that you must go through the step of adding prior transactions.

The account is entered in the Account field. The first transaction date is entered as the Statement Start Date and the session date is entered automatically in the Statement End Date field and the Reconciliation Date field. These dates will advance by one month when you have finished reconciling the bank account for the current month. The dates are correct, so do not change them.

We need to add the opening and closing bank statement balances.

Click   the **Statement Opening Balance field**.

Type   37238 **Press** (tab) to advance to the Statement End Balance field.

Type   45988.59 **Press** (tab) to advance to the Comment field.

Type   January Bank Reconciliation

For the first reconciliation, we need to add the outstanding transaction from the previous period. A deposit of $1 177 appears on the bank statement but not in the ledger report. The deposit was made at the end of December, too late to be included in the December bank statement, so we need to add it now. Adding prior transactions in the Account Reconciliation Journal does not create a journal entry and does not affect the ledger balance. The step is necessary only to create a match between the bank statement and the current ledger.

Click   **Add Prior Outstanding** to see the confirmation message:

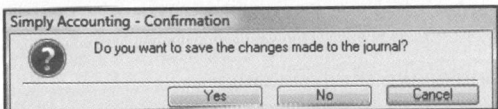

You must save the changes to the journal to continue. If you have not yet entered the account balances and dates, you will not see this message.

WARNING!
The first time you complete a reconciliation for any account, you must complete this step (click Add Prior Outstanding) even if there are no outstanding prior transactions. If there are no prior transactions to add, click OK from the Add Outstanding Transactions screen.

Click   **Yes** to continue and open the Add Outstanding Transactions window:

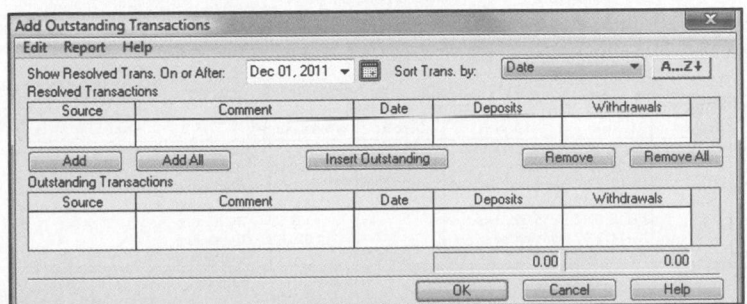

If there are no prior transactions that you need to insert, click OK at this stage to return to the journal.

If you have transactions in Simply Accounting that precede the bank statement starting date, they will appear in the upper portion of the screen, in the Resolved Transactions section. If they have been resolved, you can leave them there. If, however, some of them were outstanding, not included in the previous bank statement, you can add them to the lower Outstanding Transactions section by selecting them and choosing Add.

If we had entered February 1 as the statement starting date, all the January transactions would appear in the Resolved Transactions section. We would then include them all as outstanding transactions by clicking Add All.

We need to add one outstanding transaction. It preceded the first entry in Simply Accounting on January 1 so it will not be in the transactions list automatically. We can add these types of items directly to the Outstanding Transactions section.

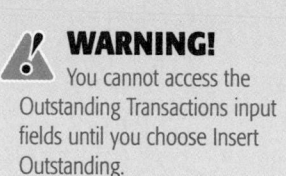

WARNING!

You cannot access the Outstanding Transactions input fields until you choose Insert Outstanding.

Click   **Insert Outstanding** to place the cursor in the Source field for Outstanding Transactions.

Type   5117 to enter the client's cheque number as the Source.

Press   (tab) to move to the Comment field. We will enter the client's name.

Type   Twilight Theatre **Press** (tab) to move to the Date field.

December 31, 2011, is entered as the default date, the last date from the previous statement period. This date is correct, so you do not need to change it. You can enter a different date if necessary.

Press   (tab) to move to the Deposits column.

Type   1177 **Press** (tab).

If there are other outstanding prior transactions, enter them in the same way.

If there are no prior transactions, click OK to return to the journal.

Click   **OK** to return to the journal window.

Marking Journal Entries as Cleared

You are now ready to begin processing individual journal entries to indicate whether they have been cleared in this bank statement. That is, you must indicate whether the bank has processed the items and the amounts have been withdrawn from or deposited to the account.

The updated journal window now looks like the following:

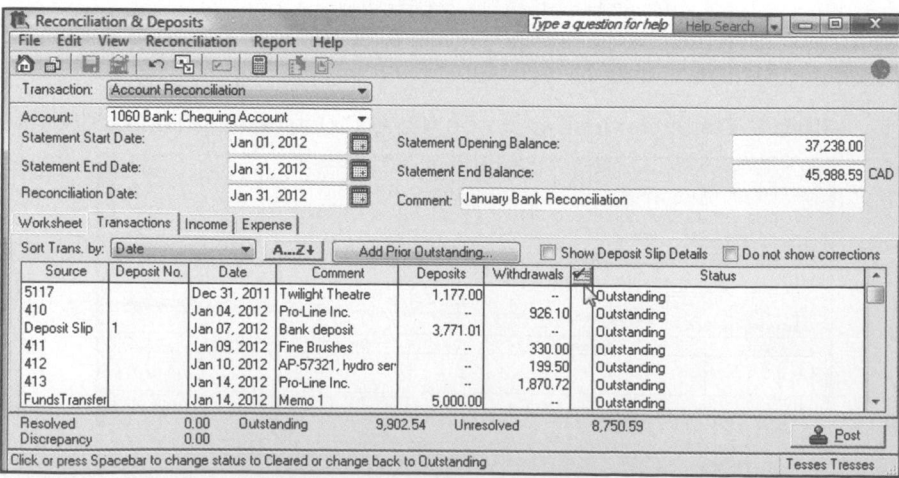

The Transactions tab is selected and all January bank account transactions are now listed, including the one we just added. The bottom section of the screen contains a summary of the transactions. Our goal is to reduce the unresolved amount to zero with no discrepancy. At this stage, a discrepancy may indicate an incorrect account balance.

The Statement End Balance should be correct because we entered it in the previous step. You can add or change it at this stage if necessary.

Showing Corrections

You can hide or show correcting journal entries in the list of transactions by clicking **Do Not Show Corrections**. Removing incorrect and reversing entries can make the reconciliation easier by increasing the match with the statement. When you hide the corrections and then clear transactions, Simply Accounting automatically applies the Reversed and Adjustment status to the original incorrect entry (Reversed status) and the reversing entry created by Simply Accounting (Adjustment status).

Group Deposits

Sometimes several cheques are deposited as a group, as they were on the weekly deposit slips. Each of these group deposits can now be cleared as a group. If you have not used the deposit slip journal to record deposits, you can define a group deposit by entering the deposit slip number for each item in the Deposit No. field beside the Source. When you clear one item in the group, the others will be cleared at the same time.

> You may want to drag the lower frame of the journal window or maximize the journal window to include more transactions on your screen at the same time.

You are now ready to mark the transactions that have been cleared, that is, the ones that appear on the bank statement.

> **Click** the Clear column  **for Cheque #5117** (click in the column), the first transaction on the list.

A checkmark appears in the Clear column , the Status has changed from Outstanding to Cleared and the Resolved Amount has increased to $1 177. As you clear each item, the Resolved and Unresolved amounts are updated.

> **Clear** the **remaining journal entries** that appear on the bank statement and scroll as necessary to display additional items.

Do not clear deposit slip #5 for $3 178.00 or the final cheque for $2 027.30.

If you mark an item as Cleared by mistake, click the  column again to return the status to Outstanding.

Your transactions list appears as follows:

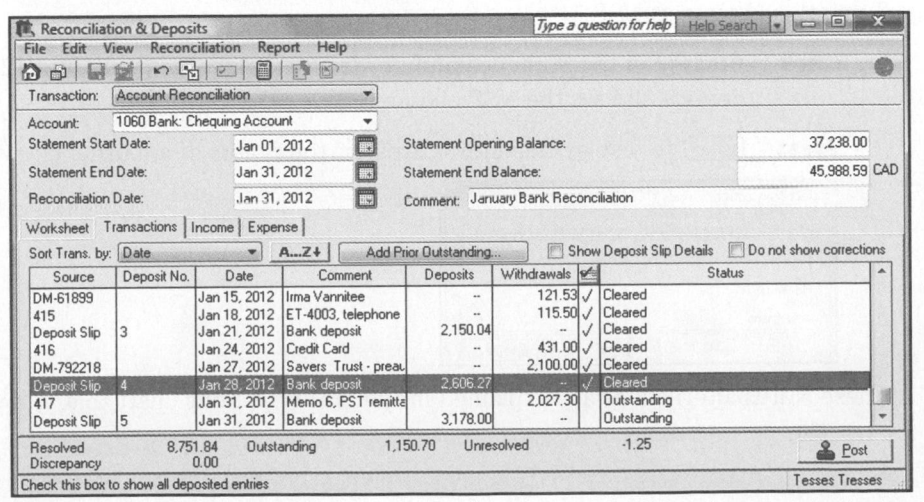

NOTES
Remember to clear the withdrawal on Jan. 27 for $2 100 to match the two bank statement entries for $600 and $1 500.

NOTES
You can click the  column heading to clear all entries on the transactions list. Then you can click an individual ✓ to restore the Outstanding status if needed.

NOTES
The Outstanding Amount is the net amount for the two outstanding items – one deposit and one cheque.

After clearing all transactions from the bank statement, the unresolved amount should be –1.25. This is the net difference for the three unmatched bank statement items: the NSF charge, the service charge and the interest. Journal entries for these items will be added later (page 598).

The next section describes the procedure for clearing transactions that are different in some way, like NSF cheques. By marking their status correctly, you will have a more accurate picture of your business transactions. Cheque #61 for $121.53 was returned as NSF and should be marked as such.

Showing Deposit Slip Details

The NSF cheque we need to mark was part of a group deposit (deposit slip #2), so it does not appear individually on the Transactions list. First we need to show the details of the deposit slips. Above the Transactions list is the **Show Deposit Slip Details** check box. This box is a toggle switch; you can hide the details when they are not required or show them if you need to change the status of a single item in the deposit group.

Click   **Show Deposit Slip Details** to add a ✓.

Press   the **down scroll arrow** ▼ until you see the items for deposit slip #2:

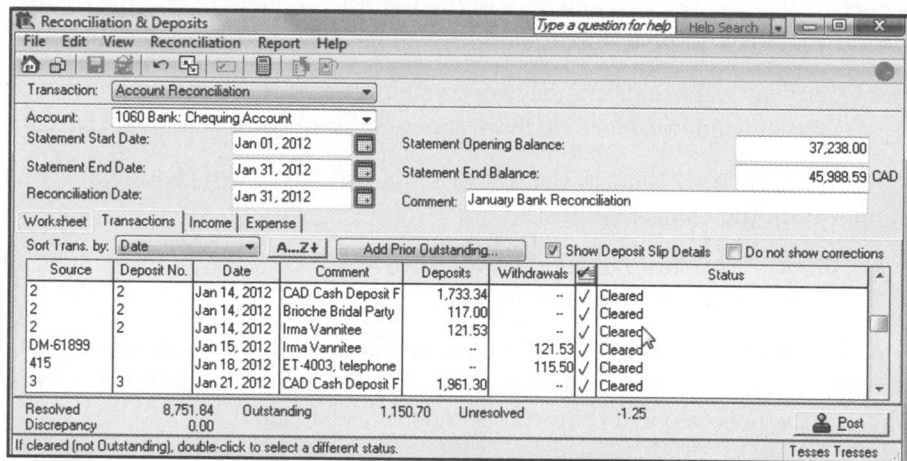

All three details, the two cheques and the cash amount on the deposit slip, are marked as Cleared when we clear the deposit.

Marking NSF Cheques

For some items — for example, NSF cheques and their reversing entries — you should add further information because they have not cleared the account in the usual way.

To mark a cheque as NSF,

Click   **Cleared** in the Status column for Irma Vannitee's cheque for $121.53 in deposit slip #2, the NSF cheque.

Press   (enter) to display the alternatives for the Status of a journal entry:

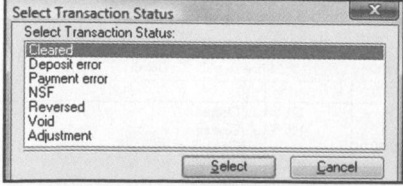

These status alternatives are explained in the Status Options chart that follows.

STATUS OPTIONS

Cleared (C)	for deposits and cheques that have been processed correctly.
Deposit Error (D)	for the adjusting journal entry that records the difference between the amount of a deposit that was recorded incorrectly and the bank statement amount for that deposit. Assign the Cleared status to the original entry for the deposit.
Payment Error (P)	for the adjusting entry that records the difference between the amount of a cheque recorded incorrectly and the bank statement amount for that cheque. Assign the Cleared status to the original entry for the cheque.
NSF (N)	for client cheques returned by the bank because there was not enough money in the client's account. Assign the Adjustment status to the adjusting entry that reverses the NSF cheque.
Reversed (R)	for cheques that are cancelled by posting a reversing transaction entry to the bank account or the Sales or Purchases journals, that is, journal entries that are corrected. Assign the Adjustment status to the reversing entry that cancels the cheque.
Void (V)	for cheques that are cancelled because of damage during printing. Assign the Adjustment status to the reversing entry that voids the cheque.
Adjustment (A)	for the adjusting or reversing entries that are made to cancel NSF, void or reversed cheques. (See the explanations for NSF, Void and Reversed above.)

Click   NSF to highlight this alternative.

Click   Select to enter it. The Cleared status changes to NSF for this item.

The final step is to change the status of the entry that reverses the payment or NSF cheque to Adjustment. The final certified cheque received in payment has been cleared normally so its status as Cleared is already correct. Changing the status does not affect the resolved and unresolved amounts. The amounts are just cleared in different ways.

> **Double click   Cleared in the Status column for Bank Debit Memo #61899,** the reversing entry.

> **Double click   Adjustment** to select this as the status.

Your updated transactions list now looks like the one shown here:

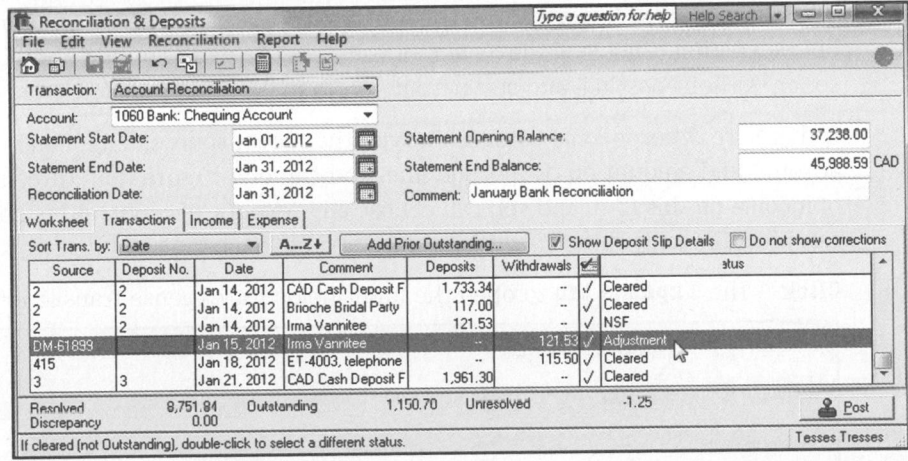

Click   Show Deposit Slip Details to restore the summary version for deposits.

The status for deposit slip #2 has changed to Cleared again. You can show the details at any time again or if you need to make corrections by clicking the check box for it again.

The resolved, unresolved and outstanding amounts, the net of deposit and withdrawal amounts are continually updated as you work through the reconciliation procedure. If you display your journal entry from the Report menu at this stage, you will see a credit to *Bank: Chequing Account* and a debit to the expense account *Reconciliation Adjustments* for $1.25, the unresolved amount at this stage — the net amount of interest and all bank charges. The expense amount total is greater than the interest amount by $1.25. The journal entries for these items will remove the unresolved amount.

Adding Account Statement Journal Entries

You are now ready to begin entering the journal information for income to this account.

Click   the **Income tab**.

The Account Reconciliation Journal now includes journal entry fields as shown:

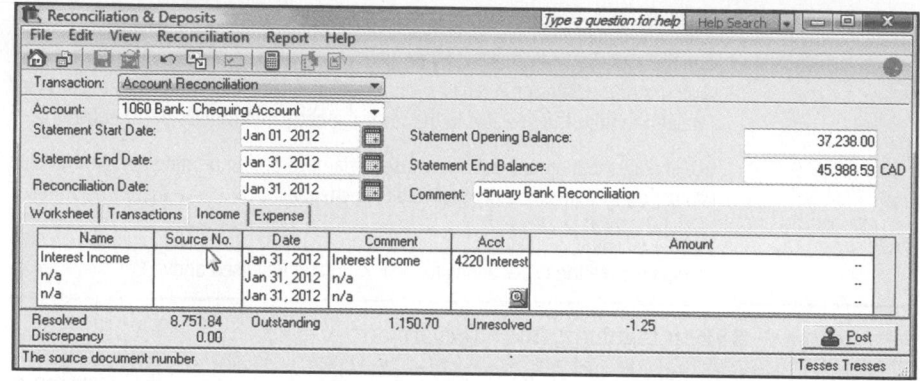

NOTES
Drag the column heading margins if necessary to see all the input columns.

The first entry for Interest Income, the income source we named earlier, is partially completed with the correct default entries for date, comment and account. You can change any of these entries by editing the contents or selecting a different account.

Click   the **Source No. field** beside Interest Revenue to advance the cursor.

Type   Bk-Stmt

Click   the **Amount field**.

Type   52.25 **Press** ⟨tab⟩. Notice that the unresolved amount — 53.50 — now matches the amount for the service fee plus the NSF charge.

NOTES
You can select a different revenue account in the reconciliation journal for these predefined incomes if this is appropriate.

You can edit these journal entries or transaction status entries at any time before posting. Choosing the Save tool will save the work you have completed so far, without posting, and still permit you to make changes later.

If there are other income categories, type the name, source, date, comment, account and amount on the second line. You can enter more than three sources of income on this form and you can choose any revenue account, although you can predefine only three linked accounts.

Click   the **Expense tab** to open the input fields for expense transactions:

NOTES
You can drag the column heading margins if necessary to see all the input columns.

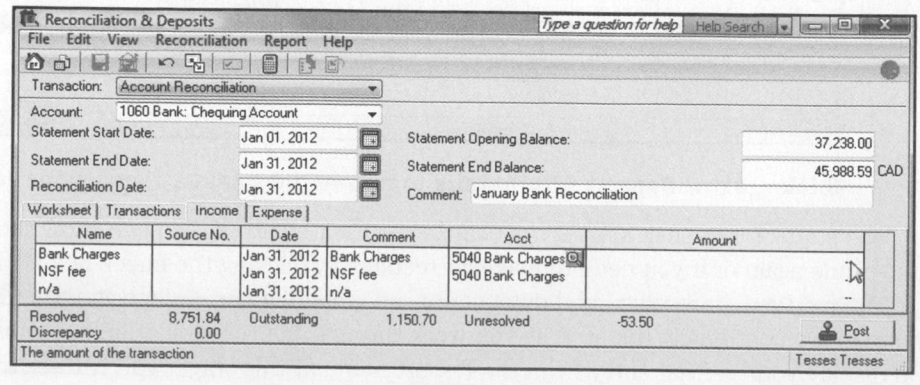

The expense transactions are also partially completed. We need to add the Source No. and the Amount. For the NSF fee, we need to change the date.

You can combine regular service charges with charges for other one-time or unusual services such as stopping a payment on a cheque or NSF fees. We have created a separate category for the NSF charge in order to track this expense. The bank statement contains the amounts for the expenses.

> **Click** the **Source No. field**. Duplicate source document codes are allowed in this journal.
>
> **Type** Bk-Stmt
>
> **Click** the **Amount field**.
>
> **Type** 23.50 **Press** (tab) to advance to the next journal line.

We can now enter the NSF service charges. You can use the same account for more than one journal entry, but you cannot choose the same expense or income category twice. The date for this charge was January 15, so we must also change the default date.

> **Click** the **Source field**. We will enter the debit memo number as the source.
>
> **Type** DM#61899 **Press** (tab).
>
> **Type** Jan 15
>
> **Click** the **Amount field**.
>
> **Type** 30 **Press** (tab).

If there are other expenses, enter the information in the same way. You can enter additional expenses and choose any expense account, although you can predefine only three linked accounts.

At this stage, your unresolved amount and discrepancy should be zero if everything is reconciled. We will look at the Worksheet to see a summary of the changes we made.

> **Click** the **Worksheet tab**:

NOTES

You can select a different expense account in the reconciliation journal for these predefined expenses if this is appropriate.

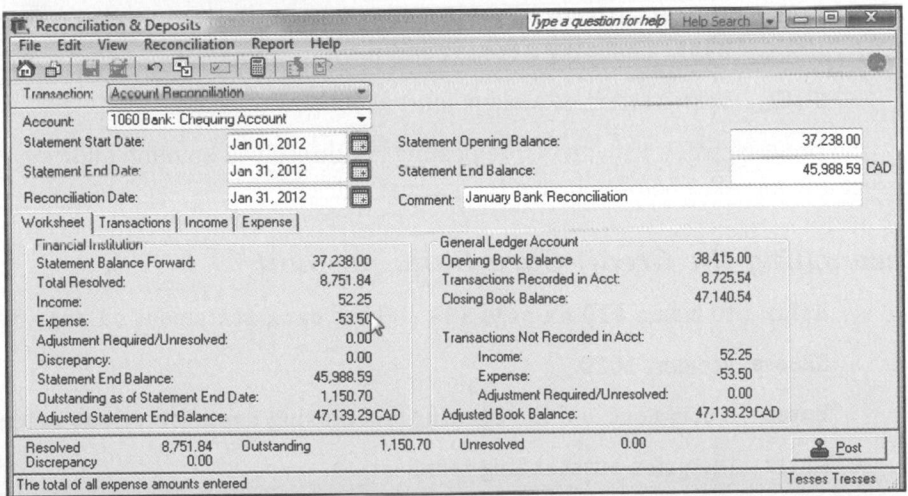

This summary shows the amounts for the bank statement and Simply Accounting records that have been entered to reconcile the differences. Both lists show the opening and closing balances and net total transaction amounts. The Account Reconciliation Journal transactions for income and expenses that were not recorded elsewhere are added to the General Ledger balance (Transactions Not Recorded In Acct), and outstanding amounts that were in the General Ledger but not on the bank statement (amount Outstanding As Of Statement End Date) are added to the Bank Statement balance. The result is a match between the two adjusted balance amounts.

You should also review the reconciliation journal entry before proceeding.

Choose the **Report menu** and **click Display Account Reconciliation Journal Entry** to display your journal entry as follows:

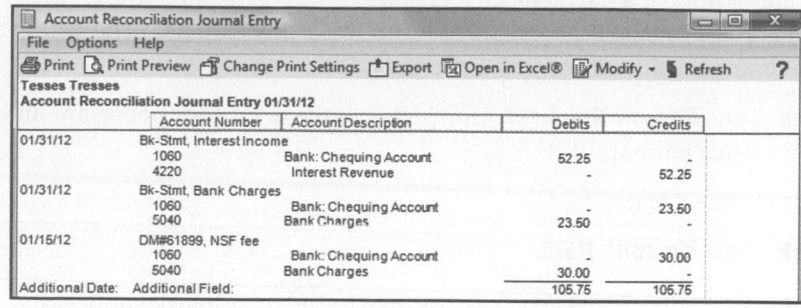

The income and expense journal entries are listed. In addition, an adjustment entry will be displayed if there is any unresolved amount.

Close the **Report window** when you have finished.

If the unreconciled amount is not zero, check your journal entries to see whether you have made an error. Click each option and tab in the journal to show your work for the corresponding part of the reconciliation procedure. Make corrections if necessary.

If you still have an unresolved amount, you can save the entry without posting and return later to try to determine whether you made a mistake or whether there was an error on the bank statement.

Any discrepancy or unresolved amount will be posted as an adjustment to the reconciliation adjustments expense account created earlier. This account should be used only for small amounts not significant enough to warrant a separate journal entry, such as differences from payroll tax rates in this text.

Click the **Save button** 💾. **Click** ☒ to close the journal without posting.

Back up the **data file. Open** the **Account Reconciliation Journal, select 1060 Bank: Chequing Account** and resume your work.

Click **Post** 👤 Post . A blank journal window appears.

The program will warn you before posting an unresolved amount, allowing you to correct any mistakes before posting the journal entries.

Reconciling the Credit Card Bank Account

Refer to **memo #10 on page 569** and the **bank statement on page 570**.

Choose **account 1080**.

Enter a **comment** and the **opening** and **closing bank statement balances**.

Enter the **prior outstanding transaction**.

Clear **all journal entries** to process the statement items.

Add journal **entries** for **service charges** and **interest**.

Add **Shortcuts** for transactions in other modules, or change modules as needed.

 Enter the **transactions for February** until the NSF cheque on Feb. 25.

Reversing NSF Cheques on Deposit Slips

In previous chapters, we reversed NSF cheques with the Reverse Receipt shortcut tool in the Adjusting receipt window of the Receipts Journal. In these cases, the bank chequing account was the linked principal bank account for the Receivables module, so the cheque was recorded (deposited) directly to this account. The reversing procedure would select this same account. For Tesses Tresses, *Undeposited Cash and Cheques* is the principal linked bank account for deposits. The NSF cheque, however, is withdrawn from *Bank: Chequing Account* — until we deposit the cheque in the bank its validity is unknown. For this situation, we need to enter a negative receipt for the paid invoice that credits *Bank: Chequing Account*. The following steps describe the procedure.

Open the **Receipts Journal**.

Choose **Brioche Bridal Customer** as the client.

Choose **1060 Bank: Chequing Account** from the drop-down list in the Deposit To field.

Click the **Cheque field** so we can enter the client cheque number.

Type NSF-986

Click the **Receipt No. field**. We will enter the bank debit number here.

Type DM-983321

Enter **February 25** as the date for the transaction.

Click the **Include Fully Paid Invoices/Deposits tool** or **choose** the **Receipt menu** and **click Include Fully Paid Invoices/Deposits**.

The two paid invoices (#468 and #487) are added to the form with the unpaid invoice. Invoice #487 was paid with the NSF cheque, so we need to select it.

Click **487** in the Invoice Or Deposit column.

Press (tab) until the cursor is in the Amount Received column for the line. We need to enter the full amount of the cheque as a negative number.

Type -126 **Press** (tab) to enter the amount.

The discount for the unpaid invoice is now selected and we need to remove it.

Press (del) to complete the entry.

Review the **journal entry**.

You will see that *Accounts Receivable* has been debited to restore the amount owing and *Bank: Chequing Account* is credited to reverse the previous deposit. Check that the discount for the unpaid invoice is not included.

Close the **journal display** and then **post** the **receipt**.

Choose **Brioche Bridal Party** again.

You will see that the invoice amount owing has been fully restored. When the payment is received, you will enter it in the usual way.

Close the **Receipts Journal** and **continue** with the **remaining transactions**.

WARNING!
Remember to delete the selected discounts for any other invoice.

NOTES
If a discount has been included with the payment, you will need to reverse it as well. Enter the amount of the discount as a negative amount in the Discount Taken field and press (tab). The cheque amount should be automatically entered as the Amount Received, with the minus sign added. You should review the entry carefully before posting and then check the Receipts Journal again for the customer to enure that the invoice has been fully restored.

Displaying Banking Reports

Click   the **Report Centre icon** 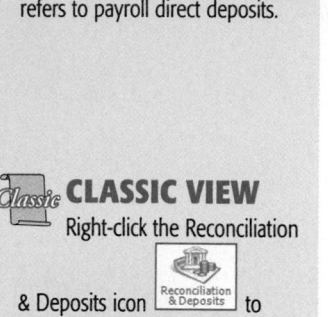 in the Home window.

Click   **Banking** to open the list of banking reports in the Report Centre:

NOTES

The Cheque Log Report was covered in Chapter 5. Refer to page 150.

For the Bank Account Transactions Report, refer to page 590.

The Direct Deposit Log refers to payroll direct deposits.

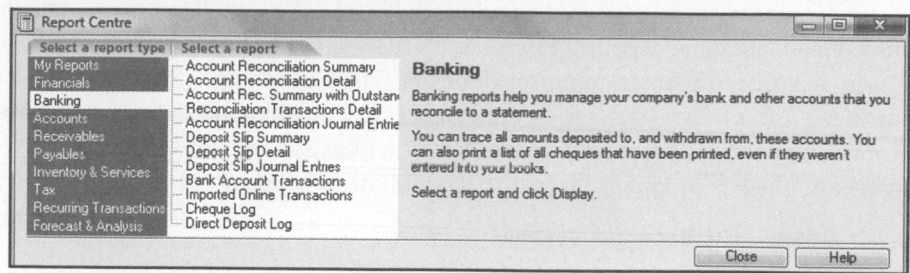

Account Reconciliation Journal

Click   **Account Reconciliation Journal Entries**. **Click Modify This Report**:

CLASSIC VIEW

Right-click the Reconciliation

& Deposits icon to select the journal. Click the

Display tool to open the report options.

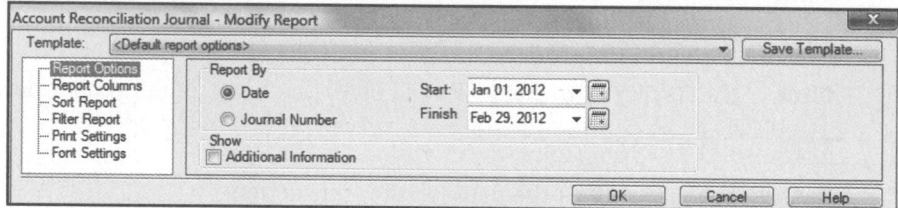

Or choose the Reports menu, choose Journal Entries and click Account Reconciliation to see the report options screen.

The journal can be prepared by selecting journal entry numbers or dates. By default, the report uses posting dates. The usual journal report customizing, sorting and filtering options are available.

Enter   the **starting** and **ending dates** (including the year) or journal numbers for the report.

Click   **OK**. **Close** the **display** when you have finished.

Deposit Slip Journal

Click   **Deposit Slip Journal Entries** and **click Modify This Report**:

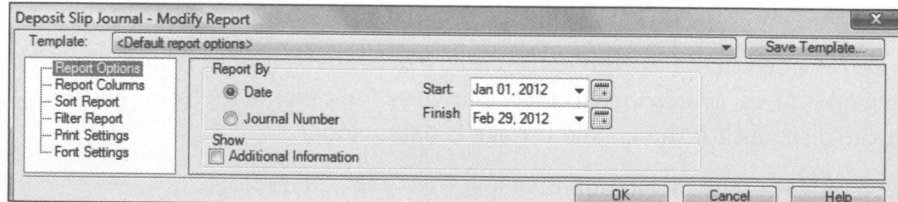

Or, from the Home window, choose the Reports menu, choose Journal Entries and click Deposit Slip to see the report options screen.

The journal can be prepared by selecting journal entry numbers or dates. By default, the report uses posting dates. The usual journal report customizing, sorting and filtering options are available.

Enter   the **starting** and **ending dates** (including the year) or journal numbers for the report.

Click   **OK**. **Close** the **display** when you have finished.

Account Reconciliation Report

Click   **Account Reconciliation Summary** to display the report sample and **click Modify This Report** to see the report options:

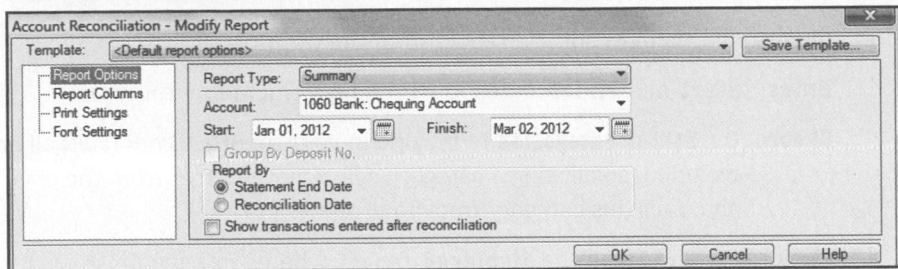

From the Home window, choose the Reports menu, then choose Banking and click Account Reconciliation Report to display the options.

Accept 1060 as the bank account or choose another account from the drop-down list for the Account field.

Enter the **start** and **end dates** (including the year). Usually these dates will coincide with the bank statement period.

Click the **Report Type list arrow**:

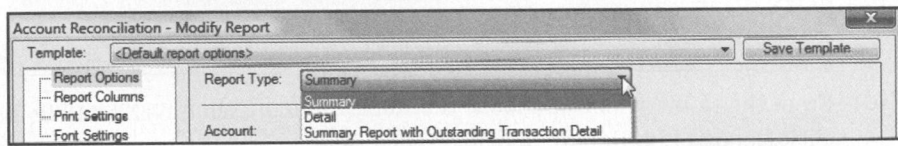

From the Report Type drop-down list, you can choose the **Summary** Report to provide totals for deposits, withdrawals, income and expense categories for the bank statements and the General Ledger account, and outstanding amounts that will reconcile the two balances. Unresolved amounts and discrepancies are also reported, if there are any. The **Detail** Report lists all journal entries with their status. You can group the Detail Report by Deposit Number. Choose **Summary Report With Outstanding Transaction Detail** to show only the total outstanding amounts and the adjusted bank and book balances. You can choose either the bank **Statement End Date** or the **Reconciliation Date** recorded in the journal for the report.

Choose the **report type** and **date (Report By) options**.

Click **OK. Close** the **displayed report** when you have finished.

Reconciliation Transaction Report

Click **Reconciliation Transactions Detail** and **click Modify This Report** to see the report options window:

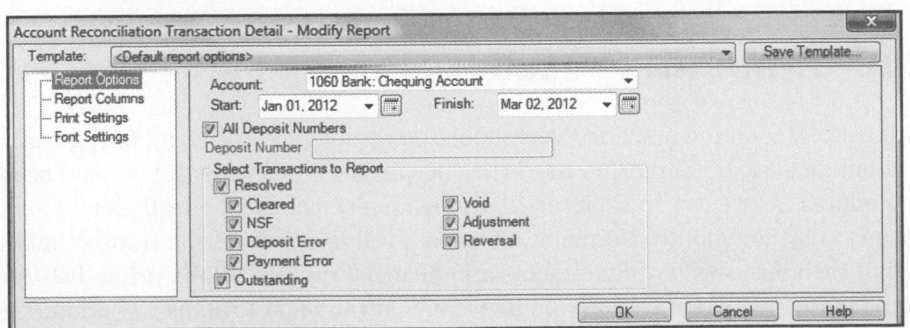

> **NOTES**
> You can display Journal reports, Invoice Lookup, and Supplier or Client Aged or Employee reports (if applicable) from the Account Reconciliation Detail Report.
> The Reconciliation Report cannot be customized except by choosing columns.

From the Home window, choose the Reports menu, then choose Banking and click Account Reconciliation Transaction Report.

The Reconciliation Transactions report will list all the transactions with their reconciliation status for the selected bank account for all the status types you chose.

Choose the **account** for the report from the drop-down list.

Enter **Start** and **Finish** dates for the report (including the year).

Choose the **Status categories** to include in your reports. By default, all are included, so clicking a category will remove the ✓ from the check box and omit this category from your report.

Click **OK** and **close** the **displayed report** when you have finished.

Deposit Slip Report

Click **Deposit Slip Summary** and **click Modify This Report**.

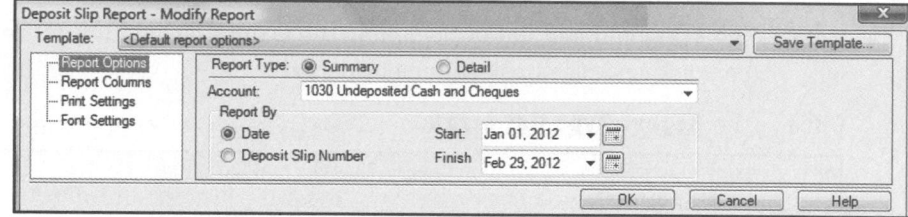

From the Home window, choose the Reports menu, then choose Banking and click Deposit Slip Report to display the options.

The Deposit Slip **Summary** Report shows the total amount on each deposit slip, while the **Detail** Report lists all cheque, bill and coin amounts separately for each deposit.

Choose the **account** for the report from the drop-down list.

You can display the report for a range of dates or deposit slip numbers. Choose the **Summary** option to see a list of totals for cash and cheques for each deposit slip. Choose **Detail** to see each item on each deposit slip and the totals.

Enter **Start** and **Finish** dates for the report (including the year).

Click **OK**. **Close** the **displayed report** and the **Report Centre** when finished.

Printing Banking Reports

Display the **report** you want to print. **Click**  or **choose** the **File menu** and **click Print** to print the report. **Close** the **Report window** when finished.

End-of-Month Procedures

There are accounting activities that should be completed at the end of regular accounting periods. Earlier we used the checklists to review fiscal year-end accounting procedures. As we saw in Chapter 12, there are also checklists for the end of each business day and month. Normally, a business will print all journal transactions at the end of each business day. Statements and financial reports will be printed at the end of each month, and all reports should be printed at the end of the fiscal period. T4s should be printed at the end of the calendar year.

Periodically, a business will clear old information from its accounting files to make space. In the manual system, it might store the details in archives or with a secured offsite backup storage provider to keep the current files manageable. Computerized systems should be similarly maintained by making backups of the data files and then clearing the information that is not required. These periodic procedures include clearing journal entries for prior periods, removing paid invoices from client and supplier records and removing suppliers and clients who no longer do business with the company.

Simply Accounting's checklists can assist with these routine procedures. You should be in the Home window.

Choose the **Business Assistant menu** and **click Checklists** to see the available lists.

Click   **Month-End Procedures** to select it and then **click Modify**.

You will see the list of routines that should be completed at the end of a month:

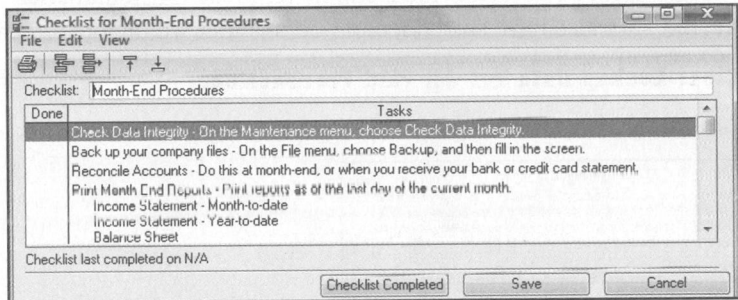

Read the task list. You have already completed some tasks on this list.

Click   the **Done column** beside the two tasks that are completed — **Back Up** and **Reconcile Accounts**. We will complete the remaining tasks before marking them.

Click   the **Home window** if part is visible or click the Simply Accounting button on the task bar to bring it to the front.

Choose the **Maintenance menu** and **click Check Data Integrity**.

If you do not see the message "Data OK," make a note of any data inconsistencies and return to your most recent backup copy of the file.

Click   **OK** to close the Integrity Summary window.

Click   the **Done column** beside **Check Data Integrity**.

Click   **Save** to return to the main checklists window. A ✓ appears in the Task In Progress column beside Month-End Procedures.

Click   **Close** to leave the Checklist window and return to the Home window.

Clearing Paid Supplier Transactions

Choose the **Maintenance menu**, then **choose Clear Data** and **Clear Paid Transactions** and **click Clear Paid Supplier Transactions**.

 **CLASSIC VIEW**
You can also click the Checklists button.

NOTES
Remember that you can print the task list for reference. Choose the File menu and click Print, click the Print tool or press `ctrl` + P to print the task list.

NOTES
You cannot clear data when you are working in multi-user mode.

PRO VERSION
You will choose Clear Paid Vendor Transactions. The term Vendor replaces Supplier.

The list of suppliers will open:

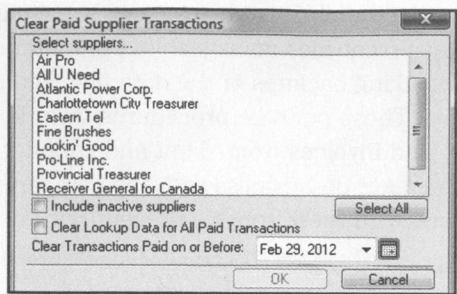

You can clear invoices for one or more suppliers at the same time. Unpaid invoices are always retained.

Enter   **Jan 31** as the last date for which you want to remove invoices.

Click   **Select All**. (To select individual suppliers, **press** `ctrl` and **click** their **names**.) We also have stored lookup details that we no longer need.

Click   **Clear Lookup Data For All Paid Transactions**.

Click   **OK**. Simply Accounting presents the warning shown here:

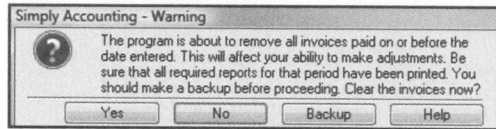

If you have selected correctly and are ready to proceed,

Click   **Yes**. When you choose to clear lookup data, you will see this warning:

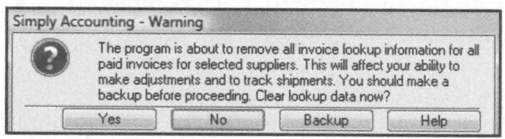

Click   **Yes** if you are certain that you should continue.

Clearing Paid Client Transactions

Choose the **Maintenance menu**, then **choose Clear Data** and **Clear Paid Transactions** and **click Clear Paid Client Transactions**:

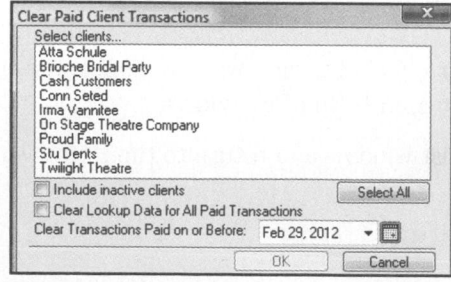

Enter   **Jan 31** as the last date for which you want to remove invoices.

Clearing client invoices is similar to clearing supplier invoices.

We will keep all transactions for February. We can clear the invoices and lookup data for Cash Customers and Atta Schule because these are not needed. You can clear paid invoices for all clients by clicking Select All.

Click   **Atta Schule**. **Press** `ctrl` and **click Cash Customers**.

Click   **Clear Lookup Data For All Paid Transactions**. **Click OK**.

The next warning is the same as the one we saw for removing supplier invoices. If you are ready, you should proceed.

Click   Yes. Again, the additional warning for lookup data is shown. If you are certain that you want to continue,

Click   Yes to remove the lookup data and return to the Home window.

Clearing Tax Reports

You should clear tax reports after filing the tax returns for the period covered by the return so that the next report will include only the current reporting period.

Choose the **Maintenance menu**, then **choose Clear Data** and **click Clear Tax Report** to display the options:

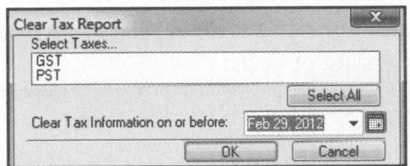

Select the tax or taxes for which you want to clear the reports or click Select All. Then enter the date. Entries on and before the date you enter will be removed.

Click   OK to see the familiar warning:

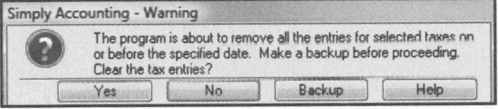

We do not want to remove any tax data because we have not submitted the returns.

Click   No to cancel and return to the Home window.

Clearing Account Reconciliation Data

Choose the **Maintenance menu**, then **choose Clear Data** and **Clear Account Rec.** and **click Clear Account Rec. Data** to display the options:

Select the account for which you want to remove the data. Then enter the date. Entries on and before the date you enter will be removed.

We do not want to remove the data at this time. If you choose to continue, you will see the familiar warning before any information is removed.

Click   Cancel to return to the Home window.

Clearing Inventory Tracking Data

Choose the **Maintenance menu**, then **choose Clear Data** and **click Clear Inventory Tracking Data** to display the following dialogue box:

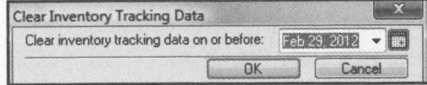

Enter   Jan 31 as the date. Entries on and before Jan 31 will be removed.

Click   OK. Again, you see the warning before any data is removed.

If you are certain that you want to proceed,

Click   Yes to delete the requested information and return to the Home window.

Clearing Lookup Data

You can clear invoice lookup data for both purchase and sales invoices together in a single step or you can clear purchase and sales invoices in separate steps. You can also clear lookup data for Remittances from this menu.

Choose the **Maintenance menu**, then **choose** Clear Data and Clear Invoice Lookup Data and **click** Clear Supplier Invoice & Client Invoice Lookup Data to display the clearing options:

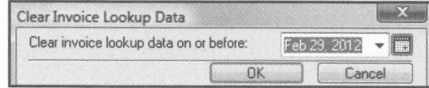

Enter   Jan 31 as the date. Entries on and before Jan 31 will be removed.

Click   OK.

Once again, you see the warning before any data is removed. If you are certain that you want to proceed,

Click   Yes to continue.

If you cleared the lookup data with the paid transactions, you will see the message stating that there is no invoice lookup data to clear. Click OK to continue.

The requested information is deleted and you will return to the Home window.

If you want to clear only purchase invoice data, choose the Maintenance menu, then choose Clear Data and Clear Invoice Lookup Data and click Clear Supplier Invoice Lookup Data to display the list of suppliers. Choose the suppliers for which you want to clear the invoices, enter the data and click OK to see the familiar warning. Click Yes to continue with clearing the data.

To remove only sales invoice data, choose the Maintenance menu, then choose Clear Data and Clear Invoice Lookup Data and click Clear Client Invoice Lookup Data. Select clients for which you want to clear the invoices, enter the date and click OK. Click Yes to continue with clearing the data.

Clearing Deposit Slip Lookup Data

Choose the **Maintenance menu**, then **choose** Clear Data and **click** Clear Lookup Data For Deposit Slips to display the options:

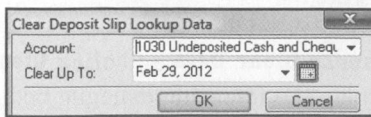

Select the account for which you want to remove the data. Then enter the date. Entries on and before the date you enter will be removed.

NOTES
If you choose to clear invoice lookup data for purchases or sales separately, you can choose to clear the data for one or more suppliers (or clients) or for all of them.

PRO VERSION
You will choose Clear Purchase Invoice and Sales Invoice Lookup Data to clear data for both sets of invoices.

PRO VERSION
You will choose Clear Purchase Invoice Lookup Data to clear data for purchase invoices. You will choose Clear Sales Invoice Lookup Data to clear data for sales invoices.

NOTES
From the Maintenance menu, Clear Data option, you can also clear lookup data for remittances, notes that you create in the Daily Business Manager, financial history and direct deposits. For each one, you can enter a date after which all data will be retained. You will be warned before any information is removed.

We do not want to remove the data at this time. If you choose to continue, you will see the familiar warning before any information is removed.

> **Click**   **Cancel** to return to the Home window.

Clearing Lookup Data for Other Payments

Lookup data for other payments are cleared separately from Purchases Journal invoices.

> **Choose** the **Maintenance menu**, then **choose Clear Data** and **click Clear Lookup Data For Other Payments** to display the clearing options:

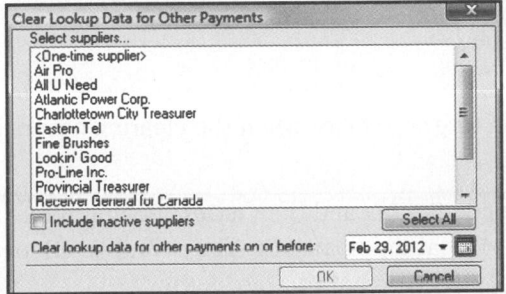

> **Enter** **Jan 31** as the date for the data you want to remove.

> **Choose** the **suppliers**. **Click Select All** to select all suppliers.

> **Click**   **OK**.

You will see the warning before any data is removed. If you want to proceed,

> **Click**   **Yes** to continue.

The requested information is deleted, and you will return to the Home window.

Automatically Clearing Data

Simply Accounting can also clear data automatically when you start a new fiscal period. Data are automatically retained for seven years.

> **Choose** the **Maintenance menu**, then **choose Clear Data** and **click Automatically Clear Data**.

The options screen shows the types of data you can clear automatically:

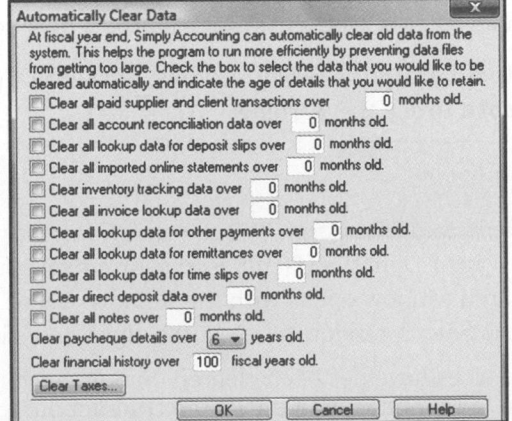

From this screen you can choose what data to clear and how many months of each type of data should be kept when the clearing occurs at the end of the fiscal period.

> **Click**   **Cancel** to return to the Home window.

NOTES
If you cleared the lookup data when you cleared the paid transactions, you will see the message stating that there is no lookup data to clear.

Automatically Clearing Tax Data

Tax information can also be cleared automatically.

> **Choose** the **Maintenance menu**, then **choose Clear Data** and **click Automatically Clear Data**. **Click** the **Clear Taxes button** to open the options screen:

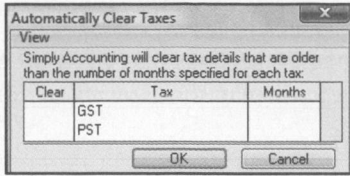

On this screen you can choose what taxes to clear and enter the number of months that you want to keep the information for these taxes when the clearing occurs at the end of the fiscal period.

> **Click** the **Clear column** beside the tax and then **enter** the number of **months** of reports you want to clear automatically. The default is 12 months.

> **Click** **Cancel** to return to the Home window.

Removing Supplier and Client Records

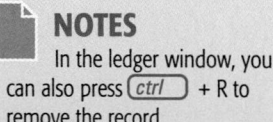

NOTES
An alternative to removing records is to mark clients or suppliers as Inactive and not include them in reports. Inactive clients and suppliers also do not appear in the drop-down lists in journals.

Sometimes you know that you will not be doing business with a client or supplier again. Removing their records reduces the length of the lists to scroll through for journal entries and saves on mailing costs. Suppliers are removed from the Suppliers window. Clients are removed from the Clients window. We will remove the client (tenant) Stu Dents because he will be moving out of the apartment after March, the date of his final cheque. First we must clear all paid transactions.

> **Choose** the **Maintenance menu**, then **choose Clear Data** and **Clear Paid Transactions** and **click Clear Paid Client Transactions**.

> **Click** **Stu Dents** on the client list.

> **Enter** **Jan 31, 2012** as the date. **Click OK**. When you see the warning,

> **Click** **Yes** to confirm. **Click Yes** to confirm removing lookup data if asked.

> **Click** **Receivables** in the Modules pane list.

> **Click** **Stu Dents** in the Home window Clients list to open the ledger record.

NOTES
In the ledger window, you can also press ⌃ *ctrl* + R to remove the record.

> **Click** the **Remove Client tool** 🔑 in the ledger window, or **choose** the **File menu** and **click Remove** to see the warning:

NOTES
There are postdated rent cheques for Stu Dents, so not all the paid transactions were cleared when January 31 was selected as the date.

You can also choose Remove Client from the Clients icon shortcuts list in the Receivables window. The Search window opens with the Remove Client option selected. Click Stu Dents in the Search window to select the client and click OK.

We selected a client for whom invoices have not been cleared. Simply Accounting will not permit you to remove a client, or supplier, with uncleared transactions.

NOTES
You can select March 1 from the Date field drop-down list. (The latest transaction date is usually on the Date field drop-down lists.)

> **Click** **OK** to return to the Receivables module window. Clear the details using March 1 as the date and then remove the client's record. If all transactions are cleared, you will see the familiar warning.

Check that you have selected the client you want before continuing.

Click   **Yes** if you have selected correctly.

Click Yes to continue if you see the message about removing lookup data. If you see the message stating that there is no lookup data, click OK to continue.

Close   the **Receivables module window** to return to the Home window.

Completing the Month-End Checklist

We will now return to the month-end checklist by marking the remaining tasks as done. The tasks relating to budgeting do not apply so we can delete them from the list and customize the list for Tesses Tresses.

Choose the **Business Assistant menu** and **click Checklists** to see the lists.

Double click   Month-End Procedures to open this list.

NOTES
Refer to page 491 for more information on removing or adding tasks in checklists.

You can also add tasks to customize the list even further. Just click on the list where you want to add a task, choose the Edit menu and click Insert (or click the Insert Item tool). Then type the task description.

Scroll down the list to the budget-related tasks.

Click   **Check Your Budget** to select this line.

Click   the **Remove Item tool** or **choose** the **Edit menu** and **click Remove**.

Click   **Yes** to confirm and select the next task. Remove it and the following one relating to budgets.

Click   the **Done column** for the remaining tasks.

Click   **Checklist Completed** to return to the opening Checklist window.

The session date appears as the Date Last Completed beside Month-End Procedures.

Click   **Close** to return to the Home window.

R E V I E W

The Student DVD with Data Files includes Review Questions and Supplementary Cases for this chapter.

OBJECTIVES

*After completing
this chapter, you
should be able to*

- ■ *plan* and *design* an accounting system for a small business
- ■ *prepare* procedures for converting from a manual system
- ■ *understand* the objectives of a computerized system
- ■ *create* company files
- ■ *set up* company accounts
- ■ *enter* settings for foreign currency transactions
- ■ *prepare* files for foreign currency transactions and importing goods
- ■ *identify* preferred customers for reduced prices
- ■ *enter* preferred customer prices and import duty rates for inventory
- ■ *finish* entering the accounting history for all modules
- ■ *insert* new accounts, suppliers, customers and employees as required
- ■ *export* reports
- ■ *use* spreadsheets for analyzing, planning and decision making
- ■ *enter* end-of-accounting-period adjustments
- ■ *perform* end-of-accounting-period closing routines
- ■ *analyze* and *interpret* comparative reports
- ■ *develop* further group interpersonal skills

INTRODUCTION

NOTES

If you change the province, remember that rules for the application of the federal Harmonized Sales Tax (HST), provincial sales taxes and payroll may vary from one province to another, and amounts in the source documents will change.

This application provides a complete accounting cycle for a merchandising business. It is a comprehensive application covering a three-month fiscal period. You will use Simply Accounting to convert a manual accounting system to a computerized accounting system and then enter transactions. The routines in this application are common to many small businesses, so they should be useful. The information in this chapter reflects the business realities in Ontario in 2010.

You may substitute information relevant to other provinces or the latest payroll and tax regulations wherever it is appropriate to do so.

Because of the length of the setup, instructions for working with the source documents are presented with those documents on page 684.

COMPANY INFORMATION

Company Profile

Flabuless Fitness, in Hamilton, Ontario, sells a wide range of fitness equipment and accessories for home and light commercial use. Stephen Reeves, the owner, opened his business a few years ago after retiring as a professional athlete, gaining business experience with another store and completing some business courses. Reeves has three employees to assist with the work in the store. They also perform other duties. One employee does the accounting, one teaches yoga classes and one delivers equipment and provides personal training services to clients. Reeves works mostly outside the store, promoting the business.

Several of the equipment suppliers offer discounts to the store for early payment. Two suppliers are located in the United States. Accounts are also set up for other supplies and services that are provided locally. The store uses a credit card for some of these purchases.

Most customers are situated in the Hamilton region, but Reeves has recently added two new customers in New York State. Prices in US dollars are entered in the ledger records so that all prices will be entered automatically in the correct amount and currency when the customer is selected. With the Canadian dollar approximately on par with the US dollar, US dollar prices are very close to Canadian dollar prices.

All account customers are given discounts for early payment and some preferred customers receive additional discounts. Individual customers usually pay by cash, debit or credit card and do not receive any discounts. Delivery is provided at a small charge and includes equipment setup and a brief demonstration on equipment use.

All items and services sold by the store are set up as inventory so that sales can be monitored. HST is charged on all sales and services, except to foreign customers. The store pays HST on all taxable purchases, including inventory purchased for resale. The exception is books, for which the store pays 5 percent GST on purchases and customers pay 5 percent at the time of sales.

The owner decided to use Simply Accounting for record keeping after a consultant prepared the report on the following pages. Reeves found an application called Hearth House in an older Simply Accounting textbook. It appeared similar in complexity and structure to Flabuless Fitness and even included complete instructions for creating the data files. Before converting the books for the store, he asked his assistant to work through this application for practice. Next she printed all the relevant business guide information and prepared the following reports to assist with the conversion on April 1, 2012:

- Income Statement
- Business Information
- Chart of Accounts
- Balance Sheet
- Post-Closing Trial Balance
- Supplier Information
- Customer Information
- Employee Information
- Inventory Information
- Accounting Procedures

 NOTES
Because of the length of the application, group work is encouraged in setting up error-free company files and completing the transactions.

NOTES
Flabuless Fitness
199 Warmup Rd., Unit 500
Hamilton, ON L8T 3B7
Tel 1: (905) 642-2348 (B-FIT)
Tel 2: (800) 448-2348 (B-FIT)
Fax: (905) 642-9100
Business No.: 245 138 121

MANAGER'S REPORT ON SIMPLY ACCOUNTING

PREPARED FOR FLABULESS FITNESS

1. Simply Accounting allows a business to process all source documents in a timely fashion. It can automatically prepare both single-period and comparative accounting reports for planning, decision making and controlling operations within the business.
2. The software eliminates some of the time-consuming manual clerical functions. For example, it can automatically prepare invoices, cheques and statements, and it can perform all the necessary mathematical calculations. Being freed from these chores, the accountant can extend her role to assume a much higher level of responsibility. For example, the accountant will have more time to spend analyzing reports with the owner and can work directly with the owner in making business decisions.
3. Simply Accounting can easily export reports to spreadsheets for further analysis, or link with the Internet, with other software programs and with suppliers and customers for interactive data exchange. When combined with the graphing, account reconciliation and budgeting features, these reports permit the owner to analyze past trends and to make better predictions about the future behaviour of the business.
4. As the business grows, the manager can divide work more meaningfully among new accounting personnel. Since Simply Accounting provides subsidiary ledgers that are linked to control accounts in the General Ledger, it automatically coordinates accounting work performed by different individuals. Customizable window backgrounds can even accommodate mood changes of the different users.
5. Simply Accounting allows the owner to exercise business controls in a number of areas.

IN GENERAL

- Access to confidential accounting records and editing capability can be restricted to authorized personnel by using passwords.
- Mechanical errors can be virtually eliminated, since journal transactions with unequal debits and credits cannot be posted. Customer, supplier, employee, inventory and jobcost names appear in full on the journal entry input forms, making errors less likely.
- The ability to preview forms, store recurring entries and look up posted invoices makes it possible to avoid errors in repeated information and to double check invoices in response to customer and supplier inquiries.
- Errors in General, Sales, Receipts, Purchases, Payments and Payroll journal entries can be corrected as adjustments or reversed. The software automatically creates and posts the reversing entries.
- Simply Accounting provides an audit trail for all journals.
- Bank account, customer, supplier and inventory records can be set up to calculate many foreign currency transactions automatically, including import duties.
- Daily Business Manager lists and checklists provide reminders of upcoming discounts, recurring entries and routine tasks.
- Business guides, accounting advice and management reports and advice all provide helpful information for running the business.
- Simply Accounting provides a directory of customers, suppliers and employees, and can create mailing labels for them.

GENERAL LEDGER

- The software provides a directory of accounts used by the business, including all linked accounts for the other ledgers in Simply Accounting.
- The information in these accounts can be used to prepare and analyze financial reports such as the Balance Sheet and Income Statement.

RECEIVABLES LEDGER

- Credit limit entries for each customer should reduce the losses from non-payment of accounts. Customers with poor payment histories can have their credit limits reduced or their credit purchase privileges removed.
- Preferred customers can be identified so that they automatically receive lower prices.
- Sales quote and order entries result in automatic Sales Journal entries when the quotes or orders are filled.
- Tax codes, payment terms and accounts are added to the customer record and automatically entered for sales when the customer is selected.
- Accounts receivable can be aged, and each customer's payment behaviour can be analyzed. This feature allows for the accurate calculation of provisions for bad debts.

PAYABLES LEDGER

- The information from the review of transactions with suppliers and from the accounts payable aged analysis can be combined with detailed cash flow reports to make payment decisions. Simply Accounting helps to predict short-term cash needs in order to establish priorities for making payments and to schedule payments to suppliers.
- The GST/HST remittance or refund is calculated automatically because of the linked GST/HST accounts in the Payables and Receivables ledgers.
- Simply Accounting purchase quote and order entries result in automatic Purchases Journal entries when quotes or orders are filled.
- The usual tax code, payment terms and expense account for a supplier can be entered in the supplier record so that they are entered automatically for purchases when the supplier is selected.

PAYROLL LEDGER

- Simply Accounting maintains employee records with both personal and payment information for personnel files.
- Paycheques for several employees can be processed as a single payroll run entry with direct payroll deposit.
- Once records are set up, the program automatically withholds employee deductions including income tax, CPP (Canada Pension Plan) and EI (Employment Insurance) and is therefore less prone to error. Updated tax tables can be obtained from Sage Software, Inc.

PAYROLL LEDGER CONTINUED

- Payroll summaries permit easy analysis of compulsory and optional payroll expenses and benefits, employee contributions and entitlements.
- Different kinds of income can be linked to different expense accounts. In addition, the wages for different employees can be linked to different expense accounts, again permitting better tracking of payroll expenses.
- Simply Accounting automatically links payroll with control accounts in the General Ledger. Remittance amounts are tracked and linked with the corresponding payroll authorities for monthly or quarterly remittance.

INVENTORY LEDGER

- The software provides an inventory summary or database of all inventory items.
- Services can be set up as inventory and tracked the same way as inventory items.
- Inventory reports flag items that need to be re-ordered, and the reports can be used to make purchase decisions.
- Import duty rates and different prices in home and foreign currencies can be set up in the ledger so they appear automatically in the journals. Additional price lists can be added.
- Inventory codes can be matched to the supplier and customer item codes so that common order forms are created automatically.
- The software calculates inventory variance costs when the items sold are out of stock and later purchased at different prices.
- Simply Accounting automatically updates inventory records for multiple locations when inventory is purchased, sold, transferred, lost, recovered or returned. It warns when you try to oversell inventory.
- Different units for stocking, selling and buying items can be saved for inventory items so that prices are automatically entered correctly for both sales and purchases. Reports can be prepared for any of the units on record.
- Inventory tracking reports can monitor sales and purchase activity on individual inventory items to see which ones are selling well and which are not. These reports can be used to determine optimum inventory buying patterns to reduce storage costs.

6. In summation, Simply Accounting provides an integrated management accounting information system with extensive built-in controls.

INCOME STATEMENT

FLABULESS FITNESS

January 1 to March 31, 2012

Revenue				▶ 5140	Depreciation: Furniture & Fixtures	80.00	
4000	GENERAL REVENUE			5150	Depreciation: Retail Premises	2 440.00	
4020	Revenue from Sales	$78 450.00		5160	Depreciation: Van	190.00	
4040	Revenue from Services	8 335.00		5180	Net Depreciation		3 160.00
4060	Sales Discounts	−965.00		5190	Delivery Expense		63.00
4100	Net Sales		$85 820.00	5200	Hydro Expense		528.00
4120	Exchange Rate Differences		−12.00	5210	Insurance Expense		1 200.00
4150	Interest Revenue		1 980.00	5220	Interest on Loan		1 240.00
4200	Freight Revenue		379.00	5230	Interest on Mortgage		5 600.00
4390	TOTAL GENERAL REVENUE		$88 167.00	5240	Maintenance of Premises		1 055.00
				5250	Supplies Used		165.00
TOTAL REVENUE			$88 167.00	5260	Property Taxes		2 700.00
				5270	Uncollectable Accounts Expense		500.00
Expense				5280	Telephone Expense		295.00
5000	OPERATING EXPENSES			5285	Van Maintenance & Operating Expense		638.00
5010	Advertising and Promotion		$ 530.00	5290	TOTAL OPERATING EXPENSES		$27 263.00
5020	Bank Charges		128.00				
5030	Credit Card Fees		1 480.00	5295	PAYROLL EXPENSES		
5040	Damaged Inventory	$ 80.00		5300	Wages		8 295.20
5050	Cost of Goods Sold: Accessories	5 195.00		5305	Salaries		22 800.00
5060	Cost of Goods Sold: Equipment	3 101.00		5310	Commissions & Bonuses		284.80
5070	Cost Variance	64.00		5320	EI Expense		998.00
5080	Freight Expense	432.00		5330	CPP Expense		1 201.00
5090	Purchase Discounts	−524.00		5340	WSIB Expense		379.00
5100	Purchases Returns & Allowances	−367.00		5360	EHT Expense		309.00
5110	Net Cost of Goods Sold		7 981.00	5370	Gp Insurance Expense		105.00
5120	Depreciation: Cash Registers	300.00		5490	TOTAL PAYROLL EXPENSES		$34 372.00
5130	Depreciation: Computer Equipment	150.00 ▶					
					TOTAL EXPENSE		$61 635.00
					NET INCOME		$26 532.00

BUSINESS INFORMATION

FLABULESS FITNESS

USER PREFERENCES: Options
Use Accounting Terms
Automatically save changes to records
Calculate record balances by session date
Automatically refresh balances
View Daily Business Manager and Checklists off
Show Company name, Advice, Session
date at startup, and Paid stamps

Transaction Confirmation Turned on

COMPANY SETTINGS: Information

Address	199 Warmup Rd., Unit 500
	Hamilton, Ontario L8T 3B7
Tel 1	(905) 642-2348 (B-FIT)
Tel 2	(800) 448-2348 (B-FIT)
Fax	(905) 642-9100
Industry	Retail

Business No. 245 138 121 RT0001
Business Province Ontario
Fiscal Start Apr 01, 2012
Earliest Transaction Apr 01, 2012
Fiscal End Jun 30, 2012

System Warn if accounts not balanced

Backup Semi-monthly; Display reminder
Scheduled, automatic backup off

Features All used

Forms Settings (Next Number)
Sales Invoices No. 3000
Sales Quotes No. 41
Receipts No. 39
Customer Deposits No. 15
Purchase Orders No. 25
Direct Deposits No. 19
Check for duplicates
Print in batches

Date Format mm-dd-yyyy and Long Dates

Logo SimData10\Setup\logos\flab.bmp

Names
Additional Field Ref. Number

Credit Card Information
Used: Visa
Payable 2250 Expense 5030

Accept:	Visa	Interac
Fee	2.5%	0%
Expense	5030	5030
Asset	1120	1120

Sales Taxes

Tax ID on forms	Track:	Purch	Sales
HST 245 138 121		2670	2650
GST 245 138 121		2670	2650

	Exempt?	Taxable?	Report?
HST	No	No	Yes
GST	No	No	Yes

Tax Codes
H: HST, taxable, 13%, not included, refundable
G: GST, taxable, 5%, not included, refundable
IN: HST, taxable, 13%, included, refundable

Foreign Currency
USD United States Dollars
Tracking Account 4120
Exchange Rate on 04/01/12 1.015

GENERAL SETTINGS No changes

PAYABLES SETTINGS
Address Hamilton, Ontario, Canada
Options: Aging periods 15, 30, 60 days
Discounts before tax Yes

Import Duty
Track import duty
Linked account 2220

RECEIVABLES SETTINGS
Address Hamilton, Ontario, Canada
Options: Aging periods 10, 30, 60 days
Interest charges 1.5% after 30 days
Statements include invoices for 31 days
Use tax code H for new customers
Discount: Payment terms 2/10, n/30
Discounts before tax No
Line Discounts Not used

Comments
On Sales Invoice Interest @ 1.5% per month
charged on accounts over 30 days.

PAYROLL SETTINGS
Names: Income and Deduction
Income 1 Salary
Income 2 Commission
Income 3 No. Clients
Income 4 Bonus
Income 5 Tuition
Income 6 Travel Exp
Deduction 1 RRSP
Deduction 2 CSB Plan
Deduction 3 Garnishee

Names: Additional Payroll
Field 1 Emergency Contact
Field 2 Contact Number
User Expense 1 Gp Insurance
Entitlement 1 Vacation
Entitlement 2 Sick Leave
Entitlement 3 PersonalDays

Incomes

Income	Type	Taxable	Vac. Pay
Regular	Hourly rate	Yes	Yes
Overtime 1	Hourly rate	Yes	Yes
Salary	Income	Yes	No
Bonus	Income	Yes	No
Commission	Income	Yes	No
No. Clients	Piece Rate	Yes	Yes
Tuition	Income	Yes	No
Travel Exp	Reimburse	No	No

Deductions
RRSP Before tax, after other deductions
CSB Plan After tax and other deductions
Garnishee After tax and other deductions

Taxes
EI factor 1.4
WSIB rate 1.29
EHT factor 0.98
QHSF Not applicable

Entitlements

Name	Track %	Max Days	Clear
Vacation	8.0%	25	No
Sick Leave	5.0%	15	No
PersonalDays	2.5%	5	No

Remittance

Payroll Liability	Payroll Authority
EI, CPP, Income Tax	Receiver General
WSIB	Workplace Safety & Insurance Board
EHT	Minister of Finance
Gp Insurance, RRSP	Ancaster Insurance
CSB	Mt. Hope Investment
Garnishee	Receiver General

Opening balance amounts: see Trial Balance

Job Categories
Sales: employees are salespersons
All employees are in Sales category

INVENTORY SETTINGS
Profit evaluation by markup
Sort inventory by number
Foreign prices from inventory records
Allow inventory levels to go below zero

ACCOUNT CLASS SETTINGS
Bank
1060 Bank: Hamilton Trust Chequing (CAD)
Next cheque no. 101
Next deposit no. 14
1080 Bank: Hamilton Trust Savings (CAD)
1140 Bank: USD Chequing (USD)
Next cheque no. 346
Cash
1030 Undeposited Cash and Cheques
Credit Card Receivable
1120 Bank: Visa and Interac
Credit Card Payable
2250 Credit Card Payable
Operating Expense Class
All postable expense accounts except COGS
subgroup (accounts 5040–5100)

LINKED ACCOUNTS FOR LEDGERS
See pages 643–648, 653–656

CHART OF ACCOUNTS

FLABULESS FITNESS

ASSETS

1000	CURRENT ASSETS [H]
1010	Test Balance Account
1030	Undeposited Cash and Cheques [A]
1060	Bank: Hamilton Trust Chequing [A]
1080	Bank: Hamilton Trust Savings [A]
1120	Bank: Visa and Interac [A]
1140	Bank: USD Chequing [A]
1150	Net Bank [S]
1200	Accounts Receivable [A]
1210	Allowance for Doubtful Accounts [A]
1220	Advances Receivable [A]
1230	Interest Receivable [A]
1240	Net Receivables [S]
1250	Purchase Prepayments
1260	Office Supplies
1265	Linen Supplies
1270	Prepaid Advertising
1280	Prepaid Insurance
1300	TOTAL CURRENT ASSETS [T]
1500	INVENTORY ASSETS [H]
1520	Accessories
1540	Fitness Equipment
1560	Books
1580	TOTAL INVENTORY ASSETS [T]
1600	CENTRE & EQUIPMENT [H]
1610	Cash Registers [A]
1620	Accum Deprec: Cash Registers [A]
1630	Net Cash Registers [S]
1640	Computer Equipment [A]
1650	Accum Deprec: Computer Equipment [A]
1660	Net Computer Equipment [S]
1670	Furniture & Fixtures [A]
1680	Accum Deprec: Furniture & Fixtures [A]
1690	Net Furniture & Fixtures [S]
1700	Retail Premises [A]
1710	Accum Deprec: Retail Premises [A]
1720	Net Retail Premises [S]
1730	Van [A]
1740	Accum Deprec: Van [A]
1750	Net Van [S]
1890	TOTAL CENTRE & EQUIPMENT [T] ▶

▶LIABILITIES

2000	CURRENT LIABILITIES [H]
2100	Bank Loan
2200	Accounts Payable
2210	Prepaid Sales and Deposits
2220	Import Duty Payable
2250	Credit Card Payable
2300	Vacation Payable
2310	EI Payable [A]
2320	CPP Payable [A]
2330	Income Tax Payable [A]
2350	Receiver General Payable [S]
2380	EHT Payable
2400	RRSP Payable
2410	CSB Plan Payable
2420	Group Insurance Payable
2430	Garnisheed Wages Payable
2460	WSIB Payable
2500	Business Income Tax Payable
2650	GST/HST Charged on Sales [A]
2670	GST/HST Paid on Purchases [A]
2750	GST/HST Owing (Refund) [S]
2790	TOTAL CURRENT LIABILITIES [T]
2800	LONG TERM LIABILITIES [H]
2820	Mortgage Payable
2890	TOTAL LONG TERM LIABILITIES [T]

EQUITY

3000	OWNER'S EQUITY [H]
3560	S. Reeves, Capital
3600	Current Earnings [X]
3690	TOTAL OWNER'S EQUITY [T]

REVENUE

4000	GENERAL REVENUE [H]
4020	Revenue from Sales [A]
4040	Revenue from Services [A]
4060	Sales Discounts [A]
4100	Net Sales [S]
4120	Exchange Rate Differences
4150	Interest Revenue
4200	Freight Revenue
4390	TOTAL GENERAL REVENUE [T] ▶

▶EXPENSE

5000	OPERATING EXPENSES [H]
5010	Advertising and Promotion
5020	Bank Charges
5030	Credit Card Fees
5040	Damaged Inventory [A]
5050	Cost of Goods Sold: Accessories [A]
5060	Cost of Goods Sold: Equipment [A]
5065	Cost of Services [A]
5070	Cost Variance [A]
5080	Freight Expense [A]
5090	Purchase Discounts [A]
5100	Purchases Returns & Allowances [A]
5110	Net Cost of Goods Sold [S]
5120	Depreciation: Cash Registers [A]
5130	Depreciation: Computer Equipment [A]
5140	Depreciation: Furniture & Fixtures [A]
5150	Depreciation: Retail Premises [A]
5160	Depreciation: Van [A]
5180	Net Depreciation [S]
5190	Delivery Expense
5200	Hydro Expense
5210	Insurance Expense
5220	Interest on Loan
5230	Interest on Mortgage
5240	Maintenance of Premises
5250	Supplies Used
5260	Property Taxes
5270	Uncollectable Accounts Expense
5280	Telephone Expense
5285	Van Maintenance & Operating Expense
5290	TOTAL OPERATING EXPENSES [T]
5295	PAYROLL EXPENSES [H]
5300	Wages
5305	Salaries
5310	Commissions & Bonuses
5320	Travel Expenses
5330	EI Expense
5340	CPP Expense
5350	WSIB Expense
5360	EHT Expense
5370	Gp Insurance Expense
5380	Employee Benefits
5490	TOTAL PAYROLL EXPENSES [T]

NOTES: The Chart of Accounts includes all accounts and Net Income. Group account types are not marked. Other account types are marked as follows: [H] Heading, [A] subgroup Account, [S] Subgroup total, [T] Total, [X] Current Earnings.

BALANCE SHEET

FLABULESS FITNESS

March 31, 2012

Assets				Liabilities			
1000	CURRENT ASSETS			▶ 2000	CURRENT LIABILITIES		
1060	Bank: Hamilton Trust Chequing	$ 77 988.00		2100	Bank Loan		$ 50 000.00
1080	Bank: Hamilton Trust Savings	108 250.00		2200	Accounts Payable		16 780.00
1120	Bank: Visa and Interac	8 635.00		2250	Credit Card Payable		220.00
1140	Bank: USD (9 350 USD)	9 500.00		2300	Vacation Payable		371.84
1150	Net Bank		$204 373.00	2310	EI Payable	$ 563.28	
1200	Accounts Receivable	17 110.00		2320	CPP Payable	824.77	
1210	Allowance for Doubtful Accounts	−800.00		2330	Income Tax Payable	1 755.60	
1220	Advances Receivable	100.00		2350	Receiver General Payable		3 143.65
1230	Interest Receivable	420.00		2380	EHT Payable		320.50
1240	Net Receivables		16 830.00	2400	RRSP Payable		350.00
1260	Office Supplies		300.00	2410	CSB Plan Payable		350.00
1265	Linen Supplies		450.00	2420	Group Insurance Payable		39.00
1270	Prepaid Advertising		180.00	2430	Garnisheed Wages Payable		200.00
1280	Prepaid Insurance		4 800.00	2460	WSIB Payable		392.51
1300	TOTAL CURRENT ASSETS		$226 933.00	2500	Business Income Tax Payable		3 600.00
				2650	GST/HST Charged on Sales	6 860.00	
1500	INVENTORY ASSETS			2670	GST/HST Paid on Purchases	−2 990.00	
1520	Accessories		7 180.00	2750	GST/HST Owing (Refund)		3 870.00
1540	Fitness Equipment		65 280.00	2790	TOTAL CURRENT LIABILITIES		$ 79 637.50
1560	Books		5 200.00				
1580	TOTAL INVENTORY ASSETS		$ 77 660.00	2800	LONG TERM LIABILITIES		
				2820	Mortgage Payable		180 000.00
1600	CENTRE & EQUIPMENT			2890	TOTAL LONG TERM LIABILITIES		$180 000.00
1610	Cash Registers	5 000.00					
1620	Accum Deprec: Cash Registers	−1 000.00		TOTAL LIABILITIES			$259 637.50
1630	Net Cash Registers		4 000.00	Equity			
1640	Computer Equipment	3 000.00		3000	OWNER'S EQUITY		
1650	Accum Deprec: Computer Equip	−1 000.00		3560	S. Reeves, Capital		$246 023.50
1660	Net Computer Equipment		2 000.00	3600	Current Earnings		26 532.00
1670	Furniture & Fixtures	2 000.00		3690	TOTAL OWNER'S EQUITY		$272 255.50
1680	Accum Deprec: Furn & Fixtures	−400.00					
1690	Net Furniture & Fixtures		1 600.00	TOTAL EQUITY			$272 555.50
1700	Retail Premises	200 000.00					
1710	Accum Deprec: Retail Premises	−5 000.00		LIABILITIES AND EQUITY			$532 193.00
1720	Net Retail Premises		195 000.00				
1730	Van	30 000.00					
1740	Accum Deprec: Van	−5 000.00					
1750	Net Van		25 000.00				
1890	TOTAL CENTRE & EQUIPMENT		$227 600.00				
	TOTAL ASSETS		$532 193.00 ▶				

POST-CLOSING TRIAL BALANCE

FLABULESS FITNESS

March 31, 2012

		Debits	Credits				Debits	Credits
1060	Bank: Hamilton Trust Chequing	$ 77 988.00		▶ 1730	Van		30 000.00	
1080	Bank: Hamilton Trust Savings	108 250.00		1740	Accum Deprec: Van			5 000.00
1120	Bank: Visa and Interac	8 635.00		2100	Bank Loan			50 000.00
1140	Bank: USD Chequing (9 350 USD)	9 500.00		2200	Accounts Payable			16 780.00
1200	Accounts Receivable	17 110.00		2250	Credit Card Payable			220.00
1210	Allowance for Doubtful Accounts		$ 800.00	2300	Vacation Payable			371.84
1220	Advances Receivable	100.00		2310	EI Payable			563.28
1230	Interest Receivable	420.00		2320	CPP Payable			824.77
1260	Office Supplies	300.00		2330	Income Tax Payable			1 755.60
1265	Linen Supplies	450.00		2380	EHT Payable			320.50
1270	Prepaid Advertising	180.00		2400	RRSP Payable			350.00
1280	Prepaid Insurance	4 800.00		2410	CSB Plan Payable			350.00
1520	Accessories	7 180.00		2420	Group Insurance Payable			39.00
1540	Fitness Equipment	65 280.00		2430	Garnisheed Wages Payable			200.00
1560	Books	5 200.00		2460	WSIB Payable			392.51
1610	Cash Registers	5 000.00		2500	Business Income Tax Payable			3 600.00
1620	Accum Deprec: Cash Registers		1 000.00	2650	GST/HST Charged on Sales			6 860.00
1640	Computer Equipment	3 000.00		2670	GST/HST Paid on Purchases		2 990.00	
1650	Accum Deprec: Computer Equipment		1 000.00	2820	Mortgage Payable			180 000.00
1670	Furniture & Fixtures	2 000.00		3560	S. Reeves, Capital			272 555.50
1680	Accum Deprec: Furniture & Fixtures		400.00				$548 383.00	$548 383.00
1700	Retail Premises	200 000.00						
1710	Accum Deprec: Retail Premises		5 000.00 ▶					

SUPPLIER INFORMATION

FLABULESS FITNESS

Supplier Name (Contact)	Address	Phone No. Fax No.	E-mail Web Site	Terms Tax ID	Expense Acct Tax Code
Ancaster Insurance (Feulle Cuvver)	718 Montgomery Dr. Ancaster, ON L9G 3H5	Tel: (905) 588-1773 Fax: (905) 588-1624	fc@ancaster.insur.ca www.ancaster.insur.ca	net 1	no tax (not exempt)
Bell Canada (Noel Coller)	100 James St. N. Hamilton, ON L8R 2K5	Tel: (905) 525-2355	www.bell.ca	net 1	5280 H
Energy Source (Manny Watts)	91 NacNab St. Hamilton, ON L8R 2L9	Tel: (905) 463-2664	watts@energysource.ca www.energysource.ca	net 1	5200 H
Feelyte Gym Accessories (Stretch Theraband)	7 Onondaga Dr. Ancaster, ON L9G 4S5	Tel: (905) 588-3846 Fax: (905) 588-7126	stretch@feelyte.com www.feelyte.com	2/10, n/30 (before tax) 466 254 108	H
Footlink Corporation (Onna Treadmill)	39 Treadwell St. Oakville, ON L6M 3K9	Tel: (905) 777-8133 Fax: (905) 777-8109	onna@footlink.com www.footlink.com	1/15, n/30 (before tax) 274 309 481	H
Minister of Finance (N.O. Money)	631 Queenston Rd. Hamilton, ON L8K 6R5	Tel: (905) 462-5555	www.gov.on.ca/fin	net 1	no tax (exempt)
Mt. Hope Investment Corp. (P. Cuniary)	122 King St. W. Hamilton, ON L8P 4V2	Tel: (905) 462-3338 Fax: (905) 461-2116	pc@mt.hope.invest.ca www.mt.hope.invest.ca	net 15	2410 no tax (exempt)
Prolife Exercisers Inc. (C. Glider) (USD supplier)	1500 Redmond Road Suite 100, Woodinville Washington 98072 USA	Tel: (509) 628-9163 Fax: (509) 629-7164	glider@prolife.ex.com www.prolife.ex.com	2/10, n/30 (before tax)	H
Receiver General for Canada		Tel 1: (800) 561-7761	www.cra-arc.gc.ca	net 1	no tax (exempt)

▶

►

SUPPLIER INFORMATION CONTINUED

Supplier Name (Contact)	Address	Phone No. Fax No.	E-mail Web Site	Terms Tax ID	Expense Acct Tax Code
Redux Home Gym Wholesalers (Bi Sepps) (USD supplier)	4900 Columbia St., #650 El Cerrito, California 94533 USA	Tel 1: (510) 525-4327 Tel 2: (800) 567-9152 Fax: (510) 526-1135	bisepps@redux.com www.redux.com	2/10, n/30 (before tax)	H
Trufit Depot (Varry Shapely)	43 Paling Ave. Hamilton, ON L8H 5J5	Tel: (905) 529-7235 Fax: (905) 529-2995	shapely@trufitdepot.ca www.trufitdepot.ca	2/5, n/30 (before tax) 244 573 650	H
Waterdown Sunoco (Mick Annick)	101 Niska Dr. Waterdown, ON L0R 2H3	Tel: (905) 622-6181 Fax: (905) 622-4777	mick@goodforcars.com www.goodforcars.com	net 1	5285 IN
Workplace Safety & Insurance Board (I.M. Hurt)	PO Box 2099 Hamilton, ON L8N 4C5	Tel: (800) 525-9100 Fax: (905) 523-1824	www.wsib.on.ca	net 1	2460 no tax (exempt)

OUTSTANDING SUPPLIER INVOICES

FLABULESS FITNESS

Supplier Name	Terms	Date	Inv/Chq No.	Amount	Tax	Total
Feelyte Gym Accessories	2/10, n/30 (before tax)	Mar. 30/12	FG-1611	$1 000	$130	$ 1 130
Footlink Corporation	1/15, n/30 (before tax)	Mar. 20/12 Mar. 21/12	FC-618 Chq 96 Balance Owing	$10 000 3 000	$1 300	$11 300 3 000 $ 8 300
Redux Home Gym Wholesalers	2/10, n/30 (before tax)	Mar. 28/12	R-914	$6 400 USD	$832 USD	$ 7 350 CAD
			Grand Total			$16 780

CUSTOMER INFORMATION

FLABULESS FITNESS

Customer Name (Contact)	Address	Phone No. Fax No.	E-mail Web Site	Terms Tax Code	Credit Limit
*Buffalo Health Clinic (Minnie Mussle)	75 Brawn Ave. Buffalo, New York 14202 USA	Tel: (716) 367-7346 Fax: (716) 367-8258	mmussle@buffalohealth.com www.buffalohealth.com Currency: USD	2/10, n/30 no tax	$15 000 ($14 000 USD)
*Chedoke Health Care (Wade Less)	13 Wellspring Dr. Hamilton, ON L8T 3B8	Tel: (905) 526-3344 Fax: (905) 525-1166	less@chedoke.healthcare.ca www.chedoke.healthcare.ca	2/10, n/30 H	$15 000
Lockport Gymnasium (B. Phatt)	62 Sweats St. Niagara Falls, New York 14301 USA	Tel: (716) 399-1489 Fax: (716) 399-2735	phatt@lockportgym.com www.lockportgym.com Currency: USD	2/10, n/30 no tax	$15 000 ($14 000 USD)
*McMaster University (Outov Shape)	Kinesiology Dept. McMaster University Hamilton, ON L8V 3M9	Tel 1: (905) 529-3000 Tel 2: (905) 529-3198 Fax: (905) 529- 3477	oshape@mcmasteru.ca www.mcmasteru.ca	2/10, n/30 H	$15 000
*Mohawk College (Phat Nomore)	Physical Education Dept. Mohawk College Hamilton, ON L8F 7F2	Tel 1: (905) 622-9250 Tel 2: (905) 622-9238 Fax: (905) 622-9729	nomore@mohawkcoll.ca www.mohawkcoll.ca	2/10, n/30 H	$15 000
Stoney Creek Sports Arena (B. Thin)	93 Workout Rd. Stoney Creek, ON L7M 5C7	Tel: (905) 838-1800 Fax: (905) 838-1278	bthin@scsa.com www.scsa.com	2/10, n/30 H	$15 000
Cash and Interac Customers	Terms: net 1	Tax code: H			
Visa Sales (for Visa customers)	Terms: net 1	Tax code: H			

NOTES: Preferred price list customers are marked with an asterisk (*). The ship-to address is the same as the mailing address for all customers.

OUTSTANDING CUSTOMER INVOICES

FLABULESS FITNESS

Customer Name	Terms	Date	Inv/Chq No.	Amount	Total
Chedoke Health Care	2/10, n/30 (after tax)	Mar. 30/12	2199	$9 040	
		Mar. 30/12	Chq 488	2 100	
			Balance Owing		$6 940
Mohawk College	2/10, n/30 (after tax)	Mar. 26/12	2194	$5 650	$5 650
Stoney Creek Sports Arena	2/10, n/30 (after tax)	Mar. 23/12	2191	$4 520	$4 520
				Grand Total	$17 110

EMPLOYEE INFORMATION SHEET

FLABULESS FITNESS

Employee	George Schwinn	Nieve Prekor	Assumpta Kisangel
Position	Shipping/Trainer	Sales/Yoga Instructor	Sales/Accounting
Address	55 Carter St. Hamilton, ON L8B 2V7	2 Meditation Circle Hamilton, ON L8B 7C1	300 Track Rd. Hamilton, ON L9G 4K8
Telephone	(905) 426-1817	(905) 527-4412	(905) 688-5778
Social Insurance No.	532 548 625	783 455 611	488 655 333
Date of Birth (mm-dd-yy)	09/18/70	03/15/73	05/24/76
Date of Hire (mm-dd-yy)	01/06/04	02/15/01	08/25/04
Federal (Ontario) Tax Exemption - TD1			
Basic Personal	$10 382 (8 943)	$10 382 (8 943)	$10 302 (8 943)
Spousal	–	–	$10 382 (7 594)
Other	–	–	$4 223 (4 216)
Total Exemptions	$10 382 (8 943)	$10 382 (8 943)	$24 987 (20 753)
Additional Federal Tax	–	$50.00	–
Employee Taxes			
Historical Income tax	$1 562.21	$2 392.08	$1 537.85
Historical EI	$217.54	$270.00	$248.96
Historical CPP	$375.20	$478.38	$438.16
Deduct EI; EI Factor	Yes; 1.4	Yes; 1.4	Yes; 1.4
Deduct CPP	Yes	Yes	Yes
Employee Income			
Advances: Historical Amount	$100.00	(use) ✓	(use) ✓
Benefits Per Period	$5.00	$12.00	$12.00
Benefits: Historical Amount	$35.00	$36.00	$36.00
Vacation Pay Owed	$371.84	(do not use)	(do not use)
Vacation Paid	$385.92	(do not use)	(do not use)
Regular Wage Rate (Hours per Period)	$16.00/hr (80 hours)	(do not use)	(do not use)
Regular Wages: Historical Amount	$8 960.00	(do not use)	(do not use)
Overtime 1 Wage Rate	$24.00/hr	(do not use)	(do not use)
Overtime 1 Wages: Historical Amount	$336.00	(do not use)	(do not use)
Salary (Hours Per Period)	(do not use)	$4 000.00 (150 Hours)	$3 600.00 (150 hours)
Salary: Historical Amount	(do not use)	$12 000.00	$10 800.00
Commission	(do not use)	(do not use)	(use) ✓ 2% (service revenue)
Commissions: Historical Amount	(do not use)	(do not use)	$285.00
No. Clients (piece rate)	$10	$10	$10
Bonus:	(use) ✓	(use) ✓	(use) ✓

▶

EMPLOYEE INFORMATION CONTINUED			
Employee	George Schwinn	Nieve Prekor	Assumpta Kisangel
Employee Income continued			
Tuition: Historical Amount	(use) ✓	(use) ✓	$440
Travel Exp.: Historical Amount	(use) ✓	$120.00	(use) ✓
Pay Periods	26	12	12
Vacation Rate	6% retained	0% not retained	0% not retained
Record Wage Expenses in	Linked Accounts	Linked Accounts	Linked Accounts
Deductions			
RRSP (Historical Amount)	$50.00 ($350.00)	$100.00 ($300.00)	$100.00 ($300.00)
CSB Plan (Historical Amount)	$50.00 ($350.00)	$100.00 ($300.00)	$100.00 ($300.00)
Garnishee (Historical Amount)	(do not use)	$200.00 ($400.00)	(do not use)
WSIB and Other Expenses			
WSIB Rate	1.29	1.29	1.02
Group Insurance (Historical Amount)	$5.00 ($35.00)	$12.00 ($36.00)	$12.00 ($36.00)
Entitlements: Rate, Maximum Days, Clear? (Historical Amount)			
Vacation	–	8%, 25 days, No (15)	8%, 25 days, No (15)
Sick Leave	5%, 15 days, No (12)	5%, 15 days, No (10)	5%, 15 days, No (8)
Personal Days	2.5%, 5 days, No (4)	2.5%, 5 days, No (2)	2.5%, 5 days, No (3)
Direct Deposit			
Yes/No	Yes	Yes	Yes
Bank, Transit, Account No.	102, 89008, 2998187	102, 89008, 3829110	102, 89008, 2309982
Percent	100%	100%	100%
Additional Information			
Emergency Contact & Number	Adrian Ingles (905) 722-0301	Alex Prekor (905) 548-2973	Martha Kisangel (905) 688-5778
T4 and RL-1 Reporting			
EI Insurable Earnings	$9 681.92	$12 000.00	$11 085.00
Pensionable Earnings	$9 716.92	$12 036.00	$11 561.00
Withheld	$2 854.95	$4 140.46	$2 824.97
Net Pay	$6 926.97	$7 979.54	$8 700.03

Employee Profiles and TD1 Information

All Employees   Flabuless Fitness pays group insurance premiums for all employees. They also are reimbursed for tuition fees when they successfully complete a university or college course. These two benefits are taxable. In addition, when they use their personal vehicles for company business, they are reimbursed for car expenses.

All employees are entitled to three weeks' vacation, ten days' sick leave and five personal days of leave per year. All three employees have sick leave and personal days that they can carry forward from the previous year. The two salaried employees take three weeks' vacation as paid time and the hourly employee receives 6 percent of his wages as vacation pay when he takes his vacation.

Starting in April, as an incentive to provide excellent customer service, all employees will receive a quarterly bonus of $10 for every completed satisfactory customer survey.

George Schwinn   is responsible for shipping, receiving, delivery and equipment setup for customers. He also works as the personal trainer in the store. He is single, so he uses only the basic tax claim amount. Every two weeks his pay, at the rate of $16 per hour, is deposited to his account. For the hours beyond 40 hours in a week, he receives an overtime rate of $24 per hour. He is owed two months of vacation pay. He contributes to his RRSP and Canada Savings Bond plan through payroll deductions. He still owes $100 from an advance of $200 for which he will pay back $50 in each of the next two pay periods.

Nieve Prekor is the store manager and yoga instructor for Flabuless Fitness, and she assists with store sales. Her monthly salary of $4 000 is deposited directly into her bank account. Prekor is married with one child but uses the basic single claim amount because her husband is also employed. Her payroll deductions include additional federal income tax for other income, wages garnisheed to pay for prior taxes owing and regular contributions to her Registered Retirement Savings Plan and Canada Savings Bonds.

Assumpta Kisangel does the accounting and manages the Payables, Receivables and Payroll in addition to sales in the store. Although she is single, she supports her infirm mother so she has the spousal equivalent claim and a caregiver amount in addition to the basic single claim amount. A commission of 2 percent of revenue from services supplements her monthly salary of $3 600 that is deposited directly into her bank account. She has RRSP and CSB contributions withheld from her paycheques.

NOTES
Wages may be garnisheed by any creditor, but the most common one is the Receiver General to pay back-taxes owing.

INVENTORY INFORMATION

FLABULESS FITNESS

Code	Description	Min Stock	CAD Prices Reg (Pref)		USD Prices Reg. (Pref)		Stock/Sell Unit	Buying Unit	Relationship	Qty on Hand	Total (Cost)
Accessories: Total asset value $7 180 (Linked Accounts: Asset 1520; Revenue 4020, COGS 5050, Variance 5070)											
A010	Body Fat Scale	2	$ 150	($ 130)	$ 145	($ 135)	unit	carton	12/carton	20	$1 100
A020	Yoga Mats	3	40	(35)	36	(32)	unit	box	10/box	60	900
A030	Dumbbells	25	2.50	(2.20)	2.25	(2.00)	kg	100kg	100/100kg	600	540
A040	Glide Slidetrak	3	90	(00)	85	(80)	each		same	20	900
A050	Heart Rate Monitor	2	90	(80)	85	(80)	unit	carton	12/carton	20	600
A060	Power Blocks	3	200	(180)	190	(180)	set		same	15	1 500
A070	Stability Balls	5	12	(10)	10	(9)	each		same	30	180
A080	Wavemaster	2	180	(165)	170	(155)	unit		same	10	950
A090	Weight Plates	25	1.50	(1.30)	1.40	(1.30)	kg	100kg	100/100kg	500	300
A100	Workout Gloves: all sizes	5	15	(13)	13	(12)	pair	box	10/box	35	210
Books: Total asset value $5 200 (Linked Accounts: Asset 1560; Revenue 4020, COGS 5050, Variance 5070) HST exempt, charge GST only											
B010	Books: Fitness Guide	2	40	(35)	35	(30)	each		same	208	5 200
Fitness Equipment: Total asset value $65 280 (Linked Accounts: Asset 1540, Revenue 4020, COGS 5060, Variance 5070)											
E010	Elliptical Exerciser: AE-200	2	2 100	(1 900)	2 000	(1 800)	unit		same	6	6 600
E020	Elliptical Exerciser: LE-400	2	2 600	(2 300)	2 500	(2 300)	unit		same	6	7 200
E030	Bicycle: Dual Action Calorie Counter	2	700	(640)	650	(600)	unit		same	12	3 600
E040	Bicycle: Recumbent R-80	2	950	(820)	900	(800)	unit		same	12	6 000
E050	Home Gym: Basic HG-1400	2	1 300	(1 150)	1 200	(1 050)	set		same	6	$3 600
E060	Home Gym: Deluxe Multi HG-1402	2	2 400	(2 100)	2 300	(2 100)	set		same	6	6 600
E070	Rowing Machine: RM-1000	3	560	(490)	520	(470)	unit		same	8	1 680
E080	Ski Exerciser: Independent SE-880	3	710	(650)	650	(590)	unit		same	12	3 600
E090	Stair Climber: Adjustable SC-A60	2	1 900	(1 700)	1 800	(1 600)	unit		same	6	4 800
E100	Treadmill: Basic T-800B	3	1 400	(1 220)	1 350	(1 200)	unit		same	12	7 200
E110	Treadmill: Deluxe T-1100D	3	2 800	(2 500)	2 700	(2 500)	unit		same	12	14 400

NOTES: No duty is charged on items imported from the United States. The duty rate is 0%.
Stocking and selling units are the same for all items.
Buying units and the relationship to stocking units are entered only when these are different from the stocking/selling units.
"Same" is entered in the relationship column when the same unit is used for all measures.

▶

▶

		CAD Prices			
Code	Description	Reg	(Pref)	Unit	Taxes

INVENTORY INFORMATION CONTINUED

Services (Linked Accounts: Revenue 4040, COGS 5065)

Code	Description	Reg	(Pref)	Unit	Taxes
S010	Personal Trainer: 1 hour	75	(70)	hour	HST (not exempt)
S020	Personal Trainer: 1/2 day	200	(190)	1/2 day	HST (not exempt)
S030	Personal Trainer: full day	400	(380)	day	HST (not exempt)
S040	Yoga Instructor: 1 hour	100	(95)	hour	HST (not exempt)
S050	Yoga Instructor: 1/2 day	200	(190)	1/2 day	HST (not exempt)

Accounting Procedures

Harmonized Sales Taxes: HST, GST and PST

HST at the rate of 13 percent is applied to all goods and services offered by Flabuless Fitness, except books. The Harmonized Sales Tax includes the provincial sales tax of 8 percent. Goods that are exempt for PST, such as books, have a different tax code applied (code G - GST @ 5%) so that the tax will be calculated correctly.

Flabuless Fitness uses the regular method for remittance of the Harmonized Sales Tax. HST and GST collected from customers are recorded as liabilities in *GST/HST Charged on Sales*. HST and GST paid to suppliers are recorded in *GST/HST Paid on Purchases* as a decrease in liability to Canada Revenue Agency (CRA). These two postable accounts are added together in the subgroup total account *GST/HST Owing (Refund)* because a single return is remitted for both taxes. The balance of HST and GST to be remitted or the request for a refund is sent to the Receiver General for Canada by the last day of the current month for the previous month.

Tax calculations will be correct only for customers and suppliers for whom the tax exempt option was set as No. The and GST and HST Reports available from the Reports menu will include transactions completed in the Sales, Purchases and General journals, but the opening historical balances will not be included. Therefore, the amounts shown in the tax reports may differ from the balances in the General Ledger accounts. You should use the General Ledger accounts to verify the balance owing (or refund due) and make adjustments to the report manually as necessary.

After the report is filed, clear the HST and GST Reports up to the last day of the previous month. Always back up your files before clearing the tax details.

The Employer Health Tax (EHT)

The Employer Health Tax (EHT) is paid by employers in Ontario to provide Ontario Health Insurance Plan (OHIP) coverage for all eligible Ontario residents. The EHT is based on the total annual remuneration paid to employees. Employers whose total payroll exceeds $400 000 must pay EHT. Although the payroll for Flabuless Fitness is less than this amount, we show the application of EHT so that you can learn how to set up the expense and make the remittances. In this application, EHT will be remitted quarterly. *EHT Payable* is set up as a liability owing to the supplier, Minister of Finance. The Remittance Payments Journal will provide you with the balance owing to the Minister of Finance when the liability is linked to this supplier.

Aging of Accounts

Flabuless Fitness uses aging periods that reflect the payment terms it provides to customers and receives from suppliers. For customers, this will be 10, 30 and 60 days, and for suppliers, 15, 30 and 60 days. Interest at 1.5 percent is charged on customer

accounts that are not paid within 30 days. Regular customer statements show interest amounts, and invoices are then prepared to add the interest to the amount owing in the ledger record.

Discounts

Flabuless Fitness offers a 2 percent discount to regular account customers if they settle their accounts within 10 days. Full payment is requested within 30 days. These payment terms are set up as defaults. When the receipt is entered and the discount is still available, the program shows the amount of the discount and the net amount owing. No discounts are given on cash or credit card sales. Customer discounts are calculated on after-tax amounts.

Some customers receive preferred customer prices that are approximately 10 percent below the regular prices. These customers are identified in the ledger records and the preferred prices are set up in the inventory ledger records.

Some suppliers also offer discounts for early settlement of accounts. Again, when the terms are entered for the supplier and payment is made before the discount period expires, the program displays the discount as available and automatically calculates a net balance owing. Payment terms vary from supplier to supplier. Most supplier discounts are calculated on before-tax amounts but some are based on after-tax amounts.

NOTES
Daily Business Manager lists are helpful for making sure that you take advantage of available discounts.

Freight

When a business purchases inventory items, the cost of any freight that cannot be directly allocated to a specific item must be charged to *Freight Expense* — a general expense that is not charged to the costs of any inventory asset account. Customers also pay for delivery and setup. HST is charged on freight for both sales and purchases (tax code H).

Bank Deposits

Deposit slips are prepared weekly when cash and cheques are received. Receipts are debited to *Undeposited Cash and Cheques* and transferred weekly to *Bank: Hamilton Trust Chequing*.

Imported Inventory

Some inventory items are imported from the United States. The bank accounts, supplier records and inventory records are modified to accommodate the foreign currency transactions and import duties automatically.

NOTES
Although import duties are not charged on the items imported by Flabuless Fitness from the United States, we show the setup of import duties and set the rates at zero so that no tax will be charged.

Business Income Tax

Flabuless Fitness pays income tax in quarterly instalments to the Receiver General based on its previous year's net income.

Purchase Returns and Allowances

A business will sometimes return inventory items to suppliers because of damage, poor quality or shipment of the wrong items. Usually a business records these returns after it receives a credit note from a supplier. The return of inventory is entered in the Purchases Journal as an inventory purchase:

- Select the item in the Item field and enter the quantity returned as a **negative** amount in the Quantity field. The program will automatically calculate a negative amount as a default in the Amount field. You cannot change the account number.
- Accept the default amount and enter other items returned to the supplier.
- Enter the appropriate tax code for each item returned.

NOTES
Purchases Returns & Allowances is a contra-expense account with a credit balance. The return creates a credit entry that will reduce total expenses.

NOTES
The sales tax rules for credits, allowances and discounts are complex. They may be different for provincial and federal taxes and they may differ from one province to another. Adjusting General Journal entries may be required to adjust the amount of tax owing and calculate the tax remittance. We have chosen to leave out the tax component for transactions of this type. Refer to Chapter 2 for more information about sales taxes.

NOTES
Sales Returns & Allowances is a contra-revenue account with a debit balance. The sales return creates a debit entry that will reduce total revenue.

NOTES
The Sales Journal entry will credit the bank account and debit Accounts Receivable.

The program will create a negative invoice to reduce the balance owing to the supplier and will reduce the applicable inventory asset accounts, the freight accounts, *GST/HST Paid on Purchases* and the quantity of items in the Inventory Ledger database.

Purchase allowances for damaged merchandise that is not returned are entered as non-inventory negative purchase invoices. Enter the amount of the allowance as a **negative** amount in the Amount field and leave the tax fields blank (i.e., treat it as non-taxable). Enter *Purchases Returns & Allowances* in the Account field.

Sales Returns and Allowances

Sometimes customers will return inventory items. Usually, a business records the return after it has issued a credit note. The return is entered in the Sales Journal as a negative inventory sale for the customer:

* Select the appropriate item in the Item field.
* Enter the quantity returned with a **negative** number in the Quantity field.
* The price of the item appears as a positive number in the Price field, and the Amount field is calculated automatically as a negative amount that should be correct. If it is not, you can change it.
* Enter the tax code for the sale and the account number for *Sales Returns & Allowances*.

The program will create a negative invoice to reduce the balance owing by the customer, and *Cost of Goods Sold* and *GST/HST Charged on Sales*. The applicable inventory asset accounts and the quantity of items in the Inventory Ledger database will be increased.

Sales allowances are entered as non-taxable, non-inventory negative sales invoices, creating a debit entry for *Sales Returns & Allowances* and a credit for *Accounts Receivable*. If the allowance is paid by cheque, enter the allowance in the Payments Journal as an Other Payment paid by cheque.

NSF Cheques

If a cheque is deposited from an account that does not have enough money to cover it, the bank returns it to the depositor as NSF (non-sufficient funds). If the cheque was in payment for a cash sale, you must process the NSF cheque through the Sales Journal because there was no Receipts Journal entry. Create a customer record if necessary and enter a positive amount for the amount of the cheque. Choose *Bank: Hamilton Trust Chequing* as the account. Choose Pay Later as the method of payment. If the customer is expected to pay the bank charges, enter these on the second invoice line as a positive amount and select the appropriate revenue account.

If the NSF cheque was deposited to a different account than the one used in the Receipts Journal, create a negative receipt to reverse the cheque. Choose Include Fully Paid Invoices. Click the invoice line that this cheque was applied to. Enter the discount taken as a negative amount. Enter the Payment Amount as a negative amount. Choose the correct bank account from the Deposit To field. Refer to page 601 and Appendix C.

Adjustments for Bad Debt

Most businesses set up an allowance for doubtful accounts or bad debts, knowing that some customers will fail to pay. The amount entered for this will be a reasonable guess at how much of the *Accounts Receivable* amount will never be collected. When the allowance is set up, a bad debts or uncollectable accounts expense account is debited and the allowance is credited (effectively reducing the net receivables balance). When a business is certain that a customer will not pay its account, the debt should be written off by crediting *Accounts Receivable* and debiting *Allowance for Doubtful Accounts*. When taxes apply, an extra step is required. Part of the original sales invoice was entered as a credit (increase) to *GST/HST Charged on Sales*. By entering the full amount and the code IN for taxes included, the GST/HST payable amount will automatically be correctly reduced. In Simply Accounting, record the write-off of the debt in the Sales Journal using the following steps:

- Select the customer whose debt will not be paid.
- Enter a source document number to identify the transaction (e.g., memo).
- Enter a **negative** amount for the total unpaid invoice in the Amount field.
- Enter *Allowance for Doubtful Accounts* in the Account field.
- Enter the tax code **IN** (taxes included).

If the customer was also charged for the NSF fees, enter this information on the next invoice line:

- Enter a **negative** amount for the total NSF charge in the Amount field.
- Enter *Allowance for Doubtful Accounts* in the Account field.
- Enter the tax code **No tax**.

Review the transaction. *Accounts Receivable* is credited (reduced) by the full amount of the invoice to remove the balance owing by this customer. *Allowance for Doubtful Accounts* has been debited (reduced) by the amount of the invoice minus taxes. *GST/HST Charged on Sales* has been debited for the tax portion of the invoice to reduce the tax liability.

After recording the write-off, "pay" both the original invoice and the write-off in the Receipts Journal. The balance will be zero and there will be no journal entry. This step removes the items from the Receipts Journal for the customer so that you can clear the paid transactions and later remove the customer's record.

Manually you would complete the entry as follows:

---

1. Set up the Allowance for Bad Debts.

Date	Particulars	Debit	Credit
04/01	5270 Uncollectable Accounts Expense	1 000.00	
	1210 Allowance for Doubtful Accounts		1 000.00

2. Customer G. Bell declares bankruptcy. Write off outstanding balance, $226, including HST.

Date	Particulars	Debit	Credit
04/30	1210 Allowance for Doubtful Accounts	200.00	
	2650 GST/HST Charged on Sales	26.00	
	1200 Accounts Receivable, G. Bell		226.00

Occasionally, a bad debt is recovered after it has been written off. When this occurs, the above procedure is reversed and the GST/HST liability must also be restored. The recovery is entered as a non-inventory sale in the Sales Journal as follows:

- Select the customer and enter the date and source document number.
- Type an appropriate comment such as "Debt recovered" in the Item Description field.
- Enter a **positive** amount for the total invoice amount in the Amount field.
- Enter the tax code **IN** (taxes included).
- Enter *Allowance for Doubtful Accounts* in the Account field.

Review the transaction. You will see that *Accounts Receivable* has been debited for the full amount of the invoice. *Allowance for Doubtful Accounts* has been credited for the amount of the invoice minus taxes. *GST/HST Charged on Sales* has been credited for the tax portion of the invoice to restore the tax liability.

As the final step, record the customer's payment in the Receipts Journal as you would record any other customer payment.

NOTES
Allowance for Doubtful Accounts is a contra-asset account that normally has a credit balance. Therefore, a debit entry from the negative amount will reduce this credit balance, reducing both the allowance and the Accounts Receivable balances.

NOTES
You would follow these steps when only part of the bad debt amount is recovered.

NOTES

In practice, a business would make these four federal tax remittances to different federal offices. Separate supplier accounts would be needed for each remittance. For this application, one supplier account and address has been used for the Receiver General to reduce the length of the supplier list.

Remittances

The Receiver General for Canada:
- Monthly EI, CPP and income tax deductions withheld from employees must be paid by the 15th of each month for the previous month.
- Monthly GST/HST owing or requests for refunds must be filed by the end of each month for the previous month.
- Business income tax is paid in quarterly instalments.
- Garnisheed wages are submitted by the 15th of each month for the previous month. A separate cheque is issued for this remittance.

The Minister of Finance:
- Quarterly Employer Health Tax (EHT) deductions must be paid by the 15th of April, July, October and January for the previous quarter.

Ancaster Insurance:
- Monthly Registered Retirement Savings Plan (RRSP) deductions withheld from employees must be paid by the 15th of the month for the previous month.
- Group insurance contributions paid by the employer must be paid by the 15th of the month for the previous month.

The Mt. Hope Investment Corporation:
- Monthly Canada Savings Bond Plan (CSB Plan) deductions withheld from employees must be paid by the 15th of the month for the previous month.

The Workplace Safety and Insurance Board:
- Quarterly Workplace Safety and Insurance Board (WSIB) assessment for employees must be paid by the 15th of the month for the previous quarter.

SUPPLEMENTARY DATA FILES FOR FLABULESS FITNESS

Detailed keystroke instructions are included for you to set up the Flabuless Fitness application files. However, the Student DVD also includes files so that you can complete segments of the application rather than having to work through it entirely. Each file stands alone so you can work through any month at your discretion.

To Enter	For (Period Covered)	Use (Backup File Name on Data CD)
Transactions:	April 1–April 30	setup\flab-apr1.cab
Transactions:	May 1–May 31	setup\flab-may1.cab
Transactions:	June 1–June 30	setup\flab-jun1.cab

INSTRUCTIONS FOR SETUP

Set up the **company accounts** in Simply Accounting using the Business Information, Chart of Accounts, Balance Sheet, Income Statement, Post-Closing Trial Balance and Supplier, Customer, Employee and Inventory Information provided above for March 31, 2012. Instructions to assist you in setting up the company accounts follow. The setup of the Inventory Ledger is given in detail. Abbreviated instructions are included for the remaining steps. Refer to the Toss for Tots (Chapter 4), Dorfmann Design (Chapter 7) and Lime Light Laundry (Chapter 9) applications if you need more detailed explanations for other ledgers. Page references for the coverage of these topics in earlier chapters are included in this chapter.

KEYSTROKES FOR SETUP

Creating Company Files

We will create the company files from scratch. Once we create the files and define the defaults, we will add the accounts, define linked accounts for all ledgers, set up additional features, create supplier, customer, employee and inventory records and add historical data.

Save your work and update your backup file frequently as you work through the setup.

Start   the **Simply Accounting program**. You should see the Select Company window.

Click   **Create A New Company**.

Click   **OK**. You will see the Setup wizard welcome screen.

Click   **Next** to open the Company Name and Address screen. The cursor is in the Name field.

Type   Flabuless Fitness (and your own name)   **Press** (tab) to advance to the Street 1 address field.

Type   199 Warmup Rd. **Press** (tab).

Type   Unit 500 **Press** (tab).

Type   Hamilton **Press** (tab).

Type   o to enter the province code (ON) and province (Ontario).

Click   the Postal Code field.

Type   18t3b7 **Press** (tab).

Type   Canada **Press** (tab).

Type   9056422348 **Press** (tab) to enter the first phone number.

Type   8004482348 **Press** (tab) to enter the second phone number.

Type   9056429100 to enter the fax number.

Click   **Next** to open the company Dates window.

The cursor is in the Fiscal Year Start field, the date on which the business begins its fiscal year. Flabuless Fitness closes its books quarterly and is beginning a new quarter in April. To be certain that you have the correct year, type the date in text style using four digits for the year. Until we change the date format, it is displayed in the short form.

Enter   the **fiscal dates** as follows:

- Fiscal Start: April 1, 2012
- Earliest Transaction date: April 1, 2012
- Fiscal End: June 30, 2012

Remember that you can edit the company information and fiscal dates later from the Setup menu, Settings option (choose Company and Information). If you later change the province, you may have to change some settings linked to the province selection.

Click   **Next**.

NOTES
Refer to page 210 for detailed instructions on creating company files.

NOTES
You cannot complete the company setup in multi-user mode. Many of the settings options are dimmed and unavailable when you are working in multi-user mode.

NOTES
Add your own name to the company name to personalize your data files.

NOTES
Because we select Ontario as the province, some defaults will be added to the data file. WCB will be renamed WSIB.

NOTES
The default date format for new companies is determined by your own computer system settings and is displayed below the date fields. This may be day, month, year or month, day, year. Entering the dates as text will result in correct fiscal dates.

Click   **Let Me Build The List Of Accounts Myself.... Click Next**.

Click   **Yes** to confirm your selection and continue to the industry type list.

Choose   **Retail** as the Industry for the business. **Click Next**.

Type   flabless to replace the default entry for the file name.

Drag through Tess in the folder name field (or the folder you last worked with).

Type   Flabless\

If you are using an alternative location for your company files, substitute the appropriate path, folder or drive in the example.

Click Browse to locate the folder you want or type the complete path in the File Location field (e.g., Type c:\SimData10\Flabless\).

Click   **Next**.

Click   **Yes** to confirm that you are creating a new folder.

Click   **Finish** to save the information. **Be patient**, and wait for Simply Accounting to finish creating the data files.

Click   **Close** to close the Setup wizard screen.

Click   **Show This Window On Startup** and **Close** to close the Welcome window.

The Home window has the name Flabless in the title bar and non-accounting term labels for the modules in the Modules pane list. The program will automatically set up defaults based on the information you have just entered.

Preparing the System

The next step involves changing the defaults. Change the defaults to suit your own work environment, such as selecting your printer or choosing forms for cheques, invoices or statements. The keystroke instructions are given for computer-generated cheques, invoices and statements. Refer to the Business Information Chart on page 616 for the company default settings.

Changing the User Preference Settings

You should make the following changes to the User Preferences from the Setup menu. Refer to Chapter 4, page 82, for assistance if necessary.

Choose   the **Setup menu** and **click User Preferences** to open the Options screen.

Click   **Use Accounting Terms** and **Automatically Save Changes To Supplier...**.

You can show Home window ledger record balances by the session date or the latest transaction date, and automatically recalculate these balances or refresh them manually when you want. Make the selections you prefer for your own use.

Click   **View**.

Click   **After Changing Session Date** for **Daily Business Manager** and for **Checklists** to turn off these features and remove the ✓s.

Click   **Show Change Session Date At Startup**.

Click   **Division** in the **Pages column** to hide the module.

Click   Time & Billing in the **Features column** to hide the module.

You do not need to hide Division and Time & Billing to finish the history because they have no linked accounts. The Transaction Confirmation Message should be selected by default.

Click   OK to save the settings and return to the Home window.

Notice that modules now have accounting term names after changing these settings. The user preference settings can be modified at any time by repeating these steps.

Changing Company Defaults

Correcting Company Information

The first steps in setting up the company data files apply to the Company module. We will work from that window.

Click OK at any time to save the settings and close the Settings window. To continue later, you can use the Settings icon to access Settings.

Click   Company in the Modules pane list to change the Home window.

Click   the Settings icon ![Settings], or **choose** the Setup menu and **click Settings**.

Click   Information.

Click   the Business No. field. Type 245 138 121 RT0001

Changing System Settings

Click   System. Use the following System settings:

- Use Cheque No. As The Source Code For Cash Purchases And Sales
- Do Not Allow Transactions Dated Before April 1, 2012
- Allow Transactions In The Future (Beyond The Session Date)
- Warn If Transactions Are More Than 7 Days In The Future
- Warn If Accounts Are Not Balanced When Entering A New Month

Changing Backup Settings

Click   Backup. Use the following Backup settings:

- Semi-monthly Backup Frequency
- Display a Backup Reminder When Closing This Company

Click   Automatically Back Up This File to remove the ✓. We do not want to schedule automatic backups for instructional files.

Changing Features Settings

Flabuless uses all features of the program except Divisions — orders, quotes and language options should be selected. Division and Packing Slips may be left unselected.

Click   Features.

Click   each feature to change its setting.

Changing Default Settings for Forms

Click   Forms to display the defaults.

CLASSIC VIEW
Division and Time & Billing are both included in the Module column.

WARNING!
Do not skip any ledger icon windows before completing the setup.

CLASSIC VIEW
You can right-click any Home window icon, and then click the Setup tool to open a Settings window. Click Company and then click Information.
If you select a journal, you will open the Linked Accounts window for the ledger. If you click a ledger icon, you will open the Settings window for the ledger.

NOTES
If you chose to hide the Division module, Division will not appear in the Features Settings window.

NOTES
Credit Cards, Sales Taxes and Currency settings require linked accounts, so we will set them after creating accounts.

Use the Forms options to set up the automatic numbering and printing of all cheques and invoices. They apply only to numerical invoices.

If you want to use automatic invoice numbering, type the next number from the source documents so the automatic numbering system can take over from the manual system. Using automatic numbering reduces the risk of typing and recording an incorrect invoice or cheque number even when you are not printing cheques and invoices through the program. For Flabuless Fitness, the next invoice is #3000.

> **Click**   1 in the **Invoices Next Form Number field**. **Type**   3000
>
> **Click**   the **Sales Quotes Next Form Number field**. **Type**   41
>
> **Click**   the **Receipts Next Form Number field**. **Type**   39
>
> **Click**   the **Customer Deposits Next Form Number field**. **Type**   15
>
> **Click**   the **Purchase Orders Next Form Number field**. **Type**   25
>
> **Click**   the **Direct Deposit Stubs Next Form Number field**. **Type**   19

Leave selected the option to verify number sequences for all forms so that the program will warn you if you skip or duplicate a number.

Click a check box to add other features or to turn off an option once it is selected. The ✓ in the appropriate boxes indicates a feature is being used.

The option to Confirm Printing/E-mail will warn you to print before posting a transaction. When printing invoices, statements or cheques, you should include the company address, unless it is already printed on your forms.

If you print or e-mail invoices and cheques through the computer, you should turn on the option to Confirm Printing/E-mail.

We want to allow batch printing, printing several forms at once after posting instead of one at a time while entering a transaction.

> **Click**   the **Print In Batches check box** for each form to add a ✓ to each box.

We should also check for duplicate numbers. This control is not selected by default.

> **Click**   the **Check For Duplicates check box for Invoices and Receipts**.

Changing Date Format Settings

> **Click**   **Date Format**.

We want to use the long date form for all dates on the screen to verify that we are entering dates correctly. For the reports, you may use either the long or short form. MM (month) should be the first entry in the Short Date Format field.

> **Choose**   **MM-dd-yyyy** from the Short Date drop-down list.
>
> **Click**   **Long Dates** as the setting for On The Screen, Use.

Adding the Company Logo

> **Click**   **Logo**. **Click Browse**. **Click Computer** in the Favorite Links section.
>
> **Double click**   **C:**. Then **double click SimData10** to open this folder.
>
> **Double click**   the **Setup folder** and **double click** the **Logos folder**.
>
> **Double click**   **Flab.bmp** to enter this file name. The logo should be added to the Logos Settings screen.

NOTES
Many invoices include the alpha or letter portion of the invoice number on the preprinted invoice form. You could then enter the next number from the numeric portion in the Invoices Number field. Alphanumeric invoice numbers, such as FF-399, cannot be increased automatically by the computer.

NOTES
If you hide Time & Billing, the next number for time slips will not be included on the Forms screen. You can leave the field blank if you are not hiding the feature.

WARNING!
Check that the short date format begins with month (MM).

NOTES
The Forms folder in your Simply Accounting Program folder is the default location when you click Browse.

Changing Default Names

Flabuless uses the additional information fields in journals. You can label these fields. However, you must use the same names for all journals. We will therefore enter a generic label for the Additional Information Field.

Click   Names:

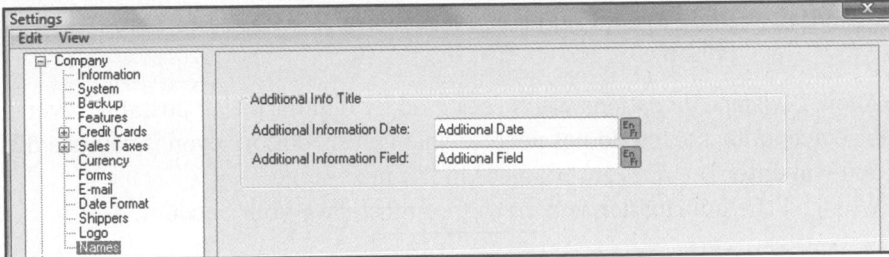

Drag through `Additional Field`.

Type   `Ref. Number`

Click   OK to save the new information and return to the Home window.

Many of the other settings require linked accounts. Therefore, we will create all the General Ledger accounts before entering the remaining settings.

Preparing the General Ledger

The next stage in setting up an accounting system involves preparing the General Ledger for operation. This stage involves

1. organizing all accounting reports and records (this step has been completed)
2. creating new accounts and adding opening balances
3. printing reports to check the accuracy of your records

Creating New Accounts

The next step is to create the accounts, including the non-postable accounts. Remember to enter the correct type of account. For postable accounts you should also indicate whether you want to omit accounts with zero balances from financial statements. You need to refer to the company Chart of Accounts on page 617 to complete this step. When we create the accounts, we will keep the Accounts window open in the background for reference.

Current Earnings is the only predefined account, and you do not need to edit it.

Refer to Format of Financial Statements (page 87) for a review of these topics if needed. Refer to the instructions in the Toss for Tots application, page 93, if you need help with creating accounts.

Click   the **Chart of Accounts icon** 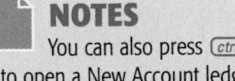 to open the Accounts window.

Click   ▣ to maximize the Accounts window.

If the accounts are not displayed by name or by type, you should change the view. Click the Display By Type tool or choose the View menu and click Type.

Click   the **Create tool** ▤ in the Accounts window tool bar or **choose** the **File menu** and **click Create**.

Drag the Ledger window to a screen position so that both the Accounts and the Ledger windows are visible. This will make it easier to monitor your progress.

Type the **account number**. Press (tab) and **type** the **account name**.

Click the correct **account type**. Remember subgroup accounts (A) must be followed by a subgroup total (S).

Click **Omit From Financial Statements If Balance Is Zero** to select this option.

Allow Division Allocations will be selected by default for all postable revenue and expense accounts, so you do not need to change this option, even if you use divisions. You will enter the account balances in the next stage.

When all the information is correct, you must save your account.

Click **Create Another** [Create Another] to save the new account and advance to a blank ledger account window.

Create the **other accounts** by repeating these procedures.

Close the **General Ledger window** when you have entered all the accounts on page 617, or when you want to end your session.

After entering all the accounts, you should check for mistakes in account number, name, type and order.

Click [✓] or **choose** the **File menu** and **click Check The Validity Of Accounts** to check for errors in account sequence such as missing subgroup totals, headings or totals. The first error is reported.

Correct the **error** and **check** the **validity** again. Repeat this step until the accounts are in logical order.

Display or **print** your updated **Chart of Accounts** at this stage to check for accuracy of account names and numbers. **Choose** the **Reports menu** and **click Display Chart of Accounts**. Compare the report with the chart on page 617 and make corrections as needed.

Entering Historical Account Balances

The opening historical balances for Flabuless Fitness can be found in the Post-Closing Trial Balance dated March 31, 2012 (page 619). All Income Statement accounts have zero balances because the books were closed at the end of the first quarter. Headings, totals and subgroup totals (i.e., the non-postable accounts) do not have balances. Remember to put any forced balance amounts into the *Test Balance Account*.

Open the account information window for **1060 Bank: Hamilton Trust Chequing**, the first account requiring a balance.

Click the **Opening Balance field**.

Type the **balance**.

Correct the **information** if necessary by repeating the above steps.

Click the **Next button** [▶] to advance to the next ledger account window.

Enter **negative numbers for accounts that decrease the total** in a group or section (e.g., *Allowance for Doubtful Accounts*, *Accum Deprec*, *GST/HST Paid on Purchases*). These account balances are indicated with a minus sign (−) in the Balance Sheet on page 618.

NOTES
We will change the account class for expense accounts when we change the class for other accounts that are used as linked accounts.

⚠ **WARNING!**
It is important to have the accounts in logical order at this stage. You will be unable to display some reports when the accounts are not in logical order, so you will not be able to check some of your work. You cannot finish the history if accounts are not in logical order.

NOTES
If you want to use the Retained Earnings linked account to enter account balance discrepancies, you must delay entering account balances until after you enter General linked accounts (page 643).

NOTES
For account 1140 Bank: USD Chequing, enter $9 500, the balance in Canadian dollars. The USD balance will be added after we set up currencies.

Repeat these **procedures** to **enter** the **balances** for the remaining accounts in the Post-Closing Trial Balance on page 619. *Test Balance Account* should have a zero balance.

Close the **Ledger window**.

After entering all account balances, you should display the Trial Balance to check them against the amounts on page 619. You can do this from the Accounts window.

Choose the **Reports menu** and **click Trial Balance**. **Click** the **Print tool**.

Close the **display** when finished. Leave the Accounts window open.

Check all **accounts** and **amounts** and **make corrections** if necessary.

Defining Account Classes

Defining bank accounts involves changing the account class to Bank and indicating the currency for the accounts and the cheque and deposit number sequences. If you use online banking, you must also enter the bank name, account numbers and Web site. We must also change the class for *Undeposited Cash and Cheques* to either Bank or Cash to use it as the linked account for receipts. Cash is the appropriate selection. Remember that the bank account class changes must be saved before we can enter the next cheque numbers. Changes are saved automatically when we open the next ledger record.

We must also define the account class for the credit card asset and the credit card payable accounts and change the account class for expense accounts. We will make all these changes before continuing the setup.

Double click **1030 Undeposited Cash and Cheques** to open the ledger.

Click the **Class Options tab**.

Choose **Cash** from the drop-down list of account classes.

Click the **Next Account button** ▶ to open the ledger for account **1060**.

Choose **Bank** from the list of account classes.

Click the **Next Deposit Number field**.

Type 14

Click the **Next Account button** ▶.

Choose **Bank** as the account class for *1080 Bank: Hamilton Trust Savings*.

Click **Chequing** (Account Type field). **Click Savings** from the list.

Click the **Next Account button** ▶ to **open** the ledger for **1120 Bank: Visa and Interac**.

Choose **Credit Card Receivable** as the account class.

Click the **Next Account button** ▶ to **open** the ledger for **1140 Bank: USD Chequing**.

Choose **Bank** as the account class.

Click the **Select Account list arrow**.

Click **2250 Credit Card Payable** to open its ledger screen at the Class Options tab screen.

Choose **Credit Card Payable** as the account class. Notice that Credit Card Receivable is not available as a class option for the liability account.

NOTES
Refer to the chart on page 616 for bank information and to page 222 for review of Bank class accounts.

NOTES
We must define 1030 Undeposited Cash and Cheques as a Bank or Cash class account in order to enter it as the linked bank account for Receivables. Cash is the most appropriate selection.
Both Bank and Cash class accounts are available in the Deposit To field for cash sales and receipts.

NOTES
To open the ledger for Credit Card Payable, you can click the Next Account button repeatedly or choose the account from the Select Account list arrow.

NOTES
Leave the account class for accounts 5040 to 5100 unchanged (set to Cost of Goods Sold class) so that you can create Gross Margin Income Statements.

NOTES
Remember that you can finish your session at any time. To continue, just open the file, accept the session date and start again from where you left off.

NOTES
Refer to the Business Information Chart on page 616 for credit card details. To review credit card setup, refer to page 224 for additional information.

NOTES
You must choose a Credit Card Payable or Bank class account as the Payable Account for cards used.

WARNING!
Although accounts in other classes appear on the Select Account list, selecting them will generate an error message when you save the entries.

NOTES
You must choose a Credit Card Receivable or Bank class account as the Asset Account for cards accepted.

NOTES
Refer to the Business Information Chart on page 616 for sales tax information. Refer to page 226 for a review of sales taxes

Click the **Select Account list arrow** again and **choose 5010 Advertising and Promotion**.

Select **Operating Expense** as the account class. **Click** ▶. **Select** the **Operating Expense** class for all postable expense accounts except the cost of goods subgroup accounts.

Close the **General Ledger window** and the **Accounts window**.

Entering Company Default Settings

Setting Up Credit Cards

Flabuless Fitness accepts Visa credit card payments from customers as well as debit cards (Interac). The store also uses a Visa card to pay for some purchases. Setting up credit cards includes naming them, identifying the linked accounts and entering fees associated with the cards. You should be in the Company module Home window.

Click the **Settings icon** [Settings] and **click Credit Cards** under Company. Click Company first if necessary.

Click **Used** to open the Credit Card Information screen for the cards that the business uses.

Click the **Credit Card Name field**.

Type Visa **Press** (tab) to move to the Payable Account field.

Press (enter) to see the list of available accounts.

Double click 2250 to add the account and move to the Expense Account field.

Press (enter) to see the account list.

Double click 5030.

Click **Accepted** to open the Credit Card Information screen for the cards that the business accepts from customers.

Click the **Credit Card Name field**.

Type Visa **Press** (tab) to advance to the Discount Fee % field.

Type 2.5 **Press** (tab) to advance to the Expense Account field.

Press (enter) to see the list of accounts available for linking.

Double click 5030 to choose and enter the account. The cursor advances to the Asset Account field.

Press (enter) to see the list of accounts available for linking.

Double click 1120 to choose and add the credit card bank account.

Enter **Interac** as the name, **0** as the %, **5030** as the Expense account and **1120** as the Asset account to set up the debit card.

Setting Up Sales Taxes

Flabuless Fitness charges and pays GST on books and HST on all other purchases. We will set up codes for these two taxes. We want to generate reports on both taxes.

Both taxes are linked to the GST/HST accounts because a single remittance to the Receiver General for Canada is made for both taxes; only the rates are different.

Click   **Sales Taxes** under Company. There are settings for tax names and codes.

Click   **Taxes** to access the Sales Tax Information screen:

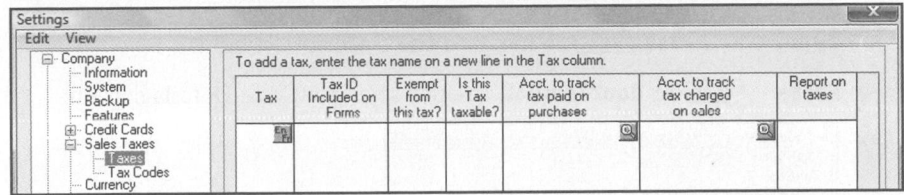

Press   (tab) to advance to the Tax field on the Taxes screen where you should enter the name of the tax. We will enter the HST first.

Type   HST **Press** (tab) to advance to the Tax ID field where we enter the business number.

Type   245 138 121 **Press** (tab) to advance to the **Exempt From This Tax?** column.

Flabuless Fitness is not tax exempt for HST, so the default, No, is correct. HST is not taxable in Ontario (no other tax is charged on HST). GST is taxable in PEI and Quebec.

Click   [icon], the **List icon for Acct To Track Tax Paid On Purchases**.

Choose **2670 GST/HST Paid on Purchases**. The cursor advances to the field for the Account To Track Taxes Charged On Sales.

Choose **2650 GST/HST Charged on Sales** from the List icon [icon] list of accounts. The cursor advances to the Report On Taxes field.

Click   No to change the default entry to Yes.

Press   (tab) so you can enter the information for GST.

Flabuless Fitness is not exempt from GST. The ID number and linked accounts are the same as for HST. GST is not taxable and the tax is refundable.

Type   GST **Press** (tab) to advance to the Tax ID field.

Type   245 138 121

Click   [icon], the **List icon for Acct To Track Tax Paid On Purchases**.

Choose **2670 GST/HST Paid on Purchases**. The cursor advances to the field for the Account To Track Taxes Charged On Sales.

Choose **2650 GST/HST Charged on Sales** from the List icon [icon] list of accounts. The cursor advances to the Report On Taxes field.

Click   No in the Report On Taxes column to change the entry to Yes.

Entering Tax Codes

Click   **Tax Codes** to open the next information screen:

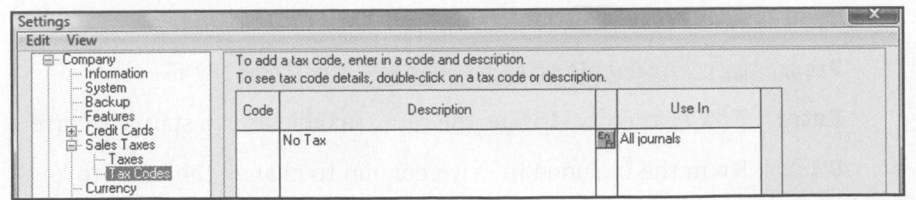

NOTES

In the Tesses Tresses application (Chapter 15) and the Village Galleries application (Chapter 14), we entered Yes for GST for Is This Tax Taxable? because PST is charged on GST in PEI and Quebec. (GST is taxable.) Clicking Yes in the Is This Tax Taxable? column for GST opens a list of taxes, and you can select the taxes that are to be charged on GST.

A single code, No Tax, is created as a default.

We need to create tax codes for sales and purchases when HST alone is charged and when only GST applies. There are also purchases with HST included, so we need a code for this situation as well (e.g., gasoline is priced with all taxes included).

Click   the **Code column** below the blank on the first line.

Type   H **Press** (tab) to move to the Description field.

Press   (enter) or **double click** to open the Tax Code Details screen:

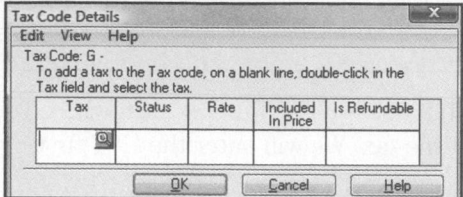

Click   the **Tax field List icon** to see the list of taxes entered.

Both taxes from the Taxes screen appear on the list.

Click   **Select** because HST is already selected and return to the Details.

Defaults are entered for the remaining fields. The **Status** is **Taxable** and the tax is **not included** — these are correct — tax is calculated and charged and is not included in the price.

Click   the **Rate field**.

Type   13

Click   **No** in the Is Refundable column to change the entry to Yes.

Click   **OK** to return to the Tax Codes screen for additional codes.

The description HST @ 13% appears beside the code H and the tax is used in all journals. You can edit the description if you want. If the tax were not refundable, non-refundable would be added to the description automatically. We are ready to enter the second code, to apply only GST.

Press   (tab) until you advance to the next line in the Code column.

Type   G **Press** (tab) to move to the Description field.

Press   (enter) to open the Tax Code Details screen.

Click   the **Tax field List icon**.

Select   **GST**. Taxable and not included are correct.

Type   5   in the **Rate field**.

Click   **No** in the Is Refundable column to change the entry to Yes.

Click   **OK** to return to the Tax Codes screen. The description GST @ 5% has been added.

Press   (tab) until you advance to the next line in the Code column, below G.

Type   IN **Press** (tab) to move to the Description field.

Press   (enter) or **double click** to open the Tax Code Details screen.

Enter   **HST** as the tax, **13%** as the rate. Taxable as the status is correct.

Click   **No** in the Included In Price column to change the entry to Yes.

Click   **No** in the Is Refundable column to change the entry to Yes.

Click   **OK** to return to the Tax Codes screen.

The description HST @ 13%, included appears beside the code IN.

Adding a Foreign Currency

Flabuless Fitness purchases some inventory items from suppliers in the United States and must set up the company files to allow transactions in USD, United States dollars. We will set up the foreign currency now because we need this information for bank account and supplier settings.

Click   **Currency** under Company to see the Currency Information window:

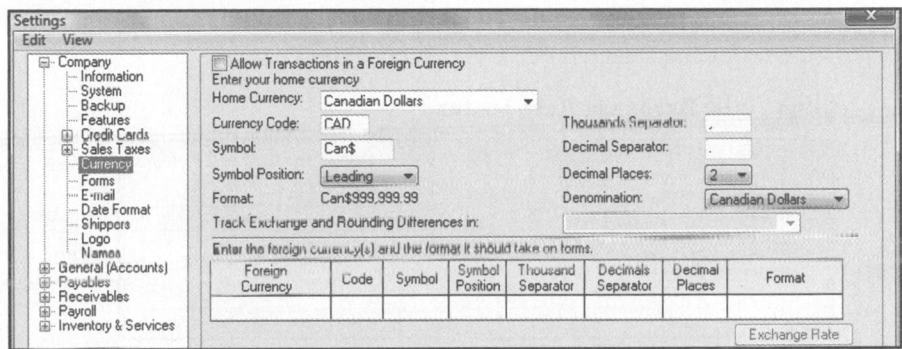

Canadian Dollars is the default in the Home Currency field, and its code, symbol, format and so on are added. You enter the currencies in the columns in the lower half of the screen, but first you must turn on the option to use other currencies.

Click   **Allow Transactions In A Foreign Currency**.

Exchange rates vary from day to day and even within the day. When purchases and payments are made at different times, they are subject to different exchange rates. We have seen these differences in the Maple Leaf Rags application (Chapter 12). Exchange rate differences may result in a gain — when the exchange rate drops before a payment is made or when the rate increases before a payment is received from a customer — or a loss — when the rate increases before a payment is made or when the rate drops before a customer makes a payment. These differences are tracked in the linked account designated on this screen. Rounding differences may also result in gains and losses because the amounts are recorded with two decimal places and exchange rates usually have several significant digits. The account for these differences may be an expense account or a revenue account. Flabuless Fitness uses a revenue account.

Click   the **list arrow** for **Track Exchange And Rounding Differences In**.

Both revenue and expense accounts are available for linking.

Click   **4120 Exchange Rate Differences** to enter the linked account.

The next step is to identify the foreign currency or currencies.

Click   the **Foreign Currency field**.

Click   the **List icon** 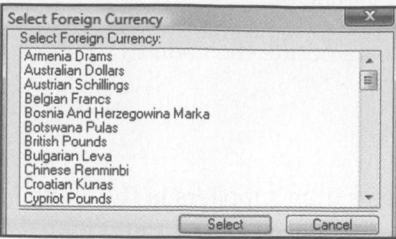 for the field to open the list of currencies:

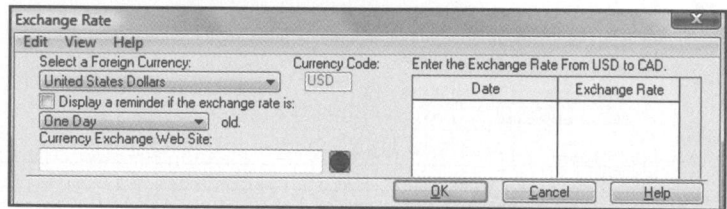

Type   U to advance to currencies beginning with U in the list. United States Dollars should be selected. If it is not,

Scroll down and **double click United States Dollars** to add it to the Currency Information screen. The currency code, symbol and format are added for the selected currency. Accept the defaults.

Click   the **Exchange Rate button**:

On this screen, we can enter the exchange rates for various dates for each currency. The selected currency is listed in the Select A Foreign Currency field. All currencies you created will be listed in the drop-down list for this field.

Click   the **Date field**.

Type   04 01 **Press** ⎡tab⎦ to advance to the Exchange Rate field.

Type   1.015

If you know the rates for other dates, you can enter them as well. Otherwise, you can enter current rates in the journals as we did in the previous chapters. These rates will be added to the list on this screen.

To ensure that you do not use an old exchange rate that is no longer accurate, you should turn on the reminder that warns if the rate is out of date. A one-day period for updating should be sufficient.

Click   **Display A Reminder If The Exchange Rate Is**.

Accept   **One Day Old** as the time interval.

Now every time you change the transaction date to one day past the rate previously used, the program will warn you and give you an opportunity to change the rate. If the rate has not changed, you can accept the old rate.

Click   **OK** to return to the Currency Settings screen.

Currency settings affect other settings — they require additional linked accounts — so they must be saved before continuing. And, now that we have added the foreign currency, we can identify the currency for the USD bank account. We must complete this step before we can choose it as the linked bank account for United States dollar transactions. At the same time we will add cheque numbers.

Click   **OK** to return to the Company module Home window.

Updating Bank Account Settings

Adding Currency to a Bank Account

We need to complete two more steps for bank accounts — identify the currency for the account, and enter the next cheque number. By default, the home currency is selected. We need to change this setting for the USD chequing account.

Click   the **Search tool** 🔍. Accounts should be selected.

Click   **1140 Bank: USD Chequing**. **Click OK** to open the ledger.

Click   the **Class Options tab** to see the current class setting — Bank.

Click   the **Currency list arrow**:

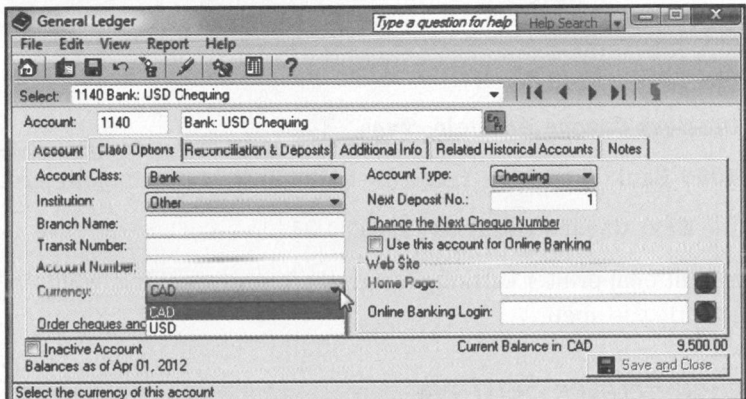

Once we identify an account as a bank account and allow foreign currency transactions, we identify the currency for the account on the Class Options tab screen.

Click   **USD**. Zero now appears as the balance amount for the USD currency.

Click   **Change The Next Cheque Number**.

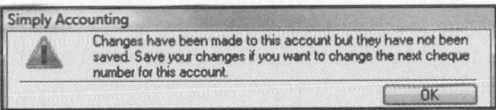

Click   **OK** to return to the ledger window so we can save the changes.

Click   the **Save tool** 💾 or **choose** the **File menu** and **click Save**:

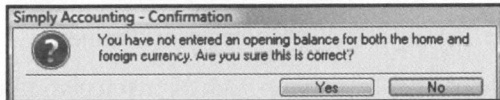

Because we have entered the balance in only the Home currency, we are asked to confirm that this is correct. It is not.

Click   **No** to return to the ledger window so we can add the USD balance.

Click   the **Account tab** to return to the Opening Balance fields. A second field has been added for the balance in USD.

Click   the **Opening Balance In USD field**. **Type** 9350

Click   the **Save tool** 💾.

You should now be able to add the next cheque number in the sequence.

Click   the **Class Options tab**.

Click   Change The Next Cheque Number to open the cheque Form settings:

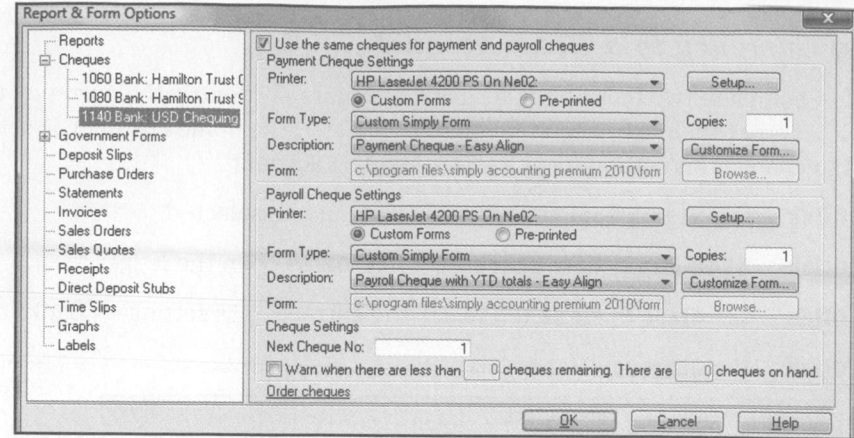

The account we started from is selected, so the cheque number field is available.

Click   the **Next Cheque No. field. Type** 346

Click   **1060 Bank: Hamilton Trust Chequing** in the left panel under Cheques.

Click   the **Next Cheque No. field. Type** 101

We will make additional printer setting changes before proceeding, while the Reports & Forms window is open.

Changing Other Printer Settings

Reports and forms settings apply only to the data file that you are using. They must be set for each data file separately and the settings are saved with each file.

Click Reports or click the form for which you want to enter settings.

Choose the printer you will be using for reports. Change the margins if necessary. Choose fonts and type sizes for the report from the lists. Click Setup to set the options for your printer if you need to change the paper size and location.

Click OK to save your settings and return to the previous Printer setting screen.

Each type of form — cheques, invoices and so on — has its own setup.

Click   Invoices to see the settings for printing invoices.

Check   that the **file locations** for the forms are correct or dimmed.

For **E-mail** and **Printed Forms**, choose generic forms such as Invoice and Purchase Order to avoid a file location error message from an incorrect file path in the Form File field. The file name field will be dimmed when you change the selection.

As you did for reports, select the printer, set the margins, font and type size to match the forms you are using. Preprinted forms were included as part of the program installation and are located in the Forms folder in the main Simply Accounting program folder. You should Show Subtotals In Invoices.

To preview invoices, you must select the **Custom Forms** and **Custom Simply Form** options.

If you want to customize and preview the invoice form, choose **User-Defined Form** as the Printed Form Description and then click Customize Form.

To print labels, click Labels and enter the size of the labels and the number that are placed across the page.

⚠ WARNING!
The entries in the Form fields should be dimmed to avoid an error message about invalid forms. When you choose the generic Description field entries Payment Cheque and Payroll Cheque, the Form field references will be dimmed.

📄 NOTES
You can change other printer settings at this stage if you want, or you can change them at any time as needed.

📄 NOTES
From the Home window, choose the Setup menu and click Reports & Forms. The printer setting options for reports are given.

📄 NOTES
Refer to Appendix G on the Student DVD if you want to customize printed invoices.

To set the printer options for cheques or other forms, click the form you want and make the necessary changes.

Click   **OK** to save the information when all the settings are correct. You can change printer settings at any time.

Close   the **Ledger window** to return to the Home window.

Entering Ledger Default Settings

General Ledger Settings

Most of the settings for the General Ledger are already correct. Flabuless is not setting up budgets or departments yet, and it does not use the additional ledger record fields. Using and showing numbers for accounts and four-digit account numbers, the default settings, are also correct for Flabuless Fitness. We need to add linked accounts.

Choose   the **Setup menu** and **click Settings** to continue entering the settings.

Defining Linked Accounts

Linked accounts are General Ledger accounts that are affected by entries in other journals. For example, recording an inventory purchase will update the Inventory Ledger, several General Ledger accounts and the balance owing to the supplier. Refer to page 229 for a review of linked accounts. Refer to page 89 for a review of the Current Earnings Account. Linked accounts are also needed for other features.

Identifying General Linked Accounts

The *Current Earnings* capital account records the changes in net income resulting from sales and expenses. At the end of the fiscal period, the net income, the balance from *Current Earnings*, is transferred to the Retained Earnings capital account — *S. Reeves, Capital* is the Retained Earnings account for Flabuless Fitness — and income and expense accounts are reset to zero to prepare for the new fiscal period.

Click   **General (Accounts)**.

If you have not yet saved the Currency settings, you will see a warning message:

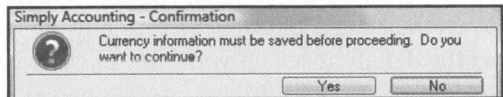

Simply Accounting - Confirmation
Currency information must be saved before proceeding. Do you want to continue?
[Yes]   [No]

Click   **Yes** to continue if you see this message. This will save the settings.

Click   **Linked Accounts under General (Accounts)**.

The General Ledger has two linked accounts. Both must be capital accounts.

GENERAL LINKED ACCOUNTS		
Retained Earnings	3560	S. Reeves, Capital
Current Earnings	3600	Current Earnings

Type   the **account number** or **select** the **account** from the drop-down list.

Payables Ledger Settings

Click   **Payables** and then **click Address**.

Enter **Hamilton**, **Ontario** and **Canada** as the default city, province and country for suppliers.

Click **Options**.

You should change the intervals for the aging of accounts. Some suppliers offer discounts for payment within 5, 10 or 15 days. Discounts from one-time suppliers are calculated on before-tax amounts.

Set the **aging** intervals at **15**, **30** and **60** days.

Click **Calculate Discounts Before Tax For One-Time Suppliers**.

Setting Up Import Duties

Although most goods imported from the United States are not subject to tariffs or import duties because of NAFTA (the North American Free Trade Agreement), you should know how to set up this feature. We will set up the program to charge duty but set the rate at zero so that no duty will be applied on purchases. You must activate the Duty option before creating supplier records so that you can indicate in the supplier records those suppliers that supply goods on which duty is charged. Without these two steps, the duty fields in the Purchases Journal will be unavailable.

Click **Duty** to access the settings we need:

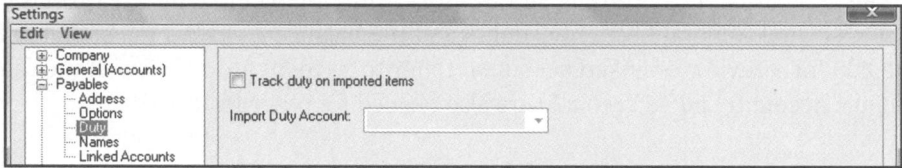

Click **Track Duty On Imported Items** to use the feature and open the linked account field.

A Payables account is linked to import duties for the liability to the Receiver General.

Click **2220 Import Duty Payable** from the Import Duty Account drop-down list.

Changing Payables Terminology

Simply Accounting chooses a set of terms that is appropriate for the type of business. These terms can be modified by the user on the Names Settings screen. For the companies in this text, we have accepted the default terms. If you want to change the terms and labels, use the following steps.

Click Names to open the settings:

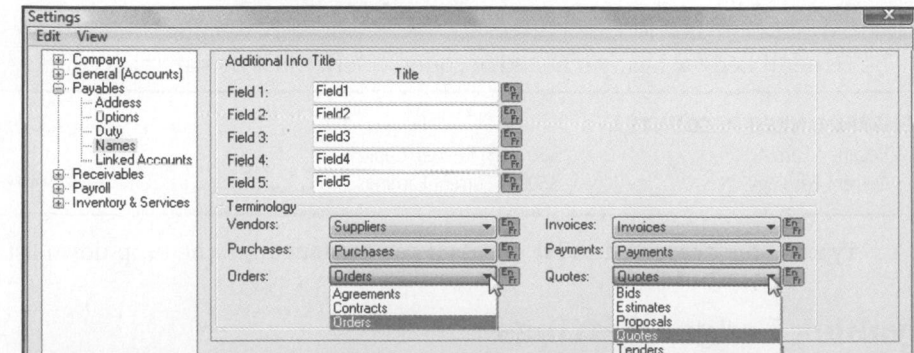

The upper part of the screen has five fields for the additional information you can add to the Payroll Ledger records. You can rename these fields if you want to use them.

The lower part of the screen has drop-down lists of terms for the various icons in the module. The names you select here will appear throughout the program as the names for icons, fields and reports. We have shown the drop-down lists of terms for Orders and Quotes. To see the terms you can choose for Vendors, Purchases and Invoices, refer to Chapter 7, page 231.

To change the terms, click the term you want to change and choose a different term from the drop-down list.

Identifying the Payables Linked Accounts

Flabuless Fitness uses *Bank: Hamilton Trust Chequing* as its principal linked bank account for all home currency cheque transactions in the subsidiary Payables and Payroll ledgers.

PAYABLES		
Bank Account to use for Canadian Dollars	1060	Bank: Hamilton Trust Chequing
Bank Account to use for United States Dollars	1140	Bank: USD Chequing
Accounts Payable	2200	Accounts Payable
Freight Expense	5080	Freight Expense
Early Payment Purchase Discount	5090	Purchase Discounts
Prepayments and Prepaid Orders	1250	Purchase Prepayments

To enter the Payables Ledger linked accounts,

Click   **Linked Accounts** to display the Linked Accounts window:

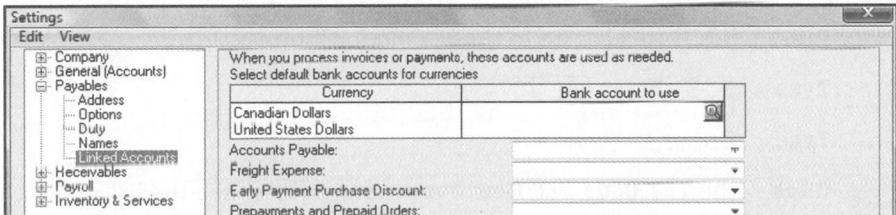

We need to identify the default General Ledger bank accounts used for payments to suppliers. Cash transactions in the Payments Journal will be posted to the bank account you select in the journal window. Bank and Cash class accounts are available in the journals, and the principal linked account defined here will be selected as the default.

You can see the list of accounts available for linking by clicking the drop-down list arrow for any linked account field. Only Bank and Cash class accounts may be used in the bank fields. That is why we needed to classify the bank accounts first.

Flabuless has two bank accounts for payments. The chequing account is the principal bank account for Canadian currency transactions, and the USD account is used for transactions in United States dollars.

You can choose a separate linked account for each currency, or you may use the Canadian dollar account for more than one currency. You can select a Home currency account as the linked account for foreign currency transactions, but you cannot select a foreign currency account as the linked account for Home currency transactions.

Click   the **List icon** 🔍 in the Bank Account To Use column for Canadian Dollars.

Click   **1060 Bank: Hamilton Trust Chequing** and **click Select**.

Click   List icon 🔍 in the Bank Account To Use column for United States Dollars.

Click   **1140 Bank: USD Chequing** and **click Select**.

NOTES
Refer to Appendix B, page A-23 for a list of the terms used for different types of industry.

CLASSIC VIEW
To add the Payables Ledger linked accounts from the Home window, right-click the Purchases or the Payments Journal icon in the Home window to select it.
    Click the Setup tool 🔧. Or choose the Setup menu, then choose Settings, Payables and Linked Accounts.

NOTES
Notice that this screen is different from the one on page 232 for Dorfmann Design that uses only one currency.

WARNING!
You cannot change the currency for an account when it is used as a linked account. You can choose a home currency account as the the linked account to use with a foreign currency. If you had not yet changed the currency for 1140 Bank: USD Chequing, you could still choose it as the linked account. However, you would then be unable to change the currency to USD.

Enter the **remaining linked accounts** from the chart on the previous page. **Type** the **account number** or **select** the **account** from the drop-down list.

Check the linked accounts carefully. To delete a linked account, click it to highlight it and press (del). You must complete this step of deleting the linked account before you can remove the account in the General Ledger from the Accounts window.

Receivables Ledger Settings

Click   **Receivables** and then **click Address**.

Enter   **Hamilton**, **Ontario** and **Canada** as the default address for customers.

Click   **Options**.

Flabuless Fitness prints the salesperson's name on all customer forms for the customer's reference in case a follow-up is required. Most customers use the tax code H, so we will use this as the default for new customers. The default tax code will be selected when we enter the customer records.

Flabuless charges 1.5 percent interest on overdue accounts after 30 days, includes paid invoices on customer statements for 31 days — this is appropriate for the monthly statements — and uses the payment terms to set the aging intervals.

Enter   **10**, **30** and **60** days as the **aging** periods.

Click   **Interest Charges** to add a ✓ and turn on the calculation.

Press   (tab) to advance to the % field for Interest Charges.

Type   1.5 **Press** (tab).

Type   30

Click   the **Tax Code For New Customers field** to see the list of tax codes.

Click   **H HST @ 13%**.

Click   **Print Salesperson On Invoices Orders & Quotes**.

Entering Discount Settings

Flabuless Fitness offers its account customers a 2 percent after-tax discount for 10 days; full payment is due in 30 days. Flabuless does not use the line discount feature.

Click   **Discount** to open the next Receivables settings screen.

Click   the **% field** of the **Early Payment Terms** section.

Type   2 **Press** (tab).

Type   10 **Press** (tab).

Type   30

Click   **Calculate Line Discounts On Invoices ...** to turn off the feature. You will see the warning:

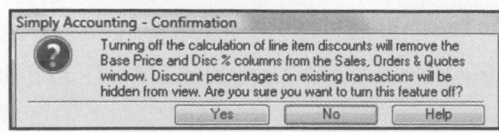

Click   **Yes** to confirm your selection.

Changing Default Comments

Click   **Comments** under Receivables.

You may add a comment or notice to all your invoices, quotes and order confirmations. You could use this feature to include payment terms, a company motto or notice of an upcoming sale. Remember that you can change the default message any time you want. You can also edit it for a particular sale or quote when you are completing the invoice. The cursor is in the Sales Invoices field.

Type   Interest @ 1.5% per month on accounts over 30 days.

Repeat this procedure to enter comments for the other forms.

Changing Receivables Terminology

Click   **Names** under Receivables:

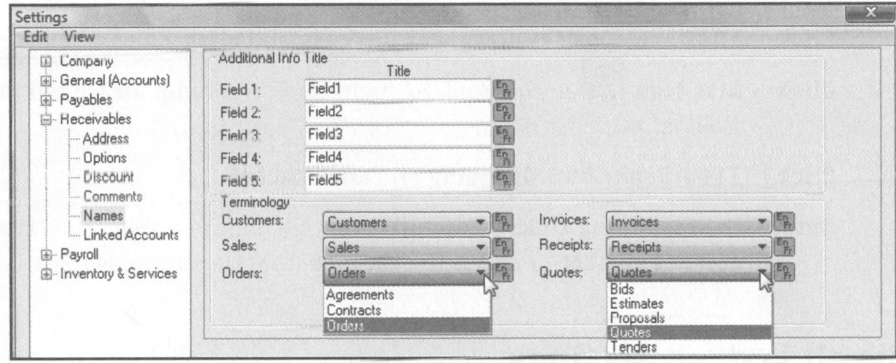

This screen has the same structure as the one for Payables additional information field names and ledger terminology.

In the screen above, we have shown the drop-down lists of terms for Orders and Quotes. The names you select here will appear throughout the program as the names for icons, fields and reports. To see the terms you can choose for Customers, Sales and Invoices, refer to Chapter 7, page 235.

To change the terms, click the term you want to change and choose a different term from the drop-down list.

Defining the Receivables Linked Accounts

The Receivables Ledger linked accounts parallel those for the Payables Ledger.

Click   **Linked Accounts** under Receivables:

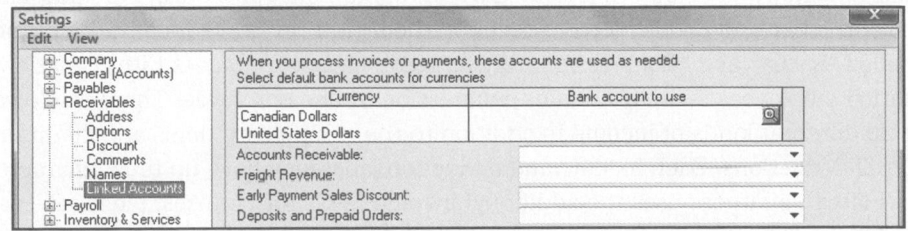

We need to identify the default General Ledger bank account used to receive payments from customers. Cash transactions in the Sales and Receipts journals will be posted to the bank account you select in the journals. The linked account will be the default but any Bank or Cash class account may be selected in the journals.

Flabuless has several bank accounts. Cheques and cash receipts are held in the *Undeposited Cash and Cheques* account and then deposited weekly to the *Bank: Hamilton Trust Chequing* account. Therefore, the default Canadian bank account for receipts is *Undeposited Cash and Cheques. Bank: USD Chequing* is the default account for foreign currency customer transactions. Although most linked accounts may be used only once, one bank account can be linked to the Payables, Receivables and Payroll ledgers.

The following accounts are required as linked accounts for the Receivables Ledger.

RECEIVABLES LINKED ACCOUNTS		
Bank Account to use for Canadian Dollars	1030	Undeposited Cash and Cheques
Bank Account to use for United States Dollars	1140	Bank: USD Chequing
Accounts Receivable	1200	Accounts Receivable
Freight Revenue	4200	Freight Revenue
Early Payment Sales Discount	4060	Sales Discounts
Deposits and Prepaid Orders	2210	Prepaid Sales and Deposits

Click   the **List icon** 🔍 in the Bank Account To Use column for Canadian Dollars.

Click   **1030 Undeposited Cash and Cheques** and **click Select**.

Click   **List icon** 🔍 in the Bank Account To Use column for United States Dollars.

Click   **1140 Bank: USD Chequing** and **click Select**.

Enter   the **remaining linked accounts** from the chart on this page. **Type** the **account number** or **select** the **account** from the drop-down list.

NOTES
The remaining accounts were introduced in Chapter 7. Refer to page 236 if you need to review these accounts.

NOTES
Refer to pages 318–324 to review payroll settings if necessary.

Payroll Ledger Settings

At this stage, we will change the settings for Payroll Names, Income, Deductions, Taxes and Entitlements. After creating supplier and employee records, we can change the Remittance and Job Category settings.

Entering Payroll Names

Because the names we use will appear on the remaining payroll setting screen, we will define them first.

Click   **Payroll** and then **click Names** in the list of Payroll options.

Click   **Incomes & Deductions** to access the first group of payroll names.

Many of the standard income types are mandatory and cannot be changed. These fields are shown in colour on a shaded background. Some of the other default names are also correct so you do not need to redefine them. You can leave Income 1 and Income 2, labelled "Salary" and "Commission," unchanged because Flabuless Fitness has two salaried employees and pays a sales commission to one employee. There is allowance for 20 different kinds of income in addition to the compulsory fields and 20 different payroll deductions. Each income and deduction label may have up to 12 characters.

Flabuless Fitness uses the additional income fields for bonuses, piece rate pay and taxable benefits (tuition fee payments) so that these incomes can be identified by name on the paycheque. The piece rate pay is based on completed favourable client surveys for the employees. Travel expenses repaid directly to employees are also entered as income but they will not be taxed.

Flabuless also has three payroll deductions at this time: RRSP — the Registered Retirement Savings Plan; CSB Plan — the Canada Savings Bond plan; and Garnishee — the wages that are withheld and submitted to the Receiver General for prior years' taxes.

Click **Income 3 in the Name Column** to highlight the contents.

Type No. Clients **Press** tab to advance to the Income 4 field.

Type Bonus **Press** tab to advance to the Income 5 field.

Type Tuition **Press** tab to advance to the Income 6 field.

Type Travel Exp. **Press** tab to advance to the Income 7 field.

Press del to remove the entry. **Press** tab to select the next field.

Delete the **remaining Income names** until they are all removed.

Press tab after deleting Income 20 to select Deduction 1 in the Deductions column.

Press tab again if necessary to select Deduction 1 in the Name column.

Type RRSP **Press** tab to advance to the second deduction Name field.

Type CSB Plan **Press** tab to highlight the next field.

Type Garnishee **Press** tab to highlight the next field.

Press del. Flabuless Fitness does not have other payroll deductions.

Press tab to select the next field. **Delete** the **remaining deductions**.

NOTES
If clicking does not highlight the field contents, drag through an entry to select it. Double clicking may open the language labels screen.

NOTES
In Chapter 9, we created Travel Expenses as a user-defined expense and issued separate cheques to the employee for them.

NOTES
For Lime Light Laundry, we used the generic Benefits field to enter all employee benefits.

NOTES
You can also press ↓ to access the next Deduction Name field instead of pressing tab.

Entering Additional Payroll Names

Flabuless Fitness keeps an emergency contact name and phone number for each employee in the personnel files. We will name these extra fields for the Payroll Ledger.

On this next screen, we also name the additional payroll expenses for Flabuless and the entitlements for employees. Flabuless has group insurance as a user-defined expense and offers sick leave and personal leave days for all employees as well as vacation days for salaried employees.

We will briefly review income, benefits and user-defined expenses.

Group insurance is classified as a benefit for employees because the premiums are paid to a third party rather than to the employee. The employer's expense for the benefit is entered as a user-defined expense. Tuition is classified as an income because it is paid to the employee through regular paycheques. The employer's expense for this benefit is recorded in the expense account linked to the income, just like wage expenses. Reimbursements may also be entered as income or as user-defined expenses, depending on how the payment is made. If we entered travel expenses as a user-defined expense, we would create a linked payable account and then issue a separate cheque to the employee to provide the reimbursement. If we repay the expense on the payroll cheque, we define it as an income — reimbursement — that is not taxable.

NOTES
You can add names to any of these fields later if you need to.

NOTES
Reimbursements are added to net pay (the amount of the paycheque), but are not added to gross pay to calculate taxes.
For Lime Light Laundry, travel expenses were set up as a user-defined expense – separate cheques were issued to the employee.

Click **Additional Payroll**.

Double click **Field1**.

Type Emergency Contact **Press** tab **twice** to highlight the next field.

Type Contact Number

Delete the **names for fields 3 to 5**.

Drag through **User Exp 1**, the Expense 1 field, to highlight the contents.

Type Gp Insurance

Delete the **remaining expenses**.

NOTES
On the Additional Payroll screen, you need to press tab twice to skip the Fr/Eng language button. If you are not using both languages, press tab once to move to the next field. On the Incomes & Deductions screen, the language button is automatically skipped when you press tab.

Drag through **Days 1**, the Entitlement 1 field, to highlight the contents.

Type Vacation **Press** (tab) **twice** to highlight the next entitlement name.

Type Sick Leave **Press** (tab) **twice** to highlight the next name.

Type PersonalDays

Delete the **remaining entitlement names**.

The Prov. Tax field is used for Quebec payroll taxes. Since we will not choose Quebec as the employees' province of taxation, the program will automatically skip the related payroll fields. WSIB is entered as the name for WCB (Workers' Compensation Board) because we selected Ontario as the business province. The field has a drop-down list of alternative names.

Entering Settings for Incomes

Click **Incomes** under Payroll.

This screen designates the types of income and the taxes that apply. By deleting the names we do not need, this list is easier to work with. As we did for Lime Light Laundry (Chapter 9), we can modify this screen by hiding the columns that apply to Quebec so that only the columns we need are on-screen at the same time.

Point to the **right column heading margin for Calc. Tax (Que.)** until the pointer changes to a two-sided arrow [⟷].

Drag the **margin to the left** until the column is hidden.

Point to the **right column heading margin for Calc. QHSF** until the pointer changes to a two-sided arrow. **Drag** the **margin to the left** until the column is hidden.

Point to the **right column heading margin for Calc. QPIP** until the pointer changes to a two-sided arrow. **Drag** the **margin to the left**.

For each type of income, you must indicate what taxes are applied and whether vacation pay is calculated on the income. Most of the information is correct. Regular and overtime hours are paid on an hourly basis, while salary and commissions are paid at designated income amounts per period. All taxes apply to these types of income at Flabuless Fitness, so these default settings are correct. Vacation pay and EI, however, are not calculated on all incomes so some of these checkmarks should be removed. In addition, we should designate the type of income for the income names that we created and the taxes that apply to them. First, we should choose the type of income because that will change the defaults that are applied.

By default, all new incomes are assigned to the Income type. This assignment is correct for Bonus, the extra annual holiday payment. The tuition fee payment is a taxable benefit paid directly to the employee, so it is classified as income. The Benefit type is used only for items such as medical or life insurance premiums that the employer pays directly to a third party on behalf of the employee. The monetary value of the premiums is added as a benefit to the employee's gross wages to determine taxes and then subtracted again to determine the net pay. The employee does not receive the actual dollar amount. If a benefit is added to net pay, it should be classified as an Income. Therefore, tuition is an Income.

Travel Expenses are **Reimbursements** and No. Clients is the name for the **Piece Rate** basis of paying bonuses. **Differential Rates** apply to different hourly rates paid at different times and are not used by Flabuless.

Click **No. Clients** to place the cursor on the correct line.

Press (tab) to move to the Type column. A List icon is added.

Click the **List icon** 🔍 to see the income types.

Click **Piece Rate** to select this type for No. Clients.

Click **Select** to add the Type to the Settings screen. **Press** (tab).

The cursor advances to the Unit of Measure field and the entry has changed to Item. The amount paid to employees is based on the number of completed surveys. Notice that the Insurable Hours checkmark was removed when we changed the type.

Type Surveys

Click **Travel Exp** to select this income line. **Press** (tab).

Click the **List icon** to see the types we can select.

Double click **Reimbursement** to enter this type on the Settings screen. All taxes are removed because this type of payment is not taxable.

We need to make some other modifications. Insurable Hours, the number of work hours, is used to determine eligibility for Employment Insurance benefits. Regular, overtime and salary paid hours are counted but commissions, bonuses and benefits are not. No work time can be reasonably attached to commissions and bonuses so they are not counted. EI is not calculated on taxable benefit income. The checkmarks for these should be removed.

Click **Commission** to select this income line.

Press (tab) **repeatedly** until the cursor is in the **Calc. Ins. Hours field**.

Click to remove the ✓, or **press** the **space bar**.

Press ⬇ **twice** to place the cursor in the **Calc. Ins. Hours field for Bonus**.

Click to remove the ✓, or **press** the **space bar**.

Press ⬇ to place the cursor in the **Calc. Ins. Hours field for Tuition**.

Click to remove the ✓, or **press** the **space bar**.

Press (shift) and (tab) together to return to the Calc. EI field for Tuition.

Click to remove the ✓, or **press** the **space bar**.

We still need to modify the entries for vacation pay. In Ontario, vacation pay is calculated on all performance-based wages. This includes the regular wages, overtime wages and piece rate pay. We need to remove the remaining ✓. The ✓ for Travel Exp has already been removed. Salaried workers receive paid time off rather than a percentage of their wages as vacation pay. We do not need to remove the ✓ for Overtime 2. If it is used later, vacation pay will be calculated on it as well.

Click **Salary** in the Income column.

Press (tab) **repeatedly** until the cursor is in the **Calc. Vac. column**.

Click to remove the ✓, or **press** the **space bar**.

Press ⬇ to place the cursor in the **Calc. Vac. field for Commission**.

Click to remove the ✓, or **press** the **space bar**.

Press ⬇ to place the cursor in the **Calc. Vac. field for No. Clients**.

Press ⬇ to place the cursor in the **Calc. Vac. field for Bonus**.

NOTES
Vacation pay is calculated on all wages. This calculation includes the piece rate pay — number of client evaluations — because it is a performance-based wage or income. Bonuses are not based on measurable performance; therefore, vacation pay is not applied to these amounts or to the other benefits.

The regulations governing vacation pay are set provincially.

> **Click**   to remove the ✓, or **press** the **space bar**.
>
> **Press**   ⏎ to place the cursor in the **Calc. Vac. field for Tuition**.
>
> **Click**   to remove the ✓, or **press** the **space bar**.

We do not need to change the Quebec tax settings. They will not be applied when we select Ontario as the province for employees. The option to **track tips** applies to payroll in Quebec, so we do not need to choose this option.

The completed Income Settings screen is shown below:

NOTES

You can modify this screen as we modified the Incomes Settings screen so that only the columns we need are on-screen. You can remove the Deduct After Tax (Que.), QHSF and QPIP columns.

Entering Tax Settings for Deductions

> **Click**   **Deductions** under Payroll.

Only the deduction names you entered earlier appear on this screen. You can calculate deductions as a percentage of the gross pay or as a fixed amount. Some deductions, like union dues, are usually calculated as a percentage of income. The Amount settings are correct for Flabuless Fitness.

All deductions are set by default to be calculated after all taxes (Deduct After Tax is checked). For CSB Plan and Garnishee, this is correct — they are subtracted from income after income tax and other payroll taxes have been deducted. However, RRSP contributions qualify as tax deductions and will be subtracted from gross income before income tax is calculated, but not before EI, CPP and so on, so you must change its setting.

> **Click**   the **Deduct After Tax column** for RRSP to remove the ✓ and change the setting to Before Tax.

The remaining settings are correct. RRSP is deducted after the other payroll taxes and vacation pay because these deductions are based on gross wages.

Defining Default Tax Rates

> **Click**   **Taxes** under Payroll.

This group of fields refers to the rate at which employer tax obligations are calculated. The factor for Employment Insurance (**EI Factor**) is correct at 1.4. The employer's contribution is set at 1.4 times the employee's contribution. In the next field, you can set the employer's rate for **WSIB** (Workplace Safety and Insurance Board) premiums. On this screen, you can enter 1.29, the rate that applies to the majority of employees. You can modify rates for individual employees in the ledger records.

The next field, **EHT Factor**, shows the percentage of payroll costs that the employer contributes to the provincial health plan. The rate is based on the total payroll costs per year; the percentage for Flabuless Fitness is 0.98 percent.

The **QHSF Factor** (Quebec Health Services Fund) applies to Quebec employees so we do not need to enter a rate for it. QHSF is similar to EHT.

> **Click**   the **WSIB Rate field**.

WARNING!

If you later change the province in the Company Information screen, the name entered for WCB does not change. You must enter the correction manually on the Additional Payroll names screen.

Type   1.29

Press   `tab` to advance to the EHT Factor field.

Type   .98

Defining Entitlements

Click   **Entitlements** under Payroll.

On this screen you can enter the rules for entitlements that apply to all or most employees. These will be added to new employee records as defaults.

Entitlements are usually linked to the number of hours worked. Employees at Flabuless Fitness are not entitled to take vacation time until they have worked for a certain period of time or to take paid sick leave immediately after being hired. The **Track Using % Hours Worked** determines how quickly entitlements accumulate. For example, 5 percent of hours worked yields about one day per month or 12 days of leave per year. Flabuless Fitness has **Maximums** for the number of days per year that an employee can take or accumulate. And finally, the days unused are not **cleared at the end of a year**. The number of days carried forward is still limited by the Maximum number of days available. The calculations are based on an eight-hour day as the default.

Flabuless Fitness gives salaried workers three weeks of vacation (8 percent) and allows a maximum of 25 days. Sick leave at 10 days per year is earned at the rate of 5 percent to the maximum of 15 days. Personal leave days (5 days) accrue at the rate of 2.5 percent for a maximum of 5 days per year. Flabuless Fitness allows two of the three weeks of vacation time and five of the 10 days of sick leave to be carried over to the following year; that is, they are not cleared at the end of the year. Personal leave days cannot be carried forward — the maximum is the same as the yearly allotment.

Click   the **Track Using % Hours Worked field for Vacation**.

Type   8 **Press** `tab` to advance to the Maximum Days field.

Type   25 **Press** `tab`.

Click   the **Track Using % Hours Worked field for Sick Leave**.

Type   5 **Press** `tab` to advance to the Maximum Days field.

Type   15 **Press** `tab`.

Click   the **Track Using % Hours Worked field for PersonalDays**.

Type   2.5 **Press** `tab` to advance to the Maximum Days field.

Type   5 **Press** `tab`.

Entering Payroll Linked Accounts

There are many linked accounts for payroll because each type of income, tax, deduction and expense that is used must be linked to a General Ledger account. The following linked accounts are used by Flabuless Fitness for the Payroll Ledger.

NOTES
EHT in Ontario applies if the total payroll is greater than $400 000. We show the entry of the EHT rates so that you can learn how to change the settings.
WSIB is the name for WCB in Ontario.
QHSF was used for Village Galleries (Chapter 14).

NOTES
Entitlements may also be given directly as a number of days without tracking hours by entering the number of days in the Maximum Days field.

NOTES
When the number of days accrued reaches the maximum, the Days Earned entries on the paycheques Entitlements tab screen will be zero.

NOTES
Refer to page 324 to review payroll linked accounts if necessary.

WARNING!
Simply Accounting will not allow you to remove an account while it is being used as a linked account. When you try to remove an account, click OK in the Warning window to return to the Accounts window. First, turn the linking function off by deleting the account in the Linked Accounts window. Then remove the account in the Accounts window. You cannot remove an account if it has a balance or if journal entries have been posted to it.

PAYROLL LINKED ACCOUNTS

INCOMES			
Principal Bank	1060 Bank: Hamilton Trust Chequing		
Vac. Owed	2300 Vacation Payable	Advances	1220 Advances Receivable
Income			
Vac. Earned	5300 Wages	Commission	5310 Commissions & Bonuses
Regular	5300 Wages	No. Clients	5310 Commissions & Bonuses
Overtime 1	5300 Wages	Bonus	5310 Commissions & Bonuses
Overtime 2	Not used	Tuition	5380 Employee Benefits
Salary	5305 Salaries	Travel Exp.	5320 Travel Expenses
DEDUCTIONS			
RRSP	2400 RRSP Payable	Garnishee	2430 Garnisheed Wages Payable
CSB Plan	2410 CSB Plan Payable		
TAXES			
Payables		**Expenses**	
EI	2310 EI Payable	EI	5330 EI Expense
CPP	2320 CPP Payable	CPP	5340 CPP Expense
Tax	2330 Income Tax Payable	WSIB	5350 WSIB Expense
WSIB	2460 WSIB Payable	EHT	5360 EHT Expense
EHT	2380 EHT Payable		
Not used	Tax (Que.), QPP, QHSF, QPIP	**Not used**	QPP, QHSF, QPIP
USER-DEFINED EXPENSES			
Payables		**Expenses**	
Gp Insurance	2420 Group Insurance Payable	Gp Insurance	5370 Gp Insurance Expense

CLASSIC VIEW
To add payroll linked accounts, you can right-click the Paycheques or the Payroll Cheque Run Journal icon in the Home window to select it.

Click the Setup tool. Or choose the Setup menu, and then choose Settings, Payroll and Linked Accounts.

If no Home window icon is selected, you can use the Setup tool icon pop-up list, choose Paycheques and click Select.

NOTES
The deleted income and deduction names do not appear on the screens for linked accounts.

NOTES
If you can use an account for more than one link, the account will be available in the drop-down list. Otherwise, once an account is selected as a linked account, it is removed from the list.

NOTES
You can add accounts from the Linked Accounts windows. Type a new number, press *enter* and choose to add the account.

Click **Linked Accounts** under Payroll then **click Incomes**.

The names here are the ones you entered in the Names windows. If you deleted a name, it will not appear here.

The linked accounts for all types of income appear together on this first screen. You must identify a wage account for each type of employee payment used by the company, even if the same account is used for all of them. Once the Payroll bank account is identified as the same one used for Payables, the program will apply a single sequence of cheque numbers for all cheques prepared from the Payables and Payroll journals.

Type the **account number** or **select** the **account** from the drop-down list.

Choose **1060 Bank: Hamilton Trust Chequing** for the Principal Bank field.

Press *tab* to advance to the next linked account field.

Choose **2300 Vacation Payable** for the Vac. Owed field.

Choose **1220 Advances Receivable** for the Advances field.

Choose **5300 Wages** for Vacation Earned, Regular and Overtime 1.

Choose **5305 Salaries** for Salaries.

Choose **5310 Commissions & Bonuses** for Commission, No. Clients and Bonus.

Choose **5380 Employee Benefits** for Tuition.

Choose **5320 Travel Expenses** for Travel Exp.

Click **Deductions** to see the next set of Payroll accounts.

Enter the **linked** payable **accounts** for **RRSP**, **CSB Plan** and **Garnishee** from the chart above.

Click **Taxes** to see the next set of Payroll linked accounts.

Enter the **linked payables accounts** for **EI**, **CPP**, **Tax**, **WSIB** and **EHT** in the Payables section and the **linked expense accounts** for **EI**, **CPP**, **WSIB** and **EHT** in the Expenses section from the chart on page 654.

Click **User-Defined Expenses** to see the final Payroll accounts.

Enter the **linked** payable **accounts** for **Gp Insurance Payable** and **Gp Insurance Expense** from the chart on page 654.

Check the **linked** payroll **accounts** against the chart on page 654.

Inventory & Services Ledger Settings

Click **Inventory & Services** to see the options for this ledger:

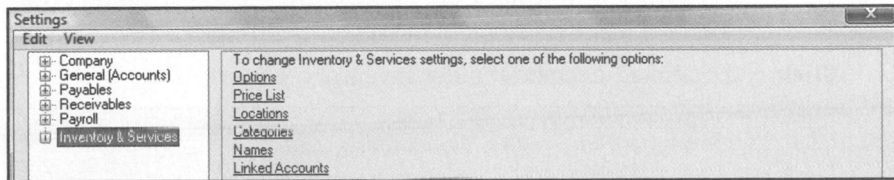

Click **Options**:

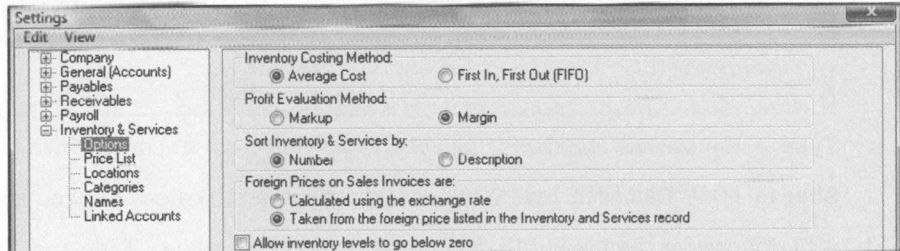

PRO VERSION
The Price List, Locations and Categories options are not available in the Pro version.
    The FIFO method of costing is also not available in the Pro version.

NOTES
The list of items you see in the Item Description field in the Sales and Purchases journals is sorted by description. The Item Number field list in these journals is sorted by number.

Inventory costs may be calculated in two ways. In the average cost method, costs are continually updated as you buy and sell at different prices. With the FIFO method, costs are tracked with the items and do not change for any one item — its historic purchase price remains as the cost price at the time of sale. Flabuless Fitness uses average costs.

Profits may be calculated on the basis of margin or markup. You can change the setting at any time, so you can prepare reports using both evaluation methods. The formulas for profit evaluation by Margin and Markup are as follows:

Margin = (Selling Price – Cost Price) x 100%/Selling Price

Markup = (Selling Price – Cost Price) x 100%/Cost Price

Flabuless Fitness uses the markup method of evaluating the profit on inventory sales, so we need to change the default setting.

Click **Markup** to change the calculation method.

If you choose to sort Inventory Ledger items by description, the product name field will appear before the product number in the Inventory Ledger input forms, and inventory selection lists will be sorted alphabetically by name. When item numbers are not used, sorting by description will make it easier to find the item you want.

Because we added a foreign currency, the option to take foreign prices for sales from the Inventory Ledger or from the exchange rate is added. The default setting to use the foreign price in the Inventory Ledger Record is correct for Flabuless Fitness. With this option, you can switch pricing methods for individual items. If you choose the exchange rate method, you cannot choose different methods for different items.

The final option is to Allow Inventory Levels To Go Below Zero. Flabuless Fitness will choose this option to permit customer sales for inventory that is backordered.

Click   **Allow Inventory Levels To Go Below Zero** to select the option.

In the Premium version, you can create additional price lists and modify price lists from this settings screen. You can also set up the locations for inventory if you have more than one place where inventory is stored or sold.

Inventory Items Linked Accounts

Flabuless Fitness currently uses only one linked account for inventory, the one for inventory adjustments or damaged merchandise. The linked accounts for the Inventory Ledger are listed here:

INVENTORY	
Item Assembly Costs	Not used
Adjustment Write-off	5040 Damaged Inventory

Click   the **Linked Accounts** under Inventory & Services:

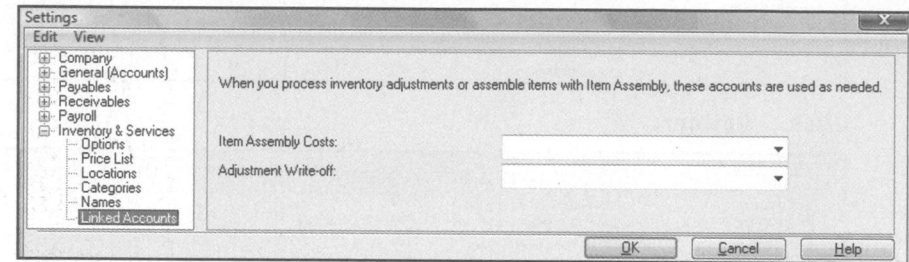

Type   the **account number** or **select** the **account** from the drop-down list.

Choose 5040 Damaged Inventory as the Adjustment Write-off linked account.

Settings options for the hidden Division module are also hidden. Time and Billing, introduced in Chapter 18, has no settings options.

Click   **OK** to save the new settings.

You will see several warnings. Because we deleted some payroll names, we are being warned that any accounts linked to these deleted fields will also be removed. The next message refers to the additional payroll names, and we are again being warned that their linked accounts will be removed. Refer to Chapter 9, page 326.

A second group of warnings relates to required account class changes for linked accounts. Refer to Chapter 7, page 236.

Read   each message **carefully** and **click Yes** in response to return to the Home window.

Preparing the Subsidiary Ledgers

We have now completed the General Ledger setup including:

1. organizing all accounting reports and records
2. creating new accounts
3. identifying linked accounts for all ledgers
4. activating additional features and entering their linked accounts

The remaining steps involve setting up the records in the subsidiary ledgers:

5. inserting supplier, customer, employee and inventory information
6. entering historical startup information
7. printing reports to check the accuracy of your records

Preparing the Payables Ledger

Use Flabuless Fitness' Supplier Information on pages 619–620 to create the supplier records and add the outstanding historical invoices. If any information is missing for a supplier, leave that field blank.

Entering Supplier Accounts

Click   **Payables** in the Modules pane list.

Click   the **Suppliers icon** Suppliers to open the Suppliers window.

Click   the **Create button** Create or **choose** the **File menu** and **click Create** or **press** ctrl + **N**. The cursor is in the Supplier field.

Enter   the supplier's **name**. On the Address tab screen, enter the **contact**, **address**, **phone**, **fax** and **tax ID** numbers, and the **e-mail** and **Web site** addresses from pages 619–620.

Click   the **Options tab**.

Enter   the **discounts**, if there are any, in the Terms fields, and the number of days in which the net amount is due. **Click Calculate Discounts Before Tax** if the discounts are before tax. Otherwise, leave the box unchecked.

You can print the contact on cheques if this is appropriate for the supplier.

Enter   the **default expense account** for the supplier if there is one.

Click   the **Taxes tab** to open the tax information screen for the supplier.

Click   the **Tax Code field list arrow** to see the codes.

For Ancaster Insurance, the selection No Tax is correct because some transactions are taxable and others are not.

It is not necessary to change Tax Exempt entries. Leaving the setting at No will make all tax codes available for a supplier. As long as the tax code in the journal is correct, taxes will be calculated correctly. You can change the tax settings at any time. You do not need to enter any details on the Statistics, Memo and Import/Export tab screens.

Correct any **errors** by returning to the field with the mistake, highlighting the errors and entering the correct information.

Enter   **historical transactions** using the keystroke instructions in the following section if the supplier has historical transactions.

Click   **Create Another** Create Another to save the record and open a blank Payables Ledger window.

Click   the **Address tab** to begin entering the next supplier record.

Entering Historical Supplier Transactions

The chart on page 620 provides the information you need to complete this stage.

Enter   the supplier's **name, address tab information, options** and **taxes**.

Click   the **Historical Transactions tab**.

Click   **Save Now**.

NOTES
For a review of the Payables Ledger setup, refer to page 237.

PRO VERSION
pro Remember that the term Vendors will replace Suppliers.

NOTES
Year to date purchases and payments are not recorded because this is a new fiscal period.

NOTES
Leaving the code as No Tax and leaving the exempt status set at No will permit you to charge taxes if needed. PST is applied to insurance in Ontario.
If taxes are not calculated correctly for a supplier or customer, check that the Ledger entries for Tax Exempt are set to No.

NOTES
Feelyte Gym Accessories is the first supplier with historical invoices.
You can refer to page 241 to review entering historical supplier invoices and payments if necessary.

Click Invoices.

Enter the **Invoice Number**, **Date**, **Pre-Tax Amount** and **Tax** for the first invoice. The default terms should be correct.

Press (tab) to advance to the next field after entering each piece of information.

When all the information is entered correctly, you must save your supplier invoice.

Click **Record** to save the invoice and to display another blank invoice for this supplier.

Repeat these steps to **enter other invoices** for this supplier.

Click **Close** to return to the Payables Ledger when you have recorded all outstanding invoices for the supplier.

Historical Payments

Click **Payments** on the Historical Transactions tab screen.

Click the **Number field**.

Enter the **cheque number** for the first payment.

Press (tab) and **enter** the **payment date** for the first payment.

Skip the **Discount fields** because discounts are taken only when the early payment is a full payment.

Click the **Amount Paid column** (on the line for the invoice being paid).

Enter the **payment amount**.

Press (tab) to advance to the next invoice if there is one. Delete any amounts or discounts that are not included in the payment.

Click **Record** to save the information and to display an updated statement for this supplier.

Repeat these steps to **enter other payments** to this supplier.

When you have recorded all outstanding payments for a supplier,

Click **Close** to return to the Payables Ledger for the supplier. Notice that the payments you have just entered have been added to the Balance field.

Click the **Create tool** [icon] to display a new blank Payables Ledger screen.

Click the **Address tab**.

Repeat these procedures to **enter** the **remaining suppliers** and their **historical transactions**.

Identifying Foreign Suppliers

In order to identify Prolife Exercisers Inc. and Redux Home Gym Wholesalers as foreign suppliers, the Options tab screen requires additional information.

Enter the supplier's **name** and **address tab information**.

Click the **Options tab**:

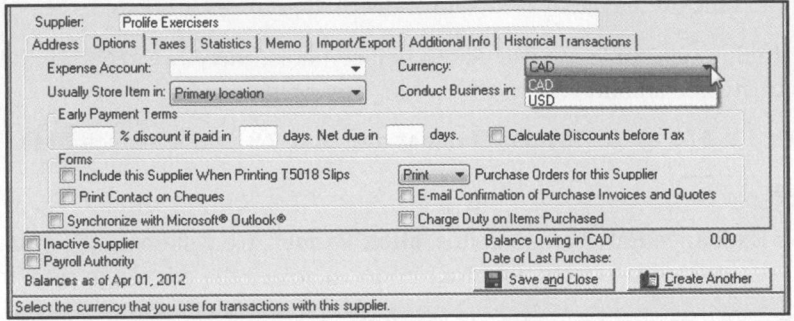

Enter   **2**% in **10** days, net **30** days as the Early Payment Terms for the supplier.

Click   **Calculate Discounts Before Tax**.

Click   the **Currency field list arrow**. **Click USD**.

Click   **Charge Duty On Items Purchased**.

You must change this Duty setting to make the duty fields in the Purchases Journal available for this supplier.

Do not enter a default expense account for inventory purchases — the linked asset account from the Inventory Ledger record is selected automatically by the program. The Balance Owing will be entered automatically by the program once you have entered historical invoices.

Click   the **Taxes tab** and **choose code H** for the foreign supplier.

Correct any **errors** by returning to the field with the mistake, highlighting the errors and entering the correct information.

Enter   **historical transactions** using the keystroke instructions in the following section if the supplier has historical transactions.

Click   **Create Another** 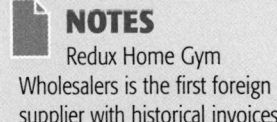 to save the record and open a blank Payables Ledger window.

Click   the **Address tab** to begin entering the next supplier record.

Invoices for Foreign Suppliers

Enter   the supplier's **name**, **address tab information**, **options** and **taxes**.

Click   the **Historical Transactions tab**. **Click Save Now**.

Click   **Invoices** on the Historical Transactions tab screen for Redux Home Gym Wholesalers:

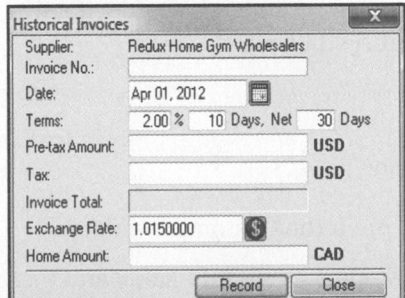

The Historical Invoices input screen for foreign suppliers has additional fields for the second currency information.

You can edit the payment terms for individual invoices if needed.

Because Redux discounts are calculated before taxes, there are separate fields for pretax and tax invoice amounts.

Enter **R-914** as the **Invoice Number** and **Mar 28** as the invoice **Date**.

Press (tab).

<table>
<tr><td>

NOTES

The Exchange Rate screen opens as soon as you enter the date. If you press (tab) after entering the date, it will open immediately. If you do not press (tab) and click the USD Amount field, it will open at that point. Click Cancel when it appears.

</td></tr>
</table>

If the Exchange Rate screen opens, **click Cancel**. We will enter the amounts in both currencies and allow the program to calculate the exchange rate.

Click the **Pretax Amount field for USD**.

Type 6400 **Press** (tab) to advance to the Tax amount field for USD.

Type 832

Click the **Home Amount field for CAD**.

Type 7350 **Press** (tab).

The exchange rate is determined automatically from these amounts.

Click **Record**.

When you have recorded all outstanding invoices for a supplier,

Click **Close** to save the invoice.

You will return to the Historical Transactions tab screen. The invoices you entered have been added to the Balance fields. Balances are displayed in both currencies. Continue by entering historical payments to this supplier if there are any, or proceed to enter the next supplier.

Click the **Create tool** 📇. **Click** the **Address tab**. **Enter** the **remaining suppliers**.

Click **Save And Close** 💾 Save and Close after adding the last supplier and then **close** the **Suppliers window**.

Display or **print** the **Supplier List** and the **Supplier Aged Detail Report**, including terms, historical differences and foreign amounts. Compare these reports with the information on pages 619–620 to check the accuracy of your work.

Preparing the Receivables Ledger

Use Flabuless Fitness' Customer Information on pages 620–621 to create the customer records and add the outstanding historical invoices. Revenue accounts are added from the inventory records so they are not needed in the customers' records. If any information is missing for a customer, leave that field blank.

Entering Customer Accounts

Click **Receivables** in the Modules pane list.

Click the **Customers icon** to open the Customers window.

Click the **Create button** or **choose** the **File menu** and then **click Create**. The cursor is in the Customer field.

Margin notes:

WARNING!
You must enter this information in the correct order for the exchange rate calculation to be made correctly.

NOTES
The Statistics tab screen shows the summary amounts in both Canadian and United States dollars.

NOTES
For a review of the Receivables Ledger setup, refer to page 244.

Enter   the customer's **name**. On the Address tab screen, enter the **contact**, **address**, **phone** and **fax numbers**, and the **e-mail** and **Web site addresses** according to page 620.

You can edit the default payment terms for individual customers or for individual historical invoices if necessary.

Click   the **Ship-To Address tab**.

The Mailing Address is already selected as the default ship-to address, so the same address will apply to both fields on invoices, orders and quotes.

Click   the **Options tab**.

Most entries on the Options tab screen are correct. Terms are entered from the default Receivables settings. Customer statements should be printed. Buffalo Health Clinic and Lockport Gymnasium are USD customers. All other customers are Canadian and use the Home currency (CAD).

Choose   **USD** from the Currency list for Buffalo Health Clinic (and for Lockport Gymnasium).

Choose   **Preferred** from the Price List field list for **Buffalo Health Clinic** and for other preferred customers (the ones marked with * in the customer information chart on page 620) to change the price list for these customers.

Change   the payment **terms** to **net 1** for **Cash and Interac**, and **Visa Sales customers**.

Click   the **Taxes tab**. For most customers, the default code H is correct.

Buffalo Health Clinic and Lockport Gymnasium, the foreign currency customers, do not pay taxes.

Select   **No Tax** as the **tax code** from the drop-down list for the US customers.

Click   the **Statistics tab**.

Enter   the **credit limit**. Enter the credit limit in both currencies for USD customers.

This is the amount that the customer can purchase on account before payments are required. If the customer goes beyond the credit limit, the program will issue a warning before posting an invoice.

The balance owing will be included automatically once you have provided the outstanding invoice information. If the customer has outstanding transactions, proceed to the next section on historical information. Otherwise,

Click   **Create Another** to save the information and advance to the next new Receivables Ledger input screen.

Click   the **Address tab**.

Entering Historical Customer Information

The chart on page 621 provides the information you need to complete this stage.

Enter   the customer's **name**, **address**, **options**, **taxes** and **credit limit**.

Click   the **Historical Transactions tab**. **Click Save Now**.

Click   **Invoices**.

NOTES
The preferred customers are:
Buffalo Health Clinic
Chedoke Health Care
McMaster University
Mohawk College

WARNING!
Do not forget to remove the discount terms for cash and credit card customer sales. Changing the ledger records will make the sales invoice terms correct automatically.

NOTES
You can refer to page 247 to review entering historical customer invoices and payments if necessary.

Enter the **invoice number**, **date** and **amount** for the first invoice. The default terms should be correct.

Press (tab) to advance to the next field after entering each piece of information.

When all the information is entered correctly, you must save the customer invoice.

Click **Record** to save the information and to display another blank invoice for this customer.

Repeat these procedures to **enter** the **remaining invoices** for the customer, if there are any.

When you have recorded all outstanding invoices for a customer,

Click **Close** to return to the Historical Transactions window for the customer.

The invoices you entered have been added to the Balance field. Continue by entering payments received from this customer, if there are any, or proceed to enter the next customer.

Click **Payments** on the Historical Transactions tab screen.

Click the **Number field**.

Enter the **cheque number** for the first payment.

Press (tab) and **enter** the **payment date** for the first payment. Again, discounts apply only to full payments made before the due dates, so you should skip the Discount fields.

Click the **Amount Paid column** (on the line for the invoice being paid).

Enter the **payment amount**.

Press (tab) to advance to the next amount if other invoices are being paid. Delete any amounts or discounts that are not included in the payment.

Click **Record** to save the information and to display an updated statement for this customer.

Repeat these procedures to **enter** the **remaining payments** from the customer.

When you have recorded all outstanding receipts from a customer,

Click **Close** to return to the Receivables Ledger window for the customer.

The payments you entered have been added to the customer's Balance field.

Click the **Create tool** 🖹 to open a new Receivables Ledger input screen.

Click the **Address tab** to prepare for entering other customers. After entering all customer records and historical data,

Click **Save And Close** 🖫 Save and Close (or ☒) after adding the last customer. **Close** the **Customers window** to return to the Home window.

Display or **print** the **Customer List** and the **Customer Aged Detail Report**, including terms and historical differences. Compare these reports with the information on pages 620–621 to check your work.

Preparing the Payroll Ledger

NOTES
For a review of the Payroll Ledger setup, refer to page 327.

Use the Flabuless Fitness Employee Information Sheet, Employee Profiles and Additional Payroll Information on pages 621–623 to create the employee records and add historical information.

We will enter the information for Flabuless Fitness employee George Schwinn.

Click   **Employees & Payroll** in the Modules pane list.

Click   the **Employees icon** in the Home window.

Click   the **Create button** or **choose** the **File menu** and **click Create**.

Entering Personal Details for Employees

The Payroll Ledger new employee information form will open at the Personal information tab screen so you can begin to enter the employee record.

The Payroll Ledger has a large number of tabs for the different kinds of payroll information. The cursor is in the Employee field. By entering the surname first, your employee lists will be in correct alphabetic order.

Type   Schwinn, George **Press** ⟨tab⟩.

Type   55 Carter St. to enter the Street address.

The default city and province, those for the store, are correct.

Click   the **Postal Code field**.

Type   18b2v7 **Press** ⟨tab⟩.

The program corrects the postal code format and advances the cursor to the Phone 1 field.

Type   9054261817

The default **Language Preference** is correctly set as English.

Click   the **Social Insurance Number (SIN) field**. You must use a valid SIN. The program has corrected the telephone number format.

Type   532548625 **Press** ⟨tab⟩.

NOTES
The program will allow you to omit the Social Insurance Number but you must enter the employee's birth date.

The cursor advances to the Birth Date field. Enter the month, day and year using any accepted date format. Birth Date is a required field and it must be correct because it is linked to CPP calculations.

Type   9-18-70 **Press** ⟨tab⟩ **twice**.

The cursor moves to the Hire Date field, which should contain the date when the employee began working for Flabuless Fitness.

Type   1-6-04

NOTES
Refer to page 297 for more information about employee terminations.

The next two fields will be used when the employee leaves the job — the date of termination and the reason for leaving that you can select from the drop-down list. The final option designates employees as active or inactive. All employees at Flabuless Fitness are active, so the default selection is correct.

We have not yet created Job Categories to identify salespersons, so we will assign employees to them later. The program will automatically enter the Date Last Paid.

NOTES
Refer to page 329 to review entering employee tax details.

NOTES
For all Flabuless Fitness employees, the total federal and provincial claim amounts are subject to indexing. Governments raise these claim amounts based on inflation and budget decisions.

WARNING!
Enter employee historical payroll details carefully. You will be unable to edit these fields after finishing the history or after making Payroll Journal entries for the employee.

They must also be correct because they are used to create T4s for tax reporting.

NOTES
The program skips the Quebec tax fields because you selected Ontario as the province of taxation and no linked accounts were entered for them.

NOTES
Refer to page 330 if you need to review entering employee income details.

Entering Employee Tax Information

Click the **Taxes tab** to advance to the next set of employee details.

This screen allows you to enter income tax–related information for an employee, including the historical amounts for the year to date. Tax Table is a required field.

Click the **Tax Table list arrow** to see the list of provinces and territories.

Click **Ontario**, the province of taxation for Flabuless Fitness employees.

Press (tab) to advance to the **Federal Claim** field.

Type 10382 **Press** (tab) to advance to the **Federal Claim Subject To Indexing**. This is the amount of personal claim minus pension and tuition/education exemption amounts.

Type 10382 **Press** (tab) to advance to the Provincial Claim field.

Provincial personal income taxes are not linked to the rates for federal income taxes, so separate **provincial claim** amounts are needed.

Type 8943 **Press** (tab).

Type 8943 **Press** (tab) to enter the Provincial Claim Amount Subject To Indexing.

The cursor advances to the **Additional Federal Tax** field. Prekor is the only employee with other income who chooses to have additional taxes withheld.

For **Prekor**, click the **Additional Fed. Tax** field and type **50**.

If an employee is insurable by EI, you must leave the box for **Deduct EI** checked. The default EI contribution factor, 1.4, for Flabuless Fitness is correct. We entered it in the Payroll Taxes Settings window (page 652).

All employees at Flabuless make CPP contributions so this check box should remain selected.

We will enter the historical income tax amounts next.

Click the **Historical Amount field** for **Income Tax**.

Type 1562.21 **Press** (tab) to advance to the EI Premiums Historical Amount field. Enter the amount of EI paid to date.

Type 217.54 **Press** (tab) to move to the CPP Contributions Historical Amount field.

Type 375.20

Entering Income Amounts for Employees

We defined all the types of income for Flabuless Fitness in the Names, Incomes & Deductions setup (page 648). All employees use the following types of income, although not all will have regular amounts and not all will be used on all paycheques:
- Advances
- Benefits
- No. Clients
- Bonus
- Tuition
- Travel Exp.

For Schwinn the following incomes are also used: Vacation (Vac.) Owed, Vacation (Vac.) Paid, Regular and Overtime 1.

For Kisangel and Prekor the following incomes are used: Salary and Commission. Because Quebec is not selected as the province of taxation, Benefits (Que) is not preselected. Advance, Benefits and Vacation checkmarks cannot be removed.

All the details you need to complete the Income tab chart are on pages 621–622.

> **Click**   the **Income tab**.

On the Income chart you can indicate the types of income that each employee receives (the **Use** column), the usual rate of pay for that type of income (**Amount Per Unit**), the usual number of hours worked (**Hours Per Period**), the usual number of pieces for a piece rate pay base (**Pieces Per Period**) and the amounts received this year before the earliest transaction date or the date used for the first paycheque (**Historical Amount**). The **Year-To-Date (YTD) Amount** is added automatically by the program based on the historical amounts you enter and the paycheques entered in the program.

Checkmarks should be entered in the Use column so that the fields will be available in the payroll journals, even if they will not be used on all paycheques.

> **Click**   **Regular** in the Income column to select the line.
>
> **Press**   `tab` to advance to the Amount Per Unit field where we need to enter the regular hourly wage rate.
>
> **Type**   16 **Press** `tab` to advance the Hours Per Period field.

The usual number of work hours in the bi-weekly pay period is 80. You can change the default amount in the Payroll journals. Salaried workers normally work 150 hours each month.

> **Type**   80 **Press** `tab` to advance to the Historical Amount field.

Historical income and deduction amounts for the year to date are necessary so that taxes and deductions can be calculated correctly and T4 statements will be accurate.

> **Type**   8960 **Press** `tab`.

The amount is entered automatically in the YTD column and the cursor advances to the Use column for Overtime 1.

> **Press**   `tab` so you can enter the overtime hourly rate.
>
> **Type**   24
>
> **Press**   `tab` **twice** to advance to the Historical Amount field. There is no regular number of overtime hours.
>
> **Type**   336

The next three income types do not apply to Schwinn, so they should not be checked. The next income that applies is No. Clients, the piece rate method of pay. There is no historical amount, but we need to enter the rate or amount per unit (survey). The remaining incomes (No. Clients, Bonus and Travel Exp.) are correctly checked. There is no fixed amount per unit or period and there are no historical amounts.

> Pressing the space bar when you are in the Use column will also add a ✓ or remove one if it is there. Pressing ⊥ will move you to the next line in the same column.
>
> **Click**   the **Use column beside Salary** to remove the ✓.
>
> **Click**   the **Use column beside Commission** to remove the ✓.
>
> **Click**   **No. Clients** in the Income column to select the line. **Press** `tab`.
>
> **Type**   10 to enter the amount received for each completed survey.

NOTES
In the chart on pages 621–622, the incomes that are used by an employee have a ✓ or an amount in the employee's column.

NOTES
Checkmarks are added by default for all incomes, deductions and expenses that have linked accounts.

WARNING!
Do not click the Use column beside Regular as that will remove the checkmark.

NOTES
If you added a linked account for Overtime 2, it will have a ✓ in the Use column and you should remove it for all employees.

NOTES
Remember that commissions must be calculated manually and entered in the Payroll journals. The Commission field in the Payroll Ledger allows only a fixed amount, not a percentage of sales, as the entry.

If employees have received vacation pay, enter this amount in the **Vac. Paid** field. Vacation pay not yet received is entered in the **Vac. Owed** field. Any advances paid to the employees and not yet repaid are recorded in the **Advances Paid** field. There is no record of advance amounts recovered.

We need to add the historical advances, benefits and vacation amounts for Schwinn. Schwinn has $100 in advances not yet repaid, and he has not used all the vacation pay he has earned this year.

Scroll   **to the top** of the list so that the information for Advance is available.

Click   the **Historical Amount column beside Advance** to move the cursor.

Type   100

Press   ⌨tab to move to the Amount Per Unit column for Benefits. The group insurance premiums paid by the employer are employee benefits.

Type   5 **Press** ⌨tab to move to the Historical Amount for Benefits.

Type   35 **Press** ⌨tab to advance to the Historical Amount for Vac. Owed.

Type   371.84 **Press** ⌨tab to advance to the Historical Vac. Paid Amount.

Type   385.92

For **Prekor**, click the Use column for Regular, Overtime 1 and Commission to remove the ✓. Enter the monthly salary and press ⌨tab. Enter 150 as the number of hours worked in the pay period. Press ⌨tab and enter the historical amount. For No. Clients, enter 10 as the amount per unit. For Travel Exp., enter 120 as the historical amount. You cannot remove the ✓ for Vac. Owed and Vac. Paid, even if they are not used.

For **Kisangel**, repeat these steps but leave Commission checked and enter the historical amount. For Tuition, enter 440 as the historical amount.

Pay Periods Per Year, another required field, refers to the number of times the employee is paid, or the pay cycle. Schwinn is paid every two weeks, 26 times per year.

Click   the **list arrow** beside the field **for Pay Periods Per Year**.

Click   **26**.

Retaining Vacation pay is normal for full-time hourly paid employees. Part-time and casual workers often receive their vacation pay with each paycheque because their work schedule is irregular. You will turn the option to retain vacation off when an employee receives the vacation pay, either when taking a vacation or when leaving the company (see page 284). If the employee is salaried and does not receive vacation pay, the option should also be turned off. For Schwinn, or any employee who receives vacation pay, leave the option to Retain Vacation checked and type the vacation pay rate in the % field.

Double click   the **% field beside Retain Vacation**.

Type   6

For **Prekor** and **Kisangel**, click Retain Vacation to remove the ✓.

Employee wages may be linked to the default expense account or to another account. Wage expenses for all Flabuless Fitness employees are linked to the default accounts entered on page 654.

Entering Default Payroll Deduction Amounts

Click   the **Deductions tab** to open the screen for payroll deductions.

On this screen, you can indicate which deductions apply to the employee, the amount normally deducted and the historical amount — the amount deducted to date this year. All deductions are selected in the Use column. These are the deductions you entered previously (page 648).

By entering deduction amounts here, they will be included automatically on the Payroll Journal input forms. Otherwise, you must enter them manually in the Journal for each pay period. Since all three employees participate in the RRSP and CSB plans, you can enter the information here so that the deductions are made automatically. You should make permanent changes by editing the employee ledger record.

If you choose to calculate deductions as a percentage of gross pay in the Payroll Settings, the Percentage Per Pay Period fields will be available.

NOTES
For one-time changes, you can edit deduction amounts in the Payroll journals on the Deductions tab or the Deductions Details screen.

Click   **RRSP** in the Deduction column to select the line.

Press   (tab). You should enter the amount that is withheld in each pay period.

Type   50 **Press** (tab) to advance the cursor to the Historical Amount field.

Type   350 **Press** (tab) to advance the cursor to the Use column for CSB Plan.

Press   (tab). Enter the amount that is to be withheld in each pay period.

Type   50 **Press** (tab) to advance the cursor to the Historical Amount field.

Type   350 **Press** (tab) to update the YTD Amount and advance to the Use column for Garnishee.

Click   the **Use column for Garnishee** to remove the ✓. Schwinn does not have wages withheld.

For **Prekor**, enter 200 as the Amount and 400 as the YTD amount for Garnishee.

The remaining deductions are not used by Flabuless Fitness. The names were deleted (page 649) so they do not appear on the chart.

Entering WSIB and Other Expenses

Click   the **WSIB & Other Expenses tab**.

The user-defined expenses we created in the Additional Payroll Names screen (page 649) and the default WSIB rate (page 652) are entered on this screen.

In Ontario, WSIB (Workplace Safety and Insurance Board) is the name for Workers' Compensation Board, so the tab is labelled WSIB. In other provinces, the tab label will be WCB & Other Expenses.

The default WSIB rate is entered from our setup information, but you can enter a different rate for an individual employee in this field. The rate is correct for Schwinn.

NOTES
Refer to page 333 to review entering WSIB (WCB) details.

NOTES
The Ontario name was changed to emphasize safety rather than compensation for accidents. WSIB (or WCB) pays workers when they have been injured on the job and are unable to work.

For **Kisangel**, enter 1.02 as the WSIB rate.

Other user-defined expenses are also added on this screen. Flabuless Fitness has only group insurance as a user-defined expense.

Click   the **Gp Insurance Amt. Per Period**. Enter the amount that the employer contributes in each pay period.

Type   5 **Press** (tab) to advance to the Historical Amount field.

Type   35

The remaining expense fields are not used by Flabuless Fitness.

Entering Employee Entitlements

We entered the default rates and amounts for entitlements as Payroll Settings (page 653), but they can be modified in the ledger records for individual employees.

We must also enter the historical information for entitlements. This historical number will include any days carried forward from the previous periods. The number of days accrued cannot be greater than the maximum number of days defined for the entitlement for an employee. The number of Net Days Accrued, the amount unused and available for carrying forward, is updated automatically from the historical information and current payroll journal entries.

Click the **Entitlements tab**.

You cannot enter information directly in the Net Days Accrued fields on the Entitlements tab screen.

Schwinn receives vacation pay instead of paid time off so the vacation entitlements details should be removed. The defaults for sick leave and personal days are correct.

Click **8.00** in the **Track Using % Hours Worked field for Vacation**.

Press (del) to remove the entry.

Press (tab) to advance to the Maximum Days field.

Press (del) to remove the entry.

Click the **Historical Days field for Sick Leave**.

Type 12

Press (↓) to advance to the Historical Days field for PersonalDays. The number of days is added to the Net Days Accrued.

Type 4 **Press** (tab) to enter the amount.

For **Kisangel** and **Prekor**, the default entries for tracking and maximum days are correct, but you must enter the Historical Days for each entitlement.

Entering Direct Deposit Information

Click the **Direct Deposit tab**.

All three employees have elected to have their paycheques deposited directly to their bank accounts. On this screen, we need to enter the bank account details. For each employee who has elected the direct deposit option, you must turn on the selection in the Direct Deposit Paycheques For This Employee check box. Then you must add the three-digit **Bank Number**, five-digit **Transit Number**, the bank Account Number and finally the amount that is deposited, or the percentage of the cheque.

Click the **Direct Deposit Paycheques For This Employee check box** to add a ✓.

Click the **Bank Number field**.

Type 102 **Press** (tab) to advance to the Transit Number field.

Type 89008 **Press** (tab) to advance to the Account Number field.

Type 2998187 **Press** (tab) **twice** to advance to the Percentage field.

Type 100

The Memo tab will not be used at this time. You could enter a note with a reminder date to appear in the Daily Business Manager, for example, a reminder to issue vacation paycheques on a specific date or to recover advances.

Entering Additional Information

Flabuless Fitness has chosen to enter the name and phone number of the person to be contacted in case of an emergency involving the employee at work. We added the names for these fields in the Payroll Settings (page 649).

Click   the **Additional Info tab** to access the fields we added for the ledger when we entered Names.

You can indicate whether you want to display any of the additional information when the employee is selected in a transaction. We do not need to display the contact information in the Payroll Journal.

Click   the **Emergency Contact field**.

Type   Adrian Ingles

Press   (tab) **twice** to move to the Contact Number field.

Type   (905) 722-0301

Entering T4 and RL-1 Reporting Amounts

The next information screen allows you to enter the year-to-date EI insurable and pensionable earnings. By adding the historical amounts, the T4 slips prepared for income taxes at the end of the year and the record of employment termination reports will also be correct.

Because there are yearly maximum amounts for CPP and EI contributions, these historical details are also needed. Totals for optional deductions are also retained in the employee record.

Click   the **T4 and RL-1 Reporting tab** to open the next screen we need to complete.

In the **Historical EI Ins. Earnings** field, you should enter the total earned income received to date that is EI insurable. The program will update this total every time you make payroll entries until the maximum salary on which EI is calculated has been reached. At that time, no further EI premiums will be deducted.

Pensionable Earnings are also tracked by the program. This amount determines the total income that is eligible for Canada Pension Plan. The Pension Adjustment amount is used when the employee has a workplace pension program that will affect the allowable contributions for personal registered pension plans and will be linked with the Canada Pension Plan. Workplace pension income is reduced when the employee also has income from the Canada Pension Plan. Since Flabuless Fitness has no company pension plan, the Pension Adjustment amount is zero.

The T4 Employee Code applies to a small number of job types that have special income tax rules.

Click   the **Historical Amounts field for EI Ins. Earnings**.

Type   9681.92

Click   the **Historical Amounts field for Pensionable Earnings**.

Type   9716.92

NOTES
Refer to page 336 to review entering employee additional information details.

NOTES
Additional information for other ledgers may also be displayed or hidden in journal transactions.

WARNING!
The Contact Number field is not predefined as a telephone number, so its format will not be corrected automatically by the program.

NOTES
Refer to page 336 if you need to review entering T4 and RL-1 reporting details.

NOTES
The EI Insurable amount is the total of gross wages, including overtime wages and vacation pay, but not benefits.
Pensionable earnings include these same incomes plus benefits.

NOTES
We will not use the remaining tax information fields for Flabuless Fitness. Flabuless Fitness does not have a company pension plan with regular payroll deductions, so there is no plan registration number. The Pension Adjustment amount is used when an employee contributes to a company pension plan and these payments reduce the amount the employee can contribute to a private registered pension plan. The company pension plan payments also affect the CPP amount received at retirement, but not CPP premiums.

Correct any employee information **errors** by returning to the field with the error. **Highlight** the **error** and **enter** the **correct information**. **Click each tab** in turn so that you can check all the information.

When all the information is entered correctly, you must save the employee record.

Click   **Create Another** 🗋 Create Another to save the record and to open a new blank employee information form.

Click   the **Personal tab** so that you can enter address information.

Repeat these procedures to **enter** other employee **records**.

Click   **Save And Close** 💾 Save and Close after entering the last record to save the record and close the Payroll Ledger.

Display or **print** the **Employee List** and the **Employee Summary Report**. Compare them with pages 621–623 to check the accuracy of your work.

Close   the **Employees window** to return to the Home window.

> **NOTES**
> You can print these reports from the Reports menu in the Employees window.

Entering Job Categories

Now that we have entered all the employees, we can set up job categories and indicate which employees are in each category.

> **NOTES**
> Refer to page 339 if you want to review the setup for job categories.

Click   the **Settings icon** 🗑 Settings. Then **click Payroll** and **Job Categories**.

On the Job Categories screen, you enter the names of the categories and indicate whether the employees in each category submit time slips and whether they are salespersons. Categories may be active or inactive. We need a new category called Sales.

Notice that if you do not create categories, the employees in the default selection <None> are salespersons so they can be selected in the Sales Journal.

Click   the **Job Category field below <None>**.

Type   Sales **Press** ⌨ tab ⌨ to add checkmarks to the next two columns and set the status to Active.

Click   **Assign Job Categories** to change the screen.

The Sales category is selected and the screen is updated with employee names. Initially, all are Employees Not In This Job Category.

You can add employee names to the category by choosing an employee and clicking **Select** or by choosing **Select All**. Once employees are in a category (the column on the right), you can remove them by selecting an employee and clicking **Remove** or clicking **Remove All** to move all names at the same time.

Click   **Select All** to place all employees in the Sales category.

Click   **OK** to save the information and return to the Home window.

Setting Up Payroll Remittances

> **NOTES**
> Refer to page 337 if you want to review payroll remittance setup.

Because we have entered all payroll settings and all suppliers, we can set up the payroll remittances information. This process has three steps: identifying the suppliers who receive payroll remittance amounts, linking the suppliers to the taxes or deductions they receive, and entering opening dates and balances. First we should designate the payroll authorities. Refer to the chart on page 616 for the Payroll remittance settings.

The suppliers to which we remit payroll taxes or other deductions are Ancaster Insurance, Minister of Finance, Mt. Hope Investment Corp., Receiver General for Canada and Workplace Safety & Insurance Board.

Click   the **Search field**.

Type   Ancaster **Click** → to open the Search Results screen.

The results show two entries: one for the supplier we want and one supplier address entry for the city of Ancaster.

Double click **Ancaster Insurance** to open the supplier's record.

Click   **Payroll Authority** to add the ✓ and change the supplier's payroll status.

Click   the **Next Supplier tool** ▶ **repeatedly** to access the record for the **Minister of Finance**, the next payroll authority.

Click   **Payroll Authority** to add the ✓ and change the supplier's payroll status.

Repeat these **steps** for the remaining payroll authorities: **Mt. Hope Investment Corp.**, **Receiver General for Canada** and **Workplace Safety & Insurance Board**.

Close   the **Payables Ledger window**. **Close** the **Search Results window**.

Click   the **Settings icon** [Settings]. Then **click Payroll** and **Remittance**.

All the payroll items that are linked to liability (remittance) accounts are listed: taxes, deductions and user-defined expenses. For each liability, we can select a supplier and enter the balance forward date and amount.

Click   the **List icon** 🔍 in the Payroll Authority column on the line for EI to see the list of suppliers we marked as Payroll Authorities.

Click   **Receiver General for Canada**.

Click   **Select** or press (enter) to return to the Remittance Settings screen.

The Receiver General for Canada appears beside EI. The cursor advances to the Balance Forward Date field for EI. We need to enter the balances owing at the time we are converting the data to Simply Accounting and the pay period covered by those amounts. These balances are in the Trial Balance on page 619. The effective date is April 1 for all liabilities.

Type   Apr 1 **Press** (tab) to advance to the Balance Forward field.

Type   563.28 **Press** (tab) to advance to the Payroll Authority field for CPP.

Enter   the remaining **Payroll Authorities**, **dates** and **balances**.

Click   **OK** to save the settings.

Preparing the Inventory Ledger

Use the Flabuless Fitness Inventory Information and chart on pages 623–624 to record details about the inventory items on hand.

Entering Inventory Records

The following keystrokes will enter the information for Flabuless Fitness' first inventory item, Body Fat Scale.

Click   **Inventory & Services** in the Modules pane list.

NOTES
Refer to the Company Information on page 616 and the Trial Balance on page 619 to complete the remittance setup.

NOTES
You can also click the Search tool 🔍 to open the Search window. Click Suppliers from the drop-down list for Select A Record Or Transaction Type To Find.
Click Ancaster Insurance and then click OK to open the supplier's record.
To open the next supplier record, you can also click the Select list arrow and click Minister of Finance.

PRO VERSION

There isn't a Build tab in the Pro version, and only two show icons will be included in the tool bar. The Show Activities tool applies only to Premium features, and the Refresh tool is used with the multi-user option in Premium.

NOTES

If you skip the Inventory icon window (Setup menu, User Preferences, View), you will see this Inventory Ledger immediately when you click the Inventory icon.

NOTES

The Inventory Description is not a required field.

WARNING!

Enter inventory details very carefully. You cannot remove an inventory record or change the Type if there is a quantity on hand. You must edit the History fields to reduce the quantity and value to zero. Then remove the item and re-enter all the details correctly.

To change the Type, close the ledger to save the changes in the history. When you open the ledger again, you may edit the Type.

WARNING!

You must enter the unit relationship information before entering the history for inventory so that purchase prices and average costs will be calculated correctly.

Click the **Inventory & Services icon** . Again, with no inventory items on file, the icon window is empty.

Click the **Create button** or **choose** the **File menu** and **click Create**:

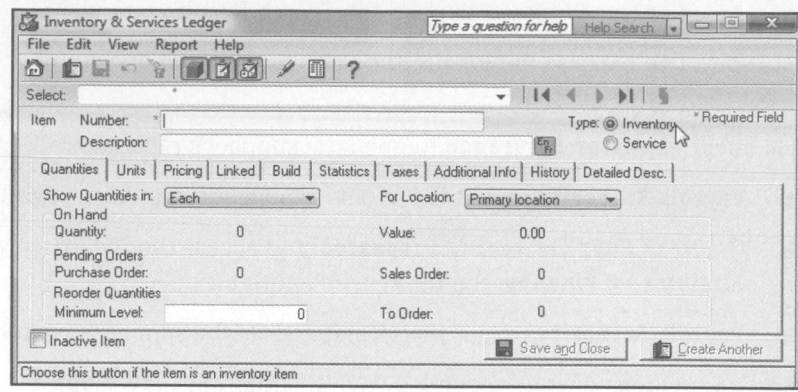

The cursor is in the Item Number field. Use this field for the code or number for the first item. When you sort inventory by description, the two item fields shown here will be reversed — the Description field will appear first. Item Number is a required field.

Type A010 **Press** (tab) to advance to the Item Description field, the field for the name of the inventory item.

Type Body Fat Scale

The Type is set correctly for this item as Inventory rather than Service.

The Show Quantities In field allows you to select the units displayed in the ledger. If you have entered different units for stocking, selling and buying, these will be available from the drop-down list. The Quantity On Hand and Value fields are updated by the program as are the Purchase Orders and Sales Orders Pending.

Click the **Minimum Level field**. Here you should enter the minimum stock level or re-order point for this inventory item.

Type 2

Click the **Units tab** to see the next information screen:

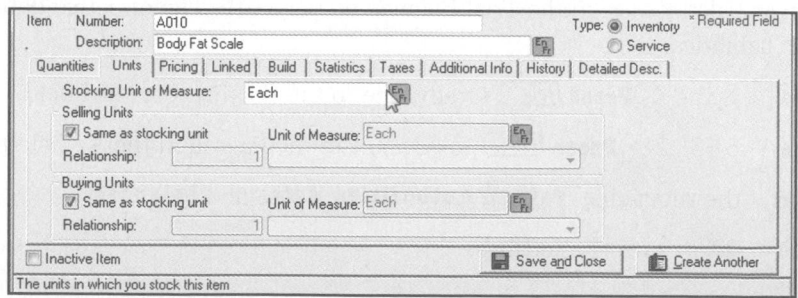

You can enter different units for items when the units for buying, stocking and selling differ. Flabuless Fitness uses the same units for stocking and selling but some buying units are different. For example, if items are purchased in dozens and stocked individually, the relationship is 12 to 1. The Stocking Unit must be changed. Body Fat Scales are purchased in cartons of 12 scales and stocked and sold individually (unit).

Double click the default entry **Each** for the Stocking Unit Of Measure.

Type Unit

Click **Same As Stocking Unit** for the **Buying Units** section to remove the ✓.

The relationship fields open to indicate how many stocking units are in each buying unit.

Press `tab` to advance to the Unit Of Measure field.

Type `Carton` **Press** `tab` **twice** to advance to the Relationship field.

Type `12` **Press** `tab`. Check that the entry is 12 Unit Per Carton. If it is not, click the drop-down list and choose this relationship.

Click the **Pricing tab** to open the next group of inventory record fields:

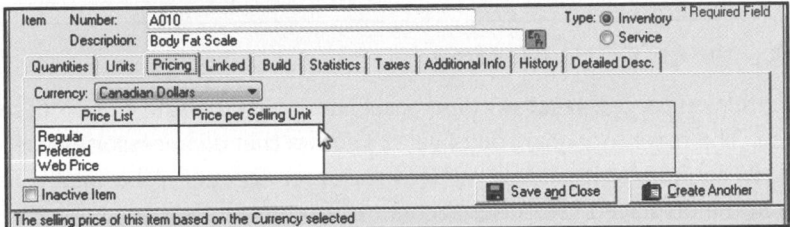

NOTES
To see the Inventory Ledger Settings, refer to page 655. You cannot change these settings while the Inventory Ledger is open.

The Currency field and foreign price fields are available only if you indicated that inventory prices should be taken from the Inventory Ledger record and not calculated using the exchange rate. The pricing option appears on the Inventory Settings screen only after you enter foreign currency information. Therefore, you must add and save currency information first. Taking prices from the ledger record is the default setting.

On the Pricing tab screen, you can enter regular, preferred and Web prices in the currencies that you have set up. If you created additional price lists, their names will also appear on this screen. The home currency (Canadian Dollars) is selected first.

NOTES
By working from the Inventory Ledger Settings, Price Lists screen, you can create new price lists and update all prices from one screen. In Chapter 18, we update inventory prices using this approach.

Click the **Regular Price Per Selling Unit field**. Here you should enter the selling price for this inventory item.

Type `150` **Press** `tab` to advance to the Preferred Selling Price field.

PRO VERSION
You cannot create additional price lists or update them globally in the Pro version.

The regular price is also entered as the default Preferred and Web Price. We do not have Web sales so we can accept the default entry for Web prices. Preferred selling prices are shown in brackets in the Inventory Information chart on page 623.

Type `130` to replace the default entry.

Choose United States Dollars from the Currency list to open USD price fields:

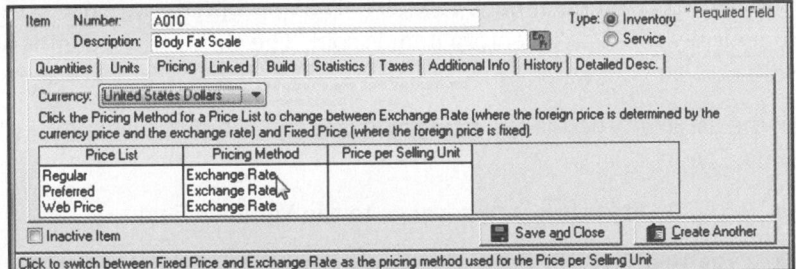

The pricing method is entered separately for each price. You can choose either Exchange Rate or Fixed Price for Regular and Preferred prices.

Click **Exchange Rate** beside Regular to change the entry to Fixed Price.

Press `tab` to advance to the Regular Price Per Selling Unit field.

Type `145` **Press** `tab` to advance to the Pricing Method field.

Click **Exchange Rate** to change the entry to Fixed Price.

Press `tab` to advance to the Preferred Price Per Selling Unit field.

Type   135 **Press** (tab).

Click   the **Linked tab** to open the linked accounts screen for the item:

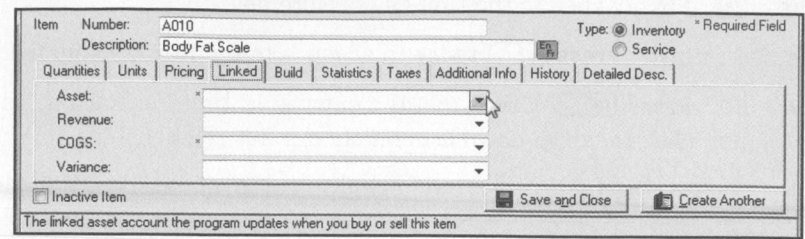

Click   the **Asset field list arrow**.

Here you must enter the **asset** account associated with the sale or purchase of this inventory item. The Inventory chart on page 623 shows that all accessories use account *1520*. All fitness equipment items use *1540* as the asset account. All available asset accounts are in the displayed list. Asset account is a required field.

> Enter the account by clicking the list arrow and choosing from the drop-down account list, or

Type   1520 **Press** (tab).

The program asks you to confirm the account class change for account 1520:

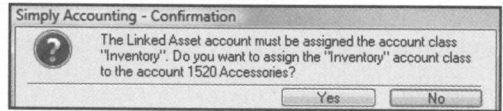

Click   **Yes** to accept the change.

The cursor advances to the **Revenue** field. Here you must enter the revenue account that will be credited with the sale of this inventory item. Again, you can display the list of revenue accounts by clicking the list arrow. Or,

Type   4020 **Press** (tab).

The cursor advances to the **C.O.G.S.** field. Here you must enter the expense account to be debited with the sale of this inventory item, normally the *Cost of Goods Sold* account. Flabuless Fitness keeps track of each inventory category separately and has different expense accounts for each category. The appropriate expense account is updated automatically when an inventory item is sold. The C.O.G.S. account is another required field.

> Click the list arrow beside the field to display the list of available expense accounts. Or,

Type   5050 **Press** (tab) to advance to the Variance field.

Click   **Yes** to accept the account class change.

Simply Accounting uses the **Variance** linked account when sales are made of items that are not in stock. If there is a difference between the historical average cost of goods remaining in stock and the actual cost when the new merchandise is received, the price difference is charged to the variance expense account at the time of the purchase. If you have not indicated a variance account, the program will ask you to identify one when you are entering the purchase.

Type   5070   or click the list arrow and choose the account.

Click   the **Build tab**.

Click   **Yes** to accept the account class change and access the Build screen:

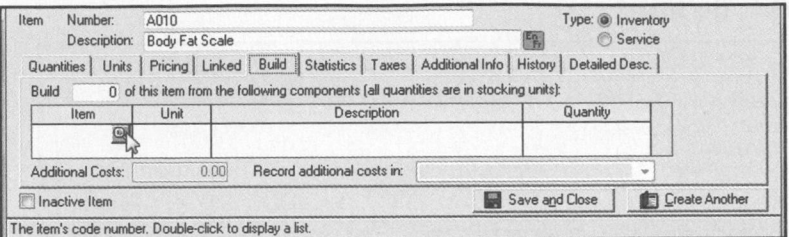

PRO VERSION
The Build tab screen is not included in the Pro version. Click the Statistics tab as the next step.

The Build feature is available in Premium but not in the Pro version. On this screen you define how this item is made or built from other inventory items. Then, in the journal, you can build the item by choosing it from the available list and entering the number of units you want to build. This screen holds the components portion of the Item Assembly Journal.

Click   the **Statistics tab** to open the next tab information screen:

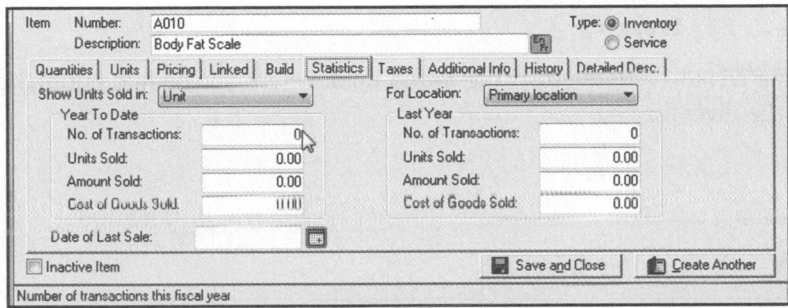

On this screen, you can enter historical information about the sale of the product. It would then be added to the inventory tracking information for reports.

The first activity field, the Date Of Last Sale, refers to the last date on which the item was sold. The next two sections contain information for the Year To Date and the previous year. Since Flabuless Fitness has not kept this information, you can skip these fields. Refer to page 380 in the Adrienne Aesthetics application (Chapter 10) for a more detailed description of these historical Statistics fields.

Click   the **Taxes tab** to input the sales taxes relating to the inventory item:

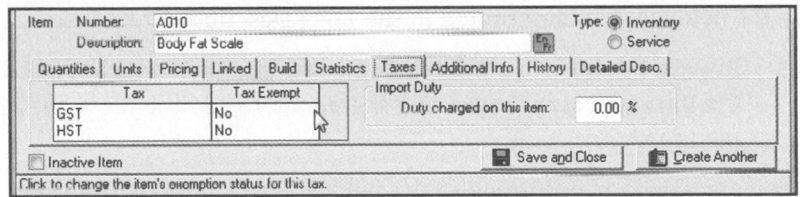

You can indicate whether the item is taxable for all the taxes you set up, provincial and federal sales taxes in this case. HST is charged on sales of all inventory items, so the default entry No for **Tax Exempt** is correct, except for Books.

The exemption settings in the ledger record do not control the tax code entered in the Sales Journal. They do prevent a tax from being applied.

For **Books: Fitness Guide**, item B010, **click No** beside **HST** for Tax Exempt to change the entry to Yes.

Duty is also entered on this screen. You must activate the duty tracking option before the duty rate field becomes available. Since no duty is charged on the imported inventory, you can leave the duty rate at 0%.

We have not added fields to the ledger record as we did for Payroll so we can skip the **Additional Info** screen.

The next step is to add the opening historical balances for the inventory items.

NOTES
To open the Duty fields in the Purchases Journal, you must activate tracking of duty information and indicate in the supplier record that duty is charged on purchases from the supplier. Rates entered in the Inventory Ledger records will appear automatically in the Purchases Journal for those items. Duty rates can also be entered in the journal if you have not entered them in the ledger records.

NOTES
When you set up multiple locations, you can enter the quantity and value for items at each location. The Primary location is the default. In Chapter 18, we add a second location for Flabuless Fitness.

WARNING!
The total opening value amounts for all items in an asset group must match the General Ledger asset account balance before you can finish entering the history.

NOTES
A picture file for the Body Fat Scale has been added to the SimData10\Setup\Logos folder with your other data files. We have not provided picture files for the remaining inventory items.

NOTES
If you add a .bmp format picture file, you will see the picture in the box beside the Long Description field. Other file formats may be used, but the pictures will not be displayed.

Click the **History tab**:

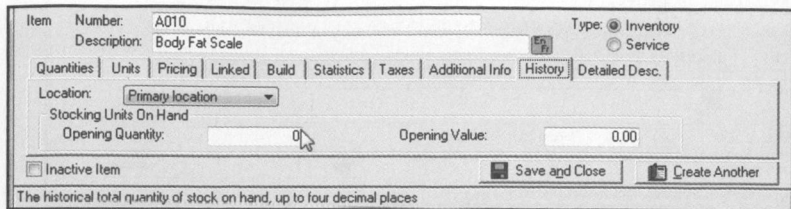

This screen has information about the starting quantities for the item at the time of conversion to Simply Accounting. The opening quantities and values are added to the quantity on hand and value on the Quantities tab screen. History is entered in stocking unit quantities (the same as selling units for Flabuless Fitness).

Click the **Opening Quantity field** to enter the opening level of inventory — the actual number of items available for sale.

Type 20 **Press** (tab).

The cursor advances to the **Opening Value** field, where you should enter the actual total cost of the inventory on hand.

Type 1100

The remaining tab allows you to enter further descriptive information.

Click the **Detailed Desc. tab**:

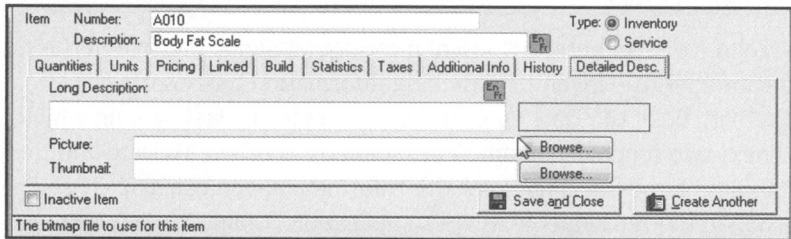

This optional information provides a detailed description of the inventory item (about 500 characters) as well as a picture in image file format.

Type the detailed item description in the Long Description text box.

Click **Browse** beside Picture. **Click Computer** and then **double click C:**, **SimData10**, **Setup**, **Logos** and **scale.bmp** to add the file name and picture.

Correct any **errors** by returning to the field with the mistake. **Highlight** the **error** and **enter** the **correct information**. **Click** the different **tabs** to see all the information that you entered.

When all the information is entered correctly, you must save your inventory record.

Click **Create Another** [Create Another] to save the record and advance to a new input screen.

Click the **Quantities tab** to prepare for entering the next item.

Repeat these procedures to **enter other** inventory **records** on page 623.

Entering Inventory Services

The final items on the inventory chart (page 624) are services that Flabuless Fitness provides. Entering services is similar to entering inventory, but there are fewer details.

You should have a blank Inventory & Services Ledger window open at the Quantities tab screen.

Click   **Service** to change the Type in the upper-right section of the screen:

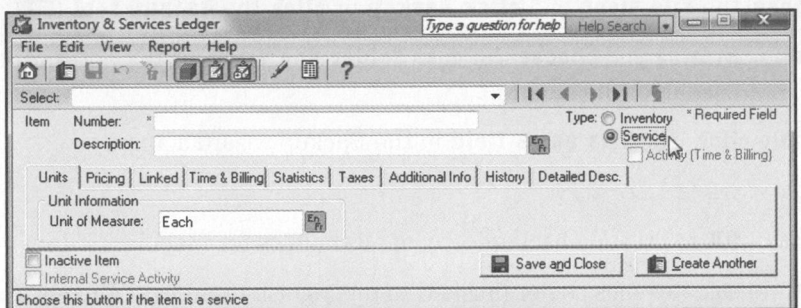

PRO VERSION
The Time & Billing tab screen is used to set up Time & Billing, a feature that is not available in the Pro version. The Activity setting and Internal Service Activity also apply to the Time & Billing feature, so they do not appear on the Pro version screen.

There are fewer tabs and fields for services because some item details do not apply. The Unit Of Measure and Selling Price have the same meaning for services as they do for inventory items. Because service items are not kept in stock or purchased, only the selling unit is applicable, there is no minimum quantity and the History tab and fields are removed. Flabuless Fitness' services are not exported, so you do not need to enter foreign prices. Only expense and revenue accounts are linked for services. The other two linked account fields do not apply and are removed for services. Remember to use *Revenue from Services* and *Cost of Services* as the linked accounts for inventory services.

Enter   the **Item Number** and **Description** and the **Unit Of Measure**.

Click   the **Pricing tab** and add **Regular** and **Preferred prices** in Canadian dollars. Select Canadian Dollars as the currency if necessary.

Click   the **Linked tab**. **Enter** the linked accounts for **Revenue (4040)** and **Expense (5065)**. Accept the account class change.

Click   the **Taxes tab**.

Most services in Ontario are subject to HST. All services offered by Flabuless Fitness are not exempt from HST, so the default is correct at No.

Click   **Create Another**   **Create Another** .

Click   the **Units tab**. **Repeat** these procedures to **enter other service records**.

Click   **Save And Close**   **Save and Close**   after entering the last service record.

Close   **Inventory & Services window** to return to the Home window.

Display or **print** the **Inventory List**, **Summary**, **Quantity** and **Price Lists** reports. Compare them with the information on pages 623–624 to check them for accuracy.

Finishing the History

The last stage in setting up the accounting system involves finishing the history for each ledger. Before proceeding, you should check the data integrity (Home window, Maintenance menu) to see whether there are any out-of-balance ledgers that will prevent you from proceeding. Correct these errors and then make a backup copy of the files.

Making a Backup of the Company Files

With the Flabuless Fitness files open, use the File menu Backup command to create a backup (refer to page 250). You may also want to create a complete working copy of the not-finished files.

WARNING!
Before you finish entering the history, make a backup copy of Flabuless Fitness company files. This is necessary if you find later that you need to correct some of the historical information. Remember, once you finish entering the history, you cannot add information for any period before the earliest transaction date.

Choose the **File menu** and **click Backup** or **click** the **Backup tool** .

Click   **Browse** and **choose** the **data folder you want** for the not-finished backup of the data file.

Double click the **File name field** in the Backup wizard screen.

Type   nf-flab

Click   **OK** to create a backup copy of all the files for Flabuless Fitness.

The "NF" designates files as not finished to distinguish them from the ones you will work with to enter journal transactions. You will return to your working copy of the file so you can finish the history.

Changing the History Status of Ledgers to Finished

Refer to page 96 and page 252 for assistance with finishing the history and correcting history errors.

Choose the **History menu** and **click Finish Entering History**.

If your amounts, account types and linked accounts are correct, you will see the warning about this step not being reversible and advising you to back up the file first.

Click   **Proceed** when there are no errors and you have backed up your files.

If you have made errors, you will not see the warning message. Instead you will see a list of errors.

Click   **Print** so that you can refer to the list for making corrections.

Click   **OK** to return to the Home window. **Make** the **corrections**, and then **try again**.

Click   **Proceed**.

The Flabuless Fitness files are now ready for you to enter transactions. The ledger icons in all module windows now appear without the open history icons. All the ledgers are ready for transactions.

Congratulations on reaching this stage! This is a good time to take a break.

Finish   your **session**. This will give you an opportunity to read the next section and the instructions before starting the source document transactions.

Entering Users and Security Passwords

Simply Accounting allows you to set up passwords for different users. The password for the system administrator (sysadmin) controls access to the system or program. Passwords for other users control viewing and editing privileges for different ledgers, journals and reports. For example, if different employees work with different accounting records, they should use different passwords.

Restricting access by setting passwords is different from hiding ledgers using the Setup menu, User Preferences, View screen. Since the View preferences are unrestricted user settings, these hidden ledgers can be restored at any time. Ledgers hidden by restricted access passwords can be accessed and restored only by opening the files with the system administrator (sysadmin) password and changing access rights.

Users and passwords are entered from the Setup menu in the Home window.

Choose the **Setup menu** and **click Set Up Users** to display the control window:

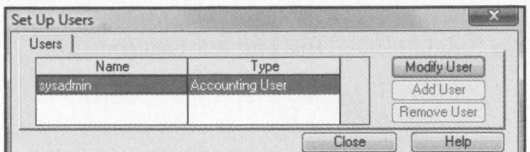

This Set Up Users window lists all users currently set up in the data files. Initially, the only user is sysadmin (system administrator). The highest level of access comes with the sysadmin password that allows the user to enter, use or modify any part of the data files, including the passwords. The sysadmin password must be set before any other passwords can be set, so this user is selected initially. You can set up passwords for additional users to allow them access to different parts of the program. Begin by adding a password for sysadmin.

Click   **Modify User** to open the Modify User password entry screen:

You cannot modify access privileges for the sysadmin because someone (the system administrator) must have full access to the data. All the rights options are dimmed. The cursor is in the Enter Password field.

You can use up to seven letters and/or numbers as the code. Passwords are case-sensitive. That is, ABC is different from abc. If you enter a password with an upper-case (capital) letter, you must use an upper-case letter each time.

Type   the **word** or **code** that you want as your password. For practice, choose a simple password such as your first name or your initials.

Press   (tab) to advance to the next field, Re-enter Password.

For security reasons, the password is never revealed on the screen — you will see an asterisk (*) or some other symbol for each letter or number that you type. As an additional precaution, Simply Accounting requires you to enter the code twice in exactly the same way.

Type   the **password** or **code** again.

If the two entries do not match, Simply Accounting generates an error message.

Click OK and try re-entering the code again. If you still do not have a match, go back to the Enter Password field and type in the code. You may have mistyped the first entry. Then re-enter the password in the Re-enter Password field.

Click   **OK** when you have entered the code twice. You will return to the Set Up Users screen.

If you have allowed read and write access to third-party products, and the password you entered is weak, the program will recommend selecting a more secure password. For practice, you can click No to continue with the easy password.

The remaining user setup option buttons are now available. If you return to the Home window, there will be one password for the data files, the one for sysadmin.

Adding Other Users

After you have added a password for the system administrator (sysadmin), you can set up additional users with unique passwords.

Each user can be allowed access to all parts of the program (full accounting rights) or access to only some of the ledgers and journals. Access to ledgers, journals and reports can be controlled separately. The Set Up Users window should be open.

Click **Add User** to open the new user setup screen again:

To give a user full access, click Full Accounting Rights below the Password section. For each ledger and journal, you can allow any of the following access levels: no access (no ✓ for Allow Access); modifying (editing) rights that include viewing; viewing rights only; or access to ledger reports. For journals, you can allow no access, enter rights (enter and look up transactions), lookup only or access to journal reports. Each ledger and journal can be controlled separately, and each user may have different access rights. Each user must have a unique name and password.

Initially, the Add User options are shown for an Accounting User for access to the ledgers and journals, but you can also restrict a user to accessing only the Time Slips. Refer to Appendix H for setting up time slip users.

The cursor should be in the User Name field.

Type the **name** of the first user.

Press (tab) **twice** to advance to the Enter Password screen.

Type the **word** or **code** that you want as your restricted usage password. You can use up to seven letters and/or numbers as the code.

Press (tab) to advance to the next field, Re-enter Password.

Type the **password** or **code** again.

Again, for security purposes, to be sure you entered the password that you intended, you must enter the same code twice. When the two entries match, you can define access rights for the first user.

To allow access, click the check boxes beside the ledger name in the appropriate columns. For example, to allow viewing access only for the General Ledger, click the Allow Access check box beside Accounts/Banking. The program adds ✓s for all columns beside Accounts/Banking. Click Modify and Reports to remove those ✓. To allow no access, leave the Allow Access check box in the first column empty.

PRO VERSION

The option to set up an Accounting Entry User or a Time Slip Entry User is not available in the Pro version. The Time & Billing module is also not listed because this is a Premium feature.

If you see a message about updating to multi-user Premium or Enterprise versions, click Do Not Show This Message Again (unless you want to upgrade).

Similarly, you can restrict access to third-party information for each user. Passwords do not serve their purpose if the user cannot view reports in Simply Accounting but can access and modify those reports in another program.

Click   OK to save the new user and return to the Set Up Users screen.

After entering all the users, return to the Home window to save all the changes.

Click   Close to return to the Home window.

Nothing has changed yet. The Home window looks the same because you are using the program as the sysadmin (system administrator).

However, the next time you open the file, the following dialogue box will appear, and you will be required to enter the password before you can open the data file:

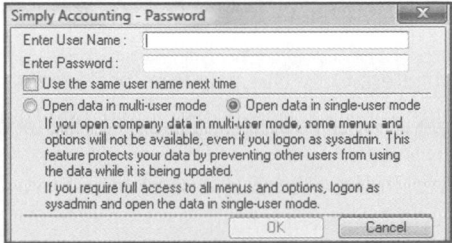

Type   the **user name**, either sysadmin or another user name. **Press** `tab`.

Type   the **password** or code for this user.

Choose   the **Single-User** or **Multi-User mode** for accessing the data file.

Click   OK.

If you enter an incorrect code, nothing happens — the Password dialogue box remains open. If you enter the sysadmin password, you will have full access to all parts of the program, including the security settings. If you have set passwords, you must enter the program using the sysadmin password in order to change the security settings and passwords. Individual users, other than the sysadmin, can change their own passwords at any time. They cannot access the passwords for other users.

If you enter as a user other than the sysadmin, and do not have full accounting rights, you will see a restricted view of the Home window.

The following Classic view Home window shows restrictions for a user, together with the access rights allocated to that user:

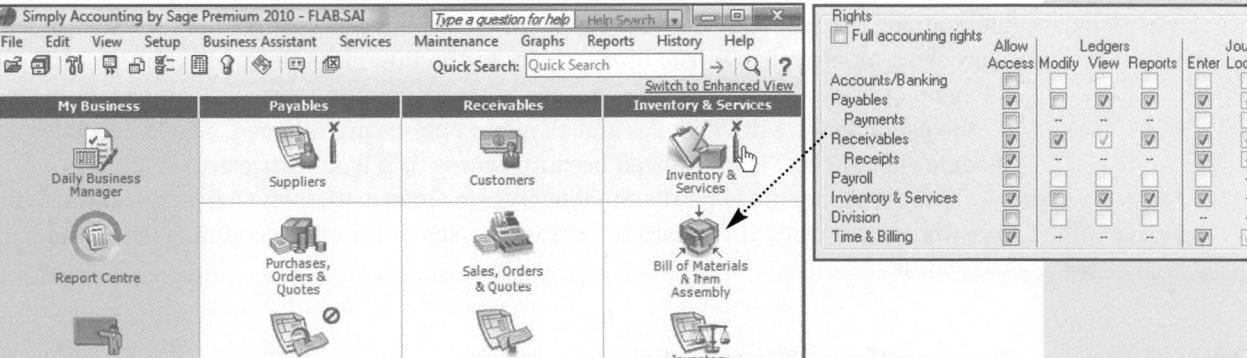

The user above can input normal sales journal entries and inventory entries, accept payments from customers and enter purchases and time slips, but cannot write cheques to suppliers, pay employees, reconcile accounts, make deposits or make General Journal entries.

PRO VERSION

pro   The Pro version is a single-user program, so the Password screen does not have the option to open in single- or multi-user mode. You will need to enter your user name and password (and, if appropriate, the option to use the same user name next time).

CLASSIC VIEW

The Classic view Home window shows all access rights on a single screen.

PRO VERSION

pro   You will not see the Time Slips icon in the Pro version, and the name of the inventory journal will be Item Assembly.

The user does not have access to the General Ledger or journals, the Payroll Ledger or journals or to the Division Ledger — their icons are missing (no ✓ appears for these ledgers in the Allow Access settings).

Only the Customers Ledger in this example can be modified. The **No Edit** symbol beside the Suppliers and Inventory & Services ledger icons means that these ledgers can be viewed but not edited (✓ for View, but not for Modify). If you open these ledgers, all fields will be dimmed.

The **No Entry** symbol [symbol] on the Payments Journal indicates no access is permitted (the user cannot write cheques — there is no ✓ for Allow Access). The Receivables (Customers & Sales) and Inventory journals are not restricted — no extra icon appears with them (✓ for Enter, Lookup and Reports).

When access to reports is restricted for any journal or ledger (no ✓ for reports), those report menu options will be dimmed.

Several main menu options are also restricted. Only the sysadmin has access to the Set Up Users menu option after passwords are set, although users can change their own passwords.

We can see the user restrictions, however, in the following illustration of two Enhanced view module windows when passwords are set.

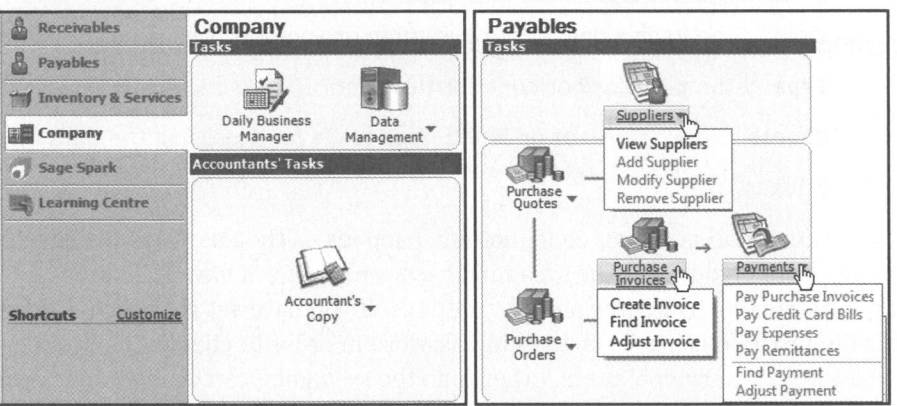

The Home window icons have not changed (no symbols are added). Modules the user cannot access — Banking and Payroll — are removed from the Modules pane list. The General Journal and Chart of Accounts icons are also removed from the Company window because the user is not permitted to access them. Access to the Payables module is limited, as we can see from the three drop-down shortcuts lists in the illustration. The user can view the supplier records but not change them — only the View shortcut is available. The user's access to the Purchases Journal is unrestricted — all menu options are still available. Access to the Payments Journal is completely denied — the user cannot write cheques and all menu options are dimmed. The Receivables module (not shown) is unchanged because access to it is unrestricted.

Refer to Appendix H on the Student DVD for information on changing and removing passwords, and using the wizard to create time-slip entry and accounting users and passwords.

Exporting Reports

Simply Accounting allows you to export reports to a specified drive and path. The files created by the program may then be used by spreadsheet or word processing programs.

Exporting files will allow you to perform additional calculations and interpret data for reporting purposes. This process of integrating Simply Accounting files with other software is an important step in making the accounting process meaningful.

The following keystrokes will export the opening Balance Sheet for Flabuless Fitness to a spreadsheet.

Display the **Balance Sheet** or the report you want to export.

Click   the **Export Report tool** ⬆ or **choose** the **File menu** and **click Export** to display the following screen:

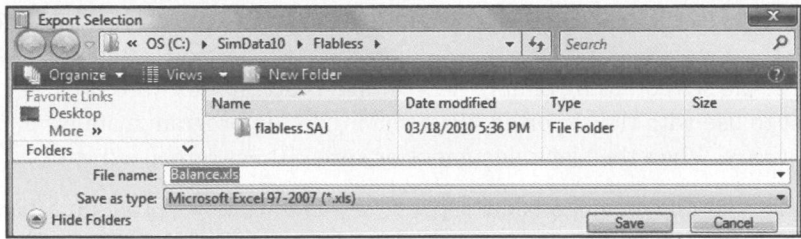

Click   the **Save As Type list arrow** to see the types of files you can create:

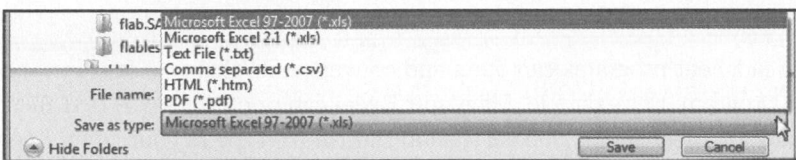

File formats available for export purposes include HTML for Web pages, Text for a word processing format file, Microsoft Excel Versions 97–2007 and 2.1, Comma Separated and PDF.

Click   **Microsoft Excel 97-2007** as the type for the Balance Sheet in the Save As Type field. Use the field list arrow to display the file type options if needed.

Choose   the **location** for your exported file. By default your working folder is selected, or the folder you used for the previous exported report.

Click   the **list arrow** for the **Save In field** to access the drive and folder you want.

Accept   the default **file name**, or **type** the **name** you want for your file. The program assigns an extension to the file name so that Microsoft Excel will recognize the new file as an Excel file.

Click   **Save**. You will return to your displayed report.

To create a text file, click Text File. To generate a file that you can view with Acrobat Reader, but not modify, click PDF.

Any Simply Accounting report that you have on display can be also be opened directly as a Microsoft Excel spreadsheet. Formulas for totals, and so on, are retained and you can then use the spreadsheet file immediately.

Display the **Simply Accounting report** you want to use in Excel.

Click   the **Open In Excel tool** 📊 or **choose** the **File menu** and **click Open In Microsoft Excel** to see the file name window:

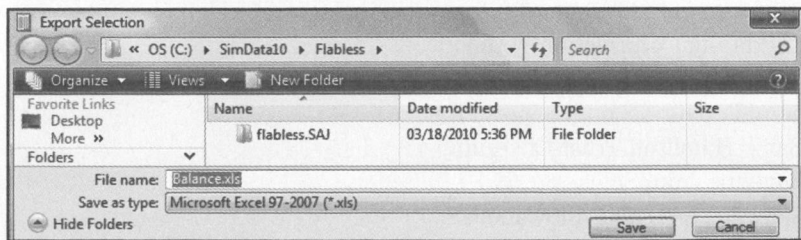

Choose a **location** for your spreadsheet data file.

> **Click**   **Save** to open the spreadsheet. Your Simply Accounting data file will remain open.
>
> **Close**   the **Excel file** when finished.

You can now work with a report that you have exported.

Using Simply Files and Reports with Other Software

Finish the session using Simply Accounting. Start the software program you want to use with the exported file, referring to the program manuals if necessary. When the blank document or spreadsheet screen appears,

Choose the File menu and click Open if this is a Windows program. Change folders if necessary to locate and then select the exported file. Be sure that the selected file type also matches the format of your exported file (e.g., .txt for a text file, or .xls for Excel).

Some spreadsheet programs can open and convert a file that was saved in the format of a different program. For example, Microsoft Excel can open (or save) text files or Comma Separated Files. Simply choose the alternative file type in your Open File (or Save File) window. Click OK. Your exported file should replace the blank document screen.

Once you have exported a financial statement as a text file, you can include it in a written report prepared with any word processing program. You can then use the features of the word processing software to enhance the appearance of the statement using format styles that are consistent with the remainder of the report. If you have exported a spreadsheet file, you can use the spreadsheet program to perform additional calculations. Then you can save the modified report as a text file or copy the cells you want to be incorporated in a word processing report. We used exported spreadsheets to create the bank statements for this text.

When working with a spreadsheet program, you can use the calculation capabilities of the spreadsheet program to make comparisons between statements from different financial periods. You might also want to use the charting or graphing features to prepare presentation materials.

Exporting reports offers advantages over re-creating the statements. Not only do you save the time of retyping, but you also ensure greater accuracy by avoiding errors made while retyping the numbers and accounts.

SOURCE DOCUMENT INSTRUCTIONS

Instructions for April

1. **Enter** the **transactions** for April using all the information provided.

2. **Print** the following **reports**:
   a. Journal Entries (All Journals) for April, including foreign amounts, corrections and additional transaction details
   b. Customer Aged Detail Report for all customers for April
   c. General Ledger account reports for
      • Bank: Hamilton Trust Chequing
      • Revenue from Sales
      • Sales Returns and Allowances
   d. Supplier Purchases Summary for Footlink Corporation, all categories, for April

3. **Export** the **Balance Sheet** as at April 30, 2012, to a spreadsheet application. **Calculate** the following **key ratios** in your spreadsheet and compare them with the ratios in the Daily Business Manager Business Performance indicators:

    a. current ratio   **b.** quick ratio

4. **Set up** a **budget** for use in May and June and **enter amounts** based on expenses and revenues for April and for the first quarter.

Instructions for May

1. **Enter** the **transactions** for May using all the information provided.

2. **Print** the following **reports**:
    a. Journal Entries (All Journals) for May, including foreign amounts, corrections and additional transaction details
    b. Supplier Aged Detail Report for all suppliers for May
    c. Employee Summary Report for all employees for the pay period ending May 31, 2012
    d. Inventory Summary Report (observe and report items that have not sold well over the two-month period)
    e. Customer Sales Summary (all customers, items and categories) for May

3. **Export** the **Comparative Balance Sheet** for April 30 and May 31, 2012, to a spreadsheet application. You will use these at the end of the quarter for three-month comparisons.

4. **Compare** May's **performance against** April's budget **forecast**.

Instructions for June

1. **Enter** the **transactions** for June using all the information provided.

2. **Print** the following **reports**:
    a. Journal Entries (All Journals) for June, including foreign amounts, corrections and additional transaction details
    b. Trial Balance, Balance Sheet and Income Statement on June 30
    c. Inventory Activity Report for Fitness Equipment (All Journals) for June
    d. Bank Transaction Report for all bank accounts from April 1 to June 30

3. **Export** the **Balance Sheet** and **Income Statement** to a spreadsheet application. Combine the Balance Sheet with the comparative one for April and May. **Compare** first- and second-quarter figures, item by item, to assess the performance of Flabuless Fitness. You may want to use Multi-period reports for this comparison.

4. **Make** a **backup copy** of your data files. **Advance** the **session date** to July 1, 2012.

5. **Print** the **Trial Balance**, **Balance Sheet** and **Income Statement** for July 1. **Compare** the end of June and the first of July **statements** and note the changes that result from Simply Accounting closing the books for the new fiscal period.

NOTES
You can restore the backup SimData10\Setup\flab-may1 to complete the transactions for May. This file does not include budget amounts.

NOTES
You can restore the backup SimData10\Setup\flab-jun1 to complete the transactions for June. This file does not include budget amounts.

PRO VERSION
Print the General Ledger Report for the bank accounts instead of the Bank Transaction Report.

WARNING!
Chapter 16, Case 8, in Appendix E on the Student DVD, has the data you need to complete the bank account reconciliation for Flabuless Fitness. You must use your data files for June 30 to complete the reconciliation, so be sure to make a backup copy before you advance the session date to the new fiscal year. (Or, use the file we provide in the SimData10\Bank folder.)

SOURCE DOCUMENTS

SESSION DATE – APRIL 15, 2012

NOTES
Edit the default purchase cost entered in the Amount field.

☐ **Purchase Order #25**   **Dated April 1, 2012**

Shipping date April 10, 2012
From Prolife Exercisers Inc.

4	E010	Elliptical Exerciser: AE-200	$ 4 200.00	USD
4	E020	Elliptical Exerciser: LE-400	4 600.00	USD
4	E100	Treadmill: Basic T-800B	2 200.00	USD
4	E110	Treadmill: Deluxe T-1100Dt	4 800.00	USD
		Freight	200.00	USD
		HST	2 080.00	USD
		Total	$18 080.00	USD

Terms: 2/10, n/30. The exchange rate is 1.015.

NOTES
Remember that receipts are deposited to Undeposited Cash and Cheques. This should be the default account.

☐ **Cash Receipt #39**   **Dated April 1, 2012**

From Stoney Creek Sports Arena, cheque #147 for $4 429.60 in payment on account including $90.40 discount for early payment. Reference invoice #2191.

☐ **Cheque Copy #101**   **Dated April 2, 2012**

To Footlink Corporation, $8 200 in payment of account including $100 discount for early payment. Reference invoice #FC-618.

☐ **Sales Order #41-DRC**   **Dated April 2, 2012**

Shipping date April 6, 2012
To Dundas Recreation Centre (use Full Add for new customer)

2	A050	Heart Rate Monitor	$ 90/	unit
60	A090	Weight Plates	1.50/	kg
2	E010	Elliptical Exerciser: AE-200	2 100/	unit
2	E020	Elliptical Exerciser: LE-400	2 600/	unit
1	E080	Ski Exerciser: Independent SE-880	710/	unit
2	E100	Treadmill: Basic T-800B	1 400/	unit
5	S010	Personal Trainer: 1 hour	75/	hour
2	S040	Yoga Instructor: 1 hour	100/	hour
		Freight (tax code H)	50	
		HST	13%	

Terms: 2/10, n/30.
Received cheque #96 for $3 000 as down payment (deposit #15) to confirm sales order.

NOTES
Dundas Recreational Centre
☐ Contact: X.S. Wayte
190 Playtime Circle
Dundas, ON L8C 2V8
Tel: (905) 466-5576
Fax: (905) 466-7284
E-mail: xswayte@ dundas.reccentre.ca
Web: www.dundas. reccentre.ca
Terms: 2/10, n/30
Credit limit: $15 000
Tax code: H

☐ **Cash Receipt #40**   **Dated April 4, 2012**

From Mohawk College, cheque #73 for $5 537 in payment of account including $113 discount for early payment. Reference invoice #2194.

☐ **Cheque Copy #346**   **Dated April 5, 2012**

To Redux Home Gym Wholesalers, $7 104 USD in payment of account including $128 discount for early payment. Reference invoice #R-914. The exchange rate is 1.028.

Sales Invoice #3000 Dated April 5, 2012

To Dundas Recreational Centre, to fill sales order #41-DRC

2	A050	Heart Rate Monitor	$ 90/ unit
60	A090	Weight Plates	1.50/ kg
2	E010	Elliptical Exerciser: AE-200	2 100/ unit
2	E020	Elliptical Exerciser: LE-400	2 600/ unit
1	E080	Ski Exerciser: Independent SE-880	710/ unit
2	E100	Treadmill: Basic T-800B	1 400/ unit
5	S010	Personal Trainer: 1 hour	75/ hour
2	S040	Yoga Instructor: 1 hour	100/ hour
		Freight (tax code H)	50
		HST	13%

Terms: 2/10, n/30.

NOTES
Remember to change the payment method to Pay Later for the sales invoice that fills the order.
If you want, you can enter Kisangel as the salesperson for all sales.

Memo #4-1 Dated April 5 2012

Re Damaged Inventory: Two (2) stability balls, item A070, were torn and damaged beyond repair. Adjust the inventory to recognize the loss.

Purchase Invoice #PE-364 Dated April 6, 2012

From Prolife Exercisers Inc., to fill purchase order #25

4	E010	Elliptical Exerciser: AE-200	$ 4 200.00	USD
4	E020	Elliptical Exerciser: LE-400	4 600.00	USD
4	E100	Treadmill: Basic T-800B	2 200.00	USD
4	E110	Treadmill: Deluxe T-1100Dt	4 800.00	USD
		Freight	200.00	USD
		HST	2 080.00	USD
		Total	$18 080.00	USD

Terms: 2/10, n/30. The exchange rate is 1.023.

Credit Card Purchase Invoice #HS-114 Dated April 6, 2012

From Hamilton Spectator (use Full Add for new vendor), $500 plus $65 HST for prepaid advertisement to run over the next 12 weeks. Purchase invoice total $565 paid in full by Visa.

NOTES
Hamilton Spectator
Contact Dawn Newsman
Wentworth St. N.
Hamilton, ON L8L 5T8
Tel: (905) 525-1800
Fax: (905) 525-1816
E-mail: newsman@
        spectator.ca
Web: www.spectator.ca
Terms: net 10
Tax code: H
Expense account: 1270

Cheque Copy #102 Dated April 6, 2012

To Feelyte Gym Accessories, $1 110 in payment of account including $20 discount for early payment. Reference invoice #FG-1611.

Memo #4-2 Dated April 7, 2012

From Visa, received monthly credit card statement for $240 including $220 for purchases up to and including April 3 and $20 annual renewal fee. Submitted cheque #103 for $240 in full payment of the balance owing.

Deposit Slip #14 Dated April 7, 2012

Prepare deposit slip for all receipts for April 1 to April 7 to deposit the funds to Bank: Hamilton Trust Chequing from Undeposited Cash and Cheques. The total deposit for the three cheques is $12 966.60.

NOTES
All deposits are made to Bank: Hamilton Trust Chequing from Undeposited Cheques and Cash.

Cash Receipt #41 Dated April 9, 2012

From Chedoke Health Care, cheque #472 for $6 759.20 in payment of account including $180.80 discount for early payment. Reference invoice #2199.

Credit Card Purchase Invoice #W-1149 Dated April 10, 2012

From Westdale Office Supplies (use Full Add for new vendor), $150 plus $19.50 HST for stationery and other office supplies for store. Purchase invoice total $169.50 paid in full by Visa.

NOTES
Westdale Office Supplies
Contact Clip Papers
26 Dalewood Ave.
Hamilton, ON L8S 1Y7
Tel: (905) 528-8199
Terms: net 30
Tax code: H
Expense account: 1260

NOTES

Hamilton District Bd of Education
Contact: Nott Skinny
10 James St. S.
Hamilton, ON L8K 4G2
Tel: (905) 461-5997
Fax: (905) 461-6936
E-mail: nskinny@hdsb.ca
Web: www.hdsb.ca
Terms: 2/10, n/30
Credit limit: $15 000
Tax code: H

Sales Invoice #3001   **Dated April 12, 2012**

To Hamilton District Bd of Education (use Full Add for new customer)

8	A040	Glide Slidetrak	$	90/ each
5	A070	Stability Balls		12 each
2	E020	Elliptical Exerciser: LE-400		2 600/ unit
2	E030	Bicycle: Dual Action Calorie Counter		700/ unit
1	E040	Bicycle: Recumbent R-80		950/ unit
		Freight		50
		HST		13%

Terms: 2/10, n/30.

Cheque Copy #347   **Dated April 13, 2012**

To Prolife Exercisers Inc., $17 760 USD in payment of account including $320 discount for early payment. Reference invoice #PE-364. The exchange rate is 1.021.

Memo #4-3   **Dated April 13, 2012**

Transfer $16 000 USD to cover the cheque to Prolife Exercisers from 1060 Bank: Hamilton Trust Chequing to Bank: USD Chequing. The exchange rate is 1.021.

Purchase Invoice #WS-6112   **Dated April 14, 2012**

From Waterdown Sunoco, $92 including HST and PST for gasoline purchase for delivery vehicle. (Use tax code IN.)

Deposit Slip #15   **Dated April 14, 2012**

Prepare deposit slip for all receipts for April 8 to April 14 to deposit the funds. One cheque for $6 759.20 is being deposited.

Memo #4-4   **Dated April 14, 2012**

Record payment for GST and HST for the period ending March 31 to the Receiver General for Canada. Issue cheque #104 in full payment.

NOTES

Enter Memo #4-5A, Memo #4-5B and so on in the Reference Number and Comment fields for the payroll remittances.

You cannot enter a date earlier than April 1 in the End of Remitting Period date field.

Memo #4-5   **Dated April 14, 2012**

Payroll Remittances: Use April 1 as the End of Remitting Period date to make the following payroll remittances in the Payments Journal.

Record payment for EI, CPP and Income Tax Payable up to April 1 to the Receiver General for Canada. Issue cheque #105 in full payment.

Record payment for Garnisheed Wages Payable up to April 1 to the Receiver General for Canada. Issue cheque #106 in full payment.

Record payment for EHT Payable up to April 1 to the Minister of Finance. Issue cheque #107 in full payment.

Record payment for RRSP Payable up to April 1 to Ancaster Insurance. Issue cheque #108 in full payment.

Record payment for CSB Payable up to April 1 to Mt. Hope Investment Corporation. Issue cheque #109 in full payment.

Record payment for Group Insurance Payable up to April 1 to Ancaster Insurance. Issue cheque #110 in full payment.

Record payment for WSIB Payable up to April 1 to Workplace Safety and Insurance Board. Issue cheque #111 in full payment.

Employee Time Summary Sheet #14   **Dated April 14, 2012**

For the Pay Period ending April 14, 2012
George Schwinn worked 80 regular hours and 2 hours of overtime in the period. Recover $50 advance. Issue payroll deposit slip DD19.

WARNING!

You must use the Paycheques Journal because the pay period and cheque dates are different from the session date.

Cash Purchase Invoice #ES-64329   **Dated April 14, 2012**

From Energy Source, $120 plus $15.60 HST paid for hydro service. Purchase invoice total $135.60. Terms: cash on receipt. Issue cheque #112 in full payment.

WARNING!

Change the tax code for Books: Fitness Guide to G for the Visa sale. Otherwise, GST may not be calculated correctly.

☐ **Credit Card Sales Invoice #3002**   **Dated April 14, 2012**

To Visa customers (sales summary)

2	A010	Body Fat Scale	$ 150/ unit	$ 300.00
40	A030	Dumbbells	2.50/ kg	100.00
3	A060	Power Blocks	200/ set	600.00
8	A070	Stability Balls	12 each	96.00
80	A090	Weight Plates	1.50/ kg	120.00
6	A100	Workout Gloves: all sizes	15/ pair	90.00
8	S020	Personal Trainer: 1/2 day	200/ 1/2 day	1 600.00
4	S030	Personal Trainer: full day	400/ day	1 600.00
8	S050	Yoga Instructor: 1/2 day	200/ 1/2 day	1 600.00
32	B010	Books: Fitness Guide (tax code G)	40 each	1 280.00
		HST	13%	793.78
		GST	5%	64.00
		Total paid by Visa		$8 243.78

☐ **Cash Receipt #42**   **Dated April 15, 2012**

From Dundas Recreational Centre, cheque #195 for $12 287.66 in payment of account including $311.99 discount for early payment. Reference invoice #3000 and deposit #15.

SESSION DATE – APRIL 30, 2012

☐ **Deposit Slip #16**   **Dated April 22, 2012**

Prepare deposit slip for all receipts for April 15 to April 22 to deposit the funds. The total deposit for the single cheque is $12 287.66.

☐ **Sales Invoice #3003**   **Dated April 22, 2012**

To Stelco Health Club (use Full Add for new preferred customer)

80	A090	Weight Plates	$1.30/ kg
3	E040	Bicycle: Recumbent R-80	820/ unit
3	E080	Ski Exerciser: Independent SE-880	650/ unit
		HST	13%

Terms: 2/10, n/30.

☐ **Cash Purchase Invoice #BC-59113**   **Dated April 22, 2012**

From Bell Canada, $80 plus $10.40 HST paid for phone service. Purchase invoice total $90.40. Terms: cash on receipt. Issue cheque #113 in full payment.

☐ **Cash Purchase Invoice #H-2012-1**   **Dated April 23, 2012**

From City of Hamilton Treasurer (use Full Add), $900 in full payment of first instalment of quarterly property tax assessment. Terms: EOM. Issued cheque #114 in full payment. Store as a monthly recurring entry. Recall the stored transaction to issue cheques #115 and #116 as postdated cheques for the next two instalments, dated May 23 and June 23.

☐ **Sales Invoice #3004**   **Dated April 28, 2012**

To Stoney Creek Sports Arena

1	A080	Wavemaster	$ 180/ unit
30	A090	Weight Plates	1.50/ kg
2	E020	Elliptical Exerciser: LE-400	2 600/ unit
2	E070	Rowing Machine: RM-1000	560/ unit
2	E110	Treadmill: Deluxe T-1100D	2 800/ unit
		Freight	30
		HST	13%

Terms: 2/10, n/30.

NOTES

Stelco Health Club
new preferred customer
Contact: Les Pound)
1 Stelco Rd.
Hamilton, ON L8P 6N6
Tel: (905) 524-1000
Fax: (905) 524-1924
E-mail: pound@
     stelcohealth.com
Web: www.stelcohealth.com
Terms: 2/10, n/30
Credit limit: $15 000
Tax code: H

NOTES

City of Hamilton Treasurer
Contact: Budd Jett
is located at 53 Main St. W.
Hamilton, ON L8P 2Z3
Tel: (905) 461-0063
Fax: (905) 461-9204
Web: www.hamilton.city.ca
Terms: net 1
Tax code: no tax (exempt)
Expense account: 5260
Use H-2012-2 and H-2012-3
as the Invoice numbers for the postdated payments for property taxes.

Credit Card Sales Invoice #3005   **Dated April 28, 2012**

To Visa customers (sales summary)

5	A020	Yoga Mats	$ 40/ unit	$	200.00
20	A030	Dumbbells	2.50/ kg		50.00
2	A050	Heart Rate Monitor	90 each		180.00
4	A060	Power Blocks	200/ set		800.00
4	E030	Bicycle: Dual Action Calorie Counter	700/ unit		2 800.00
4	E100	Treadmill: Basic T-800B	1 400/ unit		5 600.00
8	S020	Personal Trainer: 1/2 day	200/ 1/2 day		1 600.00
9	S050	Yoga Instructor: 1/2 day	200/ 1/2 day		1 800.00
18	B010	Books: Fitness Guide (tax code G)	40 each		720.00
		HST	13%		1 693.90
		GST	5%		36.00
		Total paid by Visa			$15 479.90

Employee Time Summary Sheet #15   **Dated April 28, 2012**

For the Pay Period ending April 28, 2012
George Schwinn worked 80 regular hours and 4 hours of overtime. Recover $50 advance. Issue payroll deposit slip DD20.

Memo #4-6   **Dated April 28, 2012**

Transfer $10 000 CAD to Savings account from 1120 Bank: Visa and Interac.

Cash Purchase Invoice #DMC-55   **Dated April 28, 2012**

From Dundurn Maintenance Co. (use Full Add), $300 plus $39 HST paid for cleaning and maintenance of premises. Terms: cash on receipt. Issue cheque #117 for $339 in full payment. The company bills monthly for its services so store the entry as a monthly recurring transaction.

Credit Invoice #8   **Dated April 28, 2012**

To Stelco Health Club, $50 allowance for scratched treadmill unit. Reference invoice #3003. There is no tax on the allowance. Enter a negative amount. Create new Subgroup Account 4070 Returns and Allowances. Change the customer terms to net 60; there is no discount. Delete or change the comment.

Credit Card Purchase Invoice #WS-6533   **Dated April 28, 2012**

From Waterdown Sunoco, $69 including HST for gasoline (tax code IN) and $40 plus $5.20 HST for oil change (tax code H). Purchase invoice total $114.20 charged to Visa account.

Bank Debit Memo #91431   **Dated April 30, 2012**

From Hamilton Trust, authorized withdrawals were made from the chequing account on our behalf for the following:

Bank service charges	$ 35
Mortgage interest payment	1 880
Mortgage principal reduction	120
Bank loan interest payment	420
Bank loan principal reduction	480

Memo #4-7   **Dated April 30, 2012**

Prepare the payroll for the two salaried employees, Nieve Prekor and Assumpta Kisangel. Add 2 percent of revenue from services for April as a commission to Kisangel's salary. Issue payroll deposit slips DD21 and DD22.

SESSION DATE – MAY 15, 2012

☐ **Cash Receipt #43**   **Dated May 1, 2012**

From Stelco Health Club, cheque #434 for $4 948.80 in payment of account including $102.02 discount for early payment. Reference sales invoice #3003 and credit invoice #8.

☐ **Purchase Order #26**   **Dated May 1, 2012**

Delivery date May 7, 2012
From Prolife Exercisers

4	E010	Elliptical Exerciser: AE-200	$ 4 200.00	USD
3	E020	Elliptical Exerciser: LE-400	3 450.00	USD
3	E100	Treadmill: Basic T-800B	1 650.00	USD
3	E110	Treadmill: Deluxe T-1100Dt	3 600.00	USD
		Freight	200.00	USD
		HST	1 703.00	USD
		Invoice total	$14 803.00	USD

Terms: 2/10, n/30. The exchange rate is 1.019.

☐ **Sales Invoice #3006**   **Dated May 1, 2012**

To McMaster University (preferred customer)

2	E030	Bicycle: Dual Action Calorie Counter	$ 640/ unit
2	E070	Rowing Machine: RM-1000	490/ unit
2	E080	Ski Exerciser: Independent SE-880	650/ set
2	E100	Treadmill: Basic T-800B	1 220/ unit
1	E110	Treadmill: Deluxe T-1100D	2 500/ unit
		HST	13%

Terms: 2/10, n/30.

☐ **Cash Purchase Invoice #AI-6921**   **Dated May 2, 2012**

From Ancaster Insurance, $2 592 (including PST) for six months of insurance coverage. Invoice total $2 592. Issued cheque #118 in payment.

☐ **Purchase Order #27**   **Dated May 4, 2012**

Delivery date May 12, 2012
From Feelyte Gym Accessories

1	A020	Yoga Mats (1 box of 10 mats)	$ 150.00
2	A030	Dumbbells orders of 100 kg	180.00
10	A040	Glide Slidetrak	450.00
5	A060	Power Blocks	500.00
15	A070	Stability Balls	90.00
		HST	178.10
		Invoice total	$1 548.10

Terms: 2/10, n/30.

☐ **Cash Receipt #44**   **Dated May 5, 2012**

From Stoney Creek Sports Arena, cheque #198 for $13 482.59 in payment of account, including $275.16 discount for early payment. Reference invoice #3004.

☐ **Deposit Slip #17**   **Dated May 5, 2012**

Prepare deposit slip for all receipts for April 29 to May 5 to deposit the funds. The total deposit for the two cheques is $18 431.39.

☐ **Cash Receipt #45**   **Dated May 7, 2012**

From McMaster University, cheque #1257 for $9 412.90 in payment of account, including $192.10 discount for early payment. Reference invoice #3006.

NOTES
PST is still charged separately on insurance in Ontario. PST paid is not refundable, so there is no need to track it or record it separately. It will be included with the amount for Prepaid Insurance.

☐   **Memo #5-1**   **Dated May 7, 2012**

Adjust the selling prices for item E050 (Home Gym: Basic HG-1400) to reflect the cost increase announced by the supplier. Change the prices in the Inventory Ledger. The new selling prices are

Regular Canadian dollar price	$1 500 CAD
Preferred Canadian dollar price	1 300 CAD
Regular United States dollar price	1 400 USD
Preferred United States dollar price	1 250 USD

☐   **Credit Card Purchase Invoice #WS-6914**   **Dated May 8, 2012**

From Waterdown Sunoco, $69 including HST for gasoline. Purchase invoice total $69 charged to Visa account.

☐   **Memo #5-2**   **Dated May 9, 2012**

From Visa, received monthly credit card statement for $940.70 for purchases up to and including May 3. The Visa statement showed that invoice #WS-6112 from Waterdown Sunoco on April 14 was incorrectly entered as Pay Later instead of Visa. Adjust the invoice and prepare cheque #119 for $940.70 to pay the Visa bill.

☐   **Purchase Invoice #PE-2014**   **Dated May 9, 2012**

From Prolife Exercisers, to fill purchase order #26

4	E010	Elliptical Exerciser: AE-200	$ 4 200.00	USD
3	E020	Elliptical Exerciser: LE-400	3 450.00	USD
3	E100	Treadmill: Basic T-800B	1 650.00	USD
3	E110	Treadmill: Deluxe T-1100Dt	3 600.00	USD
		Freight	200.00	USD
		HST	1 703.00	USD
		Invoice total	$14 803.00	USD

Terms: 2/10, n/30. The exchange rate is 1.0178.

☐   **Purchase Invoice #FG-1804**   **Dated May 12, 2012**

From Feelyte Gym Accessories, to fill purchase order #27

1	A020	Yoga Mats (1 box of 10 mats)	$ 150.00
2	A030	Dumbbells orders of 100 kg	180.00
10	A040	Glide Slidetrak	450.00
5	A060	Power Blocks	500.00
15	A070	Stability Balls	90.00
		HST	178.10
		Invoice total	$1 548.10

Terms: 2/10, n/30.

☐   **Sales Order #5-1-MC**   **Dated May 12, 2012**

Delivery date May 14, 2012
From Mohawk College (preferred customer)

40	A090	Weight Plates	$ 1.30/ kg
2	E030	Bicycle: Dual Action Calorie Counter	640 unit
2	E060	Home Gym: Deluxe Multi HG-1402	2 100 set
2	E090	Stair Climber: Adjustable SC-A60	1 700 unit
		HST	13%

Terms: 2/10, n/30.

☐   **Purchase Invoice #R-1031**   **Dated May 12, 2012**

From Redux Home Gym Wholesalers

2	E050	Home Gym: Basic HG-1400	$1 400.00	USD
		HST	182.00	USD
		Invoice total	$1 582.00	USD

Terms: 2/10, n/30. Free delivery. The exchange rate is 1.0195.

☐ **Employee Time Summary Sheet #16**　　　**Dated May 12, 2012**

For the Pay Period ending May 12, 2012
George Schwinn worked 80 regular hours in the period. He will receive $200 as an advance and have $50 recovered from each of the following four paycheques. Issue payroll deposit slip DD23.

☐ **Credit Card Sales Invoice #3007**　　　**Dated May 12, 2012**

To Visa customers (sales summary)

11	A020	Yoga Mats	$ 40/ unit	$ 440.00
42	A030	Dumbbells	2.50/ kg	105.00
4	A040	Glide Slidetrak	90 each	360.00
2	A050	Heart Rate Monitor	90/ unit	180.00
1	A060	Power Blocks	200/ set	200.00
2	E090	Stair Climber: Adjustable SC-A60	1 900/ unit	3 800.00
2	E110	Treadmill: Deluxe T-1100D	2 800/ unit	5 600.00
6	S020	Personal Trainer: 1/2 day	200/ 1/2 day	1 200.00
16	B010	Books: Fitness Guide	40 each	640.00
		HST	13%	1 545.05
		GST	5%	32.00
		Total paid by Visa		$14 102.05

NOTES
Remember to change the tax code for Books to G.

☐ **Deposit Slip #18**　　　**Dated May 12, 2012**

Prepare deposit slip for all receipts for May 6 to May 12 to deposit the funds. The total deposit for the single cheque is $9 412.90.

☐ **Cash Receipt #46**　　　**Dated May 13, 2012**

From Mohawk College, cheque #284 for $2 000 as down payment (deposit #16) in acceptance of sales order #5-1-MC.

☐ **Memo #5-3**　　　**Dated May 14, 2012**

Record payment for GST and HST for the period ending April 30 to the Receiver General for Canada. Issue cheque #120 in full payment. Clear the tax reports up to April 30.

☐ **Memo #5-4**　　　**Dated May 14, 2012**

Payroll Remittances: Make the following remittances for the period ending April 30. Choose Pay Remittance for payroll remittances.

☐ Record payment for EI, CPP and Income Tax Payable for April to the Receiver General for Canada. Issue cheque #121 in full payment.

☐ Record payment for Garnisheed Wages Payable for April to the Receiver General for Canada. Issue cheque #122 in full payment.

☐ Record payment for RRSP Payable to Ancaster Insurance. Issue cheque #123 in full payment.

☐ Record payment for CSB Payable to Mt. Hope Investment Corporation. Issue cheque #124 in full payment.

☐ Record payment for Group Insurance Payable for April to Ancaster Insurance. Issue cheque #125 in full payment.

NOTES
Enter Memo #5-4A, Memo #5-4B and so on in the Reference Number and Comment fields for payroll remittances. When you enter April 30 as the remittance period ending date, you will see a warning about entering transactions that apply to the previous month. You can continue or change the date to May 1.

☐ **Cheque Copy #348**　　　**Dated May 15, 2012**

To Prolife Exercisers, $14 541 USD in payment of account including $262 early payment discount. Reference invoice #PE-2014. The exchange rate is 1.020.

☐ **Memo #5-5**　　　**Dated May 15, 2012**

Transfer $15 000 USD to cover the cheque to Prolife Exercisers. Transfer money to Bank: USD Chequing from 1120 Bank: Visa and Interac Account. The exchange rate is 1.020.

☐ **Memo #5-6**   **Dated May 15, 2012**

Create new inventory item:

Item:	E065 Home Gym: Free Weight HG-1403
Selling price:	$2 800 /set Regular ($2 600 Preferred) CAD
Foreign currency price:	$2 700 Regular ($2 500 Preferred) USD
Minimum level:	1

Linked accounts:

Asset	1540 Fitness Equipment
Revenue	4020 Revenue from Sales
Expense	5060 Cost of Goods Sold: Equipment
Variance	5070 Cost Variance

☐ **Purchase Invoice #R-1047**   **Dated May 15, 2012**

From Redux Home Gym Wholesalers, new inventory item purchase

2	E065	Home Gym: Free Weight HG-1403	$3 500.00	USD
	HST		455.00	USD
	Invoice total		$3 955.00	USD

Terms: 2/10, n/30. Free delivery. The exchange rate is 1.020.

☐ **Sales Invoice #3008**   **Dated May 15, 2012**

To Mohawk College, to fill sales order #5-1-MC

40	A090	Weight Plates	$	1.30/ kg
2	E030	Bicycle: Dual Action Calorie Counter		640/ unit
2	E060	Home Gym: Deluxe Multi HG-1402		2 100/ set
2	E090	Stair Climber: Adjustable SC-A60		1 700/ unit
	HST			13%

Terms: 2/10, n/30.

SESSION DATE – MAY 31, 2012

☐ **Deposit Slip #19**   **Dated May 19, 2012**

Prepare deposit slip for the single cheque for $2 000 for May 13 to May 19.

☐ **Cash Purchase Invoice #ES-79123**   **Dated May 20, 2012**

From Energy Source, $150 plus $19.50 HST paid for hydro service. Purchase invoice total $169.50. Terms: cash on receipt. Issue cheque #126 in full payment.

☐ **Cash Purchase Invoice #BC-71222**   **Dated May 20, 2012**

From Bell Canada, $95 plus $12.35 HST paid for phone service. Purchase invoice total $107.35. Terms: cash on receipt of invoice. Issue cheque #127 in full payment.

☐ **Credit Card Purchase Invoice #M-1034**   **Dated May 21, 2012**

From Mountview Delivery (use Quick Add for the new supplier), $80 plus $10.40 HST paid for delivery services. Invoice total $90.40. Full amount paid by Visa. Enter tax code H in the Purchases Journal.

☐ **Cheque Copy #128**   **Dated May 21, 2012**

To Feelyte Gym Accessories, $1 520.70 in payment of account including $27.40 discount for early payment. Reference invoice #FG-1804.

☐ **Cheque Copy #349**   **Dated May 22, 2012**

To Redux Home Gym Wholesalers, $5 439 USD in payment of account including $98 discount for early payment. Reference invoices #R-1031 and #R-1047. The exchange rate is 1.021.

Sales Invoice #3009   **Dated May 22, 2012**

To Chedoke Health Care (preferred customer)

2	E060	Home Gym: Deluxe Multi HG-1402	2 100 set
3	S040	Yoga Instructor: 1 hour	95/ hour
2	S050	Yoga Instructor: 1/2 day	190/ 1/2 day
	HST		13%

Terms: 2/10, n/30.

Memo #5-7   **Dated May 22, 2012**

Transfer $6 000 USD to Bank: USD Chequing from 1120 Bank: Visa and Interac Account to cover the cheque to Redux. The exchange rate is 1.021.

Cash Receipt #47   **Dated May 22, 2012**

From Mohawk College, cheque #391 for $7 891.30 in payment of account with $201.86 discount for early payment. Reference invoice #3008 and deposit #16.

Cash Receipt #48   **Dated May 24, 2012**

From Chedoke Health Care, cheque #532 for $5 387.50 in payment of account including $109.95 discount for early payment. Reference invoice #3009.

Memo #5-8   **Dated May 24, 2012**

Add Charitable Donations as a payroll deduction. Since Flabuless Fitness will match employee donations, a user-defined expense is also needed.
Create new Group accounts
    2440 Charitable Donations - Employee
    2450 Charitable Donations - Employer
    5390 Charitable Donations Expense
Add Donations as new name (Setup, Settings, Payroll, Names)
    for Deduction 4 on Names, Incomes & Deductions screen
    for User-Defined Expense 2 on Names, Additional Payroll screen
Change Deduction Settings (Payroll, Deductions)
    Deduct Donations by Amount After Tax, EI, CPP, EHT And Vacation Pay
Add new payroll linked accounts (under Payroll Settings)
    2440 for Donations (Linked Accounts, Deductions)
    2450 for Donations (Linked Accounts, User-Defined Expenses, Payables)
    5390 for Donations (Linked Accounts, User-Defined Expenses, Expenses)
Enter amounts in Payroll Ledger for Deductions and WSIB & Other Expenses
    Kisangel: Check Use for the deduction; enter $20 as the deduction and the expense amount per period
    Prekor: Check Use for the deduction; enter $25 as the deduction and the expense amount per period

NOTES

To add deductions, refer to
page 648 for names
page 652 for payroll
    deductions settings
page 654 for linked accounts
page 666 for entering the
    employee deduction
page 667 for WSIB & other
    expense amounts.

Credit Card Sales Invoice #3010   **Dated May 26, 2012**

To Visa customers (sales summary)

50	A030	Dumbbells	$ 2.50/ kg	$	125.00
6	A040	Glide Slidetrak	90 each		540.00
4	A050	Heart Rate Monitor	90/ unit		360.00
2	A060	Power Blocks	200/ set		400.00
12	A100	Workout Gloves: all sizes	15/ pair		180.00
1	E040	Bicycle: Recumbent R-80	950/ unit		950.00
1	E060	Home Gym: Multi HG-1402	2 400/ set		2 400.00
4	S020	Personal Trainer: 1/2 day	200/ 1/2 day		800.00
8	S050	Yoga Instructor: 1/2 day	200/ 1/2 day		1 600.00
25	B010	Books: Fitness Guide (tax code G)	40 each		1 000.00
	HST		13%		956.15
	GST		5%		50.00
	Total paid by Visa				$9 361.15

NOTES

Remember to change the tax code for Books to G.

☐ **Employee Time Summary Sheet #17**   **Dated May 26, 2012**

For the Pay Period ending May 26, 2012
George Schwinn worked 80 regular hours in the period and 2 hours of overtime.
Recover $50 advanced and issue payroll deposit slip DD24.

☐ **Deposit Slip #20**   **Dated May 26, 2012**

Prepare deposit slip for all receipts for May 20 to May 26 to deposit the funds.
The total deposit for two cheques is $13 278.80.

☐ **Cash Purchase Invoice #DMC-68**   **Dated May 28, 2012**

From Dundurn Maintenance Co., $300 plus $39 HST paid for cleaning and
maintenance of premises. Terms: cash on receipt. Issue cheque #129 for $339 in
full payment. Recall stored transaction.

☐ **Debit Card Sales Invoice #3011**   **Dated May 28, 2012**

To Bruno Scinto (cash and Interac customer)

2	A020	Yoga Mats	$ 40/ unit	$ 80.00
2	A050	Heart Rate Monitor	90/ unit	180.00
1	E090	Stair Climber: Adjustable SC-A60	1 900/ unit	1 900.00
1	E110	Treadmill: Deluxe T-1100D	2 800/ unit	2 800.00
		HST	13%	644.80
		Invoice total paid in full		$5 604.80

Debit card #5919 7599 7543 7777. Amount deposited to Visa and Interac account.

☐ **Credit Card Purchase Invoice #WS-7823**   **Dated May 30, 2012**

From Waterdown Sunoco, $115, including HST, for gasoline and $40 plus $5.20
HST for tire repairs. Purchase invoice total $160.20 paid in full by Visa.
(Remember to change the tax code for the tire repairs.)

NOTES
Remember that if you want
to preview the customer
statement, you must choose
Custom Simply Form as the Form
Type and Statements as the
Description in the Reports and
Forms settings on the screen for
Statements.

☐ **Memo #5-9**   **Dated May 31, 2012**

Print customer statements. Prepare invoice #3012 to charge Hamilton District Bd
of Education $142.04 interest — 1.5% of the overdue amount. Terms: net 15.

☐ **Memo #5-10**   **Dated May 31, 2012**

Prepare the payroll salaries for Nieve Prekor and Assumpta Kisangel. Kisangel
took one day of personal leave. Add 2 percent of service revenue for May as a
commission to Kisangel's salary. Issue payroll deposit slips DD25 and DD26.

☐ **Bank Debit Memo #96241**   **Dated May 31, 2012**

From Hamilton Trust, authorized withdrawals were made from the chequing
account on our behalf for the following:

Bank service charges	$ 35
Mortgage interest payment	1 870
Mortgage principal reduction	130
Bank loan interest payment	400
Bank loan principal reduction	500

☐ **Purchase Order #28**   **Dated May 31, 2012**

Delivery date June 7, 2012
From Footlink Corporation

4	E030	Bicycle: Dual Action Calorie Counter	$1 200.00
2	E060	Home Gym: Deluxe Multi HG-1402	2 200.00
4	E090	Stair Climber: Adjustable SC-A60	3 200.00
		Freight	120.00
		HST	873.60
		Invoice total	$7 593.60

Terms: 1/15, n/30.

SESSION DATE – JUNE 15, 2012

☐ **Purchase Order #29**   **Dated June 1, 2012**

Delivery date June 15, 2012
From Feelyte Gym Accessories

1	A050	Heart Rate Monitor (1 carton of 12)	$360.00
20	A070	Stability Balls	120.00
2	A100	Workout Gloves: all sizes (2 boxes of 10)	120.00
		HST	78.00
		Invoice total	$678.00

Terms: 2/10, n/30.

☐ **Sales Invoice #3013**   **Dated June 3, 2012**

To Buffalo Health Clinic, New York (preferred USD customer)

2	E100	Treadmill: Basic T-800B	$1 200/ unit	USD
2	E110	Treadmill: Deluxe T-1100D	2 500/ unit	USD
		Freight	60	USD

Terms: 2/10, n/30. The exchange rate is 1.022.

☐ **Purchase Invoice #TD-1127**   **Dated June 5, 2012**

From Trufit Depot

2	E070	Rowing Machine: RM-1000	$ 420.00
2	E080	Ski Exerciser: Independent SE-880	600.00
		HST	132.60
		Invoice total	$1 152.60

Terms: 2/5, n/30. Free delivery.

☐ **Sales Invoice #3014**   **Dated June 5, 2012**

To Hamilton District Bd of Education

60	A030	Dumbbells	$ 2.50/ kg
1	E020	Elliptical Exerciser: LE-400	2 600/ unit
1	E030	Bicycle: Dual Action Calorie Counter	700/ unit
1	E060	Home Gym: Deluxe Multi HG-1402	2 400/ set
1	E100	Treadmill: Basic T-800B	1 400/ unit
		Freight	30
		HST	13%

Terms: 2/10, n/30. Allow customer to exceed credit limit.

☐ **Purchase Invoice #FC-861**   **Dated June 7, 2012**

From Footlink Corporation, to fill purchase order #28

4	E030	Bicycle: Dual Action Calorie Counter	$1 200.00
2	E060	Home Gym: Deluxe Multi HG-1402	2 200.00
4	E090	Stair Climber: Adjustable SC-A60	3 200.00
		Freight	120.00
		HST	873.60
		Invoice total	$7 593.60

Terms: 1/15, n/30.

☐ **Employee Time Summary Sheet #18**   **Dated June 9, 2012**

For the Pay Period ending June 9, 2012
George Schwinn worked 80 regular hours in the period (no overtime) and took one day of sick leave. Recover $50 advanced and issue payroll deposit slip DD27.

☐ **Cash Receipt #49**   **Dated June 9, 2012**

From Hamilton District Bd of Education, cheque #1431 for $17 673.31 in payment of account including $164.53 discount for early payment. Reference invoices #3001, #3012 and #3014.

> **NOTES**
> Taxes are not charged on freight for foreign customers.

☐ **Cheque Copy #130**   **Dated June 9, 2012**

To Trufit Depot, $1 132.20 in payment of account including $20.40 discount for early payment. Reference invoice #TD-1127.

☐ **Memo #6-1**   **Dated June 9, 2012**

From Visa, received monthly credit card statement for $319.60 for purchases made before June 3, 2012. Submitted cheque #131 for $319.60 in full payment of the balance owing.

☐ **Deposit Slip #21**   **Dated June 9, 2012**

Prepare deposit slip for the single cheque for $17 673.31 being deposited.

☐ **Credit Card Sales Invoice #3015**   **Dated June 9, 2012**

NOTES
Remember to change the tax code for Books to G.

To Visa customers (sales summary)

10	A030	Dumbbells	$ 2.50/ kg	$ 25.00
3	A050	Heart Rate Monitor	90/ unit	270.00
2	A060	Power Blocks	200/ set	400.00
2	A080	Wavemaster	180/ unit	360.00
100	A090	Weights Plates	1.50/ kg	150.00
2	E090	Stair Climber: Adjustable SC-A60	1 900/ unit	3 800.00
2	E100	Treadmill: Basic T-800B	1 400/ unit	2 800.00
8	S010	Personal Trainer: 1 hour	75/ hour	600.00
4	S020	Personal Trainer: 1/2 day	200/ 1/2 day	800.00
6	S040	Yoga Instructor: 1 hour	100/ hour	600.00
2	S050	Yoga Instructor: 1/2 day	200/ 1/2 day	400.00
24	B010	Books: Fitness Guide (tax code G)	40 each	960.00
		HST	13%	1 326.65
		GST	5%	48.00
		Total paid by Visa		$12 539.65

☐ **Memo #6-2**   **Dated June 14, 2012**

Record payment for GST and HST for the period ending May 31 to the Receiver General for Canada. Issue cheque #132 in full payment. Clear the HST Report up to May 31.

☐ **Memo #6-3**   **Dated June 14, 2012**

NOTES
Enter Memo #6-3A, Memo #6-3B and so on in the Reference Number and Comment fields for the payroll remittances.

Payroll Remittances: Make the following payroll remittances for the pay period ending May 31 in the Payments Journal.

☐ Record payment for EI, CPP and Income Tax Payable for May to the Receiver General for Canada. Issue cheque #133 in full payment.

☐ Record payment for Garnisheed Wages Payable for May to the Receiver General for Canada. Issue cheque #134 in full payment.

☐ Record payment for RRSP Payable to Ancaster Insurance. Issue cheque #135 in full payment.

☐ Record payment for CSB Payable to Mt. Hope Investment Corporation. Issue cheque #136 in full payment.

☐ Record payment for Group Insurance Payable for May to Ancaster Insurance. Issue cheque #137 in full payment.

NOTES
You cannot create the new supplier from the Pay Remittance form in the Payments Journal — you must close the Remittance Journal.
Refer to page 670 for setting up payroll authorities and remittances.

☐ Record payment for Charitable Donations Payable for May to Canadian Cancer Society. Create a new supplier record and select Payroll Authority for the supplier. Choose the new supplier in the Payroll Remittance Settings screen for both Donations entries. Include employee and employer contributions in remittance. Issue cheque #138 in full payment.

☐ **Cash Receipt #50**   **Dated June 15, 2012**

From Buffalo Health Clinic, cheque #638 for $7 460 USD in payment of account. Reference invoice #3013. The exchange rate is 1.019.

☐ **Purchase Invoice #FG-2187**   **Dated June 15, 2012**

From Feelyte Gym Accessories to fill purchase order #29

1	A050	Heart Rate Monitor (1 carton of 12)	$360.00
20	A070	Stability Balls	120.00
2	A100	Workout Gloves: all sizes (2 boxes of 10)	120.00
	HST		78.00
	Invoice total		$678.00

Terms: 2/10, n/30.

SESSION DATE – JUNE 30, 2012

☐ **Sales Invoice #3016**   **Dated June 16, 2012**

To Stelco Health Club (preferred customer)

40	A090	Weight Plates	$ 1.30/ kg
1	E050	Home Gym: Basic HG-1400	1 300/ set
1	E060	Home Gym: Deluxe Multi HG-1402	2 100/ set
	HST		13%

Terms: 2/10, n/30.

☐ **Memo #6-4**   **Dated June 16. 2012**

Transfer $30 000 from the Visa bank account to the savings account.

☐ **Memo #6-5**   **Dated June 18, 2012**

Pay $8 000 to the Receiver General for Canada for quarterly instalment of business income tax. Issue cheque #139. Create new Group account 5550 Business Income Tax Expense. (Hint: Remember Business Income Tax Payable.)

☐ **Memo #6-6**   **Dated June 18, 2012**

Create appropriate new Heading and Total accounts around the new Group account 5550 to restore the logical order of accounts.

☐ **Cash Purchase Invoice #BC-86344**   **Dated June 19, 2012**

From Bell Canada, $120 plus $15.60 HST paid for monthly phone service. Purchase invoice total $135.60. Terms: cash on receipt of invoice. Issue cheque #140 in full payment.

☐ **Cash Purchase Invoice #ES-89886**   **Dated June 19, 2012**

From Energy Source, $140 plus $18.20 HST paid for hydro service. Purchase invoice total $158.20. Terms: cash on receipt of invoice. Issue cheque #141 in full payment.

☐ **Cash Sales Invoice #3017**   **Dated June 20, 2012**

To Jim Ratter (choose Continue)

1	A010	Body Fat Scale	$150.00	$150.00
	HST		13%	19.50
	Invoice total			$169.50

Received cheque #16 in full payment.

☐ **Cheque Copy #142**   **Dated June 20, 2012**

To Footlink Corporation, $7 526.40 in payment of account including $67.20 discount for early payment. Reference invoice #FC-861.

☐ **Cheque Copy #143**   **Dated June 23, 2012**

To Feelyte Gym Accessories, $666 in payment of account including $12 discount for early payment. Reference invoice #FG-2187.

☐ **Cash Receipt #51**   **Dated June 23, 2012**

From Stelco Health Club, cheque #499 for $3 822.74 in payment of account including $78.02 discount for early payment. Reference invoice #3016.

☐ **Deposit Slip #22**   **Dated June 23, 2012**

Prepare deposit slip for two cheques totalling $3 992.24 to deposit funds.

☐ **Credit Card Sales Invoice #3018**   **Dated June 23, 2012**

NOTES
Remember to change the tax code for Books to G.

To Visa customers (sales summary)

10	A020	Yoga Mats	$ 40/ each	$ 400.00
40	A030	Dumbbells	2.50/ kg	100.00
2	A060	Power Blocks	200/ set	400.00
10	A070	Stability Balls	12 each	120.00
20	A090	Weight Plates	1.50/ kg	30.00
2	E040	Bicycle: Recumbent R-80	950/ unit	1 900.00
2	E050	Home Gym: Basic HG-1400	1 500/ set	3 000.00
2	E070	Rowing Machine: RM-1000	560/ unit	1 120.00
2	E090	Stair Climber: Adjustable SC-A60	1 900/ unit	3 800.00
4	S020	Personal Trainer: 1/2 day	200/ 1/2 day	800.00
8	S040	Yoga Instructor: 1 hour	100/ hour	800.00
4	S050	Yoga Instructor: 1/2 day	200/ 1/2 day	800.00
12	B010	Books: Fitness Guide (tax code G)	40 each	480.00
		HST	13%	1 725.10
		GST	5%	24.00
		Total paid by Visa		$15 499.10

☐ **Purchase Order #30**   **Dated June 23, 2012**

NOTES
Scandia Weights Co.
Contact: B. Fitt
i82 Nordica Lane
Hamilton, ON L8P 2G6
Tel: (905) 465-6247
Fax: (905) 466-3554
E-mail: fitt@scandiawts.com
Web: www.scandiawts.com
Terms: net 30
Tax code: H
Business No. 372 640 813

Delivery date July 10, 2012
From Scandia Weights Co. (use Full Add for the new supplier)

2	A030	Dumbbells (2 orders of 100 kg)	$ 180.00
2	A090	Weight Plates (2 orders of 100 kg)	120.00
		HST	39.00
		Purchase invoice total	$339.00

Terms: net 30.

☐ **Employee Time Summary Sheet #19**   **Dated June 23, 2012**

For the Pay Period ending June 23, 2012
George Schwinn worked 80 regular and 2 overtime hours in the period and took 1 day of sick leave. Recover $50 advanced and issue payroll deposit slip DD28.

☐ **Credit Card Purchase Invoice #WS-9855**   **Dated June 25, 2012**

From Waterdown Sunoco, $98 including HST paid for gasoline. Purchase invoice total $98 paid in full by Visa.

☐ **Memo #6-7**   **Dated June 25, 2012**

Issue a cheque to George Schwinn for vacation pay. George wants to pay for his upcoming vacation. A contract has been arranged with a local delivery company to complete deliveries during his absence. Issue cheque #144.

⚠ **WARNING!**
Remember to remove all wage and benefit amounts, deductions, user-defined expense amounts and entitlements for the vacation paycheque.
Remember to turn on the Retain option after creating the vacation paycheque.

☐ **Sales Invoice #3019**   **Dated June 25, 2012**

To Lockport Gymnasium, New York

2	E020	Elliptical Exerciser: LE-400	$2 500/ unitUSD
3	E080	Ski Exerciser: Independent SE-880	650/ unitUSD
3	E100	Treadmill: Basic T-800B	1 350/ unitUSD
		Freight	60 USD

Terms: 2/10, n/30. The exchange rate is 1.0185.

Memo #6-8 **Dated June 25, 2012**

Received Bank Debit Memo #99142 from Hamilton Trust. Cheque #16 from Jim Ratter for $169.50 was returned as NSF. Prepare a sales invoice to charge Ratter for the sales amount and add $30 in service charges for the cost of processing the cheque. Create new Group account 4220 Other Revenue. Terms: net 30.

Cash Purchase Invoice #DMC-89 **Dated June 28, 2012**

From Dundurn Maintenance Co., $300 plus $39 HST paid for cleaning and maintenance of premises. Terms: cash on receipt. Issue cheque #145 for $39 in full payment. Recall stored transaction.

Credit Card Sales Invoice #3020 **Dated June 30, 2012**

To Visa customers (sales summary)

4	A040	Glide Slidetrak	$ 90 each	$ 360.00
20	A090	Weight Plates	1.50/ kg	30.00
1	E040	Bicycle: Recumbent R-80	950/ unit	950.00
8	S010	Personal Trainer: 1 hour	75/ hour	600.00
2	S030	Personal Trainer: full day	400/ day	800.00
3	S050	Yoga Instructor: 1/2 day	200/ 1/2 day	600.00
11	B010	Books: Fitness Guide (tax code G)	40 each	440.00
		HST	13%	434.20
		GST	5%	22.00
		Total paid by Visa		$4 236.20

Memo #6-9 **Dated June 30, 2012**

Write off Jim Ratter's account because attempts to locate him were unsuccessful. The outstanding amount is considered a bad debt. Improved customer screening for payment by cheque will be implemented immediately. (See margin notes.)

Memo #6-10 **Dated June 30, 2012**

Prepare the payroll for Nieve Prekor and Assumpta Kisangel, the salaried employees. Add 2 percent of service revenue for June as a commission to Kisangel's salary. Issue payroll deposit slips DD29 and DD30.

Prepare separate payroll cheques to pay all employees for completed surveys and quarterly bonuses. Withhold 10 percent income tax. (See margin notes.)

Kisangel $300 bonus, 20 completed client surveys, $50 income tax
Prekor $250 bonus, 28 completed client surveys, $53 income tax
Schwinn $250 bonus, 26 completed client surveys, $51 income tax

Issue cheques #146, #147 and #148.

Purchase Order #31 **Dated June 30, 2012**

Delivery date July 10, 2012
From Feelyte Gym Accessories

1	A010	Body Fat Scale (carton of 12)	$	660.00
2	A020	Yoga Mats (boxes of 10)		300.00
2	A040	Glide Slidetraks		90.00
1	A050	Heart Rate Monitor (carton of 12)		360.00
20	A070	Stability Balls		120.00
2	A080	Wavemaster		190.00
2	A100	Workout Gloves: all sizes (boxes of 10)		120.00
		HST		239.20
		Purchase order total		$2 079.20

Terms: 2/10, n/30.

NOTES

You cannot reverse Ratter's NSF cheque or enter a negative receipt for it because it was a cash sale. You cannot adjust an invoice by changing the method of payment.

Entering the Bank Account in the Sales Invoice for the amount of the NSF cheque will reverse the bank deposit and restore the accounts payable.

Use Quick Add to create a new partial record for Jim Ratter. For the Ratter invoice, credit chequing account for $169.50, credit Other Revenue for $30, debit Accounts Receivable for $199.50. Refer to Accounting Procedures, page 626.

NOTES

Remember to change the tax code for Books to G.

NOTES

Use tax code IN for $169.50, the sale portion of the bad debt. Use No Tax as the code for the $30 handling charge. Remember to "pay" the account. Refer to Accounting Procedures, page 626.

NOTES

Use the Paycheques Journal to enter the piece rate pay and bonuses.

- Click Enter Taxes Manually so that you can edit the income tax amounts.
- On the Income tab screen, remove all hours, wage, salary and benefit amounts. Do not remove Vacation Accrued for Schwinn.
- On the remaining tab screens, remove entitlement hours and deduction and user-defined expense amounts.
- Click the Taxes tab.
- Click Recalculate Taxes.
- Enter the income tax amount. Do not change the EI or CPP amounts.
- Click Enter Taxes Automatically after creating the bonus cheques.

NOTES

Wellness in Print
☐ Contact: Slim Writer
29 Editorial Circle
Hamilton, ON L6G 2S6
Tel: (905) 488-1000
Terms: net 30
Tax code: G
Business No. 813 276 490

☐ **Purchase Invoice #WP-4489**   **Dated June 30, 2012**

From Wellness in Print (use Full Add for new supplier)
  100 B010   Books: Fitness Guide $ 2 500.00
           GST   125.00
           Purchase order total $2 625.00
Terms: net 30 days.

☐ **Memo #6-11**   **Dated June 30, 2012**

Increase the allowance for doubtful accounts by $500 in preparation for the next fiscal period.

☐ **Bank Credit Memo #7642**   **Dated June 30, 2012**

From Hamilton Trust, semi-annual interest was deposited to bank accounts. $155 was deposited to chequing account and $815 to the savings account. Remember interest receivable balance $420.

☐ **Bank Debit Memo #143661**   **Dated June 30, 2012**

From Hamilton Trust, authorized withdrawals were made from the chequing account on our behalf for the following:
     Bank service charges $ 35
     Mortgage interest payment   1 850
     Mortgage principal reduction   150
     Bank loan interest payment   380
     Bank loan principal reduction   520

☐ **Memo #6-12**   **Dated June 30, 2012**

Prepare quarterly adjusting entries for depreciation on fixed assets using the following amounts:
     Cash Registers $ 300
     Computer Equipment   150
     Furniture & Fixtures   80
     Retail Premises   2 450
     Van   1 875

☐ **Memo #6-13**   **Dated June 30, 2012**

Prepare adjusting entries for the following:
     Office Supplies used $ 290
     Linen Supplies used   120
     Prepaid Insurance expired   2 016
     Prepaid Advertising expired   680
     Payroll Liabilities accrued for Schwinn   680
Create a new Group liability account Accrued Payroll 2260.

REVIEW

The Student DVD with Data Files includes Review Questions and Supplementary Cases for this chapter that encourage group work and report analysis. The DVD also includes bank reconciliation and online banking for this chapter.

CHAPTER SEVENTEEN

Stratford Country Inn

OBJECTIVES

After completing this chapter, you should be able to

- **plan** and **design** an accounting system for a small business
- **prepare** a conversion procedure from manual records
- **understand** the objectives of a computerized accounting system
- **create** company files
- **set up** company accounts
- **assign** appropriate account numbers and account classes
- **choose** and **enter** appropriate settings for all ledgers
- **create** supplier, guest and employee records
- **enter** historical data and account balances in all ledgers
- **finish** entering historical data to prepare for journal entries
- **enter** accounting transactions from realistic source documents

COMPANY INFORMATION

Company Profile

NOTES

Stratford Country Inn
100 Festival Road
Stratford, ON
N5A 3G2
Tel 1: (519) 222-6066
Tel 2: (888) 272-6000
Fax: (519) 272-7960
Business No.: 767 698 321

NOTES

For the accommodation business, the terms Guest and Supplier replace Customer and Vendor.

Stratford Country Inn is situated in Ontario just outside the Stratford city limits, close to Stratford Festival Theatres. The Inn has room for approximately 50 guests, with additional cots available for families with children who want to share rooms. In addition to the theatre, which attracts most of the guests, the Inn has facilities for rowing and canoeing on the small lake area near the Thames River, and a forested area nearby is used for lovely summer walks or cross-country skiing in winter. Boxed lunches and dinners are provided for picnics on the waterfront before theatre events or for afternoons in the woods or on the lake. Many guests stay for several days at a time, and weekly rates are offered.

For an additional cost, a private consultant will pamper the guests with aromatherapy sessions. The consultant pays a rental fee to the Inn for use of her studio.

Guests come from near and far, and even a few American theatre groups have become regular visitors. The Inn prepares invoices and accepts payments in United States dollars for US accounts. For the American groups, an agency books

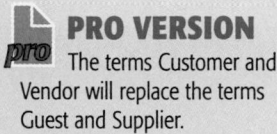

PRO VERSION
The terms Customer and Vendor will replace the terms Guest and Supplier.

group tours for a fixed price that includes theatre tickets and accommodation. Most individual guests pay by Visa or MasterCard. All guests pay HST on the services provided by the Inn. Regular guests, corporations such as colleges, universities and schools, or agencies that reserve blocks of theatre tickets and accommodation have credit accounts. Groups place a deposit to confirm their accommodation. In the event of overbooking, guests who cannot be placed at the Inn are put up at a nearby bed and breakfast at the Inn's expense.

The grounds of the Inn include conference rooms for discussions and debates about theatre performances and related topics. Buses take guests to the theatre and return them to the Inn on a scheduled basis. Meals can be included for those who want an all-inclusive package. The Inn's dining room serves all full accommodation guests and also caters to the public and to guests who choose not to take a full meal package.

The owner, manager and desk attendant look after the front office. Five additional staff cater to all the other needs of the guests.

Accounts payable have been set up for food supplies, a maintenance contract (a cleaning crew vacuums the Inn), maintenance and repairs (electrical and carpentry work), linen supplies for kitchen and guest rooms and laundry services for towels and bedding.

By June 30, the Inn was ready to convert its accounting records to Simply Accounting and had gathered the following reports to make the conversion:

- Chart of Accounts
- Post-Closing Trial Balance
- Supplier Information
- Guest Information
- Employee Information and Profiles

CHART OF ACCOUNTS

STRATFORD COUNTRY INN

ASSETS
Bank: Stratford Trust CAD Chequing
Bank: Stratford Trust USD Chequing
Bank: Credit Card
Accounts Receivable
Advances Receivable
Purchase Prepayments
Prepaid Advertising
Prepaid Insurance
Food Inventory
Linens & Towels
Blankets & Bedding
Supplies: Computer
Supplies: Office
Supplies: Dining Room
Supplies: Washroom
Computer Equipment
Accum Deprec: Computers ▶

▶Furniture & Fixtures
Accum Deprec: Furn & Fix
Vehicle
Accum Deprec: Vehicle
Country Inn & Dining Room
Accum Deprec: Inn & Dining Room
Grounds & Property

LIABILITIES
Bank Loan
Accounts Payable
Prepaid Sales and Deposits
Credit Card Payable
Vacation Payable
EI Payable
CPP Payable
Income Tax Payable
EHT Payable
Group Insurance Payable ▶

▶Tuition Fees Payable
WSIB Payable
HST Charged on Services
HST Paid on Purchases
Mortgage Payable

EQUITY
E. Prospero, Capital
Current Earnings

REVENUE
Revenue from Inn
Revenue from Dining Room
Rental Fees
Other Revenue
Exchange Rate Differences

EXPENSE
Advertising & Promotion
Bank Charges and Card Fees
COGS: Food ▶

▶Depreciation: Computers
Depreciation: Furn & Fix
Depreciation: Vehicle
Depreciation: Inn & Dining Room
Purchase Discounts
Interest Expense: Loan
Interest Expense: Mortgage
Hydro Expenses
Maintenance & Repairs
Overflow Accommodation
Telephone Expense
Vehicle Expenses
Wages: Management
Wages: General
Wages: Dining Room
EI Expense
CPP Expense
WSIB Expense
EHT Expense
Tuition Fees Expense

NOTES: Use appropriate account numbers and add subgroup totals, headings and totals to organize your Chart of Accounts as necessary. Remember to add a test balance account for the setup.

POST-CLOSING TRIAL BALANCE

STRATFORD COUNTRY INN

June 30, 2012	Debits	Credits		Debits	Credits
Bank: Stratford Trust CAD Chequing	$33 964		▶ Accum Deprec: Vehicle		10 000
Bank: Stratford Trust USD Chequing			Country Inn & Dining Room	400 000	
(2 940 USD)	3 000		Accum Deprec: Inn & Dining Room		20 000
Bank: Credit Card	12 000		Grounds & Property	200 000	
Accounts Receivable (deposit)		$ 1 000	Bank Loan		25 000
Advances Receivable	250		Accounts Payable		8 068
Prepaid Advertising	50		Credit Card Payable		395
Prepaid Insurance	400		Vacation Payable		4 946
Food Inventory	1 650		EI Payable		1 092
Linens & Towels	2 000		CPP Payable		1 759
Blankets & Bedding	3 000		Income Tax Payable		3 109
Supplies: Computer	400		EHT Payable		577
Supplies: Office	500		Group Insurance Payable		330
Supplies: Dining Room	800		WSIB Payable		1 310
Supplies: Washroom	250		HST Charged on Services		6 280
Computer Equipment	4 000		HST Paid on Purchases	3 900	
Accum Deprec: Computers		1 200	Mortgage Payable		300 000
Furniture & Fixtures	38 000		E. Prospero, Capital	-	364 898
Accum Deprec: Furn & Fix		4 200		$754 164	$754 164
Vehicle	50 000 ▶				

SUPPLIER INFORMATION

STRATFORD COUNTRY INN

Supplier Name (Contact)	Address	Phone No. Fax No.	E-mail Web Site	Terms Tax ID
Avon Maintenance Services (Ken Sparkles)	66 Kleen Road Stratford, Ontario N5A 3C3	Tel: (519) 272-4611 Fax: (519) 272-4813	www.avonservices.com	net 30 631 393 461
Bard's Linen & Towels (Jason Bard)	21 Venice Street Stratford, Ontario N5A 4L2	Tel: (519) 271-2273 Fax: (519) 271-9333	bard@bards.com www.bards.com	2/10, n/30 after tax 763 271 673
Bell Canada (Bea Heard)	30 Whisper Road Stratford, Ontario N5A 4N3	Tel: (519) 273-2355	bheard@bell.ca www.bell.ca	net 1 634 345 373
Minister of Finance	PO Box 3000, Stn A Toronto, Ontario M5C 1M2		www.gov.on.ca/fin	net 1
Perth County Hydro (Wynd Mills)	66 Power Road Stratford, Ontario N5A 4P4	Tel: (519) 272-6121	www.perthenergy.com	net 1 721 431 214
Receiver General for Canada	PO Box 20002, Stn A Sudbury, Ontario P3A 5C3	Tel: (800) 959-5525	www.cra-arc.gc.ca	net 1
Stratford Service Centre (A.L.L. Ledfree)	33 MacBeth Avenue Stratford, Ontario N5A 4T2	Tel: (519) 271-6679 Fax: (519) 276-8822	ledfree@ssc.com www.ssc.com	net 1 634 214 211
Tavistock Laundry Services (Martin Tavistock)	19 Merchant Road Stratford, Ontario N5A 4C3	Tel: (519) 271-7479 Fax: (519) 271-7888	www.tavistock.com	net 30 639 271 343
Tempest Food Wholesalers (Vita Minns)	35 Henry Avenue Stratford, Ontario N5A 3N6	Tel: (519) 272-4464 Fax: (519) 272-4600	vita@tempest.com www.tempest.com	net 30 673 421 936
Travellers' Life				
Workplace Safety & Insurance Board				
Zephyr Advertising Services (Tom DeZiner)	32 Portia Blvd. Stratford, Ontario N5A 4T2	Tel: (519) 271-6066 Fax: (519) 271-6067	tom@westwinds.com www.westwinds.com	net 1 391 213 919

LIST OF PAYROLL AUTHORITIES

STRATFORD COUNTRY INN

Supplier Name	Payroll Remittance
Receiver General for Canada	EI, CPP and Income Tax
Workplace Safety & Insurance Board	WSIB
Minister of Finance	EHT
Travellers' Life	group insurance

OUTSTANDING SUPPLIER INVOICES

STRATFORD COUNTRY INN

Supplier Name	Terms	Date	Inv/Chq No.	Amount	Total
Avon Maintenance Services	net 30	June 7/12	AM-68	$565	
	net 30	June 14/12	AM-85	565	
	net 30	June 21/12	AM-101	565	
	net 30	June 28/12	AM-127	565	
			Balance owing		$2 260
Tavistock Laundry Services	net 30	June 8/12	TL-693	$904	
	net 30	June 22/12	TL-742	904	
			Balance owing		$1 808
Tempest Food Wholesalers	net 30	June 23/12	TF-113	$2 000	
	net 30	June 30/12	TF-183	2 000	
			Balance owing		$4 000
			Grand Total		$8 068

GUEST INFORMATION

STRATFORD COUNTRY INN

Guest Name (Contact)	Address	Phone No. Fax No.	E-mail Web Site	Terms Credit Limit
Festival Club of Rosedale (Jane Birken)	3 Rosedale Valley Rd. Toronto, Ontario M5G 3T4	Tel: (416) 482-6343	janebir@conundrum.com	net 5 $6 000
Hamlet Holiday Agency (Ron Doleman)	60 Tibault Avenue Stratford, Ontario N5A 3K3	Tel 1: (519) 272-6461 Tel 2: (800) 777-7777	rdoleman@hamlet.com www.hamlet.com	net 5 $6 000
Metro Arts Appreciation Group (R. Downey)	4400 Yonge St. North York, Ontario M6L 3T4	Tel: (416) 923-8142	RDowney@artnet.com www.artnet.com	net 5 $6 000
NY Friends of Shakespeare (J. Monte)	33, 16th Avenue Buffalo, NY 13002	Tel 1: (716) 755-4992 Tel 2: (888) 755-5000	monte@aol.com	net 5 $4 000 (USD)
Waterloo University Literary Club (T. Fornello)	88 College Rd. Waterloo, Ontario N2A 3F6	Tel: (519) 431-6343	fornello4@uwo.ca	net 5 $6 000

OUTSTANDING GUEST INVOICES

STRATFORD COUNTRY INN

Guest Name	Terms	Date	Inv/Chq No.	Total
Hamlet Holiday Agency	net 30	June 30/12	Deposit #40 (Chq 317; enter a negative invoice)	$1 000

EMPLOYEE INFORMATION SHEET

STRATFORD COUNTRY INN

	Owen Othello	Clara Claudius	Mary MacBeth	Hedy Horatio	Juliet Jones	Shelley Shylock	Bud Romeo
Position	Manager	Clerk	Cook	Waiter	Concierge	Waiter	Service
Social Insurance No.	691 113 724	873 863 211	284 682 556	294 654 421	177 162 930	891 263 634	254 685 829
Address	38 Falstaff St. Stratford, ON N5A 3T3	147 King Henry St. Mary's, ON N4X 1B2	3 Bard Cr. Stratford, ON N5A 6Z8	17 Elizabeth St. Stratford, ON N5A 4Z1	5 Capella Cres. Stratford, ON N5A 5M1	29 Avon St. Stratford, ON N5A 5N5	42 Hosteller St. New Hamburg, ON N0B 2G0
Telephone	(519) 272-2191	(519) 373-6495	(519) 277-1338	(519) 278-5343	(519) 273-9122	(519) 273-5335	(519) 381-3738
Date of Birth (mm-dd-yy)	6-29-72	4-21-65	8-3-70	12-3-77	1-25-71	3-12-81	5-27-70
Date of Hire (mm-dd-yy)	3-1-99	5-2-92	6-1-02	6-1-04	1-1-03	1-1-06	12-16-01
Federal (Ontario) Tax Exemption - TD1							
Basic Personal	$10 382 (8 943)	$10 382 (8 943)	$10 382 (8 943)	$10 382 (8 943)	$10 382 (8 943)	$10 382 (8 943)	$10 382 (8 943)
Other	$4 520 (4 552)	–	$10 382 (7 594)	$3 040 (3 072)	$18 865 (16 070)	$9 960 (10 088)	$10 382 (7 594)
Total Exemptions	$14 902 (13 495)	$10 382 (8 943)	$20 764 (16 537)	$13 422 (12 015)	$29 247 (25 013)	$20 342 (19 031)	$20 764 (16 537)
Indexed Amounts	$10 382 (8 943)	$10 382 (8 943)	$20 764 (16 537)	$10 382 (8 943)	$29 247 (25 013)	$10 382 (8 943)	$20 764 (16 537)
Additional Federal Tax	–	–	–	$50.00	–	$50.00	–
Employee Taxes							
Historical Income tax	$4 110.12	$2 796.42	$3 029.01	$2 655.52	$3 345.44	$1 013.86	$1 499.66
Historical EI	$501.60	$376.20	$513.51	$329.55	$468.16	$176.36	$325.85
Historical CPP	$989.34	$721.44	$1 014.83	$621.80	$917.87	$294.49	$613.90
Employee Income							
Advances: Historical	–	–	–	$100.00	–	–	$150.00
Benefits: Historical	$3 400.00	–	–	$1 920.00	–	$3 120.00	–
Vacation Pay Owed	–	–	$1 400.57	$898.85	$1 276.85	$400.96	$888.77
Regular Wage Rate	–	–	$22.00/hr.	$14.00/hr.	$20.00/hr.	$12.00/hr.	$14.00/hr.
No. Hours Per Period	160	160	80	80	80	80	80
Wages: Historical	–	–	$22 880.00	$14 560.00	$20 800.00	$7 872.00	$14 560.00
Overtime 1 Wage Rate	–	–	$33.00/hr	$21.00/hr	$30.00/hr	$18.00/hr	$21.00/hr
Overtime 1: Historical	–	–	$462.00	$420.00	$480.00	$144.00	$252.00
Regular Salary	$3 800/mo.	$2 850/mo.	–	–	–	–	–
Salary: Historical	$22 800.00	$17 100.00	–	–	–	–	–
Commission	1% (Sales–Returns)	–	–	–	–	–	–
Pay Periods	12	12	26	26	26	26	26
Vacation Rate	4 weeks	4 weeks	6% retained	6% retained	6% retained	6% retained	6% retained
Wage Account	Management	General	Dining Room	Dining Room	General	Dining Room	General
Deductions							
Group Insurance	$30.00	$60.00	$30.00	$15.00	$30.00	$15.00	$30.00
Insurance: Historical	$180.00	$360.00	$390.00	$195.00	$390.00	$195.00	$390.00
WSIB and User-Defined Expenses							
WSIB Rate	2.55	2.55	1.70	1.70	2.55	1.70	2.55
Tuition: Historical	$3 400.00	–	–	$1 920.00	–	$3 120.00	–
Entitlements (Rate, Maximum Days, Clear, Days Accrued)							
Vacation	8%, 30, No, 20	8%, 30, No, 20	–	–	–	–	–
Sick Leave	5%, 15, No, 9	5%, 15, No, 7	5%, 15, No, 8	5%, 15, No, 9	5%, 15, No, 10	5%, 15, No, 3	5%, 15, No, 8
T4 and RL-1 Reporting							
EI Insurable Earnings	$22 800.00	$17 100.00	$23 342.00	$14 980.00	$21 280.00	$8 016.00	$14 812.00
Pensionable Earnings	$26 200.00	$17 100.00	$23 342.00	$16 100.00	$21 280.00	$11 136.00	$14 812.00
Withheld	$5 781.06	$4 254.06	$4 947.35	$3 801.87	$5 121.47	$1 679.71	$2 829.41
Net Pay	$17 018.94	$12 845.94	$18 394.65	$11 278.13	$16 158.53	$6 336.29	$12 132.59

Payroll Information

General Payroll Information   E. Prospero, the owner, has arranged group insurance for his employees, and all employees have elected to join the plan. As entitlements, all staff may take 10 days' sick leave per year, and the vacation allowances are quite generous for the industry — four weeks of paid vacation for salaried staff after three years of service and 6 percent for all hourly paid employees. As an additional benefit, employees are reimbursed for their tuition fees on completion of eligible courses. Salaried employees are paid monthly, and hourly employees are paid every two weeks. All employees are eligible for EI and pay CPP; the EI factor is 1.4. The Inn pays 0.98 percent of payroll for EHT, the provincial health tax. WSIB rates vary for different types of work performed by the employees of the Inn.

Wage expenses for the manager, the dining room staff and the remaining general employees are tracked separately in three different payroll expense accounts.

Employee Profiles and TD1 Information

E. Prospero   owns the Inn and oversees all activities. Together with family members, he fills in where needed. He does not collect a salary and is not recorded as an employee.

Owen Othello   is the salaried manager for the Inn. He welcomes guests, instructs other employees and discusses issues, problems and plans with the owner. He is single and studies part time in an MBA program. One night a week he commutes to Toronto. An education allowance — $140 per month federal and $144 provincial — and $3 400 for tuition increase his basic tax claim amounts. Othello is the salesperson for all sales, and beginning in July, he will receive a commission of 1 percent of sales.

Clara Claudius   has been with the Inn the longest and works as the desk attendant. Although her primary job is reservations clerk, she also performs the accounting for the Inn. She too is salaried. Because her husband is also fully employed, she uses only the basic single tax claim amounts. They have two young children as dependants.

Mary MacBeth   works as the cook in the dining room. As a single parent with dependent children, she is allowed to use the eligible dependant claim as the spousal equivalent for tax purposes. She is paid at an hourly rate of $22 per hour for the first 40 hours each week and $33 per hour after that.

Hedy Horatio   divides her time between waiting tables and helping the cook for her pay at the rate of $14 per hour plus $21 per hour for overtime hours. She studies part time at Conestoga College in the chef training program. The $1 920 tuition fee and the education tax claims — $140 per month federal and $144 provincial — supplement her basic single claim.

Juliet Jones   deals with requests from guests, working as the concierge and arranging for room service. She lives with and cares for her father and therefore has the eligible dependant claim plus a caregiver claim. She also has additional deductions transferred from her father ($4 260 federal and provincial) to supplement her basic single claim. Her hourly wage rate is $20 for the first 40 hours in the week and $30 for additional hours.

Shelley Shylock   waits tables in the dining room at the Inn. During the summer and festival months, she works full time for the Inn at the rate of $12 per hour and $18 for hours beyond the first 40 each week. She works part time until summer while she is a full-time student at the University of Waterloo. The education deduction of $465 ($481 provincial) per month plus tuition fees at $6 240 supplement her tax claim amounts.

NOTES
Enter entitlements as Payroll Settings and edit records for each employee as needed.

Tuition is a user-defined payroll expense and taxable benefit. The benefits for Othello, Horatio and Shylock have already been paid, so only historical amounts are entered.

Remember that WSIB is the name for WCB in Ontario.

NOTES
The claim amounts subject to indexing do not include education and tuition amounts. The amount subject to indexing is used by the program to update claim amounts when a new tax table is introduced, based on the government indexing rate.

NOTES
Federal education amounts include the monthly allowance for textbooks.

Bud Romeo   takes care of room service requests and also handles the baggage for the guests. He is married with two dependent children, so he has the spousal claim amount in addition to the basic single amount. He too is paid hourly at the rate of $14 per hour and $21 per hour for the time beyond 40 hours per week.

INSTRUCTIONS

1. Use all the information presented in this application to set up the company accounts for Stratford Country Inn in Simply Accounting using the following steps:
   a. Create company files in a new data folder for storing the company records.
   b. Enter the company information. Start a new fiscal period on July 1, 2012, and finish the period on September 30, 2012. Choose Accommodation as the industry.
   c. Enter names and printer information.
   d. Prepare the settings by changing the default settings as necessary.
   e. Organize the Balance Sheet and Income Statement accounts.
   f. Create accounts to correspond to your Balance Sheet and Income Statement. Add appropriate account numbers and types.
   g. Set up currency information for the USD transactions. The exchange rate on June 30 is 1.0185.
   h. Change the account class for bank and credit card accounts and set up the cheque sequence.
   i. Enter linked accounts for the ledgers and credit cards. The fee is 2.75 percent.
   j. Enter sales tax information and create tax codes for HST @ 13%, refundable;
   k. Enter guest, supplier and employee information. The tax code for all suppliers and guests is H, except for the suppliers that are payroll or tax authorities, and for Tempest Food Wholesalers that supplies tax exempt foods.
   l. Enter historical balances in all ledgers.
   m. Create two Job Categories: Sales (employees are salespersons) and Other (employees in this category are not salespersons). Assign Othello to Sales and all other employees to the Other category.
   n. Set up Payroll Authorities and Payroll Remittances. Add the balance forward amounts from the Trial Balance as at July 1, 2012.
   o. Back up your files.
   p. Finish entering the history for all ledgers and finish your session.

2. Using the information provided, enter the source documents for July using Simply Accounting.

3. After you have completed your entries, print the following reports:
   a. Journal Entries (All Journals) from July 1 to July 31, 2012
   b. Supplier Aged Detail Report for all suppliers on July 31, 2012
   c. Guest Aged Detail Report for all guests on July 31, 2012
   d. Employee Summary (all employees) for the pay period ending July 31, 2012
   e. Income Statement for the period ending July 31, 2012

SOURCE DOCUMENTS

Create new accounts or supplier and guest records as needed for the source documents that follow. Change session dates as needed.

WARNING!
Save your work and make backups frequently.

WARNING!
Remember to use a test balance account to check the trial balance before finishing the history for the General Ledger. Print the appropriate reports to check your work as you enter the company data.

NOTES
Guests from the United States pay taxes on their Ontario purchases because the services and goods are consumed in Ontario.

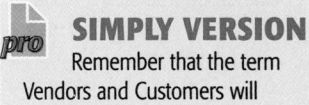

SIMPLY VERSION
Remember that the term Vendors and Customers will replace Suppliers and Guests.

Telephone: (519) 271-BARD (2273) Fax: (519) 271-9333		**Bard's** **Linen & Towels**	Website: www.bards.com E-mail: bard@bards.com

Invoice:	BLT-64	**Sold to:**	Stratford Country Inn 100 Festival Road Stratford, ON N5A 3G2
Date: July 1, 2012			

STOCK NO.	QTY.	DESCRIPTION	PRICE	AMOUNT
1601	20	Satin Sheets	35.00	700.00
1801	100	Bath Towels	10.00	1000.00
2802	100	Face Cloths	3.00	300.00

CUSTOMER COPY	Terms on Account: 2/10, N/30			**GROSS**	2000.00
Method of payment:	**On Account**	**C.O.D.**	**Credit Card**		
HST #763 271 673	✓			**HST 13%**	260.00
				TOTAL	2260.00

AVON
Maintenance
Services
66 Kleen Road, Stratford, ON N5A 3C3
Telephone (519) 272-4611
Fax: (519) 272-4813
www.avonservices.com

Invoice:	AM-148
Date:	July 1, 2012
Sold to:	Stratford Country Inn 100 Festival Road Stratford, ON N5A 3G2
Phone:	(519) 222-6066

Code	Service Description	Price
KX-55	Vacuum Premises Floor Polishing Washroom Cleaning Maintenance and repairs Recurring bi-weekly billing	1000.00

Signature:	Terms: Net 30 days	HST	130.00
E Prosper	HST #631 393 461	Amount owing	1130.00

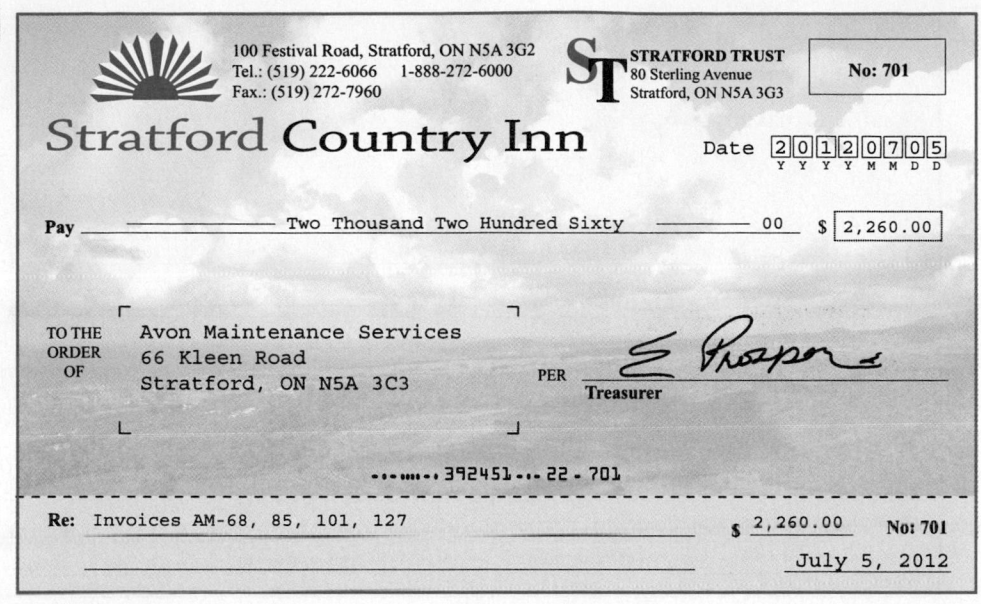

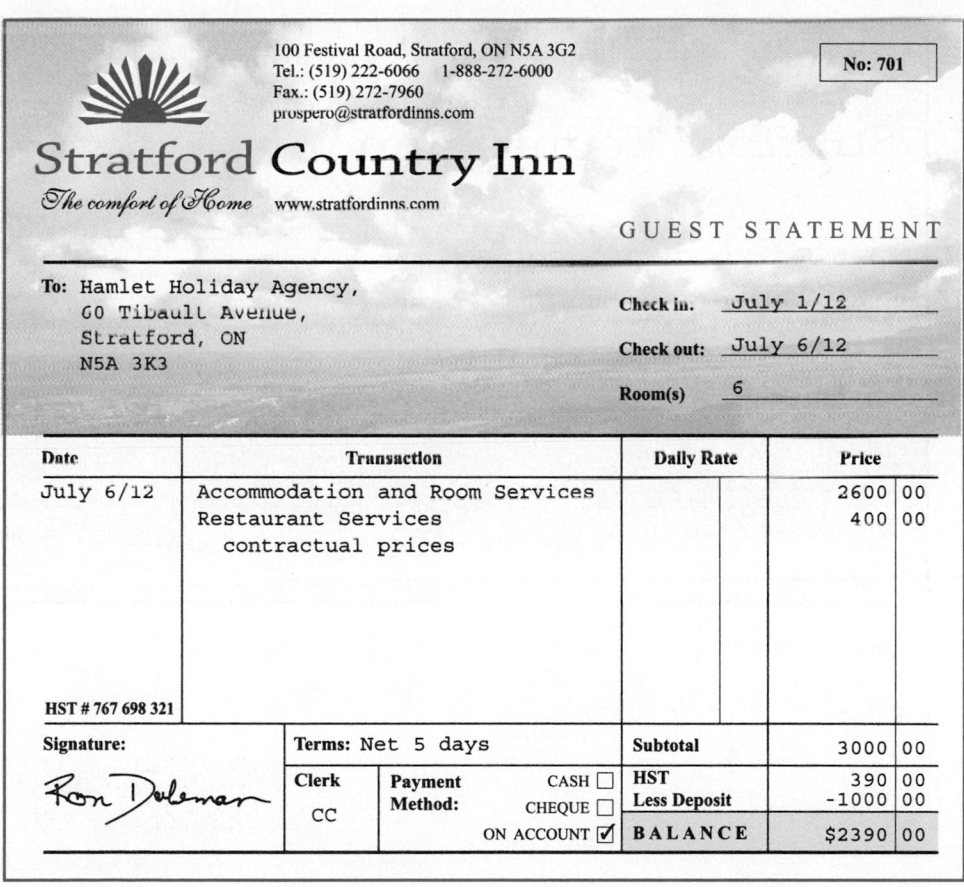

Waterloo University Literary Club
88 College Road
Waterloo, ON N2A 3F6

No: 413

Date 2 0 1 2 0 7 0 6
Y Y Y Y M M D D

Pay to the order of   Stratford Country Inn $ 1,000.00

_____ One Thousand _____ 00/100 Dollars

Waterloo Trust
550 King Street
Waterloo, ON N2A 3F8

WT

T. Fornella

Chair

⑈⑈⑈⑈ 60431 ⑈⑈ 105 ⑈⑈ 413

Re: Deposit #41 — booking rooms in Inn   No: 413

_____ $1,000.00   July 6, 2012

---

100 Festival Road, Stratford, ON N5A 3G2
Tel.: (519) 222-6066   1-888-272-6000
Fax.: (519) 272-7960

ST **STRATFORD TRUST**
80 Sterling Avenue
Stratford, ON N5A 3G3

No: 702

Stratford Country Inn

Date 2 0 1 2 0 7 0 7
Y Y Y Y M M D D

Pay _____ One Thousand Eight Hundred Eight _____ 00 $ 1,808.00

TO THE
ORDER
OF

Tavistock Laundry Services
19 Merchant Road
Stratford, ON N5A 4C3

PER *E. Prospero*

Treasurer

⑈⑈⑈⑈⑈ 392451 ⑈⑈⑈ 22 ⑈ 702

Re: Invoices TL-693, 742 $ 1,808.00   No: 702

_____   July 7, 2012

100 Festival Road, Stratford, ON N5A 3G2
Tel.: (519) 222-6066   1-888-272-6000
Fax.: (519) 272-7960
prospero@stratfordinns.com

Stratford Country Inn
The comfort of Home   www.stratfordinns.com

VISA | No: 27 V |

SALES SUMMARY
STATEMENT

Week ___ July 7, 2012 ___

Accommodation ☑
Restaurant ☑

Transaction	Amount	
Accommodation and Room Services	5,250	00
Restaurant Services	1,750	00

HST # 767 698 321

Approved:

E Prospero

Subtotal	7 000	00
Harmonized Sales Tax	910	00
VISA Receipts	7,910	00

Sold to:	Stratford Country Inn
	100 Festival Road
	Stratford, ON
	N5A 3G2

TEMPEST
Food Wholesalers

35 Henry Avenue
Stratford, ON N5A 3N6

Telephone:
(519) 272-4464
Fax:
(519) 272-4600
Website:
www.tempest.com

Billing Date: July 8, 2012
Invoice No: TF-284
Customer No.: 3423
Customer Copy

Date	Description	Charges	Payments	Amount
July 8/12	Fish and Meats	1000.00		1000.00
	Fresh Fruits	200.00		200.00
	Fresh Vegetables	200.00		200.00
	Dry Goods	200.00		200.00
	Dairy Products	200.00		200.00
	Baking Goods	200.00		200.00
	Recurring bi-weekly billing			

Terms: Net 30 days | **Subtotal** | 2000.00 |

HST #673 421 936

Signature: *E Prospero*

Overdue accounts are subject to 16% interest per year

| **HST 13%** | exempt |
| **Owing** | 2000.00 |

Invoice No: TL-798

Date: July 8, 2012

Customer: Stratford Country Inn
100 Festival Road
Stratford, ON
N5A 3G2

Phone: (519) 222-6066

TAVISTOCK
LAUNDRY
Services

19 Merchant Road
Stratford, ON
N5A 4C3

Phone: (519) 271-7479
Fax: (519) 271-7888
www.tavistock.com

HST #639 271 343

Code	Description	Price	Amount
C-11	10 Loads Sheets	40.00	400.00
C-14	5 Loads Pillow Covers	20.00	100.00
C-20	15 Loads Towels	20.00	300.00
	Recurring bi-weekly billing		

Overdue accounts are subject to a 2% interest penalty per month	Sub-total	800.00
Terms: Net 30 days	**HST**	104.00
Signature: *E Prosper*	**Total**	904.00

---

100 Festival Road, Stratford, ON N5A 3G2
Tel.: (519) 222-6066   1-888-272-6000
Fax.: (519) 272-7960

ST STRATFORD TRUST
80 Sterling Avenue
Stratford, ON N5A 3G3

No: 703

Stratford Country Inn

Date | 2 0 1 2 0 7 0 9 |
Y Y Y Y M M D D

Pay —————— Four Thousand —————— 00 $ | 4,000.00 |

TO THE ORDER OF   Tempest Food Wholesalers
35 Henry Avenue
Stratford, ON N5A 3N6

PER *E Prosper*
Treasurer

⑈⑈⑈⑈⑈ 392451 ⑈⑈ 22 · 703

Re: Invoices TF-113, 183

$ 4,000.00   **No: 703**

July 9, 2012

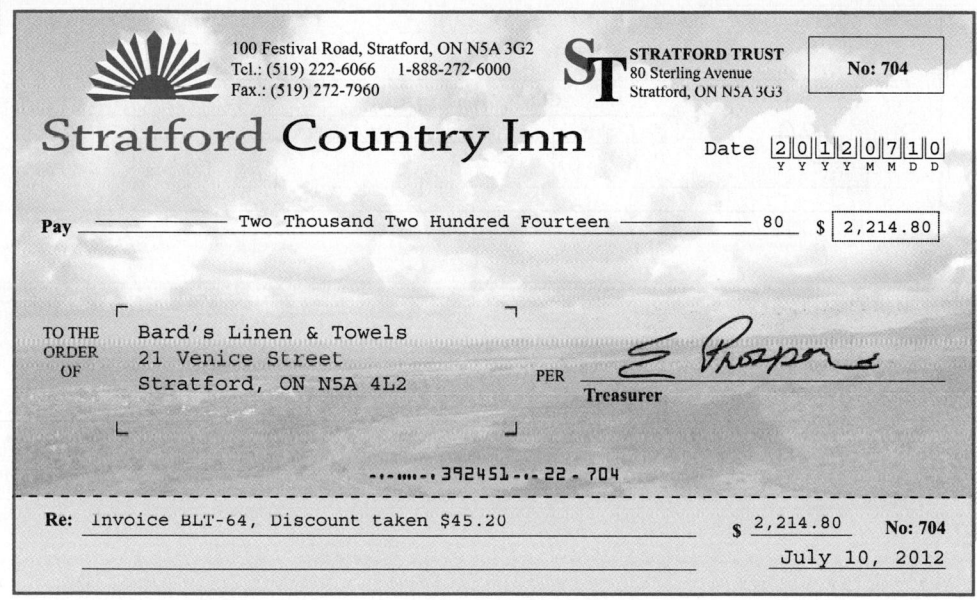

Hamlet Holiday Agency
60 Tibault Avenue,
STRATFORD, ON N5A 3K3

SB Scotia Bank
44 Welland Avenue
STRATFORD, ON N5A 3F6

No: 349

Date 2 0 1 2 0 7 1 0
      Y Y Y Y M M D D

Pay ——— Two thousand, three hundred & ninety ——— 00 $ 2,390.00

TO THE
ORDER
OF
Stratford Country Inn
100 Festival Road
Stratford, ON N5A 3G2

PER _Ron Deleman_
Treasurer

⑄⑄⑄ 64299 ⑄ 168 ⑄ 349

Re: Receipt #56 (Cheque #317)   **No: 349**
     Invoice #701 $2,390.00   July 10, 2012

---

100 Festival Road, Stratford, ON N5A 3G2
Tel.: (519) 222-6066   1-888-272-6000
Fax.: (519) 272-7960

ST STRATFORD TRUST
80 Sterling Avenue
Stratford, ON N5A 3G3

No: 704

Stratford Country Inn

Date 2 0 1 2 0 7 1 0
      Y Y Y Y M M D D

Pay ——— Two Thousand Two Hundred Fourteen ——— 80 $ 2,214.80

TO THE
ORDER
OF
Bard's Linen & Towels
21 Venice Street
Stratford, ON N5A 4L2

PER _E Prospero_
Treasurer

⑄⑄⑄ 392451 ⑄ 22 - 704

Re: Invoice BLT-64, Discount taken $45.20 $ 2,214.80   **No: 704**
                                                 July 10, 2012

33 MacBeth Avenue
Stratford, ON N5A 4T2
Tel: (519) 271-6679
Fax: (519) 276-8822
www.ssc.com

Date: July 11, 2012   **Invoice:** 1143

Customer: Stratford Country Inn
                100 Festival Road
                Stratford, ON
                N5A 3G2

Phone: (519) 222-6066

HST #634 214 211

Code	Description	Price	Amount
M-114	Lube, Oil and Filter	40.00	40.00
XF-1	Fuel	120.00	120.00
		Sub-total	160.00

APPROVAL	CUSTOMER COPY				
EP	**Cash**	**VISA**	**On Account**	**HST**	20.80
		✓		**Owing**	180.80

---

100 Festival Road, Stratford, ON N5A 3G2
Tel.: (519) 222-6066   1-888-272-6000
Fax.: (519) 272-7960

ST **STRATFORD TRUST**
80 Sterling Avenue
Stratford, ON N5A 3G3

No: 705

Stratford Country Inn

Date | 2 | 0 | 1 | 2 | 0 | 7 | 1 | 2 |
Y Y Y Y M M D D

Pay ———— Two Thousand Three Hundred Eighty ———— 00 $ 2,380.00

TO THE
ORDER
OF
    Receiver General for Canada
    PO Box 20002, Stn A
    Sudbury, ON P3A 5C3

PER *E Prosper*
Treasurer

⑈⑈⑈⑈ 392451 ⑈⑈ 22 ⑈ 706

Re: HST Remittance for June 30 $ 2,380.00   **No: 705**

July 12, 2012

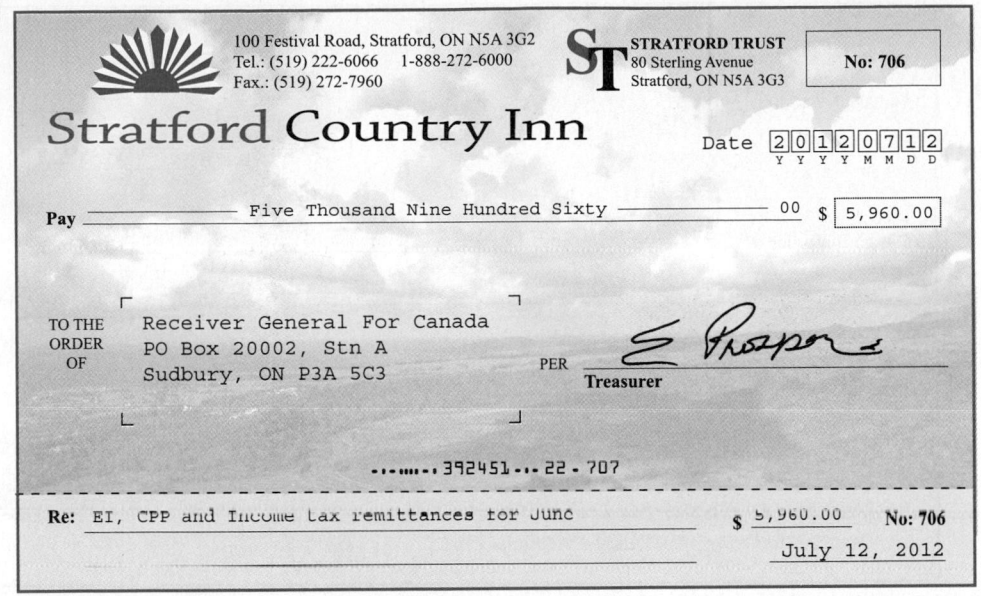

100 Festival Road, Stratford, ON N5A 3G2
Tel.: (519) 222-6066   1-888-272-6000
Fax.: (519) 272-7960

STRATFORD TRUST
80 Sterling Avenue
Stratford, ON N5A 3G3

No: 706

Stratford Country Inn

Date 2 0 1 2 0 7 1 2
Y Y Y Y M M D D

Pay ———— Five Thousand Nine Hundred Sixty ———— 00 $ 5,960.00

TO THE
ORDER
OF

Receiver General For Canada
PO Box 20002, Stn A
Sudbury, ON P3A 5C3

PER *E Prospero*
Treasurer

⑈⑆392451⑆22⑆707

Re: EI, CPP and Income tax remittances for June $ 5,960.00   No: 706
July 12, 2012

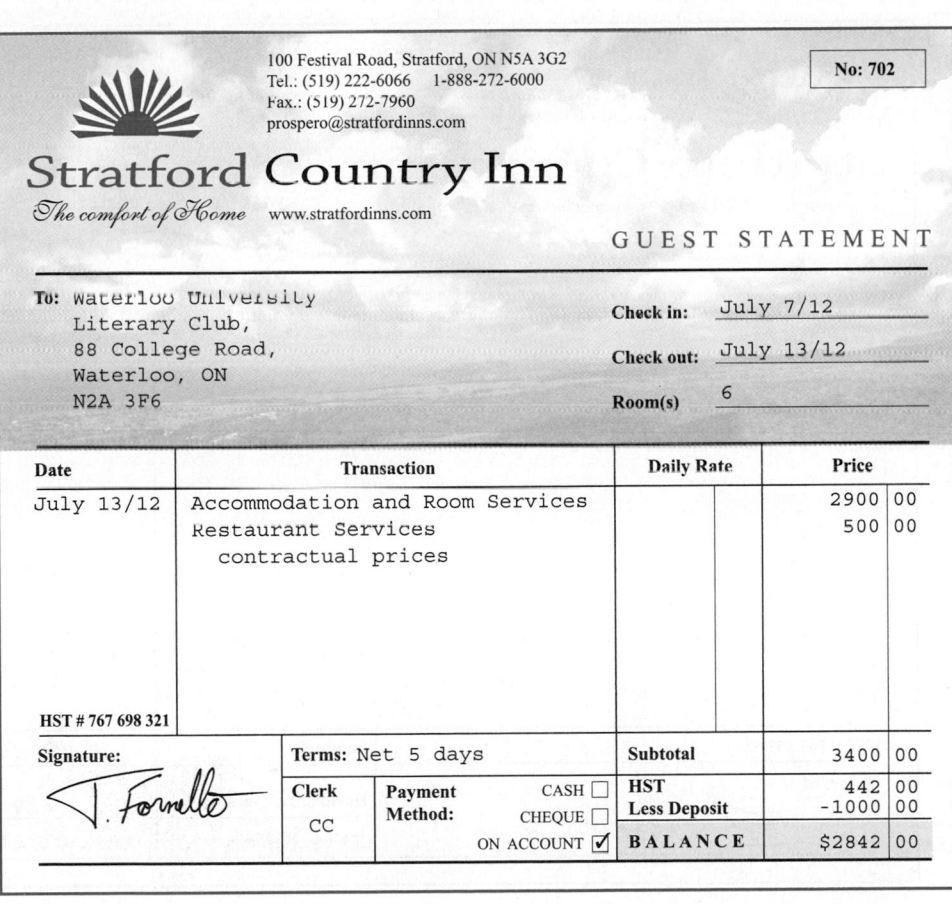

100 Festival Road, Stratford, ON N5A 3G2
Tel.: (519) 222-6066   1-888-272-6000
Fax.: (519) 272-7960
prospero@stratfordinns.com

No: 702

Stratford Country Inn
The comfort of Home   www.stratfordinns.com

GUEST STATEMENT

To: Waterloo University
Literary Club,
88 College Road,
Waterloo, ON
N2A 3F6

Check in: July 7/12
Check out: July 13/12
Room(s)   6

Date	Transaction	Daily Rate	Price	
July 13/12	Accommodation and Room Services		2900	00
	Restaurant Services		500	00
	contractual prices			

HST # 767 698 321

Signature: *J. Fornello*

Terms: Net 5 days	Subtotal	3400	00

Clerk	Payment Method:	CASH ☐	HST	442	00
CC		CHEQUE ☐	Less Deposit	-1000	00
		ON ACCOUNT ☑	**BALANCE**	$2842	00

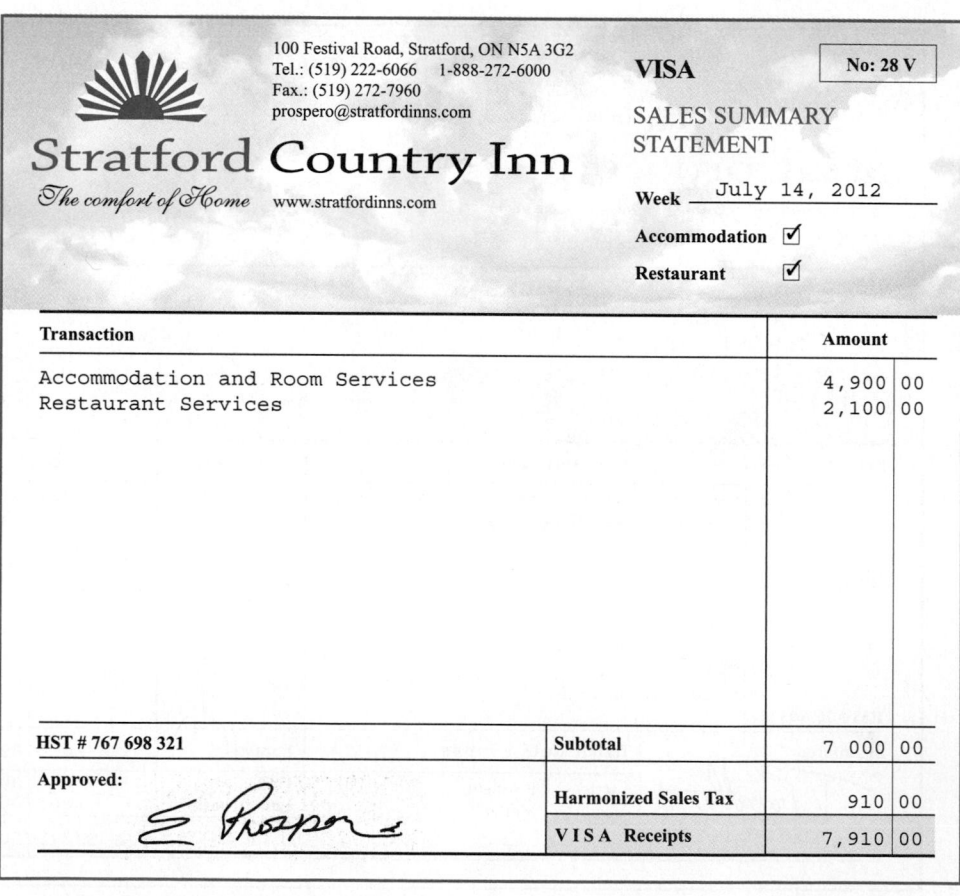

NY Friends of Shakespeare
33, 16th Avenue,
Buffalo, NY 13002

No: 137

Date 2 0 1 2 0 7 1 3
Y Y Y Y M M D D

Pay to the order of   Stratford Country Inn $ 1,000.00 (USD)

——————— One thousand ————————————— 00/100 Dollars

CB Chase Bank
    4, 12th Avenue
    Buffalo, NY 13002

J.Monte

ııı–ı–– 93937–ı 301 ıı 137

Re: Deposit #42 — booking rooms in Inn. United
States Currency. Currency Exchange 1.019 $1,000.00 (USD)   July 13, 2012

No: 137

---

100 Festival Road, Stratford, ON N5A 3G2
Tel.: (519) 222-6066   1-888-272-6000
Fax.: (519) 272-7960
prospero@stratfordinns.com

Stratford Country Inn
The comfort of Home   www.stratfordinns.com

VISA   No: 28 V

SALES SUMMARY
STATEMENT

Week   July 14, 2012

Accommodation ☑
Restaurant   ☑

Transaction	Amount	
Accommodation and Room Services	4,900	00
Restaurant Services	2,100	00

HST # 767 698 321

Approved: E. Prospero

Subtotal	7 000	00
Harmonized Sales Tax	910	00
VISA Receipts	7,910	00

100 Festival Road, Stratford, ON N5A 3G2
Tel.: (519) 222-6066   1-888-272-6000
Fax.: (519) 272-7960
prospero@stratford.com

| ET27 |

Stratford Country Inn

The comfort of Home   www.stratfordinns.com

EMPLOYEE TIME
SUMMARY SHEET

Pay period ending: July 14, 2012

Name of Employee	Regular hours	Overtime hours	Sick days
☐ Horatio, Hedy	80	0	0
☐ Jones, Juliet	80	0	1
☐ MacBeth, Mary	80	2	0
☐ Romeo, Bud	80	2	0
☐ Shylock, Shelley	80	2	0

Memo: Issue cheques #707 to #711
        Recover $100 advance from Horatio and Romeo

66 Kleen Road, Stratford, ON N5A 3C3
Telephone (519) 272-4611
Fax: (519) 272-4813
www.avonservices.com

Invoice No: AM-184

Date: July 15, 2012

Sold to: Stratford Country Inn
        100 Festival Road
        Stratford, ON
        N5A 3G2

Phone: (519) 222-6066

Code	Service Description		Price
KX-55	Vacuum Premises Floor Polishing Washroom Cleaning Maintenance and repairs Recurring bi-weekly billing * new price as described in our previous notice	*	1100.00

Signature: *E Prospero*	Terms: Net 30 days	HST	143.00
	HST #631 393 461	Amount owing	1243.00

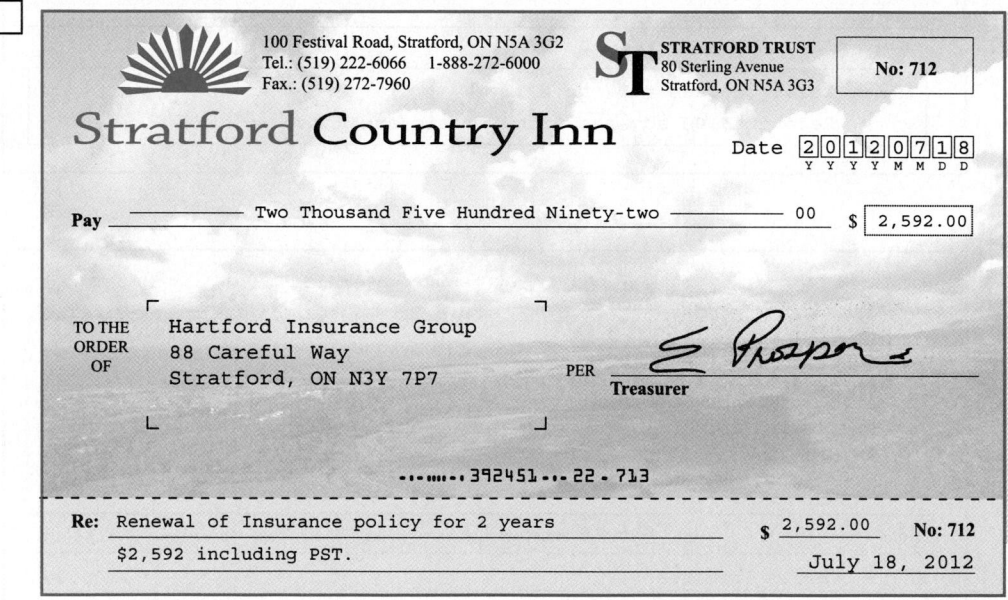

Waterloo University Literary Club
88 College Road
Waterloo, ON N2A 3F6

No: 479

Date 2 0 1 2 0 7 1 7
Y Y Y Y M M D D

Pay to the order of   Stratford Country Inn $ 2,842.00

———————————— Two Thousand Eight Hundred & Forty-two ———— 00   /100 **Dollars**

WT **Waterloo Trust**
550 King Street
Waterloo, ON N2A 3F8

J. Fornell
Chair

⑆⑈ 60431 ⑈ 105 ⑈ 479

- -

Re: Receipt #58 (Cheque #413)   **No: 479**

        Invoice #702 $2,842.00   July 17, 2012

---

100 Festival Road, Stratford, ON N5A 3G2
Tel.: (519) 222-6066   1-888-272-6000
Fax.: (519) 272-7960

ST **STRATFORD TRUST**
80 Sterling Avenue
Stratford, ON N5A 3G3

No: 712

Stratford Country Inn

Date 2 0 1 2 0 7 1 8
Y Y Y Y M M D D

Pay ———————— Two Thousand Five Hundred Ninety-two ———— 00 $ 2,592.00

TO THE
ORDER
OF

Hartford Insurance Group
88 Careful Way
Stratford, ON N3Y 7P7

PER   _E. Prosper_
Treasurer

⑆⑈ 392451 ⑈ 22 ⑈ 713

- -

Re: Renewal of Insurance policy for 2 years $ 2,592.00   **No: 712**

       $2,592 including PST.   July 18, 2012

PERTH COUNTY HYDRO
66 Power Road, Stratford,
Ontario N5A 4P4
www.perthenergy.com

Customer Care:
272-6121

CUSTOMER NAME / SERVICE ADDRESS
Stratford Country Inn 100 Festival Road Stratford, ON N5A 3G2

Date:	July 18, 2012
Account No:	3921 462 513
Invoice No:	37232

Months	Reading	Description	Net Amount
1	86527	Commercial Consumption	300.00
1		Flat Rate Charge – Water Heaters	60.00
1		Rental of Equipment	40.00
		Total Current Charges	400.00
		Previous Charges 385.20	
		Total Payments, Thank You 385.20	
		Balance Forward	0.00
		Adjustments	0.00

Paid in Full with
cheque #713 for $452
07/18/12 E Prosper

Average Daily KWh Consumption		HST #721 431 214	Due Date	HST 13%	52.00
Same Period Last Year	This Bill	After due date, a 1.5% monthly late payment interest charge will apply.	July 25/12		
269	258		Pay This Amount	TOTAL	452.00

Bell

30 Whisper Road
Stratford, ON
N5A 4N3

www.bell.ca

Account Inquiries: 273-BELL (2355)

Account Number
519-222-6066

Account Address

Stratford Country Inn
100 Festival Road
Stratford, ON
N5A 3G2

July 18, 2012

ACCOUNT SUMMARY

Current Charges	
Monthly Services (June 12 to July 12)	240.00
Equipment Rentals	50.00
Chargeable Messages	30.00
HST 634 345 373	41.60
Total Current Charges	361.60

Previous Charges	
Amount of Last Bill	323.00
Payment Received June 19 – Thank You	323.00
Adjustments	0.00
Balance Forward	0.00

Paid in Full – chq
#714 – 07/18/12
E Prosper

Invoice: BC-66431	PLEASE PAY THIS AMOUNT UPON RECEIPT ➡	$361.60

100 Festival Road, Stratford, ON N5A 3G2
Tel.: (519) 222-6066   1-888-272-6000
Fax.: (519) 272-7960
prospero@stratfordinns.com

Stratford Country Inn

The comfort of Home   www.stratfordinns.com

No: 703

GUEST STATEMENT

To: NY Friends of Shakespeare,
33, 16th Avenue,
Buffalo, NY
13002

Check in: July 14/12

Check out: July 20/12

Room(s) 8

Date	Transaction	Daily Rate	Price	
July 20/12	Accommodation and Room Services		2600	00
	Restaurant Services		400	00
	contractual prices			
	All amounts billed in			
	United States currency			
	Exchange rate: 1.0195 CAD			
HST # 767 698 321				

Signature: *J.Monte*	**Terms:** Net 5 days		**Subtotal**	3000	00
	Clerk CC	**Payment Method:** CASH ☐ CHEQUE ☐ ON ACCOUNT ☑	**HST** **Less Deposit**	390 -1000	00 00
			BALANCE	$2390	00

Festival Club of Rosedale
3 Rosedale Valley Rd.
Toronto, Ontario
M5G 3T4

No: 61

Date 2 0 1 2 0 7 2 0
    Y Y Y Y M M D D

Pay to the order of   Stratford Country Inn $ 1,000.00

——————— One Thousand ——————————————— 00 /100 **Dollars**

R **Royal Bank**
B 56 Bloor Street
Toronto, ON M5N 3G7

Jane Birker

Chairperson

⑈━━ 34298 ⑈021⑈061

Re: Deposit #43 — booking rooms in Inn

$1,000.00   July 20, 2012

No: 61

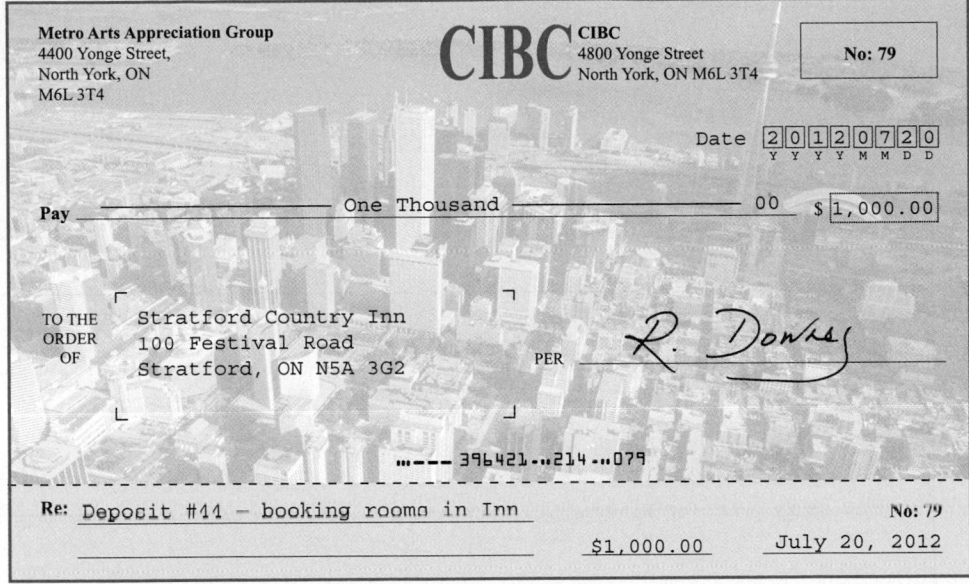

Metro Arts Appreciation Group					
4400 Yonge Street,			**CIBC** CIBC		**No: 79**
North York, ON			4800 Yonge Street		
M6L 3T4			North York, ON M6L 3T4		

Date 2 0 1 2 0 7 2 0
Y Y Y Y M M D D

Pay ———— One Thousand ———— 00 $ 1,000.00

TO THE ORDER OF
Stratford Country Inn
100 Festival Road
Stratford, ON N5A 3G2

PER R. Dowey

⑈⑈⑈⑈ 396421⑈⑈214⑈⑈079

Re: Deposit #11 — booking rooms in Inn   No: 79

$1,000.00   July 20, 2012

STRATFORD TRUST VISA
80 Sterling Avenue
Stratford, ON N5A 3G3

Statement Period			Account Number	Account Enquiries	Daily Interest Rate	Annual Interest Rate
	M D Y					
From	06/15/12		4512 6221 1384 6201	1-800-272-VISA	.05068%	18.5%
To	07/15/12					

Trans. Date	Post Date	Particulars	Amount	Bus. Exp.
06 13	06 16	Stratford Service Centre, Stratford, ON	85.00	EP
06 18	06 21	Office Supplies Unlimited, Stratford, ON	88.00	EP
06 25	06 27	Stratford Service Centre, Stratford, ON	133.00	EP
06 28	06 30	Bullrich Dept. Store #32, Stratford, ON	113.00	EP
06 28	06 30	Bullrich Dept. Store #32, Stratford, ON	24.00	EP
07 11	07 13	Stratford Service Centre, Stratford, ON	180.80	EP
06 20	06 20	Payment — Thank You	-422.00	EP

Balance $575.80 paid in Full by cheque #715 E Prosper July 21/12

Credit Limit	Opening Balance	Total Credits	Total Debits	Your New Balance
8500.00	422.00	446.00	599.80	575.80

Available Credit	Payment Due Date Month Day Year	Overlimit or Past Due	Current Due	Minimum Payment	Payment Amount
7924.20	07/24/12		57.00	57.00	575.80

100 Festival Road, Stratford, ON N5A 3G2
Tel.: (519) 222-6066   1-888-272-6000
Fax.: (519) 272-7960
prospero@stratfordinns.com

VISA | No: 29 V |

SALES SUMMARY STATEMENT

Week ___ July 21, 2012

Accommodation ☑

Restaurant ☑

Stratford Country Inn
The comfort of Home   www.stratfordinns.com

Transaction	Amount	
Accommodation and Room Services	5 000	00
Restaurant Services	1,950	00

HST # 767 698 321	Subtotal	6 950	00
Approved: *E Prospero*	Harmonized Sales Tax	903	50
	VISA Receipts	7,853	50

Sold to:	Stratford Country Inn 100 Festival Road Stratford, ON N5A 3G2	**TEMPEST** *Food Wholesalers*	**Telephone:** (519) 272-4464 **Fax:** (519) 272-4600 **Website:** www.tempest.com
Billing Date:	July 22, 2012		
Invoice No:	TF-344	35 Henry Avenue Stratford, ON N5A 3N6	
Customer No.:	3423		

Customer Copy

Date	Description	Charges	Payments	Amount
July 22 /12	Fish and Meats	1000.00		1000.00
	Fresh Fruits	200.00		200.00
	Fresh Vegetables	200.00		200.00
	Dry Goods	200.00		200.00
	Dairy Products	200.00		200.00
	Baking Goods	200.00		200.00
	Recurring bi-weekly billing			

Terms: Net 30 days	Subtotal	2000.00
HST #673 421 936		
Signature: *E Prospero*	HST 13%	exempt
Overdue accounts are subject to 16% interest per year	Owing	2000.00

Invoice No: TL-841

Date: July 22, 2012

Customer: Stratford Country Inn
100 Festival Road
Stratford, ON
N5A 3G2

Phone: (519) 222-6066

19 Merchant Road   Phone: (519) 271-7479
Stratford, ON   Fax: (519) 271-7888
N5A 4C3   www.tavistock.com

HST #639 271 343

Code	Description		Price	Amount
C-11	10 Loads Sheets	*	45.00	450.00
C-14	5 Loads Pillow Covers		20.00	100.00
C-20	15 Loads Towels		20.00	300.00
	Recurring bi-weekly billing * new prices			

Overdue accounts are subject to a 2% interest penalty per month	**Sub-total**	850.00
Terms: Net 30 days	**HST**	110.50
Signature: *E Prospon*	**Total**	960.50

Zephyr Advertising Services
32 Portia Blvd.,
Stratford, ON
N5A 4T2

Telephone (519) 271-6066
Fax (519) 271-6067
www.westwinds.com
orders: contact tom@westwinds.com

Stratford Country Inn
100 Festival Road
Stratford, ON
N5A 3G2

ZA - 6998

Date	Description	Charges	Amount
July 23, 2012	Brochures & Flyers	100.00	100.00
	Paid in full *cheque # 716* *July 23/12* *E Prospon*		
		HST	13.00
HST # 391 213 919	**Terms:** Cash on Receipt	**Total**	113.00

NY Friends of Shakespeare
33, 16th Avenue,
Buffalo, NY 13002

No: 181

Date 2 0 1 2 0 7 2 4
Y Y Y Y M M D D

Pay to the order of Stratford Country Inn $ 2,390.00 (USD)

———— Two thousand, three hundred ninety ———— 00 /100 Dollars

CB **Chase Bank**
4, 12th Avenue
Buffalo, NY 13002

J.Monte

⑈–⑈— 93937 ⑈ 301 ⑈ 181

Re: Receipt #61 — (Cheque #137) Invoice #703.
U.S. Currency. Currency Exchange 1.021 Cdn. $2,390.00 (USD)   No: 181   July 24, 2012

STRATFORD SERVICE CENTRE

33 MacBeth Avenue
Stratford, ON N5A 4T2
Tel: (519) 271-6679
Fax: (519) 276-8822
www.ssc.com

Date: July 25, 2012   **Invoice:** 1207

Customer: Stratford Country Inn
100 Festival Road
Stratford, ON
N5A 3G2

Phone: (519) 222-6066

HST #634 214 211

Code	Description	Price	Amount
R-69	Transmission—overhaul	500.00	500.00
XF-1	Fuel	100.00	100.00
		Sub-total	600.00

APPROVAL EP

CUSTOMER COPY

Cash	VISA	On Account		
	✓		HST	78.00
			Owing	678.00

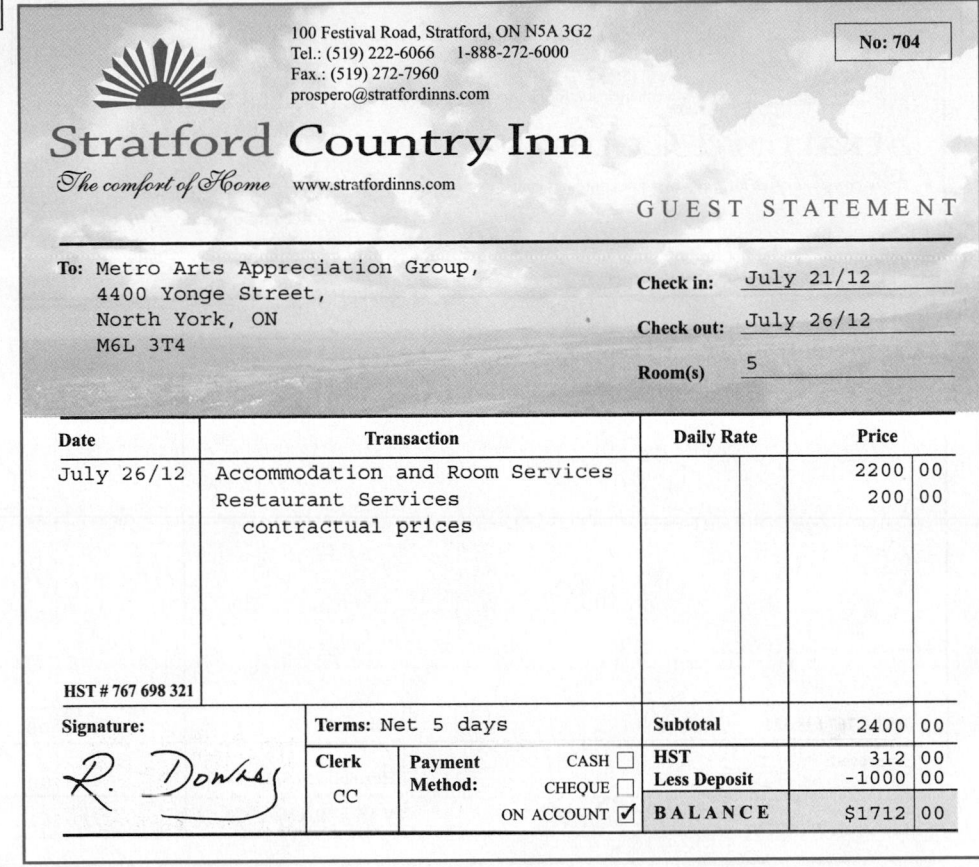

100 Festival Road, Stratford, ON N5A 3G2
Tel.: (519) 222-6066   1-888-272-6000
Fax.: (519) 272-7960
prospero@stratfordinns.com

No: 704

Stratford Country Inn
The comfort of Home   www.stratfordinns.com

GUEST STATEMENT

To: Metro Arts Appreciation Group,
4400 Yonge Street,
North York, ON
M6L 3T4

Check in: July 21/12

Check out: July 26/12

Room(s) 5

Date	Transaction	Daily Rate	Price	
July 26/12	Accommodation and Room Services		2200	00
	Restaurant Services		200	00
	contractual prices			

HST # 767 698 321

Signature:	Terms: Net 5 days		Subtotal	2400	00
R. Donkey	**Clerk** CC	**Payment Method:** CASH ☐ CHEQUE ☐ ON ACCOUNT ☑	HST Less Deposit	312 -1000	00 00
			BALANCE	**$1712**	**00**

Hamlet Holiday Agency
60 Tibault Avenue,
STRATFORD, ON N5A 3K3

SB Scotia Bank
44 Welland Avenue
STRATFORD, ON N5A 3F6

No: 393

Date 2 0 1 2 0 7 2 7
       Y Y Y Y M M D D

Pay ———————— One thousand ———————————— 00 $ 1,000.00

TO THE
ORDER   Stratford Country Inn
OF   100 Festival Road
         Stratford, ON N5A 3G2   PER   *Ron Dorleman*

⑈⑈—⑆—— 64299 ⑆ 168 ⑆ 393

Re: Deposit #45 — booking rooms in Inn   **No: 393**

$1,000.00   July 27, 2012

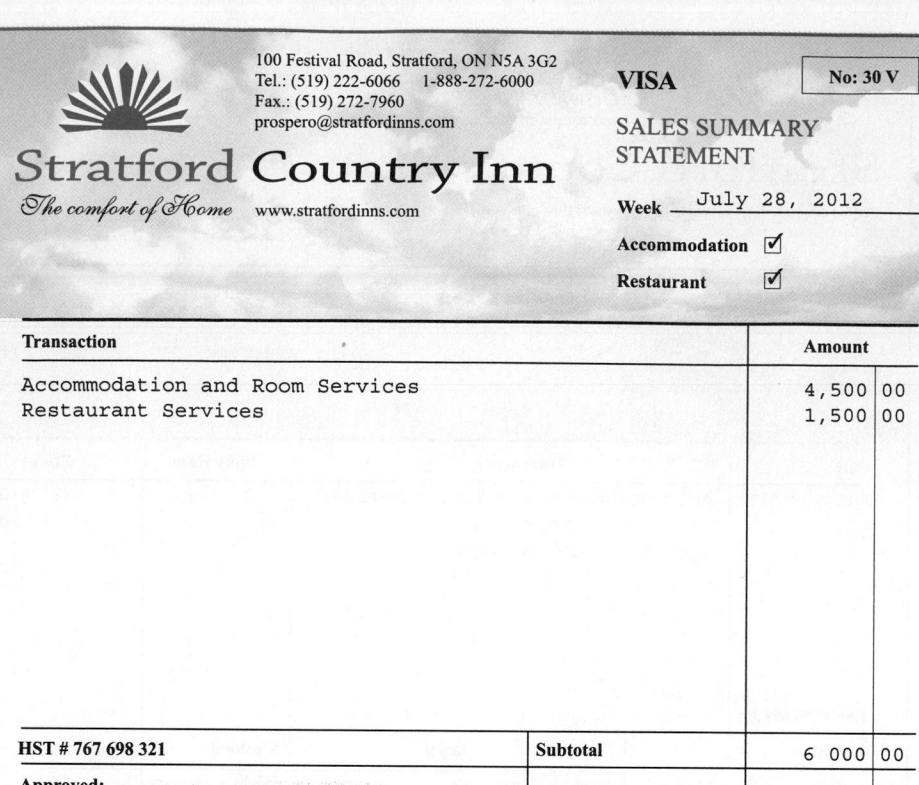

100 Festival Road, Stratford, ON N5A 3G2
Tel.: (519) 222-6066   1-888-272-6000
Fax.: (519) 272-7960
prospero@stratfordinns.com

Stratford Country Inn
The comfort of Home   www.stratfordinns.com

VISA   No: 30 V

SALES SUMMARY
STATEMENT

Week _____ July 28, 2012 _____

Accommodation ☑
Restaurant ☑

Transaction	Amount	
Accommodation and Room Services	4,500	00
Restaurant Services	1,500	00

HST # 767 698 321

Approved:

	Subtotal	6 000	00
	Harmonized Sales Tax	780	00
	VISA Receipts	6,780	00

---

100 Festival Road, Stratford, ON N5A 3G2
Tel.: (519) 222-6066   1-888-272-6000
Fax.: (519) 272-7960
prospero@stratford.com

          ET28

Stratford Country Inn
The comfort of Home   www.stratfordinns.com

E M P L O Y E E   T I M E
S U M M A R Y   S H E E T

Pay period ending: July 28, 2012

Name of Employee	Regular hours	Overtime hours	Sick days
☐ Horatio, Hedy	80	2	0
☐ Jones, Juliet	76	4	0
☐ MacBeth, Mary	80	0	0
☐ Romeo, Bud	80	0	1
☐ Shylock, Shelley	80	2	0

Memo: Issue cheques #717 to #721
          Recover $50 advance from Romeo

100 Festival Road, Stratford, ON N5A 3G2
Tel.: (519) 222-6066   1-888-272-6000
Fax.: (519) 272-7960
prospero@stratfordinns.com

No: 705

Stratford Country Inn
The comfort of Home   www.stratfordinns.com

GUEST STATEMENT

To: Festival Club of Rosedale,
3 Rosedale Valley Road,
Toronto, ON
M5G 3T4

Check in: July 26/12
Check out: July 30/12
Room(s) 6

Date	Transaction	Daily Rate	Price
July 30/12	Accommodation and Room Services		1800 00
	Restaurant Services		200 00
	contractual prices		

HST # 767 698 321

Signature: *Jane Birker*

Terms:			
Clerk CC	Payment Method:	CASH ☐ CHEQUE ☐ ON ACCOUNT ☑	

Subtotal	2000 00
HST	260 00
Less Deposit	-1000 00
BALANCE	$1260 00

100 Festival Road, Stratford, ON N5A 3G2
Tel.: (519) 222-6066   1-888-272-6000
Fax.: (519) 272-7960
prospero@stratfordinns.com

Stratford Country Inn
The comfort of Home   www.stratfordinns.com

MEMO #32

From: the owner's desk
To: Clara Claudius
July 31, 2012

1. a) Pay Owen Othello, manager, salary and sales commission for one month. Issue cheque #722.
   b) Pay Clara Claudius, desk attendant, salary for one month. Issue cheque #723.
2. Transfer $35,000 from Credit Card Bank account to Chequing account.
3. Pay quarterly balances owing as at July 1
   a) To Minister of Finance (EHT)
   b) Workplace Safety and Insurance Board (WSIB)
   c) Travellers' Life (Group Insurance)
   Issue cheques # 724, 725, 726

100 Festival Road, Stratford, ON N5A 3G2
Tel.: (519) 222-6066   1-888-272-6000
Fax.: (519) 272-7960
prospero@stratfordinns.com

Stratford Country Inn

The comfort of Home   www.stratfordinns.com

MEMO #33

From: the owner's desk
To: Clara Claudius
July 31, 2012

Prepare adjusting entries for the following:
a) Food Inventory on hand $1395
b) Write off $200 of Prepaid Insurance
c) Write off $50 of Prepaid Advertising
d) Depreciation on assets:
   Country Inn & Dining Rooom $600
   Computers $100
   Furniture & Fixtures $600
   Vehicles $800

REVIEW

The Student DVD with Data Files includes a
comprehensive supplementary case for this chapter.

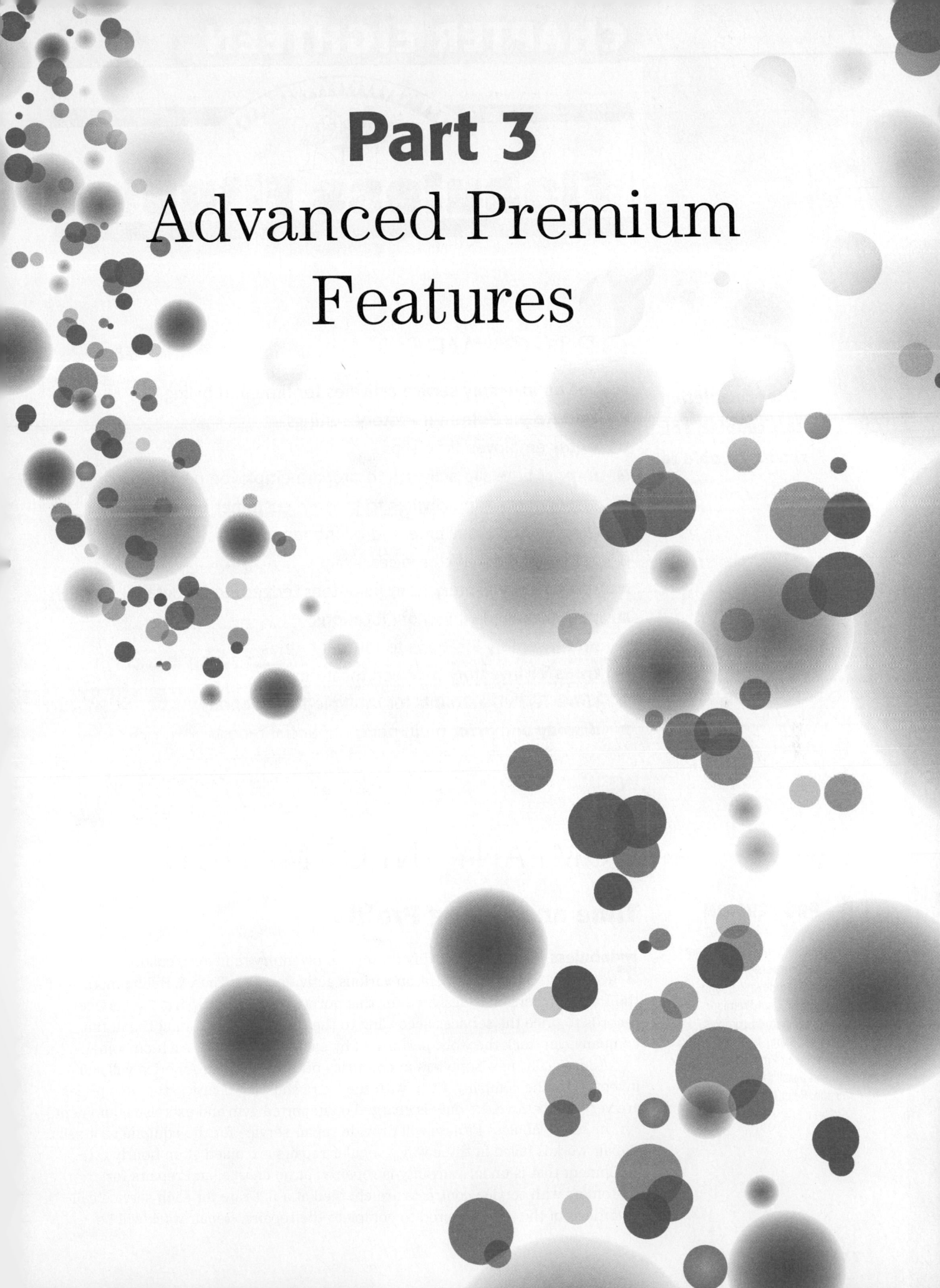

Part 3
Advanced Premium Features

CHAPTER EIGHTEEN

OBJECTIVES

**After completing
this chapter, you
should be able to**

- ■ **set up** inventory service activities for time and billing
- ■ **update** prices from Inventory Settings
- ■ **enter** employee time slips
- ■ **import** time slip activities to prepare employee paycheques
- ■ **import** time slip activities to prepare customer invoices
- ■ **display** and **print** time and billing reports
- ■ **set up** additional currencies
- ■ **build** new inventory from Inventory Ledger record details
- ■ **set up** multiple inventory locations
- ■ **add** inventory locations to journal entries
- ■ **transfer** inventory between locations
- ■ **show** related accounts for multiple fiscal periods
- ■ **display** and **print** multi-period financial reports

COMPANY INFORMATION

Time and Billing Profile

PRO VERSION
You will be unable to
complete this chapter if you are
using the Pro version.
   You can download and
install the Student Premium
version program to complete
Chapters 18 and 19. You must
uninstall your Pro version before
you can install the Student
version. Refer to page A–10.

Flabuless Fitness will modify its service inventory to invoice customers according to the time spent on various activities. The Time & Billing module of the Premium version is designed for this purpose. After modifying the service records to price the services according to the time spent providing them, the company can track the work performed by each employee for each customer.

   Additionally, new suppliers in countries outside of North America will sell inventory to the company. Even with the extra shipping charges, the new prices are very competitive. No duty is charged on imported gym and exercise equipment.

   In July, Flabuless Fitness will provide repair service for the equipment it sells. Repair work is billed in three ways: regular repairs are billed at an hourly rate; equipment that is under warranty is repaired at no charge; and repairs for customers with service contracts are charged at a flat rate for each service call regardless of the time required to complete the repairs. Repair work will be managed from a second location that Reeves is preparing to open nearby in Burlington, Ontario. The Burlington store will also sell the complete range of fitness accessories. Other inventory items can be shipped to that location if requested by customers. Two inventory locations will be set up for the two stores so that Reeves can track the inventory at each location.

Reeves hired two new employees, Yvonne Tinker and Moishe Alee. Tinker will assist Schwinn with the repairs and maintenance of exercise equipment. Tinker is also trained as a yoga instructor and can provide service as a personal trainer. Alee will work as the primary sales associate in the new store.

The company's fiscal period will be reduced to one month and customer invoice summaries will be used to reduce the number of source documents that you enter in this application.

SOURCE DOCUMENTS

SESSION DATE – JULY 1, 2012

NOTES
The wage expense credit entry that reverses the accrued payroll ensures that the correct amount from this pay period will be assigned to the previous year, adhering to the principle of recording expenses in the period in which they were incurred.

☐ **Memo #7-1**   **Dated July 1, 2012**

Prepare an adjusting entry to reverse the year-end adjustment for $680 for accrued payroll. (Debit Accrued Payroll and credit Wages.)

☑ **Memo #7-2**   **Dated July 1, 2012**

741   Change the company fiscal dates. The new fiscal end is July 31, 2012.
Change account number for 1150 Net Bank to 1190 to accommodate the new bank account for foreign currency transactions.

☑ **Memo #7-3**   **Dated July 1, 2012**

742   Add euro as a foreign currency to prepare for purchases from a new supplier in Germany. The linked account for exchange rate differences is 4120 and the exchange rate on July 1 is 1.3905.
Create new Subgroup account 1150 Bank: Euro Chequing. 1150 is a Bank class account and the next cheque number is 101.
Add 1150, the new bank account, as the linked account for Payables and Receivables bank transactions in euros.

☑ **Memo #7-4**   **Dated July 1, 2012**

744   Set up inventory locations for the two stores: Hamilton and Burlington. The Hamilton store is the primary location for inventory and the Burlington store is the secondary location for accessories and repair work.

☑ **Memo #7-5**   **Dated July 1, 2012**

745   Create new inventory service records to add services and include Time & Billing information:

Item	Description	Selling Price Reg (Pref)	Unit	Related to Time?	Billable?	Billing Basis	Rate
S060	Repair Service	$ 80 ($75)	Hour	Yes	billable	billable time	
S070	Contract Repairs	100 (90)	Service Call	No	billable	flat fee	1 call X price
S100	Warranty Repairs	0 (0)	Service Call	No	non-billable		

Linked accounts: Revenue: 4050 Revenue from Repairs (new Subgroup account)
            Expense: 5065 Cost of Services
Taxes: Charge HST on repair service work.

✓ **Memo #7-6**   **Dated July 1, 2012**

749   Edit the remaining service inventory records to add Time & Billing information and change the Canadian dollar prices.

Item	Selling Price Reg	(Pref)	Unit	Related to Time?	Relation	Billable?	Billing Basis
S010	$ 75	($ 70)	hour	yes		billable	billable time
S020	210	(195)	1/2 day	yes	3 hours/ 1/2 day	billable	billable time
S030	420	(385)	day	yes	7 hours/ day	billable	billable time
S040	100	(95)	hour	yes		billable	billable time
S050	210	(195)	1/2 day	yes	3 hours/ 1/2 day	billable	billable time

☐ **Memo #7-7**   **Dated July 1, 2012**

Create two new employee records for Yvonne Tinker and Moishe Alee. Tinker will work exclusively on customer jobs (activities) billed on the basis of time. She will be paid for the hours worked, but her minimum pay will be for 20 hours per week. Alee will be paid a monthly salary as a sales assistant in the Burlington store.

NOTES

The full TD1 claim amounts are subject to indexing.

Refer to pages 327–337 if you need assistance with entering the new employees. There is no historical information for the new employees.

Tinker and Alee will not receive the group insurance benefit or the piece rate pay (No. Clients) or Bonus initially. Those benefits will apply after they finish the probationary work period. They also have no additional deductions at this time for RRSP, CSB, Donations or Garnishee.

	Tinker, Yvonne	Alee, Moishe
Address:	499 Toolkit Dr.	551 Staefit Dr.
	Hamilton, ON L7F 2P9	Burlington, ON L5T 8H3
Telephone	(905) 458-7192	(905) 688-9101
SIN	420 011 009	128 663 887
Birthdate	06-23-80	08-31-82
Date of Hire	07-01-12	07-01-12
Job Category	Sales	Sales
Tax Table	Ontario	Ontario
Fed Claim	$10 382	$10 382
Prov Claim	($8 943)	($8 943)
Regular Wage	$16/hour	NA
# hours:	20 hours	150 hours
	(min hours in paycheque)	
Overtime Wage	$24/hour	NA
Salary	NA	$2 950 /month
Do not use	Salary, Commission	Regular, Overtime
Pay Period:	Weekly (52 per year)	Monthly (12 per year)
Vacation:	4% Retained	3 weeks (0%, not retained)
Record Wage	Expenses in: Payroll linked accounts	
WSIB Rate:	1.29	1.29
Vacation	delete entry	8%, 25 days max
Sick leave	5%, 15 days max	5%, 15 days max
Personaldays	2.5%, 5 days max	2.5%, 5 days max
Direct deposit	100% of paycheque to	100% of paycheque to
	bank #102	bank #102
	transit #89008,	transit #67752,
	account #341002	account #198823

☐ **Cash Receipt #53**   **Dated July 1, 2012**

From Lockport Gymnasium, cheque #1628 for $10 838.80 USD in full payment of account including $221.20 discount for early payment. Reference sales invoice #3019. The exchange rate is 1.021.

☐ **Memo #7-8**   **Dated July 1, 2012**

From Visa, received monthly credit card statement for $98 for purchases made before July 1, 2012. Submitted cheque #149 for $98 in full payment of the balance owing.

SESSION DATE – JULY 14, 2012

✓ **TIME SLIP #1**   **DATED JULY 7, 2012**

753 For George Schwinn

Customer	Item	Actual Time	Billable Time	Billable Amount	Payroll Time
McMaster University	S010	2 hours	1.5 hours	$105.00	2 hours
McMaster University	S070	2 hours	2 hours	90.00	2 hours
Mohawk College	S020	4 hours	4 hours	260.00	4 hours
Mohawk College	S060	2 hours	2 hours	150.00	2 hours
Mohawk College	S100	2 hours	–	–	2 hours

☐ **TIME SLIP #2**   **DATED JULY 7, 2012**

For Yvonne Tinker

Customer	Item	Actual Time	Billable Time	Billable Amount	Payroll Time
McMaster University	S050	7 hours	6 hours	$390.00	7 hours
McMaster University	S060	4 hours	3.5 hours	262.50	4 hours
Chedoke Health Care	S020	4 hours	3 hours	195.00	4 hours
Chedoke Health Care	S060	6 hours	5 hours	375.00	6 hours
Chedoke Health Care	S100	2 hours	–	–	2 hours

NOTES
Remember to enter 330 for 3.5 hours. You cannot enter decimals in the Time Slips Journal

✓ **Employee Time Summary Sheet #20**   **Dated July 7, 2012**

757 For the Pay Period ending July 7, 2012
Use time slips to prepare the paycheque for Yvonne Tinker. Issue deposit slip #31.
Pay George Schwinn for 80 regular hours in the period and 2 hours of overtime.
Recover $50 advanced and issue deposit slip #32.

✓ **Sales Invoice #3021**   **Dated July 7, 2012**

759 To McMaster University: Complete sales invoice for $847.50 plus HST from time
slip activities. Include all activities to date. Sales invoice total $957.68. Terms:
2/10, n/30.

☐ **Sales Invoice #3022**   **Dated July 7, 2012**

To Mohawk College: Complete sales invoice for $410 plus HST from time slip
activities. Include all activities to date. Sales invoice total $463.30. Terms: 2/10, n/30.

☐ **Sales Invoice #3023**   **Dated July 7, 2012**

To Chedoke Health Care: Complete sales invoice for $570 plus HST from time
slip activities. Include all activities to date. Sales invoice total $644.10. Terms:
2/10, n/30.

✓ **Memo #7-9**   **Dated July 7, 2012**

761 Create a new inventory record for a promotional fitness package that bundles
several popular fitness accessories. Create new Asset account: 1510 Promotions
when prompted.
Item: AP100 Promotional Fitness Package
Unit: package
Minimum: 0
Linked accounts: Asset 1510 Promotions Revenue 4020   COGS 5050

Currency	Regular Selling Price	Preferred Selling Price
CAD	$210	$200
USD	$200	$190
EUR	€145	€135

Tax exempt: GST Yes   HST No

Build Components: use 1 of each A010 Body Fat Scale
A020 Yoga Mats
A050 Heart Rate Monitor
A070 Stability Balls
A100 Workout Gloves: all sizes
and 5 (kg) of A030 Dumbbells

☑ **Memo #7-10**   **Dated July 7, 2012**

763 Build two packages of the new item Promotional Fitness Package (AP100).

☑ **Memo #7-11**   **Dated July 7, 2012**

NOTES
Accept the default cost prices
for items transferred.

766 The Burlington store is preparing for its official opening. Transfer the following inventory items from the Hamilton store to the Burlington store:

2	AP100	Promotional Fitness Packages
20	A020	Yoga Mats
200	A030	Dumbbells
20	A050	Heart Rate Monitors
20	A070	Stability Balls
50	B010	Books

☑ **Purchase Invoice #SW-1775**   **Dated July 10, 2012**

767 From Scandia Weights Inc. to fill purchase order #30
All items shipped to Burlington store

2	A030	Dumbbells (2 orders of 100 kg)	$180.00
2	A090	Weight Plates: (2 orders of 100 kg)	120.00
	HST		39.00
	Purchase invoice total		$339.00

Terms: net 30.

☐ **Purchase Invoice #FG-3877**   **Dated July 10, 2012**

From Feelyte Gym Accessories to fill purchase order #31
All items shipped to Burlington store

1	A010	Body Fat Scale (carton of 12)	$ 660.00
2	A020	Yoga Mats (boxes of 10)	300.00
2	A040	Glide Slidetraks	90.00
1	A050	Heart Rate Monitor (carton of 12)	360.00
20	A070	Stability Balls	120.00
2	A080	Wavemaster	190.00
2	A100	Workout Gloves: all sizes (boxes of 10)	120.00
	HST		239.20
	Purchase invoice total		$2 079.20

Terms: 2/10, n/30.

☐ **Purchase Invoice #ABS-7597**   **Dated July 10, 2012**

From ABS International (use Full Add for new foreign supplier)

5	E030	Bicycle: Dual Action Cal counter	€1 000.00
5	E040	Bicycle: Recumbent R-80	1 700.00
	Freight		100.00
	HST		364.00
	Purchase invoice total		€3 164.00

The duty rate for these items is 0%.
Terms: net 30.
The exchange rate is 1.385.
Change the default amounts.
All items shipped to the Hamilton store.

NOTES
ABS International
☐ (contact Steele Bunns)
Schumacher Str. 96
55123 Mainz, Germany
Tel: (49-6131) 468 913
Fax: (49-6131) 468 248
Currency: EUR
Terms: net 30
Tax code: H

✓ **Sales Invoice #3024**   **Dated July 10, 2012**

769   To Stoney Creek Sports Arena (from Hamilton store)

50	A030	Dumbbells	$ 2.50/ kg
2	E080	Ski Exerciser: Independent SE-880	710/ unit
2	E110	Treadmill: Deluxe T-1100D	2 800/ unit
		Freight (tax code G)	75
		HST	13%

Terms: 2/10, n/30.

Memo #7-12   **Dated July 14, 2012**

Remittances: Use the June 30 balances to make the following remittances in the Payments Journal. (See margin notes.)

☐ Record payment for GST and HST for June to the Receiver General for Canada. Issue cheque #150 in payment.

☐ Record payment for garnisheed wages payable for June to the Receiver General for Canada. Issue cheque #151 in full payment.

☐ Record payment for EI, CPP and Income Tax Payable for June to the Receiver General for Canada. Issue cheque #152 in full payment.

☐ Record payment for EHT Payable for the quarter to the Minister of Finance. Issue cheque #153 in payment.

☐ Record payment for RRSP Payable to Ancaster Insurance. Issue cheque #154 in payment.

☐ Record payment for CSB Payable to Mt. Hope Investment Corporation. Issue cheque #155 in payment.

☐ Record payment for Group Insurance Payable for June to Ancaster Insurance. Issue cheque #156 in payment.

☐ Record payment for Charitable Donations Payable for June to Canadian Cancer Society (employer and employee contributions). Issue cheque #157 in payment.

☐ **Sales Order #7-1 DRC & Deposit #17**   **Dated July 14, 2012**

Delivery date July 24, 2012 (from Hamilton store)

From Dundas Recreational Centre, to replace old gym equipment

3	E010	Elliptical Exerciser: AE-200	$2 100/ unit
3	E020	Elliptical Exerciser: LE-400	2 600/ unit
5	E030	Bicycle: Dual Action Calorie Counter	700/ unit
5	E040	Bicycle: Recumbent R-80	950/ unit
2	E050	Home Gym: Basic HG-1400	1 500/ set
		HST	13%

Terms: 2/10, n/30.

Deposit cheque #438 for $6 000 received with order.

SESSION DATE – JULY 31, 2012

☐ **Cash Receipt #54**   **Dated July 16, 2012**

From Stoney Creek Sports Arena, cheque #314 for $7 995.43 in payment of account including $163.17 discount for early payment. Reference sales invoice #3024.

☐ **Cash Purchase Invoice #BC-00124**   **Dated July 20, 2012**

From Bell Canada, $110 plus HST for one month of phone service. Purchase invoice total $124.30. Terms: cash on receipt of invoice. Issue cheque #158 in full payment.

☐ **Cash Purchase Invoice #ES-93215**   **Dated July 20, 2012**

From Energy Source, $180 plus HST for hydro service. Purchase invoice total $203.40. Terms: cash on receipt of invoice. Issue cheque #159 in full payment.

NOTES

Choose Previous Year in the report options window to make the June 30 balances available for sales tax amounts.

Choose Make Other Payment to remit the sales taxes.

Choose Pay Remittance to remit payroll taxes and deductions.

You must use July 1 as the End Of Remitting Period Date for the payroll remittances or, if you change the System Settings to allow transactions before July 1, you can enter June 30.

Clear the GST and HST reports for June 30.

TIME SLIP #3   **DATED JULY 21, 2012**

For George Schwinn

Customer	Item	Actual Time	Billable Time	Billable Amount	Payroll Time
Dundas Recreational Centre	S020	4 hours	3 hours	$210.00	4 hours
Dundas Recreational Centre	S070	1 hour	1 hour	100.00	1 hour
McMaster University	S060	3 hours	3 hours	225.00	3 hours
McMaster University	S100	2 hours	–	–	2 hours
Stoney Creek Sports Arena	S020	4.5 hours	4 hours	280.00	4.5 hours
Stoney Creek Sports Arena	S060	2 hours	2 hours	160.00	2 hours
Stoney Creek Sports Arena	S100	2 hours	–	–	2 hours

TIME SLIP #4   **DATED JULY 21, 2012**

For Yvonne Tinker

Customer	Item	Actual Time	Billable Time	Billable Amount	Payroll Time
Mohawk College	S030	16 hours	14 hours	$770.00	16 hours
Mohawk College	S050	6 hours	6 hours	390.00	6 hours
Mohawk College	S060	3 hours	3 hours	225.00	3 hours
Mohawk College	S100	6 hours	–	–	6 hours
Stelco Health Club	S020	6 hours	6 hours	390.00	6 hours
Stelco Health Club	S060	8 hours	7.5 hours	562.50	8 hours

Employee Time Summary Sheet #21   **Dated July 21, 2012**

For the Pay Period ending July 21, 2012

Edit the employee record for Yvonne Tinker. Tinker will be paid every two weeks (26 pay periods per year) and her minimum number of hours will be 40. If her contract hours from time slips are less than 40 hours, she will be paid for 40 hours. Use time slips to prepare the bi-weekly paycheque for Yvonne Tinker for the actual number of hours worked. Issue deposit slip #33.

George Schwinn worked 80 regular hours in the period and 4 hours of overtime. Issue deposit slip #34 in payment. (Add time from time slips but choose Yes to use regular hours when prompted.)

Deposit Slip #23   **Dated July 21, 2012**

Prepare deposit slip for $13 995.43 for two cheques received in previous week.

Sales Invoice #3025   **Dated July 21, 2012**

To Dundas Recreational Centre: Complete sales invoice for $310 plus HST from time slip activities. Include all activities to date. Sales invoice total $350.30. Terms: 2/10, n/30.

Sales Invoice #3026   **Dated July 21, 2012**

To McMaster University: Complete sales invoice for $225 plus HST from time slip activities. Include all activities to date. Sales invoice total $254.25 Terms: 2/10, n/30.

Sales Invoice #3027   **Dated July 21, 2012**

To Stoney Creek Sports Arena: Complete sales invoice for $440 plus HST from time slip activities. Include all activities to date. Sales invoice total $497.20. Terms: 2/10, n/30.

Sales Invoice #3028   **Dated July 21, 2012**

To Mohawk College: Complete sales invoice for $1 385 plus HST from time slip activities. Include all activities to date. Sales invoice total $1 565.05. Terms: 2/10, n/30.

☐ **Sales Invoice #3029**   **Dated July 21, 2012**

To Stelco Health Club: Complete sales invoice for $952.50 plus HST from time slip activities. Include all activities to date. Sales invoice total $1 076.33. Terms: 2/10, n/30.

☐ **Credit Card Purchase Invoice #WS-12331   Dated July 24, 2012**

From Waterdown Sunoco, $125 including HST paid for gasoline and $380 plus HST for vehicle repairs. Purchase invoice total $554.40 paid in full by Visa. Use Tax code IN for the gasoline purchase and tax code H for the repairs.

☐ **Sales Invoice #3030**   **Dated July 28, 2012**

To Dundas Recreational Centre to fill sales order #7-1 DRC (Hamilton store)

3	E010	Elliptical Exerciser: AE-200	$2 100/ unit
3	E020	Elliptical Exerciser: LE-400	2 600/ unit
5	E030	Bicycle: Dual Action Calorie Counter	700/ unit
5	E040	Bicycle: Recumbent R-80	950/ unit
2	E050	Home Gym: Basic HG-1400	1 500/ set
	HST		13%

Terms: 2/10, n/30. Allow customer to exceed credit limit.

NOTES
Do not forget to change the payment method for invoice #3030.

☐ **TIME SLIP #5**   **DATED JULY 31, 2012**

For George Schwinn

Customer	Item	Actual Time	Billable Time	Billable Amount	Payroll Time
McMaster University	S010	4 hours	4 hours	$280.00	4 hours
McMaster University	S070	2 hours	2 hours	90.00	2 hours
Stelco Health Club	S020	4 hours	4 hours	260.00	4 hours
Stelco Health Club	S060	2.5 hours	2.5 hours	187.50	2.5 hours
Mohawk College	S060	3.5 hours	3.5 hours	262.50	3.5 hours
Mohawk College	S100	2 hours	–	–	2 hours

☐ **TIME SLIP #6**   **DATED JULY 31, 2012**

For Yvonne Tinker

Customer	Item	Actual Time	Billable Time	Billable Amount	Payroll Time
Dundas Recreational Centre	S010	14 hours	13 hours	$975.00	14 hours
Dundas Recreational Centre	S070	2 hours	2 hours	100.00	2 hours
Mohawk College	S020	10 hours	9 hours	585.00	10 hours
Stelco Health Club	S040	9 hours	8 hours	760.00	9 hours
Stelco Health Club	S100	6 hours	–	–	6 hours

NOTES
Remember to enter 230 for 2.5 hours and 330 for 3.5 hours.

☐ **Sales Invoice #3031**   **Dated July 31, 2012**

To McMaster University: Complete sales invoice for $370 plus HST from time slip activities. Include all activities to date. Sales invoice total $418.10. Terms: 2/10, n/30.

☐ **Sales Invoice #3032**   **Dated July 31, 2012**

To Mohawk College: Complete sales invoice for $847.50 plus HST from time slip activities. Include all activities to date. Sales invoice total $957.68. Terms: 2/10, n/30.

☐ **Sales Invoice #3033**   **Dated July 31, 2012**

To Stelco Health Club: Prepare sales invoice for $1 207.50 plus HST from time slip activities for all activities to date. Sales invoice total $1 364.48. Terms: 2/10, n/30.

☐ **Sales Invoice #3034**   **Dated July 31, 2012**

To Dundas Recreational Centre: Sales invoice for $1 075 plus HST from time slip activities for all activities to date. Sales invoice total $1 214.75. Terms: 2/10, n/30.

NOTES
Remember to change the tax code for Books to G for invoices #3035 and #3036.

WARNING!
This is the first sale from the Burlington store, so you must change the default location.

Bank Debit Memo #143661   **Dated July 31, 2012**

From Hamilton Trust, authorized withdrawals were made from the chequing account on our behalf for the following:

Bank service charges	$ 35
Mortgage interest payment	1 850
Mortgage principal reduction	150
Bank loan interest payment	380
Bank loan principal reduction	520

Credit Card Sales Invoice #3035   **Dated July 31, 2012**

To Visa customers (sales summary). Sold from Hamilton store.

1	A010	Body Fat Scale	$ 150/ unit	$ 150.00
2	A100	Workout Gloves: all sizes	15/ pair	30.00
1	E110	Treadmill: Deluxe T-1100D	2 800/ unit	2 800.00
2	S010	Personal Trainer: 1 hour	75/ hour	150.00
2	S030	Personal Trainer: full day	420/ day	840.00
6	S040	Yoga Instructor: 1 hour	100/ hour	600.00
1	S050	Yoga Instructor: 1/2 day	210/ 1/2 day	210.00
4	S060	Repair Service	80/ hour	320.00
11	B010	Books: Fitness Guide (tax code G)	40 each	440.00
		GST	5%	22.00
		HST	13%	663.00
		Total paid by Visa		$6 225.00

Debit Card Sales Invoice #3036   **Dated July 31, 2012**

To Interac customers (sales summary). Sold from Burlington store.

1	A010	Body Fat Scale	$150/ unit	$150.00
1	A020	Yoga Mats	40/ unit	40.00
6	A070	Stability Balls	12 each	72.00
2	A100	Workout Gloves: all sizes	15/ pair	30.00
2	S010	Personal Trainer: 1 hour	75/ hour	150.00
1	S040	Yoga Instructor: 1 hour	100/ hour	100.00
1	S050	Yoga Instructor: 1/2 day	210/ 1/2 day	210.00
12	B010	Books: Fitness Guide (tax code G)	40 each	480.00
		GST	5%	24.00
		HST	13%	97.76
		Total paid by Interac		$1 353.76

Memo #7-13   **Dated July 31, 2012**

Prepare the payroll for Nieve Prekor, Assumpta Kisangel and Moishe Alee, the salaried employees. Add 2 percent of service revenue for July as a commission to Kisangel's salary. Issue deposit slips #35, #36 and #37.

Memo #7-14   **Dated July 31, 2012**

Interest earned but not yet received for bank accounts for July is $295.

Memo #7-15   **Dated July 31, 2012**

Prepare month-end adjusting entries for depreciation on fixed assets using the following amounts:

Cash registers	$100
Computer equipment	50
Furniture & fixtures	25
Retail premises	810
Van	625

☐ **Memo #7-16**   **Dated July 31, 2012**

Prepare end-of-period adjusting entries for the following:

Office Supplies used	$ 100
Linen Supplies used	60
Prepaid Insurance expired	812
Prepaid Advertising expired	100
Payroll Liabilities accrued	1 540

☑ **Memo #7-17**   **Dated July 31, 2012**

769   With two stores open and increased expenses, the prices for all inventory items
will be raised. All Regular prices (Canadian and US) will increase by 10 percent.
All preferred prices (Canadian and US) will increase by 5 percent. Round all
prices to the nearest dollar amount.

☑ **Memo #7-18**   **Dated July 31, 2012**

776   Print all financial reports for the fiscal period.
Back up the data files.
Start a new fiscal year. Do not clear old data.
Change the fiscal end to August 31, 2012.

KEYSTROKES

Modifying Company Information

Changing Fiscal Dates

Open   **SimData10\Time\flab-time.SAI** to access the data files for this
chapter.

Accept **July 1, 2012** as the session date.

Click   **Company** in the Modules pane list to open the Company window.

Enter   **Memo 7-1** to reverse the year-end payroll adjusting entry.

Click   the **Settings icon** , then **click Information**, or **choose** the **Setup**
menu and **click Settings**, **Company** and **Information**.

This will access the fields for fiscal dates:

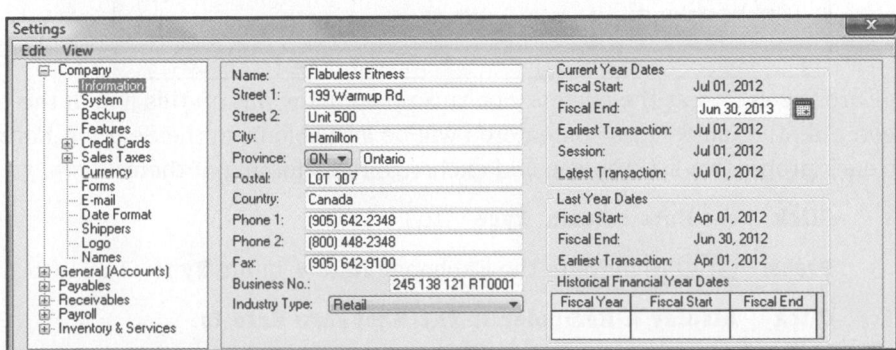

Most fiscal dates cannot be changed. Only the fiscal end can be edited. After
starting a new fiscal period, the fiscal end is updated to one year past the new fiscal
start because this period is most commonly used. Flabuless, however, will use a one-
month fiscal period to allow for more frequent performance review.

Drag through Jun 30, 2013 in the Fiscal End field.

Type   07-31-2012

Leave the Settings window open so you can add the currency.

Adding a Foreign Currency

The Premium version of Simply Accounting allows more than one foreign currency. Setting up additional currencies is similar to adding the first one. We will add the euro as the second foreign currency because a new supplier in Germany will provide some inventory items.

Click   **Currency** to open the Currency Information window:

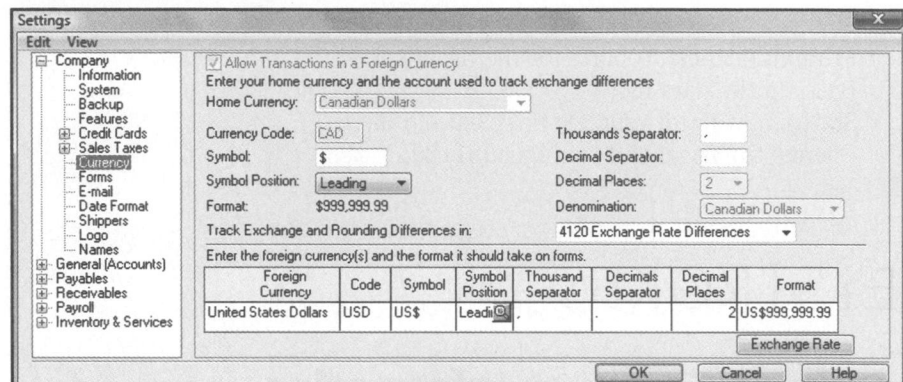

The currency added previously and its linked account for exchange rate differences are entered. You can select a different linked account, but you must use the same linked account for all currencies.

Click   the **Foreign Currency column** below United States Dollars. **Click** the **List icon** 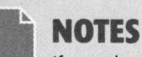 to see the currency selection list.

Click   **Euro** and then **click Select** to return to the Currency window and add the codes and symbols.

Click   the **Exchange Rate button**:

NOTES
If you choose United States Dollars from the Select A Foreign Currency list, you will see a list of all the dates and exchange rates you have already used.

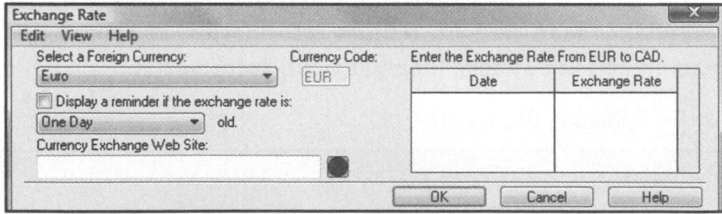

Euro is selected as the currency because the cursor was on this line in the previous screen. All other currencies you entered will be available from the Select A Foreign Currency drop-down list. You can add exchange rates for any of them.

Click   the **Date column. Type** Jul 1

Press   `tab` to move to the Exchange Rate column. **Type** 1.3905

Click   **Display A Reminder If The Exchange Rate Is**.

The ✓ is added and we will use the default **One Day** as our reminder period.

Click   **OK** to return to the Settings screen. **Click OK** to return to the Home window.

Adding a Foreign Bank Account

Before using the currency in transactions, we need to create a new bank account for euro transactions.

Click   the **Chart of Accounts icon** ![Chart of Accounts] to open the Accounts window.

Change the account **number for 1150 Net Bank**, the bank Subtotal account, to 1190 if you have not already done so.

Click   the **Create tool** ![Create] to open a new ledger window and **add** the new account **1150 Bank: Euro Chequing**.

Click   **Subgroup Account** to change the Type if necessary.

Click   the **Class Options tab**.

Choose **Bank** from the Account Class drop-down list.

Click   the **Currency list arrow** to see the options.

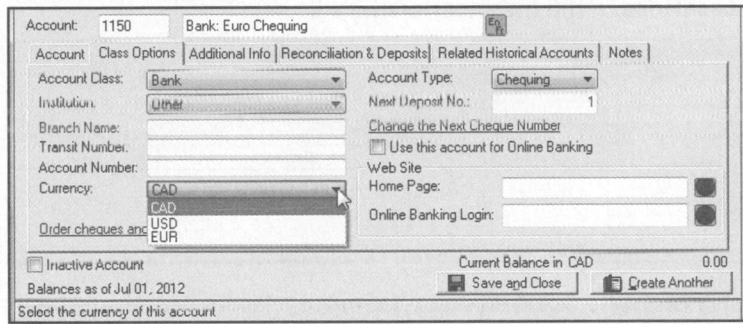

NOTES
You can click the Create tool in the Accounts window or in any ledger account window to open a new account ledger record window.

Click   **EUR**. We must save the account before adding the cheque number.

Click   the **Save tool** ![Save].

Click   **Change The Next Cheque Number** to open the Reports & Forms settings.

Click   the **Next Cheque No. field** near the bottom of the form.

Type   101 **Click OK** to save the number and return to the ledger window.

Close   the **Ledger window** and then **close** the **Accounts windows**.

Adding Linked Bank Accounts

We need to identify the new account as the linked account for euro transactions.

Choose the **Setup menu**. Then **choose Settings, Payables** and **Linked Accounts**:

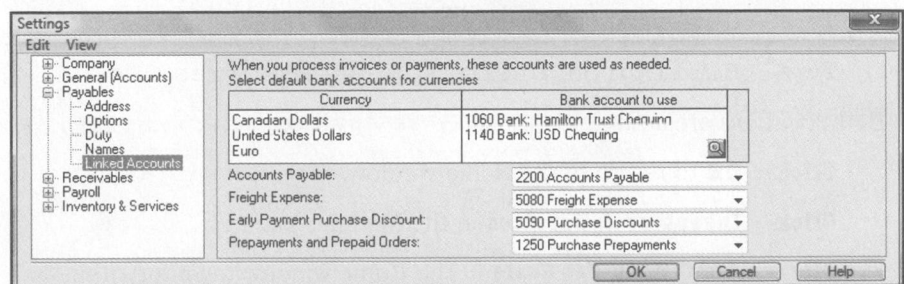

Click   the **Bank Account To Use column** beside Euro.

Click   the **List icon** ![List]. Notice that only the Canadian and Euro bank accounts can be selected as the Euro currency bank account.

Double click 1150.

Click **Receivables** and **Linked Accounts**.

Click the **Bank Account To Use column** beside Euro.

Type 1150 **Press** (tab). Leave the Settings window open.

Entering Inventory Locations

Before leaving the Settings window, we will add the two stores as the locations for the business and for inventory. Items can be purchased for and sold from either store. Adjustments can also be made for the separate locations. The number of items in each store can, therefore, be monitored. If needed, items can be transferred from one location to another.

> **Click** **Inventory & Services** in the Settings modules list.

> **Click** **Locations** in the Inventory settings list:

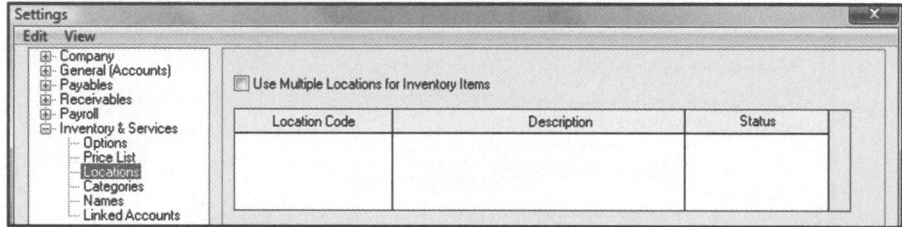

> **Click** **Use Multiple Locations For Inventory Items** to activate the option:

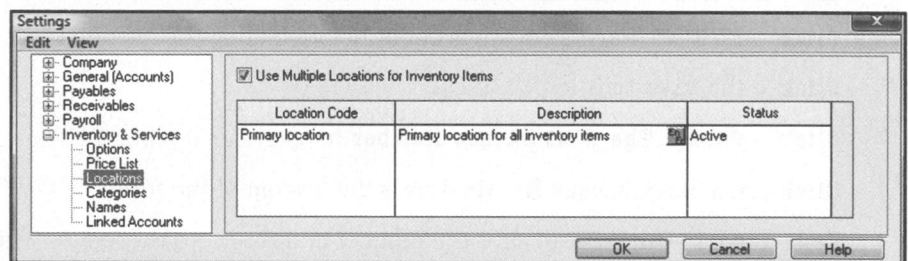

The Code and Description fields are now available; we can enter the two stores. We will accept the default description for the first location.

> **Press** (tab) **twice** to select Primary Location.

> **Type** Hamilton to replace the default name.

> **Click** the next line of the **Location Code field** for the next store.

> **Type** Burlington **Press** (tab).

> **Type** Burlington Store for accessories

Both locations are active.

> **Click** **OK** to return to the Home window.

> **Click** **Inventory & Services** in the Modules pane list.

> **Click** **A010 Body Fat Scale** in the Home window Inventory Item list.

The Quantities tab screen includes a Location field.

> **Click** the **For Location field list arrow** to see the two locations you entered:

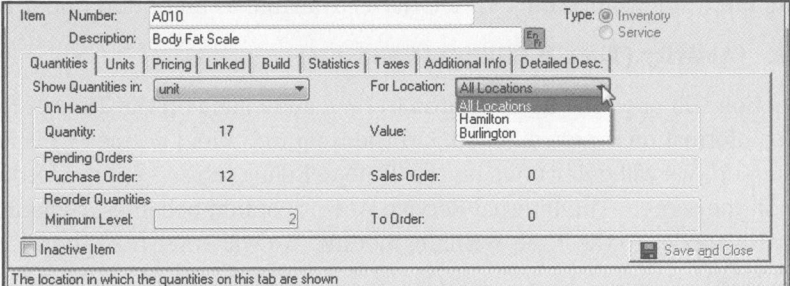

NOTES
You can set separate minimum levels for each location. When you select a location, the Minimum Level field becomes available for that location. When All Locations are shown, the field is dimmed.

Choose Hamilton from the For Location drop-down list to display the quantity at that store. **Choose Burlington** from the For Location drop-down list.

Initially, all the stock is at the primary location, the Hamilton store. The quantity at the Hamilton store is the same as the quantity for the All Locations selection. The quantity at the Burlington store is zero.

Close the **Ledger window** to return to the Inventory & Services module window.

Time and Billing

Many businesses that provide services use time as the basis for billing customers. Law firms, consulting businesses and service businesses that complete maintenance and repair work are just a few examples. In addition, these businesses may keep track of how much time each employee spends on a particular job and then compare this with the standard number of hours expected for that type of work. Some jobs can be billed at a flat rate and some, such as warranty repairs or work performed for other departments of the same company, may be provided at no charge. In each of these cases, it is still important to know how much time was spent on the job. Businesses might also want to track non-billable and non-payroll times such as for lunch breaks when an employee is at a customer site.

The Time & Billing module in Simply Accounting tracks these kinds of activities by integrating the Payroll, Inventory and Sales ledgers.

Setting Up Time and Billing Activities

Before recording the services provided by employees to customers, that is, filling in time slips, we must modify the inventory records so that we can apply time and billing. First we will create the new services. We will work from the Inventory module.

Choose Add Inventory & Service from the Inventory & Services icon drop-down shortcuts list to open a new record for inventory.

Type S060 **Press** (tab). **Type** Repair Service **Press** (tab).

Click **Service** as the Type of item to modify the form for service items:

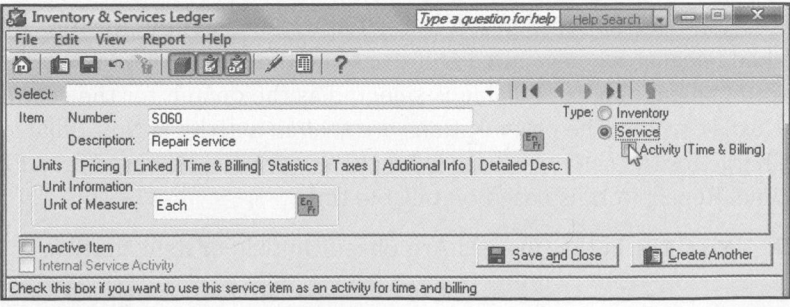

The Units tab window appears and Activity is available as an option under Service.

> **Click**   **Activity (Time & Billing)** to add a ✓.

This selection will open the fields related to time and billing on the Time & Billing tab. The Units information is now dimmed and the Required Field notice (*) is added back to the screen. We will enter units on the Time & Billing tab screen, as instructed by the message on the screen. The Internal Service Activity option becomes available because this also applies to the Time & Billing module. We will enter the other item information first.

> **Click**   the **Pricing tab** to open the Canadian dollar (home currency) price list.
>
> **Click**   the **Regular Price Per Selling Unit field**.
>
> **Type**   80   **Press** (tab) to advance to the Preferred Selling Price field.
>
> **Type**   75
>
> **Click**   the **Linked tab**.
>
> **Click**   the **Revenue account field**. We will add the new account.
>
> **Type**   4050 Revenue from Repairs   **Press** (tab) and **click Add** to start the Add An Account wizard with the name and number added.
>
> **Click**   **Next three times** to accept the defaults until you see the **Subgroup And Group Accounts** screen.
>
> **Click**   **Yes** because this account is a Subgroup account.
>
> **Accept**   the **remaining defaults** to finish creating the account.
>
> **Click**   the **Expense field** and **type**   5065
>
> **Click**   the **Time & Billing tab** to see the next group of fields to be set up:

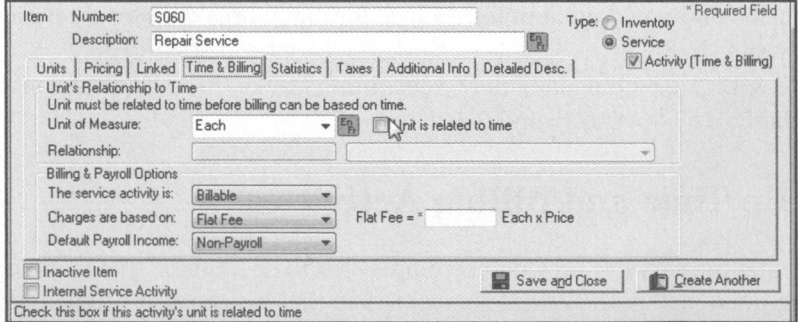

This screen has all the details that relate to the Time & Billing module. On this screen we must define the unit that the price is based on, indicate whether the unit is based on time and then add the relationship between the time and the unit of measure.

> **Click**   the **list arrow beside Each** in the Unit Of Measure field.
>
> **Click**   **Hour**.

This Unit is automatically recognized as related to time, and the Relationship fields are now dimmed because we have already indicated a time unit. The next group of fields defines the billing options. Billable is selected as the default for the service activity and this is correct. The other options are that an activity is Non-Billable or that there is No Charge for the activity. Charges for the service can be based on a Flat Fee or on Billable Time. Repair work is based on billable time.

> **Click**   **Flat Fee** in the Charges Are Based On field or its list arrow.

Click   Billable Time to change the entry.

The next option allows the time worked on the activity to be credited directly to an employee's paycheque. You can choose whether the time should be charged to the default payroll income account or to overtime. The non-payroll option may be selected if the work is completed by salaried employees. All services offered by Flabuless Fitness are provided by the regular employees at the regular hourly wage rate.

Click   Non-Payroll in the Default Payroll Income field or its list arrow.

Click   Regular to complete the Time & Billing tab screen as shown here:

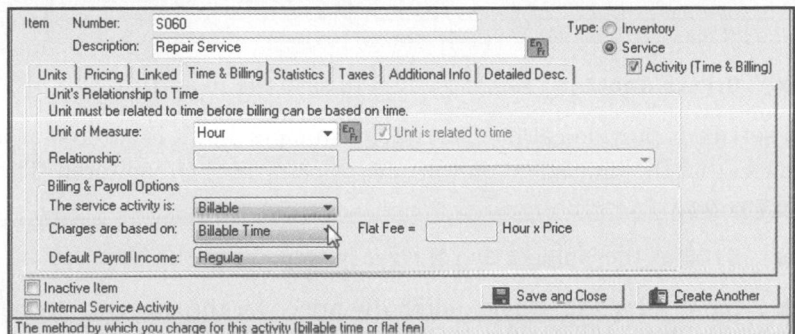

Click   the **Taxes tab**. The defaults are correct. HST is charged, so the service is not tax exempt for HST. (You can indicate the service is exempt for GST if you want.)

Click   Create Another [Create Another] to save the record.

You are now ready to enter the next service. Service and Activity (Time & Billing) remain selected from the previous entry and are correct.

Enter   S070 as the Number and **Contract Repairs** as the Description.

Click   the **Pricing tab** and **enter 100** as the Regular Price Per Selling Unit and **90** as the Preferred Price.

Click   the **Linked tab** and **enter 4050** as the Revenue account and **5065** as the Expense account.

Click   the **Time & Billing tab**.

Enter   Service Call as the Unit Of Measure.

The service is priced at a flat rate, so the unit is not related to time. Service Call is not recognized as a unit of time so the ✓ is not added. Billable is also the correct choice but we need to enter the rate. Notice that Flat Fee = ___ Service Call x Price is entered as the field label. This means that we must enter a number, not a price. The price will be calculated as the number of completed service calls multiplied by the price that is taken from the Pricing tab fields.

The flat rate for this service is one times the price; each service call is priced at $100 ($90 for preferred customers).

Click   the **field beside Flat Fee =**.

Type   1

Choose   Regular as the Default Payroll Income category.

Only HST applies to the service, but you can accept the default tax information of no exemptions, so the record is complete.

Your Time & Billing screen should look like the one shown here:

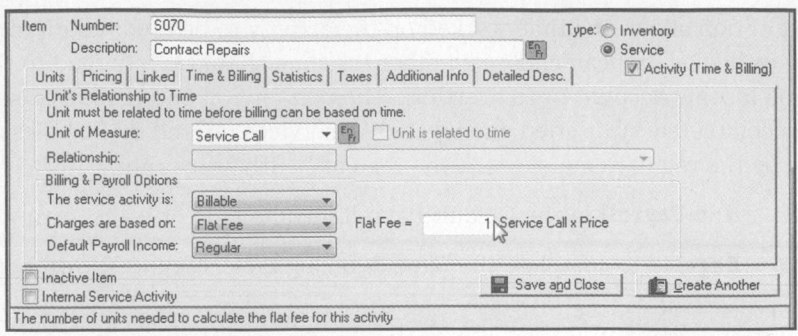

Click   Create Another to save the record.

The final service is provided at no charge to customers, but it is entered as an inventory item so that the time spent on warranty repairs can be monitored. The price will be entered as zero.

> **Enter   S100** as the Number and **Warranty Repairs** as the Description.

> **Click   the Pricing tab**. Do not enter any prices for the warranty service so that the prices will remain at zero.

> **Click   the Linked tab** and **enter 4050** as the Revenue account and **5065** as the Expense account.

> **Click   the Time & Billing tab.**

> **Enter   Service Call** as the Unit Of Measure.

The service call for warranty work is not related to time because there is no charge for this service. We must indicate that the work is not billable. In addition, employees are paid at their usual wage rate for completing warranty work, even though the customer does not pay, so we must change the payroll category.

> **Click   the list arrow beside Billable**. **Click Non-Billable** to change the entry.

> **Choose   Regular** as the Default Payroll Income category to complete the record:

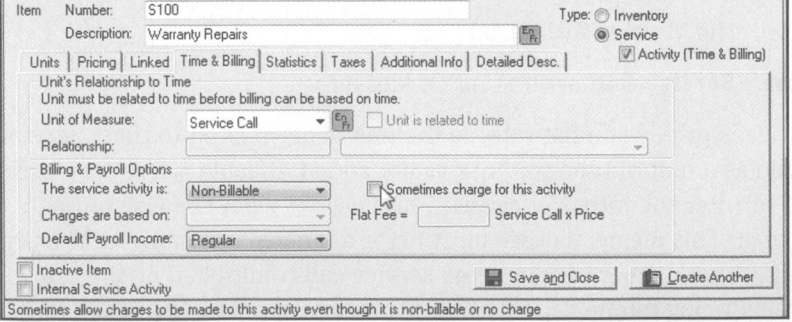

Another option for services that are normally not billed is to **sometimes charge**. When you choose the No Charge or Non-Billable options, this category becomes available. The pricing options are the same as for billable activities. You can relate the unit to time and enter the number of hours or minutes per unit, or enter a flat fee for the exceptional price. Prices are taken from Price fields on the Pricing tab screen.

> **Click   Save And Close** to save the record and return to the Inventory & Services module window.

Adding Time and Billing Information to Services

You are now ready to edit the remaining service records to apply time and billing.

Scroll down the Inventory Item list in the Inventory & Services module window.

Click **S010 Personal Trainer: 1 hour** in the Home window list of items and services to open the record.

Click the **Time & Billing tab** to open the Time & Billing screen.

All the fields are dimmed because we still need to mark the service as an Activity for time and billing.

Click **Activity (Time & Billing)** to open the extra fields.

Hour was already entered as the Unit for the service. Most selections are already correct — this unit is automatically recognized as a unit related to time. The service is Billable and charges are based on Billable Time. We need to select the payroll income.

Choose **Regular** as the Default Payroll Income category.

The next service, **S020 Personal Trainer: 1/2 day**, requires additional information to indicate how many hours are in the 1/2 day. The service will still be billed at an hourly rate, but the rate is lower when a longer time period is purchased.

Click the **Next Item tool** 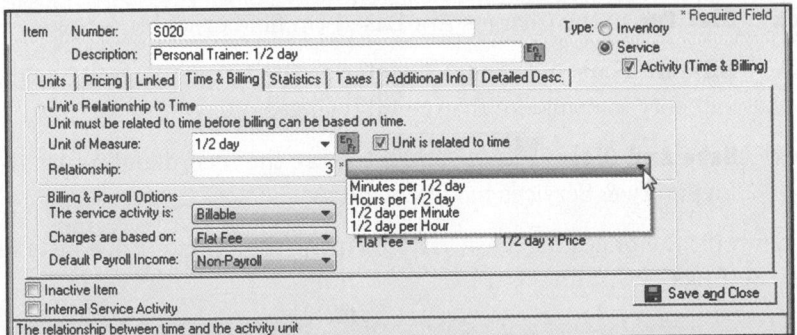 to open the record for **S020**.

Click **Activity (Time & Billing)**.

Click **Unit Is Related To Time** to add a ✓ and open the relationship fields.

Each one-half day is based on three billable hours of activity, so the relationship is entered as 3 hours per 1/2 day. The relationship field is a required field when the unit is not Hour or Minute and you indicate that it is related to time.

Click the **first Relationship field**.

Type 3

Click the **list arrow beside the second Relationship field** to see the list:

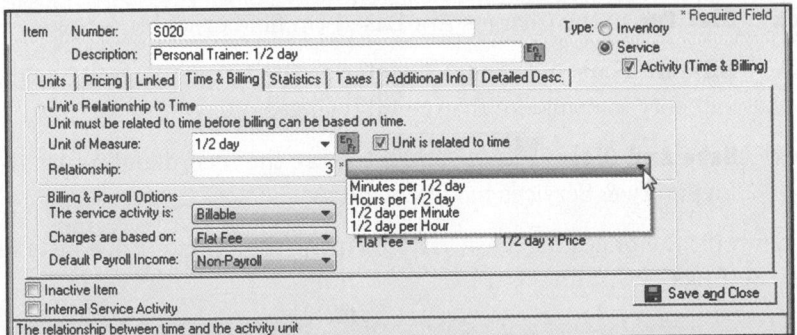

The relationship can be based on the number of hours or minutes per unit, or the number of units per hour or minute.

Click **Hours Per 1/2 Day**.

The next option is correct — the activity is Billable. However, it is charged on the basis of time, not at a flat rate. We need to change the entry for Charges Are Based On.

Click **Flat Fee** in the Charges Are Based On field or its list arrow.

Click **Billable Time** and then **choose Regular** as the Default Payroll Income category to complete the record changes.

Click   the **Next Item tool** to open the record for **S030 Personal Trainer: full day**.

Click   **Activity (Time & Billing)**.

Click   **Unit Is Related To Time** to add a ✓ and open the relationship fields.

Each full day is based on seven billable hours of activity, so the relationship is entered as seven hours per day.

Enter   **7** in the first Relationship field.

Choose   **Hours Per Day** from the second Relationship field list.

Click   **Flat Fee** in the Charges Are Based On field or its list arrow.

Click   **Billable Time** and **choose Regular** as the Default Payroll Income category to complete the record changes.

Click   the **Next Item tool** to open the record for **S040 Yoga Instructor: 1 hour**.

Click   **Activity (Time & Billing)**.

Again, because Hour is the unit, most of the default details are correct.

Choose   **Regular** as the Default Payroll Income category.

Click   the **Next Item tool** to open **S050 Yoga Instructor: 1/2 day**.

Click   **Activity (Time & Billing)**.

Click   **Unit Is Related To Time**.

Each 1/2 day is based on three billable hours of activity, so the relationship is entered as 3 hours per 1/2 day.

Click   the **first Relationship field**. **Type**   3

Click   the **list arrow beside the second Relationship field**.

Click   **Hours Per 1/2 Day**.

Click   **Flat Fee** in the Charges Are Based On field or its list arrow.

Click   **Billable Time** and **choose Regular** as the Default Payroll Income category to complete the record changes.

Click   **Save And Close** [Save and Close] to save the record and return to the Inventory & Services module window.

We will now edit the prices for these services using the Update Price Lists feature in the Inventory Settings.

Updating Service Activity Prices

NOTES
Price increases and decreases may be entered as amounts or percentages relative to the reference price.

The Premium version allows you to define additional price lists and to update all prices from one screen. This feature is available as one of the settings for the Inventory Ledger. You can change prices one item at a time from this location or, if prices are raised by a fixed percentage for one or more items or services, you can make the price changes globally. You can also set the prices in one list relative to the prices in another list by indicating the increase or decrease.

Click   the **Settings icon** [Settings]. **Click Price List** to see the Price List Settings:

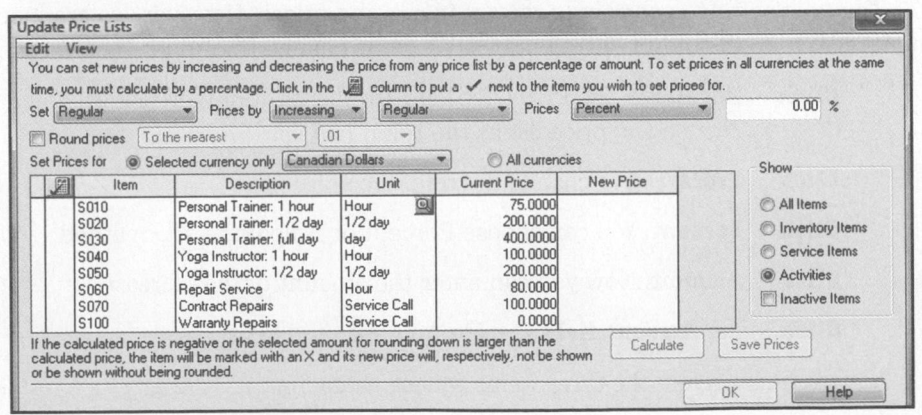

On this screen, you can define new price lists. You cannot remove or modify the three predefined price list names. If you want to create a new price list, you can type the new price list name below Web Price in the Description column and click Update Price Lists to open the item list. We need to update Regular and Preferred prices.

Click the **Update Price Lists button**:

The inventory list opens with all items and services listed. You can display the list of all items, only inventory items, only service items or only activities.

You can select the items whose prices you want to update globally. You can set the prices in one list relative to another list by increasing or decreasing the reference prices by a fixed percentage or amount. Then you can round off the prices to the nearest unit — ranging from 0.0001 dollar to 1 000 dollars. You can make the price changes for one currency or for all currencies at the same time. You can also enter or edit individual prices in the new price column, so you can also use this list to enter price changes manually for several inventory items on a single screen, without opening each ledger record separately. If you have different units for stocking and selling, you can select the unit as well.

You can Round Prices if you want to work with even amounts. Choose the direction for rounding off the price — up to the nearest, down to the nearest or to the nearest unit. Choose the nearest unit you want to round to from the drop-down list.

We will work from the smaller list of Activities. When you are changing a large number of prices, it is more efficient to work from the Price List screen.

Click **Activities** in the Show list on the right-hand side of the screen:

NOTES
Click an item to select it. Then click the list icon that opens beside the entry in the Unit column to see the different units you can choose.

The Regular prices are shown. We will edit these first. We will change the prices directly by entering the revised price in the New Price column. The prices for S010 and S040 are correct.

Click   **S020** and **press** (tab) until the cursor is in the New Price column.

Type   210

Press   ⊥ to place the cursor in the New Price column for activity S030.

Type   420

Press   ⊥ **twice** to place the cursor in the New Price column for activity S050.

Type   210   Your price list should now look like the following one:

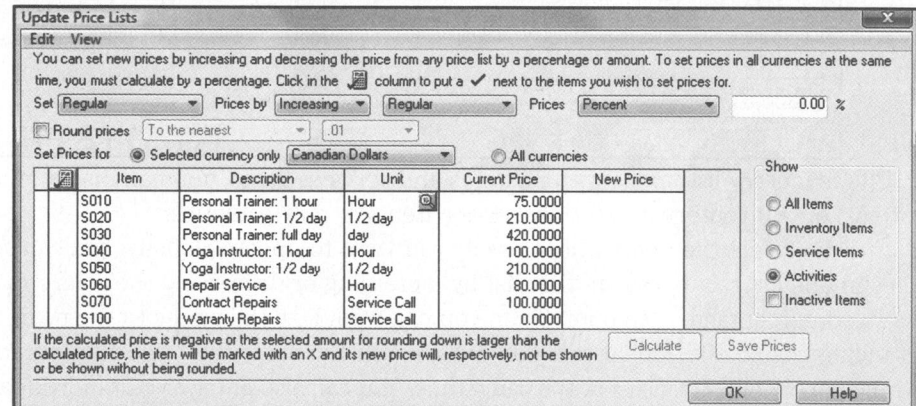

Click   the **Save Prices button** to save this set of prices and update the list:

The new prices have become the current prices.

We will update the preferred prices using the global update method. The price for three items is increasing by the fixed amount of $5, relative to the old preferred prices. The current settings would set the **Regular** prices by **Increasing** the **Regular** prices by a **percentage**, so we must change these settings. First, we must select the price list we want to change — the preferred prices.

Click   **Regular** in the Set field and **select Preferred** to place this price list on the screen.

The next setting is correct — we are increasing prices. However, we are increasing them relative to the old preferred prices. We must change the Prices By reference list.

Click   **Regular** in the Prices By field (to the right of Increasing). You can choose any price list as the reference list.

Click   **Preferred** to change the reference price list.

Click   **Percent**. You can choose Percent or Amount as the method.

Click   **Amount**. Now you can enter the amount of the increase.

Click   the **Amount field** (beside Amount) and **type**   5

Now we must select the three items we are changing.

Click   the **Select Item column** 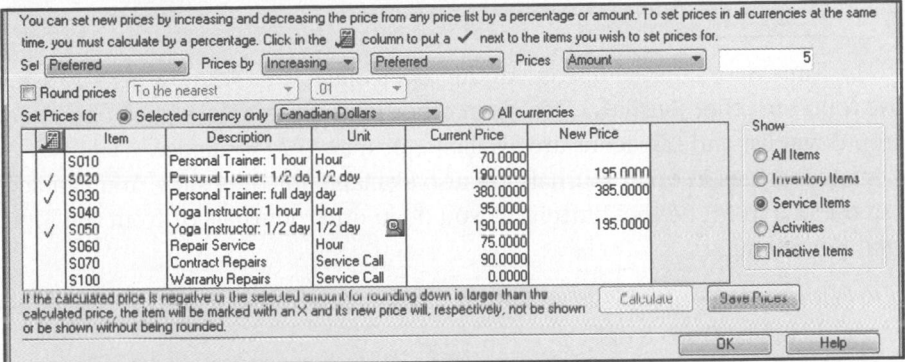 beside **S020** to add a ✓ and choose the item for global updating.

Press   ⊕ to place the cursor in the Select column for activity S030.

Click   to add a ✓ beside S030.

Press   ⊕ **twice** to place the cursor in the Select column for activity S050.

Click   to add a ✓ beside S050.

Click   **Calculate** to apply the formula we entered and update the list as shown:

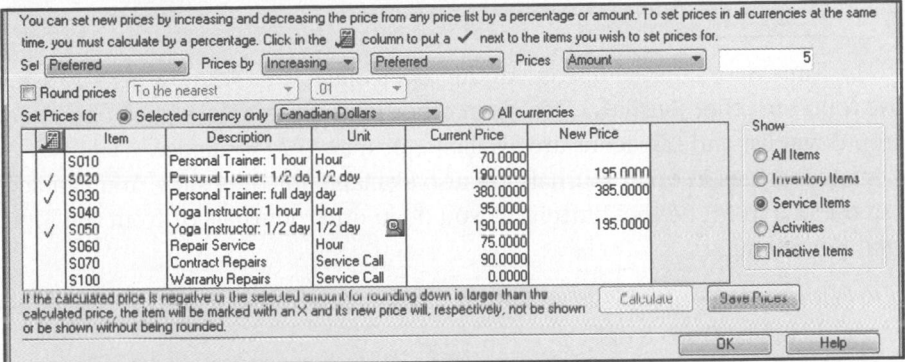

If the new prices are correct, you can save them. If not, you can edit individual prices, apply a different formula or round the prices.

Click   **Save Prices**. The new prices move to the Current Price column.

Click   **OK** to return to the Settings window. **Click OK** again to save all the changes and return to the Home window.

Click   **Employees & Payroll** in the Modules pane list.

Create   the **two new employee records**. Then **enter** the **cash receipt** and the **Visa payment**) and **change** the **session date to July 14**.

Preparing Time Slips

After setting up the service records to mark the activities and enter the billing information, you can track the amount of time that each employee works for each customer at each activity by completing Time Slips.

Time slips for employees may be entered from the Receivables module window or from the Employees & Payroll module window. These alternatives are illustrated in the partial Home windows below:

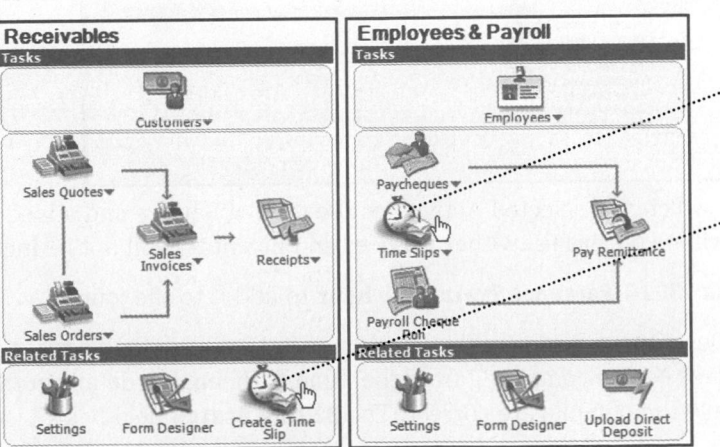

Click the **Create A Time Slip icon** in the Receivables module Related Tasks pane, or the **Time Slips icon** in the Payroll module Tasks pane:

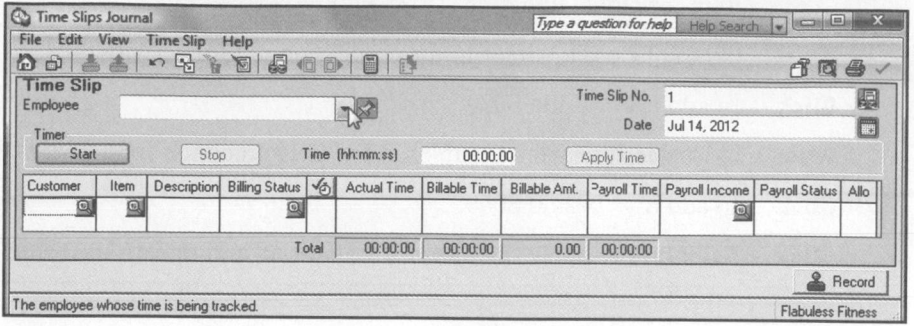

The Time Slips Journal opens. All the tool icons in this window are the same as those found in other journals. Also, as in other journals, employees can be selected from a drop-down list and List icons are available for many of the fields.

Many features in other journals are also available for time slips. You can access these options from the tool buttons as you do in other journals or from the Time Slip menu. For example,

- Click the Store tool ▣ and enter a name and frequency to store the time slip as a recurring transaction.
- Click the Look Up Time Slip tool ▣ to look up a time slip just as you look up purchases or sales invoices.
- Click the Adjust Time Slip tool ▣ to adjust a time slip after recording. You cannot adjust a time slip for selecting the wrong employee.

The Time Slips number is updated automatically by the program. Its starting number is taken from the Forms Settings, just like the next number for other forms. If the Time & Billing module is not hidden, the Next Number field for Time Slips is included in the Forms Settings screen. The number is correct.

The first time slip is for Schwinn. His first job was completed for McMaster University, a preferred customer.

Click the **Employee list arrow** and **choose George Schwinn**.

Enter **July 7** in the Date field for the Time Slip.

Click the **Customer field List icon** ▣ and **select McMaster University**.

Click the **Item field List icon** ▣ to see the Select Activity list:

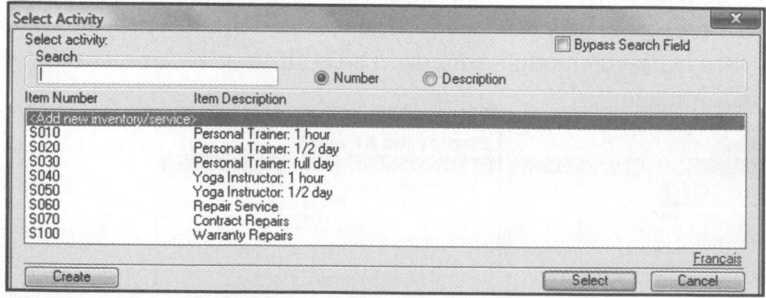

All services for which you selected Activity as the type of Service and added time and billing details will be on this list. Other services and inventory will not be included.

Double click S010 Personal Trainer: 1 hour to add it to the journal.

The Item and Description fields are the usual ones for inventory and service transactions. The next field is completed from the Time & Billing tab details in the ledger record. Usually the defaults are correct. The **Billing Status** field has a List icon and a selection list. Activities may be Billable, Non-Billable or provided at No Charge. You can change the default entry if needed.

If an activity is billable, you can use the **Timer** in this window to track the time worked on the activity. A checkmark in the **Stopwatch column** indicates that you can use the timer. Some businesses track all time spent for a customer. For example, if a customer phoned for advice, and telephone advice was a billable activity, you could start the timer at the beginning of the phone call and then stop at the end to have an accurate measure of the duration of the call.

To use the timer, click the Stopwatch column for the customer and activity if the ✔ is not already there. Click the Start button. The counter will keep time in seconds until you click Stop. You can use this measurement as the actual time for the activity by clicking Apply Time.

Time is entered as the number of hours, minutes and seconds (hhmmss). The simplest way to explain the format for entering time is with a few examples. The following chart summarizes the examples and outlines some of the rules:

EXAMPLES OF TIME ENTRIES IN THE TIME SLIPS JOURNAL

Entering This Number	Records This Time
1 or 01 or 100 or 10000	Records 1 hour
001 or 0001 or 000100	Records 1 minute
00001 or 000001	Records 1 second
130 or 0130 or 013000	Records 1.5 hours (1 hour and 30 minutes)
0110 or 110 or 11000	Records 1 hour and 10 minutes
1030 or 103000	Records 10 hours and 30 minutes
11515 or 011515	Records 1 hour, 15 minutes and 15 seconds
995959	Records 99 hours, 59 minutes and 59 seconds

RULES FOR TIME ENTRIES IN THE TIME SLIPS JOURNAL

- You can enter up to six digits (hhmmss). A one- or two-digit number is always interpreted as the number of hours (zero minutes, zero seconds). The remaining missing digits are always assumed to be zero.
- For a three-digit entry, the first number represents hours and the next two represent the minutes.
- For a four-digit number, the first two numbers represent hours and the next two represent minutes.
- For a five-digit number, the first number represents the number of hours, the next two, minutes, and the final two, seconds.
- For a six-digit entry, the first two numbers represent hours, the next two, minutes, and the last two, seconds.
- You can omit seconds and minutes if they are zero. Leading zeros are not needed for hours.
- The times allowed on a line for one activity range from the shortest time of 1 second, entered as 000001 or 00001, to the longest, 99 hours, 59 minutes and 59 seconds, entered as 995959.

There are three columns for time: the **Actual Time** spent at the activity; the **Billable Time** or amount of time that the customer pays for; and the **Payroll Time** or hours the employee is paid for. Sometimes the customer is billed for fewer hours than the job actually required. For example, if an estimate has been given and the work is much more complex than anticipated, a business will usually not bill the customer for the full amount in the interest of good customer relations. At other times, the customer may be charged for more time than the activity requires. For example, a job may have a minimum time component, such as one hour of labour. Most companies will want to keep track of all times so that they can revise their prices to reflect their true costs.

Schwinn spent two hours completing the first job (actual time); the customer will pay for 1.5 hours of work (billable time); and Schwinn will be paid for two hours of work for this job (payroll time).

Click the **Actual Time field**.

NOTES
If there is no checkmark in the Stopwatch column, clicking will add it. Clicking will also remove the checkmark once it is there.

NOTES
Notice that decimals are not allowed for the time entries. You must enter the hours, minutes and seconds as whole numbers.

NOTES
The best way to learn the formats for entering times is to enter different numbers and observe how Simply Accounting records them in the journal.

NOTES
An employee may be paid for the actual number of hours, the billable number of hours or some other time agreed on between the employee and the employer. For example, the pay may be limited to a maximum number of hours for a specific job to encourage efficient work habits.

NOTES
Remember that a single digit represents the number of hours.

Type 2 **Press** (tab). Your journal now looks like the one below:

The program enters 02:00:00, the actual time, as the billable time and the payroll time. The price (**Billable Amt.**) is the billable time multiplied by the price from the ledger for that time unit, 2 hours multiplied by the preferred hourly rate of $70. Notice that the **Payroll Status** is Not Paid. You can edit the billable time, the billable amount, the payroll time and payroll income category for individual activities. We need to change the billable time to 1.5 hours, 1 hour and 30 minutes. The billable time is already selected.

Type 130 **Press** (tab) to update the billable amount to $105.

Click the **Customer list icon** and **select McMaster University** for the second activity.

Click the **Item list icon** and **select S070 Contract Repairs**.

Click the **Actual Time column**.

Type 2 **Press** (tab).

This time the flat rate is entered and you cannot edit the billable time. However, you can edit the billable amount. The next activity is for another customer.

Click the **Customer list icon**. **Select Mohawk College**.

Click the **Item list icon** and **select S020 Personal Trainer: 1/2 day**.

Click the **Actual Time column**.

Type 4 **Press** (tab).

For this ledger record, recall that we entered 3 hours as the usual number of hours in the 1/2 day of activity. The hourly rate was determined as the Preferred Selling Price divided by the usual number of hours — $195 divided by 3 or $65. Thus the amount for 4 hours is 4 x $65 or $260.

Click the **Customer list icon** and **select Mohawk College** for the fourth activity.

Click the **Item list icon** and **select S060 Repair Service**.

Click the **Actual Time column**.

Type 2 **Press** (tab).

Repair service work is billed at a straight hourly rate so the amount is the billable time multiplied by the hourly rate for the preferred customer.

Click the **Customer list icon** and **select Mohawk College** for the final activity.

Click the **Item list icon** and **select S100 Warranty Repairs**.

Click   the **Actual Time column**.

Type   2 **Press** ⌐tab⌐.

No amount is entered because the activity is non-billable, but the hours are added to the employee's payroll time. The journal is complete and should look like the one below:

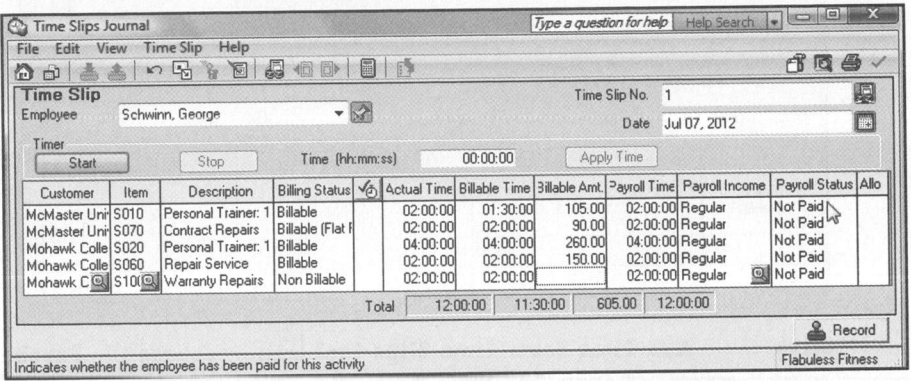

Check   the **time slip** carefully before recording and **correct mistakes**.

You can also allocate time slips details to projects or divisions, either on the basis of percent or time.

Click the Allo column for the activity line to open the Allocation screen:

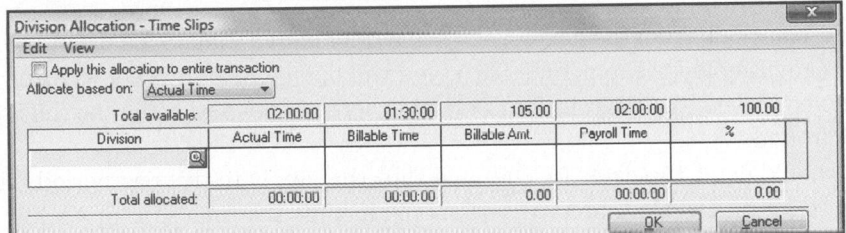

Choose the division and the amount of time for that activity that is allocated to the division. Click OK to return to the journal when finished.

Click   the **Record button** ⌐ Record ⌐ to save the entry.

Complete Time Slip #2 and then **close** the **Time Slips Journal**.

Add   a **shortcut** for the **Time Slips Journal**. **Choose Create Time Slip** under the Time & Billing heading.

Paying Employees from Time Slips

When activities are set up in the Inventory and Services Ledger, and time slips are entered for employees, Simply Accounting tracks the hours worked so you can use the summary of these time slips to prepare paycheques.

We will use this method to prepare the paycheque for the new employee, Yvonne Tinker, because these activities are her primary responsibility. We need to use the Paycheques Journal because the pay date does not match the session date.

Open   the **Paycheques Journal**.

Enter   **July 7** as the Date and the Period Ending date.

Choose **Tinker** from the Employee list and **press** ⟨tab⟩ to enter her information:

Click   the **Add Time From Time Slips tool** 🔄 or **choose** the **Paycheque menu** and **click Add Time From Time Slips**.

The Payroll Hour Selection screen opens:

When you begin from the Employees & Payroll module Time Slips drop-down shortcut (Pay Employee From Time Slip), you will open a Search window. After you select the employee, the Payroll Hour Selection screen opens with the Payroll Journal in the background.

You should enter the dates for the time slips that apply to this pay period. Tinker has worked for one week; therefore, you should include the time slips up to July 7.

These dates are entered as the defaults because we already entered July 7 as the period ending date and July 1 is the date Tinker was hired.

Click   **OK** to return to the journal.

The number of hours is updated as shown in the following completed journal entry:

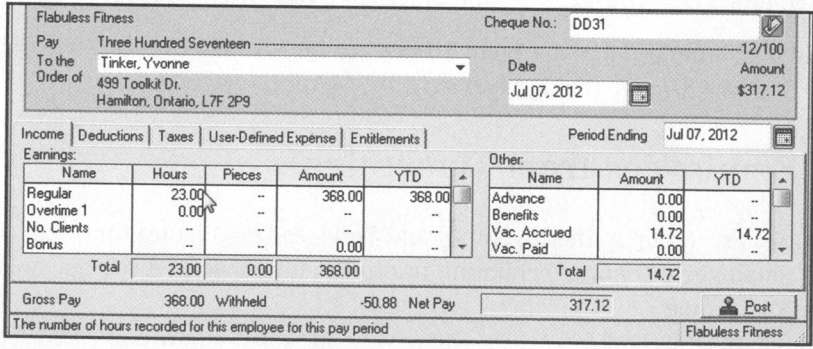

You can edit the number of hours as usual if necessary, and you can add advances or other deductions if they are appropriate.

Review the **journal entry** and, when you are certain that it is correct,

Click   **Post** to save the transaction. **Click Yes** to continue.

Choose **Schwinn** from the Employee list and press ⟨tab⟩ to enter his default payroll information.

Click   the **Add Time From Time Slips tool** 🔄 or **choose** the **Paycheque menu** and **click Add Time From Time Slips**:

Again, the time slip period matches the pay period for the employee.

> **Click**   **OK** to see the warning:

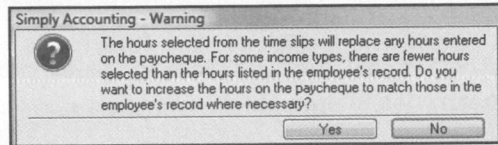

For Schwinn, the hours worked exceed the hours on his time slip for the various customer jobs because he also performs other duties at the store. You have the option of accepting the Time Slip information or increasing the hours to match the default in the employee records. For Schwinn, the Payroll Ledger entry is the correct one.

> **Click**   **Yes** to increase the number of hours and return to the journal. The number of Regular hours remains unchanged at 80 hours.
>
> **Click**   the **Overtime 1 field** and add the overtime hours by **typing**   2.
>
> **Click**   the **Advance field** and **accept** the **default** because only $50 remains to be repaid.
>
> **Review** the **journal entry** and make corrections if necessary.
>
> **Click**   **Post**. **Click Yes** to continue and save the transaction.
>
> **Close**   the **Payroll Journal**.

The program will update the Payroll Hours Selection dates for the next paycheque, and the Payroll Status on these Time Slips.

> **Click**   the **Create Time Slip shortcut** to open the Time Slips Journal.
>
> **Click**   the **Look Up Time Slips tool** ⬚.
>
> **Type**   2   in the Time Slip Number field and **click OK** to see Tinker's time slip.

You should see that the employee has been paid — Paid appears in the Payroll Status column for each job completed by this employee. You cannot use this time slip information for payroll again.

> **Click**   the **Look Up Time Slips tool** ⬚ and **enter 1** in the Time Slip Number field. **Click OK** to see Schwinn's time slip.

His payroll status too is marked as Paid because we added time from the time slips, even though the hours were not used to determine his pay.

> **Close**   the **Time Slips Journal**.

Preparing Sales Invoices from Time Slips

When sales invoices are prepared for mailing to customers, the activities from the time slips can be added directly to the invoices without re-entering each activity.

> **Click**   **Receivables** in the Modules pane list, if necessary.
>
> **Click**   the **Sales Invoices icon** `Sales Invoices▾` to open the Sales Journal.
>
> **Choose McMaster University** as the customer. Invoice and Pay Later are correct.

Enter   **July 7, 2012** as the invoice date.

Time slip activities may be entered using the tool shown below or the Sales menu option:

Click   the **Add Time Slip Activities tool** 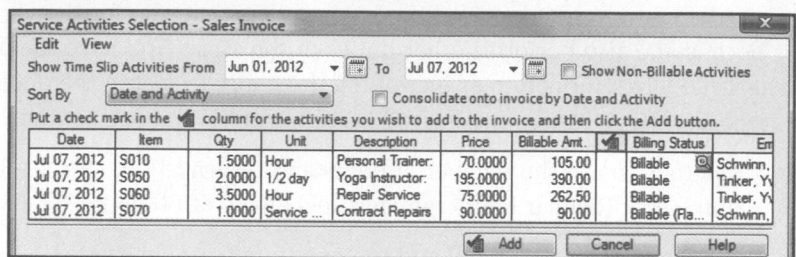 or **choose** the **Sales menu** and **click Add Time Slip Activities** to open the activities list for this customer:

NOTES
If necessary, scroll or change the column width to see all the columns.

NOTES
By showing non-billable activities, you can include Warranty Repair hours on the selection list. Non-billable activities are not added to the sales invoice.

NOTES
Clicking the Add Activity column heading, will select all the activities in the list. Then you can click any activity to deselect it if you need to.

NOTES
You can edit the amount billed to the customer in the Sales Journal by changing the Amount or the Price. You can also choose a different account number for the sales.

Services provided to the customer by all employees will be listed, and you can also include Non-Billable Activities by clicking its check box. You may need to scroll to see the information in all columns. You can Sort the list By Date And Activity, the default, By Employee And Activity or By Activity. You can also Consolidate the list By Date And Activity, combining the amounts for each activity on the same date. You can select all the activities for the invoice, or omit some if they are incomplete or come after the billing date. All activities should be included in the invoice for McMaster University.

Enter   **Jul 1 2012** and **Jul 7 2012** as the date range in the Show Time Slip Activities From and To date fields. (You need to add the year.)

Click   the **Add Activity column** for the first activity, S010. Only activities with a ✓ in this column are added to the sales invoice.

Click   the **Add Activity column** for the remaining activities.

Click   the **Add button** to return to the completed Sales Journal:

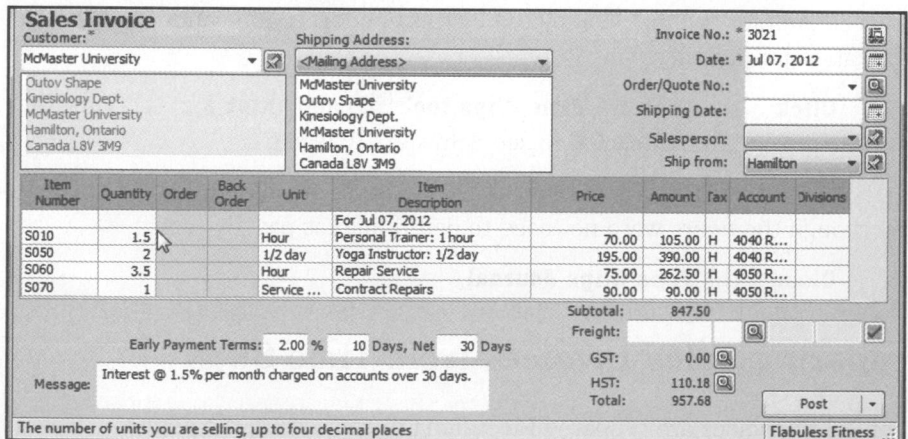

The activities are now added to the journal. Notice that the Quantity refers to the units in the ledger — for S050, the customer pays for two one-half day units of three hours each. For S070, the flat-rate service call, the quantity is one. You can add other regular services or inventory to the sales invoice if they were sold to the same customer; you do not need to create a separate invoice for them.

You should review the journal entry before posting it.

Choose the **Report menu** and **click Display Sales Journal Entry**:

Flabuless Fitness Sales Journal Entry 07/07/2012 (J6)			
Account Number	Account Description	Debits	Credits
1200	Accounts Receivable	957.68	-
2650	GST/HST Charged on Sales	-	110.18
4040	Revenue from Services	-	495.00
4050	Rervenue from Repairs	-	352.50
Additional Date:	Ref. Number:	957.68	957.68

NOTES
If the information in the Time Slip was incorrect, close the Sales Journal without posting the invoice and adjust the Time Slip. Then re-enter the sales invoice.

The journal entry is like other sales journal entries. The correct tax amounts are recorded, based on Ledger record information. HST is charged on all the services provided by Flabuless Fitness.

Close the **report** when you have finished viewing it.

Make corrections if necessary.

To correct the activities, click 🔄 to return to the Service Activities Selection list. Previously selected activities are shown as Invoiced in the Billing Status column. Clicking the Add Activity column 🗒 will remove the ✓ and restore the status to billable so you can select a different group of activities.

Click **Post** [Post ▾] to save the journal entry.

Enter the next **two sales invoices** by adding activities from the time slips and then **close** the **Sales Journal**.

Building New Inventory

Instead of assembling inventory using the Item Assembly method, you can set up the inventory assembly components as part of the ledger record and then use this information to build an item using the Bill of Materials method. We will create the new inventory Promotional Fitness Package, including the items or materials that make up the package.

Choose Inventory & Services from the Modules pane list.

Choose Add Inventory & Service from the Inventory & Services icon shortcuts list to open the Inventory Ledger for new Service Activity items. The cursor is in the Item Number field.

Type AP100 **Press** (tab).

Type Promotional Fitness Package

Click **Inventory** as the Type to modify the form for the inventory item.

The Units tab screen is displayed. All units are the same for this package.

Double click Each and **type** Package

Click the **Quantities tab**. The Minimum level is correct at 0.

Click the **Pricing tab** to access the price fields.

On the Pricing tab screen, you can enter regular and preferred prices in all the currencies that you have set up. Canadian prices are shown initially.

Click the **Regular Price Per Selling Unit field**.

Type 210 **Press** (tab) to advance to the Preferred Price field.

Type 200

Choose United States Dollars from the Currency list.

Foreign prices for Flabuless Fitness are fixed, so we need to change the default setting. Clicking the entry will change the setting.

Click   **Exchange Rate** beside Regular to change the setting to Fixed Price.

Press   `tab` to advance to the Regular Selling Price for United States Dollars.

Type   200 **Press** `tab` to advance to the Preferred Pricing Method.

Click   **Exchange Rate** to change the setting to Fixed Price. **Press** `tab`.

Type   190

Choose   **Euro** from the currency list.

Click   **Exchange Rate** beside Regular to change the setting to Fixed Price.

Press   `tab` to advance to the Regular Price for Euro.

Type   145 **Press** `tab` to advance to the Preferred Pricing Method.

Click   **Exchange Rate** to change the setting. **Press** `tab`. **Type** 135

Click   the **Linked tab** to open the linked accounts screen.

Click   the **Asset field**.

Type   1510 Promotions **Press** `tab`. We need to add the account.

Click   **Add** and **press** `tab` to open the Add Account wizard.

Accept   the remaining **defaults** for the account and **click Yes** to change the account class.

Press   `tab` to advance to the Revenue account field.

Type   4020 **Press** `tab` to advance to the COGS account field.

Type   5050

The variance linked account is not needed for this item.

Click   the **Taxes tab** to see the sales taxes relating to the inventory.

The default entry No for Tax Exempt is correct — HST is charged on the sale of this item. Duty is not charged on this item because it is not purchased.

Click   the **Build tab** to see the information screen that we need for entering the assembly or building components for inventory items:

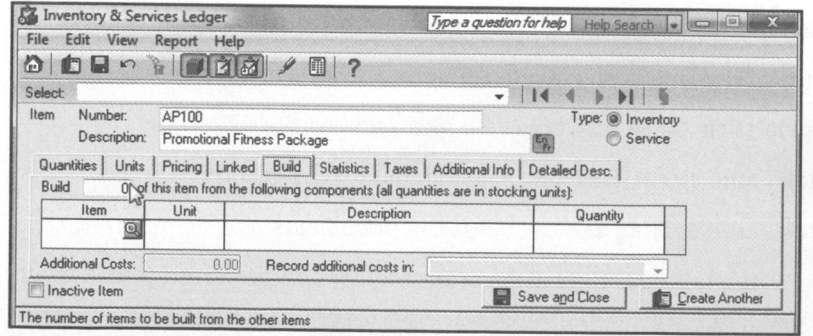

On this screen, we enter the relationship between the new inventory and its components, that is, how many new items we are building and how many of each input item this number of units requires. This is very similar to the Item Assembly Journal, except that we are only defining the building process at this stage. The actual building or assembly still takes place in the journal. One package is created from the set of accessories — we build one package at a time.

The components are listed here again for reference:

1	A010 Body Fat Scale
1	A020 Yoga Mats
1	A050 Heart Rate Monitor
1	A070 Stability Balls
1	A100 Workout Gloves: all sizes
5 kg	A030 Dumbbells

Click   the **Build field** to enter the default number of packages being assembled from the set of components.

Type   1 **Press** (tab) to advance to the Item (number) field.

Click   the **List icon** and **select A010 Body Fat Scale** to enter the first item.

The cursor advances to the Quantity field after entering the unit and description. Here you need to enter the number of Body Fat Scales included in each Promotional Fitness Package. We are defining the unit relationship between the assembled item and its components. One component item is used to make the package.

Type   1 **Press** (tab) to advance to the second Item line.

Enter   the **next four components** and **enter 1** as the quantity for each. For **A030, enter 5** as the quantity.

The Additional Costs and its linked account field (Record Additional Costs In) became available once we entered the number of units to build. These fields have the same meaning as they do in the Item Assembly Journal. However, in the Premium version, costs are entered in the ledger record and separate assembly linked accounts can be defined for each item. There are no additional costs associated with creating the package so we should leave these fields blank.

Click   the **Quantities tab**. The quantity on hand remains at zero until we build the item in the journal.

Correct any **errors** by returning to the field with the mistake. **Highlight** the **error** and **enter** the **correct information. Click** the different **tabs** to see all the information that you entered.

When all the information is entered correctly, you must save the record.

Click   **Save And Close** [💾 Save and Close] to save the record.

Building an Inventory Item in the Journal

The quantity of Promotional Fitness Packages is still zero. In order to create stock of the package for sale, we must build the item in the Bill of Materials & Item Assembly Journal.

The Build From Bill Of Materials Journal is shown by the hand pointer below:

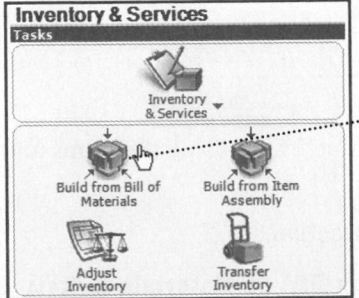

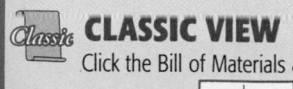
Click the **Build From Bill Of Materials icon** to open the journal:

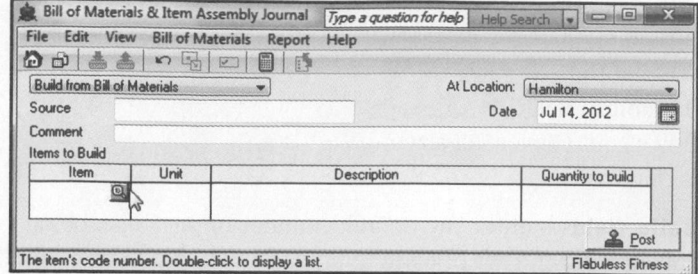

In the Premium version, you can assemble new inventory items either by using the Item Assembly method that we used in previous applications, or the Bill of Materials method that follows.

The journal resembles the lower half of the Build From Item Assembly Journal screen, the Assembled Items section, but without components and costs (see page 382). Information for the upper half of that screen — for components and costs — is located in the ledger record. The default location is Hamilton.

Click the **Source field**.

Type Memo 7-10 **Press** (tab) to advance to the Date field.

Type 7-7 **Press** (tab) **twice** to advance to the Comment field.

Type Create promotional packages **Press** (tab). The cursor moves to the Item field.

Click the **List icon** to open the selection list:

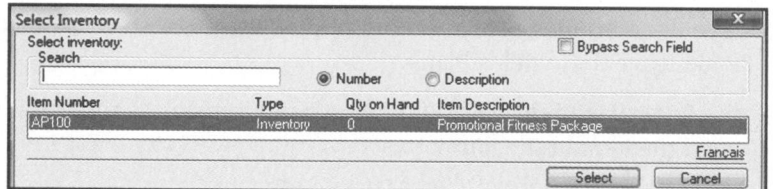

All the items for which you have added build information will be listed on this screen. Because we have entered these details only for the Promotional Fitness Package, it is the only one listed.

Double click AP100 to add it to the journal.

The unit and description are added for the package and the default quantity is 1. The quantity is selected so we can change it. We are creating two packages.

Type 2 to complete the journal entry as shown:

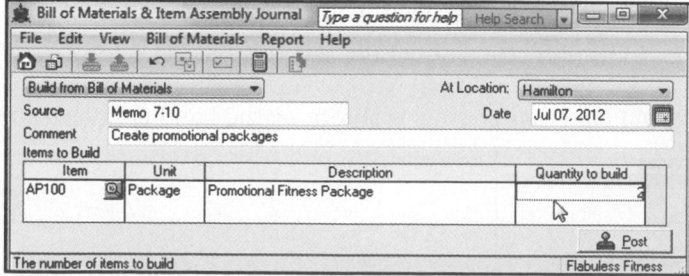

If you have other items to build, you can continue by choosing the items and entering a quantity for each of them.

Review your **work** before posting the transaction.

Choose the **Report menu** and **click Display Bill Of Materials & Item Assembly Journal** to display the journal transaction:

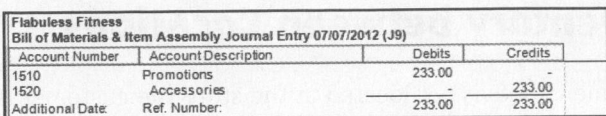

The asset account balances have been updated by the transaction, just as they are in an Item Assembly transaction. Compare this journal entry with the one on page 384. The inventory quantities are also updated from the transaction — the quantity of packages increases and the quantities for the other items decrease. Any additional costs would be credited to the linked cost account and debited to the assembled item asset account.

Close   the **journal display** and **make corrections** if necessary.

If there is not enough inventory of any item in stock to complete the build, you will see an error message asking you to reduce the quantity to build:

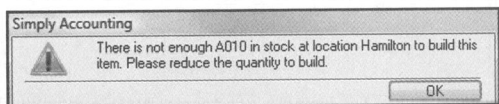

Click OK and reduce the number of units you are building.

Click   **Post** [Post] to save the entry.

Click the Item list icon to see that the number of promotional packages has been changed to two. Click Cancel to close this screen without making a selection.

You can now sell the package just like any other inventory item.

Multiple Levels of Build

You can use a built item just like any other single inventory item. The process is the same when you are selling the item or using it as a component to build other inventory. We created an additional built item to illustrate the following multiple build.

Nested building components are common in construction work. When you use a built item as a component for a second-stage build, you select it on the Build tab screen just like other inventory. When you are building the new second-stage item in the Bill of Materials Journal, the built component may be out of stock. In this case, Simply Accounting provides the following message:

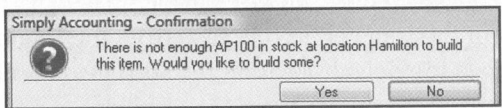

You can now build the primary item, the built component, as part of the same journal transaction.

Click Yes to continue with the additional build:

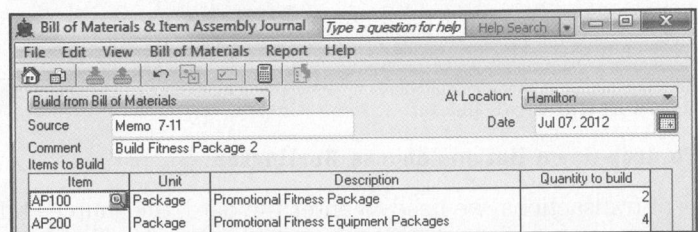

Simply Accounting will add the out-of-stock item to the Bill of Materials Journal as the first item to build. The number of units built will be those required to complete the secondary build.

Close   the **journal**. Leave the Inventory & Services window open.

Transferring Inventory between Locations

Sometimes the item a customer wants is not located at the store the customer is visiting. When this occurs, items can be transferred from another location where the stock is available. In Simply Accounting, the option to transfer items is available in the Inventory Adjustments & Transfers Journal, accessed from the Transfer Inventory icon in the Inventory & Services module window:

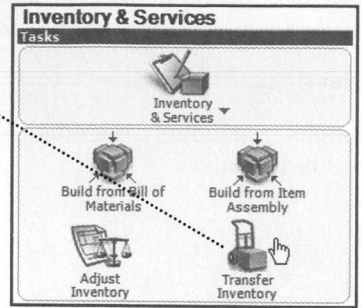

CLASSIC VIEW

Click the Inventory Adjustments & Transfers icon to open the journal. Choose Transfer Between Locations from the drop-down transactions list if necessary.

Click   the **Transfer Inventory icon** to open the journal with Transfer Between Locations, the type of transaction we need, already selected:

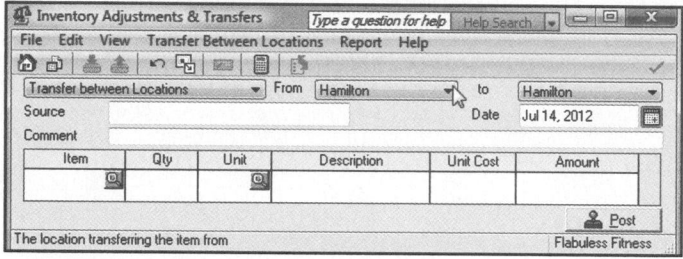

This is the same journal we used for other inventory adjustments in previous chapters, but there is no field for account numbers. When multiple locations are used, the transfers between locations are made in this journal as well. You can select the type of transaction from the transactions drop-down list as shown:

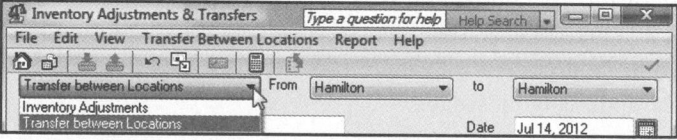

We need to indicate the direction of the transfer, in this case from the Hamilton store to the Burlington store. Hamilton is the default location for both fields because it is the primary location. This is correct as the From location.

Click   the **From** drop-down list to see both locations:

NOTES

Both locations are listed in the From and the To location drop-down lists because items may be transferred from either location to the other.

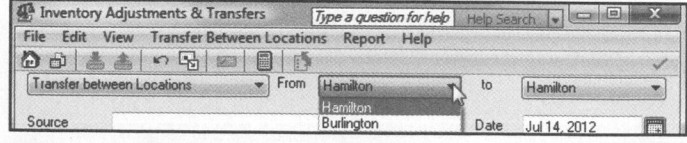

Click   **Hamilton** in the From list.

Click   the **To drop-down list** and **choose Burlington**.

As for other types of transactions, we need to enter the date, the source and a comment. Then we will enter the items that are being moved.

Click   the **Source field**.

Type   Memo 7-11 **Press** ⌞tab⌟ to move to the Date field.

Enter   **July 7** as the date of the inventory move.

Click   the **Comment field**.

Type   Move inventory to Burlington store

Press   `tab` to advance to the Item code field. A list of items is available, as it is for inventory fields in other journals.

You can access the inventory list by pressing `enter` in the Item field, double clicking the field or clicking the List icon.

Click   the **List icon** and **select AP100**, the first item on the transfer list.

Press   `tab` to move to the Qty (quantity) field.

Type   2

Enter   the **remaining items** in the same way to complete the entry as shown:

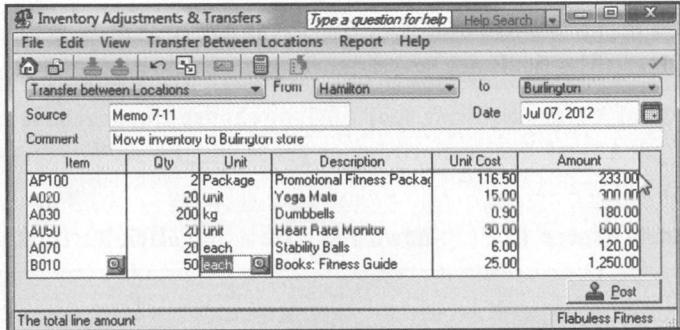

When you record (post) the transfer, the inventory at the two locations will be updated — the quantity at the Hamilton store is reduced and the quantity at the Burlington store is increased. You can see the changes that you made by accessing the ledger records for the items and choosing the locations on the Quantity tab screen. However, no journal entry results from this transaction and you cannot look up or adjust the entry, so check it carefully before posting. When you are certain that the transaction is correct, you must save it.

NOTES
The successful recording message for the transfer does not include a journal entry number

Click   Post 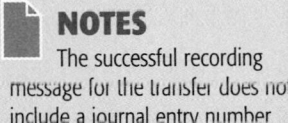 to save the entry. **Close** the **journal** to return to the Inventory Home window.

To correct the transfer after posting, you should repeat the transfer but reverse the direction of the movement of goods — enter the original From location in the To location field and the original To location in the From location field. Refer to Appendix C, page A–34.

Adding Location Information for Purchases

Now that we have multiple locations for inventory, we must indicate which location the inventory is taken from or sent to when we make purchases, sales and adjustments. By choosing the correct location, we can accurately keep track of the quantity on hand at each store.

The purchase order from Scandia Weights should be delivered to the Burlington store.

Open   the **Purchases Journal** (click the Create Purchase Invoice shortcut).

Choose PO #30 in the order number field and **press** `tab`.

The order is placed on-screen as an Invoice:

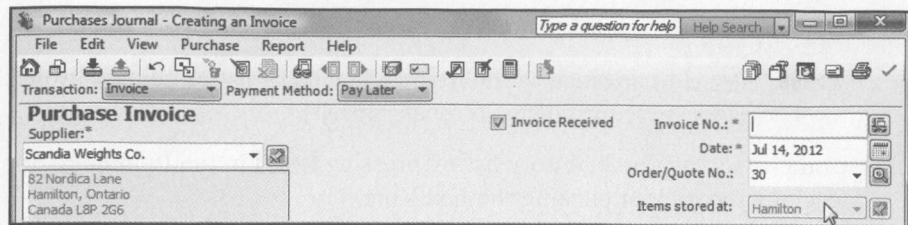

When the order was entered, locations were not set up. The location field (Items Stored At) is dimmed and unavailable. Hamilton, the primary location, is entered, and this is not correct. We need to edit the order to change the location before filling it.

Choose **Order** from the Transaction drop-down list to restore the purchase order. **Click Yes** to confirm that you are discarding the invoice.

Choose **PO #30** in the Quote/Order field list. **Press** (tab) to place the order on the screen. The fields are still dimmed and cannot be edited.

Click the **Adjust Purchase Order tool** 🔳, or **choose** the **Purchase menu** and **click Adjust Purchase Order** or **press** (ctrl) + **A**. We can now modify the order.

Click the **Items Stored At drop-down list arrow** and **click Burlington**:

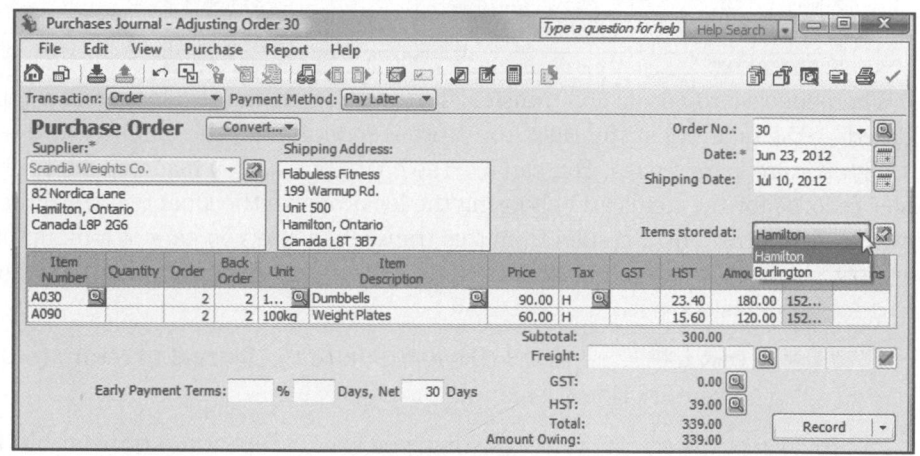

Enter **Jul 10 12** as the purchase order date.

We can now fill the order.

Choose **Invoice** from the Transaction drop-down list or **choose** **Convert This Purchase Order To A Purchase Invoice** from the Convert drop-down list.

Simply Accounting shows you the following confirmation message:

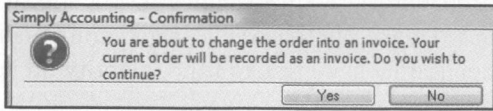

Click **Yes** to confirm that you are changing the order to an invoice.

Click the **Fill Backordered Quantities tool** 🔳, or **choose** the **Purchase menu** and **click Fill Backordered Quantities**.

Add **SW-1775** as the invoice number to complete the transaction.

Review your **journal entry**. Location details are not included in the journal entry, but the inventory records will be correctly updated.

Close the **display** when finished.

⚠️ **WARNING!**
You must change the date for the purchase order. The original purchase order was placed on June 23. You cannot continue with this date because it precedes July 1, the date in the Do Not Allow Transactions Dated Before (Company, System Settings) field.

Click   **Post** ⬚Post⬚ to save the entry when you are certain that it is correct.

Click   **OK** to confirm that the order has been filled and **click Yes** to confirm successful posting.

Adjust   **purchase order #31**. **Add Burlington** as the **location** and **enter July 10** as the **Date**. **Fill** the order and **add FG-3877** as the invoice number.

Enter   the **purchase from ABS International**, after using Full Add to enter the new European vendor and then **close** the **Purchases Journal**.

Entering Locations in the Sales and Other Journals

All journals that use inventory items also have a location field. In the Sales Journal, you choose the location from the Ship From drop-down list as shown:

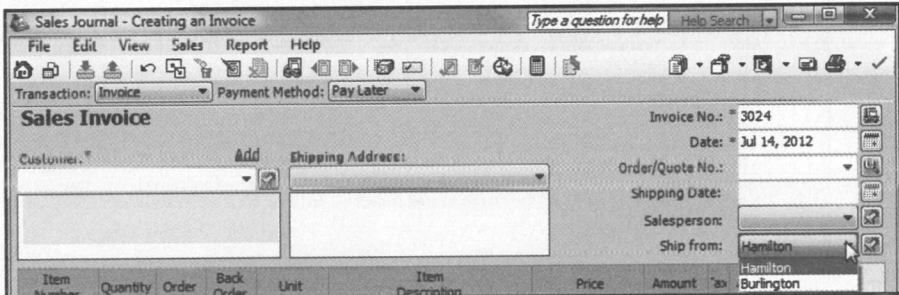

For inventory adjustments, that is, losses or movement of inventory stock for in-store use, choose the location from the At Location drop-down list as shown:

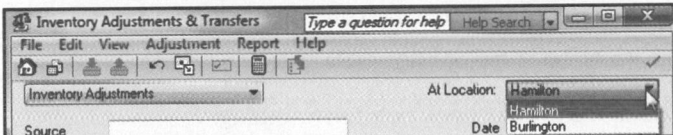

For building items from item assembly or from a bill of materials, enter the location in the At Location field as shown:

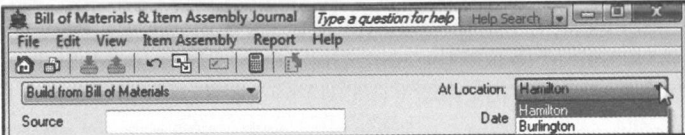

If the location you chose does not have sufficient stock of any items needed to complete the build or assembly, you will see the following message:

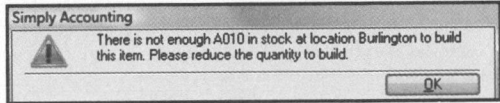

You can transfer inventory to the required location or choose a smaller quantity.

Enter   the **remaining transactions** for July up to memo #7-17.

Updating Inventory Prices

At the end of the month, all inventory prices must be increased. Rather than changing each record for regular and preferred prices in both Canadian and US dollars, we will use the Update Price List method that we used earlier to edit the activity prices. This method is more efficient when many prices must be changed or when they are changed by a fixed amount or percentage. In this case, we are increasing regular prices by 10 percent. The feature also allows us to round off the prices automatically.

Click the **Settings icon** .

Click **Inventory & Services** and then **click Price List**.

Click **Update Price Lists**.

Click **Inventory Items** to restrict the list to the ones we need.

Click the **select item column heading** to select all items as shown:

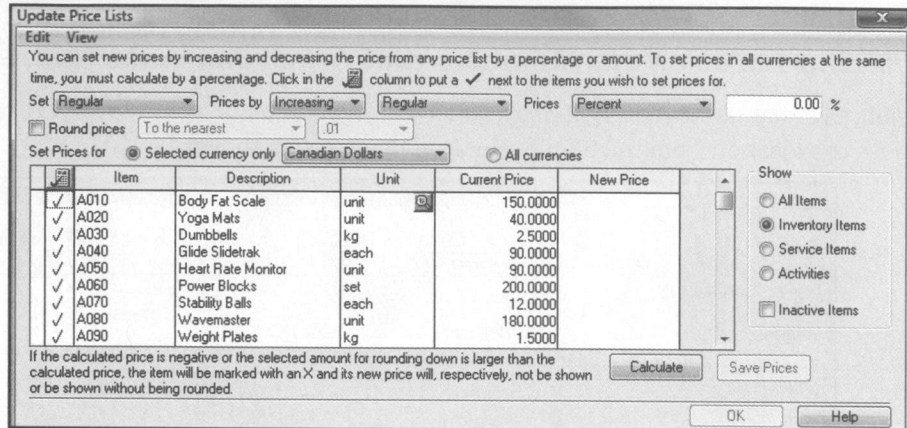

The upper part of the screen has the rules for the change. We are increasing Canadian Regular prices by a fixed percentage, so these entries are already correct. The entry shows that we are setting prices for the selected currency only (Canadian dollars). We need to enter a percentage and the rule for rounding prices.

Click **0.00** in the % field. **Type** 10

Press (tab) to move to the check box for rounding.

Click the **Round Prices check box** to add a ✓ and open the next field we need.

You can round up, round down or round to the nearest amount. We want to round to the nearest dollar, so we just need to add the unit. One cent (.01) is the default entry. The units range from one ten-thousandth of a dollar (.0001) to one thousand dollars (1 000.00).

Click the list arrow beside the unit with .01 (one cent) as the default entry.

Choose 1.00 (one dollar) as the unit. Your settings should match the following:

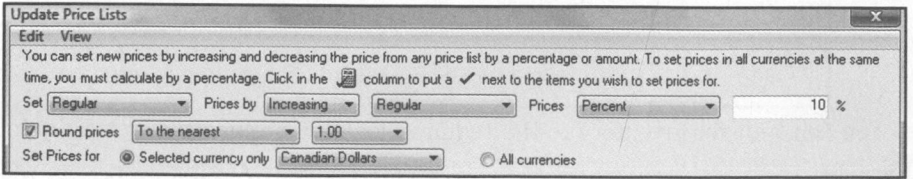

Click **Calculate** to update the prices and add them to the New Price column.

We can now still edit individual prices — they have not yet been saved. For A030 and A090, the lower-priced items, the new prices are too high.

Click **3.00** in the New Price column for A030.

Type 2.75

Change the **price** for **A090** from 2.00 to **1.75**.

Click   Save Prices to transfer the new prices to the Current Price column.

Now we need to update the preferred Canadian prices and the US dollar prices. We will set Preferred Canadian prices by increasing preferred Canadian prices by 5 percent and rounding to the nearest dollar. The increase, 10 percent, and the rounding rules are still entered from the previous update. All items remain selected.

Click   the **Set drop-down list arrow** and **select Preferred**.

Press   ⬚ tab ⬚ **twice** to move to the second price list field — the reference list.

Click   the **drop-down list arrow** and **select Preferred**.

Click   **10** in the % field and **type** 5 Your settings should be like the ones shown in the following screen:

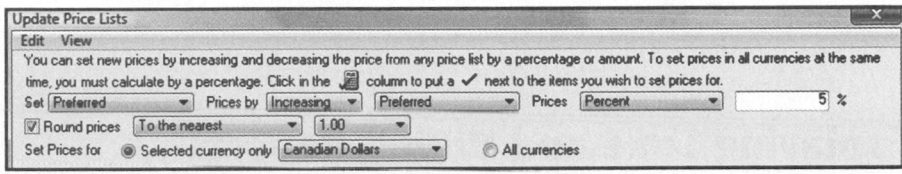

Click   Calculate to update all prices.

This time, some prices actually went down as a result of rounding to the nearest dollar. We will edit these prices, for items A030 and A090.

Click   **2.00** in the New Price column for A030.

Type   2.30

Change the **price** for **A090** from 1.00 to **1.40**.

Click   Save Prices to transfer the new prices to the Current Price column.

We will update the preferred US dollar prices next because most settings are already correct. We will set Preferred US dollar prices by increasing preferred US dollar prices by 5 percent and rounding to the nearest dollar. We need to change the selected currency.

Click   Canadian in the Selected Currency Only field to display the list.

Choose   United States Dollars to change the selection as shown:

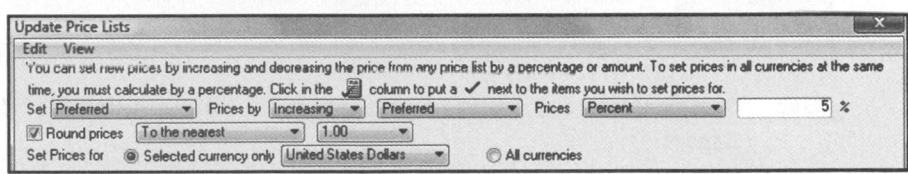

Click   Calculate to update all prices.

Click   **2.00** in the New Price column for A030 so you can change this price.

Type   2.1

Change the **price** for **A090** from 1.00 to **1.40**. **Click Save Prices**.

The final change is for Regular US dollar prices. These prices should be set by increasing regular US dollar prices by 10 percent and rounding to the nearest dollar.

Choose Regular in the Set price field.

Choose Regular in the next price reference field.

Click   **5** in the % field and **type** 10

> **NOTES**
> Notice that you can change the pricing method for foreign currency prices as well on the Update Price Lists screen.

Your settings should match the ones we show here:

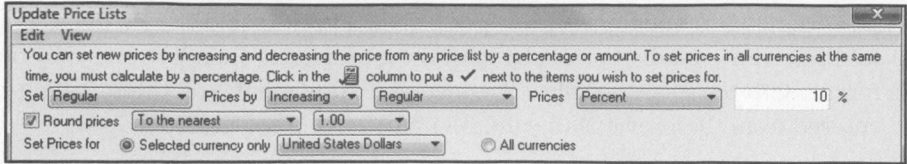

Click   **Calculate** to update all prices.

Click   **2.00** in the New Price column for A030 so you can change this price.

Type   2.40

Change the **price** for **A090** from 2.00 to **1.50**. **Click Save Prices**.

Click   **OK** to return to the Settings screen and **click OK** again to return to the Home window.

Displaying Time and Billing Reports

The various Time and Billing reports provide different ways of organizing the same information. You can view the reports by customer, by employee and by activity.

Customer Time and Billing Report

Click   the **Report Centre icon** in the Home window. **Click Time & Billing**. **Click** the ⊞ beside **Billing** and beside **Payroll** to expand the list of available reports:

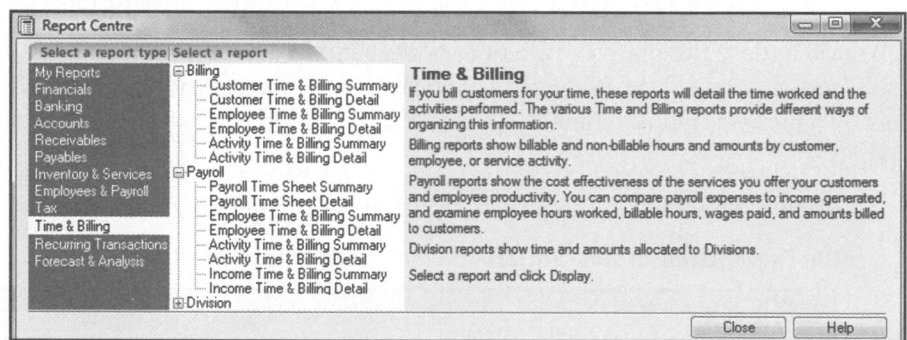

Click   **Customer Time & Billing Summary** under **Billing**. **Click Modify This Report**:

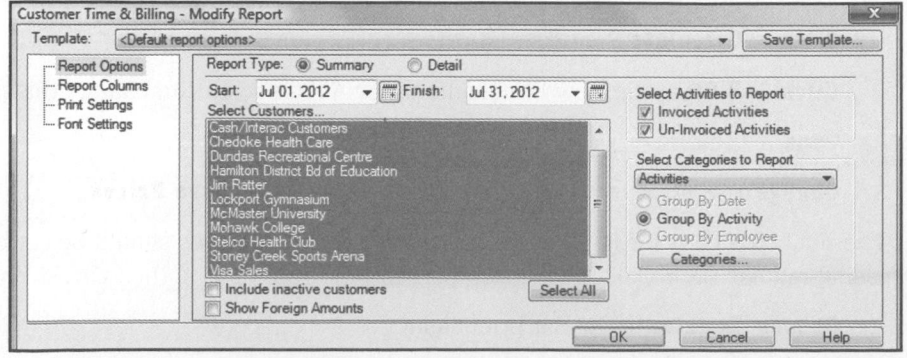

Time and Billing reports by customer show the time and billed amounts organized by customer. Summary and Detail reports are available. **Detail** reports include a report line for each activity or employee on each time slip while the **Summary** reports show only the totals for each selected category (activity or employee). You can select one or more customers for inclusion in the report. The reports will include columns for several billing details — actual time spent on activities, billable time, billable percentage (the proportion of the total time worked for which the customer was charged), billable amounts and invoiced amounts. In addition, if you changed the prices for any of the services, the report will show these changes as amounts written down or up. In the report, the invoiced amounts will then be different from the billable amounts. The effective billable percentage shows the relation between the invoiced amount and the billable amount. The non-billable time, no-charge time, amounts written down or up as percentages of the billable amounts are not in the default report, but you can add them by customizing the report columns. The default columns may also be removed. The report details can also be grouped — by date, by activity or by employee.

You can include **invoiced activities** (bills have been sent) or **uninvoiced activities** (bills have not been created and sent) or both.

The next decision for the report relates to the **categories** you want to include. You can report on the time spent according to the **activities** performed for the customer, or according to the **employee** who completed the work or both. In all cases, the categories are shown for each customer you selected.

Enter	**Start** and **Finish dates** for the report (including the year).
Choose	the **customers** for the report. **Press** and **hold** `ctrl` and **click** the **customer names** to begin a new selection. Then **click Select All** to include all customers.
Choose	the **invoicing details** for the report. **Click** a **detail** to remove a ✓ or to add it.
Click	the **Select Categories To Report list arrow** to select activities or employees or both.
Click	the **Categories button** to open the secondary selection list.

If you choose Activity, you will see the list of activities:

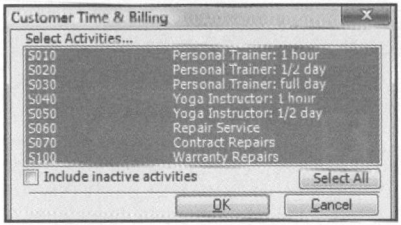

If you choose Employees as the category, you must select from the employee list. If you choose both Activity and Employees, you must choose from lists for both.

Initially, all activities are selected and clicking will change the selection. The selection acts like a toggle switch. To begin a new selection of activities,

Click	**Select All** to clear all selections.
Press	and **hold** `ctrl` and **click** the **activities** you want in the report to begin a new selection. Then **click Select All** to include all activities.
Click	**OK** to return to the report options screen.
Click	**OK** to see the report.

The report shows the amount of time worked for each customer according to the activity, employee or both, depending on the category you selected.

Close	the **report** when you have finished.

NOTES

Remember that Select All acts as a toggle switch. Initially, all items (or customers) are selected. Clicking Select All will clear the selection. If no items or a few items are selected, clicking Select All will include all items.

NOTES

When you select two categories, you can group the report details by either one.

Employee and Activity Time and Billing Reports

The other two Time and Billing reports are similar to the Time By Customer Report, except that they organize the amounts by employee or by activity. The first options screen for the **Employee Time & Billing Report** (Summary or Detail) will show the Employee list, and the second selection screen will list the customers, the activities or both, depending on the category you choose. The Time by Employee Report shows the time and billed amounts for each employee for each customer, each activity or both, depending on the categories you choose.

Similarly, the first options screen for the **Activity Time & Billing Report** (Summary or Detail) will show the Activity list, and the second selection screen will list the customers, the employees or both, depending on the category you choose. The Time by Activity Report shows the time and the billed amounts for each activity for each customer or by each employee or both, depending on the category you choose.

Other report options are the same as they are for the Time by Customer Report, and both reports are available as a Summary or a Detail report.

Payroll Time Sheet Reports

The Time Sheet Report provides a summary of the hours of each income category that is on the time sheets. The number of hours of non-payroll, regular payroll and overtime for each employee can be included.

Click   Payroll Time Sheet Summary under **Payroll. Click Modify This Report:**

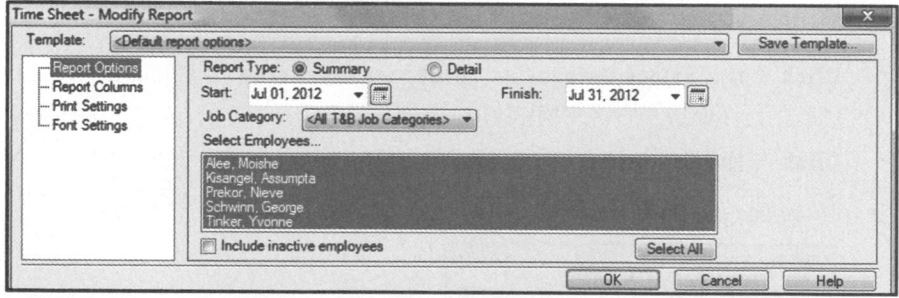

The **Summary** Report will provide the total number of hours in each payroll category (Non-payroll, Regular and Overtime 1 — the payroll category in the ledger record for the activity) for each employee selected for each time period during the report interval. The **Detail** Report will show the number of hours in each payroll category for each time sheet.

You can customize the report by selecting columns for the payroll category. Non-payroll, Regular and Overtime 1 columns may be selected.

Enter   Start and **Finish dates** for the report (including the year).

Choose the **employees** for the report. **Press** and **hold** ⌊ctrl⌋ and **click** the **employee names** to begin a new selection. Then **click Select All** to include all employees.

Click   OK to display the report.

Close   the **report** when you have finished.

Employee Time and Billing Payroll Reports

The remaining Payroll Time reports provide information about the cost effectiveness of the service activities by comparing the labour costs with the income generated — the amount billed to the customer. Employee productivity is also measured by examining the actual hours, billable hours, payroll hours, wages paid and invoiced amounts.

Click   Employee Time & Billing Summary under **Payroll**.

Click   Modify This Report:

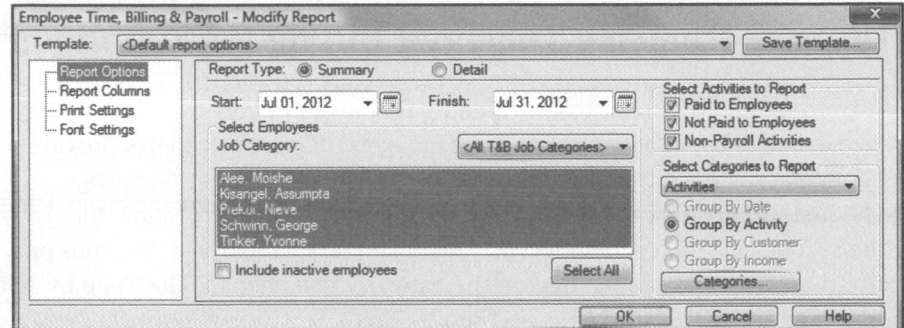

Summary and Detail reports are available. **Detail** reports include a report line for each time sheet entry while the **Summary** reports show only the totals for each selected category. You can select one or more employees for inclusion in the report. The reports will include several time and billing **details** — actual time spent on activities, payroll time, billable time, billable amounts, the actual payroll expense and the productivity ratio (the billable amount compared to the payroll expense) can be included. The effective productivity ratio percentage shows the relation between the invoiced amount and the payroll expense amount. Payroll percentage (payroll time as a proportion of actual time) and billable percentage (the proportion of the total time worked for which the customer was charged) can be added to the report when you customize the report by selecting these time and billing details (report columns). The default report columns may be included or removed.

The report can include **activities** for which you have **paid** the employees, activities that have **not yet been paid**, activities that are **non-payroll** or all three payroll details.

The next decision for the report relates to the **categories** you want to include. You can report on the time spent according to the **activity** performed by the employee, according to the **customer** for whom the work was completed, or according to the **income** (that is, regular, non-payroll or overtime) or any two of these three categories. In all cases, the categories are shown for each employee you selected.

When you choose two categories for the report, you can group report details by one of them — select from date, activity, customer or income.

Enter   Start and **Finish dates** for the report (including the year).

Choose the **employees** for the report. **Press** and **hold** (ctrl) and **click** the **employee names** to begin a new selection. Then **click Select All** to include all employees.

Choose the **payroll details**. **Click** a **detail** to add or to remove a ✓.

Choose the **categories** for the report from the drop-down list.

Click the **Categories button** to open the secondary selection list.

If you select the Activities category, you will see the complete list of all services defined as activities in the ledger.

Choose the **activities** for the report. **Press** and **hold** `ctrl` and **click** the **activity names** to begin a new selection. Then **click Select All** to include all activities.

Click **OK** to return to the report options screen.

Click **OK** to see the report. By default the report will print in landscape orientation (sideways on the page) so that all details can fit on a line.

Close the **report** when you have finished.

Activity and Income Time and Billing Payroll Reports

These two reports are similar to the Time by Employee Report except that they organize amounts by activity or by income category. The three reports provide essentially the same information but organize the details in different ways.

The first options screen for the **Time by Activity Report** will show the Activity list, and the second selection screen will list the customers, employees, incomes or any two of these that you select, depending on the category you choose. The Time by Activity Report shows the same details as the Time by Employee Report but lists them for each activity for each customer, each employee, each income or any two of these, depending on the categories you choose.

Similarly, the first options screen for the **Time by Income Report** will show the income list, and the second selection screen will list the customers, the employees, activities or any two of these three, depending on the category you choose. The Time by Income Report shows the same details as the Time by Employee Report but lists them for each activity for each customer, by each employee, each activity or any two of these, depending on the categories you choose.

Other report options are the same as they are for the Time by Employee Report, and both reports are available as a Summary or a Detail report.

Multiple Fiscal Periods and Reports

After you have accumulated two fiscal periods of financial data, you can produce historical reports for these additional periods. Data for the current and previous years are always available, unless you have cleared the information.

Print the **financial reports** for July (Income Statement, Balance Sheet, Trial Balance, Supplier and Customer Aged reports, Employee Summary Report and Inventory Summary and Quantity reports).

Prepare a **list** of inventory items that should be ordered.

Choose the **Maintenance menu** and **click Start New Year** to begin a new fiscal year.

Choose Yes when asked if you want to Back Up Your Data Files Before Beginning The New Fiscal Year and follow the backup instructions.

Choose No when asked if you want to clear the old data.

The Update Locking Date screen opens.

Enter **08/01/12** as the new date. **Click OK** to update the earliest transaction.

Choose the **Setup menu**, then **click Settings**, **Company** and **Information**:

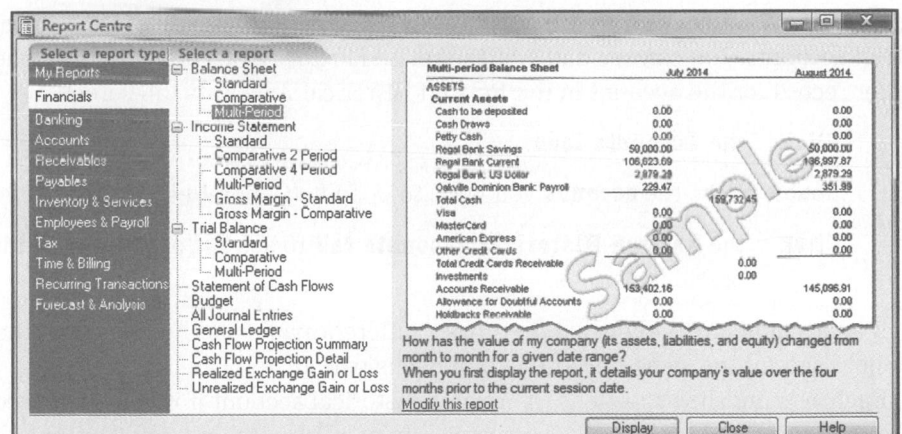

Notice that the first fiscal period, April 1 to June 30, 2012, is now listed in the section for Historical Financial Year Dates.

Drag through the **Fiscal End date**.

Type   08-31-12   **Click OK** to save the date and return to the Home window.

Multi-Period Financial Reports

Multiple-period reports are available for the Balance Sheet, Income Statement and Trial Balance. All are accessed from the Financials list of reports.

Click   the **Report Centre icon**.

Click   **Financials** to expand this list of reports.

Click   the ⊞ beside **Balance Sheet**, **Income Statement** and **Trial Balance** to expand the Select A Report list. **Click Multi-Period** under **Balance Sheet** as shown:

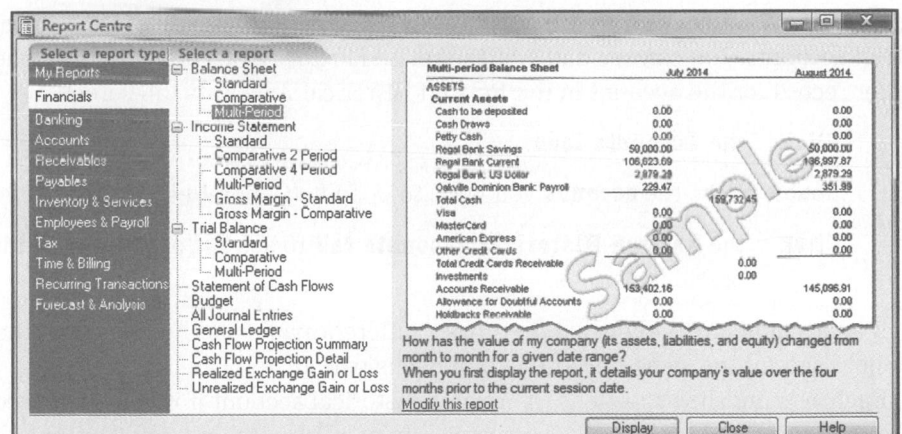

> **NOTES**
> From the Home window, choose the Reports menu, Financials, Multi-Period Reports, and click Balance Sheet, Income Statement or Trial Balance.

Click   **Modify This Report**:

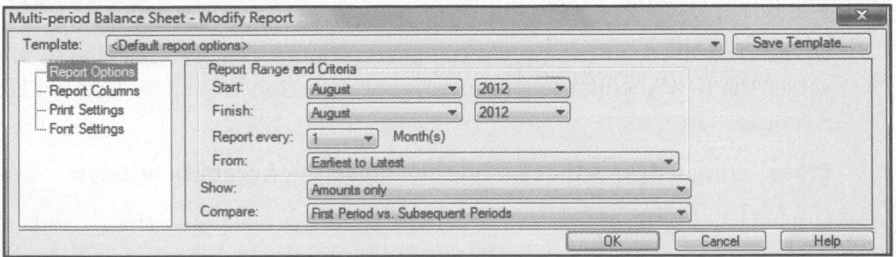

> **NOTES**
> Dates before the previous fiscal period that are eligible for the report will show in the Historical Financial Year Dates section of the Company Information screen on this page.

From the Home window, choose the Reports menu, then choose Financials and Multi-Period Reports and click Balance Sheet to see the report options.

NOTES
The Pro version stores up to seven years of historical financial data; the Premium version stores up to 99 years of data.

The regular financial reports available in comparative form compare two fiscal periods or dates. Reports for the previous fiscal period are also available in regular reports. The multi-period reports show more than two periods and can include multiple fiscal periods before the previous one.

For Flabuless Fitness, monthly data can be viewed in a single report for April, the first month for which we entered financial data in Simply Accounting, to July.

There are several options for displaying the report. You can show the balances for each month for any interval ranging from one to 12 months. The report can be ordered from the earliest period to the latest or from latest to earliest. You can show Amounts Only, Difference In Percentage or Difference In Amounts, just as you do for regular comparative reports. And you can compare the first period with each subsequent period, or you can compare each period with subsequent periods.

After choosing the options for the report,

Click   **OK** to see the report.

Close   the **report** when you have finished.

The **Income Statement** and **Trial Balance** are available for the same periods as the Balance Sheet. They have the same report options. To see these reports,

Click   **Multi-Period under Income Statement** (or **Trial Balance**) and then **click Modify This Report**.

Choose   the **report options** and **click OK**.

Close   the **report** when you have finished. **Close** the **Report Centre**.

Related Historical Accounts

Because we have advanced to the next (third) fiscal period, we can see the list of related accounts. You can see and edit the related historical accounts in the General Ledger record for the account in the Related Historical Accounts tab screen.

Click   the **Accounts icon**.

Double click   the **account** you want to open its General Ledger record.

Click   the **Related Historical Accounts tab** to see the accounts used in previous periods.

If an account currently being used has a different name and number than the account used for the same purpose in a previous period, you can link them.

Each account shows itself as the related historical account if it has been used for more than two fiscal periods. Each account can be related to only one account. Therefore, if the account is already related to itself, you cannot select it again. Instead, you can link a new account to the old one.

Open the record for the previously used account. Select a fiscal year and then select the new account from the account selection list in the Related Historical Accounts tab.

Close   the **Ledger window** and then **close** the **Accounts window**.

If you have used different accounts for the same purpose over the periods and you have related them, you can add the related accounts to the Account List. To see the report of related account numbers,

Choose the **Reports menu**, then **choose Lists** and **click Accounts**.

Click   **Include Related Historical Accounts** and then **click OK** to see the
report.

The report will list all General Ledger accounts with the current information and
the accounts that were used for those same purposes in previous fiscal periods — the
information that is stored in the General Ledger Related Historical Accounts tab fields.

Close   the **report** when you have finished.

Close   the **Home window** to exit the Simply Accounting program.

R E V I E W

The Student DVD with Data Files includes Review
Questions and Supplementary Cases for this chapter.

OBJECTIVES

After completing this chapter, you should be able to

- **activate** departmental accounting
- **create** departments
- **add** departments to accounts, vendors and clients
- **add** departments in journal entries
- **apply** line discounts in sales journal entries
- **display** and **print** department reports

COMPANY INFORMATION

Company Profile

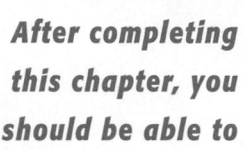
Able & Associates Inc. is a partnership of two chartered accountants, Count and Memor Able. They began their practice in Huntsville, Ontario, two years ago, shortly after receiving their C.A. designations. They each invested capital to start up the office. By relying extensively on electronic communications, remote access to client computers and frequent phone calls, they are able to serve clients throughout a large geographic area. Only occasional on-site meetings are required and local clients often come to their office. Most of their revenue comes from auditing and preparing regular financial statements and income tax returns for small business clients. They share office space and office expenses, including a full-time office assistant. Count works in the office full time, but Memor is there only four days a week, spending the other day working in a small family business. Thus, they allocate their joint expenses using a 60/40 percent division.

Most of the clients have contracts with Able & Associates and pay fees on a monthly basis. These clients are entitled to a discount of 2 percent of their fees if they pay within 10 days of the invoice date. Full payment is requested within 30 days. One-time clients do not receive discounts. Some regular vendors also offer discounts for early payment.

On March 31, at the end of the fiscal period, they decided to use the departmental accounting feature in Simply Accounting to track their financial performance. Payroll taxes were remitted at year-end. To prepare for allocating opening account balances to departments, all opening account balances were transferred to unallocated accounts in the corresponding financial statement section. The following business information was used to set up the accounts:

- Chart of Accounts
- Post-Closing Trial Balance and Statement of Opening Account Balances
- Vendor Information
- Client Information
- Employee Information
- Accounting Procedures

CHART OF POSTABLE ACCOUNTS

ABLE & ASSOCIATES INC.

ASSETS
- 10800 Bank: Chequing
- 11000 Investments
- 11200 Prepaid Association Dues
- 11400 Prepaid Subscriptions
- 11600 Prepaid Insurance
- 12000 Accounts Receivable
- 13400 Office Supplies
- 14400 Office Equipment
- 14800 Office Furniture
- 15000 Library ▶

▶LIABILITIES
- 21000 Bank Loan
- 22000 Accounts Payable
- 22500 Visa Payable
- 23000 EI Payable
- 23100 CPP Payable
- 23200 Income Tax Payable
- 24200 WSIB Payable
- 26500 HST Charged on Services
- 26700 HST Paid on Purchases

EQUITY
- 34500 Invested Capital: C. Able ▶

- ▶34800 Invested Capital: M. Able
- 35500 Retained Earnings
- 36000 Current Earnings

REVENUE
- 41000 Revenue from Services
- 41500 Revenue from Interest
- 41800 Other Revenue
- 42000 Sales Discounts

EXPENSE
- 51200 Association Dues
- 51300 Bank and Card Fees ▶

- ▶51400 Interest Expense
- 51500 Insurance Expense
- 51600 Publicity and Promotion
- 51800 Purchase Discounts
- 52000 Subscriptions
- 52200 Telephone Expense
- 52400 Rent
- 54000 Salaries
- 54100 EI Expense
- 54200 CPP Expense
- 54300 WSIB Expense

NOTES: The Chart of Accounts includes only postable accounts and the Current Earnings account. Able & Associates use five-digit account numbers for the General Ledger accounts.

POST-CLOSING TRIAL BALANCE

ABLE & ASSOCIATES INC.

April 1, 2012	Debits	Credits			Debits	Credits
10800 Bank: Chequing	$ 21 300		▶ 21000 Bank Loan			$ 15 000
11000 Investments	44 000		22000 Accounts Payable			2 260
11200 Prepaid Association Dues	2 800		22500 Visa Payable			1 400
11400 Prepaid Subscriptions	1 500		26500 HST Charged on Services			2 200
11600 Prepaid Insurance	4 500		26700 HST Paid on Purchases		1 640	
12000 Accounts Receivable	2 260		34500 Invested Capital: C. Able			33 000
13400 Office Supplies	1 800		34800 Invested Capital: M. Able			22 000
14400 Office Equipment	12 000		35500 Retained Earnings			28 740
14800 Office Furniture	8 000				$104 600	$104 600
15000 Library	4 800	▶				

STATEMENT OF ACCOUNT OPENING BALANCES

ABLE & ASSOCIATES INC.

April 1, 2012	Debits	Credits			Debits	Credits
19500 Unassigned Assets	$102 960	▶	29500 Unassigned Liabilities			$ 19 220
			39500 Unassigned Capital			83 740
					$102 960	$102 960

Note: The true account balances are shown for the regular postable accounts in the Trial Balance. The three unassigned accounts in the Statement of Opening Balances are temporary holding accounts. The temporary balance in these accounts is the sum of all balances for that section of the Balance Sheet (which temporarily have zero balances). These balances will be transferred back to the regular accounts to set up the departmental opening balances.

VENDOR INFORMATION

ABLE & ASSOCIATES INC.

Vendor Name (Contact)	Address	Phone No. Fax No.	E-mail Web Site	Terms Tax ID
Bell Canada (Yap Long)	500 Central Line Huntsville, Ontario P1F 2C2	Tel: (705) 466-2355	yap.l@bell.ca www.bell.ca	net 1
Muskoka Maintenance (M. Handimann)	72 Spoiler St. Huntsville, Ontario P1P 2B8	Tel: (705) 469-0808 Fax: (705) 469-6222	handimann@yahoo.com	2/10, n/30 295 416 822
Northlands Office Mgt. (Hi Bilding)	59 Condor St. Huntsville, Ontario P1D 4F4	Tel: (705) 283-9210 Fax: (705) 283-2310	bilding@northlands.com	net 1
Office Plus (B. Laser)	4 Paper Corners Huntsville, Ontario P1E 1G1	Tel: (705) 466-3335	www.officeplus.ca	1/15, n/30 822 101 500
Receiver General for Canada	Sudbury Tax Services Office PO Box 20004 Sudbury, ON P3A 6B4	Tel 1: (800) 561-7761 Tel 2: (800) 959-2221	www.cra-arc.gc.ca	net 1

OUTSTANDING VENDOR INVOICES

ABLE & ASSOCIATES INC.

Vendor Name	Terms	Date	Invoice No.	Amount	Total
Office Plus	1/15, n/30	Mar. 21/12	OP-2339	$2 260	$2 260

CLIENT INFORMATION

ABLE & ASSOCIATES INC.

Client Name (Contact)	Address	Phone No. Fax No.	E-mail Web Site	Terms Credit Limit
Adrienne Aesthetics (Adrienne Kosh)	65 Bytown Ave. Ottawa, Ontario K2C 4R1	Tel 1: (613) 722-9876 Tel 2: (613) 722-8701 Fax: (613) 722-8000	a.kosh@adrienneaesthetics.com www.adrienneaesthetics.com	2/10, n/30 $10 000
Flabuless Fitness (Stephen Reeves)	199 Warmup Rd., Unit 500 Hamilton, Ontario L8T 3B7	Tel: (905) 642-2348 Fax: (905) 642-9100	sreeves@flabfit.com www.flabfit.com	2/10, n/30 $10 000
Gorgeous Gifts (Gitte Gurlosi)	600 First St. Huntsville, Ontario P1L 2W4	Tel: (705) 462-1203 Fax: (705) 462-3394	gg@ggifts.com www.ggifts.com	2/10, n/30 $10 000
Truman Tires (Tyrone Truman)	600 Westminster St. London, Ontario N6P 3B1	Tel: (519) 729-3733 Fax: (519) 729-7301	tt@trumantires.com www.trumantires.com	2/10, n/30 $10 000

OUTSTANDING CLIENT INVOICES

ABLE & ASSOCIATES INC.

Client Name	Terms	Date	Invoice No.	Amount	Total
Adrienne Aesthetics	2/10, n/30	Mar. 25/12	843	$2 260	$2 260

ABLE & ASSOCIATES INC.

Tryin, Reelie (Office Assistant)

Social Insurance No.	429 535 644	Total Federal (Ontario) Tax Exemption - TD1 $10 382 (8 943)
Address	200 Water St. #301 Huntsville, Ontario P1H 2L8	Employee Income (Reg. hours) Salary $3 800 /month (150 hours)
Telephone	(705) 446-2190	
Date of Birth (mm-dd-yy)	04-04-78	WSIB Rate 0.89
EI, CPP & Income Tax	Calculations built into Simply Accounting program	

Accounting Procedures

Taxes (HST)

Able & Associates Inc. is a professional service business using the regular method of calculating HST. HST, at the rate of 13 percent, is charged on all services and paid on purchases. The difference between the HST charged and HST paid is remitted to the Receiver General for Canada quarterly.

Departments

Able & Associates has two departments, one for each partner. The division of most assets is 60 percent and 40 percent, to be consistent with their initial investments in the partnership and their time in the office.

Discounts for Early Payments

Able & Associates offers discounts to regular clients if they pay their accounts within 10 days. Full payment is expected in 30 days. No discounts are allowed on partial payments. Different discounts are applied occasionally for clients in special circumstances. These are entered as line discounts for the sales.

Some vendors with whom Able & Associates has accounts set up also offer discounts for early payments.

> **NOTES**
> Able & Associates Inc. pays GST at the rate of 5 percent on subscriptions to professional journals and other books purchased for the business.

INSTRUCTIONS

1. **Set up two departments** for Able & Associates.

2. **Record entries for the source documents** in Simply Accounting. Transactions indicated with a ✓ in the completion box beside the source document have step-by-step keystroke instructions on the pages indicated.

3. **Print** the following **reports and graphs** after you have finished making your entries. Instructions for departmental reports begin on page 799.

   a. Comparative Balance Sheet with Departments for April 1 and April 30.
   b. Income Statement with Departments for April 1 to April 30.
   c. Departmental Income Statement.
   d. Journal Report for April 1 to April 30 for all journals.

NOTES
This exercise has few source documents so we use a single session date for all transactions.

NOTES
Remember to reverse the usual liability entries for HST Paid on Purchases because this account normally has a debit balance.

NOTES
You will be unable to allocate the payment to Office Plus because more than one department is involved and you cannot select accounts for the payments. As for the cash purchase, you can choose only one bank account, so this amount also remains unallocated.

SOURCE DOCUMENTS

SESSION DATE — APRIL 30, 2012

✓ **Memo #1**   **Dated April 1/12**

786   Create two departments for Able & Associates:
      1001: C. Able   2001: M. Able

✓ **Memo #2**   **Dated April 1/12**

788   Assign accounts to departments. Invested Capital accounts are used by the department named in the account. All accounts are used by both departments.

✓ **Memo #3**   **Dated April 1/12**

789   Assign departmental opening account balances by transferring the unassigned balances from the chart below. Add linked accounts and then finish the history.

	Department	1001: C. Able	2001: M. Able	Source
10800	Bank: Chequing	$ 12 780	$ 8 520	Debit from Unassigned Assets
11000	Investments	26 500	17 500	Debit from Unassigned Assets
11200	Prepaid Association Dues	1 400	1 400	Debit from Unassigned Assets
11400	Prepaid Subscriptions	900	600	Debit from Unassigned Assets
11600	Prepaid Insurance	2 700	1 800	Debit from Unassigned Assets
12000	Accounts Receivable	2 260		Debit from Unassigned Assets
13400	Office Supplies	1 080	720	Debit from Unassigned Assets
14400	Office Equipment	7 200	4 800	Debit from Unassigned Assets
14800	Office Furniture	4 000	4 000	Debit from Unassigned Assets
15000	Library	2 400	2 400	Debit from Unassigned Assets
21000	Bank Loan	9 000	6 000	Credit from Unassigned Liabilities
22000	Accounts Payable	1 356	904	Credit from Unassigned Liabilities
22500	Visa Payable	840	560	Credit from Unassigned Liabilities
26500	HST Charged on Services	1 320	880	Credit from Unassigned Liabilities
26700	HST Paid on Purchases	984	656	Debit from Unassigned Liabilities
34500	Invested Capital: C. Able	33 000		Credit from Unassigned Capital
34800	Invested Capital: M. Able		22 000	Credit from Unassigned Capital
35500	Retained Earnings	17 244	11 496	Credit from Unassigned Capital

✓ **Memo #4**   **Dated April 1/12**

792   Clients: Assign C. Able to Adrienne Aesthetics and M. Able to Flabuless Fitness. The remaining clients are associated with both departments.

✓ **Cash Purchase Invoice #NO-2012-4**   **Dated April 3/12**

793   From Northlands Office Mgt., $1 400 plus $182 HST for rental of office suite. Invoice total, $1 582 paid by cheque #3011. $840 (60 percent) of the expense should be assigned to C. Able and $560 (40 percent) to M. Able.

✓ **Cash Receipt #48**   **Dated April 4/12**

794   From Adrienne Aesthetics, cheque #3101 for $2 214.80, including $45.20 discount in full payment of invoice #843. Assign all amounts to C. Able.

✓ **Sales Invoice #851**   **Dated April 5/12**

795   To Adrienne Aesthetics, $5 800 plus $754 HST for auditing financial statements and $900 plus $117 HST for monthly accounting fee. Invoice total $7 243.30. Terms: 2/10, n/30. Additional 5 percent discount applies to the fee for auditing, by special arrangement with client. Adrienne Aesthetics is C. Able's client.

☐ **Cheque Copy #3012**   **Dated April 5/12**

To Office Plus, $2 237.40, including $22.60 discount in full payment of invoice #OP-2339. (You cannot assign these amounts — see margin notes.)

☐ **Cash Sales Invoice #852**   **Dated April 10/12**

To Truman Tires, $1 000 plus $130 HST for monthly fee for accounting assistance. Assign $600 (60%) of the fee to C. Able and $400 (40%) to M. Able. Received cheque #2900 for $1 107.40 in full payment, including 2% discount for early payment. (See margin notes.)

NOTES
For the sale to Truman Tires, enter 600 as the amount for account 41000 - 1001, and on the second line, enter 400 as the amount for account 41000 - 2001. The amounts for Bank: Chequing, Sales Discounts and HST will remain unallocated.

☐ **Sales Invoice #853**   **Dated April 14/12**

To Flabuless Fitness, $5 000 plus HST for preparing special financial reports for potential investors and $700 plus HST for monthly accounting fee. Invoice total $5 876 (with discount). Terms: 2/10, n/30. Additional 10 percent discount applies to the fee for preparing financial reports. Assign 100% of all amounts to M. Able.

☐ **Sales Invoice #854**   **Dated April 20/12**

To Gorgeous Gifts, $3 000 plus $390 HST for assistance with response to Canada Revenue Agency audit and $500 plus $65 HST for monthly accounting fee. Invoice total $3 955. Terms: 2/10, n/30. Assign $1 800 plus $300 (60%) of revenue amounts to C. Able and $1 200 and $200 (40%) to M. Able.

☐ **Cash Purchase Invoice #BC-233008**   **Dated April 22/12**

From Bell Canada, $400 plus $52 HST for monthly telephone and Internet service for one multi-line office telephone, two mobile phones and networked Internet service. Invoice total, $452 paid by cheque #3013. Assign $240 (60%) of expense amount to C. Able and $160 (40%) to M. Able.

☐ **Purchase Invoice #OP-5102**   **Dated April 25/12**

From Office Plus, $3 000 plus $390 HST for new boardroom table and chairs (Office Furniture account). Invoice total $3 390. Terms: 1/15, n/30. Assign $1 800 (60%) of the asset account amount to C. Able and $1 200 (40%) to M. Able. (See margin notes.)

NOTES
For the purchase from Office Plus, enter 1800 as the amount for account 14800 - 1001, and on the second line, enter 1200 as the amount for account 14800 - 2001. The amounts for Accounts Payable and HST will remain unallocated.

☐ **Memo #5**   **Dated April 25/12**

Remit the HST owing to the Receiver General as at March 31. Issue cheque #3014. Assign $1 320 for HST Charged on Services and $984 for HST Paid (60% of HST amounts) to C. Able and $880 for HST Charged on Services and $656 for HST Paid (40%) to M. Able.

☐ **Cash Sales Invoice #855**   **Dated April 30/12**

To various one time clients, $6 000 plus $780 HST for personal income tax preparation. Total cash received $6 780 deposited to bank account. Assign $3 600 (60%) of revenue amount to C. Able and $2 400 (40%) to M. Able.

☑ **Memo #6**   **Dated April 30/12**

796

Prepare payroll for Tryin, office assistant. Issue cheque #3015. Assign 60% of all amounts to C. Able and 40% to M. Able.

☐ **Memo #7**   **Dated April 30/12**

The following transactions appeared on the monthly bank statement for the bank chequing account. Assign 60% of all amounts to C. Able and 40% to M. Able.

	Amounts for C. Able	Amounts for M. Able
Bank charges $60	$ 36	$ 24
Bank Loan principal $300	180	120
Bank Loan interest $200	120	80
Interest on Chequing account $60	36	24
Interest from Investments $180	108	72
Bank net withdrawal $320	192	128

☐   **Memo #8**   **Dated April 30/12**

Enter the adjustments for supplies used and prepaid expenses expired in April. Assign all amounts as indicated in the following summary. Create new Group Expense account 52600 Supplies Used.

	Amounts for C. Able	Amounts for M. Able
Office Supplies $100	$ 60	$ 40
Prepaid Insurance $500	300	200
Prepaid Association Dues $400	200	200
Prepaid Subscriptions $250	150	100

KEYSTROKES

Departmental Accounting

Most companies are divided into departments such as sales, marketing, service, finance, human resources and manufacturing. And most companies want to track the costs and performance of these departments separately. The departmental accounting feature in Simply Accounting permits more detailed company reporting and analysis.

Unlike projects that work only through journal entries, departments are connected to all ledgers and journals. Departments can be associated with individual accounts, vendors and clients, and you can choose departments for accounts in journal entries.

Each account may be used by only one department or by more than one department. For example, automotive parts in a car dealership will be used by the service department but not by the human resources or sales departments. Other accounts, such as a bank account, may be connected to all departments. Similarly, individual vendors, such as a car-parts vendor, may be linked to a specific department while others, such as utility providers, are linked to all departments. Clients, too, may be connected to specific departments. When you set up these connections, the departmental links are added to journal entries automatically, and you can generate detailed reports with departmental information.

Departmental account balances are generated when you add departmental information to journal entries, but they cannot be added as opening account balances in the ledgers. Therefore, ideally, you will add departmental information when you create company files so that you can have departmental information for all accounts. You can also choose to use departments only for income statement accounts and start using departments at the beginning of a fiscal period when these accounts have zero balances.

Setting Up Departments

Open   SimData10\Able\able. Enter April 30, 2012 as the session date.

The history for the company files is not finished. Some linked accounts are missing and the ledgers are not balanced. (See margin notes.)

Creating Departments

Before using departmental accounting, you must activate the feature and create the departments. The feature is not turned on by default, and you can add departments to an existing Simply Accounting data file.

⚠ **WARNING!**
You cannot remove departments once you add them and use them, so you should back up data files before adding departments.

📄 **NOTES**
If you are working from backups, you should restore SimData10\able1.CAB to SimData10\Able\able.

📄 **NOTES**
The history for the data set must remain unfinished for now. Accounts Receivable and Accounts Payable accounts are needed in journal entries (to add opening department balances – see page 789), so they have not yet been entered as linked accounts. In addition, Accounts Receivable and Accounts Payable begin with zero balances. As a result, these opening balances do not match the totals of the historical client and vendor invoices.

Click the **Settings icon** , and then **click General (Accounts)** and **Departments**:

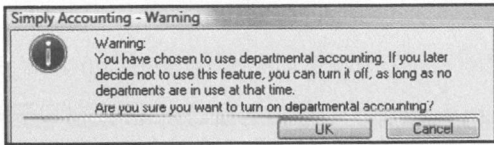

Click **Use Departmental Accounting** to see the warning:

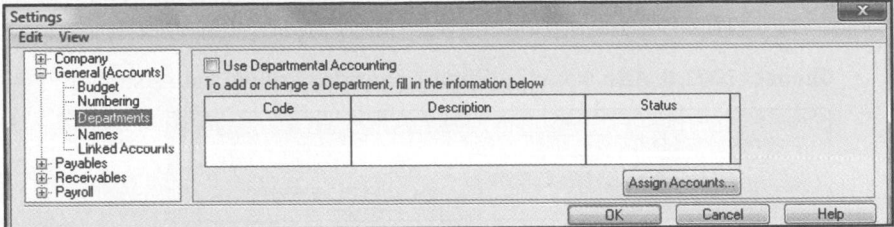

Adding departments is not a reversible step, unless the departments have not yet been used.

Click Cancel if you are not working with a separate copy of the data file. Make a backup first.

Click **OK** to return to the Departments Settings screen.

For each department you want, you must assign a four-digit code and a name.

Click the **Code field**.

Type 1001 **Press** (tab) to advance to the Description field. The Status is automatically set as Active.

Type C. Able

Unused departments can have their status set to Inactive by clicking Active.

Click the **Code field** on the next line. **Type** 2001

Press (tab) to advance to the Description field. **Type** M. Able

Click the **Assign Accounts button** to open the next screen:

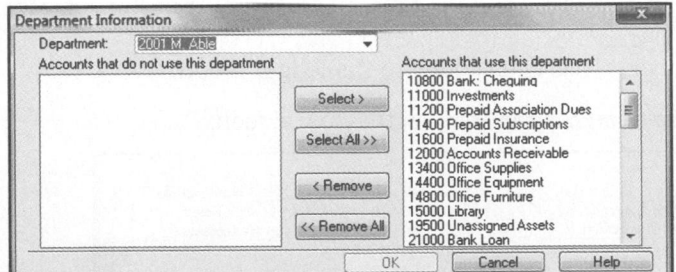

From this screen, you can indicate which accounts use the departments. The cursor was on M. Able in the previous screen, so this department is selected. You can select departments from the drop-down list in the Department field.

Initially, all accounts use all departments. You can select accounts that are to be removed for a department.

The two investment accounts are separated according to the partner, so we should assign each one only to its correct department. That is, we can remove *34500 Capital Investments: C. Able* for M. Able and remove *34800 Capital Investments: M. Able* for C. Able. We are working with the M. Able department first.

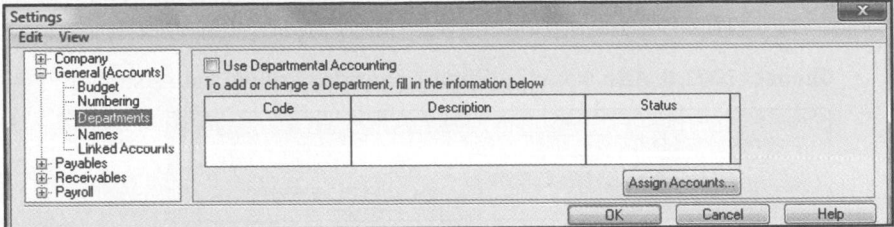

WARNING!
The Department Code must be a four-digit number. No letters or other characters are allowed.

NOTES
Able & Associates uses five-digit account numbers.

Scroll down the list of Accounts That Use This Department.

Click **34500 Invested Capital: C. Able** to select the account.

Click **Remove.** The account moves to the list of Accounts That Do Not Use This Department on the left side of the screen.

Choose **1001 C. Able** from the Department drop-down list as shown:

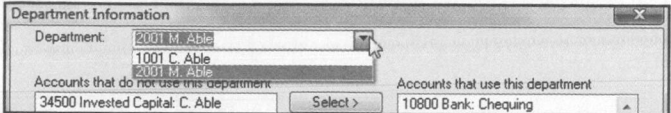

Click **34800 Invested Capital: M. Able** to select the account.

Click **Remove.**

To move an account back to the "Use" list, click it again and then click Select.

Click an account that you want to change and then press and hold (ctrl). Click the next account until all the accounts you want are included.

Click the Remove button to shift the selected accounts to the other column.

Click Remove All to shift all the accounts to the "Do Not Use" column.

If only a few accounts use a department, it is easier to place them all on the "Do Not Use" side and then move the few to the "Use" side.

Reverse this procedure to move an account from the "Do Not Use" to the "Use" side. Click the account on the "Do Not Use" side and then click the Select button.

Click **OK** to return to the Settings window. **Click OK** to return to the Home window.

Adding Departments to Accounts

Instead of adding department information to accounts from the Department Information window, you can add departments in the account ledger record directly.

Click **Company** in the Modules Pane list. **Click** the **Chart of Accounts icon.**

Double click 34500 Invested Capital: C. Able in the list of accounts to open the General Ledger.

A new tab, Departments, has been added to the ledger record.

Click the **Departments tab** to open the new screen:

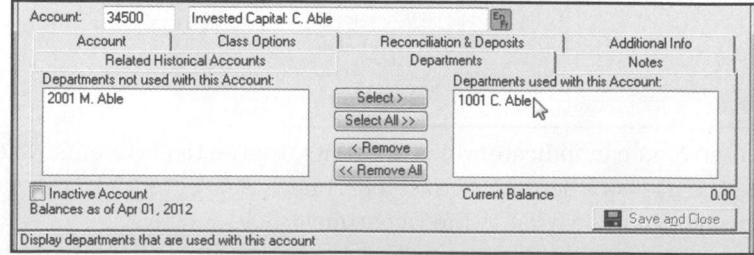

Notice that 2001 M. Able is located on the left side under Departments Not Used With This Account because we moved it earlier on the Settings screen. 1001 C. Able is in the Departments Used With This Account column.

On this screen, you can designate the departments that the account uses. You can modify these selections at any time. You can see that this screen is the same as the one for Department Information, except that now we are "moving" the department instead of the account. However, in the General Ledger, you change the information for only one account at a time.

Click a department to select it or press <u>ctrl</u> and click more than one department if you want to select additional departments. Clicking Select will add the department to the account. Clicking Remove will remove a selected department from the account and place it on the "Not Used" side. Remove All and Select All will move all departments at once to the other side.

Close   the **Ledger window**. **Close** the **Accounts window**.

Adding Opening Departmental Balances

When you create a new company data file and add general ledger accounts, you must enter the opening account balances as well, but you cannot split these balances among the departments. However, when you are entering transactions and have set up departments, you can choose a department from any Account field that allows you to select an account. We will use this approach to enter the opening departmental balances for all accounts. Initially we placed the total for all Balance Sheet accounts in the "unassigned" placeholder accounts for each section. When we transfer these amounts back to their appropriate accounts through General Journal entries, we can also assign departments.

After entering the transfers, the three unassigned accounts should all have zero balances and your Trial Balance should match the one on page 781.

Click   the **General Journal icon** 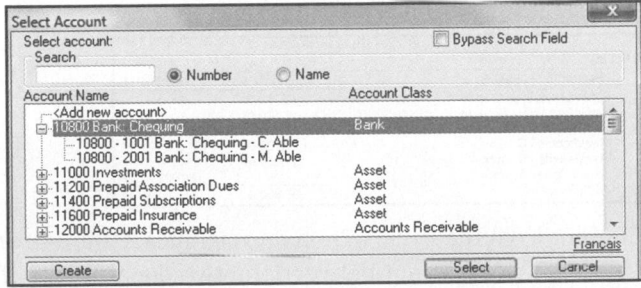.

Enter   **Memo 3A** as the Source, and **enter April 1** as the date.

Click   the **Comment field** and **type** `Transfer opening asset account balances to departments`

Click   the **Account field List icon** 🔍 to see the modified Select Account list.

Each account has a ⊞ icon added to indicate additional information is available. When you click the ⊞, all departments used by that account will be listed, so you can select a department for the transaction.

Click   the ⊞ **icon** beside **10800 Bank: Chequing**:

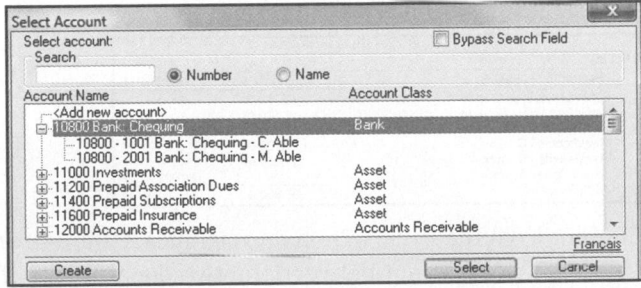

The modified list now shows the departments connected with the account.

Bank: Chequing has both departments available for a journal transaction. If you click the ⊞ beside *34500 Capital Investments: C. Able*, you will see that you can select only the one department that we assigned to it.

Click   **10800 - 1001 Bank: Chequing - C. Able**.

Click   **Select** to return to the journal with the cursor in the Asset field.

Type   `12780` to enter the portion of the asset for this department.

Click   the **Account field list icon** again.

Double click   **10800 - 2001 Bank: Chequing - M. Able**. The cursor advances to the Credits field.

Type   –8520   (add a minus sign to the amount). **Press** (tab). The amount moves to the Debits column because we typed the minus sign.

Click   the **Account field** and **type**   19500

Press   (tab) to enter the total balance for the asset as a credit entry.

Notice that the accounts with departments all use the same format: account number, space, hyphen, space, department number. We can use this format to enter account numbers directly in a journal without using the Select Account list. You can omit the spaces when typing these numbers. Simply Accounting will add them.

Click   the **Account field** on the next blank line.

Type   11000–1001

Press   (tab) to enter the account and advance to the Debits field.

Type   26500

Click   the **Account field** and **type**   11000–2001

Press   (tab) and **type**   –17500   to move the amount to the Debits field.

Click   the **Account field** and **type**   19500   **Press** (tab) to enter the credit amount. At this stage, your journal entry should look like the one below:

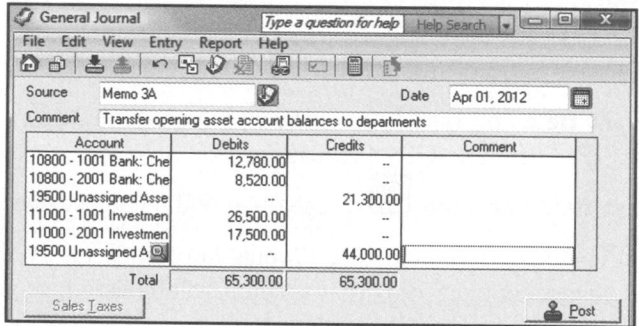

Before continuing, we will review the journal entry.

Press   (ctrl) + **J** to open the journal display:

Able & Associates Inc. General Journal Entry 04/01/2012 (J1)			
Account Number	Account Description	Debits	Credits
10800 - 1001	Bank: Chequing - C. Able	12,780.00	-
10800 - 2001	Bank: Chequing - M. Able	8,520.00	-
19500	Unassigned Assets	-	21,300.00
11000 - 1001	Investments - C. Able	26,500.00	-
11000 - 2001	Investments - M. Able	17,500.00	-
19500	Unassigned Assets	-	44,000.00
Additional Date:	Additional Field:	65,300.00	65,300.00

The journal entry is different from the usual one in one significant way — we were able to divide the balance in each asset account between the two departments. These separate amounts can be added to the standard financial reports and will enable us to produce separate reports for each department.

Close   the **journal display**.

Enter   the **remaining asset account balance transfers** from memo #3 on page 784.

Review   the **journal entry** again to verify that the total debits and credits match the initial account balance for *Unassigned Assets*.

Post   the **journal entry** after entering all the asset account balances.

Enter   the **liability account balance transfers** from memo #3 on page 784 as the second journal entry.

Review   the **transaction** and then **post** it when the amounts are correct.

Enter   the **capital account balance transfers** from memo #3 on page 784 as the third journal entry.

Review   the **transaction** and then **post** it when the amounts are correct.

Close   the **General Journal** to return to the Company module window.

Compare   your **Trial Balance** with the one on page 781 and make corrections if needed.

We are now ready to finish the history for the company files. If you entered the amounts correctly, the account balances for *Accounts Receivable* and *Accounts Payable* should match the historical invoice balances. However, we must still add the missing essential linked accounts.

Finishing the History

To access *Accounts Receivable* and *Accounts Payable* as postable accounts in the General Journal, we did not enter them as linked accounts. To finish the history, you must add these essential linked accounts.

Click   the **Settings icon** . **Click Payables** in the left panel of the Settings window and then **click Linked Accounts**.

Enter   **22000 Accounts Payable** as the linked account for Accounts Payable.

Enter   **22000 Accounts Payable** as the linked account for Prepayments and Prepaid Orders.

Click   **Receivables** in the left panel of the Settings window and then **click Linked Accounts**.

Enter   **12000 Accounts Receivable** as the linked account for Accounts Receivable.

Enter   **12000 Accounts Receivable** as the linked account for Deposits and Prepaid Orders.

Click   **OK** to save the settings.

Choose   the **History menu** and **click Finish Entering History**.

Click   **Backup** and continue to back up the not-finished file. **Click OK** when the backup is complete.

Click   **Proceed** to finish the history.

NOTES
Do not enter sales tax information when prompted for the HST accounts.

NOTES
Remember you can adjust General Journal entries after posting. Refer to page 47.

WARNING!
If you try to finish the history now, you will see the error message that the essential linked accounts are missing.

WARNING!
Make a backup copy of the not-finished file so you can correct opening balance amounts later if necessary.

Adding Departments to Client Records

If some clients or vendors deal with only one department, you can add this information to the ledger record. C. Able has Adrienne Aesthetics as an exclusive client, and Flabuless Fitness deals only with M. Able.

> **Click**   **Receivables** in the Modules pane list. **Click Adrienne Aesthetics** in the Clients List pane to open the record at the Address tab screen.

A Department field is added to the Address tab screen.

> **Click**   the **Department list arrow** to see the drop-down list of departments:

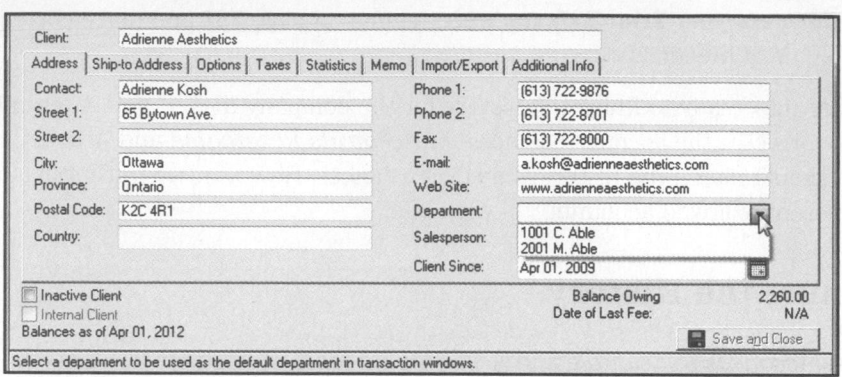

> **Click**   **1001 C. Able** to select the department.

Next we need to select the departmental revenue account as the client's default.

> **Click**   the **Options tab** so you can change the default revenue account.

> **Click**   the **Revenue Account field list arrow** to see the expanded account list:

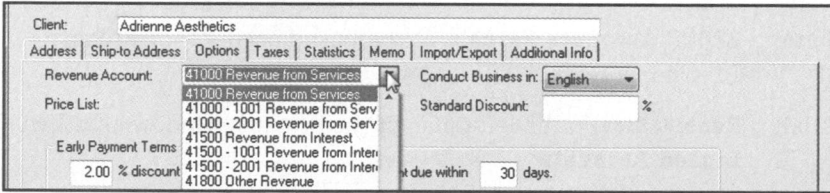

By selecting the departmental account in the ledger record, department information will be added as the default when you sell to this client.

> **Choose**   **41000 - 1001 Revenue from Services - C. Able** from the account list.

> **Click**   the **Next Client tool** ▶ to open the record for Flabuless Fitness.

> **Choose**   **41000 - 2001 Revenue from Services - M. Able** from the Revenue Account list.

> **Click**   the **Address tab** and **enter 2001 M. Able** in the Department field.

> **Click**   **Save And Close** 💾 Save and Close .

The remaining clients work with both departments so we cannot add one department exclusively for them.

Adding Departments to Vendor Records

If a vendor is connected exclusively with one department, you can add the department to the vendor record, just as you do for clients. At this time, all vendors are used by both departments so we will not add departments to the records.

If you want to add departments to vendor records, open the Payables module window and then open the vendor record. The Department field has been added to the Address tab screen.

Click the Department field list arrow to see the departments and click the one you want.

On the Options tab screen, choose the departmental account as the default for expenses.

Repeat this procedure for other vendors. Close the last vendor record.

Adding Departments to Journal Transactions

Entering Departments for Purchases

Adding departmental details to purchases involves selecting the appropriate departmental General Ledger subaccount instead of the main one.

Before proceeding, you should create shortcuts for the journals in other modules.

Create **shortcuts** to create and pay vendor invoices, to create paycheques and to create General Journal entries.

Click the **Pay Vendor Invoices shortcut** to open the journal.

Choose **Make Other Payment** from the transaction (Pay) list.

Choose **Northlands Office Mgt.** as the vendor. **Press** (tab). The default general Rent account and tax code are added from the vendor's record.

Enter **April 3** as the payment date.

Click the **List icon** 🔍 beside *Rent* to open the Select Account screen. **Click** the ⊞ icon beside **52400 Rent**:

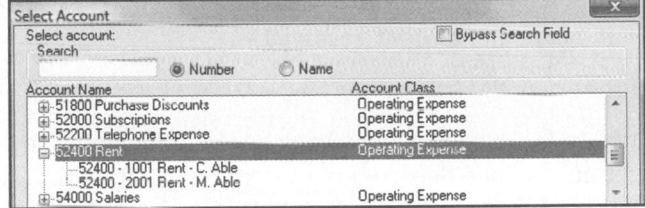

Department subaccounts are added, just as they were in the General Journal.

Click **52400 - 1001 Rent - C. Able**. **Press** (enter) to add the account for C. Able's share.

Click the **Amount field. Type** 840

Click the second journal line **account field List icon.**

Choose **52400 - 2001 Rent - M. Able**. **Press** (enter) to add the account for M. Able's share.

Click the **Amount field. Type** 560

Enter line **Descriptions**, **Source** and **Comment** to complete the entry.

Choose the **Report** menu and **click Display Payments Journal entry**:

Able & Associates Inc. Payments Journal Entry 04/03/2012 (J4)			
Account Number	Account Description	Debits	Credits
26700	HST Paid on Purchases	182.00	-
52400 - 1001	Rent - C. Able	840.00	-
52400 - 2001	Rent - M. Able	560.00	-
10800	Bank: Chequing	-	1,582.00
Additional Date:	Additional Field:	1,582.00	1,582.00

The rental expense amount has been shared between the two departments, but the other amounts have not. Because no single department is linked to the vendor, and the other accounts for the transaction are not accessible, they remain unallocated.

Close the **journal display** to return to the journal.

Click the **From bank account list arrow**:

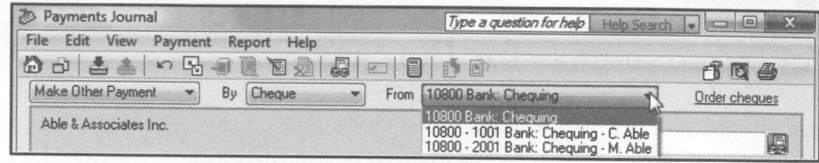

You can change the default bank account for this payment, but you can choose only one account for the single cheque. A complete allocation requires access to both bank department subaccounts. Therefore, you cannot allocate the bank amount.

Make **corrections** if necessary. **Post** the **transaction** and **close** the **journal**.

Entering Departments for Receipts

Restore the **Receivables module** as the Home window if necessary.

Click the **Receipts Journal icon** Receipts▼ to open the journal.

Choose Adrienne Aesthetics. **Press** ⎾tab⏌ to add the outstanding invoice.

Enter **Apr 4 12** as the date and **enter 3101** as the client's cheque number.

Accept the **discount taken** and **amount received**.

Press ⎾ctrl⏌ + **J** to review the transaction.

All amounts are allocated to C. Able except the bank account amount. The accounts are allocated because we set up a unique department link for the client in the ledger record. The allocated amounts are those for the default linked accounts for the journal. In this case, we can also allocate the bank amount because only one department is involved and we can access the account.

Close the **display** to return to the journal.

Click the **Deposit To bank account list arrow**:

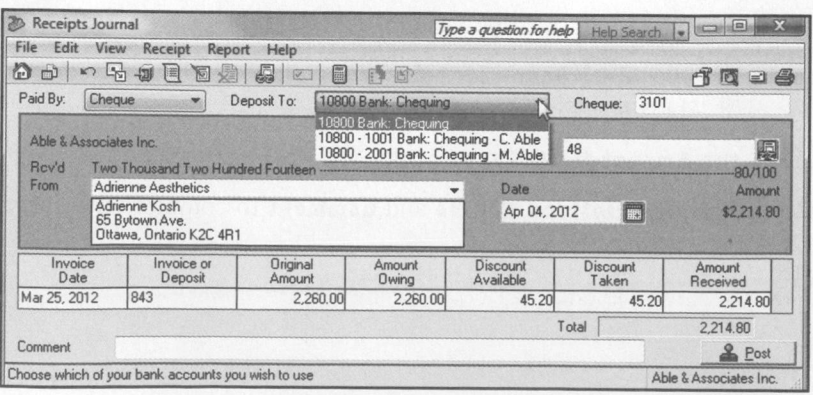

Click   **10800 - 1001 Bank Chequing - C. Able** to update the journal entry.

Press   ⌐ctrl⌐ + **J** to review the transaction:

Able & Associates Inc. Receipts Journal Entry 04/04/2012 (J5)			
Account Number	Account Description	Debits	Credits
10800 - 1001	Bank: Chequing - C. Able	2,214.80	-
42000 - 1001	Sales Discounts - C. Able	45.20	-
12000 - 1001	Accounts Receivable - C. Able	-	2,260.00
Additional Date:	Additional Field:	2,260.00	2,260.00

The entry is now completely allocated and it is correct. All amounts, including the discount, are attributed to C. Able's department.

Close   the **display** to return to the journal.

Make   **corrections** if necessary and **post** the **transaction**.

Close   the **Receipts Journal**.

Entering Departments for Sales

Click   the **Client Invoices icon** Client Invoices▼ to open the Fees journal.

Choose **Adrienne Aesthetics**. **Press** ⌐tab⌐ to add the client's default record details.

Enter   **April 5** as the date. This time the default revenue account is correct:

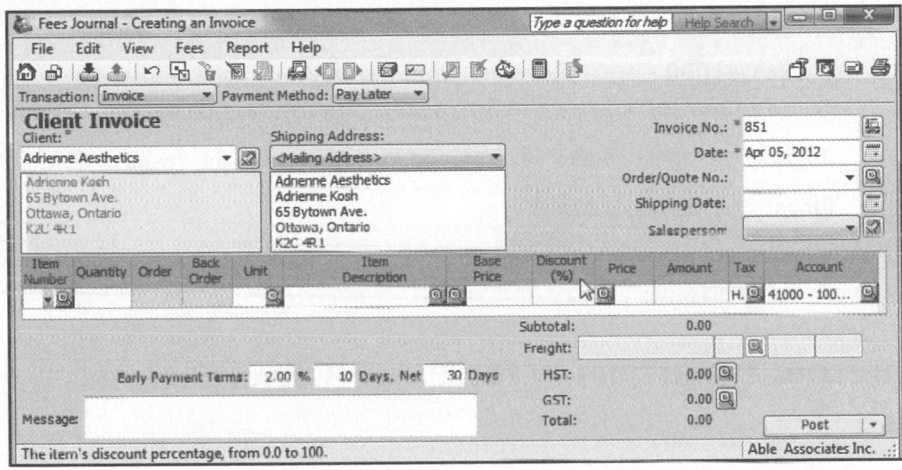

The account is taken from the record because a single department is linked to the client and we added this as the default revenue account.

Two columns — **Base Price** and **Disc. %** — have been added to the journal. These fields allow us to add discounts that apply only to a single invoice line, so you can enter different discount rates for each invoice line. Able & Associates offers discounts for special circumstances. For part of this invoice, a 5 percent discount applies.

Entering Line Discounts

Click   the **Item Description field**.

Type   prepare audited financial statements

Press   ⌐tab⌐ to advance to the Base Price field.

Type   5800

Press   ⌐tab⌐ to advance to the Discount % field.

Type   5

Press (tab) to apply the amount of the discount — $290.00 — and add $5 510, the new discounted unit price, to the Price field.

To have the amount entered automatically, you can enter the quantity for the line.

Click   the **Quantity field**. **Type** 1 **Press** (tab) to update the line.

The discounted amount, $5 510, is now entered as the amount.

Press   (ctrl) + **J** to review the transaction as we have entered it so far:

Able & Associates Inc. Fees Journal Entry 04/05/2012 (J6)			
Account Number	Account Description	Debits	Credits
12000 - 1001	Accounts Receivable - C. Able	6,226.30	-
26500 - 1001	HST Charged on Services - C. Able	-	716.30
41000 - 1001	Revenue from Services - C. Able	-	5,510.00
Additional Date:	Additional Field:	6,226.30	6,226.30

Again, all amounts are allocated correctly because we have a single department linked to the record. Notice that the discount is taken directly to reduce revenue; it is not linked to the sales discount account used for early payments.

Close   the **display** to return to the journal and complete the entry.

Click   the **Item Description field**. **Type** monthly fee

Click   the **Amount field**. No discount applies to this service.

Type   900

Press   (tab) **twice** to add the tax code and advance to the Account field.

Choose 41000 - 1001 Revenue from Service - C. Able. The default account appears only for the first invoice line, so we must add it here.

Review the **entry**, **make corrections** and then **post** the **transaction**.

Close   the **Sales Journal**.

Enter   the **payment** to Office Plus and continue with the **transactions** up to the payroll entry on April 30.

Entering Departments for Payroll Transactions

Payroll amounts are allocated to departments differently from amounts in other journals. If an employee works only with one department, you can add the department to the employee's ledger record.

Click   the **Create Paycheque shortcut** to open the journal.

Choose Tryin, Reelie. **Press** (tab) to add the employee's default record details.

All Payroll Journal accounts are linked accounts, so you cannot choose the department subaccounts to enter allocations. Instead, you can open the Department Allocation screens from the Paycheque menu as shown:

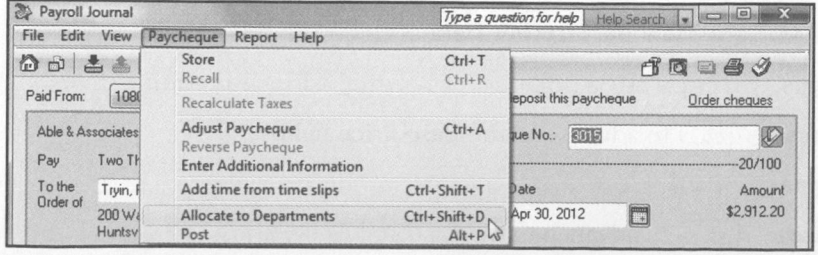

Choose the **Paycheque menu** and **click Allocate To Departments** or **click** the **Allocate Amounts To Departments tool**.

The tool at the far right-hand side of the tool bar opens the Allocation screen :

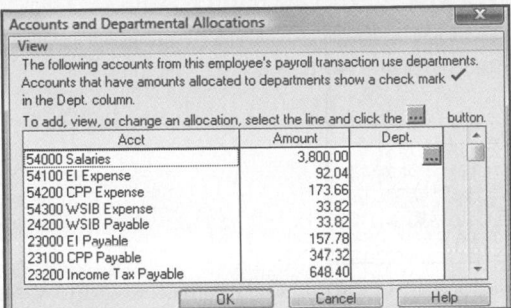

All accounts used in the journal entry are listed, and you can allocate one or more of them, or all, in the same way, or you can use different percentages or amounts.

Click   the **Department Detail button** 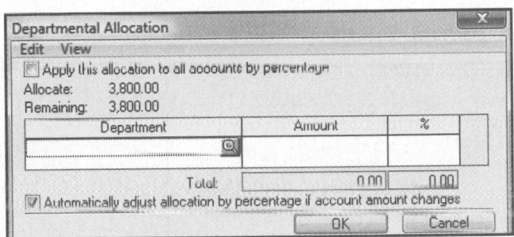 (in the Dept. column) for Salaries:

This screen is similar to the one we use to enter division allocations. You can select one or more departments for each journal entry amount. And you can apply the same allocation to all accounts, just as we did for divisions in Chapter 13. Payroll amounts for the Ables are allocated by percentage, but you can allocate by amount if you prefer. You do not need to allocate the entire amount for an account. We want the same breakdown to apply to all amounts.

Click   the **Department List icon** 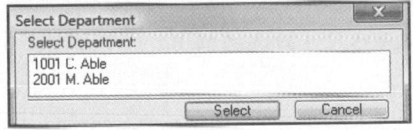 to see the list of departments:

Click   **1001 C. Able. Click Select** to add the department.

Press   (tab) **twice** to advance to the % (percentage) field.

Type   60 **Press** (tab) to advance to the Department field again.

Press   (enter) and **enter M. Able** for the rest of the allocation.

Press   (tab) and **accept** the **default entry** — 40 percent.

Click   **Apply This Allocation To All Accounts By Percentage**.

Click   **OK** to return to the account list screen. A ✓ has been added to each account in the Dept. column.

Click   **10800 Bank Chequing** to select the account line.

Click   the **Dept. Detail button** 🔲 for this account:

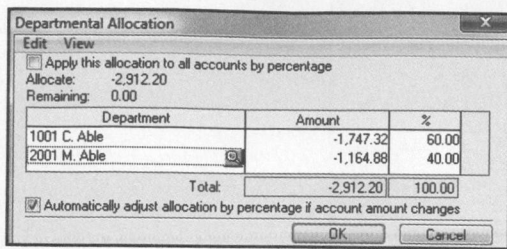

You can see that the same 60–40 allocation is applied. But in this window, you have the option to change the allocation for the single account without affecting the others.

Click   **OK** to accept the amounts already entered (or Cancel).

Click   **OK** again to return to the journal and review the entry.

Press   ⌨ctrl + **J** to view the journal entry:

Able & Associates Inc.			
Payroll Journal Entry 04/30/2012 (J15)			
Account Number	Account Description	Debits	Credits
54000 - 1001	Salaries - C. Able	2,280.00	-
54000 - 2001	Salaries - M. Able	1,520.00	-
54100 - 1001	EI Expense - C. Able	55.22	-
54100 - 2001	EI Expense - M. Able	36.82	-
54200 - 1001	CPP Expense - C. Able	104.20	-
54200 - 2001	CPP Expense - M. Able	69.46	-
54300 - 1001	WSIB Expense - C. Able	20.29	-
54300 - 2001	WSIB Expense - M. Able	13.53	-
10800 - 1001	Bank: Chequing - C. Able	-	1,747.32
10800 - 2001	Bank: Chequing - M. Able	-	1,164.88
23000 - 1001	EI Payable - C. Able	-	94.67
23000 - 2001	EI Payable - M. Able	-	63.11
23100 - 1001	CPP Payable - C. Able	-	208.39
23100 - 2001	CPP Payable - M. Able	-	138.93
23200 - 1001	Income Tax Payable - C. Able	-	389.04
23200 - 2001	Income Tax Payable - M. Able	-	259.36
24200 - 1001	WSIB Payable - C. Able	-	20.29
24200 - 2001	WSIB Payable - M. Able	-	13.53
Additional Date:	Additional Field:	4,099.52	4,099.52

All amounts are automatically applied in the 60–40 ratio for the two departments.

Close   the **display** to return to the journal.

Make   **corrections** if necessary and **post** the **transaction**.

Close   the **Paycheques Journal**.

Enter   the final **two General Journal entries** with allocations for all accounts.

Handling Unallocated Amounts

We saw that the amounts for some accounts in the journals were not allocated. Most of the affected accounts are Balance Sheet accounts and many users prefer to apply departmental accounting only to Income Statement accounts to avoid these incomplete entries. Unallocated amounts can also leave Departmental Balance Sheets out of balance as some amounts will not be included. For example, in a purchase of assets, the asset account was allocated but the HST account was not.

To prepare complete Departmental reports without unallocated amounts, you can enter General Journal adjusting entries to transfer the balances from the main account to the correct departmental subaccount. You can see that this could be a time-consuming exercise as you would have to first determine all the appropriate amounts. Furthermore, the linked *Accounts Receivable* and *Accounts Payable* accounts are not accessible as postable accounts. You would still be unable to allocate these amounts. For this exercise, we will not enter the adjustments for unallocated amounts.

NOTES
In the Accountants' Edition of Simply Accounting, all accounts are available for posting. Your accountant would be able to make these adjustments for you by working with an accountant's copy of your data file. Refer to Chapter 12.

Department Reports

Many of the standard Simply Accounting reports can have department information added to them. In addition, the primary financial statements, the Balance Sheet, Income Statement and Trial Balance are available as departmental reports. As before, we will work from the Report Centre.

Click   the **Report Centre icon** in the Home window.

Click   **Financials** to open the list of financial reports.

Click   the ⊞ **beside Balance Sheets** to expand this list.

Click   the ⊞ **beside Income Statement** to expand this list.

Click   the ⊞ **beside Trial Balance** to expand this list:

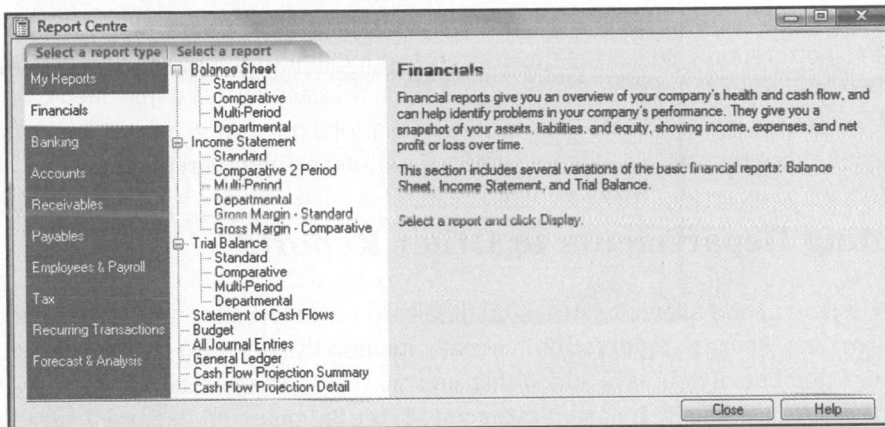

You can prepare a Departmental version of each of these reports.

Displaying Departmental Balance Sheets

If you want Balance Sheet information for each department, you should prepare the Departmental Balance Sheet.

Click   **Departmental** under **Balance Sheet**. **Click Modify This Report**:

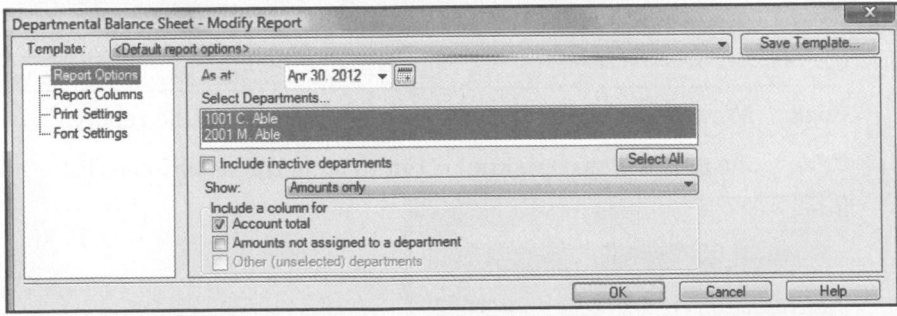

From the Home window, choose the Reports menu, then choose Financials and Departmental Reports and click Balance Sheet to see the report options.

You can report on one or more departments or all departments. The departments are shown as column headings, so you have a complete Balance Sheet for each department you selected. Remember that the Balance Sheet for each department separately may not balance if some amounts were not allocated.

Reports can include **Amounts** only or each amount as a **Percentage Of The Total**. You can also add **extra columns** for the total amount for each account, for amounts not

NOTES
Including unallocated amounts and totals will provide balanced reports.

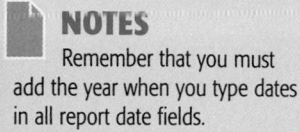

assigned to any department and for the total amount for other departments not included in the report.

Choose the **departments** you want to include.

Choose the **Amounts** or **Percentage** option.

Choose the **additional columns** you want

Enter the **date** for the report (including the year) and **click OK**.

Close the **display** when you have finished.

Departmental Income Statement and Trial Balance Reports

Departmental Income Statements and Departmental Trial Balances are also available. The Departmental Income Statement is probably the most frequently used of these reports.

For both reports, select the departments to include in the report and choose whether you want to include amounts that are not assigned to a department. You can show amounts only or add the percentage of the total amount in your reports. In other respects, these reports are like the standard non-departmental reports.

Adding Departments to Other Reports

Many other reports allow departmental details to be added after you set up and use departments. **Journal reports** automatically include the department number with the account numbers if you have added that information to the journal transaction.

The **Balance Sheet**, **Income Statement**, **Trial Balance** and **General Ledger** all have a **Show Departments** check box added. Division reports also have this option.

Access the **report options** in the usual way from the Report Centre or from the Reports menu.

The Show Departments option is shown in the Balance Sheet Options window:

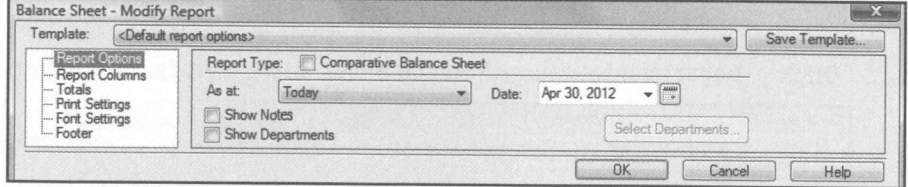

Click **Show Departments** to have the details added to the report.

Click the **Select Departments button** to open the department list:

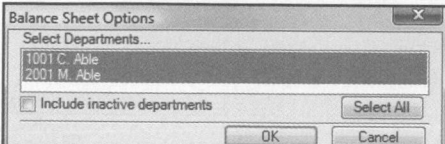

Select the **departments** you want to add to the report.

Click **OK** to return to the initial Balance Sheet Options window.

Choose other **report options** in the usual way and **click OK** to see the report.

Close the **display** when you have finished.

Department information can also be added to client and vendor reports. The Vendor Aged and Aged Overdue reports and the Pending Purchase Order Report allow you to group the vendors by department for the report. The Client Aged and Aged Overdue reports and the Pending Sales Order Report have the same option for grouping clients by department.

The following Vendor Aged Report Options screen shows this option:

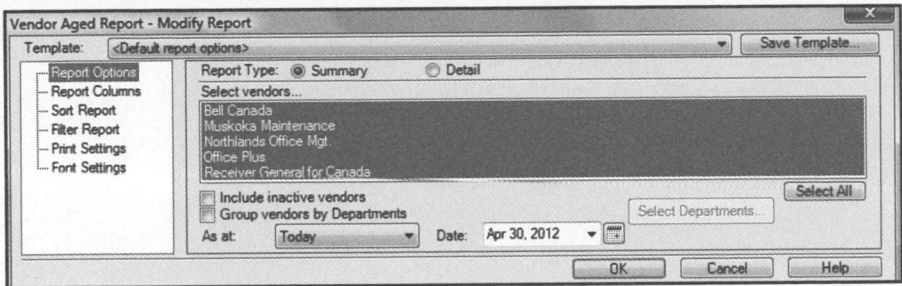

Click   **Group Vendors By Departments** to select the option.

Click   the **Select Departments button** to open the department list.

Select   the **departments** you want to add to the report.

You can include or omit vendors that do not have an assigned department.

Click   **OK** to return to the Vendor Aged Report Options screen.

Choose other **report options** in the usual way.

Click   **OK** to see the report.

Close   the **display** when you have finished.

Close   the **Report Centre** if it is open.

REVIEW

The Student DVD with Data Files includes Review Questions and Supplementary Cases for this chapter.

Part 4
Appendices

Installing Simply Accounting

INSTALLING SIMPLY ACCOUNTING FROM THE PROGRAM CD

The instructions for installation that follow refer to the regular Premium version of the program, but most steps for installing the program are the same for all versions. Margin notes outline the differences for the Pro version and for the Student (Premium) version.

STUDENT VERSION
Instructions for downloading, installing and activating the Student version begin on page A–10.

NOTES
From the Computer window, you can right-click D: and click Autoplay to start the autorun feature and show the Installation screens on this page.

The Simply Accounting Student version is now available only as a download from the Simply Accounting Web site. Special instructions for downloading, installing and registering the Student version begin on page A–10.

Start your **computer** and the **Windows program**.

Close any **other programs** that you have running before beginning.

Insert the **Simply Accounting program CD** in the CD/DVD drive.

Installation from the CD/DVD drive should begin immediately.

Many computers have drive D: as the CD/DVD drive, so we will use that in the keystrokes that follow.

First you must choose the language you want for the installation instructions:

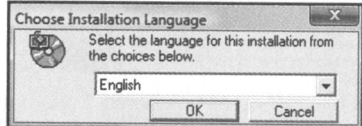

Accept **English** or **choose French** from the drop-down list.

Click **OK**. The following options screen appears to begin the installation:

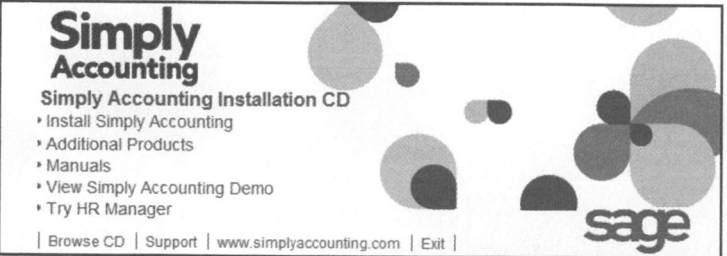

If you have any other programs running, click Exit, close the other programs and start again.

Click **Install Simply Accounting**. If installation does not begin immediately, follow the boxed instructions on page A-3.

IF INSTALLATION DOES NOT BEGIN IMMEDIATELY

You can install the program from the Windows opening screen or desktop. Many computers have drive D: as the CD/DVD drive, so we will use that drive in the keystrokes that follow. (For drive D:, substitute the drive letter for your CD/DVD drive.)

Click the **Start icon** on the task bar to open the Search field.

Click the **Start Search text box** 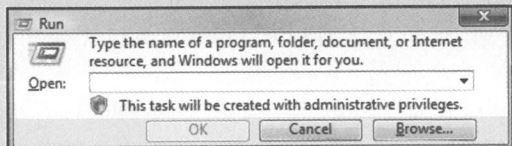.

Type run and **press** ⌨ *(enter)* to open the Run window:

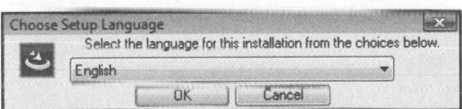

Click the **Open** field if necessary to place the cursor. You can type the name of the program you want directly in the Open field of the Run window.

Type d:\Simply\setup or **d:\launch.exe** in the Open field and **click OK**.

If you start with the **launch** program, you will open the Choose Installation Language screen (first screen on the previous page). If you start with the **setup** program, you will start with the Choose Setup Language screen (first screen following this box).

If you need to locate the program, **click Browse** in the Run window to find the Simply Accounting program CD. (Click Computer, then double click the Simply Accounting CD). **Click launch** (or **launch.exe**) and then **click Open** to return to the Run window with launch(.exe) added to the Open field.

Click OK to start the install procedure with the Choose Installation Language screen.

If you double click **launch(.exe)** or the **Simply folder** and **setup(.exe)** on the CD's list of files, the installation may begin directly.

Wait for the Choose Setup Language selection screen to appear:

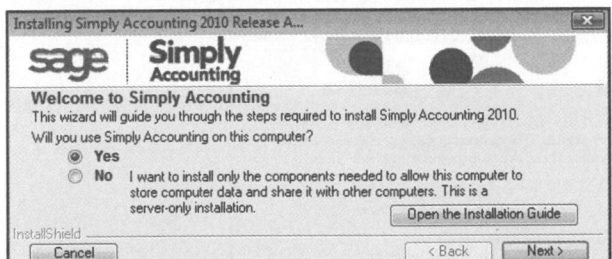

Click your **language preference** and **click OK**:

The Components Installation – the No option – applies when you are working on a network that has the program already installed. Clicking Open The Installation Guide will explain these options in detail. Most users will need the full installation. If you are working on a stand-alone computer, or you are installing the program to a network server, choose Yes to install the full stand-alone version.

Do not install the Components version if you are working with this text. Choose Yes to install the full stand-alone version.

WARNING!
Install the full version. Do not install only the components.

Choose Yes and **click Next** to install the complete version of the program:

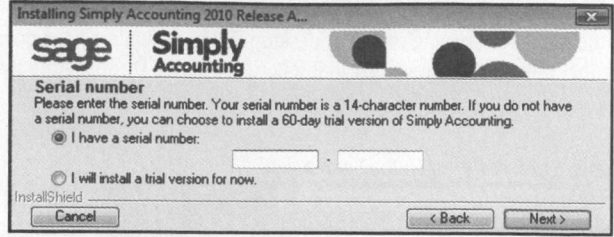

You must enter the serial number exactly as it appears on the program package or CD case before you can continue. For all copies of the **Student version**, the serial number is **242P2U2-1000001**. For regular or retail Pro and Premium versions, each copy has a unique serial number.

The cursor is in the Serial Number field, ready for you to enter the number.

Type   your **Serial Number** in the space provided.

Click   **Next** to advance to the license agreement:

Read   the **agreement**, and if you accept the agreement, **click I Agree** to begin installing the program.

The screen you see next will depend on which firewall program you are using. Simply Accounting uses the Connection Manager program to access data files. If you have a firewall installed on your computer, you must allow this program to access your data. If you do not allow access through your firewall, you cannot open your data files.

If you are using the Microsoft Windows firewall, you will see this screen:

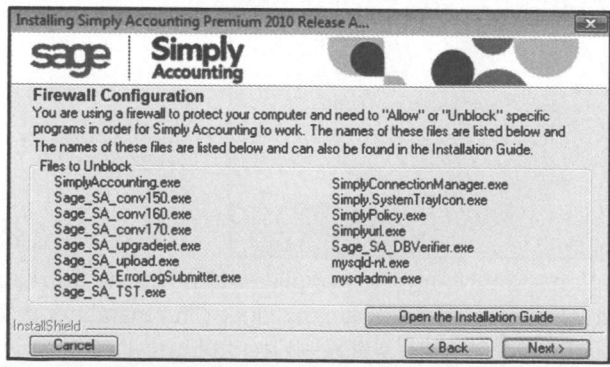

Click   **Open The Installation Guide** for help with firewall settings. **Close** the **Help window**.

You may see a list of files. If a firewall prompt does not appear automatically, you may need to configure your firewall manually to allow access to all the listed programs.

Or, you may see this screen, asking to configure the firewall automatically:

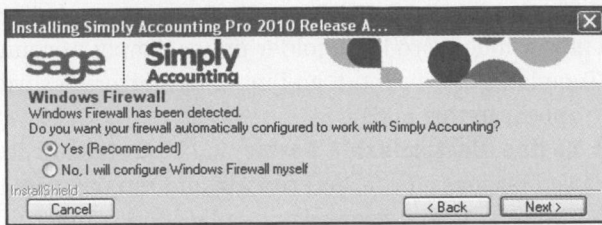

Click **Next**. Now you must choose the location for your program:

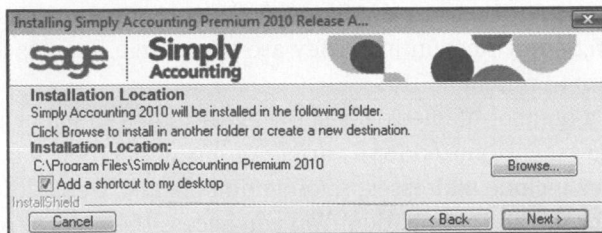

By default, the program will add a shortcut to your desktop. If you do not want a shortcut, click Add A Shortcut To My Desktop to remove the ✓.

Click **Next** to accept the default location, C:\Program Files\Simply Accounting Premium 2010.

To choose another folder, click Browse and choose an existing folder from the pop-up window, or type an alternative location in the Browse window. Click OK.

Simply Accounting will automatically create the folder for you.
You must now choose the program components you want to install:

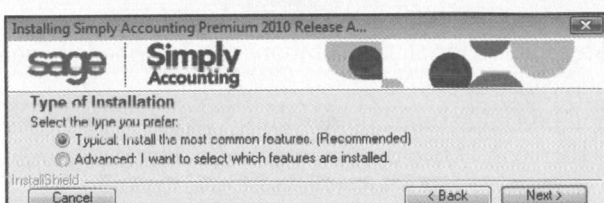

The default option, Typical, will provide all the basic components you need. If you want to omit some features, you must choose the Advanced option. Leave the default selection unchanged.

Click **Next** to proceed to the screen confirming your installation choices:

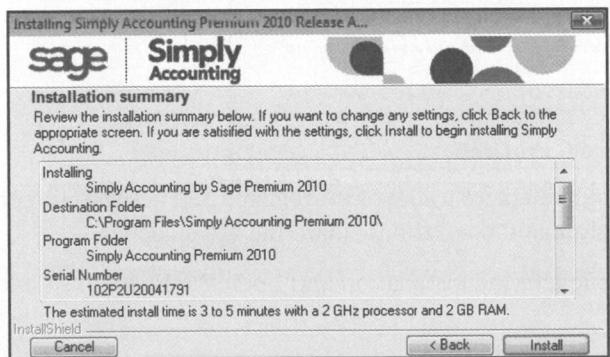

By default, all components are selected for installation as follows:

- **Simply Accounting Program**: the Simply Accounting program that you will need to perform the accounting transactions for your company. It will be placed in the main Simply Accounting Premium 2010 folder in the Program Files folder or the folder location you selected.
- **Sample Data**: complete records for a sample company — Universal Construction. They will be placed in Public\Public Documents\ Simply\2010\Samdata.

- **Templates**: predefined charts of accounts and settings for a large number of business types. These files will be stored in a folder under Simply Accounting Premium 2010 called Template. The skeleton and inteplus starter files with only charts of accounts also appear in this folder.
- **Crystal Reports Print Engine**, **Customizable Forms** and **Management Reports**: a variety of commonly used business forms and reports and the program to access and print them. The reports and forms will be placed in a folder under Simply Accounting Premium 2010 called Forms.
- **Microsoft Office Documents**: a variety of Microsoft Office documents designed for integrated use with Simply Accounting. They are placed in a Reports folder under Simply Accounting Premium 2010.
- **New Business Guide**: a number of checklists showing the steps to follow in setting up a new business, customized for a variety of business types in different provinces. These guides include addresses, phone numbers and Web addresses that you can contact for further information. You can access the guides from the Simply Accounting Business Assistant menu or from the Programs list.
- **Manuals** & **Tutorials**: documentation and videos to help you learn the program.
- **Add-in for Microsoft Outlook**: a program link that connects your data with Microsoft Outlook.

Click   Install. As the installation continues, you will see the progress:

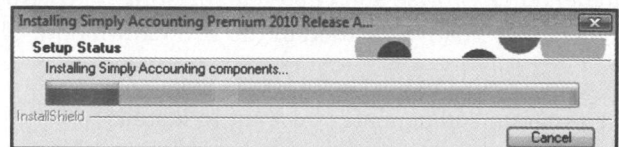

The Install program creates folders for all the components described above and installs the add-in link for Microsoft Outlook.

In addition, the installation procedure adds names in the Programs list for the Simply Accounting program, Microsoft Office documents, Help, data repair utilities and the New Business Guide.

The next option is to view the ReadMe file, or start the program, or both:

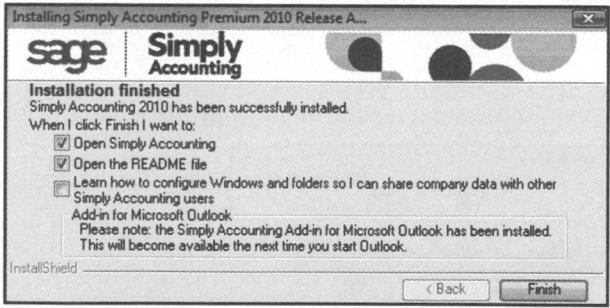

We will start the program immediately so we can register and activate the program. The options to start the program and open the ReadMe file are selected.

Click   Finish to complete the installation and open the ReadMe screen.

Registering and Activating Simply Accounting

Read   the **information** about recent changes to the program that may not yet be documented elsewhere.

Close   the **ReadMe screen** to see the Registration message:

NOTES
You can customize these reports and forms to suit your own business needs .

PRO VERSION
The Microsoft Outlook Add-in is not available in the Pro version.

STUDENT VERSION
Proceed to page A–15 for assistance with activating the Student version.

WARNING!
Wait for the Setup window to close after you close the ReadMe window. This may take some time.

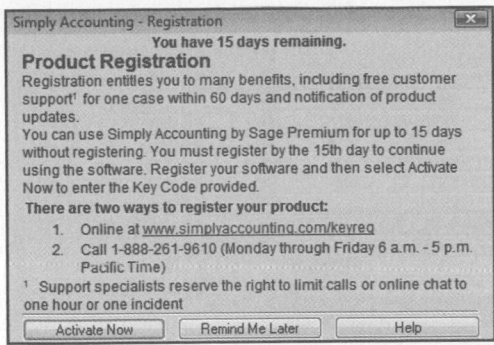

If you choose Remind Me Later, open a data file, choose the Help menu and click Enter Key Code to see the screen shown above. This reminder message will also appear each time you start the program until you complete the activation.

Until you register and activate the program, you will be allowed to use the program for a limited number of days. If you have already registered and have the activation codes, skip the next step.

Have your product serial number ready for the registration. You can register online or by telephone. The telephone number is provided. To register online, start your Internet connection. Enter the Web address given on the registration information screen or double click the Web address on this screen. Follow the instructions provided. Print a copy of the codes screen for reference.

When you register, you will provide the serial number from the program package or CD and receive a client ID number, a key code number and a payroll ID number. These numbers will be linked to the serial number you provided and cannot be used for a different copy of the program.

Click   **Activate Now** to start the activation procedure:

Enter   your **Company Name** and the **Client ID** provided by Sage Software for the program you have registered.

If you have installed a previous version of Simply Accounting, your company name and client ID may be entered automatically.

You can retrieve the key code online, the default selection. To do this,

Start   your **Internet connection** and **click OK**.

You will be connected to the Simply Accounting Web site and the client ID and serial number will be uploaded from your program to create a key code. The key code will be added to your program automatically.

If you already have the key code, you can enter it on this screen.

Click   **Use This Key Code** to open the Key Code fields.

Enter   the **Key Code** provided by Sage Software for this program.

⚠ WARNING!

The Company Name must match the name you use to register the program with Sage.

Enter all numbers exactly as they are given to you, including spaces and punctuation.

PRO VERSION
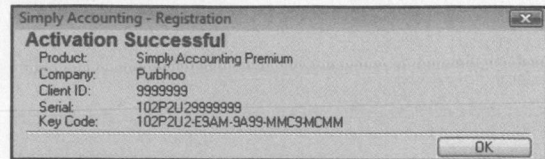
You will see an additional screen about upgrading to the Premium version of Simply Accounting. Close this screen to continue.

NOTES
Instructions for starting Simply Accounting are included in Chapter 1 of this text, beginning on page 7.

NOTES
If you have not activated the program yet, you can activate the program from the Help menu. Choose Enter Key Code from the Help menu to open the You Have XX Days Remaining screen shown on page A-7.

NOTES
Always Check For Updates At Startup has a ✓ beside it that indicates the automatic update feature is on. Click the option to remove the ✓ and turn off the option. Click OK to continue.

STUDENT VERSION
You will not see the payroll activation option or screens because payroll is already activated.

Enter all names and numbers exactly as they are given to you, including spaces and punctuation. The key code is not case sensitive. If you make a mistake, the program will warn you and you can re-enter the details.

Click   OK.

When you have completed the registration, you will see the confirmation screen:

Click   OK to continue to Simply Accounting's Welcome screen:

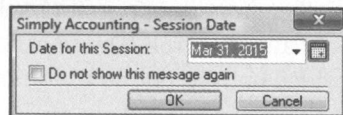

Click   Open The Sample Company…. Click OK to continue to the Session Date window:

Click   OK to accept the default session date.

You can now view a short video to learn more or access this video later from the Help menu. These are some of the options on the Getting Started screen.

Click   Close to close the Getting Started window.

If you see an information screen about payroll services, close this window.

If you see a message about automatic updates, read the sidebar Notes and refer to page A–10. **Do not turn on** the **update feature** (remove the ✓).

Unlocking the Payroll Features

We will unlock and activate the Payroll module before proceeding. You will not need to unlock payroll in the Student version of the program.

Choose the **Help menu** and **click Unlock Auto Payroll** as shown:

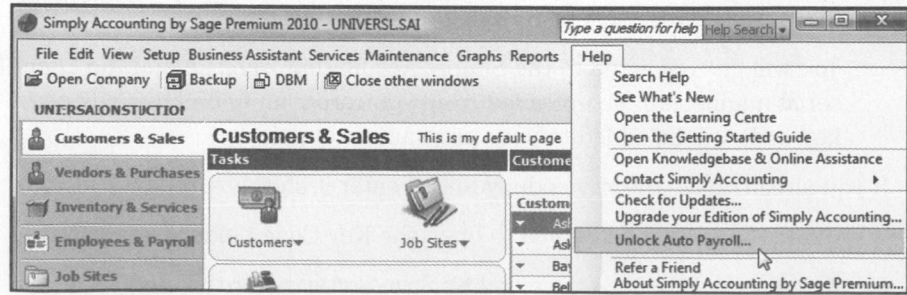

An information screen about payroll services for Simply Accounting opens:

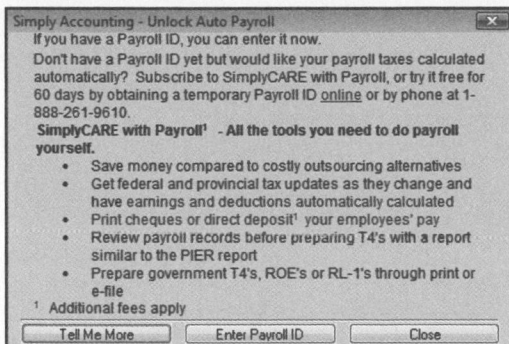

This screen advises you that you need a payroll ID and subscription to the Simply Accounting Payroll Plan — a fee-based service — to use the payroll features in the program. To learn more about the payroll plan or to subscribe, click Tell Me More.

Click   Enter Payroll ID:

Your client ID number will be entered from the activation procedure.

You must enter the payroll ID number provided for your program registration. The default selection is to retrieve the payroll ID online.

Click   OK. (Be sure that you have started your Internet connection.)

The payroll ID will be downloaded directly to your program.

If you have the number already, you can enter it directly.

Click   the **Payroll ID field** and **type** the **number** provided, exactly as it is given to you. The code is not case sensitive.

If the activation is successful, you will see the following message:

> **Simply Accounting**
>
> **Thank you for subscribing to SimplyCARE.**
>
> OK

Click   OK to continue.

After you have activated your program and unlocked the payroll, you can retrieve these codes automatically by selecting the online options if you need to reinstall the program.

You can now use all features of the program.

Click    to close the Simply Accounting Home window.

Click   Exit to close the Simply Accounting installation screen unless you want to install other programs or documents.

Click    to close the Control Panel window if it is open.

⚠ WARNING!
Do not remove the program CD before clicking Exit on the opening Simply Accounting Installation screen (see the illustration on page A-2).

Turning Off Automatic Updates

When you start Simply Accounting, you may see a message about automatic program updates:

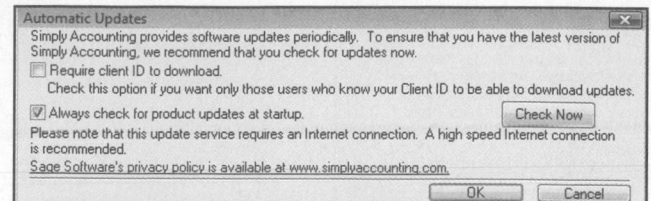

You can download updates automatically or periodically when needed. If you are working with the data files in this text, you should not update the program beyond the version we use, which is Release A. Therefore, you should turn off the automatic update option.

Click   **Always Check For Product Updates At Startup** to remove the ✓ and turn off the automatic update option.

Click   **OK** to continue accessing your data files.

If the message about updates does not appear automatically, you should check that the updates are turned off from the Help menu (refer to the screen on page A–8).

Choose the **Help menu** and **click Check For Updates** to see the screen above.

You can also use this approach to turn on automatic updates later, after you have finished the applications in this text.

DOWNLOADING, INSTALLING AND ACTIVATING THE STUDENT VERSION

The Student Premium version of Simply Accounting must be downloaded from the Sage Simply Accounting Web site. The actual installation is the same as it is for the regular retail CD version of the program, so we will not repeat those steps here. Instead, we will demonstrate the steps involved in downloading the program and extracting the program files to start the installation. Because activating or registering the Student version is different from the activation of the regular retail version, we also provide detailed instructions for that process. These instructions begin on page A–15.

Downloading the Student Version Program

Start   your **Internet connection** and **open** your **Web browser**.

Type   www.simplyaccounting.com/downloads/student in the Web address field.

Press (enter):

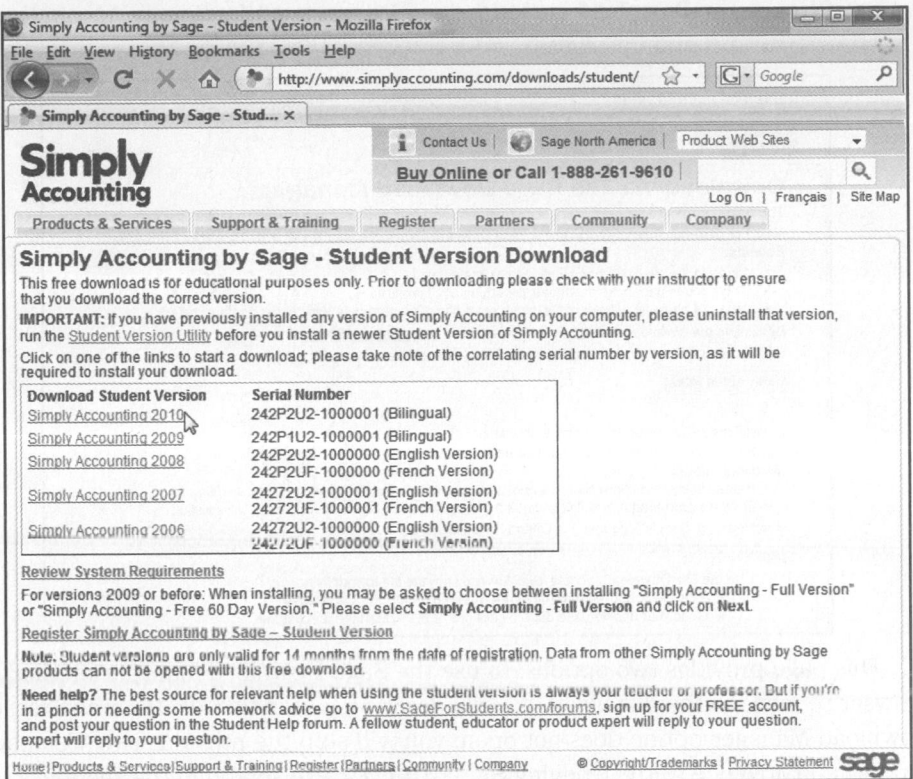

NOTES
You can also access this Web page from the main Simply Accounting Web site — <www.simplyaccounting.com>.
From this site, follow the links for Partners > Educational Partner Program > For Students > Downloads.

WARNING!
Several versions are available for downloading from this site, so be sure to select the correct version.

Several versions can be downloaded from this site, so be sure to select the right one.

Click   Simply Accounting 2010 to open an instruction page:

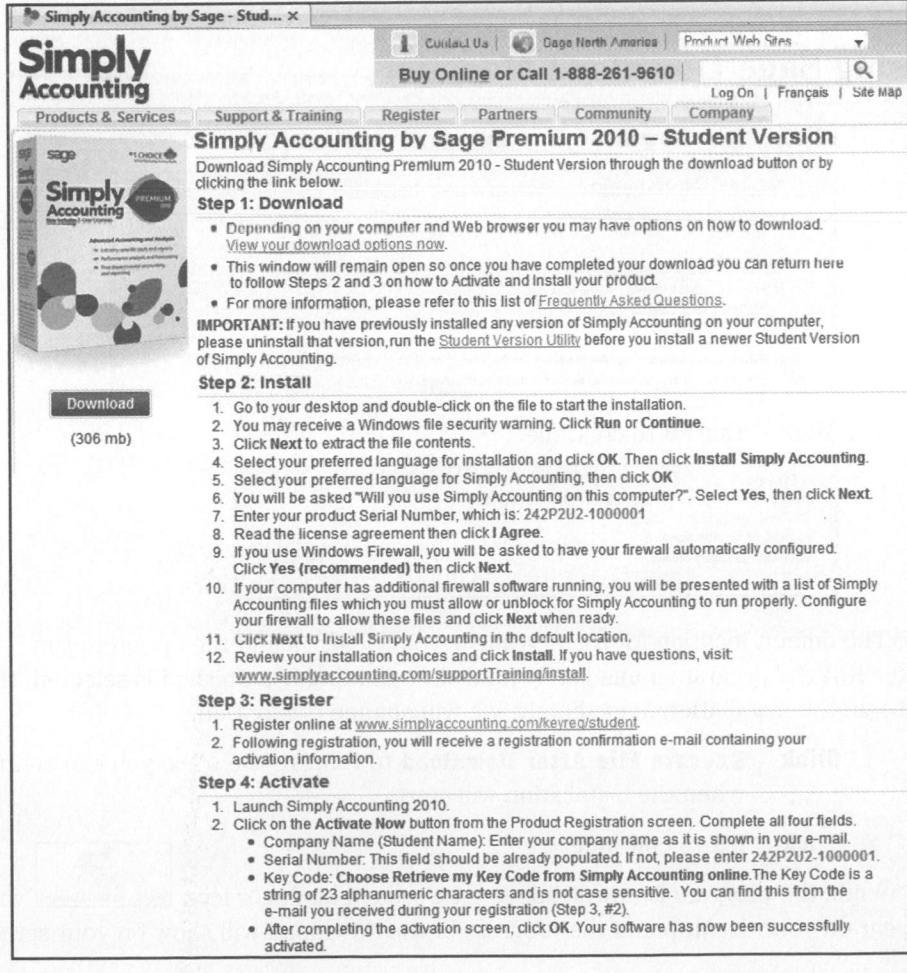

Click   the **Download button** below the image of the Simply Accounting program package:

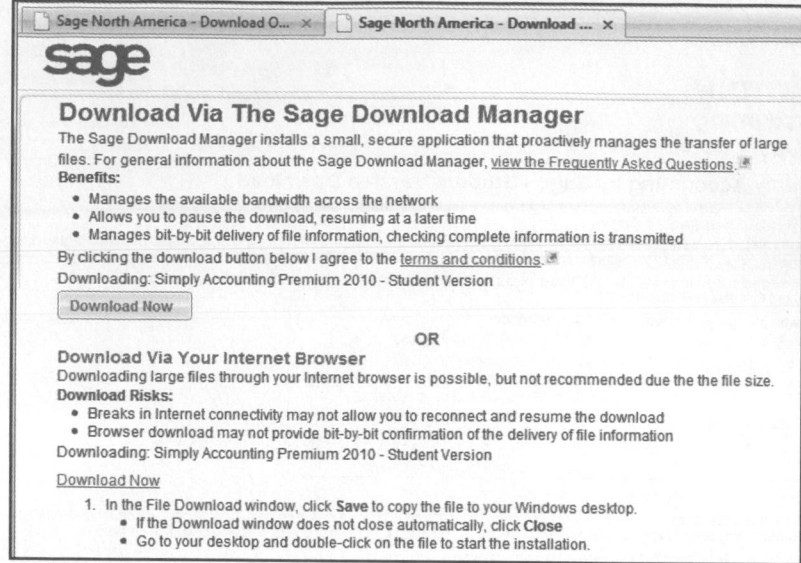

This page provides two options: to use the Sage Download Manager or your Internet browser to manage the download. We will describe both methods. If for any reason the Download Manager option does not open, you will skip the previous two Web page screens and advance to the Opening SA_2010ACP1.exe screen in the section Downloading through Your Internet Browser on page A–13 as soon as you click the Simply Accounting 2010 program link on page A–11. Dedicated Web pages are sometimes discontinued so we show the browser alternative as well.

Using Sage Download Manager

Click   the **Download Now button**:

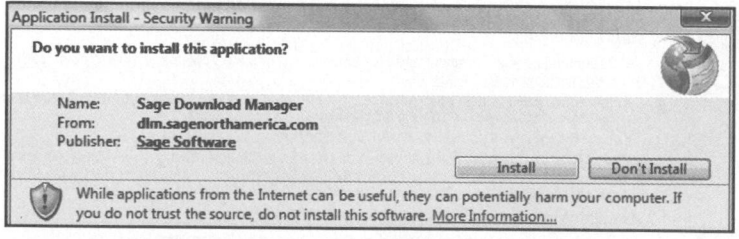

Click   **Install** to continue:

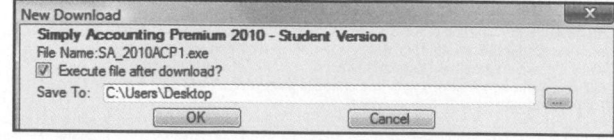

The default location for the new file is your desktop and the option to run (execute) the program immediately after downloading has finished is selected, that is, to begin the installation immediately. We will change this option.

Click   **Execute File After Download** to remove the ✓ so you can control when the installation will start.

Click   **OK** to continue.

While the program is downloading, a Download Manager icon ![Sage Download Manager] will appear on your desktop and the progress of the download will show on your screen:

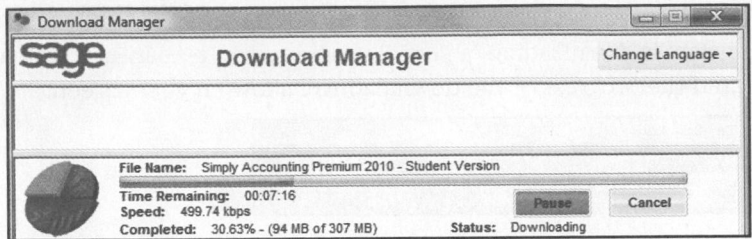

After the file has been downloaded, you should see 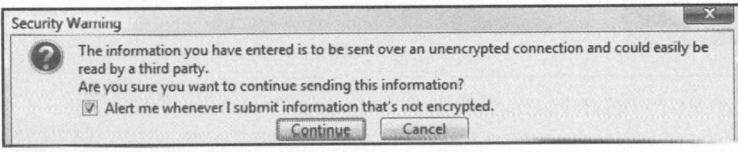 (the Simply Accounting program icon) on your desktop. You can close your Web browser and Internet connection now, unless you want to install and activate your program immediately.

Downloading through Your Internet Browser

Using the Internet browser is the second method of placing the program on your computer. This option appears on the lower half of the Download Manager screen, after "Or." If for some reason the Download Manager option is not available, you may advance to this step immediately when you choose Simply Accounting 2010 from the opening downloads/student page.

Click   the **Download Now underlined link** in the Download Via Your Internet Browser section. You may see this security warning:

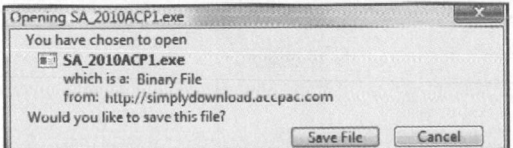

Click   **Continue**:

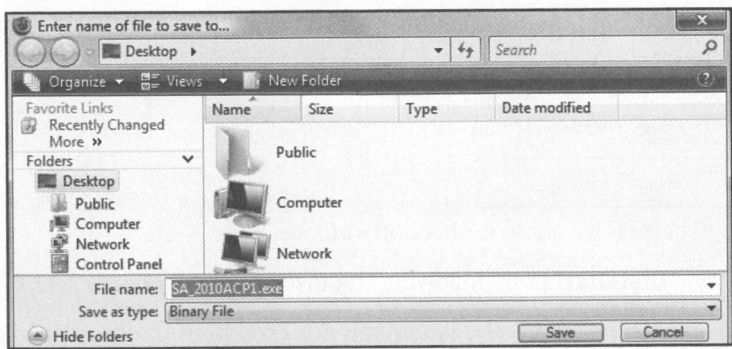

Your browser settings may have the option to open this file or to save it. You should save the file.

Click   **Save File** or **Save** to open the file location screen:

Choose   the **location** for the downloaded file. Desktop is the usual default and you can accept this choice.

Click   **Save**.

While the program is downloading, a partial program icon 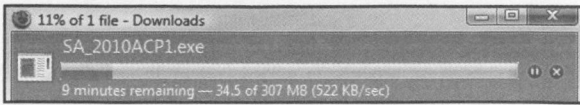 will appear on your desktop and the progress of the download will show on your screen:

After the file has been downloaded, you should see 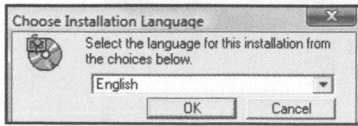 (the Simply Accounting program icon) on your desktop. You can close your Web browser and Internet connection now, unless you want to install and activate your program immediately.

Beginning the Installation

When you are installing the downloaded Student version from SA_2010ACP1.exe, you must run it to extract the program files before the installation begins.

Double click the **Simply Accounting program icon** .

Click   **OK** to continue and open the Simply Accounting InstallShield Wizard:

> **STUDENT VERSION**
> It may take several minutes for all the program files to be extracted from the SA_2010ACP1.exe file before you see the installation screens.

Click   **Next** to begin extracting the program files.

Again, the progress of the file extraction will display on your screen:

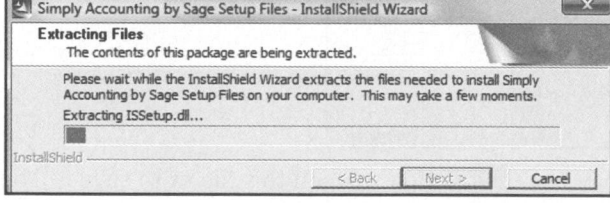

Wait   for the extraction to finish. The Next button will be available as soon as the files are ready to be installed.

Click   **Next** to begin the installation with the Choose Installation Language screen:

This is the same screen we show in this appendix on page A–2.

Continue the **installation** by following the instructions on pages A–2 to A–6.

Type   242P2U2-1000000 when you are prompted to enter the serial number. (This serial number applies to all copies of the Student version program.)

Activating the Student Version

When you start the Student version of Simply Accounting, you will see this message:

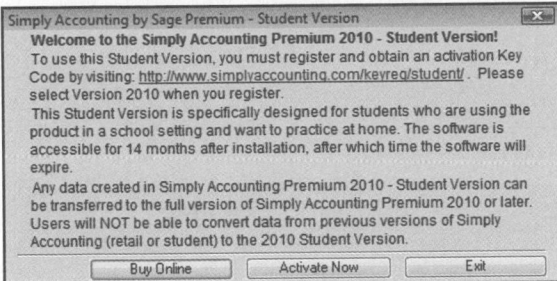

You must activate the program before you can use it. There is no trial period.

Do not click the **Activate Now button** yet.

If you click Activate Now at this stage, you will open the Activation screen that requires you to enter the key code (page A–17), and you do not have it yet. Instead, you should go to the Web site from the previous screen that includes a direct link to the activation site. If you are at the Activation screen on page A–16 and you do not have the key code, see the instruction in the Student version sidebar note.

Start   your **Internet connection**.

Click   **www.simplyaccounting.com/keyreg/student/** — the underlined Web address link in the Welcome screen to open the Student Version Registration window for Simply Accounting:

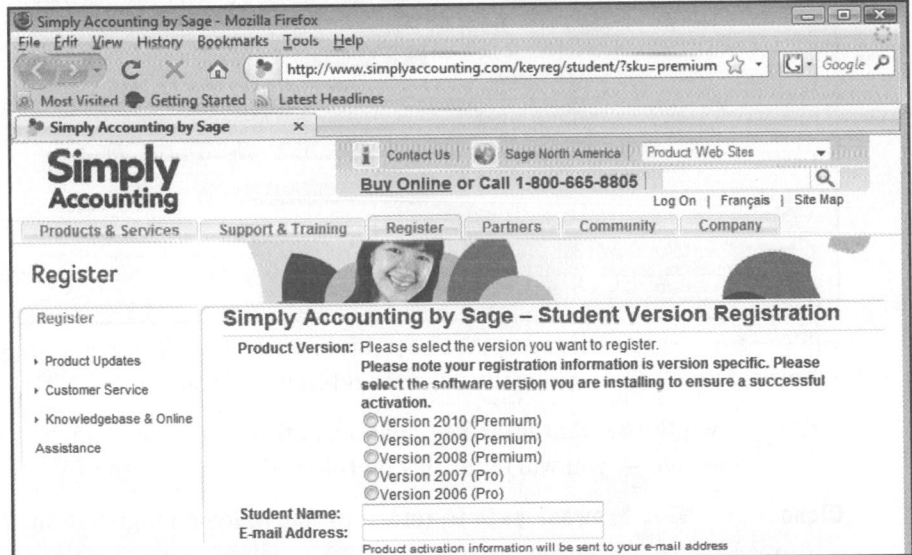

If your browser is open, you can type the address in the Address bar. Type <www.simplyaccounting.com/keyreg/student/> in the browser Address bar.

The required fields for your registration are included on the first part of this screen.

Click   **Version 2010 (Premium)** to select the version included with this text.

Enter   **your own name** in the Student Name field.

Enter   your **e-mail address** in the E-Mail Address field.

You will receive an e-mail from Sage with the serial number and key code. Keep these numbers for reference.

The remaining fields are optional, but it is helpful for Sage to have these details. These optional fields are shown on this next screen:

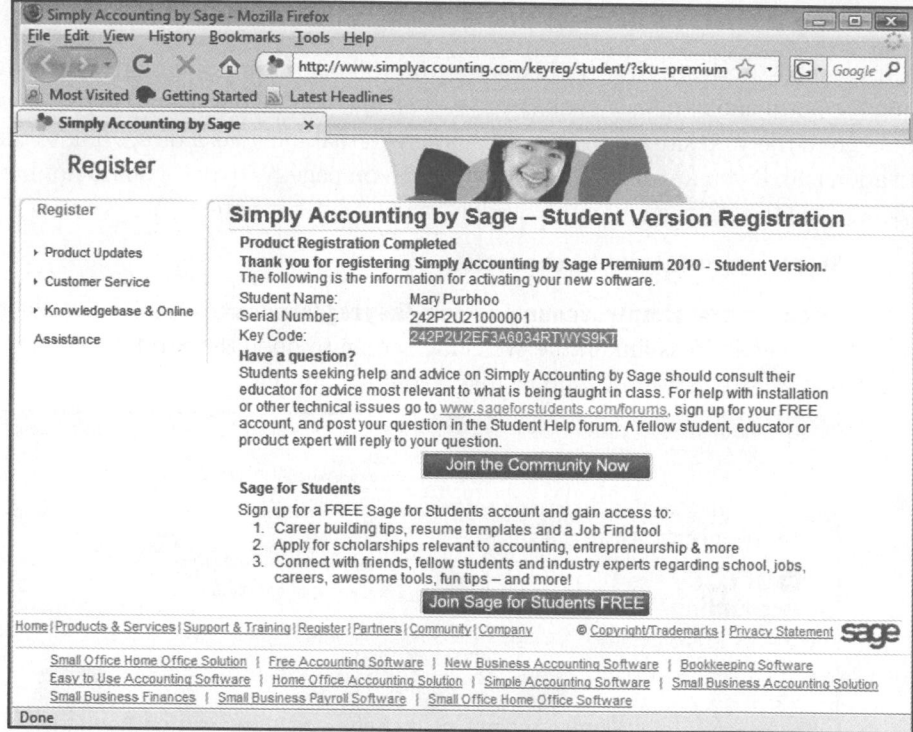

Click   Submit when you have finished:

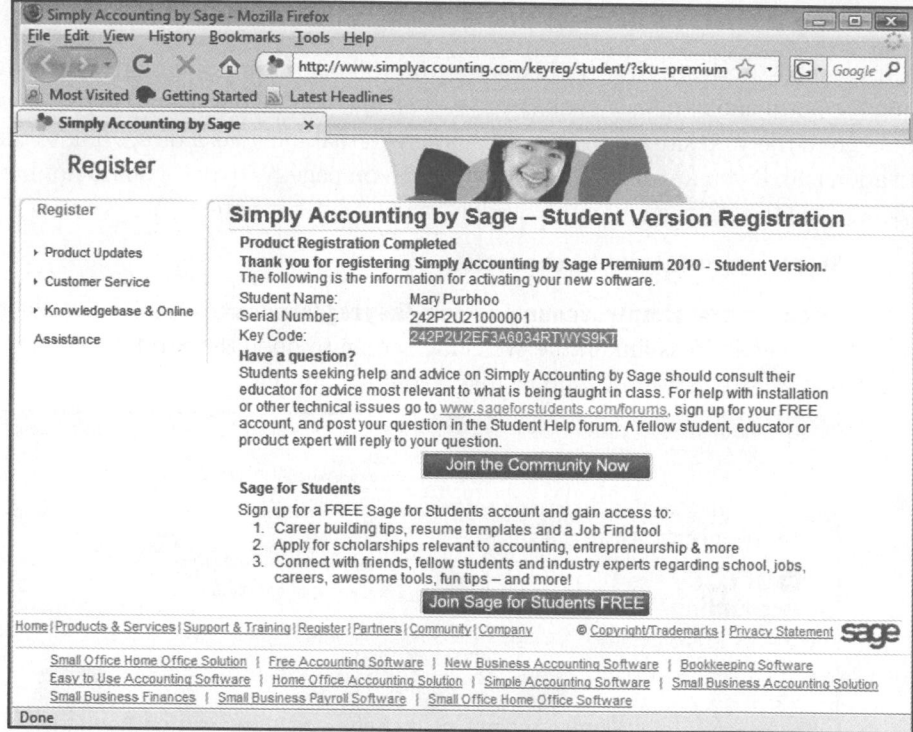

You will see a message confirming the successful registration. The key code you need is on this screen. You can print the page for reference if you want.

Write   down the **23 character key code** from this screen or from your e-mail message — you will enter this on the Activation screen.

Close   your **Web browser page** to return to the Welcome registration screen.

Click   Activate Now to open the Student Version Activation screen:

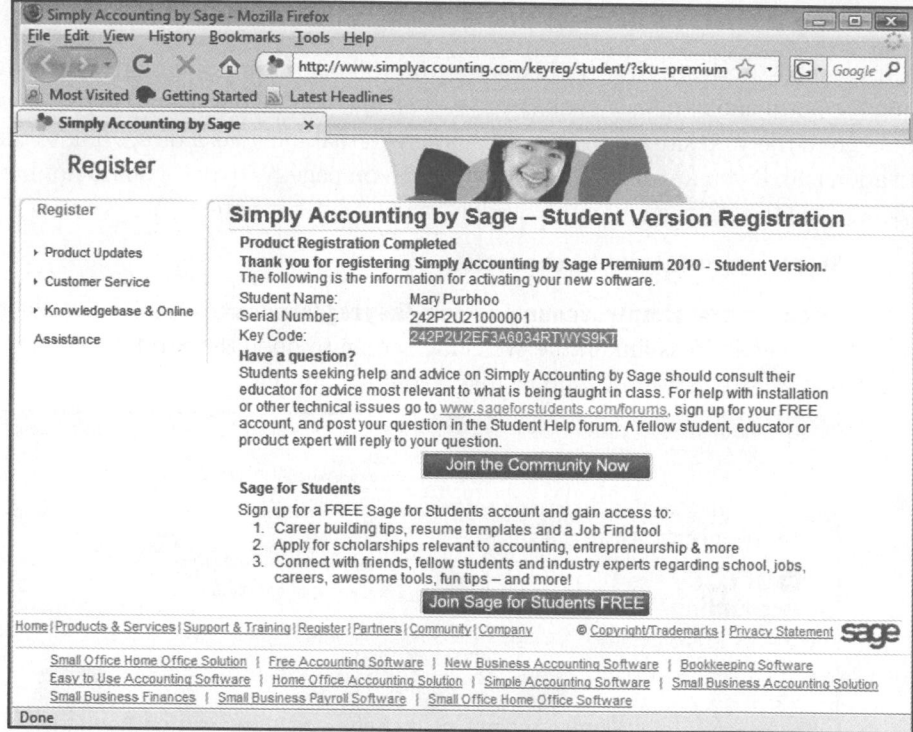

Type   **your name** in the Company Name field.

Click   the **first Key Code field**.

Type   the **23 character key code** from the Sage Registration screen.

Click   **OK**. Your Simply Accounting Welcome screen opens and you can now use the program for 14 months.

Click   **Exit** to close the Simply Accounting Installation screen unless you want to install other programs or documents.

Student Version Expired Error Message

If you have had any previous version of Simply Accounting installed on your computer, you may see this "expired" message when you try to activate the Student version:

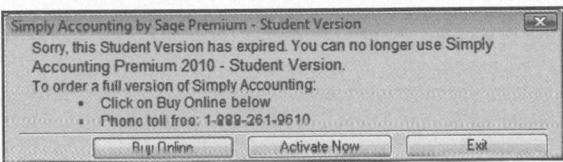

Click   **Exit** to close this window and **uninstall** the **Student 2010 version**.

This "expired" message is triggered by program registration file information from a previous program installation. If you see this message, you may have previously installed a version of the Simply Accounting program. You must uninstall that program before you can install the current Simply Accounting 2010 program.

Click   **Exit** to close this window and **uninstall** the **Student 2010 version** and any other version of Simply Accounting you have installed.

Use   the **Control Panel Programs – Uninstall A Program** function (Add/Remove Programs in Windows XP) to uninstall the program properly.

If you have already uninstalled all other Simply Accounting programs and you still see this message when you try to activate the Student version, you will need to uninstall the Student version program again and then run the Student Version Utility.

Uninstall the **Simply Accounting 2010 Student version program**.

Start   your **Internet connection** and **open** your **Web browser** if necessary.

Type   www.simplyacounting.com/downloads/student in the Web address field. **Press** (enter).

Click   the **Student Version Utility program link** on this Web page to download this program to your desktop.

Double click the **desktop icon StudentVerCleanUp.exe** to run this program.

You will see this confirmation when the program has finished:

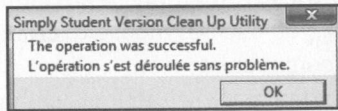

Click   **OK**.

You should now be able to install and activate Simply Accounting version 2010 by following the instructions on page A–10.

Windows Basics, Shortcuts & Terms

WINDOWS BASICS

This section explains the Windows terms and procedures commonly used in the text.

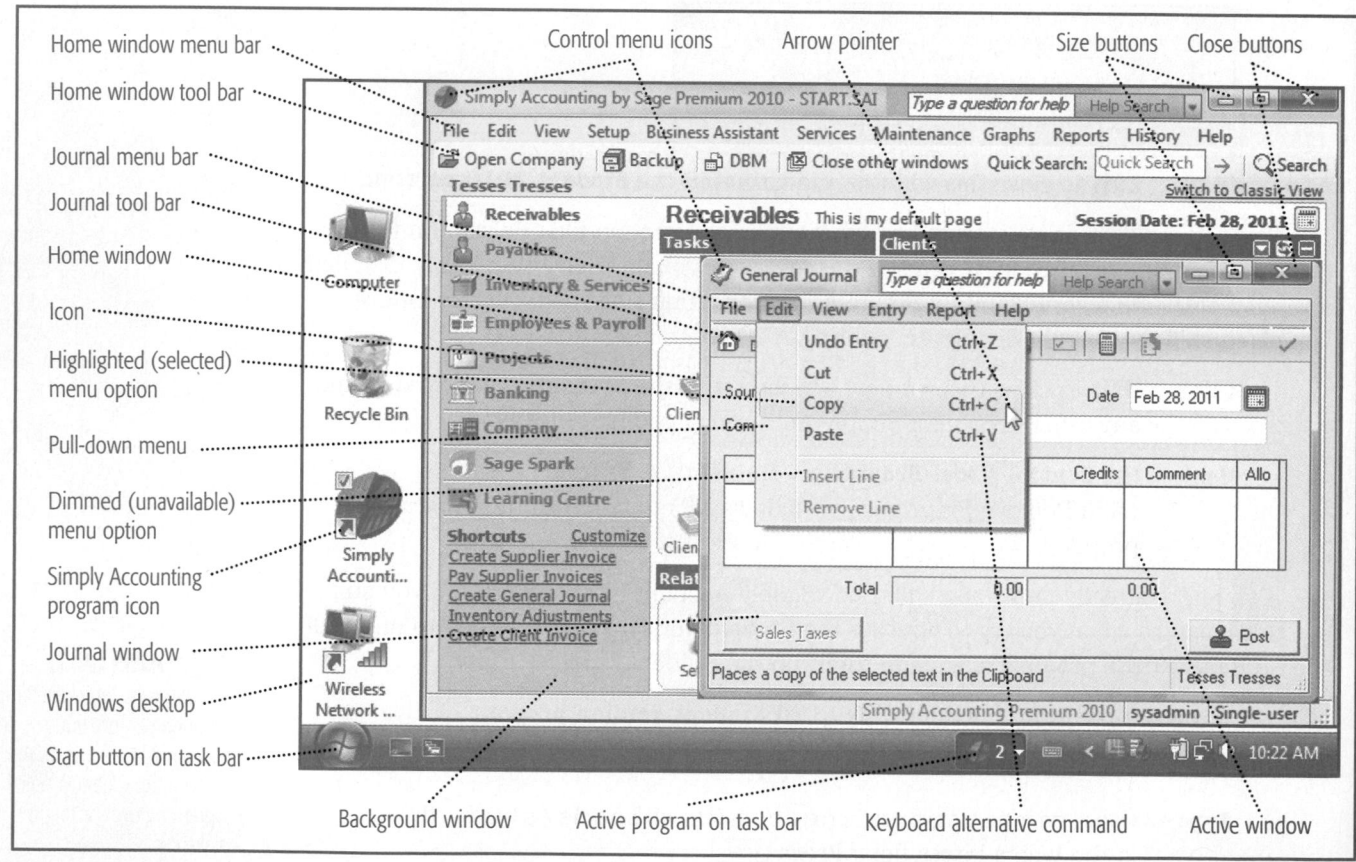

The illustration above shows the Simply Accounting program on the Windows Vista desktop. The General Journal is open and active with the Home window in the background. The Journal's Edit menu is pulled down and Copy is selected.

The **mouse** is used to move the cursor. When you move the mouse, an **arrow** or **pointer** moves to indicate cursor placement. If you **click** (press) the left mouse button, the cursor will move to the location of the arrow (if this is a legitimate place for the cursor to be at the time). That is, you use the mouse to **click** (point to and click) a screen location, item on a list, command or icon.

The arrow or pointer changes shape depending on what actions you may perform. When you are moving the mouse, it appears as an arrow or hand pointer. When you are in a field that can accept text, it appears as a long **I-shaped bar**. Clicking will change it to an insertion point — a flashing vertical line in a text

> **NOTES**
> In Windows XP, the Computer icon is labelled My Computer and the Start button includes the Start label.

field. When the computer is processing information and you are unable to perform any action, you will see an **hourglass** or a **spinning wheel**. This is your signal to wait.

Dragging refers to the method of moving the mouse while holding the left button down. As you drag through the options in a menu, each one will be successively highlighted or darkened. Dragging through text will highlight it. Point to the beginning of the text to be highlighted. Then click and hold the mouse button down while moving through the entire area that you want to highlight. Release the mouse button at the end of the area you want to highlight. You can highlight a single character or the entire contents of a field. The text will remain highlighted and can be edited by typing new text. Delete text by pressing the Backspace key or (del). Clicking a different location will remove the highlighting.

To **double click** means to press the left mouse button twice quickly. This action can be used as a shortcut for opening and closing windows. Double clicking an icon or file name will open it. Double clicking the Control Menu icon will close the window. The Simply Accounting files are set up to open journals and windows with a single click instead of a double click.

The **active window** is the one that you are currently working in. If you click an area outside the active window that is part of a background window, that window will move to the foreground. To return to a previous window, click any part of it that is visible. If the window you need is completely hidden, you can restore it by clicking its button on the task bar. Click ▭ to reduce (minimize) an active window to a task bar button.

An **icon** is a picture form of your program, file name or item. **Buttons** are icons or commands surrounded by a box frame. In Simply Accounting, clicking the Home window tool button ⌂ will bring the Home window to the front and make it active.

The **menu bar** is the line of command group headings at the top of each window. Each menu contains one or more commands or selections (the **pull-down menu**) and can be accessed by clicking the menu name. Each window has different menu selections, and the options in the pull-down menus may differ. To choose an option from the menu, click the menu name and then scroll to **highlight** the option and click to **select** it. If an option is dimmed, you will be unable to highlight or select it.

Some menus are **cascading menus**. When the menu option you want has an arrow, ▶, it has a second level of menu choices. To select from a cascading menu, click the menu bar name and point to the first-level menu option. When the next level of the menu appears, click the selection that you need.

You can **select multiple items** from a screen or list. Click the first item to select it. Then press and hold (ctrl) while you click each of the other items you want to select. The items previously selected will remain selected. If the items are in a list and you want to select several items in a row, click the first item and then press and hold (shift) while clicking the last item that you want to include. All the items between the two will also be selected. To change your selection, click somewhere else.

The **Control Menu icon** is situated in the upper left-hand corner of each window. The icon looks different for different programs and windows. It has its own pull-down menu, including the Close and Size commands. To close windows, you can double click this icon, choose Close from its pull-down menu or click the **Close button** ☒ in the upper right-hand corner of the window.

Size buttons are located in the upper right-hand corner of the window. Click ▣ (**Maximize**) to make the window full screen size or ▭ (**Minimize**) to reduce the window to a task bar button. If the window is full screen size or smaller than usual, restore it to its normal size with the ▣ (**Restore**) button.

You can also change the size of a window by dragging. Point to a side. When the pointer changes to a two-sided arrow ↔ or ↕, drag the window frame to its new size.

When a window contains more information than can fit on the screen at one time, the window will contain **scroll arrows** (▼, ▲, ▶ or ◀) in any corner or direction next to the hidden information (bottom or right sides of the window). Click the arrow and hold the mouse button down to scroll the screen in the direction of the arrow you are on.

Input fields containing data may have a **drop-down** or **pop-up list** from which to select. A **list arrow** beside the field ▼ indicates that a list is available. When you click the arrow, the list appears. Click an item on the list to add it to the input field directly.

SHORTCUTS

Using the Keyboard Instead of a Mouse

All Windows software applications are designed to be used with a mouse. However, there may be times when you prefer to use keyboard commands to work with a program because it is faster. There are also times when you need to know the alternatives to using a mouse, as when the mouse itself is inoperative. It is not necessary to memorize all the keyboard commands. A few basic principles will help you to understand how they work, and over time you will use the ones that help you to work most efficiently. Some commands are common to more than one Windows software program. For example, *ctrl* + C (press and hold the Control key while you press C) is commonly used as the copy command and *ctrl* + V as the paste command. Any selected text or image will be copied or pasted when you use these commands.

The menu bar and the menu choices can be accessed by pressing *alt*. The first menu bar item will be highlighted. Use arrow keys, ⬆ and ⬇, to move up and down through the pull-down menu choices of a highlighted menu item or ⬅ and ➡ to go back and forth to other menu items. Some menu choices have direct keyboard alternatives or shortcuts. If the menu item has an underlined letter, pressing *alt* together with the underlined letter will access that option directly. For example, *alt* + F (press *alt*, and while holding down *alt*, press F) accesses the File pull-down menu. Then pressing O (the underlined letter for Open) will give you the dialogue box for opening a new file. Some tool buttons in Simply Accounting have a direct keyboard command, and some menu choices also have a shortcut keyboard command. When available, these direct keystrokes are given with the tool button name or to the right of a menu choice. For example, *alt* + *f4* is the shortcut for closing the active window or exiting from the Simply Accounting program when the Home window is the active window.

To cancel the menu display, press *esc*.

In the Simply Accounting Home window, you can use the arrow keys to move among the ledger and journal icons. Press *alt*, *alt* and ➡ to highlight the first icon, and then use the arrow keys to change selections. Each icon is highlighted or selected as you reach it and deselected as you move to another icon.

To choose or open a highlighted or selected item, press *enter*.

When input fields are displayed in a Simply Accounting window, you can move to the next field by pressing *tab* or to a previous field by pressing *shift* and *tab* together. The *tab* key is used frequently in this workbook as a quick way to accept input, advance the cursor to the next field and highlight field contents to prepare for immediate editing. Using the mouse while you input information requires you to remove your hands from the keyboard, while the *tab* key does not.

A summary of keyboard shortcuts used in Simply Accounting is included on page A-21.

NOTES
The illustration on page A-18 shows several keyboard alternative commands in the pull-down Edit menu.

SUMMARY OF BASIC KEYBOARD SHORTCUTS

Shortcut	Resulting Action
ctrl + A	**Adjust**, begin the Adjust a Posted Entry function.
ctrl + B	Bring the **Home window** to the front.
ctrl + C	**Copy** the selected text.
ctrl + E	Look up the **Previously Posted Invoice** (from a journal lookup window).
ctrl + F	**Search**, begin the search function.
ctrl + J	**Display** the **journal entry** report.
ctrl + K	**Track shipment** from a previously posted invoice lookup screen.
ctrl + L	Look up a **previously posted transaction** (from the journal window).
ctrl + N	Look up the **next posted Invoice** (from a journal lookup window).
ctrl + N	Open a **new record** window (from a ledger icon or ledger record window).
ctrl + P	**Print**, open the print dialogue box.
ctrl + R	**Recall** a stored journal entry (from a journal window when an entry is stored).
ctrl + R	**Remove** the account record, or remove the quote or order (from ledger, quote or order window).
ctrl + S	Access the **Save As** function from the Home window (Home window, File menu) to save the data file under a new name. Keep the new file open.
ctrl + S	**Save** changes to a record; keep the ledger window open (from any ledger window).
ctrl + T	**Store** the current journal entry (open the Store dialogue box).
ctrl + V	**Paste** the selected text at the cursor position.
ctrl + X	**Cut** (delete) the selected text.
ctrl + Z	**Undo** the most recent change.
alt + C	**Create another** record; saves the record you are creating and opens a new record form to create another new record.
alt + N	**Save and close**; save the new record and close the ledger.
alt + P	**Post** the journal entry or record the order or quote.
alt + **f4**	**Close** the active window (if it has a close button). Closes the program if the Home window is active.
alt + the underlined character on a button	**Select** the button's action. An alternative to clicking the button and/or pressing **enter**.
alt	Access the first item on the **menu bar**.
alt + **alt**	Select the **first icon** in the Home window.
tab	Advance the cursor to the **next field**.
shift + **tab**	Move the cursor to the **previous field**.
Click	**Move** the cursor or **select** an item or entry.
shift + Click	Select **all** the items between the first item clicked and the last one.
ctrl + Click	Select this item **in addition** to ones previously selected.
enter	**Choose** the selected item or action.
Double click	**Select** an entire word or field contents. In fields with lists, open the selection list.
→	**Move right** to the next icon to select it or to the next character in text.
←	**Move left** to the next icon to select it or to the next character in text.
↓	**Move down** to the next icon or entry in a list to select it.
↑	**Move up** to the previous icon or entry in a list to select it.

ACCOUNTING VS NON-ACCOUNTING TERMS

We have used accounting terms in this workbook because they are familiar to students of accounting, and because we needed to provide a consistent language for the book. The most frequently used non-accounting terms are included here for reference and comparison, in case you want to leave the non-accounting terms selected (Home window, Setup menu, User Preferences, Options screen — see page 82).

The chart shows the terms used for the Pro version and for the Premium version when the Other Industry type is selected. For other industries in the Premium version, the terms in the chart on the following page — Terminology Used for Different Types of Industries — will replace the Non-accounting Terms for Payables and Receivables. For example, you may see Providers and Expenses or Supporters and Revenues. The term Suppliers generally replaces Vendors.

SUMMARY OF EQUIVALENT TERMS

MAJOR TERMS	ACCOUNTING TERMS	NON-ACCOUNTING TERMS
	Journal Entries	Transaction Details
	Payables	Vendors & Purchases
	Receivables	Customers & Sales
	Post	Process

DETAILED LIST: LOCATION	ACCOUNTING TERMS	NON-ACCOUNTING TERMS
Setup menu – Settings screen	Payables	Vendors & Purchases
	Receivables	Customers & Sales
Setup menu, User Preferences, View screen – Modules/Pages	Payables (Classic View)	Vendors & Purchases
	Receivables (Classic View)	Customers & Sales
Graphs menu	Payables	Unpaid Purchases
	Receivables	Unpaid Sales
Reports menu and Report Centre – Financials	General Ledger	Transactions by Account
Report Centre – Financials	All Journal Entries	All Transactions
Reports menu and Report Centre	Payables	Vendors & Purchases
	Receivables	Customers & Sales
Reports menu	Journal Entries	Transaction Details
Reports menu – Management Reports	Payables	Vendors & Purchases
	Receivables	Customers & Sales
All Icon window menus	Journal	Transactions
Accounts ledger window	General Ledger	Chart of Accounts Records
Vendors ledger window	Payables Ledger	Vendor Records
Customers ledger window	Receivables Ledger	Customer Records
All journals (button and menu)	Post	Process

TERMS AND INDUSTRY TYPES

In the Premium version, the terms and labels change when you select different types of industries (Setup menu, Settings, Company, Information screen — see page 76). The chart on the following page summarizes the terms you will see when you apply different industry types. You can change the default industry terminology on the Settings, Names screens for the Payables and Receivables modules.

TERMINOLOGY USED FOR DIFFERENT TYPES OF INDUSTRIES

INDUSTRY	TERMS OR LABELS USED IN RECEIVABLES LEDGER				
	Customers	**Sales Invoices**	**Sales Quotes**	**Sales Orders**	**Sales Journal – Invoice**
Pro version (all)	Customers	Sales Invoices	Sales Quotes	Sales Orders	Sales Journal – Invoice
Premium Version					
Accommodation	Guest	Charges	Sales Quotes	Sales Orders	Sales Journal – Charge
Agriculture	Customers	Customer Invoices	Customer Quotes	Customer Orders	Revenues Journal – Invoice
Construction/ Contractor	Customers	Bills	Estimates	Contracts	Sales Journal – Bill
Educational Service	Clients	Statements	Client Quotes	Client Orders	Fees Journal – Statement
Entertainment	Customers	Sales Invoices	Sales Quotes	Sales Orders	Sales Journal – Invoice
Food & Beverage	Guest	Charges	Sales Quotes	Sales Orders	Sales Journal – Charge
Manufacturing/ Industrial	Customers	Sales Invoices	Sales Quotes	Sales Orders	Sales Journal – Invoice
Medical Dental	Patients	Statements	Patient Quotes	Patient Orders	Fees Journal – Statement
Non–profit	Supporters	Statements	Supporter Quotes	Supporter Orders	Revenues Journal – Statement
Other	Customers	Sales Invoices	Sales Quotes	Sales Orders	Sales Journal – Invoice
Personal Service	Clients	Client Invoices	Client Quotes	Client Orders	Revenues Journal – Invoice
Professional Service	Clients	Client Invoices	Client Quotes	Client Orders	Fees Journal – Invoice
Real Estate/ Property	Clients	Statements	Client Quotes	Client Orders	Revenues Journal – Statement
Retail	Customers	Sales Invoices	Sales Quotes	Sales Orders	Sales Journal – Invoice
Service	Clients	Client Invoices	Client Quotes	Client Orders	Revenues Journal – Invoice
Transportation	Customers	Sales Invoices	Sales Quotes	Sales Orders	Sales Journal – Invoice

INDUSTRY	TERMS OR LABELS USED IN PAYABLES LEDGER				
	Vendors	**Purchase Invoices**	**Purchase Quotes**	**Purchase Orders**	**Purchases Journal – Purchase Invoice**
Pro version (all)	Vendors	Purchase Invoices	Purchase Quotes	Purchase Orders	Purchases Journal – Invoice
Premium Version					
Accommodation	Suppliers	Invoices	Purchase Quotes	Purchase Orders	Purchases Journal – Invoice
Agriculture	Suppliers	Purchase Invoices	Purchase Quotes	Purchase Orders	Purchases Journal – Invoice
Construction/ Contractor	Suppliers	Invoices	Quotes	Orders	Purchases Journal – Invoice
Educational Service	Suppliers	Invoices	Purchase Quotes	Purchase Orders	Purchases Journal – Invoice
Entertainment	Suppliers	Supplier Invoices	Supplier Quotes	Supplier Orders	Expenses Journal – Invoice
Food & Beverage	Suppliers	Invoices	Purchase Quotes	Purchase Orders	Purchases Journal – Invoice
Manufacturing/ Industrial	Suppliers	Purchase Invoices	Purchase Quotes	Purchase Orders	Purchases Journal – Invoice
Medical Dental	Suppliers	Invoices	Supplier Quotes	Supplier Orders	Expenses Journal – Invoice
Non–profit	Providers	Invoices	Provider Quotes	Provider Orders	Expenses Journal – Invoice
Other	Vendors	Purchase Invoices	Purchase Quotes	Purchase Orders	Purchases Journal – Invoice
Personal Service	Suppliers	Supplier Invoices	Supplier Quotes	Supplier Orders	Expenses Journal – Invoice
Professional Service	Vendors	Vendor Invoices	Vendor Quotes	Vendor Orders	Expenses Journal – Invoice
Real Estate/ Property	Suppliers	Invoices	Supplier Quotes	Supplier Orders	Expenses Journal – Invoice
Retail	Suppliers	Purchase Invoices	Purchase Quotes	Purchase Orders	Purchases Journal – Invoice
Service	Suppliers	Supplier Invoices	Supplier Quotes	Supplier Orders	Expenses Journal – Invoice
Transportation	Vendors	Purchase Invoices	Purchase Quotes	Purchase Orders	Purchases Journal – Invoice

Terms for Project   Project (for Other, Service, Personal Service, Professional Service, Transportation and all industries in Pro version),
Division (for Accommodation, Education, Entertainment, Food, Manufacturing and Retail),
Crops (for Agriculture), Job Site (for Construction), Partner (for Medical), Fund (for Non-profit), Property (for Real Estate)

APPENDIX C

Correcting Errors after Posting

We all make mistakes. This appendix outlines briefly the procedures you need to follow for those rare occasions when you have posted a journal entry incorrectly and you need to reverse it manually. In most cases, you can use the Adjust Journal Entry or Reverse Entry procedures to make corrections.

Obviously, you should try to detect errors before posting. Reviewing journal entries should become routine practice. The software also has built-in safeguards that help you avoid mistakes. For example, outstanding invoices cannot be overpaid and employee wages and payroll deductions are calculated automatically. Furthermore, names of accounts, customers, vendors, employees and inventory items appear in full, so that you may check your journal information easily.

Before making a reversing entry, consider the consequences of not correcting the error. For example, misspelled customer names may not be desirable, but they will not influence the financial statements. After making the correction in the ledger, the newly printed statement will be correct (the journal will retain the original spelling). Sometimes, however, the mistake is more serious. Financial statements will be incorrect if amounts or accounts are wrong. Payroll tax deductions will be incorrect if a wage amount or linked account is incorrect. GST/HST and PST remittances may be incorrect as a result of incorrect tax codes or sales or purchase amounts. Discounts will be incorrectly calculated if an invoice or payment date is incorrect. Some errors also originate from outside sources. For example, purchase items may be incorrectly priced by the vendor.

NOTES
Adjusting entry procedures are shown on:
    page 47 – General Journal
    page 133 – Purchases
    page 135 – Other Payments
    page 143 – Payments
    page 189 – Sales
    page 281 – Paycheque
    page 296 – Payroll Run
             Entry
Reversing entry procedures are explained on:
    page 49 – General Journal
    page 144 – Purchases
    pages 184 and 601
             – Receipts
    page 283 – Payroll
    page 252 – Historical
             invoices

For audit purposes, prepare a memo explaining the error and the correction procedure. A complete reversing entry is often the simplest way to make the corrections for a straightforward audit trail. With Simply Accounting's one-step reversing entry feature from the Adjust Entry window, the reversing entry is made automatically. This feature is available for General Journal entries, paycheques, sales, purchases, receipts and for most payments. Choose Adjust Invoice from the pull-down menu under the corresponding transaction menu, or click the Adjust Invoice tool in the journal. Then make the corrections if possible, or choose Reverse Entry from the pull-down menu under the corresponding transaction menu or click the Reverse tool. Under all circumstances, you should follow Generally Accepted Accounting Principles. Simply Accounting will create the reversing entry automatically. Reports will include the correct entries after you post the adjusted journal entry. Including the original and reversing entries in reports is optional.

However, this feature is not available for all journals. And when the journal entry deposit account for a receipt is not the bank account (because the deposit was made later) you need to reverse a receipt to record an NSF cheque. Therefore, we will illustrate the procedure for reversing entries in all journals.

Reversing entries in all journals have several common elements. In each case, you should use an appropriate source number that identifies the entry as reversing (e.g., add ADJ or REV to the original source number). You should use the original posting date and add a comment. Make the reversing entry as illustrated on the following pages. Display the journal entry, review it carefully and, when you are certain it is correct, post it. Next, you must enter the correct version of the transaction as a new journal entry with an appropriate identifying source number (e.g., add COR to the original source number).

Reversing entries are presented for each journal. Only the transaction portion of each screen is shown because the remaining parts of the journal screen do not change. The original and reversing entry screens and their corresponding journal displays are included. Explanatory notes appear beside each set of entries.

GENERAL JOURNAL: Original Entry

Account	Debits	Credits	Comment	Allo
1360 Marble Inventory	400.00	--	marble for inventory contracts	
2670 GST Paid on Purchases	20.00	--	GST paid @ 5%	
2120 A/P - Marblehead Suppliers	--	420.00	terms: net 30	
Total	420.00	420.00		

Reversing Entry

Account	Debits	Credits	Comment	Allo
2120 A/P - Marblehead Suppliers	420.00	--	reversing AP amount	
2670 GST Paid on Purchases	--	20.00	reversing GST paid amount	
1360 Marble Inventory	--	400.00	reversing inventory amount	
Total	420.00	420.00		

PURCHASES JOURNAL (NON-INVENTORY): Original Entry

Item Number	Quantity	Order	Back Order	Unit	Item Description	Price	Tax	HST	Amount	Account	Divisions
					equipment rentals		H	78.00	600.00	5110 ...	[Multiple Divisions]

Subtotal:	600.00
Freight:	
Early Payment Terms: % Days, Net 15 Days	
HST:	78.00
Total:	678.00

Purchases Journal Entry 12/14/12 (J24)					
Account Number	Account Description	Division	Debits	Credits	Division Amt
2670	HST Paid on Purchases		78.00	-	
5110	Tool Rentals		600.00	-	
		- Sales Division			120.00
		- Service Division			480.00
2200	Accounts Payable		-	678.00	
Additional Date:	Additional Field:		678.00	678.00	

Reversing Entry

Item Number	Quantity	Order	Back Order	Unit	Item Description	Price	Tax	HST	Amount	Account	Divisions
					reversing equipment rentals		H	-78.00	-600.00	5110 ...	[Multiple Divisions]

Subtotal:	-600.00
Freight:	
Early Payment Terms: % Days, Net 15 Days	
HST:	-78.00
Total:	-678.00

GENERAL JOURNAL

Use the same accounts and amounts in the reversing entry as in the original entry.

Accounts that were debited should be credited and accounts that were credited originally should be debited.

Click the Sales Taxes button if you used this screen. Choose the tax code and, if necessary, enter the Amount Subject To Tax with a minus sign.

Repeat the allocation using the original percentages.

The General Journal display is not shown because it basically looks the same as the journal input form.

You can use the Adjust Entry or Reverse Entry features instead. See page 47 and page 49.

PURCHASES JOURNAL

The only change you must make is that positive amounts in the original entry become negative amounts in the reversing entry (place a minus sign before the amount in the Amount field).

Similarly, negative amounts, such as for GST/HST Paid in GST/HST remittances, must be changed to positive amounts (remove the minus sign).

If freight was charged, enter the amount of freight with a minus sign.

Use the same accounts and amounts in the reversing entry as in the original entry. Tax amounts change automatically.

Repeat the allocation with the original percentages.

You can use the Adjust Invoice and Reverse Invoice options instead (page 133 and page 144). Reversing a paid invoice will generate a credit note.

Remember to "pay" the incorrect and reversing invoices to remove them from the Payments Journal and later clear them.

OTHER PAYMENTS

The only change you must make is that positive amounts in the original entry become negative amounts in the reversing entry (place a minus sign before the amount in the Amount field).

Similarly, negative amounts, such as for GST/HST Paid in GST/HST remittances, must be changed to positive amounts (remove the minus sign).

Use the same accounts and amounts in the reversing entry as in the original entry. Tax amounts change automatically.

Repeat the allocation with the original percentages.

You can use the Adjust Invoice and Reverse Invoice options instead (page 135).

If you see a message about using the next cheque number with a negative amount, click No and enter a memo number or other reference in the cheque number field.

Purchases Journal Entry 12/14/12 (J25)

Account Number	Account Description	Division	Debits	Credits	Division Amt
2200	Accounts Payable		678.00	-	
2670	HST Paid on Purchases		-	78.00	
5110	Tool Rentals		-	600.00	
		- Sales Division			-120.00
		- Service Division			-480.00
Additional Date:	Additional Field:		678.00	678.00	

PAYMENTS JOURNAL — OTHER PAYMENTS: Original Entry

Acct	Description	Amount	Tax	HST	Allo
5150 Telephone Expense	telephone service	200.00	H	26.00	✓

Subtotal	200.00
Tax	26.00
Total	226.00

Payments Journal Entry 12/16/12 (J26)

Account Number	Account Description	Division	Debits	Credits	Division Amt
2670	HST Paid on Purchases		26.00	-	
5150	Telephone Expense		200.00	-	
		- Sales Division			80.00
		- Service Division			120.00
1050	Bank: Chequing CAD		-	226.00	
Additional Date:	Additional Field:		226.00	226.00	

Reversing Entry

Acct	Description	Amount	Tax	HST	Allo
5150 Telephone Expense	reversing telephone invoice	-200.00	H	-26.00	✓

Subtotal	-200.00
Tax	-26.00
Total	-226.00

Payments Journal Entry 12/17/12 (J27)

Account Number	Account Description	Division	Debits	Credits	Division Amt
1050	Bank: Chequing CAD		226.00	-	
2670	HST Paid on Purchases		-	26.00	
5150	Telephone Expense		-	200.00	
		- Sales Division			-80.00
		- Service Division			-120.00
Additional Date:	Additional Field:		226.00	226.00	

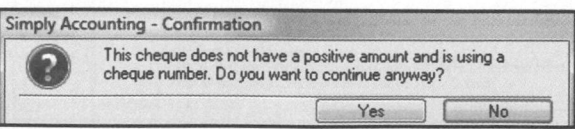

Simply Accounting - Confirmation

This cheque does not have a positive amount and is using a cheque number. Do you want to continue anyway?

[Yes] [No]

PAYROLL REMITTANCES

Payroll remittance entries cannot be reversed. You must make corrections in the Adjustments column of the Remittance Journal if incorrect amounts were remitted. When you enter an amount in the Adjustments column, the program warns you with the message shown here.

Positive remittance adjustment amounts create expense account entries — they do not affect the payable amounts in the ledger. You must make additional General Journal adjusting entries so that the final ledger amounts are correct.

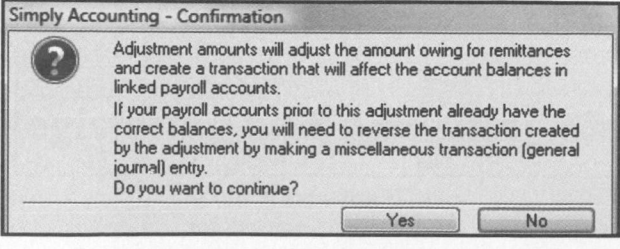

Simply Accounting - Confirmation

Adjustment amounts will adjust the amount owing for remittances and create a transaction that will affect the account balances in linked payroll accounts.

If your payroll accounts prior to this adjustment already have the correct balances, you will need to reverse the transaction created by the adjustment by making a miscellaneous transaction (general journal) entry.

Do you want to continue?

[Yes] [No]

PAYMENTS: Original Entry

Due Date	Invoice or Prepayment	Original Amount	Amount Owing	Discount Available	Discount Taken	Payment Amount
Jan 12, 2013	MT-1521	856.54	856.54	17.13	17.13	839.41
					Total	839.41

Payments Journal Entry 12/18/12 (J27)			
Account Number	Account Description	Debits	Credits
2200	Accounts Payable	856.54	-
1050	Bank: Chequing CAD	-	839.41
5130	Purchase Discounts	-	17.13
Additional Date:	Additional Field:	856.54	856.54

Reversing Entry

Due Date	Invoice or Prepayment	Original Amount	Amount Owing	Discount Available	Discount Taken	Payment Amount
Dec 27, 2012	MT-1142	678.00	0.00	0.00	0.00	
Jan 12, 2013	MT-1521	856.54	0.00	0.00	-17.13	-839.41
					Total	-839.41

Payments Journal Entry 12/18/12 (J28)			
Account Number	Account Description	Debits	Credits
1050	Bank: Chequing CAD	839.41	-
5130	Purchase Discounts	17.13	-
2200	Accounts Payable	-	856.54
Additional Date:	Additional Field:	856.54	856.54

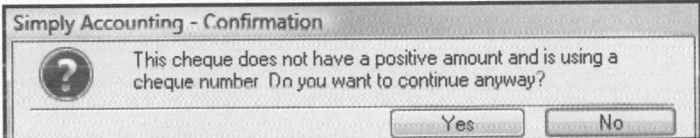

Simply Accounting – Confirmation

This cheque does not have a positive amount and is using a cheque number. Do you want to continue anyway?

[Yes]   [No]

CREDIT CARD PAYMENTS: Original Entry

Credit Card Payable Account Balance:	235.00
Additional Fees and Interest:	20.00
Payment Amount:	220.00

Payments Journal Entry 12/19/12 (J29)			
Account Number	Account Description	Debits	Credits
2250	Credit Card Payable	200.00	-
5040	Credit Card Fees	20.00	-
1050	Bank: Chequing CAD	-	220.00
Additional Date:	Additional Field:	220.00	220.00

Reversing Entry

Credit Card Payable Account Balance:	35.00
Additional Fees and Interest:	-20.00
Payment Amount:	-220.00

Payments Journal Entry 12/19/12 (J30)			
Account Number	Account Description	Debits	Credits
1050	Bank: Chequing CAD	220.00	-
2250	Credit Card Payable	-	200.00
5040	Credit Card Fees	-	20.00
Additional Date:	Additional Field:	220.00	220.00

PAYMENTS

Click the Include Fully Paid Invoices tool button.

The change you must make is that positive amounts in the original entry become negative amounts in the reversing entry.

If a discount was taken, click the invoice line for the payment being reversed in the Discount Taken field. Type the discount amount with a minus sign. Press _tab_ to enter the payment amount. The minus sign will be added.

If no discount was taken, click the invoice line for the payment being reversed in the Payment Amount field. Type a minus sign and the amount.

Click No if you see the warning about posting a negative cheque amount and enter another reference number instead.

This will restore the original balance owing for the invoice.

If you have already cleared the paid invoice, prepare a new Purchases Journal entry for the amount of the payment (non-taxable) to restore the balance owing. Enter a positive amount in the Amount field for the amount of the cheque and the Bank account in the Account field (to avoid entering the expense twice). On the next line, enter the discount amount (positive) with the Purchase Discounts account in the Account field. This will debit the Bank and Purchase Discounts accounts and credit Accounts Payable.

You can also use the Adjust Payment tool or the Reverse Payment feature. (See page 143 and page 184.)

CREDIT CARD PAYMENTS

Enter the same amounts as in the original entry.

Add a minus sign to the Additional Fees And Interest amount and to the Payment Amount in the reversing entry.

Enter a memo number or other reference in the cheque number field to avoid using a cheque number for a negative amount.

INVENTORY PURCHASES

Change positive quantities in the original entry to negative ones in the reversing entry (place a minus sign before the quantity in the Quantity field).

Similarly, change negative quantities, such as for returns, to positive ones (remove the minus sign).

Add a minus sign to the freight amount if freight is charged.

Use the same accounts and amounts in the reversing entry as in the original entry. Tax amounts are corrected automatically.

Repeat the allocation using the original percentages.

You can use the Adjust Invoice and Reverse Invoice options instead (page 133 and page 144).

Remember to "pay" the incorrect and reversing invoices to remove them from the Payments Journal and later clear them.

SALES JOURNAL

For inventory sales, change positive quantities in the original entry to negative ones in the reversing entry (place a minus sign before the quantity in the Quantity field). Similarly, change negative quantities, such as for returns, to positive ones (remove the minus sign).

For non-inventory sales, change positive amounts in the original entry to negative amounts in the reversing entry (place a minus sign before the amount in the Amount column).

Add a minus sign to the freight amount if freight is charged. Add the salesperson.

Use the same accounts and amounts in the reversing entry as in the original entry, and the same method of payment.

Repeat the allocation using the original percentages.

You can use the Adjust Invoice and Reverse Invoice options instead (page 189). Reversing a paid invoice will generate a credit note.

Remember to "pay" the incorrect and reversing invoices to remove them from the Receipts Journal and later clear them.

INVENTORY PURCHASES: Original Entry

Item Number	Quantity	Order	Back Order	Unit	Item Description	Price	Tax	HST	Amount	Account	Divisions
T104	20			Each	P205/75R15 Tires	56.00	H	145.60	1,120.00	1400 ...	
T108	20			Each	P185/60R15 Tires	48.00	H	124.80	960.00	1400 ...	

Subtotal:	2,080.00	
Freight:	200.00 H	26.00 ☑
HST:	296.40	
Total:	2,576.40	

Early Payment Terms: 2.00 % 10 Days, Net 30 Days

Purchases Journal Entry 12/14/12 (J31)

Account Number	Account Description	Division	Debits	Credits	Division Amt
1400	Winter Tires		2,080.00	-	
2670	HST Paid on Purchases		296.40	-	
5065	Freight Expense		200.00	-	
		- Sales Division			200.00
2200	Accounts Payable		-	2,576.40	
Additional Date:	Additional Field:		2,576.40	2,576.40	

Reversing Entry

Item Number	Quantity	Order	Back Order	Unit	Item Description	Price	Tax	HST	Amount	Account	Divisions
T104	-20			Each	P205/75R15 Tires	56.00	H	-145.60	-1,120.00	1400 ...	
T108	-20			Each	P185/60R15 Tires	48.00	H	-124.80	-960.00	1400 ...	

Subtotal:	-2,080.00	
Freight:	-200.00 H	-26.00 ☑
HST:	-296.40	
Total:	-2,576.40	

Early Payment Terms: 2.00 % 10 Days, Net 30 Days

Purchases Journal Entry 12/14/12 (J32)

Account Number	Account Description	Division	Debits	Credits	Division Amt
2200	Accounts Payable		2,576.40	-	
1400	Winter Tires		-	2,080.00	
2670	HST Paid on Purchases		-	296.40	
5065	Freight Expense		-	200.00	
		- Sales Division			-200.00
Additional Date:	Additional Field:		2,576.40	2,576.40	

SALES JOURNAL (INVENTORY AND NON-INVENTORY): Original Entry

Item Number	Quantity	Unit	Item Description	Price	Amount	Tax	Account	Divisions
CL08	2	tube	Protection Cream: dbl action 60 ml	25.00	50.00	GP	4020 Reve...	Sales
CL05	1	jar	Masks: herb 100 ml	40.00	40.00	GP	4020 Reve...	Sales
			consultation		150.00	G	4040 Reve...	Service

Subtotal:	240.00		
Freight:	10.00 G	0.50	☑
GST:	12.50		
RST:	6.30		
Total:	268.80		

Early Payment Terms: 2.00 % 5 Days, Net 30 Days

Message:

Sales Journal Entry 02/14/2012 (J22)

Account Number	Account Description	Division	Debits	Credits	Division Amt
1200	Accounts Receivable		268.80	-	
5060	Cost of Goods Sold		42.00	-	
		- Sales			42.00
1310	Creams and Lotions		-	42.00	
2640	RST Payable		-	6.30	
2650	GST Charged on Sales		-	12.50	
4020	Revenue from Sales		-	90.00	
		- Sales			90.00
4040	Revenue from Services		-	150.00	
		- Service			150.00
4080	Freight Revenue		-	10.00	
		- Sales			10.00
Additional Date:	Additional Field:		310.80	310.80	

Reversing Entry

Item Number	Quantity	Unit	Item Description	Price	Amount	Tax	Account	Divisions
CL08	-2	tube	Protection Cream: dbl action 60 ml	25.00	-50.00	GP	4020 Reve...	Sales
CL05	-1	jar	Masks: herb 100 ml	40.00	-40.00	GP	4020 Reve...	Sales
			consultation		-150.00	G	4040 Reve...	Service

Subtotal: -240.00
Freight: -10.00 G   -0.50 ✓
Early Payment Terms: 2.00 % 5 Days, Net 30 Days
GST: -12.50
RST: -6.30
Message:
Total: -268.80

Sales Journal Entry 02/14/2012 (J23)					
Account Number	Account Description	Division	Debits	Credits	Division Amt.
1310	Creams and Lotions		42.00	-	
2640	RST Payable		6.30	-	
2650	GST Charged on Sales		12.50	-	
4020	Revenue from Sales		90.00	-	
		- Sales			-90.00
4040	Revenue from Services		150.00	-	
		- Service			-150.00
4080	Freight Revenue		10.00	-	
		- Sales			-10.00
1200	Accounts Receivable		-	268.80	
5060	Cost of Goods Sold		-	42.00	
		- Sales			42.00
Additional Date:	Additional Field:		310.80	310.80	

DEPOSITS or PREPAYMENTS: Original Entry

Invoice Date	Invoice or Deposit	Original Amount	Amount Owing	Discount Available	Discount Taken	Amount Received
Dec 13, 2012	130	4,725.66	4,725.66	94.51		

Deposit Reference No. 18
Deposit Amount 500.00
Total 500.00

Receipts Journal Entry 12/14/12 (J33)			
Account Number	Account Description	Debits	Credits
1050	Bank: Chequing CAD	500.00	-
2150	Prepaid Sales and Deposits	-	500.00
Additional Date:	Additional Field:	500.00	500.00

Reversing Entry

Invoice Date	Invoice or Deposit	Original Amount	Amount Owing	Discount Available	Discount Taken	Amount Received
Dec 13, 2012	130	4,725.66	4,725.66	94.51		
	Deposits					
	18	500.00	500.00			500.00

Deposit Reference No. 19
Deposit Amount 0.00
Total -500.00

Receipts Journal Entry 12/14/12 (J34)			
Account Number	Account Description	Debits	Credits
2150	Prepaid Sales and Deposits	500.00	-
1050	Bank: Chequing CAD	-	500.00
Additional Date:	Additional Field:	500.00	500.00

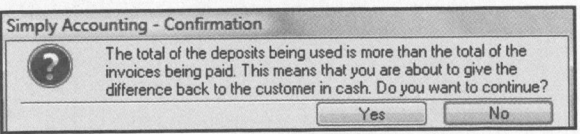

Simply Accounting - Confirmation
The total of the deposits being used is more than the total of the invoices being paid. This means that you are about to give the difference back to the customer in cash. Do you want to continue?
Yes   No

RECEIPTS

Click ⬚, the Include Fully Paid Invoices tool.

Change positive amounts in the original entry to negative amounts in the reversing entry.

If a discount was taken, click the invoice line for the payment being reversed in the Discount Taken field. Type the discount amount with a minus sign. Press tab to enter the payment amount. The minus sign will be added. Type a minus sign and enter the amount for the deposit.

If no discount was taken, click the invoice line for the payment being reversed in the Payment Amount field. Type a minus sign with the amounts for both invoices and deposits.

This will restore the original balance owing for the invoice.

If you have already cleared the invoice, make a new Sales Journal entry for the payment amount (non-taxable) to restore the balance owing. Enter both the cheque and discount amounts as positive amounts and enter the Bank and Sales Discounts accounts instead of Revenue.

You can use the Adjust Receipt and Reverse Receipt options instead (page 184).

If an NSF cheque uses a different bank account from the deposit entry, you must reverse the receipt manually. Choose the Bank account in the Deposit To field.

PAYROLL JOURNAL

Redo the original incorrect entry but DO NOT POST IT!

Click the Enter Taxes Manually tool to open all the deduction fields for editing.

Type a minus sign in front of the number of hours (regular and overtime) or in front of salary, commission and bonus amounts and piece rate quantity. Press tab to update all amounts, including vacation pay (change them to negative amounts).

For the Advance field, change the sign for the amount. Advances should have a minus sign in the reversing entry and advances recovered should be positive amounts. ▶

RECEIPTS WITH DEPOSITS: Original Entry

Invoice Date	Invoice or Deposit	Original Amount	Amount Owing	Discount Available	Discount Taken	Amount Received
Dec 13, 2012	130	4,725.66	4,725.66	94.51	94.51	4,631.15
	Deposits					
	18	500.00	500.00			500.00

Deposit Reference No. 19		Deposit Amount	0.00
		Total	4,131.15

Receipts Journal Entry 12/14/12 (J34)			
Account Number	Account Description	Debits	Credits
1050	Bank: Chequing CAD	4,131.15	-
2150	Prepaid Sales and Deposits	500.00	-
4150	Sales Discounts	94.51	-
1200	Accounts Receivable	-	4,725.66
Additional Date:	Additional Field:	4,725.66	4,725.66

Reversing Entry

Invoice Date	Invoice or Deposit	Original Amount	Amount Owing	Discount Available	Discount Taken	Amount Received
Dec 01, 2012	102	791.00	0.00	0.00		
Dec 13, 2012	130	4,725.66	0.00	0.00	-94.51	-4,631.15
	Deposits					
	18	500.00	0.00			-500.00

Deposit Reference No. 19		Deposit Amount	0.00
		Total	-4,131.15

Receipts Journal Entry 12/15/12 (J37)			
Account Number	Account Description	Debits	Credits
1200	Accounts Receivable	4,725.66	
1050	Bank: Chequing CAD	-	4,131.15
2150	Prepaid Sales and Deposits	-	500.00
4150	Sales Discounts	-	94.51
Additional Date:	Additional Field:	4,725.66	4,725.66

PAYROLL JOURNAL: Original Entry

Income | Deductions | Taxes | User-Defined Expense | Entitlements   Period Ending Dec 14, 2012

Earnings:

Name	Hours	Pieces	Amount	YTD
Regular	80.00	--	1,280.00	31,360.00
Overtime 1	5.00	--	120.00	936.00
Piece Rate	--	10.00	50.00	50.00
Bonus	--	--	100.00	100.00
Total	85.00	10.00	1,550.00	

Other:

Name	Amount	YTD
Advance	100.00	100.00
Benefits	50.00	50.00
Vac. Accrued	58.00	1,911.00
Vac. Paid	0.00	
Tot.	208.00	

Gross Pay 1,600.00   Withheld   -462.27   Net Pay   1,187.73   &Post

Income | Deductions | Taxes | User-Defined Expense | Entitlements

Deductions:

Name	Amount	YTD
CSB	100.00	100.00
Union Dues	16.00	324.96
Total	116.00	

Income | Deductions | Taxes | User-Defined Expense | Entitlements

CPP/QPP	72.54	QPIP
EI	25.09	
Tax	248.64	
Tax (Que)		

Income | Deductions | Taxes | User-Defined Expense | Entitlements

Amount per pay period

Medical	20.00

Income | Deductions | Taxes | User-Defined Expense | Entitlements

The number of hours worked in this pay period: 80.00

	Days Earned	Days Released
Vacation		
Sick Leave	0.50	1.00
Personal Day	0.25	

Payroll Journal Entry 12/14/12 (J38)

Account Number	Account Description	Debits	Credits
1120	Advances Receivable	100.00	-
5310	General Wages	1,458.00	-
5320	Piece Rate Wage Expense	50.00	-
5330	Commissions and Bonuses	100.00	-
5350	Medical Benefit Expense	20.00	-
5410	EI Expense	35.13	-
5420	CPP Expense	72.54	-
5430	WSIB Expense	54.40	-
5460	EHT Expense	15.68	-
1050	Bank: Chequing CAD	-	1,187.73
2300	Vacation Payable	-	58.00
2310	EI Payable	-	60.22
2320	CPP Payable	-	145.08
2330	Income Tax Payable	-	248.64
2350	Medical Payable	-	20.00
2390	EHT Payable	-	15.68
2400	CSB Payable	-	100.00
2410	Union Dues Payable	-	16.00
2460	WSIB Payable	-	54.40
Additional Date:	Additional Field:	1,905.75	1,905.75

Reversing Entry

Income | Deductions | Taxes | User-Defined Expense | Entitlements — Period Ending Dec 14, 2012

Earnings:

Name	Hours	Pieces	Amount	YTD
Regular	-80.00	--	-1,280.00	28,800.00
Overtime 1	-5.00	--	-120.00	696.00
Piece Rate	--	-10.00	-50.00	-50.00
Bonus	--	--	-100.00	-100.00
Total	-85.00	-10.00	-1,550.00	

Other:

Name	Amount	YTD
Advance	-100.00	-100.00
Benefits	-50.00	-50.00
Vac. Accrued	-58.00	1,795.00
Vac. Paid	0.00	--
Tot.	-208.00	

Gross Pay -1,600.00 Withheld 462.27 Net Pay -1,187.73 [Post]

Income | **Deductions** | Taxes | User-Defined Expense | Entitlements

Deductions:

Name	Amount	YTD
CSB	-100.00	-100.00
Union Dues	-16.00	292.96
Total	-116.00	

Income | Deductions | **Taxes** | User-Defined Expense | Entitlements

CPP/QPP	-72.54	QPIP
EI	-25.09	
Tax	-248.64	
Tax (Que)		

Income | Deductions | Taxes | **User-Defined Expense** | Entitlements

Amount per pay period

Medical	-20.00

Income | Deductions | Taxes | User-Defined Expense | **Entitlements**

The number of hours worked in this pay period: -80.00

	Days Earned	Days Released
Vacation		
Sick Leave	1.50	
Personal Day		

Payroll Journal Entry 12/14/12 (J38)

Account Number	Account Description	Debits	Credits
1050	Bank: Chequing CAD	1,187.73	-
2300	Vacation Payable	58.00	-
2310	EI Payable	60.22	-
2320	CPP Payable	145.08	-
2330	Income Tax Payable	248.64	-
2350	Medical Payable	20.00	-
2390	EHT Payable	15.68	-
2400	CSB Payable	100.00	-
2410	Union Dues Payable	16.00	-
2460	WSIB Payable	54.40	-
1120	Advances Receivable	-	100.00
5310	General Wages	-	1,458.00
5320	Piece Rate Wage Expense	-	50.00
5330	Commissions and Bonuses	-	100.00
5350	Medical Benefit Expense	-	20.00
5410	EI Expense	-	35.13
5420	CPP Expense	-	72.54
5430	WSIB Expense	-	54.40
5460	EHT Expense	-	15.68
Additional Date:	Additional Field:	1,905.75	1,905.75

PAYROLL JOURNAL CONTINUED

▶Click the Deductions tab and edit each deduction amount by typing a minus sign in front of it.

Click the Taxes tab. Check the amounts for CPP, EI and Tax with the original journal entry because these amounts may be incorrect (the employee may have reached the maximum contribution since the original entry, or may have entered a different tax bracket). Change the amounts to match the original entry if necessary. The Employee Detail Report will provide the amounts entered for each paycheque.

Click the User-Defined Expenses tab. Change the original positive amounts to negative by adding a minus sign.

Click the Entitlements tab. Add a minus sign to the number of hours worked. You cannot enter a negative number for days released so you must edit the number of days earned. Click the number in the Days Earned field for the entitlements taken. Add back the number of days released from the original entry. For example, change 0.5 to 1.5 if 1 day was taken.

Repeat the allocation with the original percentages.

Remember to click the Calculate Taxes Automatically button before you make the correct payroll entry.

The year-to-date balances will be restored.

You can use the Adjust Cheque option or Reverse Cheque instead to reverse and correct the Paycheque or Payroll Run journal entry (see page 281 and page 283). Using the reverse cheque approach may be safer, as payroll transactions are complex.

NOTES

When you are reversing a direct deposit entry, you must confirm that a negative amount is entered as the net deposit. Click No and enter another reference number in the cheque/deposit number field.

ITEM ASSEMBLY JOURNAL

Re-enter the assembly as you did originally.

Type a minus sign in front of each quantity in the Qty field in both the Assembly Components and Assembled Items sections.

Also type a minus sign in front of the amount for Additional Costs.

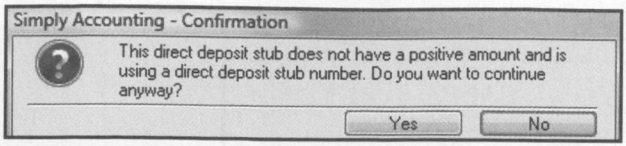

ITEM ASSEMBLY JOURNAL: Original Entry

Assembly Components

Item	Qty	Unit	Description	Unit Cost	Amount
T110	20	Each	P195/65R16 Tires	50.00	1,000.00
W107	20	Each	Chrome-Steel R16 Wheels	35.00	700.00
				Additional Costs	250.00
				Total	1,950.00

Assembled Items

Item	Qty	Unit	Description	Unit Cost	Amount
WHP1	5	pkg	Tires/Wheels/Winter Pkg	390.00	1,950.00
				Total	1,950.00

Bill of Materials & Item Assembly Journal Entry 12/12/12 (J32)

Account Number	Account Description	Debits	Credits
1420	Winter-Holiday Tire Packages	1,950.00	-
1360	Wheels	-	700.00
1400	Winter Tires	-	1,000.00
5045	Assembly Costs	-	250.00
Additional Date:	Additional Field:	1,950.00	1,950.00

Reversing Entry

Assembly Components

Item	Qty	Unit	Description	Unit Cost	Amount
T110	-20	Each	P195/65R16 Tires	50.00	-1,000.00
W107	-20	Each	Chrome-Steel R16 Wheels	35.00	-700.00
				Additional Costs	-250.00
				Total	-1,950.00

Assembled Items

Item	Qty	Unit	Description	Unit Cost	Amount
WHP1	-5	pkg	Tires/Wheels/Winter Pkg	390.00	-1,950.00
				Total	-1,950.00

Bill of Materials & Item Assembly Journal Entry 12/12/12 (J38)

Account Number	Account Description	Debits	Credits
1360	Wheels	700.00	-
1400	Winter Tires	1,000.00	-
5045	Assembly Costs	250.00	-
1420	Winter-Holiday Tire Packages	-	1,950.00
Additional Date:	Additional Field:	1,950.00	1,950.00

ADJUSTMENTS JOURNAL: Original Entry

Item	Qty	Unit	Description	Unit Cost	Amount	Acct	Allo
T107	-2	Each	P185/65R15 Tires	40.00	-80.00	5100 Invenl	√
				Total	-80.00		

Inventory Adjustments Journal Entry 12/10/12 (J41)					
Account Number	Account Description	Division	Debits	Credits	Division Amt
5100	Inventory Adjustment		80.00	-	
		- Service Division			80.00
1400	Winter Tires		-	80.00	
Additional Date:	Additional Field:		80.00	80.00	

Reversing Entry

Item	Qty	Unit	Description	Unit Cost	Amount	Acct	Allo
T107	2	Each	P185/65R15 Tires	40.00	80.00	5100 Invenl	√
				Total	80.00		

Inventory Adjustments Journal Entry 12/11/12 (J42)					
Account Number	Account Description	Division	Debits	Credits	Division Amt
1400	Winter Tires		80.00	-	
5100	Inventory Adjustment		-	80.00	
		- Service Division			-80.00
Additional Date:	Additional Field:		80.00	80.00	

TRANSFER FUNDS JOURNAL: Original Entry

Currency:	JPY ▼	Exchange Rate: 0.0100000 $
Transfer from:	1050 Bank: Chequing CAD ▼	
Transfer to:	1060 Bank: Foreign Currency ▼	
Amount:	100,000 JPY	
Comment:	transfer to cover cheque	

Reversing Entry

Currency:	JPY ▼	Exchange Rate: 0.0100000 $
Transfer from:	1060 Bank: Foreign Currency ▼	
Transfer to:	1050 Bank: Chequing CAD ▼	
Amount:	100,000 JPY	
Comment:	reverse funds transfer entry	

General Journal 12/14/12 to 12/14/12						
		Account Number	Account Description	Debits	Credits	Foreign A...
12/14/12	J42	FundsTransfer, transfer to cover cheque				
		1060	Bank: Foreign Currency	1,000.00	-	¥100,000
		1050	Bank: Chequing CAD	-	1,000.00	¥100,000
1 Japanese Yen equals 0.0100000 Canadian Dollars						
12/14/12	J43	FundsTransfer, reverse funds transfer entry				
		1050	Bank: Chequing CAD	1,000.00	-	¥100,000
		1060	Bank: Foreign Currency	-	1,000.00	¥100,000
1 Japanese Yen equals 0.0100000 Canadian Dollars				2,000.00	2,000.00	

ADJUSTMENTS JOURNAL

Change the sign for the quantity in the Qty field (positive to negative or negative to positive).

Repeat the allocation using the original percentages.

TRANSFER FUNDS JOURNAL

The easiest way to reverse the transfer is to enter the same amounts but switch the bank accounts. Enter the original Transfer From account in the Transfer To field. Enter the original Transfer To account in the Transfer From field.

There is no journal entry to review. You can see the reversal in the General Journal Report. The two related General Journal Report entries are shown here.

For foreign currency transfers, use the same exchange rate for both the original and the reversing transfer.

You can also use the Adjust Entry or Reverse Entry procedure for the transfer in the General Journal. When you look up transactions, the transfer entry is included. You can select it and then adjust it or reverse it like any other General Journal transaction (page 47 and page 49).

BILL OF MATERIALS JOURNAL

Change the sign for the quantity in the Quantity To Build field (positive to negative or negative to positive).

Notice that the journal entries are the same as those for the Item Assembly Journal transactions on page A-32.

BILL OF MATERIALS JOURNAL: Original Entry

Items to Build

Item	Unit	Description	Quantity to build
AP200	Each	Starter package	2

Bill of Materials & Item Assembly Journal Entry 08/01/2012 (J2)

Account Number	Account Description	Debits	Credits
1510	Promotions	92.00	-
1520	Accessories	-	42.00
1560	Books	-	50.00
Additional Date:	Ref. Number:	92.00	92.00

Reversing Entry

Items to Build

Item	Unit	Description	Quantity to build
AP200	Each	Starter package	-2

Bill of Materials & Item Assembly Journal Entry 08/01/2012 (J3)

Account Number	Account Description	Debits	Credits
1520	Accessories	42.00	-
1560	Books	50.00	-
1510	Promotions	-	92.00
Additional Date:	Ref. Number:	92.00	92.00

TRANSFER INVENTORY JOURNAL

You cannot enter a negative quantity in the Transfer Inventory Journal.

Enter the transaction in the same way as the original one with one change – switch the locations for the From and To fields. Enter the original From location in the To field and the original To location in the From field.

No journal entry results from this transaction. However, the inventory ledger records will be updated for both locations.

TRANSFER INVENTORY JOURNAL: Original Entry

Transfer between Locations   From   Hamilton   to   Burlington
Source   Memo 52   Date   Aug 01, 2012
Comment   inventory transfer to new store

Item	Qty	Unit	Description	Unit Cost	Amount
B010	50	each	Books	25.00	1,250.00
A030	100	kg	Dumbbells	0.90	90.00

Reversing Entry

Transfer between Locations   From   Burlington   to   Hamilton
Source   Memo 53   Date   Aug 01, 2012
Comment   reversing inventory transfer

Item	Qty	Unit	Description	Unit Cost	Amount
B010	50	each	Books	25.00	1,250.00
A030	100	kg	Dumbbells	0.90	90.00

Working in Multi-User Mode

WORKING IN MULTI-USER MODE

The Premium and Enterprise versions are available in multi- and single-user versions. The Pro version allows only a single user to access the data file at once.

In multi-user mode, several people can access and work with a data file at the same time. Some features and functions are not available in multi-user mode. These restrictions are described in the text whenever they apply. Access to some aspects of the program may be restricted to the system administrator (sysadmin).

Accessing Data Files

Multi-user versions allow more than one user to access the data files at the same time, with or without passwords. When no users and passwords are set up for a data file, access to the file is the same for multi- and single-user mode. The data file opens in single-user mode. Once the data file is open, you can switch to multi-user mode from the File menu.

If you try to open a data file that is currently used by another user in single-user mode, you will see the following error message:

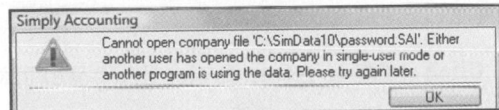

Click **OK** to close the message.

Only one person at a time can work with a data file in single-user mode, so you must switch the status of the open file to multi-user.

Choose the **File menu** and **click Switch To Multi-User Mode**.

If you have not entered users, the Add Users wizard will begin (see the instructions in Appendix H, page A-102 on the Student DVD). Otherwise, you will see the following warning:

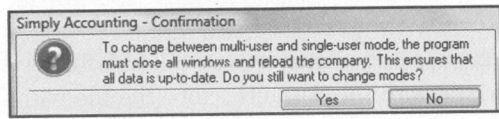

Click **Yes** to proceed.

No changes are apparent in the Home window, but some menu options are dimmed because they are not available in multi-user mode. All Refresh tools in the ledger and journal windows will be available and no longer dimmed.

If users and passwords have been set up for the program, you will see the following screen when you open the data file:

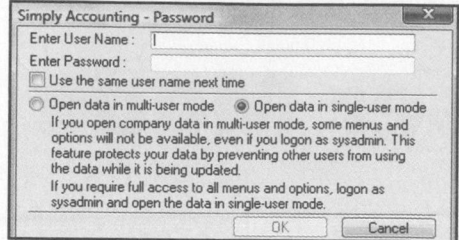

Enter your user name and password; choose whether you want to work in single-user or multi-user mode and then click OK. Passwords are case sensitive. That is, you must type the password in upper- or lower-case letters, exactly as the password was created initially. For more information on creating and using passwords, refer to Chapter 16, page 680 and Appendix H on the Student DVD.

If another user is already working with the data file when you try to access it in single-user mode, you will see the following warning:

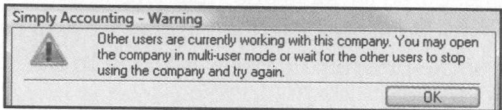

You must open the data file in multi-user mode, wait until the other users have finished or, if only one person is using the file, switch that user's file to multi-user mode.

Click   OK to return to the Select Company window.

To switch to single-user mode at any time:

Choose the **File menu** and **click Switch To Single-User Mode**.

If other users are currently using the file, you will see the following warning:

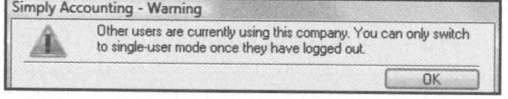

Click   OK to return to the Home window.

If you are working in multi-user mode, your user name and "Multi-user" will appear in the right-hand corner of the status bar as shown:

When you close a data file in multi-user mode, you will see the following closing message about backups:

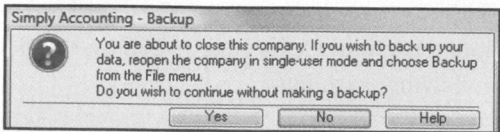

Before making a backup, you must switch to single-user mode. If other users are still working with the data file, close the file without making a backup.

Click   Yes to close the file without making a backup.

Restrictions in Multi-User Mode

Some aspects of the program are unavailable when you are working in multi-user mode. You will be unable to change the settings for any modules, clear data, make or restore backups, save the file under a different name, import or export records or transactions, update price lists, merge records, use data base checking and repair utilities, modify checklists, remove or modify user settings and passwords (although you can create new users). You can export GIFI reports and upload direct deposit files but not T4s or ROEs. You can change the session date, but you cannot start a new year.

Refreshing Data in Multi-User Mode

In multi-user mode, different users can work with and modify the same data file at the same time. Therefore, the program allows you to automatically refresh the data set with changes made by other users or to refresh the data set only when the Refresh option is selected. You can refresh lists, Home window record balances or both. All ledger, journal and report windows include Refresh tools that allow you to update the data periodically. If you want the program to update the data continually, you can change this preference setting for individual users.

NOTES
The Automatically Refresh Lists setting does not apply to all users. It is set by individual users.

Choose the **Setup menu**, then **choose User Preferences** and **click Options**:

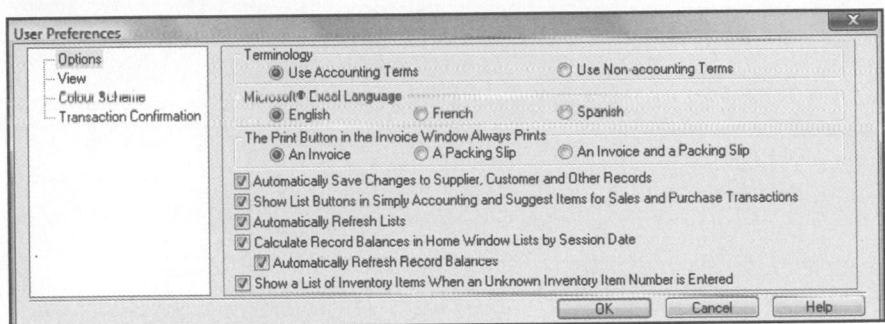

Click   Automatically Refresh Lists to change the setting.

Click   OK to save the change.

Refresh Tools

All journals have the **Refresh Lists** tool in the tool bar. This tool applies to the multi-user mode — different users use, access and modify the company data files simultaneously. Clicking the Refresh Lists tool ensures that you use the most recent version of the data set — the one that exists after all changes from all users have been applied.

NOTES
In single-user mode, the Refresh Report tool will update an open report with data you added (such as journal entries or record changes) since you displayed the report initially.

All report windows include the **Refresh Report** tool icon. In multi-user mode, the journal entry number is omitted from the journal display (different users may be creating journal entries at the same time so the number is not known for certain until after posting).

The **Refresh Invoices** tool in the Payments and Receipts journals ensures that the list of outstanding invoices for a vendor or customer is the current one, after applying the changes made by other users.

The **Refresh Data** tool in the icon windows looks the same as the Refresh Report icon and serves the same purpose — updating accounts (vendors, customers, employees or inventory) with changes made by other users. It appears just before the Select A Report tool in all ledger icon windows. The icon is dimmed in single-user mode and when you are creating a new ledger record.

In ledger windows, the **Refresh Record tool** updates the ledger record with changes made by other users. The tool is located on the Select account line in the ledger and looks the same as the Refresh Report tool.

INDEX

A

abbreviations, *2, 77*
Able & Associates Inc.
   accounting procedures, *783*
   company information, *780–783*
   department reports, *799–801*
   departments, *792–798*
   discounts for early payments, *783*
   opening departmental balances, *789–791*
   setting up departments, *786–789*
   source documents, *784–786*
access rights, *681–682*
accommodation business, *703*
   see also Stratford Country Inn
account balances
   historical account balances, *95–96, 634–635*
   opening balance, *95, 221, 789–791*
   opening departmental balances, *789–791*
   Test Balance Account, *221, 252*
account classes
   bank accounts, *222–224*
   credit card accounts, *223*
   default selection, *46, 94*
   defining, *635–636*
   expense accounts, *224*
   generally, *222*
   Gross Margin Income Statement, *397*
   recording changes in, *223*
account groups, *87–88*
account input fields, *82*
Account List, *59*
Account List Report, *59*
account numbers
   banks, *335*
   changing account numbers, *96*
   expanded account numbering, *219, 229*
   four-digit account numbers, *41*
   no number entered, *94*
   number of digits, *82*
   Numbering option, *81–82*
   in Premium version, *41*
   in Pro version, *81*
account reconciliation
   Account Reconciliation Journal, *592–600*
   bank statement reconciliation, *590–600*
   cheque number as source code for cash expenses and revenues, *79*
   clearing data, *607*
   credit card accounts, *600*
   generally, *587*
   linking reconciliation accounts, *588–590*

naming reconciliation accounts, *588–590*
   online reconciliation, *581, 587–588*
   turning on feature, *587–588*
Account Reconciliation Journal, *592–600, 602*
Account Reconciliation Report, *603*
Account reports, *52*
   see also general reports
accountants, *492–493, 493–495*
accountant's copy, *490–491*
Accountants' Edition, *493, 798*
accounting
   accounting terms, *A–22, 11, 82*
   accrual-basis accounting, *78*
   cash-basis accounting, *78*
accounts
   see also Chart of Accounts; specific accounts
   account classes. *See* account classes
   account numbers. *See* account numbers
   account types, *46, 86, 92*
   Accounts window, *92–96*
   Add an Account wizard, *674*
   allocation of balance, *46*
   Check Validity of Accounts tool, *93*
   deleting accounts, *61*
   departments, adding, *788–789*
   editing an account, *92*
   financial statement, omission from, *46*
   General Ledger accounts, *90–92*
   graphs, *64–65*
   historical account balances, *95–96*
   new accounts. *See* new accounts
   organization of accounts, *41, 86, 88*
   postable accounts, *88*
   preset accounts, *92–93*
   record balances, *82*
   removal, if linked, *230*
   Skeleton accounts, *89–90*
   zero balances, *61*
Accounts Ledger, *45*
accrual-basis accounting, *78*
activation of program, *A–6–A–8, A–15–A–17*
Activity Time and Billing Payroll Reports, *776*
Activity Time and Billing Reports, *774*
adjusting entries. *See* adjustments
adjustments
   see also corrections after posting; corrections before posting
   bad debts, *626–627*
   cash purchases, *133*
   closing adjusting entries, *102*
   corrections after posting, *A–33*
   inventory adjustments, *374–375*
   paycheques, *292*
   payroll entries, *281–283*
   payroll remittances, *287*
   Payroll Run entry, *296–297*
   posted entry, *47–49*
   posted invoice, *133–135*
   posted payment, *143–144*
   posted Sales Journal entry, *189–190*
   posting of adjusted entries, *49*
   sales quotes, *424–425*
   shortcuts, *47*
   showing or omitting in reports, *58, 60*
   time slips, *757, 761*
Adrienne Aesthetics
   accounting procedures, *357*

company information, *352–358*
   Forecast & Analysis Reports, displaying, *397–400*
   instructions, *358–359*
   inventory items, *376–386*
   Inventory module, *373–375*
   inventory purchases, accounting for, *370–373*
   inventory reports, displaying, *389–397*
   inventory sales, accounting for, *366–370*
   promotional gift packages, *357–358*
   purchase returns, *388–389*
   sales returns, *387–388*
   selling to preferred customers, *386–387*
   source documents, *359–366*
Advice, *16–17, 83*
Aged Detail Report, *253*
Aged Overdue Payables Reports, *148*
Aged Overdue Receivables Reports, *194*
aging of accounts, *624–625*
Air Care Services
   accounting procedures, *158–159*
   adjustment of posted Sales Journal entry, *189–190*
   cash flow reports, *197–199*
   cash sales, entering, *177–179*
   company information, *155–159*
   credit card sales, entering, *187–188*
   customer information, editing, *186–187*
   customer reports, *191–202*
   customizing the sales invoice, *170–171*
   instructions, *159*
   new customer, *179–183*
   NSF cheques, *184–185*
   open invoice accounting for receivables, *158*
   opening data files, *166*
   previewing invoices, *171–172*
   recalling a stored sales entry, *191*
   receipts, accounting for, *173–177*
   reversing a receipt, *184–185*
   sales, accounting for, *166–173*
   shortcuts for other transactions, *190–191*
   source documents, *160–165*
   storing a recurring sales entry, *188*
   tax reports, *196–197*
Alberta
   see also Dorfmann Design; Helena's Academy; Missoni Marbleworks
   provincial medical plan premiums, *264, 277*
   PST (Provincial Sales Tax), *29*
allocations
   apply allocations, *82*
   balance of account, *46*
   Balance Sheet accounts, *520, 533*
   cost allocations, *520–524*
   departments, and unallocated amounts, *798*
   division reports, *531–534*
   divisions, *517–520*
   freight expenses, *526*
   incomplete allocations message, *530*
   Inventory Adjustments Journal, *518*
   other journals, *530–531*
   Payroll Journal, *530–531*
   project allocation option, *220*
   in Sales Journal, *527–529*

file extensions, *213*
file locations, *6–7*
formats for export purposes, *683*
  with other software, *684*
  path, *8*
  personalization of files, *76*
  picture files, *676*
  read-only files, *4*
  Skeleton file, *72, 86–87*
  starter files, *72, 86–87*
financial institution services, *25, 110*
Financial reports, *52, 53, 776–778*
  see also general reports
financial statements, *41, 46, 87–89*
Finish History option, *96–97*
finishing a session, *20, 65–66*
finishing the history, *96–97, 677–678, 791*
fiscal periods
  advancing to new fiscal period, *102*
  changing, *741–742*
  comparative statements, *56*
  earlier fiscal periods, *105–106*
  ending a fiscal period, *102–106*
  fiscal end date, *77*
  fiscal start date, *77, 105*
  multiple fiscal periods, and reports, *776–779*
  previous fiscal periods, *51*
  shorter than one year, *77*
  starting new fiscal period, *102–105*
Fiscal Year-End Procedures, *492*
Flabuless Fitness
  account classes, defining, *635–636*
  accounting procedures, *624–628*
  bank accounts, *641–643*
  company default settings, *636–643*
  company files, creation of, *629–630*
  company information, *613–628, 741–742*
  credit cards, setting up, *636*
  exporting reports, *682–684*
  finishing the history, *677–678*
  fiscal dates, changing, *741–742*
  foreign bank account, adding, *743*
  foreign currency, adding, *639–640, 742–744*
  General Ledger, *633–636, 643*
  instructions for setup, *628*
  Inventory & Services Ledger, *655–656, 671–677*
  inventory locations, entering, *744–745*
  inventory prices, updating, *769–772*
  job categories, *670*
  ledger default settings, entering, *643–656*
  linked bank accounts for foreign
    currency transactions, *743–744*
  Manager's Report on Simply Accounting, *614–615*

multiple fiscal periods, and reports, *776–779*
  new accounts, creating, *633–635*
  new inventory, building, *761–765*
  Payables Ledger, *643–646, 657–660*
  Payroll Ledger, *648–655, 663–670*
  payroll remittances, *670–671*
  printer settings, *642–643*
  Receivables Ledger, *646–648, 660–662*
  sales taxes, *636–639*
  security passwords, *678–682*
  service activity prices, updating, *750–753*
  services, adding time and billing to, *749–750*
  source documents, *684–685, 686–702, 733–741*
  subsidiary ledgers, preparing, *656–677*
  supplementary data files, *628*
  the system, preparation of, *630–633*
  tax codes, entering, *637–639*
  time and billing profile, *732–733*
  time and billing reports, displaying, *772–776*
  time and billing setup, *745–753*
  time slips, *753–761*
  transfer of inventory between locations, *766–772*
  users, entering, *678–682*
folders
  change folders, *20*
  new folder, *20, 74, 678*
Forecast & Analysis Reports
  Customer Analysis Report, *398*
  displaying, *397–400*
  multiple fiscal periods, *192*
  Product Analysis Report, *398–399*
  Sales Receipts by Payment Method
    Reports, *399*
  Sales Synopsis Report, *399*
foreign currency
  adding, *639–640, 742–744*
  additional currencies, and linked
    accounts, *236*
  bank accounts, adding to, *641–642*
  exchange rate reports, *495–496*
  exchange rates, *478, 480, 486, 487–488, 489, 640, 660*
  multiple foreign currencies, *742*
  pricing method, changing, *771*
  setup, *659*
  suppliers' use of, *240*
  transferring foreign funds, *488*
foreign customers
  exchange rates, *478, 480*
  receipts, entering, *480–481*
  sales to, *478–479*
foreign purchases. *See* foreign suppliers
foreign suppliers
  exchange rates, *486, 487–488*
  foreign supplier record, *485–487*
  and GST, *486*
  identifying, *658–659*
  import duties, *524–526*
  import duty remittances, *530*
  invoices for, *659–660*
  payments to, *481, 487–488*
  purchases from, *485–487*
forms
  batch printing, *217*
  cheque Form settings, *223*
  commonly used forms, *4*
  company address, adding, *217*
  customizable forms, *4*

default settings, *217, 631–632*
  Form Numbers, *217*
  Forms folder, *219*
  language, *80*
  payroll form settings, *340–341*
  verify sequence numbers, *217*
freight expenses, *357, 372, 457–458, 505, 526, 625*
French, *80, 518*
Full Add, *126, 179–180*
future-dated transactions, *105*

G

General Journal
  Adjust Journal Entry, *40*
  Banking module, *40*
  corrections after posting, *A–25*
  corrections before posting, *44*
  displaying, *59–60*
  entering transactions, *40–45*
  foreign funds transfer, *489*
  opening, *12*
  posting, *44–45*
  Reverse Entry tool, *49*
  review of entry, *44*
  sales taxes, entering, *138–140*
General Ledger
  budget amounts, entering, *551–553*
  changing settings, *229*
  editing accounts, *91–92*
  entering General Ledger accounts, *90–92*
  finishing General Ledger history, *96–97*
  General Ledger Report, *57–58*
  general linked accounts, *643*
  linked accounts, *643*
  modifying accounts in, *220*
  new accounts, *93–95, 220–221, 633–635*
  preparing, *89–90, 219–220, 633–636*
  report, *475, 590, 591*
  settings, *643*
general reports
  see also reports
  Account List Report, *59*
  Balance Sheet, *54–55*
  Chart of Accounts, *58–59*
  displaying general reports, *51*
  Expenses and Net Profit as % of
    Revenue, *63–64*
  General Journal, *59–60*
  General Ledger Report, *57–58*
  generally, *51–54*
  graphing, *62–65*
  Income Statement, *56–57*
  Revenues by Account, *64*
  Trial Balance, *57*
Getting Started screen, *10*
GIFI code, *46, 90, 91*
go-back symbol, *47*
Goods and Services Tax. *See* GST (Goods
  and Services Tax)
graphs
  budget reports, *557–559*
  copying, *63*
  customer reports, *200–202*
  and Customers window, *191*
  default start and finish dates, *63*
  Expenses and Net Profit as % of
    Revenue, *63–64*
  Expenses by Account, *64–65*
  Expenses vs Budget graphs, *558–559*
  general reports, *62–65*
  Payables by Aging Period Charts, *153*

Inventory Adjustments Journal, *390–391, 518*
Inventory Ledger. *See* Inventory & Services Ledger
Inventory Lists, *389*
Inventory Quantity Reports, *391–392*
inventory reports
    Adjustments Journal, *390–391*
    Customer Sales Reports, *396–397*
    displaying, *389–397*
    generally, *389*
    Gross Margin Income Statement, *397*
    Grouped Inventory Lists, *390*
    Inventory Lists, *389*
    Inventory Quantity Reports, *391–392*
    Inventory Sales Reports, *394*
    Inventory Statistics Reports, *393–394*
    Inventory Summary Reports, *391*
    Inventory Tracking Reports, *393–397*
    Inventory Transaction Reports, *394–395*
    Item Assembly Journal, *390*
    management reports, *399–400*
    Price Lists, *392–393*
    printing, *400*
    Supplier Purchases Reports, *395–396*
Inventory Sales Reports, *394*
Inventory Statistics Reports, *393–394*
Inventory Summary Reports, *391*
Inventory Tracking Reports, *393–397*
Inventory Transaction Reports, *394–395*
invoices
    see also purchase invoices; sales invoices
    clear paid invoices, *104*
    e-mail, *505*
    Paid Stamp, *84*
    previewing, *505*
    print, *82, 505*
Item Assembly Journal, *A–32, 382–386, 390*

J

job categories, *328–329, 339–341, 350–351, 670*
Job Site, *167*
journals
    see also specific journals
    adding division details to journal reports, *533–534*
    Additional Information feature, *44*
    allocations, *530–531*
    batch printing from, *560*
    in Classic View, *138*
    customization, *84, 171*
    departments, adding, *793–798*
    displaying all journal entries, *150*

    displaying reports, *452*
    for hidden modules, *151*
    hiding optional fields, *84*
    icons, *13*
    journal activities, *11*
    journal entries, preparing for, *250–252*
    reports, and departments, *800*
    shortcuts, *44, 120*
    Windows Calculator tool, *42*

K

keyboard shortcuts, *A–20–A–21*
keystrokes, *6, 39, 102–106*
    see also setup; shortcuts

L

labels. *See* mailing labels
language, *80, 82, 85, 518*
Learning Centre, *11, 13, 14*
ledgers
    see also specific ledgers
    in Classic View, *138*
    default settings, entering, *643–656*
    hidden, *52*
    history status, change to finished, *678*
    icon, *11, 13*
    names, *13, 522*
    open history symbol, *74*
    preparing, *86–96, 219–250*
Lime Light Laundry
    accounting procedures, *315–316*
    company information, *309–316*
    Employee Ledger records, *327–337*
    finishing payroll history, *341*
    instructions, *316*
    job categories, *339–341*
    linking remittances to suppliers, *338–339*
    payroll setup, *317–343*
    salesperson reports, *350–351*
    source documents, *343–349*
line discounts, *646, 795–796*
line of credit, *405, 421, 450*
linked accounts
    additional currencies, use of, *236*
    assembly costs accounts, *762*
    changing, *229*
    Classic View, *229*
    credit card accounts, *225*
    currency, changes in, *645*
    essential linked accounts, *236*
    foreign currency transactions, *743–744*
    General Ledger, *643*
    general linked accounts, *229–230, 643*
    inventory, *375, 378, 656, 762*
    linked revenue account, *379*
    new accounts, creating, *643*
    payables linked accounts, *120, 231–232, 645–646*
    payroll, *324–327, 325–326, 326, 653–655*
    prepayments, *232*
    receivables, *170, 235–237, 647–648*
    reconciliation accounts, *588–590*
    removal, restricted, *230*
    Retained Earnings, *634*
    setup, *229–237*
    taxes, *227*
    vacation pay, *277*
    variance linked account, *674*
    wage accounts, *277*

logo, *81, 218–219, 219, 632, 683*
Long Date Format, *19, 167, 218*
Long Dates text option, *18, 39, 78*
lookup data
    clearing, *608*
    deposit slip lookup data, clearing, *608–609*
    for other payments, clearing, *609*
Lookup tool, *123, 144, 184, 481–484*
lost files, *21*
lower Tasks pane, *11*

M

mailing labels
    customers, *200*
    employee mailing labels, *303*
    printing, *152–153, 200, 303*
    suppliers, *152–153*
main menu bar, *11*
Maintenance menu, *50, 253*
management reports
    cash flow reports, *198–199*
    and Customers window, *191*
    displaying, *61–62*
    division management reports, *534*
    inventory, *399–00*
    overdue payments, *152*
    payroll, *308*
    and Report Centre, *191*
    supplier reports, *151–152*
Manitoba
    see also Adrienne Aesthetics; Air Care Services
    PST (Provincial Sales Tax), *29*
manuals, *4*
Maple Leaf Rags Inc.
    accountant's copy, *490–491, 492–493*
    accountant's journal entries, importing, *493–495*
    accounting procedures, *457–458*
    company information, *453–458*
    credit card bill payments, *470–472*
    exchange rate reports, *495–496*
    foreign customers, *478–479, 480–481*
    foreign suppliers, *485–487, 487–488*
    instructions, *458*
    looking up and tracking purchases, *485*
    looking up invoices to track shipments, *481–484*
    monitoring routine activities, *491–495*
    opening data files, *467*
    source documents, *458–466*
    supplier's Web site, accessing, *473–475*
    tax remittances, *475–477*
    tracking sales, *467–470*
    transferring foreign funds, *488–490*
margin, *655*
markup, *655*
maximizing the Home window, *40*
medical benefits, *276, 320*
medical companies, *416, 432*
    see also Andersson Chiropractic Clinic
medical contributions, *277*
Microsoft Excel documents, *679, 683*
Microsoft Excel language option, *82*
Microsoft Office Word, *679*
Microsoft Outlook, *130, 182, 245, 484*
Missoni Marbleworks
    accounting procedures, *34*
    adjusting a posted entry, *47–49*
    advancing the session date, *49–51*
    company information, *32–34*

Q

QHSF Factor, *323, 652*
QHSF (Quebec Health Services Fund), *321, 538*
QPIP (Quebec Parental Insurance Plan), *321, 538*
QST (provincial sales tax), *29, 540*
Quebec
    see also Village Galleries
    CSST (La Commission de la Santé et de la Sécurité du Travail), *538*
    payroll taxes, *319*
    QHSF Factor, *323*
    QHSF (Quebec Health Services Fund), *321, 538*
    QPIP (Quebec Parental Insurance Plan), *321, 538*
    QST (provincial sales tax), *29, 540*
    Relevé 1 Slips, *299–300, 336–337, 669–670*
Quick Add, *126, 179*
quill pen symbol, *12, 74*
quotes
    customization of columns, *432*
    patient quotes, *422–425*
    purchase quotes, *415–417, 432*
    removal of, *450–451*
    reports, *451–452*
    sales quotes, *422–425, 433*

R

read-only files, *4, 19*
Recalculate Taxes tool, *283*
receipts
    accounting for, *173–177*
    on accounts with deposits, *433–434*
    customer, changing, *185*
    Find Receipt, *184*
    foreign customer receipts, entering, *480–481*
    negative receipts (NSF cheques), *566*
    partial payments, *175–176*
    reversing a receipt, *184–185*
    for sales with deposits on orders, *440–441*
Receipts Journal
    additional transaction information, *422*
    in Classic View, *173, 185*
    corrections after posting, *A–30*
    corrections before posting, *177*
    customer deposits, *426–428, 434*
    departments, adding, *794–795*
    displaying, *195*
    foreign customers, *480–481*
    opening, *173*
    posting, *177*
    review of entry, *176–177*
    tabbing order, *174*

receivables. *See* sales
Receivables by Aging Period graph, *200*
Receivables by Customer graph, *201*
Receivables Due vs Payables Due graph, *202*
Receivables Ledger
    customer accounts, entering, *244–247, 660–661*
    default comments, *235, 647*
    default settings, *233–234*
    discount settings, *234, 646*
    historical customer information, *661–662*
    linked accounts, *170, 235–237, 647–648*
    payment terms, *169*
    preparing, *660–662*
    receivables terminology, changing, *647*
    sales quotes, *423*
    settings, *233–234, 646–648*
    Statistics tab, *246*
    Taxes tab, *246*
    terminology, changing, *235*
Receivables module window, *10–12*
Receiver General for Canada, *24, 288, 473*
Reconciliation and Deposits Journal, *39, 580–586, 586*
Reconciliation Transaction Report, *603–604*
Record of Employment Report, *299–300*
recurring transactions
    due, and Daily Business Manager, *444–445*
    Payroll Journal entries, *278*
    purchases, *121–122*
    Random frequency, *151*
    recurring frequency options, *121*
    Recurring Transactions Report, *151*
    removing, *447–448*
    sales, *188*
Recurring Transactions Report, *151*
Refresh Lists option, *82*
Refresh tool, *40, 91, 173*
registered charities. *See* Toss for Tots
registration
    details, *14*
    instructions, *A–6–A–8*
    validation codes, *7*
Related Tasks pane, *11*
Relevé 1 Slips, *299–300, 336–337, 669–670*
reminders, *79, 83*
Remittance Journal, *288–289*
removal
    alternative to records removal, *610*
    customer records, *610–611*
    of linked accounts, *230*
    orders, *450–451*
    quotes, *450–451*
    recurring transactions, *447–448*
    supplier records, *610–611*
reports
    see also specific reports
    Account reports, *52*
    all journal entries, in single report, *150, 195*
    analysis, *51*
    Banking reports, *52*
    banking reports, *602–604*
    budget reports, *555–557*
    cash flow reports, *197–199*
    commonly used reports, *4*
    corrections, showing or omitting, *58, 60, 149, 185*

customer reports, *191–195*
customization, *60–61*
defaults, *53, 54–55, 56*
department reports, *799–801*
departments, adding, *800–801*
division reports, *531–534*
drill-down reports, *61–62*
exchange rate reports, *495–496*
exporting reports, *682–684*
filtering, *60*
Financial reports, *52, 53*
Forecast & Analysis Reports, *397–400*
general reports, *51–61*
inventory reports, *389–397*
journal reports, *452*
Modify This Report option, *54, 55*
multi-period reports, *52, 777–778*
multiple fiscal periods, *776–779*
orders, *451–452*
and other software, *684*
payroll reports, *304–308*
previous fiscal periods, *51*
printing, *62*
quotes, *451–452*
Recently Viewed Reports, *11*
related historical accounts, *778–779*
Remittance Report, *290*
Report Centre, *11, 13, 52–54, 146*
Reports drop-down list, *11*
Reports menu, *52*
Reports pane, *11, 52–54*
salesperson reports, *350–351*
supplier reports, *146–152*
tax reports, *196–197*
This Week To Date option, *80*
time and billing reports, *772–779*
year for all date fields, *54*
restoring default settings, *66*
restoring from backup, *20–23*
retail industry, *366*
retail sales taxes. *See* PST (Provincial Sales Tax)
Retained Earnings accounts, *89, 229, 634*
returns
    generally, *358*
    purchase returns, *388–389*
    sales returns, *387–388*
revenue accounts, *168, 246, 379, 552*
Revenues by Account, *64*
reversals
    NSF cheques, *184–185, 601*
    paycheques, *283*
    posted purchase entry, *144–145*
    resulting entries, *145*
    Reverse Entry tool, *49*
    reversing entry after posting, *49*
    sales invoices, *388*
ROI (return on investment), *399*
rounding errors, *169, 469*
routine activities, monitoring, *491–495*
RRSP contributions, *322, 333*
RT extension, *216*

S

Sage Download Manager, *A–12–A–13*
Sage Software payroll ID code, *273*
Sage Spark Online Billing program, *14*
salaried workers, *274*
sales
    see also customers; Receivables Ledger
    accounting for, *166–173*
    cash sales. *See* cash sales
    credit card sales. *See* credit card sales
    debit cards, *436–437*